Additional information for Professors:

- 10 NEW videos included with this edition, including:

  – Motivation and the Container Store

  – Commitment and Pike Place Fish Market

  – Money & Ethics

  – Executive Excess

  – Leadership, Power, and Influence and HP CEO Carly Fiorina

  – Corporate Culture and SAS Institute

See the Information Center of the Online Learning Center at www.mhhe.com/mcshane3e for a complete list and description, or the end of the text for the Video case summaries.

- Over 40 self-assessments and interactivities can be found on the Student Interactive Study Guide on CD-Rom. The end-of-chapter text exercises include a CD icon to indicate which are included on the CD. See the Instructor's Manual, or the Instructor's Center of the OLC for a description of each exercise.

- See the Walkthrough and preceding Preface to get an in-depth look at the content and structural changes, and all of the features and supplements available with McShane/Von Glinow, **ORGANIZATIONAL BEHAVIOR, 3E**

organizational behavior

3e

Emerging Realities for the Workplace Revolution

organizational behavior *3e*

Steven L. McShane
The University of Western Australia

Mary Ann Von Glinow
Florida International University

McGraw-Hill Irwin

Boston   Burr Ridge, IL   Dubuque, IA   Madison, WI   New York   San Francisco   St. Louis
Bangkok   Bogotá   Caracas   Kuala Lumpur   Lisbon   London   Madrid   Mexico City
Milan   Montreal   New Delhi   Santiago   Seoul   Singapore   Sydney   Taipei   Toronto

ORGANIZATIONAL BEHAVIOR:
EMERGING REALITIES FOR THE WORKPLACE REVOLUTION

Published by McGraw-Hill/Irwin, a business unit of The McGraw-Hill Companies, Inc., 1221 Avenue of the Americas, New York, NY 10020. Copyright © 2005, 2003, 2000 by The McGraw-Hill Companies, Inc. All rights reserved. No part of this publication may be reproduced or distributed in any form or by any means, or stored in a database or retrieval system, without the prior written consent of The McGraw-Hill Companies, Inc., including, but not limited to, in any network or other electronic storage or transmission, or broadcast for distance learning. Some ancillaries, including electronic and print components, may not be available to customers outside the United States.

This book is printed on acid-free paper.

1 2 3 4 5 6 7 8 9 0 WCK/WCK 0 9 8 7 6 5 4

ISBN   0-07-293147-7

Vice president and editor-in-chief: *Robin J. Zwettler*
Editorial director: *John E. Biernat*
Executive editor: *John Weimeister*
Senior developmental editor: *Christine Scheid*
Executive marketing manager: *Ellen Cleary*
Producer, Media technology: *Mark Molsky*
Senior project manager: *Kari Geltemeyer*
Production supervisor: *Debra R. Sylvester*
Lead designer: *Pam Verros*
Photo research coordinator: *Judy Kausal*
Photo researcher: *Amelia Bethea*
Supplement producer: *Betty Hadala*
Senior digital content specialist: *Brian Nacik*
Cover illustration: *© Masterfile*
Interior illustrations: *© Photodisc*
Typeface: *10/12 New Aster*
Compositor: *ElectraGraphics, Inc.*
Printer: *Quebecor World Versailles Inc.*

Library of Congress Cataloging-in-Publication Data

McShane, Steven Lattimore.
    Organizational behavior : emerging realities for the workplace revolution / Steven L. McShane, Mary Ann Von Glinow.— 3rd ed.
      p. cm.
    Includes indexes.
    ISBN 0-07-293147-7 (alk. paper) — ISBN 0-07-111163-8 (international ed. : alk. paper)
    1. Organizational behavior. I. Von Glinow, Mary Ann Young, 1949– II. Title
HD58.7.M42 2005
    658—dc22
                                        2003070638

www.mhhe.com

ABOUT THE AUTHORS

Steven L. McShane

Steven L. McShane is Professor of Management in the Graduate School of Management at the University of Western Australia (UWA). He has also served on the business faculties at Simon Fraser University and Queen's University in Canada. Steve receives high teaching ratings from MBA and doctoral students both in Perth, Australia, and in Singapore, where he also teaches for UWA.

Steve earned his PhD from Michigan State University in organizational behavior, human resource management, and labor relations. He also holds a Master of Industrial Relations from the University of Toronto and an undergraduate degree from Queen's University in Canada. Steve has served as president of the Administrative Sciences Association of Canada (the Canadian equivalent of the Academy of Management) and director of graduate programs in the business faculty at Simon Fraser University.

Steve is also the author of *Canadian Organizational Behavior,* 5th edition (McGraw-Hill, 2004), Canada's best-selling OB textbook. He is co-author with Professor Tony Travaglione of *Organisational Behaviour on the Pacific Rim* (McGraw-Hill, 2003), which became the second best-selling OB book in that region within its first year of publication. Steve has published several dozen articles and conference papers on informal and structural knowledge management, the socialization of new employees, gender bias in job evaluation, wrongful dismissal, media bias in business magazines, emotions in decision making, and other diverse topics.

Along with teaching and writing, Steve enjoys his leisure time swimming, bodyboard surfing, canoeing, skiing, and traveling with his wife and two daughters.

Mary Ann Von Glinow

Dr. Von Glinow is Director of the Center for International Business Education and Research (CIBER) and Professor of Management and International Business at Florida International University. Previously on the Business School faculty of the University of Southern California, she has an MBA and PhD in Management Science from The Ohio State University. Dr. Von Glinow was the 1994–95 President of the Academy of Management, the world's largest association of academicians in management and is a Fellow of the Academy, and the Pan Pacific Business Association. She sits on eleven editorial review boards and numerous international panels. She teaches in executive programs in Latin America, Central America, the Caribbean region, Asia, and the U.S. She is Department Editor for the *Journal of International Business Studies.*

Dr. Von Glinow has authored over 70 journal articles and eleven books. Her most recent includes *Organizational Learning Capability* by Oxford University Press, 1999 (in Chinese and Spanish translation) which won a Gold Book Award from the Ministry of Economic Affairs in Taiwan in 2002. She heads an international consortium of researchers delving into "Best International Human Resource Management Practices," and her research in this arena won an award from the American Society for Competitiveness' Board of Trustees.

Mary Ann consults to a number of domestic and multinational enterprises, and serves as a mayoral appointee to the Shanghai Institute of Human Resources in China. Since 1989, she has been a consultant in General Electric's "Workout" and "Change Acceleration Program" including "Coaching to Management." Her clients have included Asia Development Bank, American Express, Burger King, Pillsbury, The Aetna, State of Florida, TRW, Rockwell Int'l, Motorola, N.Y. Life, Amoco, Lucent, and Joe's Stone Crabs, to name a few.

Dedicated with love and devotion to Donna,
and to our wonderful daughters,
Bryton and Madison
—S.L.M.

To my family and my virtual,
globally-distributed family!
—M.A.V.G.

BRIEF CONTENTS

CONTENTS

CHAPTER 9

Foundations of Team Dynamics   264

CHAPTER 10

Developing High-Performance Teams   294

CHAPTER 13

Conflict and Negotiation in the Workplace   386

CHAPTER 14

Leadership in Organizational Settings   414

PART FOUR

Organizational Processes   443

CHAPTER 15

Organizational Structure and Design   444

CHAPTER 16

Organizational Culture   474

PREFACE

Welcome to a new era of organizational behavior! Virtual teams are replacing committees. Values and self-leadership are replacing command-and-control supervision. Knowledge is replacing infrastructure. Companies are looking for employees with emotional intelligence, not just technical smarts. Globalization has become the mantra of corporate survival. Co-workers aren't down the hall; they're at the other end of an Internet connection located somewhere else on the planet.

Organizational Behavior, Third Edition, is written in the context of these emerging workplace realities. This edition explains how emotions guide employee motivation, attitudes, and decisions; how values have become the new resource to shape workplace behavior; how a person's social identity relates to team dynamics, stereotyping, and organizational culture; and how appreciative inquiry has become one of the emerging strategies for organizational change. This book also presents the new reality that organizational behavior is not just for managers; it is relevant and useful to anyone who works in and around organizations.

GLOBAL ORIENTATION

Love it or hate it, globalization is part of the emerging reality of organizations. The opening chapter of *Organizational Behavior,* Third Edition, reflects this situation by introducing the topic of globalization in the context of OB concepts. Global issues are also highlighted throughout this book—cross-cultural values and ethics (Chapter 2), job satisfaction and emotional responses in different societies (Chapter 4), the relevance of motivation concepts across cultures (Chapter 5), attitudes toward money in various cultures (Chapter 6), employee stress from overwork in Japan (Chapter 7), cross-cultural issues in the success of self-directed work teams and the prevalence of virtual teams (Chapter 10), problems with cross-cultural communication (Chapter 11), cultural values and expectations as a factor in the preferred influence tactics (Chapter 12), cross-cultural conflict (Chapter 13), preferred leadership styles across cultures (Chapter 14), and cross-cultural issues in organizational change (Chapter 17) are just some examples.

To further emphasize the emerging reality of globalization, every chapter has one or more *Global Connections* features that link OB concepts to organizational incidents around the world. For example, you will read how an increasing number of young people in Japan are dramatically altering the traditional employment relationship by becoming "freeters," how a German advertising and Web design firm is gaining attention by adopting a no-nonsense "back to work" corporate culture, how nonverbal communication narrowly avoided a potentially deadly incident during the war in Iraq, how employees in Argentina are saving their jobs by taking over the businesses abandoned by their employers, and how people throughout Asia are trying out new forms of team building.

LINKING THEORY WITH REALITY

Every chapter of *Organizational Behavior*, Third Edition, is filled with real-life examples to make OB concepts more meaningful and reflect the relevance and excitement of this field. For example, you will read how Wall Street brokerage firms are putting employees into teams for better customer service, how Hewlett-Packard created a more performance-oriented corporate culture by acquiring Compaq, how the president of New York's Central Park Conservancy improved her perceptions of employees by literally walking in their shoes, how high-involvement cross-functional teams assisted the dramatic turnaround of Nissan Motor Company, and how Pixar Animation Studios designed its new campus headquarters to improve employee communications.

These real-life stories appear in many forms. Every chapter of this book is filled with photo captions and in-text anecdotes about work life in this new millennium. Each chapter also includes *Connections*, a special feature that "connects" OB concepts with real organizational incidents. Case studies in each chapter and video case studies in each part also connect OB concepts to the emerging workplace realities. These stories provide representation across the United States and around the planet. Moreover, these examples cover a wide range of industries—from software to government, and from small businesses to the Fortune 500.

ORGANIZATIONAL BEHAVIOR KNOWLEDGE FOR EVERYONE

Another distinctive feature of *Organizational Behavior*, Third Edition, is that it is written for everyone in organizations, not just "managers." The new reality is that people throughout the organization—systems analysts, production employees, accounting professionals—are assuming more responsibilities as companies remove layers of bureaucracy and give nonmanagement staff more autonomy over their work. Consequently, the philosophy of this book is that everyone who works in and around organizations needs to understand and make use of organizational behavior knowledge.

CONTEMPORARY THEORY FOUNDATION

Organizational Behavior, Third Edition, has a solid foundation of contemporary and classic scholarship. You can see this in the references. Each chapter is based on dozens of articles, books, and other sources. The most recent literature receives thorough coverage, resulting in what we believe is the most up-to-date organizational behavior textbook available. These references also reveal that we reach out to information systems, marketing, and other disciplines for new ideas. At the same time, this textbook is written for students, not the scholars whose work is cited. Consequently, you will read about the conceptual and applied implications of leading research, but not detailed descriptions of those studies. Also, the names of researchers or their affiliations are rarely mentioned in the text. The philosophy of this textbook is to present OB scholarship in ways that students will remember long after the final examination.

Organizational Behavior was the first textbook in this field to discuss workplace emotions, social identity theory, appreciative inquiry, search conferences, the employee-customer-profit chain model, and several other groundbreaking topics. This edition continues to present innovative and contemporary ideas, including the latest knowledge on individualism-collectivism, innate drives theory, Schwartz's values model, counterproductive work behaviors, learning orientation, virtual teams, workaholism, executive coaching, emotions in decision making, and several other topics.

CHANGES TO THE THIRD EDITION

Organizational Behavior, Third Edition, is the result of reviews over the past three years by more than 140 organizational behavior scholars and teachers in several countries. This feedback, along with a continuous scan of relevant literature, has resulted in numerous improvements. First, you will notice significant changes to the textbook structure. Guided by extensive reviewer feedback, the chapters are more clearly organized around individual, team, and organizational levels of analysis. The early chapters focus on individual differences, with the more stable characteristics (values, personality) presented before the more fluid characteristics (emotions, attitudes). This edition also has two chapters on teams; integrates decision making, creativity, and employee involvement into one chapter; moves employment and career topics closer to related material throughout the textbook; and moves organizational change to the book's final chapter.

Along with structural improvements, this edition presents more experiential learning support than ever before. In particular, this edition nearly doubles the number of self-assessments and includes a CD where students can complete these assessments more efficiently. *Organizational Behavior* is one of the few books with comprehensive cases, and this edition further supports instructor requests for more of these lengthier cases. You will also find several new cases and team exercises in each chapter of the book.

Almost every chapter has been substantially updated with new conceptual and anecdotal material. Here are some of the most significant improvements within each chapter of this edition:

- *Chapter 1: Introduction to the Field of Organizational Behavior*—The section on trends in OB now includes discussion of corporate social responsibility, as well as completely rewritten subsections on globalization and information technology in the context of organizational behavior. The systematic research anchor now recognizes grounded theory methodology, and the chapter adds new information on telecommuting as well as OB and the bottom line
- *Chapter 2: Individual Behavior, Values, and Personality*—This completely rewritten chapter places the most stable individual differences (values, personality) near the beginning of the book. It also includes groundbreaking research on individualism and collectivism, Schwartz's model (which dominates current values literature), a new section on values congruence, and new information on counterproductive work behaviors. This chapter also includes updated information on ethical principles and employee competencies.
- *Chapter 3: Perception and Learning in Organizations*—This completely rewritten chapter logically combines perceptions and learning. Minimizing stereotyping bias, practicing self-fulfilling prophecy, and empathy are revised and updated based on new literature. Social identity theory is also updated here to reflect the rapidly growing OB literature on this subject.

■ *Chapter 4: Workplace Emotions and Attitudes*—This significantly revised chapter offers the most up-to-date definition and model of emotions, emotional labor, and emotional intelligence. The chapter also introduces groundbreaking ideas from neurology and evolutionary psychology on the dual rational-emotional processes in attitudes and behavior. This edition also includes the exit-voice-loyalty-neglect (EVLN) model of job satisfaction, important new research on the relationship between job satisfaction and job performance, new information on effects of surface versus deep acting emotional labor on emotional dissonance, and updated information on organizational commitment.

■ *Chapter 5: Motivation in the Workplace*—Innate drives theory, one of the most important conceptual developments in employee motivation, is introduced in this chapter. This edition also has a new section on organizational justice, including full discussion on procedural justice as a source of motivation. Executive coaching and the integration of goal setting with feedback are also new features of this chapter.

■ *Chapter 6: Applied Performance Practices*—This appropriately renamed chapter includes a new section on empowerment, updated information on self-leadership in practice, and discussion of the balanced scorecard.

■ *Chapter 7: Work-Related Stress and Stress Management*—This popular chapter includes new information on workaholism, as well as updates on the job burnout model, work hours as a stressor, and work–life balance.

■ *Chapter 8: Decision Making and Creativity*—Based on the preferences of reviewers, this completely rewritten chapter integrates decision making, creativity, and employee involvement, and precedes our discussion of team dynamics. The chapter includes new information on the dual rational-emotional processes in decision making, in both identifying problems and making choices. It also presents a new model of employee involvement in decision making, new information on implicit favorite and information processing distortion in decision making, and more explicit identification and critique of the "rational" and "bounded rationality" decision-making processes.

■ *Chapter 9: Foundations of Team Dynamics*—The topic of teams is now split into two chapters with new material, as requested by several reviewers. This chapter includes new details about the potential benefits of teams as well as Belbin's team roles. It also updates coverage of types of teams, team composition, and task interdependence.

■ *Chapter 10: Developing High-Performance Teams*—This new chapter integrates the topics of self-directed work teams, virtual teams, team trust, team decision making, and team building. It provides the latest knowledge on virtual teams, including why they exist and how to design them more effectively. The chapter also updates information on constructive conflict in team decision making as well as challenges to self-directed work teams.

■ *Chapter 11: Communicating in Teams and Organizations*—This chapter is reorganized for a more logical flow of topics from interpersonal to organizational-level concepts. It also updates the sections on direct communication with top management, the effect of information technologies on the organizational grapevine, and communication issues in work space design.

- *Chapter 12: Power and Influence in the Workplace*—This chapter offers an entirely new presentation and orientation on the types of influence in the workplace. It also adds a new section on contingencies of influence tactics, and it improves the connection between influence and organizational politics. The chapter also describes how *guanxi* in Asia and *blat* in Russia serve as influence tactics through the exchange process.

- *Chapter 13: Conflict and Negotiation in the Workplace*—This chapter introduces new information on constructive versus socioemotional conflict. The chapter also offers new information on conflict management styles, time deadlines in negotiation, and third-party conflict resolution.

- *Chapter 14: Leadership in Organizational Settings*—This chapter introduces new research on cross-cultural issues in leadership, including findings from the GLOBE leadership project. It updates information on integrity, emotional intelligence, and other leadership competencies. It also updates writing about implicit leadership theory, the debate on transformational versus charismatic leadership, and how women and men are evaluated as leaders.

- *Chapter 15: Organizational Structure and Design*—This chapter offers new information on divisional structures, including the general decline of geographic divisional structures. It also includes updated information on network structures as well as centralization-decentralization.

- *Chapter 16: Organizational Culture*—Along with numerous updated references and examples, this chapter revises information on ethics and corporate culture. It also incorporates information on organizational socialization.

- *Chapter 17: Organizational Change*—This chapter features several structural changes to streamline the information and improve the flow of topics. In particular, it has a new section on three approaches to organizational change (action research, appreciative inquiry, parallel learning structures). The chapter updates information on creating an urgency to change, search conferences as a change process, types of change agents, the action research approach to organizational change, and the appreciative inquiry approach to organizational change. This chapter also completes the book with an overview of strategies for personal development in organizational settings.

SUPPORTING THE LEARNING PROCESS

The changes described above refer only to the text material. *Organizational Behavior*, Third Edition, also has improved technology supplements, cases, videos, team exercises, and self-assessments. The detailed Walkthrough on the following pages highlights the many learning features available to you and your students with *Organizational Behavior*.

STUDENT-FOCUSED LEARNING FEATURES

With its core philosophy being "OB is for everyone," every chapter of **Organizational Behavior** is filled with innovative features and exercises to help students learn and apply the knowledge they've gained from chapter material.

LEARNING OBJECTIVES

A topical guide for the student, **Learning Objectives** tell them what they should and will know after completing the chapter.

chapter 1

chapter 2

chapter 3

chapter 4

chapter 5

chapter 6

chapter 7

chapter 8

chapter 9

Individual Behavior, Values, and Personality

Learning Objectives

After reading this chapter, you should be able to:

■ Diagram the MARS model.

■ Describe three basic ways to match individual competencies to job requirements.

■ Identify five types of individual behavior in organizations.

■ Define values and explain why values congruence is important.

■ Define the six main values that vary across cultures.

■ List four ethical principles.

■ Explain how moral intensity, ethical sensitivity, and the situation influence ethical behavior.

■ Identify the "Big Five" personality dimensions.

■ Summarize the personality concepts behind the Myers-Briggs Type Indicator.

■ Explain how personality relates to Holland's model of vocational choice.

It is no accident that the Container Store is a runaway leader in the hypercompetitive retail business. The Dallas-based seller of customized storage products pays attention to several key drivers to ensure that employees provide unflagging customer service. The Container Store begins by carefully selecting job applicants who are conscientious and embrace customer service values. To attract and keep this talent, the company pays 50 percent or more than typical retail salaries and maintains a respectful culture. "We are absolute wild-eyed fanatics when it comes to only hiring great people," says president and CEO Kip Tindell, who cofounded the Container Store with partner and chairman Garrett Boone. "One of our Foundation Principles™ is that one great person is equal to three good people in terms of business productivity."

Once hired, full-time employees receive 241 hours of training during their first year, compared to under a dozen hours for frontline staff at most other retailers. This training provides more than specialized skills and knowledge to analyze customer storage needs. It also teaches fundamental values that encourage employees to go beyond the customer's short-term expectations. "Helping people is an obligation on our part," says Boone. "It's not a religious imperative. It's an ethical imperative to really help that person to the best of your ability."

The Container Store also motivates employees beyond generous pay and benefits. Team members in each store collectively set goals and provide supportive feedback in the daily "huddle." Employees also call in to a special celebration voice mail system to tell stories about co-workers who went above and beyond the call of duty. To create a sense of ownership and involvement, employees receive ongoing information about the company and have a lot of freedom to make decisions. "A funny thing happens when you take the time to educate your employees, pay them well, and treat them as equals," says Kip Tindell. "You end up with extremely motivated and enthusiastic people."[1] ■

The Container Store is a role model for applying the key drivers of employee performance in customer service.

OPENING VIGNETTE

Each chapter begins with an engaging **opening vignette** that sets the stage for the chapter. These brief but interesting case studies introduce students to critical issues, challenge their preconceptions, and highlight some of today's hottest companies.

When Rewards Go Wrong

There is an old saying that "what gets rewarded, gets done." But what companies reward isn't always what they had intended for employees to do. Here are a few dramatic examples:

- Stock options are supposed to motivate executives to improve corporate performance. Instead, they seem to motivate some leaders to inflate stock values through dodgy accounting practices. For example, according to U.S. government authorities, HealthSouth founder and former CEO Richard Scrushy demanded that his accounting staff artificially prop up profits at the nation's largest outpatient medical provider. When some employees urged him to abandon these questionable schemes, Scrushy refused, reportedly saying "Not until I sell my stock!" HealthSouth narrowly avoided bankruptcy after the company's true financial health became public.
- Integrated steel companies often rewarded managers for increased labor efficiency. The lower the labor hours required to produce a ton of steel, the larger the manager's bonus. Unfortunately, steel firms usually didn't count the work of outside contractors in the formula, so the reward system motivated managers to hire expensive contractors in the production process. By employing more contractors, the cost of production actually increased, not decreased.
- Toyota rewards its dealerships based on customer satisfaction surveys, not just car sales. What Toyota discovered, however, is that this motivates dealers to increase satisfaction scores, not customer satisfaction. One Toyota dealership received high ratings because it offered

U.S. government authorities claim that stock options motivated former HealthSouth CEO Richard Scrushy (shown) and other executives to engage in dodgy accounting practices rather than improve stockholder value for the long term.

CONNECTIONS

Connections boxes connect OB concepts with real organizational incidents.

GLOBAL CONNECTIONS

Providing the student with a link to the international arena, **Global Connections** boxes go beyond the borders of the United States to show how companies in other countries are tackling emerging workplace realities.

Protesting Unfair "Fat Cat" Pay in the United Kingdom

Cats have become an increasingly common sight at corporate annual general meetings throughout the United Kingdom. More precisely, dozens of people have been dressing up as "fat cats" in business suits as a way of protesting the generous paychecks of British executives. Labor unions are behind many of these antics, but institutional investors and private shareholders are also expressing their feelings of unfairness by voting against executive remuneration.

Over half of GlaxoSmithKline's shareholders opposed a U.S.$35 million golden parachute that chief executive Jean-Pierre Garnier would be paid if fired from the pharmaceutical giant. A larger percentage of shareholders also opposed or abstained from voting for overly generous pay packages for executives at advertising group WPP and engineering group BAE Systems. Whitbread is under pressure to change contracts of its senior executives after the National Association of Pension Funds called on shareholders to abstain from voting on executive remuneration packages at the British bakery giant.

Critics say there is plenty of reason for the theatrics and shareholder unrest against executive pay. John Weston was ousted as chief executive of BAE Systems after the company lost more than $1 billion and its stock price hit a 10-year low. In spite of these failings, Weston was sent out the door with a U.S.$2.3 million payout and nearly $6 million pension guarantee. Corus chief executive Sir Brian Moffat was awarded a 130 percent pay increase soon after the Anglo-Dutch metals group announced huge financial losses and a 12-month pay

British protesters express their anger over unfair executive pay by dressing as "fat cats" in business suits outside the company's annual general meetings.

freeze for its workforce. "How do Corus bosses explain their wage freeze for workers while gifting fortunes to themselves?" asks Paul Flynn, the member of Parliament in South Wales, where Corus has cut back or closed steel production.

Sources: J. Boxell, "Investor Protest Threatens to Force Whitbread to Cut Executive Contracts," *Financial Times* (London), June 18, 2003, p. 25; W. Wallace, "British Shareholders Battle 'American-Style' Exec Pay," *Los Angeles Times*, June 2, 2003, Part 3, p. 5; "Handfuls of Protesters Decrying 'Fat Cat' Paycheques," *Canadian Press*, May 25, 2003; "Heads, They Win," *The Guardian* (London), May 9, 2003; "Bosses' Pay Sparks Anger," *BBC News*, April 5, 2002.

END-OF-CHAPTER MATERIAL GEARED TOWARD APPLICATION

SELF-ASSESSMENTS

Experiential exercises and **self-assessments** represent an important part of the active learning process. *Organizational Behavior*, Third Edition, offers one or two **team exercises** in every chapter. Many of these learning activities are not available in other organizational behavior textbooks, such as "Where in the World are We?" (Chapter 8) and "A Cross-Cultural Communication Game" (Chapter 11). This edition has nearly **four dozen self-assessments** in the book or on the student CD. The CD icon shown above signals that the assessment can be found interactively on the Student CD-Rom. The self-assessments featured personalize the meaning of several organizational behavior concepts, such as workaholism, corporate culture preferences, self-leadership, empathy, stress, creative disposition, and tolerance of change.

SELF-ASSESSMENT EXERCISE 6.4

ASSESSING YOUR SELF-LEADERSHIP

Purpose This exercise is designed to help you understand self-leadership concepts and to assess your self-leadership tendencies.

Instructions Indicate the extent to which each statement in this instrument describes you

very well or does not describe you at all. plete each item honestly to get the best est of your level of overall self-leadership as scores on each of the subscales.

SELF-ASSESSMENT EXERCISE 6.5

STUDENT EMPOWERMENT SCALE

Purpose This exercise is designed to help you understand the dimensions of empowerment and to assess your level of empowerment as student.

Instructions Empowerment is a concept that applies to people in a variety of situations. This instrument is specifically adapted to your

position as a student at this college or u sity. Indicate the extent to which you ag disagree with each statement in this instru then request the results, which provide an all score as well as scores on each of the fo mensions of empowerment. Complete each honestly to get the best estimate of your le empowerment.

TEAM EXERCISES

TEAM EXERCISE 7.3

STAGE FRIGHT!

Purpose This exercise is designed to help you to diagnose a common stressful situation and determine how stress management practices apply to this situation.

Background Stage fright—including the fear of public speaking—is one of the most stressful experiences many people have in everyday life. According to some estimates, nearly three-quarters of us frequently get stage fright, even when speaking or acting in front of a small audience. Stage fright is an excellent topic for this team activity on stress management because the psychological and physiological symptoms of stage fright are really symptoms of stress. In other words, stage fright is the stress experience in a specific context involving a public audience. Based on the personal experiences of team members, your team is asked to identify the symptoms of stage fright and to determine specific stress management activities that effectively combat stage fright.

Instructions

- *Step 1*—Students are organized into teams, typically four to six students per team. Ideally, each team should have one or more people who acknowledge that they have experienced stage fright.
- *Step 2*—Each team's first task is to identify the symptoms of stage fright. The best way

to organize these symptoms is to l three categories of stress outco scribed in the textbook: physiolog chological, and behavioral. The stage fright symptoms may be diffe the stress outcomes described in book, but the three broad categor be relevant. Teams should be pre identify several symptoms and t one or two specific examples of st symptoms based on personal exper team members. (Please remember vidual students are not required to their experiences to the entire clas

- *Step 3*—Each team's second task i tify specific strategies people coul applied to minimize stage fright. categories of stress management in the textbook will likely provide template in which to organize th stage fright management activiti team should document several str minimize stage fright and be able one or two specific examples to some of these strategies.
- *Step 4*—The class will congregate each team's analysis of symptoms tions to stage fright. This informa then be compared to the stress e and stress management practices tively.

SELF-ASSESSMENT EXERCISE 7.4

TIME STRESS SCALE

Purpose This self-assessment is designed to help you to identify your level of time-related stress.

Instructions Read each of the following

cerns of social comparison. However, cussion will focus on the time stress s

1. Yes No Do you plan to slov

DISCUSSION QUESTIONS

Discussion Questions

1. Identify three reasons why motivating employees is becoming increasingly challenging.
2. Harvard Business School professors Lawrence and Nohria recently proposed four fundamental human drives. Relate these innate drives to Maslow's needs hierarchy theory and Alderfer's ERG theory. How are they similar? How do they differ?
3. Use all three components of expectancy theory to explain why some employees are motivated to show up for work during a snowstorm whereas others make no effort to leave their home.
4. What are the limitations of expectancy theory in predicting an individual's work effort and behavior?
5. Several service representatives are upset that the newly hired representative with no previous experience will be paid $1,000 a year above the usual starting salary in the pay range. The department manager explained that the new hire

would not accept the entry-level rate, so company raised the offer by $1,000. All five r currently earn salaries near the top of the s ($10,000 higher), although they all started the minimum starting salary a few years ear Use equity theory to explain why the five ser representatives feel inequity in this situatio

6. Using your knowledge of the characteristics effective goals, establish two meaningful go related to your performance in this class.
7. When do employees prefer feedback fr nonsocial rather than social sources? Expl why nonsocial sources are preferred un these conditions.
8. Inequity can occur in the classroom as well in the workplace. Identify classroom situati in which you experienced feelings of inequ What can instructors do to maintain an e ronment that fosters both distributive and p cedural justice?

BUSINESS WEEK CASE STUDIES

Found at the end of each chapter, *BusinessWeek* **case studies** introduce the online full-text article and provide critical thinking questions for class discussion or assignments. These cases encourage students to understand and diagnose real-world issues using organizational behavior knowledge. For example, one case study challenges students to analyze how specific collaborative technology at Lockheed Martin Aeronautics facilitates virtual teams (Chapter 10). Another case study asks students to identify the influence tactics used to deter a manager at TAP Pharmaceutical Products from blowing the whistle on corporate wrongdoing (Chapter 12).

CASE STUDY 7.2

RETHINKING THE RAT RACE

BusinessWeek Long work hours. They have become a badge of honor, a sign of status and importance. The harder you work, the higher your rise on the corporate ladder. Rather than free us from work, technology has eroded the boundaries between work and leisure. Even if Americans can't bring themselves to take more official time off from the job, they will increasingly demand that the job be more accommodating to their personal time. They may work until midnight, but they also want the right to surf the Web at work or spend more time chatting with co-workers.

This *Business Week* case study looks at shifting expectations regarding hours of work and work–life balance. This article speculates about whether office life in the future will mix work and leisure together as much as these two are getting mixed together at home. Read through this *Business Week* article at www.mhhe. mcshane3e and prepare for the discussion tions below.

Discussion Questions

1. What are the main reasons presented in article why Americans work so many each year?

2. In your opinion, will the blurring of and leisure at home and in the work increase or decrease stress levels? Ex your answer.

Source: D. Brady, "Rethinking the Rat Race," *Business* August 26, 2002, p. 142.

CASE STUDY 5.1

BUDDY'S SNACK COMPANY

By Russell Casey, Clayton State University, and Gloria Thompson, University of Phoenix

Buddy's Snack Company is a family-owned company located in the Rocky Mountains. Buddy Forest started the business in 1951 by selling homemade potato chips out of the back of his pickup truck. Nowadays, Buddy's is a $36 million snack food company that is struggling to regain market share lost to Frito-Lay and other fierce competitors. In the early 1980s, Buddy passed the business on to his son, Buddy Jr., who is currently grooming his son, Mark, to succeed himself as head of the company.

Six months ago, Mark joined Buddy's Snacks as a salesperson and after four months was quickly promoted to sales manager. Mark recently graduated from a local university with an M.B.A. in marketing, and Buddy Jr. was hoping that Mark would be able to implement strategies that could help turn the company around. One of Mark's initial strategies was to introduce a new sales performance management system. As part of this approach, any salesperson who receives a below-average performance rating was required to attend a mandatory coaching session with his/her supervisor. Mark Forest is hoping that these coaching sessions will motivate his employees to increase their sales. This case describes the reaction of three salespeople who have been required to attend a coaching session because of their low performance over the previous quarter.

Lynda Lewis

Lynda is a hard worker who takes pride in her work ethic. She has spent a lot of time reading the training material and [viewing] the training [techniques], viewing training [material on her own] time, and accompanying [other sales on] their calls. Lynda has no pr

failure to make quota during this pa results not from lack of effort but jus in the economy. She is hopeful that turn around in the next quarter.

Lynda is upset with Mark for hav tend the coaching session because thi time in three years that her sales quo been met. Although Lynda is willing ever it takes to be successful, she is that the coaching sessions will be hel urday. Doesn't Mark realize that Ly raise three boys by herself and that we an important time for her family Lynda is a dedicated employee, she how manage to rearrange the family's

Lynda is now very concerned abo efforts are being perceived by Mark she exceeded the sales quota from th quarter yet had not received a "tha "good job" for those efforts. The en ence has left Lynda unmotivated and ing her future with the company.

Michael Benjamin

Michael is happy to have his job Snack Company, although he really sales work that much. Michael accept sition because he felt that he would work hard and would have a lot of fre ing the day. Michael was sent to coach because his customer satisfaction re low; in fact, they were the lowest in th Michael tends to give "canned" pr [to each customer rather than]

CHAPTER CASES AND ADDITIONAL END-OF-TEXT CASES

Every chapter includes at least one short **case study** that challenges students to diagnose issues and apply ideas from that chapter. Additional comprehensive cases appear at the end of the book. Several cases are new to this book and are written by instructors around the United States and from other countries. Other cases, such as Arctic Mining Consultants, are classics that have withstood the test of time.

SUMMARY AND KEY TERMS

Chapter Summary

Money and other financial rewards are a fundamental part of the employment relationship. They potentially fulfill existence, relatedness, and growth needs. Money generates emotions and attitudes which vary across cultures. People (particularly men) also tend to identify themselves in terms of their wealth.

Organizations reward employees for their membership and seniority, job status, competencies, and performance. Membership-based [rewards] [at]tract job applicants and seniority-b[ased] [re]duce turnover, but these reward [also] discourage turnover among those [with poor] performance. Rewards based on [job status] maintain internal equity and motiv[ate employees to] compete for promotions. However, [such] rewards are inconsistent with mark[et forces,] encourage employees to compete [with others,] and can lead to organizational polit[ics. Competency-] based rewards are becoming increas[ingly popular be-]

cause they improve workforce flexibility and are consistent with the emerging idea of employability. But competency-based rewards tend to be subjectively measured and can result in higher costs as employees spend more time learning new skills.

Awards/bonuses, commissions, and other individual performance-based rewards have existed for centuries and are widely used. Many companies are [shifting to team-based rewards such as gainsharing.]

Key Terms

autonomy, p. 187
balanced scorecard, p. 180
employee stock ownership plan (ESOP), p. 179
empowerment, p. 191
gainsharing plan, p. 179
job characteristics model, p. 186
job design, p. 184
job enlargement, p. 189
job enrichment, p. 189
job evaluation, p. 176
job feedback, p. 187
job rotation, p. 188

job specialization, p. 184
mental imagery, p. 194
motivator-hygiene theory, p. 186
open-book management, p. 179
profit-sharing plans, p. 179
scientific management, p. 185
self-leadership, p. 193
self-talk, p. 194
skill variety, p. 187
stock options, p. 179
task identity, p. 187
task significance, p. 187

INSTRUCTOR SUPPLEMENTS

Organizational Behavior, Third Edition, includes a variety of **supplemental materials** to help instructors prepare and present the material in this textbook more effectively.

INSTRUCTOR'S CD-ROM

The **Instructor's CD-Rom** contains the **Instructor's Manual,** the **Computerized Test Bank, PowerPoint presentation,** and additional downloads of **art from the text.** Written by Steve McShane, the IM includes the learning objectives, glossary of key terms, a chapter synopsis, complete lecture outline with thumbnail images of corresponding PowerPoint slides, suggested solutions to the end-of-chapter discussion questions, and comments on photo caption critical thinking questions. It also includes teaching notes for the chapter case(s), additional cases, team exercises, and self-assessments and transparency masters. Many chapters include supplemental lecture notes and suggested videos. The Test Bank includes more than 2,400 multiple-choice, true/false, and essay questions. Steve McShane wrote all questions, the majority of which have been tested in class examinations. Each question identifies the relevant page reference and difficulty level.

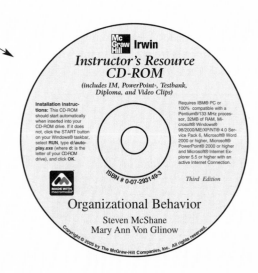

POWERPOINT

Organizational Behavior includes a complete set of **PowerPoint Presentation** files, with at least 18 slides relating to each chapter. These slides have received high praise for their clean design, use of graphics, and inclusion of some photos from the textbook.

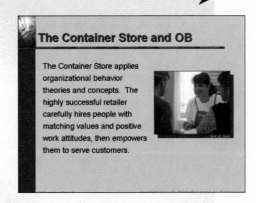

The Container Store and OB

The Container Store applies organizational behavior theories and concepts. The highly successful retailer carefully hires people with matching values and positive work attitudes, then empowers them to serve customers.

VIDEOS (ISBN: 0-07-293150-7)

The new video collection features PBS and CBC footage, and original business documentaries that relate to examples and cases in the text.

VIDEO DVD (ISBN: 0-07-294694-6)

To give professors more choice in delivery of the video footage, the entire video collection for *Organizational Behavior* can be found on the **Video DVD.**

ONLINE LEARNING CENTER

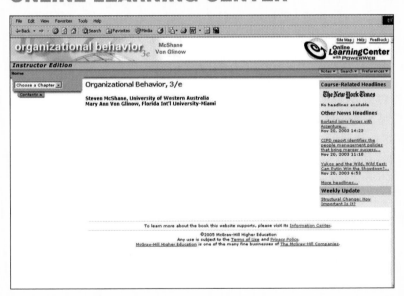

www.mhhe.com/mcshane3e

The **Instructor Center** of the Online Learning Center (OLC) is a one-stop shopping website with additional course materials, supplements, links, and exercises found chapter by chapter. With the addition of our newly integrated PowerWeb feature, students and professors alike have access to peer-reviewed content, including up-to-date articles from leading periodicals and journals, current news, and weekly updates with accompanying assessments, exercises, and study tips. Ask your sales representative how you can obtain access to the PowerWeb feature for your students.

STUDENT SUPPLEMENTS

ONLINE LEARNING CENTER

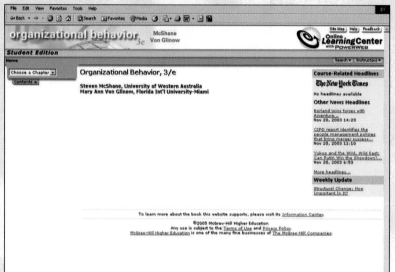

The **Online Learning Center** (OLC) is a website that follows the text chapter by chapter, with additional materials and quizzes that enhance the text and/or classroom experience. As students read the book, they can go online to take self-grading quizzes, review material, or work through interactive exercises. OLCs can be delivered in multiple ways—professors and students can access them directly through the textbook website, through PageOut, or within a course management system (e.g., WebCT, Blackboard, TopClass, or e College).

STUDENT INTERACTIVE STUDY GUIDE ON CD-ROM

The **Student CD-ROM,** packaged free with each text, encourages students to think critically and to be active learners. This added-value feature includes:

· Interactive self-assessment modules that support hands-on learning and encourage students to evaluate their own personality characteristics and preferences.

· Chapter summaries.

· Interactive chapter quizzes.

· Flashcards to test vocabulary knowledge.

· A link to the Online Learning Center to accompany *Organizational Behavior*.

McGRAW-HILL'S POWER WEB

Harness the assets of the Web by keeping current with PowerWeb! This online resource provides high-quality, peer-reviewed content including up-to-date articles from leading periodicals and journals, current news, weekly updates, interactive exercises, Web research guide, study tips, and much more! Ask your sales representative how to incorporate PowerWeb into your course by accessing the Premium content area on the Online Learning Center

ACKNOWLEDGMENTS

Organizational Behavior, Third Edition, symbolizes the power of teamwork. More correctly, it symbolizes the power of a *virtual team* with Mary Ann Von Glinow in Miami, Steve McShane in Perth, Australia, and in Singapore, and members of the editorial crew from Chicago, New York City, and Michigan.

Superb virtual teams require equally superb team members, and we were fortunate to have this in our favor. Executive editor John Weimeister led the way with enthusiasm and foresight, while clearing the way of any challenges. Christine Scheid (Senior Developmental Editor) demonstrated amazingly cool coordination skills as the authors pushed the deadline limits so students have the latest OB knowledge. The keen copyediting skills of Carole Schwager made *Organizational Behavior*, Third Edition, incredibly error-free. Kari Geltemeyer, our Senior Project Manager, met the challenge of a tight production schedule. Pam Verros delivered an elegant design with a textbook cover that captures the global and future-focus themes of this textbook. Amy Bethea triumphed to deliver the many photos that the authors had selected for this edition. Thanks to you all. This has been an exceptional team effort!

As was mentioned earlier, more than 140 instructors around the world reviewed parts or all of *Organizational Behavior*, Third Edition, or its regional editions over the past three years. Their compliments were energizing, and their suggestions significantly improved the final product. The following people from American colleges and universities provided the most recent feedback for improvements specifically for *Organizational Behavior*, Third Edition:

Carole Barnett
University of New Hampshire

Joy Benson
University of Illinois–Springfield

Greg Bier
Stephens College

Weldon Blake
Bethune Cookman College

Antonia Bos
Tusculum College

James Breaugh
University of Missouri–St. Louis

Holly Buttner
University of North Carolina–Greensboro

Michael Camarata
Marywood University

Sandra Deacon Carr
Boston University

Beth Chung
San Diego State University

Roger Dean
Washington & Lee University

George Dodge
Clearwater Christian College

Sally Dresdow
University of Wisconsin–Green Bay

Richard Feltman
San Diego State University

Marilyn Fox
Minnesota State University–Mankato

Janice Gates
Western Illinois University

Ronald Humphrey
Virginia Commonwealth University

Rusty Juban
Dallas Baptist University

Dong Jung
San Diego State University

Tom Kolenko
Kennesaw State University

Susan Manring
Elon College

Jennifer Martin
York College of Pennsylvania

Linda Morable
Richland College

Emile Pilafidis
University of La Verne

Liz Ravlin
University of South Carolina

Pete Richardson
Southwest Missouri State University

Jill Roberts
Campbellsville University

Lena Rodriguez
San Diego State University

Michael Shaner
St. Louis University

Jason Shaw
University of Kentucky–Lexington

Tracy Sigler
Northern Kentucky University

Vikki Sitter
Milligan College

Randall Sleeth
Virginia Commonwealth University

Maryalice Smith
Tarrant County College–NE

Gary Stark
University of Minnesota–Duluth

Pat Stubblebine
Miami University–Oxford

Bill Turnley
Kansas State University

Matthew Valle
Elon College

Andrew Ward
Emory University

The authors would also like to extend our sincerest thanks to the many instructors in the United States and other countries who contributed cases and exercises to this edition of *Organizational Behavior:*

Jeffrey Bagraim
University of Cape Town, South Africa

Hazel Bothma
University of Cape Town, South Africa

Sharon Card
Saskatchewan Institute of Applied Science & Technology

Russell Casey
Clayton State University

Mary Gander
Winona State University

Cheryl Harvey
Wilfrid Laurier University

Lisa Ho
Louis Vuitton, Singapore

Joseph Kavanaugh
Sam Houston State University

Cynthia Larson-Daugherty
National University

Carolynn Larson-Garcia
Assesso

Henry S. Maddux III
Sam Houston State University

Rosemary Maellaro
University of Dallas

Fiona McQuarrie
University College of the Fraser Valley

Aneil Mishra
Wake Forest University

Karen Mishra
Wake Forest University

Kim Morouney
Wilfrid Laurier University

Harry Gene Redden
Sam Houston State University

Christina Stamper
Western Michigan University

Gloria Thompson
University of Phoenix

William Todorovic
University of Waterloo

Joseph C. Santora
Essex County College and TSTDCG, Inc.

James C. Sarros
Monash University

Steve would also like to extend special thanks to his students for sharing their learning experiences and assisting with the development of the three organizational behavior textbooks in the United States, Canada, and the Pacific Rim. These students include officers attending his MBA classes at SAFTI Military Institute's Command and Staff College in Singapore and MBA students at the University of Western Australia's Graduate School of Management in Perth. Steve is also very grateful to his colleagues at the Graduate School of Management who teach organizational behavior, including: Gail Broady, Renu Burr, Stacy Chappell, Catherine Jordan, Sandra Kiffin-Petersen, Chris Perryer, David Plowman, and Chris Taylor. These wonderful people listen patiently to his ideas, diplomatically correct his wayward thoughts, and share their experiences using the American or Pacific Rim editions of this book in Perth (Australia), Jakarta (Indonesia), Manila (Philippines), Shanghai (People's Republic of China), and Singapore. Finally, Steve is forever indebted to his wife Donna McClement and to their wonderful daughters, Bryton and Madison. Their love and support give special meaning to Steve's life.

Mary Ann would like to thank the many, many students who have used and hopefully enjoyed this book. I've been stopped on my campus and at occasional meetings by students who tell me that they recognize my picture and wanted to thank me! There are a few that have actually asked for my autograph! (Note, that didn't happen when I was President of the Academy of Management!) Thus it is to the students that I acknowledge many thanks, particularly for making this learning venture fun and exciting. Also, I would like to thank the faculty and staff at Florida International University, who have been very supportive of this effort. By far and away, my coauthor Steve McShane is the penultimate scholar. He has boundless energy and a mind that doesn't seem to quit, particularly with those late night or early morning emails! Steve is also the techno-wizard behind this edition. Finally I would like to thank my family—John, Rhoda, Lauren, Lindsay, and Christy—as well as some very special people in my life—Janet, Peter, Bill, Karen, Jerry, Barbara, Kate, Joanne, Mary, Linda, and Steve. I know I never get a chance to thank them enough, so thank you my friends! I also thank Emma, Zack, Molly, and Googun, my babies! A final note of thanks goes to my CIBER family: Tita, Sonia, Juan, Elsa, and KK—you are simply the best! Thank you all, for being there for me!

Steven L. McShane
Mary Ann Von Glinow

Introduction

Introduction to the Field of Organizational Behavior

Learning Objectives

After reading this chapter, you should be able to:

■ Define organizational behavior and give three reasons for studying this field of inquiry.

■ Discuss how globalization influences organizational behavior.

■ Summarize the apparent benefits and challenges of telecommuting.

■ Identify changes in the workforce in recent years.

■ Describe employability and contingent work.

■ Explain why values have gained importance in organizations.

■ Define corporate social responsibility and argue for or against its application in organizations.

■ Identify the five anchors on which organizational behavior is based.

■ Diagram an organization from an open systems view.

■ Define knowledge management and intellectual capital.

■ Identify specific ways that organizations acquire and share knowledge.

D o you Google? So many people use the ubiquitous search engine that its name has become part of our Internet language. In fact, Google's 10,000 servers process more than 200 million search queries in 90 languages every day, over half of them from users outside the United States. Google's success is even more amazing because this profitable company of 1,000 employees began just a few years ago (1998) in the dorm rooms of Stanford University graduate students Larry Page and Sergey Brin (shown in photo).

Google is a living laboratory where continuous experimentation and customer feedback are part of the knowledge creation process. Google engineers are expected to devote a quarter of their time to new ideas. Ten full-time staff scan the constant flow of user e-mails and redirect this vital feedback throughout the company. When Google scientist Krishna Bharat created a prototype of a dynamic news service, a beta version was publicly released just a few months later. With extensive public feedback and further development, Google News has become a runaway hit with several versions around the planet. "A public trial helps you go fast," explains Marissa Mayer, an engineer who worked on the Google News project. "If it works, it builds internal passion and fervor. It gets people thinking about the problem."

Google's focus on employees is almost as intense as its focus on technology. The Googleplex (Google's

Google founders Larry Page and Sergey Brin have leveraged the power of organizational behavior to create the world's leading Internet search engine as well as one of the best places to work.

headquarters) is a unique oasis, complete with Lava Lamps, rubber exercise balls, and free gourmet meals. The company boasts work–life balance, generous health benefits, and a team-based environment where employees work in "high density clusters remarkably reflective of our server setup, with three or four staffers sharing spaces with couches and dogs." Every Friday, employees gather to hear about the company's performance during the previous week. "We want everyone to know exactly how the company's doing, exactly where we stand in relation to our goals," says Craig Silverstein, Google's director of technology and first employee hired after Page and Brin.

Google carefully selects new recruits. "We are definitely growing slower than we would otherwise because of our stringent hiring standards," Silverstein admits. The result is a geeky culture that reflects the beliefs of its founders. "These are people who think they are creating something that's the best in the world," says Peter Norvig, a Google engineering director. "And that product is changing people's lives."[1] ∎

Google has become a powerful force on the Internet, but its real power comes from the company's effective application of organizational behavior theories and concepts. More than ever, organizations are relying on these ideas and practices to remain competitive. For example, Google employees are driven by a strong corporate culture derived from company founders Larry Page and Sergey Brin. The company encourages creativity and knowledge sharing. It motivates employees through perks and exciting work opportunities, and it engages in careful person–job matching.

This book is about people working in organizations. Its main objective is to help you understand behavior in organizations and to work more effectively in organizational settings. Organizational behavior knowledge is not only for managers and leaders. It is relevant and useful to anyone who works in and around organizations. In this chapter, we introduce you to the field of organizational behavior, outline the main reasons why you should know more about it, highlight some of the organizational trends influencing the study of organizational behavior, describe the fundamental perspectives behind the study of organizations, and introduce the concept that organizations are knowledge and learning systems.

The Field of Organizational Behavior

organizational behavior (OB)
The study of what people think, feel, and do in and around organizations.

Organizational behavior (OB) is the study of what people think, feel, and do in and around organizations. OB scholars systematically study individual, team, and structural characteristics that influence behavior within organizations. By saying that organizational behavior is a field of study, we mean that scholars have been accumulating a distinct knowledge about behavior within organizations—a knowledge base that is the foundation of this book.

By most estimates, OB emerged as a distinct field around the 1940s.[2] However, its origins can be traced much further back in time. The Greek philosopher Plato wrote about the essence of leadership. Aristotle, another respected philosopher, addressed the topic of persuasive communication. The writings of Chinese philosopher Confucius in 500 B.C. are beginning to influence contemporary thinking about ethics and leadership. In 1776, Adam Smith advocated a new form of organizational structure based on the division of labor. One hundred years later, German sociologist Max Weber wrote about rational organizations and initiated discussion of charismatic leadership. Soon after, Frederick Winslow Taylor introduced the systematic use of goal setting and rewards to motivate employees. In the 1920s, Elton Mayo and his colleagues conducted productivity studies at Western Electric's Hawthorne plant in the United States. They reported that an informal organization—employees casually interacting with others—operates alongside the formal organization. OB has been around for a long time; it just wasn't organized into a unified discipline until after World War II.

What Are Organizations?

Organizations have existed for as long as people have worked together. Massive temples dating back to 3500 B.C. were constructed through the organized actions of many people. Craftspeople and merchants in ancient Rome formed guilds, complete with elected managers. And more than 1,000 years ago, Chinese factories were producing 125,000 tons of iron a year.[3] We have equally impressive examples of contemporary organizations, ranging from Wal-Mart, the world's largest and most successful retailer, to Google, the world's leading search engine. "A company is one of humanity's most amazing inventions," says Steven Jobs, CEO of Apple Computer and Pixar Animation Studios. "It's totally abstract. Sure, you have to build something with bricks and mortar to put the people in, but basically a company is this abstract construct we've invented, and it's incredibly powerful."[4]

By any standard, Wal-Mart is an awesome phenomenon. The world's largest retailer generates annual global sales exceeding $240 billion and employs nearly 1.5 million people from Minneapolis to Mexico City (shown in photo). According to one consultant's report, the company's persistent drive for efficiency accounts for one-eighth of U.S. productivity growth in recent years. Wal-Mart has had its share of discrimination lawsuits and complaints about unpaid work hours. Still, the retailer that grew up and remains headquartered in Bentonville, Arkansas, is also the most admired company in America. How much bigger can Wal-Mart get? Plenty, according to CEO Lee Scott. "Could we be two times larger?" asks Scott. "Sure. Could we be three times larger? I think so."[5] In your opinion, what organizational behavior concepts described in this book would have the greatest influence on the success of Wal-Mart and other mammoth organizations?

• structured pattern
  interaction
• coordinated tasks
• working toward
  some purpose

So, what are these powerful constructs that we call **organizations?** They are groups of people who work interdependently toward some purpose.[6] Organizations are not buildings or other physical structures. Rather, they consist of people who interact with each other to achieve a set of goals. Employees have structured patterns of interaction, meaning that they expect each other to complete certain tasks in a coordinated way—in an *organized* way.

Organizations have a purpose, whether it's producing oil from oil sands or selling books on the Internet. Some scholars and students alike are skeptical about the relevance of goals in a definition of organizations.[7] They argue that an organization's mission statement may be different from its true goals. Also, they question the assumption that all organizational members believe in the same goals. These points may be true, but imagine an organization without goals: it would consist of a mass of people wandering around aimlessly without any sense of direction. Overall, organizations likely have a collective sense of purpose, even though this purpose is not fully understood or agreed upon.

Why Study Organizational Behavior?

Organizational behavior seems to get more respect from people who have been in the workforce a while than from students who are just beginning their careers. Many of us specialize in accounting, marketing, information systems, and other fields with corresponding job titles, so it's understandable that students focus on these career paths. After all, who ever heard of a career path leading to a "vice-president of OB" or a "chief OB officer"?

Even if organizational behavior doesn't have its own job title, most people eventually come to realize that this field is a potential gold mine of valuable knowledge. The fact is, everyone in the workforce needs to understand, predict, and influence behavior (both our own and that of others) in organizational settings (see Exhibit 1.1). Marketing students learn marketing concepts and computer science students learn about circuitry and software code. But everyone benefits from organizational behavior knowledge to address the people issues when trying to apply marketing, computer science, and other ideas.

• understand
• research
• predict
• influence

Understanding, Predicting, and Influencing   Each one of us has an inherent need to understand and predict the world in which we live.[8] Much of our time is spent working in or around organizations, so the concepts offered in this and other OB textbooks will help you to partially satisfy that innate drive. The knowledge presented in this book also gives you the opportunity to question and rebuild your personal theories that have developed through observation and experience. Look at the "It All Makes Sense" self-assessment at the end of this chapter. How many of the statements are true? Even if you correctly answer most of them, the information you will read in this book can further develop and crystallize your personal beliefs so that they more accurately model and predict organizational behavior.

It's nice to understand and predict organizational events, but most of us want to influence the environment in which we live. Whether you are a marketing specialist or a computer engineer, OB knowledge will help you to influence organizational events by understanding and applying concepts in motivation, communication, conflict, team dynamics, and other topics. Indeed, some scholars emphasize that the usefulness of OB research depends on more than just understanding and predicting behavior. It also depends on the degree to which practitioners can interpret research results and apply them.[9]

This book takes the view that organizational behavior knowledge is for everyone—not just managers. As organizations reduce layers of management and delegate more responsibilities to the rest of us, the concepts described in this book will become increasingly important for anyone who works in and around organizations. We all need to understand organizational behavior and to master the practices that influence organizational events. That's why you won't find very much emphasis here on "management." Yes, organizations will continue to have managers ("adult supervision," as young employees cynically call them), but their roles have changed. More important, the rest of us are now expected to manage ourselves. As one forward-thinking organizational behavior scholar wrote many years ago: Everyone is a manager.[10]

OB and the Bottom Line   So far, our answer to the question "Why study OB?" has focused on how OB knowledge benefits you as an individual. But organizational behavior knowledge is also important for the organization's financial health. A recent study of more than 700 firms calculated that companies applying performance-based rewards, employee communication, work–life balance, and other organizational behavior ideas have three times the level of financial success as companies without these OB practices. Moreover, the study provides evidence that OB practices *cause* better financial performance, not the other way around. This finding is not new to Warren Buffett and other financial gurus who, for many years, have considered the organization's leadership and quality of employees as two of the best predictors of the firm's financial potential.[11]

Organizational Behavior Trends

There has never been a better time to learn about organizational behavior. The pace of change is accelerating, and most of the transformation is occurring in the workplace. Let's take a brief tour through five trends in the workplace: globalization, information technology, the changing workforce, emerging employment relationships, and workplace values and ethics.

Globalization

Betty Coulter is a typical 21-year-old American college or university grad. She wears the latest jeans and is a faithful fan of the hottest American TV shows. At least, that's what Betty will say, if asked, when you call her about a broken appliance. In reality, Betty is Savitha Balasubramanyam, an employee at a call center in Bangalore, India. "It doesn't matter if I'm really Betty or Savitha," says Balasubramanyam with a well-practiced American accent. "What matters is that at the end of the day I've helped the customer."[12]

Welcome to the world of globalization! Whether they are software giants in Europe or call centers in India, competitors are just as likely to be located in a distant part of the world as within your country. SAP, the German software giant, is the leader in enterprise software. Wipro Technologies, India's largest software company, routinely wins multimillion-dollar contracts from the likes of General Electric, Home Depot, and Nokia. CustomerAsset, where Savitha Balasubramanyam works, provides seamless customer service—including American accent!—from India's technology hub.

globalization
Economic, social, and cultural connectivity (and interdependence) with people in other parts of the world.

Globalization refers to economic, social, and cultural connectivity with people in other parts of the world. It is all about the ongoing process of increasing interdependence with each other around the planet, whether through trading goods and services, sharing knowledge, or interacting with people from different cultures and locations in the world.[13] Organizations globalize when they extend their activities to other parts of the world, actively participate in other markets, and compete against organizations located in other countries. Many firms have had "international" operations for many years, but these were usually import-export businesses or fairly independent subsidiaries that served local markets. Globalization, on the other hand, connects and coordinates these geographically dispersed segments so they serve global customers and compete against other global businesses.[14]

Consider Starbucks, the Seattle-based coffee merchant that has grown from 116 stores in North America to a global brand with 4,600 stores in 21 countries on four continents. Starbucks carefully emphasizes the global tradition of coffee drinking, not its American roots. "It's not an American theme," argues Starbucks chairman Howard Schultz. "It has a universal language because the relevancy of Starbucks, the third place (home and office are the first two places), the quality of the coffee, the social atmosphere, the romance—all of these things are as relevant in Singapore and China as they are in Zurich or Seattle."[15]

Implications for Organizational Behavior   Globalization influences several aspects of organizational behavior—some good, some not so good. Globalization is applauded for increasing organizational efficiency and providing a broader net to attract valuable knowledge and skills. It potentially opens up new career opportunities and provides a greater appreciation of diverse needs and perspectives.

But globalization also presents new challenges.[16] The debate about whether globalization makes developing countries wealthier or poorer adds a new ethical dimension to corporate decisions.[17] Firms also need to adjust their organizational structures and forms of communication to assist their global reach. Globalization adds more diversity to the workforce, which affects the organization's culture and introduces new forms of values-based conflict among employees.

- greater efficiencies + knowledge sources
- ethical issues about economies of developing countries
- new organizational structure + communication
- greater workforce diversity
- more competitive pressure, demands on employees

Globalization is also identified as one of the main sources of increased competitive pressures, mergers, and market volatility. These environmental conditions, in turn, reduce job security, increase work intensification, and demand more work flexibility from employees. Thus, globalization might partly explain why many of us now work longer hours, have heavier workloads, and experience more work–family conflict (due mainly to lack of time to fulfill both obligations) than at any time in recent decades (see Chapter 7).[18] "Any company, whether international or not, has to look at the way globalization has impacted the way we work," warns an executive at the global health care company GlaxoSmithKline. "And even if you're not global, there's a competitor or customer somewhere who is."[19]

Lastly, globalization influences the study of organizational behavior. We cannot assume that organizational behavior practices are equally effective around the world, so scholars are paying more attention to cross-cultural differences.[20] In the Best Practices Project, for instance, over three dozen scholars are discovering human resource management practices based on companies around the globe. Another consortium of scholars, called Project GLOBE, is studying leadership and organizational practices across dozens of countries.[21] These global investigations have become increasingly necessary as we discover the complex effects of values and other differences across cultures.

Globalization has important implications for how we learn about organizational behavior. The best performing companies may be in Finland, Brazil, or Singapore, not just in Houston or San Francisco. That's why this book presents numerous examples from around the planet. We want you to learn from the best, no matter where their headquarters is located.

Information Technology and OB

By day, Nana Frimpong is the official woodcarver for King Otumfuo Osei Tutu II in the royal Asante court of Ghana, West Africa. But when he isn't carving stools for the king, Frimpong sells his wares over the Internet. Demand from international buyers is so strong that he now employs a staff of 15 carvers. In this country of 19 million people and only 100,000 telephones, Frimpong is somewhat of a celebrity and role model of the country's potential prosperity. "There are a lot of Nana Frimpongs in the Asante nation," says King Tutu. "Many can be helped through the Internet."[22]

Whether we write computer code in California or make wooden stools in Ghana, the Internet and other forms of information technology are changing our lives. They are connecting people around the planet and allowing small businesses in developing countries to compete in the global marketplace. Within organizations, information technology blurs the temporal and spatial boundaries between individuals and the organizations that employ them. It redesigns jobs, reshapes the dynamics of organizational power and politics, and creates new standards for competitive advantage through knowledge management.[23] Information technology also generates new communication patterns unheard of a decade or two ago. While attending a meeting, some employees now carry on parallel conversations: They talk to the group verbally while communicating wirelessly through a personal digital assistant (PDA) to specific people in the same room! Two other emerging work activities attributed to information technology are telecommuting and virtual teams.

"Can't talk now. I'm in a seminar about improving communication with technology."

(© 2001 Ted Goff. www.tedgoff.com. Used with permission.)

Telecommuting   Up to a point, Karen Dunn Kelley follows a familiar routine as a mother and busy executive. She puts her school-aged children on the bus, feeds breakfast to her 19-month-old before handing him off to a nanny, then heads off to the office. But Kelley's daily commute is different from most; it's just a short walk from her house to the office over her garage. Furthermore, Kelley is an executive with Houston-based AIM Management Group, yet the home office where she oversees 40 staff and $75 billion in assets is located in Pittsburgh.[24]

Karen Dunn Kelley is among the tens of millions of people who practice **telecommuting** (also called *teleworking)*—an alternative work arrangement where employees work at home or a remote site, usually with a computer connection to the office. According to one estimate, 27 percent of American employees consider themselves teleworkers; 75 percent of these people work at home under informal arrangements and the others have a formal structured arrangement with equipment supplied by the employer. Terrorist attacks and SARS outbreaks have further pushed employees to work at home. "Our [company's] operations weren't affected in the slightest degree by SARS," says Microsoft Taiwan spokeswoman Zoe Cherng. "I believe working from home will be a trend in the future."[25]

Many companies applaud the benefits of telecommuting. AT&T estimates that by avoiding daily travel, telecommuters are about 10 percent more productive than before they started working from home. It also estimates that by not driving a car to and from work, AT&T employees prevented 70,000 tons of carbon dioxide from being emitted into the air. The city of Austin, Texas, also encourages its employees to telecommute as a way of reducing air pollution. Over two-thirds of Nortel Network's employees in the United Kingdom say they feel more empowered by working at home. Other studies report that

telecommuting
Working from home, usually with a computer connection to the office; also called teleworking.

Telecommuting is taking Europe by storm. More than 20 million Europeans (about 12 percent of the workforce) currently work from home at least once each week, more than double the number two years ago. Employees in Finland have the highest rate of telecommuting in Europe (16.8 percent of the workforce), followed by Sweden (15.2 percent) and the Netherlands (14.5 percent). France, Spain, Luxembourg, and Portugal have the lowest percentage of telecommuting population. Experts expect even more European teleworkers in the future as European Union member countries adopt the European Flexible Working Directive, which allows employees with children under six to apply for flexible working arrangements.[28] In your opinion, what factors would explain differences in the levels of telecommuting across Europe?

telecommuters have higher job satisfaction and less work–family conflict than do employees who do not telecommute. Sun Microsystems estimates that it saves $50 million annually because telecommuting reduces the need for office space.[26]

In spite of these benefits, teleworkers face a number of real or potential challenges.[27] One recent university study revealed that family relations suffer if employees lack sufficient space and resources for a home office. Over half of teleworkers surveyed in one study cited lack of recognition as a disadvantage of working from home, although empirical research has not yet found an adverse effect of telecommuting on career progression or performance evaluations. Loneliness is another common complaint, particularly among teleworkers who rarely visit the office. "The part of the day I most looked forward to was the few minutes of talking to the counterperson at the bagel store," admits Charles Gallo, a telecommuting computer programmer in New York City. Overall, organizational behavior scholars will continue to have several issues to investigate as more people around the world become teleworkers.

Virtual Teams   Information technology also facilitates the development of virtual teams. **Virtual teams** are cross-functional groups that operate across space, time, and organizational boundaries with members who communicate mainly through information technologies.[29] There is currently a flurry of research activity regarding the types of work best suited to virtual teams and the conditions that facilitate and hinder their effectiveness. Some conclusions are beginning to emerge from these preliminary studies.

One observation is that virtual teams are still teams, first and foremost, so their dynamics are similar to those of co-located teams (whose members are located in the same physical area). For example, team development and subgroup cliques are found in virtual teams in ways similar to co-located teams. However, virtual teams require different strategies to build trust and deal with members who are not pulling their weight. Virtual teamwork also calls for unique leadership skills, such as greater empathy and persuasive tactics. Information technology is a critical feature of virtual teams because it represents the lifeline of their existence.[30] These and other virtual team issues will be discussed more fully in Chapter 10.

virtual teams
Cross-functional teams that operate across space, time, and organizational boundaries with members who communicate mainly through information technologies.

The Changing Workforce

Walk into Malek's Bakery in Rochester, New York, and you might think you have entered a United Nations building. In the kitchen are bakers Hoang Ngo from Vietnam, Ideliso Olivares from Cuba, and Joe Vigh from Romania.

Working on the front counter are two women from Germany and the Czech Republic. The popular bakery is owned and operated by Lea Malek, a native of Hungary.[31] Like Malek's Bakery, most companies in the United States have a multicultural workforce because of the country's increasing demographic diversity. Minorities represent over one quarter of the American workforce, and this is projected to increase substantially over the next few decades. The Hispanic population is one of the fastest growing groups in the United States and has replaced African-Americans as the second largest ethnic group.[32] Within the next 50 years, one in four Americans will be Hispanic, 14 percent will be African-American, and 8 percent will be Asian-American. By 2060, non-Hispanic whites will be a minority.

Exhibit 1.2 illustrates the primary and secondary dimensions of workforce diversity. The primary categories—gender, ethnicity, age, race, sexual orientation, and mental/physical qualities—represent personal characteristics that influence an individual's socialization and self-identity. The secondary dimensions are those features that we learn or have some control over throughout our lives, such as education, marital status, religion, and work experience.

Scholars are increasingly troubled by attempts to distinguish people by their ethnicity. Some point out that interracial marriages make ethnic distinctions both difficult and inappropriate. Others warn that distinguishing people by their ethnicity merely reinforces stereotyping. In particular, there is a risk that non-white Americans are viewed as "perpetual foreigners," even though their families moved to this country generations ago. "I've been told a million times, 'Your English is so good! Where are you from?'" says Anne Xuan Clark, a Seattle resident whose ancestors are Vietnamese and Irish. Clark comes from California, but that doesn't satisfy some acquaintances. "No, where are you *really* from?" they ask again.[33]

Another form of diversity is the increasing representation of women in the workforce. Women now represent nearly 50 percent of the paid workforce, compared to just 20 percent a few decades ago. Gender-based shifts continue to occur within occupations. For example, women represented only 17 percent of accountants in the United States in the 1960s. Today, over half of the accountants are women. Only 9 percent of medical school students in 1970 were women. They now account for 43 percent of medical school enrollments.[34]

Age cohorts represent another primary dimension of workforce diversity.[35] Baby boomers—people born between 1946 and 1964—have somewhat different values and expectations in the workplace than Generation-X employees—those born between 1965 and 1979.[36] According to several writers, a typical baby boomer tends to expect and desire more job security (at least, at this stage in his or her life). In contrast, Gen-Xers are typically less loyal to one organization and, in return, expect less job security. Gen-Xers tend to be motivated more by workplace flexibility and the opportunity to use new technology. Baby boomers seem more workaholic to improve their economic and social status. Some writers are starting to describe how Generation-Y employees (those born after 1980) expect plenty of responsibility and involvement in their employment relationship. While these statements certainly don't apply to everyone in each cohort, they reflect the fact that different generations have different values and expectations.[37]

EXHIBIT 1.2

Primary and
secondary
dimensions of
workforce diversity

Primary dimension

Secondary dimension

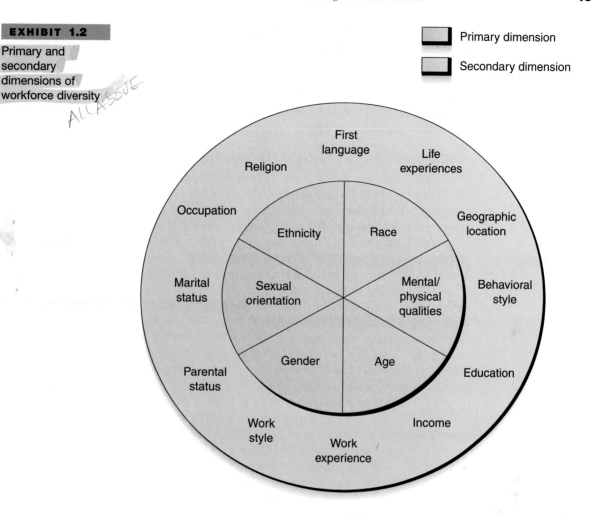

Sources: Adapted from M. Loden, *Implementing Diversity* (Chicago: Irwin, 1996); S. Bradford, "Fourteen Dimensions of Diversity: Understanding and Appreciating Differences in the Workplace," in *1996 Annual: Volume 2 Consulting,* ed. J. W. Pfeiffer (San Diego: Pfeiffer and Associates, 1996), pp. 9–17.

Implications for Organizational Behavior   Diversity presents both opportunities and challenges in organizations. To be sure, the relationship between workforce diversity and the effectiveness of a team or organization is very complex. In some circumstances and to some degree, diversity can become a competitive advantage by improving decision making and team performance on complex tasks.[38] For many businesses, a diverse workforce is also necessary to provide better customer service in the global marketplace. "We go out of our way to recruit from a melting pot of nationalities," says an executive at Amadeus, a developer of worldwide airline reservation software near Nice, France. "We believe that our product is superior because of the different cultures of the people developing it."[39]

Along with its benefits, workforce diversity presents new challenges.[40] For instance, there are situations in which diverse groups are less effective, although we are still trying to learn about the contingencies of diversity. Discrimination is another ongoing concern. Women have represented a large portion of the workforce for the past two decades, yet they are still underrepresented in senior positions. Racism still raises its ugly head from time to time. We will explore these issues more closely under various topics, such as stereotyping (Chapter 3), team dynamics (Chapters 9 and 10), and conflict management (Chapter 13).

Emerging Employment Relationships

The changing workforce, new information and communication technology (ICT), and globalization have fueled substantial changes in employment relationships. Employees face increasing turbulence in their work and employment relationships due to mergers, corporate restructuring, and privatization of government-managed organizations.[41] From this turbulence, a "new deal" employment relationship called **employability** has emerged that replaces the implied guarantee of lifelong employment in return for loyalty.

> **employability**
>
> An employment relationship in which people perform a variety of work activities rather than hold specific jobs, and are expected to continuously learn skills that will keep them employed.

Employability requires employees to perform a variety of work activities rather than hold specific jobs, and they are expected to continuously learn skills that will keep them employed. From this perspective, individuals must anticipate future organizational needs and develop new competencies that match those needs. Corporate leaders claim that employability is necessary so that organizations can adapt to the rapidly changing business environment. However, employability also has implications for job design, organizational loyalty, workplace stress, and other topics in this book.[42] This is already apparent in Japan, where companies are tearing down the long-established lifetime employment practices in favor of a more performance-oriented arrangement. Global Connections 1.1 describes how many young Japanese have responded to this employability trend by becoming "freeters."

Contingent Work   Another employment shift is the increasing percentage of the workforce in **contingent work.** Contingent work includes any job in which the individual does not have an explicit or implicit contract for long-term employment, or one in which the minimum hours of work can vary in a nonsystematic way. By some estimates, more than 15 percent of the U.S. workforce is employed in some sort of contingent work arrangement. Experts predict that this percentage will continue to rise.[43]

> **contingent work**
>
> Any job in which the individual does not have an explicit or implicit contract for long-term employment, or one in which the minimum hours of work can vary in a nonsystematic way.

Who are these contingent workers? A small, but highly publicized, cadre of professional contingent workers are known as "free agents." Free agents possess valued competencies, so they tend to get desired work in the marketplace. They are usually confident in their independence and are unlikely to be interested in permanent employment.[44] A much larger group of contingent workers, called "temporary temporaries," accept temporary work because they are unable to find permanent employment. Some have outdated skills; others lack work experience. Temporary temporaries accept contingent work to meet basic economic needs, gain work experience, and find leads to permanent employment.

Contingent work has increased in recent years because companies want greater flexibility in terms of the number of people or skill set employed.[45] Information technology also makes it easier for people in some professions to contract out their services without worrying about commuting or travel.

Japan's Rising Tide of Freeters

Imagine a free-and-easy lifestyle with short work hours, minimal stress, and just enough money to shop, play, and maybe even save a little. There are no company obligations, no deadlines to worry about, and relatively little income tax to pay. Sound good? Mika Onodera thinks so. "Living as a freeter, I get more freedom and I like that," says the 28-year-old bakery employee in downtown Tokyo. "Although I cut back on my spending, I have enough money to go out with friends and live comfortably."

Onodera is one of more than 2 million "freeters" in Japan, more than double the number a decade ago. Freeters are young people, including university graduates, who scrape by with low-paying part-time jobs as convenience store clerks, restaurant waiters, building cleaners, and so on. They don't really try too hard to find permanent jobs, don't worry at all about long-term careers, and think job-hopping is a badge of honor. Onodera, for example, is on her fifth job in as many years. Onodera shares an apartment with her sister, but many freeters still live with their parents. Some freeters were pushed into this situation by high unemployment, but many have chosen this lifestyle.

Freeter comes from the English word "free" and the German-origin word "arbeiter," which means casual work. You don't have to look far in Japan for inspiration to become a freeter. Japanese culture traditionally praises people who live to work (rather than the other way around), yet the country's bookshelves are filling up with bestsellers such as *Why Do We Work?*, *Job-Switching King*, *Manual for a Happy Jobless Life*, and *Timetable for Quitting a Company*.

Corporate and government leaders are getting worried that the rising tide of freeters will undermine the country's economic development. Several Japanese government departments have already developed a counterattack, including a program to inculcate in elementary school pupils the importance of full-time jobs, funding for more school counselors, and support for young entrepreneurs who want to start their own businesses.

Sources: Y. Hani, "We Can Work It Out," *Japan Times,* July 13, 2003; "Editorial: Clearing Career Paths," *Asahi Shimbun,* June 19, 2003; "Officials Worry as Younger Japanese Embrace 'Freeting,'" *Taipei Times,* June 4, 2003, p. 12.

More than 2 million young Japanese have become "freeters," with low expectations and little desire to climb the corporate ladder or follow the "live to work" pattern of their parents.

Another reason for the increasing number of contingent workers is that employers offer them few benefits and little job security, so they reduce payroll costs. However, some critics suggest that contingent workers have less

Job Security vs. Employability

- Security
- permanent vs temporary
- company manages vs. self manage
- high vs low skill development

training and work experience, which leads to low-quality products or services and increases accident rates.[46]

Workplace Values and Ethics

The opening story in this chapter mentioned that the success of Google is partly attributed to its values and its careful hiring of people with compatible values. **Values** represent stable, long-lasting beliefs about what is important in a variety of situations that guide our decisions and actions. They are evaluative standards that help us define what is right or wrong, or good or bad, in the world.[47] Values dictate our priorities, our preferences, and our desires. They influence our motivation and decisions. "Ninety-nine percent of what we say is about values," advises Anita Roddick, founder of the Body Shop.[48]

Cultural, personal, professional, and organizational values have been studied by organizational behavior scholars for several decades.[49] *Cultural values,* which we discuss in Chapter 2 (along with personal and ethical values), represent the dominant prescriptions of a society. They are usually influenced by religious, philosophical, and political ideologies. *Personal values* incorporate cultural values, as well as other values socialized by parents, friends, and personal life events. Professional values are held either formally or informally by members of a professional group, such as doctors, engineers, and architects. *Organizational values,* discussed in Chapter 16 on **organizational culture,** are widely and deeply shared by people within the organization.[50]

Importance of Values in the Workplace   Values are not new to organizational behavior, but the popularity of this topic has increased noticeably in recent years. One reason is that corporate leaders are looking for better ways to guide employee decisions and behavior. Today's increasingly educated and independent workforce resents the traditional "command-and-control" supervision, and financial rewards are far from perfect. Values represent a potentially powerful way to keep employees' decisions and actions aligned with corporate goals. Values represent the unseen magnet that pulls employees in the same direction. They foster a common bond and help to ensure that everyone in the organization—regardless of job or rank—has aligned goals.[51]

A second reason for the recent interest in values is that globalization has raised our awareness of and sensitivity to differences in values across cultures. Global organizations face the challenge of ensuring that employees make consistent decisions and actions around the world even though they may have diverse cultural values. Reinforcing a common organizational culture isn't easy, because some organizational values may conflict with some individual and societal values.[52]

The third reason why values have gained prominence is that organizations are under increasing pressure to engage in ethical practices and corporate social responsibility. **Ethics** refers to the study of moral principles or values that determine whether actions are right or wrong and outcomes are good or bad (see Chapter 2). We rely on our ethical values to determine "the right thing to do." Ethical behavior is driven by the moral principles we use to make decisions. These moral principles represent fundamental values. Unfortunately, a lot of people give executives low grades on their ethics report cards these

values
Stable, long-lasting beliefs about what is important in a variety of situations, that guide our decisions and actions

organizational culture
The basic pattern of shared assumptions, values, and beliefs governing the way employees within an organization think about and act on problems and opportunities.

ethics
The study of moral principles or values that determine whether actions are right or wrong and outcomes are good or bad.

corporate social responsibility (CSR)

An organization's moral obligation towards its stakeholders.

stakeholders

Shareholders, customers, suppliers, governments, and any other groups with a vested interest in the organization.

days.[53] The failures of Enron Energy and WorldCom represented two of the largest bankruptcies in American history. More importantly, they have become icons of unethical and possibly illegal conduct by corporate executives.

Corporate Social Responsibility   Over 30 years ago, economist Milton Friedman pronounced that "there is one and only one social responsibility of business—to use its resources and engage in activities designed to increase its profits."[54] Friedman is a respected scholar, but this argument was not one of his more popular—or accurate—statements. Today, any business that follows Friedman's advice will face considerable trouble in the marketplace. Indeed, few people agree with Friedman. According to a recent large survey, more than 70 percent say that business executives have a responsibility to take into account the impact their decisions have on employees, local communities, and the country. In other words, the public expects organizations to engage in corporate social responsibility.[55]

Corporate social responsibility (CSR) refers to an organization's moral obligation toward all of its stakeholders. **Stakeholders** are the shareholders, customers, suppliers, governments, and any other groups with a vested interest in the organization.[56] As part of corporate social responsibility, many companies have adopted the *triple bottom line* philosophy. This means that they try to support or "earn positive returns" in the economic, social, and environmental spheres of sustainability. Firms that adopt the triple bottom line aim to survive and be profitable in the marketplace (economic), but they also intend to maintain or improve conditions for society (social) as well as the physical environment.[57]

More than ever, companies in the United States and elsewhere are coming under scrutiny for their CSR practices. Shareholders, job applicants, current employees, and suppliers are increasingly deciding whether to associate with an organization based on how well it applies virtuous values. "People increasingly prefer to work for or do business with what is deemed to be a socially responsible company," says Nick Wright, London-based head of corporate responsibility at investment bank UBS Warburg.[59]

Not surprisingly, two-thirds of 1,000 chief executives surveyed around the world said corporate social responsibility was vital to the profitability of any company. The problem, according to a study by PricewaterhouseCoopers, is that only 24 percent of the surveyed executives publicly report on their social responsibility practices.[60] McDonald's, Rio Tinto, Nike, Nestlé, and several other companies are beginning to

At Tom's of Maine, employees are encouraged to pay attention to their values, not just corporate goals. "It's management by values and objectives, not just management by objectives," says Tom Chappell, who co-founded the personal care products with his wife, Kate Chappell (both shown in photo). Chappell explains that objectives are the domain of the mind, whereas values are the domain of the heart. "Values bring the whole person to work," he explains. "We employ the whole person, the mind and the soul." Tom Chappell helped to establish The Saltwater Institute, a foundation that helps CEOs and entrepreneurs integrate their personal values with their workplace decisions.[58] How can companies integrate values-based decision making and leadership into the organization?

produce CSR reports or sustainability reviews that assess (or at least discuss) the company's progress toward triple bottom-line goals. Still, critics point out that some of these corporate report cards lack the depth to properly analyze corporate good deeds.[61]

Fortunately, a few companies have pushed the intensity of CSR evaluation beyond public relations. For instance, Vancouver City Savings Credit Union retains an independent, external social auditor to report on the inclusivity, embeddedness, and continuous improvement of its social and environmental performance. The auditor considers how well VanCity genuinely engages its stakeholders, integrates corporate social responsibility into all its operations and policymaking, and applies what it learns to improve future performance on the triple bottom line. "If companies take a chance, and take their corporate strategy in a new direction—one that respects people, the environment, and the bottom line—they will profit in ways they never dreamed of," advises Dave Mowat, CEO of the Canadian financial institution.[62]

The Five Anchors of Organizational Behavior

Globalization, information and communication technology, the changing workforce, emerging employment relationships, and workplace values are just a few of the trends that we will explore in this textbook. To understand these and other topics, organizational behavior scholars rely on a set of basic beliefs or knowledge structures (see Exhibit 1.3). These conceptual anchors represent the way that OB researchers think about organizations and how they should be studied. Let's look at each of these five beliefs that anchor the study of organizational behavior.

The Multidisciplinary Anchor

Organizational behavior is anchored around the idea that the field should develop from knowledge in other disciplines, not just from its own isolated research base.[63] In other words, OB should be multidisciplinary. The upper part of Exhibit 1.4 identifies the traditional disciplines from which organizational

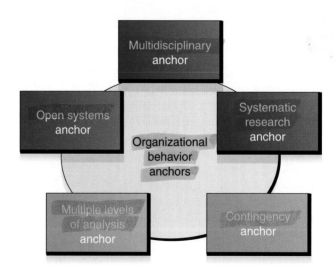

EXHIBIT 1.4	

Multidisciplinary anchor of organizational behavior

Discipline	Relevant OB topics
Traditional disciplines	
Psychology	Drives, perception, attitudes, personality, job stress, emotions, leadership
Sociology	Team dynamics, roles, socialization, communication patterns, organizational power, organizational structure
Anthropology	Corporate culture, organizational rituals, cross-cultural dynamics, organizational adaptation
Political science	Intergroup conflict, coalition formation, organizational power and politics, decision making, organizational environments
Economics	Decision making, negotiation, organizational power
Industrial engineering	Job design, productivity, work measurement
Emerging disciplines	
Communications	Knowledge management, electronic mail, corporate culture, employee socialization
Information systems	Team dynamics, decision making, knowledge management
Marketing	Knowledge management, creativity, decision making
Women's studies	Organizational power, perceptions

behavior knowledge has developed. For instance, sociologists have contributed to our knowledge of team dynamics, organizational socialization, organizational power, and other aspects of the social system. The field of psychology has aided our understanding to most issues relating to individual and interpersonal behavior. Recently, the subfield of evolutionary psychology has contributed new ideas about the origins of human drives and behavior, including innate human drives, social orientations, and cognitive and affective (thinking and feeling) processes.[64]

The bottom part of Exhibit 1.4 identifies some of the emerging fields from which organizational behavior knowledge is acquired. The communications field helps us to understand the dynamics of knowledge management, electronic mail, corporate culture, and employee socialization. Information systems scholars are exploring the effects of information technology on team dynamics, decision making, and knowledge management. Marketing scholars have enhanced our understanding of job satisfaction and customer service, knowledge management, and creativity. Women's studies scholars are studying perceptual biases and power relations between men and women in organizations.

The true test of OB's multidisciplinary anchor is how effectively OB scholars continue to transfer knowledge from traditional and emerging disciplines. History suggests that fields of inquiry tend to become more inwardly focused as they mature.[65] However, some OB scholars have recently argued that OB is hardly inwardly focused. Instead, it probably suffers from a "trade deficit"— importing far more knowledge from other disciplines than is exported to other disciplines. This occurs because many OB scholars are have been trained in other fields (e.g., psychology, sociology) and merely replicate research from those fields in an organizational context. By borrowing heavily from other fields, OB runs the risk of perpetually lagging behind other disciplines and having little of its own knowledge to offer. Thus, while willingly importing ideas from other fields, OB scholars perhaps need to focus more of their research on topics that are unique to organizational behavior.[66]

The Systematic Research Anchor

A second anchor for organizational behavior researchers is their belief in the value of studying organizations through systematic research methods. Traditionally, scholars have relied on the **scientific method** by forming research questions, systematically collecting data, and testing hypotheses against those data. Typically, this approach relies on quantitative data (numeric information) and statistical procedures to test hypotheses. The idea behind the scientific method is to minimize personal biases and distortions about organizational events.

More recently, OB scholars have also adopted a **grounded theory** approach to developing knowledge. Grounded theory is a process of developing a theory through the constant interplay between data gathering and the development of theoretical concepts. This dynamic and cyclical view of the research process allows for observation, participation, and other qualitative methods in the data collection process, rather than just quantitative data collection (i.e., numeric data).[67] Appendix A at the end of this book provides an overview of research design and methods commonly found in organizational behavior studies.

The Contingency Anchor

"It depends" is a phrase that OB scholars often use to answer a question about the best solution to an organizational problem. The statement may seem evasive, yet it reflects an important way of understanding and predicting organizational events, called the **contingency approach.** This anchor states that a particular action may have different consequences in different situations. In other words, no single solution is best in all circumstances.[68]

Many early OB theorists proposed universal rules to predict and explain organizational life, but there are usually too many exceptions to make these "one best way" theories useful. For example, in Chapter 14 we will learn that leaders should use one style (e.g., participation) in some situations and another style (e.g., direction) in other situations. Thus, when faced with a particular problem or opportunity, we need to understand and diagnose the situation and select the strategy most appropriate *under those conditions.*[69]

Although contingency-oriented theories are necessary in most areas of organizational behavior, we should also be wary about carrying this anchor to an extreme. Some contingency models add more confusion than value over universal ones. Consequently, we need to balance the sensitivity of contingency factors with the simplicity of universal theories.

The Multiple Levels of Analysis Anchor

This textbook divides organizational behavior topics into three levels of analysis: individual, team, and organization (see Exhibit 1.5). The individual level includes the characteristics and behaviors of employees as well as the thought

---

scientific method

A set of principles and procedures that help researchers to systematically understand previously unexplained events and conditions.

grounded theory

A process of developing theory through the constant interplay between data gathering and the development of theoretical concepts

contingency approach

The idea that a particular action may have different consequences in different situations.

EXHIBIT 1.5

Three levels of
analysis in
organizational
behavior

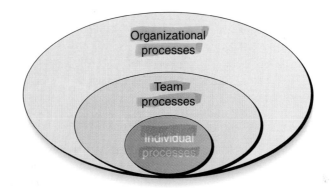

EXHIBIT 1.5

Three levels of analysis in organizational behavior

processes that are attributed to them, such as motivation, perceptions, personalities, attitudes, and values. The team level of analysis looks at the way people interact. This includes team dynamics, decisions, power, organizational politics, conflict, and leadership. At the organizational level, we focus on how people structure their working relationships and on how organizations interact with their environments.

Although an OB topic is typically pegged into one level of analysis, it usually relates to multiple levels.[70] For instance, communication is located in this book as a team (interpersonal) process, but we also recognize that it includes individual and organizational processes. Therefore, you should try to think about each OB topic at the individual, team, and organizational levels, not just at one of these levels.

The Open Systems Anchor

Hewlett-Packard may have lots of buildings and equipment, but CEO Carly Fiorina says that her job is to nurture something that is alive. "I think that a company is a living system," says Fiorina. "It is an organism, it is operating in other living systems, and a leader has to think about the company as a living, breathing system."[71] Carly Fiorina is describing the fifth anchor of organizational behavior—the view that organizations are **open systems.**

open systems

Organizations that take their sustenance from the environment and, in turn, affect that environment through their output.

Organizations are open systems because they take their sustenance from the environment and, in turn, affect that environment through their output. A company's survival and success depend on how well employees sense environmental changes and alter their patterns of behavior to fit those emerging conditions.[72] In contrast, a closed system has all the resources needed to survive without dependence on the external environment. Organizations are never completely closed systems, but monopolies operating in very stable environments can ignore customers and others for a fairly long time without adverse consequences.

As Exhibit 1.6 illustrates, organizations acquire resources from the external environment, including raw materials, employees, financial resources, information, and equipment. Inside the organization are numerous subsystems, such as processes (communication and reward systems), task activities (production, marketing), and social dynamics (informal groups, power dynamics). With the aid of technology (such as equipment, work methods, and information), these subsystems transform inputs into various outputs. Some outputs (e.g., products and services) may be valued by the external environment,

constant process (handwritten)

EXHIBIT 1.6

Open systems view
of organizations

whereas other outputs (e.g., employee layoffs, pollution) have adverse effects. The organization receives feedback from the external environment regarding the value of its outputs and the availability of future inputs. This process is cyclical and, ideally, self-sustaining, so that the organization may continue to survive and prosper.

External Environment and Stakeholders   It is almost a cliché to say that most organizations today operate in more dynamic, fast-paced environments than they did a few decades ago. To illustrate how fast organizations are changing, consider this: In the 1920s, companies stayed on the S&P 500 stock exchange list an average of 67 years. Today, the average company life cycle on the S&P 500 is about 12 years. In other words, your grandparents could work for the same organization all of their lives, whereas you will likely outlive two or three companies.[73] Similarly, the most valued companies in America today—such as Cisco Systems, Electronic Arts, and Microsoft—were either junior start-ups or nonexistent 20 years ago. And unless these firms anticipate and adapt to continual change, few of them will be around 20 years from now.

As open systems, successful organizations monitor their environments and take appropriate steps to maintain a compatible fit with the new external conditions. Recent studies reveal that successful organizations adapt quickly to those rapidly changing environments.[74] They develop a dynamic capability—the ability to change their outputs and transformational processes that produce those outputs—to maintain a close alignment with the external environment. This does not mean that successful organizations rapidly change all of the time. On the contrary, some firms change too quickly, such as by offering products, services, or customer experiences long before the public wants them. The point here is that organizations need to adapt to changing environments, but not so much that they overspend their resources or overshoot stakeholder needs.

Stakeholders represent a central part of the internal and external environment. As mentioned earlier, these include any person or entity with a vested interest in the organization. Stakeholders influence the firm's access to inputs and ability to discharge outputs. And unless they pay attention to the needs of all stakeholders, organizational leaders may find their business in trouble. For instance, leaders may put their organization at risk if they pay attention only to shareholders and ignore the broader corporate social responsibility.[75] We see this stakeholder misalignment when job applicants avoid companies that ignore corporate social responsibility and when organizations fail to treat their employees and suppliers with respect.

Systems as Interdependent Parts   The open systems anchor states that organizations consist of many internal subsystems that need to be continuously aligned with each other. As companies grow, they develop more and more complex subsystems that must coordinate with each other in the process of transforming inputs to outputs.[76] These interdependencies can easily become so complex that a minor event in one subsystem may amplify into serious unintended consequences elsewhere in the organization.

The open systems anchor is an important way of viewing organizations. However, it has traditionally focused on physical resources that enter the organization and are processed into physical goods (outputs). This was representative of the industrial economy but not of the "new economy," where the most valued input is knowledge.

Knowledge Management

Organizational behavior scholars have built on the open system anchor to create an entire subfield of research dedicated to the dynamics of knowledge management. **Knowledge management** is any structured activity that improves an organization's capacity to acquire, share, and use knowledge in ways that improve its survival and success.[77] The knowledge that resides in an organization is called its **intellectual capital,** which is the sum of everything that an organization knows that gives it competitive advantage—including its human capital, structural capital, and relationship capital.[78]

knowledge management
Any structured activity that improves an organization's capacity to acquire, share, and use knowledge in ways that improve its survival and success.

intellectual capital
The sum of an organization's human capital, structural capital, and relationship capital.

■ *Human capital*—This is the knowledge that employees possess and generate, including their skills, experience, and creativity.

■ *Structural capital*—This is the knowledge captured and retained in an organization's systems and structures. It is the knowledge that remains after all the human capital has gone home.

■ *Relationship capital*—This is the value derived from an organization's relationships with customers, suppliers, and other external stakeholders who provide added value for the organization. For example, this includes customer loyalty as well as mutual trust between the organization and its suppliers.[79]

Knowledge Management Processes

Intellectual capital represents the *stock* of knowledge held by an organization. This stock of knowledge is so important that some companies try to measure its value.[80] But knowledge management is much more than the organization's stock of knowledge. It is a *process* that develops an organization's capacity to acquire, share, and use knowledge more effectively. This process is often called **organizational learning** because companies must continuously learn about their various environments in order to survive and succeed through adaptation.[81] The "capacity" to acquire, share, and use knowledge means that companies have established systems, structures, and organizational values that support the knowledge management process. Let's look more closely at some of the strategies companies use to acquire, share, and use knowledge.

organizational learning

The knowledge management process in which organizations acquire, share, and use knowledge to succeed.

Knowledge Acquisition   Knowledge acquisition includes the organization's ability to extract information and ideas from its environment as well as through insight. One of the fastest and most powerful ways to acquire knowledge is through **grafting**—hiring individuals or acquiring entire companies. For instance, graphics chip maker ATI Technologies picked up plenty of knowledge by hiring the most experienced Nortel staff who were recently laid off. "Nortel is the company with the skill sets that ATI is looking for," says an ATI executive.[82] Knowledge also enters the organization when employees learn about the external environment. Wal-Mart executives do this by systematically shopping at competitor stores every week. More commonly, employees acquire external knowledge by meeting with vendors, attending seminars and conferences, and learning directly from clients.[83] A third knowledge acquisition strategy is through experimentation. Companies receive knowledge through insight as a result of research and other creative processes (see Chapter 10).[84]

grafting

The process of acquiring knowledge by hiring individuals or buying entire companies.

individual learning

experimentation

communication

Knowledge Sharing   Many organizations are reasonably good at acquiring knowledge, but they waste this resource by not effectively disseminating it. As several executives have lamented: "I wish we knew what we know." Studies report that knowledge sharing is usually the weakest link in knowledge management.[85] Valuable ideas sit idly—rather like unused inventory—or remain hidden "silos of knowledge" throughout the organization. One organizational unit might apply useful ideas to improve performance or customer service, whereas a nearby unit has not discovered these better procedures.

Organizations need better communication to improve knowledge sharing (see Chapter 11). Some companies encourage knowledge sharing through **communities of practice.** These are informal groups bound together by shared expertise and passion for a particular activity or interest.[86] Great Harvest Bread Co. applies this idea by encouraging its 140 highly autonomous franchisees to participate in the company's learning community. This community consists of casual visits, telephone calls, and e-mails to other Great Harvest franchisees. "We had an epiphany a long time ago," says Tom McMakin, chief operating officer of the Dillon, Montana, company. "Owners profit more from each other's experiences than from the 'wisdom' of a central world headquarters."[87]

communities of practice

Informal groups bound together by shared expertise and passion for a particular activity or interest.

AWARENESS

empowerment

Knowledge Use   Acquiring and sharing knowledge are wasted exercises unless knowledge is effectively put to use. To do this, employees must realize that the knowledge is available and that they have enough freedom to apply it. This requires a culture that supports experiential learning (see Chapter 3).

Organizational Memory

Intellectual capital can be lost as quickly as it is acquired.[88] Corporate leaders need to recognize that they are the keepers of an **organizational memory.** This unusual metaphor refers to the storage and preservation of intellectual capital. It includes information that employees possess as well as knowledge embedded in the organization's systems and structures. It includes documents, objects, and anything else that provides meaningful information about how the organization should operate.

How do organizations retain intellectual capital? One way is by keeping good employees. While many high-tech companies laid off an unprecedented number of people to cut costs during the recent "tech wreck," Apple Computer held on to its talent. "Our main asset is human talent, and we cannot afford to lose it," explains Apple's chief financial officer, Fred Anderson.[90] A second strategy is to systematically transfer knowledge before employees leave. This occurs when new recruits apprentice with skilled employees, thereby acquiring knowledge that is not documented.

A third organizational memory strategy is to transfer knowledge into structural capital.[91] This includes bringing out hidden knowledge, organizing it, and putting it in a form that can be available to others. This is what the organizing committee for the Sydney Olympics (SOCOG) did. SOCOG received mostly informal and anecdotal information from the Atlanta Olympics on how to run this type of event. To ensure that cities hosting future Olympics would have more knowledge, every division and functional area within SOCOG was asked to complete an extensive template of how they set up their operations. This resulted in 90 manuals that document everything from organizational structure and stakeholders to staffing and budgets.[92]

A few years ago, Evercare (formerly Helmac) decided to move its headquarters and manufacturing from Flint, Michigan, to Waynesboro, Georgia. The move nearly killed the manufacturer of Lint Pic-up products because none of Evercare's production employees wanted to leave Flint. So, when the company's executives arrived in Georgia to set up production, they struggled to rebuild the company's manufacturing and distribution systems from scratch. "Nothing was documented," recalls manufacturing vice president John Moore, shown here with vice president of distribution Barbara Tomaszewski. "All of the knowledge, all of the practices were built in people's heads." The good news was that the rebuilt company seems stronger because employees did not learn some of the past practices that didn't work.[89] How could other companies minimize this loss of organizational memory in similar situations?

Before leaving the topic of organizational memory and knowledge management, you should know that successful companies also *unlearn*. Sometimes it is appropriate for organizations to selectively forget certain knowledge.[93] This means that they should cast off the routines and patterns of behavior that are no longer appropriate. Employees need to rethink their perceptions, such as how they should interact with customers and which is the "best way" to perform a task. As we shall discover in Chapter 17, unlearning is essential for organizational change.

The Journey Begins

This chapter gives you some background about the field of organizational behavior. But it's only the beginning of our journey. Throughout this book, we will challenge you to learn new ways of thinking about how people work in and around organizations. We begin this process in Chapter 2 by presenting a basic model of individual behavior, then introducing over the next six chapters various stable and mercurial characteristics of individuals that relate to elements of the individual behavior model. Next, this book moves to the team level of analysis. We begin by examining a basic model of team effectiveness and specific features of high-performance teams, then we consider decision making and creativity, communication, power and politics, conflict and negotiation, and leadership in team settings. Finally, we shift our focus to the organizational level of analysis, where the topics of organizational structure, organizational culture, and organizational change are examined in detail.

Chapter Summary

Organizational behavior is a relatively young field of inquiry that studies what people think, feel, and do in and around organizations. Organizations are groups of people who work interdependently toward some purpose. OB concepts help us to predict and understand organizational events, adopt more accurate theories of reality, and influence organizational events. This field of knowledge also improves the organization's financial health.

There are several trends in organizational behavior. Globalization requires corporate decision makers to be sensitive to cultural differences; it seems to be associated with the recent rise in job insecurity, work intensification, and other sources of work-related stress. Information technology blurs the temporal and spatial boundaries between individuals and the organizations that employ them. It has contributed to the growth of telecommuting—an alternative work arrangement where employees work at home or a remote site, usually with a computer connection to the office. Information technology is also a vital ingredient in virtual teams—cross-functional groups that operate across space, time, and organizational boundaries.

Another trend in organizations is the increasingly diverse workforce. Diversity potentially improves decision making, team performance, and customer service, but it also presents new challenges. A fourth trend is the employment relationships that have emerged from the changing workforce, information and communication technology, and globalization forces. Employment relationship trends include employability and contingent work. Values and ethics represent the fifth trend. In particular, companies are learning to apply values in a global environment, and they are under pressure to abide by ethical values and higher standards of corporate social responsibility.

Organizational behavior scholars rely on a set of basic beliefs to study organizations. These anchors include beliefs that OB knowledge should be multidisciplinary and based on systematic research, that organizational events usually have contingencies, that organizational behavior can be viewed from three levels of analysis (individual, team, and organization), and that organizations are open systems.

The open systems anchor suggests that organizations have interdependent parts that work together to continually monitor and transact with the external environment. They acquire resources from the environment, transform them through technology, and return outputs to the environment. The external environment consists of the natural and social conditions outside the organization. External environments are generally highly turbulent today, so organizations must become adaptable and responsive.

Knowledge management develops an organization's capacity to acquire, share, and use knowledge in ways that improve its survival and success. Intellectual capital is knowledge that resides in an organization, including its human capital, structural capital, and relationship capital. It is a firm's main source of competitive advantage. Organizations acquire knowledge through grafting, individual learning, and experimentation. Knowledge sharing occurs mainly through various forms of communication. Knowledge sharing includes communities of practice, networks where people share their expertise and passion for a particular activity or interest. Knowledge use occurs when employees realize that the knowledge is available and that they have enough freedom to apply it. Organizational memory refers to the storage and preservation of intellectual capital.

Key Terms

communities of practice, p. 24

contingency approach, p. 20

contingent work, p. 14

corporate social responsibility (CSR), p. 17

employability, p. 14

ethics, p. 16

globalization, p. 8

grafting, p. 24

grounded theory, p. 20

intellectual capital, p. 23

knowledge management, p. 23

open systems, p. 21

organizational behavior (OB), p. 4

organizational culture, p. 16

organizational learning, p. 24

organizational memory, p. 25

organizations, p. 6

scientific method, p. 20

stakeholders, p. 17

telecommuting, p. 10

values, p. 16

virtual teams, p. 11

Discussion Questions

1. A friend suggests that organizational behavior courses are useful only to people who will enter management careers. Discuss the accuracy of your friend's statement.

2. Look through the list of chapters in this textbook and discuss how globalization could influence each organizational behavior topic.

3. Corporate social responsibility is one of the hottest issues in corporate boardrooms these days, partly because it is becoming increasingly important to employees and other stakeholders. In your opinion, why have stakeholders given CSR more attention recently? Does abiding by CSR standards potentially cause companies to have conflicting objectives with some stakeholders in some situations?

4. "Organizational theories should follow the contingency approach." Comment on the accuracy of this statement.

5. Employees in the water distribution unit of a large city were put into teams and encouraged to find ways to improve efficiency. The teams boldly crossed departmental boundaries and areas of management discretion in search of problems. Employees working in other parts of the city began to complain about these intrusions. Moreover, when some team ideas were implemented, the city managers discovered that a dollar saved in the water distribution unit may have cost the organization two dollars in higher costs elsewhere. Use the open systems anchor to explain what happened here.

6. After hearing a seminar on knowledge management, a mining company executive argues that this perspective ignores the fact that mining companies could not rely on knowledge alone to stay in business. They also need physical capital (such as digging and ore processing equipment) and land (where the minerals are located). In fact, these two may be more important than what employees carry around in their heads. Discuss the merits of the mining executive's comments.

7. At a recent seminar on information technology, you heard a consultant say that over 30 percent of U.S. companies use software to manage documents and exchange information, whereas firms in Europe are just beginning to adopt this technology. Based on this, the consultant concluded that "knowledge management in Europe is at its beginning stages." In other words, few firms in Europe practice knowledge management. Comment on this consultant's statement.

8. BusNews Corporation is the leading stock market and business news service. Over the past two years, BusNews has experienced increased competition from other news providers. These competitors have brought in Internet and other emerging computer technologies to link customers with information more quickly. There is little knowledge within BusNews about how to use these computer technologies. Based on the knowledge acquisition processes for knowledge management, explain how BusNews might gain the intellectual capital necessary to become more competitive in this respect.

CASE STUDY 1.1

PFIZER-PHARMACIA MERGER

Christina Stamper, Western Michigan University

In July 2002, Pfizer, Inc., announced the acquisition of Pharmacia Corporation, which would create the largest pharmaceutical company in the world with a projected $48 billion in annual revenue and a research budget of more than $7 billion. The CEO of Pfizer, Hank McKinnell, stated, "The combination brings together two young, strong, broad and complementary product portfolios, enhanced research and development pipelines and outstanding sales and marketing organizations." However, before the companies could operate as one entity, their merger had to be approved by both the European Union and the U.S. Federal Trade Commission to ensure there were no violations of antitrust laws. During the ensuing nine months required to gain the approval of both organizations, employees at Pharmacia were increasingly concerned about their future employment with the company. This concern was especially intense in Kalamazoo, Michigan, where Pharmacia was the largest employer in the area with approximately 7,300 total workers.

Pfizer announced that it would seek $2.5 billion in total cost savings as a result of the merger. This created speculation in the Kalamazoo area that much of these cost savings would result from reduced labor costs due to downsizing, as well as the complete closure of one or more local operations. Pharmacia had several business sites in Kalamazoo County, including manufacturing in Portage; human and animal research and development operations in Kalamazoo, Portage, and Richland; and allergy diagnostic operations in Kalamazoo.

While other employees in Pharmacia were worried about their financial futures, the 1,250 research scientists at the "Discovery" research and development site held a bit more hope for their jobs. There was ample evidence that this site, which focused on creating drugs for infectious and central nervous system diseases, was considered by many to be one of the most effective in the industry. Therefore, many employees at this site, in addition to community leaders, thought that Mr. McKinnell would retain this operation almost intact, since he had stated the importance of improving Pfizer's drug "pipeline," a term used to describe the process of testing, developing, and producing the drug for market.

In April 2003, when it was announced that the merger would occur in the next few months, the anxiety about job loss in the community hit a fever pitch. In addition to the Pharmacia employees who could potentially lose jobs and thus their income, community leaders were concerned about the "trickle-down" effect on other area businesses that provide products and services to these consumers, as well as the effect on the tax bases of the local communities (a loss estimated to be around $9.3 million per year). There was so much concern that local governmental and business leaders joined forces to create a $635 million incentive plan to offer Pfizer to keep local jobs. Even state government officials stepped in to try to keep jobs in the area.

After meeting with Michigan's governor Jennifer Granholm to discuss state Medicaid laws designed to reduce drug costs (which would be unfavorable to Pfizer), Mr. McKinnell stated:

> It's clear that Michigan has a budget problem. We respect that and we're certainly willing to work with the state to resolve that problem. We need to make sure that the state understands the complexity of our business and how that is related to what we do in Michigan and around the world. Almost every state has a need to control spending. We just think there are smart ways to do it and dumb ways to do it.

Some in the press interpreted Mr. McKinnell's statements as an attempt to coerce Michigan's government leaders into removing the Medicaid policies, using local jobs as leverage.

On April 22, a senior vice president at Pfizer sent the Kalamazoo city commissioners, Portage city council, and other local government bodies a memo warning of "mass layoffs" in each of their communities. This memo was sent as required by the federal Worker Adjustment Retraining and Notification Act (WARN), which is designed to give communities ample notice when facing substantial layoffs of local jobs. The memo stated that "the number of affected employees cannot be estimated at this time, but it is anticipated that the number of terminated employees will reach the threshold numbers for mass layoff under the regulations cited." A "mass layoff" is defined by WARN as affecting at least 500 employees.

The reaction to the memos in the local community was strong. Regarding possible losses to the city and surrounding areas, Kalamazoo's mayor, Robert Jones (a retired Pharmacia scientist), was quoted in the local press: "It is as serious as it gets. We have seen in this state cities with major manufacturers that pull out and leave brownfields, how devastating it can be to those cities." Kalamazoo city manager Pat DiGiovanni described various situations that could occur, including seeking a financial bailout from the state of Michigan or possible bankruptcy of the city if Pfizer were to close down operations.

On April 24, Pfizer CEO Hank McKinnell made an unscheduled trip to the Kalamazoo area to try to address the concerns raised by the memo. In meetings with local officials, he stated that there would be a reduction in jobs in the area, including those at the downtown Kalamazoo Discovery site. At a quickly organized press conference, Mr. McKinnell stated, "Most jobs will stay here, that's No. 1. There will be no change to most jobs on (the Kalamazoo research) site. There will be some movement of jobs from here to elsewhere . . . and there will be movement of jobs from elsewhere to here." He was quoted as saying that the memo was "a really bad idea," which gave the impression that Pfizer was pulling out of downtown Kalamazoo. Further, he stated:

> [The memo] created a great deal of uncertainty and pain, frankly, not only within the people working on this site and their families but within the community. In my discussion of how we might respond to what was an unfortunate accident, which we take full responsibility for and apologize for . . . it seemed to me the best way to do that would be for me to come to Kalamazoo and talk to the senior leaders on this site.

In addition, he assured city leaders that Pfizer would not pull out of the Discovery site, and that there would "be research people in downtown Kalamazoo. It will be different because we need to fit our capability elsewhere. But we are not going to put plywood over the windows and close the doors."

On April 29, employees were notified about the reorganization decisions made by Pfizer. Kalamazoo was designated as the primary drug-safety evaluation site, meaning the animal research operations in Richland would grow. Portage would also see growth in its manufacturing site, becoming Pfizer's largest site in the country. However, the research and development work at the Discovery site in downtown Kalamazoo would be halted or moved to other sites in St. Louis, Missouri, and Ann Arbor, Michigan. A Pfizer representative declined to estimate how many total employees would lose their jobs, but estimates have reached about 2,000 for the Kalamazoo area. Mr. DiGiovanni, the city manager, stated that, "All in all, we did better than I think people expected. There are a lot more hurting communities (worldwide) today than Kalamazoo, Michigan."

Pfizer officials argue that their decision to base two global centers (drug safety and manufacturing) in the Kalamazoo area indicates a strong local commitment and good organizational citizenship. However, quotes from former Pharmacia employees imply something different:

Look, there was blood on the floor when they (Pfizer) got done with Kalamazoo. The core mission-critical functions of a pharmaceutical company is [sic] drug discovery, clinical development, manufacturing, and sales and marketing. Ten years ago they were all present in Kalamazoo. Today we've lost discovery, clinical development, and sales and marketing. We've retained manufacturing, but in the long run that is vulnerable because of cheaper offshore manufacturing capability.

You save so much money based on the elimination of jobs without considering the skills here. Our skills are better than that of those who retained their jobs elsewhere.

They told us they would look over the operations and take the best from each company. And we thought, well, everything here works great, even better than what they [Pfizer] have, so they'll keep us. We had much more in the pipeline then they did. You would think they would have thought since they were buying this world-class operation that they'd want to keep it together, but instead they're breaking it up . . . It would be like buying a machine that works really well and taking it apart and giving it all new parts. It's not going to work as well.

Discussion Questions

1. Did Hank McKinnell handle the Medicare situation and WARN memo in an ethical manner? What would you have done if you were in Mr. McKinnell's place?

2. What is your opinion about how Pfizer is acting as an "organizational citizen"? What

has the company done that has shown good or inadequate social responsibility?

3. What factors should have been considered in Pfizer's decision to restructure its newly merged organization? Do you think it made good decisions? What would you have done differently with regard to laying off employees?

Sources: "Pfizer Facts," *Kalamazoo Gazette,* April 29, 2003; "Pfizer Ups Ante with Pharmacia Deal," *Mergers and Acquisitions* 37, no. 9 (September 2002), pp. 15–16; J. Bennett, "Michigan Will Become Heart of Pfizer," *Detroit Free Press,* April 30, 2003; E. Finnerty, "Pfizer Notification Gives Kalamazoo Officials Reason to Speculate," *Kalamazoo Gazette,* April 23, 2003; E. Finnerty, "Researchers Say Pfizer's Choices Create Bitterness," *Kalamazoo Gazette,* May 4, 2003; "Pfizer Job Decisions Next Week," *Kalamazoo Gazette,* April 22, 2003; D. Haar, "CEO Strong-Arming States over Medicaid Policies," *Hartford (CT) Courant,* April 25, 2003; L. Jarvis,"Pfizer Redefines Role as Pharma Juggernaut with Pharmacia Deal," *Chemical Market Reporter* 262, no. 3 (July 22–29, 2002), pp. 1–10; A. Jones, "Downtown to Lose Drug Discovery Research and Medical Development," *Kalamazoo Gazette,* April 30, 2003; A. Jones, "It's Good-Bye Pharmacia, Day One for New Pfizer," *Kalamazoo Gazette,* April 16, 2003; J. Prichard, "Pfizer to Transfer Some Michigan Jobs, Add Others," *Associated Press State and Local Wire,* April 30, 2003; J. C. Parikh, "Pfizer Workers Sort Out Feelings about Job Loss," *Kalamazoo Gazette,* May 5, 2003; L. J. Sellers, "Pfizer Buys Another Marketing Partner," *Pharmaceutical Executive* 22, no. 8 (August 2002), p. 16; L. Turner, "Pfizer Chief Apologizes, Says Most Jobs Will Stay," *Kalamazoo Gazette,* April 25, 2003; L. Turner, "Pfizer Jobs Will Remain in Kalamazoo, but Now the Debate Begins. Are Those Jobs Vital or Expendable?" *Kalamazoo Gazette,* May 1, 2003.

CASE STUDY 1.2

ANCOL CORPORATION

Paul Sims was delighted when Ancol Corporation offered him the job of manager at its Lexington, Kentucky, plant. Sims was happy enough managing a small metal stamping plant with another company, but the invitation to apply for the plant manager job at one of the leading metal fabrication companies was irresistible. Although the Lexington plant was the smallest of Ancol's 15 operations, the plant manager position was a valuable first step in a promising career.

One of Sims's first observations at Ancol's Lexington plant was that relations between employees and management were strained. Taking a page from a recent executive seminar he had attended on building trust in the workplace, Sims ordered the removal of all time clocks from the plant. Instead, the plant would assume that employees had put in their full shift. This symbolic gesture, he believed, would establish a new level of credibility and strengthen relations between management and employees at the site.

Initially, the 250 production employees at the Lexington plant appreciated their new freedom. They felt respected and saw this gesture as a sign of positive change from the new plant manager. Two months later, however, problems started to appear. A few people began showing up late, leaving early, or taking extended lunch breaks. Although this represented only about 5 percent of the employees, others found the situation unfair. Moreover, the increased absenteeism levels were beginning to have a noticeable effect on plant productivity. The problem had to be managed.

Sims asked supervisors to observe and record when the employees came or went and to discuss attendance problems with those abusing their privileges. But the supervisors had no previous experience keeping attendance and many lacked the necessary interpersonal skills to discuss the matter with subordinates. Employees resented the reprimands, so relations with supervisors deteriorated. The additional responsibility of keeping track of attendance also made it difficult for supervisors to complete their other responsibilities. After just a few months, Ancol found it necessary to add another supervisor position and reduce the number of employees assigned to each supervisor.

But the problems did not end there. Without time clocks, the payroll department could not deduct pay for the amount of time that employees were late. Instead, a letter of reprimand was placed in the employee's personnel file. However, this required yet more time and additional skills from the supervisors. Employees did not want these letters to become a permanent record, so they filed grievances with their labor union. The number of grievances doubled over six months, requiring even more time for union officials and supervisors to handle these disputes.

Nine months after removing the time clocks, Paul Sims met with union officials, who agreed that it would be better to put the time clocks back in. Employee–management relations had deteriorated below the level when Sims had started. Supervisors were overworked. Productivity had dropped due to poorer attendance records and increased administrative workloads.

A couple of months after the time clocks were put back in place, Sims attended an operations meeting at Ancol's headquarters in Cincinnati. During lunch, Sims described the time clock incident to Liam Jackson, Ancol's plant manager in Portland, Oregon. Jackson looked surprised, then chuckled. He explained that the previous manager at his plant had done something like that with similar consequences six or seven years earlier. The manager had left some time ago, but Jackson heard about the earlier time clock incident from a supervisor during a recent retirement party.

"I guess it's not quite like lightning striking the same place twice," said Sims to Jackson. "But it sure feels like it."

Discussion Questions

1. Use the systems theory model to explain what happened when Ancol removed the time clocks.

2. What changes should occur to minimize the likelihood of these problems in the future?

Source: © Copyright 2000 Steven L. McShane. This case is based on actual events, but names and some facts have been changed to provide a fuller case discussion.

CASE STUDY **1.3**

PLANET STARBUCKS

BusinessWeek The Starbucks coffee shop on Sixth Avenue and Pine Street in downtown Seattle sits serene and orderly, but not long ago it was the center of attention by antiglobalization protesters. As Starbucks caffeinates the world, it must increasingly address the dynamics of its size and global reach. The coffee chain is expanding into other countries at a time when American cities are becoming saturated. But with this expansion come new challenges and risks. Meanwhile, the company's dramatic growth, along with workforce changes over the past decade, have affected employee morale, motivation, and burnout.

This *Business Week* case study looks at the globalization of Starbuck's Corporation as well as the new challenges it faces in the United States. The article describes the problems and opportunities the company has experienced overseas. It also details some of the workforce issues in the United States. Read through this *Business Week* article at www.mhhe.com/mcshane3e and prepare for the discussion questions below.

Discussion Questions

1. What are the main problems that Starbucks faces as it becomes a global organization?

2. This article identifies issues that Starbucks is experiencing with employees in the United States. What are these issues and, in your opinion, what are the main causes of these problems?

Source: S. Holmes, "Planet Starbucks," *Business Week,* September 9, 2002, p. 100.

HUMAN CHECKERS

Purpose This exercise is designed to help students understand the importance and application of organizational behavior concepts.

Materials None, but the instructor has more information about the team's task.

Instructions

- *Step 1*—Form teams with six students. If possible, each team should have a private location where team members can plan and practice the required task without being observed or heard by other teams.
- *Step 2*—All teams will receive special instructions in class about the team's assigned task. All teams have the same task and will have the same amount of time to plan and practice the task. At the end of this planning and practice, each team will be timed while completing the task in class. The team that completes the task in the least time wins.
- *Step 3*—No special materials are required or allowed for this exercise. Although the task is not described here, students should learn the following rules for planning and implementing the task:

  Rule 1—You cannot use any written form of communication or any props to assist in the planning or implementation of this task.

  Rule 2—You may speak to other students on your team at any time during the planning and implementation of this task.

  Rule 3—When performing the task, you must move only in the direction of your assigned destination. In other words, you can only move forward, not backward.

  Rule 4—When performing the task, you can move forward to the next space, but only if it is vacant (see Exhibit 1).

  Rule 5—When performing the task, you can move forward two spaces, if that space is vacant. In other words, you can move around a student who is one space in front of you to the next space if that space is vacant (see Exhibit 2).

- *Step 4*—When all teams have completed their task, the class will discuss the implications of this exercise for organizational behavior.

EXHIBIT 1

EXHIBIT 2

Discussion Questions

1. Identify organizational behavior concepts that the team applied to complete this task.

2. What personal theories of people and work teams were applied to complete this task?

3. What organizational behavior problems occurred and what actions were (or should have been) taken to solve them?

IT ALL MAKES SENSE

Purpose This exercise is designed to help you understand how organizational behavior knowledge can help you to understand life in organizations.

Instructions Read each of the statements below and circle whether each statement is true or false, in your opinion. The class will consider the answers to each question and discuss the implications for studying organizational behavior. After reviewing these statements, the instructor will provide information about the most appropriate answer. (Note: This activity may be done as a self-assessment or as a team activity.)

1. True False A happy worker is a productive worker.
2. True False Decision makers tend to continue supporting a course of action even though information suggests that the decision is ineffective.
3. True False Organizations are more effective when they prevent conflict among employees.
4. True False It is better to negotiate alone than as a team.
5. True False Companies are most effective when they have a strong corporate culture.
6. True False Employees perform better without stress.
7. True False Effective organizational change always begins by pinpointing the source of its current problems.
8. True False Female leaders involve employees in decisions to a greater degree than do male leaders.
9. True False People in Japan value group harmony and duty to the group (high collectivism) more than do Americans (low collectivism).
10. True False Top-level executives tend to exhibit a Type A behavior pattern (i.e., hard-driving, impatient, competitive, short-tempered, strong sense of time urgency, rapid talkers).
11. True False Employees usually feel overreward inequity when they are paid more than co-workers performing the same work.

TELEWORK DISPOSITION ASSESSMENT

Purpose This exercise is designed to help you assess the extent to which you possess the personal characteristics most suitable for telecommuting.

Instructions This instrument asks you to indicate the degree to which you agree or disagree with each of the statements provided. You need to be honest with yourself to make a reasonable estimate of your locus of control. The results provide a rough indication of how well you would adapt to telework. Please keep in mind that this scale considers only your personal characteristics. Other factors, such as organizational, family, and technological systems support, must also be taken into account.

 After studying the preceding material, be sure to check out our website at
www.mhhe.com/mcshane3e
for more in-depth information and interactivities that correspond to this chapter.

Individual Behavior and Processes

Individual Behavior, Values, and Personality

Learning Objectives

After reading this chapter, you should be able to:

■ Diagram the MARS model.

■ Describe three basic ways to match individual competencies to job requirements.

■ Identify five types of individual behavior in organizations.

■ Define values and explain why values congruence is important.

■ Define the six main values that vary across cultures.

■ List four ethical principles.

■ Explain how moral intensity, ethical sensitivity, and the situation influence ethical behavior.

■ Identify the "Big Five" personality dimensions.

■ Summarize the personality concepts behind the Myers-Briggs Type Indicator.

■ Explain how personality relates to Holland's model of vocational choice.

*I*t is no accident that the Container Store is a runaway leader in the hypercompetitive retail business. The Dallas-based seller of customized storage products pays attention to several key drivers to ensure that employees provide unflagging customer service. The Container Store begins by carefully selecting job applicants who are conscientious and embrace customer service values. To attract and keep this talent, the company pays 50 percent or more than typical retail salaries and maintains a respectful culture. "We are absolute wild-eyed fanatics when it comes to only hiring great people," says president and CEO Kip Tindell, who cofounded the Container Store with partner and chairman Garrett Boone. "One of our Foundation Principles™ is that one great person is equal to three good people in terms of business productivity."

Once hired, full-time employees receive 241 hours of training during their first year, compared to under a dozen hours for frontline staff at most other retailers. This training provides more than specialized skills and knowledge to analyze customer storage needs. It also teaches fundamental values that encourage employees to go beyond the customer's short-term expectations.

The Container Store is a role model for applying the key drivers of employee performance in customer service.

"Helping people is an obligation on our part," says Boone. "It's not a religious imperative. It's an ethical imperative to really help that person to the best of your ability."

The Container Store also motivates employees beyond generous pay and benefits. Team members in each store collectively set goals and provide supportive feedback in the daily "huddle." Employees also call in to a special celebration voice mail system to tell stories about co-workers who went above and beyond the call of duty. To create a sense of ownership and involvement, employees receive ongoing information about the company and have a lot of freedom to make decisions. "A funny thing happens when you take the time to educate your employees, pay them well, and treat them as equals," says Kip Tindell. "You end up with extremely motivated and enthusiastic people."[1] ∎

The Container Store applies several key concepts that are the drivers of individual behavior and performance. Employee motivation is supported through rewards and recognition. Selection and training ensure that staff members are able to perform the tasks. The Container Store's strong customer service values provide clear role perceptions to keep employees steered in the right direction. And as Garrett Boone stated, these values also maintain solid ethical standards throughout the company.

This chapter begins by presenting a basic model of individual behavior and results (called the MARS model) and outlining the main types of behavior in the workplace. The next section looks closely at values, including Schwartz's model of personal values, issues relating to values congruence, the dynamics of cross-cultural values, and key features of ethical values in the workplace. In the latter part of this chapter, we examine the relationship between personality and behavior, the five-factor model of personality, the Myers-Briggs Type Indicator, and other personality characteristics that are often discussed in organizational behavior research. The chapter closes by examining Holland's theory of personality and career fit.

MARS Model of Individual Behavior and Results

Why do individuals behave the way they do and perform well or poorly in the workplace? This question has been the Holy Grail of much research in organizational behavior, and it is the focus of the next six chapters in this book. As you might imagine, OB scholars have looked at numerous variables drawn from several disciplines and theoretical perspectives to understand the dynamics of individual behavior. Over the next few pages, we begin the journey to understand these dynamics by presenting a basic model of individual behavior (called the MARS model) and outlining the main types of behavior in organizational settings. Then, we set out to examine the main individual difference topics underlying the MARS model, beginning with two of the most stable influences: values and personality.

The MARS model, illustrated in Exhibit 2.1, is a useful starting point to understanding the drivers of individual behavior and results. The model highlights the four factors that directly influence an employee's voluntary behavior and resulting performance—motivation, ability, role perceptions, and situational factors. These four factors are represented by the acronym "MARS" in the model's name.[2]

The MARS model shows that these four factors have a combined effect on individual performance. If any factor weakens, employee performance will decrease. For example, enthusiastic salespeople (motivation) who understand their job duties (role perceptions) and have sufficient resources (situational factors) will not perform their jobs as well if they lack sufficient knowledge and sales skill (ability). Thus, the Container Store and other companies that excel in customer service pay attention to all four factors in the MARS model.

Exhibit 2.1 also shows that the four factors in the MARS model are influenced by several other individual variables that we will discuss over the next few chapters. Personality and values are the most stable characteristics,[3] so we look at them later in this chapter. Emotions, attitudes, and stress are much more fluid characteristics, whereas individual perceptions and learning usually lie somewhere between. Each of these factors relates to the MARS model

EXHIBIT 2.1   MARS model of individual behavior and results

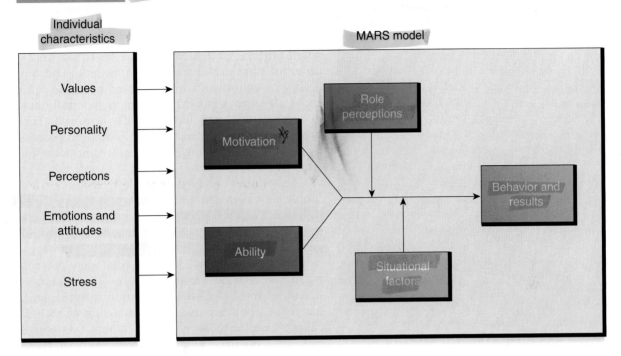

in various ways. For example, personal values affect an employee's motivation through emotions and tend to shape role perceptions through the perceptual process. Learning influences an employee's ability, role perceptions, and motivation, as we shall learn in Chapter 3. Before examining these individual characteristics, let's briefly introduce the four elements of the MARS model, followed by an overview of the different types of individual behavior and results in the workplace.

Employee Motivation

Motivation represents the forces within a person that affect his or her direction, intensity, and persistence of voluntary behavior.[4] *Direction* refers to the fact that motivation is goal-oriented, not random. People are motivated to arrive at work on time, finish a project a few hours early, or aim for many other targets. *Intensity* is the amount of effort allocated to the goal. For example, two employees might be motivated to finish their project a few hours early (direction), but only one of them puts forth enough effort (intensity) to achieve this goal. Finally, motivation involves varying levels of *persistence,* that is, continuing the effort for a certain amount of time. Employees sustain their effort until they reach their goal or give up beforehand. Chapter 5 looks more closely at the conceptual foundations of employee motivation, and Chapter 6 considers some applied motivation practices.

Ability

Employee abilities also make a difference in behavior and task performance. **Ability** includes both the natural aptitudes and learned capabilities required to successfully complete a task. *Aptitudes* are the natural talents that help

motivation
The forces within a person that affect his or her direction, intensity, and persistence of voluntary behavior

ability
Both the natural aptitudes and learned capabilities required to successfully complete a task.

Fly-fishing is barely known in Chiang Mai, Thailand, but lure manufacturers have flocked there for some of the world's best fish fly making. "Chiang Mai is to fly tying what Silicon Valley is to computers," says an executive at Targus Fly & Feather, a Mesa, Arizona, company with large fly-making operations in Thailand. Local residents have a high level of finger dexterity, thanks to centuries of making local handicrafts, and this aptitude is well-suited to fish fly tying. Even so, Kwanruen Thanomrungruang (shown in photo) and other employees require two months of training and don't become fully proficient at fly tying for up to two years.[5] Which of the three person–job matching strategies would be most effective for fly-tying companies in Thailand?

competencies
Skills, knowledge, aptitudes, and other characteristics of people that lead to superior performance.

employees learn specific tasks more quickly and perform them better. For example, you cannot learn finger dexterity; rather, some people have a more natural ability than others to manipulate small objects with their fingers. There are many different physical and mental aptitudes, and our ability to acquire skills is affected by these aptitudes. *Learned capabilities* refer to the skills and knowledge that you have actually acquired. This includes the physical and mental skills you possess as well as the knowledge you acquire and store for later use.

Employee Competencies Skills, knowledge, aptitudes, and other personal characteristics that lead to superior performance are typically bunched together into the concept of **competencies**.[6] Competencies are generic, meaning that they are relevant for a wide variety of jobs. For instance, Ericsson, the Swedish telecommunications giant, has a "competence triangle" consisting of technical/professional competencies, human competencies, and business competencies. Each of these generic groups has a set of more specific competencies. Ericsson lists teamwork, communications, cultural awareness, and other competencies necessary for social interaction in its human competency category.[7]

Most large organizations spend a lot of money finding out the key competencies for superior work performance, but the competency perspective has a few problems.[8] One concern is disagreement whether competencies include only knowledge and abilities or also include personal values and personality traits. Another concern is that some companies describe competencies so broadly that they are difficult to measure or understand in practical terms. Last, most firms try to identify a single cluster of competencies, yet researchers increasingly believe that alternative combinations of competencies may be equally successful. In other words, companies hire people with one set of skills and abilities, yet job applicants with a different set of personal characteristics would be equally effective in the job.

Person–Job Matching Three basic methods are used to match individuals and their competencies with job requirements.[9] One strategy is to select applicants whose existing competencies best fit the required tasks. This includes comparing each applicant's competencies with the requirements of the job or work unit. A second approach is to provide training so employees develop required skills and knowledge.

The third person–job matching strategy is to redesign the job so employees are only given tasks within their capabilities. This approach was applied recently at AT&T's customer service operations in Dallas. Employees were feeling overwhelmed by the variety of products they sold—analog and digital cable, Internet, HDTV, home theater, and so on. "Our employees just said 'Help! This is way too complex, we're trained on three things and we need help!'" says Lucy Noonan, AT&T's system's VP of customer care and sales. AT&T's solution was to create more specialized jobs so employees had to master just one product at a time. "Once they've been trained on video cable they get to go to the next level and master high-speed," Noonan explains. "And only until they master that can they then sell telephony."[10]

Role Perceptions

Shaare Zedek Medical Center in Jerusalem has become a role model for mass casualty preparedness. This expertise is partly due to the fact that the hospital has treated hundreds of victims of suicide bombings over the past three years, and partly because it has worked at creating highly efficient work processes. Efficiency is vital, because trauma victims have the best chance of survival during the first "golden hour" after the event. As soon as a bomb explodes, ambulances are dispatched, off-duty employees rush to the hospital, the emergency room is cleared of nonessential patients, and security checks are processed. Frequent practice drills, as well as the real bombings, ensure that everyone knows what to do and how to do it in the least amount of time. "It's really like a well-oiled machine and everyone knows what his job is," says Uri Schwartz, Shaare Zedek's director of public relations.[11]

Emergency room staff at Shaare Zedek Medical Center are like a "well-oiled machine" not just because they have the right competencies. They have also developed accurate **role perceptions** to achieve desired behavior and results.[12] Employees have accurate role perceptions when they understand the specific tasks assigned to them, the relative importance of those tasks, and the preferred behaviors to accomplish those tasks. Shaare Zedek's ambulance drivers, for example, know when to race off to the scene of a bombing, which procedures to follow on the scene for each type of injury, and which victims to take first to the hospital. In other words, they know which skills and knowledge to apply and what priorities to follow.

How do organizations improve role perceptions? One strategy is to ensure that employees understand their required responsibilities and to show how these goals relate to organizational goals. Employees also clarify their role perceptions as they work together over time and receive frequent and meaningful performance feedback. To apply these practices, companies such as Textron, Inc., conduct performance reviews that focus on goals and role perceptions. "You should tell employees what you expect of them from day one," advises an executive at the aircraft manufacturing and financial services company. "Employees know exactly what their objectives are and how they relate to business units and, ultimately, the entire enterprise."[13]

Situational Factors

In addition to the employee's motivation, ability, and role perceptions, the situation in which the person works also influences his or her behavior and job performance. Situational factors include conditions beyond the employee's

---

role perceptions
A person's beliefs about the specific tasks assigned to them, their relative importance, and the preferred behaviors to accomplish those tasks.

[handwritten margin notes:]
- Time
- People
- Budget
- Work facilities

immediate control that constrain or facilitate his or her behavior and performance.[14] Some situational characteristics—such as consumer preferences and economic conditions—originate from the external environment and, consequently, are beyond the employee's and organization's control. However, some situational factors—such as time, people, budget, and physical work facilities—are controlled by others in the organization. Corporate leaders need to carefully arrange these conditions so employees can achieve their performance potential. Lockheed Martin's jet fighter production facility does this by asking employees to identify obstacles created by management that prevent them from performing effectively.[15]

Motivation, ability, role perceptions, and situational factors affect all conscious workplace behaviors and their performance outcomes. In the next section, we introduce the five categories of behavior in organizational settings.

Types of Individual Behavior in Organizations

People engage in many different types of behavior in organizational settings. Exhibit 2.2 highlights the five types of behavior discussed most often in the organizational behavior literature: task performance, organizational citizenship, counterproductive work behaviors, joining and staying with the organization, and work attendance.

Task Performance

The most obvious category of individual behaviors in the workplace are those that support the organization's objectives. Goal-directed behaviors under the individual's control that support organizational objectives are known as **task performance**.[16] These include physical behaviors as well as mental processes leading to behaviors. For example, foreign exchange traders make decisions and take actions to exchange currencies. Employees in most jobs have more than one performance dimension. Foreign exchange traders, for example, must be able to identify profitable trades, work cooperatively with clients and co-workers in a stressful environment, assist in training new staff, and work on special telecommunications equipment without error. Some are more im-

task performance
Goal-directed behaviors under the individual's control that support organizational objectives.

EXHIBIT 2.2

Types of work-related behavior

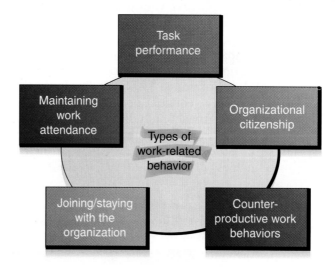

portant than others, but only by considering all performance dimensions can we fully evaluate an employee's contribution to the organization.

Exhibiting Organizational Citizenship

organizational citizenship
Behaviors that extend beyond the employee's normal job duties.

Normally, Ghadeer Rassoul's morning commute takes a leisurely 30 minutes. But these are not normal times for Rassoul, an executive at JAWWAL, the Palestinian cellular telephone provider. With bombed-out roads and military checkpoints along the way, many people wouldn't risk daily travel between Nablus, where Rassoul lives, and JAWWAL's offices in Ramallah. Rassoul, on the other hand, makes the extra effort. She leaves home at 3 A.M. (before curfew ends) and travels by donkey for two hours over old trails between villages that locals have used for decades. Then, she walks through hilly paths for half a mile to arrive at JAWWAL headquarters.[17]

Ghadeer Rassoul's extraordinary efforts to get to work each day go well beyond normal job expectations. Instead, they fall into a category of behaviors collectively known as organizational citizenship. **Organizational citizenship** refers to behaviors that extend beyond the employee's normal job duties.[18] These activities include helping others without selfish intent, being actively involved in organizational activities, avoiding unnecessary conflicts, performing tasks beyond normal role requirements and, as Ghadeer Rassoul does every day, gracefully tolerating impositions.

These organizational citizenship behaviors are highly related to each other and are caused by the same factors.[19] Throughout this book, we will identify the factors that explain why some employees are good organizational citizens and others are not. Later in this chapter, for example, we learn that people with a conscientiousness personality trait have higher organizational citizenship. In Chapter 5, we learn that organizational citizenship is higher among employees who believe the company is treating them fairly.

A traveler from the Middle East had an unusual request when he recently took his family to the Four Seasons hotel in Washington, D.C. "'My kids haven't seen Santa Claus since we've arrived,' he lamented to the Four Seasons staff. Going beyond the call of duty, assistant front office manager Liliana Vidal-Quadras found an employee and costume to play Santa for a few hours. It's this extra effort that makes the Four Seasons one of the top luxury hotels in the world. While the pay is adequate, Four Seasons employees mainly engage in organizational citizenship because they are treated fairly and have high conscientiousness.[20] In what other ways would Four Seasons employees demonstrate organizational citizenship?

Counterproductive Work Behaviors

counterproductive work behaviors (CWBs)
Voluntary behaviors that are potentially harmful to the organization's effectiveness.

Whereas most managers evaluate employee performance based on their task performance and organizational citizenship behaviors, some pay more attention to **counterproductive work behaviors (CWBs).**[21] CWBs are voluntary behaviors that have the potential to harm the organization by directly affecting its functioning or property or by hurting employees in a way that will reduce their effectiveness. Scholars have recently identified five categories of CWBs: abuse of others (e.g., insults and nasty comments), threats (threatening harm), work avoidance (e.g., tardiness), work sabotage (doing work incorrectly), and overt acts (theft). Notice from this list that CWBs include both acts of commission (deliberately harming the organization and its employees) and acts of omission (ignoring or avoiding actions that would benefit colleagues and the organization).[22]

Several factors that influence counterproductive behaviors are described throughout this book. For instance, stress is a known cause of workplace violence and aggression (Chapter 7). Perceptions of organizational injustice predict theft, sabotage, and failure to comply with rules and directives from management (Chapter 5). CWBs are also associated with personality traits such as Machiavellianism, which is described in Chapter 12.

Joining and Staying with the Organization

Task performance, organizational citizenship, and the lack of counterproductive work behaviors are obviously important for the organization's success. But what many corporate leaders are chanting about these days is the need to attract and keep talented employees. The simple fact is that if qualified people don't join and stay with the organization, none of these performance-related behaviors would occur.

The importance of hiring and keeping qualified people is obvious when we consider the consequences of not having enough employees to perform the work. An extreme example is the nursing shortage in the United States and many other countries. Nursing school enrollment has been falling at a time when hospitals are expanding capacity to handle the aging population. The resulting nursing shortage feeds on itself by causing active nurses to burn out and leave the profession. Many hospitals make up for the shortfall by offering hiring bonuses. University Hospital in Augusta, Georgia, for instance, offers some nursing students $5,000 scholarships in return for a commitment to work at the hospital on graduation. However, these incentives are not a long-term solution. "We have had nursing shortages before, but this one isn't like the others . . . and it's not going to go away," warns Lois Bock, director of nursing recruitment at the Cleveland Clinic Foundation.[23]

Beyond avoiding staff shortages, effective organizations continuously search out the most qualified people. As consulting firm McKinsey and Company highlighted in its report *The War for Talent*, organizations need to acquire knowledge by hiring the best employees. A more recent McKinsey report concludes that successful companies win the talent war by applying many of the ideas in this book—building trust and loyalty, having visionary leaders, offering enriched jobs, financially rewarding performance.[24]

Keeping Talented Employees   The war for talent includes keeping the best people, not just hiring them. As we learned in Chapter 1, much of an organization's intellectual capital is the knowledge employees carry around in their heads. Long-service employees, in particular, have valuable information about work processes, corporate values, and customer needs. Very little of this is documented anywhere. Thus, knowledge management involves keeping valuable employees with the organization. "At 5 P.M., 95% of our assets walk out the door," says an executive at SAS Institute, a leading statistics software firm. "We have to have an environment that makes them want to walk back in the door the next morning."[25]

The problem is that many employees don't return the next morning. Over half of 500 executives surveyed worldwide identified retaining talented employees as the top people issue in the company. Even with recent layoffs in some industries, the emerging employability attitude toward work and continuing shortages in some industries (e.g., information technology, nursing) will keep turnover rates near record levels.[26]

Why do people quit their jobs? Traditionally, OB scholars have identified low job satisfaction as main cause of turnover. **Job satisfaction** is a person's evaluation of his or her job and work context (see Chapter 4). Employees become dissatisfied with their employment relationship, which motivates them to search for and join another organization with better conditions. While job dissatisfaction builds over time and eventually affects turnover, scholars have recently suggested that specific "shock events" need to be considered.[27] These events, such as the boss's unfair decision or a conflict episode with a coworker, create strong emotions that engage employees in the process of thinking about and searching for alternative employment.

job satisfaction
A person's evaluation of his or her job and work context.

Maintaining Work Attendance

Along with attracting and retaining employees, organizations need everyone to show up for work at scheduled times. American business leaders might complain that approximately 2 percent of the U.S. workforce is absent from scheduled work each day, but this absenteeism rate is low by world standards. In contrast, absenteeism in Sweden exceeds 6 percent and in the Persian Gulf country of Bahrain, absenteeism among Bahraini employees is as high as 15 percent.[28] Companies with high absenteeism have difficulty making products or providing services because key people are missing from the work process.

What causes people to be absent from work? Situational factors—such as severe weather or car breakdown—certainly influence work attendance. Recognizing this, Xerox minimizes absenteeism by giving all employees free flu shots and health screenings. When their car breaks down or child is sick, Xerox employees are encouraged to do their work from home.[29] Factors that affect ability are also a source of absenteeism, such as when employees are incapacitated by illness or injury. Motivation is a third factor. Employees who experience job dissatisfaction or work-related stress are more likely to be absent or late for work because taking time off is a way to temporarily withdraw from stressful or dissatisfying conditions. Absenteeism is also higher in organizations with generous sick leave because this benefit limits the negative financial impact of taking time away from work.[30]

Several individual factors shown earlier with the MARS model influence the direct causes of these five types of workplace behavior. The remainder of this chapter looks closely at two of the most stable factors: values and personality.

values
Stable, long-lasting beliefs about what is important in a variety of situations, that guide our decisions and actions

Values in the Workplace

The opening story to this chapter describes how the Container Store hires employees with customer service values and relies on a values-based business model, in which organizational decisions and actions are consciously directed by a clear set of core values. **Values** are stable, evaluative beliefs that guide our

Cultivating Values at New Zealand's The Warehouse

Who is the most successful discount retailer on planet Earth? Most people would probably say Wal-Mart or the French giant Carrefour. Yet the best of the breed may be The Warehouse, which sells lots of cheap stuff in dozens of distinctive big red box stores throughout New Zealand. *Forbes* magazine praised The Warehouse as "easily one of the best retail operations in the entire world." The *Wall Street Journal* rated it as the second best performing small-cap company in the Asia-Pacific region.

What is so special about The Warehouse? Founder Stephen Tindall will gladly tell you that "people first" values is the main reason for the company's success. "We have discovered that our policies of putting team members first . . . makes them feel good about the business they work for," explains Tindall. "This feel-good attitude enables our team members to put the customers first and to provide exceptional service to them."

The Warehouse extends its "feel good" values to the community and environment. It has adopted Sweden's "Natural Step" sustainable development process to reduce dependence on nonrenewable substances. The company's timber procurement policy restricts purchases to timber furniture products that demonstrate sustainability of the resources used. It has commissioned an independent social audit, the results of which appear in annual reports.

Perhaps the strongest symbol of The Warehouse's values in action is that it aims to eliminate landfill waste by 2020. To achieve this daunting "zero waste" objective, 29 stores have odorless worm farms to digest all of the organic refuse from the premises. Eight of The Warehouse stores have already achieved the zero waste goal.

"People first" and social responsibility values have made The Warehouse in New Zealand one of the world's top-rated discount retailers.

Sources: "Waste Plan: Handle with Care," *New Zealand Herald,* March 4, 2002; J. Doebele, "Kiwi Category Killer," *Forbes,* August 20, 2001; S. Fea, "Tindall Pushes Zero Waste," *Southland Times* (Chistchurch, NZ), May 11, 2001, p. 3; "Warehouse Grasps the Bigger Picture," *New Zealand Herald,* January 4, 2001; M. Alexander, "Warehouse Boss Just Loves Seeing Red," *Sunday Star-Times* (Auckland, NZ), December 31, 2000; J. E. Hilsenrath, "Value Creators: In the Company of Asia's Superheroes," *Asian Wall Street Journal,* December 8, 2000, p. P3.

---

preferences for outcomes or courses of action in a variety of situations.[31] They are perceptions about what is good or bad, right or wrong. Values don't just represent what we want; they state what we "ought" to do—socially desirable ways to achieve our needs. They influence our choice of goals and the means for achieving those goals. Indeed, without values to guide us, it would be difficult to make any decisions. As we read in Global Connections 2.1, the Warehouse in New Zealand has become incredibly successful, based, in part, on its values-based model of doing business.

value system

An individual's values arranged in a hierarchy of preferences.

People arrange values into a hierarchy of preferences, called a **value system.** Some individuals value new challenges more than they value conformity. Others value generosity more than frugality. Each person's unique value system is developed and reinforced through socialization from parents, religious institutions, friends, personal experiences, and (as we shall learn later in this chapter) the society in which he or she lives. As such, a person's hierarchy of values is stable and long lasting. For example, one study found that value systems of a sample of adolescents were remarkably similar 20 years later as adults.[32]

VALUES
ImportANt b/c:
• EthicAl VAlues
• Guide employee behAvior
• GlobAlizAtion rAises AwAreness of vAlues differences
• Influence perceptions, decisions, behAvior

In Chapter 1, we learned that values research is gaining prominence in organizational behavior. Organizations are under increasing pressure to apply ethical values in their business practices. Values are also replacing direct supervision as a more acceptable way to guide employee behavior. Moreover, globalization has raised our awareness of and sensitivity to differences in values across cultures. Beyond these current issues, values are important because they influence so much of what we experience in organizational settings, such as perceptions, decision making, leadership behavior, and organizational citizenship.[33]

Types of Values

Values come in many forms, and scholars have devoted considerable attention to organizing them into coherent groups. The model in Exhibit 2.3, developed and tested by social psychologist Shalom Schwartz, has received considerable research support across more than 40 countries.[34] Schwartz reduced dozens of personal values into these 10 broader domains of values and further organized these domains into four clusters structured around two higher order bipolar dimensions.

EXHIBIT 2.3   Schwartz's values circumplex

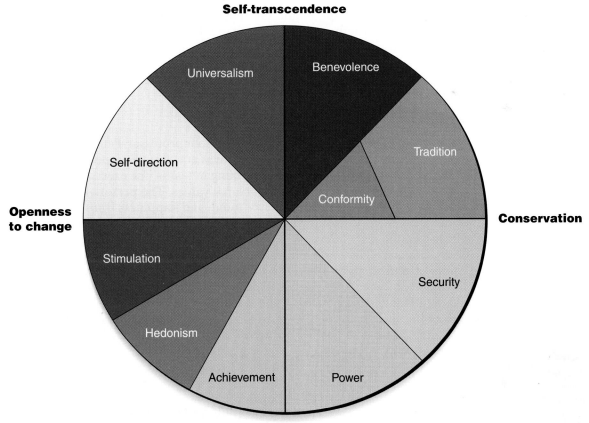

One dimension in Schwartz's model has openness to change at one extreme and conservation at the other extreme. Openness to change represents the extent to which a person is motivated to pursue innovative ways; it corresponds to the values of self-direction (independent thought and action) and stimulation (excitement and challenge). Conservation, the opposite end of this dimension, is the extent to which a person is motivated to preserve the status quo. Conservation is associated with the values of conformity (adherence to social norms and expectations), security (safety and stability), and tradition (moderation and preservation of the status quo).

The other bipolar dimension in Schwartz's model ranges from self-enhancement to self-transcendence. Self-enhancement—how much a person is motivated by self-interest—is related to the values of achievement (pursuit of personal success) and power (dominance over others). Self-transcendence, the other extreme of this dimension, refers to the motivation to promote the welfare of others and nature. It relates to the values of benevolence (concern for others in one's life) and universalism (concern for the welfare of all people and nature).

The dimensions of values identified in Schwartz's model are most commonly discussed as individual values, but values also apply to organizations, professions, societies, and other entities. Furthermore, we need to distinguish *espoused values* from *enacted values*. Espoused values represent the values that we want others to believe we abide by. Individuals, organizations, professions, and other groups might say they value environmentalism, creativity, and politeness, whether or not they really do value these things in practice. Values are socially desirable, so people create a positive public image by claiming to believe in values that others expect them to embrace. Enacted values, on the other hand, represent the values-in-use. They are values we actually rely on to guide our decisions and actions.[35]

Values Congruence

A few years ago, Copenhagen Business School professor Peter Pruzan held a seminar on workplace values with executives at a large European-based multinational manufacturing company. Working in teams, the executives developed a list of their five most important personal values. The personal values list included honesty, love, beauty, peace of mind, and happiness (most of which fall under the categories of universalism and benevolence in Exhibit 2.3). In the afternoon, the teams developed a list of the enacted (not espoused) values of their company. The company values list included success, efficiency, power, competitiveness, and productivity (most of which are represented by achievement and power in Exhibit 2.3). In other words, the organization's values were almost completely opposite to the executives' personal values. After an embarrassing silence, the CEO briefly spoke, announcing that he would consider resigning. He said that he had actively constructed a monster, a corporate Frankenstein![36]

values congruence
A situation wherein two or more entities have similar value systems.

The CEO of the European firm didn't resign, but he and his executive team learned an important lesson: They need to pay much more attention to the congruence of personal and organizational values. **Values congruence** refers to situations where two or more entities have similar value systems. In the example of the European manufacturer, the organization's value system was incongruent with the value systems of its employees. Unfortunately, significant

[handwritten margin notes:
Consequences of Incongruence:
• incompatible decisions
• lowers satisfaction
• increased stress + turnover

Benefits of Incongruence:
• Better decision making
• enhanced problem definition
• prevents "corporate cults"]

incongruence between personal and organization values seems to be common. In one study, 76 percent of the managers believed that a conflict exists between their own ethical beliefs and their company's values. Another investigation found that managers saw substantial differences between their personal values and organizational practices. MBA students in the United States anticipate (and have experienced) values incongruence; a recent survey estimated that half of them feel that they will have to make business decisions that conflict with their personal values.[37]

Incongruence between the value systems of employees and their organization has a number of consequences. Values are guideposts, so employees whose values differ markedly from the organization's values might make decisions incompatible with the organization's goals. Incongruence also leads to lower job satisfaction and organizational commitment, as well as higher stress and turnover among employees. "To work for a company whose ideals aren't consistent with mine—that would be torture," says Humphrey Wong, a senior research scientist at Kodak. Wong enjoys working at Kodak in Rochester, New York, because he seldom experiences conflict between his personal values and the values that his employer supports.[38]

Does this mean that the most successful organizations perfectly align employee values with the organization's values? Not at all! While a comfortable degree of values congruence is necessary for the reasons noted above, organizations also benefit from some level of values *incongruence*. As we will learn in Chapter 8, employees with diverse values offer different perspectives on issues, which may lead to better decision making. The conflict resulting from values incongruence among employees can sharpen everyone's thinking about the definition of the problem and the rationale for preferred choices. Moreover, too much congruence can create a "corporate cult" that potentially undermines creativity, organizational flexibility, and business ethics (see Chapter 16).[39]   *["group thing"]*

Values congruence applies to more than employees and companies within one country. It also relates to the compatibility of the organization's values with the prevailing values of the society in which it conducts business.[40] This fact is particularly important as information technology and globalization increase the frequency of cross-cultural interaction. For example, an organization from one society that tries to impose its value system on employees located in another culture may experience higher employee turnover and have more difficult relations with the communities in which the company operates. SC Johnson was aware of this need for values congruence for its Australian business. The American household products firm is "a family company with family values." But Australians generally like to separate their work from their personal lives, so SC Johnson's solution tweaked its values somewhat. "You can't sell that family company idea in Australia, so we position it as family values with work/life balance," explains an SC Johnson executive.[41] Let's look more closely at cross-cultural values.

Values Across Cultures

Anyone who has worked long enough in other countries will know that values differ across cultures. Some cultures value group decisions, whereas others think that the leader should take charge. Meetings in Germany usually start on time, whereas they might be half an hour late in Brazil without much concern.

South Korean Culture Meets American Values in Montgomery, Alabama

Residents of Montgomery, Alabama, are taking a lot more interest in Korean culture these days. That's because the South Korean automobile giant Hyundai Motor Company is building its first American manufacturing plant in the area. Montgomery City Library has ordered more books and tapes on Korean culture and language. Auburn University is oversubscribed for its luncheons on Korean and business etiquette. Some residents are even taking classes to learn the difficult Korean language.

Hyundai is also helping people to learn about Korean values. Every American employee hired completes a 16-hour course in Korean culture. American executives at Hyundai have already been immersed in Korean and Hyundai values with a week-long trip to Ulsan, South Korea. The education includes eating Korean food, learning about Korean history, and touring Hyundai's main manufacturing operations in Ulsan (where almost half of the one million residents work for the Korean automaker).

Hyundai executives also say they are adjusting their practices in Ulsan to fit American culture. However, Hyundai's reflection of Korea's high power distance culture—which reveres hierarchy and power of executives—may be difficult to leave behind. Hyundai's swankiest office in Montgomery is reserved for Hyundai chairman Chung Mong-Koo when he occasionally visits. The company even flies over his exclusive limousine before his arrival. When a Korean-born Hyundai executive was asked if he had met Chairman Chung during one of his visits to Montgomery, he quickly replied: "He is too high. I could not personally speak with him."

Jim Crate, foreign editor for Detroit-based *Automotive News*, says Montgomery residents will likely see Hyundai's practices clash with American values in a variety of ways. "It's a very Korean company," Crate says. "They will have to evolve in coming to America."

Sources: B. Clanton, "It's a Job to Fill 1,600 Jobs," *Montgomery Advertiser*, August 19, 2003, p. B8; B. Clanton, "At Home with Hyundai: Part 2—Culture Shock," *Montgomery Advertiser*, June 2, 2003; B. Clanton, "Execs Sop Up Korean Culture," *Montgomery Advertiser*, April 14, 2003 p. A1; B. Clanton, "Hyundai Plant Ignites Interest," *Montgomery Advertiser*, September 17, 2002; T. Kleffman, "Company Faces Culture Clash," *Montgomery Advertiser*, April 3, 2002.

Hyundai Motor Company says its business practices in South Korea (shown in photo) will be adapted at its new plant in Alabama to more closely suit American values.

We need to understand differences in cultural values to avoid unnecessary conflicts and misunderstandings between people from different countries. That's why, as Global Connections 2.2 describes, American employees at Hyundai's new manufacturing facility in Montgomery, Alabama, are learning about Korean values, and why Hyundai executives are adapting their Korean business practices to be more compatible with American culture.

Individualism and Collectivism

individualism

The extent to which a person values independence and personal uniqueness.

No cross-cultural values have attracted more attention—or controversy and misunderstanding—than individualism and collectivism. **Individualism** is the extent to which we value independence and personal uniqueness. Highly individualist people value personal freedom, self-sufficiency, control over their own lives, and appreciation of the unique qualities that distinguish them from others. This value relates most closely to the self-direction dimension shown earlier in Exhibit 2.3. **Collectivism** is the extent to which we value our duty to groups to which we belong, and to group harmony. Highly collectivist people define themselves by their group membership and value harmonious relationships within those groups.[42] Collectivism is located within the conservation range of values (security, tradition, conformity) in Exhibit 2.3.

collectivism

The extent to which people value duty to groups to which they belong, and to group harmony.

You might think from these definitions that individualism and collectivism are opposites. Until recently, many scholars thought so, too, but the two concepts are actually unrelated, according to research studies.[43] Some people and cultures have both high individualism and high collectivism, for example.

How individualistic and collectivistic are Americans? Exhibit 2.4 shows that Americans with European heritage are relatively more individualistic than people in most other countries. Only people in some South American countries (such as Chile and Peru) are apparently more individualistic. Exhibit 2.4 also

EXHIBIT 2.4

Individualism and collectivism in selected countries

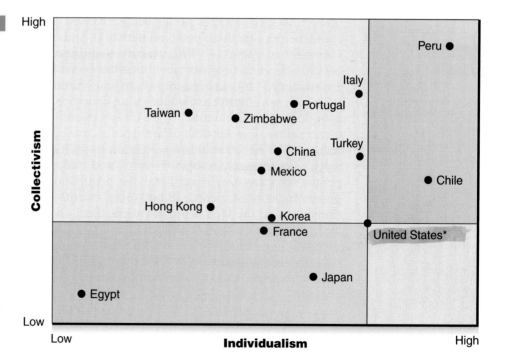

Source: Based on information in D. Oyserman, H. M. Coon, and M. Kemmelmeier, "Rethinking Individualism and Collectivism: Evaluation of Theoretical Assumptions and Meta-Analyses," *Psychological Bulletin* 128 (2002), pp. 3–72. The countries shown here represent only a sample of those in Oyserman's meta-analysis.

NOTE: The United States includes studies from both the United States and Canada and refers only to people with European heritage in those countries.

shows that European-Americans are relatively low in collectivism, whereas people in Italy, Taiwan, Peru, Zimbabwe, and most other countries have higher collectivism.

One notable observation in Exhibit 2.4 is that people in Japan are *less* collectivist than most cultures. This is a stark contrast to statements in many cross-cultural books that Japan is one of the most collectivist countries on the planet! The problem was that a major study more than 20 years ago identified Japan as collectivist, but it measured collectivism in a way that bears little resemblance to how the concept is usually defined.[44] Subsequent studies have reported that Japan is relatively low on the collectivist scale (as Exhibit 2.4 reveals), but these persistent results have been slow to replace the old views on this matter.

Other Cross-Cultural Values

Organizational scholars have studied many other values in cross-cultural research, but four of them are most prominent: power distance, uncertainty avoidance, achievement versus nurturing orientation, and long- versus short-term orientation.[45]

power distance
The extent to which people accept unequal distribution of power in a society.

■ *Power distance*—**Power distance** is the extent that people accept unequal distribution of power in a society. Those with high power distance accept and value unequal power, whereas those with low power distance expect relatively equal power sharing. In high power distance cultures, employees are comfortable receiving commands from their superiors, and resolving conflicts through formal rules and authority. In contrast, people in low power distance cultures prefer being involved in decisions and resolving conflicts more through personal networks and coalitions.[46]

uncertainty avoidance
The degree to which people tolerate ambiguity or feel threatened by ambiguity and uncertainty.

■ *Uncertainty avoidance*—**Uncertainty avoidance** is the degree to which people tolerate ambiguity (low uncertainty avoidance) or feel threatened by ambiguity and uncertainty (high uncertainty avoidance). Employees with high uncertainty avoidance value structured situations where rules of conduct and decision making are clearly documented. They usually prefer direct rather than indirect or ambiguous communications.

■ *Achievement versus nurturing orientation*—Achievement-oriented cultures value assertiveness, competitiveness, and materialism.[47] They appreciate people who are tough and favor the acquisition of money and material goods. In contrast, people in nurturing-oriented cultures emphasize relationships and the well-being of others. They focus on human interaction and caring rather than competition and personal success.

■ *Long-term versus short-term orientation*—People in different cultures also differ in their long- or short-term orientation. Those with a long-term orientation anchor their thoughts more in the future than in the past and present. They value thrift, savings, and persistence, whereas those with a short-term orientation place more emphasis on the past and present, such as respect for tradition and fulfilling social obligations.

Exhibit 2.5 provides the best estimate of how Americans compare to some other cultures on these four values. In general, Americans have a low power distance and a short-term orientation. They are moderately achievement-oriented and have a moderate level of uncertainty avoidance (i.e., they tolerate ambiguity to some extent). This information provides the best comparison available of these values across cultures, but it is far from ideal. The informa-

EXHIBIT 2.5

Comparison of the United States with selected countries on cultural values

Country	Power distance	Uncertainly avoidance	Achievement vs. nurturing orientation	Long- vs. short-term orientation
China	High	Medium	Medium	Long-term
France	High	High	Medium	Short-term
Japan	Medium	High	Achievement	Long-term
Netherlands	Low	Medium	Nurturing	Medium
Russia	High	High	Nurturing	Short-term
United States	Low	Medium	Achievement	Short-term

Sources: Based on G. Hofstede, "Cultural Constraints in Management Theories," *Academy of Management Executive* 7 (1993), pp. 81–94; G. Hofstede, "The Cultural Relativity of Organizational Practices and Theories," *Journal of International Business Studies* 14 (Fall 1983), pp. 75–89. For the "achievement vs. nurturing orientation" and long- vs. short-term orientation" scales, "medium" indicates that the country is near the middle of the two poles of the dimension.

tion for the first three scales was collected from IBM employees worldwide more than a quarter century ago, and the fourth scale is based on a student sample. It is possible that neither IBM employees nor students represent the general population.[48]

One concern with all cross-cultural values research is the assumption that everyone in a society has similar cultural values. This may be true in a few countries, but not in culturally diverse societies such as the United States. Consistent with this concern, research has found a wide range of long- versus short-term orientation within the United States, Australia, and Chile. By attributing certain values to an entire society, we are engaging in a form of stereotyping that limits our ability to understand the more complex reality of that society.[49]

Ethical Values and Behavior

ethics
The study of moral principles or values that determine whether actions are right or wrong and outcomes are good or bad.

Our discussion of values would be incomplete without examining the dynamics of ethics in the workplace. **Ethics** refers to the study of moral principles or values that determine whether actions are right or wrong and outcomes are good or bad. We introduced the concept of ethics in Chapter 1 because it has become such an important issue in society and, consequently, in our study of organizational behavior. People rely on their ethical values to determine "the right thing to do." Employees and customers value companies and their leaders with ethical values. Indeed, surveys indicate that the employer's integrity is as important to most employees as their income.[50]

Unfortunately, the number and magnitude of incidents involving corporate wrongdoing is raising serious questions about the ethical values of many corporate leaders. Accounting fraud seems to top the list, with the best known scams at WorldCom, Enron, and Qwest in the United States; food retailer Royal Ahold in the Netherlands; and business conglomerate SK Group in South Korea. Swedish construction group NCC fired several managers for supporting a cartel in the construction industry. Several Wall Street brokerages paid record fines for deliberately biasing research in order to attract new business. Painting firms in Ohio and a chemical firm in Florida have allegedly been bribing government officials. Little wonder that barely half of U.S. employees recently surveyed believe that senior leaders are people of high personal integrity.[51]

Four Ethical Principles

To better understand the ethical dilemmas facing organizations, we need to consider the various ethical principles that people rely on to make decisions. Philosophers and other scholars have identified several ethical principles incorporating different values and logical foundations, but most of these can be condensed down to four basic groups—utilitarianism, individual rights, distributive justice, and care.[52] You might prefer one principle over the others based on your personal values. However, all four principles should be actively considered to put important ethical issues to the test.

utilitarianism
The moral principle stating that decision makers should seek the greatest good for the greatest number of people when choosing among alternatives.

individual rights principle
The moral principle stating that every person is entitled to legal and human rights.

distributive justice principle
The moral principle stating that people who are similar should be rewarded similarly, and those dissimilar should be rewarded differently in proportion to those differences.

care principle
The moral principle stating that we should benefit those with whom we have special relationships.

- *Utilitarianism*—**Utilitarianism** advises us to seek the greatest good for the greatest number of people. In other words, we should choose the option providing the highest degree of satisfaction to those affected. This is sometimes known as a *consequential principle* because it focuses on the consequences of our actions, not on how we achieve those consequences. One problem with utilitarianism is that it is almost impossible to evaluate the benefits or costs of many decisions, particularly when many stakeholders have wide-ranging needs and values. Another problem is that most of us are uncomfortable engaging in behaviors that seem, well, unethical, to attain results that are ethical.

- *Individual rights*—The **individual rights principle** reflects the belief that everyone has entitlements that let them act in a certain way. Some of the most widely cited rights are freedom of movement, physical security, freedom of speech, fair trial, and freedom from torture.[53] The individual rights principle includes more than legal rights; it also includes human rights that everyone is granted as a moral norm of society. For example, access to education and knowledge isn't a legal requirement everywhere, but most of us believe that it is a human right. One problem with individual rights is that certain individual rights may conflict with others. The shareholders' right to be informed about corporate activities may ultimately conflict with an executive's right to privacy, for example.

- *Distributive justice*—The **distributive justice principle** suggests that people who are similar in relevant ways should receive similar benefits and burdens; those who are dissimilar should receive different benefits and burdens in proportion to their dissimilarity. For example, we expect that two employees who contribute equally in their work should receive similar rewards, whereas those who make a lesser contribution should receive less. A variation of this principle says that inequalities are acceptable where they benefit the least well off in society. Thus, employees in risky jobs should be paid more if this benefits others who are less well off. One problem with the distributive justice principle is that it is difficult to agree on who is "similar" and what factors are "relevant." Most of us agree that race and gender should not be relevant when distributing paychecks. But should rewards be determined purely by an employee's performance, or should effort, seniority, and other factors also be taken into account?

- *Care*—The **care principle** states that the morally correct action is one that expresses care in protecting the special relationships that individuals have with each other. Whereas distributive justice emphasizes impartiality, the care principle emphasizes partiality—favoring those with whom we have special relationships. The idea behind the ethic of care is that our self-perception is based on relationships with others. Consequently, our self-esteem and self-worth are influenced by how well we support and nurture those relationships.[54] The challenge of the care principle is that it can degenerate into unjust favoritism, such as the "old boy's" network. This, in effect, conflicts with both distributive justice and utilitarianism.

Moral Intensity, Ethical Sensitivity, and Situational Influences

Along with ethical principles and their underlying values, we need to consider three other factors that influence ethical conduct in the workplace: the moral intensity of the issue, the individual's ethical sensitivity, and situational factors.

moral intensity
The degree to which an issue demands the application of ethical principles.

Moral intensity is the degree to which an issue demands the application of ethical principles. The higher the moral intensity, the more that ethical principles should provide guidance to resolve the issue. Stealing from your employer is usually considered high on moral intensity, whereas borrowing a company pen for personal use is much lower on the scale. Several factors influence the moral intensity of an issue, such as the extent to which the issue clearly produces good or bad consequences, the extent to which others in the society think it is good or evil, how quickly it affects people, how close the decision maker feels to the issue, and how much control the person has over the issue.[55]

ethical sensitivity
A personal characteristic that enables people to recognize the presence and determine the relative importance of an ethical issue.

Even if an issue has high moral intensity, some employees might not recognize its ethical importance because they have low ethical sensitivity. **Ethical sensitivity** is a personal characteristic that enables people to recognize the presence and determine the relative importance of an ethical issue.[56] Ethically sensitive people are not necessarily more ethical. Rather, they are more likely to recognize whether an issue requires ethical consideration; that is, they can more accurately estimate the moral intensity of the issue. Ethically sensitive people tend to have higher empathy. They also have more information about the specific situation. For example, accountants would be more ethically sensitive regarding the appropriateness of specific accounting procedures than would someone who has not received training in this profession.

The third important factor explaining why good people do bad things is the situation in which the unethical conduct occurs. A few recent surveys have reported that employees regularly experience corporate pressure that leads to selling beyond the customers' needs, lying to the client, or making unrealistic promises. Other surveys have found that most employees believe they experience so much pressure that it compromises their ethical conduct. For instance, nearly two-thirds of the managers in one academic study stated that pressure from top management causes people further down in hierarchy to compromise their beliefs, whereas 90 percent of top management disagreed with this statement.[57] The point here is not to justify unethical conduct. Rather, we need to recognize the situational factors that influence wrongdoing so that organizations can correct these problems in the future.

Cultural Differences in Business Ethics

When Harry Gould Jr. visited Gould Paper's manufacturing plants in France, he asked his French counterpart to show him the books (financial statements). The French executive casually asked "Which books do you want to see?" The executive kept three sets of records—one for his family, one for the revenue collector, and the real one. "[The French executive] didn't think anything about that," Gould recalls. "There's a cultural mindset that has no bearing on the reality we are used to here in the United States."[58]

As Harry Gould discovered, corporate decision makers face a larger set of ethical dilemmas when they enter the global marketplace. The French executive saw little wrong with having three sets of financial records, whereas most Americans would consider this practice of falsifying information highly unethical. This isn't an isolated example. Several years ago, the United States made bribery at home or abroad a criminal offense for American companies, whereas it was a legitimate tax deduction in Australia, Germany, Netherlands, and several other countries until recently.[59] Various studies have identified differences across cultures regarding attitudes toward software piracy, padding résumés, and a host of other ethical issues.[60]

Do these studies suggest that people in some countries have fewer ethical values? Probably not. Research indicates that fundamental ethical principles are fairly similar across cultures, but people interpret the moral intensity of specific situations differently in their situation.[61] False financial reporting may be more common in France than in the United States, for example, because French businesspeople might believe it is widely practiced and has little adverse effect on anyone. Americans, on the other hand, are more likely to view false financial reporting as unethical because they believe it has adverse consequences. Thus, financial reporting likely has higher moral intensity in the United States than in some other cultures.

When Jim Churchman (shown in photo) searched out MBA programs, he was looking for more than courses that develop technical skills; he was also looking for an MBA with a strong ethics orientation. "A leader should make decisions not just from the numbers standpoint, but from an ethical standpoint as well," says the group manager at Sprint in Overland Park, Kansas. Churchman and other prospective students increasingly expect college business programs to place more emphasis on ethics. Some companies are also demanding that business educators improve ethical values in their graduates. "Ethics responsibility doesn't just happen," suggests Fred Verinder, a top ethics officer at Blue Cross Blue Shield. "It must start with the college freshman, and thus far it has been the missing link at most schools. They must make students aware that they'll face not just career challenges but ethical choices."[64] In your opinion, to what degree can university business programs improve the ethical conduct of people enrolled in those programs?

Supporting Ethical Behavior

Most large and medium-size organizations in the United States, Canada, United Kingdom, and several other countries apply one or more strategies to improve ethical conduct. Ethical codes of conduct are the most common. Ninety-five percent of the Fortune 500 companies in the United States and 57 percent of the 500 largest U.K. companies now have codes of ethics.[62] Ethical codes establish the organization's ethical standards and signal to employees that the company takes ethical conduct seriously. However, written ethics codes alone won't prevent wrongdoing in the workplace. After all, Enron had a well-developed code of ethical conduct, but that document didn't prevent senior executives from engaging in wholesale accounting fraud, resulting in the energy company's bankruptcy.[63]

To supplement ethics codes, many firms provide

ethics training. For instance, more than 75,000 defense systems workers at Boeing Company recently attended a four-hour class on ethics.[65] Boeing had been denied military contracts after executives were caught stealing information from a competitor, and this training was supposed to avoid future cases of wrongdoing. The session mainly provided details about the company's ethics code and directed employees to online primers on ethics and ethical challenges. Other companies offer more active ethics training, in which they analyze case studies involving ethical conduct.

United Technologies Corporation goes further than many companies to instill ethical values in its employees. The defense and engineering goliath relies on more than 150 ethics officers dispersed throughout the company to distribute the company's code of ethics, educate staff, and answer questions about ethical dilemmas. United Technologies also relies on a highly confidential and active ombuds office that investigates and acts on information about wrongdoing.[66]

Aside from these programs and practices, one of the strongest influences on the moral fiber of an organization is the ethical conduct of its leaders.[67] As we will learn in Chapter 14, effective leaders have integrity in the eyes of followers. By the same token, leaders must demonstrate authentic ethical conduct to be effective. They do this by focusing on the organization's shared vision in a culture of openness and dialogue. By acting with the highest standards of moral conduct, leaders not only gain support and trust from followers; they role model the ethical standards that employees are more likely to follow.

Personality in Organizations

Ethical, cross-cultural, and other values are relatively stable characteristics, so they are an important influence on individual behavior. Another individual characteristic that has long-term stability is personality. In fact, there is considerable evidence that values and personality traits are interrelated and reinforce each other.[68] The final section of this chapter examines the key features of personality, the dominant models of personality, the effect of personality on workplace behavior, and how personality relates to vocational choice.

personality

The relatively stable pattern of behaviors and consistent internal states that explain a person's behavioral tendencies.

Personality refers to the relatively stable pattern of behaviors and consistent internal states that explain a person's behavioral tendencies.[69] Personality has both internal and external elements. External traits are the observable behaviors that we rely on to identify someone's personality. For example, we can see that a person is extroverted by the way he or she interacts with other people. The internal states represent the thoughts, values, and genetic characteristics that we infer from the observable behaviors.

We say that personality explains behavioral *tendencies* because individuals' actions are not perfectly consistent with their personality profile in every situation. Personality traits are less evident in situations where social norms, reward systems, and other conditions constrain our behavior.[70] For example, talkative people remain relatively quiet in a library where "no talking" rules are explicit and strictly enforced.

The Origins of Personality

Over the next few pages, we will look at personality traits and trait models that add value to our knowledge of individual behavior in organizations. However, behind these trait categories is a battle among psychologists regarding the origins of personality.[71] Some scholars staunchly believe that personality is based purely on genetic code. They point to evidence that personality traits are connected to specific parts of the brain and chemical activities in the body. Evolutionary psychologists have taken this perspective a step further by explaining how personality has been shaped by generations of social evolution. Other psychologists, without denying some effects of genetics, argue that the environment in which we live influences our personality. Our personality is, at least in part, developed through early childhood socialization. To a small degree, personality can also evolve through socialization and life experiences later in life.[72]

Personality and Organizational Behavior

At one time, scholars often explained employee behavior in terms of personality traits and companies regularly administered personality tests to job applicants. This changed in the 1960s when researchers reported that the relationship between personality and job performance is very weak.[73] They cited problems with measuring personality traits and explained that the connection between personality and performance exists only under very narrowly defined conditions. Companies stopped using personality tests due to concerns that these tests might unfairly discriminate against visible minorities and other identifiable groups.

Over the past decade, personality has regained some of its credibility in organizational settings.[74] Recent studies have reported that certain personality traits predict certain work-related behaviors, stress reactions, and emotions fairly well under certain conditions. Scholars have reintroduced the idea that effective leaders have identifiable traits and that personality explains some of a person's positive attitudes and life happiness. Personality traits seem to help people find the jobs that best suit their needs.[75] Personality is still considered a relatively poor selection test, but this hasn't stopped many companies from using personality tests and assessments to hire executives. For instance, Carly Fiorini had to complete a two-hour, 900-question personality test as part of the process to select her as Hewlett-Packard's new chief executive.[76] With these caveats in mind, let's look at the main personality traits and dimensions currently studied in organizational settings.

The Big Five Personality Dimensions

Since the days of Plato, scholars have been trying to develop lists of personality traits. About 100 years ago, a few personality experts tried to catalogue and condense the many personality traits that had been described over the years. They found thousands of words in *Roget's Thesaurus* and *Webster's Dictionary* that represented personality traits. They aggregated these words into 171 clusters, then further shrunk them down to five abstract personality dimensions. Using more sophisticated techniques, recent investigations identified the same five dimensions—known as the **Big Five personality dimensions**.[77] These five dimensions, represented by the handy acronym CANOE, are outlined in Exhibit 2.6 and described below:

- *Conscientiousness*—**Conscientiousness** refers to people who are careful, dependable, and self-disciplined. Some scholars argue that this dimension also includes the will to achieve. People with low conscientiousness tend to be careless, less thorough, more disorganized, and irresponsible.

"Big Five" personality dimensions
The five abstract dimensions representing most personality traits: conscientiousness, agreeableness, neuroticism, openness to experience, and extroversion (CANOE)

conscientiousness
A "Big Five" personality dimension that characterizes people who are careful, dependable, and self-disciplined.

Dimension	People who score "high" on this dimension tend to be more:
Conscientiousness	Careful, dependable, self-disciplined
Agreeableness	Courteous, good-natured, empathic, caring
Neuroticism	Anxious, hostile, depressed
Openness to experience	Sensitive, flexible, creative, curious
Extroversion	Outgoing, talkative, sociable, assertive

- *Agreeableness*—This includes the traits of being courteous, good-natured, empathic, and caring. Some scholars prefer the label of "friendly compliance" for this dimension, with its opposite being "hostile noncompliance." People with low agreeableness tend to be uncooperative, short-tempered, and irritable.
- *Neuroticism*—Neuroticism characterizes people with high levels of anxiety, hostility, depression, and self-consciousness. In contrast, people with low neuroticism (high emotional stability) are poised, secure, and calm.
- *Openness to experience*—This dimension is the most complex and has the least agreement among scholars. It generally refers to the extent to which people are sensitive, flexible, creative, and curious. Those who score low on this dimension tend to be more resistant to change, less open to new ideas, and more fixed in their ways.
- *Extroversion*—**Extroversion** characterizes people who are outgoing, talkative, sociable, and assertive. The opposite is **introversion,** which refers to those who are quiet, shy, and cautious. Introverts do not necessarily lack social skills. Rather, they are more inclined to direct their interests to ideas than to social events. Introverts feel quite comfortable being alone, whereas extroverts do not.

extroversion
A "Big Five"
personality dimension
that characterizes
people who are
outgoing, talkative,
sociable, and
assertive.

introversion
A "Big Five"
personality dimension
that characterizes
people who are quiet,
shy, and cautious.

Several studies have found that these personality dimensions affect work-related behavior and job performance.[78] Champions of organizational change (people who effectively gain support for new organizational systems and practices) seem to be placed along the positive end of the five personality dimensions described above.[79] People with high emotional stability tend to work better than others in high-stressor situations. Those with high agreeableness tend to handle customer relations and conflict-based situations more effectively.

Conscientiousness has taken center stage as the most valuable personality trait for predicting job performance in almost every job group. Conscientious employees set higher personal goals for themselves, are more motivated, and have higher performance expectations than do employees with low levels of conscientiousness. High-conscientiousness employees tend to have higher levels of organizational citizenship and work better in workplaces that give employees more freedom than in traditional "command and control" workplaces. Employees with high conscientiousness, as well as agreeableness and emotional stability, also tend to provide better customer service, which explains why this trait is important at the Container Store, described at the beginning of this chapter.[80]

Myers-Briggs Type Indicator

More than half a century ago, the mother and daughter team of Katherine Briggs and Isabel Briggs-Myers developed the **Myers-Briggs Type Indicator (MBTI),** a personality inventory designed to identify individuals' basic preferences for perceiving and processing information. The MBTI builds on the personality theory proposed in the 1920s by Swiss psychiatrist Carl Jung that identifies the way people prefer to perceive their environment as well as obtain and process information. Jung suggested that everyone is either extroverted or introverted in orientation and has particular preferences for perceiving (sensing or intuition) and judging or deciding on action (thinking or feeling). The MBTI is designed to measure these as well as a fourth dimension relating to how people orient themselves to the outer world (judging versus perceiving).[81] Extroversion and introversion were discussed earlier, so let's examine the other dimensions:

- *Sensing/intuition*—Some people like collecting information through their five senses. Sensing types use an organized structure to acquire factual and preferably quantitative details. In contrast, intuitive people collect information nonsystematically. They rely more on subjective evidence as well as their intuition and sheer inspiration. Sensers are capable of synthesizing large amounts of seemingly random information to form quick conclusions.
- *Thinking/feeling*—Thinking types rely on rational cause-effect logic and the scientific method (see Chapter 1) to make decisions. They weigh the evidence objectively and unemotionally. Feeling types, on the other hand, consider how their choices affect others. They weigh the options against their personal values more than rational logic.
- *Judging/perceiving*—Some people prefer order and structure in their relationship with the outer world. These judging types enjoy the control of decision making and want to resolve problems quickly. In contrast, perceiving types are more flexible. They like to spontaneously adapt to events as they unfold and want to keep their options open.

The MBTI questionnaire combines the four pairs of traits into 16 distinct types. For example, ESTJ is one of the most common types for managers, meaning that they are extroverted, sensing, thinking, and judging types. Each of the 16 types has its strengths and weaknesses. ENTJs are considered natural leaders, ISFJs have a high sense of duty, and so on. These types indicate people's preferences, not the way they necessarily behave all of the time.

Effectiveness of the MBTI   Is the MBTI useful in organizations? Many business leaders think so. The MBTI is one of the most widely used personality tests in work settings.[82] For example, City Bank & Trust in Oklahoma (now part of BancFirst) used the MBTI to help executives understand each other after the merger of several smaller banks. "[MBTI] really was a breakthrough as far as us being able to have empathy for one another," says Bill Johnstone, who was City Bank & Trust president at the time.[83] The MBTI is equally popular for career counseling and some executive coaching.

Yet, in spite of its popularity, evidence regarding the effectiveness of the MBTI and Jung's psychological types is mixed.[84] The MBTI does a reasonably good job of measuring Jung's psychological types. The MBTI predicts preferences for information processing in decision making and preferences for particular occupations. However, other evidence is less supportive regarding the MBTI's ability to predict job performance. One possible exception is that some MBTI dimensions are associated with some emotional intelligence dimensions (see Chapter 4).[85] Overall, the MBTI seems to improve self-awareness for career development and mutual understanding, but it probably should not be used in selecting job applicants.

Other Personality Traits

The Big Five personality dimensions and the MBTI don't capture every personality trait. We will discuss a few others where they fit specific topics in later chapters, such as positive and negative affectivity (Chapter 4), Type A and Type B behavior patterns (Chapter 7), and Machiavellianism (Chapter 12). Two other personality traits that you should know are locus of control and self-monitoring.

locus of control
A personality trait referring to the extent to which people believe events are within their control.

Locus of Control   **Locus of control** refers to a generalized belief about the amount of control people have over their own lives. Individuals who feel that they are very much in charge of their own destiny have an *internal locus of control;* those who think that events in their life are due mainly to fate/luck or powerful others have an *external locus of control*. Locus of control is a generalized belief, so people with an external locus can feel in control in familiar situations (such as opening a door or serving a customer). However, their underlying locus of control would be apparent in new situations in which control over events is uncertain.

People perform better in most employment situations when they have a moderately strong internal locus of control. They tend to be more successful in their careers and earn more money than their external counterparts. Internals are particularly well suited to leadership positions and other jobs requiring initiative, independent action, complex thinking, and high motivation. Internals are also more satisfied with their jobs, cope better in stressful situations, and are more motivated by performance-based reward systems. This last point was supported in a recent study of Hong Kong bank tellers. Tellers with an internal locus of control had more positive work attitudes following a promotion than did tellers with a more external locus of control.[86]

self-monitoring
A personality trait referring to an individual's level of sensitivity to the expressive behavior of others and the ability to adapt appropriately to these situational cues

Self-Monitoring   **Self-monitoring** refers to an individual's level of sensitivity to the expressive behavior of others and the ability to adapt appropriately to these situational cues. High self-monitors can adjust their behavior quite easily and therefore show little stability in other underlying personality traits. In contrast, low self-monitors are more likely to reveal their moods and personal characteristics, so predicting their behavior from one situation to the next is relatively easy.[87] The self-monitoring personality trait has been identified as a significant factor in many organizational activities. Employees who are high self-monitors tend to be better at social networking, interpersonal conversations, and leading people. They are also more likely than low self-monitors to be promoted within the organization and to receive better jobs elsewhere.[88]

Self-monitoring, locus of control, conscientiousness, and the many other personality traits help us to understand individual behavior in organizations. One fairly successful application of personality is in the area of vocational choice.

Personality and Vocational Choice

Getting laid off was a mixed blessing for Aubrey Witherspoon. Although people rarely want to lose a job, Witherspoon didn't particularly enjoy his work processing insurance application forms at Royal & SunAlliance. After completing career interest tests as part of his outplacement, Witherspoon discovered "that I'm more of a people person. I'm not much of a clerical person." He put that feedback to use and is now much happier talking to people all day as a customer service representative at ALLTEL in Charlotte, North Carolina.[89]

Aubrey Witherspoon and many other people have discovered that a career

While working as a Navy diver, Dan Porzio prepared for his next career in financial planning. But he was far from happy in his new field, so he took a job selling cellular telephones. Still unhappy, Porzio moved into the investment industry, where he worked for three years. During that time, he visited a career counselor and discovered why he lacked interest in his work. "I thought those other jobs were ones that I wanted to do but I found out I was doing things that didn't jive with my character," Porzio explains. With that knowledge in hand, Porzio found a job that fit his personality as captain of the Annabelle Lee riverboat in Richmond, Virginia (shown in photo).[92] Aside from receiving career counseling, how can we determine whether a job fits our personality and values?

is not just about matching your skills with job requirements. It is a complex alignment of personality, values, and competencies with the requirements of work and characteristics of the work environment. Witherspoon may have been talented at processing applications, but his personality and values were more aligned with working with people.

John Holland, a career development scholar, was an early proponent of this notion that career success depends on the degree of *congruence* between the person and his or her work environment.[90] Holland argued that people can be classified into different types relating to their personality and that they seek out and are more satisfied in work environments that are congruent with their particular profile. Thus, congruence refers to the extent that someone has the same or similar personality type as the environment in which he or she is working. Some research has found that high congruence leads to better performance, satisfaction, and length of time in that career, but other studies are less supportive of the model.[91]

Holland's Six Types   Holland's theory classifies both individual personalities and work environments into six categories: realistic, investigative, artistic, social, enterprising, and conventional.

EXHIBIT 2.7	Holland's six types of personality and work environment		
Holland type	**Personality traits**	**Work environment characteristics**	**Sample occupations**
Realistic	Practical, shy, materialistic, stable	Work with hands, machines, or tools; focus on tangible results	Assembly worker; dry cleaner, mechanical engineer
Investigative	Analytic, introverted, reserved, curious, precise, independent	Work involves discovering, collecting, and analyzing; solving problems	Biologist, dentist, systems analyst
Artistic	Creative, impulsive, idealistic, intuitive, emotional	Work involves creation of new products or ideas, typically in an unstructured setting	Journalist, architect, advertising executive
Social	Sociable, outgoing, conscientious, need for affiliation	Work involves serving or helping others; working in teams	Social worker, nurse, teacher, counselor
Enterprising	Confident, assertive, energetic, need for power	Work involves leading others; achieving goals through others in a results-oriented setting	Salesperson, stockbroker, politician
Conventional	Dependable, disciplined, orderly, practical, efficient	Work involves systematic manipulation of data or information	Accountant, banker, administrator

Sources: Based on information in D. H. Montross, Z. B. Leibowitz, and C. J. Shinkman, *Real People, Real Jobs* (Palo Alto, CA: Davies-Black, 1995); J. H. Greenhaus, *Career Management* (Chicago: Dryden, 1987).

Exhibit 2.7 defines these types of people and work environments and suggests sample occupations representing those environments. Few people fall squarely into only one of Holland's classifications. Instead, Holland refers to a person's degree of *differentiation;* that is, the extent to which the individual fits into one or several types. A highly differentiated person is aligned with a single category, whereas most people fit into two or more categories.

Since most people fit into more than one personality type, Holland developed a model shaped like a hexagon with each personality type around the points of the model. *Consistency* refers to the extent that a person is aligned with similar types, which are next to each other in the hexagon, whereas dissimilar types are opposite. For instance, the enterprising and social types are next to each other in Holland's model, so individuals with both enterprising and social personalities have high consistency.

Practical Implications of Holland's Theory   Does Holland's theory work? It is certainly the most popular vocational fit model in existence and is the basis of much career counseling. Although some of the research supports Holland's general premises, scholars are concerned with specific aspects of the model. One problem is that Holland's personality types represent only the Big Five personality dimensions of openness and extroversion, even though other personality dimensions should be relevant to vocational fit.[93] Another limitation is that Holland's hexagon doesn't represent the true relationships among the six types because some opposing categories are less opposite than others. There are also doubts about whether Holland's model can be generalized to other cultures. Aside from these concerns, Holland's model seems to explain individual attitudes and behavior to some extent, and it is the dominant model of career testing today.[94]

Personality and values lay some of the foundation for our understanding of individual behavior in organizations. However, people are, of course, also influenced by the environments in which they live and work. These environments are perceived and learned, the two topics presented in the next chapter.

Chapter Summary

Individual behavior is influenced by motivation, ability, role perceptions, and situational factors (MARS). Motivation consists of internal forces that affect the direction, intensity, and persistence of a person's voluntary choice of behavior. Ability includes both the natural aptitudes and learned capabilities required to successfully complete a task. Role perceptions are a person's beliefs about what behaviors are appropriate or necessary in a particular situation. Situational factors are environmental conditions that constrain or facilitate employee behavior and performance.

Five types of behavior are discussed most often in the organizational behavior literature. Task performance represents physical behaviors as well as mental processes that support the organization's objectives. Organizational citizenship refers to behaviors that extend beyond the employee's normal job duties. Counterproductive work behaviors are voluntary and potentially harm the organization by directly affecting its functioning or property, or by hurting employees in a way that will reduce their effectiveness. Joining and staying with the organization is a fourth category of work-related behavior. The fifth type of work-related behavior is work attendance.

Values are stable, evaluative beliefs that guide our preferences for outcomes or courses of action in a variety of situations. They influence our decisions and interpretation of what is ethical. People arrange values into a hierarchy of preferences, called a value system. Shalom Schwartz grouped the dozens of individual values described by scholars over the years into 10 broader domains, which are further reduced to four quadrants of a circle. Organizations need to pay attention to values congruence—the similarity of values across systems (such as individual with organizational values).

Six values that differ across cultures are individualism, collectivism, power distance, uncertainty avoidance, achievement versus nurturing orientation, and long- versus short-term orientation. Four values that guide ethical conduct are utilitarianism, individual rights, distributive justice, and care. Three other factors that influence ethical conduct are the extent that an issue demands ethical principles (moral intensity), the person's ethical sensitivity to the presence and importance of an ethical dilemma, and situational factors that cause people to deviate from their moral values. Companies improve ethical conduct through a code of ethics, ethics training, ethics ombuds offices, and the conduct of corporate leaders.

Personality refers to the relatively stable pattern of behaviors and consistent internal states that explain a person's behavioral tendencies. Psychologists continue to debate the origins of personality, but most believe it is shaped by both heredity and environmental factors. Most personality traits are represented within the Big Five personality dimensions (CANOE): conscientiousness, agreeableness, neuroticism, openness to experience, and extroversion. Conscientiousness is a relatively strong predictor of job performance.

The Myers-Briggs Type Indicator measures how people prefer to focus their attention, collect information, process and evaluate information, and orient themselves to the outer world. Another popular personality trait in organizational behavior is locus of control, which is a generalized belief about the amount of control people have over their own lives. Another trait, called self-monitoring, refers to an individual's level of sensitivity and ability to adapt to situational cues. Holland developed a model of vocational choice that defines six personalities and their corresponding work environments.

Key Terms

ability, p. 39

Big Five personality dimensions, p. 58

care principle, p. 54

collectivism, p. 51

competencies, p. 40

conscientiousness, p. 58

counterproductive work behaviors (CWBs), p. 43

distributive justice principle, p. 54

ethical sensitivity, p. 55

ethics, p. 53

extroversion, p. 59

individualism, p. 51

individual rights principle, p. 54

introversion, p. 59

job satisfaction, p. 45

locus of control, p. 61

moral intensity, p. 55

motivation, p. 39

Myers-Briggs Type Indicator (MBTI), p. 60

organizational citizenship, p. 43

personality, p. 57

power distance, p. 52

role perceptions, p. 41

self-monitoring, p. 61

task performance, p. 42

uncertainty avoidance, p. 52

utilitarianism, p. 54

values, p. 45

values congruence, p. 48

value system, p. 46

Discussion Questions

1. An insurance company has high levels of absenteeism among the office staff. The head of office administration argues that employees are misusing the company's sick leave benefits. However, some of the mostly female staff members have explained that family responsibilities interfere with work. Using the MARS model, as well as your knowledge of absenteeism behavior, discuss some of the possible reasons for absenteeism here and how it might be reduced.

2. You notice that sales representatives in the Pacific Northwest made 20 percent fewer sales to new clients over the past quarter than salespeople located elsewhere in the United States. Use the MARS model to provide possible explanations explain why the performance of the Pacific Northwest sales reps was lower than elsewhere.

3. Most large organizations spend a lot of money identifying the key competencies for superior work performance. What are the potential benefits and pitfalls associated with identifying competencies? Are there alternatives to selecting employees rather than by identifying their competencies?

4. This chapter discussed the concept of values congruence in the context of an employee's personal values with the organization's values. But values congruence also relates to the juxtaposition of other pairs of value systems. Explain how values congruence is relevant with respect to organizational versus professional values.

5. People in a particular South American country have high power distance and high collectivism. What does this mean, and what are the implications of this information when you (a senior executive) visit employees working for your company in that country?

6. "All decisions are ethical decisions." Comment on this statement, particularly by referring to the concepts of moral intensity and ethical sensitivity.

7. In some countries, drivers ignore the lines on the road. It is common to see three or four rows of cars moving quickly along a street or highway where the lines indicate there should be just two rows of vehicles. They also honk their horns whenever approaching other vehicles. In other countries, drivers stay within the indicated lines and honk their horns only when there is a risk of accident. Are drivers in one country more ethical than in the other country? Why or why not?

8. Look over the four pairs of psychological types in the Myers-Briggs Type Indicator and identify the personality type (i.e., four letters) that would be best for a student in this course. Would this type be appropriate for students in other fields of study (e.g., biology, fine arts)?

HEADING FOR THE BIG APPLE

By Jeffrey Bagraim, University of Cape Town

It has been three months since Julius Goodman sat back in his chair and reflected on his great career success. On his desk, fresh out of its envelope, was confirmation that he was being transferred from his employer's regional office in Cape Town, South Africa, to BigCo's head office in New York for five years. "Watch me take a bite out of the Big Apple," he remembered musing to himself.

Julius had been sure that this assignment, as vice-president of marketing for a new product division, would be the ticket to his promotion to the Executive Management Team. He had been sure his wife, Stella, and two children, Dave (aged 15) and Mark (aged 13), would be ecstatic. It was "a dream come true."

Julius had been selected because he seemed to have all the attributes that would enable someone to work well abroad. He was well known in the Cape Town office for his global perspective on business issues, and he always thought about the "big picture" when making decisions. Others enjoyed working with him, and he displayed an uncommon sensitivity to the individual needs of the diverse team that reported to him. He had a reputation as a developer of people and as someone who thrived on change and uncertainty at work and in life. He particularly enjoyed participating in BigCo's global benchmarking exercise and embraced BigCo's objective of developing a world-class South African operation. His flexibility, people skills, and general management ability had flagged him for future promotion. Now he was being given the opportunity to prove himself, and he knew it.

He remembered how he had returned home at 7 P.M. to tell his wife and sons about his good fortune, and he smiled when he remembered how excited they had been. It took several weeks for the reality of the impending transition to sink in.

At first, his family joked about the move and set agendas for what they would do when they arrived in New York, but as time wore on they began asking practical questions. Stella began asking questions he could not answer: What would happen to their beloved pet, Goliath (a Great Dane)? How would she break the news to her colleagues at the charity where she did voluntary work every morning? Would they have to sell their home and furniture?

The questioning process started a bit later for Dave and Mark. At first they wanted to know only one thing: When would they visit Disneyland? After a while, frustrated by the ambiguous answers Julius gave them, they turned their attention to practical concerns: What would happen to their studies? Where would they go to school? What would become of their sports training? How would they cope in the winter? In all, they were very excited but they did begin to entertain some regret about the being uprooted from their school, their friends, and their brand new car, which they shared.

Anyway, the family was sure about one thing: They would fit into the America way of life without any trouble. After all, American culture was very familiar to them. They even joked about how they were learning American English. On reflection, Julius realized that his family had relied on television to ensure a successful transition. It would not be sufficient.

Julius refused to attend any of BigCo's training programs that had been designed to prepare executive for cross-national transfers. He was usually eager to attend training courses, but he was under tremendous time pressure. After looking over the course content he felt sure that learning about issues such as stress management, business etiquette in different countries, financial management, and self-awareness would be a waste of his time. He discouraged Stella from attending the spouse program. He was convinced that such training was a low priority given the massive task Stella was facing in preparing the family for the move. After all, they were moving to America not China. How different could America be?

Julius had read that General Motors spent more than $500,000 a year on cross-cultural training for the approximately 150 employees and their families who are transferred abroad every year. He knew that several BigCo executives who had transferred had later applied to return home long before their assignments were completed. He was thankful that he had been selected for an American assignment. He could scarcely imagine the difficulties that faced those being transferred to places with a completely different language and culture. He was sure that his transition into American life would be smooth and painless.

The first few days in New York were exciting. The family felt like they were on holiday. Everything was as they had dreamed it to be—the streets were thronging with people, the variety of goods on offer was amazing, and the people were friendly and open. Julius found his fellow workers at the New York office to be both friendly and brimming with useful advice. He took a few days off to sort himself out and dedicated this time to finding a permanent place to live. He could not believe what a complicated decision choosing a neighborhood was, and he was mystified by the seemingly archaic rental agreement he was asked to sign. Choosing a school for his children was equally difficult, and he was concerned that they would need a long time to adjust to the American school system. Everything was so different.

Julius and his family soon began to miss all the things that they were used to at home in Cape Town. They missed cricket and rugby. They missed Peppermint Crisps, fish paste, and Mrs. Balls' Chutney, but most of all they missed their family and friends. New York may be the Big Apple, but finding a decent-tasting chocolate bar or friends to replace those back home was impossible. They missed home, and he had not even begun work yet. The few days he had anticipated to "sort himself out" kept on being extended.

Julian began work after a two-week settling-in period and soon realized that working life in the New York office was very different from that in the Cape Town office. He found his American colleagues to be very brash and aggressive; he was not used to their individualistic, independent approach to solving problems. He was not used to the bluntness they displayed in meetings and the urgency with which they approached their work. The consultative, time-intensive decision-making approach he was used to was simply not going to be appropriate with his rather impatient and assertive colleagues. He also wondered about their short-term orientation and their rationalistic manner of approaching issues. Julius was convinced that his consensus-building approach to decision making would add value, but he knew that he had to prove himself before attempting to introduce new approaches to decision making. Overall, he was impressed by his colleagues' drive, tenacity, and ability to work hard, although he sometimes suspected that the long hours they put in were not as productive as they could have been. It seemed that they were trying very hard to impress the CEO. They may have called the CEO by his first name, but they respected his position of authority and his power.

Since his first day at work, Julius enjoyed the casual manner in which people interacted and the casual dress code that the New York office promoted. Nevertheless, he knew that interpersonal competition was intense and that everyone had to watch his or her own back. Julius also soon realized that the labor laws that had protected him in South Africa did not exist in America. He saw his colleagues being fired without all the formalities and inquiries that he had taken for granted as part of his working life. Julius began to change; he became tense and more competitive, friendly but on guard. This was proving to be a very stressful assignment. He had to make it work. This assignment could sink him. The pressure built up and he began to work longer and longer.

To add to his woes, his family seemed to be having an increasingly difficult time. Stella found it difficult to make friends and began to feel very isolated. She found that she had little in common with the American women who lived nearby, and the South African New Yorkers she met were working extremely long hours and could rarely meet with her. She found it hard not to work (immigration laws prevented her from working). Though she did not have the same degree of fear that she had in South Africa, she actually began to miss some of the "real problems" in South Africa, everything here seemed less important, less serious, and she missed her car. Before coming to New York, she had not used public transportation since her childhood; now she traveled on the underground trains every day.

She also wondered that there were no seasons for fruit and vegetables . . . everything was available year-round. These were not problems but they added to her sense of dislocation.

On a social level, both Julius and Stella had heard that America was very informal. They found that this was a great simplification of reality. Dining out was often a formal affair and going out to dinner in a suit seemed very strange to Julius. Both of them were startled by the meticulous punctuality of their friends, but they soon adjusted. The widespread ignorance about South Africa among people they met was initially funny, then irritating. Some people were very knowledgeable about South Africa, but many were extremely ignorant, "Do you know Joey Stewart, he's been in Algeria for six years, you must know him? Do you have lions roaming near Cape Town?"

Despite all their difficulties, Julius and his family remained convinced that the transfer to New York had been a positive experience. New York was an exciting place and they were going to go home in only a few years! Of course, the excitement of the first few days did wear off—reality was more of a culture shock than they had anticipated, but the worst was over and they could now begin to enjoy what the city had to offer. Clearly, the holiday was over and it would take a very long time (if not forever) to feel like a "New Yorker." Perhaps he should have attended that training course after all.

Discussion Questions

1. In selecting someone for a foreign assignment, what criteria would you set in the selection process?

2. What factors should organizations consider when trying to facilitate the smooth cross-cultural transitions of their employees?

3. What are the cultural characteristics of American national culture that affect organizational behavior in American organizations?

4. What are the benefits to a global organization of encouraging employees to accept foreign assignments (cross-cultural exchanges)?

5. In which countries are employees *most like* employees in your country and in which countries are employees the *least like* those in your country?

6. How would you describe your own national culture and why is it often very difficult to identify your own national culture?

CASE STUDY 2.2

PUSHING PAPER CAN BE FUN

A large American city government was putting on a number of seminars for managers of various departments throughout the city. At one of these sessions, the topic discussed was motivation—how we can get public servants motivated to do a good job? The plight of a police captain became the central focus of the discussion:

> I've got a real problem with my officers. They come on the force as young, inexperienced rookies, and we send them out on the street, either in cars or on a beat. They seem to like the contact they have with the public, the action involved in crime prevention, and the apprehension of criminals. They also like helping people out at fires, accidents, and other emergencies.

> The problem occurs when they get back to the station. They hate to do the paperwork, and because they dislike it, the job is frequently put off or done inadequately. This lack of attention hurts us later on when we get to court. We need clear, factual reports. They must be highly detailed and unambiguous. As soon as one part of a report is shown to be inadequate or incorrect, the rest of the report is suspect. Poor reporting probably causes us to lose more cases than any other factor.

> I just don't know how to motivate them to do a better job. We're in a budget crunch and I have absolutely no financial rewards at my disposal. In fact, we'll probably have to lay some people off in the near future. It's hard for me to make the

job interesting and challenging because it isn't—it's boring, routine paperwork, and there isn't much you can do about it.

Finally, I can't say to them that their promotions will hinge on the excellence of their paperwork. First of all, they know it's not true. If their performance is adequate, most are more likely to get promoted just by staying on the force a certain number of years than for some specific outstanding act. Second, they were trained to do the job they do out in the streets, not to fill out forms. All through their career it is the arrests and interventions that get noticed.

Some people have suggested a number of things, like using conviction records as a performance criterion. However, we know that's not fair—too many other things are involved. Bad paperwork increases the chance that you lose in court, but good paperwork doesn't necessarily mean you'll win. We tried setting up team competitions based upon the excellence of the reports, but the officers caught on to that pretty quickly. No one was getting any type of reward for winning the competition, and they figured why should they bust a gut when there was no payoff.

I just don't know what to do.

Discussion Questions

1. What performance problems is the captain trying to correct? p. 42

2. Use the MARS model of individual behavior and performance to diagnose the possible causes of the unacceptable behavior.

3. Has the captain considered all possible solutions to the problem? If not, what else might be done?

Source: T. R. Mitchell and J. R. Larson Jr., *People in Organizations*, 3rd ed. (New York: McGraw-Hill, 1987), p. 184. Used with permission.

CASE STUDY 2.3

AFTER ENRON: THE IDEAL CORPORATION

BusinessWeek Jack Stack, the CEO from Springfield, Missouri, who popularized open-book management in the 1980s, is concerned about the changing attitudes of America's emerging business leaders. Rather than focusing on the needs of all stakeholders and the potential value that employees can contribute, the new executives seemed more interested in their own pocketbooks. The strategy isn't to grow the business; it seems to be to raise stockholder value, sell out, and get out of town. Stack's ideas about ethics and empowerment were out of favor—until the dot-com bubble burst and Enron created a more sobering awareness of Stack's views.

This *Business Week* case study looks at the changing landscape of business in an era when ethics is becoming important again. It describes the messages that Jack Stack, Alfred P. West, and other executives are communicating that will improve ethical decision making. Read through this *Business Week* article at www.mhhe.com/mcshane3e and prepare for the discussion questions below.

Discussion Questions

1. What corporate changes are identified in this article that will emphasize more ethical decision making in organizations?

2. In this article, Larry Johnston, CEO of Albertson's Inc., says: "A lot of companies simply looked at performance in assessing their leaders. There have to be two dimensions to leadership: performance and values. You can't have one without the other." What does Johnston mean by this statement, and what are its implications for hiring corporate leaders who are ethical?

3. This article mentions that "transparency" will help improve corporate ethics. What does "transparency" mean, and how will ethics improve through this condition?

Source: J. A. Byrne, "After Enron: The Ideal Corporation," *Business Week*, August 26, 2002, p. 68.

COMPARING CULTURAL VALUES

Purpose   This exercise is designed to help you determine the extent to which students hold similar assumptions about the values that dominate in other countries.

Instructions   The names in the left column represent labels that a major consulting project identified with businesspeople in a particular country, based on its national culture and values. These names appear in alphabetical order. In the right column are the names of countries, also in alphabetical order, corresponding to the labels in the left column.

- *Step 1*—Working alone, students will connect the labels with the countries by relying on their perceptions of these countries. Each label is associated with only one country, so each label will be connected to only one country, and vice versa. Draw a line to connect the pairs, or put the label number beside the country name.
- *Step 2*—The instructor will form teams of four or five students. Members of each team will compare their results and try to reach consensus on a common set of connecting pairs.
- *Step 3*—Teams or the instructor will post the results for all to see the extent of students' common opinions about businesspeople in

EXHIBIT	Values labels and country names, listed alphabetically

Value label	Country name
1. Affable humanists	Australia
2. Ancient modernizers	Brazil
3. Commercial catalysts	Canada
4. Conceptual strategists	China
5. Efficient manufacturers	France
6. Ethical statesmen	Germany
7. Informal egalitarians	India
8. Modernizing traditionalists	Netherlands
9. Optimistic entrepreneurs	New Zealand
10. Quality perfectionists	Singapore
11. Rugged individualists	Taiwan
12. Serving merchants	United Kingdom
13. Tolerant traders	United States

Source: Based on R. Rosen, P. Digh, M. Singer, and C. Phillips, *Global Literacies* (New York: Simon & Schuster, 2000).

other cultures. Class discussion can then consider the reasons why the results are so similar or different, as well as the implications of these results for working in a global work environment.

ETHICS DILEMMA VIGNETTES

Purpose   This exercise is designed to make you aware of the ethical dilemmas people face in various business situations, as well as the competing principles and values that operate in these situations.

Instructions   The instructor will form teams of four or five students. Team members will read each vignette below and discuss possible actions for each vignette. Then, relying on *consensus*, each team should choose a preferred course of

action. Teams should be prepared to (a) clearly describe their course of action and (b) justify their action using logic and ethical principles.

Vignette 1   At work you use many different software packages. Several weeks ago your supervisor ordered a new package for you that several of your colleagues are currently using. The software is now late in arriving. The package would aid you tremendously in completing your current project, but it is not absolutely necessary. Earlier today your supervisor brought her copy of the software to you and suggested that you copy it onto your computer for use until your copy arrives. You know that the software is licensed to be installed onto only one computer. **What would you do in this situation?**

Vignette 2   You are the owner of a highly rated talk radio station in a large Midwest city. The popular radio personality on the morning phone-in show, Judy Price, is married to John Price, an attorney who recently entered state politics. He was elected and is quickly becoming a prominent lawmaker with controversial, but generally popular, ideas for reform. The radio station's Board of Directors is increasingly concerned that the station's perceived objectivity would be compromised if Ms. Price remains on air as a news commentator while her husband holds such a public position in the state. Some co-workers doubt that Judy Price would publicly criticize her husband or his policies, although they don't know for certain. Ms. Price says that her job comes first and that any attempt to remove her would represent a form of discrimination. There are no other on-air positions available for her at this station. **What would you do in this situation?**

Vignette 3   James Ngoyen and Stephen Brolin spent several months negotiating with a potential client in another country about buying one of the company's products. Ngoyen is head of marketing for this product and will soon retire; Brolin will be promoted into Ngoyen's job. The client agreed in principle to sign a contract, representing one of the company's largest sales to a single source. The company has suffered through a prolonged recession and, without this contract, the company would have to lay off up to 20 percent of the employees who produce this specific product. Last month, Brolin suddenly had a serious illness and will likely take permanent disability leave. In his place, the company promoted Naomi Green, a highly capable marketing professional who was slated for promotion to a similar position in one of the company's other product areas. Ngoyen and Green met the client to finalize the contract, which would be signed a few days later. However, soon after returning from that trip, Ngoyen received a disturbing note from the client, indicating that it would not sign the contract if the account was managed by Naomi Green or any other woman. The note said that women did not usually hold such positions in the client's country, and the arrangement was causing distress. The client would sign the contract if a male manager were placed in charge of the product? **What would you do in this situation?**

Vignette 4   While on a trip out of town on business you had dinner with your sister. Your company has a policy of reimbursing dinner expenses up to $50 per meal. The total cost for this meal for both you and your sister was $35.70. The cost of your meal alone was $16.30. You know that others in your company routinely submit claims for dinner expenses for nonbusiness parties. **What would you do in this situation?**

Sources: Vignette 1 and 4 are adapted from R. R. Radtke, "The Effects of Gender and Setting on Accountants' Ethically Sensitive Decisions," *Journal of Business Ethics* 24 (April 2000), pp. 299–312. Vignettes 2 and 3 are written by Steven L. McShane and are based on true events.

IDENTIFYING YOUR SELF-MONITORING PERSONALITY

Purpose   This self-assessment is designed to help you to estimate your level of self-monitoring personality.

Instructions   The statements in this scale refer to personal characteristics that might or might not be characteristic of you. Mark the box indicating the extent that the statement is true or false as a characteristic of you. This exercise is completed alone so students assess themselves honestly without concerns of social comparison. However, class discussion will focus on the relevance of self-monitoring personality in organizations.

Self-Monitoring Scale

Indicate the degree to which you think the following statements are true or false.	Very False	Somewhat False	Slightly More False than True	Slightly More True than False	Somewhat True	Very True
1. In social situations, I have the ability to alter my behavior if I feel that something else is called for............	☐	☐	☐	☐	☐	☐
2. I am often able to read people's true emotions correctly through their eyes...............................	☐	☐	☐	☐	☐	☐
3. I have the ability to control the way I come across to people, depending on the impression I wish to give them..	☐	☐	☐	☐	☐	☐
4. In conversations, I am sensitive to even the slightest change in the facial expression of the person I'm conversing with......................................	☐	☐	☐	☐	☐	☐
5. My powers of intuition are quite good when it comes to understanding others' emotions and motives...............	☐	☐	☐	☐	☐	☐
6. I can usually tell when others consider a joke in bad taste, even though they may laugh convincingly.....	☐	☐	☐	☐	☐	☐
7. When I feel that the image I am portraying isn't working, I can readily change it to something that does........	☐	☐	☐	☐	☐	☐
8. I can usually tell when I've said something inappropriate by reading the listener's eyes.................................	☐	☐	☐	☐	☐	☐
9. I have trouble changing my behavior to suit different people and different situations....................................	☐	☐	☐	☐	☐	☐
10. I have found that I can adjust my behavior to meet the requirements of any situation I find myself in............	☐	☐	☐	☐	☐	☐
11. If someone is lying to me, I usually know it at once from that person's manner of expression.........................	☐	☐	☐	☐	☐	☐
12. Even when it might be to my advantage, I have difficulty putting up a good front......................................	☐	☐	☐	☐	☐	☐
13. Once I know what the situation calls for, it's easy for me to regulate my actions accordingly.............................	☐	☐	☐	☐	☐	☐

Source: R. D. Lennox and R. N. Wolfe, "Revision of the Self-Monitoring Scale," *Journal of Personality and Social Psychology* 46 (June 1984), pp. 1348–64. The response categories in this scale have been altered slightly due to limitations with the original scale responses.

INDIVIDUALISM–COLLECTIVISM SCALE

Purpose This self-assessment is designed to help you to identify your level of individualism and collectivism.

Instructions This scale consists of several statements, and you are asked to indicate how well each statement describes you. Read each statement in this self-assessment and select the response that best indicates how the statement describes you. You need to be honest with yourself to receive a reasonable estimate of your level of individualism and collectivism.

IDENTIFYING YOUR LOCUS OF CONTROL

Purpose This self-assessment is designed to help you to estimate the extent to which you have an internal or external locus of control personality.

Instructions This instrument asks you to indicate the degree to which you agree or disagree with each of the statements provided. You need to be honest with yourself to ascertain a reasonable estimate of your locus of control. The results show your relative position in the internal–external locus continuum and the general meaning of this score.

MATCHING HOLLAND'S CAREER TYPES

Purpose This self-assessment is designed to help you to understand Holland's career types.

Instructions Holland's theory identifies six different types of work environments and occupations in which people work. Few jobs fit purely in one category, but all have a dominant type. Your task is to determine the Holland type that you believe best fits each of the occupations presented in the instrument. While completing this self-assessment, you can open your book to the exhibit describing Holland's six types.

After studying the preceding material, be sure to check out our website at
www.mhhe.com/mcshane3e
for more in-depth information and interactivities that correspond to this chapter.

chapter 3

Perception and Learning in Organizations

Learning Objectives

After reading this chapter, you should be able to:

■ Outline the perceptual process.

■ Explain how we perceive ourselves and others through social identity.

■ Outline the reasons why stereotyping occurs and the perceptual problems it creates.

■ Describe three ways to minimize the adverse effects of stereotyping.

■ Describe the attribution process and two attribution errors.

■ Summarize the self-fulfilling prophecy process.

■ Explain how empathy and the Johari Window can help improve our perceptions.

■ Define learning.

■ Describe the A-B-C model of behavior modification and the four contingencies of reinforcement.

■ Describe the three features of social learning theory.

■ Summarize the four components of Kolb's experiential learning model.

As president of the Central Park Conservancy, Regina Peruggi normally spends most of her time digging around New York City for donations to maintain the world-famous park. For one week, however, she was swinging a pick ax, seeding grass, and literally digging the earth as a groundskeeper in the park. The role switch was filmed by BBC/PBS as part of the series *Back to the Floor,* which drops executives from atop the corporate ladder to the lowest rung. The idea is for executives to get a reality check on what front-line employees face every day.

Peruggi knew that gardening in Central Park is hard physical labor, but she did not anticipate some of the other realities. For example, grounds staff spend up to three hours each day picking up trash even though some of them are expert horticulturalists. "You're really wasting the talent of somebody like John, who really knows horticulture, who could be doing horticulture all day long," she says. Peruggi also realized the dangers that her staff face from drug dealers in some parts of the park. "I learned things I could never have learned any other way," she admits.

Rather than waiting for film crews to arrive, some executives step into the shoes of their employees as a regular routine. David Neeleman, the founder of New York–based JetBlue, works in the trenches each month with his baggage handlers and ticket takers. "With other aviation companies, upper-level management doesn't like to mingle with employees," says Fred Ramos, JetBlue's ground-operations supervisor. "But David wants to be smack in the middle of everything."

Regina Peruggi, president of New York's Central Park Conservancy, got her perceptions back in focus by spending a week working on the front line.

At Domino's Pizza, sending the CEO back to the front lines isn't good enough. The Ann Arbor, Michigan, company has developed a week-long Pizza Prep School where its administrative and management staff receive 20 hours of classroom instruction in operating a pizza store along with 24 hours of hands-on experience. The experience gives everyone a better understanding of how their decisions affect the company's retail outlets. Pizza Prep School has been so successful that J. Walter Thompson, the company that provides marketing services to Domino's, is also sending its account executives through the program. "If you know the ins and outs of the operation of a pizza store, you can develop marketing programs from an operational perspective," says a J. Walter Thompson executive.[1] ■

perception
The process of receiving information about and making sense of the world around us.

Whether by working in someone else's job or paying attention to what others are saying, people throughout the organization need to develop better ways to perceive the world around them and learn about the consequences of their actions. **Perception** is the process of receiving information about and making sense of the world around us. It entails deciding which information to notice, how to categorize this information, and how to interpret it within the framework of our existing knowledge. This chapter begins by describing the perceptual process, that is, the dynamics of selecting, organizing, and interpreting external stimuli. Social identity theory, which has recently become a leading perceptual theory in organizational behavior, is introduced. Next, we look at the dynamics of stereotyping, including ways of minimizing stereotype biases in the workplace. Attribution, self-fulfilling prophecy, and other perceptual issues are then discussed, followed by an overview of empathy and Johari Window as general strategies to minimize perceptual problems.

The opening vignette also considers the topic of learning because executives working the front lines learn about what employees and customers experience every day. Indeed, it is difficult to discuss perceptions without also referring to the knowledge and skills learned from those perceptions. That's why perceptions and learning are combined in this chapter. The latter part of this chapter introduces the concept of learning as well as the related concepts of tacit and explicit knowledge. We then look at the elements of behavior modification, social learning theory, and experiential learning.

The Perceptual Process

The Greek philosopher Plato wrote long ago that we see reality only as shadows reflected on the rough wall of a cave.[2] In other words, reality is filtered through an imperfect perceptual process. This imperfect process, which is illustrated in Exhibit 3.1, begins when environmental stimuli are received through our senses. Most stimuli are screened out; the rest are organized and interpreted based on various information processing activities. The resulting

EXHIBIT 3.1

Model of the perceptual process

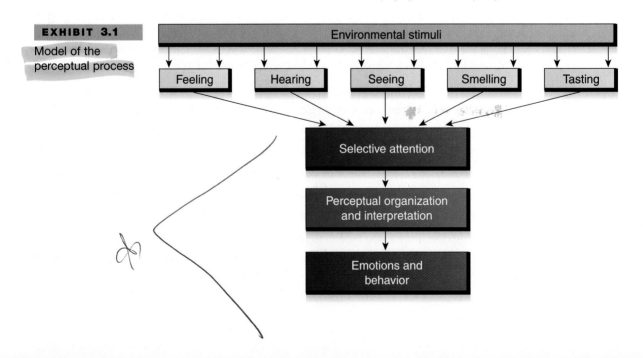

perceptions influence our emotions and behavior toward those objects, people, and events.[3]

Selective Attention

Our five senses are constantly bombarded with stimuli. Some things are noticed, but most are screened out. A nurse working in postoperative care might ignore the smell of recently disinfected instruments or the sound of co-workers talking nearby. Yet a small flashing red light on the nurse station console is immediately noticed because it signals that a patient's vital signs are failing. This process of filtering information received by our senses is called **selective attention.**

One influence on selective attention is the size, intensity, motion, repetition, and novelty of the target (including people). The red light on the nurse station console receives attention because it is bright (intensity), flashing (motion), and a rare event (novelty). As for people, we would notice two employees having a heated debate if co-workers normally don't raise their voices (novelty and intensity). Notice that selective attention is also influenced by the context in which the target is perceived. You might be aware that a client has a German accent if the meeting takes place in Dallas, but not if the conversation took place in Germany, particularly if you had been living there for some time. On the contrary, it would be your accent that would be noticed!

Characteristics of the Perceiver   Selective attention depends on more than the object and context. It is also affected by characteristics of the perceiver. We tend to remember information that is consistent with our values and attitudes and ignore information that is inconsistent with them. For example, interviewers who develop positive feelings toward a job applicant early in the interview tend to subsequently screen out negative information about that candidate.[4] In extreme cases, our emotions screen out large blocks of information that threaten our beliefs and values. This phenomenon, called *perceptual defense,* protects our self-esteem and may be a coping mechanism to minimize stress in the short run.[5]

Selective attention is also affected by our expectations.[6] An African proverb says: "It is on the regular path we take that the wild beast attacks." In other words, through experience, we are conditioned to anticipate routine events. Unique events are excluded from our thoughts—until it is too late. In organizational settings, expectations prevent decision makers from seeing opportunities and competitive threats. For this reason, experts urge us to develop *splatter vision*—taking everything in as a whole while focusing on nothing. Truck drivers learn to expect the unexpected, such as a child darting out onto the road. Jet fighter pilots constantly check their peripheral vision, not just what's ahead of them. Police detectives try to avoid forming theories too early in criminal investigations with few leads or suspects. "When you get a theory, it can put blinders on to what really happened," explains one detective, referring to a homicide where there were few leads or suspects.[7]

Perceptual Organization and Interpretation

After selecting stimuli, we usually simplify and "make sense" of them. This involves organizing the information into general categories and interpreting it. We rely on perceptual grouping principles to organize people and objects into

selective attention
The process of filtering information received by our senses.

recognizable and manageable patterns or categories. This *perceptual grouping* occurs in a number of ways. It occurs when we make assumptions about people based on their similarity or proximity to others. It also occurs when we think we see trends in otherwise ambiguous information. Another form of perceptual grouping is closure, such as filling in missing information about what happened at a meeting that you missed (e.g., who was there, where it was held).

Perceptual grouping helps us to make sense of the workplace, but it can also inhibit creativity and open-mindedness. It puts blinders on our ability to organize and interpret people and events differently. Perceptual grouping is influenced by our broader assumptions and beliefs, known as mental models.

Mental Models   Communications guru Marshall McLuhan once wrote that people wear their own set of idiosyncratic goggles. In his colorful way, McLuhan was saying that each of us holds a unique view of what the world looks like and how it operates. These idiosyncratic goggles are known as **mental models.**[8] Mental models are the broad worldviews or "theories-in-use" that people rely on to guide their perceptions and behaviors. For example, most of us have a mental model about attending a college lecture or seminar. We have a set of assumptions and expectations about how people arrive, arrange themselves in the room, ask and answer questions, and so forth. We can create a mental image of what a class would look like in progress.

Mental models help us to make sense of our environment, but they may blind us from seeing that world in different ways.[9] For example, accounting professionals tend to see corporate problems in terms of accounting solutions, whereas marketing professionals see the same problems from a marketing perspective. Mental models also block our recognition of new opportunities. How do we change mental models? It's a tough challenge. After all, we developed models from several years of experience and reinforcement. The most important way to minimize the perceptual problems with mental models is to constantly question them. We need to ask ourselves about the assumptions we make. Working with people from diverse backgrounds is another way to break out of existing mental models. Colleagues from different cultures and areas of expertise tend to have different mental models, so working with them makes your assumptions more obvious.

mental models
The broad worldviews or "theories in-use" that people rely on to guide their perceptions and behaviors.

Social Identity Theory

social identity theory
A conceptual framework based on the idea that how we perceive the world depends on how we define ourselves in terms of our membership in various social groups.

The perceptual process is an interactive dynamic between our self-perceptions and perceptions of others. In other words, how we perceive the world depends on how we define ourselves. This connection between self-perception and perception of others is explained through **social identity theory.**[10] According to social identity theory, people maintain a *social identity* by defining themselves in terms of the groups to which they belong and have an emotional attachment. For instance, someone might have a social identity as an American, a graduate of the University of Vermont, and an employee at IBM (see Exhibit 3.2). Everyone engages in this social categorization process because it helps to make sense of where we fit within the social world.

Along with a social identity, people have a *personal identity*—characteristics that make them unique and distinct from people in any particular group. For instance, an unusual achievement that distinguishes you from other people

EXHIBIT 3.2

Self-perception and
social perception
through social
identity

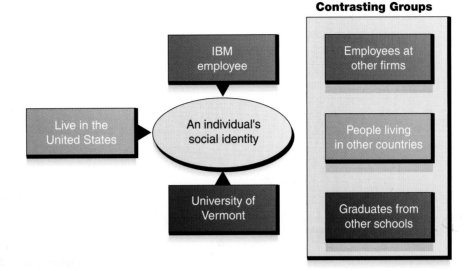

typically becomes a personal identity characteristic (e.g., "I'm probably the only one in this class who has trekked through Malaysia's Cameron Highlands!"). The difference between personal and social identity is that personal identity refers to something about you as an individual without reference to a larger group. Social identity, on the other hand, defines you in terms of characteristics of the group. By perceiving yourself as an IBM employee, you are actually assigning characteristics to yourself that are also characteristics of IBM employees in general.

People adopt degrees of personal and social identity, depending on the situation.[11] Let's say that you and other students in your organizational behavior class are similar with respect to race, age, and other observable characteristics. In this context, your self-concept might be dominated by your personal identity, that is, your unique accomplishments. On the other hand, if you are a computer science student in a class consisting mostly of business students, then your group membership—your social identity—would likely dominate your self-perception. In this situation, you would define yourself more by your field of specialization ("I'm in the computer science program") than by any personal identity characteristics. As your membership in a distinguishing social group becomes known to others, they, too, would likely identify you by that feature.

Social identity is a complex combination of many memberships arranged in a hierarchy of importance. Which groups are emphasized in our social identity? One determining factor is how obvious our membership is in the group. We define ourselves by our sex, race, age, and other observable characteristics because other people easily identify our membership in those groups. Thus, if one of your demographic features is uncommon in a particular setting, you are more likely to partly define yourself by that feature when in that setting. It is difficult to ignore your gender in a class where most other students are the opposite gender, for example. In that context, gender tends to become a stronger defining feature of your social identity than in social settings where there are many people of the same gender.

Although observable demographics are usually part of our social identity, a much more important influence is the status of the group in society. Most of us want to have a positive self-image, so we identify with groups that have higher status or respect. Medical doctors usually define themselves in terms of their profession because of its high status, whereas people in low-status jobs are less likely to do so. Some people define themselves in terms of where they work because their employer has a favorable reputation in the community; other people never mention where they work because the firm is known for its poor customer service or ethical conduct.[12]

Perceiving Others Through Social Identity

Social identity theory doesn't just explain how we develop self-perceptions. It also explains the dynamics of *social perception*—how we perceive others. In particular, it describes how and why we categorize others into homogeneous and often less favorable groups. Social identity is a *comparative* process, meaning that we define ourselves in terms of our differences with people who belong to other groups. By defining yourself as someone who attends this college, you probably make comparisons to people who attend other colleges. To simplify this comparison process, we tend to *homogenize* people within social categories. We think that people within our college (or sex or race, etc.) share certain traits, and people in comparison groups share a different set of traits. This may be partly true, but we further exaggerate these differences. You can see an extreme form of this comparison process when executives describe their competitors or students refer to people at other colleges, particularly just before a football game against the other college.

Comparison and homogenization explain why we perceptually group other people and overgeneralize their traits. But we also tend to develop less positive (or sometimes downright negative) images of people outside our social identity groups. Why do we disparage people who are different from us? Here's the answer: We are motivated to support our self-esteem by identifying ourselves with groups that have positive characteristics. To maintain this favorable social identity, we usually construct favorable images of our own social identity groups and, as a result, less favorable images of people belonging to other social categories. This is particularly true when the other groups are in competition and conflict with our social identity groups. The negative image of opponents preserves our self-image while the threat exists.[13]

To summarize, the social identity process explains how we perceive ourselves and others. We partly identify ourselves in terms of our membership in social groups. This comparison process includes creating a homogeneous image of our own social groups and different homogeneous images of people in other groups. We also tend to assign more favorable features to our own groups and less favorable features to other groups. This perceptual process makes our social world easier to understand. However, it also becomes the basis for stereotyping people in organizational settings, which we discuss next.

stereotyping
The process of assigning traits to people based on their membership in a social category.

Stereotyping in Organizational Settings

Stereotyping is an extension of social identity theory and a product of our natural process of organizing information. It is the process of assigning traits to people based on their membership in a social category.[14] In other words, stereotypes define people by the demographic or other observable groups to which they belong. The stereotyping process begins when we develop social categories and assign traits that are difficult to observe. For instance, students might form a stereotype that professors are both intelligent and absent-minded. Personal experiences shape stereotypes to some extent, but we mostly adopt stereotypes provided to us within our culture (from socialization and movie characters, for instance).[15]

Next, people are assigned to one or more social categories based on easily observable information about them, such as their gender, appearance, or physical location. Observable features allow us to assign people to a social group quickly and without much investigation. Last, the cluster of traits linked to the social category is assigned to people identified as members of that group. For example, we subconsciously assume that professors are absentminded, at least until we know them better.

Why Stereotyping Occurs

Stereotyping occurs for three reasons.[16] First, trying to absorb the unique constellations of attributes about each person we meet is a huge cognitive challenge; there is too much information to remember. Instead, we rely on a natural process called *categorical thinking*—grouping people and objects into preconceived categories that are stored in our long-term memory. This categorization process is the basis of stereotyping. Second, we have a strong need to understand and anticipate how others will behave. We don't have much information when first meeting someone, so we rely heavily on stereotypes to fill in the missing pieces.

Last, stereotyping enhances our self-perception and social identity. Recall from social identity theory that our self-perception is developed by defining ourselves in terms of membership in certain social groups and contrasting them with other groups. To define yourself as an American male, for instance, you tend to rely on stereotypes of females and of people from other cultures. To enhance our self-concept, we tend to emphasize the positive aspects of the groups to which we belong and to emphasize the negative aspects of contrasting groups. This creates less favorable images of other groups, which involves subconsciously assigning inaccurate traits to people in those different groups. Moreover, researchers recently discovered that we are particularly motivated to use negative stereotypes toward people who hurt our self-esteem.[17]

Problems with Stereotyping

Early writers warned that stereotypes were almost completely incorrect or, at best, exaggerated the traits of people in the stereotyped groups. Scholars now take a more moderate view. They say that stereotypes generally have some inaccuracies, some overestimation or underestimation of real differences, and some degree of accuracy.[18] Still, stereotyping causes numerous problems. For instance, Global Connections 3.1 describes how sex-role stereotyping as well as occupational stereotyping explains the paucity of women around the world who embark on engineering and technology careers.

One problem is that stereotypes do not accurately describe every person in that social category. For instance, research has found that people with physical disabilities are stereotyped as being quiet, gentle-hearted, shy, insecure, dependent, and submissive.[19] Although this may be true of some people, it is

Social Identity and Stereotypes Discourage Women from Engineering

Alarm bells are ringing around the world regarding the chronic underrepresentation of women in engineering, science, and information technology. Over half of undergraduate university students in the United States, Canada, and Australia are women, yet only about 20 percent of them complete computer science and engineering degrees. "Women are still in the minority here," says Azar Mouzari, a fourth-year student of electrical engineering at the University of Ottawa, Canada. "You can feel it. When I went into a class of 40 or 50, there were only three or four women."

One problem is that perceptions of engineering and information technology (IT) don't fit the self-images that women want for themselves. "If you ask a woman to characterize a typical IT professional, she is likely to describe a young man with excess facial hair, sitting behind a computer all day munching pizza and guzzling Coke," quips Ann Swain, chief executive of the Association of Technology Staffing Companies in the United Kingdom. This concern is supported by a recent Australian report, which concluded that "the image of the industry is a major problem and is putting girls off."

Sex-role stereotyping is another perceptual barrier to women entering engineering and technology. "Stereotyping is already occurring in children as young as five," warns Marie-Noelle Barton, director of the Women in Science and Engineering Campaign (Wise) in the United Kingdom. "Girls are given Barbie dolls to play with whilst boys are handed action hero-type transformers that convert from dinosaurs to mechanical planes," says Azizan Baharuddin, a professor at the University of Malaya in Kuala Lumpur, Malaysia. "The idea that boys' toys are geared towards engineering and technicality is too one-sided." Gloria Nsomba, head of marketing at Malawi Telecoms, says that women in that African country are further discouraged because they are "perceived not to be intelligent enough to tackle" engineering and similar male-dominated careers.

Sex-role stereotyping also causes many women to have lower self-confidence in their ability to complete engineering

University of Ottawa student Azar Mouzari, shown here with Dean Tyseer Aboulnasr, and other women are underrepresented in engineering programs partly because of stereotyping and self-perceptions.

and technology courses. Even though female and male engineering students receive similar grades, women are more likely to leave these programs when they receive low grades. "Guys that aren't doing well will blame the prof, or the book, or the class that sucks," says Justyna Krzysiak, an engineering student at the University of Calgary, Canada. "Girls tend to blame themselves more. They'll say 'I'm just not smart enough to be an engineer,' or, 'this isn't really for me.'" The guys stay because they blame the situation, the female students leave because they blame themselves.

Sources: A. Swain, "Easing a Skills' Shortage—Women in IT," *Guardian* (London), March 13, 2003, p. 6; Z. Idris, "Three Who Found Joy in Science," *New Straits Times* (Kuala Lumpur, Malaysia), August 5, 2002, p. 6; "Pre-schooler Science Blow," *Electronics Times,* July 2002, p. 3; G. Nsomba, "The Status of Women—The Struggle against Hostile Customs," *All Africa,* March 11, 2002; J. Sinclair, "Breaking Down the Barriers," *The Age* (Melbourne), January 30, 2002; M. Orton, "'You Feel Very Isolated,'" *Ottawa Citizen,* July 25, 2002; R. Ross, "System Favors the Few, the Male," *Toronto Star,* May 20, 2002, p. E1; H. Sokoloff, "'Geek' Culture Turns Women Off Computer Studies: Report," *National Post* (Canada), March 19, 2002, p. A1; D. Rucker, "Barrier Breakers," *Oilweek,* April 2, 2001, p. 30ff.

certainly not characteristic of everyone who has a physical disability. Another concern is that stereotypes cause us to ignore or misinterpret information that is inconsistent with the stereotype.[20] If we meet a professor with a good short-term memory, we tend to ignore that observation unless we notice several times that this person is not absentminded.

A more serious problem with stereotyping is that it lays the foundation for prejudice and intentional or unintentional (systemic) discrimination.[21]

prejudice
The unfounded negative emotions and attitudes toward people belonging to a particular stereotyped group.

Prejudice refers to unfounded negative emotions and attitudes toward people belonging to a particular stereotyped group. For instance, the Alaskan Governor's Commission on Tolerance heard of physical attacks against Native Americans as well as slurs against a city worker because of his sexual orientation. In a recent survey of more than 8,000 teenagers in Hong Kong, most boys said that it was "unthinkable" for men to have female bosses. (Most teenage girls in that study thought it was OK for men to have female bosses.)[22]

Even when people try to minimize prejudicial attitudes, they might engage in *unintentional (systemic) discrimination*, which limits the opportunities of qualified employees and job applicants. Unintentional discrimination occurs when decision makers rely on stereotypes to establish notions of the "ideal" person in specific roles.[23] A person who doesn't fit the ideal is likely to receive a less favorable evaluation. This is increasingly apparent in recent age discrimination claims. Recruiters say they aren't biased against older job applicants, yet older workers have a much more difficult time gaining employment even though research indicates they are well qualified.

Minimizing Stereotyping Bias

If stereotyping is such a problem, shouldn't we try to avoid this process altogether? Unfortunately, it's not that simple. Most scholars agree that categorizing information (including stereotyping people) is a natural process related to the mechanics of brain functioning.[24] In other words, it's a hardwired activity that we can't completely avoid. Moreover, as previously mentioned, stereotyping minimizes mental effort, fills in missing information, and is part of the social identity process.[25] The good news is that while we might not be able to prevent the *activation* of stereotypes, we can minimize the *application* of stereotypic information in our decisions and actions. Three strategies for minimizing the *application* of stereotyping are diversity awareness training, meaningful interaction, and decision-making accountability.

Diversity Awareness Training   Organizations can minimize the adverse consequences of stereotyping through diversity awareness training. Most diversity programs educate employees about the organizational benefits of diversity and the problems with stereotyping. Many try to dispel myths about people from visible minority and other demographic groups. Some sessions rely on role playing and exercises to help employees discover the subtle, yet pervasive effects of stereotyping in their decision making and behavior.[26] Diversity training does not correct deep-rooted prejudice; it probably doesn't even change stereotypes in tolerant people. What diversity training can potentially do, however, is to increase our sensitivity to equality and motivate us to block inaccurate perceptions arising from ingrained stereotypes.

Although diversity awareness training can potentially reduce our reliance on stereotypes, some training sessions potentially reinforce rather than weaken stereotyping. Specifically, by teaching employees about cross-cultural values, diversity training replaces popular stereotypes with "sophisticated stereotyping."[27] The problem with this sophisticated stereotyping is that many societies are quite diverse, so images of an entire culture may not apply to specific people within that culture (see Chapter 2). Unfortunately, employees do not learn this point in diversity sessions, so they develop overly simplistic beliefs about people from other cultures.

Meaningful Contact Through the UPS Community Internship Program

Mark Colvard had a dilemma—whether to accommodate a driver who needed time off to help an ailing family member. Under company rules, the driver wasn't eligible, and other drivers might complain if the time off was granted. Nevertheless, Colvard decided to take some heat by giving the driver two weeks off.

Colvard had recently spent a month as part of UPS's Community Internship Program (CIP), immersed in community projects in the immigrant border town of McAllen, Texas, and living in austere accommodations nearby. By working closely with local residents, Colvard developed a better understanding of other people's needs. Without that experience, Colvard's decision might have gone the other way.

"The interns return to work—if not changed people—people with changed perspectives," says Cal Darden, senior vice president of U.S. Operations for UPS, the world's largest parcel delivery company. "It's remarkable how far an experience like CIP, one that places you in the other guy's shoes, can help you see that your real job as a leader is helping other employees achieve and succeed."

Launched in 1968, CIP accepts 50 people each year out of a pool of 2,400 up-and-coming UPS managers to work in community projects in McAllen, in an Appalachian mountain community near Chattanooga, Tennessee, and on the Lower East Side of New York City. The program helps UPS managers gain awareness of the conditions that affect all communities, understand the driving societal factors and why many challenges exist, become sensitive to life conditions that may be affecting their employees and how those make them feel, and become involved in their communities once they return home.

Nancy Bottoms served as a CIP intern in McAllen by tutoring children, helping build houses, and assisting in a local drug abuse program. She says that the experience changed her approach to leadership. "Now I tend to step back, to look harder at how I respond to people," says the UPS district air manager in Kansas. "My employees would say that I talk with them more and do more to get them involved in our community. "

Sources: J. J. Salopek, "Just Like Me," *Training & Development* 56 (October 2002), p. 52; C. Darden, "Delivering on Diversity Leadership: A Walk in the Other Guy's Shoes," Speech to the Southern Institute of Ethics Diversity Management Network, February 25, 2003; L. W. Johnson, "UPS Trains Managers Using Community Service," *Atlanta Business Chronicle,* September 17, 2001.

---

contact hypothesis
A theory stating that the more we interact with someone, the less we rely on stereotypes to understand that person.

Meaningful Interaction Another potentially effective way to minimize the adverse effects of stereotyping is to have people interact with each other. This practice is based on the **contact hypothesis,** which says that the more we interact with someone, the less we rely on stereotypes to understand that person.[28] The contact hypothesis sounds simple, but it really works only under certain conditions. Specifically, participants must have close and frequent interaction working toward a shared goal where they need to rely on each other (i.e., cooperate rather than compete with each other). The contact hypothesis works best when everyone has equal status and is engaged in a meaningful task. An hour-long social gathering between executives and front-line employees does not satisfy this condition. Neither does an activity where executives give the commands and employees follow those orders, even though both groups are technically working together. Under the right conditions, the contact hypothesis can have a profound influence on the attitudes and stereotypes that people have toward others. As Connections 3.2 describes, UPS has been practicing a unique form of contact hypothesis for more than 30 years.

We also need to keep in mind that meaningful contact with people from different backgrounds usually *does not* change our stereotypes; rather, it tends to minimize our *application* of those stereotypes. For instance, working closely with an accountant on an important project probably won't change your stereotype of accountants, but you would develop more accurate perceptions of that specific accountant. The explanation for this is that stereotypes are difficult to alter because they are heavily influenced by socialization and cultural images.

Decision-Making Accountability   A third way to minimize the biasing effects of stereotyping is to hold decision makers accountable for the information they rely on and the criteria they use to make choices in organizational decisions.[29] Whether selecting job applicants or handing out preferred assignments, decisions tend to be swayed by discriminatory stereotypes unless decision makers are forced to actively search for and evaluate information. Accountability encourages this active information processing process and, consequently, motivates decision makers to set aside stereotypic perceptions in favor of more accurate information.

Attribution Theory

attribution process
The perceptual process of deciding whether an observed behavior or event is caused largely by internal or by external factors.

Earlier in this chapter (in Global Connections 3.1), we read that female engineering students tend to blame themselves for poor performance in school, whereas male students tend to blame external causes. This process of assigning credit or blame to yourself or the situation is called the **attribution process**—deciding whether an observed behavior or event is caused primarily by internal or external factors.[30] Internal factors originate from within a person, such as the individual's ability or motivation. We make an *internal attribution* by believing that an employee performs the job poorly because he or she lacks the necessary competencies or motivation. External factors originate from the environment, such as lack of resources, other people, or just luck. An *external attribution* would occur if we believe that the employee performs the job poorly because he or she doesn't receive sufficient resources to do the task.

How do people determine whether to make an internal or external attribution about a co-worker's excellent job performance or a supplier's late shipment? Basically, they rely on the three attribution rules shown in Exhibit 3.3. Internal attributions are made when the observed individual behaved this way in the past (high consistency), he or she behaves like this toward other people or in different situations (low distinctiveness), and other people do not behave this way in similar situations (low consensus). On the other hand, an external attribution is made when there is low consistency, high distinctiveness, and high consensus.

The following example will help to clarify the three attribution rules. Suppose that an employee is making poor-quality products one day on a particular machine. We would probably conclude that there is something wrong with the machine (an external attribution) if the employee has made good-quality products on this machine in the past (low consistency), the employee makes good-quality products on other machines (high distinctiveness), and other employees have recently had quality problems on this machine (high consensus). We would make an internal attribution, on the other hand, if the employee usually makes poor-quality products on this machine (high consistency), other employees produce good-quality products on this machine (low consensus), and the employee also makes poor-quality products on other machines (low distinctiveness).[31]

Attributions influence most, if not all, voluntary behaviors and decisions.[32] Students who make internal attributions about their poor performance are more likely to drop out of their programs. Executives make more strategic decisions when they have internal attributions about the causes of the firm's poor performance. Our satisfaction with work accomplishments is influenced to a large degree by whether we take credit for those accomplishments or

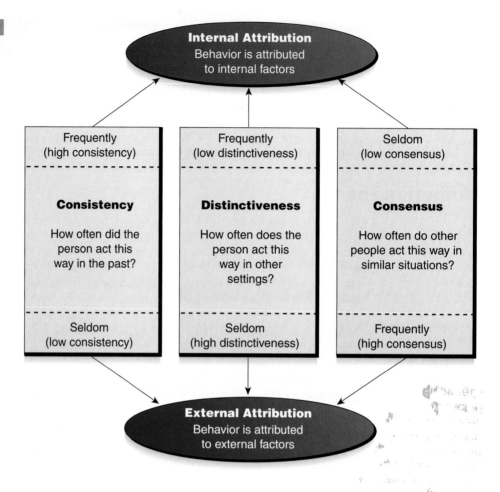

attribute the success to external causes. Even viewing others as leaders is affected by our attribution of their accomplishments (see Chapter 14).

Attribution Errors

fundamental attribution error
The tendency to attribute the behavior of other people more to internal than to external factors.

The attribution process is far from perfect. The most fundamental error we make in attribution is called (not surprisingly) **fundamental attribution error.** This refers to the tendency to attribute the behavior of other people more to internal than external factors. If an employee is late for work, observers are more likely to conclude that the person is lazy than to think that external factors may have caused this behavior. Fundamental attribution error occurs where there is limited information about the situational factors affecting other people. The person performing the behavior is naturally more sensitive to situational influences. This can lead to disagreement over the degree to which employees should be held responsible for their poor performance or absenteeism.[33] The observer blames the employee's lack of motivation or ability, whereas the employee does not feel responsible because the behavior seems to be due to factors beyond his or her control.

self-serving bias
A perceptual error whereby people tend to attribute their favorable outcomes to internal factors and their failures to external factors.

Another attribution error, known as **self-serving bias,** is the tendency to attribute our favorable outcomes to internal factors and our failures to external factors. Simply put, we take credit for our successes and blame others or the situation for our mistakes. The existence of self-serving bias in corporate life has been well documented. One recent example is a study that monitored a small government organization as it introduced a performance management system. The study found that 90 percent of the employees who received lower-than-expected performance ratings blamed this on their supervisor, the organization, the appraisal system, or other external causes. Only a handful blamed themselves for the unexpected results.[34]

Aside from these errors, attributions vary from one person to another based on personal values and experiences. For instance, female managers are less likely than male managers to make internal attributions about their job performance.[35] Overall, we need to be careful about personal and systematic biases in the attribution process within organizations.

Self-Fulfilling Prophecy

When Henry Quadracci started Quad/Graphics in the 1970s, he could afford only inexperienced employees, many of whom had low self-esteem. "When they come into the employment office, they're not looking at the stars," Quadracci observed. "They're looking at their shoes." But Quadracci saw the potential of these new hires, and continually treated them as winners. The strategy worked. Quad/Graphics employees develop confidence and exceptional performance, and this has made the printing firm one of the largest and most successful in America.[36]

Henry Quadracci has been relying on the **self-fulfilling prophecy.** Self-fulfilling prophecy occurs when our expectations about another person cause that person to act in a way that is consistent with those expectations.[37] In other words, our perceptions can influence reality. Exhibit 3.4 illustrates the four steps in the self-fulfilling prophecy process using the example of a supervisor and subordinate.[38]

self-fulfilling prophecy
Occurs when our expectations about another person cause that person to act in a way that is consistent with those expectations.

1. *Expectations formed*—The supervisor forms expectations about the employee's future behavior and performance. These expectations are sometimes inaccurate, because first impressions are usually formed from limited information.

EXHIBIT 3.4

The self-fulfilling prophecy cycle

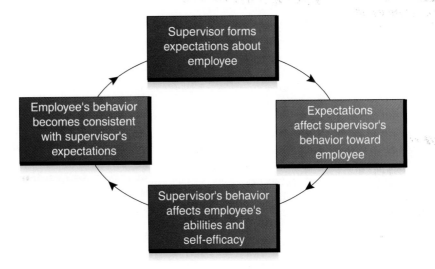

2. *Behavior toward the employee*—The supervisor's expectations influence his or her treatment of employees.[39] Specifically, high-expectancy employees (those expected to do well) receive more emotional support through nonverbal cues (e.g., more smiling and eye contact), more frequent and valuable feedback and reinforcement, more challenging goals, better training, and more opportunities to demonstrate their performance.

3. *Effects on the employee*—The supervisor's behaviors have two effects on the employee. First, through better training and more practice opportunities, a high-expectancy employee learns more skills and knowledge than a low-expectancy employee. Second, the employee becomes more self-confident, which results in higher motivation and willingness to set more challenging goals.[40]

4. *Employee behavior and performance*—With higher motivation and better skills, high-expectancy employees are more likely to demonstrate desired behaviors and better performance. The supervisor notices this, which supports his or her original perception.

learning orientation
The extent that an organization or individual supports the learning process, particularly opportunities to acquire knowledge through experience and experimentation.

Self-Fulfilling Prophecies in Practice

Employees are more likely to be victims of negative self-fulfilling prophecy than beneficiaries of positive self-fulfilling prophecy. For instance, research has found that women score lower on math tests in situations where people around them convey a negative stereotype of women regarding math tests. Women perform better on these tests when they are not exposed to this negative self-fulfilling prophecy.[41] How can organizations harness the power of positive self-fulfilling prophecy? Researchers initially recommended that leaders should become aware of the self-fulfilling prophecy effect and learn how to exhibit contagious enthusiasm. Unfortunately, these training programs have had limited success, partly because leaders have difficulty maintaining positive perceptions toward employees who, in their mind, aren't very good.[42]

More recently, experts have recommended a three-pronged approach in which leaders develop positive self-fulfilling prophecies by creating a learning orientation, applying appropriate leadership styles, and building self-efficacy in employees.[44] First, leaders need to develop a **learning orientation;** that is, they need to appreciate the value of the employee learning, not just accomplishing tasks. They do this by accepting reasonable mistakes as a natural part of the learning process. Second, leaders need to apply appropriate leadership behaviors to all

Five years ago, by his own admission, Jamarr Myers (left in photo) was a troubled kid headed in the wrong direction. Today, the 19-year-old is a service team leader, supervising 30 to 40 cashiers at a Wegmans grocery store in Rochester, New York. How did Myers so dramatically turn his life around? He says a major factor was that Wegmens' management showed its belief in him through its Work–Scholarship Connection program. This program, which now involves dozens of employees, provides practical and emotional support to students who are at risk of dropping out of school. When Myers joined the program, his friends joked that he would be "a janitor or pushing carts," Myers recalls. "But they believe now. If it hadn't been for this program, I wouldn't be here."[43] Explain the dynamics of self-fulfilling prophecy in the Work–Scholarship Connection and similar programs.

employees. In other words, they practice the contingency approach to leadership that we will learn about in Chapter 14. For employees who are new to the position or task, this would usually include providing frequent, objective feedback and creating a positive relationship by showing support.

Self-fulfilling prophecies succeed mainly due to the employee self-efficacy, so the third strategy is to teach leaders how to increase **self-efficacy.** Self-efficacy refers to a person's belief that he or she has the ability, motivation, and resources to complete a task successfully.[45] People with high self-efficacy have a "can-do" attitude toward a specific task and, more generally, toward other challenges in life. Leaders can increase employee self-efficacy by showing employees that they possess the necessary knowledge and skills, by displaying confidence in the employee's competencies, and by having employees observe others similar to themselves performing the tasks effectively.

self-efficacy

A person's belief that he or she has the ability, motivation, and resources to complete a task successfully.

Other Perceptual Errors

Self-fulfilling prophecy, attribution, and stereotyping are processes that both assist and interfere with the perceptual process. Four other well-known perceptual errors in organizational settings are primacy effect, recency effect, halo effect, and projection bias.

Primacy Effect

primacy effect

A perceptual error in which we quickly form an opinion of people based on the first information we receive about them.

The **primacy effect** relates to the saying that "first impressions are lasting impressions." It is our tendency to quickly form an opinion of people based on the first information we receive about them.[46] This rapid perceptual organization occurs because we need to make sense of the world around us. Moreover, we tend to categorize people fairly quickly because this is easier on the brain cells than remembering every detail about a person. For example, if we first meet someone who avoids eye contact and speaks softly, we might conclude that the person lacks self-confidence. It is easier to remember the person has low self-confidence than to recall the specific behaviors exhibited during the first encounter.

Unfortunately, first impressions—particularly negative first impressions—are difficult to change. The problem is that after categorizing someone as lacking self-confidence, we tend to select subsequent information that supports our first impression and screen out information that opposes that impression. Negative impressions tend to "stick" more than positive impressions because negative characteristics are more easily attributed to the person, whereas positive characteristics are often attributed to the situation.[47]

Recency Effect

recency effect

A perceptual error in which the most recent information dominates one's perception of others.

The **recency effect** occurs when the most recent information dominates our perception of others.[48] This effect is stronger than the primacy effect when there is a long delay between the time when the first impression is formed and the person is evaluated. In other words, the most recent information has the greater influence on our perception of someone when the first impression has worn off with the passage of time.

The recency effect is found in performance appraisals, for which supervisors must recall every employee's performance over the previous year. Recent

(*DILBERT reprinted by permission of United Feature Syndicate, Inc.*)

performance information dominates the evaluation because it is the most easily recalled. Some employees are well aware of the recency effect and use it to their advantage by getting their best work on the manager's desk just before the performance appraisal is conducted.

Halo Error

halo error

A perceptual error whereby our general impression of a person, usually based on one prominent characteristic, colors the perception of other characteristics of that person.

Halo error occurs when our general impression of a person, usually based on one prominent characteristic, colors our perception of other characteristics of that person.[49] If we meet a client who speaks in a friendly manner, we tend to infer a host of other favorable qualities about that person. If a colleague doesn't complete tasks on time, we tend to view his or her other traits unfavorably. In each case, one trait important to the perceiver forms a general impression, and this impression becomes the basis for judgments about other traits. Halo error is most likely to occur when concrete information about the perceived target is missing or we are not sufficiently motivated to search for it.[50] Instead, we use our general impression of the person to fill in the missing information.

Halo error has received considerable attention in research on performance appraisal ratings.[51] Consider the situation in which two employees have the same level of work quality, quantity of work, and customer relations performance, but one tends to be late for work. Tardiness might not be an important factor in work performance, but the supervisor has a negative impression of employees who are late for work. Halo error would cause the supervisor to rate the tardy employee lower on *all* performance dimensions because the tardiness created a negative general impression of that employee. The punctual employee would tend to receive higher ratings on *all* performance dimensions even though his or her performance level is really the same as that of the tardy employee. Consequently, halo error distorts our judgments and can result in poor decision making.

Projection Bias

projection bias

A perceptual error in which an individual believes that other people have the same beliefs and behaviors that we do.

Projection bias occurs when we believe other people have the same beliefs and behaviors that we do.[52] If you are eager for a promotion, you might think that others in your position are similarly motivated. If you are thinking of quitting your job, you start to believe that other people are also thinking of quitting. Projection bias is also a defense mechanism to protect our self-esteem. If we break a work rule, projection bias justifies this infraction by claiming that "everyone does it." We feel more comfortable with the thought that our negative traits exist in others, so we believe that others also have these traits.

Improving Perceptions

We can't bypass the perceptual process, but we should make every attempt to minimize perceptual biases and distortions. Earlier, we learned about diversity awareness and contact practices to minimize the adverse effects of biased stereotypes. Two other broad perceptual improvement practices are developing empathy and improving self-awareness.

empathy
A person's understanding and sensitivity to the feelings, thoughts, and situation of others.

Improving Perceptions Through Empathy

Empathy refers to a person's understanding and sensitivity to the feelings, thoughts, and situation of others. Empathy has both a cognitive (thinking) and emotional component.[53] The cognitive component, which is sometimes called *perspective taking*, represents an intellectual understanding of another person's situational and individual circumstances.[54] The emotional component of empathy refers to experiencing the feelings of the other person. You have empathy when actively visualizing the other person's situation (perspective taking), and feeling that person's emotions in that situation.

Empathizing with others is an important part of the perceptual process because it improves our sensitivity to external causes of another person's performance and behavior. This has the effect of minimizing fundamental attribution error, described earlier in this chapter. A supervisor who imagines what it's like to be a single mother, for example, would become more sensitive to the external causes of lateness and other events among these employees.

Empathy comes naturally to some people. However, the rest of us can develop empathy skills by receiving intensive feedback through coaching. Coaches attend meetings with their clients and debrief them later regarding how well they demonstrated empathy toward others in the meeting.[56] The opening story to this chapter described how people can also increase empathy with employees and customers by literally "walking in their shoes." The idea here is to improve your perceptions of other people by taking on their roles in the workplace. The more

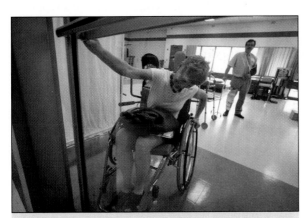

Barbara Fabiani doesn't normally have any trouble opening doors. But the New Haven, Connecticut, architect discovered that opening a door while being confined to a wheelchair presents unique challenges. "Well, that only took forever," joked Fabiani after finally getting through. Fabiani and other architects spent an afternoon at Gaylord Hospital pretending to have disabilities so they could develop a better appreciation of the physical barriers facing people with disabilities. Some participants were outfitted with arm slings and soft leg braces to simulate inability to use a leg and an arm. Several were blindfolded so they could know what it's like to live without sight. "Now, they have some sympathy and understanding of what people with these disabilities have to go through," says one of the organizers of the event.[55] How could companies organize events like this so employees have more empathy for the customers they serve?

you personally experience the environment in which other people live and work, the better you will understand and be sensitive to their needs and expectations.

Know Yourself: Applying the Johari Window

Knowing yourself—becoming more aware of your values, beliefs, and prejudices—is a powerful way to improve your perceptions.[57] Let's say that you had an unpleasant experience with lawyers and developed negative emotions toward people in this profession. Being sensitive to these emotions should enable you to regulate your behavior more effectively when working with legal professionals. Moreover, if co-workers are aware of your antipathy to lawyers, they are more likely to understand your actions and help you to be objective in the future.

Johari Window

The model of personal and interpersonal understanding that encourages disclosure and feedback to increase the open area and reduce the blind, hidden, and unknown areas of oneself.

The **Johari Window** is a popular model for understanding how co-workers can increase their mutual understanding.[58] Developed by Joseph Luft and Harry Ingram (hence the name *Johari*), this model divides information about you into four "windows"—open, blind, hidden, and unknown—based on whether your own values, beliefs, and experiences are known to you and to others (see Exhibit 3.5). The *open area* includes information about you that is known both to you and to others. For example, both you and your co-workers may be aware that you don't like to be near people who smoke cigarettes. The *blind area* refers to information that is known to others but not to you. For example, your colleagues might notice that you are embarrassed and awkward when meeting someone confined to a wheelchair, but you are unaware of this fact. Information known to you but unknown to others is found in the *hidden area*. We all have personal secrets about our likes, dislikes, and personal experiences. Finally, the *unknown area* includes your values, beliefs, and experiences that aren't known to you or others.

EXHIBIT 3.5

Johari Window

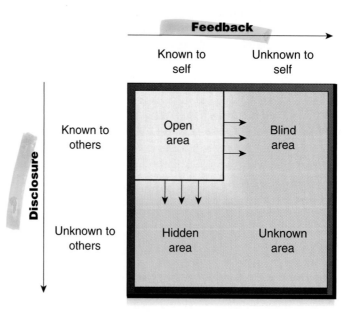

Source: Based on J. Luft, *Group Processes* (Palo Alto, CA: Mayfield, 1984).

The main objective of the Johari Window is to increase the size of the open area so that both you and colleagues are aware of your perceptual limitations. This is partly accomplished by reducing the hidden area through *disclosure*— informing others of your beliefs, feelings, and experiences that may influence the work relationship.[59] The open area also increases through *feedback* from others about your behaviors. This information helps you to reduce your blind area, because co-workers often see things in you that you do not see. Finally, the combination of disclosure and feedback occasionally produces revelations about information in the unknown area.

The Johari Window applies to some diversity awareness and meaningful contact activities that we described earlier. By learning about cultural differences and communicating more with people from different backgrounds, we gain a better understanding of their behavior. Engaging in open dialogue with co-workers also applies the Johari Window. As we communicate with others, we naturally tend to disclose more information about ourselves and eventually feel comfortable providing candid feedback to them.

The perceptual process represents the filter through which information passes from the external environment to our brain. As such, it is really the beginning of the learning process, which we discuss next.

Learning in Organizations

learning
A relatively permanent change in behavior (or behavior tendency) that occurs as a result of a person's interaction with the environment.

Learning is a relatively permanent change in behavior (or behavior tendency) that occurs as a result of a person's interaction with the environment.[60] Learning occurs when the learner behaves differently. For example, we can see that you have "learned" computer skills when you operate the keyboard and windows more quickly than before. Learning occurs when interaction with the environment leads to behavior change. This means that we learn through our senses, such as through study, observation, and experience.

Learning is essential for open systems thinking and knowledge management (see Chapter 1) because the organization's survival and success depend on employees learning about the external environment.[61] Learning also influences individual behavior and performance through three elements of the MARS model described in Chapter 2. First, people acquire skills and knowledge through learning opportunities, which gives them the competencies to perform tasks more effectively. Second, learning clarifies role perceptions. Employees develop a better understanding of their tasks and relative importance of work activities. Third, learning motivates employees. Employees are more motivated to perform certain tasks because they learn that their effort will result in desired performance. Indeed, one major consulting firm recently reported that the ability to learn new skills was one of the top five factors motivating people to accept employment with an organization.[62]

Learning Explicit and Tacit Knowledge

When employees learn, they acquire both explicit and tacit knowledge. *Explicit knowledge* is organized and can be communicated from one person to another. The information you receive in a lecture is mainly explicit knowledge because the instructor packages and consciously transfers it to you. Explicit knowledge can be written down and given to others.

tacit knowledge
Knowledge embedded in our actions and ways of thinking, and transmitted only through observation and experience.

However, explicit knowledge is really only the tip of the knowledge iceberg. Most of what we know is **tacit knowledge.**[63] You have probably said to someone: "I can't tell you how to do this, but I can show you." Tacit knowledge is not documented; rather, it is action-oriented and known below the level of consciousness. Some writers suggest that tacit knowledge also includes the organization's culture and a team's implicit norms. People know these values and rules exist, but they are difficult to describe and document. Tacit knowledge is acquired through observation and direct experience. For example, airline pilots learn to operate commercial jets more by watching experts and practicing on flight simulators than through lectures. They acquire tacit knowledge by directly experiencing the complex interaction of behavior with the machine's response.

The rest of this chapter introduces three perspectives of learning tacit and explicit knowledge: reinforcement, social learning, and direct experience. Each perspective offers a different angle for understanding the dynamics of learning.

Behavior Modification: Learning Through Reinforcement

behavior modification
A theory that explains learning in terms of the antecedents and consequences of behavior.

One of the oldest perspectives on learning, called **behavior modification** (also known as *operant conditioning* and *reinforcement theory*), takes the rather extreme view that learning is completely dependent on the environment. Behavior modification does not question the notion that thinking is part of the learning process, but it views human thoughts as unimportant intermediate stages between behavior and the environment.[64] Our experience with the environment teaches us to alter our behaviors so that we maximize positive consequences and minimize adverse consequences.[65]

A-B-C's of Behavior Modification

Behavior modification recognizes that behavior is influenced by two environmental contingencies: the antecedents that precede behavior and the consequences that follow behavior. These principles are part of the A-B-C model of behavior modification shown in Exhibit 3.6. The central objective of behavior modification is to change behavior (B) by managing its antecedents (A) and consequences (C).[66]

Antecedents are events preceding the behavior, informing employees that certain behaviors will have particular consequences. An antecedent may be a sound from your computer signaling that an e-mail has arrived or a request from your supervisor to complete a specific task by tomorrow. These antecedents let employees know that a particular action will produce particular consequences. Notice that antecedents do not cause behaviors. The computer sound doesn't cause us to open our e-mail. Rather, the sound is a cue telling us that certain consequences are likely to occur if we engage in certain behaviors.

Although antecedents are important, behavior modification mainly focuses on the *consequences* of behavior. Consequences are events following a particular behavior that influence its future occurrence. Generally speaking, people tend to repeat behaviors that are followed by a pleasant consequences and are less likely to repeat behaviors that are followed by unpleasant consequences or no consequences at all.

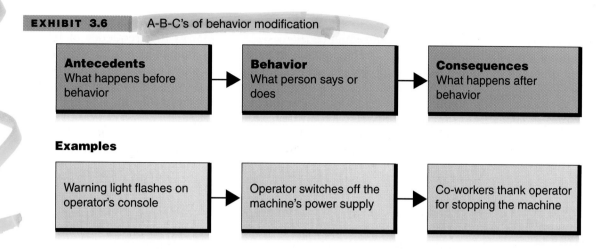

EXHIBIT 3.6	A-B-C's of behavior modification

Antecedents
What happens before behavior
→
Behavior
What person says or does
→
Consequences
What happens after behavior

Examples

Warning light flashes on operator's console
→
Operator switches off the machine's power supply
→
Co-workers thank operator for stopping the machine

Sources: Adapted from T. K. Connellan, *How to Improve Human Performance* (New York: Harper & Row, 1978), p. 50; F. Luthans and R. Kreitner, *Organizational Behavior Modification and Beyond* (Glenview, IL: Scott, Foresman, 1985), pp. 85–88.

Contingencies of Reinforcement

Behavior modification identifies four types of consequences, collectively known as the *contingencies of reinforcement,* that strengthen, maintain, or weaken behavior. Exhibit 3.7 describes these contingencies: positive reinforcement, negative reinforcement, punishment, and extinction.[67]

EXHIBIT 3.7	Contingencies of reinforcement

	Consequence is introduced	No consequence	Consequence is removed
Behavior increases or is maintained	**Positive reinforcement** Example: You receive a bonus after successfully completing an important project.		**Negative reinforcement** Example: Supervisor stops criticizing you when your job performance improves.
Behavior decreases	**Punishment** Example: You are threatened with a demotion or discharge after treating a client badly.	**Extinction** Example: Co-workers no longer praise you when you engage in dangerous pranks.	**Punishment** Example: You give up your "employee of the month" parking spot to this month's winner.

positive reinforcement
Occurs when the introduction of a consequence increases or maintains the frequency or future probability of a behavior.

negative reinforcement
Occurs when the removal or avoidance of a consequence increases or maintains the frequency or future probability of a behavior.

punishment
Occurs when a consequence decreases the frequency or future probability of a behavior.

extinction
Occurs when the target behavior decreases because no consequence follows it.

- *Positive reinforcement*—**Positive reinforcement** occurs when the *introduction* of a consequence *increases or maintains* the frequency or future probability of a behavior. Receiving a bonus after successfully completing an important project usually creates positive reinforcement because it typically increases the probability that you use those behaviors in the future.

- *Negative reinforcement*—**Negative reinforcement** occurs when the *removal or avoidance* of a consequence *increases or maintains* the frequency or future probability of a behavior. Supervisors apply negative reinforcement when they stop criticizing employees whose substandard performance has improved. When the criticism is withheld, employees are more likely to repeat behaviors that improved their performance.[68] Negative reinforcement is sometimes called *avoidance learning* because employees engage in the desired behaviors to avoid unpleasant consequences (such as being criticized by your supervisor or being fired from your job.)

- *Punishment*—**Punishment** occurs when a consequence *decreases* the frequency or future probability of a behavior. It may occur by the supervisor's introducing an unpleasant consequence or removing a pleasant consequence (see Exhibit 3.7). An example of the former would be where an employee is threatened with a demotion or discharge after treating a client badly. The latter form of punishment would occur when a salesperson must give a cherished parking spot to another employee who has higher sales performance for the month.

- *Extinction*—**Extinction** occurs when the target behavior decreases because no consequence follows it. For example, if an employee makes practical jokes that are potentially dangerous or costly, this behavior might be extinguished by discouraging others from praising the employee when he or she engages in these pranks. Behavior that is no longer reinforced tends to disappear; it becomes extinct. In this respect, extinction is a do-nothing strategy.[69]

Which contingency of reinforcement should we use in the learning process? In most situations, positive reinforcement should follow desired behaviors and extinction (do nothing) should follow undesirable behaviors. This is because there are fewer adverse consequences when applying these contingencies compared with punishment and negative reinforcement. However, some form of punishment (dismissal, suspension, demotion, etc.) may be necessary for extreme behaviors, such as deliberately hurting a co-worker or stealing inventory. Indeed, research suggests that, under certain conditions, punishment maintains a sense of equity.[70] However, punishment and negative reinforcement should be applied cautiously because they generate negative emotions and attitudes toward the punisher (e.g., supervisor) and organization.

Schedules of Reinforcement

Along with the types of consequences, behavior modification identifies the schedule that should be followed to maximize the reinforcement effect. In fact, there is some evidence that scheduling the reinforcer affects learning more than the size of the reinforcer.[71] The most effective schedule of reinforcement for learning new tasks is *continuous reinforcement*—reinforcing every occurrence of the desired behavior. Employees learn desired behaviors quickly and, when the reinforcer is removed, extinction also occurs very quickly.

The other schedules of reinforcement are intermittent. Most people get paid with a *fixed interval schedule* because they receive their reinforcement (paycheck) after a fixed period of time. A *variable interval schedule* is common for promotions. Employees are promoted after a variable amount of time. If you are given the rest of the day off after completing a fixed amount of work (e.g., stocking shelves in the store), then you would have experienced a *fixed ratio schedule*—reinforcement after a fixed number of behaviors or accomplishments. Last, companies often use a *variable ratio schedule* in which employee behavior is reinforced after a variable number of times. Salespeople experience variable ratio reinforcement because they make a successful sale (the reinforcer) after a varying number of client calls. They might make 4 unsuccessful calls before receiving an order on the fifth one, then make 10 more calls before receiving the next order, and so on.

The variable ratio schedule is a low-cost way to reinforce behavior because employees are rewarded infrequently. It is also highly resistant to extinction. Suppose your boss walks into your office at varying times of day. Chances are that you would work consistently better throughout the day than if your boss visits at exactly 11 A.M. every day. If your boss doesn't walk into your office at all on a particular day, you would still expect a visit right up to the end of the day if previous visits were random.

Behavior Modification in Practice

Everyone practices behavior modification in one form or another. We thank people for a job well done, are silent when displeased, and sometimes try to punish those who go against our wishes. Behavior modification also occurs in various formal programs to reduce absenteeism, minimize accidents, and improve task performance. When implemented correctly, the results are generally impressive.[73] For instance, VJS Foods, a British food company, reduced absenteeism by giving employees with perfect attendance each month two chances to win U.S.$500. Rhode Island shipyard Electric Boat recently awarded $2,500 to each of 20 winners drawn from a pool of 955 employees who had not called in sick for at least two years. Student attendance improved (particularly in the last hour of classes) when some Los Angeles high schools introduced a lottery-based prize to students who had no absences over the previous week.[74]

To address the growing problem of absenteeism and excessive sick leave, Mercy Medical Center in Baltimore introduced a carrot-and-stick approach based on classic behavior modification principles. Mercy's 2,000 employees are allowed nine episodes of illness each year before they risk being fired. (One "episode" can include several continuous days of absenteeism.) Bosses are encouraged to educate employees about attendance and to call staff who are out sick. Meanwhile, employees with six months of perfect attendance receive a $100 bonus. Those with one year without absenteeism have their names put in a drawing for up to $3,000.[72] What are some of the unintended consequences of applying behavior modification in this situation?

In spite of these favorable results, behavior modification has several limitations.[75] It is more difficult to apply to conceptual activities than to observable behaviors. For example, it's much easier to reward employees for good work attendance than for good problem solving. A second problem is "reward inflation," in which the reinforcer is eventually considered an entitlement. For this reason, most behavior modification programs must run infrequently and for short durations. A third problem is that the variable ratio schedule often takes the form of a lottery, which conflicts with the ethical values of some employees. Finally, behavior modification's radical "behaviorist" philosophy (that human thinking processes are unimportant) has lost followers as fairly strong evidence has indicated that people *can learn* through mental processes, such as observing others and thinking logically about possible consequences.[76] Thus, without throwing away the principles of behavior modification, most learning experts today also embrace the concepts of social learning theory.

Social Learning Theory: Learning by Observing

social learning theory

A theory stating that much learning occurs by observing others and then modeling the behaviors that lead to favorable outcomes and avoiding the behaviors that lead to punishing consequences.

Social learning theory states that much learning occurs by observing others and then modeling the behaviors that lead to favorable outcomes and avoiding behaviors that lead to punishing consequences.[77] Three related features of social learning theory are behavioral modeling, learning behavior consequences, and self-reinforcement.

Behavioral Modeling

People learn by observing the behaviors of a role model on the critical task, remembering the important elements of the observed behaviors, and then practicing those behaviors.[78] Behavioral modeling works best when the model is respected and the model's actions are followed by favorable consequences. For instance, recently hired college graduates should learn by watching a previously hired college graduate who successfully performs the task.

Behavioral modeling is a valuable form of learning because tacit knowledge and skills are mainly acquired from others in this way. Earlier in our discussion of learning, we stated that tacit knowledge is the subtle information about required behaviors, the correct sequence of those actions, and the environmental consequences (such as a machine response or customer reply) that should occur after each action. The adage that a picture is worth a thousand words applies here. It is difficult to document or verbally explain how a master baker kneads dough better than someone less qualified. Instead, we must observe these subtle actions to develop a more precise mental model of the required behaviors and the expected responses. Behavioral modeling also guides role perceptions. Leaders model the behavior that they expect from others, for example.

Behavioral Modeling and Self-Efficacy   Behavioral modeling increases self-efficacy because people gain more self-confidence after seeing someone else do it than if they are simply told what to do. This is particularly true when observers identify with the model, such as someone who is similar in age, experience, gender, and related features. You might experience this when working in a student support group. You form a "can-do" attitude when another student similar to you describes how he or she was able to perform well in a course that you are now taking. You learn not only what has to be done, but that others like you have been successful at this challenge.

Self-efficacy is also affected by initial experiences when practicing the previously modeled behavior. Observers gain confidence when the environmental cues follow a predictable pattern and there are no unexpected surprises when practicing the behavior.[79] For example, computer trainees develop a stronger self-efficacy when they click the mouse and get the same computer response as the model did when performing the same behavior. The expected response gives trainees a greater sense of control over the computer because they can predict what will happen following a particular behavior.

Learning Behavior Consequences

A second element of social learning theory says that we learn the consequences of behavior in ways other than through direct experience. In particular, we learn by logically thinking through the consequences of our actions and by observing the consequences that other people experience following their behavior. On the first point, we often anticipate desirable or adverse consequences through logic. We expect either positive reinforcement or negative reinforcement after completing an assigned task and either punishment or extinction after performing the job poorly because it is a logical conclusion based on ethical values.

We also learn to anticipate consequences by observing the experiences of other people. Civilizations have relied on this principle for centuries, by punishing civil disobedience in public to deter other potential criminals.[80] Learning behavior consequences occurs in more subtle ways in contemporary organizations. Consider the employee who observes a co-worker receiving a stern warning for working in an unsafe manner. This event would reduce the observer's likelihood of engaging in unsafe behaviors because he or she has learned to anticipate a similar reprimand following those behaviors.[81]

Self-Reinforcement

The final element of social learning theory is *self-reinforcement*. Self-reinforcement occurs whenever an employee has control over a reinforcer but doesn't "take" the reinforcer until completing a self-set goal.[82] For example, you might be thinking about taking a work break after you finish reading the rest of this chapter—and not before! You could take a break right now, but you don't use this privilege until you have achieved your goal of reading the chapter. The work break is a form of positive reinforcement that is self-induced. You use the work break to reinforce completion of a task. Numerous consequences may be applied in self-reinforcement, ranging from raiding the refrigerator to congratulating yourself for completing the task.[83] Self-reinforcement has become increasingly important because employees are given more control over their working lives and are less dependent on supervisors to dole out positive reinforcement and punishment.

Learning Through Experience

Mandy Chooi is about to meet with a lower level manager who has botched a new assignment. She is also supposed to make a strategy presentation to her boss in three hours, but the telephone won't stop ringing and she is deluged with e-mail. It's a stressful situation. Fortunately, the challenges facing the Motorola human resources executive from Beijing today are not real. Chooi is sitting in a simulation to develop and test her leadership skills. "It was hard. A lot harder than I had expected," she says. "It's surprising how realistic and demanding it is."[84]

Many organizations are shifting their learning strategy away from the classroom and toward a more experiential approach. Classrooms transfer explicit knowledge that has been documented, but most tacit knowledge and skills are acquired through experience as well as observation.[85] Experiential learning has been conceptualized in many ways, but one of the most enduring perspectives is Kolb's experiential learning model, shown in Exhibit 3.8.[86] This model illustrates experiential learning as a cyclical four-stage process.

Concrete experience involves sensory and emotional engagement in some activity. It is followed by reflective observation, which involves listening, watching, recording, and elaborating on the experience. The next stage in the learning cycle is abstract conceptualization. This is the stage in which we develop concepts and integrate our observations into logically sound theories. The fourth stage, active experimentation, occurs when we test our previous experience, reflection, and conceptualization in a particular context.

Notice from this model that experiential learning includes the polar opposites of concrete to abstract conceptualization. We need to experience concrete reality as well as form abstract concepts from that reality. Experiential learning also involves the polar opposites of active experimentation and passive reflection. People tend to prefer and operate better in some stages than in others due to their unique competencies and personality. Still, experiential learning requires all four stages in proper balance.

Experiential Learning in Practice

Learning through experience works best where there is a strong *learning orientation*.[87] As we described earlier in this chapter, organizations with a strong

EXHIBIT 3.8

Kolb's experiential learning model

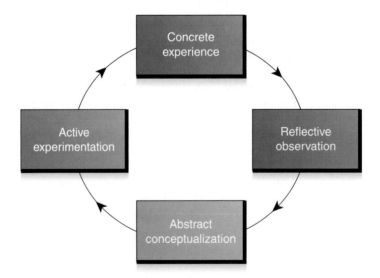

Sources: Based on information in J. E. Sharp, "Applying Kolb Learning Style Theory in the Communication Classroom," *Business Communication Quarterly* 60 (June 1997), pp. 129–34; D. A. Kolb, *Experiential Learning* (Englewood Cliffs, NJ: Prentice Hall, 1984).

The Warwick, Rhode Island, fire department recruits shown here are recapping the burning building exercise in which their task was to control the fire and save victims (including the two dummies lying on the ground). Warwick and many other communities have special learning centers in which they can "burn" buildings. Fire and police units nearby in Woonsocket also recently participated in a mock disaster in which they rescued students during school from a mock chemical accident in the area. "Woonsocket is certainly one of the better prepared communities in the state when it comes to responding to this type of situation," says an executive at the Rhode Island Emergency Management Agency, who watched the "disaster" unfold.[88] How does this emergency training exercise apply Kolb's experiential learning model?

learning orientation value knowledge management and, in particular, the generation of new knowledge as employees achieve their goals. If an employee initially fails to perform a task, then the experience might still be a valuable learning opportunity. In other words, organizations encourage employees to appreciate the process of individual and team learning, not just the performance results.

Organizations achieve a learning orientation culture by rewarding experimentation and recognizing mistakes as a natural part of the learning process. They encourage employees to take reasonable risks to ultimately discover new and better ways of doing things. Without a learning orientation, mistakes are hidden and problems are more likely to escalate or reemerge later. It's not surprising, then, that one of the most frequently mentioned lessons from the best performing manufacturers is to expect mistakes. "[Mistakes] are a source of learning and will improve operations in the long run," explains an executive at Lockheed Martin. "[They] foster the concept that no question is dumb, no idea too wild, and no task or activity is irrelevant."[89]

Action Learning   The fastest growing form of experiential learning in the workplace is called **action learning.** Action learning refers to a variety of

action learning
A variety of experiential learning activities in which employees are involved in a "real, complex, and stressful problem," usually in teams, with immediate relevance to the company.

experiential learning activities in which employees are involved in a "real, complex, and stressful problem," usually in teams, with immediate relevance to the company.[90] In action learning, the task becomes the source of learning.

Kolb's experiential learning model presented earlier is usually identified as the main template for action learning.[91] Action learning requires concrete experience with a real organizational problem. The process includes "learning meetings" in which participants reflect on their observations regarding the problem or opportunity. The action learning team is responsible for conceptualizing or applying a model to solve the problem or take the opportunity. Then the team tests the model through experimentation in the real setting. For example, an action learning team at Carpenter Technology was given the challenge to investigate the steel manufacturer's strategy for entry into India. The team investigated the opportunity, wrote up its recommendation, and participated in its implementation.[92]

Action learning is considered one of the most important ways to develop executive competencies.[93] It involves both tacit and explicit learning, forces employees to diagnose new situations, and makes them rethink current work practices. At the same time, the results of action learning potentially add value to the organization in terms of a better work process or service. For example, one of Motorola's action learning teams spent several months learning how to create and manage a software business.[94]

This chapter has introduced you to two fundamental activities in human behavior in the workplace: perceptions and learning. These activities involve receiving information from the environment, organizing it, and acting on it as a learning process. Perceptions and learning are mainly cognitive (thinking) processes, but they are influenced by—and have an influence on—the emotional side of human behavior. In the next chapter, we consider the dynamics of emotions and attitudes in the workplace.

Chapter Summary

Perception involves selecting, organizing, and interpreting information to make sense of the world. Selective attention is influenced by characteristics of the target, the target's setting, and the perceiver. Perceptual grouping principles organize incoming information. This is also influenced by our emotions, expectations, and mental models.

According to social identity theory, people perceive themselves by their unique characteristics and membership in various groups. They also develop homogeneous, and usually positive, images of people in their own groups, and usually less positive homogeneous images of people in other groups. This leads to overgeneralizations and stereotypes.

Stereotyping is the process of assigning traits to people based on their membership in a social category.

Stereotyping economizes mental effort, fills in missing information, and enhances our self-perception and social identity. However, stereotyping also lays the foundation for prejudice and intentional or unintentional discrimination. We can't prevent the activation of stereotyping, but we can minimize the application of stereotypic information in our decisions and actions. Three strategies to minimize the influence of stereotypes are diversity awareness training, meaningful interaction, and decision-making accountability.

The attribution process involves deciding whether the behavior or event is largely due to the situation (external attributions) or personal characteristics (internal attributions). Two attribution errors are fundamental attribution error and self-serving bias. Self-fulfilling prophecy occurs when our expectations about another person cause that person to act in a way that is consistent with those expectations. Leaders can create positive self-fulfilling prophecies by supporting a learning orientation, applying contingency-oriented leaderships styles, and increasing the employee's self-efficacy.

Four other perceptual errors commonly noted in organizations are primacy effect, recency effect, halo effect, and projection bias. We can minimize these and other perceptual problems through empathy and becoming more aware of our values, beliefs, and prejudices (Johari Window).

Learning is a relatively permanent change in behavior (or behavior tendency) that occurs as a result of a person's interaction with the environment. Learning is an important part of knowledge management and influences ability, role perceptions, and motivation in the MARS model of individual performance.

The behavior modification perspective of learning states that behavior change occurs by altering its antecedents and consequences. Antecedents are environmental stimuli that provoke (not necessarily cause) behavior. Consequences are events following

behavior that influence its future occurrence. Consequences include positive reinforcement, negative reinforcement, punishment, and extinction. The schedules of reinforcement also influence behavior.

Social learning theory states that much learning occurs by observing others and then modeling those behaviors that seem to lead to favorable outcomes and avoiding behaviors that lead to punishing consequences. It also recognizes that we often engage in self-reinforcement. Behavioral modeling is effective because it transfers tacit knowledge and enhances the observer's self-efficacy.

Many companies now use experiential learning because employees do not acquire tacit knowledge through formal classroom instruction. Kolb's experiential learning model is a cyclical four-stage process that includes concrete experience, reflective observation, abstract conceptualization, and active experimentation. Action learning refers to a variety of experiential learning activities in which employees solve problems or take advantage of opportunities, usually in teams, with immediate relevance to the organization.

Key Terms

action learning, p. 101
attribution process, p. 85
behavior modification, p. 94
contact hypothesis, p. 84
empathy, p. 91
extinction, p. 96
fundamental attribution error, p. 86
halo error, p. 90
Johari Window, p. 92
learning, p. 93
learning orientation, p. 88
mental models, p. 78
negative reinforcement, p. 96
perception, p. 76

positive reinforcement, p. 96
prejudice, p. 83
primacy effect, p. 89
projection bias, p. 90
punishment, p. 96
recency effect, p. 89
selective attention, p. 77
self-efficacy, p. 89
self-fulfilling prophecy, p. 87
self-serving bias, p. 86
social identity theory, p. 78
social learning theory, p. 98
stereotyping, p. 80
tacit knowledge, p. 94

Discussion Questions

1. You are part of a task force to increase worker responsiveness to emergencies on the production floor. Identify four factors that should be considered when installing a device that will get every employee's attention when there is an emergency.

2. What mental models do you have about attending a college or university lecture? Are these mental models helpful? Could any of these mental models hold you back from achieving the full benefit of the lecture?

3. Contrast "personal" and "social" identity. Do

you define yourself in terms of the university or college you attend? Why or why not? What implications does your response have for the future of your university or college?

4. During a diversity management session, a manager suggests that stereotypes are a necessary part of working with others. "I have to make assumptions about what's in the other person's head, and stereotypes help me do that," she explains. "It's better to rely on stereotypes than to enter a working relationship with someone from another culture without any idea of what they believe in!" Discuss the merits of and problems with the manager's statement.

5. At the end of an NHL hockey game the coach of the losing team was asked to explain his team's defeat. "I dunno," he begins, "we've done well in this rink over the past few years. Our busy schedule over the past two weeks has pushed the guys too hard, I guess. They're worn out. You probably noticed that we also got some bad breaks on penalties tonight. We should have done well here, but things just went against us." Use attribution theory to explain the coach's perceptions of the team's loss.

6. Describe how a manager or coach could use the process of self-fulfilling prophecy to enhance an individual's performance.

7. Describe a situation in which you used behavior modification to influence someone's behavior. What specifically did you do? What was the result?

8. Why are organizations moving toward the use of experiential approaches to learning? What conditions are required for success?

NUPATH FOODS, INC.

James Ornath read the latest sales figures with a great deal of satisfaction. The vice-president of marketing at Nupath Foods, Inc., was pleased to see that the marketing campaign to improve sagging sales of Prowess cat food was working. Sales volume of the product had increased 20 percent in the past quarter compared with the previous year, and market share was up.

The improved sales of Prowess could be credited to Denise Washington, the brand manager responsible for cat foods at Nupath. Washington had joined Nupath less than two years ago as an assistant brand manager after leaving a similar job at a consumer products firm. She was one of the few women in marketing management at Nupath and had a promising career with the company. Ornath was pleased with Washington's work and tried to let her know this in the annual performance reviews. He now had an excellent opportunity to reward her by offering the recently vacated position of market research coordinator. Although technically only a lateral transfer with a modest salary increase, the marketing research coordinator job would give Washington broader experience in some high-profile work, which would enhance her career with Nupath. Few people were aware that Ornath's own career had been boosted by working as marketing research coordinator at Nupath several years before.

Denise Washington had also seen the latest sales figures on Prowess cat food and was expecting Ornath's call to meet with her that morning. Ornath began the conversation by briefly mentioning the favorable sales figures, and then explained that he wanted Washington to take the marketing research coordinator job. Washington was shocked by the news. She enjoyed brand management and particularly the challenge involved with controlling a product that directly affected the company's profitability. Marketing research coordinator was a technical support position—a "backroom" job—far removed from the company's bottom-line activities. Marketing research was not the route to top management in most organizations, Washington thought. She had been sidelined.

After a long silence, Washington managed a weak "Thank you, Mr. Ornath." She was too bewildered to protest. She wanted to collect her thoughts and reflect on what she had done wrong. Also, she did not know her boss well enough to be openly critical. Ornath recognized Washington's surprise, which he naturally assumed was her positive response to hearing of this wonderful career opportunity. He, too, had been delighted several years earlier about his temporary transfer to marketing research to round out his marketing experience. "This move will be good for both you and Nupath," said Ornath as he escorted Washington from his office.

Washington had several tasks to complete that afternoon, but she was able to consider the day's events that evening. She was one of the top women in brand management at Nupath and feared that she was being sidelined because the company didn't want women in top management. Her previous employer had made it quite clear that women "couldn't take the heat" in marketing management and tended to place women in technical support positions after a brief term in lower brand management jobs. Obviously Nupath was following the same game plan. Ornath's comments that the coordinator job would be good for her was just a nice way of saying that Washington couldn't go any further in brand management at Nupath. Washington was now faced with the difficult decision of confronting Ornath and trying to change Nupath's sexist practices or submitting her resignation.

Discussion Questions

1. What symptom(s) exist in this case to suggest that something has gone wrong?

2. Diagnose the underlying problems that have led to these symptoms.

3. What actions should the organization take to correct these problems?

Source: Copyright © Steven L. McShane.

CASE STUDY 3.2

NO WAY TO TREAT A LADY

BusinessWeek   Melissa J. Howard's career at Wal-Mart started well, until she became store manager at a new supercenter in Indiana. Howard was shocked to learn that two new male co-managers at the store were making $15,000 more a year than her $70,000 salary and bonus, even though they had no previous experience at Wal-Mart. Then, according to Howard, a new district manager, also a man, told her flat-out that she belonged at home with her child. Howard, the only female manager at the 10 stores in his district, complained to higher-ups but got no results. Howard finally quit when her new boss pressured her to take a demotion to co-manager at a store 60 miles away.

This *Business Week* case study looks at the class action against the world's largest retailer by Melissa J. Howard and hundreds of other women who claim they have been discriminated against. The case presents some of the preliminary evidence, stories by other plaintiffs, and possible explanations of why Wal-Mart executives may have engaged in sex discrimination. Read through this *Business Week* article at www.mhhe.com/mcshane3e and prepare for the discussion questions below.

Discussion Questions

1. If the claims against Wal-Mart are true, what concepts in this chapter would help to explain Wal-Mart's discriminatory decisions and actions?

2. Assuming that the statistical data in this case regarding employment and salaries of women are accurate, what justifications might Wal-Mart executives offer to explain these numbers?

3. What initiatives would you recommend to minimize sex discrimination at Wal-Mart and similar organizations?

Source: W. Zellner, "No Way to Treat a Lady," *Business Week*, March 3, 2003, p. 63.

105

THE LEARNING EXERCISE

Purpose   This exercise is designed to help you understand how the contingencies of reinforcement in behavior modification affect learning.

Materials   Any objects normally available in a classroom will be acceptable for this activity.

Instructions   The instructor will ask for three volunteers, who are then briefed outside the classroom. The instructor will spend a few minutes briefing the remaining students in the class about their duties. Then, one of the three volunteers will enter the room to participate in the exercise. When completed, the second volunteer enters the room and participates in the exercise. When completed, the third volunteer enters the room and participates in the exercise. Your instructor will have more details at the start of this activity.

ASSESSING YOUR EMOTIONAL EMPATHY

Purpose   This exercise is designed to help you understand and to estimate your propensity for emotional empathy.

Instructions   This instrument asks you to indicate the degree to which each of the statements presented does or does not describe you very well. You need to be honest with yourself for a reasonable estimate of your level of emotional empathy. The results show your relative position along the emotional empathy continuum and the general meaning of this score.

ASSESSING YOUR PERSPECTIVE TAKING (COGNITIVE EMPATHY)

Purpose   This exercise is designed to help you understand and to estimate your propensity for perspective taking, which represents the cognitive (thinking) aspect of empathy.

Instructions   This instrument asks you to indicate the degree to which each of the statements presented does or does not describe you very well. You need to be honest with yourself for a reasonable estimate of your level of perspective taking. The results show your relative position along the perspective taking continuum and the general meaning of this score.

ASSESSING YOUR GENERAL SELF-EFFICACY

Purpose This exercise is designed to help you understand the concept of self-efficacy and to estimate your general self-efficacy.

Overview Self-efficacy refers to a person's belief that he or she has the ability, motivation, and resources to complete a task successfully. Self-efficacy is usually conceptualized as a situation-specific belief. You may believe that you can perform a certain task in one situation, although you are less confident with that task in another situation. However, there is also evidence that people develop a more general self-efficacy. This exercise helps you to estimate your general self-efficacy.

Instructions Read each of the statements below and circle the response that best fits your personal belief. Then use the scoring key in Appendix B of this book to calculate your results. This self-assessment is completed alone so that students rate themselves honestly without concerns of social comparison. However, class discussion will focus on the meaning of self-efficacy, how this scale might be applied in organizations, and the limitations of measuring self-efficacy in work settings.

New General Self-Efficacy Scale

To what extent does each statement describe you? Indicate your level of agreement by marking the appropriate response on the right.	Strongly Agree	Agree	Neutral	Disagree	Strongly Disagree
1. I will be able to achieve most of the goals that I have set for myself..........................	☐	☐	☐	☐	☐
2. When facing difficult tasks, I am certain that I will accomplish them..............................	☐	☐	☐	☐	☐
3. In general, I think that I can obtain outcomes that are important to me.........................	☐	☐	☐	☐	☐
4. I believe I can succeed at most any endeavor to which I set my mind...........................	☐	☐	☐	☐	☐
5. I will be able to successfully overcome many challenges...................................	☐	☐	☐	☐	☐
6. I am confident that I can perform effectively on may different tasks.............................	☐	☐	☐	☐	☐
7. Compared to other people, I can do most tasks very well....................................	☐	☐	☐	☐	☐
8. Even when things are tough, I can perform quite well..	☐	☐	☐	☐	☐

Source: G. Chen, S. M. Gully, and D. Eden, "Validation of a New General Self-Efficacy Scale," *Organizational Research Methods* 4 (January 2001), pp. 62–83.

After studying the preceding material, be sure to check out our website at

www.mhhe.com/mcshane3e

for more in-depth information and interactivities that correspond to this chapter.

chapter 4

Workplace Emotions and Attitudes

Learning Objectives

After reading this chapter, you should be able to:

- Define emotions and identify the two dimensions around which emotions are organized.

- Diagram the model of emotions, attitudes, and behavior.

- Identify the conditions that require and the problems associated with emotional labor.

- Describe the four dimensions of emotional intelligence.

- Summarize the effects of job dissatisfaction in terms of the exit-voice-loyalty-neglect model.

- Compare the effects of affective and continuance commitment on employee behavior.

- Describe five strategies to increase organizational commitment.

- Contrast transactional and relational psychological contracts.

*L*ayoffs and cutbacks had sapped staff morale at Cooley Dickinson Hospital in Northampton, Massachusetts, and the employee satisfaction team couldn't figure out how to improve the situation. Then, someone mentioned Fish!—a set of principles for creating positive attitudes at work. After viewing the Fish! video during a fish fry, managers and staff started celebrating birthdays, enjoying ice cream breaks, and hosting a Christmas holiday gift-wrapping service. Morale soared. "The FISH team is keeping employee satisfaction out front," says Cooley Dickinson's director of guest services. "That stuff doesn't happen by accident."

The Fish! philosophy started at Pike Place Fish Market in Seattle. Fishmongers turned a money-losing, morale-draining business into a world-famous attraction by deciding to have fun at work—largely by tossing fish around and joking with customers. Out of this turnaround came four Fish! principles: play, make their day, be there, and choose your attitude. To create an exciting workplace, employees need to learn how to play, just as the fishmongers toss fish.

Justin Hall (shown) and other staff at Pike Place Fish Market in Seattle practice their Fish! philosophy by tossing fish and joking with customers.

To "make their day," employees must interact with clients so they, too, have a positive experience. To "be there," employees need to be focused (not mentally in several places) and actively engaged to have fun. And "choose your attitude" says that everyone has the power to choose how they feel at work.

The Fish! philosophy has caught on. Human resources staff members at Scope International in Malaysia have fun with color coordination days (where they wear the same color on a particular day). Sprint Global Connections Services call center staff in Kansas City, Missouri, toss around foam toys, walk around in bunny slippers, and dance under a disco ball suspended from the ceiling. Sounds strange, but these antics helped Sprint to reduce turnover, improve productivity, and win a Call Center of the Year award. And at Matanuska Valley Federal Credit Union, staff members have a fish parade around the building's exterior before opening. "The winters here in Alaska can get pretty cold and bleak starting in October," explains a manager at the Palmer, Alaska, financial institution. "Fish! has helped boost morale and is just plain fun during those long months."[1] ∎

Whether you work at a hospital in Massachusetts, a credit union in Alaska, or a bank services group in Malaysia, your emotions and attitudes are receiving a lot more attention these days. That's because the emotions people experience and their judgments about various aspects of work make a difference in the organization's performance, customer loyalty, and employee well-being. This chapter presents the most up-to-date information available on the topic of workplace emotions and attitudes. We begin by understanding the meaning and types of emotions. This is followed by a close look at how attitudes are formed, and new thinking about how emotions influence both attitudes and behavior in the workplace.

Next, we consider the dynamics of emotional labor, including the conditions requiring and ways of supporting emotional labor. This leads into the popular topic of emotional intelligence, which presents the current perspective on the components of emotional intelligence and ways of improving this ability. Job satisfaction, the most widely studied work attitude, is then discussed. We look at job satisfaction around the world, the effects of job satisfaction on work behavior, and new findings regarding the relationship between job satisfaction and employee performance and customer satisfaction. The next section provides an overview of organizational commitment, including the types of commitment, consequences of commitment, and ways to build affective commitment. Organizational commitment is strongly influenced by trust and the psychological contract, so the final section of this chapter looks at the meaning and elements of both concepts.

Emotions in the Workplace

The tragic events of September 11, 2001, in the United States are permanently etched in our minds. The four hijacked planes, the collapse of the World Trade Center towers, and the crash into the Pentagon evoked a variety of emotions. "For us, who teach in New York City, the emotional weight of the sadness and the terror were like a mantle that we found difficult to lift for several days," recall Sumita Raghuram and Janet Marks, two faculty members at Fordham University. "Having witnessed the horror first-hand, it was not easy for us to set aside our emotions and resume our role as teachers."[2]

emotions
Psychological and physiological episodes toward an object, person, or event that create a state of readiness.

Raghuram, Marks, and most other people around the planet experienced strong emotions from the events of September 11, 2001. **Emotions** are psychological and physiological episodes experienced toward an object, person, or event that create a state of readiness.[3] There are a few key components to this definition. First, emotions are brief events or "episodes." Your anger toward a co-worker, for instance, would typically subside within a few minutes. Second, emotions are directed toward someone or something. We experience joy, fear, anger, and other emotional episodes toward tasks, customers, public speeches we present, a software program we are using, and so on. This contrasts with *moods*, which are less intense emotional states that are not directed toward anything in particular.[4]

A third feature of this definition is that we experience emotions both psychologically and physiologically. Your anger toward a co-worker would be triggered from the psychological processes of perceiving a particular situation (e.g., discovering that the co-worker may have erased several hours of your work from the computer system) and appraising that situation against your

**"Biosensors. The whole company
knows instantly when I'm displeased."**

(Copyright © Ted Goff, 2001 www.tedgoff.com. Used with permission)

values and expectations. The physiological dimension of emotions might consist of a rise in blood pressure and increased adrenalin. It also consists of facial expressions, such as pursing your lips and furrowing your brow when discovering that the computer work had been erased.

Last, emotions create a state of readiness. Emotional episodes are communications to ourselves. They make us aware of events that may affect our survival and well-being. Some emotions (e.g., anger, surprise, fear) are particularly strong "triggers" that demand our attention, interrupt our train of thought, and generate the motivation to act on the environment.[5]

Types of Emotions

People experience numerous emotions in the workplace and other settings. Some scholars have clustered all emotions into six primary categories: anger, fear, joy, love, sadness, and surprise. For example, alarm and anxiety cluster together to form the primary emotional category called fear.[6] However, emotions are more commonly organized around two or three dimensions.[7] The most widely recognized dimensional view of emotions is the Affect Circumplex Model shown in Exhibit 4.1, which organizes emotions on the basis of their pleasantness and activation (the extent that the emotion produces alertness or engagement). Fear, for example, is an unpleasant experience (i.e., we try to avoid conditions that generate fear) and has high activation (i.e., it motivates us to act). Emotions on the opposite side of the circle have the opposite effect. As we see in Exhibit 4.1, calm is the opposite to fear; it is a pleasant experience that produces very little activation in us.

Emotions, Attitudes, and Behavior

Emotions play an important role in workplace behavior. To understand the influence of emotions on behavior, we first need to understand the concept called attitudes. **Attitudes** represent the cluster of beliefs, assessed feelings, and behavioral intentions toward a person, object, or event (called an *attitude*

attitudes
The cluster of beliefs, assessed feelings, and behavioral intentions toward an object.

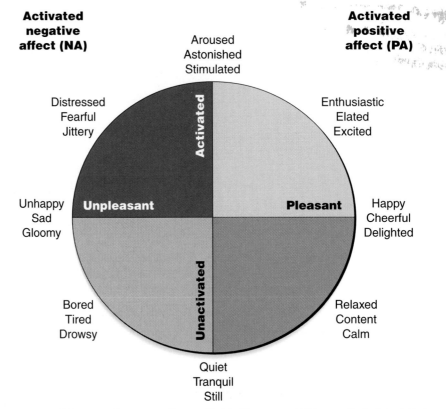

EXHIBIT 4.1

Affect circumplex model

Source: J. Larson, E. Diener, and R. E. Lucas, "Emotion: Models, Measures, and Differences," in R. G. Lord, R. J. Klimoske, and R. Kanfer (Eds.), *Emotions in the Workplace* (San Francisco: Jossey-Bass, 2002), pp. 64–113.

object).[8] Attitudes are *judgments,* whereas emotions are *experiences.* Attitudes involve logical reasoning, whereas we sense emotions. We also experience most emotions briefly, whereas our attitude toward someone or something is more stable over time. Attitudes include three components: beliefs, feelings, and behavioral intentions.

- *Beliefs*—These are your established perceptions about the attitude object—what you believe to be true. For example, you might believe that mergers result in layoffs. Or you might believe that mergers ensure survival in an era of globalization. These beliefs develop from past experience and learning.[9]
- *Feelings*—Feelings represent your positive or negative evaluations of the attitude object. Some people think mergers are good; others think they are bad. Your like or dislike of mergers represents your assessed feelings toward the attitude object.
- *Behavioral intentions*—These represent your motivation to engage in a particular behavior with respect to the attitude object. You might plan to quit rather than stay with the company during the merger. Alternatively, you might intend to e-mail senior executives that this merger was a good decision.

Until recently, scholars took the view that the three components of attitude influence behavior through a purely rational process. This rational attitude-

EXHIBIT 4.2

Model of emotions,
attitudes, and
behavior

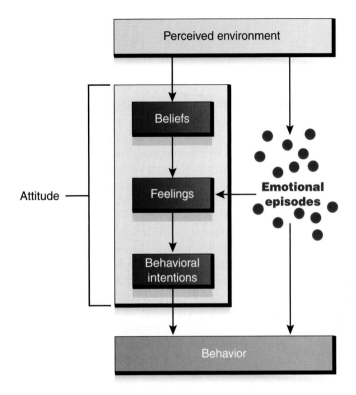

behavior model is illustrated on the left side of Exhibit 4.2. The perceived environment influences our beliefs about an attitude object. We then calculate our feelings toward the attitude object based on these beliefs. The resulting evaluative judgments (feelings) lead to behavioral intentions, and behavioral intentions lead to behavior under certain circumstances.

Let's look at each stage of this rational process more closely. First, we calculate our feelings from our beliefs. This process, known as the *expectancy-value model*, says that feelings are determined by the person's beliefs about the attitude object's expectancy of producing specific outcomes as well as by the value (good or bad) of those outcomes. Let's say that you believe (expectancy) the consequences of mergers are mostly negative (value). For example, you think they are disruptive, result in layoffs, and usually lose money for the company. Even if you recognize a couple of positive outcomes of mergers, you would likely develop negative feelings toward mergers (i.e., you dislike mergers).

Next, feelings influence your behavioral intentions. People with the same feelings may form different behavioral intentions based on their unique past experience. Suppose that your company announced that it would merge with a larger company. Employees who think mergers are bad (feelings) may intend to quit, whereas others might want to complain about the decision. People choose the behavioral intention that they think will work best for them.

Finally, behavioral intentions are better than feelings or beliefs at predicting a person's behavior.[10] Even so, scholars have reported for many years that behavioral intentions alone are relatively weak predictors of behavior. The main reason for this weak relationship is that behavioral intentions represent the motivation to act, yet the other three factors in the MARS model—ability, role perceptions, and situational factors—also influence individual behavior (see Chapter 2). You might intend to write a letter complaining about the announced merger, but a heavy workload and family obligations prevent you from completing this intended task.

Linking Emotions to Attitudes and Behavior   Notice that the rational model —which has dominated attitude research for decades—does not mention emotions in either attitude formation or the prediction of behavior. This neglect dates back to Plato, Descartes, and other philosophers who urged scholars to separate emotion from reasoning. Today, we know that the rational attitude model is incomplete because it ignores emotions. Indeed, evidence is mounting that emotions play an important role in understanding both attitudes and behavior.[11]

So, where do emotions fit in? Neuroscience provides some guidance here. Neuroscientists report that our perceptions of the external world are routed to two parts of the brain—the emotional center and the rational center.[12] The expectancy-value attitude model represents the rational brain center process. The emotional center also receives the perceptual information, but it processes it much faster and with less precision. The incoming information produces emotional episodes that are tagged to the information. Imagine hearing that the organization where you work will soon merge with a larger competitor. Upon hearing this announcement, you might immediately experience surprise, optimism, anger, excitement, or other emotions. The emotional center tagged emotions to the announcement indicating that the situation threatens or supports your survival and well-being.

The right side of Exhibit 4.2 offers a simplified presentation of how emotions get integrated with the rational process and influence behavior. The emotional center generates emotions regarding the attitude object based on a "quick and dirty" assessment of perceived environment information (e.g., you are surprised, excited, or angry upon hearing the merger announcement). Those emotions are then transmitted to the rational center, which is more slowly analyzing the information. The emotional markers influence your judgment about the announcement and shape your feelings toward the attitude object. If you experience anxiety and irritation when hearing the merger announcement, then you would likely develop negative feelings toward it.[13]

You can see how emotions affect our workplace attitudes. When performing our jobs or interacting with co-workers, we experience a variety of emotions that shape our longer term feelings toward the company. The more emotions that are positive, the more we form positive attitudes toward the organization and various aspects of it. The opening story to this chapter described how Sprint, Cooley Dickenson Hospital, Scope International, and numerous other firms use the Fish! package to improve morale by injecting more fun at work. Connections 4.1 looks at other means by which organizations have created positive emotions. In each case, the idea is to generate emotional episodes that result in favorable judgments about the organization.

One last observation about the attitude model in Exhibit 4.2 relates to the arrow directly from the emotional episodes to behavior. This indicates that people react to their emotions, not just their judgments (attitudes). When upset, an employee might stomp out of a meeting, bang a fist on the desk, or burst into tears. When overjoyed, an employee might embrace a co-worker or

Serious Fun: Companies Want Employees to Experience Positive Emotions

Richer Sounds holds a world record for retail sales per square foot, but the British hi-fi store chain is equally well known for being a fun place to work. Everyone receives a monthly allowance to socialize with co-workers after work. Headquarters is filled with wacky artwork, including a life-size image of Elvis. And when selling stereo equipment gets too stressful, Richer Sounds has several holiday homes scattered from Venice to St. Tropez where staff can stay for free. "The idea is to make work fun," says John Clayton, recruitment and training director at Richer Sounds.

Fun at work? It sounds like an oxymoron. But to attract and motivate valuable talent, companies are finding creative ways to generate positive emotions in the workplace. Employees at First National Bank of Bar Harbor, Maine, hold golf putting tournaments in the lobby. PJI Holdings, a Malaysian engineering services company, recently treated its staff to a fun-frolicking day at a lagoon theme park near Kuala Lumpur, complete with team competitions (telematches) and a talent show. Staff at The Horn Group's Boston office recently organized a photographic scavenger hunt around the city. MDS Nordion employees in Ottawa, Canada, hold an annual winter carnival that includes relay races, mock sumo wrestling, and sleigh rides. "There's always something fun like that going on," says an executive at the world's leading supplier of medical isotopes.

Positive emotions are so important at Isle of Capri Casinos that the company includes fun as one of its corporate objectives. Recently the Biloxi, Mississippi, casino company held a scavenger hunt in which teams of managers were assigned unusual missions, such as creatively getting an admission ticket from the Houston Space Station box office, a fresh paw print of a large dog, a copy of a Flying Burrito Brothers album, and a photo of a parrot at a local zoo. To achieve these tasks,

This scavenger hunt is just one of the ways that Isle of Capri Casinos and other companies are creating a fun-oriented workplace to attract and motivate employees.

each team received a survival kit containing $500 cash, keys to a minivan, T-shirts, maps, cameras, and other gear.

These fun and games may seem silly, but some corporate leaders are deadly serious about their value. "It's pretty simple," explains an executive at Quebecor. "If you want to make the most money, you must attract the best people. To get the best people, you must be the most fun."

Sources: J. Clayton, "Richer Sounds: A Sound Footing," *Employee Benefits,* August 4, 2003, p. 33; J. P. Crane, "Some Companies Betting on Fun Activities Can Help Retain Workers, Build Satisfaction," *Boston Globe,* July 27, 2003, p. G1; C. Curtis, "Creative Workplace Practices Abound in Maine," *Portland (Maine) Press Herald,* June 27, 2003; "Splashing Fun at Staff Day," *New Straits Times* (Kuala Lumpur, Malaysia), April 24, 2003; "Richer Sounds—Hi-Fi Retailer: All Singing to the Same Tune," *Sunday Times* (London), March 2, 2003; "Isle of Capri Casinos, Inc. Creates Real-Life Employee 'Survivor' Event," *PR Newswire,* January 21, 2003, P. Chisholm, "Redesigning Work," *Maclean's,* March 5, 2001, pp. 34–38; J. Elliott, "All Work and No Play Can Chase Workers Away," *Edmonton Journal,* February 28, 2000.

---

break into a little dance. Even minor emotions cause us to change facial expressions and other subtle behaviors. These actions are not carefully thought out. They are fairly automatic emotional responses that serve as coping mechanisms in that situation.[14]

cognitive dissonance

A psychological tension that occurs when people perceive an inconsistency between their beliefs, feelings, and behavior.

Cognitive Dissonance   Emotions and attitudes usually lead to behavior, but behavior sometimes influences our attitudes through the process of **cognitive dissonance.**[15] Cognitive dissonance occurs when we perceive an inconsistency between our beliefs, feelings, and behavior. This inconsistency creates an uncomfortable tension (dissonance) that we are motivated to reduce by changing one or more of these elements. Behavior is usually the most difficult element to change, particularly when it is known to everyone, was done voluntarily, and can't be undone. Thus, we usually change our beliefs and feelings to reduce the inconsistency.

Emotions and Personality   Our coverage of the dynamics of workplace emotions wouldn't be complete unless we mentioned that a person's emotions are also partly determined by that person's personality, not just workplace experiences. **Positive affectivity (PA)** is the tendency to experience positive emotional states. It is very similar to extroversion, described in Chapter 2 as a characteristic of people who are outgoing, talkative, sociable, and assertive. In contrast, some people are high on **negative affectivity (NA),** which is the tendency to experience negative emotions.[16] Employees with high NA tend to be more distressed and unhappy because they focus on the negative aspects of life.

To what extent do these personality traits influence emotions and behavior? Some research reports that PA and NA employees differ in their attendance, turnover, and reactions to job satisfaction. NA is also associated with various stages of job burnout (see Chapter 7).[17] However, other evidence suggests that PA and NA have relatively weak effects on work-related attitudes.[18] Overall, it seems that PA and NA influence emotions and attitudes in the workplace, but their effects are not as strong as situational factors.

positive affectivity (PA)
The tendency to experience positive emotional states.

negative affectivity (NA)
The tendency to experience negative emotions.

Managing Emotions at Work

The Elbow Room Café is packed and noisy on this Saturday morning. A customer at the restaurant in Vancouver, Canada, half shouts across the room for more coffee. A passing waiter scoffs: "You want more coffee, get it yourself!" The customer only laughs. Another diner complains loudly that he and his party are running late and need their food. This time, restaurant manager Patrick Savoie speaks up: "If you're in a hurry, you should have gone to McDonald's." The diner and his companions chuckle.

To the uninitiated, the Elbow Room Café is an emotional basket case, full of irate guests and the rudest staff on the West Coast. But it's all a performance—a place where guests can enjoy good food and play out their emotions about dreadful customer service. "It's almost like coming to a theater," says Savoie, who spends much of his time inventing new ways to insult the clientele.[19]

Whether giving the most insulting service at Elbow Room Café in Vancouver or the friendliest service at Sprint's call center in Kansas City, Missouri, employees are usually expected to manage their emotions in the workplace. **Emotional labor** refers to the effort, planning, and control needed to express organizationally desired emotions during interpersonal transactions.[20] When interacting with co-workers, customers, suppliers, and others, employees are expected to abide by *display rules*. These rules are norms requiring employees to display certain emotions and withhold others.

emotional labor
The effort, planning, and control needed to express organizationally desired emotions during interpersonal transactions.

Conditions Requiring Emotional Labor

Most employees are expected to engage in some level of emotional labor. People experience more emotional labor when their jobs require frequent and long durations of voice or face-to-face contact with clients and others.[21] For

[Handwritten margin notes: Emotional labor higher when job requires: long display emotions, varitey [variety] emotions, more intense emotions. Influenced by culture + other situational factors]

instance, caregivers at a nursing home must show courtesy, promote positive emotions, and control the emotions of residents while hiding their own fatigue, anger, and other true emotions. Emotional labor is also more challenging where the job requires employees to display a variety of emotions (e.g., anger as well as joy) and intense emotions (e.g., showing delight rather than smiling weakly). Bill collectors face these challenges. They must learn to show warmth to anxious first-time debtors and irritation (but not anger) toward debtors who seem indifferent to their financial obligations.[22]

Jobs vary in the extent that employees must abide by the display rules. "Smile: we are on stage" is one of the most important rules that employees learn at the Ritz-Carlton in San Francisco.[23] The extent that someone must follow display rules also depends on the power and personal relationship of the person receiving the service. You would closely follow display rules when meeting the owner of a client's organization, whereas more latitude might be possible when serving a friend. There are also cross-cultural differences in emotional display norms and values. One survey reported that 83 percent of Japanese believe it is inappropriate to get emotional in a business context, compared with 40 percent of Americans, 34 percent of French, and 29 percent of Italians. In other words, Italians are more likely to accept or tolerate people who display their true emotions at work, whereas this would be considered rude or embarrassing in Japan.[24]

Emotional Dissonance

Comedian George Burns once said: "The secret to being a good actor is honesty. If you can fake *that,* you've got it made." Burns's humor highlights the fact that most of us have difficulty hiding our true emotions all of the time. Instead, emotions "leak" out as voice intonations, posture, and in other subtle ways.[25] The problem is particularly true of anger, which is one of the most difficult emotions to control. This conflict between required and true emotions is called **emotional dissonance,** and it is a significant cause of stress and job burnout (see Chapter 7).[26] Emotional dissonance is most common where employees must display emotions that are quite different from their true feelings and where emotional display rules are highly regulated.

emotional dissonance
A conflict between a person's required and true emotions.

Does emotional dissonance always create stress? Not necessarily. A recent study revealed that stress and burnout levels depend on whether employees manage the emotional labor requirements through surface acting or deep acting.[27] George Burns was referring to *surface acting*—thinking through and acting out behaviors that reflect the required emotions even though you hold quite different emotions. An example of surface acting would be smiling at a customer even though you feel irritated by that person. Surface acting is stressful because you have to act out behaviors while holding back your true emotions that are incompatible with those behaviors.

Deep acting, on the other hand, involves changing your emotions to meet the job requirements. Rather than feeling irritated by a particular customer, you apply strategies that make you less irritated and generally happier to work with this person. For example, you might think that the customer is irritating due to personal problems and that you might help make the individual's life a little better through good service. Thus, rather than having a conflict between your required and true emotions, deep acting involves shifting your true

Japanese Employees Learn Service with a Smile

Hiroshi Ieyoshi and three dozen other gas station attendants are gathered for some tough after-hours training. They're learning how to smile. "It's easy to say you should smile at the customers," says Ieyoshi, the earnest 33-year-old pump manager after the 90-minute seminar. "But to be honest, it all depends on how I feel at the moment."

Ieyoshi isn't the only one who has trouble smiling at customers. In Japanese culture, hiding your emotions is considered a virtue because lack of expression minimizes conflict and avoids drawing attention to the individual.

Leading the smile revolution is Yoshihiko Kadokawa, president of the Smile Amenity Institute and author of *The Power of a Laughing Face.* The former retail executive discovered that even in this dour society, the friendliest clerks consistently have the highest sales. "I have found, through my surveys, that sales personnel could beef up sales by as much as 20% each day by just smiling more at their customers," says Kadokawa.

McDonald's Corporation puts such a premium on smiling faces in Japan that the company screens out those who are too poker-faced. While applicants describe a pleasant experience, interviewers evaluate whether their faces reflect the pleasure they're discussing. McDonald's wants all of its employees to provide the friendly service at the price stated on the menu: "Smiles, 0 yen."

In spite of the cultural barriers, some Japanese employees have acquired a natural ability to smile as much as Westerners. In the class with gas station attendants, Kutaro Matsunaga stands out. But he has been practicing for a long time. "My name means 'happy man,' and I always want to make my customers happy," explains Matsunaga, with a smile.

Sources: S. Kakuchi, "Put on a Happy Face," *Asian Business* 36 (March 2000), p. 56; V. Reitman, "Learning to Grin—And Bear It," *Los Angeles Times,* February 22, 1999, p. A1.

Students at the Smile Amenity Institute practice smiling (right) with instructor Yoshihiko Kadokawa (left).

emotions so they are more compatible with the required emotions. Not only does this reduce stress; it also creates a sense of accomplishment if your performance is effective.

Supporting Emotional Labor

Many organizations support emotional labor by teaching employees the subtle behaviors that express appropriate emotions. This occurs at some airlines where flight attendants and check-in staff complete videotaped exercises and receive feedback on their emotional labor. The feedback helps them to learn the subtle art of expressing organizationally desired emotions. Earlier, we mentioned that people in Japan traditionally expect a narrow range of emotional displays. But this is changing as companies discover that employee smiles are good for business. Global Connections 4.2 describes how some Japanese companies are sending their employees to "smile school," where they learn the fine art of displaying pleasant emotions.

Along with training, some corporate leaders believe that the best way to support emotional labor is by hiring employees with the natural tendency to display desired emotions. For example, when CiCi's Pizza opens new stores, it looks for job applicants with a "happy, cheery" attitude. The Plano, Texas, franchise restaurant believes that it is easier to teach new skills than attitudes. "We hire for attitude and train for skill," says Mike Lemmons, who owns several CiCi's Pizza franchises.[28] In some respects, this means that CiCi's and other companies look for people with well-developed emotional intelligence, which we discuss next.

Emotional Intelligence

Each year, the U.S. Air Force hires about 400 recruiters, and each year up to 100 of them are fired for failing to sign up enough people for the service. Selecting and training 100 new recruiters costs $3 million, not to mention the hidden costs of their poor performance. So Rich Handley, head of Air Force recruiting, decided to give 1,200 recruiters a new test that measured how well they manage their emotions and the emotions of others. He discovered that the top recruiters were better at asserting their feelings and thoughts, empathizing with others, feeling happy in life, and being aware of their emotions in a particular situation. The next year, Handley selected new recruiters partly on their results on this emotions test. The result: Only eight recruiters got fired or quit a year later.[29]

To select the best recruiters, the U.S. Air Force considers more than the cognitive intelligence of job applicants; it also looks at their **emotional intelligence (EI).** EI is the ability to perceive and express emotion, assimilate emotion in thought, understand and reason with emotion, and regulate emotion in oneself and others.[30] In other words, EI represents a set of competencies that allow us to perceive, understand, and regulate emotions in ourselves and in others. These *emotional competencies* are learned capabilities based on emotional intelligence that lead to superior performance.

Exhibit 4.3 illustrates the most recent and most popular EI model, developed by psychologist and journalist Daniel Goleman and his colleagues. According to Goleman's model, EI can be organized into four dimensions representing the recognition of emotions in ourselves and in others, as well as the regulation of emotions in ourselves and in others. Each dimension consists of a set of emotional competencies that people must possess to fulfill that dimension of emotional intelligence.[31]

- *Self-awareness*—Self-awareness refers to having a deep understanding of one's own emotions as well as strengths, weaknesses, values, and motives. Self-aware people are in touch with their feelings and know what feels right to them. In other words, they effectively recognize their intuition or gut instincts.
- *Self-management*—This represents how well we control or redirect our internal states, impulses, and resources. It includes keeping disruptive impulses in check, displaying honesty and integrity, being flexible in times of

emotional intelligence (EI)
The ability to perceive and express emotion, assimilate emotion in thought, understand and reason with emotion, and regulate emotion in oneself and others.

EXHIBIT 4.3

Emotional
Intelligence
Competencies
Model

	Self (personal competence)	Other (social competence)
Recognition of emotions	**Self-Awareness** Emotional self-awareness Accurate self-assessment Self-confidence	**Social Awareness** Empathy Organizational awareness Service
Regulation of emotions	**Self-Management** Emotional self-control Transparency Adaptability Achievement Initiative Optimism	**Relationship Management** Inspirational leadership Influence Developing others Change catalyst Conflict management Building bonds Teamwork and collaboration

Sources: D. Goleman, R. Boyatzis, and A. McKee, *Primal Leadership* (Boston: Harvard Business School Press, 2002), Chapter 3; D. Goleman, "An EI-Based Theory of Performance," in *The Emotionally Intelligent Workplace,* ed. C. Cherniss and D. Goleman (San Francisco: Jossey-Bass, 2001), p. 28.

change, maintaining the drive to perform well and seize opportunities, and remaining optimistic even after failure. Self-management involves an inner conversation that guides our behavior.

- *Social awareness*—Social awareness is mainly about *empathy*—having understanding and sensitivity to the feelings, thoughts, and situation of others (see Chapter 3). This includes cognitively understanding another person's situational circumstances (called perspective taking) as well as actually experiencing the other person's feelings (called emotional empathy). By being empathic, people are also able to know a customer's needs and expectations, even when unstated. Social awareness extends beyond empathy for other individuals; it also includes being organizationally aware, such as sensing office politics and understanding social networks.

- *Relationship management*—This dimensions of EI refers to managing other people's emotions. At this time, Goleman and his colleagues link relationship management with a wide variety of concepts that look more like performance outcomes than competencies. They include inspiring others, influencing people's beliefs and feelings, developing others' capabilities, managing change, resolving conflict, cultivating relationships, and supporting teamwork and collaboration. Each of these challenges requires competencies relating to communication and other forms of social interaction.

The four dimensions of emotional intelligence are not independent of each other. On the contrary, most EI writers agree that these dimensions roughly form a hierarchy of levels of emotional intelligence.[32] Relationship management is the highest level of EI because it requires all three other dimensions. In other words, someone who masters relationship management would have a high degree of emotional intelligence because he or she must also have sufficiently high levels of the other three dimensions. Self-awareness is the lowest level of EI because it does not require the other dimensions; instead it is a prerequisite for the other three dimensions. Self-management and social awareness are somewhere in the middle of the EI hierarchy. Some writers imply that social awareness is the higher of the two, but this is less clear.

EI has its roots in the social intelligence literature introduced more than 80 years ago, but scholars spent most of this time focused on cognitive intelligence (IQ).[33] Now, the U.S. Air Force and others are realizing that EI is an important set of competencies in the performance of most jobs. As we described in Chapter 2, people perform better when their aptitudes—including general intelligence—match the job requirements. But most jobs also involve social interaction, so employees also need emotional intelligence to work effectively in social settings. The evidence fairly strongly indicates that emotional intelligence makes a difference in organizations. Studies have reported that people with high EI scores are better at interpersonal relations, perform better in jobs requiring emotional labor, and are more successful in many aspects of job interviews. Teams whose members have high emotional intelligence initially perform better than teams with low EI.[34]

Improving Emotional Intelligence   Emotional intelligence is related to several personality traits described in Chapter 2, including extroversion, conscientiousness, agreeableness, emotional stability, and low neuroticism.[35] Still, EI can be learned to some extent. Endpoint Research, a Canadian firm specializing in pharmaceutical and biotechnology clinical trials, has put all 65 of its employees through the EI assessment so they can develop their weak areas. Methodist Hospitals of Dallas has also introduced emotional intelligence training to its management group, with the CEO front-and-center participating in the program.[36]

These training programs may help, but people don't develop emotional intelligence just by learning about its dimensions. They require personal coaching, plenty of practice, and frequent feedback. Emotional intelligence also increases with age; it is part of the process called maturity.[37] Overall, emotional intelligence offers considerable potential, but we also have a lot to learn about its measurement and effects on people in the workplace.

Our discussion so far laid the foundations of emotions and attitudes, but scholars are also interested in specific attitudes in the workplace. The next two sections of this chapter look at two of the most widely studied attitudes: job satisfaction and organizational commitment.

Executives at ANZ Banking Group learned that they were above average on financial and operational activities but needed improvement with values and social competencies. So, with the guidance of McKinsey & Company, the Australian financial institution introduced a training program in which thousands of ANZ managers learned about emotional intelligence and how to apply these competencies to create "caring, connected relationships between employees at ANZ, as well as the bank's millions of customers," explains an ANZ executive. "This transformation is an ongoing journey, which realizes the importance of engaging employees on both an emotional and intellectual level."[38] Looking at the four dimensions of emotional intelligence, why is it important for managers to have a high emotional intelligence?

Job Satisfaction

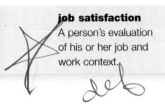

job satisfaction
A person's evaluation of his or her job and work context.

Job satisfaction is undoubtedly the most widely studied attitude in organizational behavior. **Job satisfaction** represents a person's evaluation of his or her job and work context.[39] It is an *appraisal* of the perceived job characteristics, work environment, and emotional experiences at work. Satisfied employees have a favorable evaluation of their job, based on their observations and emotional experiences. Job satisfaction is really a collection of attitudes about specific facets of the job.[40] Employees can be satisfied with some elements of the job while simultaneously dissatisfied with others. You might like your co-workers but be less satisfied with workload or other aspects of the job.

How satisfied are we at work? National surveys indicate that over 85 percent of Americans have been satisfied with their jobs for the past decade or more. However, this level may have slipped somewhat recently, mainly due to downsizings and lack of work–life balance.[41] Exhibit 4.4 shows that Americans also have the fourth-highest job satisfaction ratings in a survey of 39 countries (22 of which are shown here). Only employees in Denmark, India, and Norway say they are happier at work. Another survey found that Ameri-

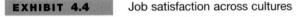

EXHIBIT 4.4   Job satisfaction across cultures

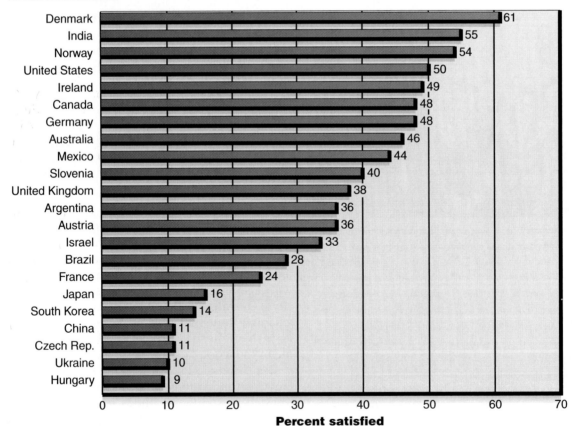

Source: Based on Ipsos-Reid survey of 9,300 employees in 39 countries in middle of Year 2000. See "Ipsos-Reid Global Poll Finds Major Differences in Employee Satisfaction Around the World," Ipsos-Reid News Release, January 8, 2001. A sample of 22 countries across the range are shown here, including all of the top scoring countries.

cans had the third highest job satisfaction, after Brazilians and Canadians, among the 10 largest economies in the world.[42]

Do these surveys mean that we have high job satisfaction? Well, maybe, but probably not as high as these statistics suggest. The problem is that surveys often use a single direct question, such as "How satisfied are you with your job?" Many dissatisfied employees are reluctant to reveal their feelings in a direct question because this is tantamount to admitting that they made a poor job choice and are not enjoying life. One indication of inflated overall satisfaction ratings is that between 30 and 50 percent of Americans (depending on the survey) say that they either are looking for another job or would leave if offered a similar job with slightly higher pay! Other surveys also show that employees rate almost all aspects of the job lower than their overall score. We also need to keep in mind that cultural values make it difficult to compare job satisfaction across countries.[43] People in China, South Korea, and Japan tend to subdue their emotions in public, so they probably avoid extreme survey ratings such as "very satisfied."

Job Satisfaction and Work Behavior

Annette Verschuren, president of The Home Depot Canada, pays a lot of attention to job satisfaction. "I can tell you within two seconds of entering a store whether morale is good," says Verschuren. The main reason for her interest is that job satisfaction is a key driver to corporate success. "With an unhappy workforce you have nothing and you will never be great," Verschuren warns.[44]

Home Depot Canada, Xerox, Sears, Roebuck and Co., and a flock of other organizations are paying a lot more attention to job satisfaction these days. In some firms, executive bonuses depend partly on employee satisfaction ratings. The reason for this attention is simple: Job satisfaction affects many of the individual behaviors introduced in Chapter 2. A useful template to organize and understand the consequences of job dissatisfaction is the **exit-voice-loyalty-neglect (EVLN) model.** As the name suggests, the EVLN model identifies four ways that employees respond to dissatisfaction:[45]

exit-voice-loyalty-neglect (EVNL) model
The four ways, as indicated in the name, employees respond to job dissatisfaction.

- *Exit:* Exit refers to leaving the situation, including searching for other employment, actually leaving the organization, or transferring to another work unit. Employee turnover is a well-established outcome of job dissatisfaction, particularly for employees with better job opportunities elsewhere. Recent evidence also suggests that exit is linked to specific "shock events," such as a conflict episode or an important violation of your expectations.[46] These shock events produce more than just dissatisfaction; they generate strong emotions that energize employees to think about and search for alternative employment.
- *Voice:* Voice refers to any attempt to change, rather than escape from, the dissatisfying situation. Voice is often researched purely as a positive or constructive response, such as directly trying to solve the problem with management or actively helping to improve the situation. However, voice can also be more confrontational, such as by filing formal grievances.[47] In the extreme, some employees might engage in counterproductive behaviors to get attention and force changes in the organization. Thus, voice might be more correctly viewed as either constructive or destructive.

■ *Loyalty:* Loyalty has been described in different ways.[48] The most widely held view is that "loyalists" are employees who respond to dissatisfaction by patiently waiting—some say "suffering in silence"—for the problem to work itself out or get resolved by others.[49]

■ *Neglect:* Neglect includes reducing work effort, paying less attention to quality, and increasing absenteeism and lateness. It is generally considered a passive activity that has negative consequences for the organization. Research clearly establishes that dissatisfied employees tend to have higher absenteeism;[50] the relationship between satisfaction and job performance is more complex, as we will discuss below.

Which of the four EVLN alternatives do employees use? It depends on the person and situation. One determining factor is the availability of alternative employment. With poor job prospects, employees are less likely to use the exit option. Employees who identify with the organization (organizational commitment, which we discuss later) are also more likely to use voice rather than exit. Personality is another influence on the choice of action. People with high conscientiousness are less likely to engage in neglect and more likely to engage in voice (as are people high in extraversion and low in neuroticism). Some experts suggest that employees differ in their EVLN behavior depending on whether they have high or low collectivism. Finally, past experience influences our choice of action. Employees who were unsuccessful with voice in the past are more likely to engage in exit or neglect when experiencing job dissatisfaction in the future.[51]

Job Satisfaction and Performance

One of the oldest beliefs in the business world is that "a happy worker is a productive worker." Is this statement true? Organizational behavior scholars have waffled on this question for the past century. In the 1980s, they concluded that job satisfaction has a weak or negligible association with task performance.[52] Now, the evidence suggests that the popular saying may be correct after all. Citing problems with the earlier studies, a groundbreaking analysis recently concluded that there is a *moderate* relationship between job satisfaction and job performance. In other words, happy workers are more productive workers *to some extent.*[53]

The moderate relationship between job satisfaction and performance begs the next question: Why isn't the relationship stronger? There are many reasons, but let's look at the three most common ones.[54] One argument is that general attitudes (such as job satisfaction) don't predict specific behaviors very well. As we learned with the EVLN model, job dissatisfaction doesn't always result in lower job effort (neglect). Instead, some employees continue to work productively while they complain (voice), look for another job (exit), or patiently wait for the problem to be fixed (loyalty).

A second explanation is that job performance leads to job satisfaction (rather than vice versa), but only when performance is linked to valued rewards. Higher performers receive more rewards and, consequently, are more satisfied than low-performing employees who receive fewer rewards. The connection between job satisfaction and performance isn't stronger because many organizations do not reward good performance. The third explanation is that job satisfaction might influence employee motivation, but this has little influence on performance in jobs where employees have little control over their job output (such as assembly line work). This point is consistent with recent evidence that the job satisfaction–performance relationship is strongest in complex jobs, where employees have more freedom to perform their work or to slack off.[55]

Job Satisfaction and Customer Satisfaction

Along with the job satisfaction–performance relationship, corporate leaders are making strong statements that happy employees make happy customers. "It just seems common sense to me that if you start with a happy, well-motivated workforce, you're much more likely to have happy customers," explains Virgin Group founder Richard Branson. Betty Gilliam says the same principle applies in health care. "Our front line is our bottom line," says Gilliam, an executive at The Care Group, an Indianapolis-based network of cardiologists and primary care physicians. "If our employees are satisfied, then our patients are satisfied."[56]

Fortunately, these views are supported by recent studies in marketing and organizational behavior. Marketing experts, in particular, have developed a model that relates employee satisfaction to customer satisfaction and profitability. As shown in Exhibit 4.5, this "employee-customer-profit chain" model suggests that increasing employee satisfaction and loyalty results in higher customer perceptions of value, which improves the company's profitability.[57]

There are two main reasons why job satisfaction has a positive effect on customer service.[58] First, job satisfaction affects a person's general mood. Employees who are in a good mood are more likely to display friendliness and positive emotions, which puts customers in a better mood. Second, satisfied employees are less likely to quit their jobs, and longer service employees have more experience and better skills to serve clients. Lower turnover also gives

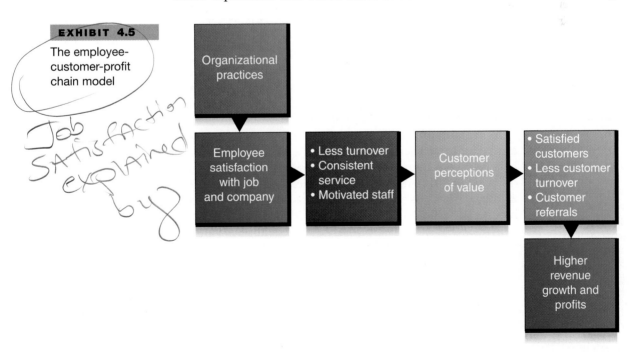

EXHIBIT 4.5

The employee-customer-profit chain model

Roger Greene (wearing goggles in photo) isn't taking any chances on poor customer service. The CEO and founder of Ipswitch Inc. has taken all 130 employees—plus one guest each—on a four-day cruise in the Bahamas. The cruise is the Lexington, Virginia, software maker's way of thanking employees for steady financial performance. It's also consistent with Greene's larger objective to keep employees happy so they will continue to provide exceptional customer service. Ipswitch employees also get five weeks of paid time off, child and elder care, domestic partner benefits, and a concierge service. "If employees are treated well," Greene explains, "they will treat the customers well, and then the profits will come."[60] Along with job satisfaction, what other work attitude described in this chapter might explain why a trip to the Bahamas increases customer service?

customers the same employees to serve them, so there is more consistent service. There is some evidence that customers build their loyalty to specific employees, not to the organization, so keeping employee turnover low tends to build customer loyalty.[59]

Before leaving this topic, it's worth mentioning that job satisfaction does more than improve work behaviors and customer satisfaction. Job satisfaction is also an ethical issue that influences the organization's reputation in the community. People spend a large portion of their time working in organizations, and many societies now expect companies to provide work environments that are safe and enjoyable. Indeed, employees in several countries closely monitor ratings of the best companies to work for, an indication that employee satisfaction is a virtue worth considerable goodwill to employers. This virtue is apparent when an organization has low job satisfaction. The company tries to hide this fact and, when morale problems become public, corporate leaders are usually quick to improve the situation.

Organizational Commitment

Organizational commitment refers to the employee's emotional attachment to, identification with, and involvement in a particular organization.[61] Organizational behavior scholars call this *affective commitment* because it refers to the individual's feelings toward the organization. Affective commitment is called organizational loyalty when the organization is the target of the individual's commitment. However, affective commitment can also refer to loyalty toward co-workers, customers, or a profession.[62] In this book, we will concentrate mainly on the employee's overall commitment to the organization.

Along with affective commitment, employees have varying levels of **continuance commitment**.[63] Continuance commitment occurs when employees believe it is in their own personal interest to remain with the organization. In other words, this form of commitment is a calculative bond with the organization, rather than an emotional attachment. For example, you may have met people who do not particularly identify with the organization where they work but feel bound to remain there because it would be too costly to quit. Continuance commitment is this motivation to stay because of the high cost of leaving.[64]

Is organizational loyalty declining? It is, according to some surveys, whereas others suggest that employee loyalty remains fairly strong (at least, in the United States) even in these times of job insecurity. One survey reports that about 30 percent of Americans have strong loyalty to their organization, up from 24 percent a few years ago. On a global comparison, one study indicates that Americans have the seventh highest level of loyalty out of 32 coun-

organizational commitment
The employee's emotional attachment to, identification with, and involvement in a particular organization.

continuance commitment
A calculative decision to remain with an organization because quitting would be costly.

tries. Another global poll of 360,000 people estimates that employees in Brazil, Spain, and Germany are the most loyal, whereas their counterparts in the United Kingdom, China, and Japan have the lowest loyalty scores. Americans are around the middle of the pack in that loyalty study.[65]

Consequences of Organizational Commitment

Corporate leaders have good reason to pay close attention to employee loyalty because it can be a significant competitive advantage. Employees with high levels of affective commitment are less likely to quit their jobs and be absent from work. Organizational commitment also improves customer satisfaction because long-tenure employees have better knowledge of work practices, and clients like to do business with the same employees. Employees with high affective commitment also have higher work motivation and organizational citizenship, as well as somewhat higher job performance.[66]

However, employees can have too much affective commitment. One concern is that organizational loyalty results in low turnover, which limits the organization's opportunity to hire new employees with new knowledge and fresh ideas. Another concern is that loyalty results in conformity, which can undermine creativity and ethical conduct. For instance, a former executive at Arthur Andersen claims that one reason for the accounting firm's downfall was that it created a cultlike level of employee loyalty where no one questioned or second-guessed top management's decisions.[67]

Consequences of Continuance Commitment   A more common problem than developing too much affective commitment are company practices that support continuance commitment. Many firms tie employees financially to the organization through low-cost loans, stock options, or deferred bonuses. Anglo Irish Bank relies on "loyalty bonuses" to reduce turnover of new staff. People who are hired at the Irish bank receive half of their bonus after 12 months of employment and the other half six months later. "The hope," says an Anglo Irish Bank executive, "is to keep them a little longer." Polaroid and AMR Corporation (parent of American Airlines) got in hot water with employees and shareholders when they tried to pay executives large "stay-put" bonuses when these firms were on the brink of bankruptcy.[68]

These "golden handcuffs" usually do reduce turnover, but they also increase continuance commitment, not affective commitment. Research suggests that employees with high levels of continuance commitment have *lower* performance ratings and are *less* likely to engage in organizational citizenship behaviors! Furthermore, unionized employees with high continuance commitment are more likely to use formal grievances, whereas employees with high affective commitment engage in more constructive problem solving when employee–employer relations sour.[69] Although some level of financial connection may be necessary, employers should not confuse continuance commitment with employee loyalty. Employers still need to win employees' hearts (affective commitment) beyond tying them financially to the organization (continuance commitment).

Building Organizational Commitment

There are almost as many ways to build organizational loyalty as topics in this textbook, but the following list of activities is most prominent in the literature.[70]

■ *Justice and support*—Affective commitment is higher in organizations that fulfill their obligations to employees and abide by humanitarian values, such as fairness, courtesy, forgiveness, and moral integrity.[71] These values relate to the concept of organizational justice that we discuss in the next chapter. Similarly, organizations that support employee well-being tend to cultivate higher levels of loyalty in return.[72]

■ *Job security*—Layoff threats are one of the greatest blows to employee loyalty, even among those whose jobs are not immediately at risk.[73] Building commitment doesn't require lifetime employment guarantees, but firms should offer enough job security that employees feel some permanence and mutuality in the employment relationship. Xilinx, SaskTel, and Southwest Airlines have fiercely loyal employees partly because these companies have avoided layoffs throughout their histories.[74]

■ *Organizational comprehension*—Affective commitment is a person's identification with the company, so it makes sense that this attitude is strengthened when employees are connected to organizational events and people. Specifically, employees become more loyal when communication processes keep them informed about what is happening in the company (see Chapter 11) and when they have opportunities to interact with co-workers across the organization.[75]

■ *Employee involvement*—Employees feel that they are part of the organization when they make decisions that guide the organization's future.[76] Through participation, employees begin to see how the organization is a reflection of their decisions. In this way, involvement strengthens the company as part of the employee's social identity. Employee involvement also builds loyalty because giving this power is a demonstration of the company's trust in its employees.

■ *Trusting employees*—**Trust** is a psychological state comprising the intention to accept vulnerability based upon positive expectations of the intent or behavior of another person.[77] Trust means putting faith in the other person or group. It is also a reciprocal activity: To receive trust, you must demonstrate trust. Trust is important for organizational commitment because it touches the heart of the employment relationship. Employees identify with and feel obliged to work for an organization only when they trust its leaders. We will discuss trust more fully in the context of high-performance teams (Chapter 10).

trust
A psychological state comprising the intention to accept vulnerability based upon positive expectations of the intent or behavior of another person.

Look closely at some of the recommendations above (job security, humanitarian values, trust) and you will see that one of the key influences on organizational commitment is the employment relationship. In particular, affective commitment is sensitive to fulfillment and violation of the psychological contract, which we look at in the last section of this chapter.

Psychological Contracts

Karl Morris once believed that organizations would repay hard work and loyalty with long-term employment. Not any more. The manager at Quokka Sports lost his job when the San Francisco pioneer in Internet-based sports programming filed for bankruptcy. "I had a reputation I would sacrifice . . . anything [for Quokka]," says Morris. "I'd run through the fire for these guys, and they shot me down."[78]

Quokka employees experienced the shock of having their psychological contract violated. This isn't unusual. According to one university study, 24 percent of employees are "chronically" angry at work, mostly because they feel their employer violated basic promises and didn't fulfill the psychological contract.[79] The **psychological contract** refers to the individual's beliefs about the terms and conditions of a reciprocal exchange agreement between that person and another party. This is inherently perceptual, so one person's understanding of the psychological contract may differ from the other party's understanding. In employment relationships, psychological contracts consist of beliefs about what the employee is entitled to receive and is obliged to offer the employer in return.[80] For example, Karl Morris believed that his psychological contract included long-term employment in return for hard work.

psychological contract
The individual's beliefs about the terms and conditions of a reciprocal exchange agreement between that person and another party.

Types of Psychological Contracts

Psychological contracts vary in many ways. One of the most fundamental differences is the extent to which they are transactional or relational.[81] As Exhibit 4.6 describes, *transactional contracts* are primarily short-term economic exchanges. Responsibilities are well defined around a fairly narrow set of obligations that do not change over the life of the contract. People hired in temporary positions and as consultants tend to have transactional contracts. To some extent, new employees also form transactional contracts until they develop a sense of continuity with the organization.

Relational contracts, on the other hand, are rather like marriages; they are long-term attachments that encompass a broad array of subjective mutual obligations. Employees with a relational psychological contract are more willing to contribute their time and effort without expecting the organization to pay back this debt in the short term. Relational contracts are also dynamic, meaning that the parties tolerate and expect that mutual obligations are not necessarily balanced in the short run. Not surprisingly, organizational citizenship

EXHIBIT 4.6

Types of psychological contracts in employment

Contract characteristics	Transactional contracts	Relational contracts
Focus	Economic	Economic and socioemotional
Time frame	Closed-ended and short-term	Open-ended and indefinite
Stability	Static	Dynamic
Scope	Narrow	Pervasive
Tangibility	Well-defined	More subjective

Source: Based on information in D. M. Rousseau and J. M. Parks, "The Contracts of Individuals and Organizations," *Research in Organizational Behavior* 15 (1993), pp. 1–43.

behaviors are more likely to prevail under relational than transactional contracts. Permanent employees are more likely to believe they have a relational contract.

Psychological Contracts Across Cultures and Generations

Psychological contracts are influenced by the social contexts in which the contracting process occurs.[82] In other words, they vary across cultures and groups of employees based on their unique cultures and cohort experiences. For instance, employees in the United States expect some involvement in company decisions (i.e., they have low power distance), whereas employees in Taiwan and Mexico are more willing to accept arbitrary orders from their supervisors (i.e., they have high power distance).

Psychological contracts also seem to vary across generations of employees. Earlier generation employees grew up with "organization man" expectations in which dedicated employees worked in secure jobs with steady promotions through the hierarchy. They often devoted their entire lives to the same company, put in regular hours, and rarely thought about changing employers.[83] The implicit contract was that if you are loyal to the company and perform your job reasonably well, the company will be loyal to you by providing job security and managing your career development. But the emerging employment relationship of employability removes job security (see Chapter 1), so these older employees are feeling betrayed because their psychological contract has been violated.[84]

However, some scholars suggest that job security has less value to Generation-X and Generation-Y employees than to baby boomers. Workforce newcomers have mainly experienced a psychological contract based on employability and are comfortable with weaker job security. "Employees are developing the view that their only job security in the future must be based on their ability and their competence," says Gary L. Howard, a Motorola vice president, "and not on keeping a job at some particular company."[85]

Psychological contracts are changing, as is the entire field of organizational behavior, by embracing new knowledge about emotions in the workplace. Emotional brain centers, emotional labor, emotional intelligence, and other topics in this chapter were unheard of a decade ago. Now, they are essential reading to improve our grasp of the complex dynamics of employee attitudes and behavior. You will discover several references to emotions-related concepts throughout this book, including the next chapter on employee motivation.

When the global recession hit Egypt's economy, a lot of high-paying jobs with fancy offices and even fancier titles evaporated. Yet professional headhunters say that Egyptian university graduates have been slow to adjust their psychological contract expectations. "The job demands today are much more sophisticated than they used to be, and yet we are finding people who are unwilling to adapt," says Hussein Rushdy (shown in photo), managing director of SkillRate Advisors. As an example, Rushdy recently tried to recruit Egyptian university graduates for sales positions at major companies, but only one in five were willing to apply. "We're not talking about selling chocolates here," says an astonished Rushdy. "We mean multinationals like P&G, Citibank, and AIG Insurance, who need high-caliber sales associates and can't find them because culturally there is a certain taboo associated with sales."[86] Along with cultural values, what other factors influence the willingness or resistance of people to change their psychological contract?

Chapter Summary

Emotions are psychological and physiological episodes experienced toward an object, person, or event that create a state of readiness. Emotions are typically organized into a bipolar circle (circumplex) based on their pleasantness and activation. Emotions differ from attitudes, which represent the cluster of beliefs, feelings, and behavioral intentions toward a person, object, or event. Beliefs are a person's established perceptions about the attitude object. Feelings are positive or negative evaluations of the attitude object. Behavioral intentions represent a motivation to engage in a particular behavior with respect to the target.

Attitudes have traditionally been studied as a rational process of analyzing the value and expectancy of outcomes of the attitude object. Thus, beliefs predict feelings, which predict behavioral intentions, which predict behavior. But this traditional perspective overlooks the role of emotions, which have an important influence on attitudes and behavior. Emotions typically form before we think through situations, so they influence this rational attitude formation process. Emotions also affect behavior directly.

Behavior sometimes influences our subsequent attitudes through cognitive dissonance. People also have the personality traits of positive or negative affectivity, which affect their emotions and attitudes.

Emotional labor refers to the effort, planning, and control needed to express organizationally desired emotions during interpersonal transactions. This is more common in jobs with frequent and lengthy customer interaction, where the job requires a variety of emotions displayed, and where employees must abide by the display rules. Emotional labor creates problems because true emotions tend to leak out, and conflict between expected and true emotions (emotional dissonance) causes stress and burnout. However, stress from emotional dissonance can be minimized through deep acting rather than surface acting.

Emotional intelligence is the ability to perceive and express emotion, assimilate emotion in thought, understand and reason with emotion, and regulate emotion in oneself and others. This concept includes four components arranged in a hierarchy: self-awareness, self-management, social awareness, and relationship management. Emotional intelligence can be learned to some extent, particularly through personal coaching.

Job satisfaction represents a person's evaluation of his or her job and work context. Satisfaction depends on the level of discrepancy between what people expect to receive and what they experience. Although surveys indicate Americans are highly satisfied with their jobs, these results may be somewhat inflated by the use of single-item questions and cultural differences. The exit-voice-loyalty-neglect model outlines four possible consequences of job dissatisfaction. Job satisfaction has a moderate relationship with job performance and with customer satisfaction. Job satisfaction is also a moral obligation in many societies.

Affective organizational commitment (loyalty) refers to the employee's emotional attachment to, identification with, and involvement in a particular organization. This contrasts with continuance commitment, which is a calculative bond with the organization. Affective commitment improves motivation and organizational citizenship, and somewhat higher job performance, whereas continuance commitment is associated with lower performance and organizational citizenship. Companies build loyalty through justice and support, some level of job security, organizational comprehension, employee involvement, and trust.

The psychological contract refers to the individual's beliefs about the terms and conditions of a reciprocal exchange agreement between that person and another party. Transactional psychological contracts are primarily short-term economic exchanges, whereas relational contracts are long-term attachments that encompass a broad array of subjective mutual obligations. Psychological contracts seem to vary across cultures as well as across generations of employees.

Key Terms

attitudes, p. 111
cognitive dissonance, p. 115
continuance commitment, p. 126
emotional dissonance, p. 117

emotional intelligence (EI), p. 119
emotional labor, p. 116
emotions, p. 110
exit-voice-loyalty-neglect (EVLN) model, p. 123

job satisfaction, p. 122

negative affectivity (NA), p. 116

organizational (affective) commitment, p. 126

positive affectivity (PA), p. 116

psychological contract, p. 129

trust, p. 128

Discussion Questions

1. After a few months on the job, Susan has experienced several emotional episodes ranging from frustration to joy about the work she has been assigned. Use the attitude model to explain how these emotions affect Susan's level of job satisfaction with the work itself.

2. A recent study reported that college instructors are frequently required to engage in emotional labor. Identify the situations in which emotional labor is required for this job. In your opinion, is emotional labor more troublesome for college instructors or for telephone operators working at a 911 emergency service?

3. "Emotional intelligence is more important than cognitive intelligence in influencing an individual's success." Do you agree or disagree with this statement? Support your perspective.

4. Describe a time when you effectively managed someone's emotions. What happened? What was the result?

5. The latest employee satisfaction survey in your organization indicates that employees are unhappy with some aspects of the organization. However, management tends to pay attention to the single-item question asking employees to indicate their overall satisfaction with the job. The results of this item indicate that 86 percent of staff members are very or somewhat satisfied, so management concludes that the other results refer to issues that are probably not important to employees. Explain why management's interpretation of these results may be inaccurate.

6. "Happy employees create happy customers." Discuss.

7. What factors influence an employee's organizational loyalty?

8. This chapter argues that psychological contracts vary across cultures and generations. Identify some of the psychological contract expectations around which younger and older employees differ.

CASE STUDY 4.1

DIANA'S DISAPPOINTMENT: THE PROMOTION STUMBLING BLOCK

By Rosemary Maellaro, University of Dallas

Diana Gillen had an uneasy feeling of apprehension as she arrived at the Cobb Street Grille corporate offices. Today she was meeting with her supervisor, Julie Spencer, and regional director, Tom Miner, to learn the outcome of her promotion interview for the district manager position. Diana had been employed by this casual dining restaurant chain for 12 years and had worked her way up from waitress to general manager. Based on her track record, she was the obvious choice for the promotion; and her friends assured her that the interview process was merely a formality. Diana was still anxious,

though, and feared that the news might not be positive. She knew she was more than qualified for the job, but that didn't guarantee anything these days.

Nine months ago, when Diana interviewed for the last district manager opening, she thought her selection for the job was inevitable. She was shocked when that didn't happen. Diana was so upset about not getting promoted then that she initially decided not to apply for the current opening. She eventually changed her mind—after all, the company had just named her Restaurant Manager of the Year and entrusted her with managing their flagship location. Diana thought her chances had to be really good this time.

A multiunit management position was a desirable move up for any general manager and was a goal to which Diana had aspired since she began working in the industry. When she had not been promoted the last time, Julie, her supervisor, explained that her people skills needed to improve. But Diana knew that explanation had little to do with why she hadn't gotten the job—the real reason was corporate politics. She heard that the person they hired was some superstar from the outside—a district manager from another restaurant company who supposedly had strong multiunit management experience and a proven track record of developing restaurant managers. Despite what she was told, she was convinced that Tom, her regional manager, had been unduly pressured to hire this person, who had been referred by the CEO.

The decision to hire the outsider may have impressed the CEO, but it enraged Diana. With her successful track record as a store manager for the Cobb Street Grille, she was much more capable, in her opinion, of overseeing multiple units than someone who was new to the operation. Besides, district managers had always been promoted internally from the store manager ranks and she was unofficially designated as the next one to move up to a district position. Tom had hired the outside candidate as a political maneuver to put himself in a good light with management, even though it meant overlooking a loyal employee like her in the process. Diana had no patience with people who made business decisions for the wrong reasons. She worked very hard to avoid politics—and it especially irritated her when the political actions of others negatively impacted her.

Diana was ready to be a district manager nine months ago, and thought she was even more qualified today—provided the decision was based on performance. She ran a tight ship, managing her restaurant completely by the book. She meticulously adhered to policies and procedures and rigorously controlled expenses. Her sales were growing, in spite of new competition in the market, and she received relatively few customer complaints. The only number that was a little out of line was the higher turnover among her staff.

Diana was not too concerned about the increasing number of terminations, however; there was a perfectly logical explanation for this. It was because she had high standards—for herself and her employees. Any employee who delivered less than 110 percent at all times would be better off finding a job somewhere else. Diana didn't think she should bend the rules for anyone, for whatever reason. A few months ago, for example, she had to fire three otherwise good employees who decided to try a new customer service tactic—a so-called innovation they dreamed up—rather than complying with the established process. As the general manager, it was her responsibility to make sure that the restaurant was managed strictly in accordance with the operations manual and she could not allow deviations. This by-the-book approach to managing had served her well for many years. It got her promoted in the past and she was not about to jinx that now. Losing a few employees now and then—particularly those who had difficulty following the rules—was simply the cost of doing business.

During a recent store visit, Julie suggested that Diana might try creating a friendlier work environment because she seemed aloof and interacted with employees somewhat mechanically. Julie even told her that she overheard employees refer to Diana as the "Ice Maiden" behind her back. Diana was surprised that Julie brought this up because her boss rarely criticized her. They had an unspoken agreement: since Diana was so technically competent and always met her financial targets, Julie didn't need to give her much input. Diana was happy to be left alone to run her restaurant without needless advice.

At any rate, Diana rarely paid attention to what employees said about her. She wasn't about to let something as childish as a silly name cause her to modify a successful management strategy. What's more, even though she had recently lost more than the average number of employees due to "personality differences" or "miscommunications" over her directives, her superiors did not seem to mind when she consistently delivered strong bottom-line results every month.

As she waited in the conference room for the others, Diana worried that she was not going to get this promotion. Julie had sounded different in the voicemail message she left to inform her about this meeting, but Diana couldn't put her finger on exactly what it was. She would be very angry if she was passed over again and wondered what excuse they would have this time.

Then her mind wandered to how her employees would respond to her if she did not get the promotion. They all knew how much she wanted the job and she cringed at how embarrassed she would be if she didn't get it. Her eyes began to mist over at the sheer thought of having to face them if she was not promoted today.

Julie and Tom entered the room then and the meeting was under way. They told Diana, as kindly as they could, that she would not be promoted at this time; one of her colleagues would become the new district manager. She was incredulous. The individual who got promoted had only been with the company three years—and Diana had trained her! She tried to comprehend how this happened, but it did not make sense. Before any further explanation could be offered,

she burst into tears and left the room. As she tried in vain to regain her composure, Diana was overcome with crushing disappointment.

Discussion Questions

1. Within the framework of the emotional intelligence domains of self-awareness, self-management, social awareness, and relationship management, discuss the various factors that might have led to Diana's failure to be promoted.

2. What competencies does Diana need to develop to be promotable in the future? What can the company do to support her developmental efforts?

Source: Reprinted with permission of Rosemary Maellaro.

CASE STUDY 4.2

THE BIG SQUEEZE ON WORKERS

BusinessWeek The post-dot-com recession has the distinction of being the first economic downturn in which productivity increased rather than decreased. The reason? The high risk of unemployment has enabled many firms to change the psychological contract in their favor. Employees are working harder and longer than ever by taking on the tasks of co-workers who lost their jobs. Companies are also shifting to just-in-time contingent workers, complete with a more bare-bones psychological contract.

This *Business Week* case study looks at the most recent jobless recovery and the new job expectations of people who are holding on to their jobs. It also examines the increasing use of contract work and the employment conditions for those workers. Read through this *Business Week* article at www.mhhe.com/mcshane3e and prepare for the discussion questions below.

Discussion Questions

1. What are the main forces that allow employers to change the psychological contract in their favor?

2. In your opinion, what effect would longer hours, averted overtime pay, and other changes in employment expectations have on the type of psychological contract employees adopt?

3. How will these employment changes affect affective organizational commitment?

Source: M. Conlin, "The Big Squeeze on Workers," *Business Week*, May 13, 2002, p. 96.

TEAM EXERCISE 4.3

RANKING JOBS ON THEIR EMOTIONAL LABOR

Purpose This exercise is designed to help you understand the jobs in which people tend to experience higher or lower degrees of emotional labor.

Instructions

- *Step 1*—Individually rank order the extent that the jobs listed below require emotional labor. In other words, assign a "1" to the job you believe requires the most effort, planning, and control to express organizationally desired emotions during interpersonal transactions. Assign a "10" to the job you believe requires the least amount of emotional labor. Mark your rankings in column 1.
- *Step 2*—The instructor will form teams of four or five members and each team will rank order the items based on consensus (not simply averaging the individual rankings). These results are placed in column 2.
- *Step 3*—The instructor will provide expert ranking information. This information should be written in column 3. Then, students calculate the differences in columns 4 and 5.
- *Step 4*—The class will compare the results and discuss the features of jobs with high emotional labor.

Occupational Emotional Labor Scoring Sheet

Occupation	(1) Individual Ranking	(2) Team Ranking	(3) Expert Ranking	(4) Absolute Difference of 1 and 3	(5) Absolute Difference of 2 and 3
Bartender	6				
Cashier	10				
Dental hygienist	5				
Insurance adjuster	4				
Lawyer	1				
Librarian	7				
Postal clerk	8				
Registered nurse	2				
Social worker	3				
Television announcer	9				
			TOTAL		
				Your score	Team score

why?

(The lower the score, the better)

SELF-ASSESSMENT EXERCISE 4.4

SCHOOL COMMITMENT SCALE

Purpose This self-assessment is designed to help you understand the concept of organizational commitment and to assess your commitment to the college or university you are currently attending.

Overview The concept of commitment is as relevant to students enrolled in college or university courses as it is to employees working in various organizations. This self-assessment adapts a popular organizational commitment instrument so it refers to your commitment as a student to the school where you are attending this program.

Instructions Read each of the statements below and circle the response that best fits your personal belief. Then use the scoring key in

Appendix B of this book to calculate your results. This self-assessment is completed alone so that students rate themselves honestly without concerns of social comparison. However, class discussion will focus on the meaning of the different types of organizational commitment and how well this scale applies to the commitment of students toward the college or university they are attending.

School Commitment Scale

To what extent does each statement describe you? Indicate your level of agreement by marking the appropriate response on the right.	Strongly Agree	Moderately Agree	Slightly Agree	Neutral	Slightly Disagree	Moderately Disagree	Strongly Disagree
1. I would be very happy to complete the rest of my education at theis school..........	☐	☐	☐	☐	☐	☐	☐
2. One of the difficulties of leaving this school is that there are few alternatives.........	☐	☐	☐	☐	☐	☐	☐
3. I really feel as if this school's problems are my own...............	☐	☐	☐	☐	☐	☐	☐
4. Right now, staying enrolled at this school is a matter of necessity as much as desire....	☐	☐	☐	☐	☐	☐	☐
5. I do not feel a strong sense of belonging to this school............	☐	☐	☐	☐	☐	☐	☐
6. It would be very hard for me to leave this school right now even if I wanted to.............	☐	☐	☐	☐	☐	☐	☐
7. I do not feel emotionally attached to this school.............	☐	☐	☐	☐	☐	☐	☐
8. To much of my life would be disrupted if I decided to move to a different school now..........	☐	☐	☐	☐	☐	☐	☐
9. I do not feel like part of the "family" at this school...............	☐	☐	☐	☐	☐	☐	☐
10. I feel that I have too few options to consider leaving this school............................	☐	☐	☐	☐	☐	☐	☐
11. This school has a great deal of personal meaning for me......	☐	☐	☐	☐	☐	☐	☐
12. If I had not already put so much of myself into this school, I might consider completing my education elsewhere...........	☐	☐	☐	☐	☐	☐	☐

Source: Adapted from J. P. Meyer, N. J. Allen, and C. A. Smith, "Commitment to Organizations and Occupations: Extension and Test of a Three-Component Model," *Journal of Applied Psychology* 78 (1993), pp. 538–551.

DISPOSITIONAL MOOD SCALE

Purpose This self-assessment is designed to help you understand mood states or personality traits of emotions and to assess your own mood or emotion personality.

Instructions This self-assessment consists of several words representing various emotions that you might have experienced. For each word presented, indicate the extent to which you have felt this way generally across all situations *over the past six months*. You need to be honest with yourself to receive a reasonable estimate of your mood state or personality trait on these scales. The results provide an estimate of your level on two emotional personality scales. This instrument is widely used in research, but it is only an estimate. You should not assume that the results are accurate without a more complete assessment by a trained professional.

After studying the preceding material, be sure to check out our website at

www.mhhe.com/mcshane3e

for more in-depth information and interactivities that correspond to this chapter.

chapter 5

Motivation in the Workplace

Learning Objectives

After reading this chapter, you should be able to:

■ Compare and contrast Maslow's needs hierarchy theory with Alderfer's ERG theory.

■ Describe Lawrence and Nohria's four innate drives and explain how these drives influence motivation and behavior.

■ Summarize McClelland's learned needs theory, including the three needs he studied.

■ Discuss the practical implications of needs-based motivation theories.

■ Diagram the expectancy theory model and discuss its practical implications for motivating employees.

■ Describe the characteristics of effective goal setting and feedback.

■ Summarize the equity theory model, including how people try to reduce feelings of inequity.

■ Identify the factors that influence procedural justice, as well as the consequences of procedural justice.

*B*ernard McCourt recognized the speaker on his voice mail but was still surprised. Governor Mitt Romney rang to thank the Massachusetts Highway Department manager for a job well done. A resident had called the governor's office, praising McCourt's crew for fixing a culvert, so Romney telephoned McCourt directly to express his compliments. "It certainly is appreciated when you hear from the person at the top," said McCourt, who has replayed Romney's voice mail message for his wife and some skeptical co-workers.

Governor Mitt Romney and other organizational leaders are discovering that one of the best ways to motivate employees is good old-fashioned praise and recognition. Stock options have evaporated and incentive plans often backfire. But for most employees, a few words of appreciation create a warm glow of satisfaction and a renewed energy. "Five to 10 percent of employees leave a company because of money," explains Christopher Owen, CEO of Meriwest Credit Union in San Jose, California. "Most of the time it's because they don't feel they are being recognized."

Julie Hans holds up the award coupons that Progress Energy employees give to one another as recognition for their good work and support.

Many companies have introduced formal programs that encourage peer recognition for a job well done. At Virgin Trains, the British rail service, employees nominate one another for monthly "Great Service Awards." Nationwide Insurance employees in Columbus, Ohio, use the Intranet to recommend co-workers who have gone above and beyond their job for a "You Got Caught" award. Nominated employees receive an e-mail, and everyone who gets "caught" is treated to a lunch celebration. Employees at Progress Energy in Raleigh, North Carolina, receive a booklet of coupons resembling currency. The coupons are distributed—up to $25 per award—to colleagues as a show of gratitude. "Everybody needs encouragement, and everybody needs their work to be recognized," says Julie Hans, a member of the Progress Energy's communications department.

While peer recognition is important, Massachusetts Highway Department manager Bernard McCourt and many other employees respond best to recognition from senior executives. Sara DeCarlo realized this, so the group circulation director at Ziff Davis Media convinced her publisher to personally congratulate staff who accomplish a major task. "If someone does a great job, why not recognize that?" DeCarlo reasons.[1] ■

motivation

The forces within a person that affect his or her direction, intensity, and persistence of voluntary behavior.

During these times of uncertainty and global competitiveness, motivating employees has become more important than ever. **Motivation** refers to the forces within a person that affect his or her direction, intensity, and persistence of voluntary behavior.[2] Motivated employees are willing to exert a particular level of effort (intensity), for a certain amount of time (persistence), toward a particular goal (direction). Even when people have clear work objectives, the right skills, and a supportive work environment, they must have sufficient motivation to achieve work objectives.

Most employers—92 percent of them, according to one recent survey[3]— agree that motivating employees has become more challenging. One reason is that globalization has dramatically changed the jobs that people perform and resulted in numerous forms of corporate restructuring and downsizing. These actions have significantly damaged the levels of trust and commitment necessary for employees to exert effort beyond the minimum requirements.[4] Some organizations have completely given up on employees motivating themselves and, instead, rely on pay-for-performance and layoff threats. These strategies may have some effect (both positive and negative), but they do not capitalize on the employee's motivational potential.

A second problem is that as companies flatten their hierarchies to reduce costs, they can no longer rely on supervisors to practice the old "command-and-control" methods of motivating employees. This is probably just as well, because direct supervision is incompatible with the values of today's educated workforce. Still, many businesses have not discovered other ways to motivate employees.

Last, employee needs are changing. Younger generations of employees are bringing different expectations to the workplace than their baby boomer counterparts. Many companies apparently aren't changing quickly enough to address this new reality. A recent survey reported that more than 40 percent of employees aged 25 to 34 sometimes or frequently feel demotivated compared to 30 percent of 35 to 44-year-olds and just 18 percent of 45 to 54-year-olds.[5] Workforce diversity and globalization have added to this complexity because diverse employees typically have diverse values. Recall from Chapter 2 that values represent stable, long-lasting beliefs that guide a person's preferences for outcomes or courses of action in a variety of situations. These values influence what we want, what we need, and what organizations should and should not do to fulfill those needs.

In this chapter, we look at the prominent theories of motivation in organizational settings. We begin by looking at needs-based motivation theories, including Maslow's needs hierarchy, Alderfer's ERG theory, innate drives theory, and McClelland's learned needs theory. Next, this chapter details expectancy theory, which applies a rational decision perspective to the topic of motivation. The third section of this chapter covers the key elements of goal setting and feedback, including the topics of multisource feedback and executive coaching. In the final section, we look at organizational justice, including the dimensions and dynamics of equity theory and procedural justice.

needs

Deficiencies that energize or trigger behaviors to satisfy those needs.

Needs-Based Theories of Motivation

Most contemporary theories recognize that motivation begins with individual needs and their underlying drives. **Needs** are deficiencies that energize or trigger behaviors to satisfy those needs. At some point in your life, you might have a strong need for food and shelter. At other times, your social needs may be unfulfilled. Unfulfilled needs create a tension that makes us want to find ways to reduce or satisfy those needs. The stronger your needs, the more motivated you are to satisfy them. Conversely, a satisfied need does not motivate.[6] In this section, we will look at two popular needs hierarchy theories: an emerging theory of innate drives, and a theory of learned needs.

Needs Hierarchy Theory

One of the earliest and best-known needs-based theories is **needs hierarchy theory.** Developed by psychologist Abraham Maslow, this theory condenses the numerous needs that scholars have identified into a hierarchy of five basic categories.[7] At the bottom are *physiological needs,* which include the need to satisfy biological requirements for food, air, water, and shelter. Next are *safety needs*—the need for a secure and stable environment and the absence of pain, threat, or illness. *Belongingness* includes the need for love, affection, and interaction with other people. *Esteem* includes self-esteem through personal achievement as well as social esteem through recognition and respect from others. At the top of the hierarchy is *self-actualization,* which represents the need for self-fulfillment—a sense that the person's potential has been realized.

Maslow recognized that we are motivated simultaneously by several needs, but behavior is mostly motivated by the lowest unsatisfied need at the time. As the person satisfies a lower level need, the next higher need in the hierarchy becomes the primary motivator. This is known as the **satisfaction-progression process.** Even if a person is unable to satisfy a higher need, he or she will be motivated by it until it is eventually satisfied. Physiological needs are initially the most important and people are motivated to satisfy them first. As they become gratified, safety needs emerge as the strongest motivator. As safety needs are satisfied, belongingness needs become most important, and so forth. The exception to the satisfaction-progression process is self-actualization; as people experience self-actualization, they desire more rather than less of this need.

Maslow's needs hierarchy is one of the best-known organizational behavior theories and is still widely cited in professional publications.[8] However, scholars have mostly dismissed Maslow's theory because it is much too rigid to explain the dynamic and unstable characteristics of employee needs.[9] Researchers have found that individual needs do not cluster neatly around the five categories described in the model. Moreover, gratification of one need level does not necessarily lead to increased motivation to satisfy the next higher need level.

ERG Theory

ERG theory was developed by organizational behavior scholar Clayton Alderfer to overcome the problems with Maslow's needs hierarchy theory.[10] ERG theory groups human needs into three broad categories: existence, relatedness, and growth. (Notice that the theory's name is based on the first letter of each need.) As Exhibit 5.1 illustrates, *existence* needs correspond to Maslow's physiological and safety needs. *Relatedness* needs refer mainly to Maslow's belongingness needs. *Growth* needs correspond to Maslow's esteem and self-actualization needs.

Existence needs include a person's physiological and physically related safety needs, such as the need for food, shelter, and safe working conditions.

---

needs hierarchy theory

Maslow's motivation theory of five instinctive needs arranged in a hierarchy, whereby people are motivated to fulfill a higher need as a lower one becomes gratified.

satisfaction-progression process

A process whereby people become increasingly motivated to fulfill a higher need as a lower need is gratified.

ERG theory

Alderfer's motivation theory of three instinctive needs arranged in a hierarchy, in which people progress to the next higher need when a lower one is fulfilled, and regress to a lower need if unable to fulfill a higher one.

existence needs

A person's physiological and physically related safety needs, such as the need for food, shelter, and safe working conditions.

Comparing Maslow's needs hierarchy and Alderfer's ERG theory

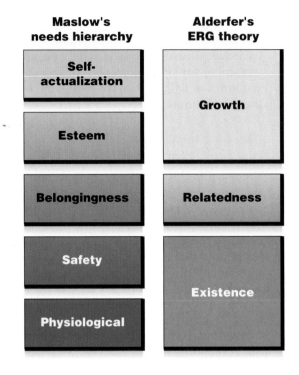

Maslow's needs hierarchy

Alderfer's ERG theory

relatedness needs
A person's needs to interact with other people, receive public recognition, and feel secure around other people.

growth needs
A person's needs for self-esteem through personal achievement as well as for self-actualization.

frustration-regression process
A process whereby a person who is unable to satisfy a higher need becomes frustrated and regresses to the next lower need level.

Relatedness needs include a person's need to interact with other people, receive public recognition, and feel secure around people (i.e., interpersonal safety). **Growth needs** consist of a person's self-esteem through personal achievement as well as the concept of self-actualization presented in Maslow's model.

ERG theory states that an employee's behavior is motivated simultaneously by more than one need level. Thus, you might try to satisfy your growth needs (such as by completing an assignment exceptionally well) even though your relatedness needs aren't completely satisfied. However, ERG theory applies the satisfaction-progression process described in Maslow's needs hierarchy model, so lower needs tend to dominate a person's motivation until they are satisfied. As existence needs are satisfied, for example, relatedness needs become more important.

Unlike Maslow's model, however, ERG theory includes a **frustration-regression process,** whereby those who are unable to satisfy a higher need become frustrated and regress back to the next lower need level. For example, if existence and relatedness needs have been satisfied, but growth need fulfillment has been blocked, we become frustrated and relatedness needs will again emerge as the dominant source of motivation.

ERG theory has received better research support than Maslow's needs hierarchy, mainly because human needs cluster more neatly around the three categories proposed by Alderfer than the five categories in Maslow's hierarchy. The combined processes of satisfaction-progression and frustration-regression also provide a more complete explanation of why employee needs change over time.[11] However, scholars increasingly doubt that human beings inherently have the same needs hierarchy.[12] Instead, some argue that people prioritize their needs around their personal values (see Chapter 2). Others suggest that people change their needs priority as they alter their personal and social identity. Specifically, employees tend to be driven by growth needs when they see themselves as unique (personal identity) and by relatedness needs when they define themselves in terms of their group memberships (social identity). In summary, people might have a needs hierarchy, but it is probably not hardwired in human nature, as ERG theory and Maslow's needs hierarchy theory assume.

Innate Human Drives

Although many scholars now doubt that people have a predetermined needs hierarchy, they have not abandoned the notion that needs are part of human nature. On the contrary, a recent groundswell of interest in evolutionary psychology has led some scholars to investigate the extent to which needs are based on innate drives, that is, hardwired into our genes and manifested as conscious emotions that influence rational calculations.[13] Various evolutionary theories have been used to explain the development of innate drives, including Darwin's "survival of the fittest" view that the human species adapted innate drives that improved future prospects of survival and regeneration. In other words, drives represent the human adaptive advantage.[14] They have evolved with the environment and with the development of human physical and social capabilities to ensure survival of the species.

Four Fundamental Drives   The search for innate human drives is still in its infancy, but Harvard Business School professors Paul Lawrence and Nitkin Nohria recently proposed four fundamental human drives that provide an initial foundation: the drive to acquire, to bond, to learn, and to defend.[15]

- *Drive to acquire*—This is the drive to seek, take, control, and retain objects and personal experiences. The drive to acquire extends beyond basic food and water; it includes the need for relative status and recognition in society. Thus, it is the foundation of competition and the basis of our need for esteem. Lawrence and Nohria suggest that the drive to acquire is insatiable because the purpose of human motivation is to achieve a higher position than others, not just to fulfill one's physiological needs.[16]
- *Drive to bond*—This is the drive to form social relationships and develop mutual caring commitments with others. It also explains why people form social identities by aligning their self-image with various social groups (see Chapter 3). Research indicates that people invest considerable time and effort forming and maintaining relationships without any special circumstances or ulterior motives.[17] Moreover, people fairly consistently experience negative emotions when relationships are dissolved, such as when the business shuts down or co-workers are laid off. The drive to bond motivates people to cooperate and, consequently, is a fundamental ingredient in the success of organizations and the development of societies.
- *Drive to learn*—This is the drive to satisfy one's curiosity, to know and understand ourselves and the environment around us. When observing something that is inconsistent with or beyond our current knowledge, we experience a tension that motivates us to close that information gap. The drive to learn fulfills our need for personal and social identity (see Chapter 3) and is related to the higher order needs of growth and self-actualization described earlier.

When SABMiller recently closed the Olympia Brewery in Tumwater, Washington, it did more than shut down the last major brewery in the Pacific Northwest. The plant closing also stirred up deep emotions as employees anticipated the loss of camaraderie and social bonds. "We're in shock," says Dale Johnson, a yard truck driver who has worked at Olympia for the past 20 years. "This place isn't like a job to me—it's like family." Evolutionary psychologists say that people have an innate drive to bond, so layoffs and plant closures create negative emotions as social relations are torn apart. "The saddest thing for me will be when the brewery whistle blows for the last time," says Ted Norton, who worked in Olympia's keg house for more than 27 years. Norton and his son, also an Olympia brewery employee, are shown here with memorabilia from Olympia brewery's heyday.[18] How would the other three innate human drives be affected by layoffs?

■ *Drive to defend*—This is the drive to protect ourselves physically and socially. Probably the first drive to develop, it creates a "fight-or-flight" response in the face of personal danger. The drive to defend goes beyond protecting our physical self. It includes defending our relationships, our acquisitions, and our belief systems. The drive to defend is always reactive—it is triggered by threat. In contrast, the other three drives are always proactive—we actively seek to improve our acquisitions, relationships, and knowledge.[19]

How do these innate drives translate into motivation and behavior? Evolutionary psychologists rely on neuroscience research indicating that our perceptions of the external world are routed to two parts of the brain—the emotional center and the rational center.[20] The emotional center, which operates faster than the rational center, relies on the innate drives to code the relevance and strength of the perceived information. Situations that violate or support these drives receive emotional markers (fear, excitement, anger, etc.). The emotionally coded information is transmitted to the rational center of the brain where it is evaluated in the context of memory and competencies. The rational center then makes a conscious choice that motivates behavior.[21]

Innate drives speed up the decision-making process because the emotional markers created by these drives highlight the alternative actions to avoid and the alternatives to favor. Emotional markers also become the conscious sources of human motivation. For example, suppose that your department has just received a new computer system that you are eager to try out (drive to learn), but your boss has restricted use of the new equipment. Your boss's interference sets off emotional markers (anger, frustration) that demand your attention and energize you to remove that barrier. Thus, to get rid of the anger or frustration, you boldly ask your boss to let you use the new equipment. You can see that emotional intelligence, which we discussed in Chapter 4, plays an important role in this process. Emotional intelligence competencies operate in the rational center to temper the emotional impulses and direct our effort toward socially acceptable behavior.

Research clearly supports the notion that the brain processes information both emotionally and rationally. However, we are still a long way from knowing whether the four drives described by Lawrence and Nohria are innate and whether they exist more or less equally in everyone. We should also remember that there is considerable debate about various evolutionary psychology theories, including whether these theories can ever be adequately tested.[22] However, this emerging model of human motives provides a useful template for understanding the origins of human motivation and the relevance of emotions in the motivation process.

Theory of Learned Needs

The needs-based models described so far look at the individual's primary or instinctive needs and their relative importance in life. However, people also have secondary needs or drives that are learned and reinforced through childhood learning, parental styles, and social norms. Several learned needs can motivate us at the same time. Psychologist David McClelland devoted his career to studying three secondary needs that he considered particularly important sources of motivation: need for achievement, need for affiliation, and need for power.

Need for Achievement (nAch)   People with a strong **need for achievement (nAch)** want to accomplish reasonably challenging goals through their own effort. They prefer working alone rather than in teams and they choose tasks with a moderate degree of risk (i.e., neither too easy nor impossible to complete). High nAch people also desire unambiguous feedback and recognition for their success. Money is a weak motivator among these achievement-oriented people, except when it provides feedback and recognition.[23] In contrast, employees with a low nAch perform their work better when money is used as an incentive.

Successful entrepreneurs tend to have a high nAch, possibly because they establish challenging goals for themselves and thrive on competition.[24] Corporate and team leaders should have a somewhat lower nAch because they must delegate work and build support through involvement (characteristics not usually found in high achievers). However, high nAch people may perform well in large companies where they are given considerable independence—as though they are running their own business.[25]

Need for Affiliation (nAff)   The **need for affiliation (nAff)** refers to a desire to seek approval from others, conform to their wishes and expectations, and avoid conflict and confrontation. People with a strong nAff want to form positive relationships with others. They try to project a favorable image of themselves and take other steps to be liked by others. Moreover, high nAff employees actively support others and try to smooth out conflicts that occur in meetings and other social settings. High nAff employees tend to be more

need for achievement (nAch)
A learned need in which people want to accomplish reasonably challenging goals through their own efforts, like to be successful in competitive situations, and desire unambiguous feedback regarding their success.

need for affiliation (nAff)
A learned need in which people seek approval from others, conform to their wishes and expectations, and avoid conflict and confrontation.

effective than those with a low nAff in coordinating roles, such as helping diverse departments work on joint projects. They are also more effective in sales positions where the main task is cultivating long-term relations with prospective customers. More generally, employees with high nAff prefer working with others rather than alone, tend to have better attendance records, and tend to be better at mediating conflicts.

Although people with a high nAff are more effective in many jobs requiring social interaction, they tend to be less effective at allocating scarce resources and making other decisions that potentially generate conflict. For example, research has found that executives with a high nAff tend to be indecisive and are perceived as less fair in the distribution of resources. Thus, people in these decision-making positions must have a relatively low need for affiliation so that their choices and actions are not biased by a personal need for approval.[26]

Need for Power (nPow)   The **need for power (nPow)** refers to a desire to control one's environment, including people and material resources. People with a high nPow want to exercise control over others and are concerned about maintaining their leadership position. They frequently rely on persuasive communication (see Chapter 12), make more suggestions in meetings, and tend to publicly evaluate situations more frequently. Some people have a high need for *personalized power*. They enjoy their power for its own sake and use it to advance their career and other personal interests. It is a symbol of status and a tool to fulfill personal needs more than a delicate instrument to serve stakeholders. Others mainly have a high need for *socialized power*. They want power as a means to help others, such as improving society or increasing organizational effectiveness.[27]

Corporate and political leaders have a high nPow, which motivates them to influence others—an important part of the leadership process (see Chapter 14).[28] However, McClelland argues that effective leaders should have a high need for socialized rather than personalized power. They have a high degree of altruism and social responsibility and are concerned about the consequences of their own actions on others. In other words, leaders must exercise their power within the framework of moral standards. The ethical guidance of their need for power develops follower trust and respect for the leader, as well as commitment to the leader's vision.[29]

Learning Needs   McClelland argued that achievement, affiliation, and power needs are learned rather than instinctive. Accordingly, he developed training programs that strengthen these needs. In his achievement motivation program, trainees practice writing achievement-oriented stories after reading others and practice achievement-oriented behaviors in business games. They also complete a detailed achievement plan for the next two years and form a reference group with other trainees to maintain their newfound achievement motive style.[30]

These programs seem to work. For example, participants attending a need for achievement course in India subsequently started more new businesses, had greater community involvement, invested more in expanding their businesses, and employed twice as many people as nonparticipants. Research on similar achievement-motive courses for North American small-business owners reported dramatic increases in the profitability of the participants' businesses.

The marginal definition:

need for power (nPow)
A learned need in which people want to control their environment, including people and material resources, to benefit either themselves (personalized power) or others (socialized power).

Practical Implications of Needs-Based Motivation Theories

Needs-based theories of motivation offer several recommendations. First, corporate leaders need to balance the drive to acquire (competition) with the drive to bond (cooperation). To achieve this balance, Lawrence and Nohria recommend financial and symbolic rewards that emphasize both individual achievement and teamwork.[31] Organizations also need to support the drive to learn by giving employees opportunities to experience novel situations and practice new skills. As for the drive to defend, corporate leaders need to minimize unnecessary threats to the personal safety, well-being, and social relationships that employees value.

Needs-based theories also suggest that different people have different needs at different times. Some employees are ready to fulfill growth needs, whereas others are still struggling to satisfy their minimum existence needs. Needs also change as people enter new stages of their life, so rewards that motivate people at one time may have less motivational value in later years. The recommendation from this is to offer employees a choice of rewards. Farm Fresh Supermarkets accomplishes this by awarding points to employees who receive positive feedback on customer comment cards. When employees accumulate enough points, they can pick their preferred gift. "We have a catalog they can buy merchandise out of," explains Ron Dennis, president of the Virginia Beach, Virginia-based grocery chain. "There are several hundred items in there, and they can get everything from a T-shirt to a toaster oven, coffee maker, and a vacuum cleaner." These gifts are valued more than standardized rewards because employees choose gifts that they value the most.[32]

Executives at EnCana Corporation know that money isn't the only way to motivate employees. But this point became vividly clear soon after the Calgary-based energy company launched its "High-Five" recognition program. The program gave employees and managers the right to recommend any deserving colleague for a high-five card, which is redeemable for $5.00. But rather than cashing in their cards for money, many employees displayed the cards in their offices. The visible symbol of recognition was apparently worth more to many people than the cash value of the card.[34] Under what conditions would the recognition from these cards motivate employees more than their monetary value?

Last, needs-based theories warn us against relying too heavily on financial rewards as a source of employee motivation.[33] While money does motivate employees to some extent, there are potentially more powerful sources of motivation, such as challenging assignments, learning opportunities, and praise from colleagues and corporate leaders.

Expectancy Theory of Motivation

Our earlier discussion of innate drives emphasized the role of emotions in human motivation, but we noted that people also engage in a rational process to direct their effort. This rational process is best represented by a popular perspective of motivation called expectancy theory. **Expectancy theory** is based on the idea that work effort is directed toward behaviors that people believe will lead to desired outcomes.[35] Through experience, we develop expectations about whether we can achieve various levels of job performance. We also develop expectations about whether job performance and work behaviors lead to particular outcomes. Finally, we naturally direct our effort toward outcomes that help us fulfill our needs.

Expectancy Theory Model

The expectancy theory model is presented in Exhibit 5.2. The key variable of interest in expectancy theory is *effort*—the individual's actual exertion of energy. An individual's effort level depends on three factors: effort-to-performance (E→P) expectancy, performance-to-outcome (P→O) expectancy, and outcome valences (V). Employee motivation is influenced by all three components of the expectancy theory model. If any component weakens, motivation weakens.

E→P Expectancy   The **effort-to-performance (E→P) expectancy** is the individual's perception that his or her effort will result in a particular level of performance. Expectancy is defined as a *probability*, and therefore ranges from 0.0 to 1.0. In some situations, employees may believe that they can unquestionably accomplish the task (a probability of 1.0). In other situations, they expect that even their highest level of effort will not result in the desired performance level (a probability of 0.0). For instance, unless you are an expert skier, you probably aren't motivated to try some of the black diamond ski runs at Vail. The reason is a very low E→P expectancy. Even your best effort won't get you down the hill feet first! In most cases, the E→P expectancy falls somewhere between these two extremes.

P→O Expectancy   The **performance-to-outcome (P→O) expectancy** is the perceived probability that a specific behavior or performance level will lead to specific outcomes. This probability is developed from previous learning. For example, students learn from experience that skipping class either ruins their chance of a good grade or has no effect at all. In extreme cases, employees may believe that accomplishing a particular task (performance) will *definitely* re-

effort-to-performance (E-to-P) expectancy
The individual's perceived probability that his or her effort will result in a particular level of performance.

performance-to-outcome (P-to-O) expectancy
The perceived probability that a specific behavior or performance level will lead to specific outcomes.

EXHIBIT 5.2

Expectancy theory of motivation

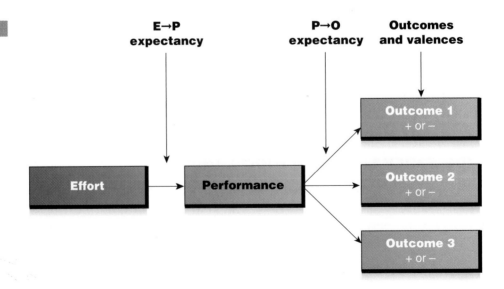

sult in a particular outcome (a probability of 1.0), or they may believe that this outcome will have *no effect* on successful performance (a probability of 0.0). More often, the P→O expectancy falls somewhere between these two extremes.

One important issue in P→O expectancies is which outcomes we think about. We certainly don't evaluate the P→O expectancy for every possible outcome. There are too many of them. Instead, we think only about outcomes of interest to us at the time. One day, your motivation to complete a task may be fueled mainly by the likelihood of getting off work early to meet friends. Other times, your motivation to complete the same task may be based more on the P→O expectancy of a promotion or pay increase. The main point is that your motivation depends on the probability that a behavior or job performance level will result in outcomes that you think about.

Outcome Valences   The third element in expectancy theory is the **valence** of each outcome that you consider. Valence refers to the anticipated satisfaction or dissatisfaction that an individual feels toward an outcome. It ranges from negative to positive. (The actual range doesn't matter; it may be from –1 to +1, or from –100 to +100.) An outcome valence represents a person's feelings toward the outcome and is determined by the perceptions about how much the outcome will fulfill or interfere with the person's needs and drives. It is also influenced by our personal values (see Chapter 2). Outcomes have a positive valence when they are consistent with our values and directly or indirectly satisfy our needs; they have a negative valence when they oppose our values and inhibit need fulfillment. If you have a strong relatedness (social) need, for example, then you would value group activities and other events that help to fulfill that need. Outcomes that move you further away from fulfilling your social need—such as working alone from home—will have a strong negative valence.

valence
The anticipated satisfaction or dissatisfaction that an individual feels toward an outcome.

Expectancy Theory in Practice

One of the appealing characteristics of expectancy theory is that it provides clear guidelines for increasing employee motivation by altering the person's E→P expectancies, P→O expectancies, and/or outcome valences.[36] Several practical implications of expectancy theory are listed in Exhibit 5.3 and described below.

Increasing E→P Expectancies   E→P expectancies are influenced by the individual's self-efficacy. Recall from Chapter 3 that self-efficacy refers to a person's belief that he or she has the ability, motivation, and situational contingencies to complete a task successfully. People with high self-efficacy have a "can-do" attitude toward a specific task and, more generally, with other challenges in life. Some companies increase this can-do attitude by assuring employees that they have the necessary competencies, clear role perceptions, and favorable situational conditions to reach the desired levels of performance. This involves properly matching employees to jobs based on their abilities, clearly communicating the tasks required for the job, and providing sufficient resources for them to accomplish those tasks. Coaching also improves self-efficacy and, consequently, the employee's E→P expectancies regarding specific tasks. Similarly, E→P expectancies are learned, so positive feedback typically strengthens employee self-efficacy.[37] Behavior modification and behavioral modeling also tend to increase E→P expectancies in many situations.

| EXHIBIT 5.3 | Practical applications of expectancy theory |

Expectancy theory component	Objective	Applications
E→P expectancies	To increase the belief that employees are capable of performing the job successfully	• Select people with the required skills and knowledge. • Provide required training and clarify job requirements. • Provide sufficient time and resources. • Assign simpler or fewer tasks until employees can master them. • Provide examples of similar employees who have successfully performed the task. • Provide coaching to employees who lack self-confidence.
P→O expectancies	To increase the belief that good performance will result in certain (valued) outcomes	• Measure job performance accurately. • Clearly explain the outcomes that will result from successful performance. • Describe how the employee's rewards were based on past performance. • Provide examples of other employees whose good performance has resulted in higher rewards.
Valences of outcomes	To increase the expected value of outcomes resulting from desired performance	• Distribute rewards that employees value. • Individualize rewards. • Minimize the presence of countervalent outcomes.

Increasing P→O Expectancies   The most obvious ways to improve P→O expectancies are to measure employee performance accurately and distribute more valued rewards to those with higher job performance. Many organizations have difficulty putting this straightforward idea into practice. Some executives are reluctant to withhold rewards for poor performance because they don't want to experience conflict with employees. Others don't measure employee performance very well. For instance, a recent Ohio State University study reported that less than half of the 6,000 people surveyed said they know how to increase their base pay or cash bonuses. In other words, most employees and managers have a generally low P→O expectancy regarding their paychecks.[38] Chapter 6 looks at reasons why rewards aren't connected to job performance.

P→O expectancies are perceptions, so employees should *believe* that higher performance will result in higher rewards. Having a performance-based reward system is important, but this fact must be communicated. When rewards are distributed, employees should understand how their rewards have been based on past performance. More generally, companies need to regularly communicate the existence of a performance-based reward system through examples, anecdotes, and public ceremonies.

Increasing Outcome Valences   Performance outcomes influence work effort only when those outcomes are valued by employees.[39] This brings us back to what we learned from the needs-based theories of motivation, namely, that companies must pay attention to the needs and reward preferences of individual employees. They should develop more individualized reward systems so that employees who perform well are offered a choice of rewards.

Expectancy theory also emphasizes the need to discover and neutralize countervalent outcomes. These are performance outcomes that have negative valences, thereby reducing the effectiveness of existing reward systems. For example, peer pressure may cause some employees to perform their jobs at the minimum standard even though formal rewards and the job itself would otherwise motivate them to perform at higher levels.

Does Expectancy Theory Fit Reality?

Expectancy theory is one of the more difficult theories to test.[40] In spite of this challenge, it is one of the better theories for predicting work effort and motivation. For example, studies have applied expectancy theory to predict a person's motivation to use a decision support system, leave the organization, work with less effort in a group setting, and engage in organizational citizenship behaviors.[41]

Some critics have suggested that expectancy theory is culture-bound, arguing that the theory makes Western-oriented assumptions that employees have strong feelings of personal control.[42] In reality, expectancy theory does not assume that people feel complete control over their lives; on the contrary, the E→P expectancy directly varies with the employee's perceived control over the work situation. Research indicates that expectancy theory predicts employee motivation in different cultures.[43]

Another challenge is that expectancy theory seems to ignore the central role of emotion in employee effort and behavior. As we learned earlier in this and previous chapters, emotions serve an adaptive function that demand our attention and energize us to take action. The valence element of expectancy theory captures some of this emotional process, but only peripherally. Thus, theorists probably need to redesign the expectancy theory model in light of new information about the importance of emotions in motivation and behavior.[44]

Goal Setting and Feedback

goals
The immediate or ultimate objectives that employees are trying to accomplish from their work effort.

goal setting
The process of motivating employees and clarifying their role perceptions by establishing performance objectives.

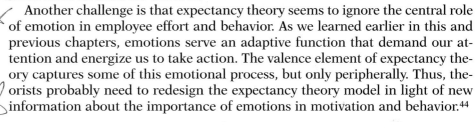

Mitel Corporation has a secret weapon to keep project deadlines on time. It's an enormous digital clock—seven feet long and one foot tall—placed in the cafeteria that measures everything from tenths of a second to days in a year. Beside the clock is a whiteboard that lists interim deadlines for all major projects at the telecommunications development company. Whenever a team misses a deadline, Mitel executives put a red slash through the date for everyone to see. Employees at the telephone equipment designer initially complained, but the results have silenced the critics. Mitel's average length of product development time has dropped from 70 to 50 weeks.[45]

Mitel and other organizations have discovered that goal setting is one of the most effective theories of motivation in organizations.[46] **Goals** are the immediate or ultimate objectives that employees are trying to accomplish from their work effort. **Goal setting** is the process of motivating employees and clarifying their role perceptions by establishing performance objectives. Goal setting potentially improves employee performance in two ways: (1) by stretching the intensity and persistence of effort and (2) by giving employees clearer role perceptions so that their effort is channeled toward behaviors that will improve work performance.

By setting specific challenging goals for its employees, CDW Corporation has become a leading provider of technology products and services to business, government, and education. "We set BHAGS—which are big, hairy, aggressive goals," says CDW president and CEO John A. Edwardson. Edwardson explains that one stretch goal was called "5432," which referred to $5 million in bonuses for $3 billion in sales by 2000. CDW employees exceeded that goal, which nearly tripled the company's revenue from three years earlier. More recently, Edwardson promised his staff that he would shave his head if they exceeded their third-quarter goals. After employees reached those objectives, Edwardson's barber joined him on stage during a pep rally to cut off his locks while a barbershop quartet sang in the background.[48] To what extent is this goal-setting process compatible with the characteristics of effective goals?

management by objectives (MBO)
A participative goal-setting process in which organizational objectives are cascaded down to work units and individual employees.

Some companies apply goal setting through a formal process known as **management-by-objectives (MBO).** There are a few variations of MBO programs, but they generally identify organizational objectives, then cascade them down to work units and individual employees. MBO also includes regular discussion of goal progress.[47] Although MBO has been criticized for creating too much paperwork, it can potentially be an effective application of goal setting.

Characteristics of Effective Goals

Goal setting is more complex than simply telling someone to "do your best." Instead, organizational behavior scholars have identified six conditions to maximize task effort and performance. These include specific goals, relevant goals, challenging goals, goal commitment, participation in goal formation (sometimes), and goal feedback.[49]

- *Specific goals*—Employees put more effort into a task when they work toward specific goals rather than "do your best" targets.[50] Specific goals have measurable levels of change over a specific and relatively short time frame, such as "reduce scrap rate by 7 percent over the next six months." Specific goals communicate more precise performance expectations, so employees can direct their effort more efficiently and reliably.
- *Relevant goals*—Goals must also be relevant to the individual's job and within his or her control. For example, a goal to reduce waste materials would have little value if employees don't have much control over waste in the production process.
- *Challenging goals*—Employees tend to process task knowledge more actively and engage in work effort more intensely and persistently when they have challenging rather than easy goals. Challenging goals also fulfill a person's achievement or growth needs when the goal is achieved.[51] Cisco Systems and other organizations emphasize "stretch goals"—goals that are challenging enough to stretch the employee's abilities and motivation toward peak performance. Stretch goals are effective if employees receive the necessary resources and are not overstressed in the process.[52]
- *Goal commitment*—Although goals should be challenging, employees also need to be committed to accomplishing goals. Thus, we need to find an optimal level of goal difficulty where the goals are challenging, yet employees are still motivated to achieve them.[53] This is the same as the E→P ex-

pectancy that we learned about in the section on expectancy theory.[54] The lower the E→P expectancy that the goal can been accomplished, the less committed (motivated) the employee is to the goal. "If a goal does not seem achievable, it's hard to get motivated because you feel as if you are failing," says Theresa Rein, head of recruiting and training company Ingeus.[55]

■ *Goal participation (sometimes)*—Goal setting is usually (but not always) more effective when employees participate in setting goals.[56] Employees identify more with goals they are involved in setting than goals assigned by a supervisor. In fact, today's workforce increasingly expects to be involved in goal setting and other decisions that affect them. Participation may also improve goal quality, because employees have valuable information and knowledge that may not be known to those who initially formed the goal. Thus, participation ensures that employees buy into the goals and have the competencies and resources necessary to accomplish them.

■ *Goal feedback*—Feedback is another necessary condition for effective goal setting.[57] **Feedback** is any information that people receive about the consequences of their behavior. Feedback lets us know whether we have achieved the goal or are properly directing our effort toward it. Feedback is also an essential ingredient in motivation because our growth needs can't be satisfied unless we receive information on goal accomplishment. Feedback is so central to goal setting that we will look more closely at it next.

feedback
Any information that people receive about the consequences of their behavior.

Characteristics of Effective Feedback

Feedback is a key ingredient in goal setting and employee performance.[58] It clarifies role perceptions by communicating what behaviors are appropriate or necessary in a particular situation. Feedback improves ability by frequently providing information to correct performance problems.[59] This is known as *corrective feedback*, because it makes people aware of their performance errors and helps them correct those errors quickly. Last, feedback is a source of motivation. It fulfills personal needs and makes people more confident that they are able to accomplish certain tasks.

Feedback is a necessary part of goal setting, so it shouldn't be surprising that many of the elements of effective goal setting also apply to effective feedback (see Exhibit 5.4). First, feedback should be *specific*. The information provided should be connected to the details of the goal, such as "you exceeded your sales quota by 5 percent last month," rather than subjective and general phrases such as "your sales are going well." Notice that specific feedback focuses on the task, not the person. This reduces the person's defensiveness when receiving negative feedback.

Second, feedback must be *relevant*, that is, it must relate to the individual's behavior rather than to conditions beyond the individual's control. This ensures that the feedback is not distorted by situational factors.[60] Third, feedback should be *timely*—available as soon as possible after the behavior or results. Timeliness helps employees see a clear association between their behavior and its consequences.

Fourth, feedback should be *sufficiently frequent*. How often is feedback "sufficiently frequent"? The answer depends on at least two contingencies. One factor is the employee's knowledge and experience with the task. Feedback is

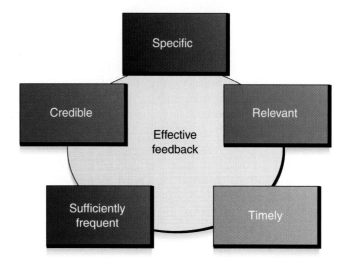

a form of reinforcement, so employees working on new tasks should receive more frequent feedback because they require more behavior guidance and reinforcement (see Chapter 3). Employees who are repeating familiar tasks can receive less frequent feedback. The second contingency is the task cycle (how long it takes to complete each task). Feedback is necessarily less frequent in jobs with a long cycle time (e.g., executives and scientists) than in jobs with a short cycle time (e.g., grocery store cashiers).

Last, feedback should be *credible*. Employees are more likely to accept feedback (particularly corrective feedback) from trustworthy and credible sources.[61] One increasingly popular way to increase feedback credibility is through multisource feedback.

Multisource Feedback   According to some estimates, almost all Fortune 500 firms rely on multisource feedback to improve the credibility and quality of information employees receive about their job performance.[62] Eighty-seven percent of firms with multisource plans give employees complete freedom to choose who will rate them. Multisource feedback is often called **360-degree feedback** because anonymous feedback is received from a full circle of people around the employee, including subordinates, peers, supervisors, and customers.[63]

Research suggests that multisource feedback provides more complete and accurate information than feedback from a supervisor alone.[64] It is particularly useful when the supervisor is unable to observe the employee's behavior or performance throughout the year. Lower level employees also feel a greater sense of fairness and open communication when they are able to provide upward feedback about their boss's performance.

Multisource feedback also creates challenges.[65] Having several people review so many other people can be expensive and time-consuming. With multiple opinions, the 360-degree process can also produce ambiguous and conflicting feedback, so employees may require guidance to interpret the results. A third concern is that peers may provide inflated rather than accurate feedback to avoid conflicts over the forthcoming year. Last, critical feedback from many people can have emotional consequences. "Initially you do take it per-

360-degree feedback
Performance feedback received from a full circle of people around an employee.

A Coach for All Seasons

Greg Ball is a great thinker, but he admits that his people skills need work. "Strategically, I'm good and logically I'm very good," says the director of communications at vaccine pharmaceutical firm Aventis Pasteur. "The people side for me is the area where I don't know the right answer." So Aventis pays an executive coach to help Ball see his work situations from different perspectives and to entertain different approaches. Executive coaching makes a lot of sense, says Ball. "If you're a professional athlete, you have a coach. I want be a professional businessperson and, therefore . . . I should have a coach, too."

Executive coaching has become the personal development tool of choice among professionals in the corporate world. Some evidence suggests that the one-on-one approach by a neutral consultant provides an effective way to clarify personal and work-related goals, and to receive honest feedback toward those goals. "You don't pay me to make you feel good," explains Marjorie Engle, an executive coach in Wichita, Kansas. "You pay me to be straight with you. I'm going to be your advocate, but I'm going to be straight with you."

Liz Sanford is one of many converts to executive coaching. "I didn't set clear expectations for people, and I had trouble with the whole facade of being in charge," says the founder of a city and transportation planning firm in Decatur, Georgia.

"Coaching is simply a relationship with someone who is paid to tell you the absolute truth," says executive coach Nancy Gerber, shown here with client Liz Sanford.

Sanford's leadership skills and confidence improved dramatically after working with personal coach Nancy Gerber. "Coaching is simply a relationship with someone who is paid to tell you the absolute truth," says Gerber.

Sources: D. Gruver, "Coaches Play No Games," *Wichita Eagle,* June 15, 2003, p. C1; C. Adams, "Coaches Offer More than Game Plan," *(Toronto) Globe & Mail,* July 8, 2002, p. C1; K. Kicklighter, "Put Me In, Coach," *Atlanta Journal and Constitution,* January 12, 2001, p. E1.

---

sonally," admits Russell Huerta, a senior accounts manager at software maker Autodesk. "[360-degree feedback] is meant to be constructive, but you have to internally battle that." Huerta manages his emotional reaction to the feedback by pretending the advice is about someone else, then learning how to improve his own behavior from that information. "It's almost an out-of-body experience, to take your mind and your emotions out of it," he recommends.[66]

executive coaching
A helping relationship using behavioral methods to assist clients in identifying and achieving goals for their professional performance and personal satisfaction.

Executive Coaching Another rapidly growing practice involving feedback and motivation is executive coaching. **Executive coaching** is defined as a helping relationship using a wide variety of behavioral methods to assist clients identify and achieve goals for their professional performance and personal satisfaction.[67] Coaching is usually conducted by an external consultant and is essentially one-on-one "just-in-time" personal development using feedback and other techniques. Coaches do not provide answers to the employee's problems. Rather, they are "thought partners" who offer more accurate feedback, open dialogue, and constructive encouragement to improve the client's performance and personal well-being. They ask provocative questions, offer perspective, and help clients clarify choices.

Connections 5.1 describes how executive coaching has a number of vocal supporters among executives and professionals. They echo preliminary research suggesting that executive coaching is more effective than behavioral modeling at helping people change their behavior and achieve their goals more quickly. Coaching is particularly useful for improving emotional intelligence, goal setting, interpersonal skills, and related activities that require specific feedback and support in a real-time work environment.[68] However, some writers also urge caution because it seems that anyone can assume the title "executive coach," and some people in these positions treat the symptoms rather than causes of executive problems.[69]

Choosing Feedback Sources   Executive coaches and multisource feedback represent two social sources of feedback, but employees can also receive feedback from nonsocial sources.[70] The job itself can be a nonsocial source of feedback. Many employees see the results of their work effort while they are making a product. Some professionals have "executive dashboards" on their computer screens that display the latest measures of sales, inventory, and other indicators of corporate success.[71] Other companies post critical performance information for employees to see. Walk into a typical call center and you will likely notice electronic displays where employees can see how many callers are waiting, the average time they have been waiting, and the length of time for each call.[72]

The preferred feedback source depends on the purpose of the information. To learn about their progress toward goal accomplishment, employees usually prefer nonsocial feedback sources, such as computer printouts or feedback directly from the job. This is because information from nonsocial sources is considered more accurate than information from social sources. Corrective feedback from nonsocial sources is also less damaging to self-esteem. This is probably just as well because social sources tend to delay negative information, leave some of it out, and distort the bad news in a positive way.[73]

When employees want to improve their self-image, they seek out positive feedback from social sources. It feels better to have co-workers say that you are performing the job well than to discover this from a computer printout.[74] Positive feedback from co-workers and other social sources mainly motivates because it fulfills relatedness as well as growth needs.

Applications and Limitations of Goal Setting and Feedback

Goal setting and feedback have a few limitations. One problem is that when goals are tied to monetary incentives, many employees tend to select easy rather than difficult goals.[75] In some cases, employees have negotiated goals with their supervisor that have already been completed! Employees with high self-efficacy and need for achievement tend to set challenging goals whether or not they are financially rewarded for their results. However, employers should typically separate goal setting from the pay-setting process to minimize the politics of goal setting.[76]

Another limitation is that we can't apply goal setting to every performance dimension of every job. We can usually find some measurable goals, but many other dimensions of job performance have complex and long-term performance outcomes that are difficult to measure. The result is that goal setting potentially focuses employees on a narrow subset of short-term performance indicators. The saying "What gets measured, gets done" applies here. Thus, goal setting may cause more performance problems in the long term that it solves in the short term.

In spite of these concerns, goals setting and feedback are widely supported by both academic literature and practitioner experience.[77] The objective nature of goal setting is particularly appreciated. For example, Payless Shoe Source replaced its traditional performance appraisal system with a simple goal-setting process that evaluated employees for exceeding, meeting, or falling short of their goals. The changeover improved performance and minimized some of the organizational politics and feelings of injustice that often accompany employee performance activities.[78] Organizational justice is, itself, an important perspective or employee motivation, which we discuss next.

Organizational Justice

Corporate leaders and OB scholars have long known that to maximize employee motivation, satisfaction, and organizational commitment, they need to treat people fairly. Although this seems simple enough, organizational justice covers several issues and has two distinct forks: distributive justice and procedural justice.[79] **Distributive justice** refers to perceived fairness in the outcomes we receive relative to our contributions and the outcomes and contributions of others. **Procedural justice,** on the other hand, refers to fairness of the procedures used to decide the distribution of resources. For example, you might feel a sense of unfairness if someone else is promoted to a job rather than you (distributive injustice), but this feeling is reduced somewhat because you also believe the decision makers had no apparent bias and seemed to consider all of the relevant information to make the decision (procedural justice). Each of these dimensions of workplace justice includes a variety of issues, which we introduce over the next few pages.

distributive justice
The perceived fairness in outcomes we receive relative to our contributions and the outcomes and contributions of others.

procedural justice
The fairness of the procedures used to decide the distributions of resources.

Distributive Justice and Equity Theory

Taiwan recently passed gender equality in the workplace legislation, but over half of the working women in that country say men get paid more for doing the same work. "It's unfair," says Hsieh Hsuen-hui, a senior trade specialist at an export company in Taipei. "Monthly salaries that male colleagues receive are about NT$10,000 higher than what I get, even though we are doing the same job." Hsieh's boss believes that men should be paid higher wages since they are more flexible when it comes to overseas business travel. Some employers openly say they pay men more because they have a greater need for income as the breadwinners. But Hsieh and other women claim that neither reason justifies the significant pay differences.[80]

Hsieh Hsuen-hui and other female professionals in Taiwan experienced the emotional tension created by feelings of distributive injustice. People apply different rules or standards to determine what is a "fair" distribution of pay and other outcomes. Some of us apply an *equality principle* in which everyone should receive the same outcomes. Some Taiwanese employers justify paying men more than women based on the *need principle* in which those with the greatest need should receive more outcomes than others with less need. Hsieh Hsuen-hui applied the most common distributive justice rule in organizational settings, known as the *equity principle*. According to this principle, outcomes should be proportional to the individual's (or group's or organization's) inputs. This reflects the distributive justice principle of ethics described in Chapter 2. Employees and organizations typically use a combination of these three principles, particularly for different situations.[81] For example, companies typically give all employees the same employee benefits (equality principle) and allow employees with heavy family demands more paid time off (need principle). However, by far the most common distributive justice principle is equity, which we discuss next.

Elements of Equity Theory   Over several decades, scholars have elaborated the equity principle through **equity theory,** which says that employees determine whether allocations are fair by comparing their own outcome/input ratio to the outcome/input ratio of some other person.[82] The outcome/input ratio is the value of the outcomes you receive divided by the value of inputs you provide in the exchange relationship. Inputs include skills, effort, experience, amount of time worked, performance results, and other employee contributions to the organization. Employees see their inputs as investments into the exchange relationship. For Hsieh Hsuen-hui, these inputs probably include her level of responsibility, effort, and other factors. Outcomes are the things employees receive from the organization in exchange for the inputs, such as pay, promotions, recognition, or an office with a window. Employees receive many outcomes and they weight each outcome and input differently, so determining the overall values isn't always easy. In the case involving Hsieh Hsuen-hui, the main outcome is the paycheck.

Equity theory states that we compare our outcome/input ratio with a comparison other.[83] In our earlier example, Hsieh Hsuen-hui compared herself with her male colleagues in similar positions. However, the comparison other may be another person, group of people, or even yourself in the past. It may be someone in the same job, another job, or another organization. Chief executives have no direct comparison within the firm, so they tend to compare themselves with their counterparts in other organizations. Some research suggests that employees frequently collect information on several referents to form a "generalized" comparison other.[84] For the most part, however, the comparison other varies from one person to the next and is not easily identifiable.

Equity Evaluation   We form an equity evaluation after determining our own outcome/input ratio and comparing this with the comparison other's ratio. Let's consider the experience of Hsieh Hsuen-hui again. Hsieh feels *underreward inequity* because her male counterparts receive higher outcomes (pay) for inputs that are, at best, comparable to what she contributes. This condition is illustrated in Exhibit 5.5 (a).

In the *equity condition,* Hsieh would believe that her outcome/input ratio is similar to the ratio of male colleagues. Specifically, if she believes that she provides the same inputs as the male senior trade specialists, then she would feel equity if both job groups received the same pay and other outcomes (see Exhibit 5.5 (b)). If the male senior trade specialists claim they make a greater contribution because they have more flexibility, then they would have feelings of equity only if they receive proportionally more pay than Hsieh and other female trade specialists. Last, it is possible that some male trade specialists experience *overreward inequity* (Exhibit 5.5 (c)). They would feel that their jobs have the same value as Hsieh's job, yet they earn more money. However, overreward inequity isn't as common as underreward inequity.

equity theory
A theory that explains how people develop perceptions of fairness in the distribution and exchange of resources.

EXHIBIT 5.5   Equity theory model

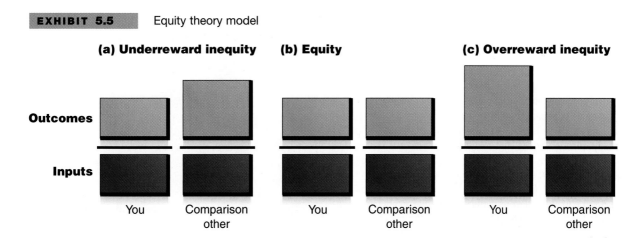

(a) Underreward inequity   **(b) Equity**   **(c) Overreward inequity**

Outcomes

Inputs

You   Comparison   You   Comparison   You   Comparison
           other   other   other

Correcting Inequity Feelings   People feel an uncomfortable emotional tension when they perceive inequity. A strong enough tension motivates employees to reduce the inequity by applying one or more of the following strategies.[85] Employees who feel underpaid sometimes *reduce their inputs* by reducing their effort, performance, and organizational citizenship if these actions don't affect their paycheck.[86] Alternatively, they might try to *increase their outcomes*, such as personally asking for a pay increase or joining a labor union to demand changes.[87] Hsieh might try to increase her outcomes by complaining to her boss or filing a complaint with the Taiwanese government through its new legislation. Some people who feel underrewarded also increase their outcomes by using company resources for personal gain.

Rather than changing their own inputs and outcomes, some people *act on the comparison other*. Employees who feel overrewarded might encourage the referent to work at a more leisurely pace. Those who feel underrewarded might subtly suggest that the overpaid co-worker should be doing a larger share of the workload. Global Connections 5.2 illustrates how attempts to change the comparison other aren't always subtle, however. British employees and shareholders are so upset with the rising pay rates of senior executives that they are protesting and voting against these exorbitant pay packages.

Equity evaluation is a subjective perceptual process, so a fourth way that employees reduce feelings of inequity is by *changing their perceptions*.[88] Over-rewarded employees typically follow this strategy because it's easier to increase their perceived inputs (seniority, knowledge, etc.) than to ask for less pay! As author Pierre Burton once said: "I was underpaid for the first half of my life. I don't mind being overpaid for the second half."[89]

If the previous strategies are ineffective, then employees sometimes *change the comparison other* to someone having a more compatible outcome/input ratio. Last, some people try to reduce inequity feelings by getting away from the inequitable situation (called *leaving the field*). Thus, equity theory explains some instances of employee turnover and job transfer. This also explains why an underrewarded employee might take more time off work even though he or she is not paid for this absenteeism.

Protesting Unfair "Fat Cat" Pay in the United Kingdom

Cats have become an increasingly common sight at corporate annual general meetings throughout the United Kingdom. More precisely, dozens of people have been dressing up as "fat cats" in business suits as a way of protesting the generous paychecks of British executives. Labor unions are behind many of these antics, but institutional investors and private shareholders are also expressing their feelings of unfairness by voting against executive remuneration.

Over half of GlaxoSmithKline's shareholders opposed a U.S.$35 million golden parachute that chief executive Jean-Pierre Garnier would be paid if fired from the pharmaceutical giant. A larger percentage of shareholders also opposed or abstained from voting for overly generous pay packages for executives at advertising group WPP and engineering group BAE Systems. Whitbread is under pressure to change contracts of its senior executives after the National Association of Pension Funds called on shareholders to abstain from voting on executive remuneration packages at the British bakery giant.

Critics say there is plenty of reason for the theatrics and shareholder unrest against executive pay. John Weston was ousted as chief executive of BAE Systems after the company lost more than $1 billion and its stock price hit a 10-year low. In spite of these failings, Weston was sent out the door with a U.S.$2.3 million payout and nearly $6 million pension guarantee.

Corus chief executive Sir Brian Moffat was awarded a 130 percent pay increase soon after the Anglo-Dutch metals group announced huge financial losses and a 12-month pay

British protesters express their anger over unfair executive pay by dressing as "fat cats" in business suits outside the company's annual general meetings.

freeze for its workforce. "How do Corus bosses explain their wage freeze for workers while gifting fortunes to themselves?" asks Paul Flynn, the member of Parliament in South Wales, where Corus has cut back or closed steel production.

Sources: J. Boxell, "Investor Protest Threatens to Force Whitbread to Cut Executive Contracts," *Financial Times* (London), June 18, 2003, p. 25; W. Wallace, "British Shareholders Battle 'American-Style' Exec Pay," *Los Angeles Times,* June 2, 2003, Part 3, p. 5; "Handfuls of Protesters Decrying 'Fat Cat' Paycheques," *Canadian Press,* May 25, 2003; "Heads, They Win," *The Guardian* (London), May 9, 2003; "Bosses' Pay Sparks Anger," *BBC News,* April 5, 2002.

Individual Differences Through Equity Sensitivity   Thus far, we have described equity theory as though everyone has the same feelings of inequity in a particular situation. The reality, however, is that people vary in their **equity sensitivity,** that is, their outcome/input preferences and reaction to various outcome/input ratios.[90] At one end of the equity sensitivity continuum are the "Benevolents"—people who are tolerant of situations where they are underrewarded. They might still prefer equal outcome/input ratios, but they don't mind if others receive more than they do for the same inputs. In the middle are people who fit the standard equity theory model. These "Equity Sensitives" want their outcome/input ratio to be equal to the outcome/input ratio of the comparison other. As the ratios become different, these people feel an uncomfortable tension. At the other end are the "Entitleds." These people feel more comfortable in situations where they receive proportionately more than others. They might accept having the same outcome/input ratio as others, but they would prefer receiving more than others performing the same work.[91]

Why are some people Benevolents and others Entitleds? Personality is one factor. Research has found that Benevolents have more of an internal locus of

equity sensitivity
A person's outcome/input preferences and reaction to various outcome/input ratios.

"O.K., if you can't see your way to giving me a pay
raise, how about giving Parkerson a pay cut?"

control, whereas Entitleds tend to have an external locus of control. Benevolents also have higher levels of conscientiousness and agreeableness.

Problems with Equity Theory   Equity theory is widely cited in the organizational behavior literature, but it has a number of limitations.[92] One concern is that the theory isn't sufficiently specific to predict employee motivation and behavior. It doesn't indicate which inputs or outcomes are most valuable, and it doesn't identify the comparison other against which the outcome/input ratio is evaluated. These vague and highly flexible elements have led some scholars to suggest that equity theory offers little value. A second problem is that equity theory incorrectly assumes people are individualistic, rational, and selfish. In reality, people are social creatures who define themselves as members of various group memberships (see social identity theory in Chapter 3). They share goals with other members of these groups and commit themselves to the norms of their groups. A third limitation is that recent studies have found that equity theory accounts for only some of our feelings of fairness or justice in the workplace. Scholars now say that procedural justice, which we look at next, is at least as important as distributive justice.

Procedural Justice

For many years, OB scholars believed that distributive justice was more important than procedural justice in explaining employee motivation, attitudes, and behavior. This belief was based on the assumption that people are driven mainly by self-interest, so they try to maximize their personal outcomes. Today, we know that people seek justice for its own sake, not just as a means to improve their paycheck. Thus, procedural justice seems to be as important as (some experts say more important than) distributive justice in explaining employee attitudes, motivation, and behavior.[93]

EXHIBIT 5.6   Components of organizational justice

Structural Rules   Procedural justice is influenced by both structural rules and social rules (see Exhibit 5.6).[94] Structural rules represent the policies and practices that decision makers should follow. The most frequently identified structural rule in procedural justice research is people's belief that they should have a "voice" in the decision process.[95] Voice allows employees to convey what they believe are relevant facts and perspectives to the decision maker, and it provides a "value-expressive" function, that is, an opportunity to speak one's mind. Other structural rules are that the decision maker is unbiased, relies on complete and accurate information, applies existing policies consistently, has listened to all sides of the dispute, and allows the decision to be appealed to a higher authority.[96]

Social Rules   Along with structural rules, procedural justice is influenced by social rules, that is, standards of interpersonal conduct between employees and decision makers. This set of rules is sometimes called *interactional justice* because it refers to how the decision maker treats employees during the process. Two social rules that stand out in the procedural justice literature are respect and accountability. Employees feel greater procedural justice when they are treated with respect. For instance, one recent study found that nonwhite nurses who experienced racism tended to file grievances only after experiencing disrespectful treatment in their attempt to resolve the racist situation. Similarly, another study found that employees with repetitive strain injuries were more likely to file workers' compensation claims after experiencing disrespectful behavior from management.[97]

The other social rule that has attracted attention is accountability. People believe that they are entitled to explanations about decisions, particularly when the results have potentially negative consequences for them. For instance, suppose a co-worker receives a better office than you do (distributive injustice). Chances are, you will feel less injustice after hearing the decision maker's explanation for that decision.

Consequences of Procedural Injustice   Procedural justice has a strong influence on our emotions and attitudes; for instance, its absence may lower organizational commitment and trust. Employees tend to experience anger toward the source of the injustice, which makes them aware of the injustice and motivates them to act on this situation. This anger generates various response behaviors that scholars categorize as either withdrawal or aggression.[98] Notice how these response behaviors are similar to the fight-or-flight responses described earlier in the chapter regarding situations that activate our drive to defend.

With respect to withdrawal, those who experience procedural injustice are less willing to comply with the higher authorities who created the injustice. If employees believe their boss relies on an unfair decision process, then those employees tend to be less motivated to follow orders in the future. Withdrawal also includes lower motivation to attend work, engage in organizational citizenship (e.g., being less helpful and tolerant of others), and perform tasks at a high standard.

Aggressive responses to procedural injustice entail a variety of counterproductive work behaviors, including sabotage, theft, conflict, and acts of violence.[99] However, most employees who experience injustice respond with milder forms of retaliation, such as showing indignation and denouncing the decision maker's competence. Research suggests that being treated unfairly undermines our self-esteem and social status, particularly when the injustice is known to others. Consequently, employees retaliate to restore their self-esteem and reinstate their status and power in the relationship with the perpetrator of the injustice. Employees also engage in these counterproductive behaviors to educate the decision maker, thereby minimizing the chance of future injustices.[100]

Organizational Justice in Practice

Throughout our discussion of organizational justice, the possibility that feelings of distributive or procedural justice or injustice can have significantly positive or negative effects on employees and the organization has been apparent. One of the clearest lessons from equity theory is that we need to continually treat people fairly in the distribution of organizational rewards. Unfortunately, this is perhaps one of life's greatest challenges because it seems that most of us have unique opinions about the value of inputs and outcomes. Decision makers need to carefully understand these dynamics along with the distribution rules—equity, equality, or need—that the organization wants to apply.

But corporate leaders need to consider more than fair distribution of rewards. They need to create a workplace where employees believe that the decision-making *process* is also fair. Research has shown that training programs can help people improve their procedural fairness. In one study, supervisors participated in role-play exercises to develop several procedural justice practices in the disciplinary process, such as maintaining the employee's privacy, giving employees some control over the process, avoiding arbitrariness, and exhibiting a supportive demeanor. Judges subsequently rated supervisors who received the procedural justice training as behaving more fairly than supervisors who did not receive the training. In another study, managers received procedural justice training through lectures, case studies, role playing, and discussion. Three months later, subordinates of the trained managers had significantly higher organizational citizenship behaviors than the subordinates of managers who did not receive procedural justice training.[101] Overall, it seems that justice can be improved in the workplace.

Chapter Summary

Motivation refers to the forces within a person that affect his or her direction, intensity, and persistence of voluntary behavior in the workplace. As a new generation of employees enters the workplace and as globalization creates a more diverse workforce, companies need to rethink their motivational practices.

Two motivation theories—Maslow's needs hierarchy and Alderfer's ERG theory—propose that employee needs change over time through a needs hierarchy. Maslow's theory groups needs into a hierarchy of five levels and states that the lowest needs are initially most important, but higher needs become more important as the lower ones are satisfied. Alderfer's ERG theory groups needs into a hierarchy of three levels: existence, relatedness, and growth. It also suggests that those who are unable to satisfy a higher need become frustrated and regress back to the next lower need level. Both Maslow's and Alderfer's theories are popular, but many scholars are now doubtful that everyone has the same.

Paul Lawrence and Nitkin Nohria proposed an evolutionary psychology theory involving four innate drives—the drive to acquire, bond, learn, and defend. These drives create emotional markers that indicate the relevance and strength of perceived information about our environments and thereby motivate us to act on those conditions. McClelland's learned needs theory argues that people have secondary needs or drives that are learned rather than instinctive, including need for achievement, need for power, and need for affiliation.

The practical implication of needs-based motivation theories is that corporate leaders need to balance the demands and influences of the different innate drives. They must also recognize that different people have different needs at different times. These theories also warn us against relying too heavily on financial rewards as a source of employee motivation.

Expectancy theory states that work effort is determined by the perception that effort will result in a particular level of performance (E→P expectancy), the perception that a specific behavior or performance level will lead to specific outcomes (P→O expectancy), and the valences that the person feels for those outcomes. The E→P expectancy increases by improving the employee's ability and confidence to perform the job. The P→O expectancy increases by measuring performance accurately, distributing higher rewards to better performers, and showing employees that rewards are performance-based. Outcome valences increase by finding out what employees want and using these resources as rewards.

Goal setting is the process of motivating employees and clarifying their role perceptions by establishing performance objectives. Goals are more effective when they are specific, relevant, and challenging; have employee commitment; and are accompanied by meaningful feedback. Participative goal setting is important in some situations. Effective feedback is specific, relevant, timely, credible, and sufficiently frequent (which depends on the employee's knowledge/experience with the task and the task cycle). Two increasingly popular forms of feedback are multisource (360-degree) assessment and executive coaching. Feedback from nonsocial sources is also beneficial.

Organizational justice consists of distributive justice (perceived fairness in the outcomes we receive relative to our contributions and the outcomes and contributions of others) and procedural justice (fairness of the procedures used to decide the distribution of resources). Equity theory, which considers the most common principle applied in distributive justice, has four elements: outcome/input ratio, comparison other, equity evaluation, and consequences of inequity. The theory also explains what people are motivated to do when they feel inequitably treated.

Equity sensitivity is a personal characteristics that explains why people react differently to varying degrees of inequity.

Procedural justice is influenced by both structural rules and social rules. Structural rules represent the policies and practices that decision makers should follow; the most frequently identified is giving employees "voice" in the decision process. Social rules refer to standards of interpersonal conduct between employees and decision makers; they are best observed by showing respect and providing accountability for decisions. Procedural justice is as important as distributive justice, and it influences organizational commitment, trust, and various withdrawal and aggression behaviors.

Key Terms   *theory's ! (Essay will be one)*

distributive justice, p. 157

effort-to-performance (E→P) expectancy, p. 148

equity sensitivity, p. 160

equity theory, p. 158

ERG theory, p. 141

executive coaching, p. 155

existence needs, p. 141

expectancy theory, p. 147

feedback, p. 153

frustration-regression process, p. 142

goals, p. 151

goal setting, p. 151

growth needs, p. 142

management-by-objectives (MBO), p. 152

motivation, p. 140

need for achievement (nAch), p. 145

need for affiliation (nAff), p. 145

need for power (nPow), p. 146

needs, p. 140

needs hierarchy theory, p. 141

performance-to-outcome (P→O) expectancy, p. 148

procedural justice, p. 157

relatedness needs, p. 142

satisfaction-progression process, p. 141

360-degree feedback, p. 154

valence, p. 149

Discussion Questions

1. Identify three reasons why motivating employees is becoming increasingly challenging.

2. Harvard Business School professors Lawrence and Nohria recently proposed four fundamental human drives. Relate these innate drives to Maslow's needs hierarchy theory and Alderfer's ERG theory. How are they similar? How do they differ?

3. Use all three components of expectancy theory to explain why some employees are motivated to show up for work during a snowstorm whereas others make no effort to leave their home.

4. What are the limitations of expectancy theory in predicting an individual's work effort and behavior?

5. Several service representatives are upset that the newly hired representative with no previous experience will be paid $1,000 a year above the usual starting salary in the pay range. The department manager explained that the new hire would not accept the entry-level rate, so the company raised the offer by $1,000. All five reps currently earn salaries near the top of the scale ($10,000 higher), although they all started at the minimum starting salary a few years earlier. Use equity theory to explain why the five service representatives feel inequity in this situation.

6. Using your knowledge of the characteristics of effective goals, establish two meaningful goals related to your performance in this class.

7. When do employees prefer feedback from nonsocial rather than social sources? Explain why nonsocial sources are preferred under these conditions.

8. Inequity can occur in the classroom as well as in the workplace. Identify classroom situations in which you experienced feelings of inequity. What can instructors do to maintain an environment that fosters both distributive and procedural justice?

BUDDY'S SNACK COMPANY

By Russell Casey, Clayton State University, and Gloria Thompson, University of Phoenix

Buddy's Snack Company is a family-owned company located in the Rocky Mountains. Buddy Forest started the business in 1951 by selling homemade potato chips out of the back of his pickup truck. Nowadays, Buddy's is a $36 million snack food company that is struggling to regain market share lost to Frito-Lay and other fierce competitors. In the early 1980s, Buddy passed the business on to his son, Buddy Jr., who is currently grooming his son, Mark, to succeed himself as head of the company.

Six months ago, Mark joined Buddy's Snacks as a salesperson and after four months was quickly promoted to sales manager. Mark recently graduated from a local university with an M.B.A. in marketing, and Buddy Jr. was hoping that Mark would be able to implement strategies that could help turn the company around. One of Mark's initial strategies was to introduce a new sales performance management system. As part of this approach, any salesperson who receives a below-average performance rating would be required to attend a mandatory coaching session with his/her supervisor. Mark Forest is hoping that these coaching sessions will motivate his employees to increase their sales. This case describes the reaction of three salespeople who have been required to attend a coaching session because of their low performance over the previous quarter.

Lynda Lewis

Lynda is a hard worker who takes pride in her work ethic. She has spent a lot of time reading the training material and learning selling techniques, viewing training videos on her own time, and accompanying top salespeople on their calls. Lynda has no problem asking for advice and doing whatever needs to be done to learn the business. Everyone agrees that Lynda has a cheery attitude and is a real "team player," giving the company 150 percent at all times. It has been a tough quarter for Lynda due to the downturn in the economy, but she is doing her best to achieve her sales targets. Lynda feels that

failure to make quota during this past quarter results not from lack of effort but just bad luck in the economy. She is hopeful that things will turn around in the next quarter.

Lynda is upset with Mark for having her attend the coaching session because this is the first time in three years that her sales quota has not been met. Although Lynda is willing to do whatever it takes to be successful, she is concerned that the coaching sessions will be held on a Saturday. Doesn't Mark realize that Lynda has to raise three boys by herself and that weekends are an important time for her family? Because Lynda is a dedicated employee, she will somehow manage to rearrange the family's schedule.

Lynda is now very concerned about how her efforts are being perceived by Mark. After all, she exceeded the sales quota from the previous quarter yet had not received a "thank you" or "good job" for those efforts. The entire experience has left Lynda unmotivated and questioning her future with the company.

Michael Benjamin

Michael is happy to have his job at Buddy's Snack Company, although he really doesn't like sales work that much. Michael accepted this position because he felt that he wouldn't have to work hard and would have a lot of free time during the day. Michael was sent to coaching mainly because his customer satisfaction reports were low; in fact, they were the lowest in the company. Michael tends to give "canned" presentations and does not listen closely to customers' needs. Consequently, Michael makes numerous errors in new sales orders, which delays shipments and loses business and goodwill for Buddy's Snack Company. Michael doesn't really care since most of his customers do not spend much money and he doesn't think it is worth his while.

The company's commission structure recently changed, so instead of selling to the warehouse stores and possibly earning a high commission, Michael is now forced to sell to lower volume convenience stores. In other words, he will have to sell twice as much product to earn the same amount of money. Michael does not think this change in commission is fair, and he feels that the coaching session will be a waste of time. He feels that the other members of the sales team are successful because they are getting all of the good leads. He doesn't socialize with others in the office and attributes others' success and promotions to "who they know" in the company rather than their hard work. He feels that no matter how much effort is put into the job, he will never be adequately rewarded.

Kyle Sherbo

For three of the last five years Kyle was the number one salesperson in the division and had hopes of being promoted to sales manager. When Mark joined the company, Kyle worked closely with Buddy Jr. to help Mark learn all facets of the business. Kyle thought this close relationship with Buddy Jr. would ensure his upcoming promotion to the coveted position of sales manager and was devastated to learn that Mark received the promotion that he thought was his.

During the past quarter, there was a noticeable change in Kyle's work habits. It had become commonplace for Kyle to be late for appointments or miss them entirely and to not return phone calls or follow up on leads. His sales performance declined dramatically, which resulted in a drastic loss of income. Although Kyle had been dedicated and fiercely loyal to Buddy Jr. and the company for many years, he is now looking for other employment. Buddy's Snacks is located in a rural community, which leaves Kyle with limited job opportunities. He was, however, offered a position as a sales manager with a competing company in a larger town, but Kyle's wife refuses to leave the area because of her strong family ties. Kyle is bitter and resentful of his current situation and now faces a mandatory coaching session that will be conducted by Mark.

Discussion Questions

1. You have met three employees of Buddy's Snacks. Explain how each employee's situation relates to equity theory.

2. Describe the three needs identified by McClelland. How are they related to worker behavior in each situation?

3. Compare and contrast the three relationships of expectancy theory. To which employee situation does each apply?

CASE STUDY 5.2

CEO COACHES

BusinessWeek By his own admission, David S. Pottruck was once a despotic leader, bulldozing other people's opinions and overruling their strategies. "I knew there was always a lot of glass being broken around me," says Pottruck, who is now co-CEO of Charles Schwab & Co. But after a performance review indicated that his peers didn't trust or like him, Pottruck began a long process of reform. Today, Pottruck's personality, management approach, and leadership style are much better, thanks to the guidance of executive coach and ex-IBM executive Terry Pearce. Although the feedback can be gut-wrenching at times, coaches offer executives meaningful and honest information about their performance, particularly the quality of their interaction with others.

This *Business Week* case study looks at the role of coaches in changing executive behavior and performance. The case describes how coaches operate, where they tend to work well, and the limitations of relying on executive coaches. Read through this *Business Week* article at www.mhhe.com/mcshane3e and prepare for the discussion questions below.

Discussion Questions

1. Why are executive coaches potentially better than performance reviews and more structured training at improving emotional intelligence and related interpersonal skills?

2. What are the limitations of executive coaches identified in this article?

A QUESTION OF FEEDBACK

Purpose This exercise is designed to help you understand the importance of feedback, including problems that occur with imperfect communication in the feedback process.

Materials The instructor will distribute a few pages of exhibits to one person on each team. The other students will require a pencil with eraser and blank paper. Movable chairs and tables in a large area are helpful.

Instructions

■ *Step 1*—The class is divided into pairs of students. Each pair is ideally located in a private area, away from other students and where one person can write. One student is given the pages of exhibits from the instructor. The other student in each pair is not allowed to see these exhibits.

■ *Step 2*—The student holding the materials will describe each of the exhibits and the other student's task is to accurately replicate each exhibit. The pair of students can compare the replication with the original at the end of each drawing. They may also switch roles for each exhibit, if they wish. If roles are switched, the instructor must distribute exhibits separately to each student so that they are not seen by the other person. Each

exhibit has a different set of limitations, as described below:

Exhibit 1—The student describing the exhibit cannot look at the other student or his or her diagram. The student drawing the exhibit cannot speak or otherwise communicate with the person describing the exhibit.

Exhibit 2—The student describing the exhibit may look at the other student's diagram. However, he or she may only say "Yes" or "No" when the student drawing the diagram asks a specific question. In other words, the person presenting the information can use only these words for feedback and only when asked a question by the writer.

Exhibit 3 (optional—if time permits)—The student describing the exhibit may look at the other student's diagram and may provide any feedback at any time to the person replicating the exhibit.

■ *Step 3*—The class will gather to debrief this exercise. This may include discussion on the importance of feedback and the characteristics of effective feedback for individual motivation and learning.

Source: © 2001 Steven L. McShane.

MEASURING YOUR EQUITY SENSITIVITY

Purpose This self-assessment is designed to help you to estimate your level of equity sensitivity.

Instructions Read each of the statements below and circle the response that you believe best reflects your position regarding each state-

ment. Then use the scoring key in Appendix B to calculate your results. This exercise is completed alone so students assess themselves honestly without concerns of social comparison. However, class discussion will focus on equity theory and the effect of equity sensitivity on perceptions of fairness in the workplace.

Equity Preference Questionnaire

To what extent do you agree or disagree that . . .	Strongly Agree	Agree	Neutral	Disagree	Strongly Disagree
1. I prefer to do as little as possible at work while getting as much as I can from my employer.........	1	2	3	4	5
2. I am most satisfied at work when I have to do as little as possible.................	1	2	3	4	5
3. When I am at my job, I think of ways to get out of work.................	1	2	3	4	5
4. If I could get away with it, I would try to work just a little bit slower than the boss expects.........	1	2	3	4	5
5. It is really satisfying to me when I can get something for nothing at work.................	1	2	3	4	5
6. It is the smart employee who gets as much as he/she can while giving as little as possible in return.........	1	2	3	4	5
7. Employees who are more concerned about what they can get from their employer rather than what they can give to their employer are the wisest..................	1	2	3	4	5
8. When I have completed my task for the day, I help out other employees who have yet to complete their tasks.................	1	2	3	4	5
9. Even if I receive low wages and poor benefits from my employer, I would still try to do my best at my job.................	1	2	3	4	5
10. If I had to work hard all day at my job, I would probably quit.................	1	2	3	4	5
11. I feel obligated to do more than I am paid to do at work.................	1	2	3	4	5
12. At work, my greatest concern is whether or not I am doing the best job I can.................	1	2	3	4	5
13. A job that requires me to be busy during the day is better than a job which allows me a lot of loafing.........	1	2	3	4	5
14. At work, I feel uneasy when there is little work for me to do.................	1	2	3	4	5
15. I would become very dissatisfied with my job if I had little or no work to do.................	1	2	3	4	5
16. All other things being equal, it is better to have a job with a lot of duties and responsibilities than one with few duties and responsibilities.................	1	2	3	4	5

Source: Reprinted from K. S. Sauleya and A. G. Bedeian, "Equity Sensitivity: Construction of a Measure and Examination of Its Psychometric Properties," *Journal of Management* vol. 26 (September 2000), pp. 885–910. Copyright © 2000, with permission from Elsevier.

MEASURING YOUR GROWTH NEED STRENGTH

Purpose This self-assessment is designed to help you to estimate your level of growth need strength.

Instructions People differ in the kinds of jobs they would most like to hold. This self-assessment gives you a chance to say just what it is about a job that is most important to you. Please indicate which of the two jobs you personally would prefer if you had to make a choice between them. In answering each question, assume that everything else about the jobs is the same. Pay attention only to the characteristics actually listed.

After studying the preceding material, be sure to check out our website at

www.mhhe.com/mcshane3e

for more in-depth information and interactivities that correspond to this chapter.

Applied Performance Practices

Learning Objectives

After reading this chapter, you should be able to:

- Explain how money and other financial rewards affect our needs, attitudes, and social identity.

- Discuss the advantages and disadvantages of the four reward objectives.

- Identify two team- and four organizational-level performance-based rewards.

- Describe five ways to improve reward effectiveness.

- Discuss the advantages and disadvantages of job specialization.

- Diagram the job characteristics model of job design.

- Identify three strategies to improve employee motivation through job design.

- Define empowerment and identify strategies to support empowerment.

- Describe the five elements of self-leadership.

- Explain how mental imagery improves employee motivation.

Not long ago, a maintenance employee stormed into the offices of Clive Beddoe, CEO and cofounder of WestJet, the discount airline headquartered in Calgary, Canada. The employee demanded to know why Beddoe was squandering money on a hamburgers and beer party for a select few at the head office. Beddoe quickly explained that he paid for the party out of his own pocket. "He was a little humbled, but I congratulated him on his attitude," Beddoe recalls. "He's like a watchdog, and he hates inequities. That's the spirit of WestJet."

The spirit of WestJet started less than a decade ago, based on the model of friendly service and flexible efficiency developed by Southwest Airlines in Dallas, Texas. Today, WestJet is North America's second most profitable airline (just below Southwest's profits) and is Canada's second largest airline, with regular routes to two dozen communities from coast to coast.

How did WestJet become so successful in such a short time? One reason is that WestJet's employees (called Westjetters) are a motivated and performance-focused bunch. Everyone is rewarded for the company's success through profit sharing and stock options. The average employee recently took home Can$9,000 based on six months of profits. Most WestJetters are also stockholders, thanks to a generous

WestJet's success is due partly to flexible employees, who are rewarded and feel empowered to serve customers effectively and efficiently.

stock ownership plan. "We've got employees who own the company, whose interests are directly aligned with the interests of the company," says WestJet chief financial officer Sandy Campbell.

Another reason for WestJet's profitability is employees who perform a variety of tasks. For example, flight attendants double as reservation agents and pilots sometimes help clean up the cabin between flights. As a result, WestJet operates with about 59 people per aircraft, compared with more than 140 at a typical full-service airline.

WestJet also avoids an intermediate layer of supervisors, giving staff more freedom to make decisions. "We empower our people to do whatever it takes to satisfy a customer in their best judgment," explains WestJet sales manager Judy Goodman. "Whatever they think is appropriate, they are free to do." This may explain why WestJet has about 20 percent market share in Canada, yet receives only 0.3 percent of all complaints submitted by airline passengers to the Canadian government.[1] ■

While many factors contribute to WestJet's success, the opening story points out that rewards, job design, empowerment, and self-leadership play a large role. This chapter looks at each of these applied performance practices. The chapter begins with an overview of the meaning of money, the different types of rewards and their objectives, and the characteristics of effective reward implementation. Next, we look at the dynamics of job design, specific job design strategies to motivate employees, and the effectiveness of recent job design interventions. We then consider the elements of empowerment as well as conditions that support empowerment. The final part of this chapter explains how employees manage their own performance through the five elements of self-leadership: personal goal setting, constructive thought patterns, designing natural rewards, self-monitoring, and self-reinforcement.

The Meaning of Money in the Workplace

Money and other financial rewards are a fundamental part of the employment relationship. Organizations distribute money and other benefits in order to align individual goals more closely with corporate objectives. Financial rewards also represent the primary (but not only) form of exchange; they compensate employees for their competencies, behaviors, and performance. This concept of economic exchange can be found across cultures. The word for "pay" in Malaysian and Slovak means to replace a loss; in Hebrew and Swedish it means making equal.[2]

But money is not just an economic medium of exchange in the employment relationship. It is a symbol with much deeper and more complex meaning.[3] It affects our needs, our emotions, and our self-perception. As one scholar wrote: "Money is probably the most emotionally meaningful object in contemporary life: only food and sex are its close competitors as common carriers of such strong and diverse feelings, significance, and strivings."[4]

Money and Employee Needs

Money is an important factor in satisfying individual needs. Money allows us to buy food and shelter (i.e., to fulfill existence needs), so it's not surprising that people value money more during and immediately after economic recessions. Money is also a symbol of status, which relates to the innate drive to acquire (see Chapter 5).[5] Financial gain also symbolizes personal accomplishments and, consequently, relates to growth needs. People with a high need for achievement are not motivated primarily by money, but they do value money as a source of feedback and a representation of goal achievement. In other words, money is a way of "keeping score" of their success. Money seems to have gained importance in people's lives. One major survey reported that compensation is one of the top three factors attracting individuals to work for an organization.[6]

Money Attitudes and Values

Money tends to create strong emotions and attitudes. Some people are preoccupied with money. Others are nervous with money and its responsibilities. One large-scale study revealed that money generates a variety of emotions, most of which are negative, such as anxiety, depression, anger, and helplessness. Money is associated with greed, avarice and, occasionally, generosity.[7]

Anyone who doubts whether money motivates should visit IKEA in Renton, Washington, on Excellence Day. Each year, the retailer hands over the entire day's sales (except sales tax) to its employees, including administration staff who also help customers during the event. A few years ago, IKEA offered a similar bonus for employees around the globe, resulting in a bonus of $1,800 for each full-time employee (prorated for part-time staff). Everyone from Stockholm, Sweden, to Sydney, Australia (shown in photo), was ecstatic about the bonus they received. "IKEA employees worked tirelessly throughout the day and well into the night, showing the same enthusiasm that has helped make the company so successful," said an IKEA executive of the worldwide bonus-day event.[8] Under what conditions would money not motivate employees?

Some OB researchers have identified several underlying attitudes toward money, collectively known as the "money ethic."[9] People with a strong money ethic believe that money is not evil; that it is a symbol of achievement, respect, and power; and that it should be budgeted carefully.

Cultural values seem to influence attitudes toward money and a money ethic. One recent study reported that people with strong Confucian work values (persistence, respect for status, thrift, and sense of shame) are more likely to carefully budget their money but are also more likely to spend it. Similarly, people in countries with a long-term orientation (such as China and Japan) give money a high priority in their lives. In contrast, Scandinavians, Australians, and New Zealanders have a strong egalitarian value that discourages people from openly talking about money or displaying their personal wealth.[10]

Money and Social Identity

People tend to define themselves in terms of their ownership and management of money. In other words, the size of our paycheck or bank account tends to influence our self-worth and self-perceptions of social status. Some individuals see themselves as hoarders or worriers of money, whereas others will tell you they are shopaholics and spendthrifts. Research on marital relationships shows that couples tend to adopt polarized roles (and, consequently, self-identities) regarding their management and expenditure of money.[11] The same polar relationships might exist in the workplace.

Men are more likely than women to emphasize money in their self-concept. One large-scale survey of people in 43 countries revealed that men attach more importance or value to money than do women in every country except India, Norway, and Transkei. Public opinion polls suggest that money has a much higher priority for men than for women.[12] Why do men identify more with money? Some writers suggest that men are more likely to believe that money equals power and that power is the path to respect. Other research has found that, compared with women, men are more confident managing their money and are more likely to use money as a tool to influence and impress others.[13]

The bottom line is that money and other financial rewards do much more than pay employees back for their contributions. They fulfill a variety of needs, influence emotions, and shape or represent a person's self-worth and social identity. This knowledge is important to remember when distributing rewards in the workplace. Over the next few pages, we look at various reward objectives and how to improve the implementation of performance-based rewards.

Reward Practices

Organizations apply a variety of rewards to attract, motivate, and retain employees. Each reward relates to specific objectives: membership and seniority, job status, competencies, and performance. Each reward objective has both advantages and disadvantages, as Exhibit 6.1 summarizes.

Membership- and Seniority-Based Rewards

Membership- and seniority-based rewards (sometimes called "pay for pulse") represent the largest part of most paychecks. Employees receive either the same wages and benefits, or these financial rewards increase with years of service. For example, the city of Bellevue, Nebraska, awards employees longevity pay of $420 per year after eight years of service. School administrators in Modesto County, California, receive pay increases based on seniority. Employees in large Japanese firms have historically received pay rates based almost completely on their age, although this system is slowly being replaced with more performance-based pay.[14]

Membership- and seniority-based rewards tend to attract job applicants with security needs, reduce stress, and sometimes improve loyalty. However, they do not directly motivate job performance; on the contrary, they discourage poor performers from seeking out work better suited to their abilities. Instead, the good performers are lured to better-paying jobs. Last, as we learned in Chapter 4, some of these rewards are golden handcuffs that potentially undermine job performance by creating continuance commitment.

Job Status–Based Rewards

Almost every organization rewards employees to some extent based on the status of the jobs they occupy. **Job evaluation** is commonly used to rate the worth or status of each job, with higher pay rates going to jobs that require more skill and effort, have more responsibility, and have more difficult work-

job evaluation
Systematically evaluating the worth of jobs within an organization by measuring their required skill, effort, responsibility, and working conditions.

EXHIBIT 6.1	Reward objectives, advantages, and disadvantages

Reward objective	Sample rewards	Advantages	Disadvantages
Membership/seniority	• Fixed pay • Most employee benefits • Paid time off	• May attract applicants • Minimizes stress of insecurity • Reduces turnover	• Doesn't directly motivate performance • May discourage poor performers from leaving • Golden handcuffs may undermine performance
Job status	• Promotion-based pay increase • Status-based benefits	• Tries to maintain internal equity • Minimizes pay discrimination • Motivates employees to compete for promotions	• Encourages political tactics to increase job worth • Creates psychological distance between employees and executives
Competencies	• Pay increase based on competency • Skill-based pay	• Improves workforce flexibility • Tends to improve quality • Consistent with employability	• Subjective measurement of competencies • Skill-based pay plans are expensive
Task performance	• Commissions • Merit pay • Gainsharing • Profit sharing • Stock options	• Motivate task performance • Attract performance-oriented applicants • Organizational rewards create an ownership culture • Pay variability may avoid layoffs during downturns	• May weaken motivation of job itself • May distance reward giver from receiver • May discourage creativity • Viewed as quick fixes, but don't solve real causes

ing conditions.[15] Organizations that don't rely on job evaluation indirectly reward job status based on surveys estimating what other companies pay for specific jobs. People in some higher status jobs are also rewarded with larger offices, company-paid vehicles, and access to exclusive dining rooms.

Job status–based pay motivates employees to compete for promotions and tries to make pay levels fair across different jobs (called *internal equity*). However, job status–based rewards have also received heavy criticism.[16] One concern is that rewarding people for the worth of their jobs is inconsistent with the model of market-responsive organizations that have few layers of hierarchy and encourage initiative in everyone. Status-based rewards motivate employees to compete with each other, rather than focusing their energy on customer service and other market needs. They also tend to reward functional specialization (e.g., marketing, finance) rather than the organization's central goals of anticipating and responding to market needs. Last, job evaluation systems motivate employees to increase their pay rate by exaggerating job duties and hoarding resources.

Competency-Based Rewards

Organizations are shifting from rewarding job status to rewarding employees for their skills, knowledge, and other competencies that lead to superior performance. For instance, Syracuse University in upstate New York replaced its 20-pay-grade hierarchy with just 7 wider pay bands. Employees now receive pay increases within each pay band partly based on how well they have acquired new knowledge and skills.[17] *Skill-based pay* is a variation of competency-based rewards.[18] The employee's pay rate depends on the number of skill modules that he or she has mastered, not on the specific job performed on a particular day.

Competency-based rewards improve workforce flexibility because they motivate employees to acquire a variety of skills that they can apply to different jobs as demands require. Product or service quality tends to improve because employees with multiple skills are more likely to understand the work process and know how to improve it.[19] Competency-based rewards are also consistent with employability because they reward employees who continuously learn skills that will keep them employed (see Chapter 1). One potential problem with competency-based pay is that measuring competencies can be subjective, particularly where they are personality traits or values.[20] Skill-based pay systems measure specific skills, so they are usually more objective and accurate. However, they are expensive because employees spend more time learning new tasks.

Performance-Based Rewards

Performance-based rewards have existed since Babylonian days in the 20th century B.C., but their popularity has increased dramatically over the past decade.[21] Some of the most popular individual, team, and organizational performance-based rewards are summarized in Exhibit 6.2 and described over the next page or two.

Individual Rewards   Individual rewards come in several forms. Many employees receive individual bonuses or awards for accomplishing a specific task or performance goal. Real estate agents and other salespeople typically earn *commissions,* in which their pay increases with sales volume. Piece-rate systems reward employees based on the number of units produced. For example, Eurofresh crop workers in Arizona get paid by the volume of tomatoes picked; lawn care staff at The Lawn Mowgul in Dallas, Texas, earn a form of piece rate (called "piecemeal") based on the number of yards cut.[22]

EXHIBIT 6.2

Types of performance-based rewards

Team Rewards   Organizations are shifting their focus from individuals to teams and, consequently, employees are finding a larger part of their total paycheck based on team performance. For the past 40 years, Wal-Mart has been awarding bonuses determined by sales at the store where employees work. Wall Street brokerage firms increasingly award bonuses based on team rather than individual performance.[23]

Rather than calculating bonuses from sales or performance, **gainsharing plans** award bonuses based on cost savings. For instance, over two-thirds of mining companies in the United States and Canada have a gainsharing bonus system, typically where mining teams receive larger bonuses for extracting more ore at lower cost. At St. Joseph's Hospital in Atlanta, Georgia, cardiac surgical teams pocket half the cost savings (up to a maximum of $2,000) of a $15,000 heart bypass operation by using less expensive sutures and avoiding opening supplies that aren't used. "We're not withholding (services)," explains the surgeon who devised the pay plan. "We're just reducing waste."[24] Gainsharing plans tend to improve team dynamics, knowledge sharing, and pay satisfaction. They also create a reasonably strong E→P expectancy (see Chapter 5) because much of the cost reduction and labor efficiency is within the team's control.[25]

A variation of gainsharing is **open-book management,** whereby employees are shown operating costs, taught how to read those financial statements, and encouraged to find ways to reduce costs. Chicago-based Artists' Frame Service practices open-book management, which includes an annual seminar on operating costs. CEO Jay Goltz shows employees a stack of 100 enlarged $1 bills, then removes most of them as he explains various expenses behind a $100 frame order: materials, office supplies, advertising, insurance, overhead, and so on.[26] Global Connections 6.1 describes how open-book practices seem to work well at Tien Wah Press's printing plants in Malaysia, Singapore, and Indonesia. Supervisors provide financial information to employees every three months, and the reward system motivates employees to suggest ideas for productivity improvement.

Organizational Rewards   WestJet Airlines, described in the opening story to this chapter, relies on two organizational-level rewards to motivate employees: profit sharing and employee stock ownership. **Profit-sharing plans** pay bonuses to employees based on the previous year's level of corporate profits. **Employee stock ownership plans (ESOPs)** encourage employees to buy shares in the company, usually at a discounted price. Employees are subsequently rewarded through dividends and market appreciation of those shares. Approximately 10 percent of the private sector U.S. workforce participates in an ESOP. Sears, Roebuck and UPS are two of the earliest companies to distribute stocks to their employees. One concern occurs where ESOPs make company pension plans too heavily weighted with company stock. If the company goes bankrupt (as occurred recently at Enron), employees lose both their jobs and a large portion of their retirement nest egg.[27]

A third organizational-level reward that has received plenty of media attention is stock options. **Stock options** give employees the right to purchase company stock at a future date at a predetermined price.[28] For example, your employer might offer you the right to purchase 100 shares at $50 anywhere between two and six years from now. If the stock price is, say, $60 two years later,

Opening the Books at Tien Wah Press

Tien Wah Press (TWP) is in a competitive business and needs to continuously improve productivity. That's why the printing company keeps its 3,000 employees in Malaysia, Singapore, and Indonesia informed about production costs and rewards them for productivity improvements.

Every three months, TWP opens its books to employees. The operations manager at each plant describes the company's performance over the previous quarter. The briefing provides details about labor costs, wages, overtime, transportation, factory overheads, building maintenance, repair and replacement consumable, paper stock balance, printing materials, and sales, as well as profit and loss.

"This briefing serves to explain to the employees how well or badly we are doing and it gives areas where the company has weaknesses that can be rectified and where its strengths are," says TWP human resource manager Datuk Kalam Azad Mohd Taib.

With this financial information, employees can see how their costs affect the company's performance. This, in turn, affects their paycheck through TWP's flexible wage system (FWS). This reward system consists of a base salary plus a merit and profit-sharing scheme (MPS). The more ideas employees offer about ways to reduce costs, the higher their future paycheck.

"The union committee is free to make a calculation on

Tien Wah Press practices open-book management by showing its financial performance every three months to employees in Malaysia, Singapore, and Indonesia.

what probable amount of MPS the employees are likely to get based on the formula given in the collective agreement," explains Kalam Azad.

Source: Based on H. Hamid, "Tien Wah's Flexi-Wage a Success," *Business Times* (Malaysia), December 7, 2000.

---

you could earn $1,000 ($10 × 100 shares) from these options, or you could wait for up to six years for the stock price to rise further. If the stock never rises above $50 during that time, you can let the options expire. The main point here is that stock options don't require employees to own stock but allow them to benefit from its increase above a threshold level.

Another organizational-level reward strategy is the **balanced scorecard.** This performance measurement system rewards people (typically executives) for improving performance on a composite of financial, customer, and internal processes, as well as employee factors. The better the measurement improvements, the larger the bonus awarded. Originally aimed at for-profit firms, the balanced scorecard has recently been introduced to nonprofit organizations. The Swedish Police Service's version of a balanced scorecard relies on surveys and objective criteria to measure customer satisfaction, police image, expected outcomes of crime investigations, perceived quality of service, and efficient use of resources.[29]

How effective are organizational-level rewards? ESOPs, stock options, and balanced scorecards tend to create an "ownership culture" in which employees feel aligned with the organization's success. According to one study, productivity rises by 4 percent annually at ESOP firms, compared to only 1.5 percent at non-ESOP firms. Balanced scorecards have the added benefit of aligning rewards to several specific measures of organizational performance.

balanced scorecard
A reward system that pays bonuses for improved results on a composite of financial, customer, internal process, and employee factors.

Profit sharing tends to create less ownership culture, but it has the advantage of automatically adjusting employee compensation with the firm's prosperity, thereby reducing the need for layoffs or negotiated pay reductions during recessions.[30]

The main problem with ESOPS, stock options, and profit sharing (less so with balanced scorecards) is that employees often perceive a weak connection between individual effort and corporate profits or the value of company shares. Even in small firms, the company's stock price or profitability is influenced by economic conditions, competition, and other factors beyond the employee's immediate control. This results in a low E→P expectancy (see Chapter 5), which weakens employee motivation. These organizational-level rewards also fail to motivate employees when profits are negligible or in "bear" markets when stock prices decline.

Improving Reward Effectiveness

Performance-based rewards have been criticized on the grounds that they undermine the intrinsic motivation for performing the job, discourage creativity, and create relationship problems. Many corporate leaders also use rewards as quick fixes, rather than carefully diagnosing the underlying causes of the undesirable behavior. For example, one company hands out cash to employees who arrive early at company meetings and fines those who arrive late. The company would be better off identifying the causes of lateness and changing the conditions, rather than using money to force a solution to the problem.[31]

These concerns do not necessarily mean that we should abandon performance-based pay. On the contrary, the top performing companies around the world are more likely to have performance-based rewards.[32] Reward systems do motivate most employees, but only under the right conditions. Here are some of the more important strategies to improve reward effectiveness.

Link Rewards to Performance   Behavior modification theory (Chapter 2) and expectancy theory (Chapter 5) both recommend that employees with better performance should be rewarded more than those with poorer performance.[33] Unfortunately, this simple principle seems to be unusually difficult to apply. One problem, according to a recent university study, is that managers rely on different criteria to evaluate employee performance. Some managers emphasize task performance, others focus on organizational citizenship, and still others place most weight on counterproductive behaviors. A Gallup survey at an American telecommunications company revealed a more devastating observation: Management's evaluation of 5,000 customer service employees was uncorrelated with the performance ratings that customers gave those employees. "Whatever behavior the managers were evaluating were irrelevant to the customers," concluded Gallup executives. "The managers might as well have been rating the employees' shoe sizes, for all the customers cared."[34]

How can we improve the pay–performance linkage? First, inconsistencies and bias can be minimized by introducing gainsharing, ESOPs, and other plans that use objective performance measures. Second, where subjective measures of performance are necessary, companies should rely on multiple sources of information. In other words, use 360-degree feedback to minimize biases from any single source (see Chapter 5). Third, companies need to apply rewards soon after the performance occurs, and in a large enough dose (such as a bonus rather than pay increase) that employees experience positive emotion when they receive the reward.[35]

Ensure that Rewards Are Relevant   Companies need to align rewards with performance within the employee's control. The more employees see a "line of sight" between their daily actions and the reward, the more they are motivated to improve performance.[36] Wal-Mart applies this principle by rewarding bonuses to top executives based on the company's overall performance, whereas frontline employees earn bonuses based on the sales volume of the store where they work. Reward systems also need to correct for situational factors. Salespeople in one region may have higher sales because the economy is stronger there than elsewhere, so sales bonuses need to be adjusted for these economic factors.

Use Team Rewards for Interdependent Jobs   Organizations should use team (or organizational) rewards rather than individual rewards when employees work in highly interdependent jobs.[37] One reason is that individual performance is difficult to measure in these situations. For example, you can't determine how well one employee in a chemical processing plant contributes to the quality of the liquid produced. It is a team effort. A second reason is that team rewards tend to make employees more cooperative and less competitive. People see that their bonuses or other incentives depend on how well they work with co-workers, and they act accordingly.

   The third reason for having team rewards is that they support employee preferences for team-based work arrangements. This was found in a study of Xerox customer service representatives. The Xerox employees assigned to teams with purely team bonuses eventually accepted and preferred a team structure, whereas those put in teams without team rewards did not adapt as well to the team structure.[38]

Ensure that Rewards Are Valued   It seems obvious that rewards work best when they are valued. Yet companies sometimes make false assumptions about what employees want, with unfortunate consequences. The solution, of course, is to ask employees what they value. Campbell Soup did this a few years ago at one of its distribution centers. Executives thought the employees would ask for more money in a special team reward program. Instead, distribution staff said the most valued reward was a leather jacket with the Campbell Soup logo on the back.[39]

Watch Out for Unintended Consequences   Performance-based reward systems sometimes have an unexpected—and undesirable—effect on employee behaviors.[40] Consider the pizza company that decided to reward its drivers for on-time delivery. The plan got more hot pizzas to customers on time, but it also increased the accident rates of its drivers because the incentive motivated them to drive recklessly.[41] Connections 6.2 describes a few other examples where reward systems had unintended consequences. The solution here is to carefully think through the consequences of rewards and, where possible, test incentives in a pilot project before applying them across the organization.

   At the beginning of this chapter, we said that money and other financial rewards have a complex effect on the needs, emotions, and social identity of em-

When Rewards Go Wrong

There is an old saying that "what gets rewarded, gets done." But what companies reward isn't always what they had intended for employees to do. Here are a few dramatic examples:

- Stock options are supposed to motivate executives to improve corporate performance. Instead, they seem to motivate some leaders to inflate stock values through dodgy accounting practices. For example, according to U.S. government authorities, HealthSouth founder and former CEO Richard Scrushy demanded that his accounting staff artificially prop up profits at the nation's largest outpatient medical provider. When some employees urged him to abandon these questionable schemes, Scrushy refused, reportedly saying "Not until I sell my stock!" HealthSouth narrowly avoided bankruptcy after the company's true financial health became public.

- Integrated steel companies often rewarded managers for increased labor efficiency. The lower the labor hours required to produce a ton of steel, the larger the manager's bonus. Unfortunately, steel firms usually didn't count the work of outside contractors in the formula, so the reward system motivated managers to hire expensive contractors in the production process. By employing more contractors, the cost of production actually increased, not decreased.

- Toyota rewards its dealerships based on customer satisfaction surveys, not just car sales. What Toyota discovered, however, is that this motivates dealers to increase satisfaction scores, not customer satisfaction. One Toyota dealership received high ratings because it offered free detailing to every customer who returned a "Very Satisfied" survey. The dealership even had a special copy of the survey showing clients which boxes to check off. This increased customer ratings, but not customer satisfaction.

- Donnelly Mirrors (now part of Magna International) introduced a gainsharing plan that motivated employees to reduce labor but not material costs. Employees at the automobile parts manufacturer knew they worked faster with sharp grinding wheels, so they replaced the expensive diamond wheels more often. This action reduced labor costs, thereby giving employees the gainsharing bonus.

U.S. government authorities claim that stock options motivated former HealthSouth CEO Richard Scrushy (shown) and other executives to engage in dodgy accounting practices rather than improve stockholder value for the long term.

However, the labor savings were easily offset by much higher costs for diamond grinding wheels.

Sources: A. Holeck, "Griffith, Ind., Native Takes Over as Steel Plant Manager," *Northwest Indiana Times,* May 25, 2003; "HealthSouth an Example of Options Gone Haywire," *Kansas City Star,* March 31, 2003; M. Romano, "Firm's Health Going South," *Modern Healthcare,* March 24, 2003, p. 4; J. A. Byrne, "How to Fix Corporate Governance," *Business Week,* May 6, 2002, p. 68; F. F. Reichheld, *The Loyalty Effect* (Boston: Harvard University Press, 1996), p. 236; D. R. Spitzer, "Power Rewards: Rewards That Really Motivate," *Management Review,* May 1996, pp. 45–50.

ployees. But money isn't the only thing that motivates people to join an organization and perform effectively. "High performers don't go for the money," warns William Monahan, CEO of Oakdale, Minnesota-based Imation Corporation. "Good people want to be in challenging jobs and see a future where they can get even more responsibilities and challenges." Rafik O. Loutfy, a Xerox research center director, agrees with this assessment. "Our top stars say they want to make an impact—that's the most important thing," he says. "Feeling they are contributing and making a difference is highly motivational for them."[42] In other words, Imation, Xerox, and other companies motivate employees mainly by designing interesting and challenging jobs, which we discuss next.

Job Design Practices

job design

The process of assigning tasks to a job, including the interdependency of those tasks with other jobs.

Organizational behavior scholars generally agree that the deepest "passion" for performing a job well comes from the work itself. **Job design** refers to the process of assigning tasks to a job, including the interdependency of those tasks with other jobs. A *job* is a set of tasks performed by one person. Some jobs have very few tasks, each requiring limited skill or effort. Other jobs entail very complex tasks requiring highly trained tradespeople or professionals. Job design is constantly shifting due to technological change and trends in psychological contracts. Employability means that employees no longer are hired into specific jobs indefinitely. Instead, they hold generic titles (associates, team members) and are expected to perform several clusters of tasks.[43]

Whether the change occurs through information technology or workforce flexibility, job design often produces an interesting conflict between the employee's motivation and ability to complete the work. To understand this issue more fully, we begin by describing early job design efforts aimed at increasing work efficiency through job specialization.

Job Design and Work Efficiency

job specialization

The result of division of labor in which each job includes a subset of the tasks required to complete the product or service.

Using a pair of tweezers, an employee at Medtronic's assembly line in Minneapolis, Minnesota, loads 275 feedthroughs—tiny needlelike components for pacemakers and neurostimulators—onto a slotted storage block. She fills a block in about 15 minutes, then places the completed block on a shelf, and loads the next block.[44] The Medtronics employee works in a job with a high degree of **job specialization.** Job specialization occurs when the work required to build a pacemaker—or any other product or service—is subdivided into separate jobs assigned to different people. Each resulting job includes a very narrow subset of tasks, usually completed in a short "cycle time." Cycle time is the time required to complete the task before starting over with a new work unit. For the Medtronics employee, the cycle time for loading each feedthrough is a few seconds.

The economic benefits of dividing work into specialized jobs have been described and applied for at least two centuries. More than 2,300 years ago, the Chinese philosopher Mencius and Greek philosopher Plato noted that division of labor improves work efficiency. In A.D. 1436, the waterways of Venice became an assembly line loading 10 galleons in just six hours. More than 200 years ago, economist Adam Smith described a small factory where 10 pin makers collectively produced as many as 48,000 pins per day because they performed specialized tasks, such as straightening, cutting, sharpening, grinding, and whitening the pins. In contrast, Smith explained that if these 10 people worked alone, they would collectively produce no more than 200 pins per day.[45]

Why does job specialization potentially increase work efficiency? One reason is that employees have fewer tasks to juggle and therefore spend less time changing activities. They also require fewer physical and mental skills to accomplish the assigned work, so less time and resources are needed for training. A third reason is that employees practice their tasks more frequently with shorter work cycles, so jobs are mastered quickly. Last, work efficiency increases because employees with specific aptitudes or skills can be matched more precisely to the jobs for which they are best suited.[46]

Scientific Management   One of the strongest advocates of job specialization was Frederick Winslow Taylor, an industrial engineer who introduced the principles of **scientific management** in the early 1900s.[47] Scientific management is the systematic partitioning of work into its smallest elements and the standardization of tasks to achieve maximum efficiency. According to Taylor, the most effective companies have detailed procedures and work practices developed by engineers, enforced by supervisors, and executed by employees. Even the supervisor's tasks should be divided: one person manages operational efficiency, another manages inspection, and another is the disciplinarian. Through scientific management, Taylor also popularized many organizational practices that are commonly found today, such as goal setting, employee training, and incentive systems.

Ample evidence suggests that scientific management has improved efficiency in many work settings. One of Taylor's earliest interventions was at a ball bearing factory where 120 women each worked 55 hours per week. Through job specialization and work efficiency analysis, Taylor increased production by two-thirds using a workforce of only 35 women working fewer than 45 hours per week. Taylor also doubled the employees' previous wages. No doubt, some of the increased productivity can be credited to improved training, goal setting, and work incentives, but job specialization also contributed to the success of scientific management.

Problems with Job Specialization   Job specialization is often applied successfully, but it doesn't always improve job performance. The reason is that job specialization ignores the effects of job content on employees.[48] Some jobs—such as loading feedthroughs at Medtronics—are so specialized that they are tedious, trivial, and socially isolating. Job specialization was supposed to let companies buy cheap, unskilled labor. Instead, many have to offer higher wages—some call it *discontentment pay*—to compensate for the job dissatisfaction of narrowly defined work.[49] Job specialization also costs more in terms of higher turnover, absenteeism, sabotage, and mental health problems. Work quality is often lower with highly specialized jobs because employees see only a small part of the process. As one observer of automobile assembly line work reports: "Often [employees] did not know how their jobs related to the total picture. Not knowing, there was no incentive to strive for quality—what did quality even mean as it related to a bracket whose function you did not understand?"[50]

Perhaps the most important reason why job specialization has not been as successful as expected is that it ignores the motivational potential of jobs. As jobs become specialized, the work tends to become easier to perform but less motivating. As jobs become more complex, work motivation increases but the ability to master the job decreases. Maximum job performance occurs somewhere between these two extremes, where most people can eventually perform the job tasks efficiently, yet the work is interesting.

scientific management

Involves systematically partitioning work into its smallest elements and standardizing tasks to achieve maximum efficiency.

Job Design and Work Motivation

Industrial engineers may have overlooked the motivational effect of job characteristics, but it is now the central focus of many job design changes. Organizational behavior scholar Frederick Herzberg is credited with shifting the spotlight when he introduced **motivator-hygiene theory.**[51] Motivator-hygiene theory proposes that employees experience job satisfaction when they fulfill growth and esteem needs (called *motivators*), and they experience dissatisfaction when they have poor working conditions, job security, and other factors related lower order needs (called *hygienes*). Herzberg argued that only characteristics of the job itself will motivate employees, whereas the hygiene factors merely prevent dissatisfaction. It might seem rather obvious to us today that the job itself is a source of motivation, but it was radical thinking when Herzberg proposed the idea in the 1950s.

Motivator-hygiene theory didn't find much research support, but Herzberg's ideas generated new thinking about the motivational potential of the job itself.[52] Out of subsequent research emerged the **job characteristics model,** shown in Exhibit 6.3.[53] The job characteristics model identifies five core job dimensions that produce three psychological states. Employees who experi-

EXHIBIT 6.3

The job characteristics model

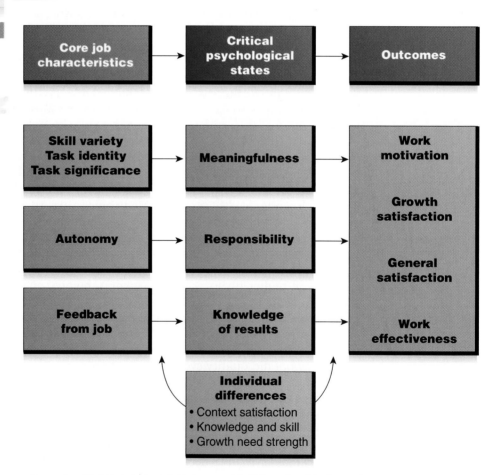

Source: From *Work Redesign* by J. R. Hackman and G. Oldham. Copyright © 1980 Pearson Education, Inc. Reprinted by permission of Pearson Education, Inc., Upper Saddle River, NJ.

skill variety
The extent to which employees must use different skills and talents to perform tasks within their job.

ence these psychological states tend to have higher levels of internal work motivation (motivation from the work itself), job satisfaction (particularly satisfaction with the work itself), and work effectiveness.

Core Job Characteristics   The job characteristics model identifies five core job characteristics (see Exhibit 6.3). Under the right conditions, employees are more motivated and satisfied when jobs have higher levels of these characteristics.

task identity
The degree to which a job requires completion of a whole or an identifiable piece of work.

■ *Skill variety*—**Skill variety** refers to the use of different skills and talents to complete a variety of work activities. For example, sales clerks who normally only serve customers might be assigned the additional duties of stocking inventory and changing storefront displays.

■ *Task identity*—**Task identity** is the degree to which a job requires completion of a whole or identifiable piece of work, such as doing something from beginning to end, or where the way one's work fits into the whole product or service is easy to see. An employee who assembles an entire computer modem rather than just soldering in the circuitry would develop a stronger sense of ownership or identity with the final product.

■ *Task significance*—**Task significance** is the degree to which the job has a substantial impact on the organization and/or larger society. For instance, Medtronic executives realize that many of their employees have low skill variety, so they have special sessions where patients give testimonials to remind staff of their task significance. "We have patients who come in who would be dead if it wasn't for us," says a Medtronic production supervisor. Little wonder that 86 percent of Medtronic employees say their work has special meaning and 94 percent feel pride in what they accomplish.[54]

■ *Autonomy*—Jobs with high levels of **autonomy** provide freedom, independence, and discretion in scheduling the work and determining the procedures to be used to complete the work. In autonomous jobs, employees make their own decisions rather than relying on detailed instructions from supervisors or procedure manuals.

■ *Job feedback*—**Job feedback** is the degree to which employees can tell how well they are doing based on direct sensory information from the job itself. Airline pilots can tell how well they land their aircraft and physicians can see whether their operations have improved the patient's health. Some research suggests that job feedback has an important effect on reducing role ambiguity and improving job satisfaction.[55]

Jousting and winemaking don't usually occur in the same place, but that doesn't stop Mike Just from practicing both crafts. The New Zealander apprenticed in Germany, where he learned the fine art of winemaking and the thrill of wearing his own set of armor at festivals in the old German castles. When not wielding his sword, Just enjoys being involved in the entire winemaking process at Lawson's Dry Hills Winery in New Zealand. "What I really like about this job is that you can start with a raw product and carry it right through to marketing the finished product, all on one site," Just explains. "We plant vines here, we pick them, we make the wine on site and bottle it, then sell them to customers who come in."[56] Based on the job characteristics model, why is Mike Just highly motivated by his work?

task significance
The degree to which
the job has a
substantial impact on
the organization
and/or larger society.

Critical Psychological States   The five core job characteristics affect employee motivation and satisfaction through three critical psychological states.[57] One of these is *experienced meaningfulness*—the belief that one's work is worthwhile or important. Skill variety, task identity, and task significance directly contribute to the job's meaningfulness. If the job has high levels of all three characteristics, employees are likely to feel that their job is highly meaningful. Meaningfulness drops as the job loses one or more of these characteristics.

Work motivation and performance increase when employees feel personally accountable for the outcomes of their efforts. Autonomy directly contributes to this feeling of *experienced responsibility*. Employees must be assigned control of their work environment to feel responsible for their successes and failures. The third critical psychological state is *knowledge of results*. Employees want information about the consequences of their work effort. Knowledge of results can originate from co-workers, supervisors, or clients. However, job design focuses on knowledge of results from the work itself.

autonomy
The degree to which a
job gives employees
the freedom,
independence, and
discretion to schedule
their work and
determine the
procedures used in
completing it.

Individual Differences   Job design doesn't increase work motivation for everyone in every situation. Employees must have the required skills and knowledge to master the more challenging work. Otherwise, job design tends to increase stress and reduce job performance. A second condition is that employees must be reasonably satisfied with their work environment (e.g., working conditions, job security, salaries) before job design affects work motivation. A third condition is that employees must have strong growth needs, since improving the core job characteristics will have little motivational effect on people who are primarily focused on existence or relatedness needs.[58]

job feedback
The degree to which
employees can tell
how well they are
doing based on direct
sensory information
from the job itself.

Increasing Work Motivation Through Job Design

Three main strategies potentially increase the motivational potential of jobs: job rotation, job enlargement, and job enrichment. This section also identifies several ways to implement job enrichment.

Job Rotation   **Job rotation** is the practice of moving employees from one job to another. Consider a large "one-hour" photo finishing retail outlet where one employee interacts with customers, another operates the photo finishing machine, and a third puts the finished product into envelopes and files them for pickup. Job rotation would call for employees to move around those three jobs every few hours or days.

job rotation
The practice of
moving employees
from one job to
another.

Moving employees around different jobs might reduce job boredom, but most organizations introduce job design mainly to develop a flexible workforce. Rotation helps employees become multiskilled, so they can fluidly shift work duties based on needs and demands. For instance, faced with cutbacks and increased workloads, Ryerson University librarians reorganized themselves from specialist to more generic jobs and rotated through four work areas.[59] A third reason for introducing job rotation is to reduce the incidence of repetitive strain injuries. Carrier Corporation uses job rotation for this reason. The air-conditioning manufacturer identified complementary jobs so employees move around to different jobs to use different muscles, thereby reducing strain on one muscle.[60]

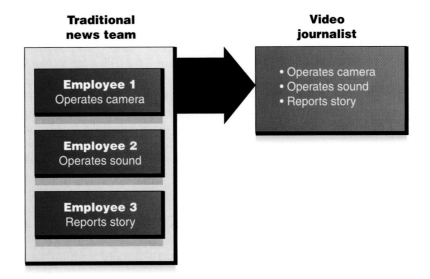

EXHIBIT 6.4

Job enlargement of video journalists

job enlargement
Increasing the number of tasks employees perform within their job.

Job Enlargement   Rather than rotating employees through different jobs, **job enlargement** combines tasks into one job. This might involve combining two or more complete jobs into one, or just adding one or two more tasks to an existing job. Either way, the job's skill variety has increased because there are more tasks to perform. For example, WestJet flight attendants have enlarged jobs because they perform a variety of tasks rather than the more narrowly defined job duties of their counterparts at the major airlines.

A recent example of job enlargement is video journalists. As Exhibit 6.4 illustrates, a traditional news team consists of a camera operator, a sound and lighting specialist, and the journalist who writes and presents or narrates the story. Now, CNN and other television networks want one video journalist to perform all of these jobs. "Look for the quick introduction of small, high quality DV cameras and laptop editing equipment, enabling us to deploy smaller reporting teams, one or two people at a time, when it makes sense," said CNN executives a few years ago in a memo to employees. "Correspondents would do well to learn how to shoot and edit . . . and smart shooters and editors will learn how to write and track." The memo also said that "CNN will always value exceptional ability, [but] the more multi-talented a newsgatherer, the more opportunity the News Group will provide that person."[61]

Job enlargement significantly improves work efficiency and flexibility. However, research suggests that simply giving employees more tasks won't affect motivation, performance, or job satisfaction. Instead, these benefits result only when skill variety is combined with more autonomy and job knowledge.[62] In other words, employees are motivated when they have a variety of tasks *and* have the freedom *and* knowledge to structure their work to achieve the highest satisfaction and performance. These job characteristics are at the heart of job enrichment.

job enrichment
Giving employees more responsibility for scheduling, coordinating, and planning their own work.

Job Enrichment   **Job enrichment** occurs when employees are given more responsibility for scheduling, coordinating, and planning their own work. Although some writers suggest that job enrichment is any strategy that increases one or more of the core job characteristics, others strongly argue that jobs are enriched only through autonomy and the resulting feelings of responsibility.[63] Two ways to enrich jobs are clustering tasks into natural groups and establishing client relationships.

Clustering tasks into natural groups stitches highly interdependent tasks into one job—for example, assembling an entire computer modem rather than just some parts of it. The video journalist job was described earlier as job enlargement because it combines several tasks. However, it is also an example of job enrichment because video journalism naturally groups tasks together to complete an entire product (i.e., a news clip). By forming natural work units, jobholders have stronger feelings of responsibility for an identifiable body of work. They feel a sense of ownership and, therefore, tend to increase job quality. Forming natural work units increases task identity and task significance because employees perform a complete product or service and can more readily see how their work affects others.

A second job enrichment strategy, called establishing client relationships, involves putting employees in *direct contact* with their clients rather than using the supervisor as a go-between. The key factor is direct communication with clients. These clients submit work and provide feedback directly to the employee rather than through a supervisor. By being directly responsible for specific clients, employees have more information and can make decisions affecting those clients.[64]

Establishing client relationships also increases task significance because employees see a line-of-sight connection between their work and consequences for customers. This was apparent among medical secretaries at a large regional hospital in Sweden after the hospital reduced its workforce by 10 percent and gave the secretaries expanded job duties. Although these employees experienced more stress from the higher workloads, some of them also felt more motivated and satisfied because they now had direct interaction with patients through shared receptionist duties. "Before, I never saw a patient; now they have a face," says one medical secretary. "I feel I have been useful when I go home. I'm tired, but at the same time I feel satisfied and pleased with myself; you feel someone needs you."[65]

Research suggests that establishing client relationships, forming natural groups, and other job enrichment interventions are generally effective. In particular, employees with high growth needs in enriched jobs have higher job satisfaction and work motivation, along with lower absenteeism and turnover. Productivity is also higher when task identity and job feedback are improved. Product and service quality tend to improve because job enrichment increases the jobholder's felt responsibility and sense of ownership over the product or service. Quality improvements are most apparent when employees complete a natural work unit or establish client relationships.[66]

Forming natural task groups and establishing client relationships are common ways to enrich jobs, but the heart of the job enrichment philosophy is to give employees more autonomy over their work. This basic idea is at the core of one of the most widely mentioned—and often misunderstood—practices, known as empowerment.

Empowerment Practices

When Clive Beddoe cofounded WestJet Airlines, he wanted to create an organization where employees had the freedom to serve customers rather than follow strict rules. Beddoe explains that most other airlines in the world have a military mindset. "You see it even in their flight uniforms and the autocratic way their companies behave," Beddoe points out. "Manuals and polices have to be followed exactly and, while that's necessary in the cockpit, it's not the best way when it comes to customer service." Beddoe emphasizes that WestJet is the opposite. "Here, we empower our employees and encourage them to be free-thinking and to do whatever it takes in whatever way they feel it's appropriate to solve customer problems."[67]

WestJet creates a work environment that makes employees feel empowered. **Empowerment** is a term that has been loosely tossed around in corporate circles and has been the subject of considerable debate among academics. However, the most widely accepted definition is that empowerment is a psychological concept represented by four dimensions: self-determination, meaning, competence, and impact of the individual's role in the organization.[68]

empowerment

A psychological concept in which people experience more self-determination, meaning, competence, and impact regarding their role in the organization.

- *Self-determination*—Empowered employees experience self-determination, which consists of freedom, independence, and discretion over their work activities.
- *Meaning*—Employees who feel empowered care about their work and believe that what they do is important.
- *Competence*—Empowered people have feelings of self-efficacy, meaning that they are confident about their ability to perform the work well and have a capacity to grow with new challenges.
- *Impact*—Empowered employees view themselves as active participants in the organization; that is, their decisions and actions have an influence on the company's success.

Empowerment consists of all four dimensions. If any dimension weakens, the employee's sense of empowerment will weaken.

From this definition, you can see that empowerment is not a personality trait, although personality might influence the extent to which someone feels empowered. People also experience degrees of empowerment, which can vary from one work environment to the next. One company that sets the standard for extreme empowerment is Semco Corporation, SA. Global Connections 6.3 describes how the Brazilian conglomerate has become world famous for giving employees complete freedom, even if their actions overrule managers and company owner Ricardo Semler.

Creating Empowerment

Chances are that you have heard corporate leaders say they are "empowering" the workforce. What these executives really mean is that they are changing the work environment to support empowerment.[69] Numerous individual, job design, and organizational factors support empowerment. At the individual level, employees must possess the necessary competencies to be able to perform the work as well as handle the additional decision-making requirements.

The Empowerment of Semco

Most executives like to say they empower their workforce, but few come close to the work arrangements at Semco Corporation, SA. "Can an organization let people do what they want, when they want and how they want?" asks Ricardo Semler, who took over his father's marine pump business in São Paulo, Brazil, 20 years ago. The answer appears to be "Yes." Today, Semco pushes the limits of empowèrment at its dozen businesses—high-tech mixing equipment, inventory control, environmental resources management, to name a few—with 3,000 employees and $160 million revenue.

Organized into small groups of 6 to 10 people, Semco employees choose their objectives every six months, hire their co-workers, work out their budgets, set their own salaries, decide when to come to work, and even elect their own bosses. Semco factory workers have chosen future factory sites management didn't like. At the head office, Semler installed hammocks so employees can snooze whenever they want.

The success of Semco's approach to empowerment was recently demonstrated when Carrefour, the French supermarket chain, hired Semco to take inventory at its 42 Brazilian hypermarkets on June 30. The assignment required 1,000 workers in 20 cities on the same day, a major challenge for any firm. Unfortunately, June 30 also turned out to be the day that Brazil played in the World Cup soccer finals. If Brazil won the game (which it did), employers could count on losing 40 percent of their employees to street celebrations. Semco managers asked employees to figure out among themselves how to work out this dilemma, which they did. Semco completed the task on time. In fact, Brazil's second largest supermarket chain asked Semco a week later to take inventory because the competitor hired for the job didn't have enough staff show up to count inventory during the World Cup final.

Semco may have radical empowerment, but Semler says that the company is "only 50 or 60 per cent where we'd like to be." Semler believes that replacing the head office with several satellite offices around São Paulo would give employees even

Ricardo Semler, shown here with staff in hammocks at head office, has taken empowerment to the extreme at Brazilian conglomerate Semco Corporation.

more opportunity for empowerment. "'If you don't even know where people are, you can't possibly keep an eye on them," Semler explains. "All that's left to judge on is performance."

Sources: S. Caulkin, "Who's in Charge Here?" *The Observer* (London), April 27, 2003, p. 9; S. Moss, "Portrait: 'Idleness Is Good,'" *The Guardian* (London), April 17, 2003, p. 8; D. Gardner, "A Boss Who's Crazy about His Workers," *Sunday Herald* (Scotland), April 13, 2003, p. 6; R. Semler, *The Seven-Day Weekend* (London: Century, 2003), Part 4, Chapter 1.

While other individual factors have been proposed (e.g., locus of control), they do not seem to have any real effect on whether employees feel empowered.[70]

Job characteristics clearly influence the dynamics of empowerment.[71] To generate beliefs about self-determination, employees must work in jobs with a high degree of autonomy with minimal bureaucratic control. To maintain a sense of meaningfulness, jobs must have high levels of task identity and task significance. And to maintain a sense of self-confidence, jobs must provide sufficient feedback.

Organizational factors also influence empowerment beliefs. Employees experience more empowerment in organizations where information and other resources are easily accessible. Empowerment also requires a learning orientation culture. In other words, empowerment flourishes in organizations that appreciate the value of the employee learning and that accept reasonable mistakes as a natural part of the learning process. Last, empowerment requires corporate leaders who trust employees and are willing to take the risks that empowerment creates. "Executives must give up control and trust the power of talent," advises Ricardo Semler, head of Semco Corporation in São Paulo, Brazil.[72]

With the right individuals, job characteristics, and organizational environment in place, empowerment can have a noticeable effect on motivation and performance. For instance, a study of bank employees concluded that empowerment improved customer service and tended to reduce conflict between employees and their supervisors. A study of nurses reported that empowerment is associated with higher trust in management, which ultimately influences job satisfaction, belief and acceptance of organizational goals and values, and effective organizational commitment.[73] Empowerment allows employees to apply their knowledge directly and with more responsiveness to problems and opportunities. It also tends to increase personal initiative because employees identify with and assume more psychological ownership of their work.

Practicing Self-Leadership

self-leadership
The process of influencing oneself to establish the self-direction and self-motivation needed to perform a task.

WestJet Airlines has been mentioned several times throughout this chapter because the company illustrates how to improve employee performance through rewards, job design, and empowerment practices. WestJet is also a symbol for another increasingly important applied performance practice, called **self-leadership.** "What occurred to me," says WestJet CEO Clive Beddoe, "is we had to overcome the inherent difficulty of trying to manage people and to hone the process into one where people wanted to manage themselves."[74]

Clive Beddoe recognizes that WestJet's success depends on employees who motivate themselves and direct their own behavior most of the time. Indeed, corporate leaders identify self-motivation as one of the most important features to look for when hiring.[75] Self-leadership refers to the process of influencing oneself to establish the self-direction and self-motivation needed to perform a task.[76] This concept includes a toolkit of behavioral activities borrowed from social learning theory (Chapter 3) and goal setting (Chapter 5). It also includes constructive thought processes that have been extensively studied in sports psychology. Overall, self-leadership takes the view that individuals mostly regulate their own actions through these behavioral and cognitive (thought) activities.

Although we are in the early stages of understanding the dynamics of self-leadership, Exhibit 6.5 identifies the five main elements of this process. These elements, which generally follow each other in a sequence, are personal goal

EXHIBIT 6.5   Elements of self-leadership

Sirius Consulting Group has been growing by leaps and bounds because it picks employees who apply self-leadership practices. "Here, you manage your own workload, set deadlines and project plans," says Siobhan MacDonald, senior account manager at the firm which matches 4,000 independent IT professionals to clients. Sirius account managers (three of whom are shown in the photo) are responsible for filing a monthly sales report and attending a brief weekly meeting, but otherwise they set their own hours. The proof of this self-leadership is in the six-figure paychecks that many account managers earn. "If you're self-motivated and a hard worker, there's no ceiling on what you can produce," MacDonald advises.[79] Along with self-set goals, what other self-leadership practices would improve the job performance of account managers?

setting, constructive thought patterns, designing natural rewards, self-monitoring, and self-reinforcement.[77]

Personal Goal Setting

The first step in self-leadership is to set goals for your own work effort. This applies the ideas we learned in Chapter 5 on goal setting, such as identifying goals that are specific, relevant, and challenging. The main difference between personal goal setting and our previous discussion is that goals are set alone, rather than assigned by or jointly decided with a supervisor. One recent study found that employees are more focused when they set their own goals. Other research reports that students who rely on personal goal setting use more effective and sophisticated learning strategies and develop stronger feelings of self-efficacy.[78]

Constructive Thought Patterns

Before beginning a task and while performing it, employees should engage in positive (constructive) thoughts about that work and its accomplishment. In particular, employees are more motivated and better prepared to accomplish a task after they have engaged in positive self-talk and mental imagery.

self-talk
Talking to ourselves about our own thoughts or actions for the purpose of increasing our self-efficacy and navigating through decisions in a future event.

Positive Self-Talk   Do you ever talk to yourself? Most of us do, according to several studies.[80] **Self-talk** refers to any situation in which we talk to ourselves about our own thoughts or actions. Some of this internal communication assists the decision-making process, such as weighing the advantages of a particular choice. Self-leadership is mostly interested in evaluative self-talk, in which you evaluate your capabilities and accomplishments.

The problem is that most evaluative self-talk is negative; we criticize much more than encourage or congratulate ourselves. Negative self-talk undermines our self-efficacy, which then undermines our potential for performing a particular task.[81] In contrast, positive self-talk creates a "can-do" belief and thereby increases motivation by raising our E→P expectancy. We often hear that professional athletes "psyche" themselves up before an important event. They tell themselves that they can achieve their goal and that they have practiced enough to reach that goal. They are motivating themselves through self-talk.

mental imagery
Mentally practicing a task and visualizing its successful completion.

Mental Imagery   You've probably heard the phrase "I'll cross that bridge when I come to it!" Self-leadership takes the opposite view. It suggests that we need to mentally practice a task and imagine successfully performing it beforehand. This process is known as **mental imagery**.[82] As you can see from this definition, mental imagery has two parts. One part involves mentally practicing the task, anticipating obstacles to goal accomplishment, and working out solutions to those obstacles before they occur. By mentally walking through the activities required to accomplish the task, we begin to see problems that may occur. We can then imagine what responses would be best for each contingency.[83]

While one part of mental imagery helps us to anticipate things that could go wrong, the other part involves visualizing successful completion of the task. We imagine the experience of completing the task and the positive results that follow. Everyone daydreams and fantasizes about being in a successful situation. You might imagine yourself being promoted to your boss's job, receiving a prestigious award, or taking time off work. This visualization increases goal commitment and motivates us to complete the task effectively.

Designing Natural Rewards

Self-leadership recognizes that employees actively craft their jobs. To varying degrees, they can alter tasks and work relationships to make the work more motivating.[84] One way to build natural rewards into the job is to alter the way a task is accomplished. People often have enough discretion in their jobs to make slight changes to suit their needs and preferences. For instance, you might try out a new software program to design an idea, rather than sketch the image with pencil. By using the new software, you are adding challenge to a task that may have otherwise been mundane.

Self-Monitoring

Self-monitoring is the process of keeping track of one's progress toward a goal. In the section on job design, we learned that feedback from the job itself communicates whether we are accomplishing the task successfully. Self-monitoring includes the notion of consciously checking that naturally occurring feedback at regular intervals. It also includes designing artificial feedback where natural feedback does not occur. Salespeople might arrange to receive monthly reports on sales levels in their territory. Production staff might have gauges or computer feedback systems installed so they can see how many errors are made on the production line. Research suggests that people who have control over the timing of performance feedback perform their tasks better than those with feedback assigned by others.[85]

Self-Reinforcement

Self-leadership includes the social learning theory concept of self-reinforcement. Self-reinforcement occurs whenever an employee has control over a reinforcer but doesn't "take" the reinforcer until completing a self-set goal (see Chapter 3).[86] A common example is taking a break after reaching a predetermined stage of your work. The work break is a self-induced form of positive reinforcement. Self-reinforcement also occurs when you decide to do a more enjoyable task after completing a task that you dislike. For example, after slogging through a difficult report, you might decide to spend time doing a more pleasant task, such as catching up on industry news by scanning websites.

Self-Leadership in Practice

It's too early to say that every component of self-leadership is useful, but evidence suggests that these practices generally improve self-efficacy, motivation, and performance. Studies in sports psychology indicate that self-set goals and constructive thought processes improve individual performance. For example, young ice skaters who received self-talk training improved their performance one year later. Self-talk and mental imagery have also improved performance of tennis players and female college swimmers. Indeed, studies show that almost all Olympic athletes rely on mental rehearsal and positive self-talk to achieve their performance goals.[87]

One study reported that new employees who practiced self-set goals and self-reinforcement had higher internal motivation. Another study found that airline employees who received constructive thought training experienced better mental performance, enthusiasm, and job satisfaction than co-workers who did not receive this training. A third study found that mental imagery helped supervisors and process engineers in a pulp and paper mill to transfer what they learned in an interpersonal communication skills class back to the job.[88]

People with a high degree of conscientiousness and internal locus of control are more likely to apply self-leadership strategies. However, one of the benefits of self-leadership is that it can be learned. Training programs have helped employees to improve their self-leadership skills. Organizations can also encourage self-leadership by providing sufficient autonomy and establishing rewards that reinforce self-leadership behaviors. Employees are also more likely to engage in self-monitoring in companies that emphasize continuous measurement of performance.[89] Overall, self-leadership promises to be an important concept and practice for improving employee motivation and performance.

Self-leadership, job design, empowerment, and rewards are valuable approaches to improving employee performance. However, performance is also affected by work-related stress. As we learn in the next chapter, too much stress is causing numerous problems with employee performance and well-being, but there are also ways to combat this epidemic.

Chapter Summary

Money and other financial rewards are a fundamental part of the employment relationship. They potentially fulfill existence, relatedness, and growth needs. Money generates emotions and attitudes which vary across cultures. People (particularly men) also tend to identify themselves in terms of their wealth.

Organizations reward employees for their membership and seniority, job status, competencies, and performance. Membership-based rewards may attract job applicants and seniority-based rewards reduce turnover, but these reward objectives tend to discourage turnover among those with the lowest performance. Rewards based on job status try to maintain internal equity and motivate employees to compete for promotions. However, job status–based rewards are inconsistent with market-responsiveness, encourage employees to compete with each other, and can lead to organizational politics. Competency-based rewards are becoming increasingly popular be-

cause they improve workforce flexibility and are consistent with the emerging idea of employability. But competency-based rewards tend to be subjectively measured and can result in higher costs as employees spend more time learning new skills.

Awards/bonuses, commissions, and other individual performance-based rewards have existed for centuries and are widely used. Many companies are shifting to team-based rewards such as gainsharing plans and to organizational rewards such as employee stock ownership plans (ESOPs), stock options, profit sharing, and balanced scorecards. ESOPs and stock options create an ownership culture, but employees often perceive a weak connection between individual performance and the organizational reward.

Financial rewards have a number of limitations, but reward effectiveness can be improved in several ways. Organizational leaders should ensure that rewards are linked to work performance, rewards are aligned with performance within the employee's control, team rewards are used where jobs are interdependent, rewards are valued by employees, and rewards have no unintended consequences.

Job design refers to the process of assigning tasks to a job, including the interdependency of those tasks with other jobs. Job specialization subdivides work into separate jobs for different people. This increases work efficiency because employees master the tasks quickly, spend less time changing tasks, require less training, and can be matched more closely with the jobs best suited to their skills. However, job specialization may reduce work motivation, create mental health problems, lower product or service quality, and increase costs through discontentment, absenteeism, and turnover.

Contemporary job design strategies reverse job specialization through job rotation, job enlargement, and job enrichment. The job characteristics model is a template for job redesign that specifies core job dimensions, psychological states, and individual differences. Organizations introduce job rotation to reduce job boredom, develop a more flexible workforce, and reduce the incidence of repetitive strain injuries. Two ways to enrich jobs are clustering tasks into natural groups and establishing client relationships.

Empowerment is a psychological concept represented by four dimensions: self-determination, meaning, competence, and impact regarding the individual's role in the organization. Individual characteristics seem to have a minor influence on empowerment. Job design is a major influence, particularly autonomy, task identity, task significance, and job feedback. Empowerment is also supported at the organizational level through a learning orientation culture, sufficient information and resources, and corporate leaders who trust employees.

Self-leadership is the process of influencing oneself to establish the self-direction and self-motivation needed to perform a task. This includes personal goal setting, constructive thought patterns, designing natural rewards, self-monitoring, and self-reinforcement. Constructive thought patterns include self-talk and mental imagery. Self-talk refers to any situation in which a person talks to himself or herself about his or her own thoughts or actions. Mental imagery involves mentally practicing a task and imagining successfully performing it beforehand.

Key Terms

autonomy, p. 187
balanced scorecard, p. 180
employee stock ownership plan (ESOP), p. 179
empowerment, p. 191
gainsharing plan, p. 179
job characteristics model, p. 186
job design, p. 184
job enlargement, p. 189
job enrichment, p. 189
job evaluation, p. 176
job feedback, p. 187
job rotation, p. 188

job specialization, p. 184
mental imagery, p. 194
motivator-hygiene theory, p. 186
open-book management, p. 179
profit-sharing plans, p. 179
scientific management, p. 185
self-leadership, p. 193
self-talk, p. 194
skill variety, p. 187
stock options, p. 179
task identity, p. 187
task significance, p. 187

Discussion Questions

1. As a consultant, you have been asked to recommend either a gainsharing plan or a profit-sharing plan for employees who work in the four regional distribution and warehousing facilities of a large retail organization. Which reward system would you recommend? Explain your answer.
2. You are a member of a team responsible for developing performance measures for your college or university department or faculty unit based on the balanced scorecard approach. Identify one performance measurement for each of the following factors: financial, customer, internal processes, and employee.
3. Alaskan Tire Corporation redesigned its production facilities around a team-based system. However, the company president believes that

employees will not be motivated unless they receive incentives based on their individual performance. Give three explanations why Alaskan Tire should introduce team-based rather than individual rewards in this setting.

4. What can organizations do to increase the effectiveness of financial rewards?

5. Most of us have watched pizzas being made while waiting in a pizzeria. What level of job specialization do you usually notice in these operations? Why does this high or low level of specialization exist? If some pizzerias have different levels of specialization than others, identify the contingencies that might explain these differences.

6. Can a manager or supervisor "empower" an employee? Discuss fully.

7. Describe a time when you practiced self-leadership to successfully perform a task. With reference to each step in the self-leadership process, describe what you did to achieve this success.

8. Can self-leadership replace formal leadership in an organizational setting?

CASE STUDY 6.1

THE REGENCY GRAND HOTEL

By Lisa Ho, under the supervision of Steven L. McShane

The Regency Grand Hotel is a five-star hotel in Bangkok, Thailand. The hotel was established 15 years ago by a local consortium of investors and was operated by a Thai general manager from its opening. The hotel is one of Bangkok's most prestigious hotels and its 700 employees enjoyed the prestige being associated with the hotel. The hotel provides good welfare benefits, above-market-rate salary, and job security. In addition, a good year-end bonus amounting to four months' salary is rewarded to employees regardless of the hotel's overall performance during the year.

Recently, the Regency was sold to a large American hotel chain that was very keen to expand its operations into Thailand. Following the acquisition announcement, the general manager decided to take early retirement when the hotel changed ownership. The American hotel chain kept all of the Regency employees, although a few were transferred to other positions. John Becker, an American with 10 years of management experience with the hotel chain, was appointed the new general manager of Regency Grand Hotel, largely because of his previous successes in integrating newly acquired hotels in the United States. In most of the previous acquisitions, Becker took over operations with poor profitability and low morale.

Becker is a strong believer in empowerment. He expects employees to go beyond guidelines/standards to consider guests' needs on a case-by-case basis. That is, employees must be guest-oriented at all times to provide excellent customer service. In his U.S. experience, Becker found that empowerment increases employee motivation, performance, and job satisfaction, all of which contribute to the hotel's profitability and customer service ratings. Soon after becoming general manager of the Regency Grand, Becker introduced the practice of empowerment, hoping to replicate the successes that he had achieved back home.

The Regency Grand Hotel had been very profitable from its opening 15 years ago. The employees always worked according to management's instructions. Their responsibility was to ensure that the instructions from their managers were carried out diligently and conscientiously. Innovation and creativity were discouraged under the previous management. Indeed, employees were punished for their mistakes and discouraged from trying out ideas that had not been approved by management. As a result, employees were afraid to be innovative and to take risks.

Becker met with the Regent's managers and department heads to explain that empowerment would be introduced in the hotel. He told them that employees must be empowered with decision-making authority so that they could use their initiative, creativity, and judgment to satisfy guest needs or handle problems effectively and efficiently. However, he stressed that the more complex issues and decisions were to be referred to superiors, who were to coach and assist rather than provide direct orders. Furthermore, Becker stressed that mistakes were allowed, but the same mistakes made more than twice would not be tolerated. He advised his managers and department heads not to discuss with him minor issues or problems and not to consult with him on minor decisions. Nevertheless, he told them that they were to discuss important or major issues and decisions with him. He concluded the meeting by asking for feedback. Several managers and department heads told him that they liked the idea and would support it, while others simply nodded their heads. Becker was pleased with the response and eager to have his plan implemented.

In the past, the Regency had emphasized administrative control, resulting in many bureaucratic procedures throughout the organization. For example, the front counter employees needed to seek approval from their manager before they could upgrade guests to another category of room. The front counter manager would then have to write and submit a report to the general manager justifying the upgrade. Soon after his meeting with managers, Becker reduced the number of bureaucratic rules at the Regency and allocated more decision-making authority to front-line employees. This action upset those who previously had decision-making power over these issues. As a result, several of these employees left the hotel.

Becker also began spending a large portion of his time observing and interacting with the employees at the front desk, lobby, restaurants, and various departments. This direct interaction with Becker helped many employees to understand what he wanted and expected of them. However, the employees had great difficulty trying to distinguish between a major and minor issue/decision. More often than not, supervisors would reverse employee decisions by stating that they were major issues requiring management approval. Employees who displayed initiative and made good decisions in satisfying the needs of guests rarely received any positive feedback from their supervisors. Eventually, most of these employees lost confidence in making decisions and reverted back to relying on their superiors for decision making.

Not long after the implementation of the practice of empowerment, Becker realized that his subordinates were consulting him more frequently than before. Most of them came to him with minor issues and consulted with him on minor decisions. He had to spend most of his time attending to his subordinates. Soon he began to feel highly frustrated and exhausted, and very often he would tell his secretary that "unless the hotel is on fire, don't let anyone disturb me."

Becker thought that the practice of empowerment would benefit the overall performance of the hotel. However, contrary to his expectation, the business and overall performance of the hotel began to deteriorate. The number of guest complaints, which had been minimal in the past, began increasing. Now a significant number of formal written complaints are filed every month, and many guests voice their dissatisfaction directly to hotel employees. The number of mistakes made by employees also began increasing. Becker was very upset when he realized that two of the local newspapers and an overseas newspaper had published negative feedback on the hotel in terms of service standards. He was most distressed when an international travel magazine voted the hotel "one of Asia's nightmare hotels."

The stress levels of the employees were continuously mounting since the introduction of the practice of empowerment. Absenteeism due to illness was increasing at an alarming rate. In addition, the employee turnover rate had reached an all-time high. The good working relationships that were established under the old management had been severely strained. The employees were no longer united and supportive of each other. They were quick to "point fingers at" or to "backstab" one another when mistakes were made and when problems occurred.

Discussion Questions

1. Identify the symptoms indicating that problems exist in this case.

2. Diagnose the problems in this case using organizational behavior concepts.

3. Recommend solutions that overcome or minimize the problems and symptoms in this case.

Note: This case is based on true events, but the industry and names have been changed.

NOW IT'S GETTING PERSONAL

BusinessWeek During this era of retrenchment and restructuring, executives are turning to statistical modeling technology to help them figure out exactly which compensation practices have the greatest impact on employee productivity and retention. Computer programs grind through workforce demographic data, looking to see if specific benefits, training programs, and incentives make any difference and, if so, to which employees. This analysis contrasts with earlier approaches that identify desirable compensation practices by finding out what the best firms do.

This *Business Week* case study looks at the new approach to estimating the value of reward systems. It illustrates some of the benefits of analyzing the return on investment of compensation practices, as well as some of the problems that some firms have experienced. Read through this *Business Week* article at www.mhhe.com/mcshane3e and prepare for the discussion questions below.

Discussion Questions

1. What is the main argument supporting the use of this new statistical approach to compensation management (called human capital management)?

2. This chapter discusses several ways to improve reward effectiveness. How does the statistical approach to compensation management relate to these recommendations?

3. Describe the main arguments against this approach to choosing employee rewards.

Source: Michelle Conlin, "Now It's Getting Personal," *Business Week,* December 16, 2002, p. 90.

IS STUDENT WORK ENRICHED?

Purpose This exercise is designed to help you to learn how to measure the motivational potential of jobs and to evaluate the extent that jobs should be further enriched.

Instructions Being a student is like a job in several ways. You have tasks to perform and someone (such as your instructor) oversees your work. Although few people want to be students most of their lives (the pay rate is too low!), it may be interesting to determine how enriched your job is as a student.

- *Step 1*—Students are placed into teams (preferably four or five people).
- *Step 2*—Working alone, each student completes both sets of measures in this exercise. Then, using the guidelines below, they individually calculate the score for the five core job characteristics as well as the overall motivating potential score for the job.
- *Step 3*—Members of each team compare their individual results. The group should identify differences of opinion for each core job characteristic. They should also note

which core job characteristics have the lowest scores and recommend how these scores could be increased.

■ *Step 4*—The entire class will now meet to discuss the results of the exercise. The instructor may ask some teams to present their comparisons and recommendations for a particular core job characteristic.

Job Diagnostic Survey

Circle the number on the right that best describes student work.	Very Little		Moderately			Very Much
1. To what extent does student work permit you to decide on your own how to go about doing the work?	1	2	3	4	5	6	7
2. To what extent does student work involve doing a whole or identifiable piece of work, rather than a small portion of the overall work process?	1	2	3	4	5	6	7
3. To what extent does student work require you to do many different things, using a variety of your skills/talents?	1	2	3	4	5	6	7
4. To what extent are the results of your work as a student likely to significantly affect the lives and well-being of other people (e.g., within your school, your family, society)?	1	2	3	4	5	6	7
5. To what extent does working on student activities provide information about your performance?	1	2	3	4	5	6	7

Circle the number on the right that best describes student work.	Very Inaccurate		Uncertain			Very Accurate
6. Being a student requires me to use a number of complex and high-level skills	1	2	3	4	5	6	7
7. Student work is arranged so that I do NOT have the chance to do an entire piece of work from beginning to end	7	6	5	4	3	2	1
8. Doing the work required of students provides many chances for me to figure out how well I am doing	1	2	3	4	5	6	7
9. The work students must do is quite simple and repetitive	7	6	5	4	3	2	1
10. The work of a student is one where a lot of other people can be affected by how well the work gets done	1	2	3	4	5	6	7
11. Student work denies me any chance to use my personal initiative or judgment in carrying out the work	7	6	5	4	3	2	1
12. Student work provides me the chance to completely finish the pieces of work I begin	1	2	3	4	5	6	7
13. Doing student work by itself provides very few clues about whether or not I am performing well	7	6	5	4	3	2	1
14. As a student, I have considerable opportunity for independence and freedom in how I do the work	1	2	3	4	5	6	7
15. The work I perform as a student is NOT very significant or important in the broader scheme of things	7	6	5	4	3	2	1

Adapted from the Job Diagnostic Survey, developed by J. R. Hackman and G. R. Oldham. The authors have released any copyright ownership of this scale (see J. R. Hackman and G. Oldham, *Work Redesign* (Reading, MA: Addison-Wesley, 1980), p. 275).

CALCULATING THE MOTIVATING POTENTIAL SCORE

Scoring Core Job Characteristics Use the following set of calculations to estimate the motivating potential score for the job of being a student. Use your answers from the Job Diagnostic Survey that you completed above.

Skill Variety (SV)

$$\frac{\text{Question } 3 + 6 + 9}{3} = \underline{\hspace{2cm}}$$

Task Identity (TI)

$$\frac{\text{Question } 2 + 7 + 12}{3} = \underline{\hspace{2cm}}$$

Task Significance (TS)

$$\frac{\text{Question } 4 + 10 + 15}{3} = \underline{\hspace{2cm}}$$

Autonomy

$$\frac{\text{Question } 1 + 11 + 14}{3} = \underline{\hspace{2cm}}$$

Job Feedback

$$\frac{\text{Question } 5 + 8 + 13}{3} = \underline{\hspace{2cm}}$$

Calculating Motivating Potential Score (MPS) Use the following formula and the results above to calculate the motivating potential score. Notice that skill variety, task identity, and task significance are averaged before being multiplied by the score for autonomy and job feedback.

$$\left(\frac{\text{SV} + \text{TI} + \text{TS}}{3}\right) \times \text{Autonomy} \times \text{Job Feedback}$$

$$\left(\frac{\underline{\hspace{0.8cm}} + \underline{\hspace{0.8cm}} + \underline{\hspace{0.8cm}}}{3}\right) + \underline{\hspace{0.8cm}} + \underline{\hspace{0.8cm}} = \underline{\hspace{0.8cm}}$$

ASSESSING YOUR SELF-LEADERSHIP

Purpose This exercise is designed to help you understand self-leadership concepts and to assess your self-leadership tendencies.

Instructions Indicate the extent to which each statement in this instrument describes you very well or does not describe you at all. Complete each item honestly to get the best estimate of your level of overall self-leadership as well as scores on each of the subscales.

STUDENT EMPOWERMENT SCALE

Purpose This exercise is designed to help you understand the dimensions of empowerment and to assess your level of empowerment as student.

Instructions Empowerment is a concept that applies to people in a variety of situations. This instrument is specifically adapted to your position as a student at this college or university. Indicate the extent to which you agree or disagree with each statement in this instrument, then request the results, which provide an overall score as well as scores on each of the four dimensions of empowerment. Complete each item honestly to get the best estimate of your level of empowerment.

WHAT IS YOUR ATTITUDE TOWARD MONEY?

Purpose This exercise is designed to help you to understand the types of attitudes toward money and to assess your attitude toward money.

Instructions Read each of the statements below and circle the response that you believe best reflects your position regarding each statement. Then use the scoring key in Appendix B to calculate your results. This exercise is completed alone so students assess themselves honestly without concerns of social comparison. However, class discussion will focus on the meaning of money, including the dimensions measured here and other aspects of money that may have an influence on behavior in the workplace.

Money Attitude Scale

To what extent do you agree or disagree that . . .	Strongly Agree	Agree	Neutral	Disagree	Strongly Disagree
1. I sometimes purchase things because I know they will impress other people.	5	4	3	2	1
2. I regularly put money aside for the future.	5	4	3	2	1
3. I tend to get worried about decisions involving money.	5	4	3	2	1
4. I believe that financial wealth is one of the most important signs of a person's success.	5	4	3	2	1
5. I keep a close watch on how much money I have.	5	4	3	2	1
6. I feel nervous when I don't have enough money.	5	4	3	2	1
7. I tend to show more respect to people who are wealthier than I am.	5	4	3	2	1
8. I follow a careful financial budget.	5	4	3	2	1
9. I worry about being financially secure.	5	4	3	2	1
10. I sometimes boast about my financial wealth or how much money I make.	5	4	3	2	1
11. I keep track of my investments and financial wealth.	5	4	3	2	1
12. I usually say "I can't afford it" even when I can afford something.	5	4	3	2	1

Sources: Adapted from J. A. Roberts and C. J. Sepulveda, "Demographics and Money Attitudes: A Test of Yamauchi and Templer's (1982) Money Attitude Scale in Mexico," *Personality and Individual Differences* 27 (July 1999), pp. 19–35; K. Yamauchi and D. Templer, "The Development of a Money Attitudes Scale," *Journal of Personality Assessment* 46 (1982), pp. 522–28.

After studying the preceding material, be sure to check out our website at

www.mhhe.com/mcshane3e

for more in-depth information and interactivities that correspond to this chapter.

chapter 7

Work-Related Stress and Stress Management

Learning Objectives

After reading this chapter, you should be able to:

■ Define stress and describe the stress experience.

■ Outline the stress process from stressors to consequences.

■ Identify the different types of stressors in the workplace.

■ Explain why a stressor might produce different stress levels in two people.

■ Discuss the physiological, psychological, and behavioral effects of stress.

■ Identify five ways to manage workplace stress.

Hong Kong physician Tom Buckley has faced many challenges, including treating victims of a devastating fire in 1996 and the bird flu outbreak in 1997. But neither of those events compared to the stress that Buckley and his colleagues experienced during the recent outbreak of atypical pneumonia, known as severe acute respiratory syndrome (SARS). "Having been through those two events, I thought it was probably impossible that there would be anything that would ever match them for stress and anxiety, but this SARS outbreak has put those into the background very much," says Buckley, who formed the SARS unit at Hong Kong's Prince of Wales Hospital and now leads the intensive care unit at Princess Margaret Hospital.

In less than five months, SARS infected 8,000 people worldwide and took the lives of more than 800 of them. The early weeks of the outbreak, centered around Hong Kong and mainland China, were particularly terrifying because no one knew how the virus spread or what medical interventions would work. Staff felt anxiety regarding their personal safety, particularly when colleagues became infected or they experienced high-risk incidents. Prince of Wales nurse Joanna Pong recalls one incident in which an elderly SARS patient suffering from dementia lowered her mask and coughed hard at Pong. "It was a scary feeling," says Pong, who fortunately did not catch the disease.

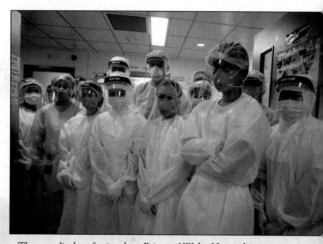

These medical professionals at Prince of Wales Hospital in Hong Kong were on the frontline treating patients with the SARS virus, which claimed more than 800 lives and created high stress levels among nurses and doctors.

Intensive care units were quickly filled beyond capacity with SARS patients. Nurses were exhausted by overwork and the challenges of wearing uncomfortable body suits, disposable surgical gowns, goggles, gloves, and tight-fitting masks throughout their shift. "Working with a mask on all day is incredibly exhausting," says Prince of Wales nurse Josephine Chung Yuen-man. "Some of my colleagues have lost a lot of weight due to all the stress."

For many medical staff, however, the greatest stress of the SARS epidemic was the isolation from loved ones. "I feel terribly lonely and cut off from other people," lamented Eric Wong, a Prince of Wales Hospital nurse in the SARS ward who spent most of his free time in the nursing quarters. "But I fear getting infected and spreading the virus on." During the epidemic, Wong avoided seeing friends and delayed his flight to New Zealand, where his wife and children live.[1] ∎

Medical staff working with SARS patients experienced high levels of stress due to concerns about personal safety, work overload, physical discomfort, heart-wrenching conflict between the needs of patients and family, and feelings of helplessness until appropriate medical treatment could be identified. But you don't have to work on the SARS ward of a hospital to experience work-related stress. According to a Gallup poll, 80 percent of Americans feel too much stress on the job; nearly half indicate that they need help coping with it. The American Institute of Stress estimates that work-related stress costs American businesses about $300 billion each year in lower productivity and higher absenteeism, turnover, alcoholism, and medical costs.[2]

Chronic work-related stress is not just an American affliction. Over half of call center staff in India feel so stressed out by the tough working conditions that they end up quitting. The Canadian Institute of Health Information reports that over one-quarter of employees in that country say they are suffering from "quite a lot" of stress. The Japanese government, which tracks job-related stress every five years, has found that the percentage of Japanese employees who feel "strong worry, anxiety or stress at work or in daily working life" has increased from 51 percent in 1982 to almost two-thirds of the population today. Nearly 20 percent of employees in the United Kingdom think their job is very or extremely stressful. In the most recent year, more than 6,000 U.K. firms paid an average of over U.S.$80,000 in stress-related damages to employees. "In human terms, depression, anxiety or a physical condition ascribed to work-related stress on average results in half a million people a year reporting stress at levels that [are] making them ill," warns U.K. Health and Safety Commission chairman Bill Callaghan.[3]

In this chapter, we look at the dynamics of work-related stress and how to manage it. The chapter begins by describing the stress experience. Next, the causes and consequences of stress are examined, along with the factors that cause some people to experience stress when others do not. The final section of this chapter looks at ways to manage work-related stress from either an organizational or individual perspective.

What Is Stress?

stress

An individual's adaptive response to a situation that is perceived as challenging or threatening to the person's well-being.

Stress is an adaptive response to a situation that is perceived as challenging or threatening to the person's well-being.[4] As we shall see, stress is the person's reaction to a situation, not the situation itself. Moreover, we experience stress when we believe that something interferes with our well-being, that is, with our innate drives and need fulfillment. Stress has both psychological and physiological dimensions. Psychologically, people perceive a situation and interpret it as challenging or threatening. This cognitive appraisal leads to a set of physiological responses, such as higher blood pressure, sweaty hands, and faster heartbeat.

We often hear about stress as a negative consequence of modern living. People are stressed from overwork, job insecurity, information overload, and the increasing pace of life. These events produce *distress*—the degree of physiological, psychological, and behavioral deviation from healthy functioning.[5] There is also a positive side of stress, called *eustress*, that refers to the healthy, positive, constructive outcome of stressful events and the stress response. Eustress is the stress experience in moderation, enough to activate and motivate people so that they can achieve goals, change their environments, and succeed in life's challenges.[6] In other words, we need some stress to survive. However, most research focuses on distress, because it is a significant concern in organizational settings. Employees frequently experience enough stress to hurt their job performance and increase their risk of mental and physical health problems. Consequently, our discussion will focus more on distress than on eustress.

General Adaptation Syndrome

general adaptation syndrome

A model of the stress experience, consisting of three stages: alarm reaction, resistance, and exhaustion.

The stress experience was first documented 50 years ago by Dr. Hans Selye, a pioneer in stress research.[7] Selye determined that people have a fairly consistent physiological response to stressful situations. This response, called the **general adaptation syndrome,** provides an automatic defense system to help us cope with environmental demands. Exhibit 7.1 illustrates the three stages of the general adaptation syndrome: alarm, resistance, and exhaustion. The line in this exhibit shows the individual's energy and ability to cope with the stressful situation.

Alarm Reaction   In the alarm reaction stage, the perception of a threatening or challenging situation causes the brain to send a biochemical message to various parts of the body, resulting in increased respiration rate, blood pressure, heartbeat, muscle tension, and other physiological responses. The individual's energy level and coping effectiveness decrease in response to the initial shock. Extreme shock, however, may result in incapacity or death because the body is unable to generate enough energy quickly enough. In most situations, the alarm reaction alerts the person to the environmental condition and prepares the body for the resistance stage.

Resistance   The person's ability to cope with the environmental demand rises above the normal state during the resistance stage because the body has activated various biochemical, psychological, and behavioral mechanisms. For example, we have a higher than normal level of adrenaline during this stage, which gives us more energy to overcome or remove the source of stress.

EXHIBIT 7.1

Selye's general adaptation syndrome

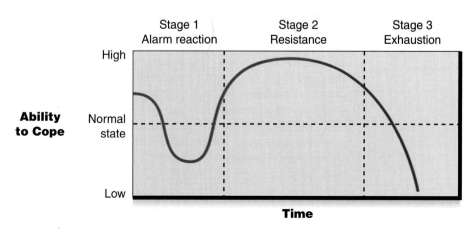

Source: Adapted from H. Selye, *The Stress of Life* (New York: McGraw-Hill, 1956).

Intense bartering and the high stakes of a wrong decision take their toll on energy traders. Many wear out after just 10 years. "The money is so good, it's worth being obsessed and not taking vacations," says Robin Conner, a 30-year-old trader at Reliant Energy in Houston, where this photo was taken. "But it can wear you out." Axia Energy trader Ken Merideth has the same feelings. "I am so burned out at the end of the day, I don't even want to make a decision about what to eat for dinner," he admits.[9] Based on your knowledge of the general adaptation syndrome, why would these energy traders "wear out" after 10 years?

However, our resistance is directed to only one or two environmental demands, so that we become more vulnerable to other challenges. This explains why people are more likely to catch a cold or other illness when they have been working under pressure.

Exhaustion   People have a limited resistance capacity and, if the source of stress persists, they will eventually move into the exhaustion stage as this capacity diminishes. In most work situations, the general adaptation syndrome process ends long before total exhaustion. Employees resolve tense situations before the destructive consequences of stress become manifest, or they withdraw from the stressful situation, rebuild their survival capabilities, and return later to the stressful environment with renewed energy. However, people who frequently experience the general adaptation syndrome have increased risk of long-term physiological and psychological damage.[8]

The general adaptation syndrome describes the stress experience, but this is only part of the picture. To effectively manage work-related stress, we must understand its causes and consequences as well as individual differences in the stress experience.

Stressors: The Causes of Stress

Stressors, the causes of stress, include any environmental conditions that place a physical or emotional demand on the person.[10] There are numerous stressors in organizational settings and other life activities. Exhibit 7.2 lists the four main types of work-related stressors: interpersonal, role-related, task control, organizational and physical environment stressors.

stressors
The causes of stress, including any environmental conditions that place a physical or emotional demand on the person.

Interpersonal Stressors

Among the four types of stressors, interpersonal stressors seem to be the most pervasive at school and work.[11] The trend toward teamwork generates interpersonal stressors because employees must interact more with co-workers. Bad bosses, office politics, and various types of interpersonal conflict also take their toll on employees. For example, one recent study found that employees experienced stress immediately after exposure to organizational politics.[12] Other interpersonal stressors include sexual harassment, workplace violence, and bullying.

Sexual Harassment   Cecylia's job as a school counselor in Radom, Poland, has been very stressful. The problem isn't her work; rather, the stress comes from the school principal's sexual advances and his treatment of her after she refused his propositions. "My refusals would infuriate him," says Cecylia. "I

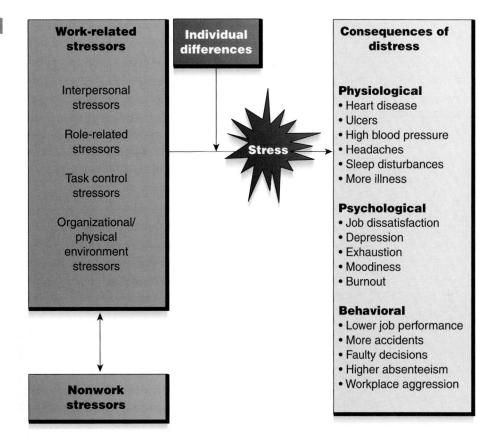

have been consistently resisting his advances, but the price I pay for my attitude is that he picks on me whenever he can."[13]

Cecylia has experienced the stress of **sexual harassment.** Sexual harassment refers to unwelcome conduct of a sexual nature that detrimentally affects the work environment or leads to adverse job-related consequences for
its victims. One form of sexual harassment, called *quid pro quo*, includes situations in which a person's employment or job performance is conditional on
unwanted sexual relations (e.g., a male supervisor threatening to fire a female
employee if she did not accept his sexual advances). Cecylia experienced the
second and more frequent form of sexual harassment, called *hostile work environment.* This includes sexual conduct that unreasonably interferes with an
individual's work performance or creates an intimidating, hostile, or offensive
working environment.[14] The definition of sexual harassment leads to compli-
cations—and interpersonal stress—because research indicates that men generally have a narrower interpretation than do women over what constitutes
hostile work environment sexual harassment.[15]

Corporate leaders increasingly recognize that sexual harassment (and other
forms of harassment) is a serious concern. But harassment is more than a
legal issue; it is a serious interpersonal stressor.[16] Victims of sexual harassment experience trauma from quid pro quo harassment and tense co-worker
relations in a hostile work environment. Moreover, they are expected to en-
dure more stress while these incidents are investigated. This is particularly
true in Japan and other countries where women who complain of harassment
are sometimes stigmatized by friends and co-workers. "Companies don't want

**sexual
harassment**

Unwelcome conduct
of a sexual nature that
detrimentally affects
the work environment
or leads to adverse
job-related
consequences for its
victims.

to hire 'dangerous women,' who make a fuss about sexual harassment," says Moeko Tanaka, the pen name of a Japanese woman who won a case of harassment against a prefecture governor.[17]

Workplace Violence   Workplace violence is a serious interpersonal stressor in most countries. In the United States, 900 employees are murdered on the job each year and 2 million others experience lesser forms of violence. A recent International Labor Organization study reported that over 60 percent of health care staff in Bulgaria, Australia, South Africa, and Portugal had experienced at least one incident of physical or psychological violence in the previous year. The most recent British Crime Survey indicates that over 600,000 people in England and Wales are physically assaulted or threatened each year at work.[18]

Employees who experience violence usually have symptoms of severe distress after the traumatic event.[19] It is not uncommon for primary victims to take long-term disability. Some never return to work. Workplace violence is also a stressor to those who observe the violence. After a serious workplace incident, counselors assist many employees, not just the direct victims. Even employees who have not directly experienced or observed violence may show signs of stress if they work in high-risk jobs.

Workplace Bullying   On the web site chat page of a local newspaper, IBM factory workers posted numerous rude and taunting remarks about their boss, a black woman. An investigation identified three IBM employees as the source of this bullying. After IBM fired the three employees, productivity at the plant soared. "A healthy business climate is built on cooperation, trust and teamwork, whether it is in a white-collar environment or on the shop floor," advises Harold Newman, IBM director of global employee relations. "Bullying is the antithesis of this."[20]

workplace bullying

Offensive, intimidating, or humiliating behavior that degrades, ridicules, or insults another person at work.

Workplace bullying (also called *workplace incivility*) refers to offensive, intimidating, or humiliating behavior that degrades, ridicules, or insults another person at work.[21] The incidence of bullying varies from one work site to the next. One study found that 40 percent of federal court employees in Michigan had experienced workplace incivility within the past five years. Two large surveys reported that 9 percent of European workers and nearly 20 percent of British workers suffered from workplace bullying over the previous 12 months. In a recent Canadian study, 12 percent of the public and service sector employees surveyed said they experienced workplace incivility, including rude behavior, name-calling, and yelling.[22] Bullying has become enough of a concern that Scandinavian countries have passed laws against it.

Research indicates that people with higher authority are more likely to engage in workplace incivility toward employees in lower positions. Women are more likely than men to be targets of bullying. Most victims experience stress and its consequences following incidents of bullying. They also have more absenteeism and, back on the job, have impaired decision making, lower work performance, and more work errors.[23]

Some organizations have taken steps to minimize the incidence of incivility. For example, Quaker Oats explicitly advises in its code of conduct that employees must treat each other with consideration, respect, and dignity. Past behavior is the best predictor of future behavior, so companies should carefully screen applicants in terms of past incidents. Feedback, particularly the 360-degree variety (see Chapter 5), lets employees know when their behavior is out of line. Last, organizations should have a grievance, mediation, or other conflict resolution process that employees trust when they become victims of workplace bullying.[24]

Role-Related Stressors

Role-related stressors include conditions where employees have difficulty understanding, reconciling, or performing the various roles in their lives. Three types of role-related stressors are role conflict, role ambiguity, and work overload. **Role conflict** refers to the degree of incongruity or incompatibility of expectations associated with the person's role.[25] Some people experience stress when they have two roles that conflict with each other (called *interrole conflict*). Nurses tend to experience interrole conflict because they struggle to maintain humanistic caring and preserve the nurse–patient relationship in a cost-efficient managed care environment controlled by others.[26] Role conflict also occurs when an employee receives contradictory messages from different people about how to perform a task (called *intrarole conflict*) or works with organizational values and work obligations that are incompatible with his or her personal values (called *person–role conflict*).[27]

Role ambiguity refers to the lack of clarity and predictability of the outcomes of one's behavior. Role ambiguity produces unclear role perceptions, which we learned in Chapter 2 has a direct effect on job performance. It is also a source of stress in a variety of situations, such as joining the organization or working in a new joint venture, because people are uncertain about task and social expectations.[28]

Work Overload   A third role-related stressor is *work overload*—working more hours and more intensely during those hours. In 1930, noted economist John Maynard Keynes predicted that by 2030 the average employee would be working a 15-hour workweek. At the time, Kellogg's, the cereal company, had switched from eight-hour to six-hour work shifts in order to employ more people during the Depression and give employees more time off.[29] But Keynes's prediction is a far cry from the number of hours employees work today. Although official paid work hours are lower than those of the early 1900s, they have moved consistently upward over the past 20 years. Equally significant, many Americans don't take their full vacation time each year, even though employees in this country already have one of the lowest levels of paid time off.[30]

Some writers claim the rising workload is due to the pressure from globalization for more efficiency, and from employees' own desire to keep up with the Joneses in wealth and consumption. Whatever the cause, it has produced higher stress levels.[31] As Global Connections 7.1 describes, work overload is such a problem in Japan that death from overwork has its own name—*karoshi*.

Task-Control Stressors

As a private driver for an executive in Jakarta, Eddy knows that traffic jams are a way of life in Indonesia's largest city. "Jakarta *is* traffic congestion," he complains. "All of the streets in the city are crowded with vehicles. It is impossible to avoid this distressing fact every day." Eddy's boss complains when traffic jams make him late for appointments. Traffic delays also require Eddy to work longer hours. "Even watching soccer on TV or talking to my wife doesn't get rid of my stress. It's driving me mad."[32]

role conflict
Incongruity or incompatibility of expectations associated with the person's role.

role ambiguity
A lack of clarity and predictability of the outcomes of one's behavior.

Karoshi: Death by Overwork in Japan

Yoichi Kawamoto typically worked eight hours each day, then stayed an extra six hours of unpaid overtime. The 52-year-old manager at a machinery firm in the southern Japanese city of Kobe also felt obliged to work Saturdays and holidays. One day, Kawamoto penned a short note, saying: "Overtime work with no pay, or not enough. Being forced to stay late," The note was written in English, presumably to hide the message from his colleagues. Kawamoto died a few days later. "His death, from a massive heart attack, was almost spontaneous," Kawamoto's wife recalls. "Those long working hours killed him."

Yoichi Kawamoto was a victim of karoshi—death from overwork. The Japanese government recorded 317 cases of karoshi in the most recent year, more than double the previous record. But experts say the karoshi death toll in Japan is probably closer to 10,000, and that up to one million white-collar employees are at risk. According to the Japanese government, employees who work more than 80 hours of overtime per month have a significantly higher risk of karoshi. Currently, more than 20 percent of male Japanese employees exceed that level of overtime.

Karoshi occurs because long work hours cause an unhealthy lifestyle, such as smoking, poor eating habits, lack of physical exercise, and sleeplessness. This results in weight gain, which, along with stressful working conditions, damages the cardiovascular system and leads to strokes and heart attacks. Long work hours also contribute to depression, which results in high suicide rates. Suicide from overwork is a form of karoshi.

Karoshi came to the public spotlight in the 1970s when Japan's economy was booming, but the country's current recession is making matters worse. Companies are laying off employees and loading the extra work onto those who remain. Performance-based expectations are replacing lifetime employment guarantees, putting further pressure on employees to work long hours. Many also blame Japan's "samurai spirit" culture, which idolizes long work hours as the ultimate symbol of company loyalty and personal fortitude. "Being exhausted is considered a virtue," explains a Japanese psychiatrist. To combat karoshi, the Japanese government has launched an advertising campaign encouraging people to call a "karoshi hotline" for anonymous help. The families of karoshi victims are also taking action by suing employers for lack of due care.

Sources: J. Ryall, "Japan Wakes Up to Fatal Work Ethic," *Scotland on Sunday,* June 15, 2003, p. 22; H. Osedo, "Japanese Workers Dying to Get Ahead," *Courier-Mail* (Brisbane, Australia), June 12, 2003, p. 19; "More than 20% of Male Japanese Employees," *Look Japan,* January 1, 2003, p. 3; Y. Liu, "Overtime Work, Insufficient Sleep, and Risk of Non-fatal Acute Myocardial Infarction in Japanese Men," *Occupational and Environmental Medicine* 59 (July 2002), pp. 447–51; D. Ibison, "Overwork Kills Record Number of Japanese," *Financial Times,* May 29, 2002, p. 12; S. Efron, "Jobs Take a Deadly Toll on Japanese," *Los Angeles Times,* April 12, 2000, p. A1.

Eddy and many other people experience stress due to a lack of task control.[33] Along with driving through congested traffic, low task control occurs where a person's work is paced by a machine or involves monitoring equipment, or where the work schedule is controlled by someone else. Many people experience stress because computers, cell phones, and other technology control their time and intrude on their private lives. Sports coaches also experience task-control stressors because they have limited direct control over the performance of their players.

The extent to which low task control is a stressor increases with the person's level of responsibility. Assembly line workers have low task control but tend to experience less stress because they also have low responsibility for those tasks. In contrast, sports coaches are under immense pressure to win games (high responsibility), yet have little control over what happens on the playing field (low task control). Similarly, Eddy (the Jakarta driver) is under pressure to get his employer to a particular destination on time, yet he has little control over traffic congestion.

Organizational and Physical Environment Stressors

Organizational and physical environment stressors come in many forms. Downsizing (reducing the number of employees) is extremely stressful to those who lose their jobs. However, layoff survivors also experience stress because of

Ken Wiley knows that logging is risky and stressful work. The tree faller in Canada's Queen Charlotte Islands, off the Alaskan coast, got badly cut when his saw kicked back on him and broke his cheekbone when hit by a falling tree. Both his father and grandfather died in logging accidents, and this photo shows him wearing a hockey jersey worn by a fellow logger who was recently killed on the job. Safety experts say the death toll could get worse because loggers are experiencing heightened stress due to organizational change and uncertainty in the industry. "There is job loss and a complete change in the way companies do business," says a government safety officer. "That is a major contributing factor in accidents . . . [with] so many things on their mind they had difficulty concentrating on the job."[37] What can forest products companies do to minimize deaths and injuries due to organizational stressors?

the reduced job security, chaos of change, additional workloads, and guilt of having a job as others lose theirs. For example, one study reported that long-term sick leave taken by surviving government employees in Finland doubled after a major downsizing.[34] "I'm finding people so overwhelmed by their work that they actually wish they had been the ones laid off," says San Diego psychotherapist Nancy Helgeson.[35]

Some stressors are found in the physical work environment, such as excessive noise, poor lighting, and safety hazards. A study of textile workers in a noisy plant found that their levels of stress measurably decreased when supplied with ear protectors. Another study reported that clerical employees experience significantly higher stress levels in noisy open offices than in quiet areas.[36] People working in dangerous work environments also potentially experience higher stress levels. For example, the opening story to this chapter described how medical staff at Prince of Wales Hospital in Hong Kong experienced stress due to the risk of infection and discomfort of their protective gear.

Work–Nonwork Stressors

The stress model shown earlier in Exhibit 7.2 has a two-way arrow, indicating that stressors from work spill over into nonwork and vice versa. There are three types of these work–nonwork stressors: time-based, strain-based, and role-based conflict.[38]

Time-Based Conflict   *Time-based conflict* refers to the challenge of balancing the time demanded by work with family and other nonwork activities. As Americans work longer hours (and more intensely during those hours), they have little time or energy left for themselves and their family. This stressor is particularly noticeable in employees who hold strong family values and weakest in people who do not value a work–life imbalance.[39] Time-based conflict relates back to the work overload stressor described earlier. Inflexible work schedules, business travel, and rotating shift schedules also take a heavy toll because they prevent employees from effectively juggling work and nonwork.[40]

Time-based conflict is more acute for women than for men because housework and child care represent a "second shift" for many women in dual-career families. Tammy Matel knows all about time-based conflict. Along with caring for three children and holding a full-time job as radio announcer in Madison,

Wisconsin, Matel was a consultant at home for Mediabase. She eventually gave up the consulting work because, even with her husband's help around the house, Matel's lack of time was hurting her marriage and relations with the children.[41]

Strain-Based Conflict   *Strain-based conflict* occurs when stress from one domain spills over to the other. Relationship problems, financial difficulties, and loss of a loved one usually top the list of nonwork stressors. New responsibilities, such as marriage, birth of a child, and a mortgage, are also stressful to most of us. Stress at work also spills over to an employee's personal life and often becomes the foundation of stressful relations with family and friends. In support of this, one study found that fathers who experience stress at work engage in dysfunctional parenting behaviors, which then lead to their children's behavior problems in school.[42]

Role Behavior Conflict   A third work–nonwork stressor, called *role behavior conflict*, occurs when people are expected to enact different work and nonwork roles. People who act logically and impersonally at work have difficulty switching to a more compassionate behavioral style in their personal lives. For example, one study found that police officers were unable to shake off their professional role when they left the job. This was confirmed by their spouses, who reported that the officers would handle their children in the same manner as they would people in their job.[43]

Stress and Occupations

Several studies have attempted to identify which jobs have more stressors than others.[44] These lists are not in complete agreement, but Exhibit 7.3 identifies a representative sample of jobs and their relative level of stressors. You should view this information with some caution, however. One problem with

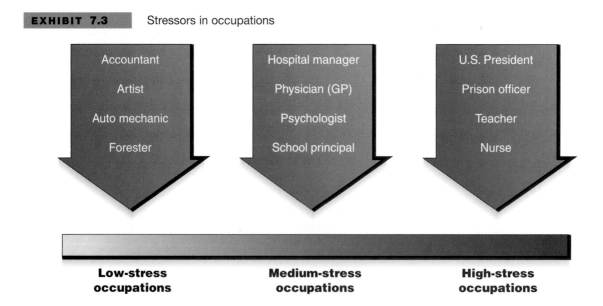

EXHIBIT 7.3   Stressors in occupations

Accountant	Hospital manager	U.S. President
Artist	Physician (GP)	Prison officer
Auto mechanic	Psychologist	Teacher
Forester	School principal	Nurse

Low-stress occupations   **Medium-stress occupations**   **High-stress occupations**

rating occupations in terms of their stress levels is that a particular occupation may have considerably different tasks and job environments across organizations and societies. A nurse's job may be less stressful in a small-town medical clinic, for instance, than in the emergency room in a large city.

Another important point to remember when looking at Exhibit 7.3 is that a major stressor to one person is insignificant to another. In this respect, we must be careful not to conclude that people in high-stressor occupations actually experience higher stress than people in other occupations. Some jobs expose people to more serious stressors, but careful selection and training can result in stress levels no different from those experienced by people in other jobs. The next section discusses individual differences in stress.

Individual Differences in Stress

Exhibit 7.2, shown earlier in this chapter, indicated that individual characteristics moderate the extent to which people experience stress or exhibit a specific stress outcome in a given situation. Two people may be exposed to the same stressor, such as having too many deadlines, yet they experience different stress levels or different stress symptoms.[45]

People exposed to the same stressors might have different stress symptoms for three reasons. First, each of us perceives the same situation differently. People who are familiar with the situation and know how to protect themselves tend to experience less stress than those who are unfamiliar or unskilled in that situation. People with high self-efficacy, for instance, are less likely to experience stress consequences in that situation because the stressor is less threatening.[46] Self-efficacy refers to a person's belief that he or she has the ability, motivation, and resources to complete a task successfully (see Chapter 3). Similarly, some people have personalities that make them more optimistic, whereas others are more pessimistic (see Chapter 4). Those with pessimistic dispositions tend to develop more stress symptoms, probably because they interpret the situation in a negative light.[47]

A second reason why some people have more stress symptoms than others in the same situation is that they have different threshold levels of resistance to a stressor. Younger employees generally experience fewer and less severe stress symptoms than older employees because they have a larger store of energy to cope with high stress levels. This explains why exercise and healthy lifestyles are discussed later in this chapter as ways to manage stress. People who exercise regularly and have healthy lifestyles (e.g., diet, sleep) are less likely to experience negative stress outcomes.

A third reason why people may experience the same level of stress and yet exhibit different stress outcomes is that they use different coping strategies.[48] Some employees tend to ignore the stressor, hoping that it will go away. This is usually an ineffective approach, which would explain why they experience higher stress levels. There is some evidence (although still inconclusive) that women cope with stress better than their male counterparts. Specifically, women are more likely to seek emotional support from others in stressful situations, whereas men try to change the stressor or use less effective coping mechanisms.[49] However, we must remember that this is not true for all women or men.

Working around honeybees is a heart-thumping experience for most of us. But Hakija Pehlic (shown here) doesn't worry when he pushes his nose through a layer of European honeybees to better determine the type of honey produced on a honeycomb frame. Pehlic, a beekeeper at Finster Honey Farms in Schuyler, New York, doesn't experience much stress in this situation because he is trained to know when it's safe to smell the honey and how to avoid getting stung. Most of the time, says Pehlic, honeybees are gentle insects that won't bother you. Maybe so, but you probably shouldn't try this at home.[50] What other individual differences would cause some people to be highly distressed in this situation whereas others would experience much less stress?

Type B behavior pattern

A behavior pattern associated with people having a low risk of coronary heart disease; type Bs tend to work steadily, take a relaxed approach to life, and be even-tempered.

Work Stress and Type A/Type B Behavior Pattern

For several years, scholars proposed that people with a **Type B behavior pattern** experience less stress in the same situation as people with a **Type A behavior pattern.** Type A people are hard-driving, competitive individuals with a strong sense of time urgency. They tend to be impatient, lose their temper, talk rapidly, and interrupt others during conversations.[51] In contrast, Type B people are less competitive and less concerned about time limitations. They tend to work steadily, take a relaxed approach to life, and be even-tempered. Although scholars are now less convinced about the importance of Type A/Type B behavior patterns in understanding work-related stress, some research continues to report that Type A people have higher job stress.[52]

Type A behavior pattern

A behavior pattern associated with people having premature coronary heart disease; type As tend to be impatient, lose their temper, talk rapidly, and interrupt others.

Work Stress and Workaholism

More than 30 years after the term was coined, workaholism has gained attention in the literature on stress and other topics. Scholars are still debating the precise definition, but they generally agree that there are several components of workaholism and different types of workaholics. The classic definition of

Workaholism: An American Addiction

Staring out from the cover of *Confessions of a Street Addict,* James Cramer looks like a dangerous man. In fact, he admits that he was an addict. "I had many of the problems you see in addicts—they can't stay away, they need more and more, they love the adrenaline and then it takes control of their lives," says Cramer.

James Cramer's "street" is Wall Street and his addiction is to his work. The cofounder of TheStreet.com and *Smart Money* magazine is a repentant workaholic who had the symptoms that scholars have associated with this affliction. He was obsessed with market trades, became a tyrant in the office whenever a stock went south, and lost touch with his family. Even casual gatherings were rated by whether they added value to his work. "You might get together with me for a drink and I would be thinking 'Why am I wasting my time?'" Cramer recalls.

Cramer has plenty of company as a workaholic in the United States. According to a large-scale study at Israel's University of Haifa, 12.7 percent of Americans are traditional workaholics, followed by 9.3 percent of Japanese workers and 8.1 percent of Israeli workers. Further down the workaholism scale are employees in Belgium (6.8 percent) and the Netherlands (6.5 percent).

There are several other telltale signs that Americans have high levels of workaholism. According to one survey, one-fifth of Americans show up to work even when sick or injured. Another survey reported that 12 percent of Americans didn't take any of their allotted vacation time last year. Americans receive an average of only 10 days vacation annually, compared with nearly a month in most other developed countries. Yet one in five Americans feel guilty about taking time off during the few days they receive. Perhaps to relieve that guilt, many Americans take along their computer, cell phone, or briefcase full of work.

"Around the world Americans are laughed at for our workaholism," says Dana Dickey, senior editor at *Conde Nast Traveler* magazine. "It is just kind of part of our culture." Dickey also thinks that the recent weak economy has increased the level of workaholism. "You don't know, you take two weeks, who knows, your desk might be given away when you get home."

Sources: K. Phillips and K. Pilgrim, "Are Americans Working Too Much?" *CNN* (Live From . . . 13:00), July 4, 2003, Transcript 070412CN.V85; K. Rives, "Many Workers Don't Take a Vacation," *(Raleigh, NC) News & Observer,* June 22, 2003; "Israel Number 3 for Workaholism: Survey," *Canadian Jewish News,* February 6, 2003; J. J. Cramer, *Confessions of a Street Addict* (New York: Simon & Schuster, 2002); J. Langton, "Wall Street Made Me a Monster," *Evening Standard,* May 27, 2002.

workaholic
A person who is highly involved in work, feels compelled to work, and has a low enjoyment of work.

workaholic is a person who is highly involved in work, feels compelled or driven to work because of inner pressures, and has a low enjoyment of work. Stereotypic workaholics exhibit compulsive behavior and are preoccupied with work, often to the exclusion and detriment of the workaholic's health, intimate relationships, and participation in child rearing.[53] As Connections 7.2 describes, Americans apparently top the list of countries with this classic form of workaholism.

Along with stereotypic workaholics, the academic literature identifies two other workaholic types: enthusiastic workaholics and work enthusiasts. *Enthusiastic workaholics* have high levels of all three components—high work involvement, drive to succeed, and work enjoyment. *Work enthusiasts* have high work involvement and work enjoyment, but low drive to succeed.[54]

Workaholism is relevant to our discussion of stress because traditional workaholics are more prone to job stress and burnout. Research has found that stereotypic workaholics tend to have a Type A behavior pattern. They have significantly higher scores on depression, anxiety, and anger than do non-workaholics, as well as lower job and career satisfaction. Workaholics of both sexes report more health complaints than do work enthusiasts.[55] There is still some debate whether the other forms of workaholism—enthusiastic workaholics and work enthusiasts—are good or bad for the individual and organization.

Consequences of Distress

The general adaptation syndrome introduced at the beginning of this chapter describes how chronic stress diminishes the individual's resistance, resulting in adverse consequences for both the employee and the organization. Let's look at the main physiological, psychological, and behavioral consequences.

Physiological Consequences

Stress takes its toll on the human body.[56] Studies have found that medical students who are anxious about their exams are more susceptible to colds and other illnesses. Many people experience tension headaches due to stress. Others get muscle pain and related back problems. These physiological ailments are attributed to muscle contractions that occur when people are exposed to stressors.

Cardiovascular disease is one of the most disturbing effects of stress in modern society.[57] Strokes and heart attacks were rare a century ago but are now among the leading causes of death in adult Americans. Stress also influences hypertension (high blood pressure). In spite of better lifestyle and medical treatment, recent evidence suggests that hypertension continues to increase, particularly among older people and non-Hispanic blacks in the United States.[58]

Medical researchers believe that the long-term effect of stress on heart disease goes something like this: Whenever people are stressed, their blood pressure goes up and down. Frequent changes in pressure cause injury to the blood vessel walls, which eventually makes them constrict and function abnormally. Over time, this leads to heart disease. Unfortunately, we often can't tell when we are physiologically stressed. For example, researchers have found that people think they are in a low-stress state when, in fact, their palms are sweating and blood pressure has risen.[59]

The most recent disturbing discovery is that stress seems to be associated with cancer. In a study of more than 60,000 people in Norway, scholars found that those with high scores on an anxiety test were 25 percent more likely to have premalignant tumors seven years later.[60]

Psychological Consequences

Stress produces various psychological consequences, including job dissatisfaction, moodiness, and depression.[61] Emotional fatigue is another psychological consequence of stress and is related to job burnout.

job burnout
The process of emotional exhaustion, cynicism, and reduced efficacy (lower feelings of personal accomplishment) resulting from prolonged exposure to stress.

Job Burnout   **Job burnout** refers to the process of emotional exhaustion, cynicism, and reduced efficacy (lower feelings of personal accomplishment) resulting from prolonged exposure to stress.[62] The phrase "job burnout" didn't exist 40 years ago; now it's heard in everyday conversations. Job burnout is a complex process that includes the dynamics of stress, coping strategies, and stress consequences. Burnout is caused by excessive demands made on people who serve or frequently interact with others. In other words, burnout is mainly due to interpersonal and role-related stressors.[63] For this reason, it is most common in helping occupations (e.g., nurses, teachers, police officers).

Exhibit 7.4 diagrams the relationship among the three components of job burnout. *Emotional exhaustion,* the first stage, plays a central role in the burn-

EXHIBIT 7.4

The job burnout
process

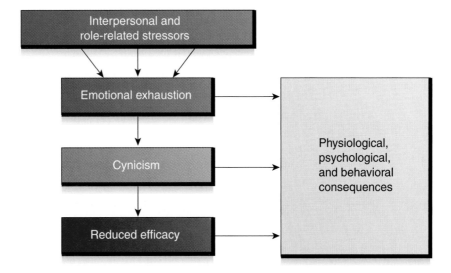

out process.[64] It is characterized by a lack of energy, tiredness, and a feeling that one's emotional resources are depleted. Emotional exhaustion is sometimes called compassion fatigue because the employee no longer feels able to give as much support and care to clients.

Cynicism (also called *depersonalization*) follows emotional exhaustion and is identified by an indifferent attitude toward work and the treatment of others as objects rather than people. Burned-out employees become emotionally detached from clients and cynical about the organization. This detachment is to the point of callousness, far beyond the level of detachment normally required in helping occupations. Cynicism is also apparent when employees strictly follow rules and regulations rather than trying to understand the client's needs and search for a mutually acceptable solution.

Reduced professional efficacy (also called *reduced personal accomplishment*), the final component of job burnout, refers to feelings of diminished confidence in the ability to perform the job well. In other words, the person's self-efficacy declines (see Chapter 3). In these situations, employees develop a

**"It's a smoke detector. The boss thinks
I might be headed for a burnout."**

sense of learned helplessness as they no longer believe that their efforts make a difference. The model shows that cynicism tends to cause reduced professional efficacy, although some experts now think lower professional efficacy and cynicism occur at the same time as a result of emotional exhaustion.[65]

Behavioral Consequences

When stress becomes distress, job performance falls and workplace accidents are more frequent. High stress levels impair our ability to remember information, make effective decisions, and take appropriate action.[66] You have probably experienced this in an exam or emergency work situation. You forget important information, make mistakes, and otherwise "draw a blank" under intense pressure.

Overstressed employees also tend to have higher levels of absenteeism. One reason is that stress makes people sick. The other reason is that absenteeism is a coping mechanism. At a basic level, we react to stress through "fight or flight." Absenteeism is a form of flight—temporarily withdrawing from the stressful situation so that we have an opportunity to reenergize. Companies may try to minimize absenteeism, but it sometimes helps employees avoid the exhaustion stage of the stress experience (see Exhibit 7.1 earlier in this chapter).[67]

Workplace Aggression   Workplace aggression is more than the serious interpersonal stressor described earlier. It is also an increasingly worrisome consequence of stress.[68] Aggression represents the fight (instead of flight) reaction to stress. In its mildest form, employees engage in verbal conflict. They "fly off the handle" and are less likely to empathize with co-workers. Occasionally, the combination of an individual's background and workplace stressors escalate this conflict into more dangerous levels of workplace hostility.

Co-worker aggression represents a relatively small proportion of workplace violence, but these behaviors are neither random nor inconsequential. Like most forms of organizational behavior, co-worker aggression is caused by both the person and the situation.[69] While certain individuals are more likely to be aggressive, we must remember that employee aggression is also a consequence of extreme stress.[70] In particular, employees are more likely to engage in aggressive behavior if they believe they have been treated unfairly, experience other forms of frustration beyond their personal control, and work in physical environments that are stressful (e.g., hot, noisy).

Managing Work-Related Stress

A recent Christmas holiday season was a nail-biter for Sharon Milligan. The 28-year-old retail director for New York fashion house Nicole Miller agonized as daily sales of the company's 14 stores fell below the previous year's numbers. She had to personally tell employees at the store in Scottsdale, Arizona, that the boutique there would be closed. A store scheduled for opening in Florida was delayed, missing a crucial weekend of holiday sales. Three days before Christmas, Milligan sat in the doctor's office with a fever and sore throat. "I just crashed," she says. Milligan flew to Jamaica the day after Christmas and slept through the first three days of her long-awaited vacation.[71]

Sharon Milligan was fortunate. She was able to manage her stress before matters got worse. Unfortunately, many of us deny the existence of our stress

until it is too late. This avoidance strategy creates a vicious cycle because the failure to cope with stress becomes another stressor on top of the one that created the stress in the first place. The solution is to discover the toolkit of effective stress management strategies identified in Exhibit 7.5, and to determine which ones are best for the situation.[72] As we look at each approach, keep in mind that the organization and employees have joint responsibility for effective stress management. Moreover, managing stress often includes more than one of these strategies.

Remove the Stressor

From this list of stress management strategies, some writers argue that the *only* way companies can effectively manage stress is by removing the stressors that cause unnecessary tension and job burnout. Other stress management strategies may keep employees "stress-fit," but they don't solve the fundamental causes of stress.[73]

One way for organizations to manage stress is to investigate the main causes of stress in their workplace. Volvo conducted a stress audit in its 500-employee research and development department in which individuals rated their jobs as high, medium, or low stress. The Swedish automobile company followed up with stress management programs. Good Hope Hospital in England also conducted an audit by asking staff to complete confidential questionnaires to identify when and how they experience stress.[74]

Another recommendation is to change the corporate culture and reward systems so they support a work–life balance and no longer reinforce dysfunctional workaholism. More generally, research has found that one of the most powerful ways to remove workplace stressors is to empower employees so that they have more control over their work and work environment (see Chapter 6).[75] Role-related stressors can be minimized by selecting and assigning employees to positions that match their competencies. Noise and safety risks are stressful, so improving these conditions would also go a long way to minimize stress in the workplace. Workplace violence and bullying can be minimized by carefully selecting employees and having clear guidelines of behavior and feedback to those who violate those standards.[76]

Employees can also take an active role in removing stressors. If stress is caused by ambiguous role expectations, for example, we might seek out more information from others to clarify these expectations. If a particular piece of work is too challenging, we might break it into smaller sets of tasks so that the overall project is less threatening or wearing. For instance, one British school board introduced a mentoring program in which teachers and school administrators were encouraged to delegate work when the workload becomes too stressful.[77] We can also minimize workplace violence by learning to identify early warning signs of aggression in customers and co-workers and by developing interpersonal skills that dissipate aggression.

A growing shortage of teachers has prompted schools throughout Wales to consider job sharing as a way to attract teachers who can't or won't work full time. "Schools would be in a win-win situation if they were to actively consider job sharing," advises education minister Jane Davidson. Mary Compton and Clare Victor, who have been sharing their teaching job at John Beddoes School in Presteigne, Wales, for the past 13 years, agree with that assessment. "[Job sharing has] had a positive effect on my family life," says Victor (left in photo). "It means that neither of us are so overworked as we would be if we were working full time. We don't get so ratty with the pupils, and have more time to prepare for lessons."[79] Along with job sharing, what other activities would encourage employees to balance their work with nonwork?

Family-Friendly and Work–Life Initiatives

Companies have introduced a variety of strategies to help employees experience a better balance between their work and personal lives. Five of the most common work–life balance initiatives are flexible work time, job sharing, telecommuting, personal leave, and child care facilities.[78]

- *Flexible work time*—Some firms are flexible on the hours, days, and amount of time employees work. For example, Kraft's work–life program gives employees the freedom to rearrange their work schedule to accommodate family events, ranging from attending children's sports activities to caring for elderly parents.[80]
- *Job sharing*—Job sharing splits a career position between two people so they experience less time-based stress between work and family. They typically work different parts of the week with some overlapping work time in the weekly schedule to coordinate activities.[81]
- *Telecommuting*—Chapter 1 described how an increasing number of employees are telecommuting. This reduces the time and stress of commuting to work and makes it easier to fulfill family obligations, such as temporarily leaving the home office to pick the kids up from school. Research suggests that telecommuters experience a healthier work–life balance.[82] However, telecommuting may increase stress for those who crave social interaction. Also, telecommuting isn't a substitute for child care.
- *Personal leave programs*—Employers with strong work–life values offer extended maternity, paternity, and personal leaves to care for a new family or take advantage of a personal experience. The U.S. Family and Medical Leave Act gives expecting mothers (and anyone considered to have an "illness") 12 weeks of unpaid, job-protected leave. However, almost every other developed nation requires employers to provide paid maternity

leave.[83] Volvo is one of the more generous companies, offering 40 weeks of paid maternity leave. Increasingly, employees require personal leave to care for elderly parents who need assistance.

■ *Child care support*—Nearly one-quarter of American employees have on-site or subsidized child care facilities. Child care support reduces stress because employees are less rushed to drop off children and less worried during the day about how well they are doing.[84]

Given the high levels of work–life conflict that we read about earlier, you would think that organizations are encouraging employees to apply these initiatives. The reality, according to some experts, is that while these practices are available, employees either feel guilty about using them or are discouraged from using them.[85] "Many organizations have all the right policies on the books," says Brad Harrington, executive director of the Boston College Center for Work and Family. "But the question is, 'Do employees feel it is acceptable to use these policies without there being negative repercussions?'" To ensure that employees actually develop a work–life balance, the top 500 managers at accounting firm RSM McGladrey, Inc., receive annual 360-degree reviews in which peers, subordinates, and managers rate how well the executive respects and encourages "balance of work and personal life priorities" among employees.[86]

Withdraw from the Stressor

Removing the stressor may be the ideal solution, but it is often not feasible. An alternative strategy is to permanently or temporarily remove employees from the stressor. Permanent withdrawal occurs when employees are transferred to jobs that better fit their competencies and values.

Temporary Withdrawal Strategies   Temporarily withdrawing from stressors is the most frequent way that employees manage stress. Marketing firm Brann Baltimore created an Aquarium Room complete with soothing blue lights, blue walls, and bubble columns. The room, which overlooks the National Aquarium in Baltimore, even has a "sandbox" so employees can dip their bare feet in the sand.[87]

Days off and vacations represent somewhat longer temporary withdrawals from stressful conditions. One study of a police and emergency response services department found that this leisure time significantly improved the employees' ability to cope with work-related stress.[88] Paid sabbaticals are offered by several employers. A four-month fully paid sabbatical is mandatory every five years at Ball Janik, a law firm in Portland, Oregon. The Australian government introduced long-service leave legislation several decades ago to enable employees "half way through their working life, to recover lost energies and to return to work relaxed and reinvigorated." Today, over two-thirds of Australian employees are eligible to receive two or three months of paid leave after 10 or 15 years of service on top of their usual annual vacation.[89]

Change Stress Perceptions

Employees often experience different levels of stress in the same situation because they perceive it differently. Consequently, stress can be minimized by changing perceptions of the situation. This does not involve ignoring risks or

When employees at Liggett-Stashower, Inc., need a short break from the daily stresses of work, they retreat to one of three theme rooms specially designed to promote creativity and relieve tension. Staff at the Cleveland advertising firm can enter the bowling room and knock down a few pins. Or they might try out the Zen room, which serves as a quiet, relaxing place to think. Behind the third door is a karaoke room (shown here) where frustrated employees can belt out tunes. "The higher the stress level, the more singing there is going on," says Kristen Flynn, a Liggett art director.[90] How does each of these rooms help employees to manage their stress?

other stressors. Rather, we can strengthen our self-efficacy and self-esteem so that job challenges are not perceived as threatening. Humor can also improve perceptions by taking some psychological weight off the situation. Several elements of self-leadership described in Chapter 6 can alter employee perceptions of job-related stressors. For example, mental imagery can reduce the uncertainty of future work activities. A study of newly hired accountants reported that personal goal setting and self-reinforcement can also reduce the stress that people experience when they enter new work settings.[91] Positive self-talk can potentially change stress perceptions by increasing our self-efficacy and developing a more optimistic outlook, at least in that situation.

Control the Consequences of Stress

Coping with workplace stress also involves controlling its consequences. For this reason, many companies have fitness centers where employees can keep in shape. Research indicates that physical exercise reduces the physiological consequences of stress by helping employees lower their respiration, muscle tension, heart rate, and stomach acidity.[92] The Robert Wood Johnson Foundation, a large health philanthropy, values physical exercise so much that its new headquarters building in Princeton, New Jersey, deliberately spread out offices. "I put on a good 2½ miles every day in walking from space to space," says Andrew Harrison, an archivist at the foundation. Another way to control the physiological consequences of stress is through relaxation and meditation. For instance, employees at AstraZeneca, a Wilmington, Delaware-based pharmaceutical company, practice a form of meditation called Qi Gong during department meetings and coffee breaks. Generally, these activities decrease the individual's heart rate, blood pressure, muscle tension, and breathing rate.[93]

Along with fitness and relaxation/meditation, many firms have shifted to the broader approach of wellness programs. These programs educate and support employees in better nutrition and fitness, regular sleep, and other good health habits. For example, the wellness program at Paychex, Inc., in Rochester, New York, offers free cholesterol screenings and counseling on diet and exercise. Park Place Entertainment Corporation in Las Vegas recently introduced a wellness program in which its 19,000 employees have free access to a wide array of wellness classes, individualized health appraisals, and health and disease prevention information.[94]

employee assistance programs (EAPs)
Counseling services that help employees overcome personal or organizational stressors and adopt more effective coping mechanisms.

Many large employers offer **employee assistance programs (EAPs)**—counseling services that help employees overcome personal or organizational stressors and adopt more effective coping mechanisms. Most EAPs are "broadbrush" programs that counsel employees on any work or personal problems. Family problems often represent the largest percentage of EAP referrals, although this varies with industry and location. EAPs can be one of the most effective stress management interventions where the counseling helps employees to understand the stressors, acquire stress management skills, and practice those stress management skills.[95]

Receive Social Support

Social support from co-workers, supervisors, family, friends, and others is one of the more effective stress management practices.[96] Social support refers to the person's interpersonal transactions with others and involves providing either emotional or informational support to buffer the stress experience.

Social support reduces stress in at least three ways.[97] First, employees improve their perception that they are valued and worthy. This, in turn, increases their self-esteem and perceived ability to cope with the stressor (e.g., "I can handle this crisis because my colleagues have confidence in me"). Second, social support provides information to help employees interpret, comprehend, and possibly remove the stressor. For instance, social support might reduce a new employee's stress because co-workers describe ways to handle difficult customers. Finally, emotional support from others can directly help to buffer the stress experience. This last point reflects the idea that "misery loves company." People seek out and benefit from the emotional support of others when they face threatening situations.[98]

Social support is an important way to cope with stress that everyone can practice by maintaining friendships. This includes helping others when they need a little support from the stressors of life. Organizations can facilitate social support by providing opportunities for social interaction among employees as well as their families. People in leadership roles also need to practice a supportive leadership style when employees work under stressful conditions and need this social support. Mentoring relationships with more senior employees may also help junior employees cope with organizational stressors.

Chapter Summary

Stress is an adaptive response to a situation that is perceived as challenging or threatening to the person's well-being. Distress represents high stress levels that have negative consequences, whereas eustress represents the moderately low stress levels needed to activate people. The stress experience, called the general adaptation syndrome, involves moving through three stages: alarm, resistance, and exhaustion. The stress model shows that stress is caused by stressors. However, the effect of these stressors depends on individual characteristics. Stress affects a person's physiological and psychological well-being and is associated with several work-related behaviors.

Stressors are the causes of stress and include any environmental conditions that place a physical or emotional demand on the person. Stressors are found in the physical work environment, the employee's various life roles, interpersonal relations, and organizational activities and conditions. Conflicts between work and nonwork obligations are a frequent source of employee stress.

Two people exposed to the same stressor may experience different stress levels because they perceive the situation differently, they have different threshold stress levels, or they use different coping strategies. Workaholics and employees with Type A behavior

patterns tend to experience more stress than do other employees.

Intense or prolonged stress can cause physiological symptoms, such as high blood pressure, ulcers, sexual dysfunction, headaches, and coronary heart disease. Behavioral symptoms of stress include lower job performance, poorer decisions, more workplace accidents, higher absenteeism, and more workplace aggression. Psychologically, stress reduces job satisfaction and increases moodiness, depression, and job burnout. Job burnout refers to the process of emotional exhaustion, cynicism, and reduced efficacy resulting from prolonged exposure to stress. It is mainly due to interpersonal and role-related stressors and is most common in helping occupations.

Many interventions are available to manage work-related stress. Some directly remove unnecessary stressors or remove employees from the stressful environment. Others help employees alter their interpretation of the environment so that it is not viewed as a serious stressor. Wellness programs encourage employees to build better physical defenses against stress experiences. Social support provides emotional, informational, and material resource support to buffer the stress experience.

Key Terms

employee assistance programs (EAPs), p. 225
general adaptation syndrome, p. 207
job burnout, p. 218
role ambiguity, p. 211
role conflict, p. 211
sexual harassment, p. 209

stress, p. 206
stressors, p. 208
Type A behavior pattern, p. 216
Type B behavior pattern, p. 216
workaholic, p. 217
workplace bullying, p. 210

Discussion Questions

1. Several websites—including www.unitedmedia.com/comics/dilbert/ and www.cartoonwork.com—use humor to describe problems that people experience at work. Scan through these and other websites and determine what types of work-related stressors are described.
2. Is being a full-time college or university student a stressful role? Why or why not? Contrast your response with other students' perspectives.

3. Prison officer and nurse are often cited as high-stress jobs, whereas accountant and forester are low-stress jobs. Why should we be careful about describing these jobs as high or low stress?
4. Two recent graduates join the same major newspaper as journalists. Both work long hours and have tight deadlines to complete their stories. They are under constant pressure to scout out new leads and be the first to report new

controversies. One journalist is increasingly fatigued and despondent and has taken several days of sick leave. The other is getting the work done and seems to enjoy the challenges. Use your knowledge of stress to explain why these two journalists are reacting differently to their jobs.

5. If you were asked to identify people who are classic workaholics, what would you look for? How would these people differ from enthusiastic workaholics?

6. A friend says that he is burned out by his job. What questions might you ask this friend to determine whether he is really experiencing job burnout?

7. What should organizations do to reduce employee stress? What is the responsibility of an employee to manage stress effectively? How might fitness programs help employees working in stressful situations?

8. A technology firm pays employees' membership fees at a local fitness facility. What is your opinion of this employer-provided benefit? Is this program an expense? An investment? Explain your perspective.

CASE STUDY 7.1

A TYPICAL DAY FOR JOE HANSEN, MANAGING DIRECTOR

By Hazel Bothma, University of Cape Town, South Africa

Meet Joe Hansen, managing director of Magical Connections, Cape Town, South Africa. Shadow him for a day and see the challenges and stressors he faces in his daily work.

Buzz. Joe turns over and switches the alarm off. It's 6:00 A.M. and he tosses with the idea of going for a run, but last night, like many before that, he stayed up working till late in the evening, so he decides to postpone it and catch another 30 minutes of sleep. Fate intervenes within minutes as he hears his 18-month-old daughter start to cry. Joe looks over at his wife and decides to let her sleep. She had to take care of their daughter last night, as he had to work until 11 P.M. Dragging himself out of bed, he fetches his wailing daughter and goes to the kitchen to prepare her bottle. While in the kitchen he balances his daughter on his lap, turns on his laptop, and grimaces as his machine shows 42 new e-mails. He thinks back to the time before e-mail and cell phones were popular. Although he would be the first to admit that he couldn't do without these new technologies, he realizes that in ways the division of boundaries between work and nonwork have become blurred. Like many of his colleagues in information technology (IT), Joe realized that separating work life from home life is difficult.

With his daughter now feeding quietly in her crib, Joe takes the opportunity to start responding to the e-mails and deleting much of the junk mail he receives. At 6:45 he jumps in the shower, still feeling tired and preparing himself for a day of work. As he combs his hair he notices the first touch of grey—38, he thinks wryly to himself, and starting to show. He wonders if his late hours and pressure from his work are to blame. It's now 7:15 and Joe needs to get to the office. No time for breakfast; instead he gulps down his second strong cup of coffee, promising himself that from tomorrow on he will make time to eat before work.

As Joe starts driving to work, the early morning traffic beginning to grow, he thinks that at least he is not on his way to the airport for one of his frequent business trips, which leave him exhausted, with piles of work to complete on his return. Hardly 10 minutes into the drive to work, his cell phone rings. Justin, one of his team managers, is requesting a meeting with him today to discuss why some of the teams are not reaching their targets. Joe thinks back to his first job at one of the major banks; teamwork was nonexistent and, with his position at the bottom of the managerial rung, he was hardly ever consulted or asked to make decisions. All this has changed, especially within the informational technology sector. Joe's company, Magical Connections, where he is managing director, has very few managers, with most of the 22 staff working in teams. A far cry to his days in the bank, when he was one of 500 employees, faceless in a hierarchical company. Many of the people that Joe worked with in the banking industry are still there. For Joe it remains a constant challenge to keep competent staff, who leave almost every two years for other IT companies or even move elsewhere in South Africa to seek work. Despite this challenge of people constantly moving in the industry, Joe does not miss the way work used to be organized in the bank, and he likes the way his company is structured. The division of labor within Magical Connection helps its progress, tasks are divided logically, and the frustration of a huge bureaucracy is something he does not miss.

As Joe walks into the office, he meets Alan, who is pacing up and down the reception floor. The company is urgently waiting for new parts from Taiwan to arrive. Alan explains that although the parts landed at the port in Durban, customs is holding them up, as some document seems to be missing. Clients who have been promised the various parts have been ringing Alan to find out where they are. Alan appears near the breaking point as he explains heatedly to Joe the pressure of having to deal with irate customers who want everything *now*. Joe is empathic with Alan as he too constantly faces pressure from all sides. After a brief meeting with Alan and brainstorming solutions to this crisis, Joe eagerly helps himself to his third cup of coffee, hoping the caffeine will perk him up. Although it's only 10 A.M., he finds a cigarette in his desk drawer and goes outside to smoke. He is well aware of the health risks, not to speak about the wrath he would face if his wife found out, but as always the day seems packed with obstacles and Joe uses this five-minute break to be on his own.

At 11, Joe sits down with one of his teams to discuss their targets. Justin starts the meeting by accusing Sharon of not performing adequately and thereby jeopardizing the team's target. Justin rants on that he is tired of having to work even harder to make up for Sharon's poor performance. As Joe sits through the meeting he realizes that Justin's antagonistic nature is not helping the meeting, and Joe is aware that the lack of good interpersonal skills of some team members only hinders the effective working of the team. Moreover, he is going to have to ascertain why Sharon is not meeting her targets. Joe makes a mental note to try to organize some training on interpersonal skills for all teams. It is imperative for Magical Connections that teams be effective, as this translates into remaining competitive at both a national and a global level. If the company is to stay afloat in this highly competitive environment, remaining competitive is a cornerstone to survival.

Dan, Joe's old school friend, phones him at 1 P.M. to invite him to lunch. Joe laughs and reminds Dan that he has not had a lunch break in the past two years. He thinks longingly of a quiet lunch—good food and company—but knows that he has too much to do. Justin is still angry about poor team performance, and Joe knows he needs to deal with this issue as soon as possible. Dan laughs back at him and tells him that as managing director he should be delegating more and enjoying some time off. He has a point, thinks Joe. Empowerment is still a relatively new concept in South Africa, but Joe knows that if he delegated more of his work to younger staff and allowed them to make more decisions, it would free up more of his time to think about long-term strategy for his company. But today is not the day for a lunch break, so a hamburger and chips from the canteen will have to do.

At 2:30, Fiona walks into his office and tells Joe of her intent to leave the company. Joe's heart sinks at the thought. She is one of the brightest staff members, and this means that again the company will have to try to attract and retain a new person. The recruitment and selection of a new person will be time-consuming, and Joe makes a mental note to start this process.

At 4, Joe finds himself lying on a table, having a massage in his office. This new idea was adopted by the company on recommendation from employees about a month ago. All employees are entitled to a 30-minute massage once a week. With gentle music floating in his office, the smell of aromatherapy oils lingering in the air, Joe feels his knots being worked under the masseur's able hands and feels the release of his tension. What a great idea this has turned out to be.

With a bulging briefcase Joe manages to leave the office at 6 P.M.—aware that his wife has been looking after their daughter all day and will now be exhausted and desperate for him to come home and help. He has about six new computer journals he needs to read, and a page of websites someone gave him that he needs to explore. Added to this Joe realizes that next week he needs to undertake a vendor computer-training course, which will keep him out of the office. The almost constant pressure to retrain and to keep abreast of the flood of information within this industry is an overwhelming feature of Joe's life.

As Joe starts his 20-minute drive home he puts a new CD on and starts humming to his favorite track. The humming soon changes to a full-throated bellow as he sings the chorus out loud and makes drumming noises on the steering wheel. However, a phone call with another work-related issue interrupts this pleasant interlude. As he ends the call, Joe thinks to himself that he is going to take his wife and daughter away this weekend. Perhaps to the mountains, where they can relax as a family and he can spend some time talking to his wife. He grins to himself, no cell phone and no laptop. Now somewhat comforted, he thinks of the challenges he faces tomorrow and in the future. Magical Connection needs to remain a company that is fast, flexible, responsive, resilient, and creative, and Joe looks forward to being one of the people leading it. Despite the challenges of his job, Joe loves his work and finds it challenging and rewarding.

Discussion Questions

1. Identify the stressors facing Joe.
2. How do you think Joe could go about managing his stress more effectively?
3. Would it be fair to argue that employees within the IT sector experience higher levels of stress than, say, employees within the banking or manufacturing sector?

Source: Reprinted with permission of Hazel Bothma.

RETHINKING THE RAT RACE

BusinessWeek Long work hours. They have become a badge of honor, a sign of status and importance. The harder you work, the higher your rise on the corporate ladder. Rather than free us from work, technology has eroded the boundaries between work and leisure. Even if Americans can't bring themselves to take more official time off from the job, they will increasingly demand that the job be more accommodating to their personal time. They may work until midnight, but they also want the right to surf the Web at work or spend more time chatting with co-workers.

This *Business Week* case study looks at shifting expectations regarding hours of work and work–life balance. This article speculates about whether office life in the future will mix work and leisure together as much as these two are getting mixed together at home. Read through this *Business Week* article at www.mhhe.com/mcshane3e and prepare for the discussion questions below.

Discussion Questions

1. What are the main reasons presented in this article why Americans work so many hours each year?
2. In your opinion, will the blurring of work and leisure at home and in the workplace increase or decrease stress levels? Explain your answer.

Source: D. Brady, "Rethinking the Rat Race," *Business Week,* August 26, 2002, p. 142.

STAGE FRIGHT!

Purpose This exercise is designed to help you to diagnose a common stressful situation and determine how stress management practices apply to this situation.

Background Stage fright—including the fear of public speaking—is one of the most stressful experiences many people have in everyday life. According to some estimates, nearly three-quarters of us frequently get stage fright, even when speaking or acting in front of a small audience. Stage fright is an excellent topic for this team activity on stress management because the psychological and physiological symptoms of stage fright are really symptoms of stress. In other words, stage fright is the stress experience in a specific context involving a public audience. Based on the personal experiences of team members, your team is asked to identify the symptoms of stage fright and to determine specific stress management activities that effectively combat stage fright.

Instructions

- *Step 1*—Students are organized into teams, typically four to six students per team. Ideally, each team should have one or more people who acknowledge that they have experienced stage fright.
- *Step 2*—Each team's first task is to identify the symptoms of stage fright. The best way

to organize these symptoms is to look at the three categories of stress outcomes described in the textbook: physiological, psychological, and behavioral. The specific stage fright symptoms may be different from the stress outcomes described in the textbook, but the three broad categories would be relevant. Teams should be prepared to identify several symptoms and to present one or two specific examples of stage fright symptoms based on personal experiences of team members. (Please remember that individual students are not required to describe their experiences to the entire class.)

- *Step 3*—Each team's second task is to identify specific strategies people could or have applied to minimize stage fright. The five categories of stress management presented in the textbook will likely provide a useful template in which to organize the specific stage fright management activities. Each team should document several strategies to minimize stage fright and be able to present one or two specific examples to illustrate some of these strategies.
- *Step 4*—The class will congregate to hear each team's analysis of symptoms and solutions to stage fright. This information will then be compared to the stress experience and stress management practices, respectively.

TIME STRESS SCALE

Purpose This self-assessment is designed to help you to identify your level of time-related stress.

Instructions Read each of the following statements and circle "Yes" or "No." Then use the scoring key in Appendix B to calculate your results. This exercise is completed alone so students assess themselves honestly without concerns of social comparison. However, class discussion will focus on the time stress scale.

1. Yes No Do you plan to slow down in the coming year?
2. Yes No Do you consider yourself a workaholic?
3. Yes No When you need more time, do

4.	Yes	No	you tend to cut back on your sleep?
	At the end of the day, do you often feel that you have not accomplished what you had set out to do?
5.	Yes	No	Do you worry that you don't spend enough time with your family or friends?
6.	Yes	No	Do you feel that you're constantly under stress trying to accomplish more than you can handle?

7.	Yes	No	Do you feel trapped in a daily routine?
8.	Yes	No	Do you feel that you just don't have time for fun any more?
9.	Yes	No	Do you often feel under stress when you don't have enough time?
10.	Yes	No	Would you like to spend more time alone?

Source: Statistics Canada's 1998 General Social Survey. Cited in P. DeMont, "Too Much Stress, Too Little Time," *Ottawa Citizen*, November 12, 1999.

SELF-ASSESSMENT EXERCISE 7.5

BEHAVIOR ACTIVITY PROFILE—THE TYPE A SCALE

Purpose   This self-assessment is designed to help you to identify the extent to which you follow a Type A behavior pattern.

Instructions   Each of us displays certain kinds of behaviors, thought patterns of personal characteristics. In this self-assessment, select the number that you feel best describes where you are between each pair of words or phrases. The best answer for each set of descriptions is the response that most nearly describes the way you feel, behave, or think. Answer these in terms of your regular or typical behavior, thoughts, or characteristics. The results show your relative position on the Type A and Type B behavior pattern continuum.

SELF-ASSESSMENT EXERCISE 7.6

WORK ADDICTION RISK TEST

Purpose   This self-assessment is designed to help you identify the extent to which you are a workaholic.

Instructions   This instrument presents several statements and asks you to indicate the extent to which each statement is true of your work habits. You need to be honest with yourself to ascertain a reasonable estimate of your level of workaholism.

SELF-ASSESSMENT EXERCISE 7.7

PERCEIVED STRESS SCALE

Purpose   This self-assessment is designed to help you to estimate your perceived general level of stress.

Instructions   The questions in this scale ask you about your feelings and thoughts during the last month. In each case, please indicate how often you felt or thought a certain way. You need to be honest with yourself to ascertain a reasonable estimate of your general level of stress.

Team Processes

Decision Making and Creativity

Learning Objectives

After reading this chapter, you should be able to:

- Diagram the rational model of decision making.

- Explain why people have difficulty identifying problems and opportunities.

- Contrast the rational model with how people actually evaluate and choose alternatives.

- Explain how emotions and intuition influence our selection of alternatives.

- Outline the causes of escalation of commitment to a poor decision.

- Describe four benefits of employee involvement in decision making.

- Identify four contingencies that affect the optimal level of employee involvement.

- Outline the four steps in the creative process.

- Describe the characteristics of employees and the workplace that support creativity.

At 9 A.M. on February 1, 2003, the NASA space shuttle *Columbia* disintegrated during reentry over Texas and other western states, killing all seven crew members. The physical cause of the accident was that *Columbia*'s left wing was damaged during liftoff by a large piece of foam debris, and the gaping hole allowed superheated gases to melt the wing's aluminum frame during reentry.

Although Columbia's disintegration was caused by a damaged wing, a special accident investigation board also concluded that NASA's damaged decision-making process resulted in several "missed opportunities" to avoid loss of life. NASA's middle management continually resisted attempts to label the foam hit as a problem. For example, a team of engineers studying the broken foam's safety risk requested new photos of *Columbia*'s wing from military satellites. That request was denied 26 minutes later without explanation. Managers also relied on a faulty simulation of the foam strike and questioned the results of tests suggesting the foam would cause damage.

The loss of the space shuttle Columbia *(shown here lifting off for its final flight) and its crew was caused by more than foam hitting the left wing; it was also due to NASA's flawed decision making.*

The accident investigation board explained that NASA managers didn't want the foam strike to be a problem because they were under intense pressure to keep the shuttle missions on track. Small pieces of foam hit the shuttle on most flights, so managers eventually viewed these events as routine. Furthermore, if the foam strike had damaged the shuttle, NASA would face the almost impossible situation of rescuing *Columbia*'s crew. In one meeting, *Columbia*'s lead flight director candidly stated: "I don't think there is much we can do, so you know it's not really a factor during the flight because there isn't much we can do about it."

The board also noted that NASA managers discouraged employee involvement. One engineer who raised concerns about the foam strike was called an "alarmist." When the team of engineers investigating the foam strike submitted their concerns, the lead flight director said in an e-mail that their "rationale was lousy." The result was decision making lacking sufficient information. "They have managers who don't know the technical background, but make decisions without asking the engineers for information," said one accident investigation board member.[1] ∎

The tragic loss of the space shuttle *Columbia* is a case study in the challenges of decision making in organizational settings. **Decision making** is a conscious process of making choices among one or more alternatives with the intention of moving toward some desired state of affairs.[2] This chapter begins by outlining the "rational" model of decision making. Then, we examine this model more critically by recognizing how people identify problems and opportunities, choose among alternatives, and evaluate the success of their decisions differently from the rational model. Bounded rationality, escalation of commitment, and intuition are three of the more prominent topics in this section. Next, we explore the role of employee involvement in decision making, including the benefits of involvement and the factors that determine the optimal level of involvement. The final section of this chapter examines the factors that support creativity in decision making, including characteristics of creative people, work environments that support creativity, and creativity activities.

The "Rational" Decision-Making Model

How do people make decisions in organizational settings? We can begin to answer this question by looking at the traditional "rational" model of decision making shown in Exhibit 8.1.[3] Throughout this chapter, we'll see that this rational model *does not* represent how people actually make decisions. However, it does provide a useful template to examine various parts of the decision process.

EXHIBIT 8.1

Rational model of decision making

1. Identify problem or opportunity
2. Choose the best decision style
3. Develop alternative solutions
4. Choose the best solution
5. Implement the selected alternative
6. Evaluate decision outcomes

Rational Decision-Making Process

According to the rational model, the first step in the decision-making process is to identify the problem or recognize an opportunity. A *problem* is a deviation between the current and the desired situation—the gap between "what is" and "what ought to be."[4] This deviation is a *symptom* of more fundamental root causes that need to be corrected.[5] An *opportunity* is a deviation between current expectations and a potentially better situation that was not previously expected. In other words, decision makers realize that certain decisions may produce results beyond current goals or expectations.

The second step is to determine the most appropriate decision style.[6] One important issue is whether this is a programmed or nonprogrammed decision.[7] A **programmed decision** follows standard operating procedures. There is no need to explore alternative solutions because the optimal solution has already been identified and documented. At many call centers, for example, staff members rely on programmed decisions in a computer database. The database narrows down the customer's problem with a set of questions, then presents a ready-made solution. In contrast, **nonprogrammed decisions** include all steps in the decision model because the problems are new, complex, or ill-defined. In these cases, decision makers must search for alternatives and possibly develop a unique solution. Programmed decisions eventually drive out nonprogrammed decisions because we rely on past solutions as problems reappear. To some extent, this is one of the problems that led to the *Columbia* disaster. NASA managers viewed the foam strikes as routine events that required only routine actions.

The third step in the rational decision model is to develop a list of possible solutions.[8] This step usually begins by searching for ready-made solutions, such as practices that have worked well on similar problems. If an acceptable solution cannot be found, then decision makers design a custom-made solution or modify an existing one. The fourth step is choosing the best alternative. In a purely rational process, this would involve identifying all factors against which the alternatives are judged, assigning weights reflecting the importance of those factors, rating each alternative on those factors, and calculating each alternative's total value from the ratings and factor weights.[9] The fifth step in the rational model is to implement the selected alternative. This is followed by the sixth step, evaluating whether the gap has narrowed between "what is" and "what ought to be." Ideally, this information should come from systematic benchmarks, so that relevant feedback is objective and easily observed.

programmed decision

Routine decisions whereby decision makers can follow standard operating procedures to select the preferred solution without the need to identify or evaluate alternative choices.

nonprogrammed decision

Unique, complex, or ill-defined situations whereby decision makers follow the full decision-making process, including a careful search for and/or development of unique solutions.

Problems with the Rational Decision-Making Model

The rational model seems so logical, yet it is rarely practiced in reality. One reason is that the rational model assumes people are efficient and logical information processing machines. But as the next few pages will reveal, people have difficulty recognizing problems; they cannot (or will not) simultaneously process the huge volume of information needed to identify the best solution; and they have difficulty recognizing when their choices have failed. The second reason why the rational model doesn't fit reality is that it focuses on logical thinking and completely ignores the fact that emotions also influence—perhaps even dominate—the decision-making process. As we shall discover in this chapter, emotions both support and interfere with our quest to make better decisions.[10] With these points in mind, let's look again at each step of decision making, but with more detail about what really happens.

Identifying Problems and Opportunities

When Albert Einstein was asked how he would save the world in one hour, he replied that he would spend the first 55 minutes defining the problem and the last 5 minutes solving it.[11] Problem identification, the first step in decision making, is arguably the most important step. But problems and opportunities do not appear on our desks as well-labeled objects. Instead, decision makers translate information into evidence that something is wrong or that an opportunity is available. As the opening story to this chapter illustrated, this translation process is filled with human bias. NASA managers did not identify the foam strike as a problem partly because the evidence was far from perfect (they didn't know whether the foam chunk had hit the wing squarely or on an angle). Still, one accident investigation board member remarked that the parking lot attendants knew a large chunk of foam flying at 1,500 miles per hour would cause damage!

The process of labeling an event or situation as a problem involves both the rational and emotional centers of the brain.[12] Recall from Chapter 4 that we process perceptual information both logically and emotionally. In a split second, the emotional center classifies situations as good or bad and assigns corresponding emotional markers (anger, surprise, delight, etc.) to the situation based on this quick evaluation. The emotional markers are then sent to the rational center where they influence the slower logical analysis of the situation. Both the emotional markers and the logical analysis determine whether you perceive something as a problem, opportunity, or irrelevant. Your emotional reaction and rational analysis of the situation also depend on which information you receive and how it is presented.

Let's say that a worried-looking colleague tells you that the company's salesperson in California just quit. You might immediately become worried or frustrated, possibly in reaction to the other person's emotional display. In other words, your emotional brain center quickly assigned these emotional markers to the news about the salesperson quitting. Meanwhile, the rational part of your brain is working through the situation and eventually concludes that this event isn't so bad after all. The salesperson's performance had been mediocre, and you already know of an excellent salesperson at another company who wants to join your company in that region. What initially felt like a problem was really an opportunity based on your rational analysis of the situation. The initial emotion of worry or frustration might have been wrong in this situation, but sometimes your emotions provide a good indicator of problems or opportunities. Later, we'll see how emotions can be valuable allies in the quest to identify problems and choose the best solution.

Perceptual Biases and Diagnostic Skill Failures

Along with weighing the emotional and rational evaluations of a situation, decision makers have to deal with imperfect perceptions. As we learned in Chapter 3, selective attention mechanisms cause relevant information to be unconsciously screened out. Moreover, employees, clients, and others with vested interests try to influence the decision maker's perceptions so that information is more or less likely to be perceived as a problem or opportunity.[13] Another perceptual challenge, also noted in Chapter 3, is that people see problems or opportunities through their *mental models*. These working models of the

Famous Missed Opportunities

Mental models create road maps that guide our decisions. Unfortunately, these maps also potentially block our ability to see emerging problems and opportunities. Here are a few famous examples:

- *L.A. Confidential* screenwriter Brian Helgeland approached Hollywood studios about a new film featuring a lowly squire in fourteenth-century England who aspires to be a knight. The squire and his street-smart colleagues (including Geoffrey Chaucer) would do battle on contemporary themes such as youth, freedom, and equality. The entire film would be set to 1970s rock music. The Hollywood studios weren't impressed. "When I pitched it, I couldn't sell it," laments Helgeland. "Some people would laugh and then say, 'What are you really here for?'" Undeterred, Helgeland eventually convinced Columbia Pictures to back the project. The film, *A Knight's Tale*, recouped its $41 million costs in just three weeks and went on to become one of the more successful films of the year.
- Graphical user interfaces, mice, windows, pull-down menus, laser printing, distributed computing, and Ethernet technologies weren't invented by Apple, Microsoft, or IBM. These essential elements of contemporary personal computing originated in the 1970s from researchers at Xerox Palo Alto Research Center (PARC). Unfortunately, Xerox executives were so focused on their photocopier business that they didn't bother to patent most of these inventions. Xerox has successfully applied some of its laser technology, but the lost value of Xerox PARC's other computing discoveries is much larger than the entire photocopier industry today.
- In 1961, William Oldendorf developed a machine that would become the foundation of modern CT scanners, replacing much more invasive procedures to diagnose the brain. But CT scanners didn't arrive until many years later because manufacturers of traditional x-ray equipment couldn't see any value in Oldendorf's discovery. A letter from one company said: "Even if it could be made to work

Brian Helgeland's film A Knight's Tale *paid for itself in just three weeks even though most Hollywood studio executives rejected the proposal.*

as you suggest, we cannot imagine a significant market for such an expensive apparatus which would do nothing but make a radiographic cross-section of a head."
- When the World Wide Web burst onto the cyberspace scene in the early 1990s, Bill Gates wondered what all the fuss was about. Even as late as 1996, the Microsoft founder lampooned investors for their love-in with companies that made Internet products. However, Gates eventually realized the error in his mental model of computing. Making up for lost time, Microsoft bought Hotmail and other Web-savvy companies and added Internet support to its Windows operating system.

Sources: "W. Oldendorf," *ASNWeb* (online), August 2003; C. Sim, "Battling the Odds," *KrisWorld* (Singapore Airlines Inflight Magazine), September 2001, pp. 8–10; B. Campbell and M. Conron, "Xerox Ready to Hit Another Home Run," *Ottawa Citizen,* June 28, 1999; O. Port, "Xerox Won't Duplicate Past Errors," *Business Week,* September 29, 1997, p. 98; T. Abate, "Meet Bill Gates, Stand-Up Comic," *San Francisco Examiner,* March 13, 1996, p. D1.

world help us to make sense of our environment, but they also perpetuate assumptions that blind us to new realities. Connections 8.1 describes how narrow mental models are the source of several famous missed opportunities.

Another barrier to effective problem identification is that decision makers have imperfect diagnostic skills.[14] A common diagnostic error is the tendency to define problems in terms of their solutions. Someone who says "The problem is that we need more control over our suppliers" has fallen into this trap. Notice that this statement focuses on a solution (controlling suppliers), whereas proper diagnosis would determine the cause of symptoms before

© 1998 Randy Glasbergen.

"My team has created a very innovative solution, but we're still looking for a problem to go with it."

(Copyright © Randy Glasbergen. Reprinted with special permission from www.glasbergen.com.)

jumping to solutions. The tendency to focus on solutions is based on the human bias for action as well as the need to reduce uncertainty.[15]

Decision makers also focus on solutions because they have a preferred set of actions that have worked well in the past. Some executives are known for cutting the workforce whenever they face problems; others introduce a new customer service program as their favorite solution to a variety of problems. The point here is that decision makers tend to look at problems from the perspective of the ready-made solutions that worked for them in the past.

Identifying Problems and Opportunities More Effectively

Recognizing problems and opportunities will always be a challenge, but the process can be improved through awareness of these perceptual and diagnostic limitations. By recognizing how mental models restrict a person's understanding of the world, decision makers learn to openly consider other perspectives of reality. Perceptual and diagnostic weaknesses can also be minimized by discussing the situation with colleagues. Decision makers discover blind spots in problem identification by hearing how others perceive certain information and diagnose problems.[16] Opportunities also become apparent when outsiders explore this information from their different mental models.

Evaluating and Choosing Alternatives

bounded rationality
Processing limited and imperfect information and satisficing rather than maximizing when choosing among alternatives.

According to the rational model of decision making, people rely on logic to evaluate and choose alternatives. This rational process assumes that decision makers have well-articulated and agreed-on organizational goals, that they efficiently and simultaneously process facts about all alternatives and the consequences of those alternatives, and that they choose the alternative with the highest payoff.

Nobel Prize–winning organizational scholar Herbert Simon questioned these assumptions half a century ago. He argued that people engage in **bounded rationality** because they process limited and imperfect information and rarely select the best choice.[17] Simon and other OB researchers subsequently demonstrated that how people evaluate and choose alternatives differs from the rational model in several ways, as illustrated in Exhibit 8.2. These

| **EXHIBIT 8.2** | Rational model assumptions versus organizational behavior findings about choosing decision alternatives |

Rational decision model assumptions	**Observations from organizational behavior**
Decision makers use goals that are clear, compatible, and agreed upon.	Decision makers use goals that are ambiguous, are in conflict, and lack consensus.
Decision makers can process information about all alternatives and their outcomes.	Decision makers have limited information-processing abilities.
Decision makers evaluate all alternatives simultaneously.	Decision makers evaluate alternatives sequentially.
Decision makers evaluate alternatives against a set of absolute standards.	Decision makers evaluate alternatives against an implicit favorite alternative.
Decision makers process factual information.	Decision makers process perceptually distorted information.
Decision makers choose the alternative with the highest payoff (maximizing).	Decision makers choose the alternative that is good enough (satisficing).

differences are so significant that even economists are now shifting from the rational model to the bounded rationality model in their theories and assumptions.[18] Let's look at these differences in terms of goals, information processing, and maximization.

Problems with Goals

We need clear goals to choose the best solution. Goals identify "what ought to be" and, therefore, provide a standard against which each alternative is evaluated. The reality, however, is that organizational goals are often ambiguous or in conflict with each other. For instance, NASA managers had conflicting goals of maintaining the highest level of safety and keeping future shuttle flights on schedule. One survey recently found that 25 percent of managers and employees felt decisions are delayed because of difficulty agreeing on what they want the decision to achieve.[19]

Problems with Information Processing

People do not make perfectly rational decisions because they don't process information very well. One problem is that decision makers can't possibly think through all of the alternatives and the outcomes of those alternatives. Consequently, they look at only a few alternatives and only some of the main outcomes of those alternatives.[20] For example, there may be dozens of computer brands to choose from and dozens of features to consider, yet people typically evaluate only a few brands and a few features.

A related problem is that decision makers typically look at alternatives sequentially rather than examining all alternatives at the same time. As a new alternative comes along, it is immediately compared to an **implicit favorite.** An implicit favorite is an alternative that the decision maker prefers and is used as a comparison against which other choices are judged. There are two problems with this sequential implicit favorite process. First, people often form an implicit favorite based on limited information long before the formal process of evaluating alternatives begins. Second, people unconsciously try to make their implicit favorite come out the winner in most comparisons.[21] They do this by distorting information and changing the importance of decision criteria.

A recent study of auditing students illustrates how people distort information and decision criteria to support their implicit favorite.[22] Students were given a detailed case and asked to determine whether a company's financial problems were "significant" enough that they should be reported in the audit. Students who decided that the company was in financial trouble distorted the available information to make the financial problems appear worse, whereas those who preferred not to report the problems minimized any reference to the negative information. Moreover, students who wanted to report the company's financial problems used a vague definition of "significant," whereas students who didn't want to report the problems used a precise and harsher definition of this criterion. In short, these students developed a preference about whether to report the company's problems, then distorted information and their decision criterion to support this preference.

Problems with Maximization

Decision makers tend to select the alternative that is acceptable or "good enough," rather than the best possible solution. In other words, they engage in **satisficing** rather than maximizing. Satisficing occurs because it isn't possible to identify every alternative, and information about available alternatives is imperfect or ambiguous. Satisficing also occurs because, as mentioned already, decision makers tend to evaluate alternatives sequentially. They evaluate alternatives one at a time against the implicit favorite and eventually select an option that is good enough to satisfy their needs or preferences.[23]

Emotions and Making Choices

Herbert Simon and other OB scholars demonstrated that the rational brain center does not evaluate alternatives nearly as well as is assumed by the rational model of decision making. However, they neglected to mention another glaring weakness with the rational model, namely, that it completely ignores the effect of emotions in human decision making. Just as both the rational and emotional brain centers alert us to problems, these processes also influence our choice of alternatives.

Scholars are just beginning to understand the effects of emotions on decision making.[24] As we learned in Chapters 4 and 5, the rational brain center processes (imperfectly, as we just learned) information about the various choices. The emotional center more quickly creates emotional markers that attract us to some alternatives and repel us from others. For instance, we pay

implicit favorite
The decision maker's preferred alternative against which all other choices are judged.

satisficing
Selecting a solution that is satisfactory, or "good enough" rather than optimal or "the best."

more attention to details when in a negative mood, possibly because a negative mood signals that there is something wrong that requires attention. In contrast, we rely on standard routines when in a positive mood, so we pay less attention to details. Specific emotions also have specific effects on our decisions. Consider anger, which tends to produce an urgent "fight" response to a threatening situation. When people experience anger, they are more likely to rely on stereotypes and other shortcuts to speed up decision making. Overall, emotions have a potentially large influence on how we evaluate alternatives.

Intuition and Making Choices

Greg McDonald felt uneasy about a suspicious-looking crack in the rock face, so the veteran miner warned a co-worker to stay away from the area. "There was no indication there was anything wrong—just a little crack," McDonald recalled. A few minutes later, the ceiling in that mineshaft 3,000 feet underground caved in. Fortunately, the co-worker had heeded McDonald's advice. "If he had been there, he would be dead," said McDonald, who was clearly shaken by the incident.[25]

The gut instinct that helped Greg McDonald save his co-worker's life is also the subject of considerable discussion in organizational behavior. Most people—whether underground miners or corporate executives—will tell you that they pay attention to their intuition when making decisions. **Intuition** is the ability to know when a problem or opportunity exists and to select the best course of action without conscious reasoning.[26] Some scholars warn us that intuition is merely wishful thinking that can have disastrous results. In spite of these warnings, most professionals and executives say they rely on intuition, particularly in combination with more rational decision making. "Often there is absolutely no way that you could have the time to thoroughly analyze every one of the options or alternatives available to you," says Ralph S. Larsen, chairman and CEO of Johnson & Johnson. "So you have to rely on your business judgment."[27] Notice that intuition rarely occurs alone. Decision makers analyze the available information, then turn to their intuition to complete the process.

Should we rely on intuition or view it with caution? The answer is both. It is true that we sometimes justify biased and nonsystematic decision making as intuition. When deciding to invest in a new business, for example, decision makers run the risk of following their emotions rather than evidence. However, there is also increasing research evidence that intuition is the conduit through which people use their tacit knowledge. Tacit knowledge is subtle information acquired through observation and experience that is not clearly understood and therefore cannot be explicitly communicated (see Chapter 3). This knowledge incorporates logical reasoning that has become habit over time. Thus, intuition allows us to draw on our vast storehouse of unconscious knowledge.[28]

Choosing Solutions More Effectively

It is very difficult to get around the human limitations of making choices, but a few strategies may help. Some companies systematically evaluate alternatives by identifying relevant factors and scoring each alternative on those criteria. For example, a cross-functional committee at Dow Chemical Company relies on a systematic evaluation process to decide which information technology projects to pursue.[29] This process potentially minimizes the implicit

intuition
The ability to know when a problem or opportunity exists and select the best course of action without conscious reasoning.

favorite and satisficing problems that occur when relying on general subjective judgments. However, there is still a risk that decision makers will bias the criteria so the preferred choice ultimately receives the highest score. Intuition also has to be taken into account within this rational process. We need to be careful that "gut feelings" are not merely perceptual distortions and false assumptions, but intuition seems to have a role in making sound choices.[30]

Another issue is how to work with our emotions when making choices. Many of us have made bad decisions in emotional haste, and many have tried to make "rational" choices when we should have paid more attention to our emotions. The first recommendation here is that we need to be constantly aware that decisions are influenced by both rational and emotional processes. With this awareness, some decision makers deliberately revisit important issues so they look at the information in different moods and have allowed their initial emotions to subside. Others practice **scenario planning,** in which they anticipate emergencies long before they occur, so that alternative courses of action are evaluated without the pressure and emotions that occur during real emergencies.[31]

> **scenario planning**
> A systematic process of thinking about alternative futures, and what the organization should do to anticipate and react to those environments.

Evaluating Decision Outcomes

Contrary to the rational model, decision makers aren't completely honest with themselves when evaluating the effectiveness of their decisions. One concern is that after making a choice, decision makers tend to support their choice by forgetting or downplaying the negative features of the selected alternative and emphasizing its positive features. This perceptual distortion, known as **postdecisional justification,** results from the need to maintain our self-esteem.[32] Postdecisional justification gives people an excessively optimistic evaluation of their decisions, but only until they receive very clear and undeniable information to the contrary. Unfortunately, it also inflates the decision maker's initial evaluation of the decision, so reality often comes as a painful shock when objective feedback is finally received.

> **postdecisional justification**
> Justifying choices by unconsciously inflating the quality of the selected option and deflating the quality of the discarded options.

Escalation of Commitment

A second problem when evaluating decision outcomes is **escalation of commitment**—the tendency to repeat an apparently bad decision or allocate more resources to a failing course of action.[33] There are plenty of escalation examples around the world. Tokyo's Metropolitan Transport Bureau promised to build a 20-mile high-speed subway loop under the city in record time and at enormous profit. Instead, the multi-billion-dollar project was seriously over budget, more than three years overdue, and won't be profitable until 2040, if ever. Denver International Airport was supposed to include a state-of-the-art automated baggage handling system. Instead, the project was eventually abandoned, causing the airport to open 16 months late and $2 billion over budget. Escalation also occurred years ago when the British government continued funding the Concorde supersonic jet long after its lack of commercial viability was apparent. To this day, some scholars refer to escalation of commitment as the "Concorde fallacy."[34]

> **escalation of commitment**
> The tendency to repeat an apparently bad decision or allocate more resources to a failing course of action.

Causes of Escalating Commitment   Why are people led deeper and deeper into failing projects? Organizational behavior scholars have identified several reasons, including self-justification, gambler's fallacy, perceptual blinders, and closing costs.

In 1997, Scotland's new parliament building had an estimated cost of £50 million (U.S.$80 million) and an estimated completion date of 2001. Instead, it will cost nearly £400 million and might be finished three years later than planned. Some writers say that elected officials didn't want to lose face over building contracts they had signed before choosing a different site (Holyrood) and doubling the building size. In spite of warnings from critics, government leaders were also extremely optimistic that the many design changes would not escalate costs. The editor of Scottish architecture journal ARCA wrote: "The Parliament building will set an all-time world record for waste of money, incompetent management and covering backsides and political reputations."[35] How can governments minimize the risk of escalation of commitment?

- *Self-justification*—Individuals try to create a positive impression of themselves (see Chapter 12), which includes the image that they make good decisions.[36] If a decision doesn't seem to be having the desired outcomes, those who made the decision pour more money and other resources into it to symbolize their confidence in their own decision-making ability. The Scottish parliament debacle seems to be partly caused by this factor. Elected officials signed contracts for a smaller building on a different site and were possibly worried that terminating those contracts would symbolize that they had made a mistake.
- *Gambler's fallacy*—Many projects result in escalation of commitment because decision makers underestimate the risk and overestimate their probability of success. They become victims of the so-called gambler's fallacy by having inflated expectations of their ability to control problems that may arise. For instance, elected officials in Scotland falsely believed that luck would be on their side in keeping costs low, even after allowing numerous design changes.
- *Perceptual blinders*—Escalation of commitment sometimes occurs because decision makers do not see the problems soon enough. Through perceptual defense (see Chapter 3), they unconsciously screen out or explain away negative information. Serious problems initially look like random errors along the trend line to success. Even when they see that something is wrong, the information is sufficiently ambiguous that it can be misinterpreted or justified.
- *Closing costs*—Even when a project's success is in doubt, decision makers will persist because the costs of ending the project are high or unknown. Terminating a major project may involve large financial penalties, a bad public image, or personal political costs.

Evaluating Decision Outcomes More Effectively

One effective way to minimize escalation of commitment and postdecisional justification is to separate decision choosers from decision evaluators. This tends to avoid the problem of saving face because the person responsible for evaluating the decision is not connected to the original decision. For example, one study found that banks were more likely to take action against bad loans after the executive responsible for signing the original loan had been transferred elsewhere.[37] In other words, the bank cut its losses only when someone else took over the loan portfolio. Similarly, elected officials in Scotland capped fees and launched an inquiry only after the original champion of the Holyrood parliament project stepped down.

A second strategy is to publicly establish a preset level at which the decision is abandoned or reevaluated.[38] This is similar to a stop-loss order in the stock market, whereby the stock is sold if it falls below a certain price. The problem with this solution is that conditions are often so complex that it is difficult to identify an appropriate point to abandon a project.[39] Finally, projects might have less risk of escalation if several people are involved. Co-workers continuously monitor each other and might notice problems sooner than someone working alone on the project. Employee involvement offers these and other benefits to the decision-making process, as we learn next.

Employee Involvement in Decision Making

Rich Kisner, a maintenance mechanic at TriMet, had several ideas that he calculated would annually save Oregon's transit agency thousands of dollars. So, when management set up a special meeting to hear employee suggestions, Kisner was there to explain how TriMet could reduce costs, such as by using less expensive lights in some areas and a special ladder to replace the more expensive bucket truck in other areas. TriMet's executives listened closely and agreed to implement many of Kisner's ideas. "Employees are the people who know their jobs best," says TriMet general manager Fred Hansen, who aims to save $3 million this year from employee suggestions

TriMet's leaders realize that in this world of rapid change and increasing complexity, they rarely have enough information to ensure the organization's success. Whether this information is about reducing costs or improving the customer experience, employee involvement can potentially solve problems or realize opportunities more effectively. **Employee involvement** (also called *participative management*) refers to the degree to which employees influence how their work is organized and carried out.[40] At the lowest level, participation involves asking employees for information. They do not make recommendations and might not even know what the problem is about. At a moderate level of involvement, employees are told about the problem and provide recommendations to the decision maker. At the highest level of involvement, the entire decision-making process is handed over to employees. They identify the problem, choose the best alternative, and implement their choice.[41]

Various levels and forms of employee involvement exist throughout every organization. Warwick International, a Welsh chemical company, encourages employees to continuously identify ways for their own operation or department to reduce costs. The ideas are presented to management, who then decides which ideas to implement. At Atlas Container's corrugated box and packaging plant in Meriden, Connecticut, employees are actively involved in discussing and deciding on machine investments, personnel issues, and other matters.[42] Global Connections 8.2 provides a particularly dramatic example of high involvement, where employees in several Argentinean companies have completely taken over day-to-day decisions after the original owners abandoned their debt-riddled companies.

Some countries require employee involvement at both the work site and corporate levels through a process of **codetermination.** In Sweden, Norway, and some other European countries, for instance, employee representatives sit on supervisory boards, making decisions about executive salaries and recommendations about the company's direction. At the same time, employers

employee involvement

The degree to which employees influence how their work is organized and carried out.

codetermination

A form of employee involvement required by some governments that typically operates at the work site as works councils and at the corporate level as supervisory boards.

High Involvement Saves Argentinean Companies

Empire Pizzeria's owners abandoned the business when they racked up huge debts, including overdue salaries and four years of back rent. Bankruptcy would have created severe hardship for the company's 30 employees because the shop is located in Buenos Aires, Argentina, a country with 22 percent unemployment and one the worst recessions in 100 years. So, employees applied a unique solution: They formed a cooperative and took over the business. "If we were not running the business, we would be out on the street," explains an Empire waiter. "Most of us are over 50 and no employer wants someone our age." The company is now settling past debts and prospering in spite of difficult times.

Over 10,000 employees at more than 160 businesses throughout Argentina are experimenting with self-management through cooperatives that operate businesses abandoned by the original owners. Most of the employee-operated businesses are manufacturing concerns, such as a tractor factory in Córdoba and a tile and ceramics plant in Patagonia. Some of them are struggling, while others are booming since employees took over.

IMPA aluminum factory is one of the success stories. Forty workers took over the factory in 1998 and, for almost one year, scraped by on U.S.$1.40 a day. Four years later, IMPA employs 172 workers, each earning $271 a month. IMPA and most other cooperatives are run by administrative councils elected by employees. Wages, future employment levels, and other important business issues are discussed at monthly meetings. Employee enthusiasm is readily apparent. "Everybody is a partner here," says Guillermo Robledo, IMPA's elected plant manager. "That's our strength, the commitment we feel to something that is our own."

One challenge is that longstanding suppliers and customers have been reluctant to work with companies run by low-level employees. "It was difficult to get started because even though the company had a reputation, people did not believe that we workers were capable of managing things," explains an employee at a cooperative that prints art books, posters, and calendars. "We had to show that the high level of quality was still intact and that the only thing missing was a few executives in the front office."

Sources: L. Rohter, "Workers in Argentina Take Over Abandoned Factories," *New York Times,* July 8, 2003; P. Moser, "In Crisis-Torn Argentina, Workers Rescue Their Factories," *Agence France Presse,* May 17, 2003; C. Fagan, "In Argentine Crisis, Workers Become Entrepreneurs to Survive," *Associated Press,* December 8, 2002; M. Valente, "Argentina: Workers' Cooperatives Revive Bankrupt Companies," *Inter Press Service,* November 29, 2002.

Empire Pizzeria in Buenos Aires, Argentina, is a symbol of how employees (including from left José Gonzalez and José Lazarte) have successfully taken over a business that the original owners abandoned under weight of debt.

must consult with employee representation committees (called works councils) regarding matters of employment staffing, work processes, and individual dismissals.[43]

Benefits of Employee Involvement

For the past half-century, organizational behavior scholars have advised that employee involvement potentially improves decision-making quality and commitment.[44] Involving employees potentially improves decision quality by recognizing problems more quickly and defining them more accurately. Employees are, in many respects, the sensors of the organization's environment. When the organization's activities misalign with customer expectations, employees are usually the first to know. Employee involvement ensures that everyone in the organization is quickly alerted to these problems.

Employee involvement can also potentially improve the number and quality of solutions generated. In a well-managed meeting, team members create *synergy* by pooling their knowledge to form new alternatives. In other words, several people working together can potentially generate more and better solutions than the same people working alone. A third benefit is that employee involvement often improves the likelihood of choosing the best alternative. This occurs because the decision is reviewed by people with diverse perspectives and a broader representation of values.

Along with improving decision quality, employee involvement tends to strengthen employee commitment to the decision. Rather than viewing themselves as agents of someone else's decision, staff members feel personally responsible for its success. Employee involvement also increases perceptions of fairness because workers participate in the allocation of resources and rewards in the project.[45] Consequently, employees are more motivated to implement the decision and are less likely to resist changes resulting from the decision. As one respected scholar recently wrote: "The new organizational realities are that top-down decision making is not sufficiently responsive to the dynamic organizational environment. Employees must be actively involved in decisions—or completely take over many decisions."[46]

Contingencies of Employee Involvement

If employee involvement is so wonderful, why don't companies leave all decisions to employees further down the hierarchy? The answer is that the optimal level of employee involvement depends on the situation. The employee involvement model, shown in Exhibit 8.3, indicates that the best level of employee involvement is contingent on the decision structure, source of decision knowledge, decision commitment, and risk of conflict in the decision process.

- *Decision structure*—At the beginning of this chapter, we learned that some decisions are programmed, whereas others are nonprogrammed. Programmed decisions are less likely to need employee involvement because the solutions are already worked out from past experience. In other words, the benefits of employee involvement increase with the novelty and complexity of the problem or opportunity.
- *Source of decision knowledge*—Subordinates should be involved in some level of decision making when the leader lacks sufficient knowledge and subordinates have additional information to improve decision quality. In

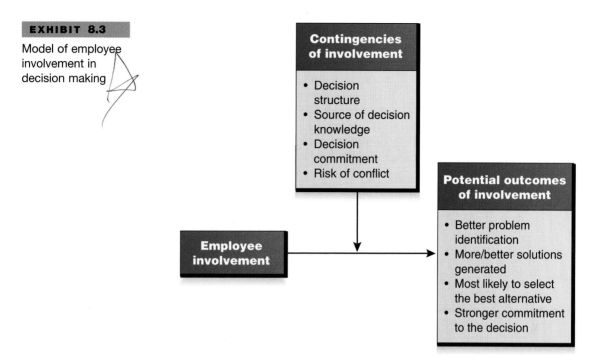

many cases, employees are closer to customers and production activities, so they often know where the company can save money, improve product or service quality, and realize opportunities. This is particularly true for complex decisions where employees are more likely to possess relevant information.[47]

■ *Decision commitment*—Participation tends to improve employee commitment to the decision. If employees are unlikely to accept a decision made without their involvement, then some level of participation is usually necessary.

■ *Risk of conflict*—Two types of conflict undermine the benefits of employee involvement. First, if employee goals and norms conflict with the organization's goals, then only a low level of employee involvement is advisable. Second, the degree of involvement depends on whether employees will reach agreement on the preferred solution. If conflict is likely, then high involvement (i.e., where employees make the decision alone) would be difficult to achieve.

Employee involvement is an important component of the decision-making process. To make the best decisions, we need to involve people who have the most valuable information and who will increase commitment to implement the decision. Another important component of decision making is creativity, which we discuss next.

Creativity

Parcel delivery might seem like a routine business, but that's not the way the folks at Yamato Transport Company see it. The Japanese company was the first to deliver customers' ski equipment to resorts and homes. To keep better track of shipments, customers receive the mobile telephone numbers of Yamato's delivery personnel, not just distribution centers. One local branch office recently started testing the use of lockers at train stations around Japan for pickup and delivery locations, notifying customers by e-mail of the delivery times.[48]

Yamato Transport is successful in Japan's fiercely competitive delivery service industry because it relies on creativity for innovative new services. **Creativity** is the development of an original product, service, or idea that makes a socially recognized contribution.[49] Although there are unique conditions for creativity that we discuss over the next few pages, it is really part of the decision-making process described earlier in the chapter. We rely on creativity to find problems, identify alternatives, and implement solutions. Creativity is not something saved for special occasions. It is an integral part of decision making.

The Creative Process Model

One of the earliest and most influential models of creativity is shown in Exhibit 8.4.[50] The first stage is *preparation*—the person's or group's effort to acquire knowledge and skills regarding the problem or opportunity.[51] Preparation involves developing a clear understanding of what you are trying to achieve through a novel solution, then actively studying information seemingly related to the topic.

The second stage, called *incubation*, is the stage of reflective thought. We put the problem aside, but our mind is still working on it in the background.[52] The important condition here is to maintain a low-level awareness by frequently revisiting the problem. Incubation does not mean that you forget about the problem or issue. Incubation assists **divergent thinking**—reframing the problem in a unique way and generating different approaches to the issue. This contrasts with *convergent thinking*—calculating the conventionally accepted "right answer" to a logical problem.[53] Divergent thinking breaks us away from existing mental models so we can apply concepts or processes from completely different areas of life. Consider the following classic example: Years ago, the experimental bulbs in Thomas Edison's lab kept falling off their fixtures until a technician wondered whether the threaded caps that screwed down tightly on kerosene bottles would work on light bulbs. They did, and the design remains to this day.[54]

Insight, the third stage of creativity, refers to the experience of suddenly becoming aware of a unique idea.[55] These flashes of inspiration don't keep a particular schedule; they might come to you at any time of day or night. They are also fleeting and can be quickly lost if not documented. For this reason, many creative people keep a journal or notebook nearby at all times, so that they can jot down these ideas before they disappear.[56] Insights are merely rough ideas. Their usefulness still requires *verification* through conscious evaluation and

creativity
Developing an original product, service, or idea that makes a socially recognized contribution.

divergent thinking
Reframing a problem in a unique way and generating different approaches to the issue.

EXHIBIT 8.4

The creative process model

experimentation. Thus, although verification is labeled the final stage of creativity, it is really the beginning of a long process of experimentation and further creativity.

Creative People and Work Environments

Minnesota Mining & Manufacturing Company (3M) introduces an average of 10 new products every week and generates 30 percent of its annual revenues from products developed within the previous four years.[57] The company achieves these impressive goals by finding creative people and putting them in an environment that encourages creative ideas. In other words, 3M executives have learned that creativity is a function of both the person and the situation.

Characteristics of Creative People   Everyone is creative, but some people seem to be more creative than others. Four of the main features of creative people are intelligence, subject-matter knowledge and experience, persistence, and inventive thinking style. First, creative people have above-average intelligence to synthesize information, analyze ideas, and apply their ideas.[58] Like the fictional sleuth Sherlock Holmes, creative people recognize the significance of small bits of information and are able to connect them in ways that no one else could imagine. Then, they have the capacity to evaluate the potential usefulness of their ideas.

Persistence is the second feature of creative people. The fact is that innovations derive more from trial and error than from intelligence and experience. Persistence drives creative people to continue developing and testing after others have given up.[59] In other words, people who develop more creative products and services are those who develop more ideas that don't work. Thomas Edison emphasized this point in his famous statement that genius is 1 percent inspiration and 99 percent perspiration. Edison and his staff discovered hundreds of ways *not* to build a light bulb before they got it right! This persistence is based on a high need for achievement and moderate or high degree of self-confidence.[60]

A third feature of creative people is that they possess sufficient knowledge and experience on the subject. Creativity experts explain that discovering new ideas requires knowledge of the fundamentals. For example, 1960s rock group the Beatles produced most of their songs only after they had played together for several years. They developed extensive experience singing and adapting the music of other people before their creative talents soared.[62]

Although knowledge and experience may be important in one sense, they can also undermine creativity because people develop mental

Jonathon Ive's creative genius is transforming the computer industry. As Apple Computer's vice-president of industrial design, Ive, along with his team, shaped the simple elegance of the iPod music appliance, the "sunflower-inspired" iMac with its flat screen rising on a stem from a dome base, the ultraslim aluminum PowerBook laptop, and, most recently, the perforated aluminum G5 tower with specialized ventilation. "He once designed a computer mouse by observing a drop of water," recalls British fashion designer Sir Paul Smith, who recently participated in selecting Ive as the British Designer of the Year. "That's lateral thinking." When Ive's team designed the colorful teardrop iMac a few years ago, they consulted with candy makers about how to ensure the uniquely translucent casing would be consistent.[61] Along with lateral thinking, what other individual characteristics probably make Jonathan Ive a creative person?

models that lead to "mindless behavior," whereby they stop questioning their assumptions.[63] This explains why some corporate leaders like to hire people from other industries and areas of expertise. For instance, Geoffrey Ballard, founder of Ballard Power Systems, hired a chemist to develop a better battery. When the chemist protested that he didn't know anything about batteries, Ballard replied: "That's fine. I don't want someone who knows batteries. They know what won't work."[64] Ballard explained that he wanted to hire people who would question and investigate what experts stopped questioning.

The fourth characteristics of creative people is that they have an inventive thinking style. Creative types are divergent thinkers and risk takers. They are not bothered about making mistakes or working with ambiguous information. They take a broad view of problems, don't like to abide by rules or status, and are unconcerned about social approval of their actions.[65]

Organizational Conditions Supporting Creativity   Hiring creative people is only part of the creativity equation. Organizations also need to maintain a work environment that supports the creative process for everyone.[66] One of the most important conditions is that the organization has a *learning orientation;* that is, leaders recognize that employees make reasonable mistakes as part of the creative process.[67] "Our beliefs are embedded in our philosophy: Failure is not fatal," explains a 3M executive in India. "Innovations are simply chance breakthroughs. And when you take a chance, there is always the possibility of a failure."[68]

Motivation from the job itself, which was discussed in Chapter 6, is another important condition for creativity.[69] Employees tend to be more creative when they believe their work has a substantial impact on the organization and/or larger society (i.e., task significance). Creativity also increases with autonomy—the freedom to pursue novel ideas without bureaucratic delays. Creativity is about changing things, and change is possible only when employees have the authority to experiment. Creativity is an ongoing learning process, so employees need access to fairly continuous feedback from the job and other sources. More generally, jobs encourage creativity when they are challenging and aligned with the employee's competencies.[70] Challenging work pushes employees to draw on their fullest potential.

Along with supporting a learning orientation and intrinsically motivating jobs, creative companies foster open communication and provide sufficient resources. They provide a reasonable level of job security, which explains why creativity suffers during times of downsizing and corporate restructuring.[71] Organizational support extends to the roles of project leaders and co-workers.[72] Project leaders must apply enough pressure to complete the project, yet give individuals and teams enough freedom and time with plenty of support. Extreme time pressures, unrealistic goals, and ongoing distractions are well-known creativity inhibitors.[73] While we need some pressure to produce, companies also need to minimize pressure when it strangles creative output. Team members and other co-workers also improve creativity when they trust each other, communicate well, and are committed to the assigned project. In contrast, creativity is undermined when co-workers criticize new ideas, are competitive against each other, and engage in political tactics to achieve personal goals.

Activities that Encourage Creativity

Along with hiring creative people and giving them a supportive work environment, organizations have introduced numerous activities that attempt to crank up the creative potential. One set of activities encourages employees to redefine the problem. One way to redefine problems is to revisit old projects. After a few months of neglect, these projects might be seen in new ways.[74] Another strategy involves asking people unfamiliar with the issue (preferably with different expertise) to explore the problem with you. You would state the objectives and give some facts, then let the other person ask questions to further understand the situation. By verbalizing the problem, listening to questions, and hearing what others think, you are more likely to form new perspectives on the issue.[75]

EDS executives don't seem to mind if James Wang (center), Jim Sugarman, and Gwendolyn Chan look like they are playing rather than working. That's because the computer service firm developed four eSpace innovation centers where playing with rubber balls, Lego blocks, and other toys are all part of the creative process. "The toys give you something to do while you're reflecting and thinking and they trigger new ideas," explains a team leader at the innovation center in Detroit. Another EDS staffer adds: "We're all about collaboration and creativity and inspiration, and the toys are props to stimulate the thought process."[77] How would this associative play improve creativity at EDS?

A second set of creativity activities, known as *associative play*, range from art classes to impromptu storytelling. Wedgwood, the Irish-based tableware company, brought together its overseas executives in a workshop where they tore up magazines, pasted up pictures, and selected music that represented what they thought the Wedgwood brand should become. Thousands of employees at Boeing Company have attended creativity classes in which they must build a stand-alone structure that can balance an egg using only 100 straws and a roll of masking tape.[76]

Another associative play activity, called *morphological analysis*, involves listing different dimensions of a system and the elements of each dimension, then looking at each combination. This encourages people to carefully examine combinations that initially seem nonsensical. Tyson Foods, the world's largest poultry producer, applied this activity to identify new ways to serve chicken for lunch. The marketing and research team assigned to this task focused on three categories: occasion, packaging, and taste. Next, the team worked through numerous combinations of items in the three categories. This created unusual ideas, such as cheese chicken pasta (taste) in pizza boxes (packaging) for concessions at baseball games (occasion). Later, the team looked more closely at the feasibility of these combinations and sent them to customer focus groups for further testing.[78]

A third set of activities that encourages creativity in organizations is known as *cross-pollination*.[79] Many creative firms mix together employees from different past projects so they share new knowledge with each other. IDEO, the California-based product design company, does this by encouraging employees to consider how features of one product they've worked on might be relevant to another. For instance, while designing a quieter fan for a computer system, designers might recall how they designed a quieter vacuum cleaner a few months earlier.[80] Cross-pollination also occurs through formal information sessions where people from different parts of the organization share their knowledge. Walt Disney Corporation encourages employees to engage in "displayed thinking" by leaving their work out in the open for others to view and comment on. Colleagues are encouraged to leave anonymous Post-it Notes with suggestions and feedback.

Cross-pollination highlights the fact that creativity rarely occurs alone. Some creative people may be individualistic, but most creative ideas are generated in formal teams and informally through other types of social interaction. This probably explains why Jonathon Ive, the award-winning designer of Apple Computer products, always refers to his team's creativity rather than anything that he alone might have thought up. "The only time you'll hear [Jonathan Ive] use the word 'I' is when he's naming some of the products he helped make famous: iMac, iBook, iPod," says one writer.[81] The next chapter introduces the main concepts in team effectiveness. Then, in Chapter 10, we learn about high-performance teams, including ways to improve team decision making and creativity.

Chapter Summary

Decision making is a conscious process of making choices among one or more alternatives with the intention of moving toward some desired state of affairs. The rational decision-making model includes identifying problems and opportunities, choosing the best decision style, developing alternative solutions, choosing the best solution, implementing the selected alternative, and evaluating decision outcomes.

Emotions, perceptual biases, and poor diagnostic skills affect our ability to identify problems and opportunities. We can minimize these challenges by being aware of the human limitations and discussing the situation with colleagues. Evaluating and choosing alternatives is often challenging because organizational goals are ambiguous or in conflict, human information processing is incomplete and subjective, and people tend to satisfice rather than maximize. Emotions shape our preferences for alternatives, and general moods support or hinder our careful evaluation of alternatives. Most people also rely on intuition to help them evaluate and choose alternatives.

Solutions can be chosen more effectively by systematically identifying and weighting the factors used to evaluate alternatives, cautiously using intuition where we possess enough tacit knowledge on the issue, and considering whether our emotions make sense in the situation. Scenario planning can help to make future decisions without the pressure and emotions that occur during real emergencies.

Postdecisional justification and escalation of commitment make it difficult to accurately evaluate decision outcomes. Escalation is mainly caused by self-justification, the gambler's fallacy, perceptual blinders, and closing costs. These problems are minimized by separating decision choosers from decision evaluators, establishing a preset level at which the decision is abandoned or reevaluated, relying on more systematic and clear feedback about the project's success, and involving several people in decision making.

Employee involvement (or participation) refers to the degree that employees influence how their work is organized and carried out. The level of participation may range from an employee providing specific information to management without knowing the problem or issue, to complete involvement in all phases of the decision process. Employee involvement may lead to higher decision quality and commitment, but several contingencies need to be considered, including the decision structure, source of decision knowledge, decision commitment, and risk of conflict.

Creativity refers to developing an original product, service, or idea that makes a socially recognized contribution. The four creativity stages are preparation, incubation, insight, and verification. Incubation assists divergent thinking, which involves reframing the problem in a unique way and generating different approaches to the issue.

Four of the main features of creative people are in-

telligence, subject-matter knowledge and experience, persistence, and inventive thinking style. Creativity is also strengthened for everyone when the work environment supports a learning orientation, the job has high intrinsic motivation, the organization provides a reasonable level of job security, and project leaders provide appropriate goals, time pressure, and resources. Three types of activities that encourage creativity are redefining the problem, associative play, and cross-pollination.

Key Terms

bounded rationality, p. 240
codetermination, p. 246
creativity, p. 250
decision making, p. 236
divergent thinking, p. 250
employee involvement, p. 246
escalation of commitment, p. 244

implicit favorite, p. 242
intuition, p. 243
nonprogrammed decision, p. 237
postdecisional justification, p. 244
programmed decision, p. 237
satisficing, p. 242
scenario planning, p. 244

Discussion Questions

1. A management consultant is hired by a manufacturing firm to determine the best site for its next production facility. The consultant has had several meetings with the company's senior executives regarding the factors to consider when making the recommendation. Discuss the decision-making problems that might prevent the consultant from choosing the best site location.

2. A developer received financial backing for a new business financial center along a derelict section of the waterfront, a few miles from the current downtown area of a large European city. The idea was to build several high-rise structures, attract large tenants to those sites, and have the city extend transportation systems out to the new center. Over the next decade, the developer believed that others would build in the area, thereby attracting the regional or national offices of many financial institutions. Interest from potential tenants was much lower than initially predicted and the city did not build transportation systems as quickly as expected. Still, the builder proceeded with the original plans. Only after financial support was curtailed did the developer reconsider the project. Using your knowledge of escalation of commitment, discuss three possible reasons why

the developer was motivated to continue with the project.

3. Ancient Book Company has a problem with new book projects. Even when others are aware that a book is far behind schedule and may engender little public interest, sponsoring editors are reluctant to terminate contracts with authors whom they have signed. The result is that editors invest more time with these projects rather than on more fruitful projects. As a form of escalation of commitment, describe two methods that Ancient Book Company can use to minimize this problem.

4. When a large insurance company decided to redesign its eating facilities at headquarters, it formed a task force of employees representing different areas of the organization. The group's mandate was to identify features of the cafeteria that would be more enjoyable for employees. Is this an effective application of employee involvement? Why or why not?

5. Employee involvement applies just as well to the classroom as to the office or factory floor. Explain how student involvement in classroom decisions typically made by the instructor alone might improve decision quality. What potential problems may occur in this process?

6. Think of a time when you experienced the creative process. Maybe you woke up with a brilliant (but usually sketchy and incomplete) idea, or you solved a baffling problem while doing something else. Describe this incident to your class and explain how the experience followed the creative process.

7. Two characteristics of creative people are that they have relevant experience and are persistent in their quest. Does this mean that people with the most experience and the highest need for achievement are the most creative? Explain your answer.

8. One feature of companies that supports creativity is that they minimize the employees' fear of failure. Why does this affect creativity and how can organizations minimize this fear? What are the limitations of this creative strategy?

CASE STUDY 8.1

EMPLOYEE INVOLVEMENT CASES

Case 1: The Sugar Substitute Research Decision

You are the head of research and development (R&D) for a major beer company. While working on a new beer product, one of the scientists in your unit seems to have tentatively identified a new chemical compound that has few calories but tastes closer to sugar than current sugar substitutes. The company has no foreseeable need for this product, but it could be patented and licensed to manufacturers in the food industry.

The sugar substitute discovery is in its preliminary stages, and considerable time and resources would be required before it would be commercially viable. This means that some resources would necessarily be taken away from other projects in the lab. The sugar substitute project is beyond your technical expertise, but some of the R&D lab researchers are familiar with that field of chemistry. As with most forms of research, the amount of research required to further identify and perfect the sugar substitute is difficult to determine. You do not know how much demand is expected for this product. Your department has a decision process for funding projects that are behind schedule. However, there are no rules or precedents about funding projects that would be licensed but not used by the organization.

The company's R&D budget is limited, and other scientists in your work group have recently complained that they require more resources and financial support to get their projects completed. Some of these other R&D projects hold promise for future beer sales. You believe that most researchers in the R&D unit are committed to ensuring company's interests are achieved.

Case 2: Coast Guard Cutter Decision Problem

You are the captain of a 200-foot Coast Guard cutter, with a crew of 16, including officers. Your mission is general at-sea search and rescue. At 2:00 this morning, while en route to your home port after a routine 28-day patrol, you received word from the nearest Coast Guard station that a small plane had crashed 60 miles offshore. You obtained all the available information concerning the location of the crash, informed your crew of the mission, and set a new course at maximum speed for the scene to commence a search for survivors and wreckage.

You have now been searching for 20 hours. Your search operation has been increasingly impaired by rough seas, and there is evidence of a severe storm building. The atmospherics associated with the deteriorating weather have made communications with the Coast Guard station impossible. A decision must be made shortly about whether to abandon the search and place your vessel on a course that would ride out the storm (thereby protecting the vessel and your crew, but relegating any possible survivors to almost certain death from exposure) or to continue a potentially futile search and the risks it would entail.

Before losing communications, you received an update weather advisory concerning the severity and duration of the storm. Although your crew members are extremely conscientious about their responsibility, you believe that they would be divided on the decision of leaving or staying.

Discussion Questions (Cases 1 and 2)

1. To what extent should your subordinates be involved in this decision? Select one of the following levels of involvement:

   - *No involvement*—You make the decision alone without any participation from subordinates.

   - *Low involvement*—You ask one or more subordinates for information relating to the problem, but you don't ask for their recommendations and might not mention the problem to them.

   - *Medium involvement*—You describe the problem to one or more subordinates (alone or in a meeting) and ask for any relevant information as well as their recommendations on the issue. However, you make the final decision, which might or might not reflect their advice.

   - *High involvement*—You describe the problem to subordinates. They discuss the matter, identify a solution without your involvement (unless they invite your ideas), and implement that solution. You have agreed to support their decision.

2. What factors led you to choose this level of employee involvement rather than the others?

3. What problems might occur if less or more involvement occurred in this case (where possible)?

Sources: The Sugar Substitute Research Decision is written by Steven L. McShane, © 2002. The Coast Guard cutter case is adapted from *The New Leadership: Managing Participation in Organizations*, V. H. Vroom and A. G. Jago, 1987. Copyright © 1987 V. H. Vroom and A. G. Jago. Reprinted with permission of the authors.

CASE STUDY 8.2

THE ART OF BRAINSTORMING

BusinessWeek — Robert Barker documents his search for the answer to the question "Where do good ideas come from?" He sought out advice from brain experts, CEOs, and people who have demonstrated their creativity through patents. Each offers advice based on his or her personal and professional experiences or findings.

Barker speaks to one of the more creative researchers at Bell Laboratories. He gets advice from recently retired Honeywell CEO Lawrence Bossidy. He finds out how Jim Brown at Honeywell discovered a popular oil change product. Barker also speaks to the head of an innovative investment firm and a highly successful advertising guru. Read through this *Business Week* article at www.mhhe.com/mcshane3e and prepare for the discussion questions that follow.

Discussion Questions

1. What characteristics of creative people are identified in this article? How are they similar to, or different from, the characteristics described in the textbook?

2. What workplace conditions and specific practices for improving or supporting creativity are identified in this article?

3. What activities or conditions that support creativity are discussed here that are not specifically mentioned in this chapter of the textbook? Are they discussed in other chapters?

Source: R. Barker, "The Art of Brainstorming," *Business Week*, August 19, 2002, pp. 168–69.

WHERE IN THE WORLD ARE WE?

Purpose This exercise is designed to help you understand the potential advantages of involving others in decisions rather than making decisions alone.

Materials Students require the unmarked map with grid marks (Exhibit 8.6) showing the United States of America. Students are not allowed to look at any other maps or use any other materials. The instructor will provide a list of communities located somewhere on Exhibit 8.6. The instructor will also provide copies of the answer sheet after students have individually and in teams estimated the locations of communities.

Instructions

- *Step 1*—Write down in Exhibit 8.5 the list of communities identified by your instructor. Then, working alone, estimate the location in Exhibit 8.6 of these communities, all of which are in the United States. For example, mark a small "1" in Exhibit 8.6 on the spot where you believe the first community is located. Mark a small "2" where you think the second community is located, and so on. Be sure to number each location clearly and with numbers small enough to fit within one grid space.
- *Step 2*—The instructor will organize students into approximately equal-sized teams

(typically five or six people per team). Working with your team members, reach a consensus on the location of each community listed in Exhibit 8.5. The instructor might provide teams with a separate copy of this map, or each member can identify the team's numbers using a different colored pen on their individual maps. The team's decision for each location should occur by consensus, not voting or averaging.

- *Step 3*—The instructor will provide or display an answer sheet, showing the correct locations of the communities. Using this answer sheet, students will count the minimum number of grid squares between the location they individually marked and the true location of each community. Write the number of grid squares in the third column of Exhibit 8.5, then add up the total. Next, count the minimum number of grid squares between the location the team marked and the true location of each community. Write the number of grid squares in the fourth column of Exhibit 8.5, then add up the total.
- *Step 4*—The instructor will ask for information about the totals and the class will discuss the implication of these results for employee involvement and decision making.

| EXHIBIT 8.5 | List of selected communities in the United States |

Community number	Community name	Individual distance in grid units from the true location	Team distance in grid units from the true location
1			
2			
3			
4			
5			
6			
7			
8			
		Total:	Total:

Source: Copyright © 2002 Steven L. McShane.

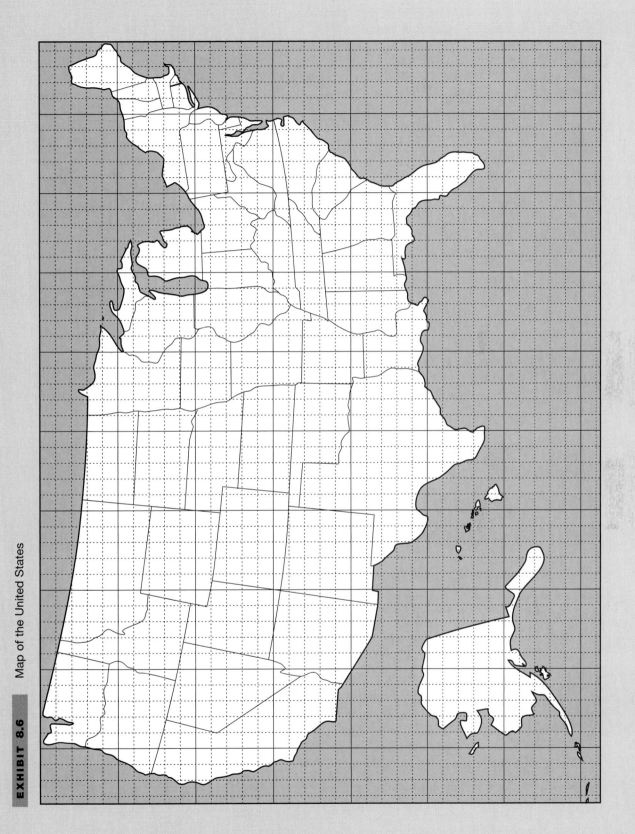

EXHIBIT 8.6 Map of the United States

TEAM EXERCISE 8.4

WINTER SURVIVAL EXERCISE

Purpose   This exercise is designed to help you understand the potential advantages of involving others in decisions rather than making decisions alone.

Instructions

- *Step 1*—Read the "Situation" below. Then, working alone, rank order the 12 items shown in the chart below according to their importance to your survival. In the "Step 1" column, indicate the most important item with "1," going through to "12" for the least important. Keep in mind the reasons why each item is or is not important.
- *Step 2*—The instructor will divide the class into small teams (four to six people). Each team will rank order the items in the "Step 2" column. Team rankings should be based on consensus, not simply averaging the individual rankings.
- *Step 3*—When the teams have completed their rankings, the instructor will provide

the expert's ranking, which can be entered in the "Step 3" column.
- *Step 4*—Each student will compute the absolute difference (i.e., ignore minus signs) between the individual ranking and the expert's ranking, record this information in the "Step 4" column, and sum the absolute values at the bottom of that column.
- *Step 5*—In the "Step 5" column, record the absolute difference between the team's ranking and the expert's ranking, and sum these absolute scores at the bottom. A class discussion will follow regarding the implications of these results for employee involvement and decision making.

Situation   You have just crash-landed somewhere in the woods of southern Manitoba or possibly northern Minnesota. It is 11:32 A.M. in mid-January. The small plane in which you were traveling crashed on a small lake. The pilot and copilot were killed. Shortly after the crash, the

EXHIBIT 8.7   Winter Survival Tally Sheet

Winter survival tally sheet					
Items	Step 1 Your individual ranking	Step 2 Your team's ranking	Step 3 Survival expert's ranking	Step 4 Difference between steps 1 and 3	Step 5 Difference between steps 2 and 3
Ball of steel wool					
Newspaper					
Compass					
Hand ax					
Cigarette lighter					
45-caliber pistol					
Section air map					
Canvas					
Shirt and pants					
Can of shortening					
Whiskey					
Chocolate bars					
Total					

(The lower the score, the better)

Your score   Team score

plane sank completely into the lake with the pilot's and copilot's bodies inside. Everyone else on the flight escaped to land dry and without serious injury.

The crash came suddenly, before the pilot had time to radio for help or inform anyone of your position. Since your pilot was trying to avoid the storm, you know the plane was considerably off course. The pilot announced shortly before the crash that you were 45 miles northwest of a small town that is the nearest known habitation.

You are in a wilderness area made up of thick woods broken by many lakes and rivers. The snow depth varies from above the ankles in windswept areas to more than knee-deep where it has drifted. The last weather report indicated that the temperature would reach 5 degrees Fahrenheit in the daytime and minus 15 degrees at night. Plenty of dead wood and twigs cover the area around the lake. You and the other surviving passengers are dressed in winter clothing appropriate for city wear—suits, pantsuits, street shoes, and overcoats. While escaping from the plane, your group salvaged the 12 items listed in Exhibit 8.7. You may assume that the number of persons in the group is the same as the number in your group, and that you have agreed to stay together.

Source: Adapted from "Winter Survival" in D. Johnson and F. Johnson, *Joining Together,* 3rd ed. (Englewood Cliffs, NJ: Prentice Hall, 1984).

TEAM EXERCISE 8.5

THE HOPPING ORANGE

Purpose This exercise is designed to help students understand the dynamics of creativity and team problem solving.

Instructions You will be placed in teams of six students. One student serves as the official timer for the team and must have a watch, preferably with stopwatch timer. The instructor will give each team an orange (or similar object) with a specific task involving use of the orange. The objective is easily understood and nonthreatening, and it will be described by the instructor at the beginning of the exercise. Each team will have a few opportunities to achieve the objective more efficiently.

TEAM EXERCISE 8.6

CREATIVITY BRAINBUSTERS

Purpose This exercise is designed to help students understand the dynamics of creativity and team problem solving.

Instructions This exercise may be completed alone or in teams of three or four people. If teams are formed, students who already know the solutions to one or more of these problems should identify themselves and serve as silent observers. When finished (or, more likely, when time is up), the instructor will review the solutions and discuss the implications of this exercise. In particular, be prepared to discuss what you needed to solve these puzzles and what may have prevented you from solving them more quickly (or at all).

1. Double-Circle Problem Draw two circles, one inside the other, with a single line and with neither circle touching the other (as shown below). In other words, you must draw both of these circles without lifting your pen (or other writing instrument).

2. Nine-Dot Problem Below are nine dots. Without lifting your pencil, draw no more than four straight lines that pass through all nine dots.

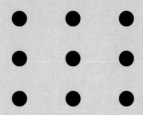

3. Nine-Dot Problem Revisited Referring to the nine-dot exhibit above, describe how, without lifting your pencil, you could pass a pencil line through all dots with three or fewer straight lines.

4. Word Search In the following line of letters, cross out five letters so that the remaining letters, without altering their sequence, spell a familiar English word.

FCIRVEEALTETITVEERS

5. Burning Ropes You have two pieces of rope of unequal lengths and a box of matches. In spite of their different lengths, each piece of rope takes one hour to burn; however, parts of each rope burn at unequal speeds. For example, the first half of one piece might burn in 10 minutes. Use these materials to accurately determine when 45 minutes has elapsed.

SELF-ASSESSMENT EXERCISE 8.7

MEASURING YOUR CREATIVE PERSONALITY

Purpose This self-assessment is designed to help you to measure the extent to which you have a creative personality.

Instructions Listed below is an adjective checklist with 30 words that may or may not describe you. Put a mark in the box beside the words that you think accurately describe you. Please *do not* mark the boxes for words that do not describe you. When finished, you can score the test using the scoring key in Appendix B. This exercise is completed alone so students assess themselves without concerns of social comparison. However, class discussion will focus on how this scale might be applied in organizations and on the limitations of measuring creativity in work settings.

Adjective Checklist

Affected ☐	Honest ☐	Reflective ☐
Capable ☐	Humorous ☐	Resourceful ☐
Cautious ☐	Individualistic ☐	Self-confident ☐
Clever ☐	Informal ☐	Sexy ☐
Commonplace ☐	Insightful ☐	Sincere ☐
Confident ☐	Intelligent ☐	Snobbish ☐
Conservative ☐	Inventive ☐	Submissive ☐
Conventional ☐	Mannerly ☐	Suspicious ☐
Dissatisfied ☐	Narrow interests ☐	Unconventional ☐
Egotistical ☐	Original ☐	Wide interests ☐

Source: Adapted from and based on information in H. G. Gough and A. B. Heilbrun Jr., *The Adjective Check List Manual* (Palo Alto, CA: Consulting Psychologists Press, 1965).

TESTING YOUR CREATIVE BENCH STRENGTH

Purpose This self-assessment is designed to help you to determine how well you engage in divergent thinking to creatively identify problems and their solutions.

Instructions This self-assessment consists of 12 questions that require divergent thinking to identify the answers. Answer each question in the space provided. When finished, look at the correct answer for each question, along with an explanation.

DECISION-MAKING STYLE INVENTORY

Purpose This self-assessment is designed to help you estimate your preferred style of decision making.

Instructions The statements in this self-assessment describe how individuals go about making important decisions. Please indicate whether you agree or disagree with each statement. Answer each item as truthfully as possible so that you get an accurate estimate of your decision-making style. This exercise is completed alone so students assess themselves honestly without concerns of social comparison. However, class discussion will focus on the decision-making style that people prefer in organizational settings.

After studying the preceding material, be sure to check out our website at
www.mhhe.com/mcshane3e
for more in-depth information and interactivities that correspond to this chapter.

Foundations of Team Dynamics

Learning Objectives

After reading this chapter, you should be able to:

■ Define teams.

■ Distinguish teams from informal groups.

■ Outline the model of team effectiveness.

■ Identify six organizational and team environmental elements that influence team effectiveness.

■ Explain the influence on team effectiveness of the team's task, composition, and size.

■ Describe the five stages of team development.

■ Identify four factors that shape team norms.

■ List six factors that influence team cohesiveness.

■ Discuss the limitations of teams.

■ Explain how companies can minimize social loafing.

A few years ago, Paul Tramontano was typical of most Wall Street brokers, single-handedly providing advice to hundreds of clients. Not anymore. The Salomon Smith Barney adviser realized that clients needed a wider variety of services than any one person can deliver, so he and two other partners formed an 11-person team, including technical specialists to complement his own focus on financial, estate planning, and advisory business. "By definition, higher-net-worth clients require different and greater levels of service," says Tramontano. "That's why I think the team approach is the model for what this industry will look like."

Firms throughout the securities industry are placing more emphasis on teams rather than individual "stars" to provide better customer service and investment performance. Almost all private-client brokers at Credit Suisse First Boston are assigned to teams. At Goldman, Sachs, accounts worth $20 million or more are handled by teams rather than individuals. Bear, Stearns and Company (shown in photo) organizes staff into specialized teams, including a relationship management team, integration team, and technology training team. When Mark Mobius was recently asked

Employees at Bear, Stearns and Company, as well as other Wall Street brokerage firms, are discovering the benefits of teamwork.

whether individual fund managers are the real "brands" for a mutual fund, the head of the Templeton Emerging Markets Fund quickly replied: "The funds are actually run by teams of people and do not depend on one person."

The challenge for Wall Street firms is to create true teams, rather than combining several lone wolves who happen to share the same office. "Most firms don't have a down payment on a clue on how to help build teams," quips the training director at one of Wall Street's largest firms.

Still, by providing team training and support, firms are starting to reap the rewards of the team approach. UBS PaineWebber brokers trained in a team development program (called "TeamWorks") generated 19 percent more revenues and 9 percent more assets than all other UBSPW advisers, whether they worked solo or on teams. The main reason for this improved performance, according to UBSPW executives, is that properly trained teams offer clients better product and service knowledge.[1] ■

Teams are replacing individuals as the basic building blocks of organizations. The opening story to this chapter described how Wall Street brokerage firms have shifted toward team-based work to better satisfy more complex client needs. SANS Fibres, the South African manufacturer of synthetic fiber and polyester polymers, relies on the team approach to eliminate waste, maximize manufacturing flow, minimize inventories, and meet customer requirements. International Steel Group's (ISG) Cleveland plant rose from the ashes of bankruptcy and quickly became profitable in part because it formed teams where employees share duties and help others across departments. "It wasn't the traditional one job for one person," says ISG executive John Mang III. "It was a team."[2]

Teams are groups of two or more people who interact and influence each other, are mutually accountable for achieving common goals associated with organizational objectives, and perceive themselves as a social entity within an organization.[3] All teams exist to fulfill some purpose, such as assembling a product, providing a service, designing a new manufacturing facility, or making an important decision. Team members are held together by their interdependence and need for collaboration to achieve common goals. All teams require some form of communication so members can coordinate and share common objectives. Team members also influence each other, although some members are more influential than others regarding the team's goals and activities.

All teams are **groups** because they consist of people with a unifying relationship. But not all groups are teams; some groups are just people assembled together without any necessary interdependence or organizationally focused objective.[4] For example, the friends you meet for lunch wouldn't be called a team because they have little or no task interdependence (each person could just as easily eat lunch alone) and no organizational purpose beyond their social interaction.

A department of employees would not be considered a team if employees perform independent tasks and have minimal interaction or coordination with each other. A department *would* be a team only if employees work together toward a common objective by sharing information, coordinating their work, and influencing each other. Although the terms "group" and "team" are used interchangeably in this book, our main focus is on teams. This is partly because most of the discussion is about groups that perform organizationally related tasks, and partly because the term "teams" has largely replaced "groups" in the business language.[5]

This chapter looks at the conditions that make teams more or less effective in organizational settings. After introducing the different types of teams in organizational settings, we present a model of team effectiveness. Most of the chapter examines each part of this model, including team and organizational environment, team design, and the team processes of development, norms, roles, and cohesiveness.

teams
Groups of two or more people who interact and influence each other, are mutually accountable for achieving common objectives, and perceive themselves as a social entity within an organization.

groups
Two or more people with a unifying relationship.

Types of Teams and Informal Groups

There are many types of teams and other groups in organizational settings. Exhibit 9.1 categorizes groups in terms of their formality (teams versus informal groups) and permanence in the organization.

Types of teams and
groups

	Permanent	**Temporary**
Formal teams	Production team Management team	Task force Skunkworks team
Informal groups	Friendship group	Community of practice

Permanent and Temporary Teams

Permanent work teams are responsible for a specific set of tasks or work processes in the organization. Wall Street securities firms rely on permanent teams because employees directly interact and coordinate work activities with each other.[6] Increasingly, production facilities are relying on high-performance teams with little or no involvement from management to complete the work processes. We will discuss these work units, known as *self-directed work teams*, in detail in Chapter 10. Management teams are also relatively permanent because these groups of people work indefinitely together for a common purpose.

Organizations also rely on relatively temporary teams, called *task forces* or *project teams*, which investigate a particular problem or opportunity and disband when the decision is made. For instance, the City of Reno, Nevada, recently formed several task forces to improve the efficiency of tree pruning, develop a kit for businesses to remove graffiti, and improve the quality of work sealing cracks on city streets. All of these projects had short-term completion dates.[7]

Skunkworks   In the early 1940s, Lockheed Corporation (now Lockheed Martin) formed a secret unit of 43 engineers and 30 shop mechanics to develop the first fighter jet to fly faster than 500 miles per hour. Located in a large circus tent outside the company's Burbank, California, production area, the group became known as the "Skonk Works" because the stench of a nearby plastic factory made the tent smell like the hidden distillery of the same name that produced moonshine in the *Li'l Abner* comic strip. The innovative Lockheed group, which is credited with numerous aerospace innovations over the years, eventually changed its name to "Skunk Works."[8]

Today, corporate leaders around the planet refer to **skunkworks** as innovative teams or work units that consist of an entrepreneurial team leader (an *innovation champion*) who borrows people and resources (called *bootlegging*) and has relatively free rein to create a product or develop a service. Skunkworks are usually physically separated from the main organization, so they

skunkworks
Cross-functional teams, usually separated from the main organization, that borrow people and resources and have relatively free rein to develop new products or services.

are independent of corporate bureaucracy. Some skunkworks are temporary teams that start up without management direction. For example, the earliest corporate Intranets started as skunkworks, championed by employees with a UNIX computer and free software from universities to create a Web server.[9]

Other skunkworks receive active management support. For instance, Vancouver City Savings Credit Union formed a special unit called VanCity Capital Corporation to provide financial support to enterprises that might get turned away from larger financial institutions. The renegade group from Canada's largest credit union has since funded several start-up ventures, including the world's largest online contact lens provider. "I like to think we are a bit of skunkworks for VanCity," says VanCity Capital president Lee Davis. "[We're] a little group of creative people outside the parent's influence who can move quickly, think outside the box, have passion and try new things."[10]

communities of practice

Groups bound together by shared expertise and passion for a particular activity or interest.

Communities of Practice   **Communities of practice** are groups bound together by shared expertise and passion for a particular activity or interest.[11] For instance, Schlumberger Ltd. has communities of practice on deep-water drilling, horizontal drilling, deviated wells, and other areas of expertise. Employees are connected to the oil-field services firm's Web portal, where they share knowledge on their daily experiences. Clarica Life Insurance Company developed an Intranet system where its 3,000 independent agents have formed communities of practice to share their expertise. Agents are also forming their own communities with customers, thereby acquiring knowledge through a stronger customer relationship.[12]

At Schlumberger and Clarica, communities of practice are formal teams that congregate in person or cyberspace to share knowledge. People who have a common passion for environmental concerns, for example, might meet twice each month over lunch to share their knowledge. Other communities interact entirely through list servers and websites where participants exchange information on specific technical issues. Many communities of practice extend beyond organizational boundaries, so they represent a source of knowledge acquisition. Along with these formal structures, many communities of practice develop informally without any particular organizational support or objectives. In other words, these communities represent a type of informal group, which we describe next.

Informal Groups

informal groups

Two or more people who form a unifying relationship around personal rather than organizational goals.

Along with formal work teams, organizations consist of **informal groups.** Informal groups are not initiated by the organization and usually do not perform organizational goals (thus they are "informal"). Instead, they exist primarily for the benefit of their members. Some informal groups, such as the group you meet for lunch, exist primarily to satisfy the drive to bond. These groups are relatively permanent because they are held together by lasting friendships and by the structure of formal teams.

Why do people belong to informal groups? Scholars have identified three main reasons. First, people often join informal groups because of the innate drive to bond. Indeed, some writers suggest that group formation is hardwired through evolutionary development of the human species.[13] As we learned in Chapter 5, people invest considerable time and effort forming and maintaining relationships without any special circumstances or ulterior motives. Similarly, social identity theory (see Chapter 3) says that we define ourselves by our group affiliations. If we belong to work teams or informal groups that are viewed favorably by others, then we tend to view ourselves more favorably. We are motivated to become members of groups that are similar to ourselves because this reinforces our social identity.[14]

A second reason why people join informal groups is that these groups accomplish tasks that cannot be achieved by individuals working alone. For example, employees will sometimes form a group (described in Chapter 12 as a *coalition*) to oppose organizational changes because they have more power when banded together than complaining separately. Last, informal groups tend to form in stressful situations because we are comforted by the physical presence of other people and are therefore motivated to be near them.[15] This explains why soldiers huddle together in battle, even though they are taught to disperse under fire. This also explains why employees tend to congregate when hearing that the company has been sold or that some people may be laid off.

Why Rely on Teams?

We began this chapter by stating that teams are replacing individuals as the basic building blocks of organizations. In fact, a survey of human resource professionals recently concluded: "Teams are now an integral part of workplace management."[16] Why all the fuss about teams? The answer to this question has a long history, dating from research on British coal mining in the 1940s to the Japanese economic miracle of the 1970s.[17]

Based on these origins, companies around the world have introduced teams because, under the right conditions, they can make better decisions, develop better products and services, and create a more energized workforce than when people work alone.[18] You can see these benefits in Connections 9.1. Bombardier's special task force quickly turned around the ailing Outboard Motor Corporation and started up a team-based production unit in Sturtevant, Wisconsin. The key observation here is that Bombardier's task force and other teams can potentially solve problems and identify opportunities quickly and effectively under the right conditions.

As a form of employee involvement (see Chapter 8), teams are generally more successful than individuals working alone at identifying problems, developing alternatives, and choosing from those alternatives. Similarly, team members can quickly share information and coordinate tasks, whereas these processes are slower and prone to more errors in traditional departments led by supervisors. And, as we learned in the opening vignette for this chapter, teams typically provide superior customer service because they provide more breadth of knowledge and expertise to customers than individual "stars" can offer. This ability to share information and respond to the external environment explains why teamwork is considered an important ingredient in knowledge management.[19]

In many situations, employees are also potentially more energized and engaged when working on teams, for at least two reasons. One reason is that employees have a drive to bond and are motivated to fulfill the goals of groups they identify with and belong to (see social identity theory in Chapter 3). Second, employees are able to perform more enriched jobs in team settings, where the task is too complex for individuals to perform alone. For example, Corning, Inc., relies on three high-performance teams to make cellular ceramic metal filters at its plant in Erwin, New York. The task is far too complex for any employee working alone, whereas team members collectively

Teamwork Revs up Production at Bombardier Marine Corporation

From 1995 to 2000, Outboard Marine Corporation's (OMC) share of the outboard engine market plummeted from 55 to just 23 percent. The maker of Evinrude and Johnson outboard motors suffered from engine quality problems and inefficient production methods. Transportation giant Bombardier Inc. purchased OMC and created a team-based transformation that surprised competitors and allies alike. (Bombardier has since sold the business to the Bombardier family and Bain Capital.)

Bombardier manufacturing executive Roch Lambert led the turnaround team, consisting of former OMC manufacturing experts as well as specialists in plant maintenance, finance, marketing, and quality control from Bombardier's other transportation operations. The team's audacious goal was to completely reconfigure OMC's manufacturing process so that, in less than one year, it would produce the highest quality Evinrude and Johnson engines ever made.

In rapid order, the turnaround team scrutinized the engine drawings, inventory system, and manufacturing process to identify faults and required changes. OMC's manufacturing operations were spread around four plants throughout the United States, which increased production costs and time. Lambert's team closed two plants and relocated production to a new building in Sturtevant, Wisconsin. Equipment was moved into the building just hours after the previous owner had moved out.

Bombardier initially selected 300 people from the 6,000 applications for the Sturtevant production facility. In particular, the company looked for "team players" with problem-solving skills, rather than looking first at work experience such as engine assembly. Built into every job was quality control, such as ensuring the previous assembler's work achieved the required standards. Bombardier's team-based approach is paying off as dealers who had abandoned the Johnson and Evinrude brands are now flocking back.

Bombardier relied on teams to transform money-losing Outboard Marine Corporation into a high-quality manufacturer of Johnson and Evinrude outboard engines.

Sources: R. Barrett, "Despite Sales, Bombardier to Stay Invested in Sturtevant," *Milwaukee Journal Sentinel,* August 27, 2003; J. Tunkieicz, "Bombardier Has More Good News of Growth," *Milwaukee Journal Sentinel,* January 11, 2003; G. Bylinsky, "Bombardier: A New Plant Saves Old Brand Names," *Fortune,* September 2, 2002, pp. 172ff; R. Barrett, "New Owner Hopes Outboard Motors Make a Splash," *Milwaukee Journal Sentinel,* January 20, 2002, p. 1D; L. Klink, "Bombardier to Hire Up to 700," *Milwaukee Journal Sentinel,* September 2, 2001, p. 32.

experience higher levels of task identity, skill variety (by rotating through jobs), autonomy, and other elements of job design by performing the entire work process.[20]

A Model of Team Effectiveness

You might have noticed that we hedged our glorification of teams by saying that they are "potentially" better than individuals "under the right conditions." We have good reason to be hesitant. Many organizations have introduced team structures that have become spectacular failures. Why are some teams effective while others fail? This question has challenged organizational re-

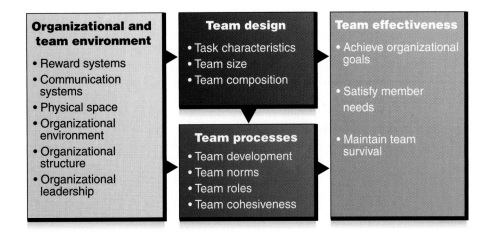

EXHIBIT 9.2

A model of team effectiveness

Organizational and team environment
- Reward systems
- Communication systems
- Physical space
- Organizational environment
- Organizational structure
- Organizational leadership

Team design
- Task characteristics
- Team size
- Team composition

Team processes
- Team development
- Team norms
- Team roles
- Team cohesiveness

Team effectiveness
- Achieve organizational goals
- Satisfy member needs
- Maintain team survival

team effectiveness
The extent to which a team achieves its objectives, achieves the needs and objectives of its members, and sustains itself over time.

searchers for some time and, as you might expect, numerous models of team effectiveness have been proposed over the years.[21]

Let's begin by clarifying what we mean by **team effectiveness.** Team effectiveness refers to how the team affects the organization, individual team members, and the team's existence.[22] First, most teams exist to serve some purpose relating to the organization or other system in which the group operates. In the opening story to this chapter, the Wall Street brokerage teams are responsible for serving clients more effectively. Some informal groups also have task-oriented (although not organizationally mandated) goals, such as sharing information in an informal community of practice.

Second, team effectiveness relies on the satisfaction and well-being of its members. People join groups to fulfill their personal needs, so effectiveness is partly measured by this need fulfillment. Finally, team effectiveness includes the team's viability—its ability to survive. It must be able to maintain the commitment of its members, particularly during the turbulence of the team's development. Without this commitment, people leave and the team will fall apart. It must also secure sufficient resources and find a benevolent environment in which to operate.

Exhibit 9.2 presents the model of team effectiveness that we will examine closely over the rest of this chapter. We begin by looking at elements of the team's and organization's environment that influence team design, processes, and outcomes.

Organizational and Team Environment

Our discussion of team effectiveness logically begins with the contextual factors that influence the team's design, processes, and outcomes.[23] There are many elements in the organizational and team environment that influence team effectiveness. Six of the most important elements are reward systems, communication systems, physical space, organizational environment, organizational structure, and organizational leadership.

- *Reward systems*—Team members tend to work together more effectively when they are at least partly rewarded for team performance.[24] This doesn't mean that everyone on the team should receive the same amount of pay based on the team's performance. On the contrary, rewards tend to work better in the United States and other Western societies when individual pay is based on a combination of individual and team performance. For instance, American Skandia rewards its best customer service representatives with an individual bonus. But recognizing that individuals rarely accomplish work alone, the U.S. operations of the Swedish insurance company also rewards the employee's team for that individual's achievement.[25]

- *Communications systems*—A poorly designed communication system can starve a team of valuable information and feedback, or it may swamp it with information overload.[26] As we will learn in Chapter 10, communication systems are particularly important when team members are geographically dispersed. Even when team members are co-located (work in the same physical space), that space should be arranged to encourage rather than discourage face-to-face dialogue.

- *Physical space*—The layout of an office or manufacturing facility does more than improve communication among team members. It also shapes employee perceptions about being together as a team and influences the team's ability to accomplish tasks. That's why Teleflex Morse, a manufacturer of gauges, steering columns, and shift controls in Lakewood Ranch, Florida, introduced a U-shaped production line system. This physical layout creates a close-knit community among production team members, allowing closer interaction with each other and making it easier to help each other when bottlenecks occur.[27]

- *Organizational environment*—Team success depends on the company's external environment. If the organization cannot secure resources, for instance, the team cannot fulfill its performance targets. Similarly, high demand for the team's output creates feelings of success, which motivates team members to stay with the team. A competitive external environment can motivate employees to work together more closely.

- *Organizational structure*—Many teams fail because the organizational structure does not support them. Teams work better when there are few layers of management and teams are given autonomy and responsibility for their work. This structure encourages interaction with team members rather than with supervisors. Teams also flourish when employees are organized around work processes rather than specialized skills. This structure increases interaction among team members.[28]

- *Organizational leadership*—Teams require ongoing support from senior executives to align rewards, organizational structure, communication systems, and other elements of team context. They also require team leaders or facilitators who provide coaching and support. Team leaders are also enablers, meaning that they ensure teams have the authority to solve their own problems and resources to accomplish their tasks.[29] Leaders also maintain a value system that supports team performance more than individual success.

Team Design Features

Putting together a team is rather like designing a mini-organization. There are several elements to consider, and the wrong combination will undermine team effectiveness. Three of the main structural elements to consider when designing teams are task characteristics, team size, and team composition. As we saw earlier in the team effectiveness model (Exhibit 9.2), these design features influence team effectiveness directly as well as indirectly through team processes. For example, the skills and diversity of team members affect team cohesiveness, but they also have a direct effect on how well the team performs its task. Similarly, the type of work performed by the team (task characteristics) may influence the types of roles that emerge, but it also has a direct effect on the satisfaction and well-being of team members.

Task Characteristics

More than a decade ago, Varian Australia introduced continuous improvement process (CIP) teams to assist productivity improvement. A recent evaluation found that while CIP teams reduced the product development cycle by up to 50 percent, most teams fell apart after a few years. One of the main problems, the company discovered, was that many CIP teams ran out of ways to improve productivity. Others gave up because they were assigned projects beyond their capability.[30]

Varian Australia and other companies have discovered that whether teams flourish or fail is partly determined by their assigned tasks or goals. Teams tend to be more effective when they work on well-structured tasks with meaningful goals within their collective knowledge and skills. Although teams may be given ill-defined assignments requiring diverse knowledge and views, they generally take longer than individuals to develop and achieve their goals when faced with these ambiguous task structures.[31]

task interdependence

The degree to which a task requires employees to share common inputs or outcomes, or to interact in the process of executing their work.

Task Interdependence   **Task interdependence** is a critically important task characteristic because it relates to the definition of teams (i.e., that they interact and influence each other and are mutually accountable). Task interdependence exists when team members must share common inputs to their individual tasks, need to interact in the process of executing their work, or receive outcomes (such as rewards) that are partly determined by the performance of others.[32] The higher the level of task interdependence, the greater the need for people to work in teams than alone.

Teams are well suited to highly interdependent tasks because people coordinate better when working together than separately. Employees also tend to be motivated and more satisfied working on teams when their tasks are highly interdependent. However, this motivation and satisfaction occurs only when team members have the same job goals, such as serving the same clients or collectively assembling the same product. In contrast, frustration is more likely to occur when each team member has unique goals (such as serving different clients) but must depend on other team members (high task interdependence) to achieve those unique goals.[33] The solution here is to ensure that task interdependence is highest when team members also share the same goals and to minimize task interdependence when employees work toward different goals.

Exhibit 9.3 illustrates the three levels of task interdependence.[34] *Pooled interdependence* is the lowest level of interdependence (other than independence), in which individuals operate independently except for reliance on a common resource or authority. Employees share a common payroll, cafeteria, and other organizational resources. In most cases, they can work well alone

EXHIBIT 9.3

Levels of task
interdependence

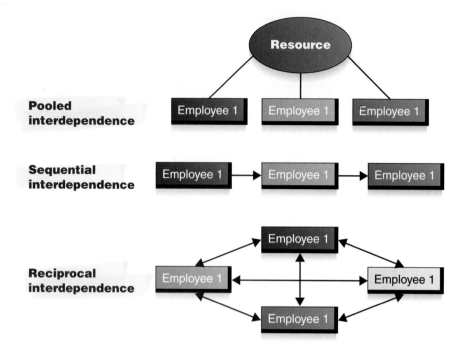

rather than in teams if pooled interdependence is the highest relationship among them.

Sequential interdependence occurs where the output of one person becomes the direct input for another person or unit. This interdependent linkage is found in fish processing plants. Fish are handled by the slitters, then passed to the gutters, who then pass their work to the slimers, who then send their work to the graders.[35] Although employees in the production line process usually work alone, they are sufficiently interdependent that Toyota and other companies create teams around these processes. *Reciprocal interdependence* represents the highest level of interdependence, in which work output is exchanged back and forth among individuals. Employees with reciprocal interdependence should almost always be organized into teams to facilitate coordination in their interwoven relationship.

Team Size

Semco SA is a conglomerate of a dozen businesses operating out of São Paulo, Brazil. Semco tries to keep work units within each business to fewer than 200 employees, which CEO Ricardo Semler reckons is as big as an organization can get without excessive controls. But within each work unit, employees directly interact with between 6 and 10 co-workers. "The maximum anyone is able to regularly deal with is a half dozen people," suggests Semler.[36]

Team size is an important concern at Semco. Some writers claim that team size should be no more than 10 people, making Semco's limit well within those guidelines. Optimal team size depends on several factors, however, such as the number of people required to complete the work and the amount of coordination needed to work together. The general rule is that teams should be large enough to provide the necessary competencies and perspectives to perform the work, yet small enough to maintain efficient coordination and meaningful involvement of each member.[37]

Larger teams are typically less effective because members consume more time and effort coordinating their roles and resolving differences. For instance, some of the continuous improvement process teams at Varian Australia (described earlier) suffered because they had more than a dozen members, making it difficult to reach agreement on ideas.[38] In these larger teams, individuals have less opportunity to participate and, consequently, are less likely to feel that they are contributing to the team's success. Larger work units tend to break into informal subgroups around common interests and work activities, leading members to form stronger commitments to their subgroup than to the larger team.

Team Composition

Houston's H-E-B Central Market is a 75,000-square-foot cornucopia of food delights. To support this customer experience, the San Antonio-based grocery retailer carefully hires job applicants who are outgoing and enjoy working in teams. Applicants begin by completing an application form and writing detailed examples of their use of teamwork and communication skills to solve problems in earlier jobs. After making the cut, prospective employees are invited back into groups of about eight people, where interviewers observe their willingness to try unusual foods and interact with others. "We want to see who can work together as a team, who's creative and who shows leadership, who's assertive and who's not," says an H-E-B executive.[39]

H-E-B Central Market has a strong team orientation, so it carefully selects people with the necessary motivation *and* competencies to work together. With respect to motivation, every member must have sufficient drive to perform the task in a team environment. Specifically, team members must be motivated to agree on the goal, work together rather than alone, and abide by the team's rules of conduct. Employees with a collectivist orientation—those who value group harmony and duty to groups to which they belong (see Chapter 2)—tend to perform better in work teams, whereas those with a low collectivist orientation tend to perform better alone.[40]

Along with the motivation to work in teams, employees must possess the skills and knowledge necessary to accomplish the team's objectives.[41] Each person needs only some of the necessary skills, but the entire group must have the full set of competencies. Team members also need to be able to work well with others. Research suggests that high-performing team members demonstrate more cooperative behavior toward others and generally have more emotional intelligence (see Chapter 4). Researchers also emphasize the importance of training employees in ways to communicate and coordinate with each other in a team environment.[42]

Team Diversity   Another important dimension of team composition is the diversity of team members.[43] **Homogeneous teams** include members with common technical expertise, demographics (age, sex), ethnicity, experiences, or values, whereas **heterogeneous teams** have members with diverse personal characteristics and backgrounds. Some forms of diversity are apparent on the surface, such as differences in sex and race. Deep-level diversity, on the other hand, refers to differences in the personalities, values, attitudes, and other psychological characteristics of team members. Surface-level diversity is apparent as soon as the team forms, whereas deep-level diversity becomes apparent over time as team members discover each other's values and beliefs.[44]

homogeneous teams

Teams that include members with common technical expertise, demographics (age, gender), ethnicity, experiences, or values.

heterogeneous teams

Teams that include members with diverse personal characteristics and backgrounds.

Automobiles on the road today are designed mostly by men, so a group of female employees at Volvo Car Corporation thought it was time for women to design a new concept car. The all-female team (shown in photo) will make all of the design and engineering decisions for the vehicle, called the "Your Concept Car." "We believe that women and men prioritize differently," says Eva-Lisa Andersson in the Swedish carmaker's Product Development Department. "This is why all the decisions on this car are being made by women." Volvo Car Corporation president Hans-Olov Olsson adds that this project is important because it "thinks along new lines and maintains a sharp focus on customer needs." Olsson also explains that the project "demonstrates the breadth and depth of women's expertise in this company."[46] Based on your knowledge of team homogeneity and heterogeneity, what are the potential advantages and limitations of an all-female product development team?

Should teams be homogeneous or heterogeneous? Both have advantages and disadvantages, so their relative effectiveness depends on the situation. Heterogeneous teams experience more conflict and take longer to develop.[45] In contrast, members of homogeneous teams experience higher satisfaction, less conflict, and better interpersonal relations. Consequently, homogeneous teams tend to be more effective on tasks requiring a high degree of cooperation and coordination, such as emergency response teams.

Although heterogeneous teams are more difficult to develop, they are generally more effective than homogeneous teams in executive groups and in other situations involving complex problems requiring innovative solutions.[47] This is because people from different backgrounds see a problem or opportunity from different perspectives. For example, one recent study found that all-male teams were less effective than mixed-gender teams on some tasks because all-male teams tended to make decisions that were too aggressive.[48]

Heterogeneous-team members also solve complex problems more easily because they usually have a broader knowledge base. A senior executive at Monsanto Corporation sums up this view: "Every time I have put together a diverse group of people, that team has always come up with a more breakthrough solution than any homogeneous group working on the same problem."[49] However, the benefits of diversity occur primarily when the team tries to reach consensus (rather than voting) and each member actively tries to understand and incorporate other members' viewpoints.

Finally, a team's diversity may give it more legitimacy or allow its members to obtain a wide network of cooperation and support in the organization. When teams represent various professions or departments, they are more likely to represent the organization's diverse interests and perspectives. Consequently, other employees are more likely to accept and support the team's decisions and actions.

Team Processes

Our discussion so far has presented two sets of elements in the team effectiveness model: (1) organizational and team environment and (2) team design. The next few pages introduce the third set of team effectiveness elements, collectively known as team processes. These processes—team development, norms, roles, and cohesiveness—are influenced by both team design and organizational and team environment factors.

Team Development

A few years ago, the National Transportation Safety Board (NTSB) in the United States studied the circumstances under which airplane cockpit crews were most likely to have accidents and related problems. What they discovered was startling: 73 percent of all incidents took place on the crew's first day, and 44 percent occurred on the crew's very first flight together. This isn't an isolated example. NASA studied fatigue of pilots after returning from multiple-day trips. Fatigued pilots made more errors in the NASA flight simulator, as one would expect. But the NASA researchers *didn't* expect the discovery that fatigued crews who had worked together made fewer errors than did rested crews who had not yet flown together.[50]

The NTSB and NASA studies reveal that team members must resolve several issues and pass through several stages of development before emerging as an effective work unit. They must get to know each other, understand their respective roles, discover appropriate and inappropriate behaviors, and learn how to coordinate their work or social activities. The longer that team members work together, the better they develop common mental models, mutual understanding, and effective performance routines to complete the work. For this reason, Budd Canada resisted union demands for a new work schedule that would create new work teams. "Even though the individual level of skills could be good, people who work together as a team regularly are always slightly ahead of a team that is put together on an ad hoc basis," explains Budd Canada executive Winston Wong.[51]

The five-stage model of team development, shown in Exhibit 9.4, provides a general outline of how teams evolve by forming, storming, norming, performing, and eventually adjourning.[52] The model shows teams progressing from one stage to the next in an orderly fashion, but the dashed lines illustrate that they might also fall back to an earlier stage of development as new members join or other conditions disrupt the team's maturity.

EXHIBIT 9.4

Stages of team development

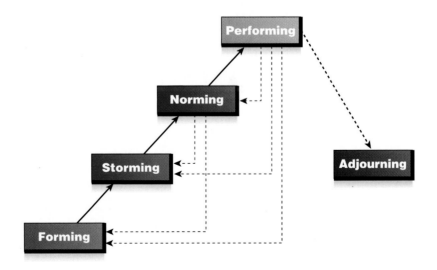

1. *Forming*—The first stage of team development is a period of testing and orientation in which members learn about each other and evaluate the benefits and costs of continued membership. People tend to be polite during this stage and will defer to the existing authority of a formal or informal leader who must provide an initial set of rules and structures for interaction. Members try to find out what is expected of them and how they will fit into the team.

2. *Storming*—The storming stage is marked by interpersonal conflict as members become more proactive and compete for various team roles. Coalitions may form to influence the team's goals and means of goal attainment. Members try to establish norms of appropriate behavior and performance standards. This is a tenuous stage in the team's development, particularly when the leader is autocratic and lacks the necessary conflict-management skills.

3. *Norming*—During the norming stage, the team develops its first real sense of cohesion as roles are established and a consensus forms around group objectives. Members develop relatively similar mental models, so they have common expectations and assumptions about how the team's goals should be accomplished. These common expectations and assumptions enable team members to interact more efficiently so they can move into the next stage, performing.[53]

4. *Performing*—The team becomes more task-oriented in the performing stage. Team members have learned to coordinate and resolve conflicts more efficiently. Further coordination improvements must occasionally be addressed, but the greater emphasis is on task accomplishment. In high-performance teams, members are highly cooperative, have a high level of trust in each other, are committed to group objectives, and identify with the team. There is a climate of mutual support in which team members feel comfortable about taking risks, making errors, or asking for help.[54]

5. *Adjourning*—Most work teams and informal groups eventually end. Task forces disband when their project is completed. Informal work groups may reach this stage when several members leave the organization or are reassigned elsewhere. Some teams adjourn as a result of layoffs or plant shutdowns. Whatever the cause of team adjournment, members shift their attention away from task orientation to a socioemotional focus as they realize that their relationship is ending.

The team development model is a useful framework for thinking about how teams develop. At the same time, we must keep in mind that it is not a perfect representation of the dynamics of team development.[55] The model does not explicitly show that some teams remain in a particular stage longer than others, and that team development is a continuous process. As membership changes and new conditions emerge, teams cycle back to earlier stages in the developmental process to regain the equilibrium or balance lost by the change (as shown by the dashed lines in Exhibit 9.4).

Team Norms

Have you ever noticed how employees in some departments almost run for the exit door the minute the workday ends, whereas people in the same jobs elsewhere almost seem to be competing for who can stay at work the longest?

These differences are partly due to **norms**—the informal rules and expectations that groups establish to regulate the behavior of their members. Norms apply only to behavior, not to private thoughts or feelings. Moreover, norms exist only for behaviors that are important to the team.[56]

Norms guide the way team members deal with clients, how they share resources, whether they are willing to work longer hours, and many other behaviors in organizational life. Some norms ensure that employees support organizational goals, whereas other norms might conflict with organizational objectives. For example, the level of employee absence from work is partly influenced by absence norms in the workplace. In other words, employees are more likely to take off work if they work in teams that support this behavior.[57]

Conformity to Team Norms   Everyone has experienced peer pressure at one time or another. Co-workers grimace if we are late for a meeting or make sarcastic comments if we don't have our part of the project completed on time. In more extreme situations, team members may try to enforce their norms by temporarily ostracizing deviant co-workers or threatening to terminate their membership. This heavy-handed peer pressure isn't as rare as you might think. One survey revealed that 20 percent of employees have been pressured by their colleagues to slack off at work. Half the time, the peer pressure occurred because colleagues didn't want to look like poor performers against their more productive co-workers.[58]

Norms are also directly reinforced through praise from high-status members, more access to valued resources, or other rewards available to the team.[59] But team members often conform to prevailing norms without direct reinforcement or punishment because they identify with the group and want to align their behavior with the team's values. This effect is particularly strong in new members because they are uncertain of their status and want to demonstrate their membership in the team. Global Connections 9.2 provides an extreme example of the consequences of team norms and conformity in organizational settings.

How Team Norms Develop   Norms develop as team members learn that certain behaviors help them function more effectively.[60] Some norms develop when team members or outsiders make explicit statements that seem to aid the team's success or survival. For example, the team leader might frequently express the importance of treating customers with respect and courtesy. A second factor triggering the development of a new norm is a critical event in the team's history. A team might develop a strong norm to keep the work area clean after a co-worker slips on metal scraps and seriously injures herself.

Team norms are most strongly influenced by events soon after the team is formed.[61] Future behaviors are shaped by the way members of a newly formed team initially greet each other, where they locate themselves in a meeting, and so on. A fourth influence on team norms is the beliefs and values that members bring to the team. For example, negotiation teams develop norms about appropriate bargaining behavior based on each member's previous bargaining experience.[62]

Troubleshooting Dysfunctional Team Norms   Although many team norms are deeply anchored, there are ways to minimize the effect of dysfunctional norms on employee behavior. One approach is to introduce performance-oriented

Elite New Zealand Prison Team's "Culture of Obedience"

Members of a special emergency response team congregated at dawn for a covert mission. The 16 hand-picked and specially trained members based at Paparua Prison, New Zealand, were supposed to reduce prison violence, prevent drugs from entering prisons, and improve prisoner compliance. But the mission on this day was different. The response team was hunting for an escapee—a rooster belonging to a member of the response team that had escaped to a neighboring farm.

This is just one of the bizarre incidents about the special unit, dubbed the "Goon Squad" by adversaries. The team worked independently of the prison officers and had its own distinctive black uniforms. Unfortunately, a government report also concluded that the team developed a distinctive set of norms, some of which violated Corrections Department policies.

A government investigation and subsequent court case heard claims that the team falsified time sheets, juggled the work roster for personal gain, borrowed department vehicles for personal use, unnecessarily intimidated inmates, consumed alcohol on duty, acted inappropriately in public, and hunted wayward roosters on company time. The special unit also conducted missions in the outside community even though its mandate was restricted to the prison. "Our focus moved to a policeman's role, which we should not have been doing," admits one former member.

None of the members complained during the unit's existence because of "a culture of obedience." For example, when one member refused to go to a party, others in the unit allegedly went to his home, restrained him, hit him over the head with an ax handle, handcuffed him, and dragged him along to the party.

"The most chilling thing about the team was an apparent fear of authority among members, leading to a culture of obedience and silence," says an executive member of the Howard League for Penal Reform. "In effect, they became a law unto themselves."

Sources: Y. Martin, " 'Goon Squad' Vote Today," *The Christchurch Press,* September 10, 2003; Y. Martin, "The Goon Squad—The Fallout Continues," *The Christchurch Press,* August 16, 2003, p. 15; Y. Martin, "Goon Squad," *The Christchurch Press,* June 9, 2001, p. 2; " 'Goon Squad' Prison Staff Disciplined," *New Zealand Press Association,* May 23, 2001; Y. Martin, "Crack Prison Team Members Guilty of Serious Misconduct," *The Christchurch Press,* May 24, 2001, p. 1.

norms as soon as the team is created. Another strategy is to select members who will bring desirable norms to the group. If the organization wants to emphasize safety, then it should select team members who already value safety.

Selecting people with positive norms may be effective in new teams, but not when adding new members to existing teams with counterproductive norms. A better strategy for existing teams is to explicitly discuss the counterproductive norm with team members using persuasive communication tactics (see Chapter 12).[63] For example, the surgical team of a small hospital had developed a norm of arriving late for operations. Patients and other hospital staff often waited 30 minutes or more for the team to arrive. The hospital CEO eventually spoke to the surgical team about their lateness and, through moral suasion, convinced team members to arrive for operating room procedures no more than five minutes late for their appointments.[64]

Team-based reward systems can sometimes weaken counterproductive norms. Unfortunately, the pressure to conform to the counterproductive norm is sometimes stronger than the financial incentive.[65] This problem occurred in the classic story of a pajama factory where employees were paid under a piece-rate system. Some individuals in the group were able to process up to 100 units per hour and thereby earn more money, but they all chose to abide by the group norm of 50 units per hour. Only after the team was disbanded did the strong performers working alone increase their performance to 100 units per hour.[66]

Finally, a dysfunctional norm may be so deeply ingrained that the best strategy is to disband the group and replace it with people having more favorable norms. Companies should seize the opportunity to introduce performance-

role
A set of behaviors that people are expected to perform because they hold certain positions in a team and organization.

oriented norms when the new team is formed, and select members who will bring desirable norms to the group.

Team Roles

Every work team and informal group has various roles that help the group to survive and achieve its objectives. A **role** is a set of behaviors that people are expected to perform because they hold certain positions in a team and organization.[68] Some roles help the team achieve its goals; other roles maintain relationships so the team survives and team members fulfill their needs. Some team roles are formally assigned to specific people. For example, team leaders are usually expected to initiate discussion, ensure that everyone has an opportunity to present their views, and help the team reach agreement on the issues discussed. But team members often take on various roles informally based on their personality and values. These role preferences are usually worked out during the storming stage of team development. However, in a dynamic environment, team members often have to fulfill various roles temporarily as the need arises.[69]

Various team role theories have been proposed over the years, but Meredith Belbin's team role theory is the most popular.[70] The model identifies nine team roles (see Exhibit 9.5) that are related to specific personality characteristics. People have a natural preference for one role or another, although they can adjust to a secondary role. Belbin's model emphasizes that all nine roles must be engaged for optimal team performance. Moreover, certain team roles should dominate over others at various stages of the team's project or activities. For example, shapers and coordinators are key figures when the team is identifying its needs, whereas completers and implementers are most important during the follow-through stage of the team's project.

How accurate is Belbin's team roles model? The evidence is mixed.[71] Research indicates that teams do require a balance of roles, and that people do tend to prefer one type of role. However, Belbin's nine roles typically boil down to six or seven roles in empirical studies. For example, the implementer and completer roles are the same or too similar to distinguish from each other. Scholars have also criticized how Belbin's roles are measured, which creates difficulty in determining the accuracy of the model. Overall, teams do have a variety of roles that must be fulfilled for team effectiveness, but we are still trying to figure out what these roles are and how to measure them.

One of the first and last tasks of the day at The Container Store is for staff to gather for the "huddle." At The Container Store outlet in White Plains, New York, floor leader Scott Buhler (holding notebook) starts the morning huddle by declaring the day's sales target. Then he asks the group about the store's vision and today's product tip. "We always highlight a product or do a quiz to make sure employees are familiar with new products," Buhler says. The Container Store institutionalized huddle sessions to educate employees, create a team environment, and reinforce norms that the company wants to instill in employees. "The spirit was to keep people on the same page," explains Garrett Boone, co-founder and chairman of the Dallas-based seller of customized storage products.[67] How do "huddles" support norms that companies want to instill in employees?

EXHIBIT 9.5

Belbin's team roles

Role label	Role description
Plant	Creative, imaginative, unorthodox. Solves difficult problems.
Coordinator	Mature, confident, a good chairperson. Clarifies goals, promotes decision making, delegates well.
Monitor (evaluator)	Sober, strategic, and discerning. Sees all options. Judges accurately.
Implementer	Disciplined, reliable, conservative, and efficient. Turns ideas into practical actions.
Completer (finisher)	Painstaking, conscientious, anxious. Searches out errors and omissions. Delivers on time.
Resource investigator	Extrovert, enthusiastic, communicative. Explores opportunities. Develops contacts.
Shaper	Challenging, dynamic, thrives on pressure. The drive and courage to overcome obstacles.
Teamworker	Cooperative, mild, perceptive, and diplomatic. Listens, builds, averts friction.
Specialist	Single-minded, self-starting, dedicated. Provides knowledge and skills in rare supply.

Sources: R. M. Belbin, *Team Roles at Work* (Oxford, UK: Butterworth-Heinemann, 1993); www.belbin.com. Reprinted with permission of Belbin Associates.

Team Cohesiveness

team cohesiveness
The degree of attraction people feel toward the team and their motivation to remain members.

Team cohesiveness—the degree of attraction people feel toward the team and their motivation to remain members—is usually an important factor in a team's success.[72] Employees feel cohesiveness when they believe the team will help them achieve their personal goals, fulfill their need for affiliation or status, or provide social support during times of crisis or trouble. Cohesiveness is an emotional experience, not just a calculation of whether to stay or leave the team. It exists when team members make the team part of their social identity (see Chapter 3). Cohesiveness is the glue or esprit de corps that holds the group together and ensures that its members fulfill their obligations.[73]

Influences on Team Cohesiveness   Several factors influence team cohesiveness: member similarity, team size, member interaction, difficult entry, team success, and external competition or challenges. For the most part, these factors influence the individual's social identity with the group and beliefs about how team membership will fulfill personal needs.[74] Several of these factors are related to our earlier discussion about why people join informal groups and how teams develop. Specifically, teams become more cohesive as they reach higher stages of development and are more attractive to potential members.

Member Similarity   Homogeneous teams become cohesive more easily than do heterogeneous teams. People in homogeneous teams have similar backgrounds and values, so they find it easier to agree on team objectives, the means to fulfill those objectives, and the rules applied to maintain group behavior. This, in turn, leads to greater trust and less dysfunctional conflict within the group.[75] In contrast, diverse teams psychologically impede cohesiveness, particularly during the early stages of development. The dilemma

With titles such as "Way of the Rat," "Brath," and "Route 666," CrossGeneration Comics Inc. is quickly emerging as the next generation in comic book publishing. One reason for CrossGen's rapid success is its emphasis on co-located teamwork. CrossGen founder Mark Alessi insists that everyone should work under one roof at the company's offices in Tampa, Florida. Within those offices, each comic book title team—consisting of a writer, penciler, inker, and colorist—has its own "quad" area, complete with high-end printing and scanning equipment. This team-oriented layout is an updated version of the famous "bullpen" that Spider-Man co-creator Stan Lee designed at Marvel Comics in the 1960s.[76] Why would CrossGen's quad system support team cohesiveness?

here is that heterogeneous teams are usually better than homogeneous teams at completing complex tasks or solving problems requiring creative solutions.

Team Size   Smaller teams tend to be more cohesive than larger teams because it is easier for a few people to agree on goals and coordinate work activities. The smallest teams aren't always the most cohesive, however. Small teams are less cohesive when they lack enough members to perform the required tasks. Thus, team cohesiveness is potentially greatest when teams are as small as possible, yet large enough to accomplish the assigned work.

Member Interaction   Teams tend to be more cohesive when team members interact with each other fairly regularly. This occurs when team members perform highly interdependent tasks and work in the same physical area.[77] Chatelain Architects encourages team interaction with an open office space consisting of low partitions and no special acoustical barriers. "We are always moving around, teaming up and working at other people's desks," says an executive at the Washington, D.C. architectural firm."[78]

Somewhat Difficult Entry   Teams tend to be more cohesive when entry to the team is restricted. The more elite the team, the more prestige it confers on its members, and the more they tend to value their membership in the unit. Existing team members are also more willing to welcome and support new members after they have "passed the test," possibly because they have shared the same entry experience. This raises the issue of how difficult the initiation for entry into the team should be. Research suggests that severe initiations can potentially lead to humiliation and psychological distance from the group, even for those who successfully endure the initiation.[79]

Trevor Pound was looking forward to lying on a Mexican beach for his thirtieth birthday. But the software engineer's crucial role in a major project at Mitel put those February vacation plans on hold. Pound barely mentioned his disappointment, but fellow team members at the communications systems firm wanted to make up for his loss. Nearly a dozen co-workers spent a weekend transforming Pound's drab gray cubicle into a colorful oasis. They brought in a five-foot-wide beach umbrella, a beach chair, a heat lamp, a ukulele, some beach toys, a dozen tropical plants, and more than 200 pounds of sand. The culprits even supplied colorful shorts and a Hawaiian-style shirt. The result: Pound celebrated his birthday in an almost tropical setting on that cold winter day. More important, the practical joke expressed the team's support for his loss of personal time.[85] How else do cohesive team members support each other?

Team Success   Cohesiveness increases with the team's level of success.[80] Individuals are more likely to attach their social identity to successful teams than to those with a string of failures. Moreover, team members are more likely to believe the group will continue to be successful, thereby fulfilling their personal goals (continued employment, pay bonus, etc.). Team leaders can increase cohesiveness by regularly communicating and celebrating the team's successes. Notice that this can create a spiral effect. Successful teams are more cohesive and, under certain conditions, higher cohesiveness increases the team's success.

External Competition and Challenges   Team cohesiveness tends to increase when members face external competition or a valued objective that is challenging.[81] This might include a threat from an external competitor or friendly competition from other teams. These conditions tend to increase cohesiveness because employees value the team's ability to overcome the threat or competition if they can't solve the problem individually. They also value their membership as a form of social support. We need to be careful about the degree of external threat, however. Evidence suggests that teams seem to be less effective when external threats are severe. Although cohesiveness tends to increase, external threats are stressful and cause teams to make less effective decisions under these conditions.[82]

Consequences of Team Cohesiveness   Every team must have some minimal level of cohesiveness to maintain its existence.[83] People who belong to high-cohesion teams are motivated to maintain their membership and to help the team perform effectively. Compared to low-cohesion teams, high-cohesion team members spend more time together, share information more frequently, and are more satisfied with each other. They provide each other with better social support in stressful situations.[84]

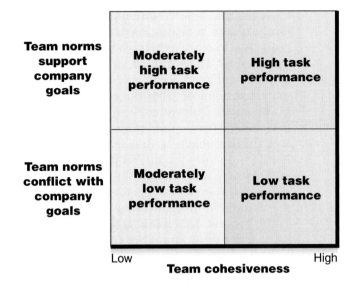

Members of high-cohesion teams are generally more sensitive to each other's needs and develop better interpersonal relationships, thereby reducing dysfunctional conflict. When conflict does arise, members tend to resolve these differences swiftly and effectively. For example, a recent study reported that cohesive recreational ice hockey teams engaged in more constructive conflict—that is, team members tried to resolve their differences cooperatively— whereas less cohesive teams engaged in more combative conflict.[86]

With better cooperation and more conformity to norms, high-cohesion teams usually perform better than low-cohesion teams.[87] However, the relationship is a little more complex. Exhibit 9.6 illustrates how the effect of cohesiveness on team performance depends on the extent that team norms are consistent with organizational goals. Cohesive teams will likely have lower task performance when norms conflict with organizational objectives, because cohesiveness motivates employees to perform at a level more consistent with group norms.[88]

The Trouble with Teams

As we explained near the beginning of this chapter, teams often have a competitive advantage over individuals working alone. This creates a problem by obscuring the fact that teams aren't always needed.[89] Sometimes, a quick and decisive action by one person is more appropriate. Some tasks are also performed just as easily by one person as by a group. "Teams are overused," admits Philip Condit, former CEO of Boeing, Inc. The aircraft manufacturer makes extensive use of teams but knows that they aren't necessary for everything that goes on in organizations. Management guru Peter Drucker agrees. "The now-fashionable team in which everybody works with everybody on everything from the beginning rapidly is becoming a disappointment," he says.[90]

A second problem is that teams take time to develop and maintain. Scholars refer to these hidden costs as **process losses**—resources (including time and energy) expended toward team development and maintenance rather than the task.[91] It is much more efficient for an individual to work out an issue

process losses
Resources (including time and energy) expended toward team development and maintenance rather than the task.

alone than to resolve differences of opinion with other people. The process loss problem becomes apparent when adding new people to the team. The group has to recycle through the team development process to bring everyone up to speed. The software industry even has a name for this. "Brooks's law" says that adding more people to a late software project only makes it later. Researchers point out that the cost of process losses may be offset by the benefits of teams. Unfortunately, few companies conduct a cost-benefit analysis to determine when to use teams or individuals.[92]

A third problem is that teams require the right environment to flourish. Many companies forget this point by putting people in teams without changing anything else. As we noted earlier, teams require appropriate rewards, communication systems, team leadership, and other conditions. Without these, the shift to a team structure could be a waste of time. At the same time, critics suggest that changing these environmental conditions to improve teamwork could result in higher costs than benefits for the overall organization.[93]

Social Loafing

social loafing
A situation in which people exert less effort (and usually perform at a lower level) when working in groups than when working alone.

Perhaps the best known limitation of teams is the risk of productivity loss due to **social loafing.** Social loafing occurs when people exert less effort (and usually perform at a lower level) when working in groups than when working alone.[94] A few experts question whether social loafing is common, but students can certainly report many instances of this problem in their team projects!

Social loafing is more likely to occur in large teams where individual output is difficult to identify. This particularly includes situations in which team members work alone toward a common output pool (i.e., they have low task interdependence). Under these conditions, employees aren't as worried that their performance will be noticed. Social loafing is less likely to occur when the task is interesting, because individuals have a higher intrinsic motivation to perform their duties. It is also less common when the group's objective is important, possibly because individuals experience more pressure from other team members to perform well. Finally, social loafing is less likely to occur among members with a strong collectivist value, because they value group membership and believe in working toward group objectives (see Chapter 2).[95]

How to Minimize Social Loafing   By understanding the causes of social loafing, we can identify ways to minimize this problem. Some of the strategies listed below reduce social loafing by making each member's performance more visible. Others increase each member's motivation to perform his or her tasks within the group.[96]

- *Form smaller teams*—Splitting the team into several smaller groups reduces social loafing because each person's performance becomes more noticeable and important for team performance. A smaller group also potentially increases cohesiveness, so that would-be shirkers feel a greater obligation to perform fully for their team.
- *Specialize tasks*—Each person's contribution is easier to see when each team member performs a different work activity. For example, rather than pooling their effort for all incoming customer inquiries, each customer service representative might be assigned a particular type of client.
- *Measure individual performance*—Social loafing is minimized when each member's contribution is measured. Of course, individual performance is

difficult to measure in some team activities, such as problem-solving projects in which the team's performance depends on one person discovering the best answer.

■ *Increase job enrichment*—Social loafing is minimized when team members are assigned more motivating jobs, such as requiring more skill variety or having direct contact with clients. However, this minimizes social loafing only if members have a strong growth need strength (see Chapter 6). More generally, however, social loafing is less common among employees with high job satisfaction.

■ *Select motivated employees*—Social loafing can be minimized by carefully selecting job applicants who are motivated by the task and have a collectivist value orientation. Those with a collectivist value are motivated to work harder for the team because they value their membership in the group.

This chapter has laid the foundation for our understanding of team dynamics. To build an effective team requires time, the right combination of team members, and the right environment. We will apply these ingredients of environment and team processes in the next chapter, which looks at high-performance teams, including self-directed teams and virtual teams.

Chapter Summary

Teams are groups of two or more people who interact and influence each other, are mutually accountable for achieving common objectives, and perceive themselves as a social entity within an organization. All teams are groups, because they consist of people with a unifying relationship; not all groups are teams, because some groups do not have purposive interaction.

Traditional departments are typically permanent work teams where employees directly interact and coordinate work activities with each other. Organizations also rely on task forces, skunkworks, communities of practice, and other teams to make decisions or complete projects. Informal groups exist primarily for the benefit of their members rather than for the organization. Teams have become popular because they tend to make better decisions, support the knowledge management process, and provide superior customer service. In many situations, employees are more energized and engaged working in teams rather than alone.

Team effectiveness includes the group's ability to survive, achieve its system-based objectives, and fulfill the needs of its members. The model of team effectiveness considers the team and organizational environment, team design, and team processes. The team or organizational environment influences team effectiveness directly, as well as through team design and

team processes. Six elements in the organizational and team environment that influence team effectiveness are reward systems, communication systems, physical space, organizational environment, organizational structure, and organizational leadership.

Three team design elements are task characteristics, team size, and team composition. Teams work best when tasks are clear, easy to implement, and require a high degree of interdependence. Teams should be large enough to perform the work, yet small enough for efficient coordination and meaningful involvement. Effective teams are composed of people with the competencies and motivation to perform tasks in a team environment. Heterogeneous teams operate best on complex projects and problems requiring innovative solutions.

Teams develop through the stages of forming, storming, norming, performing, and eventually adjourning. However, some teams remain in a particular stage longer than others, and team development is a continuous process. Teams develop norms to regulate and guide member behavior. These norms may be influenced by critical events, explicit statements, initial experiences, and members' pregroup experiences. Team members also have roles—a set of behaviors they are expected to perform because they hold certain positions in a team and organization.

Cohesiveness is the degree of attraction people feel toward the team and their motivation to remain members. Cohesiveness increases with member similarity, smaller team size, higher degree of interaction, somewhat difficult entry, team success, and external challenges. Teams need some level of cohesiveness to survive, but high-cohesive units have higher task performance only when their norms do not conflict with organizational objectives.

Teams are not always beneficial or necessary.

Moreover, they have hidden costs, known as process losses, and require particular environments to flourish. Teams often fail because they are not set up in supportive environments. Social loafing is another potential problem with teams. This is the tendency for individuals to perform at a lower level when working in groups than when alone. Social loafing can be minimized by making each member's performance more visible and increasing each member's motivation to perform his or her tasks within the group.

Key Terms

communities of practice, p. 268
groups, p. 266
heterogeneous teams, p. 275
homogeneous teams, p. 275
informal groups, p. 268
norms, p. 279
process losses, p. 285

role, p. 281
skunkworks, p. 267
social loafing, p. 286
task interdependence, p. 273
team cohesiveness, p. 282
team effectiveness, p. 271
teams, p. 266

Discussion Questions

1. Informal groups exist in almost every form of social organization. What types of informal groups exist in your classroom? Why are students motivated to belong to these informal groups?
2. What are "communities of practice"? How can they contribute to organizational performance? Individual performance?
3. You have been asked to lead a complex software project over the next year that requires the full-time involvement of approximately 100 people with diverse skills and backgrounds. Using your knowledge of team size, how can you develop an effective team under these conditions?
4. You have been put in charge of a cross-functional task force that will develop enhanced Internet banking services for retail customers. The team includes representatives from marketing, information services, customer service, and accounting, all of whom will move to the same location at headquarters for three months. Describe the behaviors you might observe during each stage of the team's development.
5. You have just been transferred from the Kansas office to the Denver office of your company, a national sales organization of electrical products for developers and contractors. In Kansas, team members regularly called customers after

a sale to ask whether the products arrived on time and whether they are satisfied. But when you moved to the Denver office, no one seemed to make these follow-up calls. A recently hired co-worker explained that other co-workers discouraged her from making those calls. Later, another co-worker suggested that your follow-up calls were making everyone else look lazy. Give three possible reasons why the norms in Denver might be different from those in the Kansas office, even though the customers, products, sales commissions, and other characteristics of the workplace are almost identical.
6. An employee at a brokerage firm recently made the following comment about his team, using a baseball metaphor: "Our team has a great bunch of people. But just like a baseball team, some people need to hit the home run, whereas others have to play catcher. Some need to be coaches and others have to be experts at fixing the equipment every day. The problem with our team is that we don't have people in some of these other jobs. As a result, our team isn't performing as well as it should." What team dynamics topic is this person mainly referring to, and what is he saying about his team in the context of that topic?
7. You have been assigned to a class project with

five other students, none of whom you have met before. To what extent would team cohesiveness improve your team's performance on this project? What actions would you recommend to build team cohesiveness among student team members in this situation?

8. "The now-fashionable team in which everybody works with everybody on everything from the beginning rapidly is becoming a disappointment." Discuss three problems associated with teams.

TREETOP FOREST PRODUCTS

Treetop Forest Products Inc. is a sawmill operation in Oregon that is owned by a major forest products company but operates independently of headquarters. It was built 30 years ago and completely updated with new machinery 5 years ago. Treetop receives raw logs from the area for cutting and planing into building-grade lumber, mostly 2-by-4 and 2-by-6 pieces of standard lengths. Higher grade logs leave Treetop's sawmill department in finished form and are sent directly to the packaging department. The remaining 40 percent of sawmill output are cuts from lower grade logs, requiring further work by the planing department.

Treetop has a general manager, 16 supervisors and support staff, and 180 unionized employees. The unionized employees are paid an hourly rate specified in the collective bargaining agreement, whereas management and support staff are paid a monthly salary. The mill is divided into six operating departments: boom, sawmill, planer, packaging, shipping, and maintenance. The sawmill, boom, and packaging departments operate a morning shift starting at 6 A.M. and an afternoon shift starting at 2 P.M. Employees in these departments rotate shifts every two weeks. The planer and shipping departments operate only morning shifts. Maintenance employees work the night shift (starting at 10 P.M.).

Each department, except packaging, has a supervisor on every work shift. The planer supervisor is responsible for the packaging department on the morning shift, and the sawmill supervisor is responsible for the packaging department on the afternoon shift. However, the packaging operation is housed in a separate building from the other departments, so supervisors seldom visit the packaging department.

This is particularly true for the afternoon shift, because the sawmill supervisor is the farthest distance from the packaging building.

Packaging Quality

Ninety percent of Treetop's product is sold on the international market through Westboard Company, a large marketing agency. Westboard represents all forest products mills owned by Treetop's parent company as well as several other clients in the region. The market for building-grade lumber is very price competitive, because there are numerous mills selling a relatively undifferentiated product. However, some differentiation does occur in product packaging and presentation. Buyers will look closely at the packaging when deciding whether to buy from Treetop or another mill.

To encourage its clients to package their products better, Westboard sponsors a monthly package quality award. The marketing agency samples and rates its clients' packages daily, and the sawmill with the highest score at the end of the month is awarded a plaque. Package quality is a combination of how the lumber is piled (e.g., defects turned in), where the bands and dunnage (packing material) are placed, how neatly the stencil and seal are applied, the stencil's accuracy, and how neatly and tightly the plastic wrap is attached.

Treetop Forest Products won Westboard's packaging quality award several times over the past few years, and received high ratings in the months that it didn't win. However, the mill's ratings have started to decline over the past couple of years, and several clients have complained about the appearance of the finished product. A few large customers switched to competitors' lumber, saying that the decision was based on the substandard appearance of Treetop's packaging when their orders arrived.

Bottleneck in Packaging

The planing and sawmilling departments have significantly increased productivity over the past couple of years. The sawmill operation recently set a new productivity record on a single day. The planer operation has increased productivity to the point where last year it reduced operations to just one (rather than two) shifts per day. These productivity improvements are due to better operator training, fewer machine breakdowns, and better selection of raw logs. (Sawmill cuts from high-quality logs usually do not require planing work.)

Productivity levels in the boom, shipping, and maintenance departments have remained constant. However, the packaging department has recorded decreasing productivity over the past couple of years, with the result that a large backlog of finished product is typically stockpiled outside the packaging building. The morning shift of the packaging department is unable to keep up with the combined production of the sawmill and planer departments, so the unpackaged output is left for the afternoon shift. Unfortunately, the afternoon shift packages even less product than the morning shift, so the backlog continues to build. The backlog adds to Treetop's inventory costs and increases the risk of damaged stock.

Treetop has added Saturday overtime shifts as well as extra hours before and after the regular shifts for the packaging department employees to process this backlog. Last month, the packaging department employed 10 percent of the workforce but accounted for 85 percent of the overtime. This is frustrating to Treetop's management, because time and motion studies recently confirmed that the packaging department is capable of processing all of the daily sawmill and planer production without overtime. Moreover, with employees earning one and a half or two times their regular pay on overtime, Treetop's cost competitiveness suffers.

Employees and supervisors at Treetop are aware that people in the packaging department tend to extend lunch by 10 minutes and coffee breaks by 5 minutes. They also typically leave work a few minutes before the end of the shift. This abuse has worsened recently, particularly on the afternoon shift. Employees who are temporarily assigned to the packaging department also seem to participate in this time loss pattern after a few days. Although they are punctual and productive in other departments, these temporary employees soon adopt the packaging crew's informal schedule when assigned to that department.

Discussion Questions

1. Based on your knowledge of team dynamics, explain why the packaging department is less productive than are other teams at Treetop.

2. How should Treetop change the nonproductive norms that exist in the packaging group?

3. What structural and other changes would you recommend that may improve this situation in the long term?

CASE STUDY 9.2

DETROIT IS CRUISING FOR QUALITY

BusinessWeek In the 1980s, Detroit automakers were widely criticized for lagging behind the Japanese in most measures of quality. Since then, Ford, General Motors, and DaimlerChrysler have all made strides in quality improvement, often borrowing methods from Japanese manufacturing. Those methods include team-based approaches such as quality circles and cross-functional teams. At the beginning of the twenty-first century, defect rates in U.S. cars are much lower, but the companies still have far to go, and they continue to rely on teams to solve—and prevent—quality problems.

This *Business Week* case study describes efforts by U.S. carmakers to improve quality. It identifies the kinds of problems that are most prevalent and gives examples of team-based solutions. Read through this *Business Week* case study at www.mhhe.com/mcshane3e and prepare for the discussion questions below.

Discussion Questions

1. What kinds of teams does the author mention in this article? How effective have they been?

2. What are some norms at U.S. automakers and their teams that may have limited their success in improving quality?

3. The article says Chrysler is forming teams for vehicle development. How might participation of employees from the design, engineering, marketing, manufacturing, and purchasing departments prevent "last-minute design changes that lead to errors later on"? What are some advantages and disadvantages of this team approach, compared with letting designers handle this process on their own?

Source: Joann Muller, "Detroit Is Cruising for Quality," *Business Week*, September 3, 2001.

CASE STUDY 9.3

TEAM TOWER POWER

Purpose   This exercise is designed to help you understand team roles, team development, and other issues in the development and maintenance of effective teams.

Materials   The instructor will provide enough Lego pieces or similar materials for each team to complete the assigned task. All teams should have identical (or very similar) amounts and types of pieces. The instructor will need a measuring tape and stopwatch. Students may use writing materials during the design stage (Step 2 below). The instructor will distribute a "Team Objectives Sheet" and "Tower Specifications Effectiveness Sheet" to all teams.

Instructions

■ *Step 1*—The instructor will divide the class into teams. Depending on class size and space available, teams may have between four and seven members, but all should be approximately equal size.

■ *Step 2*—Each team is given 20 minutes to design a tower that uses only the materials provided, is freestanding, and provides an optimal return on investment. Team members may wish to draw their tower on paper or flip chart to assist the tower's design. Teams are free to practice building their tower during this stage. Preferably, teams are assigned to their own rooms so the design can be created privately. During this stage, each team will complete the Team Objectives Sheet distributed by the instructor. This sheet requires the Tower Specifications Effectiveness Sheet, also distributed by the instructor.

■ *Step 3*—Each team will show the instructor that it has completed its Team Objectives Sheet. Then, with all teams in the same room, the instructor will announce the start of the construction phase. The time elapsed for construction will be closely monitored and the instructor will occasionally call out time elapsed (particularly if there is no clock in the room).

■ *Step 4*—Each team will advise the instructor as soon as it has completed its tower. The team will write down the time elapsed that the instructor has determined. It may be asked to assist the instructor by counting the number of blocks used and height of the tower. This information is also written on the Team Objectives Sheet. Then the team calculates its profit.

■ *Step 5*—After presenting the results, the class will discuss the team dynamics elements that contribute to team effectiveness. Team members will discuss their strategy, division of labor (team roles), expertise within the team, and other elements of team dynamics.

Source: Several published and online sources describe variations of this exercise, but there is no known origin to this activity.

TEAM ROLES PREFERENCES SCALE

Purpose   This self-assessment is designed to help you to identify your preferred roles in meetings and similar team activities.

Instructions   Read each of the statements on the next page and circle the response that you believe best reflects your position regarding each statement. Then use the scoring key in Appendix B to calculate your results for each team role. This exercise is completed alone so students assess themselves honestly without concerns of social comparison. However, class discussion will focus on the roles that people assume in team settings. This scale only assesses a few team roles.

Team Roles Preferences Scale

Circle the number that best reflects your position regarding each of these statements.	Does Not Describe Me at All	Does Not Describe Me Very Well	Describes Me Somewhat	Describes Me Well	Describes Me Very Well
1. I usually take responsibility for getting the team to agree on what the meeting should accomplish....................	1	2	3	4	5
2. I tend to summarize to other team members what the team has accomplished so far.........................	1	2	3	4	5
3. I'm usually the person who helps other team members overcome their disagreements...........................	1	2	3	4	5
4. I try to ensure that everyone gets heard on issues.............	1	2	3	4	5
5. I'm usually the person who helps the team determine how to organize the discussion..........................	1	2	3	4	5
6. I praise other team members for their ideas more than do others in the meetings............................	1	2	3	4	5
7. People tend to rely on me to keep track of what has been said in meetings...................................	1	2	3	4	5
8. The team typically counts on me to prevent debates from getting out of hand.........................	1	2	3	4	5
9. I tend to say things that make the group feel optimistic about its accomplishments.................................	1	2	3	4	5
10. Team members usually count on me to give everyone a chance to speak................................	1	2	3	4	5
11. In most meetings, I am less likely than others to "put down" the ideas of team mates...............................	1	2	3	4	5
12. I actively help team mates to resolve their differences in meetings..	1	2	3	4	5
13. I actively encourage quiet team members to describe their ideas on each issue......................................	1	2	3	4	5
14. People tend to rely on me to clarify the purpose of the meeting..	1	2	3	4	5
15. I like to be the person who takes notes or minutes of the meeting.......................................	1	2	3	4	5

Source: Copyright © 2000. Steven L. McShane.

After studying the preceding material, be sure to check out our website at
www.mhhe.com/mcshane3e
for more in-depth information and interactivities that correspond to this chapter.

Developing High-Performance Teams

Learning Objectives

After reading this chapter, you should be able to:

■ Identify the characteristics of self-directed work teams (SDWTs).

■ Describe the four conditions in sociotechnical systems theory for high-performance SDWTs.

■ Summarize three challenges to the implementation of SDWTs.

■ Explain why virtual teams have become increasingly common in organizations.

■ Describe the role of communication systems, task structure, team size, and team composition in virtual team effectiveness.

■ Summarize the three levels of trust in teams.

■ Identify five problems facing teams when making decisions.

■ Describe the five structures for team decision making.

■ Discuss the potential benefits and limitations of brainstorming.

■ Outline the four types of team building.

■ Identify three reasons why team building might fail.

Twenty years ago, Margaret Carter started selling pâté and other gourmet food products to local pubs as a way to support herself and her children following her divorce. Today, her Welsh company, the Patchwork Traditional Food Company, is a bustling operation whose 30 employees manufacture gourmet foods for clients throughout the United Kingdom and continental Europe.

Carter says that the company's two ingredients for success are making its products by hand in small batches and relying on self-directed work teams. "We've had the self-directed teams for about 15 years, and the idea is that nobody has titles and staff are empowered to make their own decisions," she says. The production team calls itself the Motley Crew; the postproduction team is known as the Musketeers.

Patchwork Traditional Food Company, the Welsh maker of pâté and other gourmet foods, relies on high-performance self-directed work teams.

Once each week, team members gather for a 59:59 meeting (which lasts no more than 59 minutes and 59 seconds) to discuss problems during the previous week and goals for the forthcoming week. Each team decides its own production schedules and work patterns, is able to recruit collectively, and is involved in everything from the design of new packaging to product development. Team members become multiskilled and eventually get rotated into the roles of team leader and communication officer.

Each team also has a daily "huddle" meeting. "In the morning everybody arrives in their various teams and the first thing they do is have something called a huddle," Carter explains. "So for 10 minutes everybody discusses the workload for the day and the issues that have arisen from the previous day." To maintain a team focus and to remove any status differences, staff conduct their morning huddle away from individual desks. "They stand in a circle away from their desks so there is no control issue," says Carter, who now spends much of her time speaking to other businesses about implementing high-performance work teams.[1] ■

Throughout the United Kingdom, the Patchwork Traditional Food Company has become a role model for high-performance work teams. Numerous organizations in North America—Harley-Davidson, TRW, Standard Motor Products, and Worthington Steel-Delta, to name a few—have also benefited from the efficiency of these work arrangements. This chapter extends our discussion of teams by focusing on high-performance teams, including self-directed work teams, virtual teams, effective decision making in teams, and team-building strategies. The chapter starts by introducing the features of self-directed work teams as well as the elements of sociotechnical systems theory, upon which these high-performance teams are based. Next, we look at the increasing popularity of virtual teams and summarize current research on how to ensure that these virtual teams are effective. We also look at the important topic of trust in virtual teams and other groups. This chapter then focuses on effective decision making in teams, including challenges and strategies to minimize problems with effective team decision making. The last section of this chapter reviews various team-building strategies.

Self-Directed Work Teams

Surrounded by tall prairie grass, Harley-Davidson's new assembly plant near Kansas City, Missouri, exemplifies the philosophy of a high-involvement organization. There are no supervisors. Instead, natural work teams of 8 to 15 employees make most day-to-day decisions through consensus. An umbrella group, representing teams and management, makes plantwide decisions. "There is more pressure on employees here because they must learn to do what supervisors did," admits Karl Eberle, vice-president and general manager of Harley-Davidson's Kansas City operations. Still, Harley-Davidson is taking employee involvement far beyond the traditional workplace. "There's a lot of work being done to empower the work force," says Eberle. "But there are very few examples of where they've taken the work force to run the factory. And that's what we've done."[2]

self-directed work teams (SDWTs)
Cross-functional work groups organized around work processes, that complete an entire piece of work requiring several interdependent tasks, and that have substantial autonomy over the execution of those tasks.

Harley-Davidson and many other organizations are following the trend toward **self-directed work teams (SDWTs).** By most estimates, over two-thirds of the medium and large organizations in North America use SDWT structures for part of their operations.[3] SDWTs complete an entire piece of work requiring several interdependent tasks and have substantial autonomy over the execution of these tasks. These teams vary somewhat from one firm to the next, but they generally have the features listed in Exhibit 10.1.[4]

First, SDWTs complete an entire piece of work, whether it's a product, a service, or part of a larger product or service. As we described in the opening vignette for this chapter, self-directed work teams at the Patchwork Traditional Food Company are responsible for the entire food manufacturing process. Second, the team—not supervisors—assigns tasks that individual team members perform. In other words, the team plans, organizes, and controls work activities with little or no direct involvement of a higher status supervisor.

Third, SDWTs control most work inputs, flow, and output. "[Teams] have total authority to make all decisions: I mean total, complete authority on every aspect of business," explains Dennis W. Bakke, cofounder and recently retired CEO of electrical power company AES Corporation.[5] Fourth, SDWTs are responsible for correcting work flow problems as they occur. In other words, the

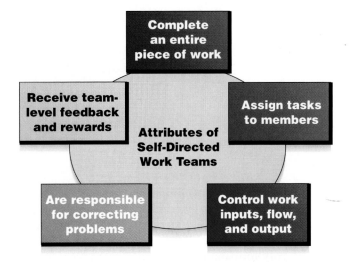

teams maintain their own quality and logistical control. For example, self-directed teams at the Collins & Aikman auto parts plant in Americus, Georgia, are responsible for quality assurance as well as safety reviews and compliance, environmental compliance, daily job assignments, and training.[6] Last, SDWTs receive team-level feedback and rewards. This recognizes and reinforces the fact that the team—not individuals—is responsible for the work, although team members may also receive individual feedback and rewards.

You may have noticed from this description that members of SDWTs have enriched and enlarged jobs (see Chapter 6). The team's work includes all the tasks required to make an entire product or provide a service. The team is also mostly responsible for scheduling, coordinating, and planning these tasks.[7] Self-directed work teams were initially designed around production processes. However, they are also found in administrative and service activities, at automobile service centers, city government administration, and customer assistance teams in courier services.[8] These service tasks are well suited to self-directed work teams when employees have interdependent tasks and decisions require the knowledge and experience of several people.[9]

Sociotechnical Systems Theory and SDWTs

How do companies create successful self-directed work teams? To answer this question, we need to look at **sociotechnical systems (STS) theory,** which is the main source of current SDWT practices. STS theory was introduced during the 1940s at Britain's Tavistock Institute, where researchers had been studying the effects of technology on coal mining in the United Kingdom.[10]

The Tavistock researchers observed that the new coal mining technology (called the "long wall" method) led to lower, not higher, job performance. They analyzed the causes of this problem and established the idea that organizations need "joint optimization" between the social and technical systems of the work unit. In other words, they need to introduce technology in a way that creates the best structure for semi-autonomous work teams. Moreover, the Tavistock group concluded that teams should be sufficiently autonomous so that they can control the main "variances" in the system. This means that the team must control the factors with the greatest impact on quality, quantity,

sociotechnical systems (STS) theory

A theory stating that effective work sites have joint optimization of their social and technological systems, and that teams should have sufficient autonomy to control key variances in the work process.

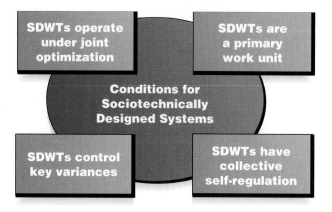

and the cost of the product or service. From this overview of STS, we can identify four main conditions for high-performance SDWTs (see Exhibit 10.2).[11]

SDWTs Are a Primary Work Unit   STS theory suggests that self-directed teams work best when they are a primary work unit, that is, they are responsible for making an entire product, providing a service, or otherwise completing an entire work process. By making an entire product or service, the team is sufficiently independent that it can make adjustments without interfering, or having interference from, other work units. At the same time, the primary work unit ensures that employees perform interdependent subtasks within their team so they have a sense of cohesiveness by working toward a common goal.[12]

SDWTs Have Collective Self-Regulation   STS theory says that teams must have sufficient autonomy to manage the work process. In STS jargon, this is called **collective self-regulation,** which means that the team can decide how to divide work among its members as well as how to coordinate that work. Collective self-regulation is a central feature in self-directed work teams and represents a team-based version of autonomy in job enrichment (see Chapter 6). In essence, this condition gives SDWTs the freedom to respond more quickly and effectively to their environment. It also motivates team members through feelings of empowerment.

SDWTs Control Key Variances   STS theory says that high-performance SDWTs have control over "key variances." These variances represent the disturbances or interruptions in the work process that affect the quality or performance of the product or service. For instance, the mixture of ingredients would be a key variance for employees in food processing because the mixture is within the team's control and it influences the quality of the final product. In contrast, introducing SDWTs offers little advantage when the primary causes of good or poor performance are mainly due to technology, supplies, or other factors beyond the team's control.

SDWTs Operate under Joint Optimization   Perhaps the most crucial feature of STS theory is **joint optimization**—the notion that the work process balances the social and technical systems to maximize the operation's effectiveness.[13] In

collective self-regulation
A feature of sociotechnical systems in which the team has autonomy to divide up work among its members as well as to coordinate that work.

joint optimization
A key requirement in sociotechnical systems theory that a balance must be struck between social and technical systems to maximize an operation's effectiveness.

Jabil Circuits relies on self-directed teams at its manufacturing operations in St. Petersburg, Florida, and Auburn Hills, Michigan. "Our manufacturing environment is team-oriented," says a Jabil Circuits' executive. "Employees are organized into teams of from three to 14 or 15 people." Each production team is responsible for a specific customer group. For example, one team makes circuit boards that go into car dashboards. Team members have a high degree of autonomy to stop production when they see quality problems. They are also cross-trained to perform several tasks so they can cover for each other.[14] What advantages and potential problems would Jabil Circuits have with this high-performance work team structure?

particular, the technological system should be implemented in a way that encourages or facilitates team dynamics, job enrichment, and meaningful feedback. This idea of joint optimization was quite radical in the 1940s, a time when many thought that technology dictated how employees should be organized. In many cases, the technology resulted in people working alone with little opportunity to directly coordinate their work or share knowledge and ideas. Sociotechnical systems theory, on the other hand, says that companies can and must introduce technology so that it supports a semi-autonomous, team-based structure.

Applying STS Theory and Self-Directed Work Teams It's not difficult to find examples of successful self-directed work teams around the world. Three years after Flexible Steel Lacing Company made the transformation to SDWTs, the Downers Grove, Illinois, manufacturer of conveyor belt fasteners reported that the time required to fill orders had dropped by 30 percent and plant productivity (sales dollar per employee) had increased by 12 percent. Beginning in the late 1990s, Canon Inc. introduced self-directed teams at all 29 of its Japanese plants. The camera and copier company claims that a team of a half-dozen people can now produce as much as 30 people in the old assembly line system.

A recent study found that car dealership service garages that organize employees into self-directed teams were significantly more profitable than service garages where employees work without a team structure. Celestica Inc., which provides manufacturing services for computer companies, dramatically improved productivity after forming permanent self-directed work teams based on a sociotechnical systems study conducted by employees. "What I like about the STS process is that the change has been driven by the employees—those responsible for execution—as opposed to management dictating how it's going to be," says a Celestica employee about the company's transition to self-directed teams.[15]

In spite of its long-term success, STS theory is not very helpful at identifying the optimal alignment of the social and technical system. Volvo's Uddevalla plant in Sweden may have demonstrated this point.[16] The Uddevalla plant replaced the traditional assembly line with fixed workstations at which teams of approximately 20 employees assemble and install components in an unfinished automobile chassis. This technological structure creates a strong team orientation, but productivity is among the *lowest* in the automobile industry because the technological design is not sufficiently flexible. (Producing a car at Uddevalla takes 50 hours versus 25 hours at a traditional Volvo plant and 13 hours at a Toyota plant.) In other words, in its attempt to accommodate the social system, Volvo's production system may have become technologically too inefficient.

Challenges to Self-Directed Work Teams

Even where sociotechnical systems theory indicates that self-directed work teams are appropriate, corporate leaders need to recognize and overcome at least three potential barriers: cross-cultural issues, management resistance, and employee and labor union resistance.

Cross-Cultural Issues   SDWTs are difficult to implement in high power distance cultures.[17] Employees in these cultures are more comfortable when supervisors give them directions, whereas low power distance employees value their involvement in decisions. Mexico has a very high power distance value system, which explains why firms have difficulty implementing self-directed work teams in that country. One study reported that Mexican employees expect managers to make decisions affecting their work, whereas SDWTs emphasize self-initiative and individual responsibility within teams. Some writers also suggest that SDWTs are more difficult to implement in cultures with low collectivism because employees are less comfortable collaborating and working interdependently with co-workers.[18]

Management Resistance   Poet Robert Frost once wrote, "The brain is a wonderful organ; it starts working the moment you get up in the morning and does not stop until you get into the office."[19] Frost's humor highlights the fact that many organizations expect employees to park their brains at the door. It's not surprising, then, to learn that supervisors and higher level managers are often the main source of resistance to the transition to self-directed work teams.[20] Their main worry is losing power when employees gain power through empowered teams. Some are concerned that their jobs will lose status, whereas others believe that they will not have any jobs at all.

Another problem is that supervisors do not know how to become "hands-off" facilitators of several work teams rather than "hands-on" supervisors of several employees. This was one of the biggest stumbling blocks to self-directed work teams at a TRW auto parts plant. Many supervisors kept slipping back into their command-and-control supervisory style. As one TRW employee explains: "One of the toughest things for some of them was to shift from being a boss to a coach, moving from saying, 'I know what's good for you' to 'How can I help you?'"[21] Research suggests that supervisors are less likely to resist self-directed work teams when they have previously worked in a high-involvement workplace and receive considerable training in their new facilitation role.[22]

Employee and Labor Union Resistance   Employees sometimes oppose SDWTs because they require new skills or appear to require more work. Many feel uncomfortable as they explore their new roles, and they may be worried that they lack the skills to adapt to the new work requirements. For instance, professional surveyors at a Swedish company reported increased stress when

When Standard Motor Products (SMP) introduced self-directed work teams at its Edwardsville, Kansas, plant, supervisors had a tough challenge replacing their command-and-control management style with something closer to a mentor or facilitator. "It wasn't easy for managers who were raised in the top-down authority model," recalls Darrel Ray, the nationally recognized consultant who worked with the auto parts company during the transition. "It is far easier to be a tyrant than it is to be a psychologist or a teacher," explains distribution manager Don Wakefield. Steve Domann was one of the managers who had difficulty adjusting. "I thought about quitting when the changes were announced," says Domann, who now oversees plant work teams as a team developer. "Some of the old management team couldn't conform to the team, but I'm glad I did."[23] In your opinion, how can organizations minimize management resistance to self-directed work teams?

their company introduced customer-focused self-directed teams.[24]

Labor unions supported the early experiments in sociotechnical change in Europe and India, but some unions in North America have reservations about SDWTs.[25] One concern is that teams improve productivity at the price of higher stress levels among employees, which is sometimes true. Another worry is that SDWTs require more flexibility by reversing work rules and removing job categories that unions have negotiated over the years. Labor union leaders are therefore concerned that regaining these hard-fought union member rights will be a difficult battle.

In spite of these challenges, self-directed work teams offer enormous potential for organizations when they are implemented under the right conditions, as specified by sociotechnical systems theory. Meanwhile, information technologies and knowledge work have enabled virtual teams to gain popularity. The next section examines this new breed of team, including strategies to create high-performance virtual teams.

Virtual Teams

Gordon Currie doesn't let a few miles get in the way of his business. Currie lives in Dawson Creek, in northern British Columbia, Canada, but clients of his Web design company are all based in the United States. What started as a hobby 12 years ago is now a global business with clients that have included Virgin Records and Hitachi. Currie's team members are even more geographically diverse than his clients. "I currently have four [team members], and I have not met face to face with any of them," confides Currie. "I have one from Sweden, two from California, and one from Australia. I went out and hired them on the Net."[26]

Gordon Currie and his colleagues are part of the growing trend toward virtual teams. **Virtual teams** are teams whose members operate across space, time, and organizational boundaries and are linked through information technologies to achieve organizational tasks.[27] As with all teams, virtual teams are groups of two or more people who interact and influence each other, are mutually accountable for achieving common goals associated with organizational objectives, and perceive themselves as a social entity within an organization (see Chapter 9).

However, virtual teams have two features that distinguish them from conventional teams. First, conventional team members are co-located (work in

virtual teams
Cross-functional teams that operate across space, time, and organizational boundaries with members who communicate mainly through information technologies.

the same physical area), whereas virtual team members are separated by distance and sometimes by time. Team members may be spread across a city or located anywhere around the planet. Second, because of their lack of co-location, members of virtual teams depend on information technologies to communicate and coordinate their work effort. Conventional teams might also use information technology, but they have the ability to communicate face to face at most times during the workday.[28]

Virtual teams may be permanent or temporary. They might operate as permanently distributed departments or as bootlegged skunkworks temporarily set up to develop a new product or service. Unlike most conventional teams, virtual teams are also differentiated in terms of their geographic, organizational, and temporal dispersion. Some virtual teams operate across organizations but within one city. Others operate within one company but across several countries, cultures, and time zones.[29]

Why Companies Form Virtual Teams

Virtual teams are one of the most significant developments in organizations over the past decade. "Virtual teams are now a reality," says Frank Waltmann, head of learning at pharmaceuticals company Novartis.[30] New information technologies offer one explanation for the frequency of virtual teams. Internet, intranets, instant messaging, virtual whiteboards, and other products have made it easier than in the past to communicate with and coordinate people at a distance. Distance isn't yet irrelevant and information technologies have not yet achieved the quality provided by face-to-face communication. Nevertheless, computer connectivity has sufficiently strengthened bonds among people in different locations to such an extent that they can now feel like a team.[31]

Andy Bearsley (left) and Matt Fox-Wilson know all about virtual teams. The New Zealand computer graphics programmers and their three employees are scattered from Auckland to Rotorua, while their clients are all located in North America. "We are fairly distributed," says Fox-Wilson. "It doesn't matter where an employee works as long as they come in once a week and they can get access to our server for source code." It initially took some convincing for North American firms to sign a contract with a team on the other side of the Pacific. But the work paid off for both parties and the duo's firm, Ambient Design, now has contracts with Adobe, Corel, and other major software firms.[33] What conditions are needed to make Ambient Design's virtual team work effectively?

The shift from production-based to knowledge-based work has also made virtual teamwork feasible. Information technologies allow people to exchange knowledge work, such as software code, product development plans, and ideas for strategic decisions. In contrast, relying on virtual teams for production work, in which people develop physical objects, is still very difficult (although not completely impossible).[32]

Information technologies and knowledge-based work make virtual teams *possible*, but two other factors—knowledge management and globalization—make them increasingly *necessary*. Knowledge has become the currency of competitive advantage, so organizations need to seek out this knowledge wherever it is available. Virtual teams represent a natural part of the knowledge management process because they encourage employees to share and use knowledge where geography limits more direct forms of collaboration. Moreover, as companies cross industry boundaries (such as when Internet providers move into the entertainment business), they must depend on virtual teams to leverage the knowledge potential across these groups.

Globalization represents the other reason why virtual teams are increasingly necessary. As we described in Chapter 1, globalization has become the new reality in many organizations. Companies are opening businesses overseas, forming tight alliances with companies located elsewhere, and serving customers who want global support. These global conditions require a correspondingly global response in the form of virtual teams that coordinate these operations.[34]

Designing High-Performance Virtual Teams

Virtual teams are a variation of teams, so the team effectiveness model in Chapter 9 provides a useful template to identify the features of high-performance virtual teams. Exhibit 10.3 outlines the key design issues for virtual teams that we discuss over the next couple of pages.

Virtual Team Environment   Reward systems, communication systems, organizational environment, organizational structure, and leadership influence the effectiveness of all teams, including virtual teams.[35] However, communication systems are particularly important because, unlike conventional teams, virtual teams cannot rely on face-to-face meetings whenever they wish. As we will learn in the next chapter, face-to-face communication transfers the highest volume and complexity of information and offers the timeliest feedback. In contrast, e-mail, telephone, and other information technologies fall far behind in their ability to exchange information. "Having a four- to five-hour discussion is hard to do by phone, especially where you need to read body language," says an executive at accounting giant PricewaterhouseCoopers.[36] Even videoconferencing, which seems similar to face-to-face meetings, actually communicates much less than we realize.

EXHIBIT 10.3	Team Design Element	Special Virtual Team Requirements
Designing high-performance virtual teams	Team environment	• Virtual teams need several communication channels available to offset lack of face-to-face communication
	Team tasks	• Virtual teams operate better with structured rather than complex and ambiguous tasks
	Team size and composition	• Virtual teams usually require smaller team size than conventional teams • Virtual team members must have skills in communicating through information technology and in processing multiple threads of conversation • Virtual team members are more likely than conventional team members to require cross-cultural awareness and knowledge
	Team processes	• Virtual team development and cohesiveness require some face-to-face interaction, particularly when the team forms

To become a high-performance virtual team, the organization needs to provide a variety of communication media so that virtual team members have the freedom to creatively combine these media to match the task demands.[37] For instance, virtual team members might rely on e-mail to coordinate routine tasks but quickly switch to videoconferences and electronic whiteboards when emergencies arise. The lack of face-to-face communication isn't all bad news for virtual teams. Working through e-mail or intranet systems can minimize status differences related to language skills. Team members whose first language is not English may be overwhelmed into silence in face-to-face meetings but have time to craft persuasive messages in cyberspace.[38]

Virtual Team Tasks   Scholars suggest that virtual teams operate best with structured tasks requiring only moderate levels of task interdependence.[39] Consider the task structure of client service engineers at BakBone Software. Each day, BakBone engineers in San Diego pick up customer support problems passed on from colleagues in Maryland and England. At the end of the workday, they pass some of these projects on to BakBone co-workers in Tokyo. The assignments sent on to Tokyo must be stated clearly because overseas co-workers can't ask questions in the middle of San Diego's night.

This structured task arrangement at BakBone works well in virtual teams. In contrast, complex and ambiguous tasks require an enormous amount of consultation and coordination in real time, which virtual teams have difficulty processing due to lack of face-to-face communication. "You don't have the time for open-ended conversation [in a virtual team]," admits BakBone engineer Roger Rodriguez. "You can't informally brainstorm with someone."[40] Generally, complex and ambiguous tasks should be assigned to co-located teams. Similarly, virtual teams should work on tasks requiring moderate levels of interdependence among team members. High levels of interdependence require more intense dialogue, so they are better assigned to co-located teams.

Virtual Team Size and Composition   The problems of team size that we learned about in Chapter 9 are amplified in virtual teams because of limited opportunities for face-to-face communication and social bonding. Even with the benefit of videoconferencing tools, team size becomes an issue at lower numbers than for conventional teams due to the limits of information technologies. High-performance virtual teams apply the team composition issues described in Chapter 9, but virtual team members also require special skills in communication systems. In particular, they need to coordinate through e-mail without creating undesirable emotions and must juggle several independent "threads" of electronic conversation (rather like the seemingly random threads in virtual chat rooms).

Virtual teams are more likely than conventional teams to include people across cultures, so team members must also be aware of cross-cultural issues. For example, one study reported that virtual teams of American and Belgian college students were easily confused by differing conventions in the use of commas versus decimal points in numbers (e.g., $2.953 million versus $2,953 million). They also experienced cultural differences in socializing. The American students were willing to engage in social communication after they completed the assignment, whereas the Belgian students were more interested in developing a relationship with their partners before beginning work on the project.[41]

Team Processes   High-performance teams apply the many recommendations in Chapter 9 regarding team development, norms, roles, and cohesiveness. Team development and cohesiveness are particular concerns because virtual teams lack the face-to-face interaction that supports these processes. For example, one recent university study found that face-to-face teams communicate better than virtual teams during the early stages of a project; only after gaining experience did virtual teams share information as openly as face-to-face teams.[42] There is no "virtual" solution to this dilemma, so many practitioners recommend that virtual team members meet face to face, particularly when the team is formed. The ability to "put a face" to remote colleagues seems to strengthen the individual's emotional bond to the team. "Even if the work of global teams will be primarily virtual, we usually start with a face-to-face meeting," explains an executive at microprocessor manufacturer Advanced Micro Devices.[43]

Team Trust

Our discussion of virtual teams would be incomplete without emphasizing the importance of trust in team dynamics. Any relationship—including the relationship among virtual team members—depends on a certain degree of trust between the parties.[44] **Trust** is a psychological state comprising the intention to accept vulnerability based on positive expectations of the intent or behavior of another person (see Chapter 4). A high level of trust occurs when the other party's actions affect you in situations where you are vulnerable, but you believe they will not adversely affect your needs.

To understand how trust relates to virtual teams, we need to understand that people experience the three levels of trust illustrated in Exhibit 10.4.

■ *Calculus-based trust*—This minimal level of trust refers to an expected consistency of behavior based on deterrence. Each party believes that the other will deliver on its promises because punishments will be administered if they fail. For example, most employees trust each other at least at a minimum level because co-workers could get fired if they attempt to undermine another employee's work effort. This ability to punish others who violate expected behavior is calculus-based trust.

trust
A psychological state comprising the intention to accept vulnerability based upon positive expectations of the intent or behavior of another person.

	Type of trust	Description
(Highest)	Identification-based trust	• Based on mutual understanding and values • Strongest when part of social identity
	Knowledge-based trust	• Based on predictability from experience • Fairly robust
(Lowest)	Calculus-based trust	• Based on deterrence • Others' fear of punishment if inconsistent

- *Knowledge-based trust*—Knowledge-based trust is grounded on the other party's predictability. This predictability develops from meaningful communication and experience with the other party. The better you know fellow team members, the more accurately you can predict what they will do in the future. Similarly, the more consistent the leader's behavior—the more he or she "walks the talk"—the more employees are willing to trust that person.[45]
- *Identification-based trust*—This third type of trust is based on mutual understanding and emotional bond between the parties. Identification occurs when one party thinks like, feels like, and responds like the other party. High-performance teams exhibit this level of trust. By sharing the same values, employees understand what to expect from each other.

Calculus-based trust is the weakest of the three because it is easily broken by a violation of expectations and the subsequent application of sanctions against the violating party. It is difficult to develop a strong level of trust based on the threat of punishment if one party fails to deliver its promises. Generally, calculus-based trust alone cannot sustain a team's relationship, particularly among members of a virtual team and with the team leader. "Trust is a basic premise of work relationships," advises a PriceWaterhouseCoopers executive. "If you manage by watching people work, then virtual teaming isn't a good choice."[46]

Knowledge-based trust is more stable than calculus-based trust because it is developed over time. Suppose that another member of your virtual team submitted documentation to you on schedule in the past, but it arrived late today. Knowledge-based trust may have been dented, but it has not been broken. Through knowledge-based trust, you "know" that this tardiness is probably an exception because it deviates from the co-worker's past actions.

Identity-based trust is the most robust of all three. Because the individual holds the same values as other team members, he or she is more likely to forgive transgressions. Social identity theory explains why this is so. Recall from Chapter 3 that social identity theory refers to the phenomenon whereby people define themselves in terms of their attachment to various groups. Having identity-based trust with team members means that we identify ourselves with that group. Consequently, we would be reluctant to acknowledge a violation of this high-level trust because it strikes at the heart of our self-image.

Dynamics of Trust in Teams   A common misconception is that team members build trust from a low level when they first join the team. According to recent studies, the opposite is actually more likely to occur. People typically join a virtual or conventional team with a high level—*not* a low level—of trust in their new teammates.[47] New members form positive expectations about work in the team and want to identify with the work unit. However, this trust is fragile because it is based on assumptions rather than well-established experience. Consequently, recent studies of virtual teams report that trust tends to decrease rather than increase over time. In other words, new team members experience trust violations, which pushes their trust to a lower level. Employees who join the team with identity-based trust tend to drop back to knowledge-based or perhaps calculus-based trust. Declining trust is particularly challenging in virtual teams because research identifies communication among team members as an important condition for sustaining trust.

Team Decision Making

So far in this chapter, we have looked at two distinctive team structures: self-directed work teams and virtual teams. In contrast, this section considers ways to build high-performance team decision making—something that occurs in all teams. Under certain conditions, teams are more effective than individuals at identifying problems, choosing alternatives, and evaluating their decisions. "Teams are the heart of the IDEO method," advises Tom Kelley, general manager of IDEO, the California industrial design firm that is renowned for its creative practices. "We believe it's how innovation and much of business take place in the world."[48] In spite of the potential benefits of teams, team dynamics can interfere with effective decision making. We begin this section by examining the main factors that restrict effective decision making and creativity in team settings. Next, we look at specific team structures that try to overcome these constraints.

Constraints on Team Decision Making

Five most common conditions that limit the effectiveness of team decision making are time constraints, evaluation apprehension, pressure to conform, groupthink, and group polarization.

Time Constraints   There's a saying that "committees keep minutes and waste hours." This reflects the fact that teams take longer than individuals to make decisions.[49] Unlike individuals, teams require extra time to organize, coordinate, and socialize. The larger the group, the more time required to make a decision. Team members need time to learn about each other and build rapport. They need to manage an imperfect communication process so that there is sufficient understanding of each other's ideas. They also need to coordinate roles and rules of order within the decision process.

production blocking
A time constraint in team decision making due to the procedural requirement that only one person may speak at a time.

Another time constraint found in most team structures is that only one person can speak at a time.[50] This problem, known as **production blocking,** causes participants to forget potentially creative ideas by the time their turn to speak arrives. Team members who concentrate on remembering their fleeting thoughts end up ignoring what others are saying, even though their statements could trigger more creative ideas.

evaluation apprehension
When individuals are reluctant to mention ideas that seem silly because they believe (often correctly) that other team members are silently evaluating them.

Evaluation Apprehension   Individuals are reluctant to mention ideas that seem silly because they believe (often correctly) that other team members are silently evaluating them.[51] This **evaluation apprehension** is based on the individual's desire to create a favorable self-presentation and need to protect self-esteem. It is most common in meetings attended by people with different levels of status or expertise, or when members formally evaluate each other's performance throughout the year (as in 360-degree feedback). Evaluation apprehension is a problem when the group wants to generate creative ideas, because innovative ideas often sound bizarre or illogical when presented, so employees are afraid to mention them in front of co-workers.

Pressure to Conform   Chapter 9 described how cohesiveness leads individual members to conform to the team's norms. This control keeps the group organized around common goals, but it may also cause team members to suppress their dissenting opinions about discussion issues, particularly when a strong team norm is related to the issue. When someone does state a point of view that violates the majority opinion, other members might punish the violator or try to prove that his or her opinion is incorrect. It's not surprising, then, that nearly half of the managers surveyed in one study say they give up in team decisions because of pressure from others to conform to the team's decision.[52] Conformity can also be subtle. To some extent, we depend on the opinions that others hold to validate our own views. If co-workers don't agree with us, then we begin to question our own opinions even without overt peer pressure.[53]

groupthink

The tendency of highly cohesive groups to value consensus at the price of decision quality.

Groupthink   **Groupthink** is the tendency of highly cohesive groups to value consensus at the price of decision quality.[54] Groupthink goes beyond the problem of conformity. There are strong social pressures on individual members to maintain harmony by avoiding conflict and disagreement. They suppress doubts about decision alternatives preferred by the majority or group leader. Team members want to maintain this harmony because their self-identity is enhanced by membership in a powerful decision-making body that speaks with one voice.[55] Team harmony also helps members cope with the stress of making crucial top-level decisions.

High cohesiveness isn't the only cause of groupthink. Groupthink is also more likely to occur when the team is isolated from outsiders, the team leader is opinionated (rather than impartial), the team is under stress due to an external threat, the team has experienced recent failures or other decision-making problems, and the team lacks clear guidance from corporate policies or procedures. Several symptoms of groupthink have been identified and are summarized in Exhibit 10.5. In general, teams overestimate their invulnerability and morality, become closed-minded to outside and dissenting information, and experience several pressures toward consensus.[56]

group polarization

The tendency of teams to make more extreme decisions than individuals working alone.

Group Polarization   **Group polarization** refers to the tendency of teams to make more extreme decisions than individuals working alone.[57] Suppose that a group of people meets to decide on the future of a new product. Individual team members might come to the meeting with various degrees of support or opposition to the product's future. Yet, by the end of the meeting, chances are that the team will agree on a more extreme solution than the average person preferred before the meeting began. One reason for the extreme preference is that team members become comfortable with more extreme positions when they realize that co-workers also generally support the same position. Persuasive arguments favoring the dominant position convince doubtful members and help form a consensus around the extreme option. Finally, individuals feel less personally responsible for the decision consequences because the decision is made by the team.

Social support, persuasion, and shifting responsibility explain why teams make more *extreme* decisions, but why do they usually make riskier decisions? The answer is that decision makers maintain overly positive emotions that create an illusion of control. They become victims of the "gambler's fallacy" that they can beat the odds. For example, team members tend to think, "This strategy might be unsuccessful 80 percent of the time, but it will work for us!" Thus, team members are more likely to favor the risky option.[58] The result of

EXHIBIT 10.5	Groupthink symptom	Description
Symptoms of groupthink	Illusion of invulnerability	The team feels comfortable with risky decisions because possible weaknesses are suppressed or glossed over.
	Assumption of morality	There is such an unquestioned belief in the inherent morality of the team's objectives that members do not feel the need to debate whether their actions are ethical.
	Rationalization	Underlying assumptions, new information, and previous actions which seem inconsistent with the team's decision are discounted or explained away.
	Stereotyping outgroups	The team stereotypes or oversimplifies the external threats upon which the decision is based; 'enemies' are viewed as purely evil or moronic.
	Self-censorship	Team members suppress their doubts in order to maintain harmony.
	Illusion of unanimity	Self-censorship results in harmonious behavior, so individual members believe that they alone have doubts; silence is automatically perceived as evidence of consensus.
	Mindguarding	Some members become self-appointed guardians to prevent negative or inconsistent information from reaching the team.
	Pressuring dissenters	Members who happen to raise their concerns about the decision are pressured to fall into line and be more loyal to the team.

Source: Based on I. L. Janis, *Groupthink: Psychological Studies of Policy Decisions and Fiascoes,* 2nd ed. (Boston: Houghton Mifflin, 1982), p. 244.

group polarization is that teams tend to choose riskier alternatives than any individual would choose.

Team Structures to Improve Creativity and Decision Making

Teams potentially make better decisions than individuals in a number of situations, but the problem just described can seriously interfere with the decision-making process. Fortunately, OB experts have identified a number of general rules and specific team structures to minimize this dilemma. One general rule is that neither the team leader nor any other participant dominates the process. This rule limits the adverse effects of conformity and lets other team members generate more creative and controversial ideas.[59] Another practice is to maintain an optimal team size. The group should be large enough that members possess the collective knowledge to resolve the problem, yet small enough that the team doesn't consume too much time or restrict individual input.[60] Team norms are also important to ensure that individuals engage in critical thinking rather than follow the group's implicit preferences.

Team structures also help to minimize the problems described over the previous few pages. Five team structures potentially improve creativity and decision making in team settings: constructive conflict, brainstorming, electronic brainstorming, Delphi technique, and nominal group technique.

constructive conflict

Occurs when team members debate their different perceptions about an issue in a way that keeps the conflict focused on the task rather than people.

Constructive Conflict   **Constructive conflict** occurs when team members debate their different perceptions about an issue in a way that keeps the conflict focused on the task rather than people. Through dialogue, participants learn about other points of view, which encourages them to reexamine their basic assumptions about a problem and its possible solution. Constructive conflict is *constructive* because the discussion brings out meaningful dialogue with minimal interpersonal conflict. This can occur if participants focus on facts and avoid statements that threaten the esteem and well-being of other team members.[61]

Some companies try to generate constructive conflict by having some team members serve as devil's advocates.[62] A devil's advocate is a team member selected to take the opposition position of the group's preference. The idea is to point out weaknesses and potential problems with the preference so that it is carefully scrutinized. This strategy sounds good in theory, but it seldom works in practice. The problem is that people selected as devil's advocates typically support the team's preferred choice more than they find problems with it.[63] If a team member supports the group's position, it is difficult for that person to take a critical role against that position.

Rather than rely on contrived dissent such as devil's advocacy, corporate leaders need to form decision-making teams that authentically engage in constructive conflict. Researchers have identified three strategies to achieve authentic constructive conflict. First, decision-making groups need to be heterogeneous.[64] As we learned in previous chapters, heterogeneous teams are better than homogeneous teams at perceiving issues and potential solutions from different perspectives.

Second, these heterogeneous team members need to meet often enough to allow meaningful discussion over contentious issues. The team's diversity won't generate constructive conflict if the team leader makes most of the decisions alone. Only through dialogue can team members better understand different perspectives, generate more creative ideas, and improve decision quality. Third, effective teams generate constructive conflict when individual members take on different discussion roles. Some participants are action-oriented, others insist on reviewing details, one or two might try to minimize dysfunctional conflict, and so on. In other words, team members cover the various roles required to support team dynamics.

Brainstorming   In the 1950s, advertising executive Alex Osborn wanted to find a better way for teams to generate creative ideas.[65] Osborn's solution, called **brainstorming,** requires team members to abide by four rules. Osborn believed that these rules encourage divergent thinking while minimizing evaluation apprehension and other team dynamics problems.

■ *Speak freely*—Brainstorming welcomes wild and wacky ideas because these become the seeds of divergent thinking in the creative process. Crazy suggestions are sometimes crazy only because they break out of the mold set by existing mental models.
■ *Don't criticize*—Team members are more likely to contribute wild and wacky ideas if no one tries to mock or criticize them. Thus, a distinctive rule in brainstorming is that no one is allowed to criticize any ideas that are presented.
■ *Provide as many ideas as possible*—Brainstorming is based on the idea that quantity breeds quality. In other words, teams generate better ideas when they generate many ideas. This relates to the belief that divergent thinking occurs after traditional ideas have been exhausted. Therefore, the group

brainstorming
A freewheeling, face-to-face meeting where team members aren't allowed to criticize, but are encouraged to speak freely, generate as many ideas as possible, and build on the ideas of others.

should think of as many possible solutions as they can and go well beyond the traditional solutions to a problem.

■ *Build on the ideas of others*—Team members are encouraged to "piggyback" or "hitchhike," that is, combine and improve on the ideas already presented. Building on existing ideas encourages the synergy of team processes that was mentioned in Chapter 8 as a benefit of employee involvement.

Brainstorming is the most popular team structure for encouraging creative ideas. Yet, for several years, organizational behavior researchers concluded that this practice is ineffective. One concern is that brainstorming rules do not completely remove evaluation apprehension; employees still know that others are silently evaluating the quality of their ideas. Moreover, brainstorming does not minimize production blocking and related time constraints. Some research also reports that individuals working alone produce more potential solutions to a problem than if they work together using brainstorming.[66]

While these past research findings seem to conclude that brainstorming is ineffective, recent evidence suggests otherwise. In particular, brainstorming tends to produce more innovative ideas (although not necessarily a greater number of ideas) than individuals working alone under certain conditions. Connections 10.1 describes how IDEO, the California-based industrial design firm, thrives on brainstorming by creating the right environment and structure to make these sessions productive. Evaluation apprehension may be a problem for brainstorming in student research experiments, but it is less of a problem at IDEO, where high-performing teams have a lot of trust and support risky thinking. IDEO's brainstorming facilitators also stretch the collective effort by pushing for more than 150 ideas in an hour.

Another problem with the earlier critiques of brainstorming is that they overlooked other benefits of brainstorming beyond the number of ideas produced. Brainstorming participants interact and participate directly, thereby increasing decision acceptance and team cohesiveness. Brainstorming rules tend to keep the team focused on the required task. There is some evidence that effective brainstorming sessions provide valuable nonverbal communication that spreads enthusiasm. Team members share feelings of optimism and excitement that may encourage a more creative climate. Clients are sometimes involved in brainstorming sessions, so these positive emotions may produce higher customer satisfaction than if people are working alone on the product.[67] Overall, brainstorming may prove more valuable to creativity than some of the earlier research studies indicated.

electronic brainstorming

Using special computer software, participants share ideas while minimizing the team dynamics problems inherent in traditional brainstorming sessions.

Electronic Brainstorming   DaimlerChrysler, Boeing, and many other firms have tried to improve team decision making through **electronic brainstorming.** With the aid of groupware (special computer software for groups), electronic brainstorming lets participants share ideas while minimizing many of the team dynamics problems described earlier. A facilitator begins the process by posting a question. Participants then enter their answers or ideas on their computer terminal. Soon after, everyone's ideas are posted anonymously and randomly on the computer screens or at the front of the room. Participants eventually vote electronically on the ideas presented. Face-to-face discussion usually follows the electronic brainstorming process.

IDEO Catches a Brainstorm

No one does brainstorming as well—or as often—as the folks at IDEO. Engineers at the California-based industrial design firm that created 3Com's Palm V and the stand-up toothpaste tube attend an average of 24 brainstorm sessions each year. A few participate in as many as 80 brainstorms annually.

IDEO's brainstorms are scheduled, face-to-face meetings that generate ideas, usually about designing products. A typical session lasts about one hour and is attended by the design team as well as other IDEO engineers with relevant skills. For instance, one brainstorming session to design better ski goggles invited engineers who knew about foam, clear plastics, and manufacturing processes. Clients are also included in some sessions.

Since its founding in 1978, IDEO has developed a clear set of brainstorming rules: defer judgment, build on the ideas of others, one conversation at a time, stay focused on the topic, and encourage wild ideas. These rules are prominently displayed throughout the meeting room and violators are given friendly reminders. A good IDEO brainstorming session produces about 100 ideas. Each idea is numbered to push for quantity and to keep track of the discussion. The creative sparks are aided by studying similar products as well as a treasure chest of unique materials brought to the session.

Newcomers at IDEO quickly discover that brainstorming requires special interpersonal skills, not just rules and props. "The skills for successful brainstorming develop in an individual over time," explains an IDEO engineer. "I consider myself a good brainstormer but only a fair facilitator. A year ago, I was a good brainstormer and a poor facilitator."

IDEO is a highly innovative product design firm thanks to teamwork, autonomy, brainstorming, and other conditions that support creativity.

Sources: R. I. Sutton, *Weird Ideas that Work* (New York: Free Press, 2002); T. Kelley, *The Art of Innovation* (New York: Currency/Doubleday, 2001), pp. 55–66; A. Hargadon and R. I. Sutton, "Building an Innovation Factory," *Harvard Business Review* 78 (May–June 2000), pp. 157–66; R. Garner, "Innovation for Fun and Profit," *Upside Magazine,* March 2000; P. Sinton, "Teamwork the Name of the Game for IDEO," *San Francisco Chronicle,* February 23, 2000; E. Brown, "A Day at Innovation U.," *Fortune,* April 12, 1999, pp. 163–65; R. I. Sutton and A. Hargadon, "Brainstorming Groups in Context: Effectiveness in a Product Design Firm," *Administrative Science Quarterly* 41 (December 1996), pp. 685–718.

Research indicates that electronic brainstorming generates more ideas than traditional brainstorming and that participants are more satisfied, motivated, and confident in the decision-making exercise than in other team structures.[68] One reason for these favorable outcomes is that electronic brainstorming significantly reduces production blocking. Participants are able to document their ideas as soon as they pop into their heads, rather than wait their turn to communicate.[69] The process also supports creative synergy because participants can easily develop new ideas from those generated by other people. Electronic brainstorming also minimizes the problem of evaluation apprehension because ideas are posted anonymously. "The equipment allows them to throw some crazy ideas out without people knowing they are the author of it," explains one executive who organized a brainstorming session.[70]

Despite these numerous advantages, electronic brainstorming is not widely used by corporate leaders. One possible reason is that it might be too structured and technology-bound for some executives. Furthermore, some decision makers may feel threatened by the honesty of statements generated through this process and by their limited ability to control the discussion. A third explanation is that electronic brainstorming may work best for certain types of decisions, but not for others. For example, electronic brainstorming may be less effective than face-to-face meetings where effective decision making is less important than social bonding and emotional interaction.[71] Overall, electronic brainstorming can significantly improve decision making under the right conditions, but more research is required to identify those conditions.

Delphi technique
A structured team decision-making process of systematically pooling the collective knowledge of experts on a particular subject to make decisions, predict the future, or identify opposing views.

Delphi Technique   The **Delphi technique** systematically pools the collective knowledge of experts on a particular subject to make decisions, predict the future, or identify opposing views (called *dissensus*).[72] Delphi groups do not meet face to face; in fact, participants are often located in different parts of the world and may not know each other's identity. Moreover, like electronic brainstorming, participants do not know who "owns" the ideas submitted. Typically, Delphi group members submit possible solutions or comments regarding an issue to the central convener. The compiled results are returned to the panel for a second round of comments. This process may be repeated a few more times until consensus or dissensus emerges. The Delphi technique helped an electricity supply company understand how to respond to customers who don't pay their bills. It was also used by rehabilitation counselors to reach consensus on rehabilitation credentialing.[73]

nominal group technique
A structured team decision-making process whereby team members independently write down ideas, describe and clarify them to the group, and then independently rank or vote on them.

Nominal Group Technique   **Nominal group technique** is a variation of traditional brainstorming and Delphi technique that tries to combine individual efficiencies with team dynamics.[74] The method is called *nominal* because participants form a group *in name only* during two stages of decision making. This process, shown in Exhibit 10.6, first involves the individual, then the group, and finally the individual again.

After the problem is described, team members silently and independently write down as many solutions as they can. During the group stage, participants describe their solutions to the other team members, usually in a round-robin format. As with brainstorming, there is no criticism or debate, although members are encouraged to ask for clarification of the ideas presented. In the final stage, participants silently and independently rank order or vote on each proposed solution. Nominal group technique encourages voting or ranking to minimize dysfunctional conflict that occurs when trying to reach consensus. Rank ordering is the first preference because this method forces each person to carefully review all of the alternatives presented.[75]

Nominal group technique tends to produce more and better quality ideas than do traditional interacting groups.[76] Due to its high degree of structure,

EXHIBIT 10.6   Exhibit 10.6 Nominal group technique

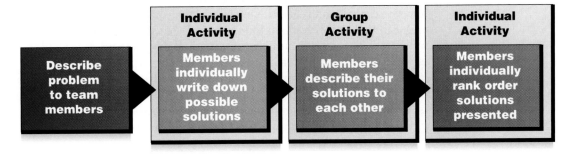

nominal group technique usually maintains a high task orientation and relatively low potential for conflict within the team. However, team cohesiveness is generally lower in nominal decisions because the structure minimizes social interaction. Production blocking and evaluation apprehension still occur to some extent.

Team Building

Before Milton Elementary School in Milton, Delaware, opened its doors for the first time, school principal Sheila Baumgardner took her new teaching and support staff to Arlington Echo Outdoor Education Center in Millersville, Maryland, for three days of team building. "The idea behind that is to develop teamwork skills since I'm bringing teachers together from buildings all over the district," Baumgardner explains. Along with walking in the woods and sharing meals together, staff spent time developing school support programs. "Our main purpose is to develop teamwork skills—camaraderie—to facilitate communication once the school year begins," she says.[77]

team building
Any formal activity intended to improve the development and functioning of a team.

Sheila Baumgardner knows that speeding up the team development process requires one of the many forms of **team building**—any formal activity intended to improve the development and functioning of a work team. By accelerating the team development process, team building indirectly tends to reshape team norms and strengthen cohesiveness. Team building is sometimes applied to newly established teams, such as Milton Elementary School, because team members are at the earliest stages of team development. However, team building is more common among existing teams that have regressed to earlier stages of team development. Team building is therefore a popular intervention when the team experiences high membership turnover or members have lost focus of their respective roles and team objectives.[78]

Types of Team Building

There are four main types of team building: role definition, goal setting, problem solving, and interpersonal processes.[79]

- *Role definition*—Role definition team building encourages team members to describe perceptions of their own role as well as the role expectations they have of other team members. After discussing these perceptions, team members revise their roles and work toward a common mental model of their respective responsibilities.[80] Role definition team building also helps everyone to understand the benefits of working together as a team and of the value of their role on the team.
- *Goal setting*—Some team-building interventions clarify the team's performance goals, increase the team's motivation to accomplish these goals, and establish a mechanism for systematic feedback on the team's goal performance. This is very similar to individual goal setting described in Chapter 5, except that the goals are applied to teams.
- *Problem solving*—This type of team building focuses on decision making, including how the team identifies problems and searches for alternatives (see Chapter 8).[81] To improve their problem-solving skills, some teams participate in simulation games that require team decisions in hypothetical situations.[82]

Asian Companies Move Team Building Outdoors

Perched on a narrow beam 25 feet above the ground, Wu Xi never stopped thinking about the possibility of falling. The 30-year-old engineer at Ericsson Cyberlab in Singapore was roped together with five colleagues as they scaled their way up an 80-foot pyramid. "I was so scared, but I couldn't give up," says Wu. "My team members held onto me very firmly and they kept encouraging me."

Throughout Asia, companies are discovering the benefits of team-building activities outside the typical office environment. Wu Xi and her co-workers climbed over rock walls, inched across planks, scaled cargo nets, and performed other daunting tasks to improve team dynamics at the Swedish telecommunication firm's Asian research unit. "We all made it to the top with lots of difficulties," explains Ericsson Cyberlab director Andreas Fasbender. "But the best part was that you could really achieve more as a team."

Outdoor team building comes in many varieties. Malaysian employees with American International Assurance recently participated in a full day of outdoor team-building activities, including a car rally treasure hunt, a "Sarong Soccer" event, and the "Twin Peak Challenge." The Empire Hotel and Country Club in Brunei has teamed up with CfBT Borneo Outdoors to offer team-building activities such as the Trust Fall, Stepping Stones, Low Ropes, Hole-in-One, Islands, and the 12/15 Wall. Petronas, Malaysia's state oil company, has held several outdoor team-building activities in recent years. "They help rein-

Employees at Ericsson Cyberlab in Singapore scale great heights to build team spirit.

force our team spirit, camaraderie and relations and improve the way we interact and communicate with each other," explains Petronas executive Azman Ibrahim.

Sources: "Team-Building Day for AIA Staff, Agents," *New Straits Times* (Malaysia), September 3, 2003; Z. Hosni, "New Team Building Site at Empire," *Borneo Bulletin,* June 18, 2003; K. Mustapha, "Stressful Bonding Exercises," *New Straits Times* (Malaysia), April 9, 2003, p. 5; D. Goh, "Firms Strike Out for Adventure Learning," *Sunday Times* (Singapore), April 8, 2001, pp. 7, 29.

---

dialogue
A process of conversation among team members in which they learn about each other's mental models and assumptions, and eventually form a common model for thinking within the team.

■ *Interpersonal processes*—This type of team building focuses on improving interpersonal processes that try to build trust and open communications among team members by resolving hidden agendas and misperceptions. This includes **dialogue** sessions where team members engage in conversations to develop a common mental model of the ideal team process. As they gain awareness of each other's models and assumptions, members eventually begin to form a common model for thinking within the team.[83] Although dialogue is potentially effective, most organizations tend to rely on wilderness team building, paintball wars, and obstacle course challenges to improve interpersonal processes.

Most interpersonal process team-building activities have distinctively American foundations, but they are becoming increasingly popular elsewhere. For example, Jan Antwerpes, a partner in a German communications consulting firm, attended an obstacle course program with his staff. "If two colleagues hold the rope for you while you're climbing 10 meters [33 feet] up, that is truly team-building. It also shows your colleagues that you care for them," says Antwerpes.[84] Global Connections 10.2 describes how these Western-style activities are also gaining acceptance in Asia.

Is Team Building Effective?

Team-building activities are being used more frequently as companies increasingly rely on teams to get the work done. Some organizations are even experimenting with offbeat team-building activities in the hope that these sessions will improve team dynamics.

Deloitte Consulting sent some of its California employees on a three-day extreme adventure race. Among other things, the experience included sleeping in garbage bags on the dew-soaked ground and huddling together in "puppy piles" to stay warm. Staffordshire County Council in England sent a team of employees to the fire brigade, where they spent the day learning to navigate through a smoke-filled room and battle a controlled towering inferno. Employees at coolsavings.com traveled to a ranch in Nevada where they practiced their team skills and strategic decision making by rounding up cattle and goats. "That one was just so unconventional that people had a really great time doing it," recalls an executive at the online promotions company. "It forced everybody to strategize together; it also forced them to work as a team, because no one was going to catch this goat on their own."[85]

Are these and more traditional team-building programs effective? Is the money well spent? So far, the answer is an equivocal "maybe." Studies suggest that some team-building activities are successful, but just as many fail to build high-performance teams.[86] One problem is that corporate leaders assume team-building activities are general solutions to general team problems. No one bothers to diagnose the team's specific needs (e.g., problem solving, interpersonal processes) because the team-building intervention is assumed to be a broad-brush solution. In reality, as we just learned, there are different types of team-building activities for different team needs. This mismatch can potentially lead to ineffective team building.[87]

Another problem is that corporate leaders tend to view team building as a one-shot medical inoculation that every team should receive when it is formed. In truth, team building is an ongoing process, not a three-day jumpstart. Some experts suggest, for example, that wilderness experiences often fail because they rarely include follow-up consultation to ensure that team learning is transferred back to the workplace.[88]

Last, we must remember that team building occurs on the job, not just on an obstacle course or in a national park. Organizations should encourage team members to reflect on their work experiences and to experiment with just-in-time learning for team development. This dialogue requires open communication, so employees can clarify expectations, coordinate work activities, and build common mental models of working together. The next chapter looks at the dynamics of communicating in teams and organizations.

Chapter Summary

Self-directed work teams (SDWTs) complete an entire piece of work requiring several interdependent tasks and have substantial autonomy over the execution of these tasks. Sociotechnical systems (STS) theory is the template typically used to determine whether SDWTs will operate effectively. STS theory identifies four main conditions for high-performance SDWTs.

First, SDWTs must be a primary work unit, that is,

they are an intactive team that makes a product, provides a service, or otherwise completes an entire work process. Second, the team must have collective self-regulation, meaning that they must have sufficient autonomy to manage the work process. Third, high-performance SDWTs have control over "key variances." This refers to the idea that teams control the disturbances or interruptions that create quality problems in the work process. Fourth, STS theory states that a balance must be struck between the social and technical systems to maximize the operation's effectiveness.

Sociotechnical systems theory has been widely supported since its origins in the 1950s. However, it is not very helpful at identifying the optimal alignment of the social and technical system. Moreover, SDWTs face several barriers to implementation. These high-performance teams tend to operate best in cultures with low power distance and high collectivism. Supervisors often resist SDWTs because of fears that empowering teams will remove the power of supervisors. Supervisors must also change from their traditional hands-on "command-and-control" style to hands-off facilitators. Employees oppose SDWTs when they worry that they lack the skills to adapt to the new work requirements. Labor unions sometimes oppose SDWTs because of the risk of higher stress and the need to remove job categories that unions have negotiated over the years.

Virtual teams are teams whose members operate across space, time, and organizational boundaries and are linked through information technologies to achieve organizational tasks. Their main differences from conventional teams is that virtual teams are not co-located and that they rely on information technologies rather than face-to-face interaction.

Virtual teams are becoming more popular because information technology and knowledge-based work makes it easier to collaborate from a distance. Virtual teams are becoming increasingly necessary because they represent a natural part of the knowledge management process. Moreover, as companies globalize, they must rely more on virtual teams than co-located teams to coordinate operations at distant sites.

Several elements in the team effectiveness model stand out as important issues for virtual teams. High-performance virtual teams require a variety of communication media, and virtual team members need to creatively combine these media to match the task demands. Virtual teams operate better with structured rather than complex and ambiguous tasks. They usually cannot maintain as large a team as is possible in conventional teams. Members of virtual teams require special skills in communication systems and should be aware of cross-cultural issues.

Virtual team members should also meet face to face, particularly when the team forms, to assist team development and cohesiveness.

Trust is important in team dynamics, particularly in virtual teams. Trust occurs when we have positive expectations about another party's intentions and actions toward us in risky situations. The minimum level of trust is calculus-based trust, which is based on deterrence. Team survival is difficult with this level of trust. Knowledge-based trust is a higher level of trust and is grounded on the other party's predictability. The highest level of trust, called identification-based trust, is based on mutual understanding and emotional bond between the parties. Most employees join a team with a high level of trust, which tends to decline over time.

Team decisions are impeded by time constraints, evaluation apprehension, conformity to peer pressure, groupthink, and group polarization. Production blocking—where only one person typically speaks at a time—is a form of time constraint on teams. Evaluation apprehension occurs when employees believe that others are silently evaluating them, so they avoid stating seemingly silly ideas. Conformity keeps team members aligned with team goals, but it also tends to suppress dissenting opinions. Groupthink is the tendency of highly cohesive groups to value consensus at the price of decision quality. Group polarization refers to the tendency of teams to make more extreme decisions than individuals working alone.

Three rules to minimize team decision-making problems are to ensure that the team leader does not dominate, maintain an optimal team size, and ensure that team norms support critical thinking. Five team structures that potentially improve team decision making are constructive conflict, brainstorming, electronic brainstorming, Delphi technique, and nominal group technique. Constructive conflict occurs when team members debate their different perceptions about an issue in a way that keeps the conflict focused on the task rather than people. Brainstorming requires team members to speak freely, avoid criticism, provide as many ideas as possible, and build on the ideas of others. Electronic brainstorming uses computer software to share ideas while minimizing team dynamics problems. Delphi technique systematically pools the collective knowledge of experts on a particular subject without face-to-face meetings. In nominal group technique, participants write down ideas alone, describe these ideas in a group, then silently vote on these ideas.

Team building is any formal activity intended to improve the development and functioning of a work team. Four team-building strategies are role definition, goal setting, problem solving, and interpersonal processes. Some team-building events succeed, but companies often fail to consider the contingencies of team building.

Key Terms

brainstorming, p. 310
collective self-regulation, p. 298
constructive conflict, p. 309
Delphi technique, p. 313
dialogue, p. 315
electronic brainstorming, p. 311
evaluation apprehension, p. 307
group polarization, p. 308
groupthink, p. 308

joint optimization, p. 298
nominal group technique, p. 313
production blocking, p. 307
self-directed work team (SDWT), p. 296
sociotechnical systems (STS) theory, p. 297
team building, p. 314
trust, p. 305
virtual teams, p. 301

Discussion Questions

1. How do self-directed work teams differ from conventional teams?
2. Advanced Telecom, Inc., has successfully introduced self-directed work teams at its operations throughout the country. The company now wants to introduce SDWTs at its plants in Thailand and Mexico. What potential cross-cultural challenges might Advanced Telecom experience as it introduces SDWTs in these high power distance countries?
3. A chicken processing company wants to build a processing plant designed around sociotechnical systems principles. In a traditional chicken processing plant, employees work in separate departments—cleaning and cutting, cooking, packaging, and warehousing. The cooking and packaging processes are controlled by separate workstations in the traditional plant. How would the company change this operation according to sociotechnical systems design?
4. What can organizations do to reduce management resistance to self-directed work teams?

5. Suppose the instructor for this course assigned you to a project team consisting of three other students who are currently taking similar courses in Ireland, India, and Brazil. All students speak English and have similar knowledge of the topic. Use your knowledge of virtual teams to discuss the problems that your team might face, compared with a team of local students who can meet face to face.
6. What can virtual teams do to sustain trust among team members?
7. Canyon Networks, Inc. sent its customer service team of 20 employees to a two-day outdoor team-building exercise. What problems might limit the effectiveness of this team-building intervention?
8. Bangalore Technologies, Inc., wants to use brainstorming with its employees and customers to identify new uses for its technology. Advise Bangalore's president about the potential benefits of brainstorming, as well as its potential limitations.

CASE STUDY 10.1

THE SHIPPING INDUSTRY ACCOUNTING TEAM

For the past five years, I have been working at McKay, Sanderson, and Smith Associates, a midsized accounting firm in Boston that specializes in commercial accounting and audits. My specialty is accounting practices for shipping companies, ranging from small fishing fleets to a couple of the big firms with ships along the East Coast.

About 18 months ago, McKay, Sanderson, and Smith Associates became part of a large merger involving two other accounting firms. These firms have offices in Miami, Seattle, Baton Rouge, and Los Angeles. Although the other two accounting firms were much larger than McKay, all three firms agreed to avoid centralizing the business around one office in Los Angeles. Instead, the new firm—called Goldberg, Choo, and McKay Associates—would rely on teams across the country to "leverage the synergies of our collective knowledge" (an often-cited statement from the managing partner soon after the merger).

The effect of the merger hit me a year ago when my boss (a senior partner and vice-president of the merged firm) announced that I would be working more closely with three people from the other two firms to become the firm's new shipping industry accounting team. The other team members were Elias in Miami, Susan in Seattle, and Brad in Los Angeles. I had met Elias briefly at a meeting in New York City during the merger but had never met Susan or Brad, although I knew that they were shipping accounting professionals at the other firms.

Initially, the shipping team activities involved e-mailing each other about new contracts and prospective clients. Later, we were asked to submit joint monthly reports on accounting statements and issues. Normally, I submitted my own monthly reports, which summarize activities involving my own clients. Coordinating the monthly report with three other people took much more time, particularly since different accounting documentation procedures across the three firms were still being resolved. Numerous e-mails and a few telephone calls were needed to work out a reasonable monthly report style.

During this aggravating process, it became apparent—to me at least—that this "teams" business was costing me more time than it was worth. Moreover, Brad in Los Angeles didn't have a clue as to how to communicate with the rest of us. He rarely replied to e-mails. Instead, he often used the telephone voice mail system, which resulted in lots of telephone tag. Brad arrives at work at 9:30 A.M. in Los Angeles (and is often late!), which is early afternoon in Boston.

I typically have a flexible work schedule from 7:30 A.M. to 3:30 P.M. so I can chauffeur my kids after school to sports and music lessons. So Brad and I have a window of less than three hours to share information.

The biggest nuisance with the shipping specialist accounting team started two weeks ago when the firm asked the four of us to develop a new strategy for attracting more shipping firm business. This new strategic plan is a messy business. Somehow, we have to share our thoughts on various approaches, agree on a new plan, and write a unified submission to the managing partner. Already, the project is taking most of my time just writing and responding to e-mails and talking in conference calls (which none of us did much before the team formed).

Susan and Brad have already had two or three "misunderstandings" via e-mail about their different perspectives on delicate matters in the strategic plan. The worst of these disagreements required a conference call with all of us to resolve. Except for the most basic matters, it seems that we can't understand each other, let alone agree on key issues. I have come to the conclusion that I would never want Brad to work in my Boston office (thank goodness, he's on the other side of the country). While Elias and I seem to agree on most points, the overall team can't form a common vision or strategy. I don't know how Elias, Susan, or Brad feels, but I would be quite happy to work somewhere that did not require any of these long-distance team headaches.

Discussion Questions

1. What type of team was formed here? Was it necessary, in your opinion?

2. Use the team effectiveness model in Chapter 9 and related information in this chapter to identify the strengths and weaknesses of this team's environment, design, and processes.

3. Assuming that these four people must continue to work as a team, recommend ways to improve the team's effectiveness.

Source: Copyright © 2004 Steven L. McShane.

THE NEW TEAMWORK

BusinessWeek Executives at Lockheed Martin Aeronautics Company in Fort Worth, Texas, are entering a new world of team dynamics. To build a new family of supersonic stealth fighter planes for the Defense Department, the defense contractor is relying on technology to encourage collaboration among up to 40,000 technical experts from more than 80 suppliers at 187 locations. This initiative is creating probably the largest and most sophisticated collectivity of virtual teams on the planet. "We're getting the best people, applying the best designs, from wherever we need them," says Mark Peden, vice-president for information systems at Lockheed Martin Aeronautics. "It's the true virtual connection."

This *Business Week* case study looks at the new trend in collaborative engineering and the resulting dynamics of virtual teams in several organizations. The article describes how technology connects team members, as well as the benefits and challenges from this emerging workplace reality. Read through this *Business Week* article at www.mhhe.com/mcshane3e and prepare for the discussion questions below.

Discussion Questions

1. What are the main reasons identified in this case study why companies are increasing their reliance on virtual teams?

2. How does the specific type of collaborative technology affect the team dynamics of virtual teams?

3. What problems and limitations are apparent when applying collaborative technology and creating virtual teams?

Source: F. Keenan and S. E. Ante, "The New Teamwork," *Business Week,* February 18, 2002.

EGG DROP EXERCISE

Purpose   This exercise is designed to help you understand the dynamics of high-performance teams.

Materials   The instructor will provide various raw materials with which to complete this task. The instructor will also distribute a cost sheet to each team and will post the rules for managers and workers. Rule violations will attract penalties that increase the cost of production.

Team Task   The team's task is to design and build a protective device that will allow a raw egg (provided by the instructor) to be dropped from a great height without breaking. The team wins if its egg does not break using the lowest priced device.

Instructions

- *Step 1*—The instructor will divide the class into teams, with approximately six people on each team. Team members will divide into roles of "managers" and "workers." The team can have as many people as they think they need for managers and workers as long as all team members are assigned to one of these roles. Please note from the cost sheet that managers and workers represent a cost to your project's budget.

- *Step 2*—Within the time allotted by the instructor, each team's managers will design the device to protect the egg. Workers and managers will then purchase supplies from the store, and workers will then build the egg protection device. Team members should read the rules carefully to avoid penalty costs.

Source: This exercise, which is widely available in many forms, does not seem to have any known origins.

THE TEAM PLAYER INVENTORY

By Theresa Kline, University of Calgary

Purpose This exercise is designed to help you estimate the extent to which you are positively predisposed to work in teams.

Instructions Read each of the statements below and circle the response that you believe best indicates the extent to which you agree or disagree with that statement. Then use the scor-

ing key in Appendix B to calculate your results for each scale. This exercise is completed alone so students assess themselves honestly without concerns of social comparison. However, class discussion will focus on the characteristics of individuals who are more or less compatible with working in high-performance work.

The Team Player Inventory

To what extent to do you agree or disagree that...?	Completely disagree	Disagree somewhat	Neither agree nor disagree	Agree somewhat	Completely agree
1. I enjoy working on team projects.	☐	☐	☐	☐	☐
2. Team project work easily allows others not to 'pull their weight'.	☐	☐	☐	☐	☐
3. Work that is done as a team is better than the work done individually.	☐	☐	☐	☐	☐
4. I do my best work alone rather than in a team.	☐	☐	☐	☐	☐
5. Team work is overrated in terms of the actual results produced.	☐	☐	☐	☐	☐
6. Working in a team gets me to think more creatively.	☐	☐	☐	☐	☐
7. Teams are used too often when individual work would be more effective.	☐	☐	☐	☐	☐
8. My own work is enhanced when I am in a team situation.	☐	☐	☐	☐	☐
9. My experiences working in team situations have been primarily negative.	☐	☐	☐	☐	☐
10. More solutions or ideas are generated when working in a team situation than when working alone.	☐	☐	☐	☐	☐

Source: T. J. B. Kline, "The Team Player Inventory: Reliability and Validity of a Measure of Predisposition towards Organizational Team Working Environments," *Journal for Specialists in Group Work*, Vol. 24 (1999), pp. 102–12. Reprinted by permission of Sage Publications, Inc.

Communicating in Teams and Organizations

Learning Objectives

After reading this chapter, you should be able to:

- Explain the importance of communication and diagram the communication process.

- Describe problems with communicating through electronic mail.

- Identify two ways in which nonverbal communication differs from verbal communication.

- Identify two conditions requiring a channel with high media richness.

- Identify four common communication barriers.

- Discuss the degree to which men and women communicate differently.

- Outline the key elements of active listening.

- Summarize four communication strategies in organizational hierarchies.

W hether debating the movement of Sully's hair in *Monsters, Inc.,* or the complex shades of blue water in *Finding Nemo,* Pixar Animation Studios' employees engage in plenty of communication. In fact, Pixar's famous attention to detail means that almost every one of the 100,000-plus frames in a full-feature animation is intensely discussed to get the "right" image. Little wonder, then, that communication was on the minds of Pixar's executives when they decided to design a new campus in Emeryville, California, a few years ago.

The original plan was to have separate buildings for designers, writers, and other specialists, but Pixar creative director John Lasseter learned that a similar design had failed at Disney long ago. Instead, Pixar created a campus that accommodates two opposing communication goals. On the one hand, the workspace should isolate the team enough that members feel connected to each other and can quickly have informal meetings. On the other hand, the workspace should not isolate the team so much that employees lose valuable knowledge from people on other teams.

Pixar Animation Studios has created a workplace that encourages communication among team members and across the organization.

With these opposing communication goals in mind, Pixar clusters teams into their own pods, offices, and meeting rooms for efficient real-time knowledge sharing. But the company also creates the "bathroom effect" in which employees are forced to see people from other work areas whenever they fetch their mail, have lunch, or visit the restroom. The building also invites staff to mingle in the central airy atrium. "It promotes that chance encounter," says Lasseter, as he waves to a co-worker several yards away. "You run into people constantly. It worked from the minute we arrived. We just blossomed here."

While Pixar's building gets people talking to each other, improv sessions in the training department get them communicating more effectively. These activities, which include telling stories and acting out wacky scenarios, challenge Pixar's staff to think quickly and work collaboratively with other team members. "If people are engaged in an exercise and need to listen to each other, respond to each other, support each other, make eye contact and create something together, chances are, that work will spill over into their relationships outside the class," explains Rebecca Stockley, an improv specialist who leads the Pixar improv sessions. Randy Nelson, the dean of Pixar University, agrees. "It's good as training in basic corporate communications and as a general lifestyle," he concludes.[1] ■

communication
The process by which information is transmitted and understood between two or more people.

John Lasseter, Steve Jobs, and other executives at Pixar Animation Studios believe in the power of communication. **Communication** refers to the process by which information is transmitted and *understood* between two or more people. We emphasize the word *understood* because transmitting the sender's intended meaning is the essence of good communication. Pixar and other large organizations require innovative strategies to keep communication pathways open. Smaller businesses may have fewer structural bottlenecks, but they, too, can suffer from subtle communication barriers.

Effective communication is vital to all organizations because it coordinates employees, fulfills employee needs, supports knowledge management, and improves decision making. First, organizations depend on the ability of people to coordinate their individual work effort toward a common goal. Information exchange is an essential part of the coordination process, allowing employees to develop common mental models that synchronize their work.[2] Second, communication is the glue that holds people together. It helps people satisfy their drive to bond (see Chapter 5) and, as part of the dynamics of social support, eases work-related stress (see Chapter 7).

Communication is also a key driver in knowledge management (see Chapter 1).[3] It brings knowledge into the organization and distributes it to employees who require that information. As such, it minimizes the "silos of knowledge" problem that undermines an organization's potential. Consider a recent incident at Intec, the Houston-based engineering and project management company. A client in Beijing advised an Intec project manager that applying certain government specifications for a pipeline would be troublesome. The Intec manager used an internal communication system (an intranet) to query colleagues about this issue. Intec engineers on three continents quickly replied with information that enabled the project manager to develop a case to the government for using different specifications. Without this knowledge, the client would not have submitted a competitive proposal.[4]

The Intec story illustrates more than the importance of communication in knowledge management; it also shows how communication influences the quality of decision making. As we noted in Chapter 8, individuals rarely have enough information alone to make decisions on the complex matters facing businesses today. Instead, problem solvers require information from co-workers, subordinates, and anyone else with relevant knowledge. In other words, effective decision makers need to communicate.

By improving decision making, knowledge management, employee needs, and coordination, workplace communication has a significant effect on organizational performance. One recent report estimated that a company's market value increases by over 7 percent when it improves its "communications integrity." Another analysis identifies the leader's communication skills as an important influence on company performance. Communication is also a key ingredient in employee satisfaction and loyalty.[5]

This chapter begins by presenting a model of the communication process and discussing several communication barriers. Next, the different types of communication channels, including computer-mediated communication, are described, followed by factors to consider when choosing a communication medium. This chapter then examines cross-cultural and gender differences in communication and strategies to improve interpersonal communication. The final sections of the chapter present some options for communicating in organizational hierarchies and describe the pervasive organizational grapevine.

At the U.S. Centers for Disease Control (CDC) in Atlanta, communication was vital in knowledge acquisition and sharing when battling the deadly SARS (severe acute respiratory syndrome) virus. By coincidence, the CDC had installed a new emergency communications center (shown in photo) just as the virus was spreading around the world. In contrast to its response to previous biothreats, such as the anthrax scare the previous year, the CDC was able to keep track of SARS developments and communicate this knowledge throughout the United States and around the world. "There was very quick communication about what we knew and didn't know," says Dr. Georges Benjamin, executive director of the American Public Health Association. "That's important because, going back to the anthrax attacks, communication is something we weren't very good at."[6] What other communication strategies would assist CDC's knowledge management process during biothreats and health alerts?

A Model of Communication

The communication model presented in Exhibit 11.1 provides a useful "conduit" metaphor for thinking about the communication process.[7] According to this model, communication flows through channels between the sender and receiver. The sender forms a message and encodes it into words, gestures, voice intonations, and other symbols or signs. Next, the encoded message is transmitted to the intended receiver through one or more communication channels (media). The receiver senses the incoming message and decodes it into something meaningful. Ideally, the decoded meaning is what the sender had intended.

In most situations, the sender looks for evidence that the other person received and understood the transmitted message. This feedback may be a formal acknowledgment, such as "Yes, I know what you mean," or indirect evidence from the receiver's subsequent actions. Notice that feedback repeats the communication process. Intended feedback is encoded, transmitted, received, and decoded from the receiver to the sender of the original message.

This model recognizes that communication is not a free-flowing conduit.[8] Rather, the transmission of meaning from one person to another is hampered by *noise*—the psychological, social, and structural barriers that distort and

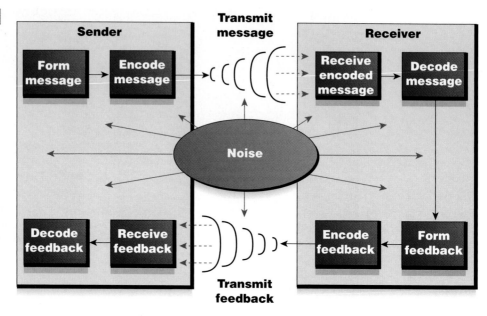

obscure the sender's intended message. If any part of the communication
process is distorted or broken, the sender and receiver will not have a common
understanding of the message.

Communication Channels

A critical part of the communication model is the channel through which information is transmitted. There are two main types of channels: verbal and
nonverbal. *Verbal communication* includes any oral or written means of transmitting meaning through words. *Nonverbal communication,* which we discuss
later, is any part of communication that does not use words.

Verbal Communication

Different forms of verbal communication should be used in different situations.
Face-to-face interaction is usually better than written methods for transmitting
emotions and persuading the receiver. This is because nonverbal cues accompany oral communications, such as voice intonations and use of silence. Moreover, in face-to-face settings, the sender receives immediate feedback from the
receiver and can adjust the emotional tone of the message accordingly.

   Written communication is more appropriate for recording and presenting
technical details. This is because ideas are easier to follow when written down
than when communicated aurally. Traditionally, written communication has
been slow to develop and transmit, but electronic mail and other computer-
mediated communication channels have significantly improved written communication efficiency.[9]

Electronic Mail

Electronic mail (e-mail) is revolutionizing the way we communicate in organizational settings.[10] Trillions of e-mail messages are transmitted each year,
and it's easy to understand their popularity. Messages are quickly formed, ed-

ited, and stored. Information can be appended and transmitted to many people with a simple click of a mouse. E-mail is asynchronous (messages are sent and received at different times), so there is no need to coordinate a communication session. This technology also allows fairly random access of information; you can select any message in any order and skip to different parts of a message.

E-mail tends to be the preferred medium for coordinating work (e.g., confirming a co-worker's production schedule) and for sending well-defined information for decision making. It tends to increase the volume of communication and significantly alter the flow of that information throughout the organization.[11] Specifically, it reduces some face-to-face and telephone communication but increases the flow of information to higher levels in the organization. Some social and organizational status differences still exist with e-mail, but they are less apparent than in face-to-face or telephone communication. E-mail also reduces many selective attention biases because it hides our age, race, weight, and other features that are observable in face-to-face meetings.

Problems with E-Mail   In spite of the wonders of e-mail, anyone who has used this communication medium knows that it also creates several problems. Perhaps the most obvious of these is that e-mail contributes to information overload. Many e-mail users are overwhelmed by hundreds of messages each week, many of which are either unnecessary or irrelevant to the receiver. This occurs because e-mails can be easily created and copied to thousands of people through group mailbox systems. For example, one KPMG consultant returned from vacation to discover nearly 1,600 e-mail messages. He e-mailed everyone saying that he wouldn't read any of the messages, so any urgent e-mails should be resent. The consultant received only seven e-mails in response.[12]

A second problem is that e-mail is an ineffective medium for communicating emotions. Notably, the emotion of sarcasm is difficult to convey through e-mail because the verbal message requires contrasting nonverbal cues. The result, as one scholar quipped, is that e-mail produces faster misunderstanding, not necessarily better communication. "Every fight that goes on [at Disney] seems to start with a misunderstanding over an e-mail," says Disney CEO Michael Eisner.[13] E-mail aficionados try to clarify the emotional tone of their messages by inserting graphic faces called emoticons, or "smileys." However, some experts warn that smileys do not easily solve the difficult task of communicating emotions through e-mail.[14]

A third problem is that e-mail seems to reduce our politeness and respect for others. This is mostly evident through the increased frequency of **flaming.** Flaming is the act of sending an emotionally charged message to others. Over half of the people questioned in one survey said they receive abusive e-mail and that men are both the most frequent victims and perpetrators.[15] The main cause of flaming is that people can post e-mail messages before their emotions subside, whereas the sender of a traditional memo or letter would have time for sober second thoughts. E-mail is also so impersonal that employees often write things that they would never say in person. Presumably, flaming and other e-mail problems will become less common as employees receive training on how to use this communication medium.[16] For example, most of us are learning rules in the largely unwritten and evolving code of conduct for

flaming
The act of sending an emotionally charged electronic mail message to others.

EXHIBIT 11.2

E-mail netiquette

E-Mail Netiquette

- **Do** fill in the "subject" line of the e-mail header with an informative description of the message.
- **Do** keep e-mail messages to fewer than 25 lines—the length of a typical computer screen.
- **Do** quote the relevant parts (but not necessarily all) of the receiver's previous message when replying to ideas in that message. (The automatic ">" indicates the original message.)
- **Do** respond to someone's e-mail (where a reply is expected) within one day for most business correspondence.
- **Do** switch from e-mail to telephone or face-to-face communication when the discussion gets too heated (flaming), the parties experience ongoing misunderstanding, or the issue becomes too complex.
- **Don't** forward private messages without the permission of the original sender.
- **Don't** send mass e-mails (using group lists) unless authorized to do so and the message definitely calls for this action.
- **Don't** send large attachments if the receiver likely has a narrow bandwidth (computer data are transmitted slowly).
- **Don't** use e-mail to communicate sensitive issues, such as disciplining someone, or to convey urgent information, such as rescheduling a meeting within the next hour.
- **Don't** write messages in ALL CAPITALS because this conveys anger or shouting. (This rule also applies to **boldface** text as e-mail software develops this feature.)
- **Don't** use emoticons excessively, and avoid them in formal business e-mails and where there is some chance that the receiver won't know their meaning.

Sources: M. Munter, P. S. Rogers, and J. Rymer, "Business E-Mail: Guidelines for Users," *Business Communication Quarterly* 66 (March 2003), pp. 26–27; M. M. Extejt, "Teaching Students to Correspond Effectively Electronically; Tips for Using Electronic Mail Properly," *Business Communication Quarterly* 61 (June 1998), pp. 57ff; K. Wasch, "Netiquette: Do's and Don'ts of E-Mail Use," *Association Management* 49 (May 1997), pp. 76, 115.

communicating on the Internet, called netiquette. Exhibit 11.2 lists a few *netiquette* rules for e-mail.

A fourth problem is that e-mail lacks the warmth of human interaction. As employees increasingly cocoon themselves through information technology, they lose the social support of human contact that potentially keeps their stress in check. Realizing this, Richard Birrer, interim president and CEO of St. Joseph's Regional Medical Center in Paterson, New Jersey, recently banned e-mail for one day in an attempt to "re-personalize the healthcare business."[17] Banning e-mail has also become a trend in the United Kingdom. As Global Connections 11.1 describes, executives at Liverpool City Council and in other British organizations believe that some things are better discussed in person than in cyberspace.

Other Computer-Mediated Communication

IBM executives weren't surprised when a recent survey indicated that IBM employees rated co-workers as one of the two most credible or useful sources of information. What *did* surprise IBM executives was that the other equally credible and important source of information was IBM's intranet.[18] Intranets, extranets, instant messaging, and other forms of computer-mediated commu-

British Organizations Ban E-mail to Rediscover Live Conversation

For the past 800 years, citizens in the port city of Liverpool, England, have relied on face-to-face communication to conduct trade and resolve their differences. But leaders at Liverpool City Council are concerned that e-mail is becoming a threat to the noble practice of dialogue among its employees. "E-mail has its advantages, but there are cases where it can be cumbersome," says David Henshaw, chief executive of Liverpool City Council. "We'd seen a doubling in internal e-mails and found a lot of e-mails were unnecessary—a lot of the stuff could be dealt with over the phone, or by getting up and walking to the person next to you."

To battle e-mail overload, Henshaw asked his employees to avoid using this medium of communication on Wednesdays. So far, Henshaw's own e-mail flow has dropped from 250 per day to just 25 on that day. The plan has its critics, however. "In business the pressure is on," says Leicestershire Chamber of Commerce chief executive Martin Traynor. "If people e-mail you in the morning, by lunch they're asking why you haven't e-mailed back." Traynor also argues that e-mail enables executives to communicate with more people who would not otherwise be accessible.

Perhaps so, but Liverpool City Council is not alone in its quest for more old-fashioned face-to-face conversation. Nestle Rowntree executives asked staff to hit the e-mail "send" button less frequently on Fridays to "reduce needless information flow across the organization." Camelot, the British lottery operator, also discouraged e-mails on the last day of the workweek unless totally, absolutely necessary. "We needed

Liverpool City Council has banned e-mail one day a week so employees can rediscover the benefits of face-to-face communication.

to make staff more aware of other forms of communication," explains Camelot spokeswoman Jenny Dowden. "If there were elements of the business where you could talk face-to-face instead of sending an e-mail, we wanted to encourage people to do that."

Sources: D. J. Horgan, "You've Got Conversation," *CIO Magazine,* October 15, 2002; "Does E-Mail Really Help Us Get the Message?" *Leicester Mercury,* August 31, 2002; J. Arlidge, "Office Staff Log Off for Email-Free Fridays," *The Observer* (London), August 12, 2001; N. Muktarsingh, "Companies Rediscover the Power of Speech," *Mail on Sunday* (London), July 22, 2001, p. 8; O. Burkeman, "Post Modern," *The Guardian* (London), June 20, 2001.

---

nication have fueled the hyperfast world of corporate information sharing.[19] Geographically dispersed work teams can coordinate their work more efficiently through instant messaging software and intranets. Suppliers are networked together so tightly through computer-mediated technology that customers see them as one organization (see Chapter 15).

Instant Messaging   *Instant messaging* appears to be the "next great thing" in technology-based communication. Very popular among Internet users under 25 year old, instant messaging connects two or more specific people and pushes the messages at each other. If you send an instant message to a coworker who is connected, your message will instantly pop up on the coworker's computer monitor (or other communications device).[20] Some companies are now experimenting with instant messaging. At financial planning firm UBS Warburg, for example, employees can log on to the instant message service that connects to dozens of other employees in a specific area of interest. A message sent within the system would instantly pop up on the computer screen of other people in that network. "No other communications technology operates in situations like that in a time-efficient manner," says a UBS Warburg executive.

Time efficiency isn't the only benefit of instant messaging. When hooked into a corporate network, instant messaging creates dozens of real-time communities of practice. For example, UBS Warburg has thousands of instant messaging channels representing different knowledge or client interests. The company's 13,000 employees connect to the channels most closely aligned with their area of work.[21] Instant messaging also has the unique benefit of accommodating several simultaneous streams of conversation. This allows employees to communicate with several people at the same time without mixing up the conversations. "No matter how good you are on the phone, the best you can do is carry on two conversations at once," says one New York City broker. "With IM, I can have six going at once . . . That allows me to get my job done and serve clients better."[22]

Nonverbal Communication

Computer-mediated communication is changing the face of organizations, but it hasn't yet replaced nonverbal communication. Nonverbal communication includes facial gestures, voice intonation, physical distance, and even silence. This communication channel is necessary where physical distance or noise prevents effective verbal exchanges and the need for immediate feedback precludes written communication. But even in close face-to-face meetings, most information is communicated nonverbally.[23] Nonverbal communication is also important in emotional labor—the effort, planning, and control needed to express organizationally desired emotions (see Chapter 4). Employees make extensive use of nonverbal cues to transmit prescribed feelings to customers, co-workers, and others.

Later in this chapter, we will discuss cross-cultural issues in communication, including how nonverbal communication misunderstandings account for some cross-cultural confusion. However, nonverbal communication is also vital in situations where two people lack a common verbal language. Global Connections 11.2 describes a memorable incident during the recent Iraq war involving coalition forces, where nonverbal communication narrowly avoided a potentially deadly incident.

Nonverbal communication differs from verbal communication in a couple of ways. First, it is less rule-bound than verbal communication. We receive a lot of formal training on how to understand spoken words, but very little on understanding the nonverbal signals that accompany those words. Consequently, nonverbal cues are more ambiguous and more susceptible to misinterpretation. Second, verbal communication is typically conscious, whereas most nonverbal communication is automatic and unconscious. We normally plan the words we say or write, but we rarely plan every blink, smile, or other gesture during a conversation. Indeed, many of these facial expressions communicate the same meaning across cultures precisely because they are hard-wired unconscious or preconscious responses to human emotions.[24] For example, pleasant emotions cause the brain center to widen the mouth, whereas negative emotions produce constricted facial expressions (squinting eyes, pursed lips, etc.).

emotional contagion
The automatic and unconscious tendency to mimic and synchronize one's own nonverbal behaviors with those of other people.

Emotional Contagion   One of the most fascinating effects of emotions on nonverbal communication is the phenomenon called **emotional contagion,** which is the automatic process of "catching" or sharing another person's emotions by

Nonverbal Gestures Help Crowd Control during Iraq War

The southern Iraqi city of Najaf is home to one of Islam's holiest sites, the Ali Mosque. The site is believed to be the final resting place of Ali, son-in-law of the prophet Mohammed. It is also home to Grand Ayatollah Ali Hussein Sistani, one of the most revered Shiites in the Muslim world and a potential supporter of U.S. efforts to introduce a more moderate government in Iraq.

One week before Saddam Hussein's regime was overthrown, Sistani sent word that he wanted to meet with senior officers of the American forces. Fearing assassination, he also asked for soldiers to secure his compound, located along the Golden Road near the mosque. But when 130 soldiers from the 101st Airborne's 2nd Battalion, 327th Infantry and their gun trucks turned onto the Golden Road to provide security, hundreds of Iraqis in the area started to get angry. Clerics tried to explain to the crowd why the Americans were approaching, but they were drowned out. The crowd assumed the Americans would try to enter and possibly attack the sacred mosque.

The chanting got louder as the quickly growing crowd approached the soldiers. Anticipating a potentially deadly situation, Lieutenant Colonel Christopher Hughes, the battalion's commander, picked up a loudspeaker and called out the unit's nickname: "No Slack Soldiers!" Then he commanded: "All No

Slack Soldiers, take a knee." According to journalists witnessing this incident, every soldier almost immediately knelt down on one knee. Hughes then called out: "All No Slack Soldiers, point your weapons at the ground." Again, the soldiers complied.

With the crowd still chanting in anger, Hughes spoke through the loudspeaker a third time: "All No Slack Soldiers, smile," he commanded. "Smile guys, everybody smile." And in this intensely difficult situation, the kneeling troops showed the friendliest smile they could muster toward the crowd.

Eyewitnesses say that these nonverbal gestures started to work; some people in the crowd smiled back at the Americans and stopped chanting. But insurgents in the crowd (apparently Hussein supporters planted to misinform the crowd), continued to yell. So Hughes spoke one more time: "All vehicles, all No Slack soldiers, calmly stand up and withdraw from this situation." And he said, "We'll go so the people understand we are not trying to hurt [them]. C'mon, Bravo, back off. Smile and wave and back off." With that, the soldiers walked backwards 100 yards, then turned around and returned to their compound.

Sources: W. Allison, "March to Mosque Provokes Worst Fears," *St. Petersburg (FL) Times*, April 4, 2003, p. 1A; *All Things Considered*, National Public Radio, April 4, 2003; R. Chilcote, "Iraqis Mistakenly Believe Soldiers Have Their Sights on a Sacred Landmark," *CNN*, April 4, 2003.

mimicking that person's facial expressions and other nonverbal behavior. Consider what happens when you see a co-worker accidentally bang his or her head against a filing cabinet. Chances are, you wince and put your hand on your own head as if *you* had hit the cabinet. Similarly, while listening to someone describe a positive event, you tend to smile and exhibit other emotional displays of happiness. While some of our nonverbal communication is planned, emotional contagion represents unconscious behavior—we automatically mimic and synchronize our nonverbal behaviors with other people.[25]

Emotional contagion serves three purposes. First, mimicry provides continuous feedback, communicating that we understand and empathize with the sender. To consider the significance of this, imagine employees remaining expressionless after watching a co-worker bang his or her head! The lack of parallel behavior conveys a lack of understanding or caring. Second, mimicking the nonverbal behaviors of other people seems to be a way of receiving emotional meaning from those people. If a co-worker is angry with a client, your tendency to frown and show anger while listening helps you share that emotion more fully. In other words, we receive meaning by expressing the sender's emotions as well as by listening to the sender's words.

Last, emotional contagion supports the drive to bond that was described in Chapter 5. By mimicking the emotions that people describe or reveal in conversations, we show that we are similar to them and share their experiences.

This display of sympathetic nonverbal behaviors communicates a collective sentiment and thereby builds social solidarity. It also strengthens team cohesiveness by providing evidence of member similarity.[26]

Choosing the Best Communication Channels

Employees perform better if they can quickly determine the best communication channels for the situation and are flexible enough to use different methods, as the occasion requires.[27] But which communication channels are most appropriate? We partly answered this question in our evaluation of the different communication channels. However, two additional contingencies worth noting are media richness and symbolic meaning.

Media Richness

Soon after Ernst & Young encouraged its employees around the globe to form virtual teams, the accounting firm realized that e-mail and voice mail weren't sufficient for these groups. "Try coming to an agreement on the verbiage of a legal contract with a team of lawyers and engineers representing multiple interests using only the telephone and e-mail," quips John Whyte, Ernst & Young's chief information officer. "You can spend weeks sorting through fragmented e-mail conversations or individual phone calls and voice mails." Now, employees discuss complex issues through special software that provides a virtual whiteboard on the computer screen and allows real-time chat (instant messaging). It's not quite as good as face-to-face meetings, but much better than the previous patchwork of e-mail and telephone calls.[28]

Ernst & Young discovered that some issues require more media richness than e-mail and telephone messages can offer. **Media richness** refers to the medium's *data-carrying capacity*—the volume and variety of information that can be transmitted.[29] Face-to-face meetings have the highest data-carrying capacity because the sender simultaneously uses multiple communication channels (verbal and nonverbal), the receiver can provide immediate feedback, and the information exchange can be customized to suit the situation. Telephone conversations would be somewhat lower in the hierarchy, and e-mail is further below telephone messages. Financial reports and other impersonal documents represent the leanest media because they allow only one form of data transmission (e.g., written), the sender does not receive timely feedback from the receiver, and the information exchange is standardized for everyone.

Exhibit 11.3 shows that rich media are better than lean media when the communication situation is nonroutine and ambiguous. Nonroutine situations require rich media because the sender and receiver have little common experience and, therefore, need to transmit a large volume of information with immediate feedback. During unexpected emergencies, for instance, you should use face-to-face meetings to coordinate work activities quickly and minimize the risk of misunderstanding and confusion. Lean media may be used in routine situations because the sender and receiver have common expectations through shared mental models.[30] Ambiguous issues, such as Ernst & Young's contract work, also require rich media because the parties must share large amounts of information with immediate feedback to resolve multiple and conflicting interpretations of their observations and experiences. For

media richness
The data-carrying capacity of a communication medium, including the volume and variety of information it can transmit.

EXHIBIT 11.3   A hierarchy of media richness

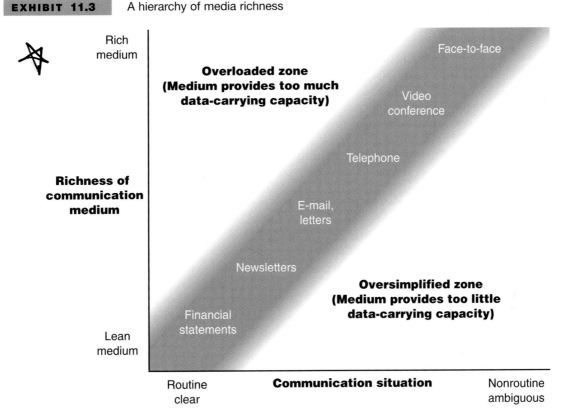

Sources: Based on R. Lengel and R. Daft, "The Selection of Communication Media as an Executive Skill," *Academy of Management Executive* 2, no. 3 (August 1988), p. 226; R. L. Daft and R. H. Lengel, "Information Richness: A New Approach to Managerial Behavior and Organization Design," *Research in Organizational Behavior,* 1984, p. 199.

instance, research indicates that product development presents several ill-defined issues, so team members work better with face-to-face communication than with leaner media.[31]

What happens when we choose the wrong level of media richness for the situation? When the situation is routine or clear, using a rich medium—such as holding a special meeting—would seem like a waste of time. On the other hand, if a unique and ambiguous issue is handled through e-mail or another lean medium, then issues take longer to resolve and misunderstandings are more likely to occur. This is the problem that employees at Ernst & Young experienced.

One last point about media richness is that we need to consider previous experience with both the media and the other person in the information exchange. People who have plenty of experience with a particular communication medium can "push" the amount of media richness normally possible through that information channel. The efficient use of a medium seems to allow more information flow for people with experience than for those who are new to the medium. Similarly, we can sometimes rely on leaner media when communicating with people who are familiar to us. This familiarity means that the sender and receiver often share common mental models, which reduces the required volume of information transmitted.[32]

Symbolic Meaning of the Medium

"The medium is the message."[33] This famous phrase by communications guru Marshall McLuhan means that the channel of communication has social consequences as much as (or perhaps more than) the content that passes through that medium. McLuhan was referring mainly to the influence of television and other "new media" on society, but this concept applies equally well to the symbolic effects of a communication medium on our interpretation of the message and the relationship between sender and receiver.

The following recent incident will help to illustrate this principle: Nearly 700 British employees at consulting firm KPMG were recently given layoff notices by e-mail. The message would have been the same whether sent by e-mail or stated by the boss in person. Moreover, KPMG defended its use of e-mail by explaining that employees had asked to receive their layoff notices through this medium. Still, the outside world swiftly condemned KPMG, not for the content of the message, but for the choice of medium through which it was sent. Even the KPMG executives who sent the layoff notices were hesitant to use e-mail when employees first suggested this medium. "I was horrified about telling staff via e-mail as I knew it would make us look callous," admitted one executive.[34] The point here is that we need to be sensitive to the symbolic meaning of the communication medium to ensure that it amplifies rather than misinterprets the meaning found in the message content.[35]

Communication Barriers (Noise)

In spite of the best intentions of sender and receiver to communicate, several barriers inhibit the effective exchange of information. As author George Bernard Shaw wrote, "The greatest problem with communication is the illusion that it has been accomplished." Four pervasive communication barriers (called "noise" earlier in Exhibit 11.1) are perceptions, filtering, language, and information overload. Later, we will also investigate cross-cultural and gender communication barriers.

Perceptions

As we learned in Chapter 3, the perceptual process determines what messages we select or screen out, as well has how the selected information is organized and interpreted. This can be a significant source of noise in the communication process if the sender and receiver have different perceptual frames and mental models. For example, a plant superintendent in a concrete block plant picked up a piece of broken brick while talking with the supervisor. This action had no particular meaning to the superintendent—just something to toy with during the conversation. Yet as soon as the senior manager had left, the supervisor ordered one half-hour of overtime for the entire crew to clean up the plant. The supervisor mistakenly perceived the superintendent's action as a signal that the plant was messy.[36]

Filtering

Some messages are filtered or stopped altogether on their way up or down the organizational hierarchy.[37] Filtering may involve deleting or delaying negative information or using less harsh words so that events sound more favorable.

Employees and supervisors usually filter communication to create a good impression of themselves to superiors. Filtering is most common where the organization rewards employees who communicate mainly positive information and among employees with strong career mobility aspirations.[38]

Language

Words and gestures carry no inherent meaning, so the sender must ensure the receiver understands these symbols and signs. In reality, lack of mutual understanding is a common reason why messages are distorted. Two potential language barriers are jargon and ambiguity.

Jargon   "Hi Jack, I've worked out a klugey solution to the UI issue," an employee e-mails to a colleague in the next cubicle. "We need to get granular on this. Unfortunately, I'm OOF next week, so you'll have to burn up a few cycles on it. I'm worried that the blue-badges on this project will go totally nonlinear when they realize the RTM date is slipping."[39]

If you understood most of the previous paragraph, you probably work at Microsoft or some other high-technology company where employees communicate through Microspeak. This **jargon**—technical language and acronyms as well as recognized words with specialized meaning in specific organizations or social groups—might baffle most of us, but it potentially increases communication efficiency when both sender and receiver understand this specialized language. Jargon also shapes and maintains an organization's cultural values as well as symbolizes an employee's identity in a group (see Chapter 3).[40]

However, jargon can also be a barrier to effective communication. One example is an incident at Sea Launch, the Long Beach, California-based multinational venture that launches satellites. During a test of a countdown protocol devised by the American staff, the Russian scientists involved with the project suddenly became moody and distant. When Sea Launch's mission

jargon
The technical language and acronyms as well as recognized words with specialized meanings in specific organizations or groups.

© 2001 Ted Goff

"That's my commendation for deciphering all the sales talk when we needed to upgrade the computer."

(Copyright © Ted Goff.)

control director Steve Thelin eventually asked why they were acting this way, the Russians complained that no one told them who "Roger" was. Everyone had a good laugh when Thelin explained that "Roger" is jargon used by the Americans to indicate that they understood what the other person in a transmission is saying.[41]

Ambiguity   Most languages—and certainly the English language—include some degree of ambiguity because the sender and receiver interpret the same word or phrase differently. If a co-worker says "Would you like to check the figures again?" the employee may be politely *telling* you to double-check the figures. But this message is sufficiently ambiguous that you may think the co-worker is merely *asking* if you want to do this. The result is a failure to communicate.

Although a communication barrier, ambiguity is sometimes used deliberately in work settings. Corporate leaders rely on metaphors and other ambiguous language to describe ill-defined or complex ideas.[42] Ambiguity is also used to avoid conveying or creating undesirable emotions. For example, one recent study reported that people rely on more ambiguous language when communicating with people who have different values and beliefs. In this case, ambiguity minimizes the risk of conflict.[43] The brokerage industry also relies on ambiguous language when advising clients to get rid of their stock in a particular company. Brokers are reluctant to use the word "sell" because it criticizes the company's performance, yet some of these companies are current or future clients. "'Hold' means 'sell,'" admits one veteran of the brokerage industry. "It's a kind of 'meta' language where you have to look into the meaning behind the word."[44]

Information Overload

On average, American office workers send and receive more than 150 messages daily through various media and spend almost 25 percent of their time processing e-mail. Little wonder that nearly half the managers in one survey acknowledged that they fairly often or regularly feel incapable of processing this "infoglut." More than 40 percent of them say that receiving so much information weakens their decision-making ability, delays important decisions, and impairs their ability to concentrate on their main tasks.[45] Communications guru Marshall McLuhan predicted this problem more than 30 years ago. "One of the effects of living with electric information is that we live in a state of information overload," said McLuhan. "There's always more than you can cope with."[46]

information overload

A condition in which the volume of information received exceeds the person's capacity to process it.

Information overload occurs when the volume of information received exceeds the person's capacity to process it. Employees have a certain *information processing capacity,* that is, the amount of information that they are able to process in a fixed unit of time. At the same time, jobs have a varying *information load,* that is, the amount of information to be processed per unit of time.[47] As Exhibit 11.4 illustrates, information overload occurs whenever the job's information load exceeds the individual's information processing capacity. Information overload creates noise in the communication system because information gets overlooked or misinterpreted when people can't process it fast enough. It has also become a common cause of workplace stress.

Information overload is minimized by increasing our information processing capacity, reducing the job's information load, or through a combination of

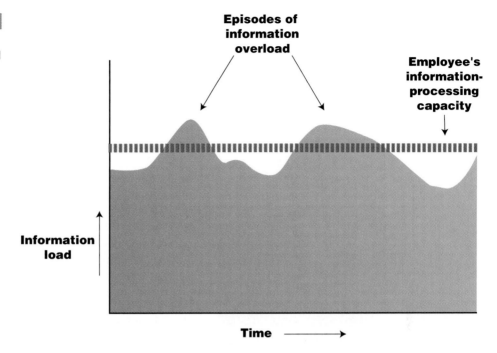

EXHIBIT 11.4

Dynamics of
information overload

both.[48] We can increase information processing capacity by learning to read faster, scanning documents more efficiently, and removing distractions that slow information processing speed. Time management also increases information processing capacity. When information overload is temporary, information processing capacity can increase by working longer hours.

We can reduce information load by buffering, summarizing, or omitting the information. *Buffering* occurs where assistants screen our messages and forward only those considered essential reading. *Summarizing* condenses information into fewer words; reading abstracts and executive summaries is more efficient than reading the entire document. *Omitting* is the practice of ignoring less important information. For example, some e-mail software programs have a filtering algorithm that screens out unwanted junk mail (spam).

Perceptions, filtering, language, and information overload are not the only sources of noise in the communication process, but they are probably the most common. Noise also occurs when we communicate across cultures or genders, both of which are discussed next.

Cross-Cultural and Gender Communication

In a world of increasing globalization and cultural diversity, organizations face new opportunities as well as communication challenges. Employees must become more sensitive and competent in cross-cultural communication. They must also overcome their reluctance to communicate with co-workers from another cultural group. These communication competencies are also gaining importance as companies increasingly work with clients, suppliers, and joint venture partners from other countries.

Language is the most obvious cross-cultural barrier.[49] Words are easily misunderstood in verbal communication, either because the receiver has a limited vocabulary or because the sender's accent makes it difficult for the receiver to understand the sound. The ambiguity of language that we discussed earlier becomes a bigger concern across cultures because sender and receiver have different values and interpretations of the language. For example, a French executive might call an event a "catastrophe" as a casual exaggeration, whereas this statement is usually taken literally as an earth-shaking event by someone in Germany.[50]

Mastering the same language improves one dimension of cross-cultural communication, but problems may still occur when interpreting voice intonation.[51] A deep voice symbolizes masculinity in North America, but African men often express their emotions using a high-pitched voice. Middle Easterners sometimes speak loudly to show sincerity and interest in the discussion, whereas Japanese people tend to speak softly to communicate politeness or humility. These different cultural norms regarding voice loudness may cause one person to misinterpret the other.

Nonverbal Differences

Nonverbal communication is more important in some cultures than in others. For example, people in Japan interpret more of a message's meaning from nonverbal cues. To avoid offending or embarrassing the receiver (particularly outsiders), Japanese people will often say what the other person wants to hear (called *tatemae*) but send more subtle nonverbal cues indicating the sender's true feelings (called *honne*).[52] A Japanese colleague might politely reject your business proposal by saying "I will think about that" while sending nonverbal signals that he or she is not really interested. This difference explains why Japanese employees may prefer direct conversation to e-mail and other media that lack nonverbal cues.

Most nonverbal cues are specific to a particular culture and may have a completely different meaning to people raised in other cultures. For example, most of us shake our head from side to side to say "No," but a variation of head shaking means "I understand" to many people in India. Filipinos raise their eyebrows to give an affirmative answer, yet Arabs interpret this expression (along with clicking one's tongue) as a negative response. Most Americans are taught to maintain eye contact with the speaker to show interest and respect, yet Native Americans, Australian Aborigines, and others learn at an early age to show respect by looking down when an older or more senior person is talking to them.[53]

Patricia Oliveira made several cultural adjustments when she moved from Brazil to Australia. One of the more humorous incidents occurred in the Melbourne office where she works. A co-worker would stick his thumbs up when asked about something, signaling that everything was OK. But the gesture had a totally different meaning to Oliveira and other people from Brazil. "He asked me why I was laughing and I had to explain that in Brazil, that sign means something not very nice," recalls Oliveira. "After that, everyone started doing it to the boss. It was really funny."[54] What other differences in cross-cultural communication would Patricia Oliveira possibly notice between Brazilians and Australians or Americans?

Even the common handshake communicates different meaning across cultures. Westerners tend to appreciate a firm handshake as a sign of strength and warmth in a friendship or business relationship. In contrast, many Asians and Middle Easterners favor a loose grip and regard a firm clench as aggressive. Germans prefer one good handshake stroke, whereas anything less than five or six strokes may symbolize a lack of trust in Spain. If this isn't confusing enough, people from some cultures view any touching in public—including handshakes—as a sign of rudeness.

Silence and Conversational Overlaps Communication includes the silence between our words and gestures. However, the meaning of silence varies from one culture to another. For instance, a recent study estimated that silence and pauses represented 30 percent of conversation time between Japanese doctors and patients, compared to only 8 percent of the time between American doctors and patients. Even though Japanese doctors and patients had shorter consultations, they said less and allowed more silence throughout the conversation.[55]

Why is there so much silence in Japanese conversations (at least, among older generation Japanese)? The listener's silence (called *haragei*) after the speaker has finished symbolizes respect and indicates that the listener is thoughtfully contemplating what has just been said.[56] Silence is an important part of communication in Japan because it preserves harmony and is more reliable than talk. Silence is shared by everyone and belongs to no one, so it becomes the ultimate form of interdependence. Moreover, Japanese value empathy, which can be demonstrated only by understanding others without using words. In contrast, most people in the United States view silence as a *lack* of communication and often interpret long breaks as a sign of disagreement.

Conversational overlaps also send different messages in different cultures. Japanese people usually stop talking when they are interrupted, whereas talking over the other person's speech is more common in Brazil and some other countries. The reason is that talking while someone is speaking to you is considered quite rude in Japan, whereas Brazilians are more likely to interpret this as the person's interest and involvement in the conversation.

Gender Differences in Communication

Popular-press books have depicted gender differences in communication to such an extent that it seems that men and women are completely different life forms. In reality, men and women have similar communication practices, but there are subtle distinctions that can occasionally lead to misunderstanding and conflict.[57] One distinction is that men are more likely than women to view conversations as negotiations of relative status and power.[58] They assert their power by directly giving advice to others (e.g., "You should do the following") and using combative language. There is also evidence that men interrupt women far more often than vice versa and that they dominate the talk time in conversations with women.

Men tend to engage in "report talk," in which the primary function of the conversation is impersonal and efficient information exchange. This may explain why men tend to quantify information (e.g., "It took us six weeks"). Women also engage in report talk, particularly when conversing with men. But conversations among women tend to have a higher incidence of relationship building through "rapport talk." Thus, women use more intensive adverbs ("I was *so happy* that he completed the report") and hedge their statements ("It seems to be . . ."). Rather than asserting status, women use indirect requests such as "Have you considered . . . ?" Similarly, women apologize more often and seek advice from others more quickly than do men. Finally, research fairly consistently indicates that women are more sensitive than men to nonverbal cues in face-to-face meetings.[59]

Both men and women usually understand each other, but these subtle differences are occasional irritants. For instance, female scientists have complained that adversarial interaction among male scientists makes it difficult for women to participate in meaningful dialogue.[60] Another irritant occurs when women seek empathy but receive male dominance in response. Specifically, women sometimes discuss their personal experiences and problems to develop closeness with the receiver. But when men hear problems, they quickly suggest solutions because this asserts their control over the situation. As well as frustrating a woman's need for common understanding, the advice actually says: "You and I are different; you have the problem and I have the answer." Meanwhile, men become frustrated because they can't understand why women don't appreciate their advice.

Improving Interpersonal Communication

Effective interpersonal communication depends on the sender's ability to get the message across and the receiver's performance as an active listener. In this section, we outline these two essential features of effective interpersonal communication.

Getting Your Message Across

This chapter began with the statement that effective communication occurs when the other person receives and understands the message. To accomplish this difficult task, the sender must learn to empathize with the receiver, repeat the message, choose an appropriate time for the conversation, and be descriptive rather than evaluative.

- *Empathize*—Recall from Chapter 3 that empathy is a person's ability to understand and be sensitive to the feelings, thoughts, and situation of others. In conversations, this involves putting yourself in the receiver's shoes when encoding the message. For instance, be sensitive to words that may be ambiguous or trigger the wrong emotional response.
- *Repeat the message*—Rephrase the key points a couple of times. The saying "Tell them what you're going to tell them; tell them; then tell them what you've told them" reflects this need for redundancy.
- *Use timing effectively*—Your message competes with other messages and noise, so find a time when the receiver is less likely to be distracted by these other matters.
- *Be descriptive*—Focus on the problem, not the person, if you have negative information to convey. People stop listening when the information attacks their self-esteem. Also, suggest things the listener can do to improve, rather than point to him or her as a problem.

Active Listening

Darryl Heustis admits that he isn't always good at listening to other people. "I've had the unique ability to start formulating my response before the person is through with the question," he says sheepishly. Fortunately, Heustis and his other colleagues at the Jerry L. Pettis Memorial VA Medical Center in Loma Linda, California, have completed training that helps them to more actively listen to what others are saying. "Now, I've learned to practice my listening skills and observation skills. I've improved at watching people carefully, looking for body language and other signals of what they're feeling."[61]

Darryl Heustis and other executives are discovering that listening is at least as important as talking. As one sage wisely wrote: "Nature gave people two ears but only one tongue, which is a gentle hint that they should listen more than they talk."[62] Listening is a process of actively sensing the sender's signals, evaluating them accurately, and responding appropriately. These three components of listening—sensing, evaluating, and responding—reflect the listener's side of the communication model described at the beginning of this chapter.[63] Listeners receive the sender's signals, decode them as intended, and provide appropriate and timely feedback to the sender. Active listeners constantly cycle through sensing, evaluating, and responding during the conversation and engage in various activities to improve these processes (see Exhibit 11.5).

Sensing   Sensing is the process of receiving signals from the sender and paying attention to them. These signals include the words spoken, the nature of the sounds (speed of speech, tone of voice, etc.), and nonverbal cues. Active listeners improve sensing by postponing evaluation, avoiding interruptions, and maintaining interest.

■ *Postpone evaluation*—Many listeners become victims of first impressions (see Chapter 3). They quickly form an opinion of the speaker's message and subsequently screen out important information. Active listeners, on

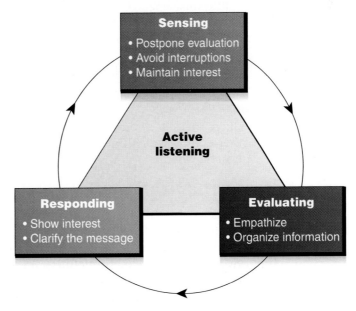

the other hand, try to stay as open-minded as possible by delaying evaluation of the message until the speaker has finished.

■ *Avoid interruptions*—Interrupting the speaker's conversation has two adverse effects on the sensing process. First, it disrupts the speaker's idea, so the listener does not receive the entire message. Second, interruptions tend to second-guess what the speaker is trying to say, which contributes to the problem of evaluating the speaker's ideas too early.

■ *Maintain interest*—As with any behavior, active listening requires motivation. Too often, we close our minds soon after a conversation begins because the subject is boring. Instead, active listeners maintain interest by taking the view—probably an accurate one—that there is always something of value in a conversation; it's just a matter of actively looking for it.

Evaluating   This component of listening includes understanding the message meaning, evaluating the message, and remembering the message. To improve their evaluation of the conversation, active listeners empathize with the speaker and organize information received during the conversation.

■ *Empathize*—Active listeners try to understand and be sensitive to the speaker's feelings, thoughts, and situation. Empathy is a critical skill in active listening because the verbal and nonverbal cues from the conversation are accurately interpreted from the other person's point of view.

■ *Organize information*—Listeners process information three times faster than the average rate of speech (450 words per minute versus 125 words per minute), so they are easily distracted. Active listeners use this spare time to organize the information into key points. In fact, it's a good idea to imagine that you must summarize what people have said after they are finished speaking.[64]

Responding   Responding, the third component of listening, refers to the listener's development and display of behaviors that support the communication process. Responsiveness is feedback to the sender, which motivates and directs the speaker's communication. Active listeners do this by showing interest and clarifying the message.

■ *Show interest*—Active listeners show interest by maintaining sufficient eye contact and sending back channel signals such as "Oh, really!" and "I see" during appropriate breaks in the conversation.

■ *Clarify the message*—Active listeners provide feedback by rephrasing the speaker's ideas at appropriate breaks ("So you're saying that . . . ?"). This further demonstrates interest in the conversation and helps the speaker determine whether you understand the message.

Communicating in Organizational Hierarchies

So far, we have focused on "micro-level" issues in the communication process, namely, the dynamics of sending and receiving information between two people in various situations. But in this era where knowledge is competitive advantage, corporate leaders also need to maintain an open flow of communication up, down, and across the organization. In this section, we discuss four "macro-level" communication strategies: work space design, newsletters/e-zines, employee surveys, and direct communication with top management.

Work Space Design

There's nothing like a wall to prevent employees from talking to each other. "So often in offices, people are stuck in little rabbit holes and you feel like you could be the only one in the building," explains Peter Lanyon, chairman of advertising firm Lanyon Phillips in Vancouver, Canada. To encourage more communication, Lanyon's new offices have adopted an open-space design. "In this space, you can see from one end to the other. You get the sense of being connected with other people." Phonak, a hearing-aid manufacturer in Warrenville, Illinois, also has very few walls to block communication. "We're in the communications business," says Phonak CEO Michael R. Jones. "We have no offices and a very open floor plan to foster communication."[65]

Do these open-space offices actually improve communication? Anecdotal evidence suggests that people do communicate more often with fewer walls between them. However, scientific research also suggests that open office design potentially increases employee stress due to the loss of privacy and personal space. According to an analysis of 13,000 employee surveys in 40 major organizations, work space primarily contributes to individual performance by providing a place to concentrate on work without distraction. The second most important influence of work space on performance is how it facilitates informal communication with co-workers.[66]

Executives at Pixar Animation Studios faced a similar dilemma, as we read in the opening vignette to this chapter. On the one hand, the film company's new building in Emeryville, California, had to create a work space where employees could focus on the project and share information within the immediate team. On the other hand, the work space had to allow sufficient interaction with people outside the team to foster creativity. The point here is that work space needs to provide a balance between its ability to give employees a place to concentrate and its influence on broader social interaction.

Newsletters and E-Zines

A decade ago, Hughes Software Systems (HSS) in India had 50 employees, a small enough group that executives could announce company news through meetings. Today, HSS employs 1,300 people, so it depends on various electronic and paper media to keep everyone informed. Employees receive hardcopy newsletters about company developments, but they also receive timely information through HSS's intranet. If that's not enough, HSS has an electronic message board called "Junk," where employees share their views on everything from the quality of cafeteria food to ways to get around the electronic blockades HSS has placed on sports websites.[67]

Hughes Software Systems and other large organizations are increasingly applying a multipronged communication strategy to share information with employees. This strategy typically includes both print-based newsletters and Web-based electronic newsletters, called e-zines. For example, Hewlett-Packard (HP) posts late-breaking company news every day in its intranet-based publication called *hpNow*. Several times each year HP employees also receive a print magazine called *Invent*, which features longer, more detailed articles. HP and other firms have discovered that one communication medium is not enough. Online sources offer instant communication, but many employees still have difficulty reading long articles on a computer screen. Print articles are slower and more costly, but they currently offer more portability and long articles are easier to read than online publications.[68]

Employee Surveys

Most of America's "best" companies to work for conduct regular employee opinion surveys. Most of them survey employees to monitor worker morale, particularly as part of broader measures of corporate performance. Other organizations use surveys to involve employees in decisions on everything from dress codes to pension plans.[69] For example, Eli Lilly & Company conducted a census of its 14,500 U.S. employees to find out what hours they prefer working. The pharmaceutical company learned that the workday it had mandated for decades was out-of-date and out-of-favor. Eli Lilly now offers flexible hours and optional compressed workweeks.[70]

management by walking around (MBWA)
A communication practice in which executives get out of their offices and learn from others in the organization through face-to-face dialogue.

Direct Communication with Top Management

"The best fertilizer in any field is that of the farmer's footsteps!" This old Chinese saying means that farmers grow the best crops by spending time in the fields to directly observe the challenges facing the crop's development. In an organizational context, senior executives can't rely on employee surveys and company newsletters alone to understand what is happening in the organization. They need to get out of the executive suite and meet directly with employees at all levels and on their turf to fully understand the issues. Nearly 40 years ago, people at Hewlett-Packard coined a phrase for this communication strategy: **management by walking around (MBWA).**[71] Richard Zuschlag, CEO of Acadian Ambulance & Air Med Services Inc. in Louisiana, practices MBWA by wandering around the company's offices and chatting with employees. "I'm a very curious person," explains Zuschlag. "Just walking around and asking a lot of my dumb questions is how I find out what's going on."[72]

Along with MBWA, executives are getting more direct communication with employees through "town hall meetings," where large groups of employees hear about a merger or other special news directly from the key decision makers. Others attend employee roundtable forums to hear opinions from a small representation of staff about various issues. Fred Hassan has done both since joining Schering-Plough as CEO. One day he has dinner with salespeople in New York; another day he meets with 11 mid-level researchers at the pharmaceutical company's headquarters in New Jersey.[74] All of these direct communication strategies potentially minimize filtering because executives listen directly to employees. They also help executives

Hiram Walker & Sons Ltd. has a stately headquarters, but CEO Ian Gourlay prefers to spend much of his time out and about. Chances are, you'll see Gourlay walking through the distillery, addressing a community reception, or attending meetings around the organization. Having the boss stop by the distillery is something of a novelty to its 400-person staff. "They find that unusual, I don't," says Gourlay, who adds that employees are becoming accustomed to seeing him and learning about him. Hiram Walker employees are also discovering the benefits of a CEO who wanders around the workplace. "He sees what we're up against and what we're trying to do," says Gary Lajoie, plant superintendent of finished goods.[73] What are the best situations for corporate leaders to meet personally with employees?

acquire a deeper meaning and quicker understanding of internal organizational problems. A third benefit of direct communication is that employees might have more empathy for decisions made further up the corporate hierarchy.

Communicating through the Grapevine

grapevine
An unstructured and informal communication network founded on social relationships rather than organizational charts or job descriptions.

Whether or not executives get out of their offices, employees will always rely on the oldest communication channel: the corporate grapevine. The **grapevine** is an unstructured and informal network founded on social relationships rather than organizational charts or job descriptions. According to some estimates, 75 percent of employees typically receive news from the grapevine before they hear about it through formal channels.[75]

Grapevine Characteristics

Research conducted several decades ago identified some unique features of the grapevine.[76] It transmits information very rapidly in all directions throughout the organization. The typical pattern is a cluster chain, whereby a few people actively transmit rumors to many others. The grapevine works through informal social networks, so it is more active where employees have similar backgrounds and are able to communicate easily. Many rumors seem to have at least a kernel of truth, possibly because rumors are transmitted through media-rich communication channels (e.g., face to face) and employees are motivated to communicate effectively. Nevertheless, the grapevine distorts information by deleting fine details and exaggerating key points of the story.

The problem with some of these earlier findings is that they might not be representative of the grapevine in this era of information technology. E-mail and instant messaging have replaced the traditional water cooler as the main place where people share gossip. Social networks have expanded as employees communicate with each other around the globe, not just around the next cubicle. Vault.com and other public websites have become virtual water coolers where anonymous comments about specific companies are posted for all to view. This technology extends gossip to anyone, not just employees connected to social networks.

Grapevine Benefits and Limitations

Should the grapevine be encouraged, tolerated, or quashed? The difficulty in answering this question is that the grapevine has both benefits and limitations. One benefit is that the grapevine helps employees make sense of their workplace when the information is not available through formal channels.[77] It is also the main conduit through which organizational stories and other symbols of the organization's culture are communicated (see Chapter 16). A third benefit of the grapevine is that this social interaction relieves anxiety.[78] This explains why rumor mills are most active during times of uncertainty. Finally, the grapevine is associated with the drive to bond. Being a recipient of gossip is a sign of inclusion, according to evolutionary psychologists. Trying to quash the grapevine is, in some respects, an attempt to undermine natural human needs for interaction.[79]

While the grapevine may be beneficial, it is not the preferred communication medium. Grapevine information is sometimes so distorted that it escalates

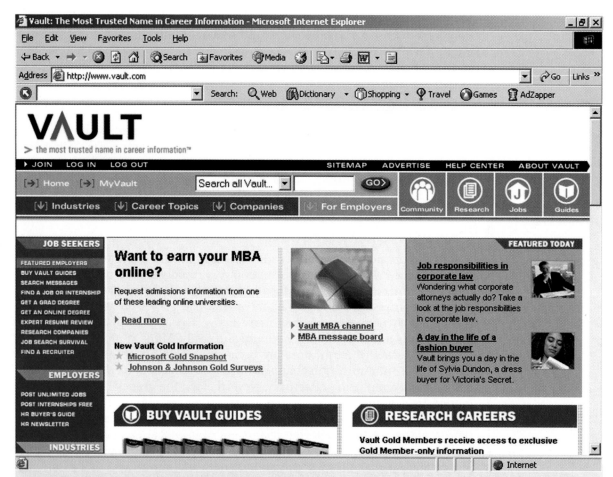

For many employees, the corporate grapevine is now connected to the Internet through Vault.com and other websites. The corporate grapevine is "no longer just four staffers huddling around a dusty water cooler," says Vault cofounder Mark Oldman. "Now there are thousands of people around the world comparing notes." Vault.com has message boards for hundreds of companies. Post some hearsay or an opinion about a particular firm and the world will know about it in seconds. "With the power of the Internet, there is more of a global and real-time flow to rumors and gossip," says Oldman. Vault.com estimates that up to 9 percent of Goldman Sachs employees check in with Vault's Goldman board during any given week. Partners at McKinsey & Company actively respond to rumors and queries posted on the consulting firm's message board at Vault.com.[80] In your opinion, how does the Internet potentially change the pattern of grapevine information and the accuracy of that information? (Source: Reprinted with permission of vault.com—The Insider Career Network.)

rather than reduces employee anxiety. This is most likely to occur when the original information is transmitted through several people rather than through one or two people. Furthermore, employees develop more negative attitudes toward the organization when management is slower than the grapevine in communicating information. For instance, 74 percent of Lakeland Electric employees say they get company information mainly through the grapevine, yet only 5 percent wanted to receive company information through this communication channel. Instead, most employees at the Florida utility listed management as their preferred source of information. The result of this discrepancy? Only 14 percent trusted the utility's management and 19 percent said the company does a good job of providing timely information to employees.[81]

What should corporate leaders do with the grapevine? City officials in Cascavel, Brazil, have banned employees from engaging in spreading office gossip, but the grapevine will always exist.[82] A better strategy is to listen to the grapevine as a signal of employee anxiety, then correct the cause of this anxiety. Some companies also listen to the grapevine and step in to correct blatant errors and fabrications. Most important, corporate leaders need to view the grapevine as a competitor, and eventually win the challenge to inform employees before they receive the news through the grapevine.

Chapter Summary

Communication refers to the process by which information is transmitted and *understood* between two or more people. Communication supports work coordination, employee well-being, knowledge management, and decision making. The communication process involves forming, encoding, and transmitting the intended message to a receiver, who then decodes the message and provides feedback to the sender. Effective communication occurs when the sender's thoughts are transmitted to and understood by the intended receiver.

Electronic mail (e-mail) is an increasingly popular way to communicate, and it has changed communication patterns in organizational settings. However, e-mail also contributes to information overload, is an ineffective channel for communicating emotions, tends to reduce politeness and respect in the communication process, and lacks the warmth of human interaction. Instant messaging is gaining popularity in organizations because it speeds up the communication process.

Nonverbal communication includes facial gestures, voice intonation, physical distance, and even silence. Employees make extensive use of nonverbal cues when engaging in emotional labor because these cues help to transmit prescribed feelings to customers, co-workers, and others. Emotional contagion refers to the automatic and unconscious tendency to mimic and synchronize our nonverbal behaviors with other people. The most appropriate communication medium depends on its data-carrying capacity (media richness) and its symbolic meaning to the receiver. Nonroutine and ambiguous situations require rich media.

Several barriers create noise in the communication process. People misinterpret messages because of perceptual biases. Some information is filtered out as it gets passed up the hierarchy. Jargon and ambiguous language are barriers when the sender and receiver have different interpretations of the words and symbols used. People also screen out or misinterpret messages due to information overload.

Globalization and workforce diversity have brought new communication challenges. Words are easily misunderstood in verbal communication and employees are reluctant to communicate across cultures. Voice intonation, silence, and other nonverbal cues have different meaning and importance in other cultures. There are also some communication differences between men and women, such as the tendency for men to exert status and engage in report talk in conversations, whereas women use more rapport talk and are more sensitive than are men to nonverbal cues.

To get a message across, the sender must learn to empathize with the receiver, repeat the message, choose an appropriate time for the conversation, and be descriptive rather than evaluative. Listening includes sensing, evaluating, and responding. Active listeners support these processes by postponing evaluation, avoiding interruptions, maintaining interest, empathizing, organizing information, showing interest, and clarifying the message.

Some companies try to encourage informal communication through work space design, although open offices run the risk of increasing stress and reducing the ability to concentrate on work. Many organizations also rely on a combination of print newsletters and intranet-based e-zines to communicate corporate news. Employee surveys are widely used to measure employee attitudes or involve employees in corporate decisions. Some executives also meet directly with employees, either through management by walking around or other arrangements, to facilitate communication across the organization.

In any organization, employees rely on the grapevine, particularly during times of uncertainty. The grapevine is an unstructured and informal network founded on social relationships rather than organizational charts or job descriptions. Although early research identified several unique features of the grapevine, some of these features may be changing as the Internet plays an increasing role in grapevine communication.

Key Terms

communication, p. 324
emotional contagion, p. 330
flaming, p. 327
grapevine, p. 345

information overload, p. 336
jargon, p. 335
management by walking around (MBWA), p. 344
media richness, p. 332

Discussion Questions

1. A city government intends to introduce electronic mail for office staff at its three buildings located throughout the city. Describe two benefits as well as two potential problems that city government employees will likely experience with this medium.

2. Instant messaging will become an increasingly popular form of information technology over the next few years. What are the advantages and disadvantages of this communication medium compared to e-mail and intranet communication?

3. Marshall McLuhan coined the popular phrase: "The medium is the message." What does this phrase mean, and why should we be aware of it when communicating in organizations?

4. Why is emotional contagion important in organizations and what effect does the increasing reliance of e-mail have on this phenomenon?

5. Under what conditions, if any, do you think it is appropriate or preferable to e-mail an employee that he or she has been laid off or fired? Aside from the symbolic concerns, what other communication problems might occur when using e-mail to layoff or fire someone?

6. Explain why men and women are sometimes frustrated with each other's communication behaviors.

7. In your opinion, has the introduction of e-mail and other information technologies increased or decreased the amount of information flowing through the corporate grapevine? Explain your answer.

8. The Bank of Key Largo (BKL) has just moved into one of the tallest buildings in Miami. Senior management is proud of its decision, because each department is neatly located on its own floor with plenty of closed offices. BKL executives have a breathtaking view from their offices on the top floor. There is even a large BKL branch at street level. Unfortunately, other tenants occupy some floors between those leased by BKL. Discuss the potential effects of this physical structure on communication at BKL.

CASE STUDY 11.1

BRIDGING THE TWO WORLDS: THE ORGANIZATIONAL DILEMMA

By William Todorovic, University of Waterloo

I had been hired by Aluminum Elements Corporation (AEC), and it was my first day of work. I was 26 years old, and I was now the manager of AEC's customer service group, which looked after customers, logistics, and some of the raw material purchasing. My superior, George, was the vice-president of the company. AEC manufactured most of its products from aluminum, the majority of which was destined for the construction industry.

As I walked around the shop floor, the employees appeared to be concentrating on their jobs, barely noticing me. Management held daily meetings, in which various production issues were discussed. No one from the shop floor was invited to these meetings, unless there was a specific problem. Later, I also learned that management had separate washrooms and separate lunchrooms, as well as other perks that floor employees did not have. Most of the floor employees felt that management, although polite on the surface, believed they had nothing to learn from the floor employees.

John, who worked on the aluminum slitter, a crucial operation required before any other operations could commence, had had a number of unpleasant encounters with George. As a result, George usually sent written memos to the floor in order to avoid a direct confrontation with John. Because the directions in the memos were complex, these memos were often more than two pages in length.

One morning, as I was walking around, I noticed that John was very upset. Feeling that perhaps there was something I could do, I approached John and asked him if I could help. He indicated that everything was just fine. From the looks of the situation, and John's body language, I felt that he was willing to talk, but John knew that this was not the way things were done at AEC. Tony, who worked at the machine next to John's, then cursed and said that the office guys only cared about schedules, not about the people down on the floor. I just looked at him; then I said that I had begun working here only last week and thought that I could address some of their issues. Tony gave me a strange look, shook his head, and went back to his machine. I could hear him still swearing as I left. Later I realized that most of the office staff were also offended by Tony's language.

On the way back to my office, Lesley, a recently hired engineer from Russia, approached me and pointed out that the employees were not accustomed to management talking to them. Management only issued orders and made demands. As we discussed the different perceptions between office and floor staff, we were interrupted by a very loud lunch bell, which startled me. I was happy to join Lesley for lunch, but she asked me why I was not eating in the office lunch room. I replied that if I was going to understand how AEC worked, I had to get to know all the people better. In addition, I realized that this was not how things were done and wondered about the nature of this apparent division between the management and the floor. In the lunchroom, the other workers were amazed to see me there, commenting that I was just new and had not learned the ropes yet.

After lunch, I asked George, my supervisor, about his recent confrontation with John. Surprised that John had gotten upset, George exclaimed, "I just wanted John to know that he did a great job, and as a result, we will be able to ship on time one large order to the West Coast. If fact, I thought I was complimenting him."

Earlier, Lesley had indicated that certain behavior was expected from management, and therefore from me. I reasoned that I do not think that this behavior works, and besides it is not what I believe or how I care to behave. For the next couple of months, I simply walked around the floor and took every opportunity to talk to the shop floor employees. Often when the employees related specific information about their workplaces, I felt that it went over my head. Frequently I had to write down the information and revisit it later. I made a point of listening to them, identifying where they were coming from, and trying to understand them. I needed to keep my mind open to new ideas. Because the shop employees expected me to make requests and demands, I made a point of not doing any of that. Soon enough, the employees became friendly and started to accept me as one of their own—or at least as a different type of a management person.

During my third month of work, the employees showed me how to improve the scheduling of jobs, especially those on the aluminum slitter. In fact, the greatest contribution was made by John, who demonstrated better ways to combine the most common slitting sizes and reduce waste by retaining some of the "common-sized" material for new orders. Seeing the opportunity, I programmed a spreadsheet to calculate and track inventory. This, in addition to better planning and forecasting, allowed us to reduce our new order turnarounds from four to five weeks to in by 10 A.M. out by 5 P.M. on the same day.

By the time I was employed for four months, I realized that staff from other departments came to me and asked me to relay messages to the shop employees. When I asked why they were delegating this task to me, they stated that I spoke the same language as the shop employees. Increasingly, I became the messenger for the office to floor shop communication.

One morning, George called me into his office and complimented me on the levels of customer service and the improvements that have been achieved. As we talked, I mentioned that we could not have done it without John's help. "He really knows his stuff, and he is good," I said. I suggested that we consider him for some type of promotion. Also, I hoped that this would be a positive gesture that would improve the communication between the office and shop floor.

George turned and pulled a flyer out of his desk; "Here is a management skills seminar. Do you think we should send John to it?"

"That is a great idea," I exclaimed. "Perhaps it would be good if he were to receive the news from you directly, George." George agreed, and after discussing some other issues, we parted company.

That afternoon, John came into my office, upset and ready to quit. "After all my effort and work, you guys are sending me for training seminars. So, am I not good enough for you?"

Discussion Questions

1. What barriers to effective communication existed in AEC? How did the author deal with these? What would you do differently?

2. Identify and discuss why John was upset at the end of the case. What do you recommend the writer should do at this time?

CASE STUDY 11.2

WATCH WHAT YOU PUT IN THAT OFFICE E-MAIL

BusinessWeek E-mail was supposed to be the communication cure for the masses—a miracle medium that would expedite projects at warp speed, facilitate multitasking, and smash corporate hierarchies. Instead, e-mail's greatest accomplishment seems to be that it has escalated office conflict to new heights. E-mail is also becoming famous for filling up our electronic mailboxes and providing a permanent record of things we should never have written down.

This *Business Week* case study looks at many problems with e-mail and outlines some of the explanations why these problems occur. Read through this *Business Week* article at www.mhhe.com/mcshane3e and prepare for the discussion questions below.

Discussion Questions

1. According to the sources described in this article, why do people tend to be ruder in e-mail messages than in face-to-face conversations?

2. Along with rudeness, what other problems with e-mail are identified in this article?

3. What does the author seem to recommend to minimize these problems with e-mail?

Source: M. Conlin, "Watch What You Put in that Office E-Mail," *Business Week,* September 30, 2002, p. 114.

TEAM EXERCISE 11.3

ANALYZING THE ELECTRONIC GRAPEVINE

Purpose This exercise is designed to help you understand the dynamics of grapevine communication.

Instructions This activity is usually conducted between classes as a homework assignment. The instructor will divide the class into teams (although this exercise can also be conducted individually). Each team will be assigned a large organization that has active posting on electronic grapevine websites such as Vault.com.

During the assignment, each team reads through recent postings of messages about the organization. Based on these raw comments, the team should be prepared to answer the following questions in the next class (or whenever the exercise is debriefed in class):

1. What are the main topics in recent postings about this organization? Are they mostly good or bad news? Why?

2. To what extent do these postings seem to present misinformation or conflicting information?

3. Should corporate leaders intervene in these rumors? If so, how?

ACTIVE LISTENING

By Mary Gander, Winona State University

Purpose This exercise is designed to help you understand the dynamics of active listening in conversations and to develop active listening skills.

Instructions For each of the four vignettes presented below, student teams (or students working individually) will compose three statements that demonstrate active listening. Specifically, one statement will indicate that you show empathy for the situation; the second asks for clarification and detail in a nonjudgmental way; the third statement will provide nonevaluative feedback to the speaker. Here are details about each of these three types of responses:

- *Showing empathy—Acknowledge feelings—* Sometimes it sounds like the speaker wants you to agree with him or her but, in reality, the speaker mainly wants you to understand how he or she feels. "Acknowledging feelings" involves taking in statements while looking at the "whole message," including body language, tone of voice, and level of arousal, and trying to determine what emotion is being conveyed. Then you let the speaker know that you realize he or she is feeling that emotion by just acknowledging it in a sentence.
- *Asking for clarification and detail while withholding your judgment and your own opinions—*This conveys that you are making an effort to understand and not just trying to push your opinions. To formulate a relevant question in asking for more clarification, you will have to listen carefully to what is said. Frame your question as someone trying to understand in more detail; often asking for a specific example is useful. This also helps the speaker evaluate his or her own opinions and perspective.
- *Providing nonevaluative feedback—feeding back the message you heard—*This will allow the speaker to determine if he or she really got the message across to you and help prevent troublesome miscommunication. It will also help the speaker become more aware of how he or she is coming across to another person (self-evaluation). Just think about what the speaker is conveying, paraphrase it in your own words, and say it back to the speaker (without judging the correctness or merit of what the speaker said), asking him or her if that is the intended meaning.

After teams (or individual students) have prepared the three statements for each vignette, the instructor will ask them to present their statements and explain how these statements satisfy the active listening criteria.

VIGNETTE 1

A colleague stops by your desk and says, "I am tired of the lack of leadership around here. The boss is so wishy-washy, he can't get tough with some of the slackers around here. They just keep milking the company, living off the rest of us. Why doesn't management do something about these guys? And *you* are always so supportive of the boss; he's not as good as you make him out to be."

VIGNETTE 2

Your co-worker stops by your cubicle, her voice and body language showing stress, frustration,

Discussion Questions
Develop three statements that respond to the speaker in this vignette by (1) showing empathy, (2) seeking clarification, and (3) providing nonevaluative feedback.

and even some fear. You know she has been working hard and has a strong need to get her work done on time and done well. You are trying to concentrate on some work and have had a number of interruptions already. She just abruptly interrupts you and says, "This project is turning out to be a mess. Why can't the other three people on my team quit fighting each other?"

VIGNETTE 3

One of your subordinates is working on an important project. He is an engineer who has good technical skills and knowledge and was selected for the project team because of that. He stops by your office and appears to be quite agitated; his voice is loud and strained, and his face has a look of bewilderment. He says, "I'm supposed to be working with four other people from four other departments on this new project, but they never listen to my ideas and seem to hardly know I'm at the meeting!"

Discussion Questions

Develop three statements that respond to the speaker in this vignette by (1) showing empathy, (2) seeking clarification, and (3) providing nonevaluative feedback.

Discussion Questions

Develop three statements that respond to the speaker in this vignette by (1) showing empathy, (2) seeking clarification, and (3) providing nonevaluative feedback.

VIGNETTE 4

Your subordinate comes into your office in a state of agitation, and asks if she can talk to you. She is polite and sits down. She seems calm and does not have an angry look on her face. However, she says, "It seems like you consistently make up lousy schedules. You are unfair and unrealistic in the kinds of assignments you give certain people, me included. Everyone else is so intimidated they don't complain but I think you need to know that this isn't right and it's got to change."

Discussion Questions

Develop three statements that respond to the speaker in this vignette by (1) showing empathy, (2) seeking clarification, and (3) providing nonevaluative feedback.

TEAM EXERCISE 11.5

CROSS-CULTURAL COMMUNICATION GAME

Purpose   This exercise is designed to develop and test your knowledge of cross-cultural differences in communication and etiquette.

Materials   The instructor will provide one set of question/answer cards to each pair of teams.

Instructions

- *Step 1*—The class is divided into an even number of teams. Ideally, each team would have three students. (Two or four student teams are possible if matched with an equal-sized team.) Each team is then paired with another team and the paired teams (Team A and Team B) are assigned a private space away from other matched teams.

- *Step 2*—The instructor will hand each pair of teams a stack of cards with the multiple-choice questions face down. These cards have questions and answers about cross-cultural differences in communication and etiquette. No books or other aids are allowed.

- *Step 3*—The exercise begins with a member of Team A picking up one card from the top of the pile and asking the question on that card to the students on Team B. The information given to Team B includes the question and all alternatives listed on the card. Team B has 30 seconds after the question and alternatives have been read to give an answer. Team B earns one point if the correct answer is given. If Team B's answer is incorrect, however, Team A earns that point. Correct answers to each question are indicated on the card and, of course, should not be revealed until the question is correctly answered or time is up. Whether or not Team B answers correctly, it picks up the next card on the pile and asks it to members of Team A. In other words, cards are read alternatively to each team. This procedure is repeated until all of the cards have been read or time has elapsed. The team receiving the most points wins.

Important Note The textbook provides very little information pertaining to the questions in this exercise. Rather, you must rely on past learning, logic, and luck to win.

Source: Copyright © 2001 Steven L. McShane.

ACTIVE LISTENING SKILLS INVENTORY

Purpose This self-assessment is designed to help you estimate your strengths and weaknesses on various dimensions of active listening.

Instructions Think back to face-to-face conversations you have had with a co-worker or client in the office, hallway, factory floor, or other setting. Indicate the extent that each item on the next page describes your behavior during those conversations. Answer each item as truthfully as possible so that you get an accurate estimate of where your active listening skills need improvement. Then use the scoring key in Appendix B to calculate your results for each scale. This exercise is completed alone so students assess themselves honestly without concerns of social comparison. However, class discussion will focus on the important elements of active listening.

ACTIVE LISTENING SKILLS INVENTORY

Circle the best response to the right that indicates the extent to which each statement describes you when listening to others.					Score
1. I keep an open mind about the speaker's point of view until he/she has finished talking..................	Not at all	A little	Some-what	Very much	_____
2. While listening, I mentally sort out the speaker's ideas in a way that makes sense to me..................	Not at all	A little	Some-what	Very much	_____
3. I stop the speaker and give my opinion when I disagree with something he/she has said...............	Not at all	A little	Some-what	Very much	_____
4. People can often tell when I'm not concentrating on what they are saying..........................	Not at all	A little	Some-what	Very much	_____
5. I don't evaluate what a person is saying until he/she has finished talking......................	Not at all	A little	Some-what	Very much	_____
6. When someone takes a long time to present a simple idea, I let my mind wander to other things...	Not at all	A little	Some-what	Very much	_____
7. I jump into conversations to present my views rather than wait and risk forgetting what I wanted to say...	Not at all	A little	Some-what	Very much	_____
8. I nod my head and make other gestures to show I'm interested in the conversation..........................	Not at all	A little	Some-what	Very much	_____
9. I can usually keep focused on what people are saying to me even when they don't sound interesting..	Not at all	A little	Some-what	Very much	_____
10. Rather than organizing the speaker's ideas, I usually expect the person to summarize them for me..	Not at all	A little	Some-what	Very much	_____
11. I always say things like "I see" or "uh-huh" so people know that I'm really listening to them..........	Not at all	A little	Some-what	Very much	_____
12. While listening, I concentrate on what is being said and regularly organize the information...........	Not at all	A little	Some-what	Very much	_____
13. While the speaker is talking, I quickly determine whether I like or dislike his/her ideas......................	Not at all	A little	Some-what	Very much	_____
14. I pay close attention to what people are saying even when they are explaining something I already know......................................	Not at all	A little	Some-what	Very much	_____
15. I don't give my opinion until I'm sure the other person has finished talking.....................................	Not at all	A little	Some-what	Very much	_____

Source: Copyright © 2000. Steven L. McShane.

After studying the preceding material, be sure to check out our website at
www.mhhe.com/mcshane3e
for more in-depth information and interactivities that correspond to this chapter.

Power and Influence in the Workplace

Learning Objectives

After reading this chapter, you should be able to:

■ Define the meaning of power and counterpower.

■ Describe the five bases of power in organizations.

■ Explain how information relates to power in organizations.

■ Discuss the four contingencies of power.

■ Explain how romantic relationships affect power dynamics in organizations.

■ Summarize the eight types of influence tactics.

■ Discuss three contingencies to consider when deciding which influence tactic to use.

■ Distinguish influence from organizational politics.

■ Describe the organizational conditions and personal characteristics that support organizational politics.

■ Identify ways to minimize organizational politics.

W orldCom, Inc. (now MCI, Inc.), was one of the world's largest telecommunications firms; now it's best known as one of the world's largest cases of accounting fraud. Two investigative reports concluded that CEO Bernie Ebbers, chief financial officer (CFO) Scott Sullivan, and a handful of other WorldCom executives initiated more than $9 billion of false or unsupported accounting entries over more than three years to overstate the company's financial well-being. How did this mammoth accounting scandal occur without anyone raising the alarm? Both reports concluded that Ebbers and Sullivan held considerable power and influence that prevented accounting staff from complaining, or even knowing, about the fraud.

Ebbers's inner circle held tight control over the flow of all financial information. Accounting groups were too geographically dispersed to share information and were discouraged by headquarters from doing so. Ebbers's group also restricted distribution of company-level financial reports and prevented sensitive reports from being prepared at all. Accountants didn't even have access to the computer files where some of the largest fraudulent entries were made. As a result, employees had to rely on Ebbers's executive team to justify the accounting entries that were requested.

Through excessive power and influence, former WorldCom CEO Bernard Ebbers (center in photo) and his inner circle of executives perpetrated one of the largest cases of accounting fraud in history.

Why didn't accounting staff ask for more information to satisfy their concerns? One reason was that CFO Scott Sullivan wielded immense personal power over employees. He was considered a "whiz kid" with impeccable integrity who had won the prestigious "CFO Excellence Award." Thus, when Sullivan's office asked staff to make questionable entries, some accountants assumed Sullivan had found an innovative—and legal—accounting loophole.

If Sullivan's expert power didn't work, other executives took a more coercive approach. Employees cited incidents where they were publicly berated for questioning headquarters's decisions and intimidated if they asked for more information. For example, when one employee in Washington, D.C., refused to alter an accounting entry, WorldCom's controller threatened to fly in from Mississippi to make the change himself. The employee changed the entry.

Ebbers had similar influence over WorldCom's board of directors. His personal charisma and intolerance of dissension produced a passive board that rubber-stamped most of his recommendations. As one report concluded: "The Board of Directors appears to have embraced suggestions by Mr. Ebbers without question or dissent, even under circumstances where its members now readily acknowledge they had significant misgivings regarding his recommended course of action."[1] ■

The WorldCom saga illustrates how power and influence can have profound consequences for employee behavior and the organization's success. Although this story has an unhappy ending, power and influence can equally influence ethical conduct and improve corporate performance. The reality is that no one escapes from organizational power and influence. They exist in every business and, according to some writers, in every decision and action.[2]

This chapter unfolds as follows: First, we define power and present a basic model depicting the dynamics of power in organizational settings. The chapter then discusses the five bases of power, as well as information as a power base. Next, we look at the contingencies necessary to translate those sources into meaningful power. Our discussion of power finishes with a look at recent studies of how office romances complicate power dynamics in organizations. The latter part of this chapter examines the various types of influence in organizational settings as well as the contingencies of effective influence strategies. The final section of this chapter looks at situations in which influence becomes organizational politics, as well as ways of minimizing politics.

The Meaning of Power

power
The capacity of a person, team, or organization to influence others.

Power is the capacity of a person, team, or organization to influence others.[3] Power is not the act of changing others' attitudes or behavior; it is only the *potential* to do so. People frequently have power they do not use; they might not even know they have power.

The most basic prerequisite of power is that one person or group believes it is dependent on another person or group for something of value.[4] This relationship is shown in Exhibit 12.1, where Person A has power over Person B by controlling something that Person B needs to achieve his or her goals. You might have power over others by controlling a desired job assignment, useful information, important resources, or even the privilege of being associated

EXHIBIT 12.1

Dependence in the power relationship

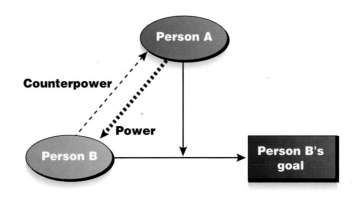

(Used with permission of Rapid Phase Ltd., www.madameve.co.za)

with you! To make matters more complex, power is ultimately a perception, so people might gain power simply by convincing others that they have something of value. Thus, power exists when others believe that you control resources that they want.[5]

Although power requires dependence, it is really more accurate to say that the parties are *interdependent*. One party may be more dependent than the other, but the relationship exists only when each party has something of value to the other. Exhibit 12.1 shows a dashed line to illustrate the weaker party's (Person B's) power over the dominant participant (Person A). This **counterpower,** as it is known, is strong enough to maintain Person A's participation in the exchange relationship. For example, executives have power over subordinates by controlling their job security and promotional opportunities. At the same time, employees have counterpower by controlling the ability to work productively and thereby creating a positive impression of the supervisor to his or her boss. Counterpower usually motivates executives to apply their power judiciously, so that the relationship is not broken.

counterpower

The capacity of a person, team, or organization to keep a more powerful person or group in the exchange relationship.

A Model of Power in Organizations

Power involves more than just dependence. As we see in Exhibit 12.2, the model of power includes both power sources and contingencies. It indicates that power is derived from five sources: legitimate, reward, coercive, expert, and referent. The model also indicates that these sources yield power only under certain conditions. The four contingencies of power include the employee's or department's substitutability, centrality, discretion, and visibility. Finally, as we will discuss later, the type of power applied affects the type of influence the powerholder has over the other person or work unit.

Sources of Power in Organizations

Over 40 years ago, social scientists John French and Bertrand Raven listed five sources of power within organizations: legitimate, reward, coercive, expert, and referent.[6] Many researchers have studied these five power bases and searched for others. For the most part, French and Raven's list remains intact.[7] The first three power bases are derived from the powerholder's position; that is, the person receives these power bases because of the specific authority or roles he or she is assigned in the organization. The latter two sources of

EXHIBIT 12.2

A model of power
within organizations

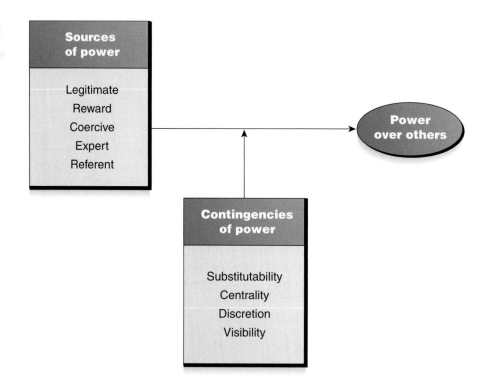

power originate from the powerholder's own characteristics. In other words, people bring these power bases to the organization.[8]

Legitimate Power

legitimate power
The capacity to influence others through formal authority.

Legitimate power is an *agreement* among organizational members that people in certain roles can request certain behaviors of others. This perceived right partly comes from formal job descriptions as well as informal rules of conduct. Executives have considerable legitimate power, but all employees also have this power based on company rules and government laws.[9] For example, an organization might give employees the right to request customer files if this information is required for their job.

Legitimate power depends on more than job descriptions. It also depends on mutual agreement from those expected to abide by this authority. Your boss's power to make you work overtime partly depends on your agreement to this power. Stories and movies about mutinies, such as *The Caine Mutiny* and *Crimson Tide*, provide extreme examples where leaders have acted outside this zone of mutual agreement. More frequently, employees question their boss's right to make them stay late or perform unsafe tasks and other activities. Thus, legitimate power is the person's authority to make discretionary decisions as long as followers accept this discretion.[10]

People in high power distance cultures (i.e., those who accept an unequal distribution of power; see Chapter 2) are more likely to comply with legitimate power than are people in low power distance cultures. Legitimate power is also stronger in some organizations than in others. A 3M scientist might continue to work on a project after being told by superiors to stop working on it because the 3M culture supports an entrepreneurial spirit, which includes ignoring your boss's authority from time to time.[11]

Crimson Tide is a riveting novel and film about the limits of legitimate power. When radical Russian nationalists threaten World War III, the nuclear submarine USS Alabama is sent to prepare for retaliation with its own nuclear arsenal. The signal to launch does come in, but a second message received soon after is incomplete before the sub goes into silent mode. The Alabama's commander, Captain Frank Ramsey (Gene Hackman, right in photo), is ready to have his crew push the button, whereas Lieutenant Commander Ron Hunter (Denzel Washington, left in photo) opposes this decision. What ensues is a mutiny that divides the loyalties of the Alabama's crew. The story illustrates how Captain Ramsay's decision and its consequences tested the limits of his legitimate power over his crew. What "mutinies" have you heard about in recent organizational settings? What commands triggered employees to refuse to obey their boss?

More generally, employees are becoming less tolerant of legitimate power. They increasingly expect to be involved in decisions rather than be told what to do. As one organizational behavior scholar states: "Command managers are an endangered species in North America. Their habitat is steadily shrinking."[12] Thus, the command style of leadership that often guided employee behavior in the past must be replaced by other forms, particularly expert and referent power, which are described below.

Reward Power

Reward power is derived form the person's ability to control the allocation of rewards valued by others and to remove negative sanctions (i.e., negative reinforcement). Managers have formal authority that gives them power over the distribution of organizational rewards such as pay, promotions, time off, vacation schedules, and work assignments. Employees also have reward power over their bosses through the use of 360-degree feedback systems (see Chapter 5). Employee feedback affects supervisors' promotions and other rewards, so they tend to behave differently toward employees after 360-degree feedback is introduced.

Coercive Power

Coercive power is the ability to apply punishment. In the opening story to this chapter, WorldCom executives demonstrated their coercive power by reprimanding employees and threatening to fire them. Employees also have coercive power, ranging from sarcasm to ostracism, to ensure that co-workers conform to team norms. Many firms rely on the coercive power of team members to control co-worker behavior.[13] Eaton Corporation's forge plant in South Bend, Indiana, may be one of them. "They say there are no bosses here," says an Eaton employee, "but if you screw up, you find one pretty fast." This situation isn't unusual. One-fifth of male and one-quarter of female Australian employees say they have been coerced by their colleagues to work less diligently.[14]

Expert Power

For the most part, legitimate, reward, and coercive power originate from the position. In contrast, *expert power* originates from within the person. It is an individual's or work unit's capacity to influence others by possessing knowledge or skills that they value. The opening story described how Scott Sullivan had expert power at WorldCom, which caused employees to unquestioningly accept his demands for dubious accounting entries. Employees are also gaining expert power as our society moves from an industrial to a knowledge-based economy.[15] The reason is that employee knowledge becomes the means of production and is ultimately outside the control of those who own the company. And without this control over production, owners are more dependent on employees to achieve their corporate objectives.

Referent Power

People have **referent power** when others identify with them, like them, or otherwise respect them. Like expert power, referent power comes from within the person. It is largely a function of the person's interpersonal skills and usually develops slowly. Referent power is usually associated with charismatic leadership. *Charisma* is often defined as a form of interpersonal attraction whereby followers develop a respect for and trust in the charismatic individual.[16]

Information and Power

Information is power.[17] This phrase is increasingly relevant in a knowledge-based economy. Information power derives from either the legitimate or expert sources of power described above and exists in two forms: (1) control over the flow and interpretation of information given to others and (2) the perceived ability to cope with organizational uncertainties.

Control over Information Flow   Not long ago, SAP, the German business-software company, introduced innovative ways for employees to receive the latest company news through their car radios, e-mail newsletters, and intranet websites. SAP employees appreciated this direct communication, but the company's middle managers objected because it undermined their power as the gatekeepers of company information.[18] Previously, SAP's middle managers were communication "traffic cops." Their job was to distribute, regulate, and filter out information throughout the organizational hierarchy. This right to

EXHIBIT 12.3

Power through the
control of
information

**Wheel formation
(centralized information flow)**

**All-channels formation
(decentralized information flow)**

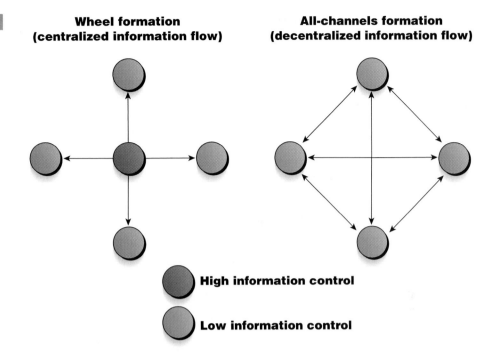

High information control

Low information control

control information flow is a form of legitimate power and is most common
in highly bureaucratic firms. The wheel formation in Exhibit 12.3 depicts this
highly centralized control over information flow. In this communication structure, employees are dependent on the information gatekeeper in the middle of
this configuration—such as the middle managers at SAP—to provide the information they require.

The problem facing these information gatekeepers is that this centralized
information control structure is incompatible with knowledge management
and high-performance work teams. Consequently, SAP and other organizations are encouraging more knowledge sharing by moving toward the all-
channels communication structure (see Exhibit 12.3) in which all employees
have relatively equal access to information. This allows employees and self-
directed work teams to make better decisions. In its purest form, the all-
channels network may seem chaotic, so large organizations with bureaucratic
cultures tend to slip back into the wheel pattern. The wheel pattern also
reemerges because, as we saw at SAP, it confers more power on those who distribute the information.[19]

Coping with Uncertainty   Organizations operate in changing environments,
so they depend on information to reduce the uncertainty of future events. The
more firms can cope with the uncertainty of future events, the more easily
they can achieve their goals.[20] Individuals and work units acquire power by
helping the organization to cope with uncertainty. Coping includes any activity that effectively deals with environmental uncertainties affecting the organization. A groundbreaking study of breweries and container companies identified three general strategies to help organizations cope with uncertainty.
These coping strategies are arranged in a hierarchy of importance, with the
first being the most powerful:[21]

- *Prevention*—The most powerful people are those who prevent environmental changes from occurring. For example, financial experts acquire power by preventing the organization from experiencing a cash shortage or defaulting on loans.
- *Forecasting*—The second most powerful people are those who can predict environmental changes or variations. In this respect, marketing specialists gain power by predicting changes in consumer preferences. Marian Salzman has considerable power, for instance, because the chief strategy officer at Euro RSCG Worldwide in New York City is a trendspotter with a solid reputation for identifying new directions in consumer behavior.[22]
- *Absorption*—People and work units also gain power by absorbing or neutralizing the impact of environmental shifts as they occur. An example is the ability of maintenance crews to come to the rescue when machines break down and the production process stops.

Contingencies of Power

Let's say that you have expert power by virtue of your ability to forecast and possibly even prevent dramatic changes in the organization's environment. Does this expertise mean that you are influential? Not necessarily. As we saw earlier in Exhibit 12.2, power bases generate power only under certain conditions. The four conditions—called the contingencies of power—include substitutability, centrality, discretion, and visibility.[23] These are not sources of power; rather, they determine the extent to which people can leverage their power bases. You may have lots of expert power, but you won't be able to influence others with this power base if the contingency factors are not in place.

Substitutability

substitutability

The extent to which people dependent on a resource have alternatives.

Substitutability refers to the availability of alternatives. Power is strongest when someone has a monopoly over a valued resource. Conversely, power decreases as the number of alternative sources of the critical resource increases. If you are the only expert in the organization on an important issue, you would be more powerful than if several people in your company possess this valued knowledge. Substitutability refers not only to other sources that offer the resource, but also to substitutions of the resource itself. For instance, labor unions are weakened when companies introduce technologies that replace the need for their union members. At one time, a strike by telephone employees would have shut down operations, but computerized systems and other technological innovations now ensure that telephone operations continue during labor strikes and reduce the need for telephone operators during normal operations. Technology is a substitute for employees and, consequently, reduces union power.

How do people and work units increase their power through nonsubstitutability? There are several ways, although not all of them are ethical. We describe some of them here for your information—not necessarily for you to practice.

- *Controlling tasks*—Governments pass laws that give certain professions an exclusive right to perform particular tasks. As an example, most countries require publicly traded corporations to have their financial statements audited by a specific accounting group (certified public accountants, chartered accountants, etc.). The simmering conflict between medical doctors and nurse practitioners is also based around the exclusive rights of doctors to perform specific medical procedures that nurse practitioners want within their mandate.

- *Controlling knowledge*—Professions control access to the knowledge of their work domain, such as through restricted enrollment in educational programs. Knowledge is also restricted on the job. Several years ago, maintenance workers in a French tobacco processing plant had become very powerful because they controlled the knowledge required to repair the tobacco machines.[24] The maintenance manuals had mysteriously disappeared and the machines had been redesigned enough that only the maintenance staff knew how to fix them if they broke down (which they often did). Knowing the power of nonsubstitutability, maintenance staff carefully avoided documenting the repair procedures and didn't talk to production employees about their trade knowledge.

- *Controlling labor*—People gain power by controlling the availability of their labor. Labor unions attempt to organize as many people as possible within a particular trade or industry so that employers have no other source of labor supply.[25] When unionized workers produce almost all of a particular product or service in a society, then the union has an easier time increasing wages. The union's power during a strike is significantly weakened when the employer can continue production through outside contractors or other non-union facilities.

- *Differentiation*—Differentiation occurs when an individual or work unit claims to have a unique resource—such as raw materials or knowledge—that the organization would want. By definition, the uniqueness of this resource means that no one else has it. The tactic here isn't so much the nonsubstitutability of the resource, but making organizational leaders believe that the resource is unique. Some people claim that consultants use this tactic. They take skills and knowledge that many consulting firms can provide and wrap them into a package (with the latest buzz words, of course) so that it looks like a service that no one else can offer.

Centrality

centrality
The degree and nature of interdependence between the powerholder and others.

While most airline employees have been restless for wage increases after years of modest gains, pilots have the most power to negotiate pay increases. "They have such power because they can ground the airline and in a couple of weeks it will have lost its profits for the entire year," says an airline investment analyst in London.[26] Airline pilots have considerable power because of their **centrality** in the organization. Centrality refers to the degree and nature of interdependence between the powerholder and others.[27] Airline pilots have high centrality because their actions affect many people and because their actions quickly affect other people. Think about your own centrality for a moment: If you decided not to show up for work or school tomorrow, how many people would be affected, and how much time would pass before they are affected? If you have high centrality, most people in the organization would be adversely affected by your absence, and they would be affected quickly.

Employees in the City of Toronto, Canada, picked an ideal time to leverage their power by going on strike in early summer. Tourism and the recreation of city residents were immediately affected by closed public swimming pools and canceled Toronto islands ferry services. A planned visit by the Pope in midsummer also put pressure on government officials to end the strike quickly. But the biggest factor was undoubtedly the stench of garbage that permeated the city. Without garbage collection, illegal dumps sprang up, and the heat of summer made living in Toronto a nightmare to many residents. "I can smell this through two doors, air conditioning, cologne and my own gym socks," quipped one resident. "I thought there was nothing stinkier than my gym socks. I was really wrong."[28] What contingencies of power gave the City of Toronto employees so much power in this strike?

Discretion

The freedom to exercise judgment—to make decisions without referring to a specific rule or receiving permission from someone else—is another important contingency of power in organizations. Consider the plight of first-line supervisors. It may seem that they have legitimate power over employees, but this power is often curtailed by specific rules. They must administer programs developed from above and follow specific procedures in their implementation. They administer rewards and punishments but must abide by precise rules regarding their distribution. Indeed, supervisors are often judged not on their discretionary skills but on their ability to follow prescribed rules and regulations. This lack of discretion makes supervisors largely powerless even though they may have access to some of the power bases described earlier in this chapter. "Middle managers are very much 'piggy-in-the-middle,'" complains a middle manager at Britain's National Health System. "They have little power, only what senior managers are allowed to give them."[29]

Visibility

Power does not flow to unknown people in the organization. Those who control valued resources or knowledge will yield power only when others are aware of these power bases, in other words, when it is visible.[30] Even someone's legitimate power has no effect until employees are aware of the person's position or status in the organization. One way to increase visibility is to take people-oriented jobs and work on projects that require frequent interaction with senior executives. "You can take visibility in steps," advises an executive at the pharmaceutical firm Searle. "You can start by making yourself visible in a small group, such as a staff meeting. Then when you're comfortable with that, seek out larger arenas."[31]

Employees also gain visibility by being, quite literally, visible. Some people strategically move into offices or cubicles where co-workers pass most often (such as closest to the elevator or office lunch room). Many professionals display their educational diplomas and awards on office walls to remind visitors of their expertise.[32] Other people play the game of "face time"—spending more time at work and showing that they are working productively. One engineer working on a color laser printer project made a habit of going to the office once each week at 2 A.M., after her boss once saw her working at that hour. "After the reaction I got from my manager I decided it was important to do that early morning work in the office," explains the engineer. "It is better to be seen here if you are going to work in the middle of the night."[33]

Another way to increase visibility is through **mentoring**—the process of learning the ropes of organizational life from a senior person within the company. Mentors give protégés more visible and meaningful work opportunities and open doors for them to meet more senior people in the organization. Mentors also teach these newcomers influence tactics supported by the organization's senior decision makers.[34]

mentoring
The process of learning the ropes of organizational life from a senior person within the company.

Networking and Power

"It's not what you know, but who you know that counts!" This often-heard statement reflects the reality that employees get ahead not just by developing their competencies, but by **networking**—cultivating social relationships with others to accomplish one's goals. Networking increases a person's power in three ways.[35] First, networks consist of people who trust each other, which increases the flow of information among those within the network. The more you network, the more likely you will receive valuable information that increases your expert power in the organization.

networking
Cultivating social relationships with others to accomplish one's goals.

Second, people tend to identify more with partners within their own networks, which increases referent power among people within each network. This network-based referent power may lead to more favorable decisions by others in the network. Finally, networking increases a person's visibility and possibly centrality, which are important contingencies of power. Networkers are better known in the organization, so their talents are more readily recognized. One recent study also found that networkers with high a self-monitoring personality tend to locate themselves in strategic positions in informal networks, so they gain centrality.[36] For example, you might be regarded as the main person who distributes information in the network or who keeps the network connected through informal gatherings.

Networking is a natural part of the informal organization, yet it can create a formidable barrier to those who are not actively connected to it.[37] Women are often excluded from powerful networks because they do not participate in golf games and other male-dominated social events. That's what Deloitte and Touche executives discovered when they investigated why so many junior female employees left the accounting and consulting firm before reaching partnership level. Deloitte and Touche now relies on mentoring, formal women's network groups, and measurement of career progress to ensure that female staff members have the same career development opportunities as their male colleagues.[38] Meanwhile, as Connections 12.1 describes, an increasing number of people in the business world are taking up golfing as a way to increase their power through networking.

Office Romance and Power

Our coverage of power in organizations would not be complete without considering the effect of workplace romance on power dynamics in organizations. The emerging reality is that many romantic relationships today are started in the workplace. A few recent surveys estimated that over 40 percent of employees in the United States and Canada have dated a co-worker, and

Golf Power

Lokendra Upadhyay is preparing for an important lesson in his MBA class at the University of Hartford. The pharmacy director at CIGNA and 18 other students are here to improve their golf swing and putting at the Pistol Creek Golf Club in Berlin, Connecticut. But today's lesson isn't just about golfing; it is also about networking on the golf course. "It's a great skill to have," says Upadhyay, who already plays golf half a dozen times a year. "A lot of deals are made on the golf course."

Americans play over 500 million rounds of golf each year, and many of those sessions result in valuable business connections and deals. Men have traditionally done most of this networking, but women are now developing their golfing skills to assist their power and influence in organizations. "We've heard so many times that a lot of business, a lot of networking and deal-making, gets done on the golf course," says Judith MacBride, a research director at the Conference Board of Canada. Her organization's research found that many women feel their career success has been restricted because they are not on the golf course with their male colleagues.

Maureen Grzelakowski agrees with that assessment. "You can be successful without knowing how to golf, but it's much more difficult," says the former high-tech executive who now owns the Oak Hills Country Club in Illinois.

To illustrate her point, Grzelakowski recalls as a Motorola executive the time she golfed on the French coast with the chief executive of a South African telecommunications company. A senior executive at rival Siemens AG didn't know how to golf and was worried about losing business to Grzelakowski, so he volunteered to caddie. Motorola and Siemens

Graduate business students at the University of Hartford take a few lessons on golfing and networking at the Pistol Creek Golf Club in Berlin, Connecticut.

wound up splitting the South African account. "He understood the importance of connecting with your customer," Grzelakowski advises.

Sources: B. Nagy, "Lesson on the Links," *Hartford Courant,* July 12, 2003; G. Burns, " 'Grass Ceiling' Impeding Women," *Chicago Tribune,* February 3, 2003, p. CN1; I. Bailey, "Golf 101: Put Down That Club, We're Making Deals Over Here," *National Post,* September 27, 2001. Rounds of golf in the United States are estimated in World Golf Foundation, *Golf 20/20: Vision for the Future,* May 2003; National Golf Course Owners Association, *2002 Rounds Played in the United States,* June 2002.

approximately half of all married couples in the United Kingdom apparently met in the workplace.[39]

Most people support the idea of forming romantic relationships at work, but many also recognize that they don't mix very well with organizational power. One concern is that co-workers tend to think employees in romantic relationships abuse their power by favoring their partner, particularly where one person in the relationship has higher status. One-third of employees in one study said that office affairs damage the work environment. Another poll found that almost 70 percent of employees disliked workplace romances between supervisors and subordinates because they can foster favoritism.[40]

Some experts say workplace romance rarely results in actual favoritism, but the Board of Commissioners in Arapahoe County, Colorado, might disagree with that assessment. A few Arapahoe County employees have complained about the romantic relationship of their boss, Tracy Baker, to a woman who reports to him. An investigation concluded that over three years Baker twice had promoted the woman from a junior position to become Baker's second-in-command, more than doubling her salary along the way. The investigation also concluded that Baker inappropriately had used department funds to entertain her and misused the e-mail system to send sexually explicit messages to her. The previous chief deputy clerk in Baker's office filed a lawsuit, claiming that Baker's office romance resulted in Baker's inappropriate behavior as well as her "loss of authority."[41]

Along with the risk or perception of favoritism, nearly one-quarter of sexual harassment cases are caused by office romances that fail. This problem can occur in one of two ways.[42] One situation occurs where one of the partners tries to continue the affair after the other partner has broken it off. The continued pursuit becomes harassment. The other situation occurs mainly in a supervisor–subordinate relationship. If the subordinate ends the relationship, the supervisor might create a hostile work environment through subtle day-to-day decisions. Even where the jilted supervisor acts appropriately, the subordinate may still feel intimidated by the former partner's power over work and career decisions.

Influencing Others

influence
Any behavior that attempts to alter another person's attitudes or behavior.

Thus far, we have focused on the sources and contingencies of power. But power is only the *capacity* to influence others. It represents the potential to change someone's attitudes and behavior. **Influence,** on the other hand, refers to any *behavior* that attempts to alter someone's attitudes or behavior.[43] Influence is power in motion. It applies one or more power bases to get people to alter their beliefs, feelings, and activities. Consequently, our interest in the remainder of this chapter is on how people use power to influence others.

Influence tactics are woven throughout the social fabric of all organizations. This is because influence is an essential process through which people coordinate their effort and act in concert to achieve organizational objectives. Some experts say that influencing others on matters of organizational value is central to the definition of leadership (see Chapter 14).[44] Influence operates down, across, and up the corporate hierarchy. Executives ensure that subordinates complete required tasks. Employees influence co-workers to help them with their job requirements. Subordinates engage in upward influence tactics so corporate leaders make decisions compatible with subordinates' needs and expectations.

Types of Influence Tactics

Organizational behavior scholars have devoted considerable attention to the various types of influence tactics found in organizational settings. Unfortunately, they do not agree on a definitive list of influence tactics. A groundbreaking study 25 years ago identified several influence strategies, but recent evidence suggests that some of them overlap.[45] The original list also seems to have a Western bias that ignores influence tactics used in non-Western cultures.[46] With these caveats in mind, let's look at the following influence tactics identified in the most recent literature (see Exhibit 12.4): silent authority, assertiveness, exchange, coalition formation, upward appeal, ingratiation and impression management, persuasion, and information control.

Silent Authority   The silent application of authority occurs where someone complies with a request because of the requester's legitimate power as well as the target person's role expectations. A frequent example occurs when you

EXHIBIT 12.4	Types of influence tactics in organizations

Influence tactic	Description
Silent authority	Influencing behavior through legitimate power without explicitly referring to that power base
Assertiveness	Actively applying legitimate and coercive power through pressure or threats
Exchange	Promising benefits or resources in exchange for the target person's compliance
Coalition formation	Forming a group that attempts to influence others by pooling the resources and power of its members
Upward appeal	Gaining support from one or more people with higher authority or expertise
Ingratiation/impression management	Attempting to increase liking by, or perceived similarity to, some targeted person
Persuasion	Using logical arguments, factual evidence, and emotional appeals to convince people of the value of a request
Information control	Explicitly manipulating someone else's access to information for the purpose of changing his or her attitudes and/or behavior

comply with your boss's request to complete a particular task. If the task is within your job scope and your boss has the right to make this request, then this influence strategy operates without negotiation, threats, persuasion, or other tactics.

Some OB experts overlook silent authority as an influence strategy, but it is the most common form of influence in high power distance cultures. Employees comply with supervisor requests without question because they respect the supervisor's higher authority in the organization. Silent authority also occurs when leaders influence subordinates through role modeling. One study reported that Japanese managers typically influence subordinates by engaging in the behaviors that they want employees to mimic.[47]

Assertiveness   In contrast to silent authority, assertiveness might be called "vocal authority" because it involves actively applying legitimate and coercive power to influence others. Assertiveness includes persistently reminding the target of his or her obligations, frequently checking the target's work, confronting the target, and using threats of sanctions to force compliance. Assertiveness typically applies or threatens to apply punishment if the target does not comply. Explicit or implicit threats range from job loss to losing face by letting down the team. Extreme forms of assertiveness include blackmailing colleagues, such as by threatening to reveal the other person's previously unknown failures unless he or she complies with your request.

Exchange   Exchange activities involve the promise of benefits or resources in exchange for the target person's compliance with your request. This tactic also includes reminding the target of past benefits or favors with the expectation that the target will now make up for that debt. The *norm of reciprocity* is a central and explicit theme in exchange strategies. According to the norm of reciprocity, individuals are expected to help those who have helped them.[48] Negotiation, which we discuss more fully in Chapter 13, is also an integral part of exchange influence activities. For instance, you might negotiate with your boss for a day off in return for working a less desirable shift at a future date. Networking is another form of exchange as an influence strategy. Active networkers build up "exchange credits" by helping colleagues in the short term for reciprocal benefits in the long term.

Networking as an influence strategy is a deeply ingrained practice in several cultures. The Chinese term *guanxi* refers to special relationships and active interpersonal connectedness. It is based on traditional Confucian values of helping others without expecting future repayment. However, modern *guanxi* seems to implicitly include long-term reciprocity, which can slip into cronyism. As a result, some Asian governments are discouraging *guanxi*-based decisions, preferring more arms-length transactions in business and government decisions.[49] *Blat* is a Russian word that also refers to special relationships or connections. Unlike *guanxi*, however, *blat* was originally associated with survival during times of scarcity and continues to have a connotation of self-interest and possible illegality.[50]

coalition

An informal group that attempts to influence people outside the group by pooling the resources and power of its members.

Coalition Formation   When people lack sufficient power alone to influence others in the organization, they might form a **coalition** of people who support the proposed change. A coalition is influential in three ways. First, it pools the power and resources of many people, so the coalition potentially has more influence than any number of people operating alone. Second, the coalition's mere existence can be a source of power by symbolizing the legitimacy of the issue. In other words, a coalition creates a sense that the issue deserves attention because it has broad support.[51] Third, a coalition taps into the power of the social identity process introduced in Chapter 3. A coalition is essentially an informal group that advocates a new set of norms and behaviors. If the coalition has a broad-based membership (i.e., its members come from various parts of the organization), then other employees are more likely to identify with that group and, consequently, accept the ideas the coalition is proposing.[52]

upward appeal

A type of coalition in which one or more members is someone with higher authority or expertise.

Upward Appeal   Have you ever had a disagreement with a colleague in which one of you eventually says "I'm sure the boss (or teacher) will agree with me on this. Let's find out!" This tactic—called **upward appeal**—is a form of coalition in which one or more members is someone with higher authority or expertise. Upward appeal ranges from a formal alliance to the perception of informal support from someone with higher authority or expertise. Upward appeal also includes relying on the authority of the firm as an entity without approaching anyone further up the hierarchy. For instance, one study reported that Japanese managers remind employees of their obligation to support the organization's objectives.[53] By reminding the target that your request is consistent with the organization's overarching goals, you are implying support from senior executives without formally involving anyone with higher authority in the situation.

ingratiation

Any attempt to increase liking by, or perceived similarity to, the targeted person.

Ingratiation and Impression Management   Upward appeals, assertiveness, and coalitions are somewhat (or very!) forceful ways to influence other people. At the opposite extreme is a "soft" influence tactic called **ingratiation.** Ingratiation includes any attempt to increase liking by, or perceived similarity to, some targeted person.[54] Flattering your boss in front of others, helping coworkers with their work, exhibiting similar attitudes (e.g., agreeing with your boss's proposal to change company policies), and seeking the other person's counsel (e.g., asking for his or her "expert" advice) are all examples of ingratiation. Ingratiation is potentially influential because this tactic increases the perceived similarity of the source of ingratiation to the target person. This similarity causes the target person to form more favorable opinions of the ingratiator. For example, if you ingratiate your boss, he or she is more likely to notice your good performance and attribute any performance problems to the situation rather than to your ability or motivation.

Notice that many ingratiation tactics are desirable behaviors that relate to organizational citizenship and information sharing.[55] However, people who are obvious in their ingratiation risk losing any influence because their behaviors are considered insincere and self-serving. The terms "apple polishing" and "brown-nosing" are applied to those who ingratiate to excess. Journalist Eric Starkman saw plenty of apple polishing several years ago when he worked at the *Detroit News*. Colleagues tried to gain favor with the newsroom boss by wearing the same clothes, including the boss's trademark suspenders and button-down shirts. "It boggled my mind how shameless some editors were," says Starkman. While subtle ingratiation may influence others, research indicates that people who engage in high levels of ingratiation are less (not more) influential and less likely to get promoted.[56]

Ingratiation is part of a larger influence tactic known as impression management. **Impression management** is the practice of actively shaping our public images.[57] Many impression management activities are done routinely to satisfy the basic norms of social behavior, such as the way we dress and how we behave toward colleagues and customers. Impression management is also a common strategy for people trying to get ahead in the workplace. For instance, almost all job applicants in a recent study relied on at least one type of impression management. An extreme example of impression management occurs when people pad their résumé. One study of 1.86 million background checks by a reference-checking firm revealed that about 25 percent of applicants falsify information about work experience and education.[58] However, as with ingratiation, employees who use too much impression management tend to be less influential because their behaviors are viewed as insincere.[59]

impression management
The practice of actively shaping one's public image.

Persuasion   **Persuasion,** one of the most frequently used influence strategies in organizations, is considered an important characteristic of leader effectiveness.[60] The literature on influence strategies has typically described persuasion as the use of reason through factual evidence and logical arguments. However, recent studies have begun to adopt a "dual process" perspective in which persuasion is influenced by both the individual's emotional reaction and rational interpretation of incoming information.[61] Thus, persuasion is an attempt to convince people by using emotional appeals as well as factual evidence and logical arguments.

persuasion
Using logical arguments, facts, and emotional appeals to encourage people to accept a request or message.

The effectiveness of persuasion as an influence tactic depends on characteristics of the persuader, message content, communication medium, and the audience being persuaded.[62] What makes one person more persuasive than another? One factor is the person's perceived expertise. Persuasion attempts are more successful when listeners believe the speaker is knowledgeable about the topic. People are also more persuasive when they demonstrate credibility, such as when the persuader does not seem to profit from the persuasion attempt and states a few points against the position.[63]

inoculation effect
A persuasive communication strategy of warning listeners that others will try to influence them in the future and that they should be wary about the opponent's arguments.

Message content is more important than the messenger when the issue is important to the audience. Persuasive message content acknowledges several points of view so the audience does not feel cornered by the speaker.[65] The message should also be limited to a few strong arguments, which are repeated a few times, but not too frequently.[66] The message content should use emotional appeals (such as graphically showing the unfortunate consequences of a bad decision), but only in combination with logical arguments so the audience doesn't feel manipulated.[67] Also, emotional appeals should always be accompanied with specific recommendations to overcome the threat. Finally, message content is more persuasive when the audience is warned about opposing arguments. This **inoculation effect** causes listeners to generate counterarguments to the anticipated persuasion attempts, which makes the opponent's subsequent persuasion attempts less effective.[68]

Two other considerations when persuading people are the medium of communication and characteristics of the audience. Generally, persuasion works best in face-to-face conversations and through other media-rich communication channels. The personal nature of face-to-face communication increases the persuader's credibility, and the richness of this channel provides faster feedback that the influence strategy is working. With respect to audience characteristics, it is more difficult to persuade people who have high self-esteem and whose targeted attitudes are strongly connected to their self-identity.[69]

Information Control   Persuasion typically involves selectively presenting information, whereas information control involves explicitly manipulating others' *access* to information for the purpose of changing their attitudes and/or behavior.[70] As described in the opening vignette for this chapter, this tactic was used by WorldCom's executive team to ensure that employees made illegal accounting entries. With limited access to vital information, accounting staff often did not realize that the entries violated accounting rules. Even employees who were suspicious had to trust explanations from headquarters that any irregularities were corrected elsewhere in the organization.

The WorldCom story is an extreme example of information control, but this influence tactic is quite common. Indeed, almost half of employees in one major survey believe people keep their colleagues in the dark about work issues if it helps their own cause.[71] Information control is frequently used as an upward influence strategy through the process of filtering (see Chapter 11).

Wearing his trademark black turtleneck and faded blue jeans, Apple Computer founder and CEO Steve Jobs is famous for stirring up crowds with evangelical fervor as he draws them into his "reality distortion field." The "Jargon Dictionary" claims the phrase originated at Apple in the 1980s to describe Jobs's peculiar knack for persuasiveness. A reality distortion field occurs when people are caught in Steve Jobs's visionary headlights and "become passionately committed to possibly insane projects, without regard to the practicality of their implementation or competitive forces in the marketplace." As one journalist wrote: "Drift too close to Jobs in the grip of one of his manias and you can get sucked in, like a wayward asteroid straying into Jupiter's gravitational zone."[64] In your opinion, how are people such as Steve Jobs so persuasive that they create a reality distortion field?

Specifically, lower level employees screen out information flowing up the hierarchy so higher level executives make decisions that are consistent with the preferences of lower level employees.

Contingencies of Influence Tactics

Now that we've covered the main strategies used to influence people, you are probably asking: Which influence tactics are best? Research has generally found that "soft" tactics such as friendly persuasion and subtle ingratiation are more acceptable than "hard" tactics such as upward appeal and assertiveness.[72] Soft tactics rely on personal power bases (expert and referent power), which tend to build commitment to the influencer's request. For example, coworkers tend to "buy in" to your ideas when you apply moderate levels of ingratiation and impression management tactics or use persuasion based on expertise. In contrast, hard influence tactics rely on position power (legitimate, reward, and coercion), so they tend to produce compliance or, worse, resistance in others. Hard tactics also tend to undermine trust, which can hurt future relationships. For example, coalitions are often successful, but their effect may be limited when the group's forcefulness is threatening.[73]

Aside from the general preference for soft rather than hard tactics, the most appropriate influence strategy depends on a few contingencies. One consideration is the influencer's power base.[74] Those with expertise may be more successful using persuasion, whereas those with a strong legitimate power base may be more successful applying silent authority. A related contingency is whether the person being influenced is higher, lower, or at the same level in the organization. Employees have some legitimate power over their boss, but they may face adverse career consequences by being too assertive with this power. Similarly, it may be more acceptable for supervisors to control information access than for employees to control what information they distribute to co-workers and people at higher levels in the organization.

A third contingency is cultural values and expectations. American managers and subordinates alike often rely on ingratiation because it minimizes conflict and supports a trusting relationship. In contrast, managers in Hong Kong and other high power distance cultures rely less on ingratiation, possibly because this tactic disrupts the more distant roles that managers and employees expect in these cultures. Instead, as we noted earlier, influence through exchange tends to be more common and effective in Asian cultures than in the United States because of the importance of interpersonal relationships (*guanxi*).[75]

The appropriateness of various influence tactics has also changed with emerging employment relationships and expectations of younger employees. Decentralizing authority, empowerment, and the increased emphasis on teams are challenging traditional applications of power through hierarchical control. Employees have gained more influence over organizational decisions, and they are increasingly wary of leaders who rely on legitimate, reward, and coercive power to control employee behavior. The general trend is toward more subtle influence tactics such as persuasion and exchange while assertiveness and silent authority will likely become less common supervisory tactics than they were a few decades ago.[76]

Gender Differences in Influence Tactics   Men and women seem to differ in their use of influence tactics. Some writers say that men are more likely than women to rely on direct impression management tactics. Specifically, men are more likely to advertise their achievements and take personal credit for successes of others reporting to them. Women are more reluctant to force the spotlight on themselves, preferring instead to share the credit with others. At the same time, women are more likely to apologize—personally take blame—even for problems not caused by them. Men are more likely to assign blame and less likely to assume it.[77]

Some research also suggests that women generally have difficulty exerting some forms of influence in organizations, and this has limited their promotional opportunities. In particular, women are viewed as *less* (not more) influential when they try to directly influence others by exerting their authority or expertise. In a study of job interviews, for example, direct and assertive female job applicants were less likely to be hired than were male applicants using the same influence tactics. Similarly, women who directly disagreed in conversations were less influential than women who agreed with the speaker.[78] These findings suggest that women may face problems applying "hard" influence tactics such as assertiveness. Instead, until stereotypes change, women need to rely on softer and more indirect influence strategies, such as ingratiation.

Influence Tactics and Organizational Politics

You might have noticed that organizational politics has not been mentioned yet, even though some of the practices or examples described over the past few pages are usually considered political tactics. The phrase was carefully avoided because, for the most part, "organizational politics" is in the eye of the beholder. I might perceive your attempt to influence our boss as normal behavior, whereas someone else might perceive your tactic as brazen organizational politics. This is why scholars mainly discuss influence tactics as behaviors and organizational politics as perceptions. The influence tactics described earlier are behaviors that might be considered organizational politics, or they might be considered normal behavior. It all depends on the observer's perception of the situation.

organizational politics
Behaviors that others perceive as self-serving tactics for personal gain at the expense of other people and possibly the organization.

When do influence tactics become organizational politics? Most scholars say that influence tactics are viewed as **organizational politics** when observers perceive that the tactics are self-serving behaviors to gain self-interests, advantages, and benefits at the expense of others and sometimes contrary to the interests of the entire organization or work unit.[79] Some influence behaviors, such as deliberately controlling the flow of information at WorldCom, are more likely to be considered political tactics. Perceptions of politics also vary with the perceiver's position and personal characteristics. Lower level employees are more likely than managers to view influence activities as organizational politics. Employees who feel they have less control over their work environment also have higher perceptions that the organization is political.[80]

While influence is sometimes beneficial to the organization, organizational politics is usually considered undesirable.[81] Indeed, employees who believe their organization is steeped in organizational politics have lower job satisfaction, organizational commitment, and organizational citizenship, as well as high levels of work-related stress. Organizational politics also increases the incidence of "neglect" behaviors, such as reducing work effort, paying less attention to quality, and increasing absenteeism and lateness (see EVLN model in Chapter 4).

Over one-third of management and nonmanagement employees recently surveyed claim that organizational politics is the most common reason for decision-making delays. Another survey estimates that business leaders spent nearly one-fifth of their time dealing with organizational politics.[82] They say this time is consumed addressing several problems created by political behaviors, such as lack of trust, reduced willingness to collaborate, reduced knowledge sharing, and misuse of organizational resources.

Conditions Supporting Organizational Politics

Organizational politics flourishes under the right conditions.[83] One of those conditions is scarce resources. When budgets are slashed, people rely on political tactics to safeguard their resources and maintain the status quo. Office politics also flourishes when resource allocation decisions are ambiguous, complex, or lack formal rules. This occurs because decision makers are given more discretion over resource allocation, so potential recipients of those resources use political tactics to influence the factors that should be considered in the decision. Organizational change encourages political behaviors for this reason. Change creates uncertainty and ambiguity as the company moves from an old set of rules and practices to a new set. During these times, employees act politically to protect their valued resources, position, and self-image.[84]

Last, organizational politics becomes commonplace when it is tolerated and transparently supported by the organization.[85] Companies sometimes promote people who are the best politicians, not necessarily the best talent to run the company. If left unchecked, organizational politics can paralyze an organization as people focus more on protecting themselves than fulfilling their roles. Political activity becomes self-reinforcing unless the conditions supporting political behavior are altered.

Personal Characteristics   Several personal characteristics affect a person's motivation to engage in organizational politics.[86] Some people have a strong need for personal as opposed to socialized power (see Chapter 5). They seek power for its own sake and use political tactics to acquire more power. People with an internal locus of control are more likely than those with an external locus of control to engage in political behaviors. This does not mean that internals are naturally political; rather, they are more likely to use influence tactics when political conditions are present because, unlike externals, they feel very much in charge of their own destiny.

Some individuals have strong **Machiavellian values.** Machiavellianism is named after Niccolò Machiavelli, the sixteenth-century Italian philosopher who wrote *The Prince*, a famous treatise about political behavior. People with high Machiavellian values are comfortable with getting more than they deserve, and they believe that deceit is a natural and acceptable way to achieve this goal. They seldom trust co-workers and tend to use cruder influence tactics, such as bypassing one's boss or being assertive, to get their own way.[87] We

Machiavellian values
The belief that deceit is a natural and acceptable way to influence others.

The Organizational Politics of Replacing Your Boss

Lyn Metcalf, chief executive of the City of South Perth, Western Australia, created the general manager's position and recommended to the city council that David Moylan was a good candidate for the job. This was a fateful recommendation because a few months later, Moylan's political tactics helped to remove Metcalf and promote Moylan to his boss's job as chief executive.

Almost as soon as Moylan was appointed general manager, he tried to convince city councilors that South Perth's administration required a major overhaul. Metcalf disagreed, saying that the organization just needed some "fine tuning" to get it running well. What Metcalf didn't know was that part of Moylan's proposed restructuring plan was to combine the chief executive position with the general manager job that Moylan had just accepted.

Soon after Moylan's appointment, Metcalf took sick leave to recover from a back operation, leaving another executive as acting CEO. Almost as soon as Metcalf took sick leave, Moylan produced a report to city councilors blaming Metcalf's leadership style and philosophy for the current problems and explaining that a new leader is needed for the proposed restructuring. During the subsequent Western Australian government inquiry into these events, Metcalf saw Moylan's report, calling it "a knife stuck well and truly in me. [It] sounds like a bit of an assassination."

Without authorization from the South Perth council, Moylan apparently took the initiative to visit Metcalf at his home during the sick leave to offer Metcalf the option of significantly reduced pay or quitting with a severance payment. Metcalf negotiated a large severance. Other city executives also left due to the proposed restructuring that Moylan orchestrated.

South Perth city general manager David Moylan was able to oust his boss, take his job, and introduce his restructuring plan through organizational politics.

The city then searched for a permanent CEO to replace Metcalf. Moylan was a frontrunner even though he lacked specialist skills for the position. Soon after, Moylan sent a memo to councilors explaining how he was the best person for the job. A few months after he was appointed general manager, Moylan moved into the chief executive's job. Less than one year later, however, Moylan was ousted when a Western Australian government inquiry concluded that his tactics were exercised without approval of elected officials.

Sources: J. Kelly, "Probe Tells of Secret Council Deals," *Sunday Times* (Perth), November 26, 2000, p. 1; J. Kelly, "Paid Off Then Promoted," *Sunday Times* (Perth), November 19, 2000, p. 5.

can see these characteristics in Global Connections 12.2, where a manager blatantly used political tactics to replace his boss as the top nonelected official of a city government.

Minimizing Organizational Politics and its Consequences

The conditions that fuel organizational politics also give us some clues about how to control dysfunctional political activities.[88] One strategy to keep organizational politics in check is to introduce clear rules and regulations to specify the use of scarce resources. Corporate leaders also need to actively support the all-channels communication structure described earlier in this chapter so that political employees do not misuse power through information control. As mentioned, organizational politics can become a problem during times of organizational change. Effective organizational change practices—particularly education and involvement—can minimize uncertainty and, consequently, politics, during the change process (see Chapter 17).

Organizational politics is either supported or punished, depending on team norms and the organization's culture. Thus, leaders need to actively manage group norms to curtail self-serving influence activities. They also need to support organizational values that oppose political tactics, such as altruism and customer focus. One of the most important strategies is for leaders to become role models of organizational citizenship rather than symbols of successful organizational politicians.

Along with minimizing organizational politics, companies can limit the adverse effects of political perceptions by giving employees more control over their work and keeping them informed of organizational events. Research has found that employees who are kept informed of what is going on in the organization and who are involved in organizational decisions are less likely to experience stress, job dissatisfaction, and absenteeism as a result of organizational politics.[89]

Chapter Summary

Power is the capacity to influence others. It exists when one party perceives that he or she is dependent on the other for something of value. However, the dependent person must also have counterpower—some power over the dominant party—to maintain the relationship.

There are five power bases. Legitimate power is an agreement among organizational members that people in certain roles can request certain behaviors of others. Reward power is derived from the ability to control the allocation of rewards valued by others and to remove negative sanctions. Coercive power is the ability to apply punishment. Expert power is the capacity to influence others by possessing knowledge or skills that they value. People have referent power when others identify with them, like them, or otherwise respect them.

Information plays an important role in organizational power. Employees gain power by controlling the flow of information that others need and by being able to cope with uncertainties related to important organizational goals.

Four contingencies determine whether these power bases translate into real power. Individuals and work units are more powerful when they are nonsubstitutable, that is, there is a lack of alternatives. Employees, work units, and organizations reduce substitutability by controlling tasks, knowledge, and labor, and by differentiating themselves from competitors. A second contingency is centrality. People have more power when they have high centrality, that is, the number of people affected is large and people are quickly affected by their actions. Discre-

tion, the third contingency of power, refers to the freedom to exercise judgment. Power increases when people have freedom to use their power. The fourth contingency, visibility, refers to the idea that power increases to the extent that a person's or work unit's competencies are known to others.

Networking involves cultivating social relationships with others to accomplish one's goals. This activity increases an individual's expert and referent power as well as visibility and possibly centrality. However, networking can limit opportunities for people outside the network, as many women in senior management positions have discovered.

Workplace romance has a complex effect on power in organizations. Co-workers tend to believe that employees in a sexual relationship will abuse their power. If the relationship ends, power imbalances between the two employees may lead to sexual harassment.

Influence refers to any behavior that attempts to alter someone's attitudes or behavior. Influence operates down, across, and up the corporate hierarchy, applies one or more power bases, and is an essential process through which people achieve organizational objectives. The most widely studied influence tactics are silent authority (influence through passive application of legitimate power), assertiveness (actively applying legitimate and coercive power), exchange (promising benefits or resources in exchange for compliance), coalition formation (a group formed to support a particular change), upward appeal (a coalition in which one or more members is someone with higher authority or expertise), ingratiation (any attempt to increase liking by, or perceived similarity to, some targeted person) and impression management (actively shaping our public images), persuasion (using logical arguments, factual evidence, and emotional appeals to convince people), and information control (explicitly manipulating access to information).

"Soft" influence tactics such as friendly persuasion and subtle ingratiation are more acceptable than "hard" tactics such as upward appeal and assertiveness. However, the most appropriate influence tactic also depends on the influencer's power base; whether the person being influenced is higher, lower, or at the same level in the organization; and the cultural values and expectations regarding influence behavior. Research also indicates that some influence tactics that are effective for men are ineffective for women.

Organizational politics refers to influence tactics that others perceive to be self-serving behaviors to gain self-interests, advantages, and benefits at the expense of others and sometimes contrary to the interests of the entire organization or work unit. Organizational politics is more prevalent when scarce resources are allocated using complex and ambiguous decisions and when the organization tolerates or rewards political behavior. Individuals with a high need for personal power, an internal locus of control, and strong Machiavellian values have a higher propensity to use political tactics.

Organizational politics can be minimized by providing clear rules for resource allocation, establishing a free flow of information, using education and involvement during organizational change, supporting team norms and a corporate culture that discourage dysfunctional politics, and having leaders who role model organizational citizenship rather than political savvy.

Key Terms

centrality, p. 365
coalition, p. 371
counterpower, p. 359
impression management, p. 372
influence, p. 369
ingratiation, p. 371
inoculation effect, p. 373
legitimate power, p. 360
Machiavellian values, p. 376

mentoring, p. 367
networking, p. 367
organizational politics, p. 375
persuasion, p. 372
power, p. 358
referent power, p. 362
substitutability, p. 364
upward appeal, p. 371

Discussion Questions

1. What role does counterpower play in the power relationship? Give an example of your own encounter with counterpower at school or work.

2. Several years ago, the major league baseball players association went on strike in September, just before the World Series started. The players' contract expired in the springtime, but they held off the strike until September when they would lose only one-sixth of their salaries. In contrast, a September strike would hurt the owners financially because they earn a larger portion of their revenue during the playoffs. As one player explained: "If we strike next spring, there's nothing stopping [the club owners] from letting us go until next June or July because they don't have that much at stake." Use your knowledge of the sources and contingencies of power to explain why the baseball players association had more power in negotiations by walking out in September rather than March.

3. You have just been hired as a brand manager of toothpaste for a large consumer products company. Your job mainly involves encouraging the advertising and production groups to promote and manufacture your product more effectively. These departments aren't under your direct authority, although company procedures indicate that they must complete certain tasks requested by brand managers. Describe the sources of power you can use to ensure that the advertising and production departments will help you make and sell toothpaste more effectively.

4. How does networking increase a person's power? What networking strategies could you initiate now to potentially enhance your future career success?

5. List the eight influence tactics described in this chapter in terms of how they are used by students to influence college instructors. Which influence tactic is applied most often? Which is applied least often, in your opinion? To what extent is each influence tactic considered legitimate behavior or organizational politics?

6. How do cultural differences impact the following influence tactics: (a) silent authority and (b) upward appeal?

7. A few years ago, the CEO of Apple Computer invited Steve Jobs (who was not associated with the company at the time) to serve as a special adviser and raise morale among Apple employees and customers. While doing this, Jobs spent more time advising the CEO on how to cut costs, redraw the organization chart, and hire new people. Before long, most of the top people at Apple were Jobs's colleagues, who began to systematically evaluate and weed out teams of Apple employees. While publicly supporting Apple's CEO, Jobs privately criticized him and, in a show of nonconfidence, sold 1.5 million shares of Apple stock he had received. This action caught the attention of Apple's board of directors, who soon after decided to replace the CEO with Steve Jobs. The CEO claimed Jobs was a conniving back-stabber who used political tactics to get his way. Others suggest that Apple would be out of business today if he hadn't taken over the company. In your opinion, were Steve Jobs's actions examples of organizational politics? Justify your answer.

8. This book frequently emphasizes that successful companies engage in knowledge management. What types of influence were described in this chapter that directly interfere with knowledge management objectives?

CASE STUDY 12.1

TRIVAC INDUSTRIES, INC.

TriVac Industries, Inc., an Akron, Ohio-based manufacturer of centralized vacuum systems, was facing severe cash flow problems due to increasing demand for its products and rapid expansion of production facilities. Steve Heinrich, TriVac's founder and majority shareholder, flew to Germany to meet with management of Rohrtech Gmb to discuss the German company's willingness to become majority shareholder of TriVac Industries in exchange for an infusion of much-needed cash. A deal was struck whereby Rohrtech would become majority shareholder while Heinrich would remain as TriVac's president. One of Rohrtech's senior executives would become the chairperson of TriVac's board of directors and Rohrtech would appoint two other board members.

This relationship worked well until Rohrtech was acquired by a European conglomerate two years later. Rohrtech's new owner wanted more precise financial information and controls placed on its holdings, including TriVac Industries, but Heinrich resented this imposition and refused to provide the necessary information. Relations between Rohrtech and TriVac Industries quickly soured to the point where Heinrich refused to let Rohrtech representatives into the TriVac Industries plant. He also instituted legal proceedings to regain control of the company.

According to the original agreement between TriVac and Rohrtech, any party who possessed over two-thirds of a company's shares could force the others to sell their shares to the majority shareholder. Heinrich owned 29 percent of TriVac's shares, whereas Rohrtech owned 56 percent. The remaining 15 percent of TriVac Industries shares were held by Tex Weston, TriVac's vice-president of sales and marketing. Weston was one of TriVac's original investors and a longtime executive at TriVac Industries, but he had remained quiet throughout most of the battle between Rohrtech and Heinrich. However, Weston finally agreed to sell his shares to Rohrtech, thereby forcing Heinrich to give up his shares. When Heinrich's bid for control failed, Rohrtech purchased all remaining shares and TriVac's board of directors (now dominated by Rohrtech) fired Heinrich as president. The board immediately appointed Weston as TriVac Industries' new president.

Searching for a New COO

Several months before Heinrich was fired as president, the chairman of TriVac's board of directors privately received instructions from Rohrtech to hire an executive search firm in New York to identify possible outside candidates for the new position of chief operating officer (COO) at TriVac Industries. The successful candidate would be hired after the conflict with Heinrich had ended (presumably with Heinrich's departure). The COO would report to the president (the person eventually replacing Heinrich) and would be responsible for day-to-day management of the company. Rohrtech's management correctly believed that most of TriVac's current managers were loyal to Heinrich, and by hiring an outsider the German firm would gain more inside control over its American subsidiary (TriVac).

The executive search firm identified several qualified executives interested in the COO position and the three candidates on the short list were interviewed by TriVac's chairman and another Rohrtech representative. One of these candidates, Kurt Devine, was vice-president of sales at an industrial packaging firm in Albany, New York, and, at 52 years old, was looking for one more career challenge before retirement. The Rohrtech representatives explained the current situation and said that they were offering stable employment after the problem with Heinrich was resolved so that the COO could help settle TriVac's problems. When Devine expressed his concern about rivalry with internal candidates, the senior Rohrtech manager stated: "We have a bookkeeper, but he is not our choice. The sales manager is capable, but he is located in California and doesn't want to move to Ohio."

One week after Heinrich was fired and Weston was appointed president, TriVac's chairman invited Devine to a meeting at a posh hotel attended by the chairman, another Rohrtech manager on TriVac's board of directors, and Weston. The chairman explained the recent events at TriVac Industries and formally invited Devine to accept the position of chief operating officer. After discussing salary and details about job duties, Devine asked the others whether he had their support as well as the support of TriVac's employees. The two Rohrtech representatives said yes, but Weston remained silent. When the chairman left the room to get a bottle of wine to toast the new COO, Devine asked Weston how long he had known about the decision to hire him. Weston replied: "Just last week when I became president. I was surprised. . . . I don't think I would have hired you."

Confrontation with Tom O'Grady

Devine began work at TriVac Industries in early October and, within a few weeks, noticed that the president and two other TriVac Industries managers were not giving him the support he needed to accomplish his work. For example, Weston would call the salespeople almost daily yet spoke to Devine only when Devine approached him first. The vice-president of sales acted cautiously toward Devine, whereas Tom O'Grady, the vice-president of finance and administration, seemed to resent his presence the most. O'Grady had been promoted from the position of controller in October and now held the highest rank at TriVac Industries below Devine. After Heinrich's departure, TriVac's board of directors had placed O'Grady in charge of day-to-day operations until Devine took over.

Devine depended on O'Grady for general operations information because he had more knowledge than anyone else about many aspects of the business. However, O'Grady provided incomplete information on many occasions and would completely refuse to educate the COO on some matters. O'Grady was also quick to criticize many of Devine's decisions and made indirect statements to Devine about his appropriateness as a COO. He also mentioned how he and other TriVac managers didn't want the German company (Rohrtech) to interfere with their company.

Devine would later learn about other things O'Grady had said and done to undermine his position. For example, O'Grady actively spoke to office staff and other managers about the problems with Devine and encouraged them to tell the president about their concerns. Devine overheard O'Grady telling another manager that Devine's memoranda were a "complete joke" and that "Devine didn't know what he was talking about most of the time." On one occasion, O'Grady let Devine present incorrect information to resellers (companies that sold TriVac products to customers) even though O'Grady knew that it was incorrect "just to prove what an idiot Rohrtech had hired."

Just six weeks after joining TriVac Industries, Devine confronted O'Grady with his concerns. O'Grady was quite candid with the COO, saying everyone felt that Devine was a "plant" by Rohrtech and was trying to turn TriVac Industries into a branch office of the German company. He said that some employees would quit if Devine did not leave because they wanted TriVac Industries to maintain its independence from Rohrtech. In a later meeting with Devine and Weston, O'Grady repeated these points and added that Devine's management style was not appropriate for TriVac Industries. Devine responded that he had not received any support from TriVac Industries since the day he had arrived even though Rohrtech had sent explicit directions to Weston and other TriVac managers that he was to have complete support in managing the company's daily operations. Weston told the two men that they should work together and that, of course, Devine was the more senior person.

Decision by TriVac's Board of Directors

As a member of TriVac's board of directors, Weston included Devine's performance on the January meeting's agenda and invited O'Grady to provide comments at that meeting. Based on this testimony, the board decided to remove Devine from the COO job and give him a special project instead. O'Grady was immediately named acting COO. The chairman and other Rohrtech representatives on TriVac's board were disappointed that events did not unfold as they had hoped, but they agreed to remove Devine rather than face the mass exodus of TriVac managers that Weston and O'Grady had warned about.

In late April, Devine attended a morning meeting of TriVac's board of directors to present his interim report on the special project. The board agreed to give Devine until mid-June to complete the project. However, the board recalled Devine into the boardroom in the afternoon and Weston bluntly asked Devine why he didn't turn in his resignation. Devine replied: "I can't think of a single reason why I should. I will not resign. I joined your company six months ago as a challenge. I have not been allowed to do my job. My decision to come here was based on support from Rohrtech and upon a great product." The next day, Weston came to Devine's office with a letter of termination signed by the chairman of TriVac's board of directors.

Discussion Questions

1. Identify the influence tactics used in this case. Which tactics were, in your opinion, incidents of organizational politics? Why?

2. What conditions seemed to support these influence tactics (and organizational politics) at Trivac?

Source: Copyright © 2002 Steven L. McShane. This case is based on true events, but dates, locations, names, and industry have been changed. Some events have also been changed or introduced for fuller case discussion.

CASE STUDY 12.2

A WHISTLE-BLOWER ROCKS AN INDUSTRY

BusinessWeek Douglas Durand was looking for new challenges when hired as vice-president for sales at TAP Pharmaceutical Products Inc. Instead, Durand experienced a gut-wrenching year in a workplace steeped with bribery and fraud. The Lake Forest, Illinois, company was lavishing doctors with perks for recommending their products and encouraging them to bilk federal and state medical programs by claiming full cost of free samples. Durand tried various ways to curtail these actions, but to no avail. Eventually, he collected evidence and became a whistle-blower.

This *Business Week* case study describes Durand's experiences at TAP Pharmaceutical Products and the process of whistle-blowing. It examines his attempts to influence salespeople and executives to stop the illegal activities, and the actions of TAP executives to discourage his complaints. Read through this *Business Week* article at www.mhhe.com/mcshane3e and prepare for the discussion questions below.

Discussion Questions

1. What influence tactics did Douglas Durand rely on to try to stop the illegal behavior at TAP Pharmaceutical Products? Were these actions successful? Why or why not?

2. What tactics did salespeople and executives at TAP Pharmaceutical Products use to influence Douglas Durand?

3. Which influence tactics, if any, identified in this case would you consider "organizational politics"? Why?

Source: C. Haddad, "A Whistle-Blower Rocks an Industry," *Business Week,* June 24, 2002, p. 126.

TEAM EXERCISE 12.3

BUDGET DELIBERATIONS

By Sharon Card, Saskatchewan Institute of Applied Science & Technology

Purpose   This exercise is designed to help you understand some of the power dynamics and influence tactics that occur across hierarchical levels in organizations.

Materials   This activity works best where one small room leads to a larger room, which leads to a larger area.

Instructions   These exercise instructions are based on a class size of about 30 students. The instructor may adjust the size of the first two groups slightly for larger classes. The instructor will organize students as follows: A few (three to four) students are assigned the position of executives. They are preferably located in a secluded office or corner of a large classroom. Another six to eight students are assigned positions as middle managers. These people will ideally be located in an adjoining room or space, allowing privacy for the executives. The remaining students represent the nonmanagement employees in the organization. They are located in an open area outside the executive and management rooms.

Rules   Members of the executive group are free to enter the space of either the middle management or nonmanagement group and to communicate whatever they wish, whenever they wish. Members of the middle management group may enter the space of the nonmanagement group whenever they wish but must request permission to enter the executive group's space. The executive group can refuse the middle management group's request. Members of the nonmanagement group are not allowed to disturb the top group in any way unless specifically invited by members of the executive group. The nonmanagement group does have the right to request permission to communicate with the middle management group. The middle management group can refuse the lower group's request.

Task   Your organization is in the process of preparing a budget. The challenge is to balance needs with the financial resources. Of course, the needs are greater than the resources. The instructor will distribute a budget sheet showing a list of budget requests and their costs. Each group has control over a portion of the budget and must decide how to spend the money over which they have control. Nonmanagement has discretion over a relatively small portion and the executive group has discretion over the greatest portion. The exercise is finished when the organization has negotiated a satisfactory budget or when the instructor calls time-out. The class will then debrief with the following questions and others the instructor might ask.

Discussion Questions

1. What can we learn from this exercise about power in organizational hierarchies?

2. How is this exercise similar to relations in real organizations?

3. How did students in each group feel about the amount of power they held?

4. How did they exercise their power in relations with the other groups?

SELF-ASSESSMENT EXERCISE 12.4

UPWARD INFLUENCE SCALE

Purpose This exercise is designed to help you understand several ways of influencing people up the organizational hierarchy as well as estimate your preferred upward influence tactics.

Instructions Read each of the statements on the next page and circle the response that you believe best indicates how often you engaged in that behavior over the past six months. Then use the scoring key in Appendix B to calculate your results. This exercise is completed alone so students assess themselves honestly without concerns of social comparison. However, class discussion will focus on the types of influence in organizations and the conditions under which particular influence tactics are most and least appropriate.

Source: C. Schriesheim and T. Hinkin, "Influence Tactics Used by Subordinates: A Theoretical and Empirical Analysis and Refinement of the Kipnis, Schmidt, and Wilkinson Subscales," *Journal of Applied Psychology* 75 (1990), pp. 246–57.

SELF-ASSESSMENT EXERCISE 12.5

PERCEPTIONS OF POLITICS SCALE (POPS)

Purpose This self-assessment is designed to help you to assess the degree to which you view your work environment as politically charged.

Instructions This scale consists of several statements that might or might not describe the school where you are attending classes. These statements refer to the administration of the school, not the classroom. Please indicate the extent to which you agree or disagree with each statement.

SELF-ASSESSMENT EXERCISE 12.6

MACHIAVELLIANISM SCALE

Purpose This self-assessment is designed to help you to assess the degree to which you have a Machiavellian personality.

Instructions Indicate the extent to which you agree or disagree that each statement in this instrument describes you. Complete each item honestly to get the best estimate of your level of Machiavellianism.

Upward Influence Scale

How often in the past 6 months have you engaged in the behaviors?	Never	Seldom	Occasionally	Frequently	Almost Always
1. I obtain the support of my co-workers in persuading my manager to act on my request............................	1	2	3	4	5
2. I offer an exchange in which I will do something that my manager wants if he or she will do what I want...............	1	2	3	4	5
3. I act very humble and polite while making my request..........	1	2	3	4	5
4. I appeal to higher management to put pressure on my manager..	1	2	3	4	5
5. I remind my manager of how I have helped him or her in the past and imply that now I expect compliance with my request...	1	2	3	4	5
6. I go out of my way to make my manager feel good about me, before asking him or her to do what I want............	1	2	3	4	5
7. I use logical arguments to convince my manager..................	1	2	3	4	5
8. I have a face-to-face confrontation with my manager in which I forcefully state what I want..............................	1	2	3	4	5
9. I act in a friendly manner toward my manager before making my request..	1	2	3	4	5
10. I present facts, figures, and other information to my manager in support of my position..........................	1	2	3	4	5
11. I obtain the support and cooperation of my subordinates to back up my request..	1	2	3	4	5
12. I obtain the informal support of higher management to back me..	1	2	3	4	5
13. I offer to make a personal sacrifice such as giving up my free time if my manager will do what I want..................	1	2	3	4	5
14. I very carefully explain to my manager the reasons for my request...	1	2	3	4	5
15. I verbally express my anger to my manager in order to get what I want..	1	2	3	4	5
16. I use a forceful manner; I try such things as demands, the setting of deadlines, and the expression of strong emotion...	1	2	3	4	5
17. I rely on the chain of command—on people higher up in the organization who have power over my supervisor..................	1	2	3	4	5
18. I mobilize other people in the organization to help me in influencing my supervisor......................................	1	2	3	4	5

After studying the preceding material, be sure to check out our website at

www.mhhe.com/mcshane3e

for more in-depth information and interactivities that correspond to this chapter.

Conflict and Negotiation in the Workplace

Learning Objectives

After reading this chapter, you should be able to:

■ Outline the conflict process.

■ Distinguish constructive from socioemotional conflict.

■ Discuss the advantages and disadvantages of conflict in organizations.

■ Identify six sources of organizational conflict.

■ Outline the five interpersonal styles of conflict management.

■ Summarize six structural approaches to managing conflict.

■ Outline four situational influences on negotiations.

■ Compare and contrast the three types of third-party dispute resolution.

To outsiders, Arthur Andersen's "One Firm" policy was solid. The Chicago-based accounting firm provided the same quality of work anywhere in the world by the same type of people trained the same way. But when Barbara Toffler joined Andersen as an ethics consultant in 1996, she discovered plenty of infighting. Arthur Andersen is now gone, the result of accounting fraud at its client Enron, but internal conflict may have contributed to the accounting firm's demise as well.

Much of the dysfunctional conflict was caused by Arthur Andersen's fee structure, which generously rewarded one engagement partner (the person in charge of the overall project) at the expense of other partners who provided services to the client. To maximize fees, executives fought over who should be the project's engagement partner and played games that would minimize the fees going to other groups. "While I was at Arthur Andersen, the fight for fees defined my existence," recalls Toffler.

While Arthur Andersen employees put up a united front during the firm's dying days (as this photo shows), the accounting firm suffered from internal battles.

In one incident, a partner demanded that he should be the engagement partner because he had made the initial connection with a client, even though the project relied mainly on expertise from Barbara Toffler's ethical practices group. The two argued all the way to the airport and in several subsequent "violent" phone arguments. In another client proposal, Toffler flew to Japan, only to spend two days of her time there negotiating through a translator with Andersen's Japanese engagement partner over how to split fees.

In a third incident, several Arthur Andersen partners met with a potential client supposedly to discuss their services. Instead, the partners openly criticized each other during the pitch so the client would spend more money on their particular specialization. A couple of partners also extended the length of their presentations so other partners would have less time to convince the client of their particular value in the project. "Eventually, I learned to screw someone else before they screwed me," says Toffler. "The struggle to win fees for your office and your group—and *not* someone else's—came to define the Firm."[1] ■

conflict
The process in which one party perceives that its interests are being opposed or negatively affected by another party.

Backstabbing and infighting over fees at Arthur Andersen illustrates the problems that can result from conflict in organizations. **Conflict** is a process in which one party perceives that its interests are being opposed or negatively affected by another party.[2] Arthur Andersen's partners experienced conflict because they saw each other as competitors vying for the same scarce resources (client fees) on projects where they had to work interdependently. This chapter looks at the dynamics of conflict in organizational settings. We begin by describing the conflict process and discussing the consequences and sources of conflict in organizational settings. Five conflict management styles are then described, followed by a discussion of the structural approaches to conflict management. The last two sections of this chapter introduce two procedures for resolving conflict: negotiation and third-party resolution.

The Conflict Process

When describing an incident involving conflict, we are usually referring to the observable part of conflict—the angry words, shouting matches, and actions that symbolize opposition. But this *manifest conflict* is only a small part of the conflict process. As Exhibit 13.1 illustrates, the conflict process begins with the sources of conflict.[3] Incompatible goals, different values, and other conditions lead one or both parties to perceive that conflict exists. We will look closely at these sources of conflict later in this chapter because understanding and changing the root causes is the key to effective conflict management.

Conflict Perceptions and Emotions

At some point, the sources of conflict lead one or both parties to perceive that conflict exists. Each party also experiences various conflict-laden emotions toward the other. For example, Barbara Toffler experienced tension and anger with other Andersen consultants who competed against her for fees.

Constructive versus Socioemotional Conflict   Is conflict always bad for organizations? Not necessarily. In Chapter 10, we learned that constructive conflict (also known as *task-related conflict*) potentially improves team decision making.[4] Constructive conflict occurs when team members debate their different perceptions about an issue in a way that keeps the conflict focused on the task

EXHIBIT 13.1

The conflict process

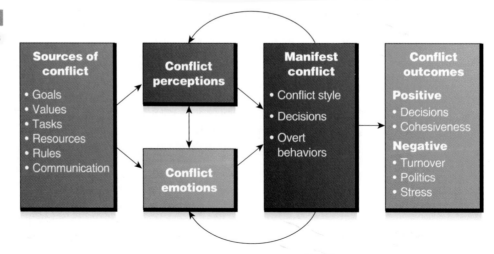

rather than people. This form of conflict is *constructive* because participants learn about other points of view, which encourages them to reexamine their basic assumptions about a problem and its possible solution. It also tests the logic of arguments presented in the debate.

Unfortunately, conflict often becomes emotional and personal. Rather than focusing on the issue, each party perceives the other party as the problem. This condition, called *socioemotional conflict,* is apparent when differences are viewed as personal attacks rather than attempts to resolve an issue. The discussion becomes emotionally charged, which introduces perceptual biases and distorts information processing.

Most research generally supports the benefits of constructive conflict and the adverse consequences of socioemotional conflict, but the situation is a little more complex than this. A major analysis of past studies recently concluded that both constructive and socioemotional conflict have a negative effect on team performance.[5] One explanation may be that any level of conflict produces negative emotions that interfere with interpersonal relationships among team members. People might make better decisions through constructive debate, but the emotions generated through this process undermine how well they work together after the debate is over. Consistent with this explanation, the recent study reported that teams with high levels of team trust and norms of openness are less likely to have negative consequences from constructive conflict. These are conditions that reduce the generation of emotions during debate. Overall, some conflict (specifically constructive conflict) can be good, but only under the right conditions.

Manifest Conflict

Conflict perceptions and emotions usually manifest themselves in the decisions and overt behaviors of one party toward the other. These conflict episodes may range from subtle nonverbal behaviors to warlike aggression. Conflict is also manifested by the style each side uses to resolve the conflict: Does one side try to defeat the other or to find a mutually beneficial solution, for example? Conflict management styles will be described later in this chapter. At this point, you should know that these styles influence each side's decisions and behaviors. Consequently, they play a critical role in determining whether the conflict will escalate or be quickly resolved.

Conflict Escalation Cycle   The conflict process in Exhibit 13.1 shows arrows looping back from manifest conflict to conflict perceptions and emotions. These loops represent the fact that the conflict process is really a series of episodes that potentially link in an escalation cycle or spiral.[6] It doesn't take much to start this conflict cycle—just an inappropriate comment, a misunderstanding, or an undiplomatic action. These behaviors communicate to the other party in a way that creates a perception of conflict. If the first party did not intend to demonstrate conflict, then the second party's response may create that perception.

If the conflict remains constructive, both parties may resolve the conflict through logical analysis. However, the communication process has enough ambiguity that a wrong look or word may trigger an emotional response by the other side and set the stage for socioemotional conflict. These distorted beliefs and emotions reduce each side's motivation to communicate, making it more difficult for them to discover common ground and ultimately resolve the conflict.[7] The parties then rely more on stereotypes and emotions to reinforce their perceptions of the other party. Some structural conditions increase the likelihood of conflict escalation. Employees who are more confrontational and less diplomatic also tend to escalate conflict.[8]

Conflict Outcomes

Angela regards herself as a nice person, but conflict with another employee put her in touch with the darker side of her personality. "I never thought I had this black spot in my soul until this person made my life hell," says the projects officer at a consulting firm. The colleague was a good friend until accusing Angela of "stealing" an important client. Relations deteriorated as the colleague responded by spreading malicious and untrue gossip about Angela. Angela complained, but her superiors didn't act on it for several months. The colleague was eventually fired.[9]

This true incident illustrates how misunderstandings and disagreements escalate into socioemotional conflict, which results in negative outcomes for the organization. "The conflict was bad for business," Angela recalls, "because it affected staff decisions and took the focus off making money." Socioemotional conflict increases frustration, job dissatisfaction, and stress. In the longer term, this leads to increased turnover and absenteeism.[10]

These symptoms are showing up among executives at the Walt Disney Company. Disney CEO Michael Eisner apparently supports an environment where executives battle each other over scarce resources. Insiders claim that several people left Disney because constant conflict wore them down.[11] At the intergroup level, conflict with people outside the team may lead to groupthink. The conflict increases cohesiveness within the group, but members value consensus so much that it undermines decision quality.[12]

Given these problems, it's not surprising that people normally associate **conflict management** with reducing or removing conflict. However,

Southwest Airlines is best known as a "fun" place to work, but the company also encourages lots of debate among its employees so that the best ideas are scrutinized. "I find it helpful to encourage people to express differing points of view and bring evidence to support their points of view to the table," says Jim Parker, Southwest's incoming CEO. Parker is shown here at left with Southwest's founder and past CEO Herb Kelleher as well as executive vice-president Colleen Barrett. "It's usually through that constructive conflict of ideas that the better idea will emerge."[13] What conditions must apply to ensure that constructive conflict is beneficial and doesn't turn into socioemotional conflict?

conflict management
Interventions that alter the level and form of conflict in ways that maximize its benefits and minimize its dysfunctional consequences.

conflict management isn't necessarily about minimizing conflict. It refers to interventions that alter the level and form of conflict in ways that maximize its benefits and minimize its dysfunctional consequences. This sometimes means increasing the level of constructive conflict. As we noted earlier and in Chapter 10, constructive conflict should be encouraged under some conditions because it potentially helps people to recognize problems, identify a variety of solutions, and better understand the relevant issues.

Conflict is also beneficial where intergroup conflict improves team dynamics within those units. Teams increase their cohesiveness and task orientation when they face an external threat. Under conditions of moderate conflict, this motivates team members to work more efficiently toward these goals, thereby increasing the team's productivity.

Sources of Conflict in Organizations

Manifest conflict is really the tip of the proverbial iceberg. What we really need to understand are the sources of this conflict, which lie under the surface. The six main conditions that cause conflict in organizational settings are shown in Exhibit 13.2.

Incompatible Goals

A common source of conflict is goal incompatibility.[14] Goal incompatibility occurs when personal or work goals seem to interfere with another person's or department's goals. This source of conflict was apparent in the infighting over fees at Arthur Andersen, described at the beginning of this chapter. It is also the main source of conflict between the original Air Canada pilots and the pilots who previously worked at Canadian Airlines (which Air Canada acquired a few years ago). As Global Connections 13.1 describes, pilots in each group want to receive the highest possible seniority to improve their career and job status. But if the former Canadian Airlines pilots get their wish to have seniority levels comparable to their previous jobs, then many Air Canada pilots will have relatively lower seniority, resulting in lower salaries and less desirable duties. The preference of Air Canada pilots is to deny any seniority to the former Canadian Airlines pilots. This battle has produced considerable manifest conflict, including fistfights on the buses taking pilots to work! The point here is that people with divergent goals are more likely to experience conflict.

Differentiation

Not long ago, a British automotive company proposed a friendly buyout of an Italian firm. Executives at both companies were excited about the opportunities for sharing distribution channels and manufacturing technologies. But the grand vision of a merged company turned to a nightmare as executives

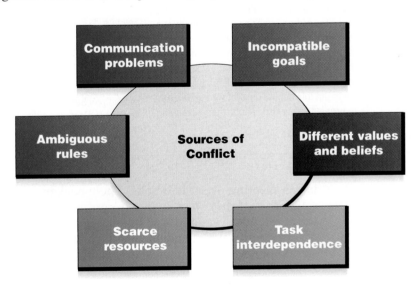

EXHIBIT 13.2

Sources of conflict in organizations

Midair Conflicts for Air Canada and Former Canadian Airlines Pilots

For almost two years after Air Canada acquired its archrival Canadian Airlines, a solid wall divided pilots from the two airlines. One door at Pearson International Airport in Toronto led to the large crew room where the 2,400 Air Canada pilots prepare for their flights. Another door further up the hallway led to a much smaller room for the 1,200 former Canadian Airlines pilots.

The physical wall dividing the two rooms is now gone, but the psychological wall of conflict is as strong as ever. "There will always be a wall there in our eyes," admits Robert Cohen, a Canadian Airlines first officer with 13 years of experience at the former airline. "We will not mingle with those people and the feeling is mutual. They [Air Canada pilots] don't even want us in their system. It's evident."

The conflict between Air Canada and former Canadian Airlines pilots is mainly a battle over seniority rights. Many Air Canada pilots believe the Canadian Airlines pilots should be placed at the bottom of the seniority list because Canadian Airlines would have gone bankrupt if Air Canada hadn't acquired it. Canadian Airlines pilots, on the other hand, believe they are entitled to the same rights and seniority because technically the two airlines merged. The outcome is critical because seniority determines the aircraft and routes pilots fly as well as their days off, vacation, pay, and pensions. "For a pilot, seniority is everything," says Peter Foster, spokesman for the Air Canada Pilots Association.

The two pilot groups tried to negotiate a single seniority list, but the effort failed after one day. A subsequent arbitration decision discounted the seniority of Canadian Airlines pilots by an average of more than nine years, which outraged the Canadian Airlines pilots. A federal labor board later agreed with Canadian Airlines pilots and a subsequent arbitration decision favored the former Canadian Airlines pilots, which angered the Air Canada pilots. Now, the federal labor board will conduct a "limited review" of the latest arbitration decision.

"This is a divisive issue and the longer it goes on, the more divisive it gets," complains Captain Rob McInnis, head of the committee acting for the former Canadian Airlines pilots. "It's our view that it's time to put this behind us, that Air Canada has much more serious problems to worry about than scrapping pilots."

Conflict between Air Canada pilots and former Canadian Airlines pilots has created tension and ill feelings as they battle over seniority rights.

Sources: S. Pigg, "Panel to Review Pilots' Seniority," *Toronto Star,* June 27, 2003, p. E1; S. Pigg, "Pilots Get New Deadlines in Dispute over Seniority," *Toronto Star,* October 4, 2002, p. C2; S. Pigg, "Pilot Seniority Issue Reopened," *Toronto Star,* July 11, 2002, p. C12; S. Pigg, "Air Canada: An Airline Divided, *Toronto Star,* June 2, 2001, p. E1; K. McArthur, "Air Canada Pilot Seniority Feelings Run High: 'Scuffles on the Crew Bus,'" *Canadian Press,* April 3, 2001; A. Swift, "Pilots for Air Canada, Canadian Airlines Begin Campaign for One Union," *Canadian Press,* January 6, 2001.

began meeting over the details. Their backgrounds and experiences were so different that they were endlessly confused and constantly apologizing to the other side for oversights and misunderstandings. At one meeting—the last as it turned out—the president of the Italian firm stood up and, smiling sadly, said, "I believe we all know what is the problem here . . . it seems your forward is our reverse; your down, our up; your right, our wrong. Let us finish now, before war is declared."[15]

These automobile executives discovered that conflict is often caused by different values and beliefs due to unique backgrounds, experiences, or training. Mergers often produce conflict because they bring together people with divergent corporate cultures. Employees fight over the "right way" to do things because of their unique experiences in the separate companies. The British and Italian automobile executives probably also experienced conflict due to different national cultures. Cultural diversity makes it difficult to understand or accept the beliefs and values that other people hold toward organizational decisions and events.

Many companies are also experiencing the rising incidence of cross-generational conflict.[16] Generation gaps have always existed, but cross-generational conflict is more common today because employees across age groups work together more than ever before. Younger and older employees have different needs, different expectations, and somewhat different values. This differentiation appears in many types of conflict. For example, younger and older employees at Techneglas Inc.'s factory in Columbus, Ohio, recently experienced conflict with each other over a proposed work schedule. Younger employees value more time off, so they wanted 12-hour shifts with bigger blocks of time off work. But many of the older Techneglas employees insisted on sticking to the current eight-hour shift schedule because it lets them work overtime with less fatigue. "The old people don't have a life," snaps one of the younger Techneglas employees. "Their jobs are their lives."[17]

Task Interdependence

Conflict tends to increase with the level of task interdependence. Task interdependence exists when team members must share common inputs to their individual tasks, need to interact in the process of executing their work, or receive outcomes (such as rewards) that are partly determined by the performance of others. The higher the level of task interdependence, the greater the risk of conflict, because there is a greater chance that each side will disrupt or interfere with the other side's goals.[18]

Other than complete independence, employees tend to have the lowest risk of conflict when working with others in a *pooled interdependence* relationship. As we described in Chapter 9, pooled interdependence occurs where individuals operate independently except for reliance on a common resource or authority. The potential for conflict is higher in *sequential interdependence* work relationships, such as an assembly line. The highest risk of conflict tends to occur in *reciprocal interdependence* situations. With reciprocal interdependence, employees are highly dependent on each other and, consequently, have a higher probability of interfering with each other's work and personal goals.

Scarce Resources

Scarce resources generate conflict because scarcity motivates people to compete with others who also need those resources to achieve their objectives.[19] Arthur Andersen partners wouldn't feud over fees, and Air Canada pilots wouldn't battle over seniority if everyone could receive what they want. The reality, however, is that Arthur Andersen consultants and Air Canada pilots must share scarce resources. The result is that each group's goals interfere with the goals of other groups because there isn't enough of the resource for everyone.

Ambiguous Rules

Ambiguous rules—or the complete lack of rules—breed conflict. This occurs because uncertainty increases the risk that one party intends to interfere with the other party's goals. Ambiguity also encourages political tactics and, in some cases, employees enter a free-for-all battle to win decisions in their favor. This explains why conflict is more common during mergers and acquisitions. Employees from both companies have conflicting practices and values, and few rules have developed to minimize the maneuvering for power and resources.[20] When clear rules exist, on the other hand, employees know what to expect from each other and have agreed to abide by those rules.

Communication Problems

Conflict often occurs due to the lack of opportunity, ability, or motivation to communicate effectively. Let's look at each of these causes. First, when two parties lack the opportunity to communicate, they tend to use stereotypes to explain past behaviors and anticipate future actions. Unfortunately, stereotypes are sufficiently subjective that emotions can negatively distort the meaning of an opponent's actions, thereby escalating perceptions of conflict. Moreover, without direct interaction, the two sides have less psychological empathy for each other.

Second, some people lack the necessary skills to communicate in a diplomatic, nonconfrontational manner. When one party communicates its disagreement in an arrogant way, opponents are more likely to heighten their perception of the conflict. Arrogant behavior also sends a message that one side intends to be competitive rather than cooperative. This may lead the other party to reciprocate with a similar conflict management style.[21] Consequently, as we explained earlier, ineffective communication often leads to an escalation in the conflict cycle.

Ineffective communication can also lead to a third problem: less motivation to communicate in the future. Socioemotional conflict is uncomfortable, so people avoid interacting with others in a conflicting relationship. Unfortunately, less communication can further escalate the conflict because there is less opportunity to empathize with the opponent's situation and opponents are more likely to rely on distorted stereotypes of the other party. In fact, conflict tends to further distort these stereotypes through the process of social identity (see Chapter 3). We begin to see competitors less favorably so that our self-identity remains strong during these uncertain times.[22]

win–win orientation
The belief that the parties will find a mutually beneficial solution to their disagreement.

The lack of motivation to communicate also explains (along with different values and beliefs, described earlier) why conflict is more common in cross-cultural relationships. People tend to feel uncomfortable or awkward interacting with co-workers from different cultures, so they are less motivated to engage in dialogue with them.[23] With limited communication, people rely more on stereotypes to fill in missing information. They also tend to misunderstand each other's verbal and nonverbal signals, further escalating the conflict.

Interpersonal Conflict Management Styles

The six structural conditions described above set the stage for conflict. The conflict process identified earlier in Exhibit 13.1 illustrated that these sources of conflict lead to perceptions and emotions. Some people enter a conflict with a **win–win orientation.** This is the perception that the parties will find a mu-

win–lose orientation

The belief that conflicting parties are drawing from a fixed pie, so the more one party receives, the less the other party will receive.

tually beneficial solution to their disagreement. They believe that the resources at stake are expandable rather than fixed if the parties work together to find a creative solution. Other people enter a conflict with a **win–lose orientation.** They adopt the belief that the parties are drawing from a fixed pie, so the more one party receives, the less the other party will receive.

Conflict tends to escalate when the parties develop a win–lose orientation because they rely on more assertive influence tactics to gain advantage. A win–lose orientation may occasionally be appropriate when the conflict really is over a fixed resource, but few organizational conflicts are due to perfectly opposing interests with fixed resources. To varying degrees, the opposing groups can gain by believing that their positions aren't perfectly opposing and that creative solutions are possible. For instance, a supplier and customer may initially think they have opposing interests—the supplier wants to receive more money for the product, whereas the customer wants to pay less money for it. Yet, further discussion may reveal that the customer would be willing to pay more if the product could be provided earlier than originally arranged. The vendor may actually value that earlier delivery because it saves inventory costs. By looking at the bigger picture, both parties can often discover common ground.

Adopting a win–win or win–lose orientation influences our conflict management style, that is, how we act toward the other person. Researchers have categorized five interpersonal styles of approaching the other party in a conflict situation. The most recent variation of this model appears in Exhibit 13.3.

EXHIBIT 13.3

Interpersonal conflict management styles

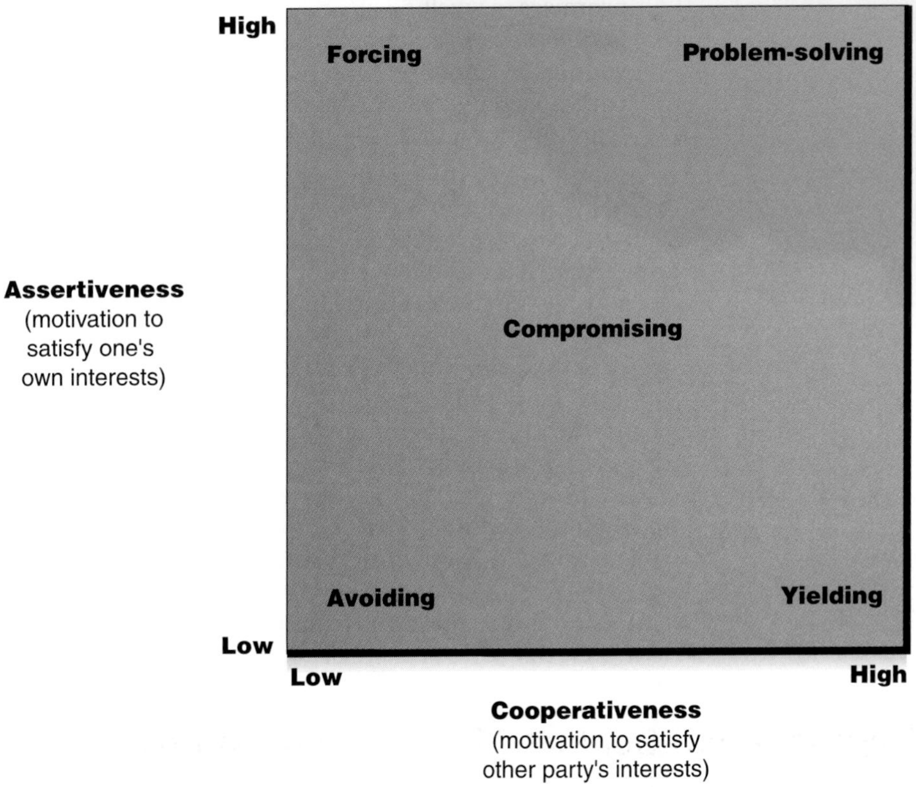

Source: C. K. W. de Dreu, A. Evers, B. Beersma, E. S. Kluwer, and A. Nauta, "A Theory-Based Measure of Conflict Management Strategies in the Workplace," *Journal of Organizational Behavior* 22 (2001), pp. 645–68. For earlier variations of this model, see T. L. Ruble and K. Thomas, "Support for a Two-Dimensional Model of Conflict Behavior," *Organizational Behavior and Human Performance* 16 (1976), p. 145.

Each conflict resolution style can be placed in a two-dimensional grid reflecting the person's degree of concern for his or her own interests and concern for the other party's interests. Problem solving is the only style that represents a purely win–win orientation. The other four styles represent variations of the win–lose approach. For effective conflict management, we should learn to apply different conflict management styles to different situations.[24]

- *Problem solving*—Problem solving tries to find a mutually beneficial solution for both parties. Information sharing is an important feature of this style because both parties collaborate to identify common ground and potential solutions that satisfy both (or all) of them.
- *Avoiding*—Avoiding tries to smooth over or avoid conflict situations altogether. It represents a low concern for both self and the other party; in other words, avoiders try to suppress thinking about the conflict. For example, some employees will rearrange their work area or tasks to minimize interaction with certain co-workers.[25]
- *Forcing*—Forcing tries to win the conflict at the other's expense. This style, which has the strongest win–lose orientation, relies on some of the "hard" influence tactics described in Chapter 12, particularly assertiveness, to get one's own way.
- *Yielding*—Yielding involves giving in completely to the other side's wishes, or at least cooperating with little or no attention to your own interests. This style involves making unilateral concessions and unconditional promises, as well as offering help with no expectation of reciprocal help.
- *Compromising*—Compromising involves looking for a position in which your losses are offset by equally valued gains. It involves matching the other party's concessions, making conditional promises or threats, and actively searching for a middle ground between the interests of the two parties.[26]

Choosing the Best Conflict Management Style

Sun Microsystems recently sued memory chipmaker Kingston Technology over exclusive rights to a new architecture in memory modules. When the court threw out Sun's complaint, Kingston cofounder David Sun had another idea; he challenged Sun Microsystems CEO Scott McNealy to a game of golf to settle their differences.[27] A golf game is an unusual way to resolve conflict, but this incident illustrates how people apply different conflict management styles. Ideally, we use different styles under different conditions, but most of us have a preferred conflict management style.

The problem-solving style is usually recognized as the preferred approach to conflict resolution. For example, the problem-solving conflict management style results in better joint venture performance.[28] The parties discuss concerns more quickly and openly, seek their partner's opinions, and explain their course of action more fully than where a non-problem-solving style is used. However, this style only works under certain conditions. Specifically, it is best when the parties do not have perfectly opposing interests and when they have enough trust and openness to share information. Problem solving is usually desirable because organizational conflicts are rarely win–lose situations. There is usually some opportunity for mutual gain if the parties search for creative solutions.[29]

You might think that avoiding is an ineffective conflict management strategy, but research suggests that it is the best approach where conflict has become socioemotional.[30] At the same time, conflict avoidance should not be a long-term solution because it increases the other party's frustration. The forcing style of conflict resolution is usually inappropriate because organizational relationships rarely involve complete opposition. However, forcing may be necessary where you know you are correct and the dispute requires a quick solution. For example, a forcing style may be necessary when the other party engages in unethical conduct because any degree of unethical behavior is unacceptable. The forcing style may also be necessary where the other party would take advantage of more cooperative strategies.

The yielding style may be appropriate when the other party has substantially more power or the

David Pottruck admits that for many years, probably dating back to his college days as a star wrestler, he had a competitive conflict management style. When someone suggested an idea contrary to his views, he would "nod and then wait for them to finish and then give them my reasons why I'm going to do something different than what they said." Now, after candid advice from a marriage counselor, the CEO of San Francisco-based brokerage firm Charles Schwab Corporation takes a much more problem-solving approach. "I tried to learn to be truly collaborative," he says, to "really sit there and listen and try to understand the opportunity for collaboration of the best of your ideas and the best of my ideas. Behaving in that way makes me a better executive."[31] Is the problem-solving (collaborative) style that Pottruck advocates here always the best approach to conflict management?

issue is not as important to you as to the other party. On the other hand, yielding behaviors may give the other side unrealistically high expectations, thereby motivating them to seek more from you in the future. In the long run, yielding may produce more conflict rather than resolve it. The compromising style may be best when there is little hope for mutual gain through problem solving, both parties have equal power, and both are under time pressure to settle their differences. However, compromise is rarely a final solution and may cause the parties to overlook options for mutual gain.

Cultural and Gender Differences in Conflict Management Styles

Cultural differences are more than just a source of conflict. Cultural background also affects the conflict management style we prefer using.[32] This is because we are more comfortable with conflict management styles that are consistent with our personal and cultural value system. Some research suggests that people with high collectivism—those who value group harmony to duty to their own groups—are motivated to maintain harmonious relations. Consequently, they tend to rely on avoidance or problem solving to resolve disagreements.[33] In contrast, people with low collectivism more frequently apply a compromising or forcing style. People with high collectivism can be just as competitive as are low collectivists with people outside their group. However, people with high collectivism are generally more likely to avoid confrontation where possible.

Some writers suggest that men and women also tend to rely on different conflict management styles.[34] Generally speaking, women pay more attention than do men to the relationship between the parties. Consequently, they tend to adopt a problem-solving style in business settings and are more willing to compromise to protect the relationship. Men tend to be more competitive and take a short-term orientation to the relationship. Of course, we must be cautious about these observations because gender has a weak influence on conflict management style.

Structural Approaches to Conflict Management

Conflict management styles refer to how we approach the other party in a conflict situation. But conflict management also involves altering the underlying structural causes of potential conflict. The main structural approaches are identified in Exhibit 13.4. Although this section discusses ways to reduce conflict, we should keep in mind that conflict management sometimes calls for increasing conflict. This occurs mainly by reversing the strategies described over the next few pages.[35]

Emphasizing Superordinate Goals

Carlos Ghosn experienced more than his share of cross-cultural conflict when French carmaker Renault made him president of its partner, Nissan Motor Company. French and Japanese executives had different expectations and work styles, which invariably resulted in cultural clashes. To minimize that conflict—and to pull the Japanese automaker out of financial trouble—Ghosn introduced a set of challenging, measurable objectives called the "Nissan Revival Plan." The plan became a superordinate goal that rallied staff and encouraged them to put aside their cultural differences. "We all knew that in order to develop a

EXHIBIT 13.4

Structural approaches to conflict management

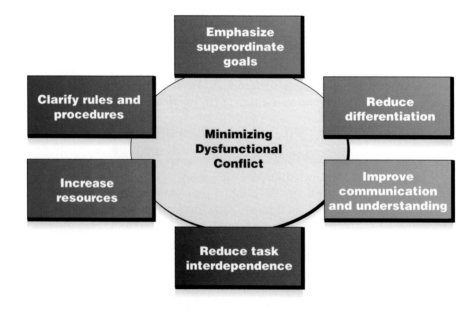

plan that would work, we would have to treat natural cultural suspicions and culture clashes as a luxury for rich people," Ghosn explained at the time.[36]

Superordinate goals are common objectives held by conflicting parties that are more important than the departmental or individual goals on which the conflict is based. By increasing commitment to corporatewide goals, employees place less emphasis and therefore feel less conflict with co-workers regarding competing individual or departmental-level goals.[37] Superordinate goals also potentially reduce the problem of differentiation because they establish a common frame of reference. Heterogeneous team members still perceive different ways to achieve corporate objectives, but superordinate goals ensure they mutually understand and agree on the objectives themselves.

Several research studies indicate that focusing on superordinate goals weakens dysfunctional conflict. One study revealed that marketing managers in Hong Kong, China, Japan, and the United States were more likely to develop a problem-solving conflict management style when executives aligned departmental goals with corporate objectives. An American study found that the most effective executive teams consistently apply a superordinate goal strategy. They frame their decisions as collaborations, thereby drawing attention and commitment away from sublevel goals.[38]

superordinate goal

A common objective held by conflicting parties that is more important than their conflicting departmental or individual goals.

Executives at Tivoli Systems discovered the importance of superordinate goals after participating in an exercise called "Paper Airplanes, Inc." Each team at the Austin, Texas, company had 30 minutes to manufacture and sell as many standard-specific planes as possible. The teams initially performed poorly because participants focused on their individual goals. "The biggest problem [was] that you couldn't just focus on your part," explains Tivoli executive Bill Jones (left in photo). Teams eventually won the exercise after their members focused on the organization's success more than their individual tasks. The exercise now represents a reminder that Tivoli employees need to focus on superordinate goals rather than departmental differences. "When things come up we refer to the exercise to help everyone get on the same page," says Brent Vance (right in photo).[39] In what others way might the Paper Airplanes exercise reduce dysfunctional conflict?

Reducing Differentiation

Another way to minimize dysfunctional conflict is to reduce the differences that produce the conflict in the first place.[40] The Manila Diamond Hotel in the Philippines accomplishes this by rotating staff across different departments. "In Manila Diamond, there is no turf mentality," explains the hotel's marketing manager. "We all work together. We even share each other's jobs whenever necessary." Similarly, Hibernia Management and Development Company, which operates a large oil platform off the coast of Newfoundland, Canada, removed the "destructive differences" between hourly and salaried personnel by putting employees on salary rather than hourly wages.[41]

Improving Communication and Understanding

Communication is critical to effective conflict management. This can range from casual gatherings among employees who rarely meet otherwise, to formal processes where differences are identified and discussed. Multinational peacekeeping forces work together more effectively when troops eat and socialize together.[42] By improving the opportunity, ability, and motivation to share information, employees develop less extreme perceptions of each other than if they rely on stereotypes and emotions. Direct communication provides a better understanding of the other person's or department's work environment and resource limitations. Ongoing communication is particularly important where the need for functional specialization makes it difficult to reduce differentiation.[43]

Some of the team-building activities described in Chapter 10 help to reduce conflict because participants learn to understand each other. Managers at the City of St. Paul, Minnesota, recently experienced the conflict-reducing benefits of a leadership development program. "You're seeing people working in the different aspects of the city and you're hearing their ideas as well, says St. Paul manager Patricia McGinn. "These are people that you will work with, so I will be able to call and say, 'I have this issue—can we talk about it?'"[44] Connections 13.2 describes another conflict-busting activity called drum circles, in which participants use drums and other percussion instruments to learn the process of working together.

Last, dialogue meetings can often help the disputing parties discuss their differences. Through dialogue, participants learn about each other's mental models and fundamental assumptions (see Chapter 10). Citizens on both sides of the nuclear debate practice this conflict management approach twice each month in Brattleboro, Vermont, located near the nuclear plant Vermont Yankee. "We're not going to agree on everything, but we hope to focus on our similarities as opposed to our differences," explains an anti–nuclear power activist who attends these meetings. "This is an attempt to start a dialogue on these issues without all the yelling, head-banging and confrontation."[45]

Reducing Task Interdependence

Conflict increases with the level of interdependence so minimizing dysfunctional conflict might involve reducing the level of interdependence between the parties. If cost effective, this might occur by dividing the shared resource so that each party has exclusive use of part of it. Sequentially or reciprocally interdependent jobs might be combined so that they form a pooled

Learning Cooperative Teamwork through the Drumbeat

Dozens of businesspeople pour into an auditorium where drums of all types—Latin American congas, African doumbeks, and Brazilian surdos—line the room. The participants anxiously take their seats. Few have played drums before, but they will all play in harmony tonight. They will learn to cooperate and coordinate through the beat of their drums. Doug Sole, the drum circle facilitator, starts by pointing randomly to individuals, asking them to play a beat that others will imitate. The rhythm intensifies as others join in, then falls apart into a cacophony.

"We're having a communication problem here," Sole interrupts. "If we all start banging our own thing, it's going to be chaos." Sole begins again, and repeats the process until the auditorium is filled with the hypnotic beat of strangers working together.

Drum circles represent a metaphor for cooperation, coordination, communication, and teamwork in nontraditional corporate structures. They focus participants on the process of working together, not just on the outcome of achieving a goal.

"In a matter of moments, perfect strangers came together in synchronistic rhythm to share a common vision," Ron Johnson recalls of his drum circle experience at Toyota Motor Sales, U.S.A., which has since set up its own drumming rooms. "Even the most cynical member of our team was blown away by the event," says an employee at Standard Bank in London, England. "It wasn't just a once off feel good, it was a reference point that we can use in the future for how excellently we work as a team and how much fun we can have doing what we do."

Sources: Drum Café website (www.drumcafe.com), August 2003; K. R. Lewis, "(Drum) Beatings Build Corporate Spirit," *Minneapolis Star Tribune,* June 3, 2003, p. E3; S. Terry, "Lost in the Rhythm," *Christian Science Monitor,* May 23, 2001, p. 11; R. Segall, "Catch the Beat," *Psychology Today,* July 2000; M. K. Pratt, "A Pound of Cure," *Fast Company,* April 2000; A. Georgiades, "Business Heeds the Beat," *Toronto Star,* August 4, 1999.

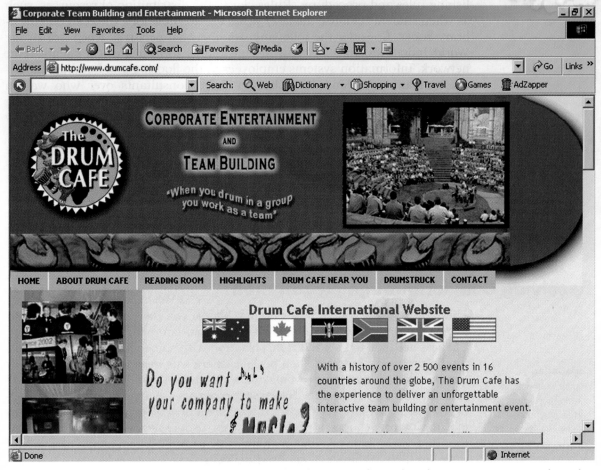

The Drum Café in Johannesburg, South Africa, and other drum circle facilitators are teaching employees how to improve cooperation and mutual understanding.

interdependence. For example, rather than having one employee serve customers and another operate the cash register, each employee could handle both customer activities alone. Buffers also help to reduce task interdependence between people. Buffers include resources, such as adding more inventory between people who perform sequential tasks. We also find human buffers in organizations—people who intervene between highly interdependent people or work units.[46]

Increasing Resources

An obvious way to reduce conflict due to resource scarcity is to increase the amount of resources available. Corporate decision makers might quickly dismiss this solution because of the costs involved. However, they need to carefully compare these costs with the costs of dysfunctional conflict arising out of resource scarcity.

Clarifying Rules and Procedures

Some conflicts arise from ambiguous decision rules regarding the allocation of scarce resources. Consequently, these conflicts can be minimized by establishing rules and procedures. Rules clarify the distribution of resources, such as when students can use the laser printer or for how long they can borrow library books. Consider the following situation that occurred when Armstrong World Industries, Inc., brought in consultants to implement a client–server network. Information systems employees at the flooring and building materials company experienced conflict with the consultants over who was in charge. Another conflict occurred when the consultants wanted to work long hours and take Friday off to fly home. Armstrong minimized these conflicts by spelling out in the contract as much as possible about each party's responsibilities and roles. Issues that were unclear or overlooked in the contract were clarified by joint discussion between two senior executives at the companies.[47]

Rules establish changes to the terms of interdependence, such as an employee's hours of work or a supplier's fulfillment of an order. In most cases, the parties affected by these rules are involved in the process of deciding these terms of interdependence. By redefining the terms of interdependence, the strategy of clarifying rules is part of the larger process of negotiation.

Resolving Conflict through Negotiation

negotiation
Occurs whenever two or more conflicting parties attempt to resolve their divergent goals by redefining the terms of their interdependence.

Think back through yesterday's events. Maybe you had to work out an agreement with other students about what tasks to complete for a team project. Chances are that you shared transportation with someone, so you had to clarify the timing of the ride. Then perhaps there was the question of who made dinner. Each of these daily events created potential conflict, and they were resolved through negotiation. **Negotiation** occurs whenever two or more conflicting parties attempt to resolve their divergent goals by redefining the terms of their interdependence.[48] In other words, people negotiate when they think that discussion can produce a more satisfactory arrangement (at least for them) in their exchange of goods or services.

As you can see, negotiation is not an obscure practice reserved for labor and management bosses when hammering out a collective agreement. Everyone negotiates—every day. Most of the time, you don't even realize that you are in negotiations.[49] Negotiation is particularly evident in the workplace because employees work interdependently with each other. They negotiate with their supervisors over next month's work assignments, with customers over the sale and delivery schedules of their product, and with co-workers over when to have lunch. And yes, they occasionally negotiate with each other in labor disputes and collective agreements.

Some writers suggest that negotiations are more successful when the parties adopt a problem-solving style, whereas others caution that this conflict management style is sometimes costly.[50] We know that any win–lose style (forcing, yielding, etc.) is unlikely to produce the optimal solution, because the parties have not shared information necessary to discover a mutually satisfactory solution. On the other hand, we must be careful about adopting an openly problem-solving style until mutual trust has been established.

The concern with the problem-solving style is that information is power, so information sharing gives the other party more power to leverage a better deal if the opportunity occurs. Skilled negotiators often adopt a *cautiously* problem-solving style at the outset by sharing information slowly and determining whether the other side will reciprocate. In this respect, they try to establish trust with the other party.[51] They switch to one of the win–lose styles only when it becomes apparent that a win–win solution is not possible or the other party is unwilling to share information with a cooperative orientation.

Bargaining Zone Model of Negotiations

The negotiation process moves each party along a continuum with an area of potential overlap called the *bargaining zone*.[52] Exhibit 13.5 displays one possible bargaining zone situation. This linear diagram illustrates a purely

EXHIBIT 13.5 Bargaining zone model of negotiations

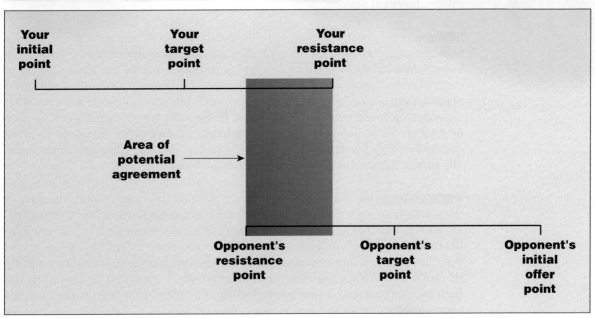

win–lose situation—one side's gain will be the other's loss. However, the bargaining zone model can also be applied to circumstances in which both sides potentially gain from the negotiations. As this model illustrates, the parties typically establish three main negotiating points. The *initial offer point* is the team's opening offer to the other party. This may be its best expectation or a pie-in-the-sky starting point. The *target point* is the team's realistic goal or expectation for a final agreement. The *resistance point* is the point beyond which the team will make no further concessions.

The parties begin negotiations by describing their initial offer point for each item on the agenda. In most cases, the participants know that this is only a starting point that will change as both sides offer concessions. In win–lose situations, neither the target nor the resistance point is revealed to the other party. However, people try to discover the other side's resistance point because this knowledge helps them determine how much they can gain without breaking off negotiations.

When the parties have a win–win orientation, the objective is to find a creative solution that keeps everyone close to their initial offer points. They hope to find an arrangement by which each side loses relatively little value on some issues and gains significantly more on other issues. For example, a supplier might want to delay delivery dates, whereas delivery times are not important to the business customer. If the parties share this information, they can quickly agree to a delayed delivery schedule, thereby costing the customer very little and gaining the supplier a great deal. On other items (financing, order size, etc.), the supplier might give something with minimal loss even though it is a significant benefit to the business customer.

Situational Influences on Negotiations

The effectiveness of negotiating depends on both the situation and the behaviors of the negotiators. Four of the most important situational factors are location, physical setting, time, and audience.

Location   It is easier to negotiate on your own turf because you are familiar with the negotiating environment and are able to maintain comfortable routines.[53] Also, there is no need to cope with travel-related stress or depend on others for resources during the negotiation. Of course, you can't walk out of negotiations as easily when on your own turf, but this is usually a minor issue. Considering these strategic benefits of home turf, many negotiators agree to neutral territory. Telephones, videoconferences, and other forms of information technology potentially avoid territorial issues, but skilled negotiators usually prefer the media richness of face-to-face meetings.[54]

Physical Setting   The physical distance between the parties and formality of the setting can influence their orientation toward each other and the disputed issues.[55] So can the seating arrangements. People who sit face to face are more likely to develop a win–lose orientation toward the conflict situation. In contrast, some negotiation groups deliberately intersperse participants around the table to convey a win–win orientation. Others arrange the seating so that both parties face a white board, reflecting the notion that both parties face the same problem or issue.

Time Passage and Deadlines   The more time people invest in negotiations, the stronger is their commitment to reaching an agreement. This increases the motivation to resolve the conflict, but it also fuels the escalation of commitment problems described in Chapter 8. For example, the more time put into negotiations, the stronger the tendency to make unwarranted concessions so that the negotiations do not fail.

Time deadlines may be useful to the extent that they motivate the parties to complete negotiations. However, time pressures are usually a liability in negotiations.[56] One problem is that time pressure inhibits a problem-solving conflict management style, because the parties have less time to exchange information or present flexible offers. Negotiators under time pressure also process information less effectively, so they have less creative ability to discover a win–win solution to the conflict. There is also anecdotal evidence that negotiators make excessive concessions and soften their demands more rapidly as the deadline approaches.

Audience Characteristics   Most negotiators have audiences—anyone with a vested interest in the negotiation outcomes, such as executives, other team members, or the general public. Negotiators tend to act differently when their audience observes the negotiation or has detailed information about the process, compared to situations in which the audience sees only the end results.[57] When the audience has direct surveillance over the proceedings, negotiators tend to be more competitive, less willing to make concessions, and more likely to engage in political tactics against the other party.[58] This "hardline" behavior shows the audience that the negotiator is working for their interests. With their audience watching, negotiators also have more interest in saving face.

Negotiator Behaviors

Negotiator behaviors play an important role in resolving conflict. Four of the most important behaviors are setting goals, gathering information, communicating effectively, and making concessions.

- *Preparation and goal setting*—Research has consistently reported that people have more favorable negotiation results when they prepare for the negotiation and set goals.[59] In particular, negotiators should carefully think through their initial offer, target, and resistance points. They need to consider alternative strategies in case the negotiation fails. Negotiators also need to check their underlying assumptions, as well as goals and values. Equally important is the need to research what the other party wants from the negotiation.
- *Gathering information*—"Seek to understand before you seek to be understood." This popular philosophy from management guru Stephen Covey applies to effective negotiations. It means that we should spend more time listening closely to the other party and asking for details.[60] One way to improve the information-gathering process is to have a team of people participate in negotiations. Asian companies tend to have large negotiation teams for this purpose.[61] With more information about the opponent's interests and needs, negotiators are better able to discover low-cost concessions or proposals that will satisfy the other side.

Paul Tellier is a master negotiator with several recommendations for making deals come together. But the CEO of transportation manufacturing giant Bombardier has one recommendation above all others: preparation. "You have to be prepared every which way about the people, the subject, and your fallback position," advises Tellier. Part of the preparation process is to anticipate and practice unexpected issues that may arise. "Before walking into the room for the actual negotiation, I ask my colleagues to throw some curve balls at me," he says.[62] In what other ways can people prepare for negotiations?

- *Communicating effectively*—Effective negotiators communicate in a way that maintains effective relationships between the parties.[63] Specifically, they minimize socioemotional conflict by focusing on issues rather than people. Effective negotiators also avoid irritating statements such as "I think you'll agree that this is a generous offer." Third, effective negotiators are masters of persuasion. This does not involve misleading the other party. Rather, as discussed in Chapter 12, persuasive negotiators structure the content of their message so that it is accepted by others, not merely understood.[64]

- *Making concessions*—Concessions are important because they (1) enable the parties to move toward the area of potential agreement, (2) symbolize each party's motivation to bargain in good faith, and (3) tell the other party of the relative importance of the negotiating items.[65] How many concessions should you make? This varies with the other party's expectations and the level of trust between you. For instance, many Chinese negotiators are wary of people who change their position during the early stages of negotiations. Similarly, some writers warn that Russian negotiators tend to view concessions as a sign of weakness, rather than a sign of trust.[66] Generally, the best strategy is to be moderately tough and give just enough concessions to communicate sincerity and motivation to resolve the conflict.[67] Being too tough can undermine relations between the parties; giving too many concessions implies weakness and encourages the other party to use power and resistance.

Third-Party Conflict Resolution

third-party conflict resolution
Any attempt by a relatively neutral person to help the parties resolve their differences.

Most of this chapter has focused on people directly involved in a conflict, yet many disputes in organizational settings are resolved with the assistance of a third party, such as your boss. **Third-party conflict resolution** is any attempt by a relatively neutral person to help the parties resolve their differences. There are generally three types of third-party dispute resolution activities: arbitration, inquisition, and mediation. These activities can be classified by their level of control over the process and control over the decision (see Exhibit 13.6).[68]

- *Arbitration*—Arbitrators have high control over the final decision, but low control over the process.[69] Executives engage in this strategy by following previously agreed rules of due process, listening to arguments from the disputing employees, and making a binding decision. Arbitration is applied as the final stage of grievances by unionized employees, but it is also becoming more common in nonunion conflicts.

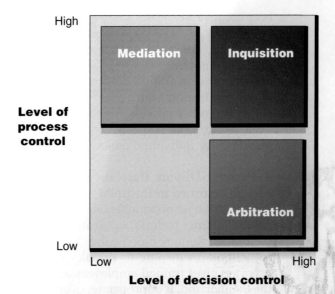

EXHIBIT 13.6

Types of third-party
intervention

- *Inquisition*—Inquisitors control all discussion about the conflict. Like arbitrators, they have high decision control because they choose the form of conflict resolution. However, they also have high process control because they choose which information to examine and how to examine it, and they generally decide how the conflict resolution process will be handled.
- *Mediation*—Mediators have high control over the intervention process. In fact, their main purpose is to manage the process and context of interaction between the disputing parties. However, the parties make the final decision about how to resolve their differences. Thus, mediators have little or no control over the conflict resolution decision.

Choosing the Best Third-Party Intervention Strategy

Team leaders, executives, and co-workers regularly intervene in disputes between employees and departments. Sometimes they adopt a mediator role; other times they serve as arbitrators. However, research suggests that people in positions of authority (e.g., managers) usually adopt an inquisitional approach whereby they dominate the intervention process as well as making a binding decision.[70] Managers like the inquisition approach because it is consistent with the decision-oriented nature of managerial jobs, gives them control over the conflict process and outcome, and tends to resolve disputes efficiently.

However, the inquisitional approach to third-party conflict resolution is usually the least effective in organizational settings.[71] One problem is that leaders who take an inquisitional role tend to collect limited information about the conflict using this approach, so their imposed decision may produce an ineffective solution to the conflict. Moreover, employees tend to think that the procedures and outcomes of inquisitions are unfair because they have little control over this approach.

Which third-party intervention is most appropriate in organizations? The answer partly depends on the situation.[72] For example, arbitration is much less popular in Hong Kong than in North America. But generally speaking, for everyday disputes between two employees, the mediation approach is usually best because this gives employees more responsibility for resolving their own disputes. The third-party representative merely establishes an appropriate context for conflict resolution. Although not as efficient as other strategies, mediation potentially offers the highest level of employee satisfaction with the conflict process and outcomes.[73] When employees cannot resolve their differences, arbitration seems to work best because the predetermined rules of evidence and other processes create a higher sense of procedural fairness. Moreover, arbitration is preferred where the organization's goals should take priority over individual goals.

Alternative Dispute Resolution   After a two-year educational leave, Michael Kenney returned to Eastman Kodak Company as a contractor, not the permanent position he previously had held. A year later, Kodak announced that Kenney's digitizing technician position would disappear and that he would soon be jobless. Kenney didn't think losing his permanent position status was fair, so he took his dispute to Kodak's Resolution Support Services program. The program gives trained employees and managers the right to hear both sides of the conflict and, if appropriate, overturn management's decision. A trained adjudicator listened to Kenney's side of the story, then, with Kenney excused, listened to the supervisor and other witnesses. The adjudicator decided that Kenney should have a permanent position because Kodak applied its educational leave policy inconsistently.[74]

alternative dispute resolution (ADR)

A third-party dispute resolution process that includes mediation, typically followed by arbitration.

Eastman Kodak joins a long list of firms that have taken third-party resolution one step further through an **alternative dispute resolution (ADR)** process. ADR combines third-party dispute resolution in an orderly sequence. ADR typically begins with a meeting between the employee and employer to clarify and negotiate their differences. If this fails, a mediator is brought in to help the parties reach a mutually agreeable solution. If mediation fails, the parties submit their case to an arbitrator, whose decision may be either binding or voluntarily accepted by the employer. Although most ADR systems rely on professions arbitrators, some firms, such as Eastman Kodak, prefer peer arbitrations, which include a panel of co-workers and managers who are not involved in the dispute.[75] Overall, ADR helps the parties solve their own problems and tends to be more conciliatory than courtroom battles.

Whether resolving conflict through third-party dispute resolution or direct negotiation, we need to recognize that many solutions come from the sources of conflict that were identified earlier in this chapter. This may seem obvious, but in the heat of conflict, people often focus on each other rather than the underlying causes. Recognizing these conflict sources is the role of effective leadership, which is discussed in the next chapter.

Chapter Summary

Conflict is the process in which one party perceives that its interests are being opposed or negatively affected by another party. The conflict process begins with the sources of conflict. These sources lead one or both sides to perceive a conflict and to experience conflict emotions. This, in turn, produces manifest conflict, such as behaviors toward the other side.

When conflict is constructive, the parties view the

conflict experience as something separate from them. Disputes are much more difficult to resolve when they produce socioemotional conflict, where the parties perceive each other as the problem. The conflict process often escalates through a series of episodes and shifts from constructive to socioemotional.

Conflict management maximizes the benefits and minimizes the dysfunctional consequences of conflict. Conflict is beneficial in the form of constructive conflict because it makes people think more fully about issues. Positive conflict also increases team cohesiveness when conflict is with another group. The main problems with conflict are that it may lead to job stress, dissatisfaction, and turnover. Dysfunctional intergroup conflict may undermine decision making.

Conflict tends to increase when people have incompatible goals, differentiation (different values and beliefs), interdependent tasks, scarce resources, ambiguous rules, and problems communicating with each other. Conflict is more common in a multicultural workforce because of greater differentiation and communication problems among employees.

People with a win–win orientation believe the parties will find a mutually beneficial solution to their disagreement. Those with a win–lose orientation adopt the belief that the parties are drawing from a fixed pie. The latter tends to escalate conflict. Among the five interpersonal conflict management styles, only problem solving represents a purely win–win

orientation. The four other styles—avoiding, forcing, yielding, and compromising—adopt some variation of a win–lose orientation. Women and people with high collectivism tend to use a problem-solving or avoidance style more than men and people with high individualism.

Structural approaches to conflict management include emphasizing superordinate goals, reducing differentiation, improving communication and understanding, reducing task interdependence, increasing resources, and clarifying rules and procedures. These elements can also be altered to stimulate conflict.

Negotiation occurs whenever two or more conflicting parties attempt to resolve their divergent goals by redefining the terms of their interdependence. Negotiations are influenced by several situational factors, including location, physical setting, time passage and deadlines, and audience. Important negotiator behaviors include preparation and goal setting, gathering information, communicating effectively, and making concessions.

Third-party conflict resolution is any attempt by a relatively neutral person to help the parties resolve their differences. The three main forms of third-party dispute resolution are mediation, arbitration, and inquisition. Managers tend to use an inquisition approach, although mediation and arbitration are more appropriate, depending on the situation. Alternative dispute resolution applies mediation, but it may also involve negotiation and eventually arbitration.

Key Terms

alternative dispute resolution (ADR), p. 408
conflict, p. 388
conflict management, p. 390
negotiation, p. 402

superordinate goals, p. 399
third-party conflict resolution, p. 406
win–lose orientation, p. 395
win–win orientation, p. 394

Discussion Questions

1. Distinguish constructive conflict from socioemotional conflict and explain where these two forms fit into the conflict escalation cycle.
2. The president of Creative Toys, Inc., read about cooperation in Japanese companies and vowed to bring this same philosophy to the company. The goal is to avoid all conflict, so that employees would work cooperatively and be happier at Creative Toys. Discuss the merits and limitations of the president's policy.
3. Conflict among managers emerged soon after a Swedish company was bought by a French com-

pany. The Swedes perceived the French management as hierarchical and arrogant, whereas the French thought the Swedes were naive, cautious, and lacking an achievement orientation. Describe ways to reduce dysfunctional conflict in this situation.
4. This chapter describes three levels of task interdependence that exist in interpersonal and intergroup relationships. Identify examples of these three levels in your work or school activities. How do these three levels affect potential conflict for you?

5. Jane was just appointed purchasing manager of Tacoma Technologies Corporation. The previous purchasing manager, who recently retired, was known for his "winner-take-all" approach to suppliers. He continually fought for more discounts and was skeptical about any special deals proposed by suppliers. A few suppliers refused to do business with Tacoma Technologies, but senior management was confident that the former purchasing manager's approach minimized the company's costs. Jane wants to try a more collaborative approach to working with suppliers. Will her approach work? How should she adopt a more collaborative approach in future negotiations with suppliers?

6. You are a special assistant to the commander-in-chief of a peacekeeping mission to a war-torn part of the world. The unit consists of a few thousand peacekeeping troops from the United States, France, and four other countries. The troops will work together for approximately one year. What strategies would you recommend to improve mutual understanding and minimize conflict among these troops?

7. Suppose that you lead one of five divisions in a multinational organization and are about to begin this year's budget deliberations at headquarters. What are the characteristics of your audience in these negotiations and what effect might they have on your negotiation behavior?

8. Managers tend to use an inquisitional approach to resolving disputes between employees and departments. Describe the inquisitional approach and discuss its appropriateness in organizational settings.

CASE STUDY 13.1

CONFLICT IN CLOSE QUARTERS

A team of psychologists at Moscow's Institute for Biomedical Problems (IBMP) wanted to learn more about the dynamics of long-term isolation in space. This knowledge would be applied to the International Space Station, a joint project of several countries that would send people into space for more than six months. It would eventually include a trip to Mars taking up to three years.

IBMP set up a replica of the Mir space station in Moscow. The team then arranged for three international researchers from Japan, Canada, and Austria to spend 110 days isolated in a chamber the size of a train car. This chamber joined a smaller chamber where four Russian cosmonauts had already completed half of their 240 days of isolation. This was the first time an international crew was involved in the studies. None of the participants spoke English as their first language, yet they communicated throughout their stay in English at varying levels of proficiency.

Judith Lapierre, a French-Canadian, was the only female in the experiment. Along with a doctorate in public health and social medicine, Lapierre studied space sociology at the International Space University in France and conducted isolation research in Antarctica. This was her fourth trip to Russia, where she had learned the language. The mission was supposed to have a second female participant from the Japanese space program, but she was not selected by IBMP.

The Japanese and Austrian participants viewed the participation of a woman as a favorable factor, says Lapierre. For example, to make the surroundings more comfortable, they rearranged the furniture, hung posters on the wall, and put a tablecloth on the kitchen table. "We adapted to our environment, whereas the Russians just viewed it as something to be endured," she explains. "We decorated for Christmas, because I'm the kind of person who likes to host people."

New Year's Eve Turmoil

Ironically, it was at one of those social gatherings, the New Year's Eve party, that events took a turn for the worse. After drinking vodka (allowed by the Russian space agency), two of the Russian cosmonauts got into a fistfight that left blood splattered on the chamber walls. At one point, a colleague hid the knives in the station's kitchen because of fears that the two Russians were about to stab each other. The two cosmonauts, who generally did not get along, had to be restrained by other men. Soon after that brawl, the Russian commander grabbed Lapierre, dragged her out of view of the television monitoring cameras, and kissed her aggressively—twice. Lapierre fought him off, but the message didn't register. He tried to kiss her again the next morning.

The next day, the international crew complained to IBMP about the behavior of the Russian cosmonauts. The Russian institute apparently took no action against any of the aggressors. Instead, the institute's psychologists replied that the incidents were part of the experiment. They wanted crew members to solve their personal problems with mature discussion, without asking for outside help. "You have to understand that Mir is an autonomous object, far away from anything," Vadim Gushin, the IBMP psychologist in charge of project, explained after the experiment had ended in March. "If the crew can't solve problems among themselves, they can't work together."

Following IBMP's response, the international crew wrote a scathing letter to the Russian institute and the space agencies involved in the experiment. "We had never expected such events to take place in a highly controlled scientific experiment where individuals go through a multistep selection process," they wrote. "If we had known . . . we would not have joined it as subjects." The letter also complained about IBMP's response to their concerns.

Informed of the New Year's Eve incident, the Japanese space program convened an emergency meeting on January 2 to address the incidents. Soon after, the Japanese team member quit, apparently shocked by IBMP's inaction. He was replaced with a Russian researcher on the international team. Ten days after the fight—a little over a month after the international team began the mission—the doors between the Russian and international crew's chambers were barred at the request of the international research team. Lapierre later emphasized that this action was taken because of concerns about violence, not the incident involving her.

A Stolen Kiss or Sexual Harassment?

By the end of the experiment in March, news of the fistfight between the cosmonauts and the commander's attempts to kiss Lapierre had reached the public. Russian scientists attempted to play down the kissing incident by saying that it was one fleeting kiss, a clash of cultures, and a female participant who was too emotional.

"In the West, some kinds of kissing are regarded as sexual harassment. In our culture it's nothing," said Russian scientist Vadim Gushin in one interview. In another interview, he explained: "The problem of sexual harassment is given a lot of attention in North America but less in Europe. In Russia it is even less of an issue, not because we are more or less moral than the rest of the world; we just have different priorities."

Judith Lapierre says the kissing incident was tolerable compared to this reaction from the Russian scientists who conducted the experiment. "They don't get it at all," she complains. "They don't think anything is wrong. I'm more frustrated than ever. The worst thing is that they don't realize it was wrong."

Norbert Kraft, the Austrian scientist on the international team, also disagreed with the Russian interpretation of events. "They're trying to protect themselves," he says. "They're trying to put the fault on others. But this is not a cultural issue. If a woman doesn't want to be kissed, it is not acceptable."

Discussion Questions

1. Identify the different conflict episodes that exist in this case. Who was in conflict with whom?

2. What are the sources of conflict for these conflict incidents?

3. What conflict management style(s) did Lapierre, the international team, and Gushin use to resolve these conflicts? What style(s) would have worked best in these situations?

4. What conflict management interventions were applied here? Did they work? What alternative strategies would work best in this situation and in the future?

Sources: The facts of this case are pieced together by Steven L. McShane from the following sources: G. Sinclair Jr., "If You Scream in Space, Does Anyone Hear?" *Winnipeg Free Press*, May 5, 2000, p. A4; S. Martin, "Reining in the Space Cowboys," *Toronto Globe & Mail*, April 19, 2000, p. R1; M. Gray, "A Space Dream Sours," *Maclean's*, April 17, 2000, p. 26; E. Niiler, "In Search of the Perfect Astronaut," *Boston Globe*, April 4, 2000, p. E4; J. Tracy, "110-Day Isolation Ends in Sullen . . . Isolation," *Moscow Times*, March 30, 2000, p. 1; M. Warren, "A Mir Kiss?" *Daily Telegraph* (London), March 30, 2000, p. 22; G. York, "Canadian's Harassment Complaint Scorned," *Toronto Globe & Mail*, March 25, 2000, p. A2; S. Nolen, "Lust in Space," *Toronto Globe & Mail*, March 24, 2000, p. A3.

THE HOUSE OF PRITZKER

BusinessWeek Just four years after the death of patriarch Jay Pritzker, one of America's wealthiest families is being torn apart by sibling rivalry and resentment. At the heart of the dispute is a rift over control of the family businesses and fortune, which include Hyatt Hotels, thousands of apartment units, industrial conglomerate Marmon Group, and stakes in Reliant Pharmaceuticals and First Health Group. Tom, the eldest son, was groomed to lead the family business and had demonstrated the ability to invest and negotiate. But even Tom could not prevent the escalating disputes among other Pritzker family members.

This *Business Week* case study examines the feud in one of America's wealthiest families. It describes the tensions that have built up in recent years and identifies the solutions that Jay Pritzker and his son, Tom, tried to use to diffuse the conflict. Read through this *Business Week* article at www.mhhe.com/mcshane3e and prepare for the discussion questions below.

Discussion Questions

1. Identify the sources of conflict that explain current relations in the Pritzker family.

2. What did Tom do to try to minimize the conflict among family members? Did any of his attempts work? Why or why not?

3. What other organizational behavior concepts seem to be relevant to this story about rivalries in the Pritzker family and its businesses?

Source: J. Weber, "The House of Pritzker," *Business Week*, March 17, 2003, p. 58.

UGLI ORANGE ROLE PLAY

Purpose This exercise is designed to help you understand the dynamics of interpersonal and intergroup conflict as well as the effectiveness of negotiation strategies under specific conditions.

Materials The instructor will distribute roles for Dr. Roland, Dr. Jones, and a few observers. Ideally, each negotiation should occur in a private area away from other negotiations.

Instructions

■ *Step 1*—The instructor will divide the class into an even number of teams of three people each, with one participant left over for each team formed (e.g., six observers if there are six teams). One-half of the teams will take the role of Dr. Roland and the other half will be Dr. Jones. The instructor will distribute roles after these teams have been formed.

■ *Step 2*—Members within each team are given 10 minutes (or another time limit stated by the instructor) to learn their roles and decide negotiating strategy.

■ *Step 3*—After reading their roles and discussing strategy, each Dr. Jones team is matched with a Dr. Roland team to conduct negotiations. Observers will receive observation forms from the instructor, and two observers will be assigned to watch the paired teams during prenegotiations and subsequent negotiations.

■ *Step 4*—As soon as Roland and Jones reach agreement or at the end of the time allotted for the negotiation (whichever comes first), the Roland and Jones teams report to the instructor for further instruction.

■ *Step 5*—At the end of the exercise, the class will congregate to discuss the negotiations.

Observers, negotiators, and instructors will then discuss their observations and experiences and the implications for conflict management and negotiation.

Source: This exercise was developed by Robert J. House, Wharton Business School, University of Pennsylvania. A similar incident is also attributed to earlier writing by R. R. Blake and J. S. Mouton.

SELF-ASSESSMENT EXERCISE 13.4

THE DUTCH TEST FOR CONFLICT HANDLING

Purpose   This self-assessment is designed to help you to identify your preferred conflict management style.

Instructions   Read each of the statements below and circle the response that you believe best reflects your position regarding each statement. Then use the scoring key in Appendix B to calculate your results for each conflict management style. This exercise is completed alone so students assess themselves honestly without concerns of social comparison. However, class discussion will focus on the different conflict management styles and the situations in which each is most appropriate.

Source: C. K. W. de Dreu, A. Evers, B. Beersma, E. S. Kluwer, and A. Nauta, "A Theory-Based Measure of Conflict Management Strategies in the Workplace," *Journal of Organizational Behavior* 22 (2001), pp. 645–68.

Dutch Test for Conflict Handling

When I have a conflict at work, I do the following:	Not at All				Very Much
1. I give in to the wishes of the other party	1	2	3	4	5
2. I try to realize a middle-of-the-road solution	1	2	3	4	5
3. I push my own point of view	1	2	3	4	5
4. I examine issues until I find a solution that really satisfies me and the other party	1	2	3	4	5
5. I avoid confrontation about our differences	1	2	3	4	5
6. I concur with the other party	1	2	3	4	5
7. I emphasize that we have to find a compromise solution	1	2	3	4	5
8. I search for gains	1	2	3	4	5
9. I stand for my own and the other's goals and interests	1	2	3	4	5
10. I avoid differences of opinion as much as possible	1	2	3	4	5
11. I try to accommodate the other party	1	2	3	4	5
12. I insist we both give in a little	1	2	3	4	5
13. I fight for a good outcome for myself	1	2	3	4	5
14. I examine ideas from both sides to find a mutually optimal solution	1	2	3	4	5
15. I try to make differences loom less severe	1	2	3	4	5
16. I adapt to the parties' goals and interests	1	2	3	4	5
17. I strive whenever possible toward a 50–50 compromise	1	2	3	4	5
18. I do everything to win	1	2	3	4	5
19. I work out a solution that serves my own as well as the other's interests as well as possible	1	2	3	4	5
20. I try to avoid a confrontation with the other	1	2	3	4	5

Leadership in Organizational Settings

Learning Objectives

After reading this chapter, you should be able to:

■ Define leadership.

■ List seven competencies of effective leaders.

■ Describe the people-oriented and task-oriented leadership styles.

■ Outline the path–goal theory of leadership.

■ Discuss the importance of Fiedler's contingency model of leadership.

■ Contrast transactional with transformational leadership.

■ Describe the four elements of transformational leadership.

■ Identify three reasons why people inflate the importance of leadership.

■ Explain how societal culture influences our perceptions of effective leaders.

■ Discuss similarities and differences in the leadership styles of women and men.

The world has changed, and so has our concept of effective leadership. Based on interviews with 6,000 executives and employees in several countries, consultants Booz Allen & Hamilton and the World Economic Forum's Strategic Leadership Project recently reported that effective leaders subordinate their own egos and, instead, nurture leadership in others throughout an organization. "I think the power and role of a leader is to release the potential of an organization," explains Richard O. Brajer, CEO of Liposcience, Inc. "This means not to take my brain and replicate it in the brains of the people around me, but to release their potential to work toward an agreed-upon direction."

"The ability to motivate and guide people toward a goal is the essence of leadership," says Robert J. Shiver, chairman and CEO of New York City–based Aerwâv Holdings, Inc. "Think of Winston Churchill, Martin Luther King, and Mahatma Gandhi, and their ability to lift the hearts and minds of people to get them focused and to drive constructive action—all in the face of great adversity."

The emerging reality is a far cry from the "command-and-control" leaders of yesteryear who took center stage and pretended to have all the answers. Mike Abrashoff discovered that the traditional leadership style is withering even in the military, where it once flourished. When Abrashoff became commander of the USS *Benfold,* the ship's 300 crew members cheered upon hearing that the former commanding officer had left. "I knew then that command and control leadership was dead," recalls Abrashoff. Instead, he interviewed every crew member and found ways to help them achieve their personal goals while also meeting the ship's objectives.

Sir Richard Branson, founder of Virgin Group, is often identified with the emerging style of leadership that motivates and guides others to become leaders.

Sir Richard Branson is often cited as a role model for the new leadership. With more than over 270 companies employing 35,000 people around the world, Branson's Virgin Group is one of the top employers of choice. Branson is viewed as a "people person" who discovers noble challenges and encourages employees to achieve them. "I've got people all over the world and it's up to me to let them test and prove themselves," says Branson.[1] ■

leadership
Influencing, motivating, and enabling others to contribute toward the effectiveness and success of the organizations of which they are members.

What is leadership? We opened this chapter by pointing out that our concept of leadership is changing, but it remains a complex issue that stirs up plenty of interest and discussion. Literature reviews indicate that the leadership concept has many definitions.[2] However, a few years ago, 54 scholars from 38 countries reached a consensus that **leadership** is the ability to influence, motivate, and enable others to contribute to the effectiveness and success of the organizations of which they are members.[3]

Leaders apply various forms of influence—from subtle persuasion to more assertiveness—to ensure application of power—to ensure that followers have the motivation and role clarity to achieve specified goals. Leaders also arrange the work environment—such as allocating resources and altering communication patterns—so that employees can achieve corporate objectives more easily. However leadership is defined, only 8 percent of executives in large firms think their organizations have enough of it.[4] Most are concerned about a lack of leadership talent.

Leadership isn't restricted to the executive suite. Anyone in the organization may be a leader.[5] Indeed, the emerging view, as we read in the opening vignette to this chapter, is that effective leaders teach and empower their employees to take leadership roles. "We're quite serious when we talk about leadership even to a bench worker on the assembly line," says an executive at General Semiconductor, a global high-technology company. "Lots of people will say, 'Oh, I'm not a leader,' but when we point out that the essence of leadership is influence, they realize everyone has leadership qualities and responsibilities."[6]

Effective self-directed work teams, for example, consist of members who share leadership responsibilities or otherwise allocate this role to a responsible coordinator. Similarly, research indicates that technology champions—employees who overcome technical and organizational obstacles to introduce technological change in their area of the organization—are most successful when they possess the traits and enact the behaviors we associate with effective leadership.[8] The point here is that anyone may be a leader at an appropriate time and place.

Newfoundland Power Inc. depends on leadership in each of its employees. "When there is a truck on the side of the road, there are two guys who are working without supervision. We trust them," explains Philip Hughes, CEO of the company that provides electricity throughout the province of Newfoundland, Canada. "Both of these guys have to have leadership qualities or nothing will happen." The power utility has dramatically improved customer service by recognizing that leadership is not restricted to the executive suite. "If there is a storm, there is no handbook or manual," Hughes explains. "The employees have to be part construction worker, part electrician and part journey person. This takes teamwork and leadership."[7] How can corporate leaders leverage the power of leadership throughout the organization?

Perspectives of Leadership

Leadership has been contemplated since the days of Greek philosophers and it is one of the most popular research topics in organizational behavior. This has resulted in an enormous volume of leadership literature, most of which can be split into the five perspectives shown in Exhibit 14.1.[9] Although some of these perspectives are currently more popular than others, each helps us to more fully understand this complex issue.

EXHIBIT 14.1

Perspectives of
leadership

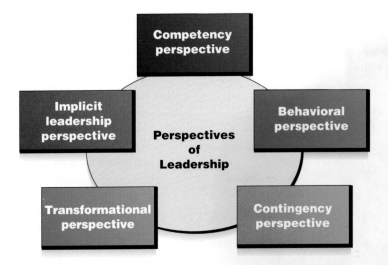

Some scholars have studied the traits or competencies of great leaders, whereas others have looked at their behaviors. More recent studies have looked at leadership from a contingency approach by considering the appropriate leader behaviors in different settings. Currently, the most popular perspective is that leaders transform organizations through their vision, communication, and ability to build commitment. Finally, an emerging perspective suggests that leadership is mainly a perceptual bias. We distort reality and attribute events to leaders because we feel more comfortable believing that a competent individual is at the organization's helm. This chapter explores each of these five perspectives of leadership. In the final section, we also look at cross-cultural and gender issues in organizational leadership.

Competency (Trait) Perspective of Leadership

Kathleen Taylor, head of worldwide operations at Four Seasons Hotels and Resorts, is highly regarded for her leadership characteristics. "There's a combination of being very intelligent with a practical sense of common sense," says her boss, Isadore Sharp, who is founder and CEO of the hotel chain. "She's very self-confident with great humility," Sharp said. "She has a great sense of fairness and sensitivity while being very direct with a high measure of integrity."[10]

Isadore Sharp's comments indicate that effective leaders possess certain characteristics. Since the beginning of recorded civilization, people have been interested in personal characteristics that distinguish great leaders from the rest of us. The ancient Egyptians demanded authority, discrimination, and justice from their leaders. The Greek philosopher Plato called for prudence, courage, temperance, and justice.[11]

For the first half of the twentieth century, organizational behavior scholars used scientific methods to determine whether certain personality traits and physical characteristics (particularly, the person's height and weight) actually distinguish leaders from lesser souls. A major review in the late 1940s concluded that no consistent list of traits could be distilled from the hundreds of studies conducted up to that time. A subsequent review suggested that a few

EXHIBIT 14.2

Seven
competencies of
effective leaders

Leadership competency	Description
Emotional intelligence	The leader's ability to perceive and express emotion, assimilate emotion in thought, understand and reason with emotion, and regulate emotion in oneself and others
Integrity	The leader's truthfulness and tendency to translate words into deeds
Drive	The leader's inner motivation to pursue goals
Leadership motivation	The leader's need for socialized power to accomplish team or organizational goals
Self-confidence	The leader's belief in his or her own leadership skills and ability to achieve objectives
Intelligence	The leader's above-average cognitive ability to process enormous amounts of information
Knowledge of the business	The leader's understanding of the company's environment to make more intuitive decisions

Sources: Most elements of this list were derived from S. A. Kirkpatrick and E. A. Locke, "Leadership: Do Traits Matter?" *Academy of Management Executive* 5 (May 1991), pp. 48–60. Several of these ideas are also discussed in: H. B. Gregersen, A. J. Morrison, and J. S. Black, "Developing Leaders for the Global Frontier," *Sloan Management Review* 40 (Fall 1998), pp. 21–32; R. J. House and R. N. Aditya, "The Social Scientific Study of Leadership: Quo Vadis?" *Journal of Management* 23 (1997), pp. 409–73.

traits are consistently associated with effective leaders, but most are unrelated to effective leadership.[12] These conclusions caused many scholars to give up their search for personal characteristics that distinguish effective leaders.

In the early 1990s, leadership experts began to reexamine the trait approach, but with more emphasis on specific *competencies*. Competencies encompass a broader range of personal characteristics—such as knowledge, skills, abilities, and values—that received less attention in the earlier studies. The recent studies coincided with the increasing popularity of competency-based practices in organizations, such as competency-based rewards described in Chapter 6.[13] The recent leadership literature identifies seven competencies that are characteristic of effective leaders.[14] These competencies are listed in Exhibit 14.2 and briefly described below.

■ *Emotional intelligence*—Effective leaders have a high level of emotional intelligence.[15] They have the ability to perceive and express emotion, assimilate emotion in thought, understand and reason with emotion, and regulate emotion in themselves and others (see Chapter 4).[16] Emotional intelligence requires a strong self-monitoring personality (see Chapter 2) because leaders must be sensitive to situational cues and readily adapt their own behavior appropriately.[17] It also requires the ability to empathize with others and possess the social skills necessary to build rapport as well as network with others. Moreover, the contingency leadership perspective described later in this chapter assumes that effective leaders are high self-monitors so they can adjust their behavior to match the situation.

■ *Integrity*—This refers to the leader's truthfulness and tendency to translate words into deeds. Integrity is sometimes called "authentic leadership" because the individual acts with sincerity. He or she has a higher moral capacity to judge dilemmas based on sound values and to act accordingly.

In Search of Leader Integrity

Greg Trantor recently stood before 500 information technology professionals under his leadership as chief information officer at Allmerica Financial Corporation and gave them the bad news: Even though the group had intensively cut costs and 42 colleagues had been laid off the year before, 65 more people would be laid off immediately. At the end of Trantor's presentation, the group applauded.

Why would employees applaud such devastating news? They were showing support to Trantor for his integrity in doing all he could to minimize the pain. "They were grateful that everything had been attempted to minimize the layoffs," explains Art Nawrocki, software assurance manager at the Worcester, Massachusetts, company. "They felt there had been honest and open communication."

The integrity of Greg Trantor and other leaders is vital for employee performance and well-being, as well as investor and customer confidence in the organization. "You need the goodwill and trust of employees," says Intel chairman Andrew Grove. "It's crucial that they have trust in you." Unfortunately, few employees in other organizations are applauding the integrity of their leaders. Only about half of employees recently surveyed in the United States said their company's top leaders had high integrity. A Gallup poll found that 73 percent of American respondents said chief executives of large corporations could not be trusted. Nearly 40 percent of British workers surveyed admitted that they do not trust their immediate boss. Half of the Australian employees recently polled said revelations about business wrongdoing had undermined their trust in employers.

This perceived lack of integrity in corporate leaders derives partly from several well-publicized incidents of leaders who betrayed employees. For instance, American Airlines executives threatened to put the company into bankruptcy protection unless employees gave up $10 billion in concessions. Meanwhile, the executives secretly set up a trust to protect their own pensions and were offered bonuses worth up to twice their salaries if they stayed through the company's difficult times. "The element of trust with senior management of

Allmerica chief information officer Greg Trantor (right) with colleagues at the financial services company which got through tough times by maintaining leader integrity.

this company has been destroyed," said the spokesperson for American Airlines's flight attendants after hearing about the secret deal.

Sources: "Workers Lack Faith in Employers," *The Age* (Melbourne, Australia), September 23, 2003; A. Sidimé, "Company Ethics on Mend," *San Antonio Express-News,* September 1, 2003; D. Gillmor, "Dan Gillmor Column," *San Jose (CA) Mercury,* May 25, 2003; K. Melymuka, "Layoff Survivors," *Computerworld,* June 9, 2003, p. 26; D. Koenig, "American Scraps Plan to Award Retention Bonuses to Top Executives," *The Tennessean,* April 19, 2003; "Four in 10 Workers 'Don't Trust' Boss," *BBC News,* October 21, 2002; J. Norman, "Ethical Fallout," *Orange County (CA) Register,* August 5, 2002.

Several large-scale studies have reported that integrity is the most important leadership characteristic. Employees want honest leaders whom they can trust.[18] The problem, as Connections 14.1 describes, is that many employees don't trust their leaders and don't think they have integrity.

- *Drive*—Leaders have a high need for achievement (see Chapter 5). This drive represents the inner motivation that leaders possess to pursue their goals and encourage others to move forward with theirs. Drive inspires an unbridled inquisitiveness and a need for constant learning.
- *Leadership motivation*—Leaders have a strong need for power because they want to influence others (see Chapter 5). However, they tend to have

a need for "socialized power" because their motivation is constrained by a strong sense of altruism and social responsibility.[19] In other words, effective leaders try to gain power so that they can influence others to accomplish goals that benefit the team or organization.

- *Self-confidence*—Kathleen Taylor at Four Seasons Hotels and other leaders believe in their leadership skills and ability to achieve objectives. They possess the self-efficacy that they are capable to lead others.[20]
- *Intelligence*—Leaders have above-average cognitive ability to process enormous amounts of information. Leaders aren't necessarily geniuses; rather, they have superior ability to analyze alternative scenarios and identify potential opportunities.
- *Knowledge of the business*—Effective leaders know the business environment in which they operate. This assists their intuition to recognize opportunities and understand their organization's capacity to capture those opportunities.

Competency (Trait) Perspective Limitations and Practical Implications

One concern with the competency perspective is that it assumes great leaders have the same personal characteristics and all of them are equally important in all situations. This is probably a false assumption; leadership is far too complex to have a universal list of traits that apply to every condition. Some competencies might not be important all the time. Moreover, research suggests that alternative combinations of competencies may be equally successful. In other words, people with two different sets of competencies might be equally good leaders.[21]

A few scholars have also warned that some personal characteristics might only influence our perception that someone is a leader, not whether the individual makes a difference to the organization's success.[22] People who exhibit integrity, self-confidence, and other traits are called leaders because they fit our stereotype of an effective leader. Or we might see a successful person, call that person a leader, and then attribute self-confidence and other unobservable traits that we consider essential for great leaders. We will discuss this perceptual distortion more fully toward the end of the chapter.

Aside from these limitations, the competency perspective recognizes that some people possess personal characteristics that offer them a higher potential to be great leaders. The most obvious implication of this is that organizations are relying increasingly on competency-based methods to hire people for future leadership positions.[23] IBM's 300-person leadership group hunts throughout the organization for people with leadership potential.[24] Leadership talents are important throughout the organization, so this recommendation should extend to all levels of hiring, not just senior executives. Companies also need to determine which behaviors represent these competencies so that employees with leadership talents are identified early for promotion.

The competency perspective of leadership does not necessarily imply that great leaders are born, not developed. On the contrary, competencies only indicate leadership potential, not leadership performance. People with these characteristics become effective leaders only after they have developed and mastered the necessary leadership behaviors. People with somewhat lower leadership competencies may become very effective leaders because they have leveraged their potential more fully. This means that companies must do more than hire people with certain competencies. They must also develop their potential through leadership development programs and practical experience in the field.

Behavioral Perspective of Leadership

In the 1940s and 1950s, scholars from Ohio State University launched an intensive research investigation to answer the question: What behaviors make leaders effective? Questionnaires were administered to subordinates, asking them to rate their supervisors on a large number of behaviors. These studies, along with similar research at the University of Michigan and Harvard University, distilled two clusters of leadership behaviors from more than 1,800 leadership behavior items.[25]

One cluster represented people-oriented behaviors. This included showing trust in and respect for subordinates, demonstrating a genuine concern for their needs, and having a desire to look out for their welfare. Leaders with a strong people-oriented style listen to employee suggestions, do personal favors for employees, support their interests when required, and treat employees as equals. The other cluster represented a task-oriented leadership style and included behaviors that define and structure work roles. Task-oriented leaders assign employees to specific tasks, clarify their work duties and procedures, ensure that they follow company rules, and push them to reach their performance capacity. They establish stretch goals and challenge employees to push beyond those high standards.

Choosing Task- versus People-Oriented Leadership

Should leaders be task-oriented or people-oriented? This is a difficult question to answer because each style has its advantages and disadvantages. People-oriented leadership is associated with higher job satisfaction among subordinates, as well as lower absenteeism, grievances, and turnover. However, job performance tends to be lower than for employees with task-oriented leaders.[26] Task-oriented leadership, on the other hand, seems to increase productivity and team unity. College students apparently value task-oriented instructors because they want clear objectives and well-prepared lectures that abide by the unit's objectives.[27]

One problem with task-oriented leadership is that it is associated with lower job satisfaction as well as higher absenteeism and turnover among subordinates. This is increasingly a concern because today's workforce is less receptive to "command-and-control" leadership. Employees want to participate in decisions rather than receive them without question.[28]

Leadership Grid
A leadership model that assesses leadership effectiveness in terms of the person's level of task-oriented and people-oriented style.

Behavioral leadership experts reported that these two styles are independent of each other. Some people are high or low on both styles, others are high on one style and low on the other, and most are somewhere between. The hypothesis that emerged was that the most effective leaders exhibit high levels of both task-oriented and people-oriented behaviors.[29] Out of this hypothesis developed a popular leadership development program, called the **Leadership Grid** (formerly known as the *Managerial Grid*).[30] Participants assess their current levels of task-oriented and people-oriented leadership, then work with trainers to achieve maximum levels of concern for both people and production (task).

The problem with the behavioral leadership perspective, as subsequent research has discovered, is it implies that high levels of both styles are best in all situations. In reality, the best leadership style depends on the situation.[31] On a positive note, the behavioral perspective laid the foundation for two of the main leadership styles—people-oriented and task-oriented—found in many contemporary leadership theories. These contemporary theories adopt a contingency perspective, which we describe next.

Contingency Perspective of Leadership

The contingency perspective of leadership is based on the idea that the most appropriate leadership style depends on the situation. Most (although not all) contingency leadership theories assume that effective leaders must be both insightful and flexible.[32] They must be able to adapt their behaviors and styles to the immediate situation. This isn't easy to do, however. Leaders typically have a preferred style. It takes considerable effort for leaders to learn when and how to alter their styles to match the situation. As we noted earlier, leaders must have a high emotional intelligence, particularly a self-monitoring personality, so they can diagnose the circumstances and match their behaviors accordingly.[33]

Path–Goal Theory of Leadership

path–goal leadership theory
A contingency theory of leadership based on expectancy theory of motivation that relates several leadership styles to specific employee and situational contingencies.

Several contingency theories have been proposed over the years, but **path–goal leadership theory** has withstood scientific critique better than the others. The theory has its roots in the expectancy theory of motivation (see Chapter 5).[34] Early research incorporated expectancy theory into the study of how leader behaviors influence employee perceptions of expectancies (paths) between employee effort and performance (goals). Based on this perspective, path–goal theory was developed and refined as a contingency leadership model.[35]

Path–goal theory states that effective leaders influence employee satisfaction and performance by making their need satisfaction contingent on effective job performance. Leaders strengthen the performance-to-outcome expectancy and valences of those outcomes by ensuring that employees who perform their jobs well have a higher degree of need fulfillment than employees who perform poorly.

servant leadership
The belief that leaders serve followers by understanding their needs and facilitating their work performance.

Effective leaders strengthen the effort-to-performance expectancy by providing the information, support, and other resources necessary to help employees complete their tasks.[36] For instance, the best performing self-directed work teams at Xerox had leaders who gave first priority to arranging organizational support for the team.[37] In other words, path–goal theory advocates **servant leadership.**[38] Servant leaders do not view leadership as a position of power; rather, they are coaches, stewards, and facilitators. Leadership is an obligation to understand employee needs and to facilitate their work performance. Servant leaders ask "How can I help you?" rather than expecting employees to serve them.

Leadership Styles   Exhibit 14.3 presents the path–goal theory of leadership. This model specifically highlights four leadership styles and several contin-

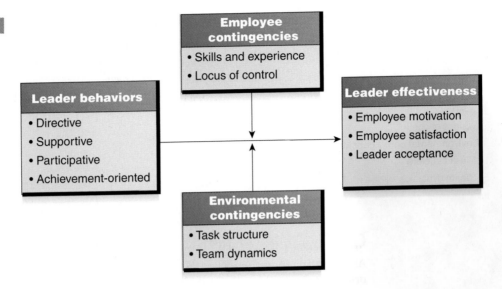

EXHIBIT 14.3

Path–goal
leadership theory

gency factors leading to three indicators of leader effectiveness. The four leadership styles are:[39]

- *Directive*—These are clarifying behaviors that provide a psychological structure for subordinates. The leader clarifies performance goals, the means to reach those goals, and the standards against which performance will be judged. It also includes judicious use of rewards and disciplinary actions. Directive leadership is the same as task-oriented leadership described earlier and echoes our discussion in Chapter 2 on the importance of clear role perceptions in employee performance.
- *Supportive*—These behaviors provide psychological support for subordinates. The leader is friendly and approachable; makes the work more pleasant; treats employees with equal respect; and shows concern for the status, needs, and well-being of employees. Supportive leadership is the same as people-oriented leadership described earlier and reflects the benefits of social support to help employees cope with stressful situations (see Chapter 7).
- *Participative*—These behaviors encourage and facilitate subordinate involvement in decisions beyond their normal work activities. The leader consults with employees, asks for their suggestions, and takes these ideas into serious consideration before making a decision. Participative leadership relates to involving employees in decisions (see Chapter 8).
- *Achievement-oriented*—These behaviors encourage employees to reach their peak performance. The leader sets challenging goals, expects employees to perform at their highest level, continuously seeks improvement in employee performance, and shows a high degree of confidence that employees will assume responsibility and accomplish challenging goals. Achievement-oriented leadership applies goal-setting theory (Chapter 5) as well as positive expectations in self-fulfilling prophecy (Chapter 3).

The path–goal model contends that effective leaders are capable of selecting the most appropriate behavioral style (or styles) for that situation. Leaders might simultaneously use more than one style at a time. For example, they might be both supportive and participative in a specific situation.

| EXHIBIT 14.4 | Selected contingencies of path–goal theory |

	Directive	Supportive	Participative	Achievement-oriented
Employee contingencies				
Skill and experience	Low	Low	High	High
Locus of control	External	External	Internal	Internal
Environmental contingencies				
Task structure	Nonroutine	Routine	Nonroutine	?
Team dynamics	Negative norms	Low cohesion	Positive norms	?

Contingencies of Path–Goal Theory

As a contingency theory, path–goal theory states that each of these four leadership styles will be effective in some situations but not in others. The path–goal leadership model specifies two sets of situational variables that moderate the relationship between a leader's style and effectiveness: (1) employee characteristics and (2) characteristics of the employee's work environment. Several contingencies have already been studied within the path–goal framework, and the model is open for more variables in the future.[40] However, we will examine only four contingencies here (see Exhibit 14.4).

Skill and Experience   A combination of directive and supportive leadership is best for employees who are (or perceive themselves to be) inexperienced and unskilled. Directive leadership gives subordinates information about how to accomplish the task, whereas supportive leadership helps them cope with the uncertainties of unfamiliar work situations. Directive leadership is detrimental when employees are skilled and experienced because it introduces too much supervisory control.

Locus of Control   Recall from Chapter 2 that people with an internal locus of control believe that they have control over their work environment. Consequently, these employees prefer participative and achievement-oriented leadership styles and may become frustrated with a directive style. In contrast, people with an external locus of control believe that their performance is due more to luck and fate, so they tend to be more satisfied with directive and supportive leadership.

Task Structure   Leaders should adopt the directive style when the task is nonroutine, because this style minimizes role ambiguity that tends to occur in these complex work situations (particularly for inexperienced employees).[41] The directive style is ineffective when employees have routine and simple tasks because the manager's guidance serves no purpose and may be viewed as unnecessarily close control. Employees in highly routine and simple jobs may require supportive leadership to help them cope with the tedious nature of the work and lack of control over the pace of work. Participative leadership is preferred for employees performing nonroutine tasks because the lack of rules and procedures gives them more discretion to achieve challenging goals.

The participative style is ineffective for employees in routine tasks because they lack discretion over their work.

Team Dynamics   Cohesive teams with performance-oriented norms act as a substitute for most leader interventions. High team cohesiveness substitutes for supportive leadership, whereas performance-oriented team norms substitute for directive and possibly achievement-oriented leadership. Thus, when team cohesiveness is low, leaders should use the supportive style. Leaders should apply a directive style to counteract team norms that oppose the team's formal objectives. For example, the team leader may need to use persuasion or assertive influence if team members have developed a norm to "take it easy" rather than get a project completed on time.

Practical Implications and Limitations of Path–Goal Theory

Path–goal theory has received considerable research support, certainly more than other contingency leadership models.[42] However, one or two contingencies (i.e., task structure) have found limited research support. Other contingencies and leadership styles in the path–goal leadership model haven't received scholarly investigation at all.[43] For example, some cells in Exhibit 14.4 have question marks because we do not yet know how those leadership styles apply to those contingencies. A recently expanded model adds new leadership styles and contingencies, but they have not yet been tested. Until further study comes along, it is unclear whether certain contingencies should be considered when choosing the best leadership style.

Another concern is that as path–goal theory expands, the model may become too complex for practical use. Although the expanded model provides a detailed representation of the complexity of leadership, it may become too cumbersome for training people in leadership styles. Few people would be able to remember all the contingencies and appropriate leadership styles for those contingencies. In spite of these limitations, path–goal theory remains a relatively complete and robust contingency leadership theory.

Other Contingency Theories

At the beginning of this chapter we noted that numerous leadership theories have developed over the years. Most of them are found in the contingency perspective of leadership. Some overlap with the path–goal model in terms of leadership styles, but most use simpler and more abstract contingencies. We will very briefly mention only two here because of their popularity and historical significance to the field.

situational leadership model
Developed by Hersey and Blanchard, suggests that effective leaders vary their style with the "readiness" of followers.

Situational Leadership Model   One of the most popular contingency theories among trainers is the **situational leadership model,** developed by Paul Hersey and Ken Blanchard.[44] The model suggests that effective leaders vary their style with the "readiness" of followers. (An earlier version of the model called this "maturity.") Readiness refers to the employee's or work team's ability and willingness to accomplish a specific task. Ability refers to the extent that the follower has the skills and knowledge to perform the task without the leader's guidance. Willingness refers to the follower's self-motivation and commitment to perform the assigned task. The model compresses these distinct concepts into a single situational condition.

The situational leadership model also identifies four leadership styles—telling, selling, participating, and delegating—that Hersey and Blanchard distinguish in terms of the amount of directive and supportive behavior provided. For example, "telling" has high task behavior and low supportive behavior. The situational leadership model has four quadrants with each quadrant showing the leadership style that is most appropriate under different circumstances.

In spite of its popularity, at least three reviews have concluded that the situational leadership model lacks empirical support.[45] Only one part of the model apparently works; namely, that leaders should use "telling" (i.e., directive style) when employees lack motivation and ability. (Recall that this is also documented in path–goal theory.) The model's elegant simplicity is attractive and entertaining, but other parts don't represent reality very well. The most recent review also concluded that the theory has logical and internal inconsistencies.

Fiedler's Contingency Model   The earliest contingency theory of leadership, called **Fiedler's contingency model,** was developed by Fred Fiedler and his associates.[46] According to this model, leader effectiveness depends on whether the person's natural leadership style is appropriately matched to the situation. The theory examines two leadership styles that essentially correspond to the previously described people-oriented and task-oriented styles. Unfortunately, Fiedler's model relies on a questionnaire that does not measure either leadership style very well.

Fiedler's model suggests that the best leadership style depends on the level of *situational control,* that is, the degree of power and influence that the leader possesses in a particular situation. Situational control is affected by three factors in the following order of importance: leader–member relations, task structure, and position power.[47] Leader–member relations is the degree to which employees trust and respect the leader and are willing to follow his or her guidance. Task structure refers to the clarity or ambiguity of operating procedures. Position power is the extent to which the leader possesses legitimate, reward, and coercive power over subordinates. These three contingencies form the eight possible combinations of *situation favorableness* from the leader's viewpoint. Good leader–member relations, high task structure, and strong position power create the most favorable situation for the leader because he or she has the most power and influence under these conditions.

Fiedler has gained considerable respect for pioneering the first contingency theory of leadership. However, his theory has faired less well. As mentioned, the leadership style scale used by Fiedler has been widely criticized. There is also no scientific justification for placing the three situational control factors in a hierarchy. Moreover, it seems that leader–member relations is actually an indicator of leader effectiveness (as in path–goal theory) rather than a situational factor. Finally, the theory considers only two leadership styles, whereas other models present a more complex and realistic array of behavior options. These concerns explain why the theory has limited empirical support.[48]

Changing the Situation to Match the Leader's Natural Style   Fiedler's contingency model may have become a historical footnote, but it does make an important and lasting contribution by suggesting that leadership style is related to the individual's personality and, consequently, is relatively stable over time. Leaders might be able to alter their style temporarily, but they tend to

leadership substitutes

A theory that identifies contingencies that either limit the leader's ability to influence subordinates or make that particular leadership style unnecessary.

use a preferred style in the long term. More recent leadership writers have also proposed that leadership styles are "hardwired" more than most contingency leadership theories assume.[49]

If leadership style is influenced by a person's personality, then organizations should engineer the situation to fit the leader's dominant style, rather than expecting leaders to change their style with the situation. A directive leader might be assigned inexperienced employees who need direction rather than seasoned people who work less effectively under a directive style. Alternatively, companies might transfer supervisors to workplaces where their dominant style fits best. For instance, directive leaders might be parachuted into work teams with counterproductive norms, whereas leaders who prefer a supportive style should be sent to departments in which employees face work pressures and other stressors.

Leadership Substitutes So far, we have looked at theories that recommend using different leadership styles in various situations. But one theory, called **leadership substitutes,** identifies contingencies that either limit the leader's ability to influence subordinates or make that particular leadership style unnecessary. When substitute conditions are present, employees are effective without a formal leader who applies a particular style. Although the leadership substitute model requires further refinement, there is general support for the overall notion that some conditions neutralize or substitute for leadership styles.[50]

The literature identifies several conditions that possibly substitute for task-oriented or people-oriented leadership. For example, performance-based reward systems keep employees directed toward organizational goals, so they probably replace or reduce the need for task-oriented leadership. Task-oriented leadership is also less important when employees are skilled and experienced. Notice how these propositions are similar to path–goal leadership theory in that directive leadership is unnecessary—and may be detrimental—when employees are skilled or experienced.[51]

Leadership substitutes have become more important as organizations remove supervisors and shift toward team-based structures. In fact, an emerging concept is that effective leaders help team members learn to lead themselves through leadership substitutes.[52] Some writers suggest that co-workers are powerful leader substitutes in these organizational structures. Co-workers instruct new employees, thereby providing directive leadership. They also provide social support, which

Employees at New Balance Athletic Shoe Inc.'s five factories in Massachusetts and Maine are competing effectively against low-wage overseas factories. They achieve this through self-directed work teams rather than supervisory control. Highly trained employees perform a half-dozen jobs, switch tasks every few minutes, and pick up the slack for one another. Employees are rewarded for technical skills, quality focus, and developing innovative ideas. The result is that New Balance plants in the United States produce a pair of shoes in 24 minutes, compared with nearly three hours in Asian factories.[53] What leadership substitutes allow employees to work effectively without direct supervision?

reduces stress among fellow employees (see Chapter 7). Teams with norms that support organizational goals may substitute for achievement-oriented leadership, because employees encourage (or pressure) co-workers to stretch their performance levels.[54]

Self-leadership has also been discussed as a potentially valuable leadership substitute in self-directed work teams.[55] Recall from Chapter 6 that self-leadership is the process of influencing oneself to establish the self-direction and self-motivation needed to perform a task.[56] It includes self-set goals, self-reinforcement, constructive thought processes, and other activities that influence the person's own motivation and behavior. As employees become more proficient in self-leadership, they presumably require less supervision to keep them focused and energized toward organizational objectives.

Transformational Perspective of Leadership

transformational leadership
A leadership perspective that explains how leaders change teams or organizations by creating, communicating, and modeling a vision for the organization or work unit, and inspiring employees to strive for that vision.

In the 1980s, so the story goes, Zhang Ruimin, the newly appointed chief executive of Haier Group, was so incensed by the poor quality of the products built at the company's factory in the Chinese port city of Qingdao that he picked up a sledgehammer and smashed several washing machines. Zhang had just taken over the state-owned appliance manufacturer and saw the need for radical change. Today, the legendary sledgehammer is displayed in a glass case on Qingdao Haier's shop floor, which has been transformed into a model of modern efficiency. Thousands of employees dressed in clean uniforms work in pristine workshops, while a fully automated logistics center and advanced research and development program help to produce superior quality appliances. Haier Group has become China's first truly multinational company with plants around the world (including North Carolina in the United States). By relying on Japanese quality control and American-style management practices, Zhang's dream of making Haier a global brand is becoming a reality.[57]

Zhang Ruimin is a **transformational leader.** Through his vision and actions, he has transformed a run-down state-owned factory into China's leading multinational enterprise. Transformational leaders such as Zhang Ruimin, Herb Kelleher (Southwest Airlines), Carly Fiorina (Hewlett-Packard), Carlos Ghosn (Renault/Nissan), and Richard Branson (Virgin) dot the corporate landscape.[58] These people are agents of change. They develop a vision for the organization or work unit, inspire and collectively bond employees to that vision, and give them a "can do" attitude that makes the vision achievable.[59]

transactional leadership
Leadership that helps organizations achieve their current objectives more efficiently, such as linking job performance to valued rewards and ensuring that employees have the resources needed to get the job done.

Transformational versus Transactional Leadership

Transformational leadership differs from transactional leadership.[60] **Transactional leadership** is "managing"—helping organizations achieve their current objectives more efficiently—by linking job performance to valued rewards or ensuring that employees have the resources needed to get the job done, for example.[61] The contingency and behavioral theories described earlier adopt the transactional perspective because they focus on leader behaviors that improve employee performance and satisfaction. In contrast, transformational leadership is about "leading"—changing the organization's strategies and culture so that they have a better fit with the surrounding environment.[62] Transformational leaders are change agents who energize and direct employees to a new set of corporate values and behaviors.

Organizations require both transactional and transformational leadership.[63] Transactional leadership improves organizational efficiency, whereas transformational leadership steers companies onto a better course of action. Transformational leadership is particularly important in organizations that require significant alignment with the external environment. Unfortunately, too many leaders get trapped in the daily managerial activities that represent transactional leadership.[64] They lose touch with the transformational aspect of effective leadership. Without transformational leaders, organizations stagnate and eventually become seriously misaligned with their environments.

Transformational versus Charismatic Leadership

One topic that has generated some confusion and controversy is the distinction between transformational and charismatic leadership.[65] Many researchers either use the words interchangeably, as if they have the same meaning, or view charismatic leadership as an essential ingredient of transformational leadership. Others take this view further by suggesting that charismatic leadership is the highest degree of transformational leadership.

However, a third group of scholars separate charismatic leadership from transformational leadership. These academics point out that charisma is a personal trait that provides referent power over followers, whereas transformational leadership is a set of behaviors that people use to lead the change process.[66] While charismatic leaders might be transformational leaders, they equally might not be. Some research points out that charismatic or "heroic" leaders easily build allegiance in followers but do not necessarily change the organization. Other research suggests that charismatic leaders produce dependent followers, whereas transformational leaders support follower empowerment, which tends to reduce dependence on the leader.[67]

It is also possible to be a transformational leader without being charismatic. Consider Alan G. Lafley, the CEO of Procter & Gamble. The word "charismatic" does not come to mind when you see Lafley in a meeting. "If there were 15 people sitting around the conference table, it wouldn't be obvious that he was the CEO," says one observer. Yet, the quiet-spoken leader has transformed the household products company and energized employees more than anyone can remember.[68] In contrast, there are many recent stories of executives who mesmerized boards of directors into hiring them with generous salaries, yet did nothing to move the corporate ship in new directions. Thus, we will focus on transformational leadership as a set of behaviors that change organizations (for good or bad), leaving charismatic leadership out of the equation.

Elements of Transformational Leadership

There are several descriptions of transformational leadership, but most include the four elements illustrated in Exhibit 14.5: creating a strategic vision, communicating the vision, modeling the vision, and building commitment to the vision.

Creating a Strategic Vision   Transformational leaders are the brokers of dreams.[69] They shape a strategic vision of a realistic and attractive future that bonds employees together and focuses their energy toward a superordinate organizational goal. Strategic vision represents the substance of transformational leadership. It reflects a future for the company or work unit that is ultimately

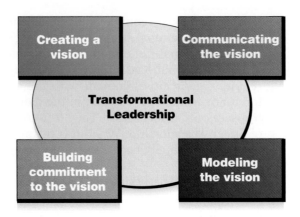

accepted and valued by organizational members. Strategic vision creates a "higher purpose" or superordinate goal that energizes and unifies employees.[70] A strategic vision might originate with the leader, but it is just as likely to emerge from employees, clients, suppliers, or other constituents. It typically begins as an abstract idea that becomes progressively clearer through critical events and discussions with staff about strategic and operational plans.[71]

There is some evidence that visions are the most important part of transformational leadership.[72] Visions offer the motivational benefits of goal setting, but they are more than mundane goals. Visions are compelling future states that bond employees and motivate them to strive for those objectives. Visions are typically described in a way that distinguishes them from the current situation, yet makes the goal both appealing and achievable.

Communicating the Vision   If vision is the substance of transformational leadership, then communicating that vision is the process. Transformational leaders communicate meaning and elevate the importance of the visionary goal to employees. They frame messages around a grand purpose with emotional appeal that captivates employees and other corporate stakeholders. Framing helps transformational leaders establish a common mental model so that the group or organization will act collectively toward the desirable goal.[73] Michael Parker, president and CEO of Dow Chemical Company, reminds anyone who works there that "Dow is about more than chemical liquids and plastic pellets." Instead, he emphasizes that "Dow is about the benefit these things bring to society in terms of cleaner drinking water and safer, more energy efficient homes and cars." Parker helps employees see their role in a different light, one that is much more meaningful and motivating.[74]

Transformational leaders also bring their visions to life through symbols, metaphors, stories, and other vehicles that transcend plain language.[75] Metaphors borrow images of other experiences, thereby creating richer meaning of the vision that has not yet been experienced. When George Cohen faced the difficult challenge of opening McDonald's restaurants in Moscow, he frequently reminded his team members that they were establishing "hamburger diplomacy." And in the mid-1800s, when ocean transportation was treacherous, Samuel Cunard emphasized that he was creating an "ocean railway." At the time, railroads provided one of the safest forms of transportation, and Cunard's metaphor reinforced the notion to employees and passengers alike that

When Karen Gilles Larson became CEO of Synovis Life Technologies (called Bio-Vascular at the time), she discovered a demoralized workforce, hitting out at each other rather than working toward a better company. So Larson met all 100 employees in the cafeteria and emphasized the need for mutual respect to turn around the beleaguered St. Paul medical products manufacturer. "We're all in a boat, and we're going to row together," she said. Over the next few years, Larson transformed Synovis by investing in research and development and diversifying the company's product range, all the while keeping employees involved and informed. Today, Synovis is one of Minnesota's top business success stories. "Now we've got cash in the bank, we're growing the revenue and profits, and it's been under her leadership," says a longtime Synovis director.[79] How might Karen Larson and other leaders communicate and model their vision in ways that would bring about meaningful change?

Cunard Steamship Lines would provide equally safe transportation across the Atlantic Ocean.[76]

Modeling the Vision   Transformational leaders not only talk about a vision; they enact it. They "walk the talk" by stepping outside the executive suite and doing things that symbolize the vision.[77] Moreover, transformational leaders are reliable and persistent in their actions. They stay on course, thereby legitimizing the vision and providing further evidence that they can be trusted. Leaders walk the talk through significant events, but they also alter mundane activities—meeting agendas, office locations, executive schedules—so they are consistent with the vision and its underlying values. To succeed as a leader, you need to act consistently with your statements, says Narayana Murthy, chairman of Infosys Technologies, one of India's largest high-technology firms. "If you don't walk the talk, you lose your credibility," he warns.[78]

Modeling the vision is important because employees and other stakeholders are executive watchers who look for behaviors to symbolize values and expectations. The greater the consistency between the leader's words and actions, the more employees will believe and follow the leader. Walking the talk also builds employee trust because trust is partly determined by the consistency of the person's actions.[80]

Building Commitment to the Vision   Transforming a vision into reality requires employee commitment. Transformational leaders build this commitment in several ways. Their words, symbols, and stories build a contagious enthusiasm that energizes people to adopt the vision as their own. Leaders demonstrate a "can do" attitude by enacting their vision and staying on course. Their persistence and consistency reflect an image of honesty, trust, and integrity. Finally, leaders build commitment by involving employees in the process of shaping the organization's vision.

Evaluating the Transformational Leadership Perspective

Transformational leaders do make a difference, according to organizational behavior studies.[81] Subordinates are more satisfied and have higher affective organizational commitment under transformational leaders. They also perform their jobs better, engage in more organizational citizenship behaviors, and make better or more creative decisions. One study also reported that organizational commitment and financial performance seem to increase in branches of a bank where the branch manager completed a transformational leadership training program.[82]

Transformational leadership is currently the most popular leadership perspective, but it faces a number of challenges. One problem is that some writers engage in circular logic by defining transformational leadership in terms of the leader's success.[83] They suggest that leaders are transformational when they successfully bring about change, regardless of whether they engage in certain behaviors we call transformational. Another concern is that the transformational leadership model seems to be universal rather than contingency-oriented. Only very recently have writers begun to explore the idea that transformational leadership is more appropriate in some situations than others.[84] For instance, transformational leadership is probably more appropriate when organizations need to adapt than when environmental conditions are stable. Preliminary evidence suggests that the transformational leadership perspective is relevant across cultures. However, there may be specific elements of transformational leadership, such as the way visions are formed and communicated, that are more appropriate in North America than other cultures.[85]

Implicit Leadership Perspective

implicit leadership theory
A theory hypothesizing that perceptual processes cause people to inflate the importance of leadership as the cause of organizational events.

The competency, behavior, contingency, and transformational leadership perspectives rest on the basic assumption that leaders "make a difference." Certainly, evidence suggests that senior executives do influence organizational performance.[86] However, leaders might have less influence than most of us would like to believe. Some leadership experts suggest that three perceptual processes cause people to inflate the importance of leadership in explaining organizational events. These processes, collectively called **implicit leadership theory**, are attribution errors, stereotyping, and the need for situational control.[87]

Attributing Leadership

People have a strong need to attribute the causes of events around them so they can feel more confident about how to control them in the future. The fundamental attribution error is a common perceptual bias in this attribution process (see Chapter 3). Fundamental attribution error is the tendency to attribute the behavior of other people to their own motivation and ability rather than the situation. In the context of leadership, it causes employees to believe that organizational events are due more to the motivation and ability of their leaders than to environmental conditions. Leaders are given credit or blame for the company's success or failure because employees do not readily see the external forces that also influence these events. Leaders reinforce this belief by taking credit for organizational successes.[88]

Stereotyping Leadership

To some extent, people rely on stereotypes to determine whether their boss is an effective leader. Each of us has preconceived notions about the features and behaviors of an effective leader. These leadership perceptions are partly based on cultural values, so an effective leader in one country might not seem so effective to employees in another country. We rely on stereotypes partly because a leader's success might not be known for months or possibly years. Consequently, employees depend on immediate information to decide whether the leader is effective. If the leader fits the mold, then employees are more confident that the leader is effective.[89]

"A year ago, I was a skinny, green-haired, skate boarding
CEO of a dot-com company. But that didn't work out."

Copyright © 2001. Randy Glasbergen. www.glasbergen.com.

Need for Situational Control

A third perceptual distortion of leadership suggests that people want to believe leaders make a difference. There are two basic reasons for this belief.[90] First, leadership is a useful way for us to simplify life events. It is easier to explain organizational successes and failures in terms of the leader's ability than by analyzing a complex array of other forces. For example, a company may fail to change quickly enough in the marketplace for many reasons, yet we tend to simplify the explanation down to the notion that the company president or some other corporate leader was ineffective.

Second, there is a strong tendency in the United States and similar cultures to believe that life events are generated more from people than from uncontrollable natural forces.[91] This illusion of control is satisfied by believing that events result from the rational actions of leaders. In short, employees feel better believing that leaders make a difference, so they actively look for evidence that this is so.

The implicit leadership perspective questions the importance of leadership, but it also provides valuable advice to improve leadership acceptance. This approach highlights the fact that leadership is a perception of followers as much as the actual behaviors and characteristics of people calling themselves leaders. Potential leaders must be sensitive to this fact, understand what followers expect, and act accordingly. Individuals who do not make an effort to fit leadership prototypes will have more difficulty bringing about necessary organizational change.[92]

Cross-Cultural and Gender Issues in Leadership

Along with the five perspectives of leadership presented throughout this chapter, we need to keep in mind that societal cultural values and practices affect what leaders do. Culture shapes the leader's values and norms, which influence his or her decisions and actions. These cultural values also shape the expectations that followers have of their leaders. This is apparent in Global Connections 14.2, which looks into the *ubuntu* values that shape the preferred leadership behaviors and style in Africa.

Leading through *Ubuntu* Values

Woven into the fabric of African society is the concept of *ubuntu*. *Ubuntu* represents a collection of values, including harmony, compassion, respect, human dignity, and collective unity. It is "that profound African sense that each of us is human through the humanity of other human beings," explains former South African president Nelson Mandela. *Ubuntu* is often described through a Zulu maxim: "umuntu ngumuntu ngabantu." Archbishop Desmond Tutu offers this translation: "We believe that a person is a person through other persons; that my humanity is caught up, bound up and inextricably in yours."

The *ubuntu* value system provides a framework for how people should lead others in Africa, whether in politics or organizations. First, *ubuntu* is about connectedness, so leaders must be comfortable with the highly participative process of making decisions through consensus. Everyone must have a chance to speak without imposed tight time restrictions. The process itself will determine the time required. This consensus process does not call for leadership abdication; rather, it requires leaders to coach, facilitate, and possibly mediate as the group moves toward mutual agreement.

Along with building consensus, *ubuntu* values a collective respect for everyone in the system. It places the good of the community above self-interest—to help others as an inherent part of your own well-being. For leaders, this condition requires the ability to provide support to followers, to mediate differences, and to serve followers rather than have followers serve leaders. The heroic leader who steps in front—and typically looks down from a higher plateau—is not consistent with *ubuntu*. Instead, leaders are respected for their wisdom and ability, so *ubuntu* selects leaders for their age and experience.

Ubuntu is "that profound African sense that each of us is human through the humanity of other human beings," explains Nelson Mandela.

Sources: L. van der Colff, "Leadership Lessons from the African Tree," *Management Decision* 41 (2003), pp. 257–61; L. van der Colff, "Ubuntu, Isivivane and Uhluhlasa: The Meaning of Leadership and Management in South Africa," *Equity-Skills News and Views* 1 (December 2002/January 2003); L. D. Krause and R. Powell, "Preparing School Leaders in Post-apartheid South Africa: A Survey of Leadership Preferences of Principals in Western Cape," *Journal of Leadership Studies* 8 (January 2002), pp. 63ff; M. P. Mangaliso, "Building Competitive Advantage from Ubuntu: Management Lessons from South Africa," *Academy of Management Executive* 15 (August 2001), pp. 23–43; Speech by President Nelson Mandela at his 80th Birthday Party, Kruger National Park, July 16, 1998.

An executive who acts inconsistently with cultural expectations is more likely to be perceived as an ineffective leader. Moreover, leaders who deviate from those values may experience various forms of influence to get them to conform to the leadership norms and expectations of the society. In other words, implicit leadership theory described in the previous section of this chapter explains differences in leadership practices across cultures.

Over the past few years, 150 researchers from dozens of countries have worked together on Project GLOBE (Global Leadership and Organizational Behavior Effectiveness) to identify the effects of cultural values on leadership.[93] The project organized countries into 10 regional clusters, of which the United States is grouped into the "Anglo" cluster with Great Britain, Australia, New Zealand, and Canada. The results of this massive investigation are just beginning to appear, but preliminary work suggests that some features of leadership are universal and some differ across cultures.

Specifically, the GLOBE Project reports that "charismatic visionary" is a universally recognized concept, and that middle managers around the world believe that it is characteristic of effective leaders. Charismatic visionary represents a cluster of concepts including visionary, inspirational, performance-orientation, integrity, and decisiveness.[94] In contrast, participative leadership is perceived as characteristic of effective leadership in low power distance cultures but less so in high power distance cultures. For instance, one study reported that Mexican employees expect managers to make decisions affecting their work. Mexico is a high power distance culture, so followers expect leaders to apply their authority rather than delegate their power most of the time.[95] In summary, there are similarities and differences in the concept and preferred practice of leadership across cultures.

Gender Differences in Leadership

Do women lead differently than men? Several writers think so. They suggest that women have an interactive style consisting of more people-oriented and participative leadership.[96] They say that women are more relationship-oriented, cooperative, nurturing, and emotional in their leadership roles. In other words, female leaders act consistently with sex role stereotypes of women in general. These writers further assert that these qualities make women particularly well suited to leadership roles at a time when companies are adopting a stronger emphasis on teams and employee involvement.

Are these stereotypes true? Do women adopt more people-oriented and participative leadership styles? The answer is no and yes, respectively. Leadership studies in field settings have generally found that male and female leaders do not differ in their levels of task-oriented or people-oriented leadership. The main explanation why men and women do not differ on these styles is that real-world jobs require similar behavior from male and female job incumbents.[97]

However, women do adopt a participative leadership style more readily than their male counterparts. Scholars suggest that women are possibly more participative because their upbringing has made them more egalitarian and less status-oriented. There is also some evidence that women have somewhat better interpersonal skills than men, and this translates into their relatively greater use of the participative leadership style. A third explanation is that subordinates expect female leaders to be more participative, based on their own sex stereotypes. Subordinates are more likely to complain (or use some other form of influence) if a female manager tries to be more autocratic than if a male does, because they expect the female executive or team leader to be participative.[98]

Evaluating Female Leaders   For several years, OB scholars warned that female leaders are evaluated slightly less favorably than equivalent male leaders, and this difference is almost completely due to sex stereotype bias. Specifically, women are evaluated negatively when they adopt a stereotypically male leadership style (i.e., autocratic) and occupy traditionally male-dominated positions. These negative evaluations suggest that women "pay the price" for entering traditionally male leadership jobs and for adopting a male-stereotypic leadership style.[99] It also lends further support to our earlier point on why women adopt a more participative style.

However, as the opening story to this chapter emphasized, the perceptions of effective leaders are shifting. Followers increasingly expect leaders to support and empower them. These leadership styles are more consistent with how many women prefer to lead and how followers stereotype female leaders. Consequently, several recent surveys reported that women are rated higher than men on most leadership dimensions, including the emerging leadership qualities of coaching, teamwork, and empowering employees.[100]

Whether women or men are better leaders depends, of course, on the individual and on specific circumstances. We should also be careful about perpetuating the apparently false assumption that women leaders are less task-oriented or more people-oriented. At the same time, both male and female leaders must be sensitive to the fact that followers have expectations about how leaders should act, and negative evaluations may go to leaders who deviate from those expectations.

Chapter Summary

Leadership is a complex concept that is defined as the ability to influence, motivate, and enable others to contribute to the effectiveness and success of the organizations of which they are members. Leaders use influence to motivate followers and arrange the work environment so that they do the job more effectively. Leaders exist throughout the organization, not just in the executive suite.

The competency perspective tries to identify the characteristics of effective leaders. Recent writing suggests that leaders have emotional intelligence, integrity, drive, leadership motivation, self-confidence, above-average intelligence, and knowledge of the business. The behavioral perspective of leadership identified two clusters of leader behavior, people-oriented and task-oriented. People-oriented behaviors include showing mutual trust and respect for subordinates, demonstrating a genuine concern for their needs, and having a desire to look out for their welfare. Task-oriented behaviors include assigning employees to specific tasks, clarifying their work duties and procedures, ensuring that they follow company rules, and pushing them to reach their performance capacity.

The contingency perspective of leadership takes the view that effective leaders diagnose the situation and adapt their style to fit that situation. The path–goal model is the prominent contingency theory that identifies four leadership styles—directive, supportive, participative, and achievement-oriented—and several contingencies relating to the characteristics of the employee and of the situation.

Two other contingency leadership theories are the situational leadership model and Fiedler's contingency theory. Research support is quite weak for both theories. However, a lasting element of Fiedler's theory is the idea that leaders have natural styles and, consequently, companies need to change the leader's environment to suit that style. Leadership substitutes identify contingencies that either limit the leader's ability to influence subordinates or make that particular leadership style unnecessary. This idea will become more important as organizations remove supervisors and shift toward team-based structures.

Transformational leaders create a strategic vision, communicate that vision through framing and use of metaphors, model the vision by "walking the talk" and acting consistently, and build commitment to the vision. This contrasts with transactional leadership, which links job performance to valued rewards and ensures that employees have the resources needed to get the job done. The contingency and behavioral perspectives adopt the transactional view of leadership.

According to the implicit leadership perspective, people inflate the importance of leadership through attribution, stereotyping, and fundamental needs for human control. Implicit leadership theory is evident across cultures because cultural values shape the behaviors that followers expect of their leaders. Cultural values also influence the leader's personal values, which, in turn, influence his or her leadership practices. The GLOBE Project data reveal that there are similarities and differences in the concept and preferred practice of leadership across cultures.

Women generally do not differ from men in the degree of people-oriented or task-oriented leadership. However, female leaders more often adopt a participative style. Research also suggests that people evaluate female leaders based on gender stereotypes, which may result in higher or lower ratings.

Key Terms

Fiedler's contingency model, p. 426
implicit leadership theory, p. 432
leadership, p. 416
Leadership Grid, p. 421
leadership substitutes, p. 427

path–goal leadership theory, p. 422
servant leadership, p. 422
situational leadership model, p. 425
transactional leadership, p. 428
transformational leader, p. 428

Discussion Questions

1. Why is it important for top executives to value and support leadership demonstrated at all levels of the organization?

2. Find two newspaper ads for management or executive positions. What leadership competencies are mentioned in these ads? If you were on the selection panel, what methods would you use to identify these competencies in job applicants?

3. Consider your favorite teacher. What people-oriented and task-oriented leadership behaviors did he or she use effectively? In general, do you think students prefer an instructor who is more people-oriented or more task-oriented? Explain your preference.

4. Your employees are skilled and experienced customer service representatives who perform non-routine tasks, such as solving unique customer problems or special needs with the company's equipment. Use path–goal theory to identify the most appropriate leadership style(s) you should use in this situation. Be sure to fully explain your answer and discuss why other styles are inappropriate.

5. Discuss the accuracy of the following statement: "Contingency theories don't work because they assume leaders can adjust their style to the situation. In reality, people have a preferred leadership style that they can't easily change."

6. Transformational leadership is currently the most popular perspective of leadership. However, it is far from perfect. Discuss three concerns with transformational leadership.

7. Identify a current political leader (e.g., president, governor, mayor) and his or her recent accomplishments. Now, using the implicit leadership perspective, think of ways that these accomplishments of the leader may be overstated. In other words, explain why they may be due to factors other than the leader.

8. You hear two people debating the merits of women as leaders. One person claims that women make better leaders than do men because women are more sensitive to their employees' needs and involve them in organizational decisions. The other person counters that although these leadership styles may be increasingly important, most women have trouble gaining acceptance as leaders when they face tough situations in which a more autocratic style is required. Discuss the accuracy of the comments made in this discussion.

CASE STUDY 14.1

JOSH MARTIN

By Joseph C. Santora, Essex County College and TSTDCG, Inc., and James C. Sarros, Monash University

Josh Martin, a 41-year-old administrator at the Center Street Settlement House, a nonprofit social service agency with 70 employees and more than $6 million in assets, sat pensively at his desk located outside the executive suite. He thought to himself, "No, it can't be. I can't have been working here for 20 years. Where did the time go?"

Martin has spent his entire adult life working at the Center Street Settlement House. He began his career there immediately after graduating from college with a degree in economics and very slowly climbed the narrow administrative ladder from his initial position as the director of a government-funded project to his current position as the deputy agency administrator. In addition, for the past five years, he has been serving as the president of the agency's for-profit construction company. He reports directly to Tom Saunders, the autocratic executive director of the agency.

Martin, a competent administrator, often gets things done through his participative leadership style. In the last few years, Martin's job responsibilities have increased exponentially. He fills many informational, decisional, and interpersonal managerial roles for the agency. Six months ago, he was given the added responsibility of processing invoices for agency vendors and consultants, authority he shares with Saunders and the agency's accountant.

Martin is rewarded handsomely for his role in the nonprofit agency. Last year, he earned $90,000, plus a liberal fringe benefits package that included an agency car, a pension plan, a medical health plan (including dental), a month's vacation, 15 paid holidays, and unlimited sick time. Although he has received an annual cost-of-living allowance (COLA), Martin has no written contractual agreement and essentially serves at the pleasure of Saunders.

Martin pays a high personal price for his attractive compensation package. He is on call, his beeper activated, 24 hours a day. Each Sunday morning, Martin attends a mandatory agency strategy meeting required of all agency managers.

Over the years, Martin has tolerated Saunders's erratic mood swings and his inattentiveness to agency details. Tension between the two men reached a high point in recent months. For example, two months ago, Martin called in sick because he was suffering from a severe bout of flu. Martin's absence forced Saunders to cancel an important meeting to supervise an agency fiscal audit. Saunders responded to Martin's absence in an irrational fashion by focusing on a small piece of tile missing from the cafeteria floor. He screamed at two employees who were eating lunch in the cafeteria.

"You see," he said, "Martin doesn't give a damn about anything in this agency. I always have to make sure things get done around here. Just look at the floor! There's a piece of tile missing!" Mary Thompson and Elizabeth Duncan, two veteran employees, seemed shocked by Saunders's reaction to the missing piece of tile. As Saunders stormed out of the cafeteria throwing his hands in the air, Mary turned to Elizabeth and whispered, "Saunders is really going off the deep end. Without Josh nothing would get done around here. I don't see how Saunders can blame Josh for every little problem. I wonder how long Josh can take this unfair treatment." Elizabeth nodded her head in agreement.

A month after this incident, Martin recommended pay increases for two employees who had received excellent performance appraisals by their supervisors. Martin believed that a 2 percent raise, admittedly only a symbolic raise, would provide motivation, would increase morale, and would not seriously jeopardize the agency's budget. When Martin proposed his recommendations for employee raises to Saunders at the Thursday weekly fiscal meeting, Saunders vehemently rejected Martin's proposal and countered it by ranting: "Everybody wants a raise around here. It's about time people started doing more work and stopped whining about money. Let's move on to the next agenda item."

Saunders closed the weekly staff meeting by saying "I'm the leader of this agency. I have to manage everything for this agency to run effectively." Phil Jones, the director of field operations, turned to Paul Lindstrom, the fiscal officer, and whispered, "Sure, Saunders is the director of this agency all right, but he couldn't manage his way out of a paper bag. Without Josh, this place would be in total chaos. Besides, at least Josh listens to us and tries to implement some of our ideas to make life simpler around here."

Martin has often contemplated resigning from the agency to seek other public sector employment. However, he believes such opportunities are rare since he is a middle-aged, white male. Besides, Saunders knows just about every agency CEO in the public sector. Martin believes that Saunders would find out that he applied for a job as soon as his résumé reached an agency personnel department. Moreover, Martin feels that his long tenure with the agency may be detrimental; most prospective employers would be suspicious of his motives for leaving the settlement house after some two decades of service.

Martin mused, "Perhaps I stayed too long at the dance." Finally, given the present economic conditions in the state, many public sector agencies would be reluctant to match his salary and benefits package—at least not in his first few years of service.

Martin is uncertain of his options at this point. On a personal note, although his wife is gainfully employed and possesses good technical skills and experience in the printing industry, Martin still needs to maintain his present standard of living to support his family, including his two college-age daughters, a $100,000 mortgage on his home, and other financial obligations. He has significant nonprofit and for-profit experience and excellent managerial and leadership skills. Yet, he wonders if there is any way out of his current situation.

Discussion Questions

1. Describe the two different leadership styles used by Josh Martin and Tom Saunders. Do these two styles tell you anything about leadership traits? Do you think there is any resolution to the organizational problems resulting from the conflicting leadership styles?

2. What are the characteristics/elements of an effective leader? Do you think Saunders is an effective leader? Why or why not? Is Martin an effective leader? Why or why not?

3. Does Josh Martin have any way out of his current situation? What would you do if you were Josh Martin?

Source: Joseph C. Santora, Essex County College & TSTDCG, Inc., and James C. Sarros, Morash University.

CASE STUDY 14.2

STAYING ON TOP

BusinessWeek Johnson & Johnson may be one of America's best run companies, but maintaining the health care giant's success will require strong leadership. Many people say that William C. Weldon, J&J's recently appointed CEO, is just the person to lead the company into the future. The leadership challenge is considerable because continuing on the company's current structure and culture may work effectively now, but probably not in the long term.

This *Business Week* case study looks at the leadership competencies and style of Johnson & Johnson's newest CEO. It describes some of the unique talents that make observers confident that Weldon is the right leader to take the company into the future. The article also highlights some of the challenges and strategies that Weldon has already applied. Read through this *Business Week* article at www.mhhe.com/mcshane3e and prepare for the discussion questions below.

Discussion Questions

1. Identify the leadership competencies that William Weldon seems to possess. How are these competencies applied to improve Johnson & Johnson's success?

2. Would you consider William Weldon a transformational leader? Why or why not?

Source: A. Barrett, "Staying on Top," *Business Week*, May 5, 2003, p. 60.

TEAM EXERCISE 14.3

LEADERSHIP DIAGNOSTIC ANALYSIS

Purpose   This exercise is designed to help students learn about the different path–goal leadership styles and when to apply each style.

Instructions

■ *Step 1*—Students individually write down two incidents in which someone had been an effective leader over them. The leader and situation might be from work, a sports team, a student work group, or any other setting where leadership might emerge. For example, students might describe how their supervisor in a summer job pushed them to reach higher performance goals than they would have done otherwise. Each incident should state the actual behaviors that the leader used, not just general statements (e.g., "My boss sat down with me and we agreed on specific targets and deadlines, then he said several times over the next few weeks that I was capable of reaching those goals.") Each incident requires only two or three sentences.

■ *Step 2*—After everyone has written their two incidents, the instructor will form small groups (typically four to five students). Each team will answer the following questions for each incident presented in that team:

1. Which path–goal theory leadership style(s) —directive, supportive, participative, or achievement-oriented—did the leader apply in this incident?
2. What conditions made this leadership style (or these styles, if more than one was used) appropriate in this situation? The team should list these contingency factors clearly and, where possible, connect them to the contingencies described in path–goal theory. (Note: The team might identify path–goal leadership contingencies that are not described in the book. These, too, should be noted and discussed.)

■ *Step 3*—After the teams have diagnosed the incidents, each team will describe to the entire class the most interesting incidents as well as its diagnosis of that incident. Other teams will critique the diagnosis. Any leadership contingencies not mentioned in the textbook should also be presented and discussed.

SELF-ASSESSMENT EXERCISE 14.4

LEADERSHIP DIMENSIONS INSTRUMENT

Purpose   This assessment is designed to help you to understand two important dimensions of leadership and to identify which of these dimensions is more prominent in your supervisor, team leader, coach, or other person to whom you are accountable.

Instructions   Read each of the statements on the next page and circle the response that you believe best describes your supervisor. You may substitute "supervisor" for anyone else to whom you are accountable, such as a team leader, CEO, course instructor, or sports coach. Then use the scoring key in Appendix B to calculate the results for each leadership dimensions. After completing this assessment, be prepared to discuss in class the distinctions between these leadership dimensions.

My supervisor . . .	Strongly Agree	Agree	Neutral	Disagree	Strongly Disagree
1. Focuses attention on irregularities, mistakes, exceptions, and deviations from what is expected of me......................	5	4	3	2	1
2. Engages in words and deeds that enhance his or her image of competence...	5	4	3	2	1
3. Monitors performance for errors needing correction..........	5	4	3	2	1
4. Serves as a role model for me...	5	4	3	2	1
5. Points out what I will receive if I do what is required.	5	4	3	2	1
6. Instills pride in being associated with him or her...............	5	4	3	2	1
7. Keeps careful track of mistakes...	5	4	3	2	1
8. Can be trusted to help me overcome any obstacle..........	5	4	3	2	1
9. Tells me what to do to be rewarded for my efforts.............	5	4	3	2	1
10. Makes me aware of strongly held values, ideals, and aspirations which are shared in common...........................	5	4	3	2	1
11. Is alert for failure to meet standards.................................	5	4	3	2	1
12. Mobilizes a collective sense of mission.............................	5	4	3	2	1
13. Works out agreements with me on what I will receive if I do what needs to be done..	5	4	3	2	1
14. Articulates a vision of future opportunities........................	5	4	3	2	1
15. Talks about special rewards for good work........................	5	4	3	2	1
16. Talks optimistically about the future..................................	5	4	3	2	1

Source: Items and dimensions are adapted from D. N. Den Hartog, J. J. Van Muijen, and P. L. Koopman, "Transactional versus Transformational Leadership: An Analysis of the MLQ," *Journal of Occupational and Organizational Psychology* 70 (March 1997), pp. 19–34. Den Hartog et al. label transactional leadership as "rational-objective leadership" and label transformational leadership as "inspirational leadership." Many of their items may have originated from B. M. Bass and B. J. Avolio, *Manual for the Multifactor Leadership Questionnaire* (Palo Alto, CA: Consulting Psychologists Press, 1989).

After studying the preceding material, be sure to check out our website at

www.mhhe.com/mcshane3e

for more in-depth information and interactivities that correspond to this chapter.

Organizational Processes

Organizational Structure and Design

Learning Objectives

After reading this chapter, you should be able to:

- Describe three types of coordination in organizational structures.

- Explain why firms can have flatter structures than previously believed.

- Discuss the dynamics of centralization and formalization as organizations get larger and older.

- Contrast functional structures with divisional structures.

- Explain why geographic divisional structures are becoming less common than other divisional structures.

- Outline the features and advantages of the matrix structure.

- Describe four features of team-based organizational structures.

- Discuss the advantages of the network structure.

- Summarize three contingencies of organizational design.

- Explain how organizational strategy relates to organizational structure.

From its beginning in 1958, W. L. Gore & Associates Inc. has maintained an organizational chart that defies traditional categorization. The Newark, Delaware-based manufacturer of fabrics (including GoreTex), electronics, and industrial and medical products was deliberately structured by founder Bill Gore as a "lattice organization" consisting of teams responsible for their own projects and work processes. "Gore is structured entirely differently from a classical organization, to encourage everyone to contribute and to be inventive and creative," explains Mike Cox, technical director of the industrial products division.

W. L. Gore & Associates Inc. has a team-based organizational structure that eliminates the traditional hierarchy.

Gore has also gone further than most organizations at eliminating job titles, supervisors, and formal hierarchies. "There is no positional power," Cox explains. "You are only a leader if teams decide to respect and follow you." In fact, anyone can start a new project simply by persuading enough people to go along with the idea. Similarly, without formal job descriptions, employees often cross functional boundaries. "We don't put people in boxes," says Gore associate Ann Gillies. "I may have a core set of HR commitments, but I also work on a purchasing project as part of a multi-functional team."

Gore's team-based structure includes a high degree of decentralized authority. Every employee has the freedom to make day-to-day decisions. Bigger issues, such as hiring and compensating staff, are decided by teams. "We make our own decisions and everything is discussed as well," explains Phyllis Tait, a medical business support leader at Gore's U.K. business unit. "For example, if I wanted to go on a course, then we would all just go into discussion and if it was good for the business, then I would get to go."

The amazing thing about Gore's structure is that it continues to operate effectively even though the company has expanded to 6,000 employees in 45 locations around the world. It does this by creating self-sufficient manufacturing facilities and limiting their size to about 200 people to maintain coordination through informal communication.[1] ∎

There is something of a revolution occurring in how organizations are structured. W. L. Gore & Associates Inc. and other companies are throwing out the old organizational charts and trying out new designs that they hope will achieve organizational objectives more effectively. **Organizational structure** refers to the division of labor as well as the patterns of coordination, communication, work flow, and formal power that direct organizational activities. An organizational structure reflects the organization's culture and power relationships.[2] Our knowledge of this subject provides the tools to engage in **organizational design,** that is, to create and modify organizational structures.

Organizational structures are frequently used as tools for change. Structures support or inhibit communication and relationships across the organization.[3] They also serve as mechanisms that either support change or make change initiatives more difficult. Structures establish new communication patterns and align employee behavior with the corporate vision. For example, Ford Motor Company restructured its many business units so that employees are closer to specific types of customers, such as luxury car buyers (Jaguar, Volvo), services (Hertz, e-commerce), and Ford's mainstream car buyers.[4]

We begin this chapter by considering the two fundamental processes in organizational structure: division of labor and coordination. This is followed by a detailed investigation of the four main elements of organizational structure: span of control, centralization, formalization, and departmentalization. The latter part of this chapter examines the contingencies of organizational design, including organizational size, technology, external environment, and strategy.

Division of Labor and Coordination

All organizational structures include two fundamental requirements: the division of labor into distinct tasks and the coordination of that labor so that employees are able to accomplish common goals.[5] Organizations are groups of people who work interdependently toward some purpose (see Chapter 1). To efficiently accomplish their goals, these groups typically divide the work into manageable chunks, particularly when there are many different tasks to perform. They also introduce various coordinating mechanisms to ensure that everyone is working effectively toward the same objectives.

Division of Labor

Division of labor refers to the subdivision of work into separate jobs assigned to different people. Subdivided work leads to job specialization, because each job now includes a narrow subset of the tasks necessary to complete the product or service (see Chapter 6). For example, designing and manufacturing an aircraft at Boeing Company requires thousands of specific tasks that are divided among thousands of people. Tasks are also divided vertically, for example, by having supervisors coordinate work while employees perform the work.

Work is divided into specialized jobs because this potentially increases work efficiency.[6] Job incumbents can master their tasks quickly because work cycles are very short. Less time is wasted changing from one task to another. Training costs are reduced because employees require fewer physical and mental skills to accomplish the assigned work. Finally, job specialization facilitates the matching of people with specific aptitudes or skills to the jobs for which they are best suited.

EXHIBIT 15.1   Coordinating mechanisms in organizations

Form of coordination	Description	Subtypes
Informal communication	Sharing information on mutual tasks; forming common mental models to synchronize work activities	• Direct communication • Integrator roles
Formal hierarchy	Assigning legitimate power to individuals, who then use this power to direct work processes and allocate resources	• Direct supervision • Corporate structure
Standardization	Creating routine patterns of behavior or output	• Standardized skills • Standardized processes • Standardized output

Source: Based on information in D. A. Nadler and M. L. Tushman, *Competing by Design: The Power of Organizational Architecture* (New York: Oxford University Press, 1997), Chap. 6; H. Mintzberg, *The Structuring of Organizations* (Englewood Cliffs, N.J.: Prentice Hall, 1979), Chap. 1; J. Galbraith, *Designing Complex Organizations* (Reading, MA: Addison-Wesley, 1973), pp. 8–19.

Coordinating Work Activities

As soon as people divide work among themselves, coordinating mechanisms are needed to ensure that everyone works in concert.[7] Every organization—from the two-person corner convenience store to the largest corporate entity—uses one or more of the following coordinating mechanisms: informal communication, formal hierarchy, and standardization (see Exhibit 15.1).

Coordination through Informal Communication   Informal communication is a coordinating mechanism in all organizations.[8] This includes sharing information on mutual tasks as well as forming common mental models so that employees synchronize work activities using the same mental road map.[9] Informal communication permits considerable flexibility because employees transmit a large volume of information through face-to-face communication and other media-rich channels (see Chapter 11). Consequently, informal communication is a vital coordinating mechanism in nonroutine and ambiguous situations.

Coordination through informal communication is easiest in small firms and work units where employees face few communication barriers. Emerging information technologies have further leveraged this coordinating mechanism in large organizations, even where employees are scattered around the globe. Larger organizations can also support informal communication by forming temporary cross-functional teams and moving team members into a common physical area (called *co-locating*). For example, **platform teams** (also called *concurrent engineering teams*) are project teams consisting of people from marketing, design, manufacturing, customer service, and other areas.[10] These employees are typically co-located to improve cross-functional coordination, whereas more formal and less flexible coordinating mechanisms are seen when product development occurs through several departments.

Larger organizations also encourage coordination through informal communication by creating *integrator roles*. Integrators are responsible for coordinating a work process by encouraging employees in each work unit to share information and informally coordinate work activities. They do not have authority over the people involved in the process, so they must rely on

platform teams
Temporary teams consisting of people from marketing, design, and other areas, who are responsible for developing a product or service.

persuasion and commitment. As an example, brand managers at Procter & Gamble coordinate work among marketing, production, and design groups.[11]

Coordination through Formal Hierarchy   Informal communication is the most flexible form of coordination, but it can be time-consuming. Consequently, as organizations grow, they develop a second coordinating mechanism in the shape of a formal hierarchy. Hierarchy assigns legitimate power to individuals, who then use this power to direct work processes and allocate resources (see Chapter 12). In other words, work is coordinated through direct supervision.

Any organization with a formal structure coordinates work to some extent through the formal hierarchy. For instance, team leaders at W. L. Gore & Associates coordinate work by ensuring that employees in their group remain on schedule and that their respective tasks are compatible with tasks completed by others in the group. At Gore, the team grants the leader authority to schedule work activities and resolve conflicts. The formal hierarchy also coordinates work among executives through the division of organizational activities. If the organization is divided into geographic areas, the structure gives the head of those regional groups legitimate power over executives responsible for production, customer service, and other activities in those areas. If the organization is divided into product groups, then the heads of those groups have the right to coordinate work across regions.

The formal hierarchy has traditionally been applauded as the optimal coordinating mechanism for large organizations. Henri Fayol, an early scholar on the subject, argued that organizations are most effective where managers exercise their authority and employees receive orders from only one supervisor. Coordination should occur through the chain of command, that is, up the hierarchy and across to the other work unit.[12] Coordination through formal hierarchy may have been popular with classic organizational theorists, but it is often a very inefficient coordinating mechanism. Later in this chapter, we will learn that there are limits to how many employees a supervisor can coordinate. Furthermore, the chain of command is rarely as fast or accurate as direct communication between employees. And, as recent scholars have warned, today's educated and individualistic workforce is less tolerant of rigid structures and legitimate power.[13]

Coordination through Standardization   Standardization—creating routine patterns of behavior or output—is the third means of coordination. Many organizations try to improve the quality and consistency of a product or service by standardizing work activities through job descriptions and procedures.[14] Standardization coordinates work that is simple and routine, but is less effective where tasks are complex and conditions are ambiguous. In these situations, companies might coordinate work by standardizing the individual's or team's goals and product or service output (e.g., customer satisfaction, production efficiency). For instance, to coordinate the work of salespeople, companies assign sales targets rather than specific behaviors.

When work activities are too complex to standardize through procedures or goals, companies often coordinate work effort by extensively training employees or hiring people who have learned precise role behaviors from educational programs. This form of coordination is used in hospital operating rooms. Surgeons, nurses, and other operating room professionals coordinate their work more through training than goals or company rules.

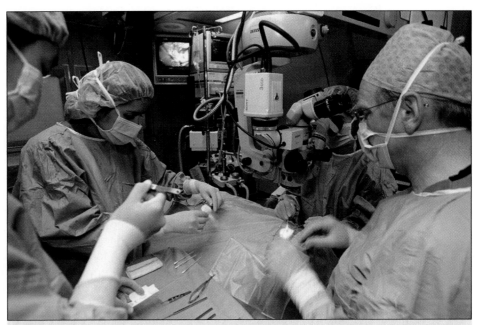

Flying to developing nations around the world, the ORBIS Flying Eye Hospital is a nonprofit service that trains local professionals and provides eye care education. Medical professionals on board the converted DC-10 also conduct an average of four eye operations each day, including the surgery on a young girl in Costa Rica shown in this photo. To some extent, these professionals coordinate their surgical work activities through informal communication. However, much of the operation occurs without discussion because team members also coordinate through standardization of skills. Through extensive training, each person has learned precise role behaviors so that his or her task activities are coordinated with others on the surgical team.[15] What other types of organizations make extensive use of standardization of skills to coordinate work?

Division of labor and coordination of work represent the two fundamental ingredients of all organizations. How work is divided, who makes decisions, which coordinating mechanisms are emphasized, and other issues are related to the four elements of organizational structure.

Elements of Organizational Structure

Every company is configured in terms of four basic elements of organizational structure. This section introduces three of them: span of control, centralization, and formalization. The fourth element—departmentalization—is presented in the next section.

Span of Control

span of control
The number of people directly reporting to the next level in the organizational hierarchy.

Span of control refers to the number of people directly reporting to the next level in the hierarchy. As we mentioned earlier, Henri Fayol strongly recommended the formal hierarchy as the primary coordinating mechanism. Consequently, he and other theorists at the time prescribed a relatively narrow span of control, typically no more than 20 employees per supervisor and 6 supervisors per manager. These prescriptions were based on the assumption that managers simply cannot monitor and control any more subordinates closely enough.

Today, we know better. The best performing manufacturing facilities currently have an average of 31 employees per supervisor. This is a much wider span of control than past scholars had recommended. Yet these operations plan to stretch this span to an average of 75 employees per supervisor over the next few years.[16]

What's the secret here? Did Fayol and others miscalculate the optimal span of control? The answer is that early scholars thought in terms of Frederick Taylor's scientific management model (see Chapter 6). They believed that employees should "do" the work, whereas supervisors and other management personnel should monitor employee behavior and make most of the decisions. This division of labor limited the span of control. It is very difficult to directly supervise 75 people. It is much easier to *oversee* 75 subordinates who are grouped into several self-directed work teams. Employees manage themselves, thereby releasing supervisors from the time-consuming tasks of monitoring behavior and making everyone else's decisions.[17]

Consolidated Diesel's manufacturing facility in Whitakers, North Carolina, illustrates this point. The plant's 1,700 employees produce 650 engines each day in four different models, each of which can be configured in any of more than 3,500 different ways. While comparable plants might have one supervisor for every 25 employees, Consolidated Diesel has one for every 100 employees. The company is able to operate with a much wider span of control because production employees are organized into self-directed work teams that are responsible for their own areas.[18]

The underlying principle here is that the span of control depends on the presence of other coordinating mechanisms. Self-directed work teams supplement direct supervision with informal communication and specialized knowledge. This also explains why dozens of surgeons and other medical professionals may report to the head surgeon in a major hospital. The head surgeon doesn't engage in much direct supervision because the standardized skills of medical staff coordinate the unit's work. A wider span of control is also possible when employees perform similar tasks or have routine jobs. In these situations, the organization relies more on standardization of work processes to coordinate work, thereby reducing the need for hands-on supervision.[19]

Tall and Flat Structures   BASF's European Seal Sands plant recently organized employees into self-directed work teams and dramatically restructured the work process. These actions did much more than increase efficiency and lower costs at the bulk chemical plant. They also chopped out several layers of hierarchy. "Seven levels of management have been cut basically to two," says a BASF executive.[20]

BASF joins a long list of companies that are moving toward flatter organizational structures. Dow Chemical has tens of thousands of employees spread throughout the world, yet the company has only six levels between the CEO and shop floor employees. Royal Mail, which delivers mail throughout Great Britain, went from 16 layers of management to 6 layers.[21] This trend toward delaying—moving from a tall to flat structure—is partly in response to the recommendations of management gurus. For example, Tom Peters challenged corporate leaders to cut the number of layers to three within a facility and to five within the entire organization.[22]

The main arguments for delayering are that it potentially cuts overhead costs and puts decision makers closer to front-line staff and information about cus-

**"Shipwrecked or not, Bradley, we
must maintain the chain of command."**

Edward Smith/Artizans.com. Reprinted with permission.

tomer needs. "Corporations have come to realize that they need to have fewer layers of management if they are to communicate daily with their organizations and if they are to become closer to the customer," advises retired Honeywell CEO Lawrence A. Bossidy.[23] However, some organizational experts warn that corporate leaders may be cutting out too much hierarchy. They argue that the much-maligned "middle managers" serve a valuable function by controlling work activities and managing corporate growth. Moreover, companies will always need hierarchy because someone has to make quick decisions and represent a source of appeal over conflicts.[24] The conclusion here is that there is an optimal level of delayering in most organizations. Flatter structures offer several benefits, but cutting out too much management can offset these benefits.

One last point before leaving this topic: The size of an organization's hierarchy depends on both the average span of control and the number of people employed by the organization. As shown in Exhibit 15.2, a tall structure has many hierarchical levels, each with a relatively narrow span of control, whereas a flat structure has few levels, each with a wide span of control.[25] Larger organizations that depend on hierarchy for coordination necessarily develop taller structures.

Centralization and Decentralization

centralization
The degree to which formal decision authority is held by a small group of people, typically those at the top of the organizational hierarchy.

Centralization and decentralization represent a second element of organizational design. **Centralization** means that formal decision-making authority is held by a small group of people, typically those at the top of the organizational hierarchy. Most organizations begin with centralized structures, as the founder makes most of the decisions and tries to direct the business toward his or her vision. But as organizations grow, they diversify and their environments become more complex. Senior executives aren't able to process all the decisions that significantly influence the business. Consequently, larger organizations tend to *decentralize*, that is, they disperse decision authority and power throughout the organization.

Microsoft is a case in point. The software giant has grown over the past quarter-century to more than 50,000 employees working on various high-tech products and services, yet almost all important decisions are still made at the

EXHIBIT 15.2   Span of control with tall and flat structures

**Tall structure/
Narrow span of control**

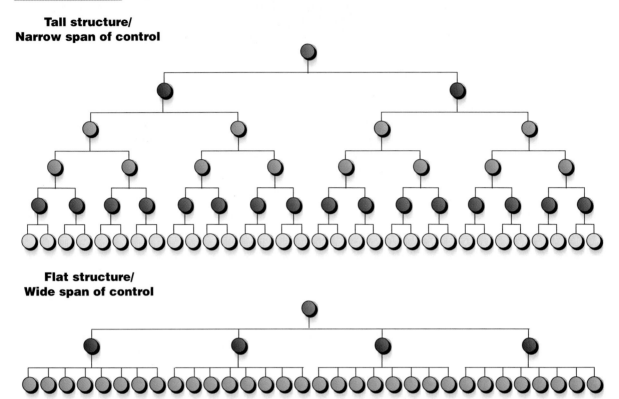

**Flat structure/
Wide span of control**

top by Bill Gates on technology and products and Steve Ballmer on sales and marketing. Sources say this centralized decision making has made Microsoft less responsive to the marketplace and has contributed to the departures of talented people who were frustrated by the process. "In our company, too many things, I think, were just having to run through two guys," says a Microsoft executive. The company is now decentralizing its structure to become more competitive.[26]

While large firms need to decentralize to some degree, they should also worry about too much decentralization. AES Corporation was renowned for pushing most decisions all the way down to the plant floor. While this highly decentralized structure helped the Arlington, Virginia, energy company to grow and respond quickly to opportunities, it also produced risky decisions by people who lacked sufficient training and experience. Those decisions, along with falling energy prices, recently plunged AES close to bankruptcy. "We took our own model to an extreme. We took it to an exaggerated level," admits AES cofounder and former chairman Roger W. Sant. AES is now moving strategic decisions further up the organizational hierarchy.[27]

The optimal level of centralization or decentralization depends on several contingencies that we will examine later in this chapter. However, we also need to keep in mind that different degrees of decentralization can occur simultaneously in different parts of the organization. Nestlé has decentralized marketing decisions to remain responsive to local markets. At the same time, the Swiss-based food company has centralized production, logistics, and supply chain management activities to improve cost efficiencies and avoid having too much complexity across the organization. "If you are too decentralized, you can become too complicated—you get too much complexity in your production system," explains Nestlé CEO Peter Brabeck.[28]

Formalization

Have you ever wondered why McDonald's hamburgers in Sarasota, Florida, look and taste the same as MacDonald's hamburgers in Singapore? The reason is that the fast-food company has engineered out variations through formalization. **Formalization** is the degree to which organizations standardize behavior through rules, procedures, formal training, and related mechanisms.[29] In other words, formalization represents the establishment of standardization as a coordinating mechanism.

McDonald's Corporation has a formalized structure because it prescribes every activity in explicit detail. Each McDonald's franchise must dole out five perfect drops of mustard, a quarter ounce of onions, and two pickles—three if they're small—on each hamburger. Drink cups are filled with ice up to a point just below the arches on their sides. Cooking and bagging fries are explained in 19 steps. Employees who work on the grill must put the hamburger patties in six rows of six patties each. A Big Mac is supposed to be assembled in 25 seconds from the time that it appears on the order screen.[30]

Older companies tend to become more formalized because work activities become routinized, making them easier to document into standardized practices. Larger companies formalize as a coordinating mechanism, because direct supervision and informal communication among employees do not operate as easily. External influences, such as government safety legislation and strict accounting rules, also encourage formalization.

Problems with Formalization   Formalization may increase efficiency, but it can also create problems. Rules and procedures reduce organizational flexibility, so employees follow prescribed behaviors even when the situation clearly calls for a customized response. Some work rules become so convoluted that organizational efficiency would decline if they were actually followed as prescribed. Labor unions sometimes call work-to-rule strikes, in which their members closely follow the formalized rules and procedures established by an organization. This tactic increases union power, because the company's productivity falls significantly when employees follow the rules that are supposed to guide their behavior.

Another concern is that although employees with very strong security needs and a low tolerance for ambiguity like working in highly formalized organizations, others become alienated and feel powerless in these structures. Finally, rules and procedures have been known to take on a life of their own in some organizations. They usurp the focus of attention from the organization's ultimate objectives of producing a product or service and serving its dominant stakeholders.

Mechanistic versus Organic Structures

We have discussed span of control, centralization, and formalization together because researchers have found that they seem to cluster together.[31] Some companies, such as McDonald's, have a **mechanistic structure,** which is

formalization
The degree to which organizations standardize behavior through rules, procedures, formal training, and related mechanisms.

mechanistic structure
An organizational structure with a narrow span of control and high degrees of formalization and centralization.

The Extreme Organic Structure of Harbinger Partners

Harbinger Partners is a "manager-free zone." That's because the business intelligence and creative services company has no bosses; everyone owns a piece of the company and is involved in making company decisions. Harbinger doesn't even have a formal headquarters, just a post office box number in St. Paul, Minnesota. The company's employees—actually, they're partners who invest up to $15,000 to join in—work either from their homes or in clients' offices.

This arrangement might give some executives sleepless nights, but not Scott Grausnick, who founded Harbinger in 1999. Instead, he deliberately created an extreme organic structure so staff could cater more effectively to customer needs while satisfying their entrepreneurial spirit. "Harbinger Partners is the perfect blend for me," says Greg Dougherty, who had contemplated starting his own consulting firm before signing up with Harbinger. "I'm an owner, yet at the same time I'm surrounded by seasoned consultants who are showing me the ropes."

Grausnick selected partners who offered high-level technical skills as well as a preference for unstructured work environments. Everyone is encouraged to think creatively about how to build the business and to take initiative. "It's a collection of very independent thinkers," says Harbinger partner Brenda Faber. "[But] we all own the business so we all have a say."

This extreme organic structure wouldn't suit every company, but it seems to work just fine at Harbinger Partners. In 1999, the company had nine partners and sales of $800,000.

Scott Grausnick looks comfortable in his backyard hammock leading Harbinger Partners, which has an extreme organic structure.

Four years later, after many high-tech services companies foundered, Harbinger has 35 partners generating revenues of $6.5 million. The company is also rated as one of the great places to work in Minnesota.

Sources: S. Brouillard, "Right at Home," *Minneapolis-St. Paul Business Journal,* August 23, 2002; D. Youngblood, "Computer Consultants Win Business with Creative Strategies," *Minneapolis Star Tribune,* July 15, 2001.

---

characterized by a narrow span of control and high degree of formalization and centralization. Mechanistic structures have many rules and procedures, limited decision making at lower levels, tall hierarchies of people in specialized roles, and vertical rather than horizontal communication flows. Tasks are rigidly defined and are altered only when sanctioned by higher authorities.

Companies with an **organic structure** have the opposite characteristics. W. L. Gore & Associates, described at the beginning of this chapter, is a clear example of an organic structure because it has a wide span of control, decentralized decision making, and little formalization. Tasks are fluid, adjusting to new situations and organizational needs. The organic structure values knowledge and takes the view that information may be located anywhere in the organization rather than among senior executives. Thus, communication flows in all directions with little concern for the formal hierarchy. Harbinger Partners is another extreme example of a company with an organic structure. As described in Connections 15.1, the business intelligence and creative services firm is completely decentralized and has minimal hierarchy and formalization.

Mechanistic structures operate best in stable environments because they rely on efficiency and routine behaviors. However, as we have emphasized through-

organic structure
An organizational structure with a wide span of control, little formalization, and decentralized decision making.

out this book, most organizations operate in a world of dramatic change. Information technology, globalization, a changing workforce, and other factors have strengthened the need for highly organic structures that are flexible and responsive to these changes. Moreover, organic structures are more consistent with knowledge management because they emphasize information sharing rather than hierarchy and status.[32]

Forms of Departmentalization

Span of control, centralization, and formalization are important elements of organizational structure, but most people think about organizational charts when the discussion of organizational structure arises. The organizational chart represents the fourth element in the structuring of organizations, called departmentalization. Departmentalization specifies how employees and their activities are grouped together. It is a fundamental strategy for coordinating organizational activities because it influences organizational behavior in the following ways.[33]

■ Departmentalization establishes the "chain of command," that is, the system of common supervision among positions and units within the organization. It establishes formal work teams, as described in Chapter 9. Departmentalization typically determines which positions and units must share resources. Thus, it establishes interdependencies among employees and subunits.

■ Departmentalization usually creates common measures of performance. Members of the same work team, for example, share common goals and budgets, giving the company standards against which to compare subunit performance.

■ Departmentalization encourages coordination through informal communication among people and subunits. With common supervision and resources, members within each configuration typically work near each other, so they can use frequent and informal interaction to get the work done.

There are almost as many organizational charts as there are businesses, but we can identify five pure types of departmentalization: simple, functional, divisional, matrix, and team-based. Few companies fit exactly into any of these categories, but they represent a useful framework for understanding more complex hybrid forms of departmentalization. Later, we will look at various forms of network structure.

Simple Structure

Most companies begin with a *simple structure*.[34] They employ only a few people and typically offer only one distinct product or service. There is minimal hierarchy—usually just employees reporting to the owners. Employees are grouped into broadly defined roles because there are insufficient economies of scale to assign them to specialized roles. Simple structures are flexible, yet they usually depend on the owner's direct supervision to coordinate work activities. Consequently, this structure is very difficult to operate under complex conditions.

The Alaska Chip Company is typical of small firms with a simple organizational structure. Alaska's newest potato chip business has minimal hierarchy and everyone has fairly loosely defined roles. Ralph Carney (shown here) cooks chips three days and delivers two days each week. Darcy Carney, his wife and cofounder, is business manager at the Anchorage firm. Darcy Carney's mother runs the office. "We're a Mom and Pop operation," says Darcy Carney.[35] *When should Alaska Chip Company discard its simple structure for another structure?*

Functional Structure

functional structure
An organizational structure that organizes employees around specific knowledge or other resources.

A **functional structure** organizes employees around specific knowledge or other resources. Employees with marketing expertise are grouped into a marketing unit, those with production skills are located in manufacturing, engineers are found in product development, and so on. Organizations with functional structures are typically centralized to coordinate their activities effectively. Standardization of work processes is the most common form of coordination used in a functional structure. Most organizations use functional structures at some level or at some time in their development.

Advantages and Disadvantages   An important advantage of functional structures is that they foster professional identity and clarify career paths. They permit greater specialization so that the organization has expertise in each area. Direct supervision is easier, because managers have backgrounds in that functional area and employees approach them with common problems and issues. Finally, functional structures create common pools of talent that typically serve everyone in the organization. This creates an economy of scale that would not exist if functional specialists were spread over different parts of the organization.[36]

Functional structures also have limitations.[37] Because people with common interests and backgrounds are grouped together, these designs tend to emphasize subunit goals over superordinate organizational goals. Employees in purchasing, accounting, engineering, and other functional units are less likely to give priority to the company's product or service than to the goals of their specific department. Unless people are transferred from one function to the next, they fail to develop a broader understanding of the business. A related concern is that functional structures emphasize differences across work units. For this reason, functional structures tend to have higher dysfunctional conflict and poorer coordination with other work units. Together, these problems require substantial formal controls and coordination when functional structures are used.

Divisional Structure

divisional structure

An organizational structure that groups employees around geographic areas, clients, or outputs.

A **divisional structure** groups employees around geographic areas, clients, or outputs (products/services). Divisional structures are sometimes called *strategic business units* (SBUs), because they are normally more autonomous than functional structures and may operate as subsidiaries rather than departments of the enterprise. Exhibit 15.3 illustrates the three pure forms of divisional structure. *Geographic divisionalized structures* organize employees around distinct areas of the country or globe. Exhibit 15.3(a) illustrates a geographic divisionalized structure similar to McDonald's Corporation's global structure. *Product/service structures* organize work around distinct outputs. Exhibit 15.3(b) illustrates this type of structure at Philips. The Dutch electronics company divides its workforce mainly into five product divisions, ranging from consumer electronics to semiconductors. *Client structures* represent the third form of divisional structure, in which employees are organized around specific customer groups. Exhibit 15.3(c) illustrates the customer-focused structure similar to one adopted by Nortel Networks.[38]

Which form of divisionalization should large organizations adopt? The answer depends mainly on the primary source of environmental diversity or uncertainty.[39] If the organization's environment is most diverse geographically, then a geographic form of divisionalization would work best. Coca-Cola, Nestlé, and many other food and beverage companies are organized mainly around geographic regions because consumer tastes and marketing strategies vary considerably around the world. Even though McDonald's makes the same Big Mac around the planet, it has more fish products in Hong Kong and more vegetarian products in India, in line with traditional diets in those countries. Philips, on the other hand, is organized around products because consumer preferences are similar within each group. Hospitals from Geneva, Switzerland, to Santiago, Chile, purchase similar medical equipment from Philips, whereas manufacturing and sales of these products are quite different from Philips's semiconductor business.

More generally, a large number of divisionalized companies are moving away from geographic structures.[40] One reason is that information technology reduces the need for local representation. Clients can purchase online and communicate with businesses from almost anywhere in the world, so local representation is less critical. Geographic structures are also waning because freer trade has reduced government intervention in some products, and consumer preferences in many product and service areas are becoming more similar (converging) around the world. The third reason for the move away from geographic divisional structures is that large companies increasingly have global business customers that demand one global point of purchase, not one in every country or region. AXA Group is moving toward global profit centers

EXHIBIT 15.3　　Three types of divisional structure

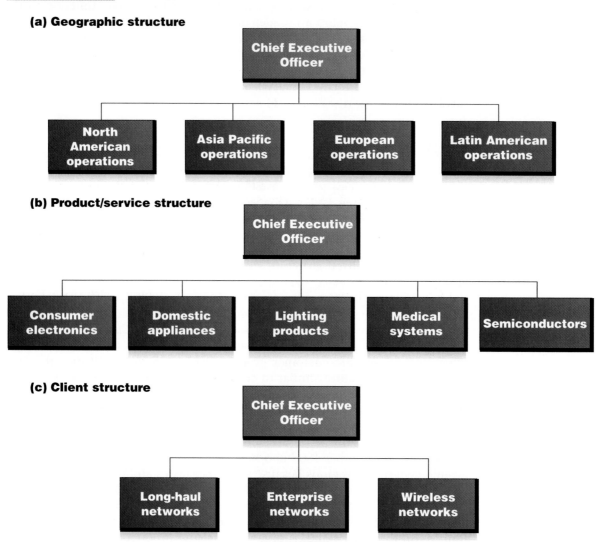

(a) Geographic structure

Chief Executive Officer

- North American operations
- Asia Pacific operations
- European operations
- Latin American operations

(b) Product/service structure

Chief Executive Officer

- Consumer electronics
- Domestic appliances
- Lighting products
- Medical systems
- Semiconductors

(c) Client structure

Chief Executive Officer

- Long-haul networks
- Enterprise networks
- Wireless networks

Note: Diagram (a) is similar to the global geographic divisional structure of McDonald's Restaurants; diagram (b) is similar to the product divisions at Philips; diagram (c) is similar to the customer-focused structure at Nortel Networks.

for its services (e.g., reinsurance) because clients increasingly expect the French-based insurer to provide global (not regional) expertise and support.[41]

Advantages and Disadvantages　　The divisional form is a building block structure, because it accommodates growth relatively easily. Related products or clients can be added to existing divisions with little need for additional learning, whereas increasing diversity may be accommodated by sprouting a new division. Organizations typically reorganize around divisional structures as they expand into distinct products, services, and domains of operation, because coordinating functional units becomes too unwieldy with increasing diversity.[42]

Organizations tend to adopt divisional structures as they grow and become more complex, but this structural configuration is not perfect. The most frequent complaint is that divisional structures duplicate and insufficiently use their resources. Another problem is that this structure creates "silos of knowledge" because functional specialists are spread throughout the various business units. Consequently, new knowledge and practices in one part of the organization are not shared elsewhere. Divisional structures also tend to reduce cooperation across groups. Nortel Networks recognized this problem, so it developed a special communication program, called "Come Together," to remind employees in each division of their responsibility to work more closely with employees from other divisions.[43]

Matrix Structure

When Wolfgang Kemna became head of SAP America, he soon discovered that the German software giant's U.S. subsidiary was too inward looking. "What I found was a highly defocused company," says Kemna. Much of the problem stemmed from SAP America's organizational structure, which was configured around the company's main product, whereas SAP actually has five main software applications—such as customer relationship management and supply chain management. Moreover, SAP's products require unique marketing and application in different industries. So, Kemna and his executive team introduced a **matrix structure** that organizes employees around both the five main software applications and various industry groups.[44]

A matrix structure overlays two organizational forms in order to leverage the benefits of both. SAP America relies on a matrix structure that balances power between its product and client groups or divisions. Some global corporations adopt a matrix structure that combines geographical with product divisions. The product-based structure allows the company to exploit global economies of scale, whereas the geographic structure keeps knowledge close to the needs of individual countries. Asea Brown Boveri (ABB) is widely known for this global matrix structure. The Swiss manufacturer of industrial electrical systems has country managers as well as managers responsible for specific product lines.[45] Many organizations also have degrees of matrix structure, meaning that each divisional group has specific responsibilities but some issues must be decided jointly across all of these groups. For instance, Citigroup's country leaders and product leaders each have specific authority, but they must work together on matters that overlap.[46]

Instead of combining two divisional structures, some matrix structures overlap a functional structure with project teams.[47] As Exhibit 15.4 illustrates, employees are assigned to a cross-functional project team, yet they also belong to a permanent functional unit (e.g., engineering, marketing) to which they return when a project is completed.

Matrix structures create the unusual situation where employees have two bosses. A project team member would report to the project leader on a daily basis, but also reports to the functional leader (engineering, marketing, etc.). Some companies give these managers equal power; more often, each has authority over different elements of the employee's or work unit's tasks.[48] Matrix structures that combine two divisionalized forms also have a dual-boss reporting system, but only for some employees. The manager of an ABB transformer plant in the United States would report to both the U.S. country manager and the global manager of ABB's transformer business. Only about 500 plant managers and group leaders at ABB have two bosses due to the matrix

matrix structure
A type of departmentalization that overlays two organizational forms in order to leverage the benefits of both.

EXHIBIT 15.4   A simplified matrix structure

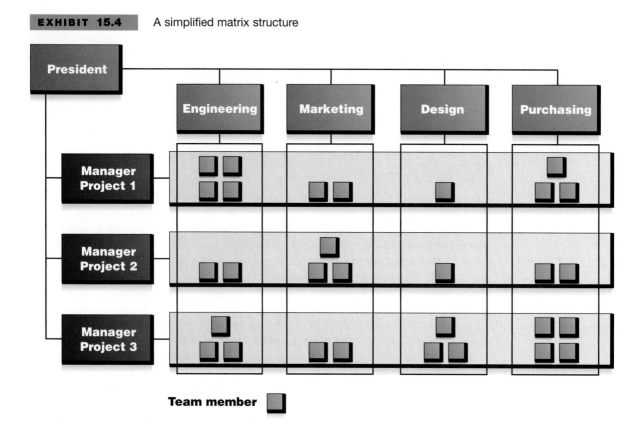

Team member ■

structure. The other 200,000 ABB employees work in direct authority structures below the matrix structure.

Advantages and Disadvantages   Matrix structures usually optimize the use of resources and expertise, making them ideal for project-based organizations with fluctuating workloads.[49] When properly managed, they improve communication efficiency, project flexibility, and innovation compared to purely functional or divisional designs. Matrix structures focus technical specialists on the goals of serving clients and creating marketable products. Yet, by maintaining a link to their functional unit, employees are able to interact and coordinate with others in their technical specialty.

In spite of these advantages, matrix structures have several well-known problems.[50] One concern is that they require more coordination than functional or pure divisional structures. The existence of two bosses can also dilute accountability. Royal Dutch/Shell has moved away from a matrix design for these reasons. Matrix structures also tend to generate conflict, organizational politics, and stress. In project-based firms, for example, project leaders must have a general management orientation and conflict resolution skills to coordinate people with diverse functional backgrounds. They also need good negotiation and persuasive communication skills to gain support from functional leaders. Employees who feel comfortable in structured bureaucracies tend to have difficulty adjusting to the relatively fluid nature of matrix structures. Stress is a common symptom of poorly managed matrix structures, because employees must cope with two managers with potentially divergent needs and expectations.

Team-Based (Lateral) Structure

About a decade ago, the Criterion Group adopted a team-based organization to improve quality and efficiency. The New Zealand manufacturer of ready-to-assemble furniture now has just one layer of eight managers between the managing director and production staff. Criterion's 140 employees are organized into self-directed work teams with their own performance indicators and activity-based costing systems.[51]

team-based organization
A type of departmentalization with a flat hierarchy and relatively little formalization, consisting of self-directed work teams responsible for various work processes.

The Criterion Group has embraced the **team-based organizational structure.** Some writers call this a *lateral structure* because, with few organizational levels, it is very flat and relies on extensive lateral communication.[52] The team-based organizational structure, which is illustrated in Exhibit 15.5, has a few distinguishing features from other organizational forms. First, it uses self-directed work teams rather than individuals as the basic building block of organizations. Second, teams are typically organized around work processes, such as making a specific product or serving a specific client group.

A third distinguishing feature of team-based organizational structures is that they have a very flat hierarchy, usually with no more than two or three management levels. The Criterion Group and other organizations delegate most supervisory activities to the team by having members take turns as the coordinator. Finally, this type of structure has very little formalization. Almost all day-to-day decisions are made by team members rather than someone further up the organizational hierarchy. Teams are given relatively few rules about how to organize their work. Instead, the executive team typically assigns output goals to the team, such as the volume and quality of product or service, or productivity improvement targets for the work process. Teams are then encouraged to use available resources and their own initiative to achieve those objectives.

Team-based structures are usually found within the manufacturing operations of larger divisionalized structures. For example, aircraft components

EXHIBIT 15.5   Team-based (lateral) structure

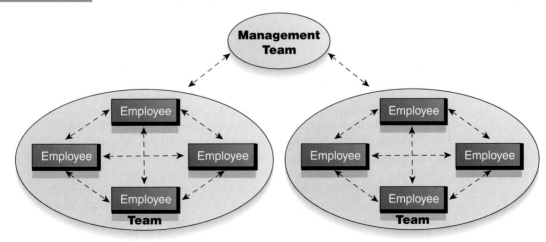

Flight Centre's Team-Based Tribal Structure

Flight Centre is ranked as one of the best places to work and is a runaway success story in the travel industry. Based in Brisbane, Australia, the travel agency has been continuously profitable in spite of the challenges facing the industry. Throughout its rapid growth, Flight Centre has maintained four layers of hierarchy and provides consistent service at each of its approximately 600 travel shops in Australia, United Kingdom, Canada, United States, and other countries.

What's the secret to Flight Centre's success? According to chief executive and cofounder Graham Turner, Flight Centre's unique "tribal" organizational structure facilitates easy replication and fuels organic growth. Each Flight Centre retail shop, as well as each administrative group, represents a family. "If you look at a family structure, then the manageable size for people to get along and understand each other is 3–7 people, and that's what we call a family," Turner explains.

Between 7 and 25 families in an area form a village with a village leader. "In a village, people co-operate with each other—the basic unit is still the family but when they need to, the families co-operate with each other," Turner says. "It might be that one store—or one family—has someone sick for a while, so another family will lend them a person until things get back to normal." As a village becomes overpopulated with Flight Centre families, it splits into smaller villages.

From 3 to 10 villages form a tribe, which is comparable to national operations and special divisions of a company. "In a tribe you've got formal functions—you've got a chief, for example. That's the level when you have to start having a bureaucracy." Flight Centre also has between 4 and 10 regional leaders who oversee several tribes (countries).

Flight Centre is highly decentralized. Each tribe (country) has control of its own recruitment, marketing, and training. Tribes also have the freedom to buy services from other Flight Centre business units, or to buy holiday packages from outside wholesalers instead. Further decentralization occurs

Flight Centre has a "tribal" structure that organizes employees around families, villages, and tribes.

down to each Flight Centre shop. The shop's team leader takes 10 percent of the shop's profit and may own up to 20 percent of the shop. The team structure is supported by a reward system in which the shop is its own profit center and employees take a share of those profits on top of their guaranteed base salary. This tribal structure seems to work well in an industry that has to pay attention to local markets and change quickly in a dynamic environment.

Sources: A. Fraser, "Chief of Flying Tribe Clips His Wings," *The Australian,* July 29, 2002, p. 31; E. Johnston, "Elf Boys," *Boss Magazine,* June 8, 2001, p. 26; S. K. Witcher, "Flight Center Founder Prides Company On Being Deliberately Unconventional," *Wall Street Journal,* December 11, 2000, p. C15; J. Palmer, "Flight Center Has an Unusual Team Culture," *Business Day* (South Africa), April 20, 2000, p. 28; M. Massey, "Travel Agency Succeeds by Going Tribal," *Business Review Weekly,* March 22, 1999, p. 69.

---

maker Pratt & Whitney has a divisionalized structure, but some of the manufacturing plants within those divisions have team-based organizational structures. Much less common are companies with a team-based structure from top to bottom. Flight Centre is a unique example of this totally team-based organization. Global Connections 15.2 describes how this Brisbane, Australia-based travel agency organizes its global operations into teams based on the concepts of families, villages, and tribes.

Advantages and Disadvantages The team-based organization represents an increasingly popular structure because it is usually more responsive and flexible.[53] Teams empower employees and reduce reliance on a managerial hierarchy, thereby reducing costs. A cross-functional team structure improves communication and cooperation across traditional boundaries. With greater autonomy, this structure also allows quicker and more informed decision making.[54] Some hospitals have shifted from functional departments to cross-functional teams for this reason. Teams composed of nurses, radiologists, anesthetists, a pharmacology representative, possibly social workers, a rehabilitation therapist, and other specialists communicate and coordinate more efficiently, therefore reducing delays and errors.[55]

One concern with team-based structures is that they can be costly to maintain due to the need for ongoing interpersonal skills training. Teamwork potentially takes more time to coordinate than formal hierarchy during the early stages of team development (see Chapter 9). Employees may experience more stress due to increased ambiguity in their roles. Team leaders also experience more stress due to increased conflict, loss of functional power, and unclear career progression ladders.[56]

Network Structures

To the outside world, Cisco Systems is one company. But the world's leading provider of business-to-business computer networks is mostly a constellation of suppliers, contract manufacturers, assemblers, and other partners connected through an intricate web of computer technology. Cisco's network springs into action as soon as a customer places an order (usually through the Internet). Suppliers send the required materials to assemblers who ship the product directly to the client, usually the same day. Seventy percent of Cisco's product is outsourced this way. In many cases, Cisco employees never touch the product. "Partnerships are key to the new world strategies of the 21st century," says a Cisco senior vice-president. "Partners collapse time because they allow you to take on more things and bring them together quicker."[57]

network structure
An alliance of several organizations for the purpose of creating a product or serving a client.

Cisco is a living example of the **network structure.** A network structure (also known as a *modular structure*) is an alliance of several organizations for the purpose of creating a product or serving a client.[58] As Exhibit 15.6 illustrates, this collaborative structure typically consists of several satellite organizations beehived around a "hub" or "core" firm. The core firm "orchestrates" the network process and provides one or two other core competencies, such as marketing or product development. For instance, Cisco mainly designs and markets new products. Nike, another network organization, mainly provides marketing expertise for its sports footwear and apparel. The core firm might be the main contact with customers, but most of the product or service delivery and support activities are farmed out to satellite organizations located anywhere in the world. Extranets (Web-based networks with partners) and other technologies ensure that information flows easily and openly between the core firm and its array of satellites.[59]

One of the main forces pushing toward a network structure is the recognition that an organization has only a few *core competencies*. A core competency is a knowledge base that resides throughout the organization and provides a strategic advantage. As companies discover their core competency, they "unbundle" noncritical tasks to other organizations that have a core competency at performing those tasks. For instance, Mitel Networks decided that its core competency is designing Internet protocol–based communications equipment, not manufacturing that equipment. Consequently, the high-technology firm in Ottawa, Canada, outsourced its manufacturing and repair business to

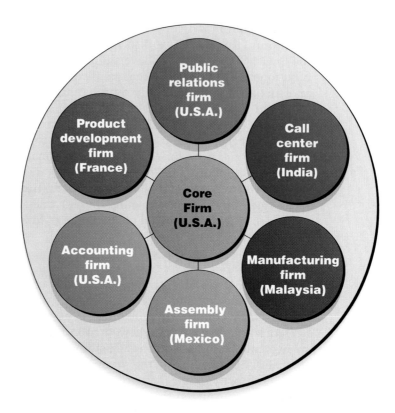

BreconRidge Manufacturing Solutions, which has a contract to manufacture Mitel products.[60]

Companies are also more likely to form network structures when technology is changing quickly and production processes are complex or varied.[61] Many firms cannot keep up with the hyperfast changes in information technology, so they outsourced their entire information systems departments to IBM, EDS, and other firms that specialize in information systems services. Similarly, many high-technology firms form networks with Celestica, Solectron, and other contract manufacturers that have expertise in these production processes.

Virtual Corporations   The network structures that exist at Cisco Systems, Mitel Networks, Nike, Dell Computer, and other firms generally perform a patterned set of tasks for all clients. When you order a computer from Dell, the network partners follow the same set of transactions as the next person who orders a computer. The specific computer configuration may change, but the relationships among the partners and the production process are fairly standardized until the partnership is reconfigured every few years.

In contrast, some network structures—known as **virtual corporations** (also called *cellular organizations*)—represent several independent companies that form unique partnership teams to provide customized products or services, usually to specific clients, for a limited time.[62] A good example of this is the British advertising firm host universal (which spells its name all lower case). It has no employees or clients, instead serving a specific project by forming a unique team of partners, who then disband when the project is finished. "At host we have no clients or employees, which enables us to pull the most

virtual corporations
Network structures representing several independent companies that form unique partnership teams to provide customized products or services, usually to specific clients, for a limited time.

effective teams together from our network without foisting redundant skills, fees and hierarchy onto clients," explains founding partner Steve Hess.[63]

Virtual corporations exist temporarily and reshape themselves quickly to fit immediate needs. When an opportunity emerges, a unique combination of partners in the alliance form a virtual corporation that works on the assignment until it is completed. Virtual corporations are self-organizing, meaning that they rearrange their own communication patterns and roles to fit the situation. The relationship among the partners is mutually determined rather than imposed by a core firm.

Advantages and Disadvantages   For several years, scholars have argued that organizational leaders must develop a metaphor of organizations as plasma-like organisms rather than rigid machines.[64] Network structures come close to the organism metaphor because they offer the flexibility to realign their structure with changing environmental requirements. If customers demand a new product or service, the core firm forms new alliances with other firms offering the appropriate resources.[65] For example, by finding partners with available plant facilities, Cisco Systems expanded its business much more rapidly than if it had built its own production facilities. When Cisco's needs change, it isn't saddled with nonessential facilities and resources. Network structures also offer efficiencies because the core firm becomes globally competitive as it shops worldwide for subcontractors with the best people and the best technology at the best price. Indeed, the pressures of global competition have made network structures more vital, and computer-based information technology has made them possible.[66]

A potential disadvantage of network structures is that they expose the core firm to market forces. Other companies may bid up the price for subcontractors, whereas the short-term cost would be lower if the company hired its own employees to provide this function. Another problem is that although information technology makes worldwide communication much easier, it will never replace the degree of control organizations have when manufacturing, marketing, and other functions are in house. The core firm can use arm's-length incentives and contract provisions to maintain the subcontractor's quality, but these actions are relatively crude compared to those used to maintain performance of in-house employees.

Contingencies of Organizational Design

Organizational theorists and practitioners are interested not only in the elements of organizational structure, but also in the contingencies that determine or influence the optimal design. In this section, we introduce four contingencies of organizational design: size, technology, environment, and strategy.

Organizational Size

Larger organizations have considerably different structures than do smaller organizations.[67] As the number of employees increases, job specialization increases due to a greater division of labor. Larger firms also have more elaborate coordinating mechanisms to manage the greater division of labor. They are more likely to use standardization of work processes and outputs to coordinate work activities. These coordinating mechanisms create an administrative hierarchy and greater formalization. Informal communication has traditionally decreased as a coordinating mechanism as organizations get larger. However, emerging computer technologies and increased emphasis on empowerment have caused informal communication to regain its importance in large firms.[68]

Larger organizations also tend to be more decentralized. As we noted earlier in this chapter, neither founders nor senior managers have sufficient time or expertise to process all the decisions that significantly influence the business as it grows. Therefore, decision-making authority is pushed down to lower levels, where incumbents are able to cope with the narrower range of issues under their control.[69]

Technology

Based on the open systems model (see Chapter 1), we know that an organization's structure needs to be aligned with its dominant technology. Two important technological contingencies that influence the best type of organizational structure are the variety and analyzability of work activities.[70] *Variety* refers to the number of exceptions to standard procedure that can occur in the team or work unit. *Analyzability* refers to the extent that the transformation of input resources to outputs can be reduced to a series of standardized steps.

Some jobs are routine, meaning that employees perform the same tasks all of the time and rely on set rules (standard operating procedures) when exceptions do occur. Almost everything is predictable. These situations, such as automobile assembly lines, have high formalization and centralization as well as standardization of work processes.

When employees perform tasks with high variety and low analyzability, they apply their skills to unique situations with little opportunity for repetition. Research project teams operate under these conditions. These situations call for an organic structure, one with low formalization, highly decentralized decision-making authority, and coordination mainly through informal communication among team members.

High-variety and high-analyzability tasks have many exceptions to routines, but these exceptions can usually be resolved through standard procedures. Maintenance groups and engineering design teams experience these conditions. Work units that fall into this category should use an organic structure, but it is possible to have somewhat greater formalization and centralization due to the analyzability of problems.

Skilled trades people tend to work in situations with low variety and low analyzability. Their tasks involve few exceptions but the problems that arise are difficult to resolve. This situation allows more centralization and formalization than in a purely organic structure, but coordination must include informal communication among the skilled employees so that unique problems can be resolved.

External Environment

The best structure for an organization depends on its external environment. The external environment includes anything outside the organization—most stakeholders (e.g., clients, suppliers, government), resources (e.g., raw materials, human resources, information, finances), competitors, and so on. Four relatively distinct characteristics of external environments influence the type of organizational structure best suited to a particular situation: dynamism, complexity, diversity, and hostility.[71]

One of Douglas Daft's first actions as Coca-Cola's CEO was to move decision making closer to local markets. The world's largest soft drink maker was slow and not exactly responsive to local needs when decisions were made out of Atlanta, so the more decentralized structure made sense in terms of the diverse consumer tastes around the planet. Still, Coke stumbled in the process as some local decision makers created marketing campaigns that threatened Coke's wholesome image. Coke's solution wasn't to centralize again. Instead, it created a global marketing group to design marketing strategy, then gave local operations freedom to develop marketing campaigns within that architecture. "We haven't swung back," insists Stephen Jones, Coke's chief marketing officer. "The local markets are still accountable, but now they have guidance, process and strategy."[73] What environmental conditions are better suited for more centralized organizational structures?

■ *Dynamic versus stable environments*—Dynamic environments have a high rate of change, leading to novel situations and a lack of identifiable patterns. Organic structures are better suited to this type of environment so that the organization can adapt more quickly to changes.[72] Network and team-based structures seem to be most effective in dynamic environments, because they usually have these features. In contrast, stable environments are characterized by regular cycles of activity and identifiable patterns of supply and demand for inputs and outputs. Events are more predictable, enabling the firm to apply rules and procedures. Thus, more mechanistic structures tend to work best under these conditions.

■ *Complex versus simple environments*—Complex environments have many elements, whereas simple environments have few things to monitor. Decentralized structures seem to be better suited to complex environments, because these subunits are close to their local environment and are able to make more informed choices.

■ *Diverse versus integrated environments*—Organizations located in diverse environments have a greater variety of products or services, clients, and regions. In contrast, an integrated environment has only one client, product, and geographic area. The more diversified the environment, the more the firm needs to use a divisionalized form aligned with that diversity. If it sells a single product around the world, a geographic divisionalized structure would align best with the firm's geographic diversity.

■ *Hostile versus munificent environments*—Firms located in a hostile environment face resource scarcity and more competition in the marketplace. Hostile environments are typically dynamic ones because they reduce the predictability of access to resources and demand for outputs. Organic structures tend to be best in hostile environments. However, when the environment is extremely hostile—such as a severe shortage of supplies or lower market share—organizations tend to temporarily centralize so that decisions can be made more quickly and executives feel more comfortable being in control.[74] Ironically, centralization may result in lower quality decisions during organizational crises, because top management has less information, particularly when the environment is complex.

organizational strategy

The way an organization positions itself in its setting in relation to its stakeholders, given the organization's resources, capabilities, and mission.

Organizational Strategy

Although size, technology, and environment influence the optimal organizational structure, these contingencies do not necessarily determine structure. Instead, there is increasing evidence that corporate leaders formulate and implement strategies that shape the characteristics of these contingencies as well as the organization's resulting structure. **Organizational strategy** refers to the way the organization positions itself in its setting in relation to its stakeholders, given the organization's resources, capabilities, and mission.[75] The idea that an organization interacts with its environment rather than being totally determined by it is known as **strategic choice.**[76] In other words, organizational leaders take steps to define and manipulate their environments, rather than letting the organization's fate be entirely determined by external influences.

strategic choice

The idea that an organization interacts with its environment rather than being totally determined by it.

The notion of strategic choice can be traced back to the work of Alfred Chandler in the early 1960s.[77] Chandler's proposal was that structure follows strategy. He observed that organizational structures follow the growth strategy developed by the organization's decision makers. Moreover, he noted that organizational structures change only after decision makers decide to do so. This recognizes that the link between structure and the contingency factors described earlier is mediated by organizational strategy.

Chandler's thesis that structure follows strategy has become the dominant perspective of business policy and strategic management. An important aspect of this view is that organizations can choose the environments in which they want to operate. Some businesses adopt a *differentiation strategy* by bringing unique products to the market or attracting clients who want customized goods and services. They try to distinguish their outputs from those provided by other firms through marketing, offering special services, and innovation. Others adopt a *cost leadership strategy*, in which they maximize productivity and are thereby able to offer popular products or services at a competitive price.[78]

The type of organizational strategy selected leads to the best organizational structure to adopt.[79] Organizations with a cost leadership strategy should adopt a mechanistic, functional structure with high levels of job specialization and standardized work processes. This is similar to the routine technology category described earlier because they maximize production and service efficiency. A differentiation strategy, on the other hand, requires more customized relations with clients. A matrix or team-based structure with less centralization and formalization is most appropriate here so that technical specialists are able to coordinate their work activities more closely with the client's needs. Overall, it is now apparent that organizational structure is influenced by size, technology, and environment, but the organization's strategy may reshape these elements and loosen their connection to organizational structure.

Chapter Summary

Organizational structure refers to the division of labor as well as the patterns of coordination, communication, work flow, and formal power that direct organizational activities. All organizational structures divide labor into distinct tasks and coordinate that labor to accomplish common goals. The primary means of coordination are informal communication, formal hierarchy, and standardization.

The four basic elements of organizational structure are span of control, centralization, formalization, and departmentalization. At one time, scholars suggested that firms should have a tall hierarchy with a narrow span of control. Today, most organizations take the opposite approach because they rely on informal communication and standardization, rather than direct supervision, to coordinate work processes.

Centralization means that formal decision authority is held by a small group of people, typically senior executives. Many companies decentralize as they become larger and more complex because senior executives lack the necessary time and expertise to process all the decisions that significantly influence the business. Companies also tend to become more formalized over time because work activities become routinized. Formalization increases in larger firms because standardization works more efficiently than informal communications and direct supervision.

A functional structure organizes employees around specific knowledge or other resources. This fosters greater specialization and improves direct supervision, but it hinders people's ability to see the organization's larger picture or to coordinate across departments. A divisional structure groups employees around geographic areas, clients, or outputs. This structure accommodates growth and focuses employee attention on products or customers rather than tasks. However, this structure creates silos of knowledge and duplication of resources.

The matrix structure combines two structures to leverage the benefits of both types of structure. How-ever, this approach requires more coordination than functional or pure divisional structures, may dilute accountability, and increases conflict. Team-based structures, which are very flat with low formalization, organize self-directed teams around work processes rather than functional specialties. A network structure is an alliance of several organizations for the purpose of creating a product or serving a client. Virtual corporations are network structures that can quickly reorganize themselves to suit the client's requirements.

The best organizational structure depends on the firm's size, technology, and environment. Generally, larger organizations are decentralized and more formalized, with greater job specialization and elaborate coordinating mechanisms. The work unit's technology—including variety of work and analyzability of problems—influences the decision to adopt an organic or mechanistic structure. The best structure also depends on whether the external environment is dynamic, complex, diverse, and hostile.

Although size, technology, and environment influence the optimal organizational structure, these contingencies do not necessarily determine structure. Rather, organizational leaders formulate and implement strategies to define and manipulate their environments. These strategies, rather than the other contingencies, directly shape the organization's structure.

Key Terms

centralization, p. 451

divisional structure, p. 457

formalization, p. 453

functional structure, p. 456

matrix structure, p. 459

mechanistic structure, p. 453

network structure, p. 463

organic structure, p. 454

organizational design, p. 446

organizational strategy, p. 468

organizational structure, p. 446

platform teams, p. 447

span of control, p. 449

strategic choice, p. 468

team-based organizational structure, p. 461

virtual corporations, p. 464

Discussion Questions

1. Why are organizations moving toward flatter structures?
2. What form of coordination is most likely to be used in a cross-functional project team?
3. Diversified Technologies, Inc. (DTI), makes four types of products, each type to be sold to different types of clients. For example, one product is sold exclusively to automobile repair shops, whereas another is used mainly in hospitals. Customer expectations and needs are surprisingly similar throughout the world. However, the company has separate marketing, product design, and manufacturing facilities in North America, Europe, Asia, and South America because, until recently, each jurisdiction had unique regulations governing the production and sales of these products. However, several governments have begun the process of deregulating the products that DTI designs and manufactures, and trade agreements have opened several markets to foreign-made products. Which form of departmentalization might be best for DTI if deregulation and trade agreements occur?

4. Why are many organizations moving away from the geographic divisional structures?

5. From an employee perspective, what are the advantages and disadvantages of working in a matrix structure?

6. Flight Centre has a team-based structure from top to bottom. Is this typical? Could such a structure exist at IBM or Intel?

7. Some writers believe that a network structure is an effective design for global competition. Is this true, or are there situations for which this organizational structure may be inappropriate?

8. Suppose that you have been hired as a consultant to diagnose the environmental characteristics of your college or university. How would you describe the school's external environment? Is the school's existing structure appropriate for this environment?

CASE STUDY 15.1

THE RISE AND FALL OF PMC AG

Founded in 1930, PMC AG is a German manufacturer of high-priced sports cars. During the early years, PMC was a small consulting engineering firm that specialized in solving difficult automotive design problems for clients. At the end of World War II, however, the son of PMC's founder decided to expand the business beyond consulting engineering. He was determined that PMC would build its own precision automobiles.

In 1948, the first PMC prototypes rolled out of the small manufacturing facility. Each copy was hand made by highly skilled craftspeople. For several years, parts and engine were designed and built by other companies and assembled at the PMC plant. By the 1960s, however, PMC had begun to design and build its own parts.

PMC grew rapidly during the 1960s to mid-1980s. The company designed a completely new car in the early 1960s, launched a lower priced model in 1970, and added a mid-priced model in 1977. By the mid-1980s, PMC had become very profitable as its name became an icon for wealthy entrepreneurs and jetsetters. In 1986, the year of highest production, PMC sold 54,000 cars. Nearly two-thirds of these were sold in North America.

PMC's Structure

PMC's organizational structure expanded with its success. During the early years, the company consisted only of an engineering department and a production department. By the 1980s, employees were divided into more than 10 functional departments representing different stages of the production process as well as upstream (e.g., design, purchasing) and downstream (e.g., quality control, marketing) activities. Employees worked exclusively in one department. For an employee to voluntarily move into another department was almost considered mutiny.

PMC's production staff were organized into a traditional hierarchy. Frontline employees reported to work group leaders, who reported to supervisors, who reported to group supervisors in each area. Group supervisors reported to production managers, who reported to production directors, who reported to PMC's executive vice-president of manufacturing. At one time, nearly 20 percent of production staff members were involved in supervisory tasks. In the early 1990s, for example, 48 group supervisors, 96 supervisors, 162 work group leaders were supervising about 2,500 frontline production employees.

PMC's Craft Tradition

PMC had a long tradition and culture that supported craft expertise. This appealed to Germany's skilled workforce because it gave employees an opportunity to test and further develop their skills. PMC workers were encouraged to master long work cycles, often as much as 15 minutes per unit. Their ideal was to build as much of the automobile as possible alone. For example, a few masters were able to assemble an entire engine. Their reward was to personally sign their name on the completed component.

The design engineers worked independently of the production department, with the result that production employees had to adjust designs to fit the available parts. Rather than viewing this as a nuisance, the production employees considered it as a challenge that would further test their well-developed craft skills. Similarly, manufacturing engineers occasionally redesigned the product to fit manufacturing capabilities.

To improve efficiency, a moving track assembly system was introduced in 1977. Even then, the emphasis on craft skills was apparent. Employees were encouraged to quickly put all the parts on the car, knowing that highly skilled troubleshooting craftspeople would discover and repair defects after the car came off the line. This was much more costly and time-consuming than assembling the vehicle correctly the first time, but it provided yet another challenging set of tasks for skilled craftspeople. And as a result, PMC vehicles were known for their few defects by the time they were sold to customers.

The End of Success?

PMC sports cars filled a small niche in the automobile market for those who wanted a true sports car just tame enough for everyday use. PMCs were known for their superlative performance based on excellent engineering technology, but they were also becoming very expensive. Japanese sports cars were not quite in the same league as PMCs, but the cost of manufacturing the Japanese vehicles was a small fraction of the cost of manufacturing a vehicle at PMC.

This cost inefficiency hit PMC's sales during the late 1980s and early 1990s. First, the German currency appreciated against the U.S. dollar, which made PMC sports cars even more expensive in the North American market. By 1990, PMC was selling half the number of cars it had sold just four years earlier. Then, the North American recession hit, driving PMC sales down further. In 1993, PMC sold just 14,000 vehicles, compared to 54,000 in 1987. And although sales rebounded to 20,000 by 1995, the high price tag put PMCs out of reach of many potential customers. It was clear to PMC's founding family that changes were needed, but they weren't sure where to begin.

Discussion Questions

1. Describe PMC's organizational structure in terms of the four organizational design features (i.e., span of control, centralization, formalization, and departmentalization.

2. Discuss the problems with PMC's current structure.

3. Identify and justify an organizational structure that, in your opinion, would be more appropriate for PMC.

Source: Written by Steven L. McShane based on information from several sources about "PMC." The company name and some details of actual events have been altered to provide a fuller case discussion.

CASE STUDY 15.2

BALLMER'S MICROSOFT

BusinessWeek It didn't take long after Bill Gates handed over Microsoft's top job to his buddy Steve Ballmer before Ballmer realized things had to change. In particular, Microsoft had become a very large organization that was not moving as quickly as it should in the marketplace. To make Microsoft more responsive, Ballmer made several changes to the organization's structure and introduced practices to ensure those structural changes worked well.

This *Business Week* case study looks at the changes that Steve Ballmer is making at Microsoft. It describes specific adjustments to the company's organizational structure, as well as coordination mechanisms to support that structure. Read through this *Business Week* article at www.mhhe.com/mcshane3e and prepare for the discussion questions below.

Discussion Questions

1. What symptoms or conditions suggested that Microsoft's current organizational structure wasn't sufficiently effective?

2. What changes did Steve Ballmer ultimately make to Microsoft's departmentalization? What problems occurred with the initial changes in departmentalization?

3. Along with changing the organizational chart, what other organizational structure changes did Steve Ballmer make at Microsoft? Do these changes seem reasonable under the circumstances?

Source: J. Greene, S. Hamm, and J. Kerstetter, "Ballmer's Microsoft," *Business Week,* June 17, 2002, pp. 66–72.

THE CLUB ED EXERCISE

By Cheryl Harvey and Kim Morouney, Wilfred Laurier University

Purpose   This exercise is designed to help you understand the issues to consider when designing organizations at various stages of growth.

Materials   Each student team should have enough overhead transparencies or flip chart sheets to display several organizational charts.

Instructions   Each team discusses the scenario presented. The first scenario is presented below. The instructor will facilitate discussion and advise teams when to begin the next step. This exercise may be continued for two class sessions.

- *Step 1*—Students are placed in teams (typically four or five people).
- *Step 2*—After reading Scenario 1 presented below, each team will design an organizational chart (departmentalization) that is most appropriate for this situation. Students should be able to describe the type of structure drawn and explain why it is appropriate. The structure should be drawn on an overhead transparency or flip chart for others to see during later class discussion. The instructor will set a fixed time (e.g., 15 minutes) to complete this task.

Scenario 1   Determined never to shovel snow again, you are establishing a new resort business on a small Caribbean island. The resort is under construction and is scheduled to open one year from now. You decide it is time to draw up an organizational chart for this new venture, called Club Ed.

- *Step 3*—At the end of the time allowed, the instructor will present Scenario 2 and each team will be asked to draw another organizational chart to suit that situation. Again, students should be able to describe the type of structure drawn and explain why it is appropriate.
- *Step 4*—At the end of the time allowed, the instructor will present Scenario 3 and each team will be asked to draw another organizational chart to suit that situation.
- *Step 5*—Depending on the time available, the instructor might present a fourth scenario. The class will gather to present their designs for each scenario. During each presentation, teams should describe the type of structure drawn and explain why it is appropriate.

Source: Adapted from C. Harvey and K. Morouney, "Organizational Design and Structure: The Club Ed Exercise," *Journal of Management Education* 22 (June 1998), pp. 425–29. Used with permission of the authors.

IDENTIFYING YOUR PREFERRED ORGANIZATIONAL STRUCTURE

Purpose   This exercise is designed to help you understand how an organization's structure influences the personal needs and values of people working in that structure.

Instructions   Personal values influence how comfortable you are working in different organizational structures. You might prefer an organization with clearly defined rules or no rules at all. You might prefer a firm where almost any employee can make important decisions, or where important decisions are screened by senior executives. Read the statements below and indicate the extent to which you would like to work in an organization with that characteristic. When finished, use the scoring key in Appendix B to calculate your results. This self-assessment is completed alone so students will complete this self-assessment honestly without concerns of social comparison. However, class discussion will focus on the elements of organizational design and their relationship to personal needs and values.

Organizational Structure Preference Scale

I would like to work in an organization where . . .					Score
1. A person's career ladder has several steps toward higher status and responsibility..............	Not at all	A little	Somewhat	Very much	_____
2. Employees perform their work with few rules to limit their discretion........................	Not at all	A little	Somewhat	Very much	_____
3. Responsibility is pushed down to employees who perform the work.......................	Not at all	A little	Somewhat	Very much	_____
4. Supervisors have few employees, so they work closely with each person..........................	Not at all	A little	Somewhat	Very much	_____
5. Senior executives make most decisions to ensure that the company is consistent in its actions...	Not at all	A little	Somewhat	Very much	_____
6. Jobs are clearly defined so there is no confusion over who is responsible for various tasks..	Not at all	A little	Somewhat	Very much	_____
7. Employees have their say on issues, but senior executives make most of the decisions...	Not at all	A little	Somewhat	Very much	_____
8. Job descriptions are broadly stated or nonexistent....................................	Not at all	A little	Somewhat	Very much	_____
9. Everyone's work is tightly synchronized around top management operating plans..........	Not at all	A little	Somewhat	Very much	_____
10. Most work is performed in teams without close supervision................................	Not at all	A little	Somewhat	Very much	_____
11. Work gets done through informal discussion with co-workers rather than through formal rules...	Not at all	A little	Somewhat	Very much	_____
12. Supervisors have so many employees that they can't watch anyone very closely................	Not at all	A little	Somewhat	Very much	_____
13. Everyone has clearly understood goals, expectations, and job duties............................	Not at all	A little	Somewhat	Very much	_____
14. Senior executives assign overall goals but leave daily decisions to front line teams.............	Not at all	A little	Somewhat	Very much	_____
15. Even in a large company, the CEO is only three or four levels above the lowest position....	Not at all	A little	Somewhat	Very much	_____

Source: Copyright © 2000. Steven L. McShane.

 After studying the preceding material, be sure to check out our website at
www.mhhe.com/mcshane3e
for more in-depth information and interactivities that correspond to this chapter.

Organizational Culture

Learning Objectives

After reading this chapter, you should be able to:

■ Describe the elements of organizational culture.

■ Discuss the importance of organizational subcultures.

■ List four categories of artifacts through which corporate culture is deciphered.

■ Identify three functions of organizational culture.

■ Discuss the conditions under which cultural strength improves corporate performance.

■ Discuss the effect of organizational culture on business ethics.

■ Compare and contrast four strategies for merging organizational cultures.

■ Identify five strategies to strengthen an organization's culture.

■ Describe the stages of organizational socialization.

■ Explain how realistic job previews assist the socialization process.

Corporate culture is one of the main drivers of employee commitment and engagement. That's what Vancouver City Savings Credit Union (VanCity)—the largest credit union in Canada—discovered when it surveyed its staff a few years ago. "Employees wanted to know the organization was truly going to live up to its values and stay true to its commitments," says Donna Wilson, VanCity's vice-president of human resources.

VanCity has relied on a strong culture of integrity and innovation for many years. For example, the company introduced Canada's first ethically screened mutual fund in 1986 and has one of North America's most thorough social responsibility audits. But the company's culture had never been written down, and VanCity's 1,500 staff needed a clearer understanding of these values. So, 130 VanCity staff—from the board of directors to employee representatives in every branch—were gathered to articulate what the organization stood for. At the end of the process, everyone agreed that VanCity had three dominant cultural values: integrity, innovation, and responsibility.

Vancouver City Savings Credit Union has reinforced its corporate culture to improve customer and employee relations.

The process didn't stop with a values statement posted in every branch. VanCity leaders meet staff in all departments and branches twice yearly to discuss the company's cultural values. VanCity's values also figure into the decision-making process. "Even on the formal business plan, notations are made where actions demonstrate the commitment to corporate values, and rewards are being given out for behaviors supporting the values," explains Donna Wilson.

Thanks to its corporate culture, VanCity is rated as one of Canada's best companies to work for, and as one of the 10 most respected businesses in British Columbia, the province where the financial institution is headquartered. "[Values] define our company clearly in the financial services market in British Columbia, and give us a national and international profile few other regionally based companies anywhere in the world enjoy," says VanCity CEO Dave Mowat.[1] ■

organizational culture
The basic pattern of shared assumptions, values, and beliefs governing the way employees within an organization think about and act on problems and opportunities.

VanCity has rediscovered the power of organizational culture. **Organizational culture** is the basic pattern of shared assumptions, values, and beliefs considered to be the correct way of thinking about and acting on problems and opportunities facing the organization. It defines what is important and unimportant in the company. You might think of it as the organization's DNA—invisible to the naked eye, yet a powerful template that shapes what happens in the workplace.[2]

This chapter begins by examining the elements of organizational culture and how culture is deciphered through artifacts. This is followed by a discussion of the relationship between organizational culture and corporate performance, including the effects of cultural strength, fit, and adaptability. Then we turn to the issue of mergers and corporate culture, followed by specific strategies for maintaining a strong organizational culture. The last section of this chapter zooms in on employee socialization, which is identified as one of the more important ways to strengthen organizational culture.

Elements of Organizational Culture

As Exhibit 16.1 illustrates, the assumptions, values, and beliefs that represent organizational culture operate beneath the surface of organizational behavior. They are not directly observed, yet their effects are everywhere. Assumptions represent the deepest part of organizational culture because they are uncon-

EXHIBIT 16.1

Elements of organizational culture

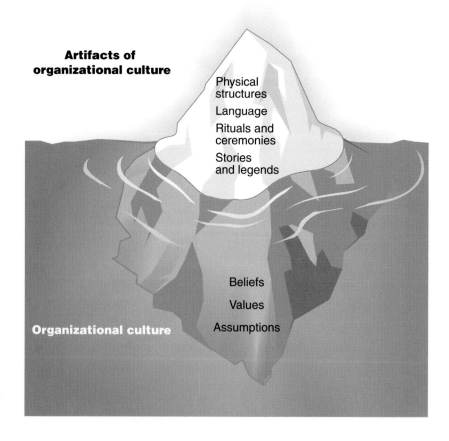

scious and taken for granted. Assumptions are the shared mental models, the broad worldviews or theories-in-use that people rely on to guide their perceptions and behaviors (see Chapter 3). At VanCity, for example, employees assume that the company's integrity to customers and staff is one of the keys to the company's survival and success. These assumptions are ingrained, taken for granted. In other companies, integrity might be appreciated but not assumed to be the essence of a successful business.

An organization's cultural beliefs and values are somewhat easier than assumptions to decipher because people are aware of them. *Beliefs* represent the individual's perceptions of reality. Values are more stable, long-lasting beliefs about what is important. They help us define what is right or wrong, or good or bad, in the world (see Chapter 2).[3] We can't determine an organization's cultural values just by asking employees and other people about them. Values are socially desirable, so what people say they value (called *espoused values*) may differ from what they truly value (*enacted values*).[4] Espoused values do not represent an organization's culture. Rather, they establish the public image that corporate leaders want to display. Enacted values, on the other hand, are values-in-use. They are the values that guide individual decisions and behavior in the workplace.

Content of Organizational Culture

Organizations differ in their cultural content; that is, the relative ordering of beliefs, values, and assumptions. Consider the following companies and their apparent dominant cultures:

- *ICICI Bank*—India's second largest bank exudes a performance-oriented culture. Its organizational practices place a premium on training, career development, goal setting, and pay-for-performance, all with the intent of maximizing employee performance and customer service. "We believe in defining clear performance for employees and empowering them to achieve their goals," says ICICI Bank executive director Kalpana Morparia. "This has helped to create a culture of high performance across the organization."[5]

- *SAS Institute*—SAS Institute has one of the most employee-friendly cultures on the planet. Located on a 200-acre campus in Cary, North Carolina, the world's largest privately held software company supports employee well-being with free on-site medical care, unlimited sick days, heavily subsidized day care, ski trips, personal trainers, inexpensive gourmet cafeterias, and tai chi classes. Unlike other software companies, SAS encourages its employees to stick to a 35-hour workweek. "You can't be a programmer 15 and 16 hours a day," says Jim Goodnight, SAS chief executive and cofounder. Little wonder that SAS Institute is rated as one of the best companies to work for.[6]

- *Wal-Mart, Inc.*—Wal-Mart's headquarters in Bentonville, Arkansas, almost screams out frugality and efficiency. The world's largest retailer has a Spartan waiting room for suppliers, rather like government office waiting areas. Visitors pay for their own soft drinks and coffee. In each of the building's inexpensive cubicles, employees sit at inexpensive desks finding ways to squeeze more efficiencies and lower costs out of suppliers as well as their own work processes.[7]

Employees at Rand Merchant Bank were recently handed a booklet entitled The Complete Book of Rules. *But instead of a long list of "do's and don'ts," all of the pages inside were blank. The message that the South African financial institution wanted to convey is that employees are empowered to make their own decisions. "We trust that in any given situation an employee who has freedom to make choices will inherently do the best for the company," explains Rand chairman Paul Harris. Empowerment practices seem to work: Rand Merchant Bank is rated the best company to work for in South Africa and tends to outperform the marketplace in terms of earnings.[8] How does Rand Merchant Bank's Book of Rules symbolize and support an empowerment culture?*

Performance-oriented. Employee-friendly. Frugal and efficient. How many corporate cultural values are there? No one knows for certain. There are dozens of individual and cross-cultural values, so there are likely as many organizational values. Some writers and consultants have attempted to classify organizational cultures into a few categories with catchy labels such as "mercenaries" and "communes." Although these typologies might reflect the values of a few organizations, they oversimplify the diversity of cultural values in organizations. Worse, they tend to distort rather than clarify our attempts to diagnose corporate culture.

Organizational Subcultures

When discussing organizational culture, we are actually referring to the *dominant culture,* that is, the themes shared most widely by the organization's members. However, organizations are also comprised of *subcultures* located throughout its various divisions, geographic regions, and occupational groups.[9] Some subcultures enhance the dominant culture by espousing parallel assumptions, values, and beliefs; others are called *countercultures* because they directly oppose the organization's core values.

Subcultures, particularly countercultures, potentially create conflict and dissension among employees, but they also serve two important functions.[10] First, they maintain the organization's standards of performance and ethical behavior. Employees who hold countercultural values are an important source of surveillance and critique over the dominant order. They encourage constructive conflict and more creative thinking about how the organization should interact with its environment. Subcultures prevent employees from blindly following one set of values and thereby help the organization to abide by society's ethical values.

The second function of subcultures is to act as spawning grounds for emerging values that keep the firm aligned with the needs of customers, suppliers, society, and other stakeholders. Companies eventually need to replace their dominant values with values that are more appropriate for the changing environment. If subcultures are suppressed, the organization may take longer to discover and adopt values aligned with the emerging environment.

artifacts
The observable symbols and signs of an organization's culture.

Deciphering Organizational Culture through Artifacts

We can't directly see an organization's cultural assumptions, values, and beliefs. Instead, as Exhibit 16.1 illustrated earlier, organizational culture is deciphered indirectly through artifacts. **Artifacts** are the observable symbols and signs of an organization's culture, such as the way visitors are greeted, the physical layout, and how employees are rewarded.[11] Understanding an organization's culture requires painstaking assessment of many artifacts because they are subtle and often ambiguous.[12] The process is very much like an anthropological investigation of a new society. Some scholars extract organizational values from the narratives of everyday corporate life.[13] Others survey employees, observe workplace behavior, and study written documents. We probably need to do all these things to accurately assess an organization's culture.

Although this book tries to present accurate examples, we should remain cautious about public statements regarding a company's culture. Most often, these statements are based on no more than a journalist's quick scan or the company's own public relations pronouncements of its espoused values. With this in mind, let's consider four broad categories of artifacts: organizational stories and legends, rituals and ceremonies, language, physical structures and symbols.

Organizational Stories and Legends

A decade ago, Southwest Airlines introduced an ad campaign with the phrase "Just Plane Smart." Unknowingly, the Dallas-based airline had infringed on the "Plane Smart" slogan at Stevens Aviation, an aviation sales and maintenance company in Greensville, South Carolina. Rather than paying buckets of money to lawyers, Stevens's chairman Kurt Herwald and Southwest CEO Herb Kelleher decided to settle the dispute with an old-fashioned arm wrestling match at a run-down wrestling stadium in Dallas. A boisterous crowd watched the "Malice in Dallas" event as "Smokin" Herb Kelleher and "Kurtsey" Herwald battled their designates, and then each other. When Kelleher lost the final round to Herwald, he jested (while being carried off on a stretcher) that his defeat was due to a cold and the strain of walking up a flight of stairs. Stevens Aviation later decided to let Southwest Airlines continue to use its ad campaign, and both companies donated funds from the event to charities.[14]

Malice in Dallas is a legendary story that almost every Southwest employee knows by heart. It is a tale that communicates one of the maverick airline's core values—that having fun is part of doing business. Stories and legends about past corporate incidents serve as powerful social prescriptions of the way things should (or should not) be done. They convey valuable knowledge throughout the organization by providing human realism to corporate expectations, individual performance standards, and the criteria for getting fired.[15] Perhaps most important, stories create emotions in listeners, which tends to improve their memory of the lesson within the story. Stories have the greatest effect at communicating corporate culture when they describe real people, are assumed to be true, and are known by employees throughout the organization. Stories are also prescriptive—they advise people what to do or not to do.[16]

We should mention that not all stories and legends are positive. On the contrary, many describe problems facing those who violate the dominant culture. Some of these anecdotes also emerge from countercultures to emphasize what is wrong with the dominant culture. General Motors (GM) employees who rejected the automaker's dominant culture liked to repeat one of these negative tales about how dozens of GM people would arrive at the airport to meet a senior executive. An executive's status was symbolized by the number of vehicles leaving the airport with the executive.[17] This story didn't just symbolize respect for authority; it highlighted the decadence and waste that characterized GM's dominant culture.

Rituals and Ceremonies

Soon after moving from IBM to Digital Equipment Corporation (acquired by Hewlett-Packard through its merger with Compaq Computer) several years ago, Peter DeLisi noticed that Digital employees seemed to fight a lot with each other. "Shouting matches were a frequent occurrence, and I came to conclude that Digital people didn't like one another," he recalls. Eventually, DeLisi learned that Digital employees didn't dislike each other; they were engaging in the ritual of "pushing back"—defending ideas until truth ultimately prevailed.[19]

"Pushing back" at Digital Computer was a ritual that reflected the firm's belief that constructive conflict is useful. **Rituals** are the programmed routines of daily organizational life that dramatize the organization's culture. Along with shouting matches at Digital, rituals include how visitors are greeted, how often senior executives visit subordinates, how people communicate with each other, and how much time employees take for lunch. **Ceremonies** are more formal artifacts than rituals. Ceremonies are planned activities conducted specifically for the benefit of an audience. This would include publicly rewarding (or punishing) employees or celebrating the launch of a new product or newly won contract.[20]

Organizational Language

The language of the workplace speaks volumes about the company's culture. How employees address co-workers, describe customers, express anger, and greet stakeholders are all verbal symbols of cultural values. Employees at the Container Store compliment each other about "being Gumby," meaning that they are being as flexible as the once-popular green toy—going outside their regular job to help a customer or another employee. (A human-sized Gumby is displayed at the retailer's headquarters.)[21]

Four Seasons Hotels and Resorts hires, trains, and rewards employees for superior customer service. Yet founder Isadore Sharp will tell you that the company's legendary service is also ingrained in Four Seasons's corporate culture. There is certainly evidence of the customer service value in stories and legends. One story recounts an incident in which rock star Rod Stewart called Four Seasons staff while he was a guest to find someone to play the bagpipes in his suite. The employees were able to find a bagpipe player, even though Stewart phoned in the request at midnight![18] In what ways do these stories and legends support organizational culture?

rituals
The programmed routines of daily organizational life that dramatize the organization's culture.

ceremonies
Planned and usually dramatic displays of organizational culture, conducted specifically for the benefit of an audience.

Organizational leaders also use phrases, metaphors, and other special vocabularies to symbolize the company's culture.[22] Of course, metaphors and catchphrases often reflect the leader's *espoused values*—the values that leaders want people to believe exist—rather than *enacted values*—the company's true values.

Language also highlights values held by organizational subcultures. For instance, consultants working at Whirlpool kept hearing employees talk about the appliance company's "PowerPoint culture." This phrase, which names Microsoft's presentation software, is a critique of Whirlpool's hierarchical culture in which communication is one way (from executives to employees). PowerPoint presentations tend be one-way conversations from the presenter to the audience, and Whirlpool employees see themselves as the audience with limited opportunity to voice opinions or concerns to senior management (the presenters).[23]

Physical Structures and Symbols

Drive up to the "Interplanetary Headquarters" of Oakley, Inc., in Foothill Ranch, California, and you get the distinct impression that the maker of ultra hip eyewear and footwear has something valuable to protect. The building entrance is framed by a round 40-foot steel armor plate. Inside, sleek pipes, watertight doors, and towering metallic walls studded with oversized bolts suggest a place that routinely repels invasion from intruders. Ejection seats from a B-52 bomber furnish the waiting area. A full-sized torpedo lies in a rack behind the receptionist's armored desk. Top-secret development labs are hidden somewhere deep inside the three bunkerlike structures connected to the main entrance area. "We've always had a fortress mentality," says an Oakley executive. "What we make is gold, and people will do anything to get it, so we protect it."[24]

Oakley, Inc., reveals its culture through the design of its interplanetary headquarters. In many organizations, the size, shape, location, and age of buildings might suggest the company's emphasis on teamwork, environmental friendliness, flexibility, or any other set of values. These structures may be deliberately designed to shape the culture, or they are incidental artifacts of the existing culture. As former British prime minister Sir Winston Churchill once said: "We shape our buildings, thereafter, they shape us."[25]

Even if the building doesn't make much of a statement, there is a treasure trove of physical artifacts inside. Desks, chairs, office space, and wall hangings (or lack of them) are just a few of the items that might convey cultural meaning. Stroll through IDEO's offices in Palo Alto, California, and you soon realize that the industrial design firm has an innovative, team-oriented, egalitarian culture. Employees have similarly sized cubicles grouped into neighborhoods facing an asymmetrical table that serves as a central "park" for the team. One employee has hung dozens of strands of beads over the doorway to her workstation. Others suspend patio umbrellas from the ceiling to reduce computer glare from the skylights. To save space, some employees hoist their bicycles overhead on pulleys.[26] Each of these artifacts alone might not say much, but put enough of them together and the company's cultural values become easier to decipher.

Organizational Culture and Performance

Does organizational culture affect corporate performance? The Container Store thinks so. Corporate culture is so important that the retailer's first employee, Barbara Anderson, has the unique job as director of company culture and education. "Every company has a culture," says Anderson. "It comes from within and it takes time to create." Herb Kelleher, the founder of Southwest Airlines, also believes that a company's culture makes a difference in the company's success: "Culture is one of the most precious things a company has, so you must work harder on it than anything else."[27] Several writers argue that a strong corporate culture is good for business because it serves three important functions.[28]

First, corporate culture is a deeply embedded form of social control that influences employee decisions and behavior.[29] Culture is pervasive and operates unconsciously. You might think of it as an automatic pilot, directing employees in ways that are consistent with organizational expectations. Second, corporate culture is the "social glue" that bonds people together and makes them feel part of the organizational experience.[30] Employees are motivated to internalize the organization's dominant culture because it fulfills their need for social identity. This social glue is increasingly important as a way to attract new staff and retain top performers.

Finally, corporate culture assists the sense-making process.[31] It helps employees understand organizational events. They can get on with the task at hand rather than spend time trying to figure out what is expected of them. Employees can also communicate more efficiently and reach higher levels of cooperation with each other because they share common mental models of reality.

Organizational Culture Strength and Fit

Each of these functions of organizational culture assumes that a strong culture is better than a weak one. A *strong organizational culture* exists when most employees across all subunits hold the dominant values. The values are also institutionalized through well-established artifacts, thereby making it difficult for those values to change. Furthermore, strong cultures are long-lasting. In many cases, they can be traced back to the beliefs and values established by the company's founder.[32] In contrast, companies have weak cultures when the dominant values are short lived and held mainly by a few people at the top of the organization.

So, can we conclude that companies with strong cultures have higher performance? Not necessarily! Studies have found only a modestly positive relationship between culture strength and success.[33] One reason for the weak relationship is that a strong culture increases organizational performance only when the cultural content is appropriate for the organization's environment (see Exhibit 16.2). When a firm's strong culture is misaligned with its environment, it is unable to effectively serve customers and other dominant stakeholders. As Global Connections 16.1 describes, Judith Mair developed a strong "back to work" culture at her German advertising and Web design firm because she believed the typical "cool" cultures at other firms contributed to their downfall. Many of the other firms had strong cultures, but they were the wrong cultures for the times.

A second reason why companies with strong cultures aren't necessarily more effective is that strong cultures lock decision makers into mental models that blind them to new opportunities and unique problems. Thus, strong cultures might cause decision makers to overlook or incorrectly define subtle misalignments between the organization's activities and the changing environment.[34] LTV, Youngstown Steel & Tube, Republic Steel, and other bankrupt steel manufacturers apparently suffered from this problem. "It was 100 years

EXHIBIT 16.2

Organizational culture and performance

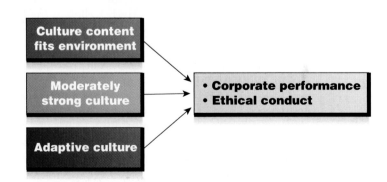

German Advertising Firm Embraces a "Back to Work" Culture

It's time to get back to work! No more pool or fooseball tables in the office. No more flexible hours. No more casual dress. No Christmas party this year . . . or any year. In a rebellion against "new economy" work practices, a small advertising and Web design firm in Cologne, Germany, is returning to a no-nonsense, disciplined corporate culture. "The office is not an amusement park," advises Judith Mair, the 30-year-old entrepreneur who started Mair & Company a few years ago with three colleagues. "Work is just work, and that's exactly what it needs to become again."

Mair & Company's businesslike culture is apparent as soon as you enter its offices. Mair and her co-workers wear company uniforms—smart blue suits when visiting clients and blue-gray tracksuits at the office. Everyone addresses each other formally, by family name. Smiling is not required; it's not even encouraged. Nonwork topics are discussed only during official five-minute breaks. The offices are Spartan: no pictures on the white walls and no personal items that would distract employees from their duties. New age gibberish from America such as "team spirit," "workflow," and "brainstorming" is strictly verboten.

The corporate culture also advocates strict working hours from 9:00 A.M. to 5:30 P.M. and minimal socializing afterward.

Weekend work is forbidden and no one is allowed to take work home. "It's dangerous if work and free time are being mixed up," Mair warns, suggesting that employees experience more stress when their company tries to take over their life beyond normal working hours.

These cultural artifacts are not dictums from the CEO. Mair & Company shifted away from the typical dot-com culture after seeing many other German Internet companies founder. They also believed that acting like a "cool" young firm by dressing in the latest fashions and having company drinks in hip bars increased employee stress. "Yeah, it's strict, but it's OK," says co-worker Vanessa Plotkin, who helped to develop the disciplined culture. "It works."

Many Germans also think Mair & Company's culture "works" in today's tough economy. Mair's recently published book about her company's culture, called *Schluss mit Lustig* (meaning "End the Fun"), has been snapped up by German business leaders looking for ways to survive in Germany's current economic slump.

Sources: K. Gehmlich, "German Businesswoman Demands End to Fun at Work," *Reuters,* July 9, 2003; K. James, "German Concern Looks at Making the Workplace Stricter and Less Friendly," *Marketplace: Minnesota Public Radio,* January 9, 2003; T. Paterson, "German Woman Boss Puts Back Clock to Outlaw Fun," *The Telegraph* (London), December 8, 2002; R. Boyes, "Germans Told: Work Is Not Fun," *The Times* (London), December 6, 2002, p. 20.

---

of integrated culture," recalls John Mang III, the ISG-Cleveland mini-mill plant manager who worked at these firms for three decades. "People in the organization are inbreds, including myself. You grew up in the culture; you didn't see anything else. You didn't typically see people even at very high levels in the steel organization coming in from the outside—even financial, executive, management. It is a culture from within so you have these rose colored glasses that everything's fine."[35]

Finally, very strong cultures tend to suppress dissenting subcultural values. In the long term, this prevents organizations from nurturing new cultural values that should become dominant values as the environment changes. In the short term, a strong culture might undermine constructive conflict (see Chapter 13). Thus, corporate leaders need to recognize that healthy organizations have subcultures with dissenting values that may produce dominant values in the future.

Adaptive Cultures

adaptive culture
An organizational culture in which employees focus on the changing needs of customers and other stakeholders, and support initiatives to keep pace with those changes.

Thus far, we have learned that strong cultures are more effective when the cultural values are aligned with the organization's environment. Also, no corporate culture should be so strong that it blinds employees to alternative viewpoints or completely suppresses dissenting subcultures. One last point to add to this discussion is that organizations are more likely to succeed when they have an adaptive culture.[36] An **adaptive culture** exists when employees focus on the changing needs of customers and other stakeholders and support initiatives to keep pace with these changes.

Organizational culture experts are starting to piece together the elements of adaptive cultures.[37] First and foremost, adaptive cultures have an external focus. Employees hold a common mental model that the organization's success depends on continuous change to support stakeholders. Nortel Networks has shifted from telephones to Internet gear. Nokia has moved from toilet paper and rubber boots to mobile telephones. These firms have maintained an adaptive culture because employees believe that change is both necessary and inevitable to keep pace with a changing external environment.

Second, employees in adaptive cultures pay as much attention to organizational processes as they do to organizational goals. They engage in continuous improvement of internal processes (production, customer service, etc.) to serve external stakeholders. Third, employees in adaptive cultures have a strong sense of ownership. They assume responsibility for the organization's performance. In other words, they believe in "it's our job" rather than "it's not my job." Fourth, adaptive cultures are proactive and quick. Employees seek out opportunities, rather than waiting for them to arrive. They act quickly to learn through discovery, rather than engaging in "paralysis by analysis."

Organizational Culture and Business Ethics

Along with other forms of performance, an organization's culture can potentially influence ethical conduct. This makes sense because, as we learned in Chapter 2, good behavior is driven by ethical values. An organization can guide the conduct of its employees by embedding ethical values in its dominant culture.

Organizational culture is also potentially a source of ethical problems when it applies excessive control over employees. All organizations require some values congruence. As explained in Chapter 2, this congruence ensures employees make decisions that are compatible with organizational objectives. Congruence also improves employee satisfaction, loyalty, and longevity (i.e., low turnover). But a few organizations imprint their cultural values so strongly on employees that they risk becoming corporate cults. They take over employee lives and rob a person's individualism.

This cultlike phenomenon was apparently one of the factors that led to the downfall of Arthur Andersen. The Chicago-based accounting firm's uniting principle, called "One Firm," emphasized consistent service throughout the world by developing Andersen employees the same way. Andersen carefully selected university graduates with compatible values, then subjected these "green beans" to a powerful indoctrination process to further imprint Andersen's culture. This production of Andersen think-alikes, called "Androids," improved service consistency, but it also undermined the ethics of individualism.[38] Thus, an organization's culture should be consistent with society's ethical values and the culture should not be so strong that it undermines individual freedom.

Merging Organizational Cultures

Corporate culture was on the minds of executives at Billiton plc in South Africa and BHP in Australia when they met to discuss a proposed merger into the world's largest mining company. "Obviously one of the questions when you get into a merger is: Is one culture going to dominate or do you create a new one?" says Tom Brown, BHP's human resources director. "Lots of mergers have failed to realize what they purported to because they failed to look at the people or culture side of the business." To ensure that the BHP-Billiton merger wasn't another casualty, the two firms set up a committee to address the cultural issues and plan integration of the two firms. The committee began by taking a "cultural swab" from both companies. What they found was two businesses in cultural transition, so it was possible to form a composite culture that takes the best of both firms.[39]

The BHP-Billiton merger started on the right track from a corporate cultural perspective. Unfortunately, it is also the exception. Mergers and acquisitions are valued at between $1 trillion and $2 trillion annually, more than the gross domestic products of many countries. Yet, more than two-thirds of these combined firms underperformed their industry peers in the following years. The main problem is that corporate leaders are so focused on the financial or marketing logistics of a merger that they fail to conduct due-diligence audits on their respective corporate cultures.[40]

"It's the people stuff that trips up mergers," says an executive at AstraZeneca U.S., one of the world's largest pharmaceutical companies after the merger of Astra AB and Zeneca Group PLC. "You can do the deal because it looks really good on paper, but if you don't engage the minds of the people from each culture, you won't get the productivity you need to be successful."[41]

The corporate world is littered with mergers that failed or had a difficult gestation because of clashing organizational cultures. The marriage of AOL with Time Warner is one of the most spectacular recent examples. In theory, the world's largest merger offered huge opportunities for converging AOL's dominance in Internet services with Time Warner's deep knowledge and assets in traditional media. Instead, the two corporate cultures mixed like oil and water. AOL's culture valued youthful, high-flying, quick deal-making. People were rewarded with stock options. Time Warner, on the other hand, had a button-down, hierarchical, and systematic culture. Executives were older and the reward was a decent retirement package (affectionately known as the "golden rubber band," because people who quit invariably returned for the retirement benefits).[42]

Bicultural Audit

bicultural audit
Diagnoses cultural relations between companies prior to a merger and determines the extent to which cultural clashes will likely occur.

Organizational leaders can minimize these cultural collisions and fulfill their duty of due diligence by conducting a bicultural audit, similar to what BHP and Billiton did prior to their merger. A **bicultural audit** diagnoses cultural relations between the companies and determines the extent to which cultural clashes will likely occur.[43] The bicultural audit process begins with interviews, questionnaires, focus groups, and observation to identify cultural differences between the merging companies. This includes carefully examining artifacts of each organization—the office layout, customer billing procedures, how decisions are made, how information is shared, and so on.

Next, the bicultural audit data are analyzed to determine which differences between the two firms will result in conflict and which cultural values provide common ground on which to build a cultural foundation in the merged organization. The final stage of the bicultural audit involves identifying strategies and preparing action plans to bridge the two organizations' cultures. Connections 16.2 describes how a potential culture clash from the merger of Hewlett-Packard and Compaq Computer was reduced (but not minimized as

Injecting "Compaq DNA" into Hewlett-Packard's Culture

Hewlett-Packard's merger with Compaq Computer was more than just the largest integration in history of two high-tech companies; it was also a monumental test of whether HP CEO Carleton Fiorina could reinvent the California firm's legendary culture, known as the "HP Way."

Soon after becoming HP's first CEO hired from outside the company, Fiorina concluded that the "HP Way has been misinterpreted and twisted as a gentle bureaucracy of entitlement instead of a performance-based meritocracy." The merger was intended, in part, to inject "a little of Compaq's DNA into the HP Way, especially speed and agility," says Jeff Clarke, head of HP's global operations and a Compaq executive at the time of the merger.

Compaq executives were wary of the merger because their company had stumbled over clashing cultures when it acquired Digital Equipment Corporation (DEC) a few years earlier. They were determined to avoid the same mistake with Hewlett-Packard. "We aggressively and thoroughly discussed the differences in culture," recalls Clarke. "We didn't do that in the DEC transaction." Clarke and HP executive Webb McKinney were in charge of dozens of integration teams, including one solely responsible for combining the two cultures. The culture integration team interviewed more than 1,500 employees at both companies then debated the cultural differences and laid out a blueprint of the new integrated culture.

Was the merger successful? Observers say that the Compaq merger has indeed injected a more aggressive culture at HP. However, it also had its share of cultural challenges. Walter Hewlett, son of founder Dave Hewlett, launched (and eventually lost) an expensive campaign to stop the merger be-

Hewlett-Packard CEO Carleton Fiorina reformulated the company's famous "HP Way" culture with more aggressive values by acquiring former rival Compaq Computer.

cause he was worried that it would damage HP's culture. Soon after the integration process began, Compaq employees in Korea posted messages such as "HP failed to understand Compaq's corporate culture," reinforced with expletives. Many employees also say that HP's kinder, gentler culture has been swept away. For instance, HP was previously one of the top 10 best companies to work for. Today, it isn't even on the list of top 100 firms.

Sources: O. de Senerpont Domis, "The HP–Compaq Way," *Daily Deal,* September 22, 2003; C. Swett, "HP Seems to Have Digested Compaq," *Sacramento Bee,* May 13, 2003, p. D1; "HP's Korean Unit Feels Strain Following Merger," *Korea Times,* September 18, 2002; B. Pimentel, "The HP–Compaq Deal: Losing Their Way?" *San Francisco Chronicle,* September 6, 2001; J. Swartz. "How Will Compaq, H-P Fit Together?" *USA Today,* September 6, 2001, p. 3B.

much as might have been possible) through a diagnosis of the corporate culture at the two companies, and the thoughtful integration of those cultures in the new combined organization.

Strategies to Merge Different Organizational Cultures

In some cases, the bicultural audit results in a decision to end merger talks because the two cultures are too different to merge effectively. For instance, GE Capital has rejected potential acquisitions when it became apparent that the other firm's cultural values were incompatible. Nortel Networks also walked away from a joint venture with Cisco Systems because it wasn't comfortable with the other firm's cultural values.[44] However, even with substantially different cultures, two companies may form a workable union if they apply the appropriate merger strategy. The four main strategies for merging different corporate cultures are assimilation, deculturation, integration, and separation (see Exhibit 16.3).[45]

EXHIBIT 16.3 Strategies for merging different organizational culture

Merger strategy	Description	Works best when:
Assimilation	Acquired company embraces acquiring firm's culture.	Acquired firm has a weak culture.
Deculturation	Acquiring firm imposes its culture on unwilling acquired firm.	Rarely works—may be necessary only when acquired firm's culture doesn't work but employees don't realize it.
Integration	Combining the two or more cultures into a new composite culture.	Existing cultures can be improved.
Separation	Merging companies remain distinct entities with minimal exchange of culture or organizational practices.	Firms operate successfully in different businesses requiring different cultures.

Source: Based on ideas in K. W. Smith, "A Brand-New Culture for the Merged Firm," *Mergers and Acquisitions* 35 (June 2000), pp. 45–50; A. R. Malekazedeh and A. Nahavandi, "Making Mergers Work by Managing Cultures," *Journal of Business Strategy,* May–June 1990, pp. 55–57.

Assimilation   Assimilation occurs when employees at the acquired company willingly embrace the cultural values of the acquiring organization. This tends to occur when the acquired company has a weak culture that is dysfunctional, whereas the acquiring company's culture is strong and focused on clearly defined values. Sun Microsystems has acquired many smaller organizations using this strategy. The California high-technology company refuses to digest larger firms because it is much more difficult to apply Sun's aggressive culture.[46] Culture clash is rare with assimilation because the acquired firm's culture is weak and employees are looking for better cultural alternatives.

Deculturation   Assimilation is rare. Employees usually resist organizational change, particularly when they are asked to throw away personal and cultural values. Under these conditions, some acquiring companies apply a *deculturation* strategy by imposing their culture and business practices on the acquired organization. The acquiring firm strips away artifacts and reward systems that support the old culture. People who cannot adopt the acquiring company's culture are often terminated.

Deculturation may be necessary when the acquired firm's culture doesn't work but employees aren't convinced of this. However, this strategy rarely works because it increases the risk of socioemotional conflict (see Chapter 13). Employees from the acquired firm resist the cultural intrusions from the buying firm, thereby delaying or undermining the merger process.

The problems of deculturation were apparent soon after AT&T's hostile takeover of NCR Corporation. AT&T antagonized NCR employees by changing NCR's name to AT&T Global Information Solutions, installing AT&T executives to run the acquired firm, and generally trying to make NCR's culture become more like AT&T's. The merger strategy failed. AT&T eventually divested NCR (which returned to its original name) after piling up nearly $4 billion in losses at the Dayton, Ohio-based cash register and computer systems company.[47]

Integration   A third strategy is to integrate the corporate cultures of both organizations. This involves combining the two or more cultures into a new composite culture that preserves the best features of the previous cultures.

Integration is slow and potentially risky, because there are many forces preserving the existing cultures. However, this strategy should be considered when the companies have relatively weak cultures or when their cultures include several overlapping values. Integration also works best when people realize that their existing cultures are ineffective and are, therefore, motivated to adopt a new set of dominant values.

Separation   A separation strategy occurs where the merging companies agree to remain distinct entities with minimal exchange of culture or organizational practices. This strategy is most appropriate when the two merging companies are in unrelated industries or operate in different countries, because the most appropriate cultural values tend to differ by industry and national culture. Distinct cultures within an organization can also lead to the separation strategy of demerging. For example, Baltimore-based Constellation Energy Group Inc. created a holding company (called BGE Corporation) to separate its slow-moving public utility business from its high-flying merchant energy firm because their cultures are so different.[48]

Changing and Strengthening Organizational Culture

Whether merging two cultures or reshaping the firm's existing values, corporate leaders need to understand how to change and strengthen the organization's dominant culture. Indeed, some organizational behavior experts conclude that the only way to ensure any lasting change is to realign cultural values with those changes. In other words, changes "stick" when they become "the way we do things around here."[49]

Changing organizational culture requires the change management toolkit that we will learn about in the next chapter (Chapter 17). Corporate leaders need to make employees aware of the urgency for change. Then they need to "unfreeze" the existing culture by removing artifacts that represent that culture and "refreeze" the new culture by introducing artifacts that communicate and reinforce the new values.

EXHIBIT 16.4

Strategies for strengthening organizational culture

Strengthening Organizational Culture

Artifacts communicate and reinforce the new corporate culture, but we also need to consider ways to further strengthen that culture. Five approaches that are commonly cited in the literature are the actions of founders and leaders, introducing culturally consistent rewards, maintaining a stable workforce, managing the cultural network, and selecting and socializing new employees (see Exhibit 16.4).

Actions of Founders and Leaders   Founders establish an organization's culture.[50] You can see this at Southwest Airlines, where founder Herb Kelleher established a culture that is both fun and efficient. Founders develop the systems and structures that support their personal values. They are also typically the visionaries whose energetic style provides a powerful role model for others to follow.

In spite of the founder's effect, subsequent leaders can break the organization away from the founder's values if they apply the transformational leadership concepts that were described in Chapter 14. Transformational leaders alter and strengthen organizational culture by communicating and enacting their vision of the future.[51] Earlier in Connections 16.2, we saw how Carly Fiorina changed Hewlett-Packard's culture because she believed HP employees hide behind their corporate culture to avoid tough decisions. "The phrase 'The HP Way' became a way of resisting change and resisting radical ideas," Fiorina explained just before HP's merger with Compaq Computer. "One of the things I've been able to do as an outsider is challenge it."[52]

Ray Anderson (shown in photo) admits that he didn't pay much attention to environmentalism when he launched Atlanta-based Interface Inc. in the 1970s. But after reading The Ecology of Commerce in 1994, Anderson's newfound environmental values have reshaped the culture of the world's largest floor covering company. "We've got a company full of people who've really bought in to that vision," says Anderson. Today, Interface has solar-powered looms, a weaving plant that uses recycled plastics, and an R&D department that experiments with hemp, sugar cane, and other renewable resources. Most of the company's 8,000 employees on four continents have received environmental training, and many of them have created environmental organizations in their communities.[53] In what ways do founders and leaders influence their organization's culture?

Introducing Culturally Consistent Rewards   Reward systems strengthen corporate culture when they are consistent with cultural values.[54] For example, Husky Injection Molding Systems has an unusual stock incentive program that supports its environmentalist culture. Employees at the plastics equipment manufacturer earn one-twentieth of a company share for each seedling they plant, one share for each month of car pooling, and so on. The idea is to align rewards to the cultural values the company wants to reinforce.

Maintaining a Stable Workforce   An organization's culture is embedded in the minds of its employees. Organizational stories are rarely written down; rituals and ceremonies do not usually exist in procedure manuals; organizational metaphors are not found in corporate directories. Thus, organizations depend on a stable workforce to communicate and reinforce the dominant beliefs and values. The organization's culture can literally disintegrate during periods of high turnover and precipitous downsizing because the corporate memory leaves with these employees.[55] Conversely, corporate leaders who want to change the corporate culture have accelerated the turnover of senior executives and older employees who held the previous culture in place.

Managing the Cultural Network   Organizational culture is learned, so an effective network of cultural transmission is necessary to strengthen the company's underlying assumptions, values, and beliefs. According to Max De Pree, former CEO of furniture manufacturer Herman Miller Inc., every organization needs "tribal storytellers" to keep the organization's history and culture alive.[56] The cultural network exists through the organizational grapevine. It is also supported through frequent opportunities for interaction so employees can share stories and reenact rituals. Senior executives must tap into the cultural network, sharing their own stories and creating new ceremonies and other opportunities to demonstrate shared meaning. Company magazines and other media can also strengthen organizational culture by communicating cultural values and beliefs more efficiently.

Selecting and Socializing Employees   People at Bristol-Myers recently noticed that executives hired from the outside weren't as successful as those promoted from within. Within a year, many quit or were fired. Ben Dowell, who runs Bristol-Myers's Center for Leadership Development, looked closely at the problem and arrived at the following conclusion: "What came through was, those who left were uncomfortable in our culture or violated some core area of our value system." From this discovery, Bristol-Myers assessed its culture—it's team-oriented, consistent with the firm's research and development roots. Now, applicants are carefully screened to ensure they have compatible values.[57]

Bristol-Myers and a flock of other organizations strengthen their corporate cultures by hiring people with beliefs, values, and assumptions similar to those cultures. They realize that a good fit of personal and organizational values makes it easier for employees to adopt the corporate culture. A good person–organization fit also improves job satisfaction and organizational loyalty because new hires with values compatible to the corporate culture adjust more quickly to the organization.[58]

Job applicants also pay attention to corporate culture during the hiring process. They realize that employees must feel comfortable with the company's values, not just the job duties and hours of work. Thus, job applicants need to look at corporate culture artifacts when deciding whether to join a particular organization. By diagnosing the company's dominant culture, they are more likely to determine whether its values are compatible with their own.

Along with selecting people with compatible values, companies maintain strong cultures through the process of organizational socialization. **Organizational socialization** refers to the process by which individuals learn the values, expected behaviors, and social knowledge necessary to assume their roles in the organization.[59] By communicating the company's dominant values, job candidates and new hires are more likely to internalize these values quickly and deeply. Socialization is an important process for absorbing corporate culture as well as helping newcomers to adjust to co-workers, work procedures,

organizational socialization
The process by which individuals learn the values, expected behaviors, and social knowledge necessary to assume their roles in the organization.

and other corporate realities. Thus, the final section of this chapter looks more closely at the organizational socialization process.

Organizational Socialization

Bill Rainford was all set for summer employment at a financial services firm in New York City. Then Microsoft called the Boston University student with the offer of a possible internship. In January, after a successful interview in Boston, Rainford flew at Microsoft's expense to Redmond, Washington, for several more interviews and a tour of the company's lush, campuslike headquarters. Microsoft even gave him a car rental so he could explore Seattle. But Rainford's real learning process occurred several months later as one of 800 interns, discovering firsthand what it's like to work at Microsoft.

"We give [interns] goals, a mentor and a manager," explains Colleen Wheeler McCreary, a senior technical recruiter for Microsoft. "They have a midpoint review and a final review. They get the full experience. We also tell them upfront during orientation that, not only is the summer internship an opportunity for them to check us out, but we are also checking them out for a possible permanent job."[60]

Microsoft Corporation successfully brings people into the organization by going beyond selecting applicants with the right competencies. It also relies on internships and other organizational socialization practices to help newcomers learn about and adjust to the company's culture, physical layout, procedures, and so on. Research indicates that the socialization process may increase or hinder job performance and job satisfaction, depending on whether the recruits are unskilled and new to the workforce or are highly skilled and have many years of work experience.[61]

Socialization as a Learning and Adjustment Process

Organizational socialization is a process of both learning and adjustment. It is a learning process because newcomers try to make sense of the company's physical workplace, social dynamics, and strategic/cultural environment. Organizational behavior research has identified six content dimensions of organizational socialization.[62] Newcomers need to learn about the organization's performance expectations, power dynamics, corporate culture, company history, and jargon. They also need to form successful and satisfying relationships with other people from whom they can learn the ropes.[63] Thus, effective socialization enables new recruits to form a cognitive map of the physical, social, and strategic/cultural dynamics of the organization without information overload.

Organizational socialization is also a process of adjustment, because individuals need to adapt to their new work environment.[64] They develop new work roles that reconfigure their social identity (see Chapter 3), adopt new team norms, and practice new behaviors. Research reports that the adjustment process is fairly rapid for many people, usually within a few months. However, newcomers with diverse work experience seem to adjust better than those with limited previous experience, possibly because they have a larger toolkit of knowledge and skills to make the adjustment possible.[65]

Newcomers absorb the organization's dominant culture to varying degrees. Some people deeply internalize the company's culture; a few others rebel against these attempts to change their mental models and values. Ideally, newcomers adopt a level of "creative individualism" in which they accept the essential elements of the organization's culture and team norms, yet maintain a healthy individualism that challenges the allegedly dysfunctional elements of organizational life.

Stages of Socialization

Socialization is a continuous process, beginning long before the first day of employment and continuing throughout one's career within the company. However, it is most intense when people move across organizational boundaries, such as when they first join a company or get transferred to an international assignment. Each of these transitions is a process that can be divided into three stages. Our focus here is on the socialization of new employees, so the three stages are called preemployment socialization, encounter, and role management (see Exhibit 16.5). These stages parallel the individual's transition from outsider, to newcomer, and then to insider.[66]

Stage 1: Preemployment Socialization   Think back to the months and weeks before you began working in a new job (or attending a new school). You actively searched for information about the company, formed expectations about working there, and felt some anticipation about fitting into that environment. The preemployment socialization stage encompasses all of the learning and adjustment that occurs prior to the first day of work in a new position.

Much of the socialization adjustment process occurs before the first day of work.[67] This is not an easy process, however. Individuals are outsiders, so they must rely on friends, employment interviews, recruiting literature, and other indirect information to form expectations about what it is like to work in the organization. Furthermore, the information exchange between applicants and employers is usually less than perfectly honest.[68] Job applicants might distort their résumés, while employers hide their blemishes by presenting overly positive images of organizational life. Job applicants avoid asking sensitive questions—about pay increases and quick promotions, for example—in order to maintain a good image to recruiters.

To make matters worse, job applicants tend to engage in postdecisional justification (see Chapter 8) during preemployment socialization. Before the first

EXHIBIT 16.5   Stages of organizational socialization

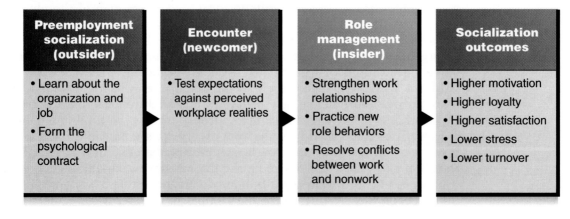

day of work, they tend to increase the importance of favorable elements of the job and justify or completely forget about some negative elements. At the same time, they reduce the perceived quality of job offers that they turned down. Employers often distort their expectations of new hires in the same way. The result is that both parties develop higher expectations of each other than they will actually experience during the encounter stage.

Stage 2: Encounter   The first day on the job typically marks the beginning of the encounter stage of organizational socialization. This is the stage in which newcomers test their prior expectations against the perceived realities. Many jobs fail the test, resulting in varying degrees of reality shock. **Reality shock** occurs when newcomers perceive discrepancies between their preemployment expectations and on-the-job reality.[69] The larger the gap, the stronger the reality shock.

reality shock
Perceived discrepancies between pre-employment expectations and on-the-job reality.

Consider Duncan McNee, a high school English and gym teacher from Brisbane, Australia, who accepted a teaching post in the United Kingdom. McNee expected a challenging new adventure teaching in another country. Instead, he was soon shocked by the severity of student behavior problems. "Even in the worst schools where I taught in Australia the kids still had some respect," says McNee. "But over here there seems to be a complete lack of it. I've had chairs being thrown around, textbooks thrown out of windows and fights."[70]

Rajit Gangadharan thought his dream had come true when offered a job at a call center in Bangalore, India. The recent business school graduate looked forward to the happy office environment, decent salary, free entertainment passes, and working with customers half a world away. But it didn't take long for Gangadharan to discover the downside of the job, including long night shifts, irregular eating habits, and few opportunities to meet his old friends. "Social life is nil in such a job," complains Gangadharan, who no longer works in a call center. A recent survey by NFO WorldGroup reports that Gangadharan is typical of call center employees in India. They are well educated and highly qualified, yet their high job expectations result in reality shock and turnover rates of 30 to 50 percent.[71] What selection and socialization strategies might help to minimize this reality shock in India's call centers?

Duncan McNee experienced reality shock because student behavior problems were much worse than he had imagined. This reality shock doesn't necessarily occur on the first day; it might develop over several weeks or even months as newcomers form a better understanding of their new work environment. Along with experiencing unmet expectations, reality shock occurs when newcomers are overwhelmed by the experience of sudden entry into a new work environment. They experience the stress of information overload and have difficulty adjusting quickly to their new role.

Reality shock is common in many organizations.[72] Unmet expectations sometimes occur because the employer is unable to live up to its promises, such as failing to provide challenging projects or resources to get the work done. Reality shock also occurs because new hires develop a distorted psychological contract through the previously described information exchange conflicts and postdecisional justification. Whatever the cause, reality shock impedes the socialization process because the newcomer's energy is directed toward managing the stress rather than learning and accepting organizational knowledge and roles.[73]

Stage 3: Role Management   During the role management stage in the social-ization process, employees settle in as they make the transition from new-comers to insiders. They strengthen relationships with co-workers and super-visors, practice new role behaviors, and adopt attitudes and values consistent with their new position and organization.

Role management also involves resolving the conflicts between work and nonwork activities. In particular, employees must redistribute their time and energy between work and family, reschedule recreational activities, and deal with changing perceptions and values in the context of other life roles. They must address any discrepancies between their existing values and those em-phasized by the organizational culture. New self-identities are formed that are more compatible with the work environment.

Improving the Socialization Process

Organizational socialization has a profound effect on individual performance, organizational commitment, and turnover, so companies should consider var-ious ways to guide this process. Two important strategies are realistic job pre-views and effectively engaging socialization agents.

Realistic Job Previews   Many companies use a "flypaper approach" to re-cruiting: They exaggerate positive features of the job and neglect to mention the undesirable elements in the hope that the best applicants will get "stuck" on the organization. In reality, as was described earlier, this strategy tends to produce a distorted psychological contract that eventually leads to lower trust and higher turnover.[74] A better approach is to give job applicants a **realistic job preview (RJP),** that is, a balance of positive and negative information about the job and work context.[75]

For example, one public transit company shows job applicants a video de-picting angry riders, knife attacks, and other abuses that bus drivers may en-dure on their routes. Applicants then meet with a union representative who explains, among other things, that new drivers are typically assigned night shifts and the poorest routes. Finally, applicants are given the opportunity to drive a bus.

Although RJPs scare away some applicants, they tend to reduce turnover and increase job performance.[76] This occurs because RJPs help applicants de-velop more accurate preemployment expectations that, in turn, minimize re-ality shock. RJPs represent a type of vaccination by preparing employees for the more challenging and troublesome aspects of work life. Moreover, appli-cants self-select themselves when given realistic information. There is also some evidence that RJPs increase organizational loyalty. A possible explana-tion for this is that companies providing candid information are easier to trust. They also show respect for the psychological contract and concern for employee welfare.[77]

Socialization Agents

Ask new employees what most helped them to adjust to their job and chances are they will mention helpful co-workers, bosses, or maybe even friends who work for the company. The fact is, a lot of organizational socialization occurs informally through these socialization agents.[78] Supervisors tend to provide technical information, performance feedback, and information about job du-

realistic job preview (RJP)
Giving job applicants a balance of positive and negative information about the job and work context.

ties. They also improve the socialization process by giving newcomers reasonably challenging first assignments, buffering them from excessive demands, and helping them form social ties with co-workers.[79]

Co-workers also are important socialization agents because they are easily accessible, can answer questions when problems arise, and serve as role models for appropriate behavior. New employees tend to receive this information and support when co-workers integrate them into the work team. Co-workers also aid the socialization process by being flexible and tolerant in their interactions with new hires.

Several organizations rely on a "buddy system," where newcomers are assigned to co-workers who provide information and social support. Every nurse who joins Children's Memorial Hospital in Chicago is assigned a mentor to help ease the transition into the new culture. ExtendMedia also has a formal buddy system, but equally valuable is the box of doughnuts put on every newcomer's desk on the first day of work. "The [doughnuts] are there to break the ice so that other people come and talk to them. We are introducing people through their stomachs," explains an executive at the interactive media company. Progressive Inc., the Mayfield, Ohio-based insurance firm, relies on current employees to recruit and socialize job applicants. "I think candidates can trust and respect people who already work here," says Jennifer Cohen, Progressive's national employment director. "They know they aren't being sold a bill of goods. They have someone to talk to about the opportunities, and they get a lot of honest information about the company."[80]

Newcomers who quickly form social relations with co-workers tend to have a less traumatic socialization experience and are less likely to quit their jobs within the first year of employment.[81] However, co-workers sometimes engage in hazing—the practice of fooling or intimidating newcomers as a practical joke or initiation ritual.

Chapter Summary

Organizational culture is the basic pattern of shared assumptions, values, and beliefs that govern behavior within a particular organization. Assumptions are the shared mental models or theories-in-use that people rely on to guide their perceptions and behaviors. Beliefs represent the individual's perceptions of reality. Values are more stable, long-lasting beliefs about what is important. They help us define what is right or wrong, or good or bad, in the world. Culture content refers to the relative ordering of beliefs, values, and assumptions.

Organizations have subcultures as well as the dominant culture. Some subcultures enhance the dominant culture, whereas countercultures have values that oppose the organization's core values. Subcultures maintain the organization's standards of performance and ethical behavior. They are also the source of emerging values that replace aging core values.

Artifacts are the observable symbols and signs of an organization's culture. Four broad categories of artifacts include organizational stories and legends, rituals and ceremonies, language, and physical structures and symbols. Understanding an organization's culture requires painstaking assessment of many artifacts because they are subtle and often ambiguous.

Organizational culture has three main functions. It is a deeply embedded form of social control. It is also the "social glue" that bonds people together and makes them feel part of the organizational experience. Finally, corporate culture helps employees make sense of the workplace.

Companies with strong cultures generally perform better than those with weak cultures, but only when the cultural content is appropriate for the organization's environment. Also, the culture should not be so strong that it drives out dissenting values that may form emerging values for the future. Organizations should have adaptive cultures so that employees focus on the need for change and support initiatives and leadership that keeps pace with these changes.

Organizational culture relates to business ethics in two ways. First, corporate cultures can support ethical values of society, thereby reinforcing ethical conduct. Second, some cultures are so strong that they rob a person's individualism and discourage constructive conflict.

Mergers should include a bicultural audit to diagnose the compatibility of the organizational cultures. The four main strategies for merging different corporate cultures are integration, deculturation, assimilation, and separation.

Organizational culture is very difficult to change. However, this may be possible by creating an urgency for change and replacing artifacts that support the old culture with artifacts aligned more with the desired future culture. Organizational culture may be strengthened through the actions of founders and leaders, introducing culturally consistent rewards, maintaining a stable workforce, managing the cultural network, and selecting and socializing employees.

Organizational socialization is the process by which individuals learn the values, expected behaviors, and social knowledge necessary to assume their roles in the organization. It is a process of both learning about the work context and adjusting to new work roles, team norms, and behaviors.

Employees typically pass through three socialization stages. Preemployment socialization occurs before the first day and includes conflicts between the organization's and applicant's need to collect information and attract the other party. Encounter begins on the first day and typically involves adjusting to reality shock. Role management involves resolving work–nonwork conflicts and settling into the workplace. To manage the socialization process, organizations should introduce realistic job previews (RJPs) and recognize the value of socialization agents in the process. RJPs give job applicants a realistic balance of positive and negative information about the job and work context. Socialization agents provide information and social support during the socialization process.

Key Terms

adaptive culture, p. 483
artifacts, p. 478
bicultural audit, p. 485
ceremonies, p. 480
organizational culture, p. 476

organizational socialization 490
realistic job preview (RJP), p. 494
reality shock, p. 493
rituals, p. 480

Discussion Questions

1. Superb Consultants submitted a proposal to analyze the cultural values of your organization. The proposal states that Superb has developed a revolutionary new survey to tap the company's true culture. The survey takes just 10 minutes to complete and the consultants say results can be based on a small sample of employees. Discuss the merits and limitations of this proposal.
2. Some people suggest that the most effective organizations have the strongest cultures. What do we mean by the "strength" of organizational culture, and what possible problems are there with a strong organizational culture?
3. The CEO of a manufacturing firm wants everyone to support the organization's dominant culture of lean efficiency and hard work. The CEO

introduced a new reward system to reinforce this culture and personally interviews all professional and managerial applicants to ensure that they bring similar values to the organization. Some employees who criticized these values had their careers sidelined until they left. Two midlevel managers were fired for supporting contrary values, such as work–life balance. Based on your knowledge of organizational subcultures, what potential problems is the CEO creating?
4. Identify at least two artifacts you have observed in your department or faculty from each of the following four broad categories: (a) organizational stories and legends; (b) rituals and ceremonies; (c) language; and (d) physical structures and symbols.

5. "Organizations are more likely to succeed when they have an adaptive culture." What can an organization do to foster an adaptive culture?

6. Acme Corporation is planning to acquire Beta Corporation, which operates in a different industry. Acme's culture is entrepreneurial and fast-paced, whereas Beta employees value slow, deliberate decision making by consensus. Which merger strategy would you recommend to minimize culture shock when Acme acquires Beta? Explain your answer.

7. Suppose you are asked by senior officers of a city government to identify ways to reinforce a new culture of teamwork and collaboration. The senior executive group clearly supports these values, but it wants everyone in the organization to embrace them. Identify four types of activities that would strengthen these cultural values.

8. Progressive, Inc., ExtendMedia, and other organizations rely on current employees to socialize new recruits. What are the advantages of relying on this type of socialization agent? What problems can you foresee (or you have personally experienced) with co-worker socialization practices?

CASE STUDY 16.1

ASSETONE BANK

AssetOne Bank is one of Asia's largest financial institutions, but it had difficulty entering the personal investment business where several other companies dominate the market. To gain entry to this market, AssetOne decided to acquire TaurusBank, a much smaller financial institution that had aggressively developed investment funds (unit trusts) and online banking in the region. Taurus was owned by a European conglomerate that wanted to exit the financial sector, so the company was quietly put up for sale. The opportunity to acquire Taurus seemed like a perfect fit to AssetOne's executives, who saw the purchase as an opportunity to finally gain a competitive position in the personal investment market. In particular, the acquisition would give AssetOne valuable talent in online banking and investment fund businesses.

Negotiations between AssetOne and Taurus-Bank occurred secretly, except for communication with government regulatory agencies, and took several months as AssetOne's executive team deliberated over the purchase. When Asset-One finally decided in favor of the acquisition, employees of both companies were notified only a few minutes before the merger was announced publicly. During the public statement, AssetOne's CEO boldly announced that Taurus-Bank would become a "seamless extension of AssetOne." He explained that, like AssetOne, Taurus employees would learn the value of detailed analysis and cautious decision making.

The comments by AssetOne's CEO shocked many employees at Taurus, which was an aggressive and entrepreneurial competitor in online banking and personal investments. Taurus was well known for its edgy marketing, innovative products, and tendency to involve employees in generating creative ideas. The company didn't hesitate to hire people from other industries who would bring different ideas to the investment and online banking business. Asset-One, on the other hand, almost completely promoted its executives from within the ranks. Every member of the senior executive team had started at AssetOne. The company also emphasized decision making at the top to maintain better control and consistency.

Frustration was apparent within a few months after the merger. Several Taurus executives quit after repeated failure of AssetOne's executive team to decide quickly on critical online banking initiatives. For example, at the time of the acquisition, Taurus was in the process of forming affinity alliances with several companies. Yet, six months later, AssetOne's executive team still had not decided whether to proceed with these partnerships.

The biggest concerns occurred in the investment fund business, where 20 of TaurusBank's 60 fund managers were lured away by competitors within the first year. Some left for better opportunities. Six fund managers left with the Taurus executive in charge of the investment fund business, who joined an investment firm that specializes in investment funds. Several employees left Taurus after AssetOne executives insisted that all new investment funds must be approved by AssetOne's executive group. Previously, Taurus had given the investment fund division enough freedom to launch new products without approval of the entire executive team.

Two years later, AssetOne's CEO admitted that the acquisition of TaurusBank did not gain the opportunities that management had originally hoped for. AssetOne had more business in this area, but many of the more talented people in investment funds and online banking had left the firm. Overall, the merged company had not kept pace with other innovative financial institutions in the market.

Discussion Questions

1. Based on your understanding of mergers and organizational culture, discuss the problems that occurred in this case.

2. What strategies would you recommend to AssetOne's executives to avoid these corporate culture clashes in future mergers and acquisitions?

Source: Copyright © 2002 Steven L. McShane.

CASE STUDY 16.2

SHAKING UP MERRILL

BusinessWeek Stan O'Neill had a tough enough time convincing employees that he was the right person to lead Merrill Lynch. O'Neill was at the Wall Street brokerage firm more than 15 years, but he kept a relatively low profile and had never held the position of broker. But that didn't stop the latest CEO at America's largest brokerage firm from attempting a more daunting task: changing its corporate culture. Merrill Lynch was most closely associated with the bull market of the 1990s and seems to have fallen the hardest after the bubble burst. O'Neill thinks the problem is partly that Merrill Lynch's corporate culture is out of step with the times.

This *Business Week* case study describes the background of Merrill Lynch CEO Stan O'Neill and examines some of the cultural changes he is making—or trying to make—at the investment firm. Read through this *Business Week* article at www.mhhe.com/mcshane3e and prepare for the discussion questions below.

Discussion Questions

1. Describe the current corporate culture as well as the culture that Stan O'Neill is trying to create at Merrill Lynch.

2. What specifically is Stan O'Neill doing to try to change Merrill Lynch's corporate culture? Do you think these actions will be successful? Why or why not?

Source: E. Thornton, A. Tergesen, and D. Welch, "Shaking Up Merrill," *Business Week*, November 12, 2001, pp. 96–102.

WEB EXERCISE 16.3

DIAGNOSING CORPORATE CULTURE PROCLAMATIONS

Purpose To understand the importance and contexts in which corporate culture is identified and discussed in organizations.

Instructions This exercise is primarily intended to a be take-home activity, although it can be completed in classes with computers and

Internet connections. The instructor will divide the class into small teams (typically four to five people per team). Each team is assigned a specific industry, such as energy, biotechnology, or computer hardware.

The team's task is to search websites of several companies in the selected industry for company statements about their corporate culture. Use the company website search engine (if it exists) to find documents with key phrases such as "corporate culture" or "company values."

In the next class, or at the end of the time allotted in the current class, students will report on their observations by answering the following three discussion questions.

Discussion Questions

1. What values seem to dominate the corporate culture of the companies you searched? Are these values similar or diverse across companies in the industry?

2. What was the broader content of the Web pages where these companies described or mentioned their corporate culture?

3. Do companies in this industry refer to their corporate culture on the websites more or less than companies in other industries searched by team in this class?

TEAM EXERCISE 16.4

TRUTH IN ADVERTISING

Purpose This team activity is designed to help you to diagnose the degree to which recruitment advertisements and brochures provide realistic previews of the job and/or organization.

Materials The instructor will bring to class either recruiting brochures or newspaper advertisements.

Instructions The instructor will place students into teams and give them copies of recruiting brochures and/or advertisements. The instructor might assign one lengthy brochure; alternatively, several newspaper advertisements may be assigned. All teams should receive the same materials so that everyone is familiar with the items and results can be compared. Teams will evaluate the recruiting material(s) and answer the following questions for each item:

Discussion Questions

1. What information in the text of this brochure/advertisement identifies conditions or activities in this organization or job that some applicants may not like?

2. If there are photographs or images of people at work, do they show only positive conditions, or do any show conditions or events that some applicants may not like?

3. After reading this item, would you say that it provides a realistic preview of the job and/or organization?

SELF-ASSESSMENT EXERCISE 16.5

CORPORATE CULTURE PREFERENCE SCALE

Purpose This self-assessment is designed to help you to identify a corporate culture that fits most closely with your personal values and assumptions.

Instructions Read each pair of the statements in the Corporate Culture Preference Scale and circle the statement that describes the organization you would prefer to work in. Then use the scoring key in Appendix B to calculate your results for each subscale. This exercise is completed alone so students assess themselves honestly without concerns of social comparison. However, class discussion will focus on the importance of matching job applicants to the organization's dominant values.

CORPORATE CULTURE PREFERENCE SCALE

I would prefer to work in an organization:

1a. Where employees work well together in teams.	OR	1b. That produces highly respected products or services.
2a. Where top management maintains a sense of order in the workplace.	OR	2b. Where the organization listens to customers and responds quickly to their needs.
3a. Where employees are treated fairly.	OR	3b. Where employees continuously search for ways to work more efficiently.
4a. Where employees adapt quickly to new work requirements.	OR	4b. Where corporate leaders work hard to keep employees happy.
5a. Where senior executives receive special benefits not available to other employees.	OR	5b. Where employees are proud when the organization achieves its performance goals.
6a. Where employees who perform the best get paid the most.	OR	6b. Where senior executives are respected.
7a. Where everyone gets their jobs done like clockwork.	OR	7b. That is on top of new innovations in the industry.
8a. Where employees receive assistance to overcome any personal problems.	OR	8b. Where employees abide by company rules.
9a. That is always experimenting with new ideas in the marketplace.	OR	9b. That expects everyone to put in 110 percent for peak performance.
10a. That quickly benefits from market opportunities.	OR	10b. Where employees are always kept informed of what's happening in the organization.
11a. That can quickly respond to competitive threats.	OR	11b. Where most decisions are made by the top executives.
12a. Where management keeps everything under control.	OR	12b. Where employees care for each other.

Source: Copyright © 2000 Steven L. McShane.

After studying the preceding material, be sure to check out our website at
www.mhhe.com/mcshane3e
for more in-depth information and interactivities that correspond to this chapter.

chapter 17

Organizational Change

Learning Objectives

After reading this chapter, you should be able to:

- Describe the elements of Lewin's force field analysis model.

- Outline six reasons why people resist organizational change.

- Discuss six strategies to minimize resistance to change.

- Outline the conditions for effectively diffusing change from a pilot project.

- Describe the action research approach to organizational change.

- Outline the "Four-D" model of appreciative inquiry and explain how this approach differs from action research.

- Explain how parallel learning structures assist the change process.

- Discuss four ethical issues in organization change.

Nissan Motor Company was on the brink of bankruptcy when French automaker Renault purchased a controlling interest and installed Carlos Ghosn as the effective head of the Japanese automaker. Along with Nissan's known problems of high debt and plummeting market share, Ghosn (pronounced "gone") saw that Nissan managers had no apparent sense of urgency to change. "Even though the evidence is against them, they sit down and they watch the problem a little bit longer," says Ghosn.

Ghosn's challenge was to act quickly, yet minimize the inevitable resistance that arises when an outsider tries to change traditional Japanese business practices. "I was non-Nissan, non-Japanese," he says. "I knew that if I tried to dictate changes from above, the effort would backfire, undermining morale and productivity. But if I was too passive, the company would simply continue its downward spiral."

To resolve this dilemma, Ghosn formed nine cross-functional teams of 10 middle managers each and gave them the mandate to identify innovative proposals for a specific area (marketing, manufacturing, etc.) within three months. Each team could form subteams with additional people to analyze specific issues in more detail. In all, more than 500 middle managers and other employees were involved in the so-called Nissan Revival Plan.

Carlos Ghosn launched a turnaround at Nissan Motor Company that saved the Japanese automaker and relied on change management practices rarely seen in Japan.

After a slow start—Nissan managers weren't accustomed to such authority or working with colleagues across functions or cultures—ideas began to flow as Ghosn stuck to his deadline, reminded team members of the automaker's desperate situation, and encouraged teams to break traditions. Three months later, the nine teams submitted a bold plan to close three assembly plants, eliminate thousands of jobs, cut the number of suppliers by half, reduce purchasing costs by 20 percent, return to profitability, cut the company's debt by half, and introduce 22 new models within the next two years.

Although risky, Ghosn accepted all of the proposals. Moreover, when revealing the plan publicly on the eve of the annual Tokyo Motor Show, Ghosn added his own commitment to the plan: "If you ask people to go through a difficult period of time, they have to trust that you're sharing it with them," Ghosn explains. "So I said that if we did not fulfill our commitments, I would resign."

Ghosn's strategy for organizational change and the Nissan Revival Plan worked. Within 12 months, the automaker had increased sales and market share and posted its first profit in seven years. The company introduced innovative models and expanded operations. Ghosn, who received high praise throughout Japan and abroad, will likely become head of Renault.[1] ■

Change is difficult enough in small firms. At Nissan Motor Company and other large organizations, it requires monumental effort and persistence. Organizational change is also very messy. The change process that Carlos Ghosn launched at Nissan seems to be smoothly executed, but it was buffeted by uncertain consequences, organizational politics, and various forms of resistance from employees and suppliers.

This chapter examines ways to bring about meaningful change in organizations. We begin by introducing Lewin's model of change and its component parts. This includes sources of resistance to change, ways to minimize this resistance, and stabilizing desired behaviors. Next, this chapter examines three approaches to organizational change—action research, appreciative inquiry, and parallel learning structures. The last section of this chapter considers both cross-cultural and ethical issues in organizational change.

Lewin's Force Field Analysis Model

force field analysis

Lewin's model of systemwide change that helps change agents diagnose the forces that drive and restrain proposed organizational change.

Social psychologist Kurt Lewin developed the force field analysis model to help explain how the change process works (see Exhibit 17.1).[2] Although developed over 50 years ago, Lewin's **force field analysis** model remains the prominent way of viewing this process.

One side of the force field model represents the *driving forces* that push organizations toward a new state of affairs. Chapter 1 described some of the driving forces in the external environment, including globalization, information technology, and a changing workforce. Along with these external forces, some corporate leaders create driving forces within the organization; they may increase competition across company departments and encourage new practices and values that the leader believes are inherently better, for instance.

The other side of Lewin's model represents the *restraining forces* that maintain the status quo. These restraining forces are commonly called "resistance to change" because they appear as employee behaviors that block the change process. Stability occurs when the driving and restraining forces are roughly in equilibrium, that is, they are of approximately equal strength in opposite directions.

EXHIBIT 17.1

Lewin's force field analysis model

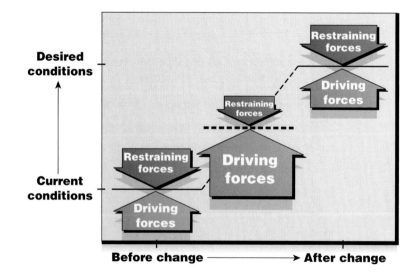

unfreezing
The first part of the change process whereby the change agent produces disequilibrium between the driving and restraining forces.

refreezing
The latter part of the change process in which systems and conditions are introduced that reinforce and maintain the desired behaviors.

Lewin's force field model emphasizes that effective change occurs by **unfreezing** the current situation, moving to a desired condition, and then **refreezing** the system so that it remains in this desired state. Unfreezing involves producing disequilibrium between the driving and restraining forces. As we will describe later, this may occur by increasing the driving forces, reducing the restraining forces, or having a combination of both. Refreezing occurs when the organization's systems and structures are aligned with the desired behaviors. They must support and reinforce the new role patterns and prevent the organization from slipping back into the old way of doing things. Over the next few pages, we use Lewin's model to understand why change is blocked and how the process can evolve more smoothly.

Restraining Forces

BP Norge, the Norwegian subsidiary of British Petroleum, faced more resistance from employees than from the infamous North Sea weather when it introduced self-directed work teams (SDWTs) on its drilling rigs. Many skeptical employees claimed that previous attempts to create SDWTs didn't work.

In his two tumultuous years as CEO, Jacques Nasser (left) heaped a lot of change on employees at Ford Motor Company. He tried to shift the automaker from engineering prowess to "cyber-savviness," from quality to efficiency, and from an old-boys' club to a performance-focused competitor. In one year, Nasser rammed through a performance review system that had taken General Electric nearly a decade to implement. The changes were too much for many Ford employees. Some engineers grumbled that quality declined; employees stung by the performance system launched age discrimination lawsuits. "When you induce change, you get a reaction," explains a senior Ford executive. "I have letters from employees congratulating us. I have letters from employees doing the opposite." In the latter group was the Ford family, who replaced Nasser with William Clay Ford (right) as CEO.[3] How can corporate leaders change their organizations quickly without experiencing the level of resistance experienced at Ford?

Others were convinced that they already had SDWTs, so why change anything? Several people complained that SDWTs required more responsibility, so they wanted more status and pay. Still others were worried that they lacked the skills to operate in SDWTs. Some BP Norge supervisors were slow to embrace SDWTs because they didn't want to give away their cherished power.[4]

BP Norge isn't the only company where employees block organizational change. In various surveys, over 40 percent of executives identify employee resistance as the most important barrier to corporate restructuring or improved performance.[5] This resistance takes many forms, including passive noncompliance, complaints, absenteeism, turnover, and collective action (e.g., strikes, walkouts). In extreme cases of resistance, such as those at Ford, Xerox, and EDS, the chief change agent eventually leaves or is pushed out.[6]

Some organizational behavior experts suggest that employee resistance is a symptom, not a problem, in the change process. In other words, change agents need to investigate and remove the causes of resistance, which are usually the underlying restraining forces.[7] For example, rather than directly dealing with incidences of passive noncompliance, leaders need to understand why employees are not changing their behavior in the desired ways. In some situations, employees may be worried about the *consequences* of change, such as how the new conditions will take away their power and status. In other situations, employees show resistance because of concerns about the *process* of change itself, such as the effort required to break old habits and learn new skills. The main reasons why people resist change are shown in Exhibit 17.2 and are described below. They include direct costs, saving face, fear of the unknown, breaking routines, incongruent systems, and incongruent team dynamics.[8]

- ◼ *Direct costs*—People tend to block actions that result in higher direct costs or lower benefits than the existing situation. For instance, Nissan suppliers actively lobbied the public and government to prevent Carlos Ghosn from implementing the Nissan Revival Plan because it threatened their highly profitable contracts with the automaker and, in some cases, put their own companies in jeopardy.

EXHIBIT 17.2

Forces resisting
organizational
change

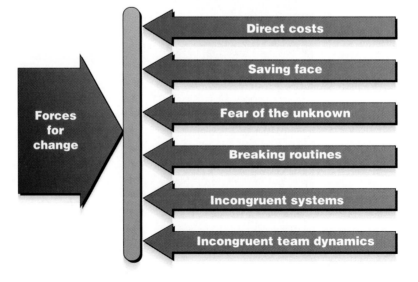

Resistance to change

▨ *Saving face*—Some people resist change as a political strategy to "prove" that the decision is wrong or that the person encouraging change is incompetent. For example, senior executives in a manufacturing firm bought a computer other than the system recommended by the information systems department. Soon after the system was in place, several information systems employees let minor implementation problems escalate to demonstrate that senior management had made a poor decision.

▨ *Fear of the unknown*—People resist change because they are worried that they cannot adopt the new behaviors. This fear of the unknown increases the *risk* of personal loss. For example, one company owner wanted sales staff to telephone rather than personally visit prospective customers. With no experience in telephone sales, they complained about the changes. Some even avoided the training program that taught them how to make telephone sales. "The salespeople were afraid of failing," explained the owner. "Each of them was very successful in the field, but they had never been exposed to a formalized telephone lead development program."[9]

▨ *Breaking routines*—Chapter 1 described how organizations need to unlearn, not just learn.[10] This means that employees need to abandon the behavioral routines that are no longer appropriate. Unfortunately, people are creatures of habit. They like to stay within their comfort zones by continuing routine role patterns that make life predictable.[11] Consequently, many people resist organizational changes that force them out of their comfort zones and require investing time and energy learning new role patterns.

▨ *Incongruent systems*—Rewards, selection, training, and other control systems ensure that employees maintain desired role patterns. Yet the organizational systems that maintain stability also discourage employees from adopting new ways.[12] The implication, of course, is that organizational systems must be altered to fit the desired change. Unfortunately, control systems can be difficult to change, particularly when they have supported role patterns that worked well in the past.[13]

▨ *Incongruent team dynamics*—Teams develop and enforce conformity to a set of norms that guide behavior (see Chapter 9). However, conformity to existing team norms may discourage employees from accepting organizational change. Team norms that conflict with the desired changes need to be altered.

Unfreezing, Changing, and Refreezing

According to Lewin's force field analysis model, effective change occurs by unfreezing the current situation, moving to a desired condition, and then refreezing the system so that it remains in this desired state. Unfreezing occurs when the driving forces are stronger than the restraining forces. This includes making the driving forces stronger, weakening or removing the restraining forces, or a combination of both.

With respect to the first option, driving forces must certainly increase enough to motivate change. Change rarely occurs by increasing driving forces alone, however, because the restraining forces often adjust to counterbalance the driving forces. It is rather like the coils of a mattress. The harder corporate leaders push for change, the stronger the restraining forces push back. This antagonism threatens the change effort by producing tension and conflict within the organization.

The preferred option is to both increase the driving forces and reduce or remove the restraining forces. Increasing the driving forces creates an urgency for change, whereas reducing the restraining forces minimizes resistance to change. "The only way to have people change is because they choose to," explains Carly Fiorina, chief executive of Hewlett-Packard. "You cannot force change onto people—not lasting change, not real change."[14]

Creating an Urgency for Change

Management guru Peter Drucker once wrote: "Every organization has to prepare for the abandonment of everything it does."[15] Consistent with Drucker's warning, we described in Chapter 1 how most organizations today operate in more dynamic, fast-paced environments than they did a few decades ago. These environmental pressures represent the driving forces that push employees out of their comfort zones. They energize people to face the risks that change creates.

In many organizations, however, external driving forces are hardly felt by anyone below the top executives' level. As we read in the opening story to this chapter, Nissan employees had no sense of urgency, no sense that the Japanese automaker would actually go bankrupt in a very short time. The problem is that corporate leaders tend to buffer employees from the external environment, yet they are surprised when change does not occur. Worse, they rely on contrived threats rather than the external driving forces to support the change effort. Thus, the change process must begin by informing employees about competitors, changing consumer trends, impending government regulations, and other driving forces.[16]

Customer-Driven Change   Shell Europe has a well-known brand name, excellent assets, and highly qualified staff, but a few years ago these three ingredients weren't achieving Shell's financial goals or fulfilling customers' needs. To make matters worse, many Shell executives believed that Shell Europe's performance was quite satisfactory. So, to create an urgency for change, the European executives were loaded onto buses and taken out to talk with customers and employees who work with customers every day. "We called these 'bus rides.' The idea was to encourage people to think back from the customer's perspective rather than from the head office," explains Pat O'Driscoll, Shell Europe's vice president of retailing. "The bus rides were difficult for a lot of people who, in their work history, had hardly ever had to talk to a customer and find out what was good and not so good about Shell from the customer's standpoint."[17]

Shell Europe is one of many organizations that have created an urgency to change through direct contact with customers. Dissatisfied customers represent a compelling driving force for change because of the adverse consequences for the organization's survival and success. Customers also provide a human element that further energizes employees to change current behavior patterns.[18]

Reducing the Restraining Forces

Effective change involves more than making employees aware of the driving forces. It also involves reducing or removing the restraining forces. Exhibit 17.3 identifies six ways to overcome employee resistance. Communication, training, employee involvement, and stress management try to reduce the re-

EXHIBIT 17.3	Methods for dealing with resistance to change		
Strategy	**Example**	**When used**	**Problems**
Communication	Customer complaint letters are shown to employees.	When employees don't feel an urgency for change or don't know how the change will affect them.	Time-consuming and potentially costly.
Training	Employees learn how to work in teams as the company adopts a team-based structure.	When employees need to break old routines and adopt new role patterns.	Time-consuming and potentially costly.
Employee involvement	Company forms a task force to recommend new customer service practices.	When the change effort needs more employee commitment, some employees need to save face, and/or employee ideas would improve decisions about the change strategy.	Very time-consuming. May also lead to conflict and poor decisions if employees' interests are incompatible with organizational needs.
Stress management	Employees attend sessions to discuss their worries about the change.	When communication, training, and involvement do not sufficiently ease employee worries.	Time-consuming and potentially expensive. Some methods may not reduce stress for all employees.
Negotiation	Employees agree to replace strict job categories with multiskilling in return for increased job security.	When employees will clearly lose something of value from the change and would not otherwise support the new conditions. Also necessary when the company must change quickly.	May be expensive, particularly if other employees want to negotiate their support. Also tends to produce compliance, but not commitment to the change.
Coercion	Company president tells managers to "get on board" the change or leave.	When other strategies are ineffective and the company needs to change quickly.	Can lead to more subtle forms of resistance, as well as long-term antagonism with the change agent.

Sources: Adapted from J. P. Kotter and L. A. Schlesinger, "Choosing Strategies for Change," *Harvard Business Review* 57 (1979), pp. 106–14; P. R. Lawrence, "How to Deal with Resistance to Change," *Harvard Business Review,* May–June 1954, pp. 49–57.

straining forces and, if feasible, should be attempted first.[19] However, negotiation and coercion are necessary for people who will clearly lose something from the change and when the speed of change is critical.

Communication   Communication is the highest priority and first strategy required for any organizational change. It reduces the restraining forces by keeping employees informed about what to expect from the change effort. Although time-consuming and costly, communication can potentially reduce fear of the unknown and develop team norms that are more consistent with the change effort. For instance, a major survey reported that high-performing organizations had strong downward communication practices in explaining and promoting major changes.

Communication improves the change process in at least two ways. First, it is the conduit through which employees typically learn about the driving forces for change. Whether through town hall meetings with senior management or by directly meeting with disgruntled customers, employees become energized to change. Second, communication clarifies an otherwise uncertain future. The more corporate leaders communicate their images of the future, the more easily employees can visualize their own role in that future.[20]

Scotiabank relied on a specific communication strategy to move employees toward a more customer-focused financial institution.[21] Employees at the Canadian financial institution participated in learning map sessions, which present a visual representation of the company's desired future. Scotiabank's corporate newsletter provided further details from the learning maps and the need for a more customer-focused company. Finally, the bank opened a toll-free telephone line so employees could receive more information on demand, as well as provide feedback about their experiences. As a result of this communication process, every Scotiabank branch in Canada implemented the bank's new sales delivery model on or ahead of schedule with strong employee buy-in.

Training   Training is an important process in most change initiatives because employees need to learn new knowledge and skills. When a company introduces a new sales database, for instance, representatives need to learn how to adapt their previous behavior patterns to benefit from the new system. Action learning, which we described in Chapter 3, is a potentially powerful form of training for organizational change because it develops management skills while discovering ways to improve the organization.[22] Coaching is a variation of training that provides more personalized feedback and direction during the learning process. Global Connections 17.1 describes how an executive at Unilever's Elida Fabergé factory in Seacroft, United Kingdom, brought about significant change by hiring team coaches to train employees. Coaching and other forms of training are time-consuming, but they help employees break routines by learning new role patterns.

Employee Involvement   The opening vignette to this chapter described how Carlos Ghosn minimized resistance to change by forming cross-functional teams to identify and recommend changes at Nissan Motor Company. Ghosn had previously implemented similar task forces to turn around failing businesses at Michelin and Renault. As a form of employee involvement, these cross-functional teams offer better solutions to problems while they minimize resistance to change by creating a psychological ownership of the decision (see Chapter 8). Rather than viewing themselves as agents of someone else's decision, participants feel personally responsible for the success of the change effort. Cross-functional task forces and other forms of employee involvement also minimize resistance to change by reducing problems of saving face and fear of the unknown.[23]

search conferences
Systemwide group sessions, usually lasting a few days, in which participants identify environmental trends and establish strategic solutions for those conditions.

While task forces can be applied in large organizations, they necessarily exclude a large portion of the workforce. **Search conferences** (or a variation called *future search conferences*), on the other hand, are a way to involve a large number of employees and other stakeholders in the change process. Search conferences are large group sessions, usually lasting a few days, in which participants identify the trends or issues and establish strategic solutions for those conditions.[24] Search conferences "put the entire system in the room," meaning that they try to involve as many employees and other stakeholders as possible associated with the organizational system.

In the corporate world, Microsoft, the U.S. Forest Service, and Peco Energy

Coaching for Change at Unilever's Elida Fabergé Factory in Seacroft

Gary Calveley announced a bold vision soon after he arrived as works director at Unilever's Elida Fabergé facility in Seacroft, United Kingdom. Calveley (who has since been promoted to logistics director at Unilever) wanted the personal care products plant to apply European quality practices, win the Best Factory award, and become the safest Unilever site in Europe. What's surprising isn't that Calveley set such audacious goals; the surprise is that the plant actually achieved them in three years!

One of the key strategies in Elida Fabergé's success was the introduction of team coaches to guide the change process. Calveley recruited Gene Toner as an independent change agent. Toner then recruited 10 people with coaching skills from sports, police, teaching, and psychology. Two were appointed from inside.

The coaching process began with "lots of tension and questioning" as employees openly wondered why they needed coaches when experts already worked on the production line. To address these doubts, Calveley worked with a theater company to produce a play portraying current and past work in the factory and how it could be improved using European quality management practices. After watching the play, coaches guided employees through the process of finding ways to turn this vision of a quality-focused factory into a reality.

The theatrical production helped employees realize that the coaches were there to guide employees toward their goals, just like sports coaches. Another contributing factor to the coaches' role was the variable pay system Calveley negotiated with the union. The new reward system tied pay increases to measurable goals in each employee's personal development plan (PDP). The coaches worked with employees

Change consultant Gene Toner (left) and plant manager Gary Calveley (right) introduced coaching to make Unilever's Elida Fabergé factory the best in Europe.

to develop these PDPs and provided feedback so they could reach them. This made the coaches a valuable ally to both employees and management in the change process.

"Once the targets had been set and people were committed to them, they started coming to the coaches," recalls one coach. "They came in early, stayed late, or came over during stoppages—it was a bit of a turnaround from being seen as a nuisance factor before." Only three employees out of the workforce of 600 didn't get a pay increase in the first year. And by the third year, the entire plant had achieved Calveley's audacious goals.

Source: Adapted from P. Baker, "Change Catalysts," *Works Management* 54 (July 2001), pp. 18–21.

---

have used search conferences to assist the change process.[25] Search conferences have been more widely used as a form of community involvement. A representation of people from upstate New York who work in the food industry participated in a search conference to consider the future of food security and related issues in the community. Citizens in Scottsdale, Arizona, were involved in a search conference to examine how to make affordable housing a reality. The state of Tasmania, Australia, held an unprecedented search conference, called Tasmania Together, involving 14,000 individuals and organizations in 60 formal community discussions. Every word uttered and submitted was entered into a database, then sorted into common topics.[26]

Search conferences potentially minimize resistance to change and assist the quality of the change process, but they also have limitations.[27] One problem is that involving so many people invariably limits the opportunity to contribute and increases the risk that a few people will dominate the process. Another concern is that search conferences generate high expectations about an ideal

To develop a meaningful strategy, the Toronto District School Board (TDSB) hosted a search conference that included students, staff, families, and community members. "This conference will bring together people who do not always have the opportunity to meet and plan for our students," said Marguerite Jackson, TDSB's director of education. "Together we will focus on collaborative planning for the future of education in our City." During the three-day event, small teams of participants looked at perceived societal, economic, technological, political, and environmental trends. These trends were then organized into themes plastered on colored paper across an entire wall. According to the organizers, the search conference enabled a large number of diverse people to discover their common ground and to work on creating the future they envision together.[28] What conditions would make search conferences most effective for organizational change?

future state that is difficult to satisfy in practice. Furthermore, some executives forget that search conferences and other forms of employee involvement require follow-up action. If employees do not see meaningful decisions and actions resulting from these meetings, they begin to question the credibility of the process and are more cynical of similar change strategies in the future.

Stress Management   Organizational change is a stressful experience for many people because it threatens self-esteem and creates uncertainty about the future. Communication, training, and employee involvement can reduce some of these stressors. However, research indicates that companies also need to introduce stress management practices to help employees cope with the changes.[29] For instance, stress management minimizes resistance by removing some of the direct costs and fear of the unknown of the change process. Stress also saps energy, so minimizing stress potentially increases employee motivation to support the change process.

Wachovia Corporation was aware of the need for stress management when it merged with First Union Corporation. The Charlotte, North Carolina-based financial institution had a 1-800 number that employees and other stakeholders could call for updates on the merger process. It also dispatched 400 middle and upper-level managers called "ambassadors" to keep everyone informed. Wachovia offered special sessions to help employees deal with change and stress. Shortly after the merger was announced, the company sent out a memo reminding people about the company's employee assistance counseling service.[30]

Negotiation   As long as people resist change, organizational change strategies will require some influence tactics. Recall from Chapter 12 that influence refers to any *behavior* that attempts to alter someone's attitudes or behavior.

Negotiation is a form of exchange, in which the promise of benefits or resources is exchanged for the target person's compliance with influencer's request. This strategy potentially activates those who would otherwise lose from the change. However, it merely gains compliance rather than commitment to the change effort, so it might not be effective in the long term.

Coercion   If all else fails, leaders rely on coercion to change organizations. Coercion, which refers to the assertive influence tactic described in Chapter 12, can include persistently reminding people of their obligations, frequently monitoring behavior to ensure compliance, confronting people who do not change, and using threats of sanctions to force compliance. Firing people who will not support the change is an extreme step, but it is not uncommon. According to some reports, nearly two-thirds of large company turnarounds include the replacement of some or all senior management.[31]

Replacing staff is a radical form of organizational "unlearning" (see Chapter 1), because replacing executives removes knowledge of the organization's past routines. This potentially opens up opportunities for new practices to take hold.[32] At the same time, coercion is a risky strategy because survivors (employees who are not fired) may have less trust in corporate leaders and engage in more political tactics to protect their own job security. Forcing people to leave isn't always necessary, even during times of radical change. One of the notable features of the turnaround at Nissan Motor Company, for example, was that few executives were replaced. More generally, various forms of coercion may change behavior through compliance, but it won't develop commitment to the change effort (see Chapter 12).

Refreezing the Desired Conditions

Unfreezing and changing behavior patterns won't result in lasting change. People are creatures of habit, so they easily slip back into past patterns. Therefore, leaders need to refreeze the new behaviors by realigning organizational systems and team dynamics with the desired changes.[33] This stabilization does not occur automatically; rather, organizational leaders must continuously stabilize the desired behaviors.

If the change process is supposed to encourage efficiency, then rewards should be realigned to motivate and reinforce efficient behavior.[34] At Nissan Motor Company, described at the beginning of this chapter, Carlos Ghosn replaced seniority-based pay with performance-based reward systems to refreeze employee behaviors consistent with this performance orientation. Feedback systems help employees learn how well they are moving toward the desired objectives and provide a permanent architecture to support the new behavior patterns in the long term. "I'm a firm believer that you change what you measure," says Carol Lavin Bernick, president of the Alberto-Culver Company North America.[35]

Strategic Visions, Change Agents, and Diffusing Change

Kurt Lewin's force field analysis model provides a rich understanding of the dynamics of organizational change. But it overlooks three other ingredients in effective change processes: strategic visions, change agents, and diffusing change.

Strategic Visions

Every successful change requires a clear, well-articulated vision of the desired future state. This vision provides a sense of direction and establishes the critical success factors against which the real changes are evaluated. It also minimizes employee fear of the unknown and provides a better understanding about what behaviors employees must learn for the future state.[36] Although some executives say that strategic visions are too "fluffy," most executives in large organizations believe a clear vision of the proposed change is the most important feature of successful change initiatives.[37]

Change Agents

Every organizational change, whether large or small, requires one or more change agents. A **change agent** is anyone who possesses enough knowledge and power to guide and facilitate the change effort. Change agents come in different forms, and more than one person is often required to serve these different roles. Transformational leaders are the primary agents of change because they form a vision of the desired future state, communicate that vision in ways that are meaningful to others, behave in ways that are consistent with the vision, and build commitment to the vision (see Chapter 14).[38] Transformational leaders are the architects who shape the overall direction for the change effort and motivate employees to achieve that objective.

Organizational change also requires transactional leaders who implement the change by aligning the behavior of individual employees on a day-to-day basis with the organization's new goals.[39] If a company wants to provide better customer service, then supervisors and other transactional leaders need to arrange rewards, resources, feedback, and other conditions that support better customer service behaviors in employees. Consultants from either inside or outside the organization represent a third change agent role. Consultants typically bring unique expertise to the change process through a toolkit of change processes, some of which we introduce later in this chapter. Finally, just as employees are encouraged to become leaders anytime and anywhere (see Chapter 14), they also assist the change process as role models for others to follow in the change process. Indeed, as companies rely increasingly on self-directed work teams, most employees are change agents from time to time.

Richard Manning (shown in photo) had his work cut out for him when Hanson plc, the British building materials giant, wanted to integrate seven recently acquired companies into a single corporate entity, creating the largest brick maker in North America. As head of North American operations in Charlotte, North Carolina, Manning began his task as a change agent by talking to every employee. "I was determined to saturate these people with information about what we were doing. And not just what we were doing but why we were doing it, and how it would benefit them and the customer and the company," he says. Manning also advised employees to be ready for more change as he shakes up the industry. "The brick industry hasn't been used to change," Manning notes. "We're changing the concept of relationships and products within this industry."[40] Of what value is a corporate vision when changing Hanson's North American operations?

Diffusion of Change

Change agents often test the transformation process with a pilot project, and then diffuse what has been learned from this experience to other parts of the organization. Unlike centralized, systemwide changes, pilot projects are more flexible and less risky.[41] The pilot project approach also makes it easier to select organizational groups that are most ready for change, which increases the pilot project's success.

But how do we ensure that the change process started in the pilot project is adopted by other segments of the organization? The MARS model introduced in Chapter 2 offers a useful template to organize the answer to this question. First, employees are more likely to adopt the practices of a pilot project when they are motivated to do so.[42] This occurs when they see that the pilot project is successful and people in the pilot project receive recognition and rewards for changing their previous work practices. As a form of transfer of training, diffusion also requires supervisor support and reinforcement of the desired behaviors. More generally, change agents need to minimize the sources of resistance to change that we discussed earlier in this chapter.

Second, employees must have the ability—the required skills and knowledge—to adopt the practices introduced in the pilot project. According to innovation diffusion studies, people adopt ideas more readily when they have an opportunity to interact and learn from others who have already applied the new practices.[43] Thus, pilot projects get diffused when employees in the original pilot are dispersed to other work units as role models and knowledge sources.

Third, pilot projects get diffused when employees have clear role perceptions; that is, they understand how the practices in a pilot project apply to them even though in a completely different functional area. For instance, accounting department employees won't easily recognize how they can adopt quality improvement practices developed by employees in the production department. The challenge here is for change agents to provide guidance that is neither too specific, because it might not seem relevant to other areas of the organization, nor too abstract, because this makes the instructions too vague. Finally, employees require supportive situational factors, including the resources and time necessary to adopt the practices demonstrated in the pilot project.

Three Approaches to Organizational Change

Thus far, we have looked at the dynamics of change that occur every day in organizations. However, organizational change agents and consultants also apply various approaches to various approaches to organizational change. This section introduces three of the leading approaches to organizational change: action research, appreciative inquiry, and parallel learning structures.

Action Research Approach

action research
A data-based, problem-oriented process that diagnoses the need for change, introduces the intervention, and then evaluates and stabilizes the desired changes.

Along with introducing the force field model, Kurt Lewin recommended an action research approach to the change process. **Action research** takes the view that meaningful change is a combination of action orientation (changing attitudes and behavior) and research orientation (testing theory).[44] On the one hand, the change process needs to be action-oriented because the ultimate goal is to bring about change. An action orientation involves diagnosing current problems and applying interventions that resolve those problems. On the other hand, the change process is a research study because change agents apply a conceptual framework (such as team dynamics or organizational

| EXHIBIT 17.4 | The action research process |

culture) to a real situation. As with any good research, the change process involves collecting data to diagnose problems more effectively and to systematically evaluate how well the theory works in practice. In other words, action research embraces the notion of organizational learning and knowledge management (see Chapter 1).[45]

Within this dual framework of action and research, the action research approach adopts an open systems view. It recognizes that organizations have many interdependent parts, so change agents need to anticipate both the intended and unintended consequences of their interventions. Action research is also a highly participative process because open systems change requires both the knowledge and commitment of members within that system. Indeed, employees are essentially co-researchers as well as participants in the intervention. Overall, action research is a data-based, problem-oriented process that diagnoses the need for change, introduces the intervention, and then evaluates and stabilizes the desired changes (see Exhibit 17.4).[46]

- *Establish client–consultant relationship*—Action research usually assumes that the change agent originates outside the system (such as a consultant), so the process begins by forming the client–consultant relationship. Consultants need to determine the client's readiness for change, including whether people are motivated to participate in the process, are open to meaningful change, and possess the abilities to complete the process. Many change management consultants prefer to adopt the role of process consultant rather than that of technical expert. **Process consultation** is a method of helping people within the system solve their own problems by making them aware of organizational processes, the consequences of those processes, and the means by which they can be changed.[47]

- *Diagnose the need for change*—Action research is a problem-oriented activity that carefully diagnoses the problem through systematic analysis of the situation. Organizational diagnosis identifies the appropriate direction for the change effort by gathering and analyzing data about an ongoing system, such as through interviews and surveys of employees and other stakeholders.[48] Organizational diagnosis also includes employee involvement in agreeing on the appropriate change method, the schedule for these actions, and the expected standards of successful change.

- *Introduce intervention*—This stage in the action research model applies one or more actions to correct the problem. It may include any of the prescriptions mentioned in this textbook, such as building more effective

process consultation

Involves helping the organization solve its own problems by making it aware of organizational processes, the consequences of those processes, and the means by which they can be changed.

teams, managing conflict, building a better organizational structure, or changing the corporate culture. An important issue is how quickly the changes should occur.[49] Some experts recommend *incremental change* in which the organization fine-tunes the system and takes small steps toward a desired state. Others claim that *quantum change* is often required, in which the system is overhauled decisively and quickly. Quantum change, as at Nissan Motor Company (see the opening vignette to this chapter), is usually traumatic to employees and offers little opportunity for correction. But incremental change is also risky when the organization is seriously misaligned with its environment, thereby threatening its survival.

■ *Evaluate and stabilize change*—Action research recommends evaluating the effectiveness of the intervention against the standards established in the diagnostic stage. Unfortunately, even when these standards are clearly stated, the effectiveness of an intervention might not be apparent for several years or might be difficult to separate from other factors. If the activity has the desired effect, then the change agent and participants need to stabilize the new conditions. This refers to the refreezing process that we described earlier. Rewards, information systems, team norms, and other conditions are redesigned so that they support the new values and behaviors.

The action research approach has dominated organizational change thinking ever since it was introduced in the 1940s. However, some experts complain that the problem-oriented nature of action research—in which something is wrong that must be fixed—focuses on the negative dynamics of the group or system rather than its positive opportunities and potential. This concern with action research has led to the development of a more positive approach to organizational change, called appreciative inquiry.

Appreciative Inquiry Approach

appreciative inquiry

An organizational change process that directs attention away from the group's own problems and focuses participants on the group's potential and positive elements.

Appreciative inquiry tries to break out of the problem-solving mentality by reframing relationships around the positive and the possible.[50] It takes the view that organizations are creative entities in which people are capable of building synergy beyond their individual capabilities. To avoid dwelling on the group's own shortcomings, the process usually directs its inquiry toward successful events and successful organizations. This external focus becomes a form of behavioral modeling, but it also increases open dialogue by redirecting the group's attention away from its own problems. Appreciative inquiry is especially useful when participants are aware of their "problems" or already suffer from enough negativity in their relationships. The positive orientation of appreciative inquiry enables groups to overcome these negative tensions and build a more hopeful perspective of their future by focusing on what is possible.

Exhibit 17.5 outlines the "Four-D" model of appreciative inquiry, which was developed in Harare, Zimbabwe, by a group working with the U.S. Agency for International Development and Save the Children Fund.[51] The process begins with *discovery*—identifying the positive elements of the observed events or organization. This might involve documenting positive customer experiences elsewhere in the organization. Or it might include interviewing members of another organization to discover its fundamental strengths. As participants discuss their findings, they shift into the *dreaming* stage by envisioning what might be possible in an ideal organization. By directing their attention to a

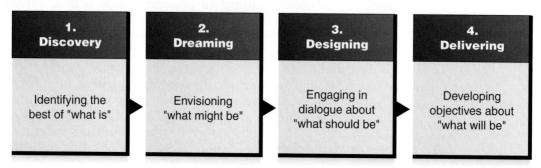

EXHIBIT 17.5   The appreciative inquiry process

1. Discovery	2. Dreaming	3. Designing	4. Delivering
Identifying the best of "what is"	Envisioning "what might be"	Engaging in dialogue about "what should be"	Developing objectives about "what will be"

Sources: Based on J. M. Watkins and B. J. Mohr, *Appreciative Inquiry: Change at the Speed of Imagination* (San Francisco: Jossey-Bass, 2001), pp. 25, 42–45; D. Whitney and C. Schau, "Appreciative Inquiry: An Innovative Process for Organization Change," *Employment Relations Today* 25 (Spring 1998), pp. 11–21; F. J. Barrett and D. L. Cooperrider, "Generative Metaphor Intervention: A New Approach for Working with Systems Divided by Conflict and Caught in Defensive Perception," *Journal of Applied Behavioral Science* 26 (1990), p. 229.

theoretically ideal organization or situation, participants feel safer revealing their hopes and aspirations than if they were discussing their own organization or predicament.

As participants make their private thoughts public to the group, the process shifts into the third stage, called *designing*. Designing involves the process of dialogue (see Chapter 10), in which participants listen with selfless receptivity to each other's models and assumptions and eventually form a collective model for thinking within the team.[52] In effect, they create a common image of what should be. As this model takes shape, group members shift the focus back to their own situation. In the final stage of appreciative inquiry, called *delivering*, participants establish specific objectives and direction for their own organization based on their model of what will be.

Appreciative Inquiry in Practice   Appreciative inquiry is a relatively new approach to organization change, but it has already generated several success stories. For example, AVON Mexico applied appreciative inquiry to develop employment opportunities for women in the top ranks. A team of employees and consultants interviewed people for their stories illustrating best practices in gender equality at AVON Mexico. These stories were presented at two-day sessions, and participants built on these best practices to discover how AVON could extend these experiences. Over the next few years, the company won the Catalyst award for gender equality, its profit increased dramatically (attributed partly to the appreciative inquiry process), and women found their way into more senior positions at AVON Mexico.[53] Connections 17.2 describes how two other organizations successfully applied appreciative inquiry principles.

Appreciative inquiry has gathered much interest among organizational change scholars and practitioners. Indeed, one problem with this approach is that its popularity has led some consultants to label anything with a positive orientation as a form of appreciative inquiry. Another concern is that research has not yet examined the contingencies of this approach.[54] Specifically, we don't yet know the conditions in which appreciate inquiry is the best approach to organizational change, and under what conditions it is less effective. Overall, appreciative inquiry has much to offer the organizational change process, but we are just beginning to understand its potential and limitations.

Changing for the Better by Appreciating the Positive

Green Mountain Coffee Roasters tripled its sales force and doubled its plant size in the late 1990s, which required the Waterbury, Vermont, company to focus more on improving its efficiency and best practices. But CEO Bob Stiller didn't want to follow the usual route of searching out weaknesses in work processes. "You have 99% customer satisfaction and the first thing everybody says is let's look at that 1%," Stiller observes.

Instead, Stiller took a positive approach through appreciative inquiry. He encouraged employees to identify what they do best and to build on those strengths. Another Green Mountain Coffee Roasters executive involved in the process explains: "We identified the one best path in each process, and asked, 'Why don't we do this with everything?'" This positive process resulted in lower costs, better cash flow, and better order entry and delivery systems.

The Hunter Douglas Windows Fashion Division (WFD) in Broomfield, Colorado, also experienced the benefits of appreciative inquiry. Employee turnover was rising while productivity and motivation were falling due to WFD's rapid expansion, reorganization to accommodate that growth, and movement of senior leaders to other areas of Hunter Douglas. When WFD's new leaders brought in consultants to reinstill a sense of community among employees and build leadership within the organization, appreciative inquiry was the recommended solution.

A WFD advisory team spent a week learning about the Four-D process, then communicated this appreciative inquiry process to employees through a series of town hall meetings. The discovery phase consisted of more than 500 interviews with employees, customers, suppliers, and community members. These results were reviewed at an "Appreciative Summit," where WFD employees worked through the dreaming, designing, and delivering stages.

A second wave of interviews became background data for a subsequent search conference-type of strategic planning summit. WFD executives say that appreciative inquiry improved productivity and cross-departmental collaboration and created a "can-do" attitude toward the company's quality management initiative. "Historically, American businesses look at problem-solving with a mind set of 'what's wrong,'" says a Hunter Douglas executive. "If you look at everything else that's right, 17 production lines are working well."

Sources: T. Kinni, "Exploit What You Do Best," *Harvard Management Update,* August 2003, pp. 3–4; D. Whitney and A. Trosten-Bloom, *The Power of Appreciative Inquiry: A Practical Guide to Positive Change* (San Francisco: Berrett-Koehler, 2003); A. Trosten-Bloom, "Case Study: Hunter Douglas Window Fashions Division," in *Appreciative Inquiry: Change at the Speed of Imagination,* ed. J. M. Watkins and B. J. Mohr (San Francisco: Jossey-Bass, 2001), pp. 176–80; M. LeJeune, "Companies Turning to 'Appreciative Inquiry' to Ask Staff What's Right," *Boulder County Business Report* 18 (February 1999), p. 7.

Appreciative inquiry helped the Hunter Douglas Windows Fashion Division in Colorado reduce employee turnover and improve work effectiveness.

Parallel Learning Structure Approach

Parallel learning structures are highly participative arrangements, composed of people from most levels of the organization who follow the action research model to produce meaningful organizational change. They are social structures developed alongside the formal hierarchy with the purpose of increasing the organization's learning.[55] Ideally, parallel learning structure participants are sufficiently free from the constraints of the larger organization so that they can more effectively solve organizational issues.

Royal Dutch/Shell relied on a parallel learning structure to introduce a more customer-focused organization.[56] Rather than trying to change the entire organization at once, executives held week-long "retail boot camps" with six country teams of frontline people (e.g., gas station managers, truck drivers, marketing professionals). Participants learned about competitive trends in their regions and were taught powerful marketing tools to identify new opportunities. The teams then returned home to study their market and develop proposals for improvement.

Four months later, boot camp teams returned for a second workshop where each proposal was critiqued by Royal Dutch/Shell executives. Each team had 60 days to put its ideas into action, then return for a third workshop to analyze what worked and what didn't. This parallel learning process did much more than introduce new marketing ideas. It created enthusiasm in participants that spread contagiously to their co-workers, including managers above them, when they returned to their home countries.

Cross-Cultural and Ethical Issues in Organization Change

One significant concern with organizational change originating from North America is that it potentially conflicts with cultural values in some other countries.[57] A few OB writers point out that change practices in the United States assume a linear model of change, as shown earlier in the force field analysis, that is punctuated by tension and overt conflict. Indeed, some organizational change practices encourage the open display of conflict. But these assumptions are incompatible with cultures that view change as a natural cyclical process with harmony and equilibrium as the objectives.[58]

For instance, people in many Asian countries try to minimize conflict in order to respect others and save face.[59] These concerns do not mean that Western-style change interventions are necessarily ineffective elsewhere. Rather, it suggests that we need to develop a more contingency-oriented perspective with respect to the cultural values of its participants.

Some organizational change practices also raise ethical concerns.[60] One ethical concern is threats to the privacy rights of individuals. The action research model is built on the idea of collecting information from organizational members, yet this requires employees to provide personal information and emotions that they may not want to divulge. The scientific nature of the data collection exercise may mislead employees into believing that their information is confidential when, in reality, executives can sometimes identify opinions of individual employees.[61]

A second ethical concern is that some change activities potentially increase management's power by inducing compliance and conformity in organizational members. This power shift occurs because change creates uncertainty and reestablishes management's position in directing the organization. Moreover, action research is a systemwide activity that requires employee participation rather than allowing individuals to get involved voluntarily. Indeed, one of the challenges of organizational change consultants is to "bring onside" those who are reluctant to engage in the process.

A third concern is that some organizational change interventions undermine the individual's self-esteem. The unfreezing process requires participants to disconfirm their existing beliefs, sometimes including their own competence at certain tasks or interpersonal relations. Some specific change practices involve direct exposure to personal critique by co-workers as well as public disclosure of one's personal limitations and faults.

A fourth ethical concern is the change management consultant's role in the change process. Ideally, consultants should occupy "marginal" positions with the clients they are serving. This means that they must be sufficiently detached from the organization to maintain objectivity and avoid having the client become too dependent on them.[62] However, some consultants tend to increase rather than decrease clients' dependence for financial gain. Others have difficulty maintaining neutrality because they often come to the situation with their own biases and agendas.

Organization change is a complex process with a variety of approaches and issues. Many corporate leaders have promised more change than they were able to deliver because they underestimated the time and challenges involved with this process. Indeed, most organizations operate in hyperfast environments that demand continuous and rapid adaptation. Successful organizations have mastered the complex dynamics of moving people through the continuous process of change.

Personal Change for the Road Ahead

In this last section of this textbook, we thought it would be a good idea to shift attention from organizational change to a few practical ideas for personal change for the road ahead. Whether you are just starting your career or are already well along the trail, the following thoughts should help you improve both your prospects and long-term career satisfaction. These points do not cover everything you need to remember about developing your career. Instead, they highlight some of the key strategies that will help you along the road ahead.

Understand Your Needs and Values

Developing yourself in organizational settings begins by understanding your personal needs and values.[63] "If you're in the wrong career, it doesn't matter if the economy is good or bad, you're still unhappy," advises Atlanta career consultant Deborah R. Brown.[64]

How do you know what type of career is most fulfilling for you? To answer this question, you need to complete self-assessments of your vocational interests and recount experiences that you enjoyed. Holland's occupational choice model presented in Chapter 2 helps to align your personality and interests with the work environment. It may also be useful to get feedback from others regarding activities that they notice you like or dislike. This applies the Johari

The recent economic downturn put a damper on job prospects for many business graduates, but Andrew Wang is philosophical. "It's not fun, but at least it forces you to figure out what it is you really want to do," says the graduating MBA student at UCLA's Anderson School of Management. So, rather than jumping into a dot-com start-up, Wang is thinking about joining a company more aligned with his personal interests. "I've had this lifelong interest in cycling, so I'm now looking at the recreational industry for product-management positions," he says. "I've learned [they] don't pay as well, but you're doing something that you like."[65] How can you tell when a particular career path fulfills your personal needs?

Window model described in Chapter 3, whereby you learn more about yourself through information presented by close associates.

Understand Your Competencies

Knowing yourself also involves knowing what you are capable of doing.[66] In Chapter 2, we learned that each of us has a set of aptitudes—natural talents that help us learn specific tasks more quickly and perform them better. Although we might visualize our future as an engineering wizard or president of the United States, we need to take our potential abilities into account. The more careers are aligned with personal competencies, the more we develop a strong sense of self-efficacy—the "can-do" attitude that further empowers our career. Self-assessments, performance results, and constructive feedback from friends can help us to identify our capabilities. Also, keep in mind that employers look beyond technical skills to generic competencies, such as communication, problem solving, and interpersonal relations. Indeed, some recruiters say they pay more attention to these foundations and assume employees will develop job-specific skills at work.

Set Career Goals

Soon after Mary Morse joined Autodesk as a software engineer, the manager above her immediate supervisor asked Morse to draw up a list of short-term and long-term career goals. Then, the manager at the California software firm provided Morse with a list of training courses, both inside and outside the company, that would help her meet those career objectives. The manager also spoke to Morse's immediate supervisor to ensure she would have time to complete those courses.[67]

Mary Morse was lucky. She joined an organization that helps employees identify and achieve their career goals. But we usually can't count on others to guide our career development. We need to set our own goals to realize our potential and ultimately fulfill our needs. Goal setting is a powerful way to motivate and achieve results, and this applies as much to careers as to any other activity. Career goals are benchmarks against which we evaluate our progress and identify strategies to develop our competencies.

Career consultant Barbara Moses emphasizes that career goal setting is a fundamental element in becoming a "career activist." It involves writing your own script rather than waiting for someone to write it for you, being vigilant by identifying and preparing for opportunities, and becoming an independent agent by separating your self-identity from your job title, your organization, or what other people think you should be.[68]

Maintain Networks

A survey by Drake Beam Morin revealed that 64 percent of the 7,435 people in the placement firm's executive career transition programs found new employment through networking. As one successful job hunter advises: "Be prepared, know your story, and network, network, network."[69] Several research studies have confirmed that networking is an increasingly important feature of your career success. In particular, people with large, nonredundant networks tend to be more successful job seekers and receive greater organizational rewards. One important piece of advice is to network in areas beyond your current sphere of work. The reason is that careers change much more than in the past, so you need to establish connections to other fields where you may someday find yourself.[70]

Get a Mentor

Thus far, our discussion has emphasized self-leadership in career development (see Chapter 6). We need to set our own goals, motivate ourselves for career advancement, and visualize where we want to go. But personal development in organizational settings also benefits from the help of others. Mentoring is the process of learning the ropes of organizational life from a senior person within the company (see Chapter 12). Mentors give protégés more visible and meaningful work opportunities, and they also provide ongoing career guidance. You might think of them as a career coach because they provide ongoing advice and feedback.[71]

Organizational Behavior: The Journey Continues

Nearly 100 years ago, industrialist Andrew Carnegie said: "Take away my people, but leave my factories, and soon grass will grow on the factory floors. Take away my factories, but leave my people, and soon we will have a new and better factory." Carnegie's statement reflects the message woven throughout this textbook that organizations are not buildings, or machinery, or financial assets. Rather, they are the people in them. Organizations are human entities— full of life, sometimes fragile, always exciting.

Chapter Summary

Lewin's force field analysis model states that all systems have driving and restraining forces. Change occurs through the process of unfreezing, changing, and refreezing. Unfreezing produces disequilibrium between the driving and restraining forces. Refreezing realigns the organization's systems and structures with the desired behaviors.

Restraining forces are manifested as employee resistance to change. The main reasons why people resist change are direct costs, saving face, fear of the unknown, breaking routines, incongruent organizational systems, and incongruent team dynamics. Resistance to change may be minimized by keeping employees informed about what to expect from the change effort (communicating); teaching employees valuable skills for the desired future (training); involving them in the change process; helping employees cope with the stress of change; negotiating trade-offs with those who will clearly lose from the change effort; and using coercion (sparingly and as a last resort).

Organizational change also requires driving forces. This means that employees need to have an urgency to change, fostered by their awareness of the environmental conditions that demand change in the organization. The change process also requires refreezing the new behaviors by realigning organizational systems and team dynamics with the desired changes.

Every successful change requires a clear, well-articulated vision of the desired future state. Strategic visions are guided by a change agent—anyone who possesses enough knowledge and power to guide and facilitate the change effort. Change agents rely on transformational leadership to develop a vision, communicate that vision, and build commitment to the vision of a desirable future state. The change process also often applies a diffusion process in which change begins as a pilot project and eventually spreads to other areas of the organization.

Organizational change agents and consultants apply various approaches to organizational change. Action research has been the dominant approach over the past half-century. Action research is a highly participative, open systems approach emphasizing that meaningful change is a combination of action orientation (changing attitudes and behavior) and research orientation (testing theory). It is a data-based, problem-oriented process that diagnoses the need for change, introduces the intervention, and then evaluates and stabilizes the desired changes.

Another approach is appreciative inquiry, which focuses participants on the positive and possible. It tries to break out of the problem-solving mentality that dominates organizational change through the action research model. The four stages of appreciative inquiry are discovery, dreaming, designing, and delivering. A third approach, called parallel learning structures, relies on social structures developed alongside the formal hierarchy with the purpose of increasing the organization's learning. They are highly participative arrangements, composed of people from most levels of the organization who follow the action research model to produce meaningful organizational change.

One significant concern with organizational changes originating from the United States is that they potentially conflict with cultural values in some other countries. Moreover, organizational change practices can raise one or more ethical concerns, including increasing management's power over employees, threatening individual privacy rights, undermining individual self-esteem, and making clients dependent on the change consultant.

Five strategies that assist personal development in organizational settings are understanding your needs and values, understanding your competencies, setting career goals, maintaining networks, and getting a mentor.

Key Terms

action research, p. 515

appreciative inquiry, p. 517

change agent, p. 514

force field analysis, p. 504

parallel learning structure, p. 520

process consultation, p. 516

refreezing, p. 505

search conferences, p. 510

unfreezing, p. 505

Discussion Questions

1. Chances are that the school you are attending is currently undergoing some sort of change to adapt more closely to its environment. Discuss the external forces that are driving these changes. What internal drivers for change also exist?

2. Use Lewin's force field analysis to describe the dynamics of organizational change at Nissan Motor Company (opening vignette to this chapter).

3. Employee resistance is a *symptom*, not a *problem*, in the change process. What are some of the real problems that may underlie employee resistance?

4. Senior management of a large multinational corporation is planning to restructure the organization. Currently, the organization is decentralized around geographical areas so that the executive responsible for each area has considerable autonomy over manufacturing and sales. The new structure will transfer power to the executives responsible for different product groups; the executives responsible for each geographic area will no longer be responsible for manufacturing in their area but will retain control over sales activities. Describe two types of

resistance senior management might encounter from this organizational change.

5. Web Circuits, Inc., is a Singapore-based manufacturer of computer circuit boards for high-technology companies. Senior management wants to introduce value-added management practices to reduce production costs and remain competitive. A consultant has recommended that the company start with a pilot project in one department and, when successful, diffuse these practices to other areas of the organization. Discuss the advantages of this recommendation and identify three ways (other than the pilot project's success) to make diffusion of the change effort more successful.

6. Suppose that you are vice-president of branch services at the Bank of East Lansing. You notice that several branches have consistently low customer service ratings even though there are no apparent differences in resources or staff characteristics. Describe an appreciative inquiry process in one of these branches that might help to overcome these problems.

7. This chapter suggests that some organizational change activities face ethical concerns. Yet several consultants actively use these processes because they believe they benefit the organization and do less damage to employees than appears on the surface. For example, some activities try to open up the employee's hidden area (see the Johari Window in Chapter 3) so that there is better mutual understanding with co-workers. Discuss this argument and identify where you think organizational change interventions should limit this process.

8. Career activism is a concept that is gaining interest because it emphasizes managing your own development in organizations. What concepts introduced throughout this book are compatible with the career activist concept? In what ways might a person be a career activist?

THE EXCELLENT EMPLOYEE

By Mary Gander, Winona State University

Emily, who has the reputation of being an excellent worker, is a machine operator in a furniture manufacturing plant that has been growing at a rate of between 15 percent and 20 percent each year for the past decade. New additions have been built onto the plant, new plants opened in the region, workers hired, new product lines developed, lots of expansion, but no significant changes have occurred in overall approach to operations, plant layout, ways of managing workers, or the design processes. Plant operations as well as organizational culture are rooted in traditional Western management practices and logic, based largely on the notion of mass production and economies of scale. Over the past four years, the company has been growing in number and variety of products produced and in market penetration; however, profitability has been flattening and showing signs of decline. Therefore, in developing their strategic plans, management is beginning to focus on production operations (internal focus) rather than mainly focusing on new market strategies, new

products, and new market segments (external focus). They hope to get manufacturing costs down and improve consistency of quality and ability to meet delivery times while decreasing inventory and increasing flexibility.

One of several new programs initiated by management in this effort to improve flexibility and lower costs was to cross-train workers. However, when a representative from Human Resources explained this program to Emily's supervisor, Jim, he reluctantly agreed to cross-train most of his workers, but *not* Emily.

Jim explained to the Human Resources person that Emily works on a machine that is very complex and not easy to effectively operate. She has to "babysit" it much of the time. He has tried many workers on it, tried to train them, but Emily is the only one who can consistently get product through the machine within specification and still meet production schedules. When anyone else tries to operate the machine, which performs a key function in the manufacturing process, it ends up either being a big bottleneck

525

or producing excessive waste, which creates a lot of trouble for Jim.

Jim goes on to explain that Emily knows this sophisticated and complicated machine inside and out after running it for five years. She likes the challenge, she says it makes the day go by faster, too. She is meticulous in her work, a very skilled employee who really cares about the quality of her work. Jim told the HR person that he wished all of his workers were like Emily. In spite of the difficulty of running this machine, Emily can run it so well that product piles up at the next workstation downstream in the production process—no one can keep up with her!

Jim was adamant about keeping Emily on this machine and not cross-training her. The HR person was frustrated. He could see Jim's point but he had to follow executive orders: "Get these people cross-trained."

Around the same period, a university student was doing a field study in the section of the plant where Emily worked. In her interview, Emily told the student that, in spite of the fact that the plant had some problems with employee morale and excessive employee turnover, she really liked working there. She liked the piecerate pay system very much and hoped that she did not have to participate in the recent "Program of the Month," which was having operators learn each other's jobs. She told the student that it would just create more waste if they tried to have other employees run her machine. She told him that other employees had tried to learn how to operate her machine but couldn't do it as well as she could.

Emily seemed to take a special liking for the student and began to open up to him. She told him that her machine really didn't need to be so difficult and touchy to operate; with a couple of rather minor design changes in the machine and better maintenance, virtually anyone could run it. She had tried to explain this to her supervisor a couple of years ago, but he just told her to "do her work and leave operations to the manufacturing engineers." She also said that if workers upstream in the process would spend a little more time and care to keep the raw material in slightly tighter specifications, it would go through her machine much more easily and trouble-free, but they were too focused on going fast and making more piecerate pay. Emily expressed a lack of respect for the managers, who couldn't see this, and even joked about how "managers didn't know anything."

Discussion Questions

1. Identify the sources of resistance to change in this case.

2. Discuss whether this resistance is justified or could be overcome.

3. Recommend ways to minimize resistance to change in this incident or in future incidents.

Source: Copyright © 2002, Mary J. Gander. Adapted from "Case of the Excellent Worker," a paper presented at the 2002 Annual Meeting of the Decision Sciences Institute. This short case is based on actual events but names have been changed to maintain anonymity.

CASE STUDY 17.2

WILL JEFF IMMELT'S NEW PUSH PAY OFF FOR GE?

BusinessWeek Since he ascended to GE's top job two years ago, Jeffrey R. Immelt has tried to turn the $132 billion giant into a truly customer-focused organization. The GE revolution dubbed "At the Customer, For the Customer" is an attempt to provide customers better service—in many cases, going beyond the call of duty. For example, scores of "black belt" GE quality experts have helped client organizations to improve work efficiency, even if it means reduced revenue in the short term for GE as a supplier.

This *Business Week* case study looks at how Jeff Immelt is changing GE and the methods he is using to make those changes. The article describes the new customer-focused strategy that GE employees are applying to improve the company's long-term success. It also details some of the problems this change effort faces inside and outside of GE. Read through this *Business Week* article at www.mhhe.com/mcshane3e and prepare for the discussion questions below.

Discussion Questions

1. What driving forces have motivated GE CEO Jeff Immelt to introduce the "At the Customer, For the Customer" change initiative?

2. What change management practices have been implemented to support the new customer-focused culture and strategy at GE? Do they seem to be successful, in your opinion?

3. What resistance to this change is described in this case? What other sources of resistance might be occurring at GE that are not mentioned in this article?

Source: D. Brady, "Will Jeff Immelt's New Push Pay Off for GE?" *Business Week,* October 13, 2003, pp. 94–97.

TEAM EXERCISE 17.3

STRATEGIC CHANGE INCIDENTS

Purpose This exercise is designed to help you to identify strategies to facilitate organizational change in various situations.

Instructions

■ *Step 1*—The instructor will place students into teams, and each team will be assigned one of the scenarios presented below.

■ *Step 2*—Each team will diagnose its assigned scenario to determine the most appropriate set of change management practices. Where appropriate, these practices should (a) create an urgency to change, (b) minimize resistance to change, and (c) refreeze the situation to support the change initiative. Each of these scenarios is based on real events.

■ *Step 3*—Each team will present and defend its change management strategy. Class discussion regarding the appropriateness and feasibility of each strategy will occur after all teams assigned the same scenario have presented. The instructor will then describe what the organizations actually did in these situations.

Scenario 1: Greener Telco The board of directors at a large telephone company wants its executives to make the organization more environmentally friendly by encouraging employees to reduce waste in the workplace. There are also expectations by government and other stakeholders for the company to take this action and be publicly successful. The goal of this initiative is to significantly reduce the use of paper, refuse, and other waste throughout the company's many widespread offices. Unfortunately, a survey indicates that employees do not value environmental objectives and do not know how to "reduce, reuse, recycle." As the executive responsible for this change, you have been asked to develop a strategy that might bring about meaningful behavioral change toward these environmental goals. What would you do?

Scenario 2: Go Forward Airline A major airline had experienced a decade of turbulence, including two bouts of bankruptcy protection, 10 chief executives, and morale so low that employees had ripped company logos off their uniforms out of embarrassment. Service was terrible and the airplanes rarely arrived or left the terminal on time. This was costing the airline significant amounts of money in passenger layovers. Managers were paralyzed by anxiety and many had been with the firm so long that they didn't know how to set strategic goals that worked. One-fifth of all flights were losing money and the company overall was near financial collapse (just three months to defaulting on payroll obligations). The newly hired CEO and you must get employees to quickly improve operational efficiency and customer service. What actions would you take to bring about these changes in time?

TOLERANCE OF CHANGE SCALE

Purpose This exercise is designed to help you understand how people differ in their tolerance of change.

Instructions Read each of the statements on the next page and circle the response that best fits your personal belief. Then use the scoring key in Appendix B of this book to calculate your results. This self-assessment is completed alone so students rate themselves honestly without concerns of social comparison. However, class discussion will focus on the meaning of the concept measured by this scale and its implications for managing change in organizational settings.

TOLERANCE OF CHANGE SCALE

To what extent does each statement describe you? Indicate your level of agreement by marking the appropriate response on the right.	Strongly Agree	Moderately Agree	Slightly Agree	Neutral	Slightly Disagree	Moderately Disagree	Strongly Disagree
1. An expert who doesn't come up with a definite answer probably doesn't know too much	☐	☐	☐	☐	☐	☐	☐
2. I would like to live in a foreign country for a while	☐	☐	☐	☐	☐	☐	☐
3. There is really no such thing as a problem that can't be solved	☐	☐	☐	☐	☐	☐	☐
4. People who fit their lives into a schedule probably miss most of the joy of living	☐	☐	☐	☐	☐	☐	☐
5. A good job is one where it is always clear what is to be done and how it is to be done	☐	☐	☐	☐	☐	☐	☐
6. It is more fun to tackle a complicated problem than to solve a simple one	☐	☐	☐	☐	☐	☐	☐
7. In the long run, it is possible to get more done by tackling small, simple problems rather than large, complicated ones	☐	☐	☐	☐	☐	☐	☐
8. Often the most interesting and stimulating people are those who don't mind being different and original	☐	☐	☐	☐	☐	☐	☐
9. What we are used to is always preferable to what is unfamiliar	☐	☐	☐	☐	☐	☐	☐
10. People who insist on a yes or no answer just don't know how complicated things really are	☐	☐	☐	☐	☐	☐	☐
11. A person who leads an even, regular life in which few surprises or unexpected happenings arise really has a lot to be grateful for	☐	☐	☐	☐	☐	☐	☐
12. Many of our most important decisions are based on insufficient information	☐	☐	☐	☐	☐	☐	☐
13. I like parties where I know most of the people more than ones where all or most of the people are complete strangers	☐	☐	☐	☐	☐	☐	☐
14. Teachers or supervisors who hand out vague assignments give one a chance to show initiative and originality	☐	☐	☐	☐	☐	☐	☐
15. The sooner everyone acquires similar values and ideals, the better	☐	☐	☐	☐	☐	☐	☐
16. A good teacher is one who makes you wonder about your way of looking at things	☐	☐	☐	☐	☐	☐	☐

Source: Adapted from S. Budner, "Intolerance of Ambiguity as a Personality Variable," *Journal of Personality* 30 (1962), pp. 29–50.

Case 1: Aegis Electronic Group, Inc.

**By Cynthia Larson-Daugherty, National University,
and Carolynn Larson-Garcia, Assesso**

Aegis Electronic Group, Inc., is a small southern California company that was incorporated in 1989. Engaged in selling a highly technical line, Aegis distributes industrial imaging products and videoconferencing applications. The company employs 12 people (6 sales members, 4 operations, 1 general manager, and an active president/owner).

Aegis has experienced long periods of profitable growth; however, by 2001, the technology sector and the economic downturns brought attention to internal processes and events that had been given quick fixes in the past. Liz Carnes, president and owner, and her core management team started seriously evaluating the company's direction and processes.

With the strength of a core sales team in place, Aegis was able to minimize the impact of the technology sector downturn in 2001 and 2002. With a highly technical product line, about a year of training is needed for a salesperson to start producing at a profitable level. As a result, a new sales trainee absorbs production time from each member of the sales team by a buddy system, where the trainee shadows current team members over a period of months.

This methodology had historically worked very well. The combination of a market downturn and changes in the sales team can have a dramatic impact on Aegis.

With economic, market, and internal changes afoot, specifically sales team turnover, management decided to experiment with new business strategies that included revamping traditional management practices of reviewing the business plan and adjusting where needed, as well as implementing organizational development initiatives.

The company had run successfully over several years with a core management team: Liz, the president/owner; Lynn, general manager (GM) and sales team manager; and Samantha, the operations manager. Organizational roles were examined with a focus on Lynn. Lynn had started with the company two years after its incorporation. Over her tenure she has done everything from answer phones to help land large accounts. As the company grew, she continued to learn and perform a variety of functions, primarily managing the staff that was brought on board. Lynn became the "go-to" person over the years because she had served in every role in the organization at one time or another. This was very helpful at times, particularly when the sales team and operations group would butt heads. Of her many roles, Lynn's ability to promote and maintain both productivity and company morale had been key. However, it was time to have her focus on exploring new markets and identify another person as a sales team manager.

During the review of Lynn's role, other items surfaced. As a result, five initiatives were piloted in 2002 and 2003: hire a dedicated sales manager, explore new markets, hire more sales staff, explore sales training alternatives, and implement companywide meetings/team building.

Hire a Sales Manager and Explore New Markets

The goal of hiring a sales manager was to allow Lynn more time to focus on exploring new markets for the company. Lynn had focused on the company for so long that bringing in fresh ideas and perspective was deemed appropriate. In addition, Lynn had always been involved in coordinating the new salesperson training, which took away time from her other duties.

An internal sales team member who had been with the company for about five years was asked if he would be interested in the position. He declined, indicating that he felt better suited to stay in his current position and continue generating sales rather than moving into management. As a result, the company sought external candidates with a sales management background. Bill was hired because he had more than a decade of middle-management sales experience with large to medium-sized companies planning sales force activities, and he possessed some technical product line knowledge. He was only the second person brought in as manager who did not gain the position as an internal promotion. The previous person left the management position because of a spouse relocation.

Bill was given Lynn's office since it was right next to the sales team and she moved to a smaller office located centrally to the president, operations, and the sales team. Lynn turned the sales team over to Bill, and she started focusing on exploring new markets.

Hire More Sales Staff and Explore Sales Training Alternatives

The nature of Aegis's highly technical product line has historically required a significant investment in employee training. The typical new hire has had several years of sales experience; however, most have limited knowledge of Aegis's product line. Although a formal training program was created to help expedite and improve the process, the generation of sales is slowed by the company's payroll investment in the employee and the sales force time needed to support the trainee. The result in turnover can have a tremendous impact on the company. The strategy in the past has been a two-pronged approach. First, management developed and is continually improving an effort to create an organizational environment and compensation package that will encourage retention. Second, recognizing that employee turnover is a natural part of the employment relationship, the company regularly recruits, hires, and trains new sales team members. This two-pronged approach has yielded some success; however, during the last two years the company peaked at 15 employees, the majority being sales staff, and has had as few as 10.

Review of the training process and materials led the company to realize that having one person coordinate trainees might be the best approach with others supplementing support on an ad hoc basis. Bill, as the new sales manager, would be the person responsible for training.

Implement Monthly Companywide Meetings/Team Building

Starting in January 2003, the company implemented a plan that included a series of monthly companywide meetings/team building sessions. The goal was to get new hires assimilated into the company, unite everyone to a common company mission and purpose, and create an environment that encouraged and promoted retention and collaboration. The meetings would also be a forum to provide both sales and operations information about what's going on in the organization while clarifying the direction of the company as well as addressing specific issues.

The Initial Results of the Organizational Changes

Bill, the new sales manager, spent a great deal of time his first three months in his office reviewing materials and planning for the future. This was his role as a middle manager in his previous job at a medium-sized company. He did not spend much time on the sales floor. He periodically had weekly meetings in an effort to get updates on what was happening. Lynn spoke to Bill initially about spending more time on the sales floor and interacting with the team on a more regular basis. She also asked him to move the hiring process along for new sales staff. In addition, she coached him on the importance of making decisions at a faster pace. She provided an example that in lieu of writing a memo or sending an e-mail in a 12-person company, on most occasions walking over and talking to people is more effective. He recognized he may be still operating as though he were in a larger organization and made the effort to move more quickly. Lynn started spending more time with Bill and the sales team to make sure he was being supported and things progressed at a faster pace.

Lynn and Liz were able to identify Arizona as another location that would allow for increased company profitability and decrease cost-of-living expenses. Planning was in progress.

The initial monthly companywide meetings/team building sessions were implemented. The first session fostered increased camaraderie among the sales team and opened up communication between sales and operations. Since Lynn had given her duties as sales manager to Bill, communication between sales and operations had weakened. Lynn had previously bridged any gap between sales and operations since she oversaw sales and Samantha, the operations manager, reported directly to her. Samantha pointed out that since the change in management paperwork regarding credit approvals was not being completed prior to shipping product, and that salespeople were now walking directly into the receiving area to check on their orders rather than waiting until the product had been logged as received. Bill explained that he was trying to find ways to work with the sales team to provide quicker answers for the customers, and he was not trying to bypass existing procedures but to expedite service. He explained that he just wanted to get delivery answers and products to customers faster to increase satisfaction.

The conversation at the first session was fairly positive, and having employees share their history and how they joined the company appeared to open up communication. The session ended on a positive note with employees asking about the date and time of the next session.

At the suggestion of Liz, the second companywide meeting/team building session would focus on reviewing and revamping the core mission and values of the company in addition to aligning company employees and generating suggestions for improving operations and sales. The result was employee alignment on a new company mission statement, "Service. Integrity. Profitability." A great deal of conversation during the session focused on the meaning of integrity, honesty, and trust. It became clear that these were core foundation principles of the company.

The session also revealed some underlying tension between sales and operations. In an effort to avoid an "us against them" situation at the session, the two areas were asked to come up with suggestions to improve current methods. The operations manager and the sales manager would then discuss the suggestions back at the office, and the group would reconvene when the managers had developed some solutions. This option seemed to be palatable for everyone at the session.

Bill and Samantha met once after the session to discuss the suggestions. However, each continued to meet individually with Lynn. Although Lynn encouraged them to meet with each other and problem solve together, weeks passed and she received no joint documentation.

Future team-building sessions were put on hold. Bill was still learning the customer base and product line, so that hiring qualified candidates and training new hires was difficult for him. As a result, most new hires were still going through Lynn, and the existing sales staff continued to go to her to get information. The new hires brought on board were being passed around and trained by those sales team members who had more experience. Lynn, unable to dedicate her time to exploring new markets since she was still the go-to person and frustrated with the growing conflict between sales and operations, recognized this was not the most effective approach. She suggested that Bill move onto the sales floor to shadow the sales force and sell to some customers in order to shorten his learning curve and take on more quickly and effectively some of the sales manager tasks. Seeing time passing with minimal results, Lynn moved to the sales floor to help train new hires and also generate sales for the company.

Status

Nine months into the "piloted" initiatives, the company has maintained stability. However, the following events occurred:

- Bill, the sales manager, moved onto the sales floor where he mainly performed duties as a sales team member. After two months, he left the organization amicably to explore other opportunities.

- The sales manager, who had moved onto the floor and was serving primarily as a sales team member for the past two months, left the organization amicably to explore other opportunities.
- Lynn now manages the sales team, including training a new salesperson who joined the company.
- Liz, Lynn, and Samantha are assessing the events of the last nine months and lessons learned. They continue to explore opening another office in Arizona and new distribution opportunities.

When sitting down to assess the past nine months and how to move forward, Liz commented, "I view things from the perspective that we can't learn sometimes unless we fail, we mostly learn from our failures."

Note: This is a case based on actual events, but with the exception of the company president, names have been changed to maintain personal anonymity.

Case 2: Arctic Mining Consultants

Tom Parker enjoyed working outdoors. At various times in the past, he had worked as a ranch hand, high steel rigger, headstone installer, prospector, and geological field technician. Now 43, Parker is a geological field technician and field coordinator with Arctic Mining Consultants. He has specialized knowledge and experience in all nontechnical aspects of mineral exploration, including claim staking, line cutting and grid installation, soil sampling, prospecting, and trenching. He is responsible for hiring, training, and supervising field assistants for all of Arctic Mining Consultants' programs. Field assistants are paid a fairly low daily wage (no matter how long they work, which may be 12 hours or more) and are provided meals and accommodation. Many of the programs are operated by a project manager who reports to Parker.

Parker sometimes acts as a project manager, as he did on a job that involved staking 15 claims near Eagle Lake, Alaska. He selected John Talbot, Greg Boyce, and Brian Millar, all of whom

had previously worked with him, as the field assistants. To stake a claim, the project team marks a line with flagging tape and blazes along the perimeter of the claim, cutting a claimpost every 500 yards (called a "length"). The 15 claims would require almost 60 miles of line in total. Parker had budgeted seven days (plus mobilization and demobilization) to complete the job. This meant that each of the four stakers (Parker, Talbot, Boyce, and Millar) would have to complete a little over seven "lengths" each day. The following is a chronology of the project.

Day 1

The Arctic Mining Consultants crew assembled in the morning and drove to Eagle Lake. From there, they were flown by helicopter to the claim site. On arrival, they set up tents at the edge of the area to be staked and agreed on a schedule for cooking duties. After supper, they pulled out the maps and discussed the job—how long it would take, the order in which the areas were to be staked, possible helicopter landing spots, and areas that might be more difficult to stake.

Parker pointed out that with only a week to complete the job, everyone would have to average 7½ lengths per day. "I know that is a lot," he said, "but you've all staked claims before and I'm confident that each of you is capable of it. And it's only for a week. If we get the job done in time, there's a $300 bonus for each man." Two hours later, Parker and his crew members had developed what seemed to be a workable plan.

Day 2

Millar completed 6 lengths, Boyce 6 lengths, Talbot 8, and Parker 8. Parker was not pleased with Millar's or Boyce's production. However, he didn't make an issue of it, thinking that they would develop their "rhythm" quickly.

Day 3

Millar completed 5½ lengths, Boyce 4, and Talbot 7. Parker, who was nearly twice as old as the other three, completed 8 lengths. He also had enough time remaining to walk over and check the quality of stakes that Millar and Boyce had completed, then walk back to his own area for helicopter pickup back to the tent site.

That night Parker exploded with anger. "I thought I told you that I wanted 7½ lengths a day!" he shouted at Boyce and Millar. Boyce said that he was slowed down by unusually thick underbrush in his assigned area. Millar said that he had done his best and would try to pick up the pace. Parker did not mention that he had inspected their work. He explained that as far as he was concerned, the field assistants were supposed to finish their assigned area for the day, no matter what.

Talbot, who was sharing a tent with Parker, talked to him later. "I think that you're being a bit hard on them, you know. I know that it has been more by luck than anything else that I've been able to do my quota. Yesterday I only had 5 lengths done after the first seven hours and there was only an hour before I was supposed to be picked up. Then I hit a patch of really open bush, and was able to do 3 lengths in 70 min-

utes. Why don't I take Millar's area tomorrow and he can have mine? Maybe that will help."

"Conditions are the same in all of the areas," replied Parker, rejecting Talbot's suggestion. "Millar just has to try harder."

Day 4

Millar did 7 lengths and Boyce completed 6½. When they reported their production that evening, Parker grunted uncommunicatively. Parker and Talbot did 8 lengths each.

Day 5

Millar completed 6 lengths, Boyce 6, Talbot 7½, and Parker 8. Once again Parker blew up, but he concentrated his diatribe on Millar. "Why don't you do what you say you are going to do? You know that you have to do 7½ lengths a day. We went over that when we first got here, so why don't you do it? If you aren't willing to do the job then you never should have taken it in the first place!"

Millar replied by saying that he was doing his best, that he hadn't even stopped for lunch, and that he didn't know how he could possibly do any better. Parker launched into him again: "You have got to work harder! If you put enough effort into it, you will get the area done!"

Later Millar commented to Boyce, "I hate getting dumped on all the time! I'd quit if it didn't mean that I'd have to walk 50 miles to the highway. And besides, I need the bonus money. Why doesn't he pick on you? You don't get any more done than me; in fact, you usually get less. Maybe if you did a bit more he wouldn't be so bothered about me."

"I only work as hard as I have to," Boyce replied.

Day 6

Millar raced through breakfast, was the first one to be dropped off by the helicopter, and arranged to be the last one picked up. That evening the production figures were Millar 8¼ lengths, Boyce 7, and Talbot and Parker 8 each. Parker remained silent when the field assistants reported their performance for the day.

Day 7

Millar was again the first out and last in. That night, he collapsed in an exhausted heap at the table, too tired to eat. After a few moments, he announced in an abject tone, "Six lengths. I worked like a dog all day and I only got a lousy 6 lengths!" Boyce completed 5 lengths, Talbot 7, and Parker 7¼.

Parker was furious. "That means we have to do a total of 34 lengths tomorrow if we are to finish this job on time!" With his eyes directed at Millar, he added: "Why is it that you never finish the job? Don't you realize that you are part of a team, and that you are letting the rest of the team down? I've been checking your lines and you're doing too much blazing (clearing underbrush) and wasting too much time making picture-perfect claim posts! If you worked smarter, you'd get a lot more done!"

Day 8

Parker cooked breakfast in the dark. The helicopter dropoffs began as soon as morning light appeared on the horizon. Parker instructed each assistant to complete 8 lengths and, if they finished early, to help the others. Parker said that he would finish the other 10 lengths. Helicopter pickups were arranged for one hour before dark.

By noon, after working as hard as he could, Millar had completed only 3 lengths. "Why bother," he thought to himself, "I'll never be able to do another 5 lengths before the helicopter comes, and I'll catch the same amount of abuse from Parker for doing 6 lengths as for 7½." So he sat down and had lunch and a rest. "Boyce won't finish his 8 lengths either, so even if I did finish mine, I still wouldn't get the bonus. At least I'll get one more day's pay this way."

That night, Parker was livid when Millar reported that he had completed 5½ lengths; Parker had done 10¼ lengths, and Talbot had completed 8. Boyce proudly announced that he finished 7½ lengths, but sheepishly added that Talbot had helped him with some of it. All that remained were the 2½ lengths that Millar had not completed.

The job was finished the next morning and the crew demobilized. Millar has never worked for Arctic Mining Consultants again, despite being offered work several times by Parker. Boyce sometimes does staking for Arctic, and Talbot works full time with the company.

Source: © Copyright. Steven L. McShane and Tim Neale. This case is based on actual events, but names and some characteristics have been changed to maintain anonymity.

Case 3: Big Screen's Big Failure

By Fiona McQuarrie, University College of the Fraser Valley

Bill Brosnan stared at the financial statements in front of him and shook his head. The losses from *Conquistadors,* the movie that was supposed to establish Big Screen Studios as a major Hollywood power, were worse than anyone had predicted. In fact, the losses were so huge that Brosnan's predecessor, Buck Knox, had been fired as a result of this colossal failure. Brosnan had wanted to be the head of a big movie production company for as long as he could remember, and he was thrilled to have been chosen by the board of directors to be the new president. But he had never expected that the first task in his dream

job would be to deal with the fallout from one of the most unsuccessful movies ever.

The driving force behind *Conquistadors* was its director, Mark Frazier. Frazier had made several profitable movies for other studios and had a reputation as being a maverick with a "vision." He was a director with clearly formulated ideas of what his movies should look like, and he also had no hesitations about being forceful with producers, studios, actors, and technical staff to ensure that his ideas came to life as he had envisioned them. For several years, while Frazier had been busy on other projects, he had also been writing a script about two Spanish aristocrats in the sixteenth century going to America to find riches and gold and encountering many amazing adventures on their travels. Frazier was something of an amateur historian, which led to his interest in the real-life stories of the Spanish conquistadors and bringing those stories to life for a twenty-first century audience. But he also felt that creating a successful epic would establish him as a serious writer and filmmaker in the eyes of Hollywood, some of whose major powers had dismissed his past work as unimaginative or cliché.

At the time Big Screen Studios approached Frazier to see if he would be interested in working for them, the company was going through something of a rough spot. Through several years of hard work and mostly profitable productions, Buck Knox, the president of Big Screen, had established Big Screen as a studio that produced cost-efficient and profitable films. The studio also had a good reputation for being supportive of the creative side of filmmaking; actors, writers, directors, and producers generally felt that Big Screen trusted them enough to give them autonomy to make decisions appropriate for their productions. (Other studios had reputations for keeping an overly tight rein on production budgets and for dictating choices based on cost rather than artistic considerations.) However, in the last two years Big Screen had invested in several major productions—a musical, a horror film, and the sequel to a wildly successful film adaptation of a comic book— that for various reasons had all performed well below expectations. Knox had also heard through the grapevine that several of the studio's board members were prepared to join together to force him out of the presidency if Big Screen did not come up with a hit soon.

Knox knew that Frazier was being wooed by several other studios for his next project, and he decided to contact Frazier to see if he was interested in directing any of the productions Big Screen had in development. After hearing Knox's descriptions of the studio's potential projects, Frazier said, "What I'd really be interested in doing is directing this script I've been writing." He described the plot of *Conquistadors* to Knox, and Knox was enchanted by the possibilities—two strong male lead characters, a beautiful woman the men encountered in South America whose affections they fought over, battles, sea voyages, and challenging journeys over mountains and through jungles. However, Knox could also see that this movie might be extremely expensive to produce. He expressed this concern to Frazier, who replied, "Yes, but it will be an investment that will pay off. I know this movie will work. I've mentioned it to two other studios and they are interested in it. I would prefer to make it with Big Screen, but if I have to, I will go somewhere else to get it made. That is how strongly I believe in it. However, any studio I work with has to trust me. I want adequate financial support from the studio, I want final approval over casting, and I won't make the film if I don't get final cut." ("Final cut" means the director, not the studio, edits the version of the movie that is released to theaters, and that the studio cannot release a version of the movie that the director does not approve.)

Knox told Frazier that he would get back to him later that week and asked Frazier not to commit to any other project until then. He spent several days mulling over the possibilities. Like Frazier, he believed that *Conquistadors* could be a huge success. It certainly sounded like it had more potential than anything else Big Screen had in development. However, Knox was still concerned about the potential cost, and the amount of control over the project that Frazier was demanding. Frazier's reputation as a maverick meant that he likely would not compromise on his demands. Knox was also concerned about his own vulnerability if the movie failed. On the other hand, Big Screen needed a big hit, and it needed one soon. Big Screen would look very bad if it turned down *Conquistadors* and the movie became a gigantic hit for some other studio. Frazier had a respectable track record of producing moneymakers, so even though he might be difficult to work with, the success of the film would probably balance out any problems during its creation. At the end of the week, Knox phoned Frazier and told him that Big Screen was willing to produce *Conquistadors*. Frazier thanked Knox, and added, "This film is going to redeem me, and it's going to redeem Big Screen as well."

Preproduction on the film started almost immediately, after Frazier and the studio negotiated a budget of $50 million. This was slightly higher than Knox had anticipated, but he believed this was not an excessive amount to permit Frazier to realize the grand vision the film needed. Knox further reassured himself by assigning John Connor, one of his trusted vice-presidents, to act as the studio's liaison with Frazier and to be executive producer on the film. Connor was a veteran of many years in the movie production industry and was experienced in working with directors and budgets. Knox trusted Connor to be able to make Frazier contain costs within the agreed-upon limits.

The first major problem the film encountered involved casting. The studio gave Frazier final approval over casting as he had requested. The first actor Frazier signed was Cole Rogan, a famous action star, to be one of the male leads. The studio did not object to this choice; in fact, Knox and Connor felt that Rogan was an asset because he had a reputation as a star who could "open" a film (in other words, audiences would come to a movie just because he was in it). However, Frazier then decided to cast Frank Monaco as the other male lead. Monaco had made only a few films to date, and those were fluffy romantic comedies. Frazier said that Monaco would bring important qualities of vulnerability and innocence to the role, to contrast with Rogan's rugged machismo. However, Knox told Connor, he saw two major problems with Monaco's casting: Monaco had never proven himself in an epic adventure role, and he was an accomplished enough actor that he would make the rather wooden Rogan look bad. Knox told Connor to suggest to Frazier that Rogan's role be recast. Unfortunately, it turned out that Frazier had signed Rogan to a "pay or play" deal, meaning that if the studio released Rogan from the project without using his services, the studio would have to pay him a considerable sum of money. Knox was somewhat bothered that Frazier had made this deal with Rogan without consulting either him or Connor, but he told Connor to instruct Frazier to release Rogan and recast the role, and the studio would just have to accept the payment to Rogan as part of the production costs. Although Frazier complained, he did as

the studio asked and chose as a replacement Marty Jones, an actor who had had some success in films but mostly in supporting roles. However, Jones was thrilled to be cast in a major role, and after Connor saw Jones's audition, he told Knox that Jones would probably be capable of convincingly playing the part.

A few weeks after casting was completed, Connor called Knox and asked to see him immediately. "Buck," he told him once he arrived at Knox's office, "we have a really big problem." Connor said that Frazier was insisting the majority of the production be filmed in the jungles of South America, where most of the action took place, rather than on a studio soundstage or in a more accessible location that resembled the South American locale. Not only that, but Frazier was also insisting that he needed to bring along most of the crew that had worked on his previous films, rather than staffing the production locally. "Why does he want that? That's going to cost a hell of a lot," Knox said. "I know," Connor said, "but he says it's the only way that the film is going to work. He says it just won't be the same if the actors are in a studio or in some swamp in the southern U.S. According to him, the actors and the crew need to be in the real location to truly understand what the conquistadors went through, and audiences won't believe it's a real South American jungle if the film isn't made in one."

Knox told Connor that Frazier had to provide an amended budget to reflect the increased costs before he would approve the location filming. Connor took the request to Frazier, who complained that the studio was weakening on its promise to support the film adequately, and added that he might be tempted to take the film to another studio if he was not allowed to film on location in South America. After a few weeks, he produced an amended budget of $75 million. Knox was horrified that the budget for *Conquistadors* had nearly doubled by half in a few weeks. He told Connor that he would accept the amended budget only under two conditions: one, that Connor would go on the location shoot to supervise the production and to ensure that costs stayed within the amended budget, and two, that if the costs exceeded Frazier's estimates, he would have to pay any excess himself.

Frazier again complained that the studio was attempting to compromise his vision, but he grudgingly accepted the modified terms.

Frazier, Connor, and the cast and crew then headed off to the South American jungles for a scheduled two-month shoot. Immediately it became apparent that there was more trouble. Connor, who reported daily to Knox, told him after two weeks had passed that Frazier was shooting scenes several times over—not because the actors or the crew were making mistakes, or because there was something substantially wrong with the scenes, but because the output just didn't meet his artistic standards. This attention to detail meant that the filming schedule was nearly a week behind after only the first week's work. Also, because the filming locations were so remote, the cast and crew were spending nearly four hours of a scheduled seven-hour workday traveling to and from location, leaving only three hours during which they could work at regular pay rates. Work outside those hours meant they had to be paid overtime, and as Frazier's demanding vision required shooting 10 or 12 hours each day, the production was incurring huge overtime costs. As if that wasn't bad enough, the "rushes" (the finished film produced each day) showed that Monaco and Jones didn't have any chemistry as a pair, and Gia Norman, the European actress Frazier had cast as the love interest, had such a heavy accent that most of her lines couldn't be understood.

Knox told Cannon that he was coming to the location right away to meet with Frazier. After several days of very arduous travel, Knox, Cannon, and Frazier met in the canvas tent that served as the director's "office" in the middle of the jungle. Knox didn't waste any time with pleasantries. "Mark," he told Frazier, "there is no way you can bring this film in for the budget you have promised or within the deadline you agreed to. David has told me how this production is being managed, and it's just not acceptable. I've done some calculations, and at the rate you are going, this picture is going to cost $85 million and have a running time of four and a half hours. Big Screen is not prepared to support that. We need a film that's a commercially viable length, and we need it at a reasonable cost."

"It needs to be as long as it is," replied Frazier, "because the story has to be told. And if it has to cost this much, it has to cost this much. Otherwise it will look like crap and no one will buy a ticket to see it."

"Mark," replied Knox, "we are prepared to put $5 million more into this picture, and that is it. You have the choice of proceeding under those terms, and keeping David fully apprised of the costs so that he can help you stay within the budget. If you don't agree to that, you can leave the production, and we will hire another director and sue you for breach of contract."

Frazier looked as though he was ready to walk into the jungle and head back to California that very minute, but the thought of losing his dream project was too much for him. He muttered, "OK, I'll finish it."

Knox returned to California, nursing several nasty mosquito bites, and Cannon stayed in the jungle and reported to him regularly. Unfortunately, from Cannon's reports, it didn't seem like Frazier was paying much attention to the studio's demands. Cannon estimated that the shoot would run three months rather than two, and that the total cost of the shoot would be $70 million. This left only $10 million of the expanded budget for postproduction, distribution, and marketing, which was almost nothing for an epic adventure. To add to Knox's problems, he got a phone call from Richard Garrison, the chairman of Big Screen's board of directors. Garrison had heard gossip about what was going on with *Conquistadors* in the jungles of South America, and he wanted to know what Knox was going to do to curb Frazier's excesses. Knox told Garrison that Frazier was operating under clearly understood requirements, and that Cannon was on the set to monitor the costs. Unfortunately, Knox thought, Cannon was doing a good job of reporting, but he didn't seem to be doing much to correct the problems he was observing.

Frazier eventually came back to California after three and a half months of shooting and started editing the several hundred hours of film he had produced. Knox requested that Frazier permit Cannon or himself to participate in the editing, but Frazier retorted that permitting that would infringe on his right to final cut, and he refused to allow anyone associated with the studio to be present in the editing room. Knox scheduled a release date for the film in six months' time and asked the studio's publicity department to start working on an ad campaign for the film, but not much could be done on either of these tasks without at least a rough cut of the finished product.

Three weeks into the editing, Cannon called Knox. "I heard from Mark today," he said. "He wants to do some reshoots." "Is that a problem?" Knox asked. "No," said Cannon, "most of it is interior stuff that we can do here. But he wants to add a prologue. He says that the story doesn't make sense without more development of how the two lead characters sailed from Spain to America. He wants to hire a ship."

"He wants to WHAT?" exclaimed Knox.

"He wants to hire a sailing ship, like the conquistadors traveled on. There's a couple of tall ships that would do, but he wants one in particular that he says is the most historically accurate. It's in drydock in Mexico, and it would cost at least a million to make it seaworthy and sail it up to southern California. And that's on top of the cost of bringing the actors and crew back for a minimum of a week. I suggested to him that we try some special effects or computerized animation for the scenes of the ship on the ocean, and shoot the shipboard scenes in the studio, but he says that won't be the same and it needs to be authentic."

At this point, Knox was ready to drive over to the editing studios and take care of Frazier himself. Instead, he called Garrison and explained the situation. "I won't commit any more money to this without the board's approval. But we've invested $80 million into this already, so is a few more million that much of a deal if it gets the damn thing finished and gets Frazier out of our hair? If we tell him no, we'll have to basically start all over again, or just dump the whole thing and kiss $80 million goodbye." At the other end of the line, Garrison sighed and said, "Do whatever you have to do to get it done."

Knox told Cannon to authorize the reshoots, with a schedule of two months and the expectation that Frazier would have a rough cut of the film ready for the studio executives to view in three months. However, because of the time Frazier had already spent in editing, Knox had to postpone the film's release date, which meant changing the publicity campaign as well—and releasing the film at the same time that one of

Big Screen's major competitors was releasing an adventure that was considered a surefire hit. However, Knox felt he had no choice. If he didn't enforce some deadline, Frazier might sit in the editing room and tinker with his dream forever.

Cannon supervised the reshoots and reported that they went as well as could be expected. The major problem was that Gia Norman had had plastic surgery on her nose after the first shoot was completed, and she looked considerably different than she had in the jungles of South America. However, creative lighting, makeup, and costuming managed to minimize the change in her appearance. By all accounts, the (very expensive) sailing ship looked spectacular in the rushes, and Frazier was satisfied that his vision had been sufficiently dramatized.

Amazingly, Frazier delivered the rough cut of the film at the agreed-upon time. Knox, Cannon, Garrison, and the rest of the studio's executives crowded into the screening room to view the realization of Frazier's dream. Five-and-a-half hours later, they were in shock. No one could deny that the movie looked fantastic, and that it was an epic on a grand scale, but there was no way the studio could release a five-and-a-half hour film commercially—moreover, Frazier had agreed to produce a movie that was at most two-and-a-half hours long. Knox was at his wits' end. He cornered Garrison in the hallway outside the screening room. "Will you talk to Mark? He won't listen to me, he won't listen to David. But we can't release this. It won't work." Garrison agreed, and contacted Frazier the next day. He reported back to Knox that Frazier, astonishingly, had agreed to cut the film to two hours and fifteen minutes. Knox, heartened by this news, proceeded with the plans for the film's release date, which by now was a month away, and got the publicity campaign going.

Two days before the scheduled release date, Frazier provided an advance copy of his shortened version of *Conquistadors* for a studio screening. Knox had asked him to provide a copy sooner, but Frazier said that he could not possibly produce anything that quickly. As a consequence, the version of the film that the studio executives were seeing for the first time was the version that had already had thousands of copies duplicated for distribution to movie theaters all across North America. In fact, those copies were on their way by courier to the theaters as the studio screening started.

At the end of the screening, the studio executives were stunned. Yes, the movie was shorter, but now it made no sense. Characters appeared and disappeared randomly, the plot was impossible to follow, and the dialogue did not make sense at several key points in the small parts of plot that were discernible. The film was a disaster. Several of the executives present voiced the suspicion that Frazier had deliberately edited the movie this way to get revenge on the studio for not "respecting" his vision and forcing him to reduce the film's length. Others suggested that Frazier was simply a lunatic who never should have been given so much autonomy in the first place.

Knox, Garrison, and Cannon held a hastily called meeting the next morning. What could the studio do? Recall the film and force Frazier to produce a more coherent shorter version? Recall the film and release the five-and-a-half hour version? Or let the shorter version be released as scheduled and hope that it wouldn't be too badly received? Knox argued that the film should be recalled and Frazier should be forced to produce the product he agreed to produce. Cannon said that he thought Frazier had been doing his best to do what the studio wanted, based on what Cannon saw on the set, and that making Frazier cut the movie so short compromised the vision that Frazier wanted to achieve. He said the studio should release the long version and present it as a "special cinematic event." Garrison, as chairman of the board, listened to both sides, and after figuring out the costs of recalling and/or reediting the film—not to mention the less tangible costs of further worsening the film's reputation—said, "Gentlemen, we really don't have any choice. *Conquistadors* will be released tomorrow."

Knox immediately canceled the critics' screenings of *Conquistadors* scheduled for that afternoon, so that bad reviews would not appear on the day of the film's release. Despite that preemptive step and an extensive advertising campaign, *Conquistadors* was a complete and utter flop. On a total outlay of $90 million, the studio recouped less than $9 million. The reviews of the film were terrible, and audiences stayed away in droves. The only place *Conquistadors* was even close to successful was in some parts of Europe, where film critics said the edited version was an example of how American studios' crass obsession with making money made them compromise the work of a genius. The studio attempted to capitalize on this small note of hope by releasing the five-and-a-half hour version of *Conquistadors* for screening at some overseas film festivals and cinema appreciation societies. However, the revenues from these screenings were so small that they made no difference to the overall financial results.

Three months after *Conquistadors* was released, Garrison called Knox in and told him he was fired. Garrison told Knox the board appreciated what a difficult production *Conquistadors* had been to manage, but that the costs of the production had been unchecked to a degree that the board no longer had confidence in Knox's ability to operate Big Screen Studios efficiently. Cannon was offered a very generous early retirement package, and accepted it. The board then hired Bill Brosnan, a vice-president at another studio, as Knox's replacement.

After reviewing *Conquistadors*' financial records and the notes that Knox had kept throughout the production, Brosnan was determined that a disaster like this would not undermine his career as it had Knox's. But what could he do to ensure this would not happen?

Case 4: Keeping Suzanne Chalmers

Thomas Chan hung up the telephone and sighed. The vice-president of software engineering at Advanced Photonics Inc. (API) had just spoken to Suzanne Chalmers, who called to arrange a meeting with Chan later that day. She didn't say what the meeting was about, but Chan almost instinctively knew that Suzanne was going to quit after working at API for the past four years. Chalmers is a software engineer in Internet Protocol (IP), the software that directs fiber-optic light through API's routers. It was very specialized work, and Suzanne was one of API's top talents in that area.

Thomas Chan had been through this before. A valued employee would arrange a private meeting. The meeting would begin with a few pleasantries, then the employee announces that he or she wants to quit. Some employees say they are leaving because of the long hours and stressful deadlines. They say they need to decompress, get to know the kids again, or whatever. But that's not usually the real reason. Almost every organization in this industry is scrambling to keep up with technological advances and the competition. Employees would just leave one stressful job for another one.

Also, many of the people who leave API join a start-up company a few months later. These start-up firms can be pressure cookers where everyone works 16 hours each day and has to perform a variety of tasks. For example, engineers in these small firms might have to meet customers or work on venture capital proposals rather than focus on specialized tasks related to their knowledge. API now has over 6,000 employees, so it is easier to assign people to work that matches their technical competencies.

No, the problem isn't the stress or long hours, Chan thought. The problem is money—too much money. Most of the people who leave are millionaires. Suzanne Chalmers is one of them. Thanks to generous stock options that have skyrocketed on the stock markets, many employees at API have more money than they can use. Most are under 40 years old, so they are too young to retire. But their financial independence gives them less reason to remain with API.

The Meeting

The meeting with Suzanne Chalmers took place a few hours after the telephone call. It began like the others, with the initial pleasantries and brief discussion about progress on the latest fiber-optic router project. Then, Suzanne made her well-rehearsed statement: "Thomas, I've really enjoyed working here, but I'm going to leave Advanced Photonics." Suzanne took a breath, then looked at Chan. When he didn't reply after a few seconds, she continued: "I need to take time off. You know, get away to recharge my

batteries. The project's nearly done and the team can complete it without me. Well, anyway, I'm thinking of leaving."

Chan spoke in a calm voice. He suggested that Suzanne should take an unpaid leave for two or maybe three months, complete with paid benefits, then return refreshed. Suzanne politely rejected that offer, saying that she needs to get away from work for a while. Thomas then asked Suzanne whether she was unhappy with her work environment—whether she was getting the latest computer technology to do her work and whether there were problems with co-workers. The workplace was fine, Susanne replied. The job was getting a bit routine, but she had a comfortable workplace with excellent co-workers.

Chan then apologized for the cramped workspace, due mainly to the rapid increase in the number of people hired over the past year. He suggested that if Suzanne took a couple of months off, API would give her special treatment with a larger work space with a better view of the park behind the campuslike building when she returned. She politely thanked Chan for that offer, but it wasn't what she needed. Besides, it wouldn't be fair to have a large workspace when other team members work in small quarters.

Chan was running out of tactics, so he tried his last hope: money. He asked whether Suzanne had higher offers. Suzanne replied that she regularly received calls from other companies, and some of them offered more money. Most were start-up firms that offered a lower salary but higher potential gains in stock options. Chan knew from market surveys that Suzanne was already paid well in the industry. He also knew that API couldn't compete on share option potential. Employees working in start-up firms sometimes saw their shares increase by 5 or 10 times their initial value, whereas shares at API and other large firms increased more slowly. However, Chan promised Suzanne that he would recommend that she receive a significant raise—maybe 25 percent more—and more stock options. Chan added that Chalmers was one of API's most valuable employees and that the company would suffer if she left the firm.

The meeting ended with Chalmers promising to consider Chan's offer of higher pay and stock options. Two days later, Chan received her resignation in writing. Five months later, Chan learned that after a few months traveling with her husband, Chalmers joined a start-up software firm in the area.

(Source: © 2001 Steven L. McShane.)

Case 5: Magic Cable

By Joseph Kavanaugh, Henry S. Maddux III, and Harry Gene Redden, Sam Houston State University

"I think I've found what I'm looking for," Gary Roberts said.

"Oh yeah, what is that?" Jim Handley asked, as he handed Roberts a pair of vice grip pliers.

"I'm thinking I might have found a way out of this dump. No more tile dust, no more 40-mile-an-hour winds blowing through the plant, and no more Al Wright for me," Roberts replied.

Wright, the plant manager, and Roberts, journeyman maintenance mechanic for Tile-Elite, had been at odds for years. Roberts had been hired during a manufacturing plant expansion at Tile-Elite and Wright had promised Roberts a production supervisor's job upon its completion. However, when the expansion was completed and the last production line was ready to produce, Wright told Roberts to forget the supervisor's job because he was more valuable to the company as a maintenance mechanic.

"I know what I said, Gary, but I think you're going to be a mechanic here even if you stay 20 years," Wright had stated at the time.

After that encounter, Wright and Roberts had mixed like oil and water and that was almost five years ago. Roberts had to admit that he was probably more valuable to the company as a maintenance mechanic in the short run, but he had been looking at the long run. He wanted to be more involved in the production process. He had just turned 40, was recently divorced, and had been involved in maintenance of some type ever since his military service in Vietnam 20 years earlier. While working full-time at his previous job, Roberts completed his bachelor's degree in business. His major had been management and it had taken him six long years to graduate. He had then wanted a position where he could use his management education. The company for which he was working while going to school had promised him a supervisor's position when he graduated, but that promise had evaporated when the company went bankrupt during the oil recession of the 1980s.

During his years with Tile-Elite, Roberts had searched for another company that would give him a chance as a supervisor, but it seemed no one wanted a man his age with minimal management experience. The oil recession had left the employment market flooded with unemployed managers with significant supervisory experience. Consequently, Roberts decided he would stick with what he knew best, maintenance, because jobs were more plentiful and the pay was reasonably good.

"Magic Cable, in Fresno, is looking for a maintenance mechanic. I've got an interview tomorrow morning," Roberts said to Handley.

"I've seen their plant over on Cook Street, behind the county barn, but I've never been in it. What do they build there?" Handley asked.

"Shoot, I don't know and I don't really care. All machines are alike. Just some are bigger than other ones, so my job will be basically the same. What I want is better working conditions and a chance for advancement. I'd even take a slight cut in pay to get out of here," Roberts answered.

"I understand where you're coming from but don't tell Magic Cable that. Well, good luck tomorrow, Gair. I hope you get that job," Handley said as he closed his toolbox and started moving toward the time clock.

Roberts hated it when Handley called him "Gair." It sounded so condescending. The only reason he hadn't said something was because Jim was such a good friend and he had taught him a lot.

Magic Cable was just two miles farther from Roberts's home than Tile-Elite. The facility was considerably smaller, but the grounds were kept neat and trimmed and Roberts considered that a good sign. The parking was also directly in front of the plant, and that would be good during bad weather.

"I've got a good feeling about this place," Roberts mused to himself as he drove through the gate.

After parking in a vacant visitors parking space, Roberts gathered his résumé and the completed employment application, took a couple of deep breaths, and headed toward the door labeled "Personnel." Once inside, all he saw was a doorbell mounted on a wall, a door with a peephole and mail slot, and a poster that displayed a picture of the building and a narrative describing the company's history. The poster was on the outside wall opposite the bell. Above the doorbell was a small sign: "Ring for Personnel." There was also a sign below the button: "We are **NOT** accepting applications." The word **"NOT"** was hanging loose so it could be removed if need be. "Lucky I've got an appointment," Roberts thought.

After pushing the button produced no sound, Roberts said out loud to himself, "Just my luck. The stupid thing is broken and no one even knows I'm here."

Almost immediately the door opened partially and a neatly dressed young woman stuck her head out and asked, "Gary Roberts?" Roberts nodded his head in reply. "Bill Lindsey, the manufacturing engineer, will be right with you," she added before shutting the door again.

"Great, more waiting," Roberts thought. After looking around the sparsely furnished lobby for a minute, Roberts occupied himself by reading the narrative written on the poster. It said Magic Cable had been started in a small warehouse in Oakland in 1977 by a group of friends with a good idea. They started manufacturing throttle and drive cables for outdoor equipment. The business grew very fast and in 1979 the plant was moved to Fresno. Now they were producing push–pull cables for automotive and aircraft purposes with a workforce consisting of about 300 employees.

Just as Roberts completed reading the poster,

the inside door swung open a second time and a tall, gray-haired man in an open-collared shirt emerged.

"Hi, I'm Bill Lindsey, the manufacturing engineer. You must be Gary Roberts. Come in here." As Roberts edged through door, Lindsey added "We need to go up and meet Bob Walters. He's our manufacturing manager. We'll both be interviewing you." And with that Lindsey turned to go up the set of stairs to his right. "Have you ever met Bob Walters?"

Roberts remembered seeing Bob Walters's name on the list of people who started Magic Cable. "No sir, I haven't," he answered.

"He's kind of rough around the edges, so don't let him run you off," Lindsey said with a wry smile. Roberts smiled back and said that he wouldn't.

Lindsey and Roberts went up one flight of stairs and proceeded down the hall. One wall of the corridor was glass and Roberts was able to see the entire production floor. The floor was organized into small production cells. Each group of operators in a work cell was busy at their machines doing their individual tasks. He noticed that many of the workers were female and seemed to represent various minorities.

"They really look overworked, don't they?" Lindsey asked while showing a slight sarcastic smile. Roberts noticed Lindsey walked with a slight limp. He had to make a conscious effort to walk slowly and not pass him. "He must be disabled somehow," Roberts thought to himself. Magic Cable appeared to be very different from the ceramic tile plant with all of its dust, heat, noisy conveyors, and frantic production pace. Gary Roberts had his second good feeling about Magic Cable.

As the pair approached the third office Gary noticed the expression on Bill Lindsey's face change. It became somber, almost showing agony. Lindsey turned and knocked on the door facing the hall. Roberts maintained his position behind Lindsey while they both stood quietly and waited to be acknowledged.

"Bill, ya'll come on in," the man inside the office said. As Lindsey and Roberts entered the office, Bob Walters rose so he could shake Roberts's hand. "This is Gary Roberts, Bob. He's here to interview for the mechanic position."

"Great, have a seat, Gary," Walters gestured to an empty office chair across from his desk. He was a good bit taller than Roberts and appeared to be in his middle fifties. He was dressed Western style and had an air of arrogance in his manner and speech, which gave Gary an uneasy feeling.

"First, Gary, tell me why you want to leave Tile-Elite," Walters said. In reply, Roberts described the working conditions at Tile-Elite, explained that there was no overtime, and stated that there was little chance for advancement. He purposely omitted his feeling about Al Wright, the plant manager. Walters sat almost motionless and listened.

"What about the people you work for?" Walters asked, expecting Roberts to add to his explanation. So Roberts related that he and management had had some differences, but said that he preferred not to expound upon them. Walters seemed satisfied with that explanation. He knew Gary's boss personally and understood the problems. He also knew that if Gary had said there were no problems, he would have been lying and there was no room at Magic Cable for a liar.

Walters began to explain what Magic Cable had to offer a plant employee. He compared Magic Cable to the tile plant. Magic Cable's working conditions were fairly pleasant; the building was air conditioned, clean, and reasonably quiet. Maintenance always got overtime because they were required to work six shifts of 10 hours each per week, with no exceptions. If the production floor was not working, maintenance people could always find something to do. The hourly pay was not quite up to Tile-Elite's level, but Walters explained that Roberts could expect to catch up in salary after a 90-day probationary period. Magic Cable paid an incentive bonus every three months and the maintenance department was included in that program.

"I've got one final question," Walters added. "How do you feel working with women? We have around 150 women on first shift and about 100 on second shift, so if there's going to be a problem in that area, I need to know it now."

"It's not a problem for me. I don't believe in dating anyone where I work," Roberts replied.

"Great, as far as I'm concerned you've got the job if you want it. What do you think, Bill?" Walters said, after turning to face Lindsey.

"Sounds great to me. Gary, you ready for work?" Lindsey asked.

"Let me give Tile-Elite a week's notice and I'll be here with bells on," Roberts answered, smiling broadly.

Roberts loved his new job. When people asked him what he did at Magic Cable, he would reply that he was semiretired. The work was easy, the machines were simple, and the 60 hours a week did wonders for his bank account. On the sixth day, Saturday, most of his time was spent in the machine shop teaching himself to run the machines. He had some small conflicts with the way things were run, but nothing serious. The most significant difference was that he wanted to be given formal training relating to the new electronics being integrated into production processes. However, Magic Cable had not shown any interest in providing that training. Roberts hoped that attitude would change. He knew he had to have patience.

As the months passed, the machine repair procedures became routine. As a result, the days became rather boring and the sixth 10-hour shift of every week felt more like 20 hours. Roberts suggested to his maintenance supervisor that the mechanics should take turns being off on Saturday. That would give everyone some recreational time and save Magic Cable some money.

When the lead man voiced the proposal to Walters, he went ballistic. He did not bother with relaying his reply through the supervisor; he came to the floor himself to find Roberts. As the manager quickly strode through the maintenance shop gate with the lead man right behind him, Roberts thought to himself, "Uh-oh!"

Walters stopped in front of the workbench where Roberts was putting seals in a gearbox. He pointed his finger at the mechanic, and said in a rather terse manner, "When you came to work here you agreed to work six 10-hour shifts a week and that is what you are going to work. The choice is not yours. If you do not want to live up to your agreement, you need to load up your toolbox and move on."

Roberts had no reply, other than a rather weak "Yes, sir." With that response, Walters immediately turned and left the maintenance shop without speaking another word.

For the next two years Roberts and the other members of the maintenance department worked within the work schedule guidelines set by Walters. Although some weekends off would have been nice, the steadiness of the overtime enabled them to have a higher standard of living. One mechanic purchased a newer and larger home and Roberts purchased the new sports car he had been wishing for.

Then one Monday morning a new production supervisor, Dale Wood, met Roberts at the time clock just inside the plant door. He appeared to be a different type of person from Walters. Wood handed Roberts a white sheet of paper folded in half so that the print was covered. As he did this, he said, "This memo outlines the new policy covering the work schedule of the maintenance department and machine shop. Rick Tanal is over the maintenance department and the machine shop from now on. He broke the news to me this morning and told me to pass it on to you and the other guys."

Tanal was the plant manager. He was a retired major from the military and had a terrible attitude toward the guys, but he was sweet as sugar to the women. One indicator of his personality was that he would shoot armadillos and rabbits while hunting on the company deer lease with his .458 Magnum rifle (elephant gun) and then brag to everyone as to how many pieces they were blown into. Roberts disliked him immensely and did not try to hide it. His "big me, little you" attitude had caused more than a few problems and clashes with male employees. His favorite reply, when asked about something the company had promised but had not delivered, was "You got that in writing?" The hourly personnel had not signed a contract so their answer was always "no." His typical comment was that if the promise was not in writing, it was not binding.

Roberts opened the folded sheet and read the memo. It stated that as of the previous Friday evening the maintenance department and the machine shop were not part of engineering any more; they were now a part of the production department. The memo also stated that the personnel in those two departments would be limited to 40 hours a week of work for an indefinite period. As he read the memo, Roberts's temperature skyrocketed. He yelled, almost screamed, several very vulgar words and made several derogatory statements concerning Tanal

and his parentage as he headed for the production office.

When Roberts got to Tanal's office he did not even knock on the door. He rushed in through the doorway, causing the plant manager to abruptly stop a telephone conversation in midsentence.

Holding the memo up in Tanal's face he asked, "What the hell is this crap?"

"New orders from the front office," Tanal replied, smiling slightly. Tanal said goodbye to the party on the other end of the phone line and hung up.

"This is not what I agreed on when I went to work here. Bob Walters said that overtime was a requirement of the job. When I tried to get him to cut the hours back, he threatened to fire me," Roberts almost yelled.

"That is in the past and has nothing to do with what is required at this time," Tanal answered. "You and the rest of the department need to learn how to live on 40 hours a week," he continued. "If you had been doing that all along, you would not be hurt by the cutback in working hours."

"I don't know who the hell you think you are, but don't tell me how to live. I spend as I see fit, whether I make my money here . . . or somewhere else." Roberts paused, and then added, "I'll tell you what, I'll give you a week, unless you don't want it, then I'm out of here."

"Are you saying that you quit?" Tanal asked.

"That's what I'm saying. I don't want to work for a thief, and I consider you a thief," Gary stated.

"A thief. How do you get that?" Tanal asked.

"Whenever you take something away you promised without discussing it, you're stealing and that's what you did. As far as I'm concerned, you stole my overtime hours from me, which amounts to about half of my check," Roberts returned.

Tanal did not have a chance to reply to this conjecture because Roberts turned on his heel and exited the office.

Roberts worked his last week grudgingly. He did not want to stay at Magic Cable, but he said he would, so he did. By the end of the week, he had secured a job as a line mechanic for a local bottling plant, loaded his toolboxes in his truck, and moved on.

Case 6: Perfect Pizzeria

Perfect Pizzeria in Southville, deep in southern Illinois, is the chain's second-largest franchise. The headquarters is located in Phoenix, Arizona. Although the business is prospering, it has employee and managerial problems.

Each operation has one manager, an assistant manager, and from two to five night managers. The managers of each pizzeria work under an area supervisor. There are no systematic criteria for being a manager or becoming a manager trainee. The franchise has no formalized training period for the manager. No college education is required. The managers for whom the case observer worked during a four-year period were relatively young (ages 24 to 27), and only one had completed college. They came from the ranks of night managers, assistant managers, or both. The night managers were chosen for their ability to perform the duties of the regular employees. The assistant managers worked a two-hour shift during the luncheon period five days a week to gain knowledge about bookkeeping and management. Those becoming managers remained at that level unless they expressed interest in investing in the business.

The employees were mostly college students, with a few high school students performing the less challenging jobs. Because Perfect Pizzeria was located in an area with few job opportunities, it had a relatively easy task of filling its employee quotas. All the employees, with the exception of the manager, were employed part-time. Consequently, they earned only the minimum wage.

The Perfect Pizzeria system is devised so that food and beverage costs and profits are set up according to a percentage. If the percentage of food unsold or damaged in any way is very low, the manager gets a bonus. If the percentage is high, the manager does not receive a bonus; rather, he or she receives only his or her normal salary.

There are many ways in which the percentage can fluctuate. Because the manager cannot be in the store 24 hours a day, some employees make up for their paychecks by helping themselves to the food. When a friend comes in to order a pizza, extra ingredients are put on the friend's pizza. Occasional nibbles by 18 to 20 employees throughout the day at the meal table also raise the percentage figure. An occasional bucket of sauce may be spilled or a pizza accidentally burned. Sometimes the wrong size of pizza may be made.

In the event of an employee mistake or a burned pizza by the oven person, the expense is supposed to come from the individual. Because of peer pressure, the night manager seldom writes up a bill for the erring employee. Instead, the establishment takes the loss and the error goes unnoticed until the end of the month when the inventory is taken. That's when the manager finds out that the percentage is high and that there will be no bonus.

In the present instance, the manager took retaliatory measures. Previously, each employee was entitled to a free pizza, salad, and all the soft drinks he or she could drink for every 6 hours of work. The manager raised this figure from 6 to 12 hours of work. However, the employees had received these 6-hour benefits for a long time. Therefore, they simply took advantage of the situation whenever the manager or the assistant was not in the building. Although the night managers theoretically had complete control of the operation in the evenings, they did not command the respect that the manager or assistant manager did. That was because night managers received the same pay as the regular employees, could not reprimand other employees, and were basically the same age or sometimes even younger than the other employees.

Thus apathy grew within the pizzeria. The manager and his workers, who started out to be a closely knit group, grew further apart. The manager made no attempt to alleviate the problem, because he felt it would iron itself out. Either the employees who were dissatisfied would quit or they would be content to put up with the new regulations. As it turned out, there was a rash of employee dismissals. The manager had no problem in filling the vacancies with new workers, but the loss of key personnel was costly to the business.

With the high turnover, the manager found he had to spend more time in the building, supervising and sometimes taking the place of inexperienced workers. This was in direct violation of the franchise regulation, which stated that a manager would act as a supervisor and at no time take part in the actual food preparation. Employees were not placed under strict supervision with the manager working alongside them. The operation no longer worked smoothly because of differences between the remaining experienced workers and the manager concerning the way in which a particular function should be performed.

Within a two-month period, the manager was again free to go back to his office and leave his subordinates in charge of the entire operation. During this two-month period, in spite of the differences between experienced workers and the manager, the unsold/damaged food percentage had returned to the previous low level and the manager received a bonus each month. The manager felt that his problems had been resolved and that conditions would remain the same, since the new personnel had been properly trained.

It didn't take long for the new employees to become influenced by the other employees. Immediately after the manager had returned to his supervisory role, the unsold/damaged food percentage began to rise. This time the manager took a bolder step. He cut out any benefits that the employees had—no free pizzas, salads, or drinks. With the job market at an even lower

ebb than usual, most employees were forced to stay. The appointment of a new area supervisor made it impossible for the manager to "work behind the counter," because the supervisor was centrally located in Southville.

The manager tried still another approach to alleviate the rising unsold/damaged food percentage problem and maintain his bonus. He placed a notice on the bulletin board, stating that if the percentage remained at a high level, a lie detector test would be given to all employees. All those found guilty of taking or purposefully wasting food or drinks would be immediately terminated. This did not have the desired effect on the employees, because they knew if they were all subjected to the test, all would be found guilty and the manager would have to dismiss all of them. This would leave him in a worse situation than ever.

Even before the following month's percentage was calculated, the manager knew it would be high. He had evidently received information from one of the night managers about the employees' feelings toward the notice. What he did not expect was that the percentage would reach an all-time high. That is the state of affairs at the present time.

Source: J. E. Dittrich and R. A. Zawacki, *People and Organizations* (Plano, TX: Business Publications, 1981), pp. 126–128. Used by permission of McGraw-Hill/Irwin.

Case 7: Two Men and a Truck International

By Aneil Mishra and Karen Mishra, Wake Forest University

Mary Ellen Sheets, CEO of Two Men and a Truck International (TMT), sits in her office, pondering the future of "her baby"—the local moving company she built that is now ranked number 7 in the moving industry. Her motto is "Movers who care," and she is very proud of the fact that both TMT International and her fran-

chisees all demonstrate care and concern for their customers in their daily work as well as in special circumstances, such as providing trucks for victims of the recent flood in North Carolina. Can TMT maintain its image as a caring, trusted company as it grows the company into the twenty-first century?

The Beginning

Mary Ellen started the first and only local moving company with her "men," sons Brig and Jon, and a truck, a $350 find that got them started. In the early 1980s, her sons wanted to earn college tuition money in the summer. They placed an ad in the local Okemos, Michigan, paper, *The Towne Courier*, with copy written by their mother which simply said "Two Men and a Truck." She also drew a simple logo for the business—a stick figure of two happy men driving a truck. The business did well and when Brig and Jon returned to Northern Michigan University in the fall, people kept calling to have their moves done. She decided to keep operating the business by hiring two men to help her with the moving.

By May 1985, she bought a "new" truck. After work each day as a systems analyst for the State of Michigan, she would return home, listen to her answering machine, and schedule moves for Joe and Elmer, her two movers. She would charge the customer $25 an hour, pay each "man" $10 an hour, and use the rest for gas money and placing classified ads. During these early "Joe and Elmer" days, she also utilized some unique practices, including not leaving any contact information with the customer after a move in case the movers happened to damage something. She also was pulled over by a Michigan State Trooper on Interstate 96 for failing to have the proper license to drive a truck. At the end of her first full year in business, she had made a $1,000 profit. Not wanting to have to figure out how to pay taxes on the income, she simply gave the money away, writing ten $100 checks to charitable organizations.

As she grew the business, working out of her home and running it by herself, she began to change the way the business operated, focusing her attention on the customer. Russ Scott, owner of the Genessee County franchise, was one of her first professional movers, and he remembers using a "14-foot truck, no ramp and one appliance dolly. Back then, there was no calling in sick. There was no on-call. There was no safety net. If there was a job booked and if we worked 14 days straight, we worked 14 days straight. It didn't happen often, but that is how it was. It was very personal. That was my truck, those were my moves, and that is how everybody looked at it. We wore several hats in those first few years. Also, we didn't focus on the dollars and cents. We focused more on the service and what we had to offer the customer, not what

we could get from the customer and it has gotten us an awful long ways. If we damaged a $200 chair, then Mary Ellen felt that we owed that customer a $200 chair, not $.60 on the pound, as the industry standard. That went a long way toward building credibility and trust with our customers. Decisions were always made that a change has to benefit 80 percent of the system" in order to be implemented.

When Mary Ellen's son Jon took over the Lansing franchise, he found that Mary Ellen had given all of the profits away to local charities—anyone that called asking for a donation. He quickly put a stop to that, saying, "You have to get this company in good shape financially." Once he did, the Lansing franchise continued to give to the community, including helping to pay for the fountain in front of Lugnut Park, where the Lansing Lugnuts (minor league baseball team) play.

System Growth and Expansion

By 1994, TMT (www.twomen.com) had grown to 35 franchisees and Mary Ellen was still doing everything herself—the newsletter, the annual meeting, visiting franchises, and doing the books. She knew the franchisees so well that she knew not only the names of their children, but the year and make of each of their trucks. In addition, Mary Ellen, having quit her job at the State of Michigan, was successfully running her own franchise in Lansing, which was growing very quickly. While the company was experiencing this tremendous growth, Mary Ellen was asked by the Michigan Republican Party to run for state Senate. She knew that she would need assistance and asked her daughter Melanie to step in as president and run the day-to-day operations of the company and her son Jon to run her franchise in Lansing.

Melanie agreed to take on the job of president even though the job paid no salary, and even though it meant giving up a job that paid $80,000 a year plus use of a company car. She did so because she realized that her mom really needed help, and not just because Mary Ellen was going to run for political office.

Melanie brought to the company her experience in sales as a pharmaceutical sales representative, as well as her experience running franchises in Georgia and Michigan. Right away, Melanie saw the need to introduce formal controls into the franchise system. Because Mary Ellen had personally brought in all the franchisees and wanted to help them grow *their* business, she was somewhat lenient in allowing the franchisees to make royalty payments when it was convenient for them. Some of the franchisees who had "grown up" with Mary Ellen wondered who this young woman was and what she was really made of. Melanie personally visited every one of the franchisees so that she could meet them and they could get to know her. Melanie felt very strongly that she needed to apply the franchise agreement fairly across all franchisees in order to protect the value of the TMT brand. Several of the franchises had become very tardy in their royalty payments, and some had stopped paying royalties altogether. In addition, she raised the royalty rate from 4 percent to 6 percent, in an industry (franchising) that has an average royalty rate of 9 percent to 10 percent. As Mary Ellen herself said, "I am probably the soft person and Melanie is the other person." Sally Degnan, training director, agrees. "Mary Ellen rules with her heart, and Melanie has a heart, but rules with her mind. We used to call her the Melanator."

In response to Melanie enforcing the franchise agreements more consistently and raising the royalty rate, six of the more disgruntled franchisees banded together, taking advantage of some loopholes in the franchise agreement, and threatened to use the TMT name and logo but not pay royalties due TMT International. Melanie invested significant sums of her own money to cover the mounting legal bills and to fight the six delinquent franchises in court in order to make sure that TMT's franchise agreement was upheld. She remembers this as particularly stressful time in her life, as she also had twin six-month-old boys to raise, and her husband was fighting a battle with cancer as well. Melanie noted that the legal costs were in excess of $600,000 and that at one point "we were so broke we just kept the heat turned down really low in the little house we were working out of. We were freezing in that house just to cut down on expenses. We had to start telling our vendors, including our attorney, that we couldn't pay them in full. We sent our attorneys $500 a month, even though we owed them several hundred thousand dollars."

The court, however, eventually upheld the TMT franchise agreement. Two of the six franchisees apologized and asked if they could return to the system while the other four were terminated. As part of the settlement, TMT and its franchises cannot operate in the state of Georgia. Since this time, Two Men and a Truck has bought the rights back for the state of Georgia and currently has 10 franchise locations operating in that state.

One of the lessons from that lawsuit was the recognition of the need to better assess prospective franchisees rather than just taking anyone with money. That is how the other brother and the other "man," Brig, came into the picture. He is the franchise recruiting director, and has brought a new level of discernment to the review of prospective franchisees. He finds that there are times to tell a prospective franchisee "Yes, we would like to take your money, but no, this will not be a good fit for us or for you." Brig also is of the philosophy that you must maintain a sense of balance between work and family. He has learned that "when I give 100 percent at work, I should be able to go home and give 100 percent to my kids as opposed to giving them the leftovers."

Mary Ellen Today

Mary Ellen knows that she has changed personally since growing this company. She admits to being "painfully shy" when she first entered the work world. Now, she is the primary PR machine for the company, appearing on CNN and *Oprah*. She writes an article for the newsletter for the franchisees and their employees called *On the Move*. She still cares about the community, preferring to do things for kids, "since they will be our customers in the future."

She otherwise allows her employees—and her children—tremendous freedom to do their jobs the way they see fit. At TMT's first strategic planning session, conducted in 1999, Mary Ellen remarked at what good ideas everyone had. There was no "but I did it this way" or "that will never work here." She sat back and listened as her employees shared their ideas enthusiastically and she gave them all a great sense of encouragement.

Daily Operations

Everyone in the home office loves working for TMT. It is a very high-energy environment where people work together with a common goal—to make TMT better each day and to serve the customer as well as possible, in line with its mission statement: "Our commitment is to continuously strive to exceed our Customer's expectations in value and high standard of satisfaction."

One way the family keeps close tabs on each other is through their weekly staff meetings. Each Tuesday morning, the staff meets to discuss what they are working on. In speaking about this, Mary Ellen remarked, "We have a joke in our company—if there is a job to be done and you make eye contact, you will get assigned to it!" Long-time employee Sue McIntosh, signage coordinator, remarked, "It's just a good place to work because they make you feel like you are important here, no matter what you do."

Maintaining this high level of energy among employees requires periods of rejuvenation in Melanie's view, and so in the spring of 2003 she instituted an Earned Sabbatical Program for all her full-time employees at the company's Lansing headquarters. The program is designed to reward employees who have been with the company full-time for six years with six straight weeks of paid time off. For more details, see http://www.twomen.com/.

Franchise Relations

TMT International works hard to maintain a positive strategic partnership with each of its franchisees. The home office does try to overcommunicate on an ongoing basis through newsletters and through its use of franchise business consultants. Franchise business consultants are assigned 20–25 franchisees that they are responsible for visiting two times each year, as well as offering ongoing communication and advice. TMT International strives to maintain consistency across franchisees, as Quincy Jones, assistant training manager, said, "Like the McDonald's of the 90s."

The franchisees' biggest problem to date has been employee retention. TMT International encourages its franchisees to raise wages, and to offer benefits and other incentives to keep good people. The home office is also encouraging the franchisees to find ways to help their employees grow with them. One example in which it assists franchisees is by tracking customer comment cards and feeding back information to each franchise so that the best movers and customer service reps can be recognized for outstanding effort. Another effort is Stick Man University, which the home office established in 1989 to provide ongoing training for franchise employees. An extensive number of courses are offered, for both new and experienced franchise employees. As Sally Degnan, the training director, describes the philosophy behind developing franchisees' employees: "You don't make the new guy walk backwards." Franchisees can also take advantage of the home office's resource library of training videos, management bestsellers, and other educational materials at any time. Sally notes that these efforts along with Stick Man University are excellent vehicles for demonstrating the home office's long-term commitment to its franchises and their employees and is a visible example of how the franchises' royalties are being used by the home office for the betterment of the entire system.

One way Jon Sorber, a member of the board and a franchisee himself, has been innovative is to create a new position for his outstanding Lansing manager, Rob Felcher. He knew that this man was ready for additional responsibility yet as a newlywed was not eager to travel as a field consultant, so he created a general manager position for him to watch over his two franchises in Grand Rapids and Lansing. One challenge frequently facing franchisees is the need to provide growth opportunities to employees who want to go beyond the initial job of mover while at the same time retaining enough movers to facilitate the franchise's rapid business growth.

One other area that TMT International is concerned about is the need to grow market share. Systemwide growth that has been exceeding 40 percent annually in recent years has yielded systemwide revenues of over $100 million for 2002 (compared to $46 million in 1999 and $31.6 million in 1998). However, a TMT franchise's typical percentage market share is still in the single digits. TMT International sees increasing market share as an enormous opportunity for growing the business, given that its biggest competitor is still the "do-it-yourselfer."

Melanie Today

Melanie views her key responsibilities at the home office to be communication and ongoing strategic planning. She is very thorough in the way she communicates with franchisees, providing them with advance memos about potential ideas that she would like to implement in order to get their feedback early on. Once she feels that there has been enough two-way communication, she will implement her idea—but not before she has had time to explain her views and assess the franchisees' acceptance of it. She is very goal-oriented and works quickly in implementing ideas, whether they are hers or someone else's.

A critical part of her communication efforts involve ensuring that franchisees are provided up-to-date information that can be used to improve customer satisfaction as well as operating and financial performance. During much of the company's history, Mary Ellen compiled much of this information, but it is now largely computerized. Each franchise now has access to market share, profit, and cost data on all franchises in the system. Melanie has ultimate responsibility for ensuring that such data are accurate and disseminated in a comprehensible and timely fashion back to all franchisees.

On the subject of strategic planning, Two Men and a Truck has 28 strategic initiatives in the works. Melanie enthusiastically promotes and participates in this program. These initiatives are in place to increase customer satisfaction, market share domestically and globally, and current franchisee profitability. Everyone at the home office is involved in at least one strategic initiative, as are several of the franchisees. These efforts must be done while keeping the focus on the company's Core Purpose and Core Values.

Melanie is also a very active member of the Young President's Organization (YPO) and shares lessons learned from experiences in this organization in each of the newsletters to franchisees. She has found this to be an invaluable outlet for exchanging ideas and being reenergized.

Mission

Our commitment is to continuously strive to exceed our customer's expectations in value and high standards of satisfaction.

Core Purpose

To be a role model in our industry.

Core Values

Integrity: To always conduct oneself with honesty and fairness.

Give Back to the Community

The Grandma Rule: To treat everyone the way you would want your Grandma treated.

Care: To have compassion for family, customers, co-workers, and community.

Be Your Best and Have Fun: To be the best professionally and personally while enjoying life and having fun.

Keys to Success

Mary Ellen feels that TMT International has been so successful, with 119 franchise locations in 25 states as of 2003, because it has selected its franchisees wisely, finding that very optimistic, positive people make the best franchisees. Melanie knows that prospective franchisees are drawn to the company by the eye-catching logo and simple but memorable name, as well as the thought of working with Mary Ellen. Those trucks catch the eyes of their moving customers as well. Once a franchise is well established, word-of-mouth referrals help grow the business. Brig commented that we are not here only to make money—but if we constantly look at our customer and make things easy for them to use our business, the money will be there. Sally Degnan agrees: "We do what we say we are going to do when we say we're going to do it and if not, we apologize for it."

The Future

■ Can the company continue to be a close-knit, family business with the growth it is experiencing?

- How can management help a franchise continue to grow without having already experienced that type of growth themselves? Can Jon's franchisees maintain their guinea pig status far ahead enough for others to learn from them?

- What will happen when Mary Ellen retires?
- Does the home office have the necessary professional talent to grow the business?
- What will happen if Melanie and her brothers decide to sell out and take the company public?

Video Summary for Part One

Google: The Search Engine that Could

Despite the demise of hundreds of Internet-based firms in recent years, the dot-com culture lives on at Google. The ubiquitous search engine has taken the world by storm, offering hyperfast search results without the clutter and commercial interference of other Web sources. This video case study takes us behind the scenes to the computer processes that make Google so popular. Google's co-founders explain how the company began and how it hopes to succeed in the future. The video case also looks at the external environment, including new competitors that might challenge Google in the future.

Discussion Questions

1. As with all organizations, Google operates as an open system. Use open systems thinking to discuss Google's current success and long-term challenges.

2. The opening chapter to this textbook highlights five trends in organizational behavior. Which of these trends are apparent in this video case study?

Video Summaries for Part Two

The Container Store

Walk into any of The Container Store locations and you'll immediately notice two things: great products and very happy and motivated employees. Indeed, *Fortune* magazine places the retailer as either the #1 or #2 among the best companies to work for in America. In this video case study, co-founders Garrett Boone and Kip Tindell tell us what makes The Container Store such a success story in employee satisfaction, motivation, and performance. The program reveals the company's cultural values and business practices that attract so many job applicants and make The Container Store a role model in superior customer service.

Discussion Questions

1. Using the MARS Model of individual behavior and performance, explain how specific practices at The Container Store increase employee performance and customer satisfaction.

2. What applied performance practices are applied at The Container Store? Are they used effectively here? Why or why not?

3. Discuss the importance of values at The Container Store. What values are important at this retailer and how do they influence employee behavior and performance?

Money and Ethics

Is business ethics an oxymoron? Although stock manipulation and other forms of business fraud have occurred for hundreds of years, Barbara Toffler, an ethics professor and former ethics consultant at Arthur Andersen, believes that business can be more ethical. Still, she acknowledges that being ethical isn't easy. Most executives know right from wrong, yet they make unethical decisions when the financial rewards and pressure to perform are high enough. This video case study documents Toffler's experience at Arthur Andersen, where greed overwhelmed ethical values. It also tells the story of grocer Stew Leonard, Sr., who was jailed for tax fraud just two years after being featured in an ethics video.

Discussion Questions

1. Identify the various strategies described in this video program to encourage ethical conduct and discourage or punish wrongdoing. Explain why each of these practices is, or is not, effective.

2. Use the expectancy theory of motivation model, discussed in Chapter 5, to explain why people engage in unethical behavior even though they know it is wrong.

Grin and Bare It (Japanese Smile School)

For many centuries, Japanese culture discouraged the use of the face as a tool for conveying emotion. The mind was all that was important, and the ideal was a face that showed no expression. In spite of these cultural foundations, research has found that contemporary Japanese shoppers spend more money in stores where employees smile more often. Japanese retailers are now sending employees to "smile school" where they learn the subtle art of displaying pleasant emotions. This video case takes us to a smile school class at a large Tokyo department store, where employees are learning how to display sincere smiles and other emotions.

Discussion Questions

1. Why has Japanese culture historically discouraged the use of face to display emotion?

2. In your opinion, why do contemporary shoppers seem to appreciate smiling employees even though Japanese cultural traditions discourage such public display?

3. Given that Japanese employees have traditionally hidden their true emotions at work, do you think Smile School will reduce emotional dissonance? Why or why not?

Pike Place Fish Market

Fifteen years ago, Pike Place Fish Market in Seattle had unhappy employees and was in financial trouble. Rather than close shop, owner John Yokoyama sought help from consultant Jim Bergquist to improve his leadership and energize the workforce. Instead of ruling as a tyrant, Yokoyama learned how to actively involve employees in the business. Soon, staff felt more empowered and gained more enjoyment from their work. They also began to actively have fun at work, including setting goals as a game, throwing fish to each other as sport, and pretending they are "world famous." Today, thanks to these and other strategies described in this video case, Pike Place *is* world famous. The little shop has become a tourist attraction and customers from California to New York call in orders.

Discussion Questions

1. Based on the model of emotions and attitudes in Chapter 4, explain how the changes at Pike Place Fish Market improved job satisfaction and reduced turnover. How did these attitude changes affect customer satisfaction?

2. Goal setting is discussed as an important activity at Pike Place. Evaluate the effectiveness of this goal setting process in the context of the characteristics of effective goals described in Chapter 5 of this textbook.

3. How is coaching applied at Pike Place, and how does this coaching influence employee performance?

Loyalty in the Workplace

Joel Baglole was chosen for a great opportunity, an internship at *The Toronto Star*, Canada's largest daily newspaper. At the end of the year, he happily accepted a job on staff, but six weeks later the prestigious *Wall Street Journal* came calling and he quit the *Star*. Is employee loyalty dead? This video case looks at the current state of loyalty and shows what companies are doing to build a more loyal workforce.

Discussion Questions

1. Which, if any, of the five strategies to build organizational commitment would be effective in this situation involving Joel Baglole?

2. Explain how Joel Baglole's psychological contract is influenced by organizational loyalty in this situation.

Stress in Japan

Stress from overwork has become an epidemic in Japan. This video program consists of two segments that illustrate the degree to which some Japanese employees are overworked, as well as the consequences of their overwork. The first segment follows a typical day of a Japanese manager, from his two-hour morning commute to his late-night working hours. The program also shows how he is under constant pressure to improve efficiency, and experiences a heavy burden and responsibility to do better. The second segment describes how karoshi—death from overwork—took the life of 23-year-old Yoshika. It reconstructs Yoshiko's work life as a graphic artist up to the time when she died suddenly on the job due to a brain hemorrhage.

Discussion Questions

1. Identify the various sources of stress (i.e., stressors) that the Japanese manager in the first segment likely experiences each day. Does he do anything to try to manage his stress?

2. What conditions led up to the karoshi death of Yoshika? Are these conditions commonly found in the country where you live?

Executive Perks

Jack Welch was an American business star as CEO of GE. Now retired, Welch is again receiving attention, but this time for the ethics of executive perks. Based on divorce papers filed by Welch's wife, GE is footing many of Welch's ongoing expenses, including a New York apartment, 24-hour access to a private jet, and a $9 million per year pension. This video case study examines the ethics of executive pay. It considers the difficulties of assessing how much executives should receive as well as the biases that exist in that process. It also refers to some of the more spectacular examples (such as former Tyco CEO Dennis Kozlowski) where executives took more than they gave back.

Discussion Questions

1. Use equity theory to evaluate the fairness of Jack Welch's retirement benefits.

2. Executive remuneration raises several ethical issues. What ethical principles and concepts apply to this discussion of executive pay?

3. Based on concepts in Chapter 12, discuss how power and influence shape executive pay checks.

Video Summaries for Part Three

Profile of Hewlett-Packard CEO Carly Fiorina

Carleton (Carly) Fiorina would much rather talk about computers than the fact she is one of the highest-placed women in corporate America. But as CEO of Hewlett-Packard. Fiorina acknowl-edges that she is still a novelty on the corporate landscape. In this video case, Fiorina discusses her career path from a philosophy major at university to corporate leader. She also acknowledges some of the challenges she faced moving up the corporate ladder and how she overcame them.

Discussion Questions

1. Identify some of the organizational politics that Fiorina experienced along the way up the corporate ladder.
2. Does Fiorina seem to think that men and women lead differently? What evidence in this program supports your opinion?
3. What personal characteristic (described in Part Two of this textbook) does Fiorina emphasize in this interview?

Delta Force & Lee Van Arsdale

The U.S. Army Special Forces unit (called Delta Force) is a special team with a unique role in antiterrorism. In this video case study, LTC Lee Van Arsdale, U.S. Army (Ret.) describes the team dynamics and elements of effective leadership that make Delta Force so effective. The former Delta Force commander recounts the demands on this unit, its high level of decision-making autonomy, and the importance of team dynamics to achieve the unit's goals

Discussion Questions

1. Why are special forces organized into teams rather than a more traditional structure of individuals reporting to a commanding officer?
2. Which leadership theory would be most appropriate for explaining effective leaders in a special forces unit?

Video Summaries for Part Four

SAS Institute

While the computer industry is known for driving employees to 24/7 work schedules, SAS Institute has a completely different culture. The Cary, North Carolina, firm values employee well-being, and demonstrates this with generous benefits and a work schedule that rarely exceeds 35 hours per week. SAS co-founder and CEO Jim Goodnight explains that the employee-friendly culture makes better business sense than many competitors realize.

Discussion Questions

1. Describe the organizational culture at SAS Institute. Is this culture appropriate for SAS's environment?
2. Describe three categories of artifacts through which organizational culture is communicated at SAS.

Hillerich & Bradsby: Makers of the Louisville Slugger

In baseball, the first name in bats is Louisville Slugger, made by Hillerich & Bradsby (H&B).

But with increased competition, H&B needed a new information system to improve information flow. In this video case study, H&B CEO John Hillerich IV describes the company's culture as well as the issues surrounding the decision to introduce a new enterprise resource planning (ERP) computer system. He recalls the challenges introducing the new system and the influence it has had on his organization.

Discussion Questions

1. Describe the organizational culture at Hillerich & Bradsby. Is this culture appropriate for the company's current environment?
2. A large part of this video describes the information and ordering systems problems that H&B experienced prior to introducing the new ERP system. What were the forces for change, as well as the forces resisting change when the new ERP system was introduced?
3. What effect has the new ERP computer system had on H&B organizational structure?

United Files for Bankruptcy

United Airlines went into bankruptcy protection one week after the Air Transportation Stabilization Board turned down the airline's request for a $1.8 billion loan guarantee. This video program reveals employee reactions to this difficult situation. United employees own 55 percent of the company, so the bankruptcy strikes a strong blow to their relationship with the company.

Discussion Questions

1. In your opinion, will United Airlines employees support or resist the changes likely to occur at the company? Why?

2. Does it seem like United Airlines corporate culture is aligned with the environment, or does the company need to change its culture to improve its future viability?

Theory Building and Systematic Research Methods

People need to make sense of their world, so they form theories about the way the world operates. A **theory** is a general set of propositions that describes interrelationships among several concepts. We form theories for the purpose of predicting and explaining the world around us.[1] What does a good theory look like? First, it should be stated as clearly and simply as possible so that the concepts can be measured and there is no ambiguity regarding the theory's propositions. Second, the elements of the theory must be logically consistent with each other, because we cannot test anything that doesn't make sense. Finally, a good theory provides value to society; it helps people understand their world better than they could without the theory.[2]

Theory building is a continuous process that typically includes the inductive and deductive stages shown in Exhibit A.1.[3] The inductive stage draws on personal experience to form a preliminary theory, whereas the deductive stage uses the scientific method to test the theory.

The inductive stage of theory building involves observing the world around us, identifying a pattern of relationships, and then forming a theory from these personal observations. For example, you might casually notice that new employees want their supervisor to give direction, whereas this leadership style irritates long-service employees. From these observations, you form a theory about the effectiveness of directive leadership. (See Chapter 14 for a discussion of this leadership style.)

EXHIBIT A.1   The theory building process

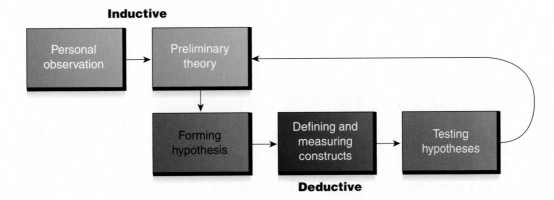

Positivism versus Interpretivism

Research requires an interpretation of reality, and researchers tend to perceive reality in one of two ways. A common view, called **positivism,** is that reality exists independent of people. It is "out there" to be discovered and tested. Positivism is the foundation for most quantitative research (statistical analysis). It assumes that we can measure variables and those variables have fixed relationships with other variables. For example, the positivist perspective says that we could study whether a supportive style of leadership reduces stress. If we find evidence of this, then someone else studying leadership and stress would "discover" the same relationship.

Interpretivism takes a different view of reality. It suggests that reality comes from shared meaning among people in that environment. For example, supportive leadership is a personal interpretation of reality, not something that can be measured across time and people. Interpretivists rely mainly on qualitative data, such as observation and nondirective interviews. They particularly listen to the language people use to understand the common meaning that people have toward various events or phenomena. For example, they might argue that you need to experience and observe supportive leadership to effectively study it. Moreover, you can't really predict relationships because the specific situation shapes reality.[4]

Most OB scholars identify themselves somewhere between the extreme views of positivism and interpretivism. Many believe that inductive research should begin with an interpretivist angle. We should enter a new topic with an open mind and search for shared meaning of people in that situation. In other words, researchers should let the participants define reality rather than let the researcher's preconceived notions shape that reality. This process involves gathering qualitative information and letting this information shape their theory.[5] After the theory emerges, researchers shift to the positivist perspective by quantitatively testing relationships in that theory.

Theory Testing: The Deductive Process

Once a theory has been formed, we shift into the deductive stage of theory building. This process includes forming hypotheses, defining and measuring constructs, and testing hypotheses (see Exhibit A.1). **Hypotheses** make empirically testable declarations that certain variables and their corresponding measures are related in a specific way proposed by the theory. For instance, to find support for the directive leadership theory described earlier, we need to form and then test a specific hypothesis from that theory. One such hypothesis might be: "New employees are more satisfied with supervisors who exhibit a directive rather than nondirective leadership style." Hypotheses are indispensable tools of scientific research, because they provide the vital link between the theory and empirical verification.

Defining and Measuring Constructs

Hypotheses are testable only if we can define and then form measurable indicators of the concepts stated in those hypotheses. Consider the hypothesis in the previous paragraph about new employees and directive leadership. To test this hypothesis, we first need to define the concepts, such as "new employees," "directive leadership," and "supervisor." These are known as **constructs,** because they are abstract ideas constructed by the researcher that can be linked to observable information. Organizational behavior scholars developed the construct called *directive leadership* to help them understand the different effects that leaders have over followers. We can't directly see, taste, or smell directive leadership; instead, we rely on indirect indicators that it exists, such as observing someone giving directions, maintaining clear performance standards, and ensuring that procedures and practices are followed.

As you can see, defining constructs well is very important, because these definitions become the foundation for finding or developing acceptable measures of those constructs. We can't measure directive leadership if we have only a vague idea about what this concept means. The better the definition is, the better our chances are of applying a measure that adequately represents that construct. However, even with a good definition, constructs can be difficult to measure, because the empirical representation must capture several elements in the definition. A measure of directive leadership must be able to identify not only people who give directions, but also those who maintain performance standards and ensure that procedures are followed.

Testing Hypotheses The third step in the deductive process is to collect data for the empirical measures of the variables. Following our directive leadership example, we might conduct a formal survey in which new employees indicate the behavior of their supervisors and their attitudes toward their supervisor. Alternatively, we might design an experiment in which people work with someone who applies either a directive or nondirective leadership style. When the data have been collected, we can use various procedures to statistically test our hypotheses.

A major concern in theory building is that some researchers might inadvertently find support for their theory simply because they use the same information used to form the theory during the inductive stage. Consequently, the deductive stage must collect new data that are completely independent of the data used during the inductive stage. For instance, you might decide to test your theory of directive leadership by studying employees in another organization. Moreover, the inductive process may have relied mainly on personal observation, whereas the deductive process might use survey questionnaires. By studying different samples and using different measurement tools, we minimize the risk of conducting circular research.

Using the Scientific Method

Earlier, we said that the deductive stage of theory building follows the scientific method. The **scientific method** is systematic, controlled, empirical, and critical investigation of hypothetical propositions about the presumed relationships among natural phenomena.[6] There are several elements to this definition, so let's look at each one. First, scientific research is systematic and controlled, because researchers want to rule out all but one explanation for a set of interrelated events. To rule out alternative explanations, we need to control them in some way, such as by keeping them constant or removing them entirely from the environment.

Second, we say that scientific research is empirical because researchers need to use objective reality—or as close as we can get to it—to test theory. They measure observable elements of the environment, such as what a person says or does, rather than relying on their own subjective opinion to draw conclusions. Moreover, scientific research analyzes these data using acceptable principles of mathematics and logic.

Finally, scientific research involves critical investigation. This means that the study's hypotheses, data, methods, and results are openly described so that other experts in the field can properly evaluate this research. It also means that scholars are encouraged to critique and build on previous research. Eventually, the scientific method encourages the refinement and eventually the replacement of a particular theory with one that better suits our understanding of the world.

Grounded Theory: An Alternative Approach

The scientific method dominates the quantitative approach to systematic research, but another approach, called **grounded theory,** dominates research using qualitative methods.[7] Grounded theory is a process of developing knowledge through the constant interplay of data collection, analysis, and theory development. It relies mainly on qualitative methods to form categories and variables, analyze relationships among these concepts, and form a model based on the observations and analysis. Grounded theory combines the inductive stages of theory development by cycling back and forth between data collection and analysis to converge on a robust explanatory model. This ongoing reciprocal process results in theory that is grounded in the data (thus the name grounded theory).

Like the scientific method, grounded theory is a systematic and rigorous process of data collection and analysis. It requires specific steps and documentation, and it adopts a positivist view by assuming that the results are generalizable to other settings. However, grounded theory also takes an interpretivist view by building categories and variables from the perceived realities of the subjects rather than from an assumed universal truth.[8] It also recognizes that personal biases are not easily removed from the research process.

Selected Issues in Organizational Behavior Research

Many issues should be considered in theory building, particularly when we use the deductive process to test hypotheses. Some of the more important issues are sampling, causation, and ethical practices in organizational research.

Sampling in Organizational Research

When finding out why things happen in organizations, we typically gather information from a few sources and then draw conclusions about the larger population. If we survey several employees and determine that older employees are more loyal to their company, then we would like to generalize this statement to all older employees in our population, not just those whom we surveyed. Scientific inquiry generally requires researchers to engage in **representative sampling**—that is, sampling a population in such a way that we can extrapolate the results of that sample to the larger population.

One factor that influences representativeness is whether the sample is selected in an unbiased way from the larger population. Let's suppose that you want to study organizational commitment among employees in your organization. A casual procedure might result in sampling too few employees from the head office and too many located elsewhere in the country. If head office employees actually have higher loyalty than employees located elsewhere, then the biased sampling would cause the results to underestimate the true level of loyalty among employees in the company. If you repeat the process again next year but somehow overweight employees from the head office, the results might wrongly suggest that employees have increased their organizational commitment over the past year. In reality, the only change may be the direction of sampling bias.

How do we minimize sampling bias? The answer is to randomly select the sample. A randomly drawn sample gives each member of the population an equal probability of being chosen, so there is less likelihood that a subgroup within that population dominates the study's results.

The same principle applies to random assignment of subjects to groups in experimental designs. If we want to test the effects of a team development training program, we need to randomly place some employees in the training group and randomly place others in a group that does not receive training. Without this random selection, each group might have different types of employees, so we wouldn't know whether the training explains the differences between the two groups. Moreover, if employees respond differently to the training program, we couldn't be sure that the training program results are representative of the larger population. Of course, random sampling does not necessarily produce a perfectly representative sample, but we do know that this is the best approach to ensure unbiased selection.

The other factor that influences representativeness is sample size. Whenever we select a portion of the population, there will be some error in our estimate of the population values. The larger the sample, the less error will occur in our estimate. Let's suppose that you want to find out how employees in a 500-person firm feel about smoking in the workplace. If you asked 400 of those employees, the information would provide a very good estimate of how the entire workforce in that organization feels. If you survey only 100 employees, the estimate might deviate more from the true population. If you ask only 10 people, the estimate could be quite different from what all 500 employees feel.

Notice that sample size goes hand in hand with random selection. You must have a sufficiently large sample size for the principle of randomization to work effectively. In our example of attitudes toward smoking, we would do a poor job of random selection if our sample consisted of only 10 employees from the 500-person organization. The reason is that these 10 people probably wouldn't capture the diversity of employees throughout the organization. In fact, the more diverse the population, the larger the sample size should be, to provide adequate representation through random selection.

Causation in Organizational Research

Theories present notions about relationships among constructs. Often, these propositions suggest a causal relationship, namely, that one variable has an effect on another variable. When discussing causation, we refer to variables as being independent or dependent. Independent variables are the presumed causes of dependent variables, which are the presumed effects. In our earlier example of directive leadership, the main independent variable (there might be others) would be the supervisor's directive or nondirective leadership style, because we presume that it causes the dependent variable (satisfaction with supervision).

In laboratory experiments (described later), the independent variable is always manipulated by the experimenter. In our research on directive leadership, we might have subjects (new employees) work with supervisors who exhibit directive or nondirective leadership behaviors. If subjects are more satisfied under the directive leaders, then we would be able to infer an association between the independent and dependent variables.

Researchers must satisfy three conditions to provide sufficient evidence of causality between two variables.[9] The first condition of causality is that the variables are empirically associated with each other. An association exists whenever one measure of a variable changes systematically with a measure of another variable. This condition of causality is the easiest to satisfy, because there are several well-known statistical measures of association. A research study might find, for instance, that heterogeneous groups (in which members come from diverse backgrounds) produce more creative solutions to problems. This might be apparent because the measure of creativity (such as number of creative solutions produced within a fixed time) is higher for teams that have a high score on the measure of group heterogeneity. They are statistically associated or correlated with each other.

The second condition of causality is that the independent variable precedes the dependent variable in time. Sometimes this condition is satisfied through simple logic. In our group heterogeneity example, to say that the number of creative solutions caused the group's heterogeneity makes no sense, because the group's heterogeneity existed before it produced the creative solutions. In other situations, however, the temporal relationship among variables is less clear. One example is the ongoing debate about

job satisfaction and organizational commitment. Do companies develop more loyal employees by increasing their job satisfaction, or do changes in organizational loyalty cause changes in job satisfaction? Simple logic does not answer these questions; instead, researchers must use sophisticated longitudinal studies to build up evidence of a temporal relationship between these two variables.

The third requirement for evidence of a causal relationship is that the statistical association between two variables cannot be explained by a third variable. There are many associations that we quickly dismiss as being causally related. For example, the number of storks in an area has a statistical association to the birth rate in that area. We know that storks don't bring babies, so something else must cause the association between these two variables. The real explanation is that both storks and birth rates have a higher incidence in rural areas.

In other studies, the third variable effect is less apparent. Many years ago, before polio vaccines were available, a study in the United States reported a surprisingly strong association between consumption of a certain soft drink and the incidence of polio. Was polio caused by drinking this pop, or did people with polio have a unusual craving for this beverage? Neither. Both polio and consumption of the pop drink were caused by a third variable: climate. The incidence of polio in the summer months and in warmer climates was higher, and people drink more liquids in these climates.[10] As you can see from this example, researchers have a difficult time supporting causal inferences, because third variable effects are sometimes difficult to detect.

Ethics in Organizational Research Organizational behavior researchers need to abide by the ethical standards of the society in which the research is conducted. One of the most important ethical considerations is the individual subject's freedom to participate in the study. For example, it is inappropriate to force employees to fill out a questionnaire or attend an experimental intervention for research purposes only. Moreover, researchers have an obligation to tell potential subjects about any potential risks inherent in the study so that participants can make an informed choice about whether to be involved.

Finally, researchers must be careful to protect the privacy of those who participate in the study. This usually includes letting people know when they are being studied as well as guaranteeing that their individual information will remain confidential (unless permission to publish identities is otherwise granted). Researchers maintain anonymity through careful security of data. The research results usually aggregate data in numbers large enough that they do not reveal the opinions or characteristics of any specific individual. For example, we would report the average absenteeism of employees in a department rather than state the absence rates of each person. When sharing data with other researchers, it is usually necessary to specially code each case so that individual identities are not known.

Research Design Strategies

Thus far, we have described how to build a theory, including the specific elements of empirically testing that theory within the standards of scientific inquiry. But what are the different ways to design a research study so that we get the data necessary to achieve our research objectives? There are many strategies, but they mainly fall under three headings: laboratory experiments, field surveys, and observational research.

Laboratory Experiments   A **laboratory experiment** is any research study in which independent variables and variables outside the researcher's main focus of inquiry can be controlled to some extent. Laboratory experiments are usually located outside the everyday work environment, such as a classroom, simulation lab, or any other artificial setting in which the researcher can manipulate the environment. Organizational behavior researchers sometimes conduct experiments in the workplace (called *field experiments*) in which the independent variable is manipulated. However, the researcher has less control over the effects of extraneous factors in field experiments than in laboratory situations.

Advantages of Laboratory Experiments   Laboratory experiments offer many advantages. By definition, this research method grants a high degree of control over extraneous variables that would otherwise confound the relationships being studied. Suppose we wanted to test the effects of directive leadership on the satisfaction of new employees. We might be concerned that employees are influenced by how much leadership is provided, not just the type of leadership style. An experimental design would allow us to control how often the supervisor exhibited this style so that this extraneous variable does not confound the results.

A second advantage of lab studies is that the independent and dependent variables can be developed more precisely than in a field setting. For example, the researcher can ensure that supervisors in a lab study apply specific directive or nondirective behaviors, whereas real-life supervisors would use a more complex mixture of leadership behaviors. By using more precise measures, we are more certain that we are measuring the intended construct. Thus, if new employees are more satisfied with supervisors in the directive leadership condition, we are more confident that the independent variable was directive leadership rather than some other leadership style.

A third benefit of laboratory experiments is that the independent variable can be distributed more evenly among participants. In our directive leadership study, we can ensure that approximately half the subjects have a directive supervisor, whereas the other half have a nondirective supervisor. In natural settings, we might have trouble finding people who have worked with a nondirective leader and, consequently, we couldn't determine the effects of this condition.

Disadvantages of Laboratory Experiments   With these powerful advantages, you might wonder why laboratory experiments are the least appreciated form of organizational behavior research.[11] One obvious limitation of this research method is that it lacks realism and, consequently, the results might be different in the real world. One argument is that laboratory experiment subjects are less involved than their counterparts in an actual work situation. This is sometimes true, although many lab studies have highly motivated participants. Another criticism is that the extraneous variables controlled in the lab setting might produce a different effect of the independent variable on the dependent variables. This might also be true, but remember that the experimental design controls variables in accordance with the theory and its hypotheses. Consequently, this concern is really a critique of the theory, not the lab study.

Finally, there is the well-known problem that participants who are aware they are being studied may act differently than they normally would. Some participants try to figure out how the researcher wants them to behave and then deliberately try to act that way. Other participants try to upset the experiment by doing just the opposite of what they believe the researcher expects. Still others might act unnaturally simply because they know they are being observed. Fortunately, experimenters are well aware of these potential problems and are usually (although not always) successful at disguising the study's true intent.

Field Surveys

Field surveys collect and analyze information in a natural environment—an office, factory, or other existing location. The researcher takes a snapshot of reality and tries to determine whether elements of that situation (including the attitudes and behaviors of people in that situation) are associated with each other as hypothesized. Everyone does some sort of field research. You might think that people from some states are better drivers than others, so you "test" your theory by looking at the way people with out-of-state license plates drive. Although your methods of data collection might not satisfy scientific standards, this is a form of field research because it takes information from a naturally occurring situation.

Advantages and Disadvantages of Field Surveys
One advantage of field surveys is that the variables often have a more powerful effect than they would in a laboratory experiment. Consider the effect of peer pressure on the behavior of members within the team. In a natural environment, team members would form very strong cohesive bonds over time, whereas a researcher would have difficulty replicating this level of cohesiveness and corresponding peer pressure in a lab setting.

Another advantage of field surveys is that the researcher can study many variables simultaneously, thereby permitting a fuller test of more complex theories. Ironically, this is also a disadvantage of field surveys, because it is difficult for the researcher to contain his or her scientific inquiry. There is a tendency to shift from deductive hypothesis testing to more inductive exploratory browsing through the data. If these two activities become mixed together, the researcher can lose sight of the strict covenants of scientific inquiry.

The main weakness with field surveys is that satisfying the conditions for causal conclusions is very difficult. One reason is that the data are usually collected at one point in time, so the researcher must rely on logic to decide whether the independent variable really preceded the dependent variable. Contrast this with the lab study in which the researcher can usually be confident that the independent variable was applied before the dependent variable occurred. Increasingly, organizational behavior studies use longitudinal research to provide a better indicator of temporal relations among variables, but this is still not as precise as the lab setting. Another reason why causal analysis is difficult in field surveys is that extraneous variables are not controlled as they are in lab studies. Without this control, there is a higher chance that a third variable might explain the relationship between the hypothesized independent and dependent variables.

Observational Research

In their study of brainstorming and creativity, Robert Sutton and Andrew Hargadon observed 24 brainstorming sessions at IDEO, a product design firm in Palo Alto, California. They also attended a dozen "Monday morning meetings," conducted 60 semistructured interviews with IDEO executives and designers, held hundreds of informal discussions with these people, and read through several dozen magazine articles about the company.[12]

Sutton and Hargadon's use of observational research and other qualitative methods was quite appropriate for their research objectives, which were to reexamine the effectiveness of brainstorming beyond the number of ideas generated. Observational research generates a wealth of descriptive accounts about the drama of human existence in organizations. It is a useful vehicle for learning about the complex dynamics of people and their activities, such as brainstorming. (The results of Sutton and Hargadon's study are discussed in Chapter 10.)

Advantages and Disadvantages of Observational Research   Participant observation takes the observation method one step further by having the observer take part in the organization's activities. This experience gives the researcher a fuller understanding of the activities compared to just watching others participate in those activities.

In spite of its intuitive appeal, observational research has a number of weaknesses. The main problem is that the observer is subject to the perceptual screening and organizing biases that we discuss in Chapter 3 of this textbook. There is a tendency to overlook the routine aspects of organizational life, even though they may prove to be the most important data for research purposes. Instead, observers tend to focus on unusual information, such as activities that deviate from what the observer expects. Because observational research usually records only what the observer notices, valuable information is often lost.

Another concern with the observation method is that the researcher's presence and involvement may influence the people he or she is studying. This can be a problem in short-term observations, but in the long term people tend to return to their usual behavior patterns. With ongoing observations, such as Sutton and Hargadon's study of brainstorming sessions at IDEO, employees eventually forget that they are being studied.

Finally, observation is usually a qualitative process, so it is more difficult to empirically test hypotheses with the data. Instead, observational research provides rich information for the inductive stages of theory building. It helps us to form ideas about the way things work in organizations. We begin to see relationships that lay the foundation for new perspectives and theory. We must not confuse this inductive process of theory building with the deductive process of theory testing.

B

Scoring Keys for Self-Assessment Activities

The following pages provide scoring keys for self-assessments that are fully presented in this textbook. Most (although not all) of these self-assessments, as well as the self-assessments that are summarized in this book, are scored on the student CD.

CHAPTER 2
Scoring Key for Self-Monitoring Scale

Scoring Instructions: Use the table below to assign numbers to each box you checked. Insert the number for each statement on the appropriate line below the table. For example, if you checked "Somewhat false" for statement 1 ("In social situations, I have the ability . . ."), you would write a "2" on the line with "(1)" underneath it. After assigning numbers for all 12 statements, add up your scores to estimate your affective and continuance school commitment.

For statement items 1, 2, 3, 4, 5, 6, 7, 8, 10, 11, 13	For statement items 9, 12
Very true = 6	Very true = 1
Somewhat true = 5	Somewhat true = 2
Slightly more true than false = 4	Slightly more true than false = 3
Slightly more false than true = 3	Slightly more false than true = 4
Somewhat false = 2	Somewhat false = 5
Very false = 1	Very false = 6

Sensitive to expressive behavior of others

$$\frac{}{(2)} + \frac{}{(4)} + \frac{}{(5)} + \frac{}{(6)} + \frac{}{(8)} + \frac{}{(11)} = \frac{}{(A)}$$

Ability to modify self-presentation

$$\frac{}{(1)} + \frac{}{(3)} + \frac{}{(7)} + \frac{}{(9)} + \frac{}{(10)} + \frac{}{(12)} + \frac{}{(13)} = \frac{}{(B)}$$

Self-monitoring total score

$$\frac{}{(A)} + \frac{}{(B)} = \frac{}{Total}$$

Interpreting your score: Self-monitoring consists of two dimensions: (1) sensitivity to expressive behavior of others and (2) ability to modify self-presentation. These two dimensions as well as the total score are defined in the following table, along with the range of scores for high, medium, and low levels of each scale.

Self-monitoring dimension and definition	Score interpretation
Sensitive to expressive behavior of others: This scale indicates the extent that you are aware of the feelings and perceptions of others, as expressed by their facial expressions, subtle statements, and other behaviors.	High: 25–36 Medium: 18–24 Low: Below 18
Ability to modify self-presentation: This scale indicates the extent to which you are adept at modifying your behavior in a way that is most appropriate for the situation or social relationship.	High: 30–42 Medium: 21–29 Low: Below 21

(continued)

Self-monitoring dimension and definition	Score interpretation
Self-monitoring total: Self-monitoring refers to an individual's level of sensitivity to the expressive behavior of others and the ability to adapt appropriately to these situational cues.	High: 55–78 Medium: 39–54 Low: Below 39

CHAPTER 3
Scoring Key for Assessing Your General Self-Efficacy

Scoring instructions: To calculate your score on the new general self-efficacy scale, use the following guideline to assign numbers to each box you checked: Strongly agree = 5; Agree = 4; Neutral = 3; Disagree = 2; Strongly disagree = 1. Then add up the numbers to determine your total score.

Interpreting your score: Self-efficacy refers to a person's belief that he or she has the ability, motivation, and resources to complete a task successfully. This particular scale is called a "general" self-efficacy scale because it estimates a person's self-efficacy in a broad range of situations. The average general self-efficacy score varies from one group of people to the next. For example, managers tend to have a somewhat higher general self-efficacy than do young undergraduate psychology students. The following table allows you to compare your general efficacy score to the range of scores among undergraduate psychology students (77 percent female; average age = 23).

General self-efficacy score	Interpretation
Above 34	High level of general self-efficacy
32–34	Above-average level of general self-efficacy
28–31	Average level of general self-efficacy
24–27	Below-average level of general self-efficacy
Below 24	Low level of general self-efficacy

CHAPTER 4
Scoring Key for School Commitment Scale

Scoring instructions: Use the following table to assign numbers to each box you checked. Insert the number for each statement on the appropriate line below the table. For example, if you checked "Moderately dis-

agree" for statement 1 ("I would be very happy . . ."), you would write a "2" on the line with "(1)" underneath it. After assigning numbers for all 12 statements, add up your scores to estimate your affective and continuance school commitment.

For statement items 1, 2, 3, 4, 6, 8, 10, 11, 12	For statement items 5, 7, 9
Strongly agree = 7	Strongly agree = 1
Moderately agree = 6	Moderately agree = 2
Slightly agree = 5	Slightly agree = 3
Neutral = 4	Neutral = 4
Slightly disagree = 3	Slightly disagree = 5
Moderately disagree = 2	Moderately disagree = 6
Strongly disagree = 1	Strongly disagree = 7

Affective commitment

$$\frac{\quad}{(1)} + \frac{\quad}{(3)} + \frac{\quad}{(5)} + \frac{\quad}{(7)} + \frac{\quad}{(9)} + \frac{\quad}{(11)} = \underline{\quad}$$

Continuance commitment

$$\frac{\quad}{(2)} + \frac{\quad}{(4)} + \frac{\quad}{(6)} + \frac{\quad}{(8)} + \frac{\quad}{(10)} + \frac{\quad}{(12)} = \underline{\quad}$$

Interpreting your affective commitment score: This scale measures both affective commitment and continuance commitment. Affective commitment refers to a person's emotional attachment to, identification with, and involvement in a particular organization. In this scale, the organization is the school you are attending. How high or low is your affective commitment? The ideal would be to compare your score with the collective results of other students in your class. You can also compare your score with the following results, which are based on a sample of employees.

Affective commitment score	Interpretation
Above 37	High level of affective commitment
32–36	Above-average level of affective commitment
28–31	Average level of affective commitment
20–27	Below-average level of affective commitment
Below 20	Low level of affective commitment

Interpreting your continuance commitment score: Continuance commitment occurs when employees believe it is in their own personal interest to remain with the organization. People with a high continuance commitment have a strong calculative bond with the organization. In this scale, the organization is the school you are attending. How high or low is your continuance commitment? The ideal would be to compare your score with the collective results of other students in your class. You can also compare your score with the following results, which are based on a sample of employees.

Continuance commitment score	Interpretation
Above 32	High level of continuance commitment
26–31	Above-average level of continuance commitment
21–25	Average level of continuance commitment
13–20	Below-average level of continuance commitment
Below 12	Low level of continuance commitment

CHAPTER 5
Scoring Key for Equity Sensitivity

Scoring instructions: To score this scale, called the Equity Preference Questionnaire (EPQ), complete the three steps below:

Step 1: Write your circled numbers for the items indicated below and add them up.

$$\overline{(1)} + \overline{(2)} + \overline{(3)} + \overline{(4)} + \overline{(5)} + \overline{(6)} + \overline{(7)}$$
$$+ \overline{(10)} = \overline{\text{Subtotal A}}$$

Step 2: The remaining items in the Equity Preference Questionnaire need to be reverse-scored. To calculate a reverse score, subtract the direct score from 6. For example, if you circled 4 in one of these items, the reverse score would be 2 (i.e., 6 – 4 = 2). If you circled 1, the reverse score would be 5 (i.e., 6 – 1 = 5). Calculate the *reverse score* for each of the items indicated below and write them in the space provided. Then calculate Subtotal B by adding up these reverse scores.

$$\overline{(8)} + \overline{(9)} + \overline{(11)} + \overline{(12)} + \overline{(13)} + \overline{(14)} + \overline{(15)}$$
$$+ \overline{(16)} = \overline{\text{Subtotal B}}$$

Step 3: Calculate the total score by summing Subtotal A and Subtotal B.

$$\overline{\text{Subtotal A}} + \overline{\text{Subtotal B}} = \overline{\text{Total}}$$

Interpreting your score: The Equity Preference Questionnaire measures the extent to which you are a "Benevolent," "Equity sensitive," or "Entitled." Generally, people who score as follows fall into one of these categories.

EPQ score	Equity preference category
59–80	Benevolents—tolerant of situations where they are underrewarded
38–58	Equity sensitives—want an outcome/input ratio equal to the ratio of the comparison other
16–37	Entitleds—want to receive proportionately more than others (i.e., like to be overrewarded)

CHAPTER 6
Scoring Key for the Money Attitude Scale

Scoring instructions: This instrument presents three dimensions with a smaller set of items from the original Money Attitude Scale. To calculate your score on each dimension, write the number that you circled in the scale to the corresponding item number in the scoring key below. For example, write the number you circled in the scale's first statement ("I sometimes purchase things . . .") on the line above "Item 1." Then add up the numbers for that dimension. The money attitude total score is calculated by adding up all scores on all dimensions.

Money attitude dimension	Calculation	Your score
Money as power/prestige	$\overline{\text{Item 1}} + \overline{\text{Item 4}} + \overline{\text{Item 7}} + \overline{\text{Item 10}} =$	___
Retention time	$\overline{\text{Item 2}} + \overline{\text{Item 5}} + \overline{\text{Item 8}} + \overline{\text{Item 11}} =$	___
Money anxiety	$\overline{\text{Item 3}} + \overline{\text{Item 6}} + \overline{\text{Item 9}} + \overline{\text{Item 12}} =$	___
Money attitude total	Add up all dimension scores =	___

Interpreting your score: The three Money Attitude Scale dimensions measured here, as well as the total score, are defined as follows:

Money as power/prestige: People with higher scores on this dimension tend to use money to influence and impress others.

Retention time: People with higher scores on this dimension tend to be careful financial planners.

Money anxiety: People with higher scores on this dimension tend to view money as a source of anxiety.

Money attitude total: This is a general estimate of how much respect and attention you give to money.

The following table shows how a sample of MBA students scored on the Money Attitude Scale. The table shows percentiles, that is, the percentage of people with the same or lower score. For example, the table indicates that a score of "12" on the retention scale is quite low because only 20 percent of students would have scored at this level or lower (80 percent scored higher). However, a score of "12" on the prestige scale is quite high because 80 percent of students score at or below this number (only 20 percent scored higher).

Percentile (% with scores at or below this number)	Prestige score	Retention score	Anxiety score	Total money score
Average score	9.89	14.98	12.78	37.64
Highest score	17	20	18	53
90	13	18	16	44
80	12	17	15	42
70	11	17	14	40
60	10	16	14	39
50	10	15	13	38
40	9	14	12	36
30	8	14	11	34
20	7	12	10	32
10	7	11	8	29
Lowest score	4	8	6	23

CHAPTER 7
Scoring Key for Time Stress Scale

Scoring instructions: To estimate how time-stressed you are, add up the number of items where you circled "Yes." Scores range from 0 to 10.

Interpreting your score: One of the major causes of stress in today's fast-paced life is the lack of time to fulfill our obligations. Severely time-stressed people are constantly under pressure to complete work, don't have enough time in the day, and feel trapped in a daily routine. Approximately 25 percent of men and 29 percent of women in their 20s are severely time-stressed. The following guidelines will help you to interpret your time-stress score.

Time stress score	Interpretation
7–10	You seem to be severely time-stressed.
5–6	You seem to be moderately time-stressed.
0–4	You seem to experience little or no time stress.

CHAPTER 8
Scoring Key for Assessing Your Creative Personality

Scoring instructions: Assign plus one (+1) point beside the following words if you put a check mark beside them: Capable, Clever, Confident, Egotistical, Humorous, Individualistic, Informal, Insightful, Intelligent, Inventive, Original, Reflective, Resourceful, Self-confident, Sexy, Snobbish, Unconventional, Wide interests.

Assign negative one (–1) point beside the following words if you put a check mark beside them: Affected, Cautious, Commonplace, Conservative, Conventional, Dissatisfied, Honest, Mannerly, Narrow interests, Sincere, Submissive, Suspicious. Words without a check mark receive a zero. Add up the total score, which will range from –12 to +18.

Interpreting your score: This instrument estimates your creative potential as a personal characteristic. The scale recognizes that creative people are intelligent, persistent, and possess an inventive thinking style. Creative personality varies somewhat from one occupational group to the next. The table below provides norms based on undergraduate and graduate university students.

Creative disposition score	Interpretation
Above +9	You have a high creative personality.
+1 to +9	You have an average creative personality.
Below +1	You have a low creative personality.

CHAPTER 9
Scoring Key for the Team Roles Preferences Scale

Scoring instructions: Write the scores circled for each item on the appropriate line (statement numbers are in brackets), and add up each scale.

Encourager ___ + ___ + ___ = ___
            (6)   (9)   (11)

Gatekeeper ___ + ___ + ___ = ___
            (4)   (10) (13)

Harmonizer ___ + ___ + ___ = ___
            (3)   (8)   (12)

Initiator ___ + ___ + ___ = ___
         (1)   (5)   (14)

Summarizer ___ + ___ + ___ = ___
           (2)   (7)   (15)

For statement items 1, 3, 6, 8, 10	For statement items 2, 4, 5, 7, 9
Completely agree = 5	Completely agree = 1
Agree somewhat = 4	Agree somewhat = 2
Neither agree nor disagree = 3	Neither agree nor disagree = 3
Disagree somewhat = 2	Disagree somewhat = 4
Completely disagree = 1	Completely disagree = 5

Interpreting your score: The five team roles measured here are different from Belbin's roles described in the textbook. However, these roles are also based on academic writing. These five roles are defined as follows, along with the range of scores for high, medium, and low levels of each role. These norms are based on results from a sample of MBA students.

Team role and definition	Interpretation
Encourager: People who score high on this dimension have a strong tendency to praise and support the ideas of other team members, thereby showing warmth and solidarity to the group.	High: 12 and above Medium: 9–11 Low: 8 and below
Gatekeeper: People who score high on this dimension have a strong tendency to encourage all team members to participate in the discussion.	High: 12 and above Medium: 9–11 Low: 8 and below
Harmonizer: People who score high on this dimension have a strong tendency to mediate intragroup conflicts and reduce tension.	High: 11 and above Medium: 9–10 Low: 8 and below
Initiator: People who score high on this dimension have a strong tendency to identify goals for the meeting, including ways to work on those goals.	High: 12 and above Medium: 9–11 Low: 8 and below
Summarizer: People who score high on this dimension have a strong tendency to keep track of what was said in the meeting (i.e., act as the team's memory).	High: 10 and above Medium: 8–9 Low: 7 and below

CHAPTER 10
Scoring Key for the Team Player Inventory

Scoring instructions: To calculate your score on the Team Player Inventory, use the table that follows to assign numbers to each box that you checked. Then add up the numbers to determine your total score.

Interpreting your score: The Team Player Inventory estimates the extent to which you are positively predisposed to working on teams. The higher your score, the more you enjoy working in teams and believe that teamwork is beneficial. The following table allows you to compare your Team Player Inventory score against the norms for this scale. These norms are derived from undergraduate psychology students.

Team player inventory score	Interpretation
40–50	You have a strong predisposition or preference for working in teams.
21–39	You are generally ambivalent about working in teams.
10–20	You have a low predisposition or preference for working in teams.

CHAPTER 11
Scoring Key for the Active Listening Skills Inventory

Scoring instructions: Use the table below to score the response you circled for each statement. Write the score for each item on the appropriate line below the table (statement numbers are in parentheses), and add up each subscale. For example, if you checked "A little" for statement 1 ("I keep an open mind . . ."), you would write a "1" on the line with "(1)" underneath it. Then calculate the overall Active Listening Inventory score by summing all subscales.

For statement items 3, 4, 6, 7, 10, 13	For statement items 1, 2, 5, 8, 9, 11, 12, 14, 15
Not at all = 3	Not at all = 0
A little = 2	A little = 1
Somewhat = 1	Somewhat = 2
Very much = 0	Very much = 3

Avoiding interruption (AI) $\dfrac{\quad}{(3)} + \dfrac{\quad}{(7)} + \dfrac{\quad}{(15)} = \dfrac{\quad}{}$

Maintaining interest (MI) $\dfrac{\quad}{(6)} + \dfrac{\quad}{(9)} + \dfrac{\quad}{(14)} = \dfrac{\quad}{}$

Postponing evaluation (PE) $\dfrac{\quad}{(1)} + \dfrac{\quad}{(5)} + \dfrac{\quad}{(13)} = \dfrac{\quad}{}$

Organizing information (OI) $\dfrac{\quad}{(2)} + \dfrac{\quad}{(10)} + \dfrac{\quad}{(12)} = \dfrac{\quad}{}$

Showing interest (SI) $\dfrac{\quad}{(4)} + \dfrac{\quad}{(8)} + \dfrac{\quad}{(11)} = \dfrac{\quad}{}$

Active listening (total score): $\dfrac{\quad}{}$

Interpreting your score: The five active listening dimensions and the overall active listening scale measured here are defined below, along with the range of scores for high, medium, and low levels of each dimension based on a sample of MBA students:

Active listening dimension and definition	Score interpretation
Avoiding interruption: People with high scores on this dimension have a strong tendency to let the speaker finish his or her statements before responding.	High: 8–9 Medium: 5–7 Low: Below 5
Maintaining interest: People with high scores on this dimension have a strong tendency to remain focused and concentrate on what the speaker is saying even when the conversation is boring or the information is well known.	High: 6–9 Medium: 3–5 Low: Below 3
Postponing evaluation: People with high scores on this dimension have a strong tendency to keep an open mind and avoid evaluating what the speaker is saying until the speaker has finished.	High: 7–9 Medium: 4–6 Low: Below 4
Organizing information: People with high scores on this dimension have a strong tendency to actively organize the speaker's ideas into meaningful categories.	High: 8–9 Medium: 5–7 Low: Below 5
Showing interest: People with high scores on this dimension have a strong tendency to use nonverbal gestures or brief verbal acknowledgments to demonstrate that they are paying attention to the speaker.	High: 7–9 Medium: 5–6 Low: Below 5
Active listening (total): People with high scores on this total active listening scale have a strong tendency to actively sense the sender's signals, evaluate them accurately, and respond appropriately.	High: Above 31 Medium: 26–31 Low: Below 26

Note: The Active Listening Inventory does not explicitly measure two other dimensions of active listening, empathizing and providing feedback. Empathizing is difficult to measure with behaviors; providing feedback involves similar behaviors as showing interest.

CHAPTER 12
Scoring Key for the Upward Influence Scale

Scoring instructions: To calculate your scores on the Upward Influence Scale, write the number circled for each statement on the appropriate line below (statement numbers are in parentheses) and add up each scale.

Assertiveness $\dfrac{\quad}{(8)} + \dfrac{\quad}{(15)} + \dfrac{\quad}{(16)} = \dfrac{\quad}{}$

Exchange $\dfrac{\quad}{(2)} + \dfrac{\quad}{(5)} + \dfrac{\quad}{(13)} = \dfrac{\quad}{}$

Coalition formation $\dfrac{\quad}{(1)} + \dfrac{\quad}{(11)} + \dfrac{\quad}{(18)} = \dfrac{\quad}{}$

Upward appeal $\dfrac{\quad}{(4)} + \dfrac{\quad}{(12)} + \dfrac{\quad}{(17)} = \dfrac{\quad}{}$

Ingratiation $\dfrac{\quad}{(3)} + \dfrac{\quad}{(6)} + \dfrac{\quad}{(9)} = \dfrac{\quad}{}$

Persuasion $\dfrac{\quad}{(7)} + \dfrac{\quad}{(10)} + \dfrac{\quad}{(14)} = \dfrac{\quad}{}$

Interpreting your score: Influence refers to any behavior that attempts to alter someone's attitudes or behavior. There are several types of influence, including the following six measured by this instrument: assertiveness, exchange, coalition formation, upward appeal, ingratiation, and persuasion. This instrument assesses your preference for using each type of influence on your boss or other people at higher levels in the organization. Each scale has a potential score ranging from 3 to 15 points. Higher scores indicate that the person has a higher preference for that particular tactic. The six upward influence dimensions measured here are defined below, along with the range of scores for high, medium, and low levels of each tactic.

Influence tactic and definition	Score interpretation
Assertiveness: Assertiveness involves actively applying legitimate and coercive power to influence others. This tactic includes persistently reminding others of their obligations, frequently checking their work, confronting them, and using threats of sanctions to force compliance.	High: 8–15 Medium: 5–7 Low: 3–4

(continued)

Influence tactic and definition	Score interpretation
Exchange: Exchange involves the promise of benefits or resources in exchange for the target person's compliance with your request. This tactic also includes reminding the target of past benefits or favors with the expectation that the target will now make up for that debt. Negotiation is also part of the exchange strategy.	High: 10–15 Medium: 6–9 Low: 3–5
Coalition formation: Coalition formation occurs when a group of people with common interests band together to influence others. This tactic pools the power and resources of many people, so the coalition potentially has more influence than each person operating alone.	High: 11–15 Medium: 7–10 Low: 3–6
Upward appeal: Upward appeal occurs when you rely on support from a higher level person to influence others. In effect, this is a form of coalition in which one or more members have higher authority or expertise.	High: 9–15 Medium: 6–8 Low: 3–5
Ingratiation: Flattering your boss in front of others, helping your boss with his or her work, agreeing with your boss's ideas, and asking for your boss's advice are all examples of ingratiation. This tactic increases the perceived similarity of the source of ingratiation to the target person.	High: 13–15 Medium: 9–12 Low: 3–8
Persuasion: Persuasion refers to using logical and emotional appeals to change others' attitudes. According to several studies, it is also the most common upward influence strategy.	High: 13–15 Medium: 9–12 Low: 3–8

CHAPTER 13
Scoring Key for the Dutch Test for Conflict Handling

Scoring instructions: Write the number circled for each item on the appropriate line (statement number is under the line), and add up each subscale.

Interpreting your score: The five conflict handling dimensions are defined as follows, along with the range of scores for high, medium, and low levels of each dimension:

Conflict-handling dimension	Calculation	Your score
Yielding	$\dfrac{}{\text{Item 1}} + \dfrac{}{\text{Item 6}} + \dfrac{}{\text{Item 11}} + \dfrac{}{\text{Item 16}} =$	____
Compromising	$\dfrac{}{\text{Item 2}} + \dfrac{}{\text{Item 7}} + \dfrac{}{\text{Item 12}} + \dfrac{}{\text{Item 17}} =$	____
Forcing	$\dfrac{}{\text{Item 3}} + \dfrac{}{\text{Item 8}} + \dfrac{}{\text{Item 13}} + \dfrac{}{\text{Item 18}} =$	____
Problem solving	$\dfrac{}{\text{Item 4}} + \dfrac{}{\text{Item 9}} + \dfrac{}{\text{Item 14}} + \dfrac{}{\text{Item 19}} =$	____
Avoiding	$\dfrac{}{\text{Item 5}} + \dfrac{}{\text{Item 10}} + \dfrac{}{\text{Item 15}} + \dfrac{}{\text{Item 20}} =$	____

Conflict-handling dimension and definition	Score interpretation
Yielding: Yielding involves giving in completely to the other side's wishes, or at least cooperating with little or no attention to your own interests. This style involves making unilateral concessions, unconditional promises, and offering help with no expectation of reciprocal help.	High: 14–20 Medium: 9–13 Low: 4–8
Compromising: Compromising involves looking for a position in which your losses are offset by equally valued gains. It involves matching the other party's concessions, making conditional promises or threats, and actively searching for a middle ground between the interests of the two parties.	High: 17–20 Medium: 11–16 Low: 4–10
Forcing: Forcing involves trying to win the conflict at the other's expense. It includes "hard" influence tactics, particularly assertiveness, to get one's own way.	High: 15–20 Medium: 9–14 Low: 4–8
Problem solving: Problem solving tries to find a mutually beneficial solution for both parties. Information sharing is an important feature of this style because both parties need to identify common ground and potential solutions that satisfy both (or all) of them.	High: 17–20 Medium: 11–16 Low: 4–10
Avoiding: Avoiding tries to smooth over or avoid conflict situations altogether. It represents a low concern for both self and the other party. In other words, avoiders try to suppress thinking about the conflict.	High: 13–20 Medium: 8–12 Low: 4–7

CHAPTER **14**
Scoring Key for Leadership Dimensions Instrument

Transactional Leadership

Scoring instructions: Add up scores for the odd numbered items (i.e., 1, 3, 5, 7, 9, 11, 13, 15). Maximum score is 40.

Interpreting your score: Transactional leadership is "managing"—helping organizations to achieve their current objectives more efficiently, such as by linking job performance to valued rewards and ensuring that employees have the resources needed to get the job done. The following table shows the range of scores for high, medium, and low levels of transactional leadership.

Transactional leadership score	Interpretation
32–40	The person you evaluated seems to be a highly transactional leader.
25–31	The person you evaluated seems to be a moderately transactional leader.
Below 25	The person you evaluated seems to display few characteristics of a transactional leader.

Transformational Leadership

Scoring instructions: Add up scores for the even-numbered items (i.e., 2, 4, 6, 8, 10, 12, 14, 16). Maximum score is 40. Higher scores indicate that your supervisor has a strong inclination toward transformational leadership.

Interpreting your score: Transformational leadership involves changing teams or organizations by creating, communicating, and modeling a vision for the organization or work unit and inspiring employees to strive for that vision. The following table shows the range of scores for high, medium, and low levels of transformational leadership.

Transformational leadership score	Interpretation
32–40	The person you evaluated seems to be a highly transformational leader.
25–31	The person you evaluated seems to be a moderately transformational leader.
Below 25	The person you evaluated seems to display few characteristics of a transformational leader.

CHAPTER **15**
Scoring Key for the Organizational Structure Preference Scale

Scoring instructions: Use the table below to assign numbers to each response you circled. Insert the number for each statement on the appropriate line below the table. For example, if you checked "Not at all" for item 1 ("A person's career ladder . . ."), you would write a "0" on the line with "(1)" underneath it. After assigning numbers for all 15 statements, add up the scores to estimate your degree of preference for a tall hierarchy, formalization, and centralization. Then calculate the overall score by summing all scales.

For statement items 2, 3, 8, 10, 11, 12, 14, 15	For statement items 1, 4, 5, 6, 7, 9, 13
Not at all = 3	Not at all = 0
A little = 2	A little = 1
Somewhat = 1	Somewhat = 2
Very much = 0	Very much = 3

Tall hierarchy (H)

$$\frac{\quad}{(1)} + \frac{\quad}{(4)} + \frac{\quad}{(10)} + \frac{\quad}{(12)} + \frac{\quad}{(15)} = \frac{\quad}{(H)}$$

Formalization (F)

$$\frac{\quad}{(2)} + \frac{\quad}{(6)} + \frac{\quad}{(8)} + \frac{\quad}{(11)} + \frac{\quad}{(13)} = \frac{\quad}{(F)}$$

Centralization (C)

$$\frac{\quad}{(3)} + \frac{\quad}{(5)} + \frac{\quad}{(7)} + \frac{\quad}{(9)} + \frac{\quad}{(14)} = \frac{\quad}{(C)}$$

Total score (mechanistic)

$$\frac{\quad}{(H)} + \frac{\quad}{(F)} + \frac{\quad}{(C)} = \frac{\quad}{Total}$$

Interpreting your score: The three organizational structure dimensions and the overall score are defined below, along with the range of scores for high, medium, and low levels of each dimension based on a sample of MBA students.

Organizational structure dimension and definition	Interpretation
Tall hierarchy: People with high scores on this dimension prefer to work in organizations with several levels of hierarchy and a narrow span of control (few employees per supervisor).	High: 11–15 Medium: 6–10 Low: Below 6

(continued)

Organizational structure dimension and definition	Interpretation
Formalization: People with high scores on this dimension prefer to work in organizations where jobs are clearly defined with limited discretion.	High: 12–15 Medium: 9–11 Low: Below 9
Centralization: People with high scores on this dimension prefer to work in organizations where decision making occurs mainly among top management rather than being spread out to lower level staff.	High: 10–15 Medium: 7–9 Low: Below 7
Total score (mechanistic): People with high scores on this dimension prefer to work in mechanistic organizations, whereas those with low scores prefer to work in organic organizational structures. Mechanistic structures are characterized by a narrow span of control and high degree of formalization and centralization. Organic structures have a wide span of control, little formalization, and decentralized decision making.	High: 30–45 Medium: 22–29 Low: Below 22

lows, along with the range of scores for high, medium, and low levels of each dimension based on a sample of MBA students.

Corporate culture dimension and definition	Score interpretation
Control culture: This culture values the role of senior executives to lead the organization. Its goal is to keep everyone aligned and under control.	High: 3–6 Medium: 1–2 Low: 0
Performance culture: This culture values individual and organizational performance and strives for effectiveness and efficiency.	High: 5–6 Medium: 3–4 Low: 0–2
Relationship culture: This culture values nurturing and well-being. It considers open communication, fairness, teamwork, and sharing a vital part of organizational life.	High: 6 Medium: 4–5 Low: 0–3
Responsive culture: This culture values its ability to keep in tune with the external environment, including being competitive and realizing new opportunities.	High: 6 Medium: 4–5 Low: 0–3

CHAPTER 16
Scoring Key for the Corporate Culture Preference Scale

Scoring instructions: In each space below, write in a "1" if you circled the statement and "0" if you did not. Then add up the scores for each subscale.

Control culture

$$\overline{(2a)} + \overline{(5a)} + \overline{(6b)} + \overline{(8b)} + \overline{(11b)} + \overline{(12a)} = \overline{\quad}$$

Performance culture

$$\overline{(1b)} + \overline{(3b)} + \overline{(5b)} + \overline{(6a)} + \overline{(7a)} + \overline{(9b)} = \overline{\quad}$$

Relationship culture

$$\overline{(1a)} + \overline{(3a)} + \overline{(4b)} + \overline{(8a)} + \overline{(10b)} + \overline{(12b)} = \overline{\quad}$$

Responsive culture

$$\overline{(2b)} + \overline{(4a)} + \overline{(7b)} + \overline{(9a)} + \overline{(10a)} + \overline{(11a)} = \overline{\quad}$$

Interpreting your score: These corporate cultures may be found in many organizations, but they represent only four of many possible organizational cultures. Also, keep in mind none of these subscales is inherently good or bad. Each is effective in different situations. The four corporate cultures are defined as fol-

CHAPTER 17
Scoring Key for the Tolerance of Change Scale

Scoring instructions: Use the table below to assign numbers to each box you checked. For example, if you checked "Moderately disagree" for statement 1 ("An expert who doesn't come up . . ."), you would write a "2" beside that statement. After assigning numbers for all 16 statements, add up your scores to estimate your tolerance for change.

For statement items 2, 4, 6, 8, 10, 12, 14, 16	For statement items 1, 3, 5, 7, 9, 11, 13, 15
Strongly agree = 7	Strongly agree = 1
Moderately agree = 6	Moderately agree = 2
Slightly agree = 5	Slightly agree = 3
Neutral = 4	Neutral = 4
Slightly disagree = 3	Slightly disagree = 5
Moderately disagree = 2	Moderately disagree = 6
Strongly disagree = 1	Strongly disagree = 7

Interpreting your score: This measurement instrument is formally known as the "tolerance of ambiguity" scale. Although it was developed 40 years ago, the instrument is still used today in research. People with a high tolerance of ambiguity are comfortable with uncertainty, sudden change, and new situations. These are characteristics of the hyperfast changes occurring in many organizations today. The table to the right indicates the range of scores for high, medium, and low tolerance for change. These norms are based on results for MBA students.

Tolerance for change score	interpretation
81–112	You seem to have a high tolerance for change.
63–80	You seem to have a moderate level of tolerance for change.
Below 63	You seem to have a low degree of tolerance for change. Instead, you prefer stable work environments.

GLOSSARY

The number(s) in parentheses indicates the chapter(s) where the term is formally defined. See the subject index for other places in the textbook where the term is discussed.

A

ability Both the natural aptitudes and learned capabilities required to successfully complete a task. (2)

action learning A variety of experiential learning activities in which employees are involved in a "real, complex, and stressful problem," usually in teams, with immediate relevance to the company. (3)

action research A data-based, problem-oriented process that diagnoses the need for change, introduces the intervention, and then evaluates and stabilizes the desired changes. (17)

adaptive culture An organizational culture in which employees focus on the changing needs of customers and other stakeholders and support initiatives to keep pace with those changes. (16)

alternative dispute resolution (ADR) A third-party dispute resolution process that includes mediation, typically followed by arbitration. (13)

appreciative inquiry An organizational change process that directs attention away from the group's own problems and focuses participants on the group's potential and positive elements. (17)

artifacts The observable symbols and signs of an organization's culture. (16)

attitudes The cluster of beliefs, assessed feelings, and behavioral intentions toward an object. (4)

attribution process The perceptual process of deciding whether an observed behavior or event is caused largely by internal or external factors. (3)

B

autonomy The degree to which a job gives employees the freedom, independence, and discretion to schedule their work and determine the procedures used in completing it. (6)

balanced scorecard A reward system that pays bonuses for improved results on a composite of financial, customer, internal process, and employee factors. (6)

behavior modification A theory that explains learning in terms of the antecedents and consequences of behavior. (3)

bicultural audit A diagnosis of cultural relations between companies prior to a merger and a determination of the extent to which cultural clashes are likely to occur. (16)

"Big Five" personality dimensions The five abstract dimensions representing most personality traits: conscientiousness, agreeableness, neuroticism, openness to experience, and extroversion (CANOE). (2)

bounded rationality Processing limited and imperfect information and satisficing rather than maximizing when choosing among alternatives. (8)

brainstorming A freewheeling, face-to-face meeting where team members aren't allowed to criticize but are encouraged to speak freely, generate as many ideas as possible, and build on the ideas of others. (10)

C

care principle The moral principle stating that we should benefit those with whom we have special relationships. (2)

centrality The degree and nature of interdependence between the powerholder and others. (12)

centralization The degree to which formal decision authority is held by a small group of people, typically those at the top of the organizational hierarchy. (15)

ceremonies Planned and usually dramatic displays of organizational culture, conducted specifically for the benefit of an audience. (16)

change agent Anyone who possesses enough knowledge and power to guide and facilitate the organizational change effort. (17)

coalition An informal group that attempts to influence people outside the group by pooling the resources and power of its members. (12)

codetermination A form of employee involvement required by some governments that typically operates at the work site as works councils and at the corporate level as supervisory boards. (8)

cognitive dissonance A psychological tension that occurs when people perceive an inconsistency between their beliefs, feelings, and behavior. (4)

collective self-regulation A feature of sociotechnical systems in which the team has autonomy to divide work among its members as well as to coordinate that work. (10)

collectivism The extent to which people value duty to groups to which they belong and to group harmony. (2)

communication The process by which information is transmitted and understood between two or more people. (11)

communities of practice Groups bound together by shared expertise and passion for a particular activity or interest. (1) (9)

competencies Skills, knowledge, aptitudes, and other characteristics of people that lead to superior performance. (2)

conflict The process in which one party perceives that its interests are being opposed or negatively affected by another party. (13)

conflict management Interventions that alter the level and form of conflict in ways that maximize its benefits and minimize its dysfunctional consequences. (13)

conscientiousness   A "Big Five" personality dimension that characterizes people who are careful, dependable, and self-disciplined. (2)

constructive conflict   Debate among team members about their different perceptions of an issue in a way that keeps the conflict focused on the task rather than people. (10)

constructs   Abstract ideas constructed by researchers that can be linked to observable information. (App. A)

contact hypothesis   A theory stating that the more we interact with someone, the less we rely on stereotypes to understand that person. (3)

contingency approach   The idea that a particular action may have different consequences in different situations. (1)

contingent work   Any job in which the individual does not have an explicit or implicit contract for long-term employment or in which the minimum hours of work can vary in a nonsystematic way. (1)

continuance commitment   A calculative decision to remain with an organization because quitting would be costly. (4)

corporate social responsibility (CSR) An organization's moral obligation toward its stakeholders. (1)

counterpower   The capacity of a person, team, or organization to keep a more powerful person or group in the exchange relationship. (12)

counterproductive work behaviors (CWBs)   Voluntary behaviors that are potentially harmful to the organization's effectiveness. (2)

creativity   Ability to develop an original product, service, or idea that makes a socially recognized contribution. (8)

D

decision making   A conscious process of making choices among one or more alternatives with the intention of moving toward some desired state of affairs. (8)

Delphi technique   A structured team decision-making process of

systematically pooling the collective knowledge of experts on a particular subject to make decisions, predict the future, or identify opposing views. (10)

dialogue   A process of conversation among team members in which they learn about each other's mental models and assumptions and eventually form a common model for thinking within the team. (10)

distributive justice   The perceived fairness in outcomes we receive relative to our contributions and the outcomes and contributions of others. (5)

distributive justice principle   The moral principle stating that people who are similar should be rewarded similarly, and those who are dissimilar should be rewarded differently in proportion to those differences. (2)

divergent thinking   Reframing a problem in a unique way and generating different approaches to the issue. (8)

divisional structure   An organizational structure that groups employees around geographic areas, clients, or outputs. (15)

E

effort-to-performance (E → P) expectancy   The individual's perceived probability that his or her effort will result in a particular level of performance. (5)

electronic brainstorming   Using special computer software, participants share ideas while minimizing the team dynamics problems inherent in traditional brainstorming sessions. (10)

emotional contagion   The automatic and unconscious tendency to mimic and synchronize one's own nonverbal behaviors with those of other people. (11)

emotional dissonance   A conflict between a person's required and true emotions. (4)

emotional intelligence (EI)   The ability to perceive and express emotion, assimilate emotion in thought, understand and reason with emotion, and regulate emotion in oneself and others. (4)

emotional labor   The effort, planning, and control needed to express organizationally desired emotions during interpersonal transactions. (4)

emotions   Psychological and physiological episodes toward an object, person, or event that create a state of readiness. (4)

empathy   A person's understanding and sensitivity to the feelings, thoughts, and situation of others. (3)

employability   An employment relationship in which people perform a variety of work activities (rather than holding specific jobs) and are expected to continuously learn skills that will keep them employed. (1)

employee assistance programs (EAPs) Counseling services that help employees overcome personal or organizational stressors and adopt more effective coping mechanisms. (7)

employee involvement   The degree to which employees influence how their work is organized and carried out. (8)

employee stock ownership plans (ESOPs)   A reward system that encourages employees to buy shares of the company. (6)

empowerment   A psychological concept in which people experience more self-determination, meaning, competence, and impact regarding their role in the organization. (6)

equity sensitivity   A person's outcome/input preferences and reaction to various outcome/input ratios. (5)

equity theory   A theory that explains how people develop perceptions of fairness in the distribution and exchange of resources. (5)

ERG theory   Alderfer's motivation theory of three instinctive needs arranged in a hierarchy, in which people progress to the next higher need when a lower one is fulfilled and regress to a lower need if unable to fulfill a higher one. (5)

escalation of commitment   The tendency to repeat an apparently bad decision or allocate more resources to a failing course of action. (8)

ethical sensitivity   A personal characteristic that enables people to recognize the presence and determine the relative importance of an ethical issue. (2)

ethics   The study of moral principles or values that determine whether actions are right or wrong and outcomes are good or bad. (1) (2)

evaluation apprehension   When individuals are reluctant to mention ideas that seem silly because they believe (often correctly) that other team members are silently evaluating them. (10)

executive coaching   A helping relationship using behavioral methods to assist clients in identifying and achieving goals for their professional performance and personal satisfaction. (5)

existence needs   A person's physiological and physically related safety needs, such as the need for food, shelter, and safe working conditions. (5)

exit-voice-loyalty-neglect (EVNL) model   The four ways, as indicated in the name, employees respond to job dissatisfaction. (4)

expectancy theory   The motivation theory based on the idea that work effort is directed toward behaviors that people believe will lead to desired outcomes. (5)

extinction   A decrease in target behavior that occurs because no consequence follows it. (3)

extroversion   A "Big Five" personality dimension that characterizes people who are outgoing, talkative, sociable, and assertive. (2)

F

feedback   Any information that people receive about the consequences of their behavior. (5)

Fiedler's contingency model   Developed by Fred Fiedler, a model that suggests that leader effectiveness depends on whether the person's natural leadership style is appropriately matched to the situation. (14)

field surveys   A research design strategy that involves collecting and analyzing information in a natural environment, an office, a factory, or other existing location. (App. A)

flaming   The act of sending an emotionally charged electronic mail message to others. (11)

force field analysis   Lewin's model of systemwide change that helps change agents diagnose the forces that drive and restrain proposed organizational change. (17)

formalization   The degree to which organizations standardize behavior through rules, procedures, formal training, and related mechanisms. (15)

frustration-regression process   A process whereby a person who is unable to satisfy a higher need becomes frustrated and regresses to the next lower need level. (5)

functional structure   An organizational structure that organizes employees around specific knowledge or other resources. (15)

fundamental attribution error   The tendency to attribute the behavior of other people more to internal than to external factors. (3)

G

gainsharing plan   A reward system in which team members earn bonuses for reducing costs and increasing labor efficiency in their work process. (6)

general adaptation syndrome   A model of the stress experience, consisting of three stages: alarm reaction, resistance, and exhaustion. (7)

globalization   Economic, social, and cultural connectivity (and interdependence) with people in other parts of the world. (1)

goals   The immediate or ultimate objectives that employees are trying to accomplish from their work effort. (5)

goal setting   The process of motivating employees and clarifying their role perceptions by establishing performance objectives. (5)

grafting   The process of acquiring knowledge by hiring individuals or buying entire companies. (1)

grapevine   An unstructured and informal communication network founded on social relationships rather than organizational charts or job descriptions. (11)

grounded theory   A process of developing theory through the constant interplay between data gathering and the development of theoretical concepts. (1) (App. A)

group   Two or more people with a unifying relationship. (9)

group polarization   The tendency of teams to make more extreme decisions than individuals working alone. (10)

groupthink   The tendency of highly cohesive groups to value consensus at the price of decision quality. (10)

growth needs   A person's needs for self-esteem through personal achievement as well as for self-actualization. (5)

H

halo error   A perceptual error whereby our general impression of a person, usually based on one prominent characteristic, colors the perception of other characteristics of that person. (3)

heterogeneous teams   Teams that include members with diverse personal characteristics and backgrounds. (9)

homogeneous teams   Teams that include members with common technical expertise, demographics (age, sex), ethnicity, experiences, or values. (9)

hypotheses   Statements making empirically testable declarations that certain variables and their corresponding measures are related in a specific way proposed by theory.

I

implicit favorite   The decision maker's preferred alternative against which all other choices are judged. (8)

implicit leadership theory   A theory hypothesizing that perceptual processes cause people to inflate the importance of leadership as the cause of organizational events. (14)

impression management   The practice of actively shaping one's public image. (12)

individualism   The extent to which a person values independence and personal uniqueness. (2)

individual rights principle   The moral principle stating that every person is entitled to legal and human rights. (2)

influence   Any behavior that attempts to alter another person's attitudes or behavior. (12)

informal groups   Two or more people who form a unifying relationship around personal rather than organizational goals. (9)

information overload   A condition in which the volume of information received exceeds the person's capacity to process it. (11)

ingratiation   Any attempt to increase liking by, or perceived similarity to, the targeted person. (12)

inoculation effect   A persuasive communication strategy of warning listeners that others will try to influence them in the future and that they should be wary of the opponent's arguments. (12)

intellectual capital   The sum of an organization's human capital, structural capital, and relationship capital. (1)

interpretivism   The view held in many qualitative studies that reality comes from shared meaning among people in that environment. (App. A)

introversion   A "Big Five" personality dimension that characterizes people who are quiet, shy, and cautious. (2)

intuition   The ability to know when a problem or opportunity exists and select the best course of action without conscious reasoning. (8)

J

jargon   The technical language and acronyms as well as recognized words with specialized meanings in specific organizations or groups. (11)

job burnout   The process of emotional exhaustion, cynicism, and reduced efficacy (lower feelings of personal accomplishment) resulting from prolonged exposure to stress. (7)

job characteristics model   A job design model that relates the motivational properties of jobs to specific personal and organizational consequences of those properties. (6)

job design   The process of assigning tasks to a job, including the interdependency of those tasks with other jobs. (6)

job enlargement   Increasing the number of tasks employees perform within their job. (6)

job enrichment   Giving employees more responsibility for scheduling, coordinating, and planning their own work. (6)

job evaluation   Systematically appraising the worth of jobs within an organization by measuring their required skill, effort, responsibility, and working conditions. (6)

job feedback   The degree to which employees can determine how well they are doing based on direct sensory information from the job itself. (6)

job rotation   The practice of moving employees from one job to another. (6)

job satisfaction   A person's evaluation of his or her job and work context. (2) (4)

job specialization   The result of division of labor in which each job includes a subset of the tasks required to complete the product or service. (6)

Johari Window   The model of personal and interpersonal understanding that encourages disclosure and feedback to increase the open area and reduce the blind, hidden, and unknown areas of oneself. (3)

joint optimization   A key requirement in sociotechnical systems theory that a balance must be struck between social and technical systems to maximize an operation's effectiveness. (10)

K

knowledge management   Any structured activity that improves an organization's capacity to acquire, share, and use knowledge in ways that improve its survival and success. (1)

L

laboratory experiment   Any research study in which independent variables and variables outside the researcher's main focus of inquiry can be controlled to some extent. (App. A)

leadership   Influencing, motivating, and enabling others to contribute to the effectiveness and success of the organizations of which they are members. (14)

Leadership Grid   A leadership model that assesses leadership effectiveness in terms of the person's level of task-oriented and people-oriented style. (14)

leadership substitutes   A theory that identifies contingencies that either limit the leader's ability to influence subordinates or make that particular leadership style unnecessary. (14)

learning   A relatively permanent change in behavior (or behavior tendency) that occurs as a result of a person's interaction with the environment. (3)

learning orientation   The extent that an organization or individual supports the learning process, particularly opportunities to acquire knowledge through experience and experimentation. (3)

legitimate power   The capacity to influence others through formal authority. (12)

locus of control   A personality trait referring to the extent to which people believe events are within their control. (2)

M

Machiavellian values   The belief that deceit is a natural and acceptable way to influence others. (12)

management by objectives (MBO)   A participative goal-setting process in which organizational objectives are cascaded down to work units and individual employees. (5)

management by walking around (MBWA)   A communication practice in which executives get out of their offices and learn from others in the organization through face-to-face dialogue. (11)

matrix structure   A type of departmentalization that overlays two organizational forms in order to leverage the benefits of both. (15)

mechanistic structure   An organizational structure with a narrow span of control and high degrees of formalization and centralization. (15)

media richness   The data-carrying capacity of a communication medium, including the volume and variety of information it can transmit. (11)

mental imagery   Mentally practicing a task and visualizing its successful completion. (6)

mental models The broad worldviews or "theories in-use" that people rely on to guide their perceptions and behaviors. (3)

mentoring The process of learning the ropes of organizational life from a senior person within the company. (12)

moral intensity The degree to which an issue demands the application of ethical principles. (2)

motivation The forces within a person that affect his or her direction, intensity, and persistence of voluntary behavior. (2) (5)

motivator-hygiene theory Herzberg's theory stating that employees are primarily motivated by growth and esteem needs, not by lower-level needs. (6)

Myers-Briggs Type Indicator (MBTI) A personality inventory designed to identify individuals' basic preferences for perceiving and processing information. (2)

N

need for achievement (nAch) A learned need in which people want to accomplish reasonably challenging goals through their own efforts, such as gaining success in competitive situations, and desire unambiguous feedback regarding their success. (5)

need for affiliation (nAff) A learned need in which people seek approval from others, conform to their wishes and expectations, and avoid conflict and confrontation. (5)

need for power (nPow) A learned need in which people want to control their environment, including people and material resources, to benefit either themselves (personalized power) or others (socialized power). (5)

needs Deficiencies that energize or trigger behaviors to satisfy those deficiencies. (5)

needs hierarchy theory Maslow's motivation theory of five instinctive needs arranged in a hierarchy, whereby people are motivated to fulfill a higher need as a lower one becomes gratified. (5)

negative affectivity (NA) The tendency to experience negative emotions. (4)

negative reinforcement The process by which the removal or avoidance of a consequence increases or maintains the frequency or future probability of a behavior. (3)

negotiation Two or more conflicting parties attempt to resolve their divergent goals by redefining the terms of their interdependence. (13)

networking Cultivating social relationships with others to accomplish one's goals. (12)

network structure An alliance of several organizations for the purpose of creating a product or serving a client. (15)

nominal group technique A structured team decision-making process whereby team members independently write down ideas, describe and clarify them to the group, and then independently rank or vote on them. (10)

nonprogrammed decision Unique, complex, or ill-defined situations whereby decision makers follow the full decision-making process, including a careful search for and/or development of unique solutions. (8)

norms The informal rules and expectations that groups establish to regulate the behavior of their members. (9)

O

open-book management Financial information is shared with employees, who are encouraged to recommend ideas that improve those financial results. (6)

open systems Organizations that take their sustenance from the environment and, in turn, affect that environment through their output. (1)

organic structure An organizational structure with a wide span of control, little formalization, and decentralized decision making. (15)

organizational behavior (OB) The study of what people think, feel, and do in and around organizations. (1)

organizational citizenship Behaviors that extend beyond the employee's normal job duties. (2)

organizational commitment The employee's emotional attachment to, identification with, and involvement in a particular organization. (4)

organizational culture The basic pattern of shared assumptions, values, and beliefs governing the way employees within an organization think about and act on problems and opportunities. (1) (16)

organizational design The process of creating and modifying organizational structures. (15)

organizational learning The knowledge management process in which organizations acquire, share, and use knowledge to succeed. (1)

organizational memory The storage and preservation of intellectual capital. (1)

organizational politics Behaviors that others perceive as self-serving tactics for personal gain at the expense of other people and possibly the organization. (12)

organizational socialization The process by which individuals learn the values, expected behaviors, and social knowledge necessary to assume their roles in the organization. (16)

organizational strategy The way an organization positions itself in its setting in relation to its stakeholders, given the organization's resources, capabilities, and mission. (15)

organizational structure The division of labor and the patterns of coordination, communication, work flow, and formal power that direct organizational activities. (15)

organizations Groups of people who work interdependently toward some purpose. (1)

P

parallel learning structures Highly participative groups constructed alongside (i.e., parallel to) the formal organization with the purpose of increasing the organization's learning and producing meaningful organizational change. (17)

path-goal leadership theory A contingency theory of leadership based on expectancy theory of motivation that relates several leadership styles to specific employee and situational contingencies. (14)

perception The process of receiving information about and making sense of the world around us. (3)

performance-to-outcome (P → O) expectancy   The perceived probability that a specific behavior or performance level will lead to specific outcomes. (5)

personality   The relatively stable pattern of behaviors and consistent internal states that explain a person's behavioral tendencies. (2)

persuasion   Using logical arguments, facts, and emotional appeals to encourage people to accept a request or message. (12)

platform teams   Temporary teams consisting of people from marketing, design, and other areas, who are responsible for developing a product or service. (15)

positive affectivity (PA)   The tendency to experience positive emotional states. (4)

positive reinforcement   The process by which the introduction of a consequence increases or maintains the frequency or future probability of a behavior. (3)

positivism   A view held in quantitative research in which reality exists independent of the perceptions and interpretations of people. (App. A)

postdecisional justification Justifying choices by unconsciously inflating the quality of the selected option and deflating the quality of the discarded options. (8)

power   The capacity of a person, team, or organization to influence others. (12)

power distance   The extent to which people accept unequal distribution of power in a society. (2)

prejudice   The unfounded negative emotions and attitudes toward people belonging to a particular stereotyped group. (3)

primacy effect   A perceptual error in which we quickly form an opinion of people based on the first information we receive about them. (3)

procedural justice   The fairness of the procedures used to decide the distribution of resources. (5)

process consultation   Helping the organization solve its own problems by making it aware of organizational processes, the consequences of those

processes, and the means by which they can be changed. (17)

process losses   Resources (including time and energy) expended toward team development and maintenance rather than the task. (9)

production blocking   A time constraint in team decision making due to the procedural requirement that only one person may speak at a time. (10)

profit sharing   A reward system that pays bonuses to employees based on the previous year's level of corporate profits. (6)

programmed decision   Routine decisions whereby decision makers can follow standard operating procedures to select the preferred solution without the need to identify or evaluate alternative choices. (8)

projection bias   A perceptual error in which an individual believes that other people have the same beliefs and behaviors that he or she does. (3)

psychological contract   The individual's beliefs about the terms and conditions of a reciprocal exchange agreement between that person and another party. (4)

punishment   A means of decreasing the frequency or future probability of a behavior through the introduction of a consequence. (3)

R

realistic job preview (RJP)   The process of giving job applicants a balance of positive and negative information about the job and work context. (16)

reality shock   Perceived discrepancies between preemployment expectations and on-the-job reality. (16)

recency effect   A perceptual error in which the most recent information dominates one's perception of others. (3)

referent power   The capacity to influence others based on the identification and respect they have for the power holder. (12)

refreezing   The latter part of the change process in which systems and conditions are introduced that reinforce and maintain the desired behaviors. (17)

relatedness needs   A person's needs to interact with other people, receive public recognition, and feel secure around other people. (5)

representative sampling   The process of sampling a population in such a way that one can extrapolate the results of that sample to the larger population. (App. A)

rituals   The programmed routines of daily organizational life that dramatize the organization's culture. (16)

role   A set of behaviors that people are expected to perform because they hold certain positions in a team and organization. (9)

role ambiguity   A lack of clarity and predictability of the outcomes of one's behavior. (7)

role conflict   Incongruity or incompatibility of expectations associated with the person's role. (7)

role perceptions   A person's beliefs about the specific tasks assigned to her or him, their relative importance, and the preferred behaviors to accomplish those tasks. (2)

S

satisfaction-progression process   A process whereby people become increasingly motivated to fulfill a higher need as a lower need is gratified. (5)

satisficing   Selecting a solution that is satisfactory, or "good enough," rather than optimal, or "the best." (8)

scenario planning   A systematic process of thinking about alternative futures and what the organization should do to anticipate and react to those environments. (8)

scientific management   The systematic partitioning of work into its smallest elements and standardizing tasks to achieve maximum efficiency. (6)

scientific method   A set of principles and procedures that help researchers to systematically understand previously unexplained events and conditions. (1) (App. A)

search conferences   Systemwide group sessions, usually lasting a few days, in which participants identify environmental trends and establish strategic solutions for those conditions. (17)

selective attention   The process of filtering information received by our senses. (3)

self-directed work teams (SDWTs)   Cross-functional work groups, organized around work processes, that complete an entire piece of work requiring several interdependent tasks and that have substantial autonomy over the execution of those tasks. (10)

self-efficacy   A person's belief that he or she has the ability, motivation, and resources to complete a task successfully. (3)

self-fulfilling prophecy   The process by which our expectations about another person cause that person to act in a way that is consistent with those expectations. (3)

self-leadership   The process of influencing oneself to establish the self-direction and self-motivation needed to perform a task. (6)

self-monitoring   A personality trait referring to an individual's level of sensitivity to the expressive behavior of others and the ability to adapt appropriately to these situational cues. (2)

self-serving bias   A perceptual error whereby people tend to attribute their favorable outcomes to internal factors and their failures to external factors. (3)

self-talk   Talking to ourselves about our own thoughts or actions for the purpose of increasing our self-efficacy and navigating through decisions in a future event. (6)

servant leadership   The belief that leaders serve followers by understanding their needs and facilitating their work performance. (14)

sexual harassment   Unwelcome conduct of a sexual nature that detrimentally affects the work environment or leads to adverse job-related consequences for its victims. (7)

situational leadership model   Developed by Hersey and Blanchard, this model suggests that effective leaders vary their style with the "readiness" of followers. (14)

skill variety   The extent to which employees must use different skills and talents to perform tasks within their job. (6)

skunkworks   Cross-functional teams, usually separated from the main organization, that borrow people and resources and have relatively free rein to develop new products or services. (9)

social identity theory   A conceptual framework based on the idea that how we perceive the world depends on how we define ourselves in terms of our membership in various social groups. (3)

social learning theory   A theory stating that much learning occurs by observing others and then modeling the behaviors that lead to favorable outcomes and avoiding the behaviors that lead to punishing consequences. (3)

social loafing   A situation in which people exert less effort (and usually perform at a lower level) when working in groups than when working alone. (9)

sociotechnical systems (STS) theory   A theory stating that effective work sites have joint optimization of their social and technological systems and that teams should have sufficient autonomy to control key variances in the work process. (10)

span of control   The number of people directly reporting to the next level in the organizational hierarchy. (15)

stakeholders   Shareholders, customers, suppliers, governments, and any other groups with a vested interest in the organization. (1)

stereotyping   The process of assigning traits to people based on their membership in a social category. (3)

stock options   A reward system that gives employees the right to purchase company shares at a future date at a predetermined price. (6)

strategic choice   The idea that an organization interacts with its environment rather than being totally determined by it. (15)

stress   An individual's adaptive response to a situation that is

perceived as challenging or threatening to the person's well-being. (7)

stressors   The causes of stress, including any environmental conditions that place a physical or emotional demand on the person. (7)

substitutability   The extent to which people dependent on a resource have alternatives. (12)

superordinate goal   A common objective held by conflicting parties that is more important than their conflicting departmental or individual goals. (13)

T

tacit knowledge   Knowledge embedded in our actions and ways of thinking and transmitted only through observation and experience. (3)

task identity   The degree to which a job requires completion of a whole or an identifiable piece of work. (6)

task interdependence   The degree to which a task requires employees to share common inputs or outcomes or to interact in the process of executing their work. (9)

task performance   Goal-directed behaviors under the individual's control that support organizational objectives. (2)

task significance   The degree to which the job has a substantial impact on the organization and/or larger society. (6)

team-based organization   A type of departmentalization with a flat hierarchy and relatively little formalization, consisting of self-directed work teams responsible for various work processes. (15)

team building   Any formal activity intended to improve the development and functioning of a team. (10)

team cohesiveness   The degree of attraction people feel toward the team and their motivation to remain members. (9)

team effectiveness   The extent to which a team achieves its objectives, achieves the needs and objectives of its members, and sustains itself over time. (9)

teams   Groups of two or more people who interact and influence each other, are mutually accountable for achieving common objectives, and perceive themselves as a social entity within an organization. (9)

telecommuting Working from home, usually with a computer connection to the office; also called *teleworking*. (1)

theory A general set of propositions that describes interrelationships among several concepts. (App. A)

third-party conflict resolution Any attempt by a relatively neutral person to help the parties resolve their differences. (13)

360-degree feedback Performance feedback received from a full circle of people around an employee. (5)

transactional leadership Leadership that helps organizations achieve their current objectives more efficiently, such as linking job performance to valued rewards and ensuring that employees have the resources needed to get the job done. (14)

transformational leadership A leadership perspective that explains how leaders change teams or organizations by creating, communicating, and modeling a vision for the organization or work unit and inspiring employees to strive for that vision. (14)

trust A psychological state comprising the intention to accept vulnerability based upon positive expectations of the intent or behavior of another person. (4) (10)

type A behavior pattern A behavior pattern associated with people having premature coronary heart disease; type A's tend to be impatient, lose their temper, talk rapidly, and interrupt others. (7)

type B behavior pattern A behavior pattern associated with people having a low risk of coronary heart disease; type B's tend to work steadily, take a relaxed approach to life, and be even-tempered. (7)

U

uncertainty avoidance The degree to which people tolerate ambiguity or feel threatened by ambiguity and uncertainty. (2)

unfreezing The first part of the change process whereby the change agent produces disequilibrium between the driving and restraining forces. (17)

upward appeal A type of coalition in which one or more members have higher authority or expertise. (12)

utilitarianism The moral principle stating that decision makers should seek the greatest good for the greatest number of people when choosing among alternatives. (2)

V

valence The anticipated satisfaction or dissatisfaction that an individual feels toward an outcome. (5)

values Stable, long-lasting beliefs about what is important in a variety of situations, which guide our decisions and actions. (1) (2)

values congruence A situation wherein two or more entities have similar value systems. (2)

value system An individual's values arranged in a hierarchy of preferences. (2)

virtual corporations Network structures representing several independent companies that form unique partnership teams to provide customized products or services, usually to specific clients, for a limited time. (15)

virtual teams Cross-functional teams that operate across space, time, and organizational boundaries with members who communicate mainly through information technologies. (1) (10)

W

win—lose orientation The belief that conflicting parties are drawing from a fixed pie, so the more one party receives, the less the other party will receive. (13)

win—win orientation The belief that the parties will find a mutually beneficial solution to their disagreement. (13)

workaholic A person who is highly involved in work, feels compelled to work, and has a low enjoyment of work. (7)

workplace bullying Offensive, intimidating, or humiliating behavior that degrades, ridicules, or insults another person at work. (7)

NOTES

CHAPTER 1

1. "Q&A with Krishna Bharat of Google News," *Google Friends Newsletter*, July 2003 (www.google.com/google friends/morejul03.html); M. A. Ostrom and M. Marshall, "Inside Google," *Mercury News* (San Jose, Calif.), May 4, 2003; K. H. Hammonds, "How Google Grows . . . and Grows . . . and Grows," *Fast Company*, 69 (April 2003), pp. 74ff; B. Keefe, "Google's Never-Ending Search," *Austin American-Statesman*, April 14, 2003, p. D1; J. Lee, "Postcards from Planet Google," *New York Times*, November 28, 2002, p. G1; Dan Rubenstein, "Google News Untouched by Human Hands," *AlterNet.org*, October 7, 2002 (originally in VUE Weekly); C. P. Taylor, "The Little Engine That Could," *Brandweek*, October 14, 2002, pp. 54–59; P. Hum, "Inside the Googleplex," *Ottawa Citizen*, July 18, 2002.

2. M. Warner, "Organizational Behavior Revisited," *Human Relations* 47 (October 1994), pp. 1151–66. The various historical sources are described in T. Takala, "Plato on Leadership," *Journal of Business Ethics* 17 (May 1998), pp. 785–98; R. Kanigel, *The One Best Way: Frederick Winslow Taylor and the Enigma of Efficiency* (New York: Viking 1997); M. Weber, *The Theory of Social and Economic Organization*, trans. A. M. Henderson and T. Parsons, (New York: Oxford University Press, 1947); G. Hofstede and M. Bond, "The Confucius Connection: From Cultural Roots to Economic Growth," *Organizational Dynamics* 16 (1988), pp. 5–21; F. J. Roethlisberger and W. J. Dickson, *Management and the Worker* (Cambridge, MA: Harvard University Press, 1939); A. Smith, *The Wealth of Nations* (London: Dent, 1910).

3. J. Micklethwait and A. Wooldridge, *The Company: A Short History of a Revolutionary Idea* (New York: Random House, 2003); L. E. Greiner, "A Recent History of Organizational Behavior," in *Organizational Behavior*, ed. S. Kerr (Columbus, OH: Grid, 1979), pp. 3–14.

4. B. Schlender, "The Three Faces of Steve," *Fortune*, November 9, 1998.

5. T. Lee, "Wal-Mart Expanding Outside U.S.," *The Tribune* (Port St. Lucie/Fort Pierce, FL), June 7, 2003; J. Useem, "One Nation under Wal-Mart," *Fortune*, March 3, 2003, pp. 65–78; W. Zellner, "No Way to Treat a Lady," *Business Week*, March 3, 2003, p. 63. Some facts were also sourced from www.walmartstores.com.

6. R. N. Stern and S. R. Barley, "Organizations as Social Systems: Organization Theory's Neglected Mandate," *Administrative Science Quarterly* 41 (1996), pp. 146–62; D. Katz and R. L. Kahn, *The Social Psychology of Organizations* (New York: Wiley, 1966), Chapter 2.

7. J. Pfeffer, *New Directions for Organization Theory* (New York: Oxford University Press, 1997), pp. 7–9.

8. P. R. Lawrence and N. Nohria, *Driven: How Human Nature Shapes Our Choices* (San Francisco: Jossey-Bass, 2002), Chapter 6.

9. S. A. Mohrman, C. B. Gibson, and A. M. Mohrman Jr., "Doing Research That Is Useful to Practice: A Model and Empirical Exploration," *Academy of Management Journal* 44 (April 2001), pp. 357–75. This view also appears in P. R. Lawrence, "Historical Development of Organizational Behavior," in *Handbook of Organizational Behavior*, ed. L. W. Lorsch (Englewood Cliffs, NJ: Prentice Hall, 1987), pp. 1–9. For a contrary view, see A. P. Brief and J. M. Dukerich, "Theory in Organizational Behavior: Can It Be Useful?" *Research in Organizational Behavior* 13 (1991), pp. 327–52.

10. M. S. Myers, *Every Employee a Manager* (New York: McGraw-Hill, 1970). The phrase "adult supervision" as a derogatory term for managers is mentioned in T. A. Stewart, "Just Think: No Permission Needed," *Fortune*, January 8, 2001, p. 190.

11. D. MacDonald, "Good Managers Key to Buffett's Acquisitions," *Montreal Gazette*, November 16, 2001; D. Yankelovich, "Got to Give to Get," *Mother Jones* 22 (July 1997), pp. 60–63. The results of the Watson Wyatt study are reported in B. N. Pfau and I. T. Kay, *The Human Capital Edge* (New York: McGraw-Hill, 2002); B. N. Pfau and I. T. Kay, "The Five Key Elements of a Total Rewards and Accountability Orientation," *Benefits Quarterly* 18 (Third Quarter 2002), pp. 7–15.

12. B. Duff-Brown, "Service Centers Booming in India," *Chicago Tribune*, July 9, 2001, p. 6; M. Landler, "Hi, I'm in Bangalore (but I Can't Say So)," *New York Times*, March 21, 2001, p. A1.

13. S. Fischer, "Globalization and Its Challenges," *American Economic Review* 93 (May 2003), pp. 1–29. For discussion of the diverse meanings of "globalization," see M. F. Guillén, "Is Globalization Civilizing, Destructive or Feeble? A Critique of Five Key Debates in the Social Science Literature," *Annual Review of Sociology* 27 (2001), pp. 235–60.

14. J. Garten, *The Mind of the CEO* (New York: Perseus, 2001), Chapter 3.

15. R. Anderson, "Starbucks: Just Getting Started," *Seattle Weekly*, April 30, 2003, p. 11; S. Holmes, "Planet Starbucks," *Business Week*, September 9, 2002; E. Van Bronhorst, "On Eve of Turning 30, Starbucks Exports Seattle 'Coffee Culture' to the Globe," *Associated Press Newswire*, September 9, 2001.

16. J. Micklethwait and A. Wooldridge, *A Future Perfect: The Challenge and Promise of Globalization*, rev. ed. (New York: Random House, 2003).

17. R. Martin, "The Virtue Matrix: Calculating the Return on Corporate Responsibility," *Harvard Business Review* 68 (March 2002).

18. C. L. Cooper and R. J. Burke (eds.), *The New World of Work: Challenges and Opportunities* (Oxford: Blackwell, 2002); C. Higgins and L. Duxbury, *The 2001 National Work–Life Conflict Study: Report One, Final Report* (Ottawa: Health Canada, March 2002); K. Sparks, B. Faragher, and C. L. Cooper, "Well-Being and Occupational Health in the

21st Century Workplace," *Journal of Occupational & Organizational Psychology* 74 (November 2001), pp. 489–510.

19. C. Kleiman, "Work Issues the Same the Whole World Over," *Seattle Times*, September 2, 2001.

20. P. R. Sparrow, "Reappraising Psychological Contracting: Lessons for the Field of Human-Resource Development from Cross-Cultural and Occupational Psychology Research," *International Studies of Management & Organization* 28 (March 1998), pp. 30–63; R. Schuler and N. Rogovsky, "Understanding Compensation Practice Variations across Firms: The Impact of National Culture," *Journal of International Business Studies* 29 (1998), pp. 159–77.

21. R. House, M. Javidan, P. Hanges, and P. Dorfman, "Understanding Cultures and Implicit Leadership Theories across the Globe: An Introduction to Project GLOBE," *Journal of World Business* 37 (Spring 2002), pp. 3–10; R. House, M. Javidan, and P. Dorfman, "Project GLOBE: An Introduction," *Applied Psychology: An International Journal* 50 (2001), pp. 489–505; M. A. Von Glinow (ed.), "Special Issue: Best Practices in IHRM: Lessons Learned from a Ten-Country/Regional Analysis," *Human Resource Management* 41 (Spring 2002).

22. R. D. Foster, "Internet Takes Ancient Craft Global," *Christian Science Monitor*, September 7, 2001, p. 7.

23. R. P. Gephart Jr., "Introduction to the Brave New Workplace: Organizational Behavior in the Electronic Age," *Journal of Organizational Behavior* 23 (2002), pp. 327–44; R. E. Rice and U. E. Gattiker, "New Media and Organizational Structuring," in *The New Handbook of Organizational Communication*, ed. F. M. Jablin and L. L. Putnam (Thousand Oaks, CA: Sage, 2001), pp. 544–81.

24. J. Gannon, "The Perfect Commute," *Post-Gazette* (Pittsburgh, PA), April 24, 2003, p. E1.

25. "Broadband-Enhanced Teleworking Options Fuel Work–Life Balance Growth for Americans," *Business Wire*, June 30, 2003; J. Ho, "Broadband Key to Communicating during Quarantine," *Taipei Times*, May 13, 2003, p. 10.

26. "Global Survey Predicts Upsurge in Telework," *e-Wire*, July 15, 2003; R. Konrad, "Sun Employees Carry 'Workplace' in Their Wallets," *Salt Lake Tribune*, May 19, 2003; S. Ursery, "Austin Fights Air Pollution with Telework Program," *American City & County* 118 (May 2003), pp. 12–13; S. R. Madsen, "The Effects of Home-Based Teleworking on Work–Family Conflict," *Human Resource Development Quarterly* 14 (Spring 2003), pp. 35–58; "AT&T Telecommute Survey Indicates Productivity Is Up," *AT&T news release*, August 6, 2002; Ipsos-Reid, *Canadian Families and the Internet*, Report to The Royal Bank of Canada, January 2002. The advantages, disadvantages, and contingencies of telecommuting are nicely detailed in L. Duxbury and C. Higgins, "Telecommute: A Primer for the Millennium Introduction," in *The New World of Work: Challenges and Opportunities*, ed. C. L. Cooper and R. J. Burke (Oxford: Blackwell, 2002), pp. 157–99.

27. K. R. Lewis, "Telecommuting Downside Can Become Pretty Deep," *Newhouse News Service*, July 9, 2003; "Boundaries between Work, Life Help Families," *MSU News Bulletin*, May 15, 2003; D. W. McCloskey and M. Igbaria, "Does 'Out of Sight' Mean 'Out of Mind'? An Empirical Investigation of the Career Advancement Prospects of Telecommuters," *Information Resources Management Journal* 16 (April–June 2003), pp. 19–34; S. Briscoe, "Home to Work," *Financial Times* (London), February 23, 2002, p. 2; N. B. Kurland and D. E. Bailey, "Telecommute: The Advantages and Challenges of Working Here, There, Anywhere, and Anytime," *Organizational Dynamics* 28 (Autumn 1999), pp. 53–68; A. Mahlon, "The Alternative Workplace: Changing Where and How People Work," *Harvard Business Review* 76 (May–June 1998), pp. 121–30.

28. J. Helin, "Finland Leads Teleworking in Europe," SAK website, July 2003 (netti.sak.fi); M. Bennett, "Law to Encourage Teleworking," *IT Week*, April 11, 2003; M. Fiutak, "Teleworking Booms in Europe," *ZDNet UK*, October 9, 2002.

29. J. Lipnack and J. Stamps, *Virtual Teams: People Working across Boundaries with Technology* (New York: John Wiley & Sons, 2001); D. J. Armstrong and P. Cole, "Managing Distances and Differences in Geographically Distributed Work Groups," in *Diversity in Work Teams: Research Paradigms for a Changing Workplace*, ed. S. E. Jackson and M. N. Ruderman (Washington, DC: American Psychological Association, 1995), pp. 187–215.

30. T. R. Kayworth and D. E. Leidner, "Leadership Effectiveness in Global Virtual Teams," *Journal of Management Information Systems* 18 (Winter 2001/2002), pp. 7–40; B. L. Kelsey, "Managing in Cyberspace: Strategies for Developing High-Performance Virtual Team," Paper presented at the 2001 Annual Conference of the Administrative Sciences Association of Canada, Organizational Behavior Division, London, Ontario, June 2001; J. S. Lureya and M. S. Raisinghani, "An Empirical Study of Best Practices in Virtual Teams," *Information & Management* 38 (2001), pp. 523–44; D. L. Duarte and N. T. Snyder, *Mastering Virtual Teams: Strategies, Tools, and Techniques That Succeed*, 2nd ed. (San Francisco: Jossey-Bass, 2000).

31. D. L. Carter, "Behind Malek's Goodies, a Melting Pot of Labor," *Democrat and Chronicle* (Rochester, NY), November 30, 2001.

32. "Managing a Multicultural Workforce," *Black Enterprise*, July 2001, p. 121; M. F. Riche, "America's Diversity and Growth: Signposts for the 21st Century," *Population Bulletin*, June 2000, pp. 3–43; C. Bowman, "BLS Projections to 2006: A Summary," *Monthly Labor Review*, November 1997, pp. 3–5.

33. F. H. Wu, *Yellow: Race in America beyond Black and White* (New York: Basic Books, 2002), pp. 79–129; F. Davila, "Prejudice Stings 'Model Minority,'" *Baltimore Sun*, July 29, 2001, p. C5; N. Glazer, "American Diversity and the 2000 Census," *The Public Interest*, June 22, 2001, pp. 3–18; S. Hepinstall, "Chinese-Americans Face Stereotyping—Survey," *Reuters English News Service*, April 25, 2001; N. Bisoondath, "There's No Place Like Home," *New Internationalist* 305 (September 1998).

34. D. Mangan, "Remember When . . . A Women Doctor Was a Rarity?" *Medical Economics* 75 (May 11, 1998), pp. 225–26; P. M. Flynn, J. D. Leeth, and E. S. Levy, "The Accounting Profession in Transition," *CPA Journal* 67 (May 1997), pp. 42–45.

35. C. Loughlin and J. Barling, "Young Workers' Work Values, Attitudes, and Behaviors," *Journal of Occupational and Organizational Psychology* 74 (2001), pp. 543–58.

36. C. Loughlin and J. Barling, "Young Workers' Work Values, Attitudes, and Behaviours," *Journal of Occupational and Organizational Psychology* 74 (November 2001), pp. 543–58; R. Zemke, C. Raines, and B. Filipczak, *Generations at Work: Managing the Clash of Veterans, Boomers, Xers, and Nexters in Your Workplace* (New York: Amacom, 2000).

37. N. Mui, "Here Come the Kids," *New York Times,* February 4, 2001, p. 1; B. R. Kupperschmidt, "Multigeneration Employees: Strategies for Effective Management," *Health Care Manager,* September 2000, pp. 65–76; S. Hays, "Generation X and the Art of the Reward," *Workforce* 78 (November 1999), pp. 44–48; B. Losyk, "Generation X: What They Think and What They Plan to Do," *The Futurist* 31 (March–April 1997), pp. 29–44.

38. T. Kochan, K. Bezrukova, S. Jackson, A. Joshi, et al., "The Effects of Diversity on Business Performance: Report of the Diversity Research Network," *Human Resource Management* 42 (2003), pp. 3–21; D. D. Frink, R. K. Robinson, B. Reithel, M. M. Arthur, et al. "Gender Demography and Organization Performance: A Two-Study Investigation with Convergence," *Group & Organization Management* 28 (March 2003), pp. 127–47; O. C. Richard, "Racial Diversity, Business Strategy, and Firm Performance: A Resource-Based View," *Academy of Management Journal* 43 (2000), pp. 164–77; G. Robinson and K. Dechant, "Building a Business Case for Diversity," *Academy of Management Executive* 11 (August 1997), pp. 21–31.

39. "Mixing Nationalities in the Workplace," *Guardian* (London), November 11, 1999, p. 23.

40. D. van Knippenberg and S. A. Haslam, "Realizing the Diversity Dividend: Exploring the Subtle Interplay between Identity, Ideology and Reality," in *Social Identity at Work: Developing Theory for Organizational Practice,* ed. S. A. Haslam, D. van Knippenberg, M. Platow, and N. Ellemers (New York: Taylor & Francis, 2003); R. J. Ely and D. A. Thomas, "Cultural Diversity at Work: The Effects of Diversity Perspectives on Work Group Processes and Outcomes," *Administrative Science Quarterly* 46 (June 2001), pp. 229–73.

41. R. J. Burke, "Organizational Transitions," in *The New World of Work: Challenges and Opportunities,* ed. C. L. Cooper and R. J. Burke (Oxford: Blackwell, 2002), pp. 3–28; F. Patterson, "Developments in Work Psychology: Emerging Issues and Future Trends," *Journal of Occupational and Organizational Psychology* 74 (November 2001), pp. 381–90.

42. W. R. Boswell, L. M. Moynihan, M. V. Roehling, and M. A. Cavanaugh, "Responsibilities in the 'New Employment Relationship': An Empirical Test of an Assumed Phenomenon," *Journal of Managerial Issues* 13 (Fall 2001), pp. 307–27; M. V. Roehling, M. A. Cavanaugh, L. M. Moynihan, and W. R. Boswell, "The Nature of the New Employment Relationship(s): A Content Analysis of the Practitioner and Academic Literatures," *Human Resource Management* 39 (2000), pp. 305–20; J. Dionne-Proulx, J-C. Bernatchez, and R. Boulard, "Attitudes and Satisfaction Levels Associated with Precarious Employment," *International Journal of Employment Studies* 6 (1998), pp. 91–114; P. Cappelli et al., *Change at Work* (New York: Oxford University Press, 1997).

43. D. G. Gallagher, "Contingent Work Contracts: Practice and Theory," in *The New World of Work: Challenges and Opportunities,* ed. C. L. Cooper and R. J. Burke (Oxford: Blackwell, 2002), pp. 115–36; K. Barker and K. Christensen (eds.), *Contingent Work: American Employment in Transition* (Ithaca, NY: ILR Press, 1998); A. E. Polivka, "Contingent and Alternative Work Arrangements, Defined," *Monthly Labor Review* 119 (October 1996), pp. 3–10; S. Nollen and H. Axel, *Managing Contingent Workers* (New York: AMACOM, 1996), pp. 4–9.

44. D. H. Pink, "Land of the Free," *Fast Company,* May 2001, pp. 125–33; S. B. Gould, K. J. Weiner, and B. R. Levin, *Free Agents: People and Organizations Creating a New Working Community* (San Francisco: Jossey-Bass, 1997); C. von Hippel, S. L. Mangum, D. B. Greenberger, R. L. Heneman, and J. D. Skoglind, "Temporary Employment: Can Organizations and Employees Both Win?" *Academy of Management Executive* 11 (February 1997), pp. 93–104; W. J. Byron, S. J., "Coming to Terms with the New Corporate Contract," *Business Horizons,* January–February 1995, pp. 8–15.

45. J. Walsh and S. Deery, "Understanding the Peripheral Workforce: Evidence from the Service Sector," *Human Resource Management Journal* 9 (1999), pp. 50ff.

46. Y-S. Park and R. J. Butler, "The Safety Costs of Contingent Work: Evidence from Minnesota," *Journal of Labor Research* 22 (Fall 2001), pp. 831–49; D. M. Rousseau and C. Libuser, "Contingent Workers in High Risk Environments," *California Management Review* 39 (Winter 1997), pp. 103–23.

47. A. Sagie and D. Elizur, "Work Values: A Theoretical Overview and a Model of Their Effects," *Journal of Organizational Behavior* 17 (1996), pp. 503–14; W. H. Schmidt and B. Z. Posner, *Managerial Values in Perspective* (New York: American Management Association, 1983).

48. Cited in T. Schubert, "STOP Bad Vibes Rising," *Management Magazine,* September 7, 2002, p. 32.

49. For early writing on values in the context of organizations, see E. H. Schein, *Organizational Culture and Leadership* (San Francisco: Jossey-Bass, 1985); G. Hofstede, *Culture's Consequences: International Differences in Work-Related Values* (Beverly Hills, CA: Sage, 1980); A. M. Pettigrew, " On Studying Organizational Cultures," *Administrative Science Quarterly* 24 (1979), pp. 570–81; G. W. England, "Personal Value Systems of American Managers," *Academy of Management Journal* 10 (1967), pp. 53–68; W. D. Guth and R. Tagiuri, "Personal Values and Corporate Strategy," *Harvard Business Review* 43 (1965), pp. 123–32.

50. L. Cooke and M. Hutchinson, "Doctors' Professional Values: Results from a Cohort Study of United Kingdom Medical Graduates," *Medical Education* 35 (2001), pp. 735–42; B. R. Agle and C. B. Caldwell, "Understanding Research on Values in Business," *Business and Society* 38 (September 1999), pp. 326–87; B. M. Meglino and E. C. Ravlin, "Individual Values in Organizations: Concepts, Controversies, and Research," *Journal of Management* 24 (May 1998), pp. 351–89.

51. The role of values as a control system is discussed in M. G. Murphy and K. M. Davey, "Ambiguity, Ambivalence and Indifference in Organisational Values," *Human Resource Management Journal* 12 (2002), pp. 17–32; T. M. Begley, "Articulating Corporate Values through Human Resource Policies,"

Business Horizons, July 2000; J. C. McCune, "Exporting Corporate Culture," *Management Review* 88 (December 1999), pp. 52–56; M. S. Fenwick, H. L. DeCieri, and D. E. Welch, "Cultural and Bureaucratic Control in MNEs: The Role of Expatriate Performance Management," *Management International Review* 39 (1999), Special Issue 3.

52. S. R. Chatterjee and C. A. L. Pearson, "Indian Managers in Transition: Orientations, Work Goals, Values and Ethics," *Management International Review* 40 (January 2000), pp. 81–95.

53. This cynicism of executive ethics is beautifully captured in D. Olive, "How Celebrity CEOs Failed to Deliver," *Toronto Star,* August 24, 2002, p. A1.

54. Cited in S. Zadek, *The Civil Corporation: The New Economy of Corporate Citizenship* (London: Earthscan, 2001), pp. 50–51.

55. Vector Research, "Analysis of the Public Opinion Poll Conducted for the Canadian Democracy and Corporate Accountability Commission," unpublished report, Toronto, 2001. F. T. McCarthy, "Doing Well by Doing Good," *Economist,* April 22, 2000.

56. M. van Marrewijk, "Concepts and Definitions of CSR and Corporate Sustainability: Between Agency and Communion," *Journal of Business Ethics* 44 (May 2003), pp. 95ff; V. M. Panapanaan, L. Linnanen, M.-M. Karvonen, and V. T. Phan, "Roadmapping Corporate Social Responsibility in Finnish Companies," *Journal of Business Ethics* 44 (May 2003), pp. 133ff; P. Bronchain (ed.), *Towards a Sustainable Corporate Social Responsibility* (Dublin, Ireland: European Foundation for the Improvement of Living and Working Conditions, 2003); Canadian Democracy and Corporate Accountability Commission, *The New Balance Sheet: Corporate Profits and Responsibility in the 21st Century, Final Report* (Toronto, January 2002); Zadek, *The Civil Corporation;* S. G. Scott and V. R. Lane, "A Stakeholder Approach to Organizational Identity," *Academy of Management Review* 25 (January 2000), pp. 43–62.

57. Zadek, *The Civil Corporation,* Chapter 9.

58. D. Keeler, "Spread the Love and Make It Pay," *Global Finance* 16 (May 2001), pp. 20ff.

59. Keeler, "Spread the Love and Make It Pay."

60. A. Maitland, "Scandals Draw Attention to 'Superficial' Measures," *Financial Times* (London), December 10, 2002, p. 1; F. Lawrence, "Social Butterflies," *The Guardian,* August 19, 2002.

61. J. Miller, "Tom's of Maine Co-founder, in Portsmouth, Relates His Philosophy," *Union Leader* (Manchester, NH), May 22, 2003, p. D8.

62. D. Mowat, "The VanCity Difference—A Case for the Triple Bottom Line Approach to Business," *Corporate Environmental Strategy* 9 (February 2002), pp. 24–29; Vancouver City Savings Credit Union, *The VanCity Social Report, 1998–99* (Vancouver: Author, 2000).

63. M. N. Zald, "More Fragmentation? Unfinished Business in Linking the Social Sciences and the Humanities," *Administrative Science Quarterly* 41 (1996), pp. 251–61.

64. For recent applications of evolutionary psychology in organizational behavior, see P. R. Lawrence and N. Nohria, *Driven: How Human Nature Shapes Our Choices* (San Francisco: Jossey-Bass, 2002); C. Loch, M. Yaziji, and C. Langen, "The Fight for the Alpha Position: Channeling Status Competition in Organizations," *European Management Journal* 19 (February 2001), pp. 16–25; B. D. Pierce and R. White, "The Evolution of Social Structure: Why Biology Matters," *Academy of Management Review* 24 (October 1999), pp. 843–53; N. Nicholson, "Evolutionary Psychology: Toward a New View of Human Nature and Organizational Society," *Human Relations* 50 (September 1997), pp. 1053–78.

65. T. S. Kuhn, *The Structure of Scientific Revolutions* (Chicago: University of Chicago Press, 1970).

66. C. Heath and S. B. Sitkin, "Big-B versus Big-O: What Is Organizational about Organizational Behavior?" *Journal of Organizational Behavior* 22 (2001), pp. 43–58.

67. A. Strauss and J. Corbin (eds.), *Grounded Theory in Practice* (London: Sage Publications, 1997); B. G. Glaser and A. Strauss. *The Discovery of Grounded Theory: Strategies for Qualitative Research* (Chicago: Aldine, 1967).

68. For an elaboration of the contingency anchor with examples from information systems, see N. S. Umanath, "The Concept of Contingency beyond 'It Depends': Illustrations from IS Research Stream," *Information & Management* 40 (July 2003), pp. 551–62. For an excellent critique of the "one best way" approach by past scholars, see P. F. Drucker, "Management's New Paradigms," *Forbes,* October 5, 1998, pp. 152–77.

69. H. L. Tosi and J. W. Slocum Jr., "Contingency Theory: Some Suggested Directions," *Journal of Management* 10 (1984), pp. 9–26.

70. D. M. Rousseau and R. J. House, "Meso Organizational Behavior: Avoiding Three Fundamental Biases," in *Trends in Organizational Behavior,* Vol. 1, ed. C. J. Cooper and D. M. Rousseau (Chichester, UK: John Wiley & Sons, 1994), pp. 13–30.

71. H. Trinca, "Her Way," *Boss Magazine,* October 9, 2000.

72. R. T. Pascale, M. Millemann, and L. Gioja, *Surfing the Edge of Chaos* (New York: Crown, 2000); P. Senge et al., *The Dance of Change* (New York: Doubleday/Currency, 1999), pp. 137–48; A. De Geus, *The Living Company* (Boston: Harvard Business School Press, 1997); A. Waring, *Practical Systems Thinking* (Boston: International Thomson Business Press, 1997); P. M. Senge, *The Fifth Discipline: The Art and Practice of the Learning Organization* (New York: Doubleday/Currency, 1990), Chapter 4; F. E. Kast and J. E. Rosenzweig, "General Systems Theory: Applications for Organization and Management," *Academy of Management Journal,* 1972, pp. 447–65.

73. R. Mitchell, "Feeding the Flames," *Business 2.0,* May 1, 2001.

74. V. P. Rindova and S. Kotha, "Continuous 'Morphing': Competing through Dynamic Capabilities, Form, and Function," *Academy of Management Journal* 44 (2001), pp. 1263–80; R. T. Pascale, M. Millemann, and L. Gioja, *Surfing on the Edge of Chaos* (London: Texere, 2000).

75. R. Martin, "The Virtue Matrix: Calculating the Return on Corporate Responsibility," *Harvard Business Review* 68 (March 2002).

76. M. L. Tushman, M. B. Nadler, and D. A. Nadler, *Competing by Design: The Power of Organizational Architecture*

(New York: Oxford University Press, 1997).

77. G. F. B. Probst, "Practical Knowledge Management: A Model That Works," *Prism* (Second Quarter 1998), pp. 17–23; G. Miles, Grant, R. E. Miles, V. Perrone, and L. Edvinsson, "Some Conceptual and Research Barriers to the Utilization of Knowledge," *California Management Review* 40 (Spring 1998), pp. 281–88; E. C. Nevis, A. J. DiBella, and J. M. Gould, "Understanding Organizations as Learning Systems," *Sloan Management Review* 36 (Winter 1995), pp. 73–85; G. Huber, "Organizational Learning: The Contributing Processes and Literature," *Organizational Science* 2 (1991), pp. 88–115.

78. H. Saint-Onge and D. Wallace, *Leveraging Communities of Practice for Strategic Advantage* (Boston: Butterworth-Heinemann, 2003), pp. 9–10; L. A. Joia, "Measuring Intangible Corporate Assets Linking Business Strategy with Intellectual Capital," *Journal of Intellectual Capital* 1 (2000), pp. 68–84; T. A. Stewart, *Intellectual Capital: The New Wealth of Organizations* (New York: Doubleday/Currency, 1997); H. Saint-Onge, "Tacit Knowledge: The Key to the Strategic Alignment of Intellectual Capital," *Strategy & Leadership* 24 (March/April 1996), pp. 10–14.

79. Relationship capital was initially called customer capital in the knowledge management literature. However, its concept is evolving to relationships among external stakeholders. For example, see D. Halloran, "Putting Knowledge Management Initiatives into Action at Motorola," Presentation by Motorola vice-president and director of human resources Dan Halloran at the Future of Business in the New Knowledge Economy Conference, March 22–23, 2000, Pan Pacific Hotel, Singapore.

80. N. Bontis, "Assessing Knowledge Assets: A Review of the Models Used to Measure Intellectual Capital," *International Journal of Management Reviews* 3 (2001), pp. 41–60; P. N. Bukh, H. T. Larsen, and J. Mouritsen, "Constructing Intellectual Capital Statements," *Scandinavian Journal of Management* 17 (March 2001), pp. 87–108.

81. There is no complete agreement on the meaning of organizational learning (or learning organization), and the relationship between organizational learning and knowledge management is still somewhat ambiguous. For discussion on this point, see B. R. McElyea, "Knowledge Management, Intellectual Capital, and Learning Organizations: A Triad of Future Management Integration," *Futurics* 26 (2002), pp. 59–65.

82. P. Tam, "Hot Jobs in a Cool Economy," *Ottawa Citizen*, April 18, 2002. The practice of grafting in knowledge management is discussed in Huber, "Organizational Learning."

83. L. Falkenberg, J. Woiceshyn, and J. Karagianis, "Knowledge Acquisition Processes for Technology Decisions," *Proceedings of the Academy of Management 2002 Annual Conference*, Technology and Innovation Management Division, pp. J1–J6.

84. A. L. Brown, "In Economic Slowdown, Wal-Mart Counts on Its Cultural Roots," *Detroit News*, June 9, 2001; L. Wah, "Behind the Buzz," *Management Review* 88 (April 1999), pp. 16–19; C. W. Wick and L. S. Leon, "From Ideas to Actions: Creating a Learning Organization," *Human Resource Management* 34 (Summer 1995), pp. 299–311; D. Ulrich, T. Jick, and M. Von Glinow, "High Impact Learning: Building and Diffusing Learning Capability," *Organizational Dynamics* 22 (Autumn 1993), pp. 52–66. This is similar to "synthetic learning" described in D. Miller, "A Preliminary Typology of Organizational Learning: Synthesizing the Literature," *Journal of Management* 22 (1996), pp. 485–505.

85. C. O'Dell and C. J. Grayson, "If Only We Knew What We Know: Identification and Transfer of Internal Best Practices," *California Management Review* 40 (Spring 1998), pp. 154–74; R. Ruggles, "The State of the Notion: Knowledge Management in Practice," *California Management Review* 40 (Spring 1998), pp. 80–89; G. S. Richards and S. C. Goh, "Implementing Organizational Learning: Toward a Systematic Approach," *The Journal of Public Sector Management* (Autumn 1995), pp. 25–31.

86. Saint-Onge and Wallace, *Leveraging Communities of Practice for Strategic Advantage*, pp. 12–13; Etienne C. Wenger and William M. Snyder, "Communities of Practice: The Organizational Frontier," *Harvard Business Review* 78 (January–February 2000), pp. 139–45; O'Dell and J. Grayson, "If Only We Knew What We Know."

87. M. Hopkins, "Zen and the Art of the Self-Managing Company," *Inc.*, November 2000, p. 55.

88. H. Beazley, J. Boenisch, and D. Harden, "Knowledge Continuity: The New Management Function," *Journal of Organizational Excellence* 22 (2003), pp. 65–81.

89. D. Cline, "On a Roll," *Augusta Chronicle*, February 2, 2003, p. D1.

90. G. Barker, "High Priest of the PC," *The Age*, April 4, 2001; N. Way, "Talent War," *Business Review Weekly*, August 18, 2000, p. 64.

91. Stewart, *Intellectual Capital*, Chapter 7.

92. B. P. Sunoo "The Sydney Challenge," *Workforce*, September 2000, pp. 70–76.

93. D. Lei, J. W. Slocum, and R. A. Pitts, "Designing Organizations for Competitive Advantage: The Power of Unlearning and Learning," *Organizational Dynamics* 27 (Winter 1999), pp. 24–38; M. E. McGill and J. W. Slocum Jr., "Unlearn the Organization," *Organizational Dynamics* 22, no. 2 (1993), pp. 67–79.

CHAPTER 2

1. S. F. Gale, "Hiking with the Honchos at the Container Store," *Workforce Management Online*, August 2003; T. Raphael, "Recruiting 'Retail Consultants' at the Container Store," *Workforce Management Online* August 2003; Take This Job and Love It!" *Successful Meetings* 52 (July 2003), p. 33; V. Barr, "A Great Place to Work and Shop," *Display & Design Ideas* 14 (August 2002), pp. 28–29; K. Tindell, "CEO Tip," *Sales & Marketing Management*, May 2002, p. 64; B. Broadway, "Good for the Soul—and for the Bottom Line," *Washington Post*, August 19, 2001, p. A1; L. Kline, "The Secret of Their Success," *D Magazine—Dallas/Fort Worth* 28 (July 2001), p. 32; J. Laabs, "Thinking Outside the Box at the Container Store," *Workforce* 80 (March 2001), pp. 34–38.

2. Thanks to senior officers in the Singapore Armed Forces for discovering the handy "MARS" acronym. Thanks

also to Chris Perryer at the University of Western Australia for pointing out that the full model should be called the "MARS BAR" because the outcomes are "behavior and results"!

3. S. Roccas, L. Sagiv, S. H. Schwartz, and A. Knafo, "The Big Five Personality Factors and Personal Values," *Personality and Social Psychology* 28 (June 2002), pp. 789–801.

4. C. C. Pinder, *Work Motivation in Organizational Behavior* (Upper Saddle River, NJ: Prentice Hall, 1998); E. E. Lawler III, *Motivation in Work Organizations* (Monterey, CA: Brooks/Cole, 1973), pp. 2–5.

5. D. D. Gray, "Thai Town Lures Makers of Fishing Hooks," *Seattle Times*, April 14, 2003.

6. J. P. Briscoe and D. T. Hall, "Grooming and Picking Leaders Using Competency Frameworks: Do They Work? An Alternative Approach and New Guidelines for Practice," *Organizational Dynamics* 28 (Autumn 1999), pp. 37–52; Hay Group et al., *Raising the Bar: Using Competencies to Enhance Employee Performance* (Scottsdale, AZ: American Compensation Association, 1996); L. M. Spencer and S. M. Spencer, *Competence at Work: Models for Superior Performance* (New York: Wiley, 1993); R. Boyatzis, *The Competent Manager: A Model for Effective Performance* (New York: John Wiley & Sons, 1982).

7. T. Hellström, "Knowledge and Competence Management at Ericsson: Decentralization and Organizational Fit," *Journal of Knowledge Management* 4 (2000).

8. R. Jacobs, "Using Human Resource Functions to Enhance Emotional Intelligence," in *The Emotionally Intelligent Workplace*, ed. C. Cherniss and D. Goleman (San Francisco: Jossey-Bass, 2001), pp. 161–63; J. Sandberg, "Understanding Human Competence at Work: An Interpretative Approach," *Academy of Management Journal* 43 (January 2000), pp. 9–25; T. Hoffmann, "The Meanings of Competency," *Journal of European Industrial Training* 23 (1999), pp. 275–85.

9. J. R. Edwards, "Person–Job Fit: A Conceptual Integration, Literature Review, and Methodological Critique," *International Review of Industrial and Organizational Psychology* 6 (1991), pp. 283–357; J. E. Hunter and R. F. Hunter, "Validity and Utility of Alternative Predictors of Job Performance," *Psychological Bulletin* 96 (1984), pp. 72–98.

10. S. Brady, "Deep in the Heart of AT&T Dallas," *Cable World*, October 7, 2002, p. 37.

11. H. L. Krieger, "Coping with It: Applebaum's Legacy," *Jerusalem Post*, September 19, 2003, p. B1.

12. The converse of this statement is that role ambiguity undermines job performance. For evidence of this, see A. Nygaard and R. Dahlstrom, "Role Stress and Effectiveness in Horizontal Alliances," *Journal of Marketing* 66 (April 2002), pp. 61–82.

13. M. Hayes, "Goal Oriented," *InformationWeek*, March 10, 2003, pp. 34ff.

14. Gary Johns discusses situational factors in terms of constraints on behavior and on the complexities of organizational research. See G. Johns, "Commentary: In Praise of Context," *Journal of Organizational Behavior* 22 (2001), pp. 31–42; Also see S. B. Bacharach and P. Bamberger, "Beyond Situational Constraints: Job Resources Inadequacy and Individual Performance at Work," *Human Resource Management Review* 5 (1995), pp. 79–102; K. F. Kane (ed.), "Special Issue: Situational Constraints and Work Performance," *Human Resource Management Review* 3 (Summer 1993), pp. 83–175.

15. J. H. Sheridan, "Lockheed Martin Corp.," *Industry Week* 247 (October 19, 1998), pp. 54–56.

16. J. P. Campbell, "The Definition and Measurement of Performance in the New Age," in *The Changing Nature of Performance: Implications for Staffing, Motivation, and Development*, ed. D. R. Ilgen and E. D. Pulakos (San Francisco: Jossey-Bass, 1999), pp. 399–429; J. P. Campbell, R. A. McCloy, S. H. Oppler, and C. E. Sager, "A Theory of Performance," in *Personnel Selection in Organizations*, ed. N. Schmitt, W. C. Borman, and Associates (San Francisco: Jossey-Bass, 1993), pp. 35–70.

17. R. El-Bakry, "Another Day at the Office," *Business Today* (Egypt), June 10, 2003.

18. D. W. Organ, "Organizational Citizenship Behavior: It's Construct Clean-Up Time," *Human Performance* 10 (1997), pp. 85–97; D. W. Organ, "The Motivational Basis of Organizational Citizenship Behavior," *Research in Organizational Behavior* 12 (1990), pp. 43–72. Early reference to organizational citizenship (extrarole behaviors) is found in C. I. Barnard, *The Functions of the Executive* (Cambridge, MA: Harvard University Press, 1938), pp. 83–84; D. Katz and R. L. Kahn, *The Social Psychology of Organizations* (New York: Wiley, 1966), pp. 337–40.

19. J. A. LePine, A. Erez, and D. E. Johnson, "The Nature and Dimensionality of Organizational Citizenship Behavior: A Critical Review and Meta-Analysis," *Journal of Applied Psychology* 87 (February 2002), pp. 52–65; L. Van Dyne and J. A. LePine, "Helping and Voice Extra-Role Behaviors: Evidence of Construct and Predictive Validity," *Academy of Management Journal* 41 (1998), pp. 108–19; R. N. Kanungo and J. A. Conger, "Promoting Altruism as a Corporate Goal," *Academy of Management Executive* 7, no. 3 (1993), pp. 37–48.

20. K. Hanson, "Perks Help Keep Four Seasons Staff Pampering Guests," *National Post*, January 13, 2001, p. D8.

21. M. Rotundo and P. Sackett, "The Relative Importance of Task, Citizenship, and Counterproductive Performance to Global Ratings of Job Performance: A Policy-Capturing Approach," *Journal of Applied Psychology* 87 (February 2002), pp. 66–80.

22. P. E. Spector and S. Fox "An Emotion-Centered Model of Voluntary Work Behavior: Some Parallels between Counterproductive Work Behavior and Organizational Citizenship Behavior," *Human Resource Management Review* 12 (2002), pp. 269–92; S. Fox, P. E. Spector, and D. Miles, "Counterproductive Work Behavior (CWB) in Response to Job Stressors and Organizational Justice: Some Mediator and Moderator Tests for Autonomy and Emotions," *Journal of Vocational Behavior* 59 (2001) pp. 291–309.

23. E. Beal, "Hospitals, Schools Work to Whittle RN Shortage," *Crain's Cleveland Business*, September 8, 2003, p. 40; T. Corwin, "Hospitals Battle Nurse Shortage," *Augusta (GA) Chronicle*, July 30, 2003, p. B1; N. M. Moore, "Outside Agencies Offer Nursing Relief, but at What Cost?" *Cleveland Sun*, May 3, 2001.

24. "War for Talent II: Seven Ways to Win," *Fast Company* 42 (January 2001); E. G. Chambers et al., "The War for Talent," *McKinsey Quarterly,* Issue 3 (1998), pp. 44–57.

25. S. M. Jacoby, "Most Workers Find a Sense of Security in Corporate Life," *Los Angeles Times,* September 7, 1998, p. B5.

26. T. Romita, "The Talent Search," *Business 2.0,* June 12, 2001; K. Dobbs, "Knowing How to Keep Your Best and Brightest," *Workforce* 80 (April 2001), pp. 56–60.

27. T. R. Mitchell, B. C. Holtom, and T. W. Lee, "How to Keep Your Best Employees: Developing an Effective Retention Policy," *Academy of Management Executive* 15 (November 2001), pp. 96–108.

28. "Absenteeism among Bahraini Employees 15%, Says Study," *Bahrain Tribune,* April 22, 2003; "Surge in Sick Leave Stumps Sweden," *Agence France Presse,* September 13, 2002; D. Smith, "Nation Fares Well in Skivers' League," *Sunday Times* (London), June 16, 2002.

29. P. Eaton-Robb, "For Employees, Solutions That Work," *Providence Journal,* January 10, 2001, p. E1. For details about the causes of absenteeism, see S. R. Rhodes and R. M. Steers, *Managing Employee Absenteeism* (Reading, MA: Addison-Welsey, 1990).

30. D. A. Harrison and J. J. Martocchio, "Time for Absenteeism: A 20–Year Review of Origins, Offshoots, and Outcomes," *Journal of Management* 24 (Spring 1998), pp. 305–50; R. D. Hackett and P. Bycio, "An Evaluation of Employee Absenteeism as a Coping Mechanism among Hospital Nurses," *Journal of Occupational & Organizational Psychology* 69 (December 1996), pp. 327–38; R. G. Ehrenberg, R. A. Ehrenberg, D. I. Rees, and E. L. Ehrenberg, "School District Leave Policies, Teacher Absenteeism, and Student Achievement," *Journal of Human Resources* 26 (Winter 1991), pp. 72–105; I. Ng, "The Effect of Vacation and Sick Leave Policies on Absenteeism," *Canadian Journal of Administrative Sciences* 6 (December 1989), pp. 18–27; V. V. Baba and M. J. Harris, "Stress and Absence: A Cross-Cultural Perspective," *Research in Personnel and Human Resources Management, Supplement* 1 (1989), pp. 317–37.

31. B. A. Agle and C. B. Caldwell, "Understanding Research on Values in Business," *Business and Society* 38 (September 1999), pp. 326–87; J. J. Dose, "Work Values: An Integrative Framework and Illustrative Application to Organizational Socialization," *Journal of Occupational and Organizational Psychology* 70 (September 1997), pp. 219–40; A. Sagie and D. Elizur, "Work Values: A Theoretical Overview and a Model of Their Effects," *Journal of Organizational Behavior* 17 (1996), pp. 503–14; S. H. Schwartz, "Are There Universal Aspects in the Structure and Contents of Human Values?" *Journal of Social Issues* 50 (1994), pp. 19–45; W. H. Schmidt and B. Z. Posner, *Managerial Values in Perspective* (New York: American Management Association, 1983); M. Rokeach, *The Nature of Human Values* (New York: Free Press, 1973).

32. D. Lubinski, D. B. Schmidt, and C. P. Benbow, "A 20-Year Stability Analysis of the Study of Values for Intellectually Gifted Individuals from Adolescence to Adulthood," *Journal of Applied Psychology* 81 (1996), pp. 443–51; M. Rokeach, *Understanding Human Values* (New York: Free Press, 1979).

33. For a recent study of values and leadership, see C. P. Egri and S. Herman, "Leadership in the North American Environmental Sector: Values, Leadership Styles, and Contexts of Environmental Leaders and Their Organizations," *Academy of Management Journal* 43 (August 2000), pp. 571–604. For other studies on the effects of values, see Meglino and Ravlin, "Individual Values in Organizations."

34. S. H. Schwartz, G. Melech, A. Lehmann, S. Burgess, M. Harris, and V. Owens, "Extending the Cross-Cultural Validity of the Theory of Basic Human Values with a Different Method of Measurement," *Journal of Cross-Cultural Psychology* 32 (September 2001), pp. 519–42; P. Stern, T. Dietz, and G. A. Guagnano, "A Brief Inventory of Values," *Educational and Psychological Measurement* 58 (December 1998), pp. 984–1001; S. H. Schwartz, "Value Priorities and Behavior: Applying a Theory of Integrated Value Systems," in *The Psychology of Values: The Ontario Symposium,* Vol. 8, ed. C. Seligman, J. M. Olson, and M. P. Zanna (Hillsdale, NJ:

Lawrence Erlbaum Associates, 1996), pp. 1–24; S. H. Schwartz, "Are There Universal Aspects in the Structure and Contents of Human Values?" *Journal of Social Issues* 50 (1994), pp. 19–45; S. H. Schwartz, "Universals in the Content and Structure of Values: Theoretical Advances and Empirical Tests in 20 Countries," *Advances in Experimental Social Psychology* 25 (1992), pp. 1–65.

35. Meglino and Ravlin, "Individual Values in Organizations"; C. Argyris and D. A. Schön, *Organizational Learning: A Theory of Action Perspective* (Reading, MA: Addison-Wesley, 1978).

36. P. Pruzan, "The Question of Organizational Consciousness: Can Organizations Have Values, Virtues and Visions?" *Journal of Business Ethics* 29 (February 2001), pp. 271–84.

37. "Scandals, Economy Alter Attitudes of Next Generation Business Leaders, MBA Student Survey Shows," *Business Wire,* May 20, 2003; S. R. Chatterjee and C. A. L. Pearson, "Indian Managers in Transition: Orientations, Work Goals, Values and Ethics," *Management International Review,* January 2000, pp. 81–95; K. F. Alam, "Business Ethics in New Zealand Organizations: Views from the Middle and Lower Level Managers," *Journal of Business Ethics* 22 (November 1999), pp. 145–53.

38. D. Turban, C. Lau, H. Ngo, I. Chow, and S. Si, "Organizational Attractiveness of Firms in the People's Republic of China: A Person–Organization Fit Perspective," *Journal of Applied Psychology* 86 (April 2001), pp. 194–206; A. E. M. Van Vianen, "Person–Organization Fit: The Match between Newcomers' and Recruiters' Preferences for Organizational Cultures," *Personnel Psychology* 53 (Spring 2000), pp. 113–49; B. A. Agle and C. B. Caldwell, "Understanding Research on Values in Business," *Business and Society* 38 (September 1999), pp. 326–87. Humphrey Wong's statement is found in B. Rand, "Job Bias Persists," *Rochester (NY) Democrat and Chronicle,* January 12, 2003.

39. D. Arnott, *Corporate Cults* (New York: AMACOM, 1999); K. M. Eisenhardt, J. L. Kahwajy, and L. J. Bourgeois III, "Conflict and Strategic Choice: How Top Management Teams Disagree," *California Management Review* 39 (Winter 1997), pp. 42–62.

40. T. A. Joiner, "The Influence of National Culture and Organizational Culture Alignment on Job Stress and Performance: Evidence from Greece," *Journal of Managerial Psychology* 16 (2001), pp. 229–42; Z. Aycan, R. N. Kanungo, and J. B. P. Sinha, "Organizational Culture and Human Resource Management Practices: The Model of Culture Fit," *Journal of Cross-Cultural Psychology* 30 (July 1999), pp. 501–26.

41. C. Fox, "Firms Go Warm and Fuzzy to Lure Staff," *Australian Financial Review,* May 15, 2001, p. 58.

42. D. Oyserman, H. M. Coon, and M. Kemmelmeier, "Rethinking Individualism and Collectivism: Evaluation of Theoretical Assumptions and Meta-Analyses," *Psychological Bulletin* 128 (2002), pp. 3–72; F. S. Niles, "Individualism-Collectivism Revisited," *Cross-Cultural Research* 32 (November 1998), pp. 315–41; C. P. Earley and C. B. Gibson, "Taking Stock in Our Progress on Individualism-Collectivism: 100 Years of Solidarity and Community," *Journal of Management* 24 (May 1998), pp. 265–304; J. A. Wagner III, "Studies of Individualism-Collectivism: Effects of Cooperation in Groups," *Academy of Management Journal* 38 (1995), pp. 152–72; H. C. Triandis, *Individualism and Collectivism* (Boulder, CO: Westview, 1995).

43. Oyserman et al., "Rethinking Individualism and Collectivism."

44. M. Voronov and J. A. Singer, "The Myth of Individualism-Collectivism: A Critical Review," *Journal of Social Psychology* 142 (August 2002), pp. 461–80; M. H. Bond, "Reclaiming the Individual from Hofstede's Ecological Analysis—A 20-Year Odyssey: Comment on Oyserman et al. (2002)" *Psychological Bulletin* 128 (2002), pp. 73–77.

45. K. L. Newman and S. D. Nolan, "Culture and Congruence: The Fit between Management Practices and National Culture," *Journal of International Business Studies* 27 (1996), pp. 753–79; G. Hofstede, "Cultural Constraints in Management Theories," *Academy of Management Executive* 7 (1993), pp. 81–94; G. Hofstede, *Culture's Consequences: International Differences in Work-Related Values* (Beverly Hills, CA: Sage, 1980).

46. M. Erez and P. Christopher Earley, *Culture, Self-Identity, and Work* (New York: Oxford University Press, 1993), pp. 126–27.

47. G. Hofstede, *Cultures and Organizations: Software of the Mind* (New York: McGraw-Hill, 1991), p. 124. Hofstede used the terms "masculinity" and "femininity" for achievement and nurturing orientation, respectively. We have adopted the latter to minimize the sexist perspective of these concepts. The achievement and nurturing orientation labels are also used in G. R. Jones, J. M. George, and C. W. L. Hill, *Contemporary Management* (New York: Irwin/Mcgraw-Hill, 1998), pp. 112–13.

48. For counterarguments, see G. Hofstede, "Attitudes, Values and Organizational Culture: Disentangling the Concepts," *Organization Studies* 19 (June 1998), pp. 477–92.

49. Voronov and Singer, "The Myth of Individualism-Collectivism"; S. S. Sarwono and R. W. Armstrong, "Microcultural Differences and Perceived Ethical Problems: An International Business Perspective," *Journal of Business Ethics* 30 (March 2001), pp. 41–56; C. J. Robertson, "The Global Dispersion of Chinese Values: A Three-Country Study of Confucian Dynamism," *Management International Review* 40 (Third Quarter 2000), pp. 253–68; J. S. Osland, A. Bird, J. Delano, and M. Jacob, "Beyond Sophisticated Stereotyping: Cultural Sensemaking in Context," *Academy of Management Executive* 14 (February 2000), pp. 65–79. The research on Canada's 13 cultural groups is found in M. Adams, *Better Happy than Rich?* (Toronto: Viking, 2001).

50. C. Savoye, "Workers Say Honesty Is Best Company Policy," *Christian Science Monitor,* June 15, 2000.

51. "National Workplace Study Shows Employees Take a Dim View of Current Leadership Ethics," Walker Information news release, September 1, 2003. For a sampling of the unethical practices mentioned here, see "Chemical Company Owners Charged with Bribery," *CNN Online,* September 18, 2003; J. Caniglia and R. Exner, "Painting Firms Bribed Inspectors, Officials Say," *Cleveland Plain Dealer,* August 8, 2003; G. Crouch, "Royal Ahold's Inquiry Ends, Finding $1.1 Billion in Errors," *New York Times,* July 2, 2003, p. C2; "SK Group Owner Jailed on Fraud, Illegal Accounting Charges," *Business Times* (Singapore), June 13, 2003; S. Craig and C. Gasparino, "Morgan Stanley Puts Settlement on 'Spin' Cycle," *Wall Street Journal,* March 31, 2003, p. C1; "Swedish Construction Group Dismisses Managers for Cartel Activities," *Associated Press,* January 31, 2002.

52. P. L. Schumann "A Moral Principles Framework for Human Resource Management Ethics," *Human Resource Management Review* 11 (Spring–Summer 2001), pp. 93–111; M. G. Velasquez, *Business Ethics,* 4th ed. (Upper Saddle River, NJ: Prentice Hall, 1998), Chapter 2.

53. R. Berenbeim, "The Search for Global Ethics," *Vital Speeches of the Day* 65 (January 1999), pp. 177–78.

54. Velasquez, *Business Ethics,* p. 123; Schumann "A Moral Principles Framework for Human Resource Management Ethics," p. 104.

55. D. R. May and K. P. Pauli, "The Role of Moral Intensity in Ethical Decision Making," *Business and Society* 41 (March 2002), pp. 84–117; B. H. Frey, "The Impact of Moral Intensity on Decision Making in a Business Context," *Journal of Business Ethics* 26 (August 2000), pp. 181–95; J. M. Dukerich, M. J. Waller, E. George, and G. P. Huber "Moral Intensity and Managerial Problem Solving," *Journal of Business Ethics* 24 (March 2000), pp. 29–38; T. J. Jones, "Ethical Decision Making by Individuals in Organizations: An Issue Contingent Model," *Academy of Management Review* 16 (1991), pp. 366–95.

56. J. R. Sparks and S. D. Hunt, "Marketing Researcher Ethical Sensitivity: Conceptualization, Measurement, and Exploratory Investigation," *Journal of Marketing* 62 (April 1998), pp. 92–109.

57. B. Stoneman and K. K. Holliday, "Pressure Cooker," *Banking Strategies,* January–February 2001, p. 13; Alam, "Business Ethics in New Zealand Organizations"; K. Blotnicky, "Is Business in Moral Decay?" *Halifax Chronicle-Herald,* June 11, 2000; D. McDougall and B. Orsini, "Fraudbusting Ethics," *CMA Management* 73 (June 1999), pp. 18–21; J. Evensen, "Ethical Behavior in Business and Life Is Its Own Reward," *Deseret News* (Salt Lake City, UT), October 19, 1997. For a discussion of the situational effects on ethical conduct, see C. J. Thompson, "A Contextualist

Proposal for the Conceptualization and Study of Marketing Ethics," *Journal of Public Policy and Marketing* 14 (1995), pp. 177–91.

58. P. Haapaniemi and W. R. Hill, "Not Just for the Big Guys!" *Chief Executive,* September 1998, pp. 62–73.

59. M. Milliet-Einbinder, "Writing Off Tax Deductibility," *OECD Observer,* April 2000, pp. 38–40; F. Rotherham, "NZ Moves to Curb Corruption by Ending Tax Deductible Bribes," *Independent Business Weekly,* June 30, 1999, p. 27.

60. T. H. Stevenson and C. D. Bodkin, "A Cross-National Comparison of University Students' Perceptions Regarding the Ethics and Acceptability of Sales Practices," *Journal of Business Ethics* 17 (January 1998), pp. 45–55; T. Jackson and M. C. Artola, "Ethical Beliefs and Management Behavior: A Cross-Cultural Comparison," *Journal of Business Ethics* 16 (August 1997), pp. 1163–73; M-K. Nyaw and I. Ignace, "A Comparative Analysis of Ethical Beliefs: A Four Country Study," *Journal of Business Ethics* 13 (1994), pp. 543–55; W. R. Swinyard, H. Rinne, and A. K. Kau, "The Morality of Software Piracy: A Cross-Cultural Analysis," *Journal of Business Ethics* 9 (1990), pp. 655–64.

61. P. F. Buller, J. J. Kohls, and K. S. Anderson, "A Model for Addressing Cross-Cultural Ethical Conflicts," *Business and Society* 36 (June 1997), pp. 169–93.

62. F. T. McCarthy, "Doing Well by Doing Good," *Economist,* April 22, 2000; Institute of Business Ethics, *Report on Business Ethics Codes 1998* (retrieved from www.ibe.org.uk).

63. T. Hatcher, "New World," *T&D,* August 2003, pp. 42ff; M. S. Schwartz, "The Nature of the Relationship between Corporate Codes of Ethics and Behavior," *Journal of Business Ethics* 32 (August 2001), pp. 247–62; J. S. Adams and A. Tashchian, "Codes of Ethics as Signals for Ethical Behavior," *Journal of Business Ethics* 29 (February 2001), pp. 199–211; M. A. Clark and S. L. Leonard, "Can Corporate Codes of Ethics Influence Behavior?" *Journal of Business Ethics* 17 (April 1998), pp. 619–30.

64. R. B. Wickman, "Interest in Ethics Courses Increases after Corporate Scandals," *Kansas City Star,* July 20, 2003; T. Pincus, "Ethics Needs to Be Instilled at Early Stage," *Chicago Sun-Times,* June 24, 2003. Also see R. Alsop, "Right and Wrong: Can Business Schools Teach Students to Be Virtuous?" *Wall Street Journal,* September 17, 2003, p. R9.

65. F. Sanchez, "Boeing Stops Work So All Employees Can Take Four-Hour Ethics Course," *Long Beach, CA: Press-Telegram,* July 31, 2003.

66. P. J. Gnazzo and G. R. Wratney, "Are You Serious about Ethics?" *Across the Board* 40 (July/August 2003), pp. 46ff; R. Osborne, "A Matter of Ethics," *Industry Week,* April 9, 2000.

67. D. R. May, T. D. Hodges, A. Y. L. Chan, and B. J. Avolio, "Developing the Moral Component of Authentic Leadership," *Organizational Dynamics* 32 (2003), pp. 247–60; R. N. Kanungo, "Ethical Values of Transactional and Transformational Leaders," *Canadian Journal of Administrative Sciences* 18 (December 2001), pp. 257–65; E. Aronson, "Integrating Leadership Styles and Ethical Perspectives," *Canadian Journal of Administrative Sciences* 18 (December 2001), pp. 244–56; M. Mendonca, "Preparing for Ethical Leadership in Organizations," *Canadian Journal of Administrative Sciences* 18 (December 2001), pp. 266–76.

68. S. Roccas, L. Sagiv, S. H. Schwartz, and A. Knafo, "The Big Five Personality Factors and Personal Values," *Personality and Social Psychology* 28 (June 2002), pp. 789–801.

69. R. T. Hogan, "Personality and Personality Measurement," in *Handbook of Industrial and Organizational Psychology,* 2nd ed, Vol. 2, ed. M. D. Dunnette and L. M. Hough (Palo Alto, CA: Consulting Psychologists Press, 1991), pp. 873–919. Also see W. Mischel, *Introduction to Personality* (New York: Holt, Rinehart, & Winston, 1986).

70. B. Reynolds and K. Karraker, "A Big Five Model of Disposition and Situation Interaction: Why a 'Helpful' Person May Not Always Behave Helpfully," *New Ideas in Psychology* 21 (April 2003), pp. 1–13; R. P. Tett and H. A. Guterman, "Situation Trait Relevance, Trait Expression, and Cross-Situational Consistency: Testing a Principle of Trait Activation," *Journal of Research in Personality* 34 (December 2000), pp. 397–423; W. Mischel and Y. Shoda, "Reconciling Processing Dynamics and Personality Dispositions," *American Review of Psychology* 49 (1998), pp. 229–58.

71. R. R. McCrae et al., "Nature over Nurture: Temperament, Personality, and Life Span Development," *Journal of Personality and Social Psychology* 78 (2000), pp. 173–86.

72. H. C. Triandis and E. M. Suh, "Cultural Influences on Personality," *Annual Review of Psychology* 53 (2002), pp. 133–60; D. C. Funder, "Personality," *Annual Review Psychology* 52 (2001), pp. 197–221; W. Revelle, "Personality Processes," *Annual Review of Psychology* 46 (1995), pp. 295–328.

73. R. M. Guion and R. F. Gottier, "Validity of Personality Measures in Personnel Selection," *Personnel Psychology* 18 (1965), pp. 135–64. Also see N. Schmitt, R. Z. Gooding, R. D. Noe, and M. Kirsch, "Meta-Analyses of Validity Studies Published between 1964 and 1982 and the Investigation of Study Characteristics," *Personnel Psychology* 37 (1984), pp. 407–22.

74. P. G. Irving, "On the Use of Personality Measures in Personnel Selection," *Canadian Psychology* 34 (April 1993), pp. 208–14.

75. K. M. DeNeve and H. Cooper, "The Happy Personality: A Meta-Analysis of 137 Personality Traits and Subjective Well-Being," *Psychological Bulletin* 124 (September 1998), pp. 197–229; M. K. Mount and M. R. Barrick, "The Big Five Personality Dimensions: Implications for Research and Practice in Human Resources Management," *Research in Personnel and Human Resources Management* 13 (1995), pp. 153–200; B. M. Bass, *Stogdill's Handbook of Leadership: A Survey of Theory and Research,* 3rd ed. (New York: Free Press, 1990); J. L. Holland, *Making Vocation Choices: A Theory of Careers* (Englewood Cliffs, NJ: Prentice Hall, 1973).

76. C. Daniels, "Does This Man Need a Shrink?" *Fortune,* February 5, 2001, pp. 205.

77. This historical review and the trait descriptions in this section are discussed in R. J. Schneider and L. M. Hough, "Personality and Industrial/Organizational Psychology," *International Review of Industrial and Organizational Psychology* 10 (1995), pp.

75–129; M. K. Mount and M. R. Barrick, "The Big Five Personality Dimensions: Implications for Research and Practice in Human Resources Management," *Research in Personnel and Human Resources Management* 13 (1995), pp. 153–200; J. M. Digman, "Personality Structure: Emergence of the Five-Factor Model," *Annual Review of Psychology* 41 (1990), pp. 417–40.

78. G. M. Hurtz and J. J. Donovan, "Personality and Job Performance: The Big Five Revisited," *Journal of Applied Psychology* 85 (December 2000), pp. 869–79; M. K. Mount, M. R. Barrick, and J. P. Strauss, "Validity of Observer Ratings of the Big Five Personality Factors," *Journal of Applied Psychology* 79 (1994), pp. 272–80; R. P. Tett, D. N. Jackson, and M. Rothstein, "Personality Measures as Predictors of Job Performance: A Meta-Analytic Review," *Personnel Psychology* 44 (1991), pp. 703–42.

79. J. M. Howell and C. A. Higgins, "Champions of Change: Identifying, Understanding, and Supporting Champions of Technological Innovations," *Organizational Dynamics*, Summer 1990, pp. 40–55.

80. T. A. Judge and R. Ilies, "Relationship of Personality to Performance Motivation: A Meta-Analytic Review," *Journal of Applied Psychology* 87 (August 2002), pp. 797–807; L. A. Witt, L. A. Burke, and M. R. Barrick, "The Interactive Effects of Conscientiousness and Agreeableness on Job Performance," *Journal of Applied Psychology* 87 (February 2002), pp. 164–69; M. Dalton and M. Wilson, "The Relationship of the Five-Factor Model of Personality to Job Performance for a Group of Middle Eastern Expatriate Managers," *Journal of Cross-Cultural Psychology*, March 2000, pp. 250–58; K. P. Carson and G. L. Stewart, "Job Analysis and the Sociotechnical Approach to Quality: A Critical Examination," *Journal of Quality Management* 1 (1996), pp. 49–64; Mount and Barrick, "The Big Five Personality Dimensions," pp. 177–78.

81. I. B. Myers, *The Myers-Briggs Type Indicator* (Palo Alto, CA: Consulting Psychologists Press, 1987); C. G. Jung, *Psychological Types*, trans. H. G. Baynes, rev. R.F.C. Hull (Princeton, NJ: Princeton University Press, 1971). (Original work published in 1921)

82. L. R. Offermann and R. K. Spiros, "The Science and Practice of Team Development: Improving the Link," *Academy of Management Journal* 44 (April 2001), pp. 376–92.

83. G. Potts, "Oklahoma City Employers Use Personality Tests to Improve Placement," *Daily Oklahoman*, February 26, 2001.

84. J. Michael, "Using the Myers-Briggs Type Indicator as a Tool for Leadership Development? Apply with Caution," *Journal of Leadership & Organizational Studies* 10 (Summer 2003), pp. 68ff; R. M. Capraro and M. M. Capraro, "Myers-Briggs Type Indicator Score Reliability across Studies: A Meta-Analytic Reliability Generalization Study," *Educational and Psychological Measurement* 62 (August 2002), pp. 590–602; W. L. Johnson et al., "A Higher Order Analysis of the Factor Structure of the Myers-Briggs Type Indicator," *Measurement and Evaluation in Counseling and Development* 34 (July 2001), pp. 96–108; W. L. Gardner and M. J. Martinko, "Using the Myers-Briggs Type Indicator to Study Managers: A Literature Review and Research Agenda," *Journal of Management* 22 (1996), pp. 45–83; M. H. McCaulley, "The Myers-Briggs Type Indicator: A Measure for Individuals and Groups," *Measurement and Evaluation in Counseling and Development* 22 (1990), pp. 181–95.

85. J. A. Edwards, K. Lanning, and K. Hooker, "The MBTI and Social Information Processing: An Incremental Validity Study," *Journal of Personality Assessment* 78 (June 2002), pp. 432–50; R. Farnsworth, E. Gilbert, and D. Armstrong, "Exploring the Relationship between the Myers-Briggs Type Indicator and the Baron Emotional Quotient Inventory: Applications for Professional Development Practices," *Proceedings of the Annual Conference of the Administrative Sciences Association of Canada, Human Resources Division* 23, no. 9 (2002), pp. 16–23; Gardner and Martinko, "Using the Myers-Briggs Type Indicator to Study Managers."

86. P. E. Spector et al, "Do National Levels of Individualism and Internal Locus of Control Relate to Well-Being? An Ecological Level International Study," *Journal of Organizational Behavior* 22 (2001), pp. 815–32; S. S. K.

Lam and J. Schaubroeck, "The Role of Locus of Control in Reactions to Being Promoted and to Being Passed Over: A Quasi Experiment," *Academy of Management Journal* 43 (February 2000), pp. 66–78; J. M. Howell and B. J. Avolio, "Transformational Leadership, Transactional Leadership, Locus of Control, and Support for Innovation: Key Predictors of Consolidated-Business-Unit Performance," *Journal of Applied Psychology* 78 (1993), pp. 891–902; D. Miller and J.-M. Toulouse, "Chief Executive Personality and Corporate Strategy and Structure in Small Firms," *Management Science* 32 (1986), pp. 1389–1409; P. E. Spector, "Behavior in Organizations as a Function of Employee's Locus of Control," *Psychological Bulletin* 91 (1982), pp. 482–97.

87. M. Snyder, *Public Appearances/ Private Realities: The Psychology of Self-Monitoring* (New York: W. H. Freeman, 1987).

88. A. Mehra, M. Kilduff, and D. J. Brass, "The Social Networks of High and Low Self-Monitors: Implications for Workplace Performance," *Administrative Science Quarterly* 46 (March 2001), pp. 121–46; M. A. Warech, J. W. Smither, R. R. Reilly, R. E. Millsap, and S. P. Reilly, "Self-Monitoring and 360–Degree Ratings," *Leadership Quarterly* 9 (Winter 1998), pp. 449–73; M. Kilduff and D. V. Day, "Do Chameleons Get Ahead? The Effects of Self-Monitoring on Managerial Careers," *Academy of Management Journal* 37 (1994), pp. 1047–60; R. J. Ellis and S. E. Cronshaw, "Self-Monitoring and Leader Emergence: A Test of Moderator Effects," *Small Group Research* 23 (1992), pp. 113–29; S. J. Zaccaro, R. J. Foti, and D. A. Kenny, "Self-Monitoring and Trait-Based Variance in Leadership: An Investigation of Leader Flexibility across Multiple Group Situations," *Journal of Applied Psychology* 76 (1991), pp. 308–15.

89. A. Veverka, "Career Tests Help Job Seekers Analyze Skills, Personality," *Charlotte Observer*, April 14, 2003.

90. J. Holland, *Making Vocational Choices: A Theory of Careers* (Englewood Cliffs, NJ: Prentice Hall, 1973).

91. A. Furnham, "Vocational Preference and P-O Fit: Reflections on Holland's Theory of Vocational Choice," *Applied Psychology: An International*

Review 50 (2001), pp. 5–29; G. D. Gottfredson and J. L. Holland, "A Longitudinal Test of the Influence of Congruence: Job Satisfaction, Competency Utilization, and Counterproductive Behavior," *Journal of Counseling Psychology* 37 (1990), pp. 389–98.

92. J. Tupponce, "Listening to Those Inner Voices," *Richmond Times-Dispatch,* May 11, 2003, p. S3.

93. Furnham, "Vocational Preference and P-O Fit"; J. Arnold, "The Psychology of Careers in Organizations," *International Review of Industrial and Organizational Psychology* 12 (1997), pp. 1–37.

94. R. A. Young and C. P. Chen, "Annual Review: Practice and Research in Career Counseling and Development—1998," *Career Development Quarterly,* December 1999, p. 98.

CHAPTER 3

1. E. Pope, "Domino's Puts Execs on the Line," *Detroit News,* August 1, 2003; J. Lynch and M. Dagostino, "Man in Motion," *People Magazine,* August 26, 2002, p. 89; "Regina Peruggi, President, Central Park Conservancy," *Public Broadcasting System,* 2002 (www.pbs.org.); S. Kapner, "Reality TV Finds New Prey (in Business)," *New York Times,* May 12, 2002, p. 12.

2. Plato, *The Republic,* trans. D. Lee (Harmondsworth, England: Penguin, 1955), Part VII, Section 7.

3. S. F. Cronshaw and R. G. Lord, "Effects of Categorization, Attribution, and Encoding Processes on Leadership Perceptions," *Journal of Applied Psychology* 72 (1987), pp. 97–106.

4. R. H. Fazio, D. R. Roskos-Ewoldsen, and M. C. Powell, "Attitudes, Perception, and Attention," in *The Heart's Eye: Emotional Influences in Perception and Attention,* ed. P. M. Niedenthal and S. Kitayama (San Diego: Academic Press, 1994), pp. 197–216.

5. D. Goleman, *Vital Lies, Simple Truths: The Psychology of Deception* (New York: Touchstone, 1985); M. Haire and W. F. Grunes, "Perceptual Defenses: Processes Protecting an Organized Perception of Another Personality," *Human Relations* 3 (1950), pp. 403–12.

6. C. N. Macrae, G. V. Bodenhausen, A. M. Schloerscheidt, and A. B. Milne, "Tales of the Unexpected: Executive Function and Person Perception," *Journal of Personality and Social Psychology* 76 (1999), pp. 200–13; J. M. Beyer et al., "The Selective Perception of Managers Revisited," *Academy of Management Journal* 40 (June 1997), pp. 716–37; C. N. Macrae and G. V. Bodenhausen, "The Dissection of Selection in Person Perception: Inhibitory Processes in Social Stereotyping," *Journal of Personality & Social Psychology* 69 (1995), pp. 397–407; J. P. Walsh, "Selectivity and Selective Perception: An Investigation of Managers' Belief Structures and Information Processing," *Academy of Management Journal* 31 (1988), pp. 873–96; D. C. Dearborn and H. A. Simon, "Selective Perception: A Note on the Departmental Identification of Executives," *Sociometry* 21 (1958), pp. 140–44.

7. J. Rupert, "We Haven't Forgotten about Her," *Ottawa Citizen,* December 6, 1999; W. Burkan, "Developing Your Wide-Angle Vision; Skills for Anticipating the Future," *Futurist* 32 (March 1998), pp. 35–38. For splatter vision applied to professional bird watchers, see E. Nickens, "Window on the Wild," *Backpacker* 25 (April 1997), pp. 28–32.

8. D. Gurteen, "Knowledge, Creativity and Innovation," *Journal of Knowledge Management* 2 (September 1998), p. 5; C. Argyris and D. A. Schön, *Organizational Learning II* (Reading, MA: Addison-Wesley, 1996); P. M. Senge, *The Fifth Discipline: The Art and Practice of the Learning Organization* (New York: Doubleday/Currency, 1990), Chapter 10; P. N. Johnson-Laird, *Mental Models* (Cambridge: Cambridge University Press, 1984). Mental models are widely discussed in the philosophy of logic. For example, see J. L. Aronson, "Mental Models and Deduction," *American Behavioral Scientist* 40 (May 1997), pp. 782–97.

9. "What Are Mental Models?" *Sloan Management Review* 38 (Spring 1997), p. 13; P. Nystrom and W. Starbuck, "To Avoid Organizational Crises, Unlearn," *Organizational Dynamics* 12 (Winter 1984), pp. 53–65.

10. S. A. Haslam, R. A. Eggins, and K. J. Reynolds, "The ASPIRe Model: Actualizing Social and Personal Identity Resources to Enhance Organizational Outcomes," *Journal of Occupational and Organizational Psychology* 76 (2003), pp. 83–113; M. A. Hogg and D. J. Terry, "Social Identity and Self-Categorization Processes in Organizational Contexts," *Academy of Management Review* 25 (January 2000), pp. 121–40; B. E. Ashforth and F. Mael, "Social Identity Theory and the Organization," *Academy of Management Review* 14 (1989), pp. 20–39; H. Tajfel, *Social Identity and Intergroup Relations* (Cambridge: Cambridge University Press, 1982). Although we have labeled this theory "social identity theory," the discussion that follows incorporates an extension of social identity theory, called self-categorization theory.

11. The interaction between personal and social identity is quite complex, as researchers are now discovering. See J. A. Howard, "Social Psychology of Identities," *Annual Review of Sociology* 26 (2000), pp. 367–93.

12. J. E. Dutton, J. M. Dukerich, and C. V. Harquail, "Organizational Images and Member Identification," *Administrative Science Quarterly* 39 (June 1994), pp. 239–63. For recent research on the selection of identity groups, see B. Simon and C. Hastedt, "Self-Aspects as Social Categories: The Role of Personal Importance and Valence," *European Journal of Social Psychology* 29 (1999), pp. 479–87.

13. J. W. Jackson and E. R. Smith, "Conceptualizing Social Identity: A New Framework and Evidence for the Impact of Different Dimensions," *Personality & Social Psychology Bulletin* 25 (January 1999), pp. 120–35.

14. C. N. Macrae and G. V. Bodenhausen, "Social Cognition: Thinking Categorically about Others," *Annual Review of Psychology* 51 (2000), pp. 93–120; S. T. Fiske, "Stereotyping, Prejudice, and Discrimination," in *Handbook of Social Psychology,* 4th ed., ed. D. T. Gilbert, S. T. Fiske, and G. Lindzey (New York: McGraw-Hill., 1998), pp. 357–411; W. G. Stephan and C. W. Stephan, *Intergroup Relations* (Boulder, CO: Westview, 1996), Chapter 1; L. Falkenberg, "Improving the Accuracy of Stereotypes within the Workplace," *Journal of Management* 16 (1990), pp. 107–18.

15. M. Billig, "Henri Tajfel's 'Cognitive Aspects of Prejudice' and the Psychology of Bigotry," *British Journal of Social Psychology* 41 (2002), pp. 171–88.

16. Macrae and Bodenhausen, "Social Cognition: Thinking Categorically about Others."

17. J. C. Turner and S. A. Haslam, "Social Identity, Organizations, and Leadership," in *Groups at Work: Theory and Research*, ed. M. E. Turner (Mahwah, NJ: Lawrence Erlbaum Associates, 2001), pp. 25–65; P. J. Oaks, S. A. Haslam, and J. C. Turner, *Stereotyping and Social Reality* (Cambridge, MA: Blackwell, 1994); L. Sinclair and Z. Kunda, "Motivated Stereotyping of Women: She's Fine if She Praised Me but Incompetent if She Criticized Me," *Personality and Social Psychology Bulletin* 26 (November 2000), pp. 1329–42.

18. F. T McAndrew et al., "A Multicultural Study of Stereotyping in English-Speaking Countries," *Journal of Social Psychology*, August 2000, pp. 487–502; S. Madon et al., "The Accuracy and Power of Sex, Social Class, and Ethnic Stereotypes: A Naturalistic Study in Person Perception," *Personality & Social Psychology Bulletin* 24 (December 1998), pp. 1304–18; Y. Lee, L. J. Jussim, and C. R. McCauley (eds.), *Stereotype Accuracy: Toward Appreciating Group Differences* (Washington, DC: American Psychological Association, 1996). For early discussion of stereotypes, see W. Lippmann, *Public Opinion* (New York: Macmillan, 1922).

19. D. L. Stone and A. Colella, "A Model of Factors Affecting the Treatment of Disabled Individuals in Organizations," *Academy of Management Review* 21 (1996), pp. 352–401.

20. C. Stangor and L. Lynch, "Memory for Expectancy-Congruent and Expectancy-Incongruent Information: A Review of the Social and Social Development Literatures," *Psychological Bulletin* 111 (1992), pp. 42–61; C. Stangor, L. Lynch, C. Duan, and B. Glass, "Categorization of Individuals on the Basis of Multiple Social Features," *Journal of Personality and Social Psychology* 62 (1992), pp. 207–18.

21. M. Hewstone, M. Rubin, and H. Willis, "Intergroup Bias," *Annual Review of Psychology* 53 (2002), pp. 575–604; Fiske, "Stereotyping, Prejudice, and Discrimination"; S. O. Gaines and E. S. Reed, "Prejudice: From Allport to DuBois," *American Psychologist* 50 (February 1995), pp. 96–103.

22. Hong Kong Equal Opportunities Commission, "EOC Research Findings on Stereotyping: A Call for Diversity," April 15, 2002; P. Porco, "Intolerance Claims Mount," *Anchorage Daily News*, July 19, 2001, p. A1.

23. J. F. Dovidio, S. L. Gaertner, K. Kawakami, and G. Hodson, "Why Can't We Just Get Along? Interpersonal Biases and Interracial Distrust," *Cultural Diversity and Ethnic Minority Psychology* 8 (May 2002), pp. 88–102; M. E. Heilman, "Sex Stereotypes and Their Effects in the Workplace: What We Know and What We Don't Know," *Journal of Social Behavior & Personality* 10 (1995), pp. 3–26.

24. K. Kawakami and J. F. Dovidio, "Implicit Stereotyping: How Reliable Is It?" *Personality and Social Psychology Bulletin* 27 (2001), pp. 212–25; J. A. Bargh, "The Cognitive Monster: The Case against the Controllability of Automatic Stereotype Effects," in *Dual Process Theories in Social Psychology*, ed. S. Chaiken and Y. Trope (New York: Guilford, 1999), pp. 361–82.

25. J. W. Sherman, A. Y. Lee, G. R. Bessenoff, and L. A. Frost, "Stereotype Efficiency Reconsidered: Encoding Flexibility under Cognitive Load," *Journal of Personality and Social Psychology* 75 (1998), pp. 589–606; C. N. Macrae, A. B. Milne, and G. V. Bodenhausen, "Stereotypes as Energy-Saving Devices: A Peek Inside the Cognitive Toolbox," *Journal of Personality and Social Psychology* 66 (1994), pp. 37–47; S. T. Fiske, "Social Cognition and Social Perception," *Annual Review of Psychology* 44 (1993), pp. 155–94.

26. L. Roberson, C. T. Kulik, and M. B. Pepper, "Using Needs Assessment to Resolve Controversies in Diversity Training Design," *Group & Organization Management* 28 (March 2003), pp. 148–74; M. Bendick Jr., M. L. Egan, and S. M. Lofhjelm, "Workforce Diversity Training: From Anti-Discrimination Compliance to Organizational Development HR," *Human Resource Planning* 24 (2001), pp. 10–25.

27. F. Glastra, M. Meerman, P. Schedler, and S. De Vries, "Broadening the Scope of Diversity Management: Strategic Implications in the Case of the Netherlands," *Relations Industrielles* (Fall 2000), pp. 698–721; J. S. Osland, A. Bird, J. Delano, and M. Jacob, "Beyond Sophisticated Stereotyping: Cultural Sensemaking in Context," *Academy of Management Executive* 14 (February 2000), pp. 65–79.

28. J. Dixon and K. Durrheim, "Contact and the Ecology of Racial Division: Some Varieties of Informal Segregation," *British Journal of Social Psychology* 42 (March 2003), pp. 1ff; S. L. Gaertner et al, "Reducing Intergroup Bias: Elements of Intergroup Cooperation," *Journal of Personality and Social Psychology* 76 (1999), pp. 388–402; S. Brickson, "The Impact of Identity Orientation Individual and Organizational Outcomes in Demographically Diverse Settings," *Academy of Management Review* 25 (January 2000), pp. 82–101; T. F. Pettigrew, "Intergroup Contact Theory," *Annual Review of Psychology* 49 (1998), pp. 65–85.

29. B. F. Reskin, "The Proximate Causes of Employment Discrimination," *Contemporary Sociology* 29 (March 2000), pp. 319–28.

30. H. H. Kelley, *Attribution in Social Interaction* (Morristown, NJ: General Learning Press, 1971).

31. J. M. Feldman, "Beyond Attribution Theory: Cognitive Processes in Performance Appraisal," *Journal of Applied Psychology* 66 (1981), pp. 127–48; H. H. Kelley, "The Processes of Causal Attribution," *American Psychologist* 28 (1973), pp. 107–28.

32. V. L. Barker, III, and P. S. Barrb, "Linking Top Manager Attributions to Strategic Reorientation in Declining Firms Attempting Turnarounds," *Journal of Business Research* 55 (2002), pp. 963–79; M. T. Dasborough and N. M. Ashkanasy, "Emotion and Attribution of Intentionality in Leader–Member Relationships," *Leadership Quarterly* 13 (October 2002), pp. 615–34; B. Weiner, "Intrapersonal and Interpersonal Theories of Motivation from an Attributional Perspective," *Educational Psychology Review* 12 (2000), pp. 1–14; J. M. Crant and T. S. Bateman, "Assignment of Credit and Blame for Performance Outcomes," *Academy of Management Journal* 36 (1993), pp. 7–27; D. R. Norris and R. E. Niebuhr, "Attributional Influences on the Job Performance–Job Satisfaction Relationship," *Academy of Management Journal* 27 (1984), pp. 424–31.

33. H. J. Bernardin and P. Villanova, "Performance Appraisal," in *Generalising from Laboratory to Field Settings,* ed. E. A. Locke (Lexington, MA: Lexington Books, 1986), pp. 43–62; and S. G. Green and T. R. Mitchell, "Attributional Processes of Leader–Member Interactions," *Organizational Behavior and Human Performance* 23 (1979), pp. 429–58.

34. P. J. Taylor and J. L. Pierce, "Effects of Introducing a Performance Management System on Employees' Subsequent Attitudes and Effort," *Public Personnel Management* 28 (Fall 1999), pp. 423–52.

35. P. Rosenthal and D. Guest, "Gender Difference in Managers' Causal Explanations for Their Work Performance: A Study in Two Organizations," *Journal of Occupational & Organizational Psychology* 69 (1996), pp. 145–51.

36. B. McElhinny, "Printing Plant Makes Its Mark," *Charleston (SC) Daily Mail,* May 6, 1997, p. D1.

37. J. M. Darley and K. C. Oleson, "Introduction to Research on Interpersonal Expectations," in *Interpersonal Expectations: Theory, Research, and Applications* (Cambridge, UK: Cambridge University Press, 1993), pp. 45–63; D. Eden, *Pygmalion in Management* (Lexington, MA: Lexington Books, 1990); L. Jussim, "Self-Fulfilling Prophecies: A Theoretical and Integrative Review," *Psychological Review* 93 (1986), pp. 429–45.

38. Similar models are presented in R. H. G. Field and D. A. Van Seters, "Management by Expectations (MBE): The Power of Positive Prophecy," *Journal of General Management* 14 (Winter 1988), pp. 19–33; D. Eden, "Self-Fulfilling Prophecy as a Management Tool: Harnessing Pygmalion," *Academy of Management Review* 9 (1984), pp. 64–73.

39. M. J. Harris and R. Rosenthal, "Mediation of Interpersonal Expectancy Effects: 31 Meta-Analyses," *Psychological Bulletin* 97 (1985), pp. 363–86.

40. D. Eden, "Interpersonal Expectations in Organizations," in *Interpersonal Expectations: Theory, Research, and Applications* (Cambridge, UK: Cambridge University Press, 1993), pp. 154–78.

41. R. P. Brown and E. C. Pinel, "Stigma on My Mind: Individual Differences in the Experience of Stereotype Threat," *Journal of Experimental Social Psychology,* in press (2003). For a general discussion of the problems with self-fulfilling prophecy, see J-F. Manzoni, "The Set-Up-to-Fail Syndrome," *Harvard Business Review* 76 (March–April 1998), pp. 101–13; J. S. Livingston, "Retrospective Commentary," *Harvard Business Review* 66 (September–October 1988), p. 125.

42. D. Eden et al., "Implanting Pygmalion Leadership Style through Workshop Training: Seven Field Experiments," *Leadership Quarterly* 11 (2000), pp. 171–210; S. Oz and D. Eden, "Restraining the Golem: Boosting Performance by Changing the Interpretation of Low Scores," *Journal of Applied Psychology* 79 (1994), pp. 744–54.

43. Adapted from B. Rand, "Companies Recognize Need to Mirror Community," *Democrat and Chronicle* (Rochester, NY), January 13, 2003.

44. S. S. White and E. A. Locke, "Problems with the Pygmalion Effect and Some Proposed Solutions," *Leadership Quarterly* 11 (Autumn 2000), pp. 389–415. This source also cites recent studies on the failure of traditional Pygmalion training. For an early application of self-efficacy in self-fulfilling prophecy, see K. S. Crawford, E. D. Thomas, and J. J. Fink, "Pygmalion at Sea: Improving the Work Effectiveness of Low Performers," *Journal of Applied Behavioral Science* 16 (1980), pp. 482–505.

45. A. D. Stajkovic and F. Luthans, "Social Cognitive Theory and Self-Efficacy: Going beyond Traditional Motivational and Behavioral Approaches," *Organizational Dynamics* 26 (Spring 1998), pp. 62–74; A. Bandura, *Self-Efficacy: The Exercise of Control* (New York: W. H. Freeman & Co., 1996); M. E. Gist and T. R. Mitchell, "Self-Efficacy: A Theoretical Analysis of Its Determinants and Malleability," *Academy of Management Review* 17 (1992), pp. 183–211; R. F. Mager, "No Self-Efficacy, No Performance," *Training* 29 (April 1992), pp. 32–36.

46. E. A. Lind, L. Kray, and L. Thompson, "Primacy Effects in Justice Judgments: Testing Predictions from Fairness Heuristic Theory," *Organizational Behavior and Human Decision Processes* 85 (July 2001), pp. 189–210; J. D. Krause and G. W. Joseph, "Decision Biases in Commercial Loan Risk Estimation," *Journal of Bank Cost & Management Accounting* 12 (1999), pp 3–10; T. W. Dougherty, D. B. Turban, and J. C. Callender, "Confirming First Impressions in the Employment Interview: A Field Study of Interview Behavior," *Journal of Applied Psychology* 79 (1994), pp. 659–65; C. L. Kleinke, *First Impressions: The Psychology of Encountering Others* (Englewood Cliffs, NJ: Prentice Hall, 1975).

47. O. Ybarra, "When First Impressions Don't Last: The Role of Isolation and Adaptation Processes in the Revision of Evaluative Impressions," *Social Cognition* 19 (October 2001), pp. 491–520.

48. D. D. Steiner and J. S. Rain, "Immediate and Delayed Primacy and Recency Effects in Performance Evaluation," *Journal of Applied Psychology* 74 (1989), pp. 136–42; R. L. Heneman and K. N. Wexley, "The Effects of Time Delay in Rating and Amount of Information Observed in Performance Rating Accuracy," *Academy of Management Journal* 26 (1983), pp. 677–86.

49. K. R. Murphy, R. A. Jako, and R. L. Anhalt, "Nature and Consequences of Halo Error: A Critical Analysis," *Journal of Applied Psychology* 78 (1993), pp. 218–25; W. H. Cooper, "Ubiquitous Halo," *Psychological Bulletin* 90 (1981), pp. 218–44.

50. T. H. Feeley, "Evidence of Halo Effects in Student Evaluations of Communication Instruction," *Communication Education* 51 (July 2002), pp. 225–36; S. Kozlowski, M. Kirsch, and G. Chao, "Job Knowledge, Ratee Familiarity, Conceptual Similarity, and Halo Error: An Exploration," *Journal of Applied Psychology,* 71 (1986), pp. 45–49.

51. C. J. Jackson and A. Furnham, "Appraisal Ratings, Halo, and Selection: A Study Using Sales Staff," *European Journal of Psychological Assessment* 17 (2001), pp. 17–24; W. K. Balzer and L. M. Sulsky, "Halo and Performance Appraisal Research: A Critical Examination," *Journal of Applied Psychology* 77 (1992), pp. 975–85.

52. R. L. Gross and S. E. Brodt, "How Assumptions of Consensus Undermine Decision Making," *Sloan Management*

Review, January 2001, pp. 86–94; G. G. Sherwood, "Self-Serving Biases in Person Perception: A Re-examination of Projection as a Mechanism of Defense," *Psychological Bulletin* 90 (1981), pp. 445–59.

53. W. G. Stephen and K. A. Finlay, "The Role of Empathy in Improving Intergroup Relations," *Journal of Social Issues* 55 (Winter 1999), pp. 729–43; C. Duan and C. E. Hill, "The Current State of Empathy Research," *Journal of Counseling Psychology* 43 (1996), pp. 261–74.

54. S. K. Parker and C. M. Axtell, "Seeing Another Viewpoint: Antecedents and Outcomes of Employee Perspective Taking," *Academy of Management Journal* 44 (December 2001), pp. 1085–1100.

55. G. Condon, "Walking in Another's Shoes," *Hartford (CT) Courant,* July 11, 2003, p. B1.

56. D. Goleman, "What Makes a Leader?" *Harvard Business Review* 76 (November–December 1998), pp. 92–102.

57. T. W. Costello and S. S. Zalkind, *Psychology in Administration: A Research Orientation* (Englewood Cliffs, NJ: Prentice Hall, 1963), pp. 45–46.

58. J. Luft, *Group Processes* (Palo Alto, CA: Mayfield Publishing, 1984). For a variation of this model, see J. Hall, "Communication Revisited," *California Management Review* 15 (Spring 1973), pp. 56–67.

59. L. C. Miller and D. A. Kenny, "Reciprocity of Self-Disclosure at the Individual and Dyadic Levels: A Social Relations Analysis," *Journal of Personality and Social Psychology* 50 (1986), pp. 713–19.

60. D. M. Harris and R. L. DeSimone, *Human Resource Development* (Fort Worth, TX: Harcourt Brace, 1994), p. 54; B. Bass and J. Vaughn, *Training in Industry: The Management of Learning* (Belmont, CA: Wadsworth, 1966), p. 8; W. McGehee and P. W. Thayer, *Training in Business and Industry* (New York: Wiley, 1961), pp. 131–34.

61. G. F. B. Probst, "Practical Knowledge Management: A Model That Works," *Prism* (Second Quarter 1998), pp. 17–23; G. Miles, Grant, R. E. Miles, V. Perrone, and L. Edvinsson, "Some Conceptual and Research Barriers to

the Utilization of Knowledge," *California Management Review* 40 (Spring 1998), pp. 281–88; E. C. Nevis, A. J. DiBella, and J. M. Gould, "Understanding Organizations as Learning Systems," *Sloan Management Review* 36 (Winter 1995), pp. 73–85; D. Ulrich, T. Jick, and M. Von Glinow, "High Impact Learning: Building and Diffusing Learning Capability," *Organizational Dynamics* 22 (Autumn 1993), pp. 52–66; G. Huber, "Organizational Learning: The Contributing Processes and Literature," *Organizational Science* 2 (1991), pp. 88–115.

62. Watson Wyatt, *Playing to Win: Strategic Rewards in the War for Talent–Fifth Annual Survey Report 2000/2001* (Washington, DC: Author, 2001).

63. E. N. Brockmann and W. P. Anthony, "Tacit Knowledge and Strategic Decision Making," *Group & Organization Management* 27 (December 2002), pp. 436–55; W. L. P. Wong and D. F. Radcliffe, "The Tacit Nature of Design Knowledge," *Technology Analysis & Strategic Management,* December 2000, pp. 493–512; I. Nonaka and H. Takeuchi, *The Knowledge-Creating Company* (New York: Oxford University Press, 1995); R. K. Wagner and R. J. Sternberg, "Practical Intelligence in Real-World Pursuits: The Role of Tacit Knowledge," *Journal of Personality and Social Psychology* 49 (1985), pp. 436–58.

64. W. F. Dowling, "Conversation with B. F. Skinner," *Organizational Dynamics,* Winter 1973, pp. 31–40.

65. R. G. Miltenberger, *Behavior Modification: Principles and Procedures* (Pacific Grove, CA: Brooks/Cole, 1997); J. Komaki, T. Coombs, and S. Schepman, "Motivational Implications of Reinforcement Theory," in *Motivation and Leadership at Work,* ed. R. M. Steers, L. W. Porter, and G. A. Bigley (New York: McGraw-Hill, 1996), pp. 34–52; H. P. Sims and P. Lorenzi, *The New Leadership Paradigm: Social Learning and Cognition in Organizations* (Newbury Park, CA: Sage, 1992), Part II.

66. F. Luthans and R. Kreitner, *Organizational Behavior Modification and Beyond* (Glenview, IL: Scott, Foresman, 1985); pp. 85–88; and T. K. Connellan, *How to Improve Human Performance* (New York: Harper & Row, 1978), pp. 48–57.

67. Miltenberger, *Behavior Modification,* Chapters 4–6.

68. T. C. Mawhinney and R. R. Mawhinney, "Operant Terms and Concepts Applied to Industry," in *Industrial Behavior Modification: A Management Handbook,* ed. R. M. O'Brien, A. M. Dickinson, and M. P. Rosow (New York: Pergamon Press, 1982), p. 117; R. Kreitner, "Controversy in OBM: History, Misconceptions, and Ethics," in *Handbook of Organizational Behavior Management,* ed. L. W. Frederiksen (New York: Wiley, 1982), pp. 76–79.

69. Luthans and Kreitner, *Organizational Behavior Modification and Beyond,* pp. 53–54.

70. K. D. Butterfield, L. K. Trevino, and G. A. Ball, "Punishment from the Manager's Perspective: A Grounded Investigation and Inductive Model," *Academy of Management Journal* 39 (1996), pp. 1479–1512; L. K. Trevino, "The Social Effects of Punishment in Organizations: A Justice Perspective," *Academy of Management Review* 17 (1992), pp. 647–76.

71. G. P. Latham and V. L. Huber, "Schedules of Reinforcement: Lessons from the Past and Issues for the Future," *Journal of Organizational Behavior Management* 13 (1992), pp. 125–49. There is strong recent interest in the timing of reinforcer and response as part of learning in animal behavior. See B. A. Williams, "Challenges to Timing-Based Theories of Operant Behavior," *Behavioural Processes* 62 (April 28, 2003), pp. 115–23; J. E. Staddon and D. T. Cerutti, "Operant Conditioning," *Annual Review of Psychology* 54 (2003), pp. 115–44.

72. S. Armour, "Sick Days May Hurt Your Bottom Line," *USA Today,* February 7, 2003, p. A1.

73. F. Luthans and A. D. Stajkovic, "Reinforce for Performance: The Need to Go Beyond Pay and Even Rewards," *Academy of Management Executive* 13 (May 1999), pp. 49–57; A. D. Stajkovic and F. Luthans, "A Meta-Analysis of the Effects of Organizational Behavior Modification on Task Performance, 1975–95," *Academy of Management Journal* 40 (1997), pp. 1122–49.

74. K. Maeshiro, "School Attendance Pays," *Los Angeles Daily News,* January 28, 2002, p. AV1; P. Eaton-Robb, "For

Employees, Solutions That Work," *Providence (RI) Journal*, January 10, 2001, p. E1; D. Behar, "Firm Launches Lottery to Beat 'Sickies' Plague," *Daily Mail* (UK), January 8, 2001, p. 27; G. Masek, "Dana Corp.," *Industry Week*, October 19, 1998, p. 48.

75. "New Warnings on the Fine Points of Safety Incentives," *Pay for Performance Report*, September 2002; G. A. Merwin, J. A. Thomason, and E. E. Sanford, "A Methodological and Content Review of Organizational Behavior Management in the Private Sector: 1978–1986," *Journal of Organizational Behavior Management* 10 (1989), pp. 39–57; T. C. Mawhinney, "Philosophical and Ethical Aspects of Organizational Behavior Management: Some Evaluative Feedback," *Journal of Organizational Behavior Management* 6 (Spring 1984), pp. 5–31.

76. J. A. Bargh and M. J. Ferguson, "Beyond Behaviorism: On the Automaticity of Higher Mental Processes," *Psychological Bulletin* 126 (2000), pp. 925–45.

77. A. Bandura, *Social Foundations of Thought and Action: A Social Cognitive Theory* (Englewood Cliffs, NJ: Prentice Hall, 1986).

78. A. Pescuric and W. C. Byham, "The New Look of Behavior Modeling," *Training & Development* 50 (July 1996), pp. 24–30; H. P. Sims Jr. and C. C. Manz, "Modeling Influences on Employee Behavior," *Personnel Journal*, January 1982, pp. 58–65.

79. L. K. Trevino, "The Social Effects of Punishment in Organizations: A Justice Perspective," *Academy of Management Review* 17 (1992), pp. 647–76; M. E. Schnake, "Vicarious Punishment in a Work Setting," *Journal of Applied Psychology* 71 (1986), pp. 343–45.

80. M. Foucault, *Discipline and Punish: The Birth of the Prison* (Harmondsworth, UK: Penguin, 1977).

81. L. K. Trevino, "The Social Effects of Punishment in Organizations: A Justice Perspective," *Academy of Management Review* 17 (1992), pp. 647–76; Schnake, "Vicarious Punishment in a Work Setting."

82. A. W. Logue, *Self-Control: Waiting until Tomorrow for What You Want Today* (Englewood Cliffs, NJ: Prentice Hall, 1995); A. Bandura, "Self-Reinforcement:

Theoretical and Methodological Considerations," *Behaviorism* 4 (1976), pp. 135–55.

83. C. A. Frayne, "Improving Employee Performance through Self-Management Training," *Business Quarterly* 54 (Summer 1989), pp. 46–50.

84. D. Woodruff, "Putting Talent to the Test," *Wall Street Journal Europe*, November 14, 2000, p. 25. The simulation events described here were experienced by the author of this article, but we reasonably assume that Mandy Chooi, who also completed the simulation, went through similar events in her simulation.

85. S. Gherardi, D. Nicolini, and F. Odella, "Toward a Social Understanding of How People Learn in Organizations," *Management Learning* 29 (September 1998), pp. 273–97; Ulrich, Jick, and Von Glinow, "High Impact Learning."

86. D. A. Kolb, R. E. Boyatzis, and C. Mainemelis, "Experiential Learning Theory: Previous Research and New Directions," in *Perspectives on Thinking, Learning, and Cognitive Styles*, ed. R. J. Sternberg and L. F. Zhang (Mahwah, NJ: Lawrence Erlbaum Associates, 2001), pp. 227–48; D. A. Kolb, *Experiential Learning* (Englewood Cliffs, NJ: Prentice Hall, 1984).

87. The learning orientation concept is the focus of current attention in marketing; see M. A. Farrell, "Developing a Market-Oriented Learning Organization," *Australian Journal of Management* 25 (September 2000); W. E. Baker and J. M. Sinkula, "The Synergistic Effect of Market Orientation and Learning Orientation," *Journal of the Academy of Marketing Science* 27 (1999), pp. 411–27.

88. D. McFadden, "This Is Only a Test," *Providence (RI) Journal-Bulletin*, May 16, 2003, p. C1; C. F. Crowley, "'No Slackers' in this Class," *Providence (RI) Journal-Bulletin*, February 11, 2003, pp. C1, C6.

89. R. Farson and R. Keyes, "The Failure-Tolerant Leader," *Harvard Business Review* 80 (August 2002), pp. 64–71; J. Jusko, "Always Lessons to Learn," *Industry Week*, February 15, 1999, p. 23.

90. R. W. Revans, *The Origin and Growth of Action Learning* (London: Chartwell Bratt, 1982), pp. 626–27.

91. V. J. Marsick, "The Many Faces of Action Learning," *Management Learning* 30 (June 1999), pp. 159–76.

92. R. M. Fulmer, P. Gibbs, and J. B. Keys, "The Second Generation Learning Organizations: New Tools for Sustaining Competitive Advantage," *Organizational Dynamics* 27 (Autumn 1998), pp. 6–20; A. L. Stern "Where the Action Is," *Across the Board* 34 (September 1997), pp. 43–47; R. W. Revans, "What Is Action Learning?" *Journal of Management Development* 15 (1982), pp. 64–75.

93. R. M. Fulmer, P. A. Gibbs, and M. Goldsmith, "Developing Leaders: How Winning Companies Keep on Winning," *Sloan Management Review*, October 2000, pp. 49–59; J. A. Conger and K. Xin, "Executive Education in the 21st Century," *Journal of Management Education* (February 2000), pp. 73–101.

94. T. T. Baldwin, C. Danielson, and W. Wiggenhorn, "The Evolution of Learning Strategies in Organizations: From Employee Development to Business Redefinition," *Academy of Management Executive* 11 (November 1997), pp. 47–58.

CHAPTER 4

1. E. D. Thompson, "Motivating Employees," *Credit Union Magazine* 69 (April 2003), p. 56; K. Mellen, "Fish! Tackles Workplace Morale," *Daily Hampshire Gazette*, February 24, 2003; S. C. Lundin, H. Paul, and J. Christensen, *Fish! Tales: Bite-Sized Stories, Unlimited Possibilities* (New York: Hyperion Press, 2002); V. Watson, "Having Fun While Improving Customer Service," Sprint News Release, June 13, 2002; S. C. Lundin, H. Paul, and J. Christensen, *Fish! A Remarkable Way to Boost Morale and Improve Results* (New York: Hyperion Press, 2000).

2. C. V. Fukami, "9/11 Montage: Professors Remember," *Academy of Management Learning & Education* 1 (September 2002), pp. 14–37.

3. The meaning of emotions is still being debated, so the definition varies somewhat across sources. The definition presented here is constructed from information in the following sources: N. M. Ashkanasy, W. J. Zerbe, C. E. J. Hartel, "Introduction: Managing Emotions in a Changing Workplace," in *Managing Emotions in the*

Workplace, ed. N. M. Ashkanasy, W. J. Zerbe, and C. E. J. Hartel (Armonk, NY: M. E. Sharpe, 2002), pp. 3–18; H. M. Weiss, "Conceptual and Empirical Foundations for the Study of Affect at Work," in *Emotions in the Workplace,* ed. R. G. Lord, R. J. Klimoski, and R. Kanfer (San Francisco: Jossey-Bass, 2002), pp. 20–63; S. Kitayama and P. M. Niedenthal, "Introduction," in *The Heart's Eye: Emotional Influences in Perception and Attention,* ed. P. M. Niedenthal and S. Kitayama (San Diego: Academic Press, 1994), pp. 6–7.

4. R. Kanfer and R. J. Klimoski, "Affect and Work: Looking Back to the Future," in *Emotions in the Workplace,* ed. R. G. Lord, R. J. Klimoski, and R. Kanfer (San Francisco: Jossey-Bass, 2002), pp. 473–90; J. M. George and A. P. Brief, "Motivational Agendas in the Workplace: The Effects of Feelings on Focus of Attention and Work Motivation," *Research in Organizational Behavior* 18 (1996), pp. 75–109.

5. R. B. Zajonc, "Emotions," in *Handbook of Social Psychology,* ed. D. T. Gilbert, S. T. Fiske, and L. Gardner (New York: Oxford University Press, 1998), pp. 591–634; K. Oatley and J. M. Jenkins, "Human Emotions: Function and Dysfunction," *Annual Review of Psychology* 43 (1992), pp. 55–85.

6. H. M. Weiss and R. Cropanzano, "Affective Events Theory: A Theoretical Discussion of the Structure, Causes, and Consequences of Affective Experiences at Work," *Research in Organizational Behavior* 18 (1996), pp. 1–74; P. Shaver, J. Schwartz, D. Kirson, and C. O'Connor, "Emotion Knowledge: Further Exploration of a Prototype Approach," *Journal of Personality and Social Psychology* 52 (1987), pp. 1061–86.

7. R. J. Larson, E. Diener, and R. E. Lucas, "Emotion: Models, Measures, and Differences," in *Emotions in the Workplace,* ed. R. G. Lord, R. J. Klimoski, and R. Kanfer (San Francisco: Jossey-Bass, 2002), pp. 64–113.

8. A. P. Brief, *Attitudes In and Around Organizations* (Thousand Oaks, CA: Sage, 1998); J. M. George and G. R. Jones, "Experiencing Work: Values, Attitudes, and Moods," *Human Relations* 50 (April 1997), pp. 393–416; J. M. Olson and M. P. Zama, "Attitudes and Attitude Change," *Annual Review of Psychology* 44 (1993), pp. 117–54. De-

bate is ongoing about whether attitudes represent only feelings or all three components described here. However, those who adopt the single-factor perspective still refer to beliefs as the cognitive *component* of attitudes. For example, see I. Ajzen, "Nature and Operation of Attitudes," *Annual Review of Psychology* 52 (2001), pp. 27–58.

9. M. D. Zalesny and J. K. Ford, "Extending the Social Information Processing Perspective: New Links to Attitudes, Behaviors, and Perceptions," *Organizational Behavior and Human Decision Processes* 52 (1992), pp. 205–46; G. Salancik and J. Pfeffer, "A Social Information Processing Approach to Job Attitudes and Task Design," *Administrative Science Quarterly* 23 (1978), pp. 224–53.

10. C. J. Armitage and M. Conner, "Efficacy of the Theory of Planned Behavior: A Meta-Analytic Review," *British Journal of Social Psychology* 40 (2001), pp. 471–99.

11. J. D. Morris, C.-M. Woo, J. A. Geason, and J.-Y. Kim, "The Power of Affect: Predicting Intention," *Journal of Advertising Research* 42 (May/June 2002), pp. 7–17; M. Perugini and R. P. Bagozzi, "The Role of Desires and Anticipated Emotions in Goal-Directed Behaviors: Broadening and Deepening the Theory of Planned Behavior," *British Journal of Social Psychology* 40 (March 2001), pp. 79ff; C. D. Fisher, "Mood and Emotions while Working: Missing Pieces of Job Satisfaction?" *Journal of Organizational Behavior* 21 (2000), pp. 185–202. For a review of the predictability of the traditional attitude model, see Armitage and Conner, "Efficacy of the Theory of Planned Behavior."

12. The rational center is mostly in the prefrontal cerebral cortex. The limbic center is typically recognized as the brain location for emotions. However, scholars now say that the emotional process is distributed rather than located in one part of the brain. See J. Schulkin, B. L. Thompson, and J. B. Rosen, "Demythologizing the Emotions: Adaptation, Cognition, and Visceral Representations of Emotion in the Nervous System," *Brain and Cognition (Affective Neuroscience)* 52 (June 2003), pp. 15–23. For discussion of brain processes and emotions, see

D. S. Massey, "A Brief History of Human Society: The Origin and Role of Emotion in Social Life," *American Sociological Review* 67 (February 2002), pp. 1–29; P. R. Lawrence and N. Nohria, *Driven: How Human Nature Shapes Our Choices* (San Francisco: Jossey-Bass, 2002), pp. 44–47, 168–70; R. Hastie, "Problems for Judgment and Decision Making," *Annual Review of Psychology* 52 (2001), pp. 653–83; A. Damasio, *The Feeling of What Happens* (New York: Harcourt, Brace, 1999).

13. Weiss and Cropanzano, "Affective Events Theory."

14. Weiss and Cropanzano, "Affective Events Theory," pp. 52–57.

15. L. Festinger, *A Theory of Cognitive Dissonance* (Evanston, IL: Row, Peterson, 1957); G. R. Salancik, "Commitment and the Control of Organizational Behavior and Belief," in *New Directions in Organizational Behavior,* ed. B. M. Staw and G. R. Salancik (Chicago: St. Clair, 1977), pp. 1–54.

16. T. A. Judge, E. A. Locke, and C. C. Durham, "The Dispositional Causes of Job Satisfaction: A Core Evaluations Approach," *Research in Organizational Behavior* 19 (1997), pp. 151–88; A. P. Brief, A. H. Butcher, and L. Roberson, "Cookies, Disposition, and Job Attitudes: The Effects of Positive Mood-Inducing Events and Negative Affectivity on Job Satisfaction in a Field Experiment," *Organizational Behavior and Human Decision Processes* 62 (1995), pp. 55–62.

17. C. M. Brotheridge and A. A. Grandey, "Emotional Labor and Burnout: Comparing Two Perspectives of 'People Work,'" *Journal of Vocational Behavior* 60 (2002), pp. 17–39; A. P. Brief and H. M.Weiss, "Organizational Behavior: Affect in the Workplace," *Annual Review of Psychology* 53 (2002), pp. 279–307; R. D. Iverson and S. J. Deery, "Understanding the "Personological" Basis of Employee Withdrawal: The Influence of Affective Disposition on Employee Tardiness, Early Departure, and Absenteeism," *Journal of Applied Psychology* 86 (October 2001), pp. 856–66.

18. C. Dormann and D. Zapf, "Job Satisfaction: A Meta-Analysis of Stabilities," *Journal of Organizational Behavior* 22 (2001), pp. 483–504;

J. Schaubroeck, D. C. Ganster, and B. Kemmerer, "Does Trait Affect Promote Job Attitude Stability?" *Journal of Organizational Behavior* 17 (1996), pp. 191–96; R. D. Arvey, B. P. McCall, T. L. Bouchard, and P. Taubman, "Genetic Differences on Job Satisfaction and Work Values," *Personality and Individual Differences* 17 (1994), pp. 21–33.

19. D. Matheson, "A Vancouver Cafe Where Rudeness Is Welcomed," Canada AM, *CTV Television*, January 11, 2000; R. Corelli, "Dishing Out Rudeness," *Maclean's*, January 11, 1999, p. 44.

20. J. A. Morris and D. C. Feldman, "The Dimensions, Antecedents, and Consequences of Emotional Labor," *Academy of Management Review* 21 (1996), pp. 986–1010; B. E. Ashforth and R. H. Humphrey, "Emotional Labor in Service Roles: The Influence of Identity," *Academy of Management Review* 18 (1993), pp. 88–115.

21. A. A. Grandey and A. L. Brauburger, "The Emotion Regulation behind the Customer Service Smile," in *Emotions in the Workplace*, ed. R. G. Lord, R. J. Klimoski, and R. Kanfer (San Francisco: Jossey-Bass, 2002), pp. 260–94; J. A. Morris and D. C. Feldman, "Managing Emotions in the Workplace," *Journal of Managerial Issues* 9 (Fall 1997), pp. 257–74.

22. J. S. Sass, "Emotional Labor as Cultural Performance: The Communication of Caregiving in a Nonprofit Nursing Home," *Western Journal of Communication* 64 (Summer 2000), pp. 330–58; R. I. Sutton, "Maintaining Norms about Expressed Emotions: The Case of Bill Collectors," *Administrative Science Quarterly* 36 (1991), pp. 245–68.

23. J. Strasburg, "The Making of a Grand Hotel," *San Francisco Chronicle*, March 25, 2001, p. B1.

24. E. Forman, "'Diversity Concerns Grow as Companies Head Overseas,' Consultant Says," *Fort Lauderdale (FL) Sun-Sentinel*, June 26, 1995.

25. J. Schaubroeck and J. R. Jones, "Antecedents of Workplace Emotional Labor Dimensions and Moderators of Their Effects on Physical Symptoms," *Journal of Organizational Behavior* 21 (2000), pp. 163–83; R. Buck, "The Spontaneous Communication of Inter-personal Expectations," in *Interpersonal Expectations: Theory, Research, and Applications* (Cambridge, UK: Cambridge University Press, 1993), pp. 227–41. The quotation from George Burns comes from the Buck source. However, this line has also been attributed to Groucho Marx.

26. W. J. Zerbe, "Emotional Dissonance and Employee Well-Being," in *Managing Emotions in the Workplace*, ed. N. M. Ashkanasy, W. J. Zerbe, and C. E. J. Hartel (Armonk, NY: M. E. Sharpe, 2002), pp. 189–214; K. Pugliesi, "The Consequences of Emotional Labor: Effects on Work Stress, Job Satisfaction, and Well-Being," *Motivation & Emotion* 23 (June 1999), pp. 125–54; A. S. Wharton, "The Psychosocial Consequences of Emotional Labor," *Annals of the American Academy of Political & Social Science* 561 (January 1999), pp. 158–76.

27. C. M. Brotheridge and A. A. Grandey, "Emotional Labor and Burnout: Comparing Two Perspectives of 'People Work,'" *Journal of Vocational Behavior* 60 (2002), pp. 17–39. This observation is also identified in N. M. Ashkanasy and C. S. Daus, "Emotion in the Workplace: The New Challenge for Managers," *Academy of Management Executive* 16 (February 2002), pp. 76–86.

28. A. Schwitzerlette, "CiCi's Pizza Coming to Beckley," *Register-Herald* (Beckley, WV), August 24, 2003.

29. T. Schwartz, "'How Do You Feel?'" *Fast Company*, June 2000, p. 296; J. Stuller, "Unconventional Smarts," *Across the Board* 35 (January 1998), pp. 22–23.

30. J. D. Mayer, P. Salovey, and D. R. Caruso, "Models of Emotional Intelligence," in *Handbook of Human Intelligence*, 2nd ed., ed. R. J. Sternberg (New York: Cambridge University Press, 2000), p. 396. This definition is also recognized in C. Cherniss, "Emotional Intelligence and Organizational Effectiveness," in *The Emotionally Intelligent Workplace*, ed. C. Cherniss and D. Goleman (San Francisco: Jossey-Bass, 2001), pp. 3–12.

31. These four dimensions of emotional intelligence are discussed in detail in D. Goleman, R. Boyatzis, and A. McKee, *Primal Leadership* (Boston: Harvard Business School Press, 2002), Chapter 3. Slight variations of this model are presented in D. Goleman, "An EI-Based Theory of Performance," in *The Emotionally Intelligent Workplace*, ed. C. Cherniss and D. Goleman (San Francisco: Jossey-Bass, 2001), pp. 27–44; R. E. Boyatzis, D. Goleman, and K. S. Rhee, "Clustering Competence in Emotional Intelligence," in *The Handbook of Emotional Intelligence*, ed. R. Bar-On and J. D. A. Parker (San Francisco: Jossey-Bass, 2000), pp. 343–62.

32. The hierarchical nature of the four EI dimensions is discussed by Goleman but is more explicit in the Salovey and Mayer model. See Mayer et al., "Models of Emotional Intelligence," pp. 396–420; J. D. Mayer and P. Salovey, "What Is Emotional Intelligence?" in *Emotional Development and Emotional Intelligence: Implications for Educators*, ed. P. Salovey and D. Sluyter (New York: Basic Books, 1997), pp. 3–31.

33. A brief history of emotional intelligence is presented in D. Goleman, "Emotional Intelligence: Issues in Paradigm Building," in *The Emotionally Intelligent Workplace*, ed. C. Cherniss and D. Goleman (San Francisco: Jossey-Bass, 2001), pp. 13–26; S. Newsome, A. L. Day, and V. M. Catano, "Assessing the Predictive Validity of Emotional Intelligence," *Personality and Individual Differences* 29 (December 2000), pp. 1005–16.

34. H. Nel, W. S. De Villiers, and A. S. Engelbrecht, "The Influence of Emotional Intelligence on Performance in a Call Center Environment," in *Conference Proceedings of the First Conference on Contemporary Management: Emotional Intelligence in Organisations*, September 1–2, 2003, ed. A. Travaglione, A. Boshoff, N. Ferres, and D. Crombia, pp. 81–90; P. J. Jordan, N. M. Ashkanasy, C. E. J. Hartel, and G. S. Hooper, "Workgroup Emotional Intelligence: Scale Development and Relationship to Team Process Effectiveness and Goal Focus," *Human Resource Management Review* 12 (2002), pp. 195–214; C.-S. Wong and K. S. Law, "The Effects of Leader and Follower Emotional Intelligence on Performance and Attitude: An Exploratory Study," *Leadership Quarterly* 13 (2002), pp. 243–74; L. T. Lam and S. L. Kirby,

"Is Emotional Intelligence an Advantage? An Exploration of the Impact of Emotional and General Intelligence on Individual Performance," *Journal of Social Psychology* 142 (February 2002), pp. 133–43; N. S. Schutte et al., "Emotional Intelligence and Interpersonal Relations," *Journal of Social Psychology* 141 (August 2001), pp. 523–36; S. Fox and P. E. Spector, "Relations of Emotional Intelligence, Practical Intelligence, General Intelligence, and Trait Affectivity with Interview Outcomes: It's Not All Just G," *Journal of Organizational Behavior* 21 (March 2000), pp. 203–20.

35. K. Van der Zee, M. Thijs, and L. Schakel, "The Relationship of Emotional Intelligence with Academic Intelligence and the Big Five," *European Journal of Personality* 16 (March/April 2002), pp. 103–25; D. Dawda and S. D. Hart, "Assessing Emotional Intelligence: Reliability and Validity of the Bar-On Emotional Quotient Inventory (EQ-i) in University Students," *Personality and Individual Differences* 28 (2000), pp. 797–812; R. R. McCrae, "Emotional Intelligence from the Perspective of the Five-Factor Model of Personality," in *The Handbook of Emotional Intelligence*, ed. R. Bar-On and J. D. A. Parker (San Francisco: Jossey-Bass, 2000), pp. 263–76.

36. J. Brown, "School Board, Employment Centers Test Emotional Intelligence," *Technology in Government* 8 (April 2001), p. 9; R. J. Grossman, "Emotions at Work," *Health Forum Journal* 43 (September–October, 2000), pp. 18–22.

37. "Emotional Intelligence (EQ) Gets Better with Age," EQi News Release, March 3, 1997.

38. C. Nader, "EQ Begins to Edge Out IQ as Desirable Quality in the Boss," *Sunday Age* (Melbourne, Australia), May 18, 2003, p. 10; ANZ Banking Group, The Journey, unpublished ANZ brochure, November 2002; L. Cossar, "IQ? But How Does Your EQ Rate?" *Business Review Weekly*, August 22, 2002, p. 68.

39. H. M. Weiss, "Deconstructing Job Satisfaction: Separating Evaluations, Beliefs and Affective Experiences," *Human Resource Management Review* 12 (2002), pp. 173–94. There is still some debate about this definition, because some definitions include emotion as an element or indicator of job satisfaction, whereas this definition views emotion as a cause of job satisfaction. For discussion of this point, see Brief and Weiss, "Organizational Behavior: Affect in the Workplace." Meanwhile, marketing scholars also refer to satisfaction as an evaluation rather than as an emotion. For example, see V. A. Zeithaml, A. Parasuraman, and L. L. Berry, "Problems and Strategies in Services Marketing," *Journal of Marketing* 49, no. 2 (1985), pp. 33–46.

40. E. A. Locke, "The Nature and Causes of Job Satisfaction," in *Handbook of Industrial and Organizational Psychology*, ed. M. Dunnette (Chicago: Rand McNally, 1976), pp. 1297–1350. Our definition takes the view that job satisfaction is a "collection of attitudes," not several "facets" of job satisfaction. For details of this issue, see Weiss, "Deconstructing Job Satisfaction."

41. F. Newport, "Most American Workers Satisfied with Their Jobs," *Gallup News Service*, August 29, 2002; T. Lemke, "Poll Data Show Americans' Long-Term Positive Attitude toward Jobs," *Washington Times*, August 28, 2001, p. B8. Evidence of recent declining job satisfaction is reported in V. Galt, "One-Third of Eloathe Their Jobs, Consultants Find," *Globe & Mail* (Toronto), January 28, 2003; Conference Board, *Special Consumer Survey Report: Job Satisfaction on the Decline* (New York: Conference Board, June 2002).

42. International Survey Research, *Employee Satisfaction in the World's 10 Largest Economies: Globalization or Diversity?* (Chicago: ISR, 2002); "Ipsos-Reid Global Poll Finds Major Differences in Employee Satisfaction Around the World," Ipsos-Reid News Release, January 8, 2001.

43. The problems with measuring attitudes and values across cultures are discussed in P. E. Spector et al., "Do National Levels of Individualism and Internal Locus of Control Relate to Well-Being? An Ecological Level International Study," *Journal of Organizational Behavior* 22 (2001), pp. 815–32; G. Law, "If You're Happy & You Know It, Tick the Box," *Management–Auckland*, 45 (March 1998), pp. 34–37.

44. M. Troy, "Motivating Your Workforce: A Home Depot Case Study," *DSN Retailing Today*, June 10, 2002, p. 29.

45. W. H. Turnley and D. C. Feldman, "The Impact of Psychological Contract Violations on Exit, Voice, Loyalty, and Neglect," *Human Relations* 52 (July 1999), pp. 895–922; M. J. Withey and W. H. Cooper, "Predicting Exit, Voice, Loyalty, and Neglect," *Administrative Science Quarterly* 34 (1989), pp. 521–39.

46. T. R. Mitchell, B. C. Holtom, and T. W. Lee, "How to Keep Your Best Employees: Developing an Effective Retention Policy," *Academy of Management Executive* 15 (November 2001), pp. 96–108. The idea of "triggering events" leading to exit is also brought forward in B. Dyck and F. A. Starke, "The Formation of Breakaway Organizations: Observations and a Process Model," *Administrative Science Quarterly* 44 (December 1999), pp. 792–822.

47. A. A. Luchak, "What Kind of Voice Do Loyal Employees Use?" *British Journal of Industrial Relations* 41 (March 2003), pp. 115–34; L. Van Dyne and J. A. LePine, "Helping and Voice Extra-Role Behaviors: Evidence of Construct and Predictive Validity," *Academy of Management Journal* 41 (1998), pp. 108–19.

48. The confusion regarding loyalty was pointed out over a decade ago in Withey and Cooper, "Predicting Exit, Voice, Loyalty, and Neglect" and is equally confusing today. In addition to the interpretation presented here, loyalty has been defined as situations where dissatisfied employees are less loyal, including engaging in fewer organizational citizenship behaviors. See Turnley and Feldman, "The Impact of Psychological Contract Violations on Exit, Voice, Loyalty, and Neglect."

49. J. Zhou and J. M. George, "When Job Dissatisfaction Leads to Creativity: Encouraging the Expression of Voice," *Academy of Management Journal* 44 (August 2001), pp. 682–96; J. D. Hibbard, N. Kumar, and L. W. Stern, "Examining the Impact of Destructive Acts in Marketing Channel Relationships," *Journal of Marketing Research* 38 (February 2001), pp. 45–61; Dyck and Starke, "The Formation of Breakaway Organizations."

50. R. D. Hackett and P. Bycio, "An Evaluation of Employee Absenteeism

as a Coping Mechanism among Hospital Nurses," *Journal of Occupational & Organizational Psychology* 69 (December 1996), pp. 327–38.

51. D. C. Thomas, K. Au, and E. C. Ravlin, "Cultural Variation and the Psychological Contract," *Journal of Organizational Behavior* 24 (2003), pp. 451–71; M. J. Withey and I. R. Gellatly, "Exit, Voice, Loyalty and Neglect: Assessing the Influence of Prior Effectiveness and Personality," *Proceedings of the Administrative Sciences Association of Canada, Organizational Behavior Division* 20 (1999), pp. 110–19; M. J. Withey and I. R. Gellatly, "Situational and Dispositional Determinants of Exit, Voice, Loyalty and Neglect," *Proceedings of the Administrative Sciences Association of Canada*, Saskatoon, Saskatchewan, June 1998.

52. B. M. Staw and S. G. Barsade, "Affect and Managerial Performance: A Test of the Sadder-but-Wiser vs. Happier-and-Smarter Hypotheses," *Administrative Science Quarterly* 38 (1993), pp. 304–31; M. T. Iaffaldano and P. M. Muchinsky, "Job Satisfaction and Job Performance: A Meta-Analysis," *Psychological Bulletin* 97 (1985), pp. 251–73; D. P. Schwab and L. L. Cummings, "Theories of Performance and Satisfaction: A Review," *Industrial Relations* 9 (1970), pp. 408–30.

53. T. A. Judge, C. J. Thoresen, J. E. Bono, and G. K. Patton, "The Job Satisfaction–Job Performance Relationship: A Qualitative and Quantitative Review," *Psychological Bulletin* 127 (2001), pp. 376–407.

54. Judge et al., "The Job Satisfaction–Job Performance Relationship," pp. 377–81.

55. Judge et al., "The Job Satisfaction–Job Performance Relationship," pp. 389, 391.

56. A. J. Schneider, "Our Front Line Is Our Bottom Line," *Stakeholder Power* (WalkerInformation newsletter), May 2003; "The Greatest Briton in Management and Leadership," *Personnel Today*, February 18, 2003, p. 20.

57. J. I. Heskett, W. E. Sasser, and L. A. Schlesinger, *The Service Profit Chain* (New York: Free Press, 1997). For recent support of this model, see D. J. Koys, "The Effects of Employee Satisfaction, Organizational Citizenship Behavior, and Turnover on Organizational Effectiveness: A Unit-Level, Longitudinal Study," *Personnel Psychology* 54 (April 2001), pp. 101–14.

58. A. J. Rucci, S. P. Kirn, and R. T. Quinn, "The Employee-Customer-Profit Chain At Sears," *Harvard Business Review* 76 (January–February 1998), pp. 83–97.

59. K. Gwinner, D. Gremier, and M. Bitner, "Relational Benefits in Services Industries: The Customer's Perspective," *Journal of the Academy of Marketing Science* 26 (1998), pp. 101–14.

60. T. Kirchofer, "Firm Takes Boat of Confidence," *Boston Herald*, March 20, 2001, p. 27.

61. R. T. Mowday, L. W. Porter, and R. M. Steers, *Employee Organization Linkages: The Psychology of Commitment, Absenteeism, and Turnover* (New York: Academic Press, 1982).

62. C. W. Mueller and E. J. Lawler, "Commitment to Nested Organizational Units: Some Basic Principles and Preliminary Findings," *Social Psychology Quarterly*, December 1999, pp. 325–46; T. E. Becker, R. S. Billings, D. M. Eveleth, and N. L. Gilbert, "Foci and Bases of Employee Commitment: Implications for Job Performance," *Academy of Management Journal* 39 (1996), pp. 464–82.

63. J. P. Meyer, "Organizational Commitment," *International Review of Industrial and Organizational Psychology* 12 (1997), pp. 175–228. Along with affective and continuance commitment, Meyer identifies "normative commitment," which refers to employee feelings of obligation to remain with the organization. This commitment has been excluded so that students focus on the two most common perspectives of commitment.

64. R. D. Hackett, P. Bycio, and P. A. Hausdorf, "Further Assessments of Meyer and Allen's (1991) Three-Component Model of Organizational Commitment," *Journal of Applied Psychology* 79 (1994), pp. 15–23.

65. Walker Information, *The Walker Loyalty Report: Loyalty in the Workplace—Topline Summary* (Indianapolis, IN: Walker Information, September 2003); "Japanese Employees Lack Commitment to Company: British Survey," *Japan Economic Newswire*, September 3, 2002; Walker Information, "Global Workforce Study Highlights Alarming Trends in Workplace Commitment and Ethics," Walker Information news release, September 18, 2000; Watson Wyatt, "Survey Says Employee Commitment Declining," News release, March 14, 2000.

66. J. P. Meyer, D. J. Stanley, L. Herscovitch, and L. Topolnytsky, "Affective, Continuance, and Normative Commitment to the Organization: A Meta-Analysis of Antecedents, Correlates, and Consequences," *Journal of Vocational Behavior* 61 (2002), pp. 20–52; M. Riketta, "Attitudinal Organizational Commitment and Job Performance: A Meta-Analysis," *Journal of Organizational Behavior* 23 (2002), pp. 257–66; F. F. Reichheld, "Lead for Loyalty," *Harvard Business Review* 79 (July–August 2001), p. 76; D. S. Bolon, "Organizational Citizenship Behavior among Hospital Employees: A Multidimensional Analysis Involving Job Satisfaction And Organizational Commitment," *Hospital & Health Services Administration*, 42 (Summer 1997), pp. 221–41; Meyer, "Organizational Commitment," pp. 203–15; F. F. Reichheld, *The Loyalty Effect* (Boston: Harvard Business School Press, 1996), Chapter 4.

67. B. L. Toffler, *Final Accounting: Ambition, Greed, and the Fall of Arthur Andersen* (New York: Broadway Books, 2003).

68. G. Gatlin, "Stay-Put Bonuses Inspire Ire," *Boston Globe*, April 28, 2003, p. 21; P. Mackey, "Old Ireland Tries New Hooks," *Computerworld*, April 23, 2001, p. 46.

69. A. A. Luchak, "What Kind of Voice Do Loyal Employees Use?" *British Journal of Industrial Relations*, in press; A. A. Luchak and I. R. Gellatly, "What Kind of Commitment Does a Final-Earnings Pension Plan Elicit?" *Relations Industrielles* 56 (Spring 2001), pp. 394–417; H. L. Angle and M. B. Lawson, "Organizational Commitment and Employees' Performance Ratings: Both Type of Commitment and Type of Performance Count," *Psychological Reports* 75 (1994), pp. 1539–51; J. P. Meyer, S. V. Paunonen, I. R. Gellatly, R. D. Goffin, and D. N. Jackson, "Organizational Commitment and Job Performance: It's the Nature of the Commitment That Counts," *Journal of Applied Psychology* 74 (1989), pp. 152–56.

70. J. P. Meyer and N. J. Allen, *Commitment in the Workplace: Theory, Research, and Application* (Thousand Oaks, CA: Sage, 1997), Chapter 4.

71. J. E. Finegan, "The Impact of Person and Organizational Values on Organizational Commitment," *Journal of Occupational and Organizational Psychology* 73 (June 2000), pp. 149–69; E. W. Morrison and S. L. Robinson, "When Employees Feel Betrayed: A Model of How Psychological Contract Violation Develops," *Academy of Management Review* 22 (1997), pp. 226–56.

72. L. Rhoades, R. Eisenberger, and S. Armeli, "Affective Commitment to the Organization: The Contribution of Perceived Organizational Support," *Journal of Applied Psychology* 86 (October 2001), pp. 825–36.

73. C. Hendry and R. Jenkins, "Psychological Contracts and New Deals," *Human Resource Management Journal* 7 (1997), pp. 38–44; D. M. Noer, *Healing the Wounds* (San Francisco: Jossey-Bass, 1993); S. Ashford, C. Lee, and P. Bobko, "Content, Causes, and Consequences of Job Insecurity: A Theory-Based Measure and Substantive Test," *Academy of Management Journal* 32 (1989), pp. 803–29.

74. M. Green, "Lessons Learnt," *Electronic News*, May 5, 2003; S. Armour, "Some Companies Choose No-Layoff Policy," *USA Today*, December 17, 2001, p. B1; "No Layoffs, Plenty of Loyalty," *Maclean's*, November 5, 2001.

75. T. S. Heffner and J. R. Rentsch, "Organizational Commitment and Social Interaction: A Multiple Constituencies Approach," *Journal of Vocational Behavior* 59 (2001), pp. 471–90.

76. A. Dastmalchian and M. Javidan, "High-Commitment Leadership: A Study of Iranian Executives," *Journal of Comparative International Management* 1 (1998), pp. 23–37.

77. D. M. Rousseau, S. B. Sitkin, R. S. Burt, et al., "Not So Different After All: A Cross-Discipline View of Trust," *Academy of Management Review* 23 (1998), pp. 393–404; R. J. Lewicki and B. B. Bunker, "Developing and Maintaining Trust in Work Relationships," in *Trust in Organizations: Frontiers of Theory and Research*, ed. R. M. Kramer and T. R. Tyler (Thousand Oaks, CA: Sage, 1996), pp. 114–39.

78. P. Stinton, "Double Disaster," *San Francisco Chronicle*, May 25, 2001, p. B1.

79. P. Kruger, "Betrayed by Work," *Fast Company*, November 1999, p. 182.

80. E. W. Morrison and S. L. Robinson, "When Employees Feel Betrayed: A Model of How Psychological Contract Violation Develops," *Academy of Management Review* 22 (1997), pp. 226–56; S. L. Robinson, M. S. Kraatz, and D. M. Rousseau, "Changing Obligations and the Psychological Contract: A Longitudinal Study," *Academy of Management Journal* 37 (1994), pp. 137–52; D. M. Rousseau and J. M. Parks, "The Contracts of Individuals and Organizations," *Research in Organizational Behavior* 15 (1993), pp. 1–43.

81. J. McLean Parks and D. L. Kidder, "'Till Death Us Do Part . . .' Changing Work Relationships in the 1990s," in *Trends in Organizational Behavior*, Vol. 1, ed. C. L. Cooper and D. M. Rousseau (Chichester, UK: Wiley, 1994), pp. 112–36.

82. Thomas, Au, and Ravlin, "Cultural Variation and the Psychological Contract"; D. M. Rousseau and R. Schalk (eds.), *Psychological Contracts in Employment: Cross-National Perspectives* (Thousand Oaks, CA: Sage, 2000); P. R. Sparrow, "Reappraising Psychological Contracting: Lessons for the Field of Human-Resource Development from Cross-Cultural and Occupational Psychology Research," *International Studies of Management & Organization* 28 (March 1998), pp. 30–63.

83. W. H. Whyte, *Organization Man* (New York: Simon & Schuster, 1956), p. 129; C. Hendry and R. Jenkins, "Psychological Contracts and New Deals," *Human Resource Management Journal* 7 (1997), pp. 38–44.

84. R. J. Burke, "Organizational Transitions," in *The New World of Work: Challenges and Opportunities*, ed. C. L. Cooper and R. J. Burke (Oxford: Blackwell, 2002), pp. 3–28; F. Patterson, "Developments in Work Psychology: Emerging Issues and Future Trends," *Journal of Occupational and Organizational Psychology* 74 (November 2001), pp. 381–90.

85. L. Uchitelle, "As Job Cuts Spread, Tears Replace Anger," *New York Times*, August 5, 2001. Psychological contract expectations of young employees are discussed in P. Herriot and C. Pemberton, "Facilitating New Deals," *Human Resource Management Journal* 7 (1997), pp. 45–56; P. R. Sparrow, "Transitions in the Psychological Contract: Some Evidence from the Banking Sector," *Human Resource Management Journal* 6 (1996), pp. 75–92.

86. Adapted from H. Mostafa, "White-Collar Blues," *Egypt Today*, July 2003.

CHAPTER 5

1. "Maximizing Your Circ Team in Tough Times," *Circulation Management* 18 (July 2003), p. 19; "Valuing the Power of Praise and Reward," *Employee Benefits*, July 2003; K. Rives, "Ways to Thank Your Colleagues," *(Raleigh, NC) News & Observer*, March 30, 2003, p. E1; J. Weiss, "Romney Offers Surprise Calls: Governor Enjoys Getting Personal to Salute Workers," *Boston Globe*, March 14, 2003, p. B1.

2. C. C. Pinder, *Work Motivation in Organizational Behavior* (Upper Saddle River, NJ: Prentice Hall, 1998); E. E. Lawler III, *Motivation in Work Organizations* (Monterey, CA: Brooks/Cole, 1973), pp. 2–5.

3. "Towers Perrin Study Finds, Despite Layoffs and Slow Economy, a New, More Complex Power Game Is Emerging between Employers and Employees," *Business Wire*, August 30, 2001.

4. T. H. Wagar, "Consequences of Work Force Reduction: Some Employer and Union Evidence," *Journal of Labor Research* 22 (Fall 2001), pp. 851–62; R. J. Burke and C. L. Cooper (eds.), *The Organization in Crisis: Downsizing, Restructuring, and Privatization* (Oxford: Blackwell Publishers, 2000); R. Burke, "Downsizing and Restructuring in Organizations: Research Findings and Lessons Learned—Introduction," *Canadian Journal of Administrative Sciences* 15 (December 1998), pp. 297–99.

5. C. Lachnit, "The Young and the Dispirited," *Workforce* 81 (August 2002), p. 18. Motivation and needs across generations are also discussed in R. Zemke and B. Filipczak, *Generations at Work: Managing the Clash of Veterans, Boomers, Xers, and Nexters in Your Workplace* (New York: Amacom, 2000); B. Losyk, "Generation X: What

They Think and What They Plan to Do," *The Futurist* 31 (March–April 1997), pp. 29–44; B. Tulgan, *Managing Generation X: How to Bring Out the Best in Young Talent* (Oxford: Capstone, 1996).

6. Pinder, *Work Motivation in Organizational Behavior*, Chapter 3.

7. A. H. Maslow, "A Theory of Human Motivation," *Psychological Review* 50 (1943), pp. 370–96; A. H. Maslow, *Motivation and Personality* (New York: Harper & Row, 1954).

8. For recent examples of Maslow's continued popularity, see M. Witzel, "Motivations that Push Our Buttons," *Financial Times*, August 14, 2002, p. 9; P. Kelley, "Revisiting Maslow," *Workspan* 45 (May 2002), pp. 50–56.

9. M. A. Wahba and L. G. Bridwell, "Maslow Reconsidered: A Review of Research on the Need Hierarchy Theory," *Organizational Behavior and Human Performance* 15 (1976), pp. 212–40.

10. C. P. Alderfer, *Existence, Relatedness, and Growth* (New York: Free Press, 1972).

11. J. P. Wanous and A. A. Zwany, "A Cross-Sectional Test of Need Hierarchy Theory," *Organizational Behavior and Human Performance* 18 (1977), pp. 78–97.

12. E. A. Locke, "Motivation, Cognition, and Action: An Analysis of Studies of Task Goals and Knowledge," *Applied Psychology: An International Review* 49 (2000), pp. 408–29; S. A. Haslam, C. Powell, and J. Turner, "Social Identity, Self-categorization, and Work Motivation: Rethinking the Contribution of the Group to Positive and Sustainable Organisational Outcomes," *Applied Psychology: An International Review* 49 (July 2000), pp. 319–39.

13. P. R. Lawrence and N. Nohria, *Driven: How Human Nature Shapes Our Choices* (San Francisco: Jossey-Bass, 2002), p. 10.

14. Lawrence and Nohria, *Driven*, p. 261.

15. Lawrence and Nohria, *Driven*, Chapters 4–7.

16. Lawrence and Nohria, *Driven*, pp. 66–68.

17. R. E. Baumeister and M. R. Leary, "The Need to Belong: Desire for Interpersonal Attachments as a Fundamental Human Motivation," *Psychological Bulletin* 117 (1995), pp. 497–529.

18. C. Clough, "Brewery's End," *The (Olympia, WA) Olympian*, June 28, 2003; J. Dodge, "Brewery Work Was a Family Tradition for This Father–Son Pair," *The (Olympia, WA) Olympian*, June 1, 2003; S. Wyland, "Most Workers Didn't See It Coming," *The (Olympia, WA) Olympian*, January 10, 2003.

19. Lawrence and Nohria, *Driven*, p. 136.

20. The emotional center is the limbic center where the innate drives reside. The rational center is the prefrontal cerebral cortex. Although signals potentially run in both directions between these brain centers, neural connections suggest a much stronger signal from the emotional center to the rational center than vice versa. See D. S. Massey, "A Brief History of Human Society: The Origin and Role of Emotion in Social Life," *American Sociological Review* 67 (February 2002), pp. 1–29; Lawrence and Nohria, *Driven*, pp. 44–47, 168–70.

21. Lawrence and Nohria, *Driven*, p. 47.

22. For critiques of various evolutionary psychology theories, see P. R. Ehrlich, "Human Natures, Nature Conservation, and Environmental Ethics," *Bioscience* 52 (January 2002), pp. 31–43; L. R. Caporael, "Evolutionary Psychology: Toward a Unifying Theory and a Hybrid Science," *Annual Review of Psychology* 52 (2001), pp. 607–28.

23. R. Amit, K. R. MacCrimmon, C. Zietsma, and J. M. Oesch, "Does Money Matter? Wealth Attainment as the Motive for Initiating Growth-Oriented Technology Ventures," *Journal of Business Venturing* 16 (March 2001), pp. 119–43; D. C. McClelland, *The Achieving Society* (New York: Van Nostrand Reinhold, 1961); M. Patchen, *Participation, Achievement, and Involvement on the Job* (Englewood Cliffs, NJ: Prentice Hall, 1970).

24. For example, see J. Langan-Fox and S. Roth, "Achievement Motivation and Female Entrepreneurs," *Journal of Occupational and Organizational Psychology* 68 (1995), pp. 209–18; H. A. Wainer and I. M. Rubin, "Motivation of Research and Development Entrepreneurs: Determinants of Company Success, Part I," *Journal of Applied Psychology* 53 (June 1969), pp. 178–84.

25. D. C. McClelland, "Retrospective Commentary," *Harvard Business Review* 73 (January–February 1995), pp. 138–39; D. McClelland and R. Boyatzis, "Leadership Motive Pattern and Long-Term Success in Management," *Journal of Applied Psychology* 67 (1982), pp. 737–43.

26. R. J. House and R. N. Aditya, "The Social Scientific Study of Leadership: Quo Vadis?" *Journal of Management* 23 (1997), pp. 409–73; D. C. McClelland and D. H. Burnham, "Power Is the Great Motivator," *Harvard Business Review* 73 (January–February 1995), pp. 126–39 (reprinted from 1976).

27. D. Vredenburgh and Y. Brender, "The Hierarchical Abuse of Power in Work Organizations," *Journal of Business Ethics* 17 (September 1998), pp. 1337–47; McClelland and Burnham, "Power Is the Great Motivator."

28. D. G. Winter, "A Motivational Model of Leadership: Predicting Long-Term Management Success from TAT Measures of Power Motivation and Responsibility," *Leadership Quarterly* 2 (1991), pp. 67–80.

29. House and Aditya, "The Social Scientific Study of Leadership: Quo Vadis?"

30. D. C. McClelland and D. G. Winter, *Motivating Economic Achievement* (New York: Free Press, 1969); D. Miron and D. McClelland, "The Impact of Achievement Motivation Training on Small Business," *California Management Review* 21 (1979), pp. 13–28.

31. Lawrence and Nohria, *Driven*, Chapter 11.

32. R. Turcsik, "The Prince of Tidewater," *Progressive Grocer*, April 15, 2003.

33. A. Kohn, *Punished by Rewards* (New York: Houghton Mifflin, 1993).

34. Human Resources Development Canada, "PanCanadian Petroleum," *Work-Life Balance in Canadian Workplaces*, July 2001. http://labour.hrdc-drhc.gc.ca/worklife/pancanadian-en.cfm.

35. Expectancy theory of motivation in work settings originated in V. H.

Vroom, *Work and Motivation* (New York: Wiley, 1964). The version of expectancy theory presented here was developed by Edward Lawler. Lawler's model provides a clearer presentation of the model's three components. P→O expectancy is similar to "instrumentality" in Vroom's original expectancy theory model. The difference is that instrumentality is a correlation, whereas P→O expectancy is a probability. See D. A. Nadler and E. E. Lawler, "Motivation: A Diagnostic Approach," in *Perspectives on Behavior in Organizations,* 2nd ed., ed. J. R. Hackman, E. E. Lawler III, and L. W. Porter (New York: McGraw-Hill, 1983), pp. 67–78; J. P. Campbell, M. D. Dunnette, E. E. Lawler, and K. E. Weick, *Managerial Behavior, Performance, and Effectiveness* (New York: McGraw-Hill, 1970), pp. 343–48; E. E. Lawler, *Motivation in Work Organizations* (Monterey, CA: Brooks/Cole, 1973), Chapter 3.

36. Nadler and Lawler, "Motivation: A Diagnostic Approach," pp. 70–73.

37. K. A. Karl, A. M. O'Leary-Kelly, and J. J. Martoccio, "The Impact of Feedback and Self-Efficacy on Performance in Training," *Journal of Organizational Behavior* 14 (1993), pp. 379–94; T. Janz, "Manipulating Subjective Expectancy Through Feedback: A Laboratory Study of the Expectancy–Performance Relationship," *Journal of Applied Psychology* 67 (1982), pp. 480–85.

38. "Most Workers Don't Know How Their Pay Raises Are Determined," Ohio State University news release, June 26, 2002. The entire report is reprinted in P. W. Mulvey et al., *The Knowledge of Pay Study* (Scottsdale, AZ: WorldatWork, 2002).

39. J. B. Fox, K. D. Scott, and J. M. Donohoe, "An Investigation into Pay Valence and Performance in a Pay-for-Performance Field Setting," *Journal of Organizational Behavior* 14 (1993), pp. 687–93.

40. W. Van Eerde and H. Thierry, "Vroom's Expectancy Models and Work-Related Criteria: A Meta-Analysis," *Journal of Applied Psychology* 81 (1996), pp. 575–86; T. R. Mitchell, "Expectancy Models of Job Satisfaction, Occupational Preference and Effort: A Theoretical, Methodological, and Empirical Appraisal," *Psychological Bulletin* 81 (1974), pp. 1053–77.

41. C. L. Haworth and P. E. Levy, "The Importance of Instrumentality Beliefs in the Prediction of Organizational Citizenship Behaviors," *Journal of Vocational Behavior* 59 (August 2001), pp. 64–75; M. L. Ambrose and C. T. Kulik, "Old Friends, New Faces: Motivation Research in the 1990s," *Journal of Management* 25 (May 1999), pp. 231–92; K. C. Snead and A. M. Harrell, "An Application of Expectancy Theory to Explain a Manager's Intention to Use a Decision Support System," *Decision Sciences* 25 (1994), pp. 499–513.

42. Elenkov, "Can American Management Concepts Work in Russia?"; N. A. Boyacigiller and N. J. Adler, "The Parochial Dinosaur: Organizational Science in a Global Context," *Academy of Management Review* 16 (1991), pp. 262–90; N. J. Adler, *International Dimensions of Organizational Behavior,* 3rd ed. (Cincinnati: South-Western, 1997), Chapter 6.

43. D. H. B. Welsh, F. Luthans, and S. M. Sommer, "Managing Russian Factory Workers: The Impact of U.S.-Based Behavioral and Participative Techniques," *Academy of Management Journal* 36 (1993), pp. 58–79; T. Matsui and I. Terai, "A Cross-Cultural Study of the Validity of the Expectancy Theory of Motivation," *Journal of Applied Psychology* 60 (1979), pp. 263–65.

44. For recent OB writing incorporating emotions in the topic of employee motivation, see E. L. Zurbriggen and T. S. Sturman, "Linking Motives and Emotions: A Test of McClelland's Hypotheses," *Personality & Social Psychology Bulletin* 28 (April 2002), pp. 521–35; P. E. Spector and S. Fox "An Emotion-Centered Model of Voluntary Work Behavior: Some Parallels between Counterproductive Work Behavior and Organizational Citizenship Behavior," *Human Resource Management Review* 12 (2002), pp. 269–92; J. Brockner and E. T. Higgins, "Regulatory Focus Theory: Implications for the Study of Emotions at Work," *Organizational Behavior and Human Decision Processes* 86 (September 2001) pp. 35–66; M. Perugini and R. P. Bagozzi, "The Role of Desires and Anticipated Emotions in Goal-Directed Behaviors: Broadening and Deepening the Theory of Planned Behavior," *British Journal of Social Psychology* 40 (March 2001), pp. 79ff.

45. David Beardsley, "This Company Doesn't Brake for (Sacred) Cows," *Fast Company* 16 (August 1998), p. 66.

46. For recent research on the effectiveness of goal setting, see L. A. Wilk and W. K. Redmon, "The Effects of Feedback and Goal Setting on the Productivity and Satisfaction of University Admissions Staff," *Journal of Organizational Behavior Management* 18 (1998), pp. 45–68; K. H. Doerr and T. R. Mitchell, "Impact of Material Flow Policies and Goals on Job Outcomes," *Journal of Applied Psychology* 81 (1996), pp. 142–52; A. A. Shikdar and B. Das, "A Field Study of Worker Productivity Improvements." *Applied Ergonomics* 26 (February 1995), pp. 21–27; M. D. Cooper and R. A. Phillips, "Reducing Accidents Using Goal Setting and Feedback: A Field Study," *Journal of Occupational & Organizational Psychology* 67 (1994), pp. 219–40.

47. T. H. Poister and G. Streib, "MBO in Municipal Government: Variations on a Traditional Management Tool," *Public Administration Review* 55 (1995), pp. 48–56.

48. J. O'Heir, "2002 Top 25 Executives: No. 10—John Edwardson," *Computer Reseller News,* November 18, 2002, p. 86; R. Kaiser, "Human Touch Selling Online," *Chicago Tribune,* September 10, 2001, p. CN1; F. Knowles, "CDW Chief Gung-Ho," *Chicago Sun-Times,* April 23, 2001, p. 51.

49. E. A. Locke and G. P. Latham, *A Theory of Goal Setting and Task Performance* (Englewood Cliffs, NJ: Prentice Hall, 1990); A. J. Mento, R. P. Steel, and R. J. Karren, "A Meta-Analytic Study of the Effects of Goal Setting on Task Performance: 1966–1984," *Organizational Behavior and Human Decision Processes* 39 (1987), pp. 52–83; M. E. Tubbs, "Goal-Setting: A Meta-Analytic Examination of the Empirical Evidence," *Journal of Applied Psychology* 71 (1986), pp. 474–83. Some practitioners rely on the acronym "SMART" goals, referring to goals that are specific, measurable, acceptable, relevant, and timely. However, this list overlaps key elements (e.g., specific goals *are* measurable and timely) and overlooks the key elements of challenging and feedback-related.

50. K. Tasa, T. Brown, and G. H. Seijts, "The Effects of Proximal, Outcome and

Learning Goals on Information Seeking and Complex Task Performance," *Proceedings of the Annual Conference of the Administrative Sciences Association of Canada, Organizational Behavior Division* 23, no. 5 (2002), pp. 11–20.

51. Locke, "Motivation, Cognition, and Action"; I. R. Gellatly and J. P. Meyer, "The Effects of Goal Difficulty on Physiological Arousal, Cognition, and Task Performance," *Journal of Applied Psychology* 77 (1992), pp. 694–704; A. Mento, E. A. Locke, and H. Klein, "Relationship of Goal Level to Valence and Instrumentality," *Journal of Applied Psychology* 77 (1992), pp. 395–405.

52. J. T. Chambers, "The Future of Business," *Executive Excellence* 17 (February 2000), pp. 3–4; K. R. Thompson, W. A. Hochwarter, and N. J. Mathys, "Stretch Targets: What Makes Them Effective?" *Academy of Management Executive* 11 (August 1997), pp. 48–60; S. Sherman, "Stretch Goals: The Dark Side of Asking for Miracles," *Fortune* 132 (November 13, 1995), pp. 231–32.

53. M. E. Tubbs, "Commitment as a Moderator of the Goal-Performance Relation: A Case for Clearer Construct Definition," *Journal of Applied Psychology* 78 (1993), pp. 86–97.

54. H. J. Klein, "Further Evidence of the Relationship between Goal Setting and Expectancy Theory," *Organizational Behavior and Human Decision Processes* 49 (1991), pp. 230–57.

55. J. Walker, "Secrets of Profitability," *Business Review Weekly* (Australia), May 15, 2003, p. 68.

56. J. Wegge, "Participation in Group Goal Setting: Some Novel Findings and a Comprehensive Model as a New Ending to an Old Story," *Applied Psychology: An International Review* 49 (2000), pp. 498–516; Locke and Latham, *A Theory of Goal Setting and Task Performance*, Chapters 6 and 7; E. A. Locke, G. P. Latham, and M. Erez, "The Determinants of Goal Commitment," *Academy of Management Review* 13 (1988), pp. 23–39.

57. R. W. Renn and D. B. Fedor, "Development and Field Test of a Feedback Seeking, Self-Efficacy, and Goal Setting Model of Work Performance," *Journal of Management* 27 (2001) pp. 563–83.

58. A. N. Kluger and A. DeNisi, "The Effects of Feedback Interventions on Performance: A Historical Review, a Meta-Analysis, and a Preliminary Feedback Intervention Theory," *Psychological Bulletin* 119 (March 1996), pp. 254–84; A. A. Shikdar and B. Das, "A Field Study of Worker Productivity Improvements," *Applied Ergonomics* 26 (1995), pp. 21–27; L. M. Sama and R. E. Kopelman, "In Search of a Ceiling Effect on Work Motivation: Can Kaizen Keep Performance 'Risin'?" *Journal of Social Behavior & Personality* 9 (1994), pp. 231–37.

59. R. Waldersee and F. Luthans, "The Impact of Positive and Corrective Feedback on Customer Service Performance," *Journal of Organizational Behavior* 15 (1994), pp. 83–95; P. K. Duncan and L. R. Bruwelheide, "Feedback: Use and Possible Behavioral Functions," *Journal of Organizational Behavior Management* 7 (Fall 1985), pp. 91–114; J. Annett, *Feedback and Human Behavior* (Baltimore: Penguin, 1969).

60. R. D. Guzzo and B. A. Gannett, "The Nature of Facilitators and Inhibitors of Effective Task Performance," in *Facilitating Work Effectiveness*, ed. F. D. Schoorman and B. Schneider (Lexington, MA: Lexington Books, 1988), p. 23; R. C. Linden and T. R. Mitchell, "Reactions to Feedback: The Role of Attributions," *Academy of Management Journal* 1985, pp. 291–308.

61. P. M. Posakoff and J. Fahr, "Effects of Feedback Sign and Credibility on Goal Setting and Task Performance," *Organizational Behavior and Human Decision Processes* 44 (1989), pp. 45–67.

62. C. Mabey, "Closing the Circle: Participant Views of a 360 Degree Feedback Programme," *Human Resource Management Journal* 11 (2001), pp. 41–53. However, one recent study reported that fewer than half of the 55 human resource executives surveyed (most from Fortune 500 companies) use 360–degree feedback. See E. E. Lawler III and M. McDermott, "Current Performance Management Practices," *WorldatWork Journal* 12 (Second Quarter 2003), pp. 49–60.

63. For discussion of multisource feedback, see L. E. Atwater, D. A. Waldman, and J. F. Brett, "Understanding and Optimizing Multisource Feedback," *Human Resource Management* 41 (Summer 2002), pp. 193–208; S. Brutus and M. Derayeh, "Multisource Assessment Programs in Organizations: An Insider's Perspective," *Human Resource Development Quarterly* 13 (July 2002), pp. 187ff; W. W. Tornow and M. London, *Maximizing the Value of 360–degree Feedback: A Process for Successful Individual and Organizational Development* (San Francisco: Jossey-Bass, 1998).

64. D. A. Waldman and L. E. Atwater, "Attitudinal and Behavioral Outcomes of an Upward Feedback Process," *Group & Organization Management* 26 (June 2001), pp. 189–205.

65. The problems with 360–degree feedback are discussed in "Perils & Payoffs of Multi-Rater Feedback Programs," *Pay for Performance Report*, May 2003, p. 1; M. A. Peiperl, "Getting 360 Degree Feedback Right," *Harvard Business Review* 79 (January 2001), pp. 142–47; A. S. DeNisi and A. N. Kluger, "Feedback Effectiveness: Can 360-Degree Appraisals be Improved?" *Academy of Management Executive* 14 (February 2000), pp. 129–39; J. Ghorpade, "Managing Five Paradoxes of 360-Degree Feedback," *Academy of Management Executive* 14 (February 2000), pp. 140–50; B. Usher and J. Morley, "Overcoming the Obstacles to a Successful 360-Degree Feedback Program," *Canadian HR Reporter*, February 8, 1999, p. 17.

66. S. Watkins, "Ever Wanted to Review the Boss?" *Investor's Business Daily*, August 10, 2001, p. A1.

67. R. R. Kilburg, *Executive Coaching: Developing Managerial Wisdom in a World of Chaos* (Washington DC: American Psychological Association, 2000), p. 65.

68. J. W. Smither et al., "Can Working with an Executive Coach Improve Multisource Feedback Ratings over Time? A Quasi-Experimental Field Study," *Personnel Psychology* 56 (Spring 2003), pp. 23–44; D. Goleman, *The Emotionally Intelligent Workplace* (San Francisco: Jossey-Bass, 2001); J. H. Eggers and D. Clark, "Executive Coaching that Wins," *Ivey Business* Journal 65 (September 2000), pp. 66ff.

69. For some of the pitfalls with executive coaching, see M. Conlin, "CEO Coaches," *Business Week*, November 11, 2002, pp. 98–104; S. Berglas, "The Very Real Dangers of Executive Coaching," *Harvard Business Review* 80 (June 2002), pp. 80–86.

70. M. C. Andrews and K. M. Kacmar, "Confirmation and Extension of the Sources of Feedback Scale in Service-Based Organizations," *Journal of Business Communication* 38 (April 2001), pp. 206–26.

71. N. Zurell, "Built for Speed," *Intelligent Enterprise*, September 3, 2002, p. 14.

72. L. Hollman, "Seeing the Writing on the Wall," *Call Center*, August 2002, p. 37.

73. M. London, "Giving Feedback: Source-Centered Antecedents and Consequences of Constructive and Destructive Feedback," *Human Resource Management Review* 5 (1995), pp. 159–88; D. Antonioni, "The Effects of Feedback Accountability on 360-Degree Appraisal Ratings," *Personnel Psychology* 47 (1994), pp. 375–90; S. J. Ashford and G. B. Northcraft, "Conveying More (or Less) Than We Realize: The Role of Impression Management in Feedback Seeking," *Organizational Behavior and Human Decision Processes* 53 (1992), pp. 310–34; E. W. Morrison and R. J. Bies, "Impression Management in the Feedback-Seeking Process: A Literature Review and Research Agenda," *Academy of Management Review* 16 (1991), pp. 522–41.

74. J. R. Williams, C. E. Miller, L. A. Steelman, and P. E. Levy, "Increasing Feedback Seeking in Public Contexts: It Takes Two (or More) to Tango," *Journal of Applied Psychology* 84 (December 1999), pp. 969–76; G. B. Northcraft and S. J. Ashford, "The Preservation of Self in Everyday Life: The Effects of Performance Expectations and Feedback Context on Feedback Inquiry," *Organizational Behavior and Human Decision Processes* 47 (1990), pp. 42–64.

75. P. M. Wright, "Goal Setting and Monetary Incentives: Motivational Tools that Can Work Too Well," *Compensation and Benefits Review* 26 (May–June, 1994), pp. 41–49.

76. F. M. Moussa, " Determinants and Process of the Choice of Goal Diffi-

culty," *Group & Organization Management* 21 (1996), pp. 414–38.

77. Some scholars suggest that goal setting is the best supported and most practical work motivation theory. See C. C. Pinder, *Work Motivation in Organizational Behavior* (Upper Saddle River, NJ: Prentice Hall, 1997), p. 384.

78. K. Gagne, "One Day at a Time," *Workspan*, February 2002, pp. 20ff.

79. D. T. Miller, "Disrespect and the Experience of Injustice," *Annual Review of Psychology* 52 (2001), pp. 527–53; R. Cropanzano and M. Schminke, "Using Social Justice to Build Effective Work Groups," in *Groups at Work: Theory and Research*, ed. M. E. Turner (Mahwah, NJ: Lawrence Erlbaum Associates, 2001), pp. 143–71; J. Greenberg and E. A. Lind, "The Pursuit of Organizational Justice: From Conceptualization to Implication to Application," in *Industrial and Organizational Psychology: Linking Theory with Practice*, ed. C. L. Cooper and E. A. Locke (London: Blackwell, 2000), pp. 72–108.

80. A. Lue, "Women Seethe over Gender Gap in Salaries," *Taipei Times*, March 6, 2003.

81. Cropanzano and Schminke, "Using Social Justice to Build Effective Work Groups."

82. R. Cropanzano and J. Greenberg, "Progress in Organizational Justice: Tunneling Through the Maze," in *International Review of Industrial and Organizational Psychology*, ed. C. L. Cooper and I. T. Robertson (New York: Wiley, 1997), pp. 317–72; R. T. Mowday, "Equity Theory Predictions of Behavior in Organizations," in *Motivation and Work Behavior*, 5th ed., ed. R. M. Steers and L. W. Porter (New York: McGraw-Hill, 1991), pp. 111–31; J. S. Adams, "Toward an Understanding of Inequity," *Journal of Abnormal and Social Psychology* 67 (1963), pp. 422–36.

83. G. Blau, "Testing the Effect of Level and Importance of Pay Referents on Pay Level Satisfaction," *Human Relations* 47 (1994), pp. 1251–68; C. T. Kulik and M. L. Ambrose, "Personal and Situational Determinants of Referent Choice," *Academy of Management Review* 17 (1992), pp. 212–37; J. Pfeffer, "Incentives in Organizations: The Importance of Social Relations," in *Organization Theory: From Chester*

Barnard to the Present and Beyond, ed. O. E. Williamson (New York: Oxford University Press, 1990), pp. 72–97.

84. T. P. Summers and A. S. DeNisi, "In Search of Adams' Other: Reexamination of Referents Used in the Evaluation of Pay," *Human Relations* 43 (1990), pp. 497–511.

85. J. S. Adams, "Inequity in Social Exchange," in *Advances in Experimental Psychology*, ed. L. Berkowitz (New York: Academic Press, 1965), pp. 157–89.

86. Y. Cohen-Charash and P. E. Spector, "The Role of Justice in Organizations: A Meta-Analysis," *Organizational Behavior and Human Decision Processes* 86 (November 2001), pp. 278–321.

87. J. Barling, C. Fullagar, and E. K. Kelloway, *The Union and Its Members: A Psychological Approach* (New York: Oxford University Press, 1992).

88. J. Greenberg, "Cognitive Reevaluation of Outcomes in Response to Underpayment Inequity," *Academy of Management Journal* 32 (1989), pp. 174–84; E. Hatfield and S. Sprecher, "Equity Theory and Behavior in Organizations," *Research in the Sociology of Organizations* 3 (1984), pp. 94–124.

89. Cited in *Canadian Business*, February 1997, p. 39.

90. M. N. Bing and S. M. Burroughs, "The Predictive and Interactive Effects of Equity Sensitivity in Teamwork-Oriented Organizations," *Journal of Organizational Behavior* 22 (2001), pp. 271–90; K. S. Sauleya and A. G. Bedeian, "Equity Sensitivity: Construction of a Measure and Examination of Its Psychometric Properties," *Journal of Management* 26 (September 2000), pp. 885–910; P. E. Mudrack, E. S. Mason, and K. M. Stepanski, "Equity Sensitivity and Business Ethics," *Journal of Occupational and Organizational Psychology* 72 (December 1999), pp. 539–60; R. P. Vecchio, "An Individual-Differences Interpretation of the Conflicting Predictions Generated by Equity Theory and Expectancy Theory," *Journal of Applied Psychology* 66 (1981), pp. 470–81.

91. The meaning of these three groups has evolved over the years. These definitions are based on W. C. King, Jr. and E. W. Miles, "The Measurement of Eq-

uity Sensitivity," *Journal of Occupational and Organizational Psychology* 67 (1994), pp. 133–42.

92. M. Wenzel, "A Social Categorization Approach to Distributive Justice: Social Identity as the Link between Relevance of Inputs and Need for Justice," *British Journal of Social Psychology* 40 (2001), pp. 315–35.

93. C. Viswesvaran and D. S. Ones, "Examining the Construct of Organizational Justice: A Meta-Analytic Evaluation of Relations with Work Attitudes and Behaviors," *Journal of Business Ethics* 38 (July 2002), pp. 193ff; J. A. Colquitt, D. E. Conlon, M. W. Wesson, L. H. Porter, and K. Y. Ng, "Justice at the Millennium: A Meta-Analytic Review of 25 Years of Organizational Justice Research," *Journal of Applied Psychology* 86 (2001), 425–45; Y. Cohen-Charash and P. E. Spector, "The Role of Justice in Organizations: A Meta-Analysis," *Organizational Behavior and Human Decision Processes* 86 (November 2001), pp. 278–321.

94. Several types of justice have been identified and there is some debate whether they represent forms of procedural justice or are distinct from procedural and distributive justice. The discussion here adopts the former view, which seems to dominate the literature. See C. Viswesvaran and D. S. Ones, "Examining the Construct of Organizational Justice: A Meta-Analytic Evaluation of Relations with Work Attitudes and Behaviors," *Journal of Business Ethics* 38 (July 2002), pp. 193ff.

95. Greenberg and Lind, "The Pursuit of Organizational Justice," pp. 79–80. For recent evidence of the voice effect, see E. A. Douthitt and J. R. Aiello, "The Role of Participation and Control in the Effects of Computer Monitoring on Fairness Perceptions, Task Satisfaction, and Performance," *Journal of Applied Psychology* 86 (October 2001), pp. 867–74.

96. L. B. Bingham, "Mediating Employment Disputes: Perceptions of Redress at the United States Postal Service," *Review of Public Personnel Administration* 17 (Spring 1997), pp. 20–30; R. Folger and J. Greenberg, "Procedural Justice: An Interpretive Analysis of Personnel Systems," *Research in Personnel and Human Re-sources Management* 3 (1985), pp. 141–83.

97. R. Hagey et al., "Immigrant Nurses' Experience of Racism," *Journal of Nursing Scholarship* 33 (Fourth Quarter 2001), pp. 389ff. K. Roberts and K. S. Markel, "Claiming in the Name of Fairness: Organizational Justice and the Decision to File for Workplace Injury Compensation," *Journal of Occupational Health Psychology* 6 (October 2001), pp. 332–47.

98. D. T. Miller, "Disrespect and the Experience of Injustice," *Annual Review of Psychology* 52 (2001), pp. 534–35; 543–45; Colquitt, Conlon, Wesson, Porter, and Ng, "Justice at the Millennium."

99. S. Fox, P. E. Spector, and D. Miles, "Counterproductive Work Behavior (CWB) in Response to Job Stressors and Organizational Justice: Some Mediator and Moderator Tests for Autonomy and Emotions," *Journal of Vocational Behavior* 59 (2001), pp. 291–309; L. Greenberg and J. Barling, "Employee Theft," in *Trends in Organizational Behavior*, Vol. 3, ed. C. L. Cooper and D. M. Rousseau (New York: Wiley, 1996), pp. 49–64.

100. D. P. Skarlicki and R. Folger, "Retaliation in the Workplace: The Roles of Distributive, Procedural, and Interactional Justice," *Journal of Applied Psychology* 82 (1997), pp. 434–43.

101. N. D. Cole and G. P. Latham, "Effects of Training in Procedural Justice on Perceptions of Disciplinary Fairness by Unionized Employees and Disciplinary Subject Matter Experts," *Journal of Applied Psychology* 82 (1997), pp. 699–705; D. P. Skarlicki and G. P. Latham, "Increasing Citizenship Behavior within a Labor Union: A Test of Organizational Justice Theory," *Journal of Applied Psychology* 81 (1996), pp. 161–69.

CHAPTER 6

1. N. de Bono, "WestJet Airlines Brings Its Discount Prices," *London Free Press*, February 2, 2002; T. Hogue, "The Little Airline that Could," *Hamilton (Ontario, CA) Spectator*, December 29, 2001, p. M2; P. Fitzpatrick, "Air Travel Complaints Soar 35%," *National Post* (Canada), November 30, 2001, p. A4; P. Verburg, "Prepare for Takeoff," *Cana-dian Business,* December 25, 2000, pp. 94–99.

2. M. C. Bloom and G. T. Milkovich, "Issues in Managerial Compensation Research," in *Trends in Organizational Behavior*, Vol. 3, ed. C. L. Cooper and D. M. Rousseau (Chichester, UK: John Wiley & Sons, 1996), pp. 23–47.

3. T. Kinni, "Why We Work," *Training* 35 (August 1998), pp. 34–39; A. Furnham and M. Argyle, *The Psychology of Money* (London: Routledge, 1998); T. L-P. Tang, "The Meaning of Money Revisited," *Journal of Organizational Behavior* 13 (March 1992), pp. 197–202.

4. Cited in T. R. Mitchell and A. E. Mickel, "The Meaning of Money: An Individual-Difference Perspective," *Academy of Management Review*, July 1999, pp. 568–78.

5. L. S. Hoon and V. K. G. Lim, "Attitudes towards Money and Work—Implications for Asian Management Style Following the Economic Crisis," *Journal of Managerial Psychology* 16 (2001), pp. 159–72; C. Loch, M. Yaziji, and C. Langen, "The Fight for the Alpha Position: Channeling Status Competition in Organizations," *European Management Journal* 19 (February 2001), pp. 16–25. For discussion of the drive to acquire, see P. R. Lawrence and N. Nohria, *Driven: How Human Nature Shapes Our Choices* (San Francisco: Jossey-Bass, 2002), Chapter 4.

6. Watson Wyatt Worldwide, *Playing to Win: Strategic Rewards in the War for Talent—Fifth Annual Survey Report 2000/2001* (Chicago: Author, 2001).

7. A. Furnham and R. Okamura, "Your Money or Your Life: Behavioral and Emotional Predictors of Money Pathology," *Human Relations* 52 (September 1999), pp. 1157–77. For a psychiatric view of the meaning of money, see M. L. Lanza, "Setting Fees: The Conscious and Unconscious Meanings of Money," *Perspectives in Psychiatric Care* 37 (April–June 2001), pp. 69–72.

8. H. Meyer, "IKEA Seattle: The Little Store that Could," *Corporate Meetings & Incentives* 21 (September 2002), pp. 16ff; J. Mayne, "Bonuses Abound," *Seattle Post-Intelligencer*, December 5, 2000, p. C5; K. Richter, "IKEA's Successful One-Day Bonus May Have Been a One-Time Deal," *Wall Street Journal Europe*, October 19, 1999, p. 4.

9. T. L-P. Tang, J. K. Kim, and T. L-N. Tang, "Endorsement of the Money Ethic, Income, and Life Satisfaction: A Comparison of Full-Time Employees, Part-Time Employees, and Non-Employed University Students," *Journal of Managerial Psychology* 17 (June 2002), pp. 442–67; T. L-P. Tang, J. K. Kim, and D. S-H. Tang, "Does Attitude toward Money Moderate the Relationship between Intrinsic Job Satisfaction and Voluntary Turnover?" *Human Relations* 53 (February 2000), pp. 213–45.

10. V. K. G. Lim, "Money Matters: An Empirical Investigation of Money, Face and Confucian Work Ethic," *Personality and Individual Differences* 35 (2003), pp. 953–70; A. K. Kau, S. J. Tan, and J. Wirtz, *Seven Faces of Singaporeans: Their Values, Aspirations, and Lifestyles* (Singapore: Prentice Hall, 1998); A. Furnham, B. D. Kirkcaldy, and R. Lynn, "National Attitudes to Competitiveness, Money, and Work among Young People: First, Second, and Third World Differences," *Human Relations* 47 (January 1994), pp. 119–32. For contrary results, see S. H. Ang, "The Power of Money: A Cross-Cultural Analysis of Business-Related Beliefs," *Journal of World Business* 35 (March 2000), pp. 43–60.

11. H. Das, "The Four Faces of Pay: An Investigation into How Canadian Managers View Pay," *International Journal of Commerce & Management* 12 (2002), pp. 18–40; O. Mellan, "Men, Women & Money," *Psychology Today* 32 (February 1999), pp. 46–50.

12. R. Lynn, *The Secret of the Miracle Economy* (London: SAE, 1991), cited in Furnham and Okamura, "Your Money or Your Life." The recent public opinion polls are cited in M. Steen, "Study Looks at What Good Employees Want from a Company," *San Jose Mercury*, December 19, 2000; J. O'Rourke, "Show Boys the Money and Tell Girls You Care," *Sydney Morning Herald*, December 10, 2000.

13. C. Nyman, "The Social Nature of Money: Meanings of Money in Swedish Families," *Women's Studies International Forum* 26 (2003), pp. 79–94; "Ladies First . . . Especially When It Comes to Worrying about Money and Health," *PR Newswire*, November 19, 2002; Steen, "Study Looks at What Good Employees Want from a Company";

Mellan, "Men, Women & Money"; V. K. G. Lim and T. S. H. Teo, "Sex, Money and Financial Hardship: An Empirical Study of Attitudes Towards Money among Undergraduates in Singapore," *Journal of Economic Psychology* 18 (1997), pp. 369–86; A. Furnham, "Attitudinal Correlates and Demographic Predictors of Monetary Beliefs and Behaviors," *Journal of Organizational Behavior* 17 (1996), pp. 375–88.

14. S. Herendeen, "Modesto Teachers Will Get Raises under New Contract," *Modesto (CA) Bee*, June 3, 2003, p. A1; C. Olson, "Papillion Mayor Ensures Longevity Pay, Other Plans," *Omaha (NE) World Herald*, February 19, 2003, p. 2B; H. Y. Park, "A Comparative Analysis of Work Incentives in U.S. and Japanese Firms," *Multinational Business Review* 4 (Fall 1996), pp. 59–70.

15. G. T. Milkovich, J. M. Newman, and C. Milkovich, *Compensation* (New York: McGraw-Hill/Irwin, 2002), Chapter 5; for a history of job evaluation, see D. M. Figart, "Equal Pay for Equal Work: The Role of Job Evaluation in an Evolving Social Norm," *Journal of Economic Issues* 34 (March 2000), pp. 1–19.

16. R. McNabb and K. Whitfield, "Job Evaluation and High Performance Work Practices: Compatible or Conflictual?" *Journal of Management Studies* 38 (March 2001), pp. 293–312; E. E. Lawler III, *Rewarding Excellence: Pay Strategies for the New Economy* (San Francisco: Jossey-Bass, 2000), pp. 30–35, 109–19; T. M. Welbourne and C. O. Trevor, "The Roles of Departmental and Position Power in Job Evaluation," *Academy of Management Journal* 43 (August 2000), pp. 761–71; M. Quaid, *Job Evaluation: The Myth of Equitable Assessment* (Toronto: University of Toronto Press, 1993).

17. "Syracuse's Restructured Flexible Pay Plan Makes Managing Employees Easier," *HR on Campus*, December 5, 2002. For discussion on why companies are shifting to competency-based pay, see R. L. Heneman, G. E. Ledford Jr., and M. T. Gresham, "The Changing Nature of Work and Its Effects on Compensation Design and Delivery," in *Compensation in Organizations: Current Research and Practice*, ed. S. Rynes and B. Gerhart (San Francisco: Jossey-Bass, 2000), pp. 195–240.

18. B. Murray and B. Gerhart, "Skill-Based Pay and Skill Seeking," *Human Resource Management Review* 10 (Autumn 2000), pp. 271–87; J. R. Thompson and C. W. LeHew, "Skill-Based Pay as an Organizational Innovation," *Review of Public Personnel Administration* 20 (Winter 2000), pp. 20–40; D-O. Kim and K. Mericle, "From Job-Based Pay to Skill-Based Pay in Unionized Establishments: A Three-Plant Comparative Analysis," *Relations Industrielles* 54 (Summer 1999), pp. 549–80; E. E. Lawler III, "From Job-Based to Competency-Based Organizations," *Journal of Organizational Behavior* 15 (1994), pp. 3–15.

19. E. E. Lawler III, G. E. Ledford Jr., and L. Chang, "Who Uses Skill-Based Pay, and Why," *Compensation and Benefits Review* 25 (March–April 1993), pp. 22–26.

20. E. E. Lawler III, "Competencies: A Poor Foundation for the New Pay," *Compensation and Benefits Review*, November–December 1996, pp. 20, 22–26.

21. E. B. Peach and D. A. Wren, "Pay for Performance from Antiquity to the 1950s," *Journal of Organizational Behavior Management*, 1992, pp. 5–26.

22. L. Spiers, "Piece by Piecemeal," *Lawn & Landscape Magazine*, August 5, 2003; J. J. Higuera, "Willcox, Ariz., Greenhouse Tomato Grower, Union Reach Contract Deals," *Arizona Daily Star*, November 21, 2002.

23. A. Daniels and C. Leonard, "Retailer Gives Out Annual Bonuses: Wal-Mart Began Tradition in 1962," *Arkansas Democrat-Gazette*, March 14, 2003, p. 33; T. Chapelle, "Facts and Fictions about Teams," *On Wall Street*, January 2003. For general discussion of team-based rewards, see Lawler, *Rewarding Excellence*, Chapter 9; J. S. DeMatteo, L. T. Eby, and E. Sundstrom, "Team-Based Rewards: Current Empirical Evidence and Directions for Future Research," in *Research in Organizational Behavior*, Vol. 20, ed. B. M. Staw and L. L. Cummings (Greenwich, CT: JAI Press, 1998), pp. 141–83.

24. "Canadian Companies Encourage Employees with Innovative Bonus Plans," *Coal International*, March/April 2002, p. 68; A. Miller, "St. Joseph's to Reward Surgeons for Savings," *Atlanta*

Journal-Constitution, January 20, 2001, p. F1.

25. K. M. Bartol and A. Srivastava, "Encouraging Knowledge Sharing: The Role of Organizational Reward Systems," *Journal of Leadership & Organizational Studies* 9 (Summer 2002), pp. 64–76; L. R. Gomez-Mejia, T. M. Welbourne, and R. M. Wiseman, "The Role of Risk Sharing and Risk Taking under Gainsharing," *Academy of Management Review* 25 (July 2000), pp. 492–507; D. P. O'Bannon and C. L. Pearce, "An Exploratory Examination of Gainsharing in Service Organizations: Implications for Organizational Citizenship Behavior and Pay Satisfaction," *Journal of Managerial Issues* 11 (Fall 1999), pp. 363–78.

26. M. E. Podmolik, "All Work and Some Play," *Crain's Chicago Business*, February 24, 2003; J. Case, "Opening the Books," *Harvard Business Review* 75 (March–April 1997), pp. 118–27; T. R. V. Davis, "Open-Book Management: Its Promise and Pitfalls," *Organizational Dynamics*, Winter 1997, pp. 7–20; J. Case, *Open Book Management: The Coming Business Revolution* (New York: Harper Business, 1995).

27. E. Wine, "US Companies Review Retirement Plans," *Financial Times* (London), February 18, 2002, p. 36. The estimated number of ESOP plans and employees are provided by the ESOP Association (www.esopassociation.org) and National Center for Employee Ownership (www.nceo.org/).

28. P. Brandes, R. Dharwadkar, and G. V. Lemesis, "Effective Employee Stock Option Design: Reconciling Stakeholder, Strategic, and Motivational Factors," *Academy of Management Executive* 17 (February 2003), pp. 77–95; J. M. Newman and M. Waite, "Do Broad-Based Stock Options Create Value?" *Compensation and Benefits Review* 30 (July 1998), pp. 78–86.

29. K. Elefalk, "The Balanced Scorecard of the Swedish Police Service: 7000 Officers in Total Quality," *Total Quality Management* 12 (2001), pp. 958–66. The background and elements of balanced scorecard are detailed in R. S. Kaplan and D. P. Norton, *The Strategy-Focused Organization* (Cambridge, MA: Harvard Business School Press, 2001).

30. S. J. Marks, "Incentives that Really Reward and Motivate," *Workforce* 80 (June 2001), pp. 108–14; "A Fair Day's Pay," *Economist*, May 8, 1999, p. 12; D. Bencivenga, "Employee-Owners Help Bolster the Bottom Line," *HRMagazine* 42 (February 1997), pp. 78–83; J. Chelius and R. S. Smith, "Profit Sharing and Employment Stability," *Industrial and Labor Relations Review* 43 (1990), pp. 256s–73s.

31. M. D. Mumford, "Managing Creative People: Strategies and Tactics for Innovation," *Human Resource Management Review* 10 (Autumn 2000), pp. 313–51; M. O'Donnell and J. O'Brian, "Performance-Based Pay in the Australian Public Service," *Review of Public Personnel Administration* 20 (Spring 2000), pp. 20–34; A. Kohn, "Challenging Behaviorist Dogma: Myths about Money and Motivation," *Compensation and Benefits Review* 30 (March 1998), pp. 27–33; A. Kohn, *Punished by Rewards* (Boston: Houghton Mifflin, 1993); B. Nelson, *1001 Ways to Reward Employees* (New York: Workman Publishing, 1994), p. 148; W. C. Hamner, "How to Ruin Motivation with Pay," *Compensation Review* 7, no. 3 (1975), pp. 17–27.

32. B. N. Pfau and I. T. Kay, "The Five Key Elements of a Total Rewards and Accountability Orientation," *Benefits Quarterly* 18 (Third Quarter 2002), pp. 7–15; B. N. Pfau and I. T. Kay, *The Human Capital Edge* (New York: McGraw-Hill, 2002); J. Pfeffer, *The Human Equation* (Boston: Harvard Business School Press, 1998). For an early summary of research supporting the motivational value of performance-based rewards, see E. E. Lawler III, *Pay and Organizational Effectiveness: A Psychological View* (New York: McGraw-Hill, 1971).

33. Lawler, *Rewarding Excellence*, pp. 77–79; S. Kerr, "Organization Rewards: Practical, Cost-Neutral Alternatives that You May Know, but Don't Practice," *Organizational Dynamics* 28 (Summer 1999), pp. 61–70.

34. M. Rotundo and P. Sackett, "The Relative Importance of Task, Citizenship, and Counterproductive Performance to Global Ratings of Job Performance: A Policy-Capturing Approach," *Journal of Applied Psychology* 87 (February 2002), pp. 66–80. For the

Gallup survey and quotation, see M. Buckingham and D. O. Clifton, *Now, Discover Your Strengths* (New York: Free Press, 2001).

35. Kerr, "Organization Rewards."

36. Lawler, *Rewarding Excellence*, p. 77; "New Survey Finds Variable Pay 'Has Yet to Deliver on Its Promise,'" *Pay for Performance Report*, March 2000, p. 1.

37. DeMatteo, Eby, and Sundstrom, "Team-Based Rewards."

38. R. Wageman, "Interdependence and Group Effectiveness," *Administrative Science Quarterly* 40 (1995), pp. 145–80.

39. "Dream Teams," *Human Resources Professional*, November 1994, pp. 17–19.

40. S. Kerr, "On the Folly of Rewarding A, While Hoping for B," *Academy of Management Journal* 18 (1975), pp. 769–83.

41. D. R. Spitzer, "Power Rewards: Rewards that Really Motivate," *Management Review*, May 1996, pp. 45–50.

42. P. M. Perry, "Holding Your Top Talent," *Research Technology Management* 44 (May 2001), pp. 26–30; "Strong Leaders Make Great Workplaces," *CityBusiness* (Minneapolis-St. Paul), August 28, 2000.

43. G. L. Dalton, "The Collective Stretch: Workforce Flexibility," *Management Review* 87 (December 1998), pp. 54–59; C. Hendry and R. Jenkins, "Psychological Contracts and New Deals," *Human Resource Management Journal* 7 (1997), pp. 38–44.

44. D. Whitford, "A Human Place to Work," *Fortune*, January 8, 2001, pp. 108–19.

45. A. Smith, *The Wealth of Nations* (London: Dent, 1910). Earlier examples are described in "Scientific Management: Lessons from Ancient History through the Industrial Revolution," www.accel-team.com.

46. M. A. Campion, "Ability Requirement Implications of Job Design: An Interdisciplinary Perspective," *Personnel Psychology* 42 (1989), pp. 1–24; H. Fayol, *General and Industrial Management*, trans. C. Storrs (London: Pitman, 1949); E. E. Lawler III, *Motivation in Work Organizations* (Monterey, CA: Brooks/Cole, 1973), Chapter 7.

47. For a review of Taylor's work and life, see R. Kanigel, *The One Best Way: Frederick Winslow Taylor and the Enigma of Efficiency* (New York: Viking, 1997). Also see C. R. Littler, "Taylorism, Fordism, and Job Design," in *Job Design: Critical Perspectives on the Labor Process*, ed. D. Knights, H. Willmott, and D. Collinson (Aldershot, UK: Gower Publishing, 1985), pp. 10–29; F. W. Taylor, *The Principles of Scientific Management* (New York: Harper & Row, 1911).

48. E. E. Lawler III, *High-Involvement Management* (San Francisco: Jossey-Bass, 1986), Chapter 6; C. R. Walker and R. H. Guest, *The Man on the Assembly Line* (Cambridge, MA: Harvard University Press, 1952).

49. W. F. Dowling, "Job Redesign on the Assembly Line: Farewell to Blue-Collar Blues?" *Organizational Dynamics*, Autumn 1973, pp. 51–67; Lawler, *Motivation in Work Organizations*, p. 150.

50. M. Keller, *Rude Awakening* (New York: Harper Perennial, 1989), p. 128.

51. F. Herzberg, B. Mausner, and B. B. Snyderman, *The Motivation to Work* (New York: Wiley, 1959).

52. S. K. Parker, T. D. Wall, and J. L. Cordery, "Future Work Design Research and Practice: Towards an Elaborated Model of Work Design," *Journal of Occupational and Organizational Psychology* 74 (November 2001), pp. 413–40. A decisive critique of Herzberg's theory is N. King, "Clarification and Evaluation of the Two Factor Theory of Job Satisfaction," *Psychological Bulletin* 74 (1970), pp. 18–31.

53. J. R. Hackman and G. Oldham, *Work Redesign* (Reading, MA: Addison-Wesley, 1980).

54. Whitford, "A Human Place to Work."

55. M. C. Andrews and K. M. Kacmar, "Confirmation and Extension of the Sources of Feedback Scale in Service-Based Organizations," *Journal of Business Communication* 38 (April 2001), pp. 206–26.

56. T. Nicholson, "The Vintage Makers—Part One," *Marlborough Express* (Fairfax, NZ), January 31, 2001.

57. G. Johns, J. L. Xie, and Y. Fang, "Mediating and Moderating Effects in Job Design," *Journal of Management* 18 (1992), pp. 657–76.

58. P. E. Spector, "Higher-Order Need Strength as a Moderator of the Job Scope–Employee Outcome Relationship: A Meta Analysis," *Journal of Occupational Psychology* 58 (1985), pp. 119–27.

59. R. M. Malinski, "Job Rotation in an Academic Library: Damned If You Do and Damned If You Don't!" *Library Trends*, March 22, 2002, pp. 673ff.

60. S. Shepard, "Safety Program at Carrier Plant in Collierville Paying Dividends," *Memphis Business Journal*, May 25, 2001, p. 38.

61. M. Grotticelli, "CNN Moves to Small-Format ENG," *Broadcasting & Cable*, May 14, 2001, p. 46.

62. N. G. Dodd and D. C. Ganster, "The Interactive Effects of Variety, Autonomy, and Feedback on Attitudes and Performance," *Journal of Organizational Behavior* 17 (1996), pp. 329–47; M. A. Campion and C. L. McClelland, "Follow-Up and Extension of the Interdisciplinary Costs and Benefits of Enlarged Jobs," *Journal of Applied Psychology* 78 (1993), pp. 339–51.

63. This point is emphasized in C. Pinder, *Work Motivation* (Glenview, IL: Scott, Foresman, 1984), p. 244; and F. Herzberg, "One More Time: How Do You Motivate Employees?" *Harvard Business Review* 46 (January–February 1968), pp. 53–62. For a full discussion of job enrichment, also see R. W. Griffin, *Task Design: An Integrative Approach* (Glenview, IL: Scott, Foresman, 1982); J. R. Hackman, G. Oldham, R. Janson, and K. Purdy, "A New Strategy for Job Enrichment," *California Management Review* 17, no. 4 (1975), pp. 57–71.

64. Hackman and Oldham, *Work Redesign*, pp. 137–38.

65. A. Hertting, K. Nilsson, T. Theorell, and U. S. Larsson, "Personnel Reductions and Structural Changes in Health Care: Work-Life Experiences of Medical Secretaries," *Journal of Psychosomatic Research* 54 (February 2003), pp. 161–70.

66. R. Saavedra and S. K. Kwun, "Affective States in Job Characteristics Theory," *Journal of Organizational Behavior* 21 (2000), pp. 131–46; P. Osterman, "How Common Is Workplace Transformation and Who Adopts It?" *Industrial and Labor Relations Review*

47 (1994), pp. 173–88; D. E. Bowen and E. E. Lawler III, "The Empowerment of Service Workers: What, Why, How, and When," *Sloan Management Review*, Spring 1992, pp. 31–39; P. E. Spector and S. M. Jex, "Relations of Job Characteristics from Multiple Data Sources with Employee Affect, Absence, Turnover Intentions, and Health," *Journal of Applied Psychology* 76 (1991), pp. 46–53; Y. Fried and G. R. Ferris, "The Validity of the Job Characteristics Model: A Review and Meta-Analysis," *Personnel Psychology* 40 (1987), pp. 287–322.

67. B. Lewis, "WestJet—A Crazy Idea that Took Off," *Vancouver Province* (Canada), October 21, 2001.

68. This definition is based mostly on G. M. Spreitzer and R. E. Quinn, *A Company of Leaders: Five Disiplines for Unleashing the Power in Your Workforce* (San Francisco: Jossey-Bass, 2001), pp. 13–21; G. M. Spreitzer, "Psychological Empowerment in the Workplace: Dimensions, Measurement, and Validation," *Academy of Management Journal* 38 (1995), pp. 1442–65. However, most elements of this definition appear in other discussions of empowerment. See, for example, S. T. Menon, "Employee Empowerment: An Integrative Psychological Approach," *Applied Psychology: An International Review* 50 (2001), pp. 153–80; W. A. Randolph, "Re-thinking Empowerment: Why Is It So Hard to Achieve?" *Organizational Dynamics* 29 (November 2000), pp. 94–107; R. Forrester, "Empowerment: Rejuvenating a Potent Idea," *Academy of Management Executive* 14 (August 2000), pp. 67–80; J. A. Conger and R. N. Kanungo, "The Empowerment Process: Integrating Theory and Practice," *Academy of Management Review* 13 (1988), pp. 471–82. Special thanks to Angus Buchanan for helping us to rediscover the details of the empowerment literature.

69. R. Forrester, "Empowerment: Rejuvenating a Potent Idea," *Academy of Management Executive* 14 (August 2000), pp. 67–90. The positive relationship between these conditions (sometimes called structural empowerment conditions) and psychological empowerment is found in H. K. S. Laschinger, J. Finegan, and J. Shamian, "Promoting Nurses' Health: Effect of Empow-

erment on Job Strain and Work Satisfaction," *Nursing Economics* 19 (March/April 2001), pp. 42–52.

70. C. S. Koberg, R. W. Boss, J. C. Senjem, and E. A. Goodman, "Antecedents and Outcomes of Empowerment," *Group and Organization Management* 24 (1999), pp. 71–91.

71. T. D. Wall, J. L. Cordery, and C. W. Clegg, "Empowerment, Performance, and Operational Uncertainty: A Theoretical Integration," *Applied Psychology: An International Review* 51 (2002), pp. 146–69; W. A. Randolph and M. Sashkin, "Can Organizational Empowerment Work in Multinational Settings?" *Academy of Management Executive* 16 (February 2002), pp. 102–16; J. Yoon, "The Role of Structure and Motivation for Workplace Empowerment: The Case of Korean Employees," *Social Psychology Quarterly* 64 (June 2001), pp. 195–206; B. J. Niehoff, R. H. Moorman, G. Blakely, and J. Fuller, "The Influence of Empowerment and Job Enrichment on Employee Loyalty in a Downsizing Environment," *Group and Organization Management* 26 (March 2001), pp. 93–113; K. Blanchard, J. P. Carlos, and A. Randolph, *The 3 Keys to Empowerment: Release the Power within People for Astonishing Results* (San Francisco: Berrett-Koehler, 1999).

72. R. Semler, *The Seven-Day Weekend* (Century: London, 2003), p. 61. The organizational factors affecting empowerment are discussed in P. A. Miller, P. Goddard, and H. K. Spence Laschinger, "Evaluating Physical Therapists' Perception of Empowerment Using Kanter's Theory of Structural Power in Organizations," *Physical Therapy* 81 (December 2001), pp. 1880–88; G. M. Spreitzer and R. E. Quinn, *A Company of Leaders: Five Disciplines for Unleashing the Power in Your Workforce* (San Francisco: Jossey-Bass, 2001); J. Godard, "High Performance and the Transformation of Work: The Implications of Alternative Work Practices for the Experience and Outcomes of Work," *Industrial & Labor Relations Review* 54 (July 2001), pp. 776–805; G. M. Spreitzer, "Social Structural Characteristics of Psychological Empowerment," *Academy of Management Journal* 39 (April 1996), pp. 483–504.

73. H. K. S. Laschinger, J. Finegan, and J. Shamian, "The Impact of Workplace Empowerment, Organizational Trust on Staff Nurses' Work Satisfaction and Organizational Commitment," *Health Care Management Review* 26 (Summer 2001), pp. 7–23; J-C. Chebat and P. Kollias, "The Impact of Empowerment on Customer Contact Employees' Role in Service Organizations," *Journal of Service Research* 3 (August 2000), pp. 66–81.

74. P. Verburg, "Prepare for Takeoff," *Canadian Business*, December 25, 2000, pp. 94–99.

75. T. Romita, "The Talent Search," *Business 2.0*, June 12, 2001.

76. C. P. Neck and C. C. Manz, "Thought Self-Leadership: The Impact of Mental Strategies Training on Employee Cognition, Behavior, and Affect," *Journal of Organizational Behavior* 17 (1996), pp. 445–67.

77. C. C. Manz and C. P. Neck, *Mastering Self-leadership: Empowering Yourself for Personal Excellence* (Englewood Cliffs, NJ: Prentice Hall, 1999); C. C. Manz, "Self-Leadership: Toward an Expanded Theory of Self-Influence Processes in Organizations," *Academy of Management Review* 11 (1986), pp. 585–600.

78. O. J. Strickland and M. Galimba, "Managing Time: The Effects of Personal Goal Setting on Resource Allocation Strategy and Task Performance," *Journal of Psychology* 135 (July 2001), pp. 357–67; P. R. Pintrich, "The Role of Goal Orientation in Self-Regulated Learning," in *Handbook of Self-Regulation*, ed. M. Boekaerts, P. R. Pintrich, and M. Zeidner (New York: Academic Press, 2000), pp. 452–502; H. P. Sims Jr. and C. C. Manz, *Company of Heroes: Unleashing the Power of Self-Leadership* (New York: Wiley, 1996).

79. R. Seymour, "Canada's Best Bosses," *Profit Magazine*, June 2001.

80. R. M. Duncan and J. A. Cheyne, "Incidence and Functions of Self-Reported Private Speech in Young Adults: A Self-Verbalization Questionnaire," *Canadian Journal of Behavioral Science* 31 (April 1999), pp. 133–36. For an organizational behavior discussion of constructive thought patterns, see J. Godwin, C. P. Neck, and J. Houghton, "The Impact of Thought

Self-Leadership on Individual Goal Performance: A Cognitive Perspective," *Journal of Management Development* 18 (1999), pp. 153–69.

81. G. E. Prussia, J. S. Anderson, and C. C. Manz, "Self-Leadership and Performance Outcomes: The Mediating Influence of Self-Efficacy," *Journal of Organizational Behavior*, September 1998, pp. 523–38.

82. Early scholars seem to distinguish mental practice from mental imagery, whereas recent literature combines mental practice with visualizing positive task outcomes within the meaning of mental imagery. For recent discussion of this concept, see C. P. Neck, G. L. Stewart, and C. C. Manz, "Thought Self-Leadership as a Framework for Enhancing the Performance of Performance Appraisers," *Journal of Applied Behavioral Science* 31 (September 1995), pp. 278–302; W. P. Anthony, R. H. Bennett III, E. N. Maddox, and W. J. Wheatley, "Picturing the Future: Using Mental Imagery to Enrich Strategic Environmental Assessment," *Academy of Management Executive* 7, no. 2 (1993), pp. 43–56.

83. L. Morin and G. Latham, "The Effect of Mental Practice and Goal Setting as a Transfer of Training Intervention on Supervisors' Self-Efficacy and Communication Skills: An Exploratory Study," *Applied Psychology: An International Review* 49 (July 2000), pp. 566–78; J. E. Driscoll, C. Cooper, and A. Moran, "Does Mental Practice Enhance Performance?" *Journal of Applied Psychology* 79 (1994), pp. 481–92.

84. A. Wrzesniewski and J. E. Dutton, "Crafting a Job: Revisioning Employees as Active Crafters of Their Work," *Academy of Management Review* 26 (April 2001), pp. 179–201; Manz, "Self-Leadership: Toward an Expanded Theory of Self-Influence Processes in Organizations."

85. M. I. Bopp, S. J. Glynn, and R. A. Henning, "Self-Management of Performance Feedback during Computer-Based Work by Individuals and Two-Person Work Teams," Paper presented at the APA-NIOSH conference, March 1999.

86. A. W. Logue, *Self-Control: Waiting until Tomorrow for What You Want Today* (Englewood Cliffs, NJ: Prentice Hall, 1995).

87. J. Bauman, "The Gold Medal Mind," *Psychology Today* 33 (May 2000), pp. 62–69; K. E. Thiese and S. Huddleston, "The Use of Psychological Skills by Female Collegiate Swimmers," *Journal of Sport Behavior*, December 1999, pp. 602–10; D. Landin and E. P. Hebert, "The Influence of Self-Talk on the Performance of Skilled Female Tennis Players," *Journal of Applied Sport Psychology* 11 (September 1999), pp. 263–82; C. Defrancesco and K. L. Burke, "Performance Enhancement Strategies Used in a Professional Tennis Tournament," *International Journal of Sport Psychology* 28 (1997), pp. 185–95; S. Ming and G. L. Martin, "Single-Subject Evaluation of a Self-Talk Package for Improving Figure Skating Performance," *Sport Psychologist* 10 (1996), pp. 227–38.

88. Morin and Latham, "The Effect of Mental Practice and Goal Setting as a Transfer of Training Intervention on Supervisors' Self-Efficacy and Communication Skills"; A. M. Saks and B. E. Ashforth, "Proactive Socialization and Behavioral Self-Management," *Journal of Vocational Behavior* 48 (1996), pp. 301–23; Neck and Manz, "Thought Self-Leadership: The Impact of Mental Strategies Training on Employee Cognition, Behavior, and Affect."

89. A. L. Kazan, "Exploring the Concept of Self-Leadership: Factors Impacting Self-Leadership of Ohio Americorps Members," *Dissertation Abstracts International* 60 (June 2000); S. Ross, "Corporate Measurements Shift from Punishment to Rewards," *Reuters*, February 28, 2000; M. Castaneda, T. A. Kolenko, and R. J. Aldag, "Self-Management Perceptions and Practices: A Structural Equations Analysis," *Journal of Organizational Behavior* 20 (1999), pp. 101–20; G. L. Stewart, K. P. Carson, and R. L. Cardy, "The Joint Effects of Conscientiousness and Self-Leadership Training on Employee Self-Directed Behavior in a Service Setting," *Personnel Psychology* 49 (1996), pp. 143–64.

CHAPTER 7

1. H. Luk, "Hong Kong's SARS-Stressed Nurses Describe Pressure, Isolation," *Associated Press*, May 22, 2003, p. 4; K. Bradsher, "SARS Takes High Toll on Nurses," *International Herald Tribune*, May 10, 2003, p. 1; N. Law, "Behind the Mask: Josephine Chung Yuen-man," *South China Morning Post* (Hong Kong), May 1, 2003, p. 5; N. Fraser, "Devoted to Care, Despite Their Fear," *South China Morning Post* (Hong Kong), April 20, 2003, p. 4.

2. S. James, "Work Stress Taking Larger Financial Toll," *Reuters*, August 9, 2003; S. Armour, "Rising Job Stress Could Affect Bottom Line," *USA Today*, July 29, 2003; "New Survey: Americans Stressed More Than Ever," *PR Newswire*, June 26, 2003; E. Galinsky, S. S. Kim, and J. T. Bond, *Feeling Overworked: When Work Becomes Too Much* (New York: Families and Work Institute, 2001); American Institute of Stress, www.stress.org.

3. "India's Call Centers Suffer High Quit Rate," *CNET Asia*, August 8, 2003; A. Derfel, "Boy, Are We Stressed Out!" *Montreal Gazette*, May 29, 2003, p. A1; I. Laing, "Too Many of Us Are Feeling the Pressure," *Newcastle Journal* (UK), January 8, 2003, p. 24; A. Smith, C. Brice, A. Collins, V. Matthews, and R. McNamara, *The Scale of Occupational Stress: A Further Analysis of the Impact of Demographic Factors and Type of Job*, Contract Research Report 311/ 2000 (Sudbury, UK: Health & Safety Executive, 2000); N. Kawakami, "Preface to Job Stress in East Asia: Exchanging Experiences among China, Japan, Korea, Taiwan and Thailand," Proceedings of the First East-Asia Job Stress Meeting, Waseda University International Conference Center, Tokyo, Japan, January 8, 2000.

4. R. S. DeFrank and J. M. Ivancevich, "Stress on the Job: An Executive Update," *Academy of Management Executive* 12 (August 1998), pp. 55–66; J. C. Quick and J. D. Quick, *Organizational Stress and Prevention Management* (New York: McGraw-Hill, 1984).

5. J. C. Quick, J. D. Quick, D. L. Nelson, and J. J. Hurrell Jr., *Preventive Stress Management in Organizations* (Washington, DC: American Psychological Association, 1997).

6. B. L. Simmons and D. L. Nelson, "Eustress at Work: The Relationship between Hope and Health in Hospital Nurses," *Health Care Management Review* 26 (October 2001), pp. 7ff.

7. H. Selye, *Stress without Distress* (Philadelphia: J. B. Lippincott, 1974).

8. S. E. Taylor, R. L. Repetti, and T. Seeman, "Health Psychology: What Is an Unhealthy Environment and How Does It Get Under the Skin?" *Annual Review of Psychology* 48 (1997), pp. 411–47.

9. G. Hassell, "Energy Trading Fast, Furious and Lucrative," *Houston Chronicle*, May 20, 2001, p. 25.

10. K. Danna and R. W. Griffin, "Health and Well-Being in the Workplace: A Review and Synthesis of the Literature," *Journal of Management*, Spring 1999, pp. 357–84; Quick and Quick, *Organizational Stress and Prevention Management*, p. 3.

11. S. E. Ross, B. C. Niebling, and T. M. Meckert, "Sources of Stress among College Students," *College Student Journal* 33 (1999), pp. 312–17; E. Narayanan, S. Menon, and P. Spector, "Stress in the Workplace: A Comparison of Gender and Occupations," *Journal of Organizational Behavior* 20 (January 1999), pp. 63–73.

12. E. Vigoda, "Stress-Related Aftermaths to Workplace Politics: The Relationships among Politics, Job Distress, and Aggressive Behavior in Organizations," *Journal of Organizational Behavior* 23 (2002), pp. 571–91. For the effects of conflict and teams on stress, see P. E. Spector and S. M. Jex, "Development of Four Self-Report Measures of Job Stressors and Strain: Interpersonal Conflict at Work Scale, Organizational Constraints Scale, Quantitative Workload Inventory, and Physical Symptoms Inventory," *Journal of Occupational Health Psychology* 3 (1998), pp. 356–67; D. F. Elloy and A. Randolph, "The Effect of Superleader Behavior on Autonomous Work Groups in a Government Operated Railway Service," *Public Personnel Management* 26 (June 1997), pp. 257ff.

13. I. A. Czerwinska, "Sexual Harassment: Men Behaving Badly," *Warsaw Voice*, March 23, 2003.

14. V. Schultz, "Reconceptualizing Sexual Harassment," *Yale Law Journal* 107 (April 1998), pp. 1683–1805. Several U.S. court cases have discussed these two causes for action, including *Lehman v. Toys 'R' Us Inc.*, 132 NJ 587; 626 A2d 445 (1993); *Meritor Savings Bank v. Vinson*, 477 Sup. Ct. 57 (1986).

15. Schultz, "Reconceptualizing Sexual Harassment." Research on gender dif-

ferences in what constitutes sexual harassment is found in M. Rotundo, D-H. Nguyen, and P. R. Sackett, "A Meta-Analytic Review of Gender Differences in Perceptions of Sexual Harassment," *Journal of Applied Psychology* 86 (October 2001), pp. 914–22.

16. L. J. Munson, C. Hulin, and F. Drasgow, "Longitudinal Analysis of Dispositional Influences and Sexual Harassment: Effects on Job and Psychological Outcomes," *Personnel Psychology,* Spring 2000, pp. 21–46; C. S. Piotrkowski, "Gender Harassment, Job Satisfaction, and Distress among Employed White and Minority Women," *Journal of Occupational Health Psychology* 3 (January 1998), pp. 33–43; L. F. Fitzgerald, F. Drasgow, C. L. Hulin, M. J. Gelfand, and V. Magley, "The Antecedents and Consequences of Sexual Harassment in Organizations: A Test of an Integrated Model," *Journal of Applied Psychology* 82 (1997), pp. 578–89; J. Barling, I. Dekker, C. A. Loughlin, E. K. Kelloway, C. Fullagar, and D. Johnson, "Prediction and Replication of the Organizational and Personal Consequences of Workplace Sexual Harassment," *Journal of Managerial Psychology* 11, no. 5 (1996), pp. 4–25.

17. H. W. French, "Fighting Sex Harassment, and Stigma, in Japan," *New York Times,* July 15, 2001, p. 1.

18. V. Di Martino, *Workplace Violence in the Health Sector: Country Case Studies* (Geneva: International Labour Organisation/International Council of Nurses, World Health Organisation and Public Services International Joint Program, 2002); United States Bureau of Justice Statistics, *Violence in the Workplace, 1993–1999* (Washington, DC: U.S. Department of Justice, December 2001); T. Budd, *Violence at Work: New Findings from the 2000 British Crime Survey.* Health and Safety Executive Occasional Paper (London: Home Office, July 2001).

19. J. Barling, A. G. Rogers, and E. K. Kelloway, "Behind Closed Doors: In-Home Workers' Experience of Sexual Harassment and Workplace Violence," *Journal of Occupational Health Psychology* 6 (July 2001), pp. 255–69; M. Kivimaki, M. Elovainio, and J. Vahtera, "Workplace Bullying and Sickness Absence in Hospital Staff," *Occupational & Environmental Medicine* 57 (October

2000), pp. 656–60; J. Barling, "The Prediction, Experience, and Consequences of Workplace Violence," in *Violence on the Job: Identifying Risks and Developing Solutions,* ed. G. R. VandenBos and E. Q. Bulatao (Washington, DC: American Psychological Association, 1996), pp. 29–49.

20. M. Meyers, "Fighting Workplace Bullying Pays Dividends," *Minneapolis Star Tribune,* January 12, 2003, p. D1.

21. H. Cowiea et al., "Measuring Workplace Bullying," *Aggression and Violent Behavior* 7 (2002), pp. 33–51; C. M. Pearson, L. M. Andersson, and C. L. Porath, "Assessing and Attacking Workplace Incivility," *Organizational Dynamics* 29 (November 2000), pp. 123–37.

22. A. Garrett, "How to Cure Bullying at Work," *Management Today,* May 2003, p. 80; D. Turner, "One in Five Staff 'Bullied' in Past 12 Months," *Financial Times* (London), October 2, 2002, p. 5; M. F. Stoeltje, "Jerks at Work," *San Antonio Express-News,* August 31, 2001, p. F1; S. Hickman, "Making Work a Better Place," *HK MBA Alumni Connections,* University of Ottawa, August 2000, p. 3.

23. Kivimaki, Elovainio, and Vahtera, "Workplace Bullying and Sickness Absence in Hospital Staff"; P. McCarthy and M. Barker, "Workplace Bullying Risk Audit," *Journal of Occupational Health and Safety, Australia and New Zealand* 16 (2000), pp. 409–18; M. O'Moore, E. Seigne, L. McGuire, and M. Smith, "Victims of Bullying at Work in Ireland," *Journal of Occupational Health and Safety* 14 (1998), pp. 569–74; G. Namie, U.S. "Hostile Workplace Survey" http://www.bullybusters.org/home/twd/bb/res/surv2000.html.

24. Pearson et al., "Assessing and Attacking Workplace Incivility."

25. R. J. House and J. R. Rizzo, "Role Conflict and Ambiguity as Critical Variables in a Model of Organizational Behavior," *Organizational Behavior and Human Performance* 7 (June 1972), pp. 467–505. Also see M. Siegall and L. L. Cummings, "Stress and Organizational Role Conflict," *Genetic, Social, and General Psychology Monographs* 12 (1995), pp. 65–95; E. K. Kelloway and J. Barling, "Job Characteristics, Role Stress and Mental Health," *Journal of Occupational Psychology* 64 (1991), pp.

291–304; R. L. Kahn, D. M. Wolfe, R. P. Quinn, J. D. Snoek, and R. A. Rosenthal, *Organizational Stress: Studies in Role Conflict and Ambiguity* (New York: Wiley, 1964).

26. M. C. Turkel, "Struggling to Find a Balance: The Paradox between Caring and Economics," *Nursing Administration Quarterly* 26 (Fall 2001), pp. 67–82.

27. G. R. Cluskey and A. Vaux, "Vocational Misfit: Source of Occupational Stress among Accountants," *Journal of Applied Business Research* 13 (Summer 1997), pp. 43–54; J. R. Edwards, "An Examination of Competing Versions of the Person–Environment Fit Approach to Stress," *Academy of Management Journal* 39 (1996), pp. 292–339; B. E. Ashforth and R. H. Humphrey, "Emotional Labor in Service Roles: The Influence of Identity," *Academy of Management Review* 18 (1993), pp. 88–115.

28. A. Nygaard and R. Dahlstrom, "Role Stress and Effectiveness in Horizontal Alliances," *Journal of Marketing* 66 (April 2002), pp. 61–82; A. M. Saks and B. E. Ashforth, "Proactive Socialization and Behavioral Self-Management." *Journal of Vocational Behavior* 48 (1996), pp. 301–23; D. L. Nelson and C. Sutton, "Chronic Work Stress and Coping: A Longitudinal Study and Suggested New Directions," *Academy of Management Journal* 33 (1990), pp. 859–69.

29. B. K. Hunnicutt, *Kellogg's Six-Hour Day* (Philadelphia: Temple University Press, 1996); J. B. Schor, *The Overworked American: The Unexpected Decline of Leisure* (New York: Basic Books, 1991).

30. K. Rives, "Many Workers Don't Take Vacation," *Raleigh (NC) News & Observer,* June 22, 2003.

31. K. Isaksson, C. Hogstedt, C., Eriksson, and T. Theorell (eds.), *Health Effects of the New Labour Market* (New York: Kluwer Academic, 2000). See also A. R. Hochschild, *The Time Bind: When Work Becomes Home and Home Becomes Work* (New York: Metropolitan Books, 1997).

32. Leo, W. S., "'Traffic Congestion Makes Me Crazy,'" *Jakarta Post,* March 18, 2003. For research on traffic congestion and stress, see G. W. Evans, R. E. Wener, and D. Phillips, "The Morning Rush Hour: Predictability

and Commuter Stress," *Environment and Behavior* 34 (July 2002), pp. 521–30; D. A. Hennessy and D. L. Wiesenthal "The Relationship between Traffic Congestion, Driver Stress and Direct versus Indirect Coping Behaviours," *Ergonomics* 40 (1997), pp. 348–61.

33. F. Kittel1 et al., "Job Conditions and Fibrinogen in 14,226 Belgian Workers: The Belstress Study," *European Heart Journal* 23 (2002), pp. 1841–48; J. M. Griffina, R. Fuhrera, S. A. Stansfeld, and M. Marmota, "The Importance of Low Control at Work and Home on Depression and Anxiety: Do These Effects Vary by Gender and Social Class?" *Social Science and Medicine* 54 (2002), pp. 783–98; J. Vahtera, M. Kivimaki, J. Pentti, and T. Theorell, "Effect of Change in the Psychosocial Work Environment on Sickness Absence: A Seven Year Follow Up of Initially Healthy Employees," *Journal of Epidemiology & Community Health* 54 (July 2000), pp. 482–83; L. D Sargent and D. J. Terry, "The Effects of Work Control and Job Demands on Employee Adjustment and Work Performance," *Journal of Occupational and Organizational Psychology* 71 (September 1998), pp. 219–36; M. G. Marmot, H. Bosma, H. Hemingway, E. Brunner, and S. Stansfeld, "Contribution of Job Control and Other Risk Factors to Social Variations in Coronary Heart Disease Incidence," *Lancet* 350 (July 26, 1997), pp. 235–39; P. M. Elsass and J. F. Veiga, "Job Control and Job Strain: A Test of Three Models," *Journal of Occupational Health Psychology* 2 (July 1997), pp. 195–211; R. Karasek and T. Theorell, *Healthy Work: Stress, Productivity, and the Reconstruction of Working Life* (New York: Basic Books, 1990).

34. M. Sverke, J. Hellgren, and K. Näswall, "No Security: A Meta-Analysis and Review of Job Insecurity and Its Consequences," *Journal of Occupational Health Psychology* 7 (July 2002), pp. 242–64; A. Tsutsumi, K. Kayaba, T. Theorell, and J. Siegrist, "Association between Job Stress and Depression among Japanese Employees Threatened by Job Loss in a Comparison between Two Complementary Job-Stress Models," *Scandinavian Journal of Work and Environmental Health* 27 (2001), pp. 146–53; R. J. Burke and C. L. Cooper (eds.), *The Organization in Crisis: Downsizing, Restructuring, and Privatization* (Oxford, UK: Blackwell, 2000); M. Kivimaki, J. Vahtera, J. Pentti, and J. E. Ferrie, "Factors Underlying the Effect of Organizational Downsizing on Health of Employees: Longitudinal Cohort Study," *BMJ: British Medical Journal* 320 (April 8, 2000), pp. 971–75.

35. M. Kinsman, "Workplace Stress on Rise as Companies Cut Payrolls," *San Diego Union-Tribune*, May 4, 2003, p. H2.

36. G. Evans and D. Johnson, "Stress and Open-Office Noise," *Journal of Applied Psychology* 85 (2000), pp. 779–83; S. Melamed and S. Bruhis, "The Effects of Chronic Industrial Noise Exposure on Urinary Cortisol, Fatigue, and Irritability: A Controlled Field Experiment," *Journal of Occupational and Environmental Medicine* 38 (1996), pp. 252–56.

37. G. Hamilton, "Death in the Woods," *Vancouver Sun*, July 24, 2002.

38. C. S. Bruck, T. D. Allen, and P. E. Spector, "The Relation between Work–Family Conflict and Job Satisfaction: A Finer-Grained Analysis," *Journal of Vocational Behavior* 60 (2002), pp. 336–53; G. A. Adams, L. A. King, and D. W. King, "Relationships of Job and Family Involvement, Family Social Support, and Work–Family Conflict with Job and Life Satisfaction," *Journal of Applied Psychology* 81 (August 1996), pp. 411–20; J. H. Greenhaus and N. Beutell, "Sources of Conflict between Work and Family Roles," *Academy of Management Review* 10 (1985), pp. 76–88.

39. R. J. Burke, "Workaholism in Organizations: The Role of Organizational Values," *Personnel Review* 30 (October 2001), pp. 637–45; D. S. Carlson, "Work–Family Conflict in the Organization: Do Life Role Values Make a Difference?" *Journal of Management*, September 2000.

40. M. Shields, "Shift Work and Health," *Health Reports* (*Statistics Canada*) 13 (Spring 2002), pp. 11–34; Higgins and Duxbury, *The 2001 National Work–Life Conflict Study*; M. Jamal and V. V. Baba, "Shiftwork and Department-Type Related to Job Stress, Work Attitudes and Behavioral Intentions: A Study of Nurses," *Journal of Organizational Behavior* 13 (1992), pp. 449–64; C. Higgins, L. Duxbury, and R. Irving, "Determinants and Consequences of Work–Family Conflict," *Organizational Behavior and Human Decision Processes* 51 (February 1992), pp. 51–75.

41. J. Newman, "Do You Work Too Hard?" *Wisconsin State Journal*, September 1, 2002, p. A1. For recent research on time-based conflict, see D. L. Nelson and R. J. Burke, "Women Executives: Health, Stress, and Success," *Academy of Management Executive* 14 (May 2000), pp. 107–21; C. S. Rogers, "The Flexible Workplace: What Have We Learned?" *Human Resource Management* 31 (Fall 1992), pp. 183–99. One somewhat different view is that time-based conflict and other work–family conflict stressors reflect the gendered assumptions about work (male) and family (female) duties. As men and women break down their gendered roles, work–family conflicts might become less troublesome. See M. Runté and A. J. Mills, "The Discourse of Work–Family Conflict: A Critique," *Proceedings of the Annual Conference of the Administrative Sciences Association of Canada, Gender and Diversity in Organizations Division* 23, no. 11 (2002), pp. 21–32.

42. E. K. Kelloway, B. H. Gottlieb, and L. Barham, "The Source, Nature, and Direction of Work and Family Conflict: A Longitudinal Investigation," *Journal of Occupational Health Psychology* 4 (October 1999), pp. 337–46; W. Stewart and J. Barling, "Fathers' Work Experiences Effect on Children's Behaviors via Job-Related Affect and Parenting Behaviors," *Journal of Organizational Behavior* 17 (1996), pp. 221–32.

43. A. S. Wharton and R. J. Erickson, "Managing Emotions on the Job and at Home: Understanding the Consequences of Multiple Emotional Roles," *Academy of Management Review* 18 (1993), pp. 457–86. For a recent discussion of role conflict and spillover between work and nonwork, see S. M. MacDermid, B. L. Seery, and H. M. Weiss, "An Emotional Examination of the Work–Family Interface," in *Emotions in the Workplace*, ed. R. G. Lord, R. J. Klimoski, and R. Kanfer (San Francisco: Jossey-Bass, 2002), pp. 402–27.

44. "Twenty Most Stressful Jobs in Britain," *The Mirror*, October 15, 2001, p. 50; Smith et al., *The Scale of Occupational Stress*; "Office Workers More Stressed than Nurses," *The Indepen-*

dent (London), August 7, 2000, p. 8; B. Keil, "The 10 Most Stressful Jobs in NYC," _New York Post_, April 6, 1999, p. 50; International Labor Office, _World Labor Report_ (Geneva: ILO, 1993), Chapter 5; Karasek and Theorell, _Healthy Work_.

45. Quick et al., _Preventive Stress Management in Organizations_, Chapter 3.

46. S. M. Jex, P. D. Bliese, S. Buzzell, and J. Primeau, "The Impact of Self-Efficacy on Stressor–Strain Relations: Coping Style as an Explanatory Mechanism," _Journal of Applied Psychology_ 86 (2001), pp. 401–9; J. Schaubroeck and D. E. Merritt, "Divergent Effects of Job Control on Coping with Work Stressors: The Key Role of Self-Efficacy," _Academy of Management Journal_ 40 (June 1997), pp. 738–54.

47. S. C. Segerstrom, S. E. Taylor, M. E. Kemeny, and J. L. Fahey, "Optimism Is Associated with Mood, Coping, and Immune Change in Response to Stress," _Journal of Personality & Social Psychology_ 74 (June 1998), pp. 1646–55.

48. K. R. Parkes, "Personality and Coping as Moderators of Work Stress Processes: Models, Methods and Measures," _Work & Stress_ 8 (April 1994) pp. 110–29; S. J. Havlovic and J. P. Keenen, "Coping with Work Stress: The Influence of Individual Differences," in _Handbook on Job Stress_ [Special Issue], ed. P. L. Perrewé, _Journal of Social Behavior and Personality_ 6 (1991), pp. 199–212.

49. B. C. Long and S. E. Kahn (eds.), _Women, Work, and Coping: A Multidisciplinary Approach to Workplace Stress_ (Montreal: McGill-Queen's University Press, 1993); E. R. Greenglass, R. J. Burke, and M. Ondrack, "A Gender-Role Perspective of Coping and Burnout," _Applied Psychology: An International Review_ 39 (1990), pp. 5–27; T. D. Jick and L. F. Mitz, "Sex Differences in Work Stress," _Academy of Management Review_ 10 (1985), pp. 408–20.

50. J. L. Hernandez, "What's the Buzz in Schuyler? Just Ask Beekeeper Finster," _Utica (NY) Observer-Dispatch_, June 23, 2003.

51. M. Friedman and R. Rosenman, _Type A Behavior and Your Heart_ (New York: Knopf, 1974). For more recent discussion, see P. E. Spector and B. J. O'Connell, "The Contribution of Personality Traits, Negative Affectivity,

Locus of Control and Type A to the Subsequent Reports of Job Stressors and Job Strains," _Journal of Occupational and Organizational Psychology_ 67 (1994), pp. 1–11; K. R. Parkes, "Personality and Coping as Moderators of Work Stress Processes: Models, Methods and Measures," _Work & Stress_ 8 (April 1994), pp. 110–29.

52. B. D. Kirkcaldy, R. J. Shephard, and A. F. Furnham, "The Influence of Type A Behavior and Locus of Control upon Job Satisfaction and Occupational Health," _Personality and Individual Differences_, in press; A. L. Day and S. Jreige, "Examining Type A Behavior Pattern to Explain the Relationship between Job Stressors and Psychosocial Outcomes," _Journal of Occupational Health Psychology_ 7 (April 2002), pp. 109–20.

53. I. Harpaz and R. Snir, "Workaholism: Its Definition and Nature," _Human Relations_ 56 (2003), pp. 291–319; C. P. Flowers and B. Robinson, "A Structural and Discriminant Analysis of the Work Addiction Risk Test," _Educational and Psychological Measurement_ 62 (June 2002), pp. 517–26; R. J. Burke, "Workaholism among Women Managers: Personal and Workplace Correlates," _Journal of Managerial Psychology_ 15 (2000), pp. 520–34; R. J. Burke, "Workaholism and Extra-work Satisfactions," _International Journal of Organizational Analysis_ 7 (1999), pp. 352–64; J. T. Spence and A. S. and Robbins, "Workaholism: Definition, Measurement and Preliminary Results," _Journal of Personality Assessment_ 58 (1992), pp. 160–78. The origin of the term "workaholism" is attributed to W. Oates, _Confessions of a Workaholic_ (New York: World, 1971).

54. R. J. Burke, "Workaholism among Women Managers: Personal and Workplace Correlates," _Journal of Managerial Psychology_ 15 (2000), pp. 520–34. Other typologies of workaholics have been proposed in B. E. Robinson, "A Typology of Workaholics with Implications for Counsellors," _Journal of Addictions & Offender Counseling_ 21 (October 2000), pp. 34ff.

55. Burke, "Workaholism among Women Managers"; B. E. Robinson, "The Work Addition Risk Test: Development of a Tentative Measure of Workaholism," _Perceptual and Motor_

Skills 88 (1999), pp. 199–210; R. J. Burke and G. MacDermid, "Are Workaholics Job Satisfied and Successful in Their Careers?" _Career Development International_ 4 (1999), pp. 277–82.

56. D. Ganster, M. Fox, and D. Dwyer, "Explaining Employees' Health Care Costs: A Prospective Examination of Stressful Job Demands, Personal Control, and Physiological Reactivity," _Journal of Applied Psychology_ 86 (May 2001), pp. 954–64; S. Cohen, D. A. Tyrrell, and A. P. Smith, "Psychological Stress and Susceptibility to the Common Cold," _New England Journal of Medicine_ 325 (August 29, 1991), pp. 654–56.

57. M. Kivimaki, P. Leino-Arjas, R. Luukkonen, H. Riihimaki et al., "Work Stress and Risk of Cardiovascular Mortality: Prospective Cohort Study of Industrial Employees," _British Medical Journal_ 325 (October 19, 2002), pp. 857–60; S. A. Everson et al., "Stress-Induced Blood Pressure Reactivity and Incident Stroke in Middle-Aged Men," _Stroke_ 32 (June 2001), pp. 1263–70; H. Bosma, R. Peter, J. Siegrist, and M. Marmot, "Two Alternative Job Stress Models and the Risk of Coronary Heart Disease," _American Journal of Public Health_ 88 (January 1998), pp. 68–74.

58. I. Hajjar and T. A. Kotchen, "Trends in Prevalence, Awareness, Treatment, and Control of Hypertension in the United States, 1988–2000," _JAMA: Journal of the American Medical Association_ 290 (July 9, 2003), pp. 199–206.

59. D. K. Sugg, "Study Shows Link between Minor Stress, Early Signs of Coronary Artery Disease," _Baltimore Sun_, December 16, 1997, p. A3.

60. "Banishing the Blues Could Cut the Chances of Cancer," _The Scotsman_, June 23, 2003.

61. R. C. Kessler, "The Effects of Stressful Life Events on Depression," _Annual Review of Psychology_ 48 (1997), pp. 191–214; H. M. Weiss and R. Cropanzano, "Affective Events Theory: A Theoretical Discussion of the Structure, Causes, and Consequences of Affective Experiences at Work," _Research in Organizational Behavior_ 18 (1996), pp. 1–74.

62. C. Maslach, W. B. Schaufeli, and M. P. Leiter, "Job Burnout," _Annual Review of Psychology_ 52 (2001), pp. 397–422; R. T. Lee and B. E. Ashforth,

"A Meta-Analytic Examination of the Correlates of the Three Dimensions of Job Burnout," *Journal of Applied Psychology* 81 (1996), pp. 123–33; R. J. Burke, "Toward a Phase Model of Burnout: Some Conceptual and Methodological Concerns," *Group and Organization Studies* 14 (1989), pp. 23–32; C. Maslach, *Burnout: The Cost of Caring* (Englewood Cliffs, NJ: Prentice Hall, 1982).

63. C. L. Cordes and T. W. Dougherty, "A Review and Integration of Research on Job Burnout," *Academy of Management Review* 18 (1993), pp. 621–56.

64. R. T. Lee and B. E. Ashforth, "A Further Examination of Managerial Burnout: Toward an Integrated Model," *Journal of Organizational Behavior* 14 (1993), pp. 3–20.

65. Maslach et al., "Job Burnout," p. 405. However, there is also recent support for the three-stage model presented here. See S. Toppinen-Tanner, R. Kalimo, and P. Mutanen, "The Process of Burnout in White-Collar and Blue-Collar Jobs: Eight-Year Prospective Study of Exhaustion," *Journal of Organizational Behavior* 23 (2002), pp. 555–70.

66. M. Jamal, "Job Stress and Job Performance Controversy: An Empirical Assessment," *Organizational Behavior and Human Performance* 33 (1984), pp. 1–21; G. Keinan, "Decision Making under Stress: Scanning of Alternatives under Controllable and Uncontrollable Threats," *Journal of Personality and Social Psychology* 52 (1987), pp. 638–44; S. J. Motowidlo, J. S. Packard, and M. R. Manning, "Occupational Stress: Its Causes and Consequences for Job Performance," *Journal of Applied Psychology* 71 (1986), pp. 618–29.

67. R. D. Hackett and P. Bycio, "An Evaluation of Employee Absenteeism as a Coping Mechanism among Hospital Nurses," *Journal of Occupational & Organizational Psychology* 69 (December 1996), pp. 327–38; V. V. Baba and M. J. Harris, "Stress and Absence: A Cross-Cultural Perspective," *Research in Personnel and Human Resources Management, Supplement 1* (1989), pp. 317–37.

68. DeFrank and Ivancevich, "Stress on the Job: An Executive Update"; Neuman and Baron, "Workplace Violence and Workplace Aggression."

69. H. Steensma, "Violence in the Workplace: The Explanatory Strength of Social (In)justice Theories," in *The Justice Motive in Everyday Life*, ed. M. Ross and D. T. Miller (New York: Cambridge University Press, 2002), pp. 149–67; L. Greenberg and J. Barling, "Predicting Employee Aggression against Coworkers, Subordinates and Supervisors: The Roles of Person Behaviors and Perceived Workplace Factors," *Journal of Organizational Behavior* 20 (1999), pp. 897–913; M. A. Diamond, "Administrative Assault: A Contemporary Psychoanalytic View of Violence and Aggression in the Workplace," *American Review of Public Administration* 27 (September 1997), pp. 228–47.

70. Neuman and Baron, "Workplace Violence and Workplace Aggression"; L. Berkowitz, *Aggression: Its Causes, Consequences, and Control* (New York: McGraw-Hill, 1993).

71. "Stressed Out: How the Big Shots Get Some Stability," *Wall Street Journal Europe*, January 18, 2001, p. 21.

72. Siegall and Cummings, "Stress and Organizational Role Conflict"; Havlovic and Keenen, "Coping with Work Stress."

73. T. Newton, J. Handy, and S. Fineman, *Managing Stress: Emotion and Power at Work* (Newbury Park, CA: Sage, 1995).

74. I. Morton, "Volvo Addresses On-the-Job Stress," *Automotive News Europe*, August 26, 2002, p. 15; N. Elkes, "Hospital Tackles Health of Stressed-Out Staff," *Birmingham Evening Mail* (UK), August 24, 2001, p. 73.

75. Burke, "Workaholism and Extra-work Satisfactions"; N. Terra, "The Prevention of Job Stress by Redesigning Jobs and Implementing Self-Regulating Teams," in *Job Stress Interventions*, ed. L. R. Murphy (Washington, DC : American Psychological Association, 1995); T. D. Wall and K. Davids, "Shopfloor Work Organization and Advanced Manufacturing Technology," *International Review of Industrial and Organizational Psychology* 7 (1992), pp. 363–98; Karasek and Theorell, *Healthy Work*.

76. J. L. Howard, "Workplace Violence in Organizations: An Exploratory Study of Organizational Prevention Techniques," *Employee Responsibilities and Rights Journal* 13 (June 2001), pp. 57–75.

77. K. Hilpern, "Boiling Over," *The Guardian* (London), March 17, 2003, p. 2.

78. C. Avery and D. Zabel. *The Flexible Workplace: A Sourcebook of Information and Research* (Westport, CT: Quorum, 2000).

79. J. Atkinson, "Job-Sharing Campaign Targets Teachers," *Western Mail*, December 28, 2002, p. 11.

80. V. Galt, "Kraft Canada Cooks Up a Tempting Workplace," *Toronto Globe & Mail*, August 5, 2002, p. B1.

81. P. Szuchman, "The Job-Share Advantage," *Working Mother* 25 (May 2002), p. 15.

82. E. J. Hill, B. C. Miller, S. P. Weiner, and J. Colihan, "Influences of the Virtual Office on Aspects of Work and Work/Life Balance," *Personnel Psychology* 51 (Autumn 1998), pp. 667–83; A. Mahlon, "The Alternative Workplace: Changing Where and How People Work," *Harvard Business Review*, May–June 1998, pp. 121–30.

83. "Driving Ambitions," *Employee Benefits*, September 6, 2002, p. 45. More than 100 countries have paid maternity leave. Among the industrialized countries, only the United States, Australia, and New Zealand do not provide this support. See T. Allard and L. Glendinning, "For Now, Aussie Mums Are Still a World Apart," *Sydney Morning Herald*, August 16, 2001; J. Satterfield, "U.S. Lags Behind Other Nations on Family Leave," *Knoxville News-Sentinel*, May 7, 2001, p. A1. For discussion of the FMLA, see S. Kim, "Toward Understanding Family Leave Policy in Public Organizations: Family Leave Use and Conceptual Framework for the Family Leave Implementation Process," *Public Productivity & Management Review* 22 (September 1998), pp. 71–87.

84. "Work/Life Balance A Key to Productivity," *Employee Benefit Plan Review*, 53 (September 1998), pp. 30–31.

85. M. Blair-Loy and A. S. Wharton, "Employees' Use of Work–Family Policies and the Workplace Social Context," *Social Forces* 80 (March 2002), pp. 813–45; C. Higgins and L. Duxbury, *The 2001 National Work–Life Conflict Study: Report One, Final Report* (Ottawa: Health Canada, March 2002).

86. M. Jackson, "Managers Measured by Charges' Work–Life Accountability

Programs Let Firms Calculate Progress," *Boston Globe*, February 2, 2003, p. G1.

87. B. Miller, "Brann Baltimore Marketing Firm's Office Gets a Fun Makeover," *Baltimore Daily Record*, October 3, 2002.

88. Y. Iwasaki, R. C. Mannell, B. J. A. Smale, and J. Butcher, "A Short-Term Longitudinal Analysis of Leisure Coping Used by Police and Emergency Response Service Workers," *Journal of Leisure Research* 34 (July 2002), pp. 311–39.

89. "How Large Firms Make Partner Sabbaticals Both Plausible and Appealing," *Partner's Report for Law Firm Owners*, June 2003, p. 1; S. Nixon, "Long-Service Leave at Risk of Being Put Out to Pasture," *Sydney Morning Herald*, April 19, 2003, p. 5; P. Paul, "Time Out," *American Demographics* 24 (June 2002).

90. S. Moreland, "Strike Up Creativity," *Crain's Cleveland Business*, April 14, 2003, p. 3.

91. A. M. Saks and B. E. Ashforth, "Proactive Socialization and Behavioral Self-Management," *Journal of Vocational Behavior* 48 (1996), pp. 301–23; M. Waung, "The Effects of Self-Regulatory Coping Orientation on Newcomer Adjustment and Job Survival," *Personnel Psychology*, 48 (1995), pp. 633–50; J. E. Maddux (ed.), *Self-Efficacy, Adaptation, and Adjustment: Theory, Research, and Application* (New York: Plenum, 1995.)

92. A. J. Daley and G. Parfitt, "Good Health—Is It Worth It? Mood States, Physical Well-Being, Job Satisfaction and Absenteeism in Members and Non-Members of British Corporate Health and Fitness Clubs," *Journal of Occupational and Organizational Psychology* 69 (1996), pp. 121–34; L. E. Falkenberg, "Employee Fitness Programs: Their Impact on the Employee and the Organization," *Academy of Management Review* 12 (1987), pp. 511–22; R. J. Shephard, M. Cox, and P. Corey, "Fitness Program Participation: Its Effect on Workers' Performance," *Journal of Occupational Medicine* 23 (1981), pp. 359–63.

93. S. Armour, "Rising Job Stress Could Affect Bottom Line," *USA Today*, July 29, 2003; "Putting the Walk in Work," *CBS News*, June 28, 2003; A. S. Sethi,

"Meditation for Coping with Organizational Stress," in *Handbook of Organizational Stress Coping Strategies*, ed. A. S. Sethi and R. S. Schuler (Cambridge, MA: Ballinger, 1984), pp. 145–65; M. T. Matteson and J. M. Ivancevich, *Managing Job Stress and Health* (New York: Free Press, 1982), pp. 160–66.

94. J. Davia, "Companies See the Benefits in Offering Wellness Programs," *Rochester (NY) Democrat and Chronicle*, July 7, 2003; R. Smith, "Park Place Entertainment Teams with Sierra Health for Wellness Program," *Las Vegas Review-Journal*, May 15, 2003.

95. J. J. L. van der Klink, R. W. B. Blonk, A. H. Schene, and F. J. H. van Dijk, "The Benefits of Interventions for Work-Related Stress," *American Journal of Public Health* 91 (February 2001), pp. 270–76; T. Rotarius, A. Liberman, and J. S. Liberman, "Employee Assistance Programs: A Prevention and Treatment Prescription for Problems in Health Care Organizations," *Health Care Manager* 19 (September 2000), pp. 24–31.

96. P. D. Bliese and T. W. Britt, "Social Support, Group Consensus, and Stressor–Strain Relationships: Social Context Matters," *Journal of Organizational Behavior* 22 (2001), pp. 425–36; B. N. Uchino, J. T. Cacioppo, and J. K. Kiecolt-Glaser, "The Relationship between Social Support and Physiological Processes: A Review with Emphasis on Underlying Mechanisms and Implications for Health," *Psychological Bulletin* 119 (May 1996), pp. 488–531; M. R. Manning, C. N. Jackson, and M. R. Fusilier, "Occupational Stress, Social Support, and the Costs of Health Care," *Academy of Management Journal* 39 (June 1996), pp. 738–50.

97. J. S. House, *Work Stress and Social Support* (Reading, MA: Addison-Wesley, 1981); S. Cohen and T. A. Wills, "Stress, Social Support, and the Buffering Hypothesis," *Psychological Bulletin* 98 (1985), pp. 310–57.

98. S. Schachter, *The Psychology of Affiliation* (Stanford, CA: Stanford University Press, 1959).

CHAPTER **8**

1. S. Jefferson, "NASA Let Arrogance on Board," *Palm Beach Post*, August 30, 2003; R. J. Smith, "NASA Culture,

Columbia Probers Still Miles Apart," *Washington Post*, August 22, 2003, p. A3; Columbia Accident Investigation Board, *Report, Volume 1* (Washington, DC: Government Printing Office, August 2003); "NASA Managers Differed over Shuttle Strike," *Reuters*, July 22, 2003; C. Gibson, "Columbia: The Final Mission," *NineMSN* (Australia), July 13, 2003.

2. F. A. Shull Jr., A. L. Delbecq, and L. L. Cummings, *Organizational Decision Making* (New York: McGraw-Hill, 1970), p. 31. Also see J. G. March, "Understanding How Decisions Happen in Organizations," in *Organizational Decision Making*, ed. Z. Shapira (New York: Cambridge University Press, 1997), pp. 9–32.

3. This model is adapted from several sources: H. Mintzberg, D. Raisinghani, and A. Théorét, "The Structure of 'Unstructured' Decision Processes," *Administrative Science Quarterly* 21 (1976), pp. 246–75; H. A. Simon, *The New Science of Management Decision* (New York: Harper & Row, 1960); C. Kepner and B. Tregoe, *The Rational Manager* (New York: McGraw-Hill, 1965); W. C. Wedley and R. H. G. Field, "A Predecision Support System," *Academy of Management Review* 9 (1984), pp. 696–703.

4. B. M. Bass, *Organizational Decision Making* (Homewood, IL: Irwin, 1983), Chapter 3; W. F. Pounds, "The Process of Problem Finding," *Industrial Management Review* 11 (Fall 1969), pp. 1–19; C. Kepner and B. Tregoe, *The Rational Manager* (New York: McGraw-Hill, 1965).

5. P. F. Drucker, *The Practice of Management* (New York: Harper & Brothers, 1954), pp. 353–57.

6. Wedley and Field, "A Predecision Support System," p. 696; Drucker, *The Practice of Management*, p. 357; L. R. Beach and T. R. Mitchell, "A Contingency Model for the Selection of Decision Strategies," *Academy of Management Review* 3 (1978), pp. 439–49.

7. I. L. Janis, *Crucial Decisions* (New York: Free Press, 1989), pp. 35–37; Simon, *The New Science of Management Decision*, pp. 5–6.

8. Mintzberg, Raisinghani, and Théorét, "The Structure of 'Unstructured' Decision Processes," pp. 255–56.

9. B. Fischhoff and S. Johnson, "The Possibility of Distributed Decision Making," in *Organizational Decision Making*, ed. Shapira, pp. 216–37.

10. The different view of emotions on decision making are discussed or emphasized in N. M. Ashkanasy and C. E. J. Hartel, "Managing Emotions in Decision-Making," in *Managing Emotions in the Workplace*, ed. N. M. Ashkanasy, W. J. Zerbe, C. E. J. Hartel (Armonk, NY: M. E. Sharpe, 2002); D. S. Massey, "A Brief History of Human Society: The Origin and Role of Emotion in Social Life," *American Sociological Review* 67 (February 2002), pp. 1–29; J. P. Forgas and J. M. George, "Affective Influences on Judgments and Behavior in Organizations: An Information Processing Perspective," *Organizational Behavior and Human Decision Processes* 86 (September 2001), pp. 3–34; N. Schwarz, "Social Judgment and Attitudes: Warmer, More Social, and Less Conscious," *European Journal of Social Psychology* 30 (2000), pp. 149–76; P. Greenspan, "Emotional Strategies and Rationality," *Ethics* 110 (April 2000), pp. 469–87.

11. A. Howard, "Opinion," *Computing*, July 8, 1999, p. 18.

12. Schwarz, "Social Judgment and Attitudes," pp. 149–76; R. Hastie, "Problems for Judgment and Decision Making," *Annual Review of Psychology* 52 (2001), pp. 653–83.

13. J. E. Dutton, "Strategic Agenda Building in Organizations," in *Organizational Decision Making*, ed. Shapira, pp. 81–107; M. Lyles and H. Thomas, "Strategic Problem Formulation: Biases and Assumptions Embedded in Alternative Decision-Making Models," *Journal of Management Studies* 25 (1988), pp. 131–45; I. I. Mitroff, "On Systematic Problem Solving and the Error of the Third Kind," *Behavioral Science* 9 (1974), pp. 383–93.

14. D. Domer, *The Logic of Failure* (Reading, MA: Addison-Wesley, 1996); M. Basadur, "Managing the Creative Process in Organizations," in *Problem Finding, Problem Solving, and Creativity*, ed. M. A. Runco (Norwood, NJ: Ablex Publishing, 1994), pp. 237–68.

15. P. C. Nutt, "Preventing Decision Debacles," *Technological Forecasting and Social Change* 38 (1990), pp. 159–74.

16. P. C. Nutt, *Making Tough Decisions* (San Francisco: Jossey-Bass, 1989).

17. H. A. Simon, "A Behavioral Model of Rational Choice," *Quarterly Journal of Economics* 69 (1955), pp. 99–118.

18. J. Conlisk, "Why Bounded Rationality?" *Journal of Economic Literature* 34 (1996), pp. 669–700; B. L. Lipman, "Information Processing and Bounded Rationality: A Survey," *Canadian Journal of Economics* 28 (1995), pp. 42–67.

19. L. T. Pinfield, "A Field Evaluation of Perspectives on Organizational Decision Making," *Administrative Science Quarterly* 31 (1986), pp. 365–88. The recent survey, conducted by Kepner-Tregoe, is described in D. Sandahl and C. Hewes, "Decision Making at Digital Speed," *Pharmaceutical Executive* 21 (August 2001), p. 62.

20. H. A. Simon, *Administrative Behavior*, 2nd ed. (New York: Free Press, 1957), pp. xxv, 80–84; and J. G. March and H. A. Simon, *Organizations* (New York: Wiley, 1958), pp. 140–41.

21. J. E. Russo, V. H. Medvec, and M. G. Meloy, "The Distortion of Information during Decisions," *Organizational Behavior & Human Decision Processes* 66 (1996), pp. 102–10; P. O. Soelberg, "Unprogrammed Decision Making," *Industrial Management Review* 8 (1967), pp. 19–29.

22. F. Phillips, "The Distortion of Criteria after Decision-Making," *Organizational Behavior and Human Decision Processes* 88 (2002), pp. 769–84.

23. H. A. Simon, *Models of Man: Social and Rational* (New York: Wiley, 1957), p. 253.

24. N. M. Ashkanasy, W. J. Zerbe, and C. E. J. Hartel, "Introduction: Managing Emotions in a Changing Workplace," in *Managing Emotions in the Workplace*, ed. Ashkanasy, Zerbe, and Hartel, pp. 3–18; Forgas and George, "Affective Influences on Judgments and Behavior in Organizations"; A. M. Isen, "An Influence of Positive Affect on Decision Making in Complex Situations: Theoretical Issues with Practical Implications," *Journal of Consumer Psychology* 11 (September 2001), pp. 75–85; E. A. Lemerise and K. A. Dodge, "The Development of Anger and Hostile Interactions" in *Handbook of Emotions*, ed. M. Lewis and J. M. Haviland-Jones (New York: Guilford Press, 2000), pp 594–606.

25. M. Lyons, "Cave-in Too Close for Comfort, Miner Says," *Saskatoon Star Phoenix*, May 6, 2002.

26. O. Behling and N. L. Eckel, "Making Sense Out of Intuition," *Academy of Management Executive* 5 (February 1991), pp. 46–54; Nutt, *Making Tough Decisions*, p. 54; H. A. Simon, "Making Management Decisions: The Role of Intuition and Emotion," *Academy of Management Executive* (February 1987), pp. 57–64; W. H. Agor, "The Logic of Intuition," *Organizational Dynamics* (Winter 1986), pp. 5–18.

27. N. Khatri, "The Role of Intuition in Strategic Decision Making," *Human Relations* 53 (January 2000), pp. 57–86; L. A. Burke and M. K. Miller, "Taking the Mystery Out of Intuitive Decision Making," *Academy of Management Executive* 13 (November 1999), pp. 91–99. The quotation is found in A. M. Hayashi, "When to Trust Your Gut," *Harvard Business Review* 79 (February 2001), pp. 59–65.

28. M. D. Lieberman, "Intuition: A Social Cognitive Neuroscience Approach," *Psychological Bulletin* 126 (2000), pp. 109–37; E. N. Brockmann and W. P. Anthony, "The Influence of Tacit Knowledge and Collective Mind on Strategic Planning," *Journal of Managerial Issues* 10 (Summer 1998), pp. 204–22; D. Leonard and S. Sensiper, "The Role of Tacit Knowledge in Group Innovation," *California Management Review* 40 (Spring 1998), pp. 112–32. For a discussion of the problems with intuition in business start-ups, see L. Broderick and M. Sponer, "The Death of Gut Instinct," *Inc.* 23 (January 2001), pp. 38–42.

29. J. Gregoire, "Leading the Charge for Change," *CIO*, June 1, 2001. Also see Y. Ganzach, A. H. Kluger, and N. Klayman, "Making Decisions from an Interview: Expert Measurement and Mechanical Combination," *Personnel Psychology* 53 (Spring 2000), pp. 1–20.

30. A. M. Hayashi, "When to Trust Your Gut," *Harvard Business Review* 79 (February 2001), pp. 59–65; E. Gubbins and B. Quinton, "Serial Entrepreneurs: They're Grrreat!" *Upstart*, January 30, 2001.

31. P. Goodwin and G. Wright, "Enhancing Strategy Evaluation in Scenario Planning: A Role for Decision Analysis," *Journal of Management*

Studies 38 (January 2001), pp. 1–16; P. J. H. Schoemaker, "Disciplined Imagination: From Scenarios to Strategic Options," *International Studies of Management & Organization* 27 (Summer 1997), pp. 43–70; K. Van Der Heijden, *Scenarios: The Art of Strategic Conversation* (New York: Wiley, 1996). The recommendation of revisiting decisions is noted in J. M. George, "Emotions and Leadership: The Role of Emotional Intelligence," *Human Relations* 53 (2000), pp. 1027–55.

32. R. N. Taylor, *Behavioral Decision Making* (Glenview, IL: Scott, Foresman, 1984), pp. 163–66.

33. D. R. Bobocel and J. P. Meyer, "Escalating Commitment to a Failing Course of Action: Separating the Role of Choice and Justification," *Journal of Applied Psychology* 79 (1994), pp. 360–63; G. Whyte, "Escalating Commitment in Individual and Group Decision Making: A Prospect Theory Approach," *Organizational Behavior and Human Decision Processes* 54 (1993), pp. 430–55; G. Whyte, "Escalating Commitment to a Course of Action: A Reinterpretation," *Academy of Management Review* 11 (1986), pp. 311–21.

34. M. Keil and R. Montealegre, "Cutting Your Losses: Extricating Your Organization When a Big Project Goes Awry," *Sloan Management Review* 41 (Spring 2000), pp. 55–68; M. Fackler, "Tokyo's Newest Subway Line a Saga of Hubris, Humiliation," *Associated Press Newswires*, July 20, 1999; P. Ayton and H. Arkes, "Call It Quits," *New Scientist*, June 20, 1998.

35. I. Swanson, "Holyrood Firms Face Grilling over Costs," *Evening News* (Edinburgh), June 6, 2003, p. 2; P. Gallagher, "New Bid to Rein in Rising Costs of Scots Parliament," *Aberdeen Press and Journal* (Scotland), June 11, 2003, p. 1; "MacDome," *Mail on Sunday*, December 16, 2001; I. Macwhirter, "Let's Build a Parliament," *The Scotsman*, July 17, 1997, p. 19.

36. F. D. Schoorman and P. J. Holahan, "Psychological Antecedents of Escalation Behavior: Effects of Choice, Responsibility, and Decision Consequences," *Journal of Applied Psychology* 81 (1996), pp. 786–93.

37. B. M. Staw, K. W. Koput, and S. G. Barsade, "Escalation at the Credit Window: A Longitudinal Study of Bank Executives' Recognition and Write-Off of Problem Loans," *Journal of Applied Psychology* 82 (1997), pp. 130–42. Also see M. Keil and D. Robey, "Turning Around Troubled Software Projects: An Exploratory Study of the Deescalation of Commitment to Failing Courses of Action," *Journal of Management Information Systems* 15 (Spring 1999), pp. 63–87.

38. W. Boulding, R. Morgan, and R. Staelin, "Pulling the Plug to Stop the New Product Drain," *Journal of Marketing Research* 34 (1997), pp. 164–76; I. Simonson and B. M. Staw, "De-escalation Strategies: A Comparison of Techniques for Reducing Commitment to Losing Courses of Action," *Journal of Applied Psychology* 77 (1992), pp. 419–26.

39. D. Ghosh, "De-escalation Strategies: Some Experimental Evidence," *Behavioral Research in Accounting* 9 (1997), pp. 88–112.

40. M. Fenton-O'Creevy, "Employee Involvement and the Middle Manager: Saboteur or Scapegoat?" *Human Resource Management Journal* 11 (2001), pp. 24–40. Also see V. H. Vroom and A. G. Jago, *The New Leadership: Managing Participation in Organizations* (Englewood Cliffs, NJ: Prentice Hall, 1988), p. 15.

41. R. C. Liden and S. Arad, "A Power Perspective of Empowerment and Work Groups: Implications for Human Resources Management Research," *Research in Personnel and Human Resources Management* 14 (1996), pp. 205–51; R. C. Ford and M. D. Fottler, "Empowerment: A Matter of Degree," *Academy of Management Executive* 9 (August 1995), pp. 21–31; R. W. Coye and J. A. Belohlav, "An Exploratory Analysis of Employee Participation," *Group & Organization Management* 20 (1995), pp. 4–17; Vroom and Jago, *The New Leadership*.

42. J. K. Smith, "Atlas Lets Its Workers Shoulder Responsibility," *Meriden (CT) Record-Journal*, August 24, 2003; S. Batley, "Staff's Bright Ideas Save Company Pounds 2m," *Daily Post* (Liverpool, UK), February 27, 2003, p. 20; P. Fengler and T. Heaps, "Aqua Purus," *Corporate Knights*, 2002 (www.corporateknights.ca).

43. J. T. Addison, "Nonunion Representation in Germany," *Journal of Labor Research* 20 (Winter 1999), pp. 73–92; G. Strauss, "Collective Bargaining, Unions, and Participation," in *Organizational Participation: Myth and Reality*, ed. F. Heller, E. Pusic, G. Strauss, and B. Wilpert (New York: Oxford University Press, 1998), pp. 97–143; D. I. Levine, *Reinventing the Workplace* (Washington, DC: Brookings, 1995), pp. 47–48.

44. For early writing supporting employee involvement, see R. Likert, *New Patterns of Management* (New York: McGraw-Hill, 1961); D. McGregor, *The Human Side of Enterprise* (New York: McGraw-Hill, 1960); C. Argyris, *Personality and Organization* (New York: Harper & Row, 1957).

45. C. L. Cooper, B. Dyck, and N. Frohlich, "Improving the Effectiveness of Gainsharing: The Role of Fairness and Participation," *Administrative Science Quarterly* 37 (1992), pp. 471–90.

46. J. P. Walsh and S-F. Tseng, "The Effects of Job Characteristics on Active Effort at Work," *Work & Occupations* 25 (February 1998), pp. 74–96; K. T. Dirks, L. L. Cummings, and J. L. Pierce, "Psychological Ownership in Organizations: Conditions under Which Individuals Promote and Resist Change," *Research in Organizational Change and Development* 9 (1996), pp. 1–23. The quotation in this paragraph is from E. E. Lawler III, *Rewarding Excellence: Pay Strategies for the New Economy* (San Francisco: Jossey-Bass, 2000), pp. 23–24.

47. J. A. Wagner III, C. R. Leana, E. A. Locke, and D. M. Schweiger, "Cognitive and Motivational Frameworks in U.S. Research on Participation: A Meta-Analysis of Primary Effects," *Journal of Organizational Behavior* 18 (1997), pp. 49–65; G. P. Latham, D. C. Winters, and E. A. Locke, "Cognitive and Motivational Effects of Participation: A Mediator Study," *Journal of Organizational Behavior* 15 (1994), pp. 49–63; Cotton, *Employee Involvement*, Chapter 8; S. J. Havlovic, "Quality of Work Life and Human Resource Outcomes," *Industrial Relations*, 1991, pp. 469–79; K. I. Miller and P. R. Monje, "Participation, Satisfaction, and Productivity: A Meta-Analytic Review," *Academy of Management Journal* 29 (1986), pp. 727–53.

48. Y. Utsunomiya, "Yamato Continues to Deliver New Ideas," *Japan Times*, July 8, 2003.

49. A. Cummings and G. R. Oldham, "Enhancing Creativity: Managing Work Contexts for the High Potential Employee," *California Management Review* 40 (Fall 1997), pp. 22–38; T. M. Amabile, *The Social Psychology of Creativity* (New York: Springer-Verlag, 1983), pp. 32–35.

50. B. Kabanoff and J. R. Rossiter, "Recent Developments in Applied Creativity," *International Review of Industrial and Organizational Psychology* 9 (1994), pp. 283–324.

51. J. R. Hayes, "Cognitive Processes in Creativity," in *Handbook of Creativity*, ed. J. A. Glover, R. R. Ronning, and C. R. Reynolds (New York: Plenum, 1989), pp. 135–45.

52. R. S. Nickerson, "Enhancing Creativity," in *Handbook of Creativity*, ed. R. J. Sternberg (New York: Cambridge University Press, 1999), pp. 392–430; A. Hiam, "Obstacles to Creativity—And How You Can Remove Them," *Futurist* 32 (October 1998), pp. 30ff.

53. R. T. Brown, "Creativity: What Are We to Measure?" in *Handbook of Creativity*, ed. Glover, Ronning, and Reynolds, pp. 3–32.

54. A. Hargadon and R. I. Sutton, "Building an Innovation Factory," *Harvard Business Review* 78 (May–June 2000), pp. 157–66.

55. For a thorough discussion of insight, see R. J. Sternberg and J. E. Davidson (eds.), *The Nature of Insight* (Cambridge, MA: MIT Press, 1995).

56. V. Parv, "The Idea Toolbox: Techniques for Being a More Creative Writer," *Writer's Digest* 78 (July 1998), p. 18; J. Ayan, *Aha! 10 Ways to Free Your Creative Spirit and Find Your Great Ideas* (New York: Crown Trade, 1997), pp. 50–56.

57. A. Chandrasekaran, "Bye, Bye Serendipity," *Business Standard*, March 28, 2000, p. 1; K. Cottrill, "Reinventing Innovation," *Journal of Business Strategy*, March–April 1998, pp. 47–51.

58. S. Taggar, "Individual Creativity and Group Ability to Utilize Individual Creative Resources: A Multilevel Model," *Academy of Management Journal* 45 (April 2002), pp. 315–30; R. J. Sternberg and L. A. O'Hara, "Creativity and Intelligence," in *Handbook of Creativity*, ed. Sternberg, pp. 251–72.

59. R. I. Sutton, *Weird Ideas that Work* (New York: Free Press, 2002), pp. 8–9, Chapter 10.

60. G. J. Feist, "The Influence of Personality on Artistic and Scientific Creativity," in *Handbook of Creativity*, ed. Sternberg, pp. 273–96; M. A. West, *Developing Creativity in Organizations* (Leicester, UK: BPS Books, 1997), pp. 10–19.

61. K. S. Brown, "The Apple of Jonathan Ive's Eye," *Investor's Business Daily*, September 19, 2003; J. Ezard "iMac Designer Who 'Touched Millions' Wins £25,000 Award," *The Guardian* (London), June 3, 2003; "Apple Design Guru Honoured," *BBC News*, June 3, 2003; N. McIntosh, "Return of the Mac," *The Guardian* (London), June 4, 2003; "Jonathan Ive: Mr iMac," *BBC News*, June 3, 2003.

62. R. W. Weisberg, "Creativity and Knowledge: A Challenge to Theories," in *Handbook of Creativity*, ed. Sternberg, pp. 226–50.

63. Sutton, *Weird Ideas that Work*, pp. 121, 153–54. For other literature on creativity and knowledge, see C. Andriopoulos, "Six Paradoxes in Managing Creativity: An Embracing Act," *Long Range Planning* 36 (2003), pp. 375–88; R. J. Sternberg, *Thinking Styles* (New York: Cambridge University Press, 1997); R. J. Sternberg, L. A. O'Hara, and T. I. Lubart, "Creativity as Investment," *California Management Review* 40 (Fall 1997), pp. 8–21.

64. T. Koppell, *Powering the Future* (New York: Wiley, 1999), p. 15.

65. D. K. Simonton, "Creativity: Cognitive, Personal, Developmental, and Social Aspects," *American Psychologist* 55 (January 2000), pp. 151–58; A. Cummings and G. R. Oldham, "Enhancing Creativity: Managing Work Contexts for the High Potential Employee," *California Management Review* 40 (Fall 1997), pp. 22–38.

66. S. Bharadwaj and A. Menon, "Making Innovation Happen in Organizations: Individual Creativity Mechanisms, Organizational Creativity Mechanisms or Both?" *Journal of Product Innovation Management* 17 (November 2000), pp. 424–34; M. D. Mumford, "Managing Creative People: Strategies and Tactics for Innovation," *Human Resource Management Review*

10 (Autumn 2000), pp. 313–51; T. M. Amabile, R. Conti, H. Coon, J. Lazenby, and M. Herron, "Assessing the Work Environment for Creativity," *Academy of Management Journal* 39 (1996), pp. 1154–84; G. R. Oldham and A. Cummings, "Employee Creativity: Personal and Contextual Factors at Work," *Academy of Management Journal* 39 (1996), pp. 607–34.

67. M. Baer and M. Frese, "Innovation Is Not Enough: Climates for Initiative and Psychological Safety, Process Innovations, and Firm Performance," *Journal of Organizational Behavior* 24 (2003), pp. 45–68. The learning orientation concept is also the focus of current attention in marketing; see M. A. Farrell, "Developing a Market-Oriented Learning Organization," *Australian Journal of Management* 25 (September 2000); W. E. Baker and J. M. Sinkula, "The Synergistic Effect of Market Orientation and Learning Orientation," *Journal of the Academy of Marketing Science* 27 (1999), pp. 411–27.

68. D. Maitra, "Livio D. Desimone: We Do Not See Failures as Failure," *Business Today* (India), June 22, 1998, p. 66.

69. C. E. Shalley, L. L. Gilson, and T. C. Blum, "Matching Creativity Requirements and the Work Environment: Effects on Satisfaction and Intentions to Leave," *Academy of Management Journal*, April 2000, pp. 215–23; R. Tierney, S. M. Farmer, and G. B. Graen, "An Examination of Leadership and Employee Creativity: The Relevance of Traits and Relationships," *Personnel Psychology* 52 (Autumn 1999), pp. 591–620; Cummings and Oldham, "Enhancing Creativity."

70. T. M. Amabile, "Motivating Creativity in Organizations: On Doing What You Love and Loving What You Do," *California Management Review* 40 (Fall 1997), pp. 39–58.

71. T. M. Amabile, "Changes in the Work Environment for Creativity during Downsizing," *Academy of Management Journal* 42 (December 1999), pp. 630–40.

72. Cummings and Oldham, "Enhancing Creativity."

73. T. M. Amabile, "A Model of Creativity and Innovation in Organizations," *Research in Organizational Behavior* 10

(1988), pp. 123–67. The survey about time pressure in advertising and marketing is summarized in "No Time for Creativity," *London Free Press*, August 7, 2001, p. D3.

74. Hiam, "Obstacles to Creativity."

75. West, *Developing Creativity in Organizations*, pp. 33–35.

76. P. Brown, "Across the Table into the Bedroom," *The Times* (London), March 1, 2001, p. D4; P. Swisher, "Soaring Creativity," *Successful Meetings* 50 (August 2001), p. 83.

77. B. Breen, "How EDS Got Its Groove Back," *Fast Company* 51 (October 2001), pp. 106–17; C. E. Ramirez, "EDS Brainstorming Team Plots Course for Future," *Detroit News*, August 27, 2001, p. 1; M. Wendland, "EDS Plots to Ignite New Ideas," *Detroit Free Press*, March 1, 2001.

78. J. Neff, "At Eureka Ranch, Execs Doff Wing Tips, Fire Up Ideas," *Advertising* Age 69 (March 9, 1998), pp. 28–29.

79. A. G. Robinson and S. Stern, *Corporate Creativity, How Innovation and Improvement Actually Happen* (San Francisco: Berrett-Koehler Publishers, 1997).

80. T. Kelley, *The Art of Innovation* (New York: Currency/Doubleday, 2001), pp. 158–62; Hargadon and Sutton, "Building an Innovation Factory."

81. K. S. Brown, "The Apple of Jonathan Ive's Eye," *Investor's Business Daily*, September 19, 2003.

CHAPTER 9

1. S. Pande, "Mark of a Brand," *Economic Times* ("Brand Equity" insert) (India), September 10, 2003, p. 1; S. Konig, "The Challenge of Teams," *On Wall Street*, August 1, 2003; T. Chapelle, "Facts and Fictions about Teams," *On Wall Street*, January 2003; www.bearstearns.com; www.globalclearing.com/primebroker/service.htm.

2. P. Haw, "Learning from Lean Principles," *Business Day* (South Africa), July 7, 2003, p. 7; E. Hart, "Manager of the Year: John Mang," *Iron & Steelmaker*, June 2003, pp. 5–7.

3. Very similar variations of this definition are found in E. Sundstrom, "The Challenges of Supporting Work Team Effectiveness," in *Supporting Work Team Effectiveness*, ed. E. Sundstrom and Associates (San Francisco: Jossey-Bass, 1999), pp. 6–9; S. G. Cohen and D. E. Bailey, "What Makes Teams Work: Group Effectiveness Research from the Shop Floor to the Executive Suite," *Journal of Management* 23 (May 1997), pp. 239–90; M. A. West, "Preface: Introducing Work Group Psychology," in *Handbook of Work Group Psychology*, ed. M. A. West (Chichester, UK: Wiley, 1996), p. xxvi; S. A. Mohrman, S. G. Cohen, and A. M. Mohrman Jr., *Designing Team-Based Organizations: New Forms for Knowledge Work* (San Francisco: Jossey-Bass, 1995), pp. 39–40; J. R. Katzenbach and K. D. Smith, "The Discipline of Teams," *Harvard Business Review* 71 (March–April 1993), pp. 111–20; M. E. Shaw, *Group Dynamics*, 3rd ed. (New York: McGraw-Hill, 1981), p. 8.

4. L. R. Offermann and R. K. Spiros "The Science and Practice of Team Development: Improving the Link," *Academy of Management Journal* 44 (April 2001), pp. 376–92. David Nadler similarly distinguishes "crowds" from "groups" and "teams." See D. A. Nadler, "From Ritual to Real Work: The Board as a Team," *Directors and Boards* 22 (Summer 1998), pp. 28–31.

5. The preference for using the term "team" rather than "group" is also discussed in Cohen and Bailey, "What Makes Teams Work"; R. A. Guzzo and M. W. Dickson, "Teams in Organizations: Recent Research on Performance and Effectiveness," *Annual Review of Psychology* 47 (1996), pp. 307–38.

6. G. E. Huszczo, *Tools for Team Excellence* (Palo Alto, CA: Davies-Black, 1996), pp. 9–15; R. Likert, *New Patterns of Management* (New York: McGraw-Hill, 1961), pp. 106–8.

7. "Employees Whose Innovations Save Money Honored by City," City of Reno, Nevada, news release, May 15, 2003.

8. The origin of skunkworks is described in T. E. Brown, "Skunk Works: A Sign of Failure, A Sign of Hope?" Paper presented at the Future of Innovation Studies conference, Eindhoven University of Technology, September 20–23, 2001. Management guru Tom Peters popularized the concept in the 1980s. See T. Peters, *Thriving on Chaos* (New York: Knopf, 1987), pp. 211–18; T. Peters and N. Austin, *A Passion for Excellence* (New York: Random House, 1985), Chapters 9 and 10.

9. R. Hertzberg, "No Longer a Skunkworks," *Internet World*, November 3, 1997.

10. M. Kane, "A Generation Removed from Crusty Capitalists," *Vancouver Sun* (British Columbia, Canada), September 8, 2003, p. D1.

11. H. Saint-Onge and D. Wallace, *Leveraging Communities of Practice for Strategic Advantage* (Boston: Butterworth-Heinemann, 2003); E. C. Wenger and W. M. Snyder, "Communities of Practice: The Organizational Frontier," *Harvard Business Review* 78 (January–February 2000), pp. 139–45; J. W. Botkin, *Smart Business: How Knowledge Communities Can Revolutionize Your Company* (New York: Free Press, 1999).

12. Saint-Onge and Wallace, *Leveraging Communities of Practice for Strategic Advantage*, Chapter 5; M. Finlay, "Panning for Gold," *ComputerUser*, July 1, 2001.

13. P. R. Lawrence and N. Nohria, *Driven: How Human Nature Shapes Our Choices* (San Francisco: Jossey-Bass, 2002); B. D. Pierce and R. White, "The Evolution of Social Structure: Why Biology Matters," *Academy of Management Review* 24 (October 1999), pp. 843–53.

14. J. C. Turner and S. A. Haslam, "Social Identity, Organizations, and Leadership," in *Groups at Work: Theory and Research*, ed. M. E. Turner (Mahwah, NJ: Lawrence Erlbaum Associates, 2001), pp. 25–65; M. A. Hogg and D. J. Terry, "Social Identity and Self-Categorization Processes in Organizational Contexts," *Academy of Management Review* 25 (January 2000), pp. 121–40.

15. A. S. Tannenbaum, *Social Psychology of the Work Organization* (Belmont, CA.: Wadsworth, 1966), p. 62; S. Schacter, *The Psychology of Affiliation* (Stanford, CA: Stanford University Press, 1959), pp. 12–19.

16. "What Makes Teams Work?" *Hrfocus*, April 2002, p. 17.

17. The British mining origins of teams are discussed in M. Moldaschl and W. G. Weber, "The 'Three Waves' of Industrial Group Work: Historical Reflections on Current Research on Group

Work," *Human Relations* 51 (March 1998), pp. 347–88. Several popular books in the 1980s encouraged teamwork, based on the Japanese economic miracle. These books include R. T. Pascale and A. G. Althos, *Art of Japanese Management* (New York: Simon & Schuster, 1982); W. Ouchi, *Theory Z: How American Management Can Meet the Japanese Challenge* (Reading, MA: Addison-Wesley, 1981).

18. G. S. Van der Vegt and O. Janssen, "Joint Impact of Interdependence and Group Diversity on Innovation," *Journal of Management* 29 (2003), pp. 729–51; C. R. Emery and L. D. Fredendall, "The Effect of Teams on Firm Profitability and Customer Satisfaction," *Journal of Service Research* 4 (February 2002), pp. 217–29.

19. J. Sapsed et al., "Teamworking and Knowledge Management: A Review of Converging Themes," *International Journal of Management Reviews* 4 (March 2002), pp. 71–85; P. Jones and J. Jordan, "Knowledge Orientations and Team Effectiveness," *International Journal of Technology Management* 16 (1998), pp. 152–61.

20. J. Y. Wiind and J. Main, *Driving Change* (New York: Free Press, 1998), pp. 139–40.

21. R. Forrester and A. B. Drexler, "A Model for Team-Based Organization Performance," *Academy of Management Executive* 13 (August 1999), pp. 36–49; M. A. West, C. S. Borrill, and K. L. Unsworth, "Team Effectiveness in Organizations," *International Review of Industrial and Organizational Psychology* 13 (1998), pp. 1–48; R. A. Guzzo and M. W. Dickson, "Teams in Organizations: Recent Research on Performance and Effectiveness," *Annual Review of Psychology* 47 (1996), pp. 307–38.

22. J. R. Hackman, R. Wageman, T. M. Ruddy, and C. L. Ray, "Team Effectiveness in Theory and in Practice," in *Industrial and Organizational Psychology: Linking Theory with Practice*, ed. C. L. Cooper and E. A. Locke (Oxford, U.K.: Blackwell, 2000), pp. 109–29; M. R. Barrick, G. L. Stewart, M. J. Neubert, and M. K. Mount, "Relating Member Ability and Personality to Work-Team Processes and Team Effectiveness," *Journal of Applied Psychology* 83 (1998), pp. 377–91; West, Borrill, and

Unsworth, "Team Effectiveness in Organizations"; Mohrman, Cohen, and Mohrman, *Designing Team-Based Organizations*, pp. 58–65; J. E. McGrath, "Time, Interaction, and Performance (TIP): A Theory of Groups," *Small Group Research* 22 (1991), pp. 147–74; G. P. Shea and R. A. Guzzo, "Group Effectiveness: What Really Matters?" *Sloan Management Review* 27 (1987), pp. 33–46.

23. J. N. Choi, "External Activities and Team Effectiveness: Review and Theoretical Development," *Small Group Research* 33 (April 2002), pp. 181–208.

24. E. E. Lawler III, *Rewarding Excellence: Pay Strategies for the New Economy* (San Francisco: Jossey-Bass, 2000), pp. 207–14; S. Sarin and V. Mahajan, "The Effect of Reward Structures on the Performance of Cross-Functional Product Development Teams," *Journal of Marketing* 65 (April 2001), pp. 35–53; J. S. DeMatteo, L. T. Eby, and E. Sundstrom, "Team-Based Rewards: Current Empirical Evidence and Directions for Future Research," *Research in Organizational Behavior* 20 (1998), pp. 141–83.

25. L. A. Yerkes, "Motivating Workers in Tough Times," *Incentive*, October 2001. pp. 120–21.

26. P. Bordia "Face-to-Face versus Computer-Mediated Communication: A Synthesis of the Experimental Literature," *Journal of Business Communication* 34 (January 1997), pp. 99–120; A. D. Shulman, "Putting Group Information Technology in Its Place: Communication and Good Work Group Performance," in *Handbook of Organization Studies*, ed. S. R. Clegg, C. Hardy, and W. R. Nord (London: Sage, 1996), pp. 357–74; J. E. McGrath and A. B. Hollingshead, *Groups Interacting with Technology* (Thousand Oaks, CA: Sage, 1994).

27. R. Shopes, "Go Teams," *Sarasota (FL) Herald-Tribune*, February 10, 2003, p. 12. Work space design and team dynamics are discussed in J. Wineman and M. Serrato, "Facility Design for High-Performance Teams," in *Supporting Work Team Effectiveness*, ed. E. Sundstrom and Associates (San Francisco: Jossey-Bass, 1999), pp. 271–98.

28. R. Wageman, "Case Study: Critical Success Factors for Creating Superb

Self-Managing Teams at Xerox," *Compensation and Benefits Review* 29 (September–October 1997), pp. 31–41; D. Dimancescu and K. Dwenger, "Smoothing the Product Development Path," *Management Review* 85 (January 1996), pp. 36–41.

29. E. F. McDonough III, "Investigation of Factors Contributing to the Success of Cross-Functional Teams," *Journal of Product Innovation Management* 17 (May 2000), pp. 221–35; A. Edmondson, "Psychological Safety and Learning Behavior in Work Teams," *Administrative Science Quarterly* 44 (1999), pp. 350–83; D. G. Ancona and D. E. Caldwell, "Demography and Design: Predictors of New Product Team Performance," *Organization Science* 3 (August 1992), pp. 331–41.

30. A. S. Sohal, M. Terziovski, and A. Zutshi, "Team-Based Strategy at Varian Australia: A Case Study," *Technovation* 23 (2003) pp. 349–57.

31. M. A. Campion, E. M. Papper, and G. J. Medsker, "Relations between Work Team Characteristics and Effectiveness: A Replication and Extension," *Personnel Psychology* 49 (1996), pp. 429–52; S. Worchel and S. L. Shackelford, "Groups under Stress: The Influence of Group Structure and Environment on Process and Performance," *Personality & Social Psychology Bulletin* 17 (1991), pp. 640–47; E. Sundstrom, K. P. De Meuse, and D. Futrell, "Work Teams: Applications and Effectiveness," *American Psychologist* 45 (1990), pp. 120–33.

32. R. Wageman, "The Meaning of Interdependence," in *Groups at Work: Theory and Research*, ed. M. E. Turner (Mahwah, NJ: Lawrence Erlbaum Associates, 2001), pp. 197–217.

33. G. S. van der Vegt, B. J. M. Emans, and E. van de Vliert, "Patterns of Interdependence in Work Teams: A Two-level Investigation of the Relations with Job and Team Satisfaction," *Personnel Psychology* 54 (Spring 2001), pp. 51–69; G. van der Vegt, B. Emans, and E. van de Vliert, "Motivating Effects of Task and Outcome Interdependence in Work Teams," *Group & Organization Management* 23 (June 1998), pp. 124–43; R. C. Liden, S. J. Wayne, and L. K. Bradway, "Task Interdependence as a Moderator of the Relation between Group Control and Perfor-

mance," *Human Relations* 50 (1997), pp. 169–81; R. Wageman, "Interdependence and Group Effectiveness," *Administrative Science Quarterly* 40 (1995), pp. 145–80; M. A. Campion, G. J. Medsker, and A. C. Higgs, "Relations between Work Group Characteristics and Effectiveness: Implications for Designing Effective Work Groups," *Personnel Psychology* 46 (1993), pp. 823–50; M. N. Kiggundu, "Task Interdependence and the Theory of Job Design," *Academy of Management Review* 6 (1981), pp. 499–508.

34. J. D. Thompson, *Organizations in Action* (New York: McGraw-Hill, 1967), pp. 54–56.

35. K. H. Doerr, T. R. Mitchell, and T. D. Klastorin, "Impact of Material Flow Policies and Goals on Job Outcomes," *Journal of Applied Psychology* 81 (1996), pp. 142–52.

36. R. Semler, *The Seven-Day Weekend* (Century: London, 2003), p. 183.

37. G. R. Hickman and A. Creighton-Zollar, "Diverse Self-Directed Work Teams: Developing Strategic Initiatives for 21st Century Organizations," *Public Personnel Management* 27 (Spring 1998), pp. 187–200; J. R. Katzenbach and D. K. Smith, *The Wisdom of Teams: Creating the High-Performance Organization* (Boston: Harvard University Press, 1993), pp. 45–47; G. Stasser, "Pooling of Unshared Information during Group Discussion," in *Group Process and Productivity*, ed. S. Worchel, W. Wood, and J. A. Simpson (Newbury Park, CA: Sage, 1992), pp. 48–67.

38. Sohal, Terziovski, and Zutshi, "Team-Based Strategy at Varian Australia," p. 353.

39. D. Huynh, "Central Market Caters to Hungry Shoppers on the Run," *Houston Chronicle*, June 1, 2001, p. 2; "Creative Hiring Replaces Yesterday's Staid Interview," *Houston Business Journal*, March 9, 2001, p. 35.

40. L. T. Eby and G. H. Dobbins, "Collectivist Orientation in Teams: An Individual and Group-Level Analysis," *Journal of Organizational Behavior* 18 (1997), pp. 275–95; P. C. Earley, "East Meets West Meets Mideast: Further Explorations of Collectivistic and Individualistic Work Groups," *Academy of Management Journal* 36 (1993), pp. 319–48.

41. Mohrman, Cohen, and Mohrman, *Designing Team-Based Organizations*, pp. 248–54; M. J. Stevens and M. A. Campion, "The Knowledge, Skill and Ability Requirements for Teamwork: Implications for Human Resources Management," *Journal of Management* 20 (1994), pp. 503–30; A. P. Hare, *Handbook of Small Group Research*, 2nd ed. (New York: Free Press, 1976), pp. 12–15.

42. S. Sonnentag, "Excellent Performance: The Role of Communication and Cooperation Processes," *Applied Psychology: An International Review* 49 (July 2000), pp. 483–97; B. Buzaglo and S. Wheelan, "Facilitating Work Team Effectiveness: Case Studies from Central America," *Small Group Research* 30 (1999), pp. 108–29; B. Schultz, "Improving Group Communication Performance: An Overview of Diagnosis and Intervention," in *Handbook of Group Communication Theory and Research*, ed. L. Frey, D. Gouran, and M. Poole (Thousand Oaks, CA: Sage, 1999), pp. 371–94; M. R. Barrick, G. L. Stewart, M. J. Neubert, and M. K. Mount, "Relating Member Ability and Personality to Work-Team Processes and Team Effectiveness," *Journal of Applied Psychology* 83 (1998), pp. 377–91.

43. D. C. Hambrick, S. C. Davison, S. A. Snell, and C. C. Snow, "When Groups Consist of Multiple Nationalities: Towards a New Understanding of the Implications," *Organization Studies* 19 (1998), pp. 181–205; F. J. Milliken and L. L. Martins, "Searching for Common Threads: Understanding the Multiple Effects of Diversity in Organizational Groups," *Academy of Management Review* 21 (1996), pp. 402–33; J. K. Murnighan and D. Conlon, "The Dynamics of Intense Work Groups: A Study of British String Quartets," *Administrative Science Quarterly* 36 (1991), pp. 165–86.

44. D. A. Harrison, K. H. Price, J. H. Gavin, and A. T. Florey, "Time, Teams, and Task Performance: Changing Effects of Surface- and Deep-Level Diversity on Group Functioning," *Academy of Management Journal* 45 (October 2002), pp. 1029–45.

45. C. M. Riordan, "Relational Demography within Groups: Past Developments, Contradictions, and New Directions," in *Research in Personnel and Human Resources Management*, Vol.

19, ed. G. R. Ferris (Greenwich, CT: JAI, 2000), pp. 131–73; K. Y. Williams, and C. A. O'Reilly, "Demography and Diversity in Organizations: A Review of 40 Years of Research," in *Research in Organizational Behavior*, Vol. 20, ed. B. M. Staw and L. L. Cummings (Greenwich, CT: JAI, 1998), pp. 77–140.

46. "Volvo Concept Car by Women, for Everybody," *Swedespeed.com*, March 7, 2003; D. Linklater, "Volvo's Gender Genre," *XTRAMSN* (online), March 4, 2003.

47. L. H. Pelled, K. M. Eisenhardt, and K. R. Xin, "Exploring the Black Box: An Analysis of Work Group Diversity, Conflict, and Performance," *Administrative Science Quarterly* 44 (March 1999), pp. 1–28; Williams and O'Reilly, "Demography and Diversity in Organizations."

48. J. A. LePine, J. R. Hollenbeck, D. R. Ilgen, J. A. Colquitt, and A. Ellis, "Gender Composition, Situational Strength, and Team Decision-Making Accuracy: A Criterion Decomposition Approach," *Organizational Behavior and Human Decision Processes* 88 (2002), pp. 445–75.

49. Linda Tucci, "Owens Drake Consulting Fosters Systematic Change," *St. Louis Business Journal*, May 25, 1998. For the importance of consensus and understanding in heterogeneous decision-making groups, see S. Mohammed and E. Ringseis, "Cognitive Diversity and Consensus in Group Decision Making: The Role of Inputs, Processes, and Outcomes," *Organizational Behavior and Human Decision Processes* 85 (July 2001), pp. 310–35.

50. The NTSB and NASA studies are summarized in J. R. Hackman, "New Rules for Team Building," *Optimize*, July 1, 2002, pp. 50–62.

51. R. Deruyter, "Budd Workers Reject Shift Change," *Kitchener-Waterloo Record*, June 1, 2002.

52. B. W. Tuckman and M. A. C. Jensen, "Stages of Small-Group Development Revisited," *Group and Organization Studies* 2 (1977), pp. 419–42. For a humorous and somewhat cynical discussion of team dynamics through these stages, see H. Robbins and M. Finley, *Why Teams Don't Work* (Princeton, NJ: Peterson's/Pacesetters, 1995), Chapter 21.

53. J. E. Mathieu and G. F. Goodwin, "The Influence of Shared Mental Models on Team Process and Performance," *Journal of Applied Psychology* 85 (April 2000), pp. 273–84; J. A. Cannon-Bowers, S. I. Tannenbaum, E. Salas, and C. E. Volpe, "Defining Competencies and Establishing Team Training Requirements," in *Team Effectiveness and Decision Making in Organizations,* ed. Guzzo, Salas, and Associates (San Francisco: Jossey-Bass, 1995), pp. 333–80.

54. A. Edmondson, "Psychological Safety and Learning Behavior in Work Teams," *Administrative Science Quarterly* 44 (1999), pp. 350–83.

55. D. L. Miller, "Synergy in Group Development: A Perspective on Group Performance," *Proceedings of the Annual ASAC Conference, Organizational Behavior Division* 17, pt. 5 (1996), pp. 119–28; S. Worchel, D. Coutant-Sassic, and M. Grossman, "A Developmental Approach to Group Dynamics: A Model and Illustrative Research," in *Group Process and Productivity,* ed. S. Worchel et al. (Newbury Park, CA: Sage, 1992), pp. 181–202; C. J. G. Gersick, "Time and Transition in Work Teams: Toward a New Model of Group Development," *Academy of Management Journal* 31 (1988), pp. 9–41.

56. D. C. Feldman, "The Development and Enforcement of Group Norms," *Academy of Management Review* 9 (1984), pp. 47–53; L. W. Porter, E. E. Lawler, and J. R. Hackman, *Behavior in Organizations* (New York: McGraw-Hill, 1975), pp. 391–94.

57. I. R. Gellatly, "Individual and Group Determinants of Employee Absenteeism: Test of a Causal Model," *Journal of Organizational Behavior* 16 (1995), pp. 469–85; G. Johns, "Absenteeism Estimates by Employees and Managers: Divergent Perspectives and Self-Serving Perceptions," *Journal of Applied Psychology* 79 (1994), pp. 229–39.

58. "Employees Terrorized by Peer Pressure in the Workplace," Morgan & Banks news release, September 2000. Also see B. Latané, "The Psychology of Social Impact," *American Psychologist* 36 (1981), pp. 343–56; C. A. Kiesler and S. B. Kiesler, *Conformity* (Reading, MA: Addison-Wesley, 1970).

59. Porter, Lawler, and Hackman, *Behavior in Organizations,* pp. 399–401.

60. Feldman, "The Development and Enforcement of Group Norms," pp. 50–52.

61. Katzenbach and Smith, *The Wisdom of Teams,* pp. 121–23.

62. K. L. Bettenhausen and J. K. Murnighan, "The Development of an Intragroup Norm and the Effects of Interpersonal and Structural Challenges," *Administrative Science Quarterly* 36 (1991), pp. 20–35.

63. R. S. Spich and K. Keleman, "Explicit Norm Structuring Process: A Strategy for Increasing Task-Group Effectiveness," *Group & Organization Studies* 10 (March 1985), pp. 37–59.

64. L. Y. Chan and B. E. Lynn, "Operating in Turbulent Times: How Ontario's Hospitals Are Meeting the Current Funding Crisis," *Health Care Management Review* 23 (June 1998), p. 7.

65. D. I. Levine, "Piece Rates, Output Restriction, and Conformism," *Journal of Economic Psychology* 13 (1992), pp. 473–89.

66. L. Coch and J. R. P. French Jr., "Overcoming Resistance to Change," *Human Relations* 1 (1948), pp. 512–32.

67. S. F. Gale, "Swanky Dinners, Trips and Everyday Praise Are Part of the Container Store's Culture," *Workforce Management,* August 2003, pp. 80–82; L. Grant, "Container Store's Workers Huddle Up to Help You Out," *USA Today,* April 30, 2002, p. B1.

68. D. Katz and R. L. Kahn, T*he Social Psychology of Organizations* (New York: John Wiley & Sons, 1966), Chapter 7; J. W. Thibault and H. H. Kelley, *The Social Psychology of Groups* (New York: John Wiley & Sons, 1959), Chapter 8.

69. S. H. N. Leung, J. W. K. Chan, and W. B. Lee, "The Dynamic Team Role Behavior: The Approaches of Investigation," *Team Performance Management* 9 (2003), pp. 84–90.

70. R. M. Belbin, *Team Roles at Work* (Oxford, UK: Butterworth-Heinemann, 1993).

71. G. Fisher, T. A. Hunter, and W. D. K. Macrosson, "Belbin's Team Role Theory: For Non-managers Also?" *Journal of Managerial Psychology* 17 (2002), pp. 14–20; J. S. Prichard and N. A. Stanton, "Testing Belbin's Team Role Theory of Effective Groups," *Journal of Management Development* 18 (1999), pp.

652–65; S. G. Fisher, T. A. Hunter, and W. D. K. Macrosson, "The Structure of Belbin's Team Roles," *Journal of Occupational and Organizational Psychology* 71 (September 1998), pp. 283–88; B. Senior, "Team Roles and Team Performance: Is There 'Really' a Link?" *Journal of Occupational and Organizational Psychology* 70 (September 1997), pp. 241–58; W. G. Broucek and G. Randell, "An Assessment of the Construct Validity of the Belbin Self-Perception Inventory and Observer's Assessment from the Perspective of the Five-Factor Model," *Journal of Occupational and Organizational Psychology* 69 (December 1996), pp. 389–405; A. Furnham, H. Steele, and D. Pendleton, "A Psychometric Assessment of the Belbin Team-Role Self-Perception Inventory," *Journal of Occupational and Organizational Psychology* 66 (1993), pp. 245–57.

72. D. Vinokur-Kaplan, "Treatment Teams that Work (and Those that Don't): An Application of Hackman's Group Effectiveness Model to Interdisciplinary Teams in Psychiatric Hospitals," *Journal of Applied Behavioral Science* 31 (1995), pp. 303–27; Shaw, *Group Dynamics,* pp. 213–26; P. S. Goodman, E. Ravlin, and M. Schminke, "Understanding Groups in Organizations," *Research in Organizational Behavior* 9 (1987), pp. 121–73.

73. J. R. Kelly and S. G. Barsade, "Mood and Emotions in Small Groups and Work Teams," *Organizational Behavior and Human Decision Processes* 86 (September 2001), pp. 99–130; S. Lembke and M. G. Wilson, "Putting the 'Team' into Teamwork: Alternative Theoretical Contributions for Contemporary Management Practice," *Human Relations* 51 (July 1998), pp. 927–44; B. E. Ashforth and R. H. Humphrey, "Emotion in the Workplace: A Reappraisal," *Human Relations* 48 (1995), pp. 97–125.

74. K. M. Sheldon and B. A. Bettencourt, "Psychological Need-Satisfaction and Subjective Well-Being within Social Groups," *British Journal of Social Psychology* 41 (2002), pp. 25–38; N. Ellemers, R. Spears, and B. Doosje, "Self and Social Identity," *Annual Review of Psychology* 53 (2002), pp. 161–86; A. Lott and B. Lott, "Group Cohesiveness as Interpersonal Attraction: A Review of Relationships with

Antecedent and Consequent Variables," *Psychological Bulletin* 64 (1965), pp. 259–309.

75. S. E. Jackson, "Team Composition in Organizational Settings: Issues in Managing an Increasingly Diverse Work Force," in *Group Process and Productivity*, ed. S. Worchel et al. (Newbury Park, CA: Sage, 1992), pp. 138–73; J. Virk, P. Aggarwal, and R. N. Bhan, "Similarity versus Complementarity in Clique Formation," *Journal of Social Psychology* 120 (1983), pp. 27–34.

76. T. S. Mulligan, "Comics' Unlikely Hero," *Los Angeles Times*, July 17, 2003, p. C1. Details of CrossGen's quad system, complete with 360-degree viewing, are also available at the company's website: www.crossgen.com.

77. M. B. Pinto, J. K. Pinto, and J. E. Prescott, "Antecedents and Consequences of Project Team Cross-Functional Cooperation," *Management Science* 39 (1993), pp. 1281–96; W. Piper, M. Marrache, R. Lacroix, A. Richardson, and B. Jones, "Cohesion as a Basic Bond in Groups," *Human Relations* 36 (1983), pp. 93–108.

78. M. Frase-Blunt, "The Cubicles Have Ears. Maybe They Need Earplugs," *Washington Post*, March 6, 2001, p. HE7.

79. J. E. Hautaluoma and R. S. Enge, "Early Socialization into a Work Group: Severity of Initiations Revisited," *Journal of Social Behavior & Personality* 6 (1991), pp. 725–48; E. Aronson and J. Mills, "The Effects of Severity of Initiation on Liking for a Group," *Journal of Abnormal and Social Psychology* 59 (1959), pp. 177–81.

80. B. Mullen and C. Copper, "The Relation between Group Cohesiveness and Performance: An Integration," *Psychological Bulletin* 115 (1994), pp. 210–27; Shaw, *Group Dynamics*, p. 215.

81. The positive and negative effects of external threats on teams is discussed in M. E. Turner and T. Horvitz, "The Dilemma of Threat: Group Effectiveness and Ineffectiveness under Adversity," in *Groups at Work: Theory and Research*, ed. M. E. Turner (Mahwah, NJ: Lawrence Erlbaum Associates, 2001), pp. 445–70.

82. M. Rempel and R. J. Fisher, "Perceived Threat, Cohesion, and Group Problem Solving in Intergroup Conflict," *International Journal of Conflict Management* 8 (1997), pp. 216–34.

83. J. M. McPherson and P. A. Popielarz, "Social Networks and Organizational Dynamics," *American Sociological Review* 57 (1992), pp. 153–70; Piper et al., "Cohesion as a Basic Bond in Groups," pp. 93–108.

84. C. A. O'Reilly III, D. F. Caldwell, and W. P. Barnett, "Work Group Demography, Social Integration, and Turnover," *Administrative Science Quarterly* 34 (1989), pp. 21–37.

85. J. Pappone, "Sometimes Life's Truly a Beach . . . ," *Ottawa Citizen*, February 3, 2000.

86. P. J. Sullivan and D. L. Feltz, "The Relationship between Intrateam Conflict and Cohesion within Hockey Teams," *Small Group Research* 32 (June 2001), pp. 342–55.

87. R. D. Banker, J. M. Field, R. G. Schroeder, and K. K. Sinha, "Impact of Work Teams on Manufacturing Performance: A Longitudinal Study," *Academy of Management Journal* 39 (1996), pp. 867–90; Vinokur-Kaplan, "Treatment Teams that Work (and Those that Don't)"; Mullen and Copper, "The Relation between Group Cohesiveness and Performance"; C. R. Evans and K. L. Dion, "Group Cohesion and Performance: A Meta-Analysis," *Small Group Research* 22 (1991), pp. 175–86.

88. K. L. Gammage, A. V. Carron, and P. A. Estabrooks, "Team Cohesion and Individual Productivity: The Influence of the Norm for Productivity and the Identifiablity of Individual Effort," *Small Group Research* 32 (February 2001), pp. 3–18; C. Langfred, "Is Group Cohesiveness a Double-Edged Sword? An Investigation of the Effects of Cohesiveness on Performance," *Small Group Research* 29 (1998), pp. 124–43.

89. E. A. Locke et al., "The Importance of the Individual in an Age of Groupism," in *Groups at Work: Theory and Research*, ed. M. E. Turner (Mahwah, NJ: Lawrence Erlbaum Associates, 2001), pp. 501–28; Robbins and Finley, *Why Teams Don't Work*, Chapter 20; "The Trouble with Teams," *Economist*, January 14, 1995, p. 61; A. Sinclair, "The Tyranny of Team Ideology," *Organization Studies* 13 (1992), pp. 611–26.

90. P. Panchak, "The Future of Manufacturing," *Industry Week* 247 (September 21, 1998), pp. 96–105; B. Dumaine, "The Trouble with Teams," *Fortune*, September 5, 1994, pp. 86–92.

91. I. D. Steiner, *Group Process and Productivity* (New York: Academic Press, 1972).

92. D. Dunphy and B. Bryant, "Teams: Panaceas or Prescriptions for Improved Performance?" *Human Relations* 49 (1996), pp. 677–99. For discussion of Brooke's law, see F. P. Brooks, *The Mythical Man-Month: Essays on Software Engineering*, 2nd ed. (Reading, MA: Addison-Wesley, 1995).

93. Q. R. Skrabec Jr., "The Myth of Teams," *Industrial Management*, September–October, 2002, pp. 25–27; R. Cross, "Looking before You Leap: Assessing the Jump to Teams in Knowledge-Based Work," *Business Horizons*, September 2000.

94. M. Erez and A. Somech, "Is Group Productivity Loss the Rule or the Exception? Effects of Culture and Group-Based Motivation," *Academy of Management Journal* 39 (1996), pp. 1513–37; S. J. Karau and K. D. Williams, "Social Loafing: A Meta-Analytic Review and Theoretical Integration," *Journal of Personality and Social Psychology* 65 (1993), pp. 681–706; J. M. George, "Extrinsic and Intrinsic Origins of Perceived Social Loafing in Organizations," *Academy of Management Journal* 35 (1992), pp. 191–202; R. Albanese and D. D. Van Fleet, "Rational Behavior in Groups: The Free-Riding Tendency," *Academy of Management Review* 10 (1985), pp. 244–55.

95. Erez and Somech, "Is Group Productivity Loss the Rule or the Exception?"; P. C. Earley, "Social Loafing and Collectivism: A Comparison of the U.S. and the People's Republic of China," *Administrative Science Quarterly* 34 (1989), pp. 565–81.

96. T. A. Judge and T. D. Chandler, "Individual-Level Determinants of Employee Shirking," *Relations Industrielles* 51 (1996), pp. 468–86; J. M. George, "Asymmetrical Effects of Rewards and Punishments: The Case of Social Loafing," *Journal of Occupational and Organizational Psychology* 68 (1995), pp. 327–38; R. E. Kidwell and N. Bennett, "Employee Propensity to Withhold Effort: A Conceptual

Model to Intersect Three Avenues of Research," *Academy of Management Review* 19 (1993), pp. 429–56; J. A. Shepperd, "Productivity Loss in Performance Groups: A Motivation Analysis," *Psychological Bulletin* 113 (1993), pp. 67–81.

CHAPTER 10

1. D. Jones, "Food Firm Expands Creating 20 Jobs," *Daily Post* (Liverpool, UK), May 29, 2003, p. 23; D. Devine, "Recipe for Making Things Happen," *Western Mail* (Wales), July 10, 2002, p. 9. www.patchwork-pate.co.uk.

2. J. Singer and S. Duvall, "High-Performance Partnering by Self-Managed Teams in Manufacturing," *Engineering Management Journal* 12 (December 2000), pp. 9–15; D. Fields, "Harley Teams Shoot for Better Bike," *Akron Beacon Journal*, June 15, 1998; M. Savage, "Harley Irons Out an Innovative Way of Working," *Milwaukee Journal Sentinel*, May 25, 1998, p. 12; L. Ziegler, "Labor's Role at New Harley Plant," National Public Radio, *All Things Considered*, February 25, 1998; C. Eberting, "The Harley Mystique Comes to Kansas City," *Kansas City Star*, January 6, 1998, p. A1. For a recent study of team cohesiveness at Harley-Davidson, see P. A. Chansler, P. M. Swamidass, and C. Cammann, "Self-Managing Work Teams: An Empirical Study of Group Cohesiveness in 'Natural Work Groups' at a Harley-Davidson Motor Company Plant," *Small Group Research* 34 (February 2003), pp. 101–20.

3. E. E. Lawler, *Organizing for High Performance* (San Francisco: Jossey-Bass, 2001); S. G. Cohen, G. E. Ledford Jr., and G. M. Spreitzer, "A Predictive Model of Self-Managing Work Team Effectiveness," *Human Relations* 49 (1996), pp. 643–76.

4. The SDT attributes discussed here are discussed in Yeatts and Hyten, *High-Performing Self-Managed Work Teams*; B. L. Kirkman and D. L. Shapiro, "The Impact of Cultural Values on Employee Resistance to Teams: Toward a Model of Globalized Self-Managing Work Team Effectiveness," *Academy of Management Review* 22 (July 1997), pp. 730–57; Mohrman et al., *Designing Team-Based Organizations*.

5. L. Rittenhouse, "Dennis W. Bakke—Empowering a Workforce with Principles," *Electricity Journal*, January 1998, pp. 48–59.

6. G. Hasek, "Zero Defects and Beyond," *Industry Week*, October 2002, p. 41.

7. P. S. Goodman, R. Devadas, and T. L. G. Hughson, "Groups and Productivity: Analyzing the Effectiveness of Self-Managing Teams," in J. P. Campbell, R. J. Campbell, and Associates (eds.), *Productivity in Organizations* (San Francisco: Jossey-Bass, 1988), pp. 295–327.

8. The automobile service centers, city government, and courier service examples of SDWTs are described in C. R. Emery and L. D. Fredendall, "The Effect of Teams on Firm Profitability and Customer Satisfaction," *Journal of Service Research* 4 (February 2002), pp. 217–29; S. Simpson, "Ilg Repaying Emotional Debt to City," *Hartford Courant*, December 15, 2001, p. B1; J. Childs, "Five Years and Counting: The Path to Self-Directed Work Teams," *Hospital Materiel Management Quarterly* 18 (May 1997), pp. 34–43.

9. D. Tjosvold, *Teamwork for Customers* (San Francisco: Jossey-Bass, 1993); D. E. Bowen and E. E. Lawler III, "The Empowerment of Service Workers: What, Why, How, and When," *Sloan Management Review*, Spring 1992, pp. 31–39.

10. E. L. Trist, G. W. Higgin, H. Murray, and A. B. Pollock, *Organizational Choice* (London: Tavistock, 1963). The origins of SDTs from sociotechnical systems research is also noted in R. Beckham, "Self-Directed Work Teams: The Wave of the Future?" *Hospital Materiel Management Quarterly* 20 (August 1998), pp. 48–60.

11. The main components of sociotechnical systems are discussed in M. Moldaschl and W. G. Weber, "The 'Three Waves' of Industrial Group Work: Historical Reflections on Current Research on Group Work," *Human Relations* 51 (March 1998), pp. 347–88; W. Niepce and E. Molleman, "Work Design Issues in Lean Production from a Sociotechnical Systems Perspective: Neo-Taylorism or the Next Step in Sociotechnical Design?" *Human Relations* 51 (March 1998), pp. 259–87.

12. E. Ulich and W. G. Weber, "Dimensions, Criteria, and Evaluation of Work Group Autonomy," in *Handbook of Work Group Psychology*, ed. M. A. West (Chichester, UK: John Wiley & Sons, 1996), pp. 247–82.

13. C. C. Manz and G. L. Stewart, "Attaining Flexible Stability by Integrating Total Quality Management and Socio-technical Systems Theory," *Organization Science* 8 (1997), pp. 59–70; K. P. Carson and G. L. Stewart, "Job Analysis and the Sociotechnical Approach to Quality: A Critical Examination," *Journal of Quality Management* 1 (1996), pp. 49–65.

14. J. King, "Employers Quickly Hire Circuit Board Assemblers," *Detroit News*, October 15, 2000, p. 1; J-A. Johnston, "The Faces of Productivity," *Tampa Tribune*, September 4, 2000, p. 7.

15. I. M. Kunii, "He Put the Flash Back in Canon," *Business Week*, September 16, 2002, p. 40; C. R. Emery and L. D. Fredendall, "The Effect of Teams on Firm Profitability and Customer Satisfaction," *Journal of Service Research* 4 (February 2002), pp. 217–29; R. Kulwiec, "Self-Managed Work Teams—Reality or Fad?" *Material Handling Management—Strategies for Top Management Supplement*, April 2001, pp. 15–22; M. Evans, T. Hamilton, L. Surtees, and S. Tuck, "The Road to a Billion," *Toronto Globe & Mail*, January 6, 2000; R. Dyck and N. Halpern, "Team-Based Organizations Redesign at Celestica," *Journal for Quality & Participation* 22 (September–October 1999), pp. 36–40.

16. L. Fuxman, "Teamwork in Manufacturing: The Case of the Automotive Industry," *International Journal of Commerce & Management* 9 (1999), pp. 103–30; P. S. Adler and R. E. Cole, "Designed for Learning: A Tale of Two Auto Plants," *Sloan Management Review* 34 (Spring 1993), pp. 85–94; J. P. Womack, D. T. Jones, and D. Roos, *The Machine that Changed the World* (New York: MacMillan, 1990).

17. B. L Kirkman and D. L Shapiro, "The Impact of Cultural Values on Job Satisfaction and Organizational Commitment in Self-Managing Work Teams: The Mediating Role of Employee Resistance," *Academy of Management Journal* 44 (June 2001), pp. 557–69; C. E. Nicholls, H. W. Lane, and

M. B. Brechu, "Taking Self-Managed Teams to Mexico," *Academy of Management Executive* 13 (August 1999), pp. 15–25.

18. C. Robert and T. M. Probst, "Empowerment and Continuous Improvement in the United States, Mexico, Poland, and India," *Journal of Applied Psychology* 85 (October 2000), pp. 643–58; B. L. Kirkman and D. L. Shapiro, "The Impact of Cultural Values on Employee Resistance to Teams: Toward a Model of Globalized Self-Managing Work Team Effectiveness," *Academy of Management Review* 22 (July 1997), pp. 730–57; C. Pavett and T. Morris, "Management Styles within a Multinational Corporation: A Five Country Comparative Study," *Human Relations* 48 (1995), pp. 1171–91; M. Erez and P. C. Earley, *Culture, Self-Identity, and Work* (New York: Oxford University Press, 1993), pp. 104–12.

19. This quotation is found at www.quoteland.com.

20. J. D. Orsburn and L. Moran, *The New Self-Directed Work Teams: Mastering the Challenge* (New York: McGraw-Hill, 2000), Chapter 11; C. C. Manz, D. E. Keating, and A. Donnellon, "Preparing for an Organizational Change to Employee Self-Management: The Managerial Transition," *Organizational Dynamics* 19 (Autumn 1990), pp. 15–26.

21. J. Jusko, "Always Lessons to Learn," *Industry Week*, February 15, 1999, pp. 23–30. For research on this issue, see G. T. Fairhurst, S. Green, and J. Courtright, "Inertial Forces and the Implementation of a Socio-technical Systems Approach: A Communication Study," *Organization Science* 6 (1995), pp. 168–85. Similar comments are reported in D. Stafford, "Sharing the Driver's Seat," *Kansas City Star*, June 11, 2002, p. D1; R. Cross, "Looking before You Leap: Assessing the Jump to Teams in Knowledge-Based Work," *Business Horizons*, September 2000.

22. M. Fenton-O'Creevy, "Employee Involvement and the Middle Manager: Saboteur or Scapegoat?" *Human Resource Management Journal* 11 (2001), pp. 24–40.

23. D. Stafford, "Sharing the Driver's Seat," *Kansas City Star*, June 11, 2002, p. D1.

24. G. Garda, K. Lindstrom, and M. Dallnera, "Towards a Learning Organization: The Introduction of a Client-Centered Team-Based Organization in Administrative Surveying Work," *Applied Ergonomics* 34 (2003), pp. 97–105.

25. R. Yonatan and H. Lam, "Union Responses to Quality Improvement Initiatives: Factors Shaping Support and Resistance," *Journal of Labor Research* 20 (Winter 1999), pp. 111–31; R. Hodson, "Dignity in the Workplace under Participative Management: Alienation and Freedom Revisited," *American Sociological Review* 61 (1996), pp. 719–38.

26. A. Ford, "Web Ace Turns Hobby into Global Winner," *Vancouver Province*, February 15, 2000.

27. J. Lipnack and J. Stamps, *Virtual Teams: People Working across Boundaries with Technology* (New York: John Wiley & Sons, 2001); A. M. Townsend, S. M. DeMarie, and A. R. Hendrickson, "Virtual Teams and the Workplace of the Future," *Academy of Management Executive* 12 (August 1998), pp. 17–29.

28. B. S. Bell and W. J. Kozlowski, "A Typology of Virtual Teams: Implications for Effective Leadership," *Group & Organization Management* 27 (March 2002), pp. 14–49.

29. Bell and Kozlowski, "A Typology of Virtual Teams"; D. L. Duarte and N. T. Snyder, *Mastering Virtual Teams: Strategies, Tools, and Techniques that Succeed*, 2nd ed. (San Francisco: Jossey-Bass, 2000), pp. 4–8.

30. S. Murray, "Pros and Cons of Technology: The Corporate Agenda: Managing Virtual Teams," *Financial Times* (London), May 27, 2002, p. 6.

31. G. Gilder, *Telecosm: How Infinite Bandwidth Will Revolutionize Our World* (New York: Free Press, 2001); J. S. Brown, "Seeing Differently: A Role for Pioneering Research," *Research Technology Management* 41 (May–June 1998), pp. 24–33.

32. Townsend, DeMarie, and Hendrickson, "Virtual Teams: Technology and the Workplace of the Future."

33. M. Foreman, "US Pays for Designers to Stay Home," *New Zealand Herald*, November 21, 2000.

34. Y. L. Doz, J. F. P. Santos, and P. J. Williamson, "The Metanational Advantage," *Optimize*, May 2002, pp. 45ff; J. S. Lureya and M. S. Raisinghani, "An Empirical Study of Best Practices in Virtual Teams," *Information & Management* 38 (2001) pp. 523–44.

35. Lureya and Raisinghani, "An Empirical Study of Best Practices in Virtual Teams"; K. Fisher and M. D. Fisher, *The Distance Manager* (New York: McGraw-Hill, 2000).

36. S. Gaspar, "Virtual Teams, Real Benefits," *Network World*, September 24, 2001, p. 45.

37. D. Robey, H. M. Khoo, and C. Powers, "Situated Learning in Cross-functional Virtual Teams," *Technical Communication*, February 2000, pp. 51–66.

38. Murray, "Pros and Cons of Technology."

39. Lureya and Raisinghani, "An Empirical Study of Best Practices in Virtual Teams."

40. S. Alexander, "Virtual Teams Going Global," *InfoWorld*, November 13, 2000, pp. 55–56.

41. S. Van Ryssen and S. H. Godar, "Going International without Going International: Multinational Virtual Teams," *Journal of International Management* 6 (2000), pp. 49–60.

42. B. J. Alge, C. Wiethoff, and H. J. Klein, "When Does the Medium Matter? Knowledge-Building Experiences and Opportunities in Decision-Making Teams," *Organizational Behavior and Human Decision Processes*, in press. Also see D. Robey, K. S. Schwaig, and L. Jin, "Intertwining Material and Virtual Work," *Information and Organization* 13 (2003), pp. 111–29; F. G. Mangrum, M. S. Fairley, and D. L. Wieder, "Informal Problem Solving in the Technology-Mediated Work Place," *Journal of Business Communication* 38 (July 2001), pp. 315–36; Robey et al., "Situated Learning in Cross-Functional Virtual Teams."

43. L. L. Bierema, J. W. Bing, and T. J. Carter, "The Global Pendulum," *T & D* 56 (May 2002), pp. 70–79.

44. Duarte and Snyder, *Mastering Virtual Teams*, pp. 139–55; S. L. Robinson, "Trust and Breach of the Psychological Contract," *Administrative Science Quarterly* 41 (1996), pp. 574–99. For a discussion of the antecedents of trust, see E. M Whitener, S. E. Brodt,

M. A. Korsgaard, and J. M. Werner, "Managers as Initiators of Trust: An Exchange Relationship Framework for Understanding Managerial Trustworthy Behavior," *Academy of Management Review* 23 (July 1998), pp. 513–30. Different foci of trust are discussed in R. D. Costigan, S. S. Ilter, and J. J. Berman, "A Multi-Dimensional Study of Trust in Organizations," *Journal of Managerial Issues* 10 (Fall 1998), pp. 303–17.

45. Whitener et al., "Managers as Initiators of Trust"; Bennis and Nanus, *Leaders*, pp. 43–55; Kouzes and Posner, *Credibility: How Leaders Gain and Lose It, Why People Demand It.* Knowledge-based trust is sometimes called "history-based trust" in the psychological literature. See R. M. Kramer, "Trust and Distrust in Organizations: Emerging Perspectives, Enduring Questions," *Annual Review of Psychology* 50 (1999), pp. 569–98.

46. S. Gaspar, "Virtual Teams, Real Benefits," *Network World*, September 24, 2001, p. 45.

47. S. L. Jarvenpaa and D. E. Leidner, "Communication and Trust in Global Virtual Teams," *Organization Science* 10 (1999), pp. 791–815; T. K. Das and B. Teng, "Between Trust and Control: Developing Confidence in Partner Cooperation in Alliances," *Academy of Management Review* 23 (1998), pp. 491–512; S. L. Jarvenpaa and D. E. Leidner, "Is Anybody Out There? The Implications of Trust in Global Virtual Teams," *Journal of Management Information Systems* 14 (1998), pp. 29–64.

48. T. Kelley, *The Art of Innovation* (New York: Currency/Doubleday, 2001), p. 69.

49. V. H. Vroom and A. G. Jago, *The New Leadership* (Englewood Cliffs, NJ: Prentice Hall, 1988), pp. 28–29.

50. R. B. Gallupe, W. H. Cooper, M. L. Grisé, and L. M. Bastianutti, "Blocking Electronic Brainstorms," *Journal of Applied Psychology* 79 (1994), pp. 77–86; M. Diehl and W. Stroebe, "Productivity Loss in Idea-Generating Groups: Tracking Down the Blocking Effects," *Journal of Personality and Social Psychology* 61 (1991), pp. 392–403.

51. B. E. Irmer and P. Bordia, "Evaluation Apprehension and Perceived Benefits in Interpersonal and Database Knowledge Sharing," *Academy of Management Proceedings*, 2002, pp. B1–B6.

52. P. W. Mulvey, J. F. Veiga, and P. M. Elsass, "When Teammates Raise a White Flag," *Academy of Management Executive* 10 (February 1996), pp. 40–49.

53. S. Plous, *The Psychology of Judgment and Decision Making* (Philadelphia: Temple University Press, 1993), pp. 200–2.

54. B. Mullen, T. Anthony, E. Salas, and J. E. Driskell, "Group Cohesiveness and Quality of Decision Making: An Integration of Tests of the Groupthink Hypothesis," *Small Group Research* 25 (1994), pp. 189–204; I. L. Janis, *Crucial Decisions* (New York: Free Press, 1989), pp. 56–63; I. L. Janis, *Groupthink: Psychological Studies of Policy Decisions and Fiascoes*, 2nd ed. (Boston: Houghton Mifflin, 1982).

55. M. E. Turner and A. R. Pratkanis, "Threat, Cohesion, and Group Effectiveness: Testing a Social Identity Maintenance Perspective on Groupthink," *Journal of Personality and Social Psychology* 63 (1992), pp. 781–96.

56. M. Rempel and R. J. Fisher, "Perceived Threat, Cohesion, and Group Problem Solving in Intergroup Conflict," *International Journal of Conflict Management* 8 (1997), pp. 216–34.

57. C. McGarty, J. C. Turner, M. A. Hogg, B. David, and M. S. Wetherell, "Group Polarization as Conformity to the Prototypical Group Member," *British Journal of Social Psychology* 31 (1992), pp. 1–20; D. Isenberg, "Group Polarization: A Critical Review and Meta-Analysis," *Journal of Personality and Social Psychology* 50 (1986), pp. 1141–51; D. G. Myers and H. Lamm, "The Group Polarization Phenomenon," *Psychological Bulletin* 83 (1976), pp. 602–27.

58. D. Friedman, "Monty Hall's Three Doors: Construction and Deconstruction of a Choice Anomaly," *American Economic Review* 88 (September 1998), pp. 933–46; D. Kahneman and A. Tversky, "Prospect Theory: An Analysis of Decision under Risk," *Econometrica* 47 (1979), pp. 263–91. The influence of gambler's fallacy in terms of emotions and evolutionary psychology is discussed in N. Nicholson, "Evolutionary Psychology: Toward a New View of Human Nature and Organizational Society," *Human Relations* 50 (September 1997), pp. 1053–78.

59. Janis, *Crucial Decisions*, pp. 244–49.

60. F. A. Schull, A. L. Delbecq, and L. L. Cummings, *Organizational Decision Making* (New York: McGraw-Hill, 1970), pp. 144–49.

61. R. Sutton, *Weird Ideas that Work* (New York: Free Press, 2002), Chapter 8; A. C. Amason, "Distinguishing the Effects of Functional and Dysfunctional Conflict on Strategic Decision Making: Resolving a Paradox for Top Management Teams," *Academy of Management Journal* 39 (1996), pp. 123–48; G. Katzenstein, "The Debate on Structured Debate: Toward a Unified Theory," *Organizational Behavior and Human Decision Processes* 66 (1996), pp. 316–32; D. Tjosvold, *Team Organization: An Enduring Competitive Edge* (Chichester, U.K.: Wiley, 1991).

62. J. S. Valacich and C. Schwenk, "Structuring Conflict in Individual, Face-to-Face, and Computer-Mediated Group Decision Making: Carping versus Objective Devil's Advocacy," *Decision Sciences* 26 (1995), pp. 369–93; D. M. Schweiger, W. R. Sandberg, and P. L. Rechner, "Experiential Effects of Dialectical Inquiry, Devil's Advocacy, and Consensus Approaches to Strategic Decision Making," *Academy of Management Journal* 32 (1989), pp. 745–72.

63. C. J. Nemeth, J. B. Connell, J. Rogers, and K. S. Brown, "Improving Decision Making by Means of Dissent," *Journal of Applied Social Psychology* 31 (2001), pp. 48–58.

64. K. M. Eisenhardt, J. L. Kahwajy, and L. J. Bourgeois III, "Conflict and Strategic Choice: How Top Management Teams Disagree," *California Management Review* 39 (Winter 1997), pp. 42–62.

65. A. F. Osborn, *Applied Imagination* (New York: Scribner, 1957).

66. B. Mullen, C. Johnson, and E. Salas, "Productivity Loss in Brainstorming Groups: A Meta-Analytic Integration," *Basic and Applied Psychology* 12 (1991), pp. 2–23.

67. R. I. Sutton and A. Hargadon, "Brainstorming Groups in Context: Effectiveness in a Product Design Firm,"

Administrative Science Quarterly 41 (1996), pp. 685–718; P. B. Paulus and M. T. Dzindolet "Social Influence Processes in Group Brainstorming," *Journal of Personality and Social Psychology* 64 (1993), pp. 575–86; Mullen, Johnson, and Salas, "Productivity Loss in Brainstorming Groups."

68. A. R. Dennis and J. S. Valacich, "Electronic Brainstorming: Illusions and Patterns of Productivity," *Information Systems Research* 10 (1999), pp. 375–77; R. B. Gallupe, A. R. Dennis, W. H. Cooper, J. S. Valacich, L. M. Bastianutti, and J. F. Nunamaker Jr., "Electronic Brainstorming and Group Size," *Academy of Management Journal* 35 (June 1992), pp. 350–69; R. B. Gallupe, L. M. Bastianutti, and W. H. Cooper, "Unblocking Brainstorms," *Journal of Applied Psychology* 76 (1991), pp. 137–42.

69. P. Bordia, "Face-to-Face versus Computer-Mediated Communication: A Synthesis of the Experimental Literature," *Journal of Business Communication* 34 (1997), pp. 99–120; J. S. Valacich, A. R. Dennis, and T. Connolly "Idea Generation in Computer-Based Groups: A New Ending to an Old Story," *Organizational Behavior and Human Decision Processes* 57 (1994), pp. 448–67; R. B. Gallupe, W. H. Cooper, M. L. Grisé, and L. M. Bastianutti, "Blocking Electronic Brainstorms," *Journal of Applied Psychology* 79 (1994), pp. 77–86.

70. G. Crone, "Electrifying Brainstorms," *National Post*, July 3, 1999, p. D11.

71. A. Pinsoneault, H. Barki, R. B. Gallupe, and N. Hoppen. "Electronic Brainstorming: The Illusion of Productivity," *Information Systems Research* 10 (1999) pp. 110–33; B. Kabanoff and J. R. Rossiter, "Recent Developments in Applied Creativity," *International Review of Industrial and Organizational Psychology* 9 (1994), pp. 283–324.

72. H. A. Linstone and M. Turoff (eds.), *The Delphi Method: Techniques and Applications* (Reading, MA: Addison-Wesley, 1975).

73. C. Critcher and B. Gladstone, "Utilizing the Delphi Technique in Policy Discussion: A Case Study of a Privatized Utility in Britain," *Public Administration* 76 (Autumn 1998), pp. 431–49; S. R. Rubin et al., "Research Directions Related to Rehabilitation Practice: A Delphi Study," *Journal of Rehabilitation* 64 (Winter 1998), p. 19.

74. A. L. Delbecq, A. H. Van de Ven, and D. H. Gustafson, *Group Techniques for Program Planning: A Guide to Nominal Group and Delphi Processes* (Middleton, WI: Green Briar Press, 1986).

75. A. B. Hollingshead, "The Rank-Order Effect in Group Decision Making," *Organizational Behavior and Human Decision Processes* 68 (1996), pp. 181–93.

76. S. Frankel, "NGT + MDS: An Adaptation of the Nominal Group Technique for Ill-Structured Problems," *Journal of Applied Behavioral Science* 23 (1987), pp. 543–51; D. M. Hegedus and R. Rasmussen, "Task Effectiveness and Interaction Process of a Modified Nominal Group Technique in Solving an Evaluation Problem," *Journal of Management* 12 (1986), pp. 545–60.

77. A. G. Dawson, "Administrators Settle into New Digs," *Delaware Coast Press*, July 16, 2003. For a history of Milton School, see www.k12.de.us/capehenlopen/mesweb/history.htm.

78. W. G. Dyer, *Team Building: Issues and Alternatives*, 2nd ed. (Reading, MA: Addison-Wesley, 1987); and S. J. Liebowitz and K. P. De Meuse, "The Application of Team Building," *Human Relations* 35 (1982), pp. 1–18.

79. Sundstrom et al., "Work Teams: Applications and Effectiveness," *American Psychologist*, p. 128; M. Beer, *Organizational Change and Development: A Systems View* (Santa Monica, CA: Goodyear, 1980), pp. 143–46.

80. Beer, *Organizational Change and Development*, p. 145.

81. T. G. Cummings and C. G. Worley, *Organization Development & Change*, 6th ed. (Cincinnati: South-Western, 1997), pp. 218–19; P. F. Buller and C. H. Bell Jr., "Effects of Team Building and Goal Setting on Productivity: A Field Experiment," *Academy of Management Journal* 29 (1986), pp. 305–28.

82. C. J. Solomon, "Simulation Training Builds Teams Through Experience," *Personnel Journal* 72 (June 1993), pp. 100–6.

83. M. J. Brown, "Let's Talk about It, Really Talk about It," *Journal for Quality & Participation* 19, no. 6, (1996), pp. 26–33; E. H. Schein, "On Dialogue, Culture, and Organizational Learning," *Organizational Dynamics*, Autumn 1993, pp. 40–51; and P. M. Senge, *The Fifth Discipline* (New York: Currency/Doubleday, 1990), pp. 238–49.

84. "German Businesswoman Demands End to Fun at Work," *Reuters*, July 9, 2003.

85. H. K. Rinella, "Working in Groups: Team Spirit," *Las Vegas Review-Journal*, August 12, 2003, p. E1; B. Oaff, "Team Games Take Turn for the Verse," *Mail on Sunday* (UK), January 28, 2001, p. 56; K. Cross, "Adventure Capital," *Business 2.0*, July 11, 2000.

86. R. W. Woodman and J. J. Sherwood, "The Role of Team Development in Organizational Effectiveness: A Critical Review," *Psychological Bulletin* 88 (1980), pp. 166–86; Sundstrom et al, "Work Teams: Applications and Effectiveness," p. 128.

87. Robbins and Finley, *Why Teams Don't Work*, Chapter 17.

88. P. McGraw, "Back from the Mountain: Outdoor Management Development Programs and How to Ensure the Transfer of Skills to the Workplace," *Asia Pacific Journal of Human Resources* 31 (Spring 1993), pp. 52–61; G. E. Huszczo, "Training for Team Building," *Training and Development Journal* 44 (February 1990), pp. 37–43.

CHAPTER **11**

1. C. Jones, "Life on the Spot," *Alameda (CA) Times-Star*, July 8, 2003; S. P. Means, "Playing at Pixar," *Salt Lake Tribune*, May 30, 2003, p. D1; G. Whipp, "Swimming against the Tide," *Daily News of Los Angeles*, May 30, 2003, p. U6; G. Whipp, "Pixar Crew Encourages Limitless Creativity and Interaction in Making Movies," *AMCTV.com*, May 28, 2003.

2. I. Nonaka and H. Takeuchi, *The Knowledge-Creating Company* (New York: Oxford University Press, 1995); C. Downs, P. Clampitt, and A. L. Pfeiffer, "Communication and Organizational Outcomes," in *Handbook of Organizational Communication*, ed. G. Goldhaber and G. Barnett (Norwood, NJ: Ablex, 1988), pp. 171–211.

3. D. Te'eni, "A Cognitive-Affective Model of Organizational Communication for Designing IT," *MIS Quarterly*

25 (June 2001), pp. 251–312; R. T. Barker and M. R. Camarata, "The Role of Communication in Creating and Maintaining a Learning Organization: Preconditions, Indicators, and Disciplines," *Journal of Business Communication* 35 (October 1998), pp. 443–67.

4. K. Melymuka, "Smarter by the Hour," *Computerworld,* June 26, 2003.

5. "What Are the Bottom Line Results of Communicating?" *Pay for Performance Report,* June 2003, p. 1; R. Maitland, "Bad Drivers," *People Management,* May 29, 2003, p. 49; T. Wanless, "Let's Hear It for Workers!" *Vancouver Province,* June 13, 2002; L. K. Lewis and D. R. Seibold, "Communication during Intraorganizational Innovation Adoption: Predicting User's Behavioral Coping Responses to Innovations in Organizations," *Communication Monographs* 63, no. 2 (1996), pp. 131–57.

6. N. Ferris, "Systems on Front Line against SARS," *Government Computer News,* June 23, 2003, p. 24; M. A. J. McKenna, "U.S. Response to 9/11 Aided War on SARS," *Atlanta Journal and Constitution,* May 11, 2003, p. A4; D. Brown, "Germ Warfare," *Washington Post,* May 6, 2003, p. C1.

7. C. E. Shannon and W. Weaver, *The Mathematical Theory of Communication* (Urbana: University of Illinois Press, 1949). For a more recent discussion, see K. J. Krone, F. M. Jablin, and L. L. Putnam, "Communication Theory and Organizational Communication: Multiple Perspectives," in *Handbook of Organizational Communication: An Interdisciplinary Perspective,* ed. F. M. Jablin, L. L. Putnam, K. H. Roberts, and L. W. Porter (Newbury Park, CA: Sage, 1987), pp. 18–40.

8. S. Axley, "Managerial and Organizational Communication in Terms of the Conduit Metaphor," *Academy of Management Review* 9 (1984), pp. 428–37.

9. J. H. E. Andriessen, "Mediated Communication and New Organizational Forms," *International Review of Industrial and Organizational Psychology* 6 (1991), pp. 17–70.

10. S. G. Jones, "Cybersociety: Computer-Mediated Communication and Community," in *Understanding Community in the Information Age,* ed. S. G. Jones (Beverley Hills, CA: Sage,

1997), pp. 10–35; F. Moore, "Storage Faces Newest Challenge—Coping with Success," *Computer Technology Review* 21 (September 2001), p. 1; S. D. Kennedy, "Finding a Cure for Information Anxiety," *Information Today,* May 1, 2001, p. 40; M. Culnan and M. L. Markus, "Information Technologies," in *Handbook of Organizational Communication: An Interdisciplinary Perspective,* ed. Jablin et al., pp. 420–43.

11. C. S. Saunders, D. Robey, and K. A. Vaverek, "The Persistence of Status Differentials in Computer Conferencing," *Human Communications Research* 20 (1994), pp. 443–72; D. A. Adams, P. A. Todd, and R. R. Nelson, "A Comparative Evaluation of the Impact of Electronic and Voice Mail on Organizational Communication," *Information & Management* 24 (1993), pp. 9–21.

12. "Does E-Mail Really Help Us Get the Message?" *Leicester Mercury* (UK), August 31, 2002, p. 15.

13. "Eisner: E-Mail Is Biggest Threat," *Associated Press,* May 12, 2000; A. D. Shulman, "Putting Group Information Technology in Its Place: Communication and Good Work Group Performance," in *Handbook of Organization Studies,* ed. S. R. Clegg, C. Hardy, and W. R. Nord (London: Sage, 1996), pp. 373–408.

14. J. Jamieson, "Net Marks 20 Years of the ;-)," *Vancouver Province,* September 20, 2002; S. Schafer, "Misunderstandings @ the Office," *Washington Post,* October 31, 2000, p. E1; M. Gibbs, "Don't Say It with Smileys," *Network World,* August 9, 1999, p. 62.

15. A. Gumbel, "How E-Mail Puts Us in a Flaming Bad Temper," *The Independent* (London), January 3, 1999, p. 14; J. Kaye, "The Devil You Know," *Computer Weekly,* March 19, 1998, p. 46; S. Kennedy, "The Burning Issue of Electronic Hate Mail," *Computer Weekly,* June 5, 1997, p. 22.

16. A. C. Poe, "Don't Touch That 'Send' Button!" *HRMagazine* 46 (July 2001), pp. 74–80. Problems with e-mail are discussed in M. M. Extejt, "Teaching Students to Correspond Effectively Electronically: Tips for Using Electronic Mail Properly," *Business Communication Quarterly* 61 (June 1998), pp. 57–67; V. Frazee, "Is E-Mail Doing More Harm than Good?" *Personnel Journal* 75 (May 1996), p. 23.

17. "A Day without E-mail?" *Modern Healthcare,* June 30, 2003, p. 36.

18. S. Stellin, "The Intranet Is Changing Many Firms from Within," *New York Times,* January 30, 2001.

19. Stellin, "The Intranet Is Changing Many Firms from Within"; A. Mahlon, "The Alternative Workplace: Changing Where and How People Work," *Harvard Business Review,* May–June 1998, pp. 121–30; C. Meyer and S. Davis, *Blur: The Speed of Change in the Connected Economy* (Reading, MA: Addison-Wesley, 1998); P. Bordia "Face-to-Face versus Computer-Mediated Communication: A Synthesis of the Experimental Literature," *Journal of Business Communication* 34 (January 1997), pp. 99–120.

20. M. McCance, "IM: Rapid, Risky," *Richmond Times-Dispatch,* July 19, 2001, p. A1; C. Hempel, "Instant-Message Gratification Is What People Want," *Ventura County Star,* April 9, 2001.

21. D. Robb, "Ready or Not . . . Instant Messaging Has Arrived as a Financial Planning Tool," *Journal of Financial Planning,* July 2001, pp. 12–14.

22. J. Black, "Why Offices Are Now Open Secrets," *Business Week,* September 17, 2003.

23. T. E. Harris, *Applied Organizational Communication: Perspectives, Principles, and Pragmatics* (Hillsdale, NJ: Lawrence Erlbaum Associates, 1993), Chapter 5; R. E. Rice and D. E. Shook, "Relationships of Job Categories and Organizational Levels to Use of Communication Channels, Including Electronic Mail: A Meta-Analysis and Extension," *Journal of Management Studies* 27 (1990), pp. 195–229; Sitkin et al., "A Dual-Capacity Model of Communication Media Choice in Organizations," p. 584.

24. P. Ekman and E. Rosenberg, *What the Face Reveals: Basic and Applied Studies of Spontaneous Expression Using the Facial Action Coding System* (Oxford, UK: Oxford University Press, 1997).

25. M. Sonnby-Borgstrom, P. Jonsson, and O. Svensson, "Emotional Empathy as Related to Mimicry Reactions at Different Levels of Information Processing," *Journal of Nonverbal Behavior* 27 (Spring 2003), pp. 3–23; S. G.

Barsade, "The Ripple Effect: Emotional Contagion and Its Influence on Group Behavior," *Administrative Science Quarterly* 47 (December 2002), pp. 644–75; E. Hatfield, J. T. Cacioppo, and R. L. Rapson, *Emotional Contagion* (Cambridge, UK: Cambridge University Press, 1993).

26. J. R. Kelly and S. G. Barsade, "Mood and Emotions in Small Groups and Work Teams," *Organizational Behavior and Human Decision Processes* 86 (September 2001), pp. 99–130.

27. R. L. Daft, R. H. Lengel, and L. K. Tevino, "Message Equivocality, Media Selection, and Manager Performance: Implications for Information Systems," *MIS Quarterly* 11 (1987), pp. 355–66.

28. I. Lamont, "Do Your Far-Flung Users Want to Communicate as if They Share an Office?" *Network World*, November 13, 2000.

29. R. Lengel and R. Daft, "The Selection of Communication Media as an Executive Skill," *Academy of Management Executive* 2 (1988), pp. 225–32; G. Huber and R. Daft, "The Information Environments of Organizations," in *Handbook of Organizational Communication: An Interdisciplinary Perspective*, ed. Jablin et al., pp. 130–64; R. Daft and R. Lengel, "Information Richness: A New Approach to Managerial Behavior and Organization Design," *Research in Organizational Behavior* 6 (1984), pp. 191–233.

30. R. E. Rice, "Task Analyzability, Use of New Media, and Effectiveness: A Multi-site Exploration of Media Richness," *Organization Science* 3 (1992) pp. 475–500; J. Fulk, C. W. Steinfield, J. Schmitz, and J. G. Power, "A Social Information Processing Model of Media Use in Organizations," *Communication Research* 14 (1987), pp. 529–52.

31. R. Madhavan and R. Grover, "From Embedded Knowledge to Embodied Knowledge: New Product Development as Knowledge Management," *Journal of Marketing* 62 (October 1998), pp. 1–12; D. Stork and A. Sapienza, "Task and Human Messages over the Project Life Cycle: Matching Media to Messages," *Project Management Journal* 22 (December 1992), pp. 44–49.

32. J. R. Carlson and R. W. Zmud, "Channel Expansion Theory and the Experiential Nature of Media Richness Perceptions," *Academy of Management Journal* 42 (April 1999), pp. 153–70.

33. M. McLuhan, *Understanding Media: The Extensions of Man* (New York: McGraw-Hill, 1964).

34. P. Nelson, "Work Practices," *Personnel Today*, November 12, 2002, p. 2; K. Griffiths, "KPMG Sacks 670 Employees by E-Mail," *The Independent* (London), November 5, 2002, p. 19.

35. S. B. Sitkin, K. M. Sutcliffe, and J. R. Barrios-Choplin, "A Dual-Capacity Model of Communication Media Choice in Organizations," *Human Communication Research* 18 (June 1992), pp. 563–98; J. Schmitz and J. Fulk, "Organizational Colleagues, Media Richness, and Electronic Mail: A Test of the Social Influence Model of Technology Use," *Communication Research* 18 (1991), pp. 487–523.

36. M. Meissner, "The Language of Work," in *Handbook of Work, Organization, and Society*, ed. R. Dubin (Chicago: Rand McNally, 1976), pp. 205–79.

37. D. Goleman, R. Boyatzis, and A. McKee, *Primal Leaders* (Boston: Harvard Business School Press, 2002), pp. 92–95.

38. M. J. Glauser, "Upward Information Flow in Organizations: Review and Conceptual Analysis," *Human Relations* 37 (1984), pp. 613–43.

39. Translation: "Hi Jack, I've worked out a rough solution to the user interface problem. We need to examine the finer details. Unfortunately, I'm away next week, so you need to devote time and energy to this problem. I'm worried that the permanent Microsoft employees on this project will get really angry when they realize that we are getting behind on the released-to-manufacturing date." See K. Barnes, "The Microsoft Lexicon," www.cinepad.com/mslex.htm; S. Greenhouse, "Braindump on the Blue Badge: A Guide to Microspeak," *New York Times*, August 13, 1998, p. C1.

40. L. Larwood, "Don't Struggle to Scope Those Metaphors Yet," *Group and Organization Management* 17 (1992), pp. 249–54; L. R. Pondy, P. J. Frost, G. Morgan, and T. C. Dandridge (eds.), *Organizational Symbolism* (Greenwich, CT: JAI Press, 1983).

41. L. Sahagun, "Cold War Foes Find Harmony in Satellite Launch Partnership," *Los Angeles Times*, July 25, 2001, p. B1.

42. M. J. Hatch, "Exploring the Empty Spaces of Organizing: How Improvisational Jazz Helps Redescribe Organizational Structure," *Organization Studies* 20 (1999), pp. 75–100; G. Morgan, *Images of Organization*, 2nd ed. (Thousand Oaks, CA: Sage, 1997); L. L. Putnam, Nelson Phillips, and P. Chapman, "Metaphors of Communication and Organization," in *Handbook of Organization Studies*, ed. Clegg et al., pp. 373–408; E. M. Eisenberg, "Ambiguity as a Strategy in Organizational Communication," *Communication Monographs* 51 (1984), pp. 227–42; R. Daft and J. Wiginton, "Language and Organization," *Academy of Management Review* 4 (1979), pp. 179–91.

43. M. Rubini and H. Sigall, "Taking the Edge Off of Disagreement: Linguistic Abstractness and Self-Presentation to a Heterogeneous Audience," *European Journal of Social Psychology* 32 (2002), pp. 343–51.

44. B. Robins, "Why 'Sell' Is Now a Four-Letter Word," *The Age* (Melbourne), June 16, 2001.

45. "2003 E-Mail Survey Reveals," *Business Wire*, June 23, 2003; T. Koski, "Reflections on Information Glut and Other Issues in Knowledge Productivity," *Futures* 33 (August 2001), pp. 483–95; C. Norton and A. Nathan, "Computer-Mad Generation Has a Memory Crash," *Sunday Times* (London), February 4, 2001; S. Bury, "Does E-Mail Make You More Productive?" *Silicon Valley North*, September 1999.

46. From "The Best of Ideas," CBC Radio program, 1967. Cited at www.mcluhan4managers.com.

47. A. Edmunds and A. Morris, "The Problem of Information Overload in Business Organisations: A Review of the Literature," *International Journal of Information Management* 20 (2000), pp. 17–28; A. G. Schick, L. A. Gordon, and S. Haka, "Information Overload: A Temporal Approach," *Accounting, Organizations & Society* 15 (1990), pp. 199–220.

48. Schick et al., "Information Overload," pp. 209–14; C. Stohl and W. C. Redding, "Messages and Message Exchange Processes," in *Handbook of*

Organizational Communication, ed. Jablin et al., pp. 451–502.

49. G. Dutton, "One Workforce, Many Languages," *Management Review* 87 (December 1998), pp. 42–47.

50. D. Woodruff, "Crossing Culture Divide Early Clears Merger Paths," *Asian Wall Street Journal,* May 28, 2001, p. 9.

51. Mead, *Cross-Cultural Management Communication,* pp. 161–62; and J. V. Hill and C. L. Bovée, *Excellence in Business Communication* (New York: McGraw-Hill, 1993), Chapter 17.

52. R. M. March, *Reading the Japanese Mind* (Tokyo: Kodansha International, 1996), Chapter 1; H. Yamada, *American and Japanese Business Discourse: A Comparison of Interaction Styles* (Norwood, NJ: Ablex, 1992), p. 34.

53. One writer explains that Aboriginal people tend to avoid conflict, so differences are discussed over an open campfire which absorbs some of the potential conflict and allows people to avoid direct eye contact. See H. Blagg, "A Just Measure of Shame?" *British Journal of Criminology* 37 (Autumn 1997), pp. 481–501. For other differences in cross-cultural communication, see R. Axtell, *Gestures: The Do's and Taboos of Body Language around the World* (New York: Wiley, 1991); P. Harris and R. Moran, *Managing Cultural Differences* (Houston: Gulf, 1987); P. Ekman, W. V. Friesen, and J. Bear, "The International Language of Gestures," *Psychology Today,* May 1984, pp. 64–69.

54. M. Griffin, "The Office, Australian Style," *Sunday Age* (Melbourne), June 22, 2003, p. 6.

55. S. Ohtaki, T. Ohtaki, and M. D. Fetters, "Doctor–Patient Communication: A Comparison of the USA and Japan," *Family Practice* 20 (June 2003), pp. 276–82.

56. H. Yamada, *Different Games, Different Rules* (New York: Oxford University Press, 1997), pp. 76–79; Yamada, *American and Japanese Business Discourse,* Chapter 2; D. Tannen, *Talking from 9 to 5* (New York: Avon, 1994), pp. 96–97; D. C. Barnlund, *Communication Styles of Japanese and Americans: Images and Realities* (Belmont, CA: Wadsworth, 1988).

57. This stereotypic notion is prevalent throughout J. Gray, *Men Are from Mars, Women Are from Venus* (New York: HarperCollins, 1992). For a critique of this view see J. T. Wood, "A Critical Response to John Gray's Mars and Venus Portrayals of Men and Women," *Southern Communication Journal* 67 (Winter 2002), pp. 201–10; D. J. Canary, T. M. Emmers-Sommer, *Sex and Gender Differences in Personal Relationships* (New York: Guilford Press, 1997), Chapter 1; M. Crawford, *Talking Difference: On Gender and Language* (Thousand Oaks, CA: Sage, 1995), Chapter 4.

58. Crawford, *Talking Difference: On Gender and Language,* pp. 41–44; Tannen, *Talking from 9 to 5;* D. Tannen, *You Just Don't Understand: Men and Women in Conversation* (New York: Ballentine Books, 1990); S. Helgesen, *The Female Advantage: Women's Ways of Leadership* (New York: Doubleday, 1990).

59. A. Mulac et al., "'Uh-Huh. What's That All About?' Differing Interpretations of Conversational Backchannels and Questions as Sources of Miscommunication across Gender Boundaries," *Communication Research* 25 (December 1998), pp. 641–68; G. H. Graham, J. Unruh, and P. Jennings, "The Impact of Nonverbal Communication in Organizations: A Survey of Perceptions," *Journal of Business Communication* 28 (1991), pp. 45–61; J. Hall, "Gender Effects in Decoding Nonverbal Cues," *Psychological Bulletin* 68 (1978), pp. 845–57.

60. P. Tripp-Knowles "A Review of the Literature on Barriers Encountered by Women in Science Academia," *Resources for Feminist Research* 24 (Spring/Summer 1995), pp. 28–34.

61. R. J. Grossman, "Emotions at Work," *Health Forum Journal* 43 (September–October, 2000), pp. 18–22.

62. Cited in K. Davis and J. W. Newstrom, *Human Behavior at Work: Organizational Behavior,* 7th ed. (New York: McGraw-Hill, 1985), p. 438.

63. The three components of listening discussed here are based on several recent studies in the field of marketing, including K. de Ruyter and M. G. M. Wetzels, "The Impact of Perceived Listening Behavior in Voice-to-Voice Service Encounters," *Journal of Service Research* 2 (February 2000), pp. 276–84; S. B. Castleberry, C. D. Shepherd, and R. Ridnour, "Effective Interpersonal Listening in the Personal Selling Environment: Conceptualization, Measurement, and Nomological Validity," *Journal of Marketing Theory and Practice* 7 (Winter 1999), pp. 30–38; L. B. Comer and T. Drollinger, "Active Empathetic Listening and Selling Success: A Conceptual Framework," *Journal of Personal Selling & Sales Management* 19 (Winter 1999), pp. 15–29.

64. S. Silverstein, "On the Job But Do They Listen?" *Los Angeles Times,* July 19, 1998.

65. H. Ditmars, "The Cold, Hard World of Advertising," *Report on Business Magazine,* September 28, 2001; "How Can You Be a Great Leader?" *Success* 48 (April 2001), pp. 28ff.

66. G. Evans and D. Johnson, "Stress and Open-Office Noise," *Journal of Applied Psychology* 85 (2000), pp. 779–83. The large study with 13,000 surveys is described in F. Russo, "My Kingdom for a Door," *Time Magazine,* October 23, 2000, p. B1.

67. M. Misra and P. Misra, "Hughes Software: Fun & Flexibility," *Business Today,* January 7, 2001, p. 182.

68. B. Sosnin, "Digital Newsletters 'E-Volutionize' Employee Communications," *HRMagazine* 46 (May 2001), pp. 99–107; G. Grates, "Is the Employee Publication Extinct?" *Communication World* 17 (December 1999/January 2000), pp. 27–30.

69. B. Schneider, S. D. Ashworth, A. C. Higgs, and L. Carr, "Design, Validity, and Use of Strategically Focused Employee Attitude Surveys," *Personnel Psychology* 49 (1996), pp. 695–705; T. Geddie, "Surveys Are a Waste of Time . . . Until You Use Them," *Communication World,* April 1996, pp. 24–26.

70. L. Girion, "Employee Inner Views," *Los Angeles Times,* September 10, 2000, p. G1.

71. The original term is "management by *wandering* around," but this has been replaced with "walking" over the years. T. Peters and R. Waterman, *In Search of Excellence* (New York: Harper and Row, 1982), p. 122; W. Ouchi, *Theory Z* (New York: Avon Books, 1981), pp. 176–77.

72. S. Bongiorni, "LSU Students Get Business Tips," *Louisiana State Times/*

Morning Advocate, November 11, 2000, p. C1.

73. T. Whipp, "Walking in the President's Shoe," *Windsor Star*, December 3, 2001.

74. J. Simons, "Is It Too Late to Save Schering?" *Fortune*, September 15, 2003, pp. 145ff.

75. "Survey Finds Good and Bad Points on Worker Attitudes," *Eastern Pennsylvania Business Journal*, May 5, 1997, p. 13.

76. G. Kreps, *Organizational Communication* (White Plains, NY: Longman, 1986), pp. 202–6; W. L. Davis and J. R. O'Connor, "Serial Transmission of Information: A Study of the Grapevine," *Journal of Applied Communication Research* 5 (1977), pp. 61–72; K. Davis, "Management Communication and the Grapevine," *Harvard Business Review* 31 (September–October 1953), pp. 43–49.

77. D. Krackhardt and J. R. Hanson, "Informal Networks: The Company behind the Chart," *Harvard Business Review* 71 (July–August 1993), pp. 104–11; H. Mintzberg, *The Structuring of Organizations* (Englewood Cliffs, NJ: Prentice Hall, 1979), pp. 46–53.

78. M. Noon and R. Delbridge, "News from behind My Hand: Gossip in Organizations," *Organization Studies* 14 (1993), pp. 23–36; R. L. Rosnow, "Inside Rumor: A Personal Journey," *American Psychologist* 46 (May 1991), pp. 484–96; C. J. Walker and C. A. Beckerle, "The Effect of State Anxiety on Rumor Transmission," *Journal of Social Behavior & Personality* 2 (August 1987), pp. 353–60.

79. N. Nicholson, "Evolutionary Psychology: Toward a New View of Human Nature and Organizational Society," *Human Relations* 50 (September 1997), pp. 1053–78.

80. J. N. Lynem, "Sex, Lies and Message Boards," *San Francisco Chronicle*, July 1, 2001, p. W1; D. E. Lewis, "Firms Try to Cope with Rumors, Gossip on Online Message Boards," *Boston Globe*, May 17, 2001; M. Schrage, "If You Can't Say Anything Nice, Say It Anonymously," *Fortune*, December 6, 1999, p. 352; S. Caudron, "Employeechat.com: Bashing HR on the Web," *Workforce* 78 (December 1999), pp. 36–42.

81. R. Rousos, "Trust in Leaders Lacking at Utility," *The Lakeland (FL) Ledger*, July 29, 2003, p. B1.

82. "Odd Spot," *The Age* (Melbourne), July 20, 2001, p. 1.

CHAPTER 12

1. *In re* WorldCom, Inc., et al., Debtors. United States Bankruptcy Court, Southern District of New York, Chapter 11, Case No. 02-15533 (Ajg) Jointly Administered Second Interim Report of Dick Thornburgh, Bankruptcy Court Examiner, June 9, 2003; Report of Investigation by the Special Investigative Committee of the Board of Directors of Worldcom, Inc. Dennis R. Beresford, Nicholas Deb. Katzenbach, C. B. Rogers, Jr., Counsel, Wilmer, Cutler & Pickering, Accounting Advisors, Pricewaterhousecoopers Llp, March 31, 2003. Also see D. S. Hilzenrath, "How a Distinguished Roster of Board Members Failed to Detect Company's Problems," *Washington Post*, June 16, 2003, p. E1; T. Catan, S. Kirchgaessner, J. Ratner, and P. T. Larsen, "Before the Fall," *Financial Times* (London), December 19, 2002, p. 17; J. O'Donnell and A. Backover "Ebbers' High-Risk Act Came Crashing Down on Him," *USA Today*, December 12, 2002, p. B1; C. Stern, "Ebbers Dominated Board, Report Says," *Washington Post*, November 5, 2002, p. E1.

2. C. Hardy and S. Leiba-O'Sullivan, "The Power behind Empowerment: Implications for Research and Practice," *Human Relations* 51 (April 1998), pp. 451–83; R. Farson, *Management of the Absurd* (New York: Simon & Schuster, 1996), Chapter 13; R. M. Cyert and J. G. March, *A Behavioral Theory of the Firm* (Englewood Cliffs, NJ: Prentice Hall, 1963).

3. For a discussion of the definition of power, see J. M. Whitmeyer, "Power through Appointment," *Social Science Research* 29 (2000), pp. 535–55; J. Pfeffer, *New Directions in Organizational Theory* (New York: Oxford University Press, 1997), Chapter 6; J. Pfeffer, *Managing with Power* (Boston: Harvard Business School Press, 1992), pp. 17, 30; H. Mintzberg, *Power In and Around Organizations* (Englewood Cliffs, NJ: Prentice Hall, 1983), Chapter 1.

4. A. M. Pettigrew, *The Politics of Organizational Decision-Making* (London: Tavistock, 1973); R. M. Emerson, "Power-Dependence Relations," *American Sociological Review* 27 (1962), pp. 31–41; R. A. Dahl, "The Concept of Power," *Behavioral Science* 2 (1957), pp. 201–18.

5. D. J. Brass and M. E. Burkhardt, "Potential Power and Power Use: An Investigation of Structure and Behavior," *Academy of Management Journal* 36 (1993), pp. 441–70; K. M. Bartol and D. C. Martin, "When Politics Pays: Factors Influencing Managerial Compensation Decisions," *Personnel Psychology* 43 (1990), pp. 599–614.

6. P. P. Carson and K. D. Carson, "Social Power Bases: A Meta-Analytic Examination of Interrelationships and Outcomes," *Journal of Applied Social Psychology* 23 (1993), pp. 1150–69; P. Podsakoff and C. Schreisheim, "Field Studies of French and Raven's Bases of Power: Critique, Analysis, and Suggestions for Future Research," *Psychological Bulletin* 97 (1985), pp. 387–411; J. R. P. French and B. Raven, "The Bases of Social Power," in *Studies in Social Power*, ed. D. Cartwright (Ann Arbor: University of Michigan Press, 1959), pp. 150–67.

7. For example, see S. Finkelstein, "Power in Top Management Teams: Dimensions, Measurement, and Validation," *Academy of Management Journal* 35 (1992), pp. 505–38.

8. G. Yukl and C. M. Falbe, "Importance of Different Power Sources in Downward and Lateral Relations," *Journal of Applied Psychology* 76 (1991), pp. 416–23.

9. G. A. Yukl, *Leadership in Organizations*, 3rd ed. (Englewood Cliffs, NJ: Prentice Hall, 1994), p. 13; B. H. Raven, "The Bases of Power: Origins and Recent Developments," *Journal of Social Issues* 49 (1993), pp. 227–51.

10. C. Hardy and S. R. Clegg, "Some Dare Call It Power," in *Handbook of Organization Studies*, ed. S. R. Clegg, C. Hardy, and W. R. Nord (London: Sage, 1996), pp. 622–41; C. Barnard, *The Function of the Executive* (Cambridge, MA: Harvard University Press, 1938).

11. I. Nonaka and H. Takeuchi, *The Knowledge-Creating Company* (New York: Oxford University Press, 1995), pp. 138–39.

12. J. A. Conger, *Winning 'em Over* (New York: Simon & Shuster, 1998), Appendix A.

13. M. L. Loughry, "Co-workers Are Watching: Performance Implications of Peer Monitoring," *Academy of Management Best Papers Proceedings 2002*, pp. O1–O6; J. A. LePine and L. Van Dyne, "Peer Responses to Low Performers: An Attributional Model of Helping in the Context of Groups," *Academy of Management Review* 26 (2001), pp. 67–84; G. Sewell, "The Discipline of Teams: The Control of Team-Based Industrial Work through Electronic and Peer Surveillance," *Administrative Science Quarterly* 43 (June 1998), pp. 397ff. For a detailed discussion of coercive and reward power in network structures, see L. D. Molm, *Coercive Power in Social Exchange* (Cambridge: Cambridge University Press, 1997).

14. "Employees Terrorized by Peer Pressure in the Workplace," Morgan & Banks news release, September 2000. The Eaton plant quotation comes from "Empowerment Torture to Some," *Tampa Tribune*, October 5, 1997, p. 6.

15. P. F. Drucker, "The New Workforce," *The Economist*, November 3, 2001, pp. 8–12; J. Ridderstale and K. Nordstrom, *Funky Business* (London: Financial Times/Prentice Hall, 2000).

16. J. D. Kudisch and M. L. Poteet, "Expert Power, Referent Power, and Charisma: Toward the Resolution of a Theoretical Debate," *Journal of Business & Psychology* 10 (Winter 1995), pp. 177–95.

17. Information was identified as a form of influence, but not power, in the original French and Raven writing. Information was added as a sixth source of power in subsequent writing by Raven, but this book takes the view that information power is derived from the original five sources. See B. H. Raven, "Kurt Lewin Address: Influence, Power, Religion, and the Mechanisms of Social Control," *Journal of Social Issues* 55 (Spring 1999), pp. 161–86; Yukl and Falbe, "Importance of Different Power Sources in Downward and Lateral Relations."

18. "Corporate Culture Instilled Online," *The Economist*, November 11, 2000.

19. D. J. Brass, "Being in the Right Place: A Structural Analysis of Individual Influence in an Organization," *Administrative Science Quarterly* 29 (1984), pp. 518–39; N. M. Tichy, M. L. Tuchman, and C. Frombrun, "Social Network Analysis in Organizations," *Academy of Management Review* 4 (1979), pp. 507–19; H. Guetzkow and H. Simon, "The Impact of Certain Communication Nets upon Organization and Performance in Task-Oriented Groups," *Management Science* 1 (1955), pp. 233–50.

20. C. S. Saunders, "The Strategic Contingency Theory of Power: Multiple Perspectives," *Journal of Management Studies* 27 (1990), pp. 1–21; D. J. Hickson, C. R. Hinings, C. A. Lee, R. E. Schneck, and J. M. Pennings, "A Strategic Contingencies' Theory of Intraorganizational Power," *Administrative Science Quarterly* 16 (1971), pp. 216–27; J. D. Thompson, *Organizations in Action* (New York: McGraw-Hill, 1967).

21. C. R. Hinings, D. J. Hickson, J. M. Pennings, and R. E. Schneck, "Structural Conditions of Intraorganizational Power," *Administrative Science Quarterly* 19 (1974), pp. 22–44.

22. V. Doctor, "Buzz Seriously . . ." *Economic Times* (India), Special "Brand Equity" Pullout, September 10, 2003, pp. 1–2. Salzman's futurology strategies are also described in M. Salzman, I. Matathia, and A. O'Reilly, *Buzz: Harness the Power of Influence and Create Demand* (New York: John Wiley & Sons, 2003).

23. Hickson et al., "A Strategic Contingencies' Theory of Intraorganizational Power"; Hinings et al., "Structural Conditions of Intraorganizational Power"; R. M. Kanter, "Power Failure in Management Circuits," *Harvard Business Review*, July–August 1979, pp. 65–75.

24. M. Crozier, *The Bureaucratic Phenomenon* (London: Tavistock, 1964).

25. M. F. Masters, *Unions at the Crossroads: Strategic Membership, Financial, and Political Perspectives* (Westport, CT: Quorum Books, 1997).

26. D. Beveridge, "Job Actions Hit World's Airlines during Year's Busiest Flying Season," *Canadian Press*, July 10, 2001; M. O'Dell, "Airlines Grounded by the Rise of Pilot Power," *Financial Times* (London), July 3, 2001.

27. Brass and Burkhardt, "Potential Power and Power Use"; Hickson et al., "A Strategic Contingencies' Theory of Intraorganizational Power," pp. 219–21; J. D. Hackman, "Power and Centrality in the Allocation of Resources in Colleges and Universities," *Administrative Science Quarterly* 30 (1985), pp. 61–77.

28. D. Wanagas, "Still Possible to Save Some Face," *National Post*, July 6, 2002; "Medical Officer of Health Orders Garbage Cleanup," *CBC News* (online), July 5, 2002; "Toronto Tourism Industry Worried Strike Will Damage Reputation," *CBC News* (online), July 5, 2002; "Toronto Strike Keeps Growing," *CBC News* (online), July 4, 2002.

29. L. Holden, "European Managers: HRM and an Evolving Role," *European Business Review* 12 (2000); Kanter, "Power Failure in Management Circuits," p. 68; B. E. Ashforth, "The Experience of Powerlessness in Organizations," *Organizational Behavior and Human Decision Processes* 43 (1989), pp. 207–42.

30. M. L. A. Hayward and W. Boeker, "Power and Conflicts of Interest in Professional Firms: Evidence from Investment Banking," *Administrative Science Quarterly* 43 (March 1998), pp. 1–22.

31. R. Madell, "Ground Floor," *Pharmaceutical Executive (Women in Pharma Supplement)*, June 2000, pp. 24–31.

32. Raven, "The Bases of Power," pp. 237–39.

33. L. A. Perlow, "The Time Famine: Toward a Sociology of Work Time," *Administrative Science Quarterly* 44 (March 1999), pp. 5–31.

34. M. C. Higgins and K. E. Kram, "Reconceptualizing Mentoring at Work: A Developmental Network Perspective," *Academy of Management Review* 26 (April 2001), pp. 264–88; B. R. Ragins, "Diversified Mentoring Relationships in Organizations: A Power Perspective," *Academy of Management Review* 22 (1997), pp. 482–521.

35. D. Krackhardt and J. R. Hanson, "Informal Networks: The Company behind the Chart," *Harvard Business Review* 71 (July–August 1993), pp. 104–11; and R. E. Kaplan, "Trade Routes: The Manager's Network of Relationships," *Organizational Dynamics*, Spring 1984, pp. 37–52.

36. A. Mehra, M. Kilduff, and D. J. Brass, "The Social Networks of High

and Low Self-Monitors: Implications for Workplace Performance," *Administrative Science Quarterly* 46 (March 2001), pp. 121ff.

37. M. Linehan, "Barriers to Women's Participation in International Management," *European Business Review* 13 (2001); R. J. Burke and C. A. McKeen, "Women in Management," *International Review of Industrial and Organizational Psychology* 7 (1992), pp. 245–83; B. R. Ragins and E. Sundstrom, "Gender and Power in Organizations: A Longitudinal Perspective," *Psychological Bulletin* 105 (1989), pp. 51–88.

38. D. M. McCracken, "Winning the Talent War for Women: Sometimes It Takes a Revolution," *Harvard Business Review,* November–December 2000, pp. 159–67; D. L. Nelson and R. J. Burke, "Women Executives: Health, Stress, and Success," *Academy of Management Executive* 14 (May 2000), pp. 107–21.

39. R. Woolnough, "No Sex Please, You're Workmates," *The Guardian* (London), June 23, 2003, p. 2; R. Dhooma, "Taking Care of Business and Pleasure," *Toronto Sun,* September 20, 1999, p. 38; E. Edmonds, "Love and Work," *Ottawa Sun,* February 14, 1999, p. S10. A variety of organizational behavior issues surrounding workplace romances are discussed in G. N. Powell and S. Foley, "Something to Talk About: Romantic Relationships in Organizational Settings," *Journal of Management* 24 (1998), pp. 421–28.

40. "Work Life," *Arizona Daily Star,* February 18, 2001, p. D1. For a discussion of perceived justice and office romance, see S. Foley and G. N. Powell, "Not All Is Fair in Love and Work: Coworkers' Preferences for and Responses to Managerial Interventions Regarding Workplace Romances," *Journal of Organizational Behavior* 20 (1999), pp. 1043–56.

41. G. Crist, "Aide to Baker to Sue County for $500,000," *Rocky Mountain News,* August 29, 2003; K. Rouse, "Another Complaint Is Filed against Clerk," *Denver Post,* July 2, 2003, p. B1; K. Rouse, "Clerk's Affair Dividing Office," *Denver Post,* November 15, 2002, p. A1; K. Rouse and G. Merritt, "After Probe, Arapahoe Wants Clerk to Resign," *Denver Post,* October 22, 2002, p. B1.

42. K. O'Brian, "Cupid Accused: Love in a Corporate Climate," *Employment Law Journal* (UK), March 2003; C. A Pierce and H. Aguinis, "A Framework for Investigating the Link between Workplace Romance and Sexual Harassment," *Group & Organization Management* 26 (June 2001), pp. 206–29; N. Nejat-Bina, "Employers as Vigilant Chaperones Armed with Dating Waivers: The Intersection of Unwelcomeness and Employer Liability in Hostile Work Environment Sexual Harassment Law," *Berkeley Journal of Employment and Labor Law,* December 22, 1999, pp. 325ff; M. Solomon, "The Secret's Out: How to Handle the Truth of Workplace Romance," *Workforce* 7 (July 1998), pp. 42–48.

43. A. Somech and A. Drach-Zahavy, "Relative Power and Influence Strategy: The Effects of Agent/Target Organizational Power on Superiors' Choices of Influence Strategies," *Journal of Organizational Behavior* 23 (2002), pp. 167–79; K. Atuahene-Gima and H. Li, "Marketing's Influence Tactics in New Product Development: A Study of High Technology Firms in China," *Journal of Product Innovation Management* 17 (2000), pp. 451–70.

44. D. Katz and R. L. Kahn, *The Social Psychology of Organizations* (New York: Wiley, 1966), p. 301.

45. The original research involving student essays is reported in D. Kipnis, S. M. Schmidt, and I. Wilkinson, "Intraorganizational Influence Tactics: Explorations in Getting One's Way," *Journal of Applied Psychology* 65 (1980), pp. 440–52. Recent studies include W. A. Hochwarter, A. W. Pearson, G. R. Ferris, P. L. Perrewe, and D. A. Ralston, "A Reexamination of Schriesheim and Hinkin's (1990) Measure of Upward Influence," *Educational and Psychological Measurement* 60 (October 2000), pp. 755–71; C. Schriesheim and T. Hinkin, "Influence Tactics Used by Subordinates: A Theoretical and Empirical Analysis and Refinement of the Kipnis, Schmidt, and Wilkinson Subscales," *Journal of Applied Psychology* 75 (1990), pp. 246–57.

46. Some of the more thorough lists of influence tactics are presented in L. A. McFarland, A. M. Ryan, and S. D. Kriska, "Field Study Investigation of Applicant Use of Influence Tactics in a Selection Interview," *Journal of Psychology* 136 (July 2002), pp. 383–98; A. Rao, K. Hashimoto, and A. Rao, "Universal and Culturally Specific Aspects of Managerial Influence: A Study of Japanese Managers," *Leadership Quarterly* 8 (1997), pp. 295–312.

47. A. Rao, K. Hashimoto, and A. Rao, "Universal and Culturally Specific Aspects of Managerial Influence: A Study of Japanese Managers," *Leadership Quarterly* 8 (1997), pp. 295–312. Silent authority as an influence tactic in non-Western cultures is also discussed in S. F. Pasa, "Leadership Influence in a High Power Distance and Collectivist Culture," *Leadership & Organization Development Journal* 21 (2000), pp. 414–26.

48. A. W. Gouldner, "The Norm of Reciprocity: A Preliminary Statement," *American Sociological Review* 25 (1960), pp. 161–78.

49. D. Tan and R. S. Snell, "The Third Eye: Exploring Guanxi and Relational Morality in the Workplace," *Journal of Business Ethics* 41 (December 2002), pp. 361–84; Y. Fan, "Questioning Guanxi: Definition, Classification, and Implications," *International Business Review* 11 (2002), pp. 543–61; D. Bell, "Guanxi: A Nesting of Groups," *Current Anthropology* 41 (February 2000), pp. 132–38.

50. S. Michailova and V. Worm, "Personal Networking in Russia and China: Blat and Guanxi," *European Management Journal* 21 (2003), pp. 509–19; A. Ledeneva, *Russia's Economy of Favors: Blat, Networking and Informal Exchange* (New York: Cambridge University Press, 1998), Chapter 5.

51. E. A. Mannix, "Organizations as Resource Dilemmas: The Effects of Power Balance on Coalition Formation in Small Groups," *Organizational Behavior and Human Decision Processes* 55 (1993), pp. 1–22; A. T. Cobb, "Toward the Study of Organizational Coalitions: Participant Concerns and Activities in a Simulated Organizational Setting," *Human Relations* 44 (1991), pp. 1057–79; W. B. Stevenson, J. L. Pearce, and L. W. Porter, "The Concept of 'Coalition' in Organization Theory and Research," *Academy of Management Review* 10 (1985), pp. 256–68.

52. D. J. Terry, M. A. Hogg, and K. M. White, "The Theory of Planned Behavior: Self-Identity, Social Identity and Group Norms," *British Journal of Social Psychology* 38 (September 1999), pp. 225ff.

53. Rao et al., "Universal and Culturally Specific Aspects of Managerial Influence."

54. D. Strutton and L. E. Pelton, "Effects of Ingratiation on Lateral Relationship Quality within Sales Team Settings," *Journal of Business Research* 43 (1998), pp. 1–12.

55. H. G. Enns, S. L. Huff, and B. R. Golden, "How CIOs Obtain Peer Commitment to Strategic IS Proposals: Barriers and Facilitators," *Journal of Strategic Information Systems* 10 (March 2001), pp. 3–14; G. Yukl, *Leadership in Organizations*, 3rd ed. (Englewood Cliffs, NJ: Prentice Hall, 1994).

56. J. Sandberg, "Office Untouchables: They Kiss Up to Boss and It Really Works," *Wall Street Journal*, July 9, 2003, p. B1; J. O'Neil, "An Investigation of the Sources of Influence of Corporate Public Relations Practitioners," *Public Relations Review* 29 (June 2003), pp. 159–69; D. Strutton, L. E. Pelton, and J. F. Tanner Jr., "Shall We Gather in the Garden: The Effect of Ingratiatory Behaviors on Buyer Trust in Salespeople," *Industrial Marketing Management* 25 (1996): 151–62; R. Thacker and S. I. Wayne, "An Examination of the Relationship between Upward Influence Tactics and Assessments of Promotability," *Journal of Management* 21 (1995), pp. 739–56.

57. A. Rao and S. M. Schmidt, "Upward Impression Management: Goals, Influence Strategies, and Consequences," *Human Relations* 48 (1995), pp. 147–67; R. A. Giacalone and P. Rosenfeld (eds.), *Applied Impression Management* (Newbury Park, CA: Sage, 1991); and J. T. Tedeschi (ed.), *Impression Management Theory and Social Psychological Research* (New York: Academic Press, 1981).

58. A. Vuong, "Job Applicants Often Don't Tell Whole Truth," *Denver Post*, May 30, 2001, p. C1. For a discussion of research on false résumés, see S. L. McShane, "Applicant Misrepresentation in Résumés and Interviews," *Labor Law Journal* 45 (January 1994), pp. 15–24.

59. M. C. Bolino and W. H. Tunley, "More Than One Way to Make an Impression: Exploring Profiles of Impression Management," *Journal of Management* 29 (2003), pp. 141–60; A. P. J. Ellis, B. J. West, A. M. Ryan, and R. P. DeShon, "The Use of Impression Management Tactics in Structured Interviews: A Function of Question Type?" *Journal of Applied Psychology* 87 (December 2002), pp. 1200–8. Also see R. C. Liden and T. R. Mitchell, "Ingratiatory Behaviors in Organizational Settings," *Academy of Management Review* 13 (1988), pp. 572–87.

60. L. A. McFarland, A. M. Ryan, and S. D. Kriska, "Field Study Investigation of Applicant Use of Influence Tactics in a Selection Interview," *Journal of Psychology* 136 (July 2002), pp. 383–98; G. Yukl and J. B. Tracey, "Consequences of Influence Tactics Used with Subordinates, Peers, and the Boss," *Journal of Applied Psychology* 77 (1992), pp. 525–35.

61. R. Buck, E. Anderson, A. Chaudhuri, and I. Ray, "Emotion and Reason in Persuasion: Applying the ARI Model and the CASC Scale," *Journal of Business Research*, in press; E. H. H. J. Das, J. B. F. de Wit, and W. Stroebe, "Fear Appeals Motivate Acceptance of Action Recommendations: Evidence for a Positive Bias in the Processing of Persuasive Messages," *Personality and Social Psychology Bulletin* 29 (May 2003), pp. 650–64; S. Fox and Y. Amichai-Hamburger, "The Power of Emotional Appeals in Promoting Organizational Change Programs," *Academy of Management Executive* 15 (November 2001), pp. 84–94; J. Dillard and E. Peck, "Persuasion and the Structure of Affect: Dual Systems and Discrete Emotions as Complementary Models," *Human Communication Research* 27 (2000), pp. 38–68.

62. A. P. Brief, *Attitudes In and Around Organizations* (Thousand Oaks, CA: Sage, 1998), pp. 69–84; K. K. Reardon, *Persuasion in Practice* (Newbury Park, CA: Sage, 1991); P. Zimbardo and E. B. Ebbeson, *Influencing Attitudes and Changing Behavior* (Reading, MA: Addison-Wesley, 1969).

63. J. J. Jiang, G. Klein, and R. G. Vedder, "Persuasive Expert Systems: The Influence of Confidence and Discrepancy," *Computers in Human Behavior* 16 (March 2000), pp. 99–109; J. A. Conger, *Winning 'Em Over: A New Model for Managing in the Age of Persuasion* (New York: Simon & Schuster, 1998); J. Cooper and R. T. Coyle, "Attitudes and Attitude Change," *Annual Review of Psychology* 35 (1984), pp. 395–426.

64. M. Hiltzik, "Apple CEO's Visions Don't Guarantee Sustained Gains," *Los Angeles Times*, April 14, 2003, p. C1; S. Gilmor, "Ahead of the Curve," *Infoworld*, January 13, 2003, p. 58. The "Jargon Dictionary" definition of reality distortion field is found at info.astrian.net/jargon/terms/r/reality-distortion_field.html.

65. E. Aronson, *The Social Animal* (San Francisco: W. H. Freeman, 1976), pp. 67–68; R. A. Jones and J. W. Brehm, "Persuasiveness of One- and Two-Sided Communications as a Function of Awareness that There Are Two Sides," *Journal of Experimental Social Psychology* 6 (1970), pp. 47–56.

66. D. G. Linz and S. Penrod, "Increasing Attorney Persuasiveness in the Courtroom," *Law and Psychology Review* 8 (1984), pp. 1–47; R. B. Zajonc, "Attitudinal Effects of Mere Exposure," *Journal of Personality and Social Psychology Monograph* 9 (1968), pp. 1–27; R. Petty and J. Cacioppo, *Attitudes and Persuasion: Classic and Contemporary Approaches* (Dubuque, IA: W. C. Brown, 1981).

67. Conger, *Winning 'Em Over*.

68. M. Pfau, E. A. Szabo, and J. Anderson, "The Role and Impact of Affect in the Process of Resistance to Persuasion," *Human Communication Research* 27 (April 2001), pp. 216–52.

69. M. Zellner, "Self-Esteem, Reception, and Influenceability," *Journal of Personality and Social Psychology* 15 (1970), pp. 87–93.

70. C. P. Egri, D. A. Ralston, C. S. Murray, and J. D. Nicholson, "Managers in the NAFTA Countries: A Cross-Cultural Comparison of Attitudes toward Upward Influence Strategies," *Journal of International Management* 6 (2000), pp. 149–71.

71. "Be Part of the Team If You Want to Catch the Eye," *Birmingham Post* (UK), August 31, 2000, p. 14.

72. L. A. McFarland, A. M. Ryan, and S. D. Kriska, "Field Study Investigation of Applicant Use of Influence Tactics in a Selection Interview," *Journal of Psychology* 136 (July 2002), pp. 383–98; Somech and Drach-Zahavy, "Relative Power and Influence Strategy"; R. C. Ringer and R. W. Boss, "Hospital Professionals' Use of Upward Influence Tactics," *Journal of Managerial Issues*

12 (Spring 2000), pp. 92–108; B. H. Raven, J. Schwarzwald, and M. Koslowsky, "Conceptualizing and Measuring a Power/Interaction Model of Interpersonal Influence," *Journal of Applied Social Psychology* 28 (1998), pp. 307–32.

73. C. M. Falbe and G. Yukl, "Consequences for Managers of Using Single Influence Tactics and Combinations of Tactics," *Academy of Management Journal* 35 (1992), pp. 638–52. The effectiveness of coalitions in marketing is described in K. Atuahene-Gima and H. Li, "Marketing's Influence Tactics in New Product Development: A Study of High Technology Firms in China," *Journal of Product Innovation Management* 17 (2000), pp. 451–70.

74. Falbe and Yukl, "Consequences for Managers of Using Single Influence Tactics and Combinations of Tactics."

75. K. R. Xin and A. S. Tsui, "Different Strokes for Different Folks? Influence Tactics by Asian-American and Caucasian-American Managers," *Leadership Quarterly* 7 (1996), 109–32; J. R. Schermerhorn Jr. and M. H. Bond, "Upward and Downward Influence Tactics in Managerial Networks: A Comparative Study of Hong Kong Chinese and Americans," *Asia Pacific Journal of Management* 8 (1991), pp. 147–58.

76. H. G. Enns, S. L. Huff, and B. R. Golden, "How CIOs Obtain Peer Commitment to Strategic IS Proposals: Barriers and Facilitators," *Journal of Strategic Information Systems* 10 (March 2001), pp. 3–14; R. C. Ringer and R. W. Boss, "Hospital Professionals' Use of Upward Influence Tactics," *Journal of Managerial Issues* 12 (Spring 2000), pp. 92–108.

77. N. Martin, "Men 'Gossip More than Women to Boost Their Egos,'" *Daily Telegraph* (London), June 15, 2001, p. P13; M. Crawford, *Talking Difference: On Gender and Language* (Thousand Oaks, CA: Sage, 1995), pp. 41–44; D. Tannen, *Talking from 9 to 5* (New York: Avon, 1995), Chapter 2, pp. 137–41, 151–52; D. Tannen, *You Just Don't Understand: Men and Women in Conversation* (New York: Ballantine Books, 1990); S. Helgesen, *The Female Advantage: Women's Ways of Leadership* (New York: Doubleday, 1990).

78. L. L. Carli, "Gender, Interpersonal Power, and Social Influence," *Journal of Social Issues* 55 (Spring 1999), pp. 81ff; E. H. Buttner and M. McEnally, "The Interactive Effect of Influence Tactic, Applicant Gender, and Type of Job on Hiring Recommendations," *Sex Roles* 34 (1996), pp. 581–91; S. Mann, "Politics and Power in Organizations: Why Women Lose Out," *Leadership & Organization Development Journal* 16 (1995), pp. 9–15.

79. E. Vigoda and A. Cohen, "Influence Tactics and Perceptions of Organizational Politics: A Longitudinal Study," *Journal of Business Research* 55 (2002), pp. 311–24; R. Cropanzano, J. C. Howes, A. A. Grandey, and P. Toth, "The Relationship of Organizational Politics and Support to Work Behaviors, Attitudes, and Stress," *Journal of Organizational Behavior* 18 (1997), pp. 159–80.

80. W. E. O'Connor and T. G. Morrison, "A Comparision of Situational and Dispositional Predictors of Perceptions of Organizational Politics," *Journal of Psychology* 135 (May 2001), pp. 301–12.

81. E. Vigoda, "Stress-Related Aftermaths to Workplace Politics: The Relationships among Politics, Job Distress, and Aggressive Behavior in Organizations," *Journal of Organizational Behavior* 23 (2002), pp. 571–91; L. A. Witt, T. F. Hilton, and W. A. Hochwarter, "Addressing Politics in Matrix Teams," *Group & Organization Management* 26 (June 2001), pp. 230–47; K. M. Kacmar and R. A. Baron, "Organizational Politics: The State of the Field, Links to Related Processes, and an Agenda for Future Research," in *Research in Personnel and Human Resources Management*, ed. G. R. Ferris (Greenwich, CT: JAI Press, 1999), pp. 1–39.

82. D. Sandahl and C. Hewes," Decision Making at Digital Speed," *Pharmaceutical Executive* 21 (August 2001), p. 62; "Notes about Where We Work and How We Make Ends Meet," *Arizona Daily Star*, February 18, 2001, p. D1.

83. M. C. Andrews and K. M. Kacmar, "Discriminating among Organizational Politics, Justice, and Support," *Journal of Organizational Behavior* 22 (2001), pp. 347–66; C. Hardy, *Strategies for Retrenchment and Turnaround: The Politics of Survival* (Berlin: Walter de Gruyter, 1990), Chapter 14.

84. S. Blazejewski and W. Dorow, "Managing Organizational Politics for Radical Change: The Case of Beiersdorf-Lechia S.A., Poznan," *Journal of World Business* 38 (August 2003), pp. 204–23.

85. G. R. Ferris, G. S. Russ, and P. M. Fandt, "Politics in Organizations," in *Impression Management in the Organization*, ed. R. A. Giacalone and P. Rosenfeld (Hillsdale, NJ: Lawrence Erlbaum Associates, 1989), pp. 143–70; H. Mintzberg, "The Organization as Political Arena," *Journal of Management Studies* 22 (1985), pp. 133–54.

86. R. J. House, "Power and Personality in Complex Organizations," *Research in Organizational Behavior* 10 (1988), pp. 305–57; L. W. Porter, R. W. Allen, and H. L. Angle, "The Politics of Upward Influence in Organizations," *Research in Organizational Behavior* 3 (1981), pp. 120–22.

87. K. S. Sauleya and A. G. Bedeian, "Equity Sensitivity: Construction of a Measure and Examination of Its Psychometric Properties," *Journal of Management* 26 (September 2000), pp. 885–910; S. M. Farmer, J. M. Maslyn, D. B. Fedor, and J. S. Goodman, "Putting Upward Influence Strategies in Context," *Journal of Organizational Behavior* 18 (1997), pp. 17–42; R. Christie and F. Geis, *Studies in Machiavellianism* (New York: Academic Press, 1970).

88. G. R. Ferris et al., "Perceptions of Organizational Politics: Prediction, Stress-Related Implications, and Outcomes," *Human Relations* 49 (1996), pp. 233–63.

89. L. A. Witt, M. C. Andrews, and K. M. Kacmar, "The Role of Participative Decisionmaking in the Organizational Politics–Job Satisfaction Relationship," *Human Relations* 53 (2000), pp. 341–57.

CHAPTER 13

1. Based on information in B. L. Tofler, *Final Accounting: Ambition, Greed, and the Fall of Arthur Andersen* (New York: Broadway Books, 2003).

2. J. A. Wall and R. R. Callister, "Conflict and Its Management," *Journal of Management* 21 (1995), pp. 515–58; D. Tjosvold, *Working Together to Get*

Things Done (Lexington, MA: Lexington Books, 1986), pp. 114–15.

3. The conflict process is described in K. W. Thomas, "Conflict and Negotiation Processes in Organizations," in *Handbook of Industrial and Organizational Psychology*, 2nd ed., Vol. 3, ed. M. D. Dunnette and L. M. Hough (Palo Alto, CA: Consulting Psychologists Press, 1992), pp. 651–718; L. Pondy, "Organizational Conflict: Concepts and Models, *Administrative Science Quarterly* 2 (1967), pp. 296–320.

4. S. Schulz-Hardt, M. Jochims, and D. Frey, "Productive Conflict in Group Decision Making: Genuine and Contrived Dissent as Strategies to Counteract Biased Information Seeking," *Organizational Behavior and Human Decision Processes* 88 (2002), pp. 563–86; L. H. Pelled, K. R. Xin, and A. M. Weiss, "No Es Como Mi: Relational Demography and Conflict in a Mexican Production Facility," *Journal of Occupational and Organizational Psychology* 74 (March 2001), pp. 63–84; L. H. Pelled, K. M. Eisenhardt, and K. R. Xin, "Exploring the Black Box: An Analysis of Work Group Diversity, Conflict, and Performance," *Administrative Science Quarterly* 44 (March 1999), pp. 1–28; K. M. Eisenhardt, J. L. Kahwajy, and L. J. Bourgeois III, "Conflict and Strategic Choice: How Top Management Teams Disagree," *California Management Review* 39 (Winter 1997), pp. 42–62; D. Tjosvold, "Conflict within Interdependence: Its Value for Productivity and Individuality," in *Using Conflict in Organizations*, ed. C. K. W. De Dreu and E. Van de Vliert (London: Sage, 1997), pp. 23–37; D. Tjosvold, *The Conflict-Positive Organization* (Reading, MA: Addison-Wesley, 1991); R. A. Baron, "Positive Effects of Conflict: A Cognitive Perspective," *Employee Responsibilities and Rights Journal* 4 (1991), pp. 25–36.

5. C. K. W. De Dreu and L. R. Weingart, "Task versus Relationship Conflict, Team Performance, and Team Member Satisfaction: A Meta-Analysis," *Journal of Applied Psychology* 88 (August 2003), pp. 587–604.

6. J. M. Brett, D. L. Shapiro, and A. L. Lytle, "Breaking the Bonds of Reciprocity in Negotiations," *Academy of Management Journal* 41 (August 1998), pp. 410–24; G. E. Martin and T. J. Bergman, "The Dynamics of Behav-

ioral Response to Conflict in the Workplace," *Journal of Occupational and Organizational Psychology* 69 (December 1996), pp. 377–87; G. Wolf, "Conflict Episodes," in *Negotiating in Organizations*, ed. M. H. Bazerman and R. J. Lewicki (Beverly Hills, CA: Sage, 1983), pp. 135–40; L. R. Pondy, "Organizational Conflict: Concepts and Models," *Administrative Science Quarterly* 12 (1967), pp. 296–320.

7. H. Witteman, "Analyzing Interpersonal Conflict: Nature of Awareness, Type of Initiating Event, Situational Perceptions, and Management Styles," *Western Journal of Communications* 56 (1992), pp. 248–80; F. J. Barrett and D. L. Cooperrider, "Generative Metaphor Intervention: A New Approach for Working with Systems Divided by Conflict and Caught in Defensive Perception," *Journal of Applied Behavioral Science* 26 (1990), pp. 219–39.

8. Wall and Callister, "Conflict and Its Management," pp. 526–33.

9. T. Wallace, "Fear & Loathing," *Boss Magazine*, April 12, 2001, p. 42.

10. C. K. W. de Dreu, P. Harinck, and A. E. M. Van Vianen, "Conflict and Performance in Groups and Organizations," *International Review of Industrial and Organizational Psychology* 14 (1999), pp. 376–405.

11. F. Rose, "The Eisner School of Business," *Fortune*, July 6, 1998, pp. 29–30. For a more favorable interpretation of conflict at Disney, see S. Wetlaufer, "Common Sense and Conflict: An Interview with Disney's Michael Eisner," *Harvard Business Review* 78 (January–February 2000), pp. 114–24.

12. M. Rempel and R. J. Fisher, "Perceived Threat, Cohesion, and Group Problem Solving in Intergroup Conflict," *International Journal of Conflict Management* 8 (1997), pp. 216–34.

13. L. Goldberg, "Southwest's New Co-Pilots," *Houston Chronicle*, April 22, 2001, p. 1.

14. R. E. Walton and J. M. Dutton, "The Management of Conflict: A Model and Review," *Administrative Science Quarterly* 14 (1969), pp. 73–84.

15. D. M. Brock, D. Barry, and D. C. Thomas, "'Your Forward Is Our Reverse, Your Right, Our Wrong': Rethinking Multinational Planning Processes in Light of National Culture,"

International Business Review 9 (December 2000), pp. 687–701.

16. For a fuller discussion of conflict across the generations, see R. Zemke and B. Filipczak, *Generations at Work: Managing the Clash of Veterans, Boomers, Xers, and Nexters in Your Workplace* (New York: Amacom, 1999).

17. T. Aeppel, "Power Generation: Young and Old See Technology Sparking Friction on Shop Floor," *Wall Street Journal*, April 7, 2000, p. A1.

18. K. Jelin, "A Multimethod Examination of the Benefits and Detriments of Intragroup Conflict," *Administrative Science Quarterly* 40 (1995), pp. 245–82; P. C. Earley and G. B. Northcraft, "Goal Setting, Resource Interdependence, and Conflict Management," in *Managing Conflict: An Interdisciplinary Approach*, ed. M. A. Rahim (New York: Praeger, 1989), pp. 161–70.

19. W. W. Notz, F. A. Starke, and J. Atwell, "The Manager as Arbitrator: Conflicts over Scarce Resources," in *Negotiating in Organizations*, ed. Bazerman and Lewicki, pp. 143–64.

20. A. Risberg, "Employee Experiences of Acquisition Processes," *Journal of World Business* 36 (March 2001), pp. 58–84.

21. Brett et al., "Breaking the Bonds of Reciprocity in Negotiations"; R. A. Baron, "Reducing Organizational Conflict: An Incompatible Response Approach," *Journal of Applied Psychology* 69 (1984), pp. 272–79.

22. T. A. Abma, "Stakeholder Conflict: A Case Study," *Evaluation and Program Planning* 23 (May 2000), pp. 199–210; J. W. Jackson and E. R. Smith, "Conceptualizing Social Identity: A New Framework and Evidence for the Impact of Different Dimensions," *Personality and Social Psychology Bulletin* 25 (January 1999), pp. 120–35.

23. D. C. Dryer and L. M. Horowitz, "When Do Opposites Attract? Interpersonal Complementarity versus Similarity," *Journal of Personality and Social Psychology* 72 (1997), pp. 592–603.

24. R. J. Lewicki and J. A. Litterer, *Negotiation* (Homewood, IL: Irwin, 1985), pp. 102–6; K. W. Thomas, "Toward Multi-dimensional Values in Teaching: The Example of Conflict Behaviors," *Academy of Management Review* 2 (1977), pp. 484–90.

25. Jehn, "A Multimethod Examination of the Benefits and Detriments of Intragroup Conflict," p. 276.

26. C. K. W. de Dreu, A. Evers, B. Beersma, E. S. Kluwer, and A. Nauta, "A Theory-Based Measure of Conflict Management Strategies in the Workplace," *Journal of Organizational Behavior* 22 (2001), pp. 645–68.

27. M. Lyster et al., "The Changing Guard," *Orange County (CA) Business Journal*, May 7, 2001, p. 31.

28. L. Xiaohua and R. Germain, "Sustaining Satisfactory Joint Venture Relationships: The Role of Conflict Resolution Strategy," *Journal of International Business Studies* 29 (March 1998), pp. 179–96.

29. Tjosvold, *Working Together to Get Things Done*, Chapter 2; D. W. Johnson, G. Maruyama, R. T. Johnson, D. Nelson, and S. Skon, "Effects of Cooperative, Competitive, and Individualistic Goal Structures on Achievement: A Meta-Analysis," *Psychological Bulletin* 89 (1981), pp. 47–62; R. J. Burke, "Methods of Resolving Superior–Subordinate Conflict: The Constructive Use of Subordinate Differences and Disagreements," *Organizational Behavior and Human Performance* 5 (1970), pp. 393–441.

30. C. K. W. De Dreu and A. E. M. Van Vianen, "Managing Relationship Conflict and the Effectiveness of Organizational Teams," *Journal of Organizational Behavior* 22 (2001), pp. 309–28.

31. "On the Record: David Pottruck," *San Francisco Chronicle*, June 15, 2003, p. 11.

32. S. Ting-Toomey, J. G. Oetzel, and K. Yee-Jung, "Self-Construal Types and Conflict Management Styles," *Communication Reports* 14 (Summer 2001), pp. 87–104; C. H. Tinsley and J. M. Brett, "Managing Workplace Conflict in the United States and Hong Kong," *Organizational Behavior and Human Decision Processes* 85 (July 2001), pp. 360–81; M. W. Morris and H-Y. Fu, "How Does Culture Influence Conflict Resolution? Dynamic Constructivist Analysis," *Social Cognition* 19 (June 2001), pp. 324–49; K. Leung and D. Tjosvold (eds.), *Conflict Management in the Asia Pacific* (Singapore: John Wiley & Sons, 1998). For an exception to these studies, see D. A. Cai and E. L. Fink, "Conflict Style Differences between Individualists and Collectivists," *Communication Monographs* 69 (March 2002), pp. 67–87.

33. C. C. Chen, X. P. Chen, and J. R. Meindl, "How Can Cooperation Be Fostered? The Cultural Effects of Individualism-Collectivism," *Academy of Management Review* 23 (1998), pp. 285–304; S. M. Elsayed-Ekhouly and R. Buda, "Organizational Conflict: A Comparative Analysis of Conflict Styles across Cultures," *International Journal of Conflict Management* 7 (1996), pp. 71–81; D. K. Tse, J. Francis, and J. Walls, "Cultural Differences in Conducting Intra- and Inter-cultural Negotiations: A Sino-Canadian Comparison," *Journal of International Business Studies* 25 (1994), pp. 537–55; S. Ting-Toomey et al., "Culture, Face Management, and Conflict Styles of Handling Interpersonal Conflict: A Study in Five Cultures," *International Journal of Conflict Management* 2 (1991), pp. 275–96.

34. N. B. Florea, M. A. Boyer, S. W. Brown, M. J. Butler, et al., "Negotiating from Mars to Venus: Gender in Simulated International Negotiations," *Simulation & Gaming* 34 (June 2003), pp. 226–48; N. Brewer, P. Mitchell, and N. Weber, "Gender Role, Organizational Status, and Conflict Management Styles," *International Journal of Conflict Management* 13 (2002), pp. 78–95.

35. E. Van de Vliert, "Escalative Intervention in Small Group Conflicts," *Journal of Applied Behavioral Science* 21 (Winter 1985), pp. 19–36.

36. L. Tischler, "Nissan Motor Company," *Fast Company* 60 (July 2002), pp. 80ff; "Nissan's Ghosn Calls Cultural Clashes 'A Luxury for the Rich,'" *PR Newswire*, January 18, 2000.

37. M. B. Pinto, J. K. Pinto, and J. E. Prescott, "Antecedents and Consequences of Project Team Cross-Functional Cooperation," *Management Science* 39 (1993), pp. 1281–97; M. Sherif, "Superordinate Goals in the Reduction of Intergroup Conflict," *American Journal of Sociology* 68 (1958), pp. 349–58.

38. X. M. Song, J. Xile, and B. Dyer, "Antecedents and Consequences of Marketing Managers' Conflict-Handling Behaviors," *Journal of Marketing* 64 (January 2000), pp. 50–66; K. M. Eisenhardt, J. L. Kahwajy, and L. J. Bourgeois III, "How Management Teams Can Have a Good Fight," *Harvard Business Review*, July–August 1997, pp. 77–85.

39. L. Mulitz, "Flying Off over Office Politics," *InfoWorld*, November 6, 2000.

40. Song, Xile, and Dyer, "Antecedents and Consequences of Marketing Managers' Conflict-Handling Behaviors."

41. "Teamwork Polishes This Diamond," *Philippine Daily Inquirer*, October 4, 2000, p. 10; "How Hibernia Helped Its Hourly Employees Make a Leap to PFP," *Pay for Performance Report*, January 2000, p. 2.

42. This strategy and other conflict management practices in joint military operations are fully discussed in E. Elron, B. Shamir, and E. Ben-Ari, "Why Don't They Fight Each Other? Cultural Diversity and Operational Unity in Multinational Forces," *Armed Forces & Society* 26 (October 1999), pp. 73–97.

43. R. J. Fisher, E. Maltz, and B. J. Jaworski, "Enhancing Communication between Marketing and Engineering: The Moderating Role of Relative Functional Identification," *Journal of Marketing* 61 (1997), pp. 54–70. For a discussion of minimizing conflict through understanding as "other point multiplicity," see T. A. Abma, "Stakeholder Conflict: A Case Study," *Evaluation and Program Planning* 23 (May 2000), pp. 199–210.

44. S. Lupak, "Leaders Show Colors at Academy," *St. Paul Pioneer Press*, July 13, 2003.

45. D. Barlow, "Group of People from Both Sides of Nuclear Issue Seeks Common Ground Out of Public Eye," *Brattleboro (VT) Reformer*, August 30, 2003. For discussion on dialogue practices, see L. Ellinor and G. Gerard, *Dialogue: Rediscovering the Transforming Power of Conversation* (New York: John Wiley & Sons, 1998); E. H. Schein, "On Dialog, Culture, and Organizational Learning," *Organizational Dynamics*, Autumn 1993, pp. 40–51.

46. P. R. Lawrence and J. W. Lorsch, *Organization and Environment* (Homewood, IL: Irwin, 1969).

47. E. Horwitt, "Knowledge, Knowledge, Who's Got the Knowledge?" *Computerworld*, April 8, 1996, pp. 80, 81, 84.

48. R. Lewicki, D. Saunders, J. Minton, and B. Barry (eds.), *Negotiation: Readings, Exercises, and Cases*, 4th ed. (New York: McGraw-Hill, 2003); D. G. Pruitt and P. J. Carnevale, *Negotiation in Social Conflict* (Buckingham, UK: Open University Press, 1993).

49. L. Edson, "The Negotiation Industry," *Across the Board*, April 2000, pp. 14–20.

50. For a critical view of the problem-solving style in negotiation, see J. M. Brett, "Managing Organizational Conflict," *Professional Psychology: Research and Practice* 15 (1984), pp. 664–78.

51. R. E. Fells, "Overcoming the Dilemmas in Walton and McKersie's Mixed Bargaining Strategy," *Industrial Relations* (Laval) 53 (March 1998), pp. 300–25; R. E. Fells, "Developing Trust in Negotiation," *Employee Relations* 15 (1993), pp. 33–45.

52. L. Thompson, *The Mind and Heart of the Negotiator* (Upper Saddle River, NJ: Prentice Hall, 1998), Chapter 2; R. Stagner and H. Rosen, *Psychology of Union–Management Relations* (Belmont, CA: Wadsworth, 1965), pp. 95–96, 108–10; R. E. Walton and R. B. McKersie, *A Behavioral Theory of Labor Negotiations: An Analysis of a Social Interaction System* (New York: McGraw-Hill, 1965), pp. 41–46.

53. J. Mayfield, M. Mayfield, D. Martin, and P. Herbig, "How Location Impacts International Business Negotiations," *Review of Business* 19 (December 1998), pp. 21–24; J. W. Salacuse and J. Z. Rubin, "Your Place or Mine? Site Location and Negotiation," *Negotiation Journal* 6 (January 1990), pp. 5–10; Lewicki and Litterer, *Negotiation*, pp. 144–46.

54. For a full discussion of the advantages and disadvantages of face-to-face and alternative negotiations situations, see M. H. Bazerman, J. R. Curhan, D. A. Moore, and K. L. Valley, "Negotiation," *Annual Review of Psychology* 51 (2000), pp. 279–314.

55. Lewicki and Litterer, *Negotiation*, pp. 146–51; B. Kniveton, *The Psychology of Bargaining* (Aldershot, UK: Avebury, 1989), pp. 76–79.

56. C. K. W. De Dreu, "Time Pressure and Closing of the Mind in Negotiation," *Organizational Behavior and Human Decision Processes* 91 (July

2003), pp. 280–95; Pruitt and Carnevale, *Negotiation in Social Conflict*, pp. 59–61; and Lewicki and Litterer, *Negotiation*, pp. 151–54.

57. B. M. Downie, "When Negotiations Fail: Causes of Breakdown and Tactics for Breaking the Stalemate," *Negotiation Journal*, April 1991, pp. 175–86.

58. Pruitt and Carnevale, *Negotiation in Social Conflict*, pp. 56–58; Lewicki and Litterer, *Negotiation*, pp. 215–22.

59. D. C. Zetik and A. F. Stuhlmacher, "Goal Setting and Negotiation Performance: A Meta-Analysis," *Group Processes and Intergroup Relations* 5 (January 2002), pp. 35–52; S. Doctoroff, "Reengineering Negotiations," *Sloan Management Review* 39 (March 1998), pp. 63–71; R. L. Lewicki, A. Hiam, and K. Olander, *Think before You Speak: The Complete Guide to Strategic Negotiation* (New York: John Wiley & Sons, 1996); G. B. Northcraft and M. A. Neale, "Joint Effects of Assigned Goals and Training on Negotiator Performance," *Human Performance* 7 (1994), pp. 257–72.

60. M. A. Neale and M. H. Bazerman, *Cognition and Rationality in Negotiation* (New York: Free Press, 1991), pp. 29–31; L. L. Thompson, "Information Exchange in Negotiation," *Journal of Experimental Social Psychology* 27 (1991), pp. 161–79.

61. Y. Paik and R. L. Tung, "Negotiating with East Asians: How to Attain "Win–Win" Outcomes," *Management International Review* 39 (1999), pp. 103–22; L. Thompson, E. Peterson, and S. E. Brodt, "Team Negotiation: An Examinaton of Integrative and Distributive Bargaining," *Journal of Personality and Social Psychology* 70 (1996), pp. 66–78.

62. B. McRae, *The Seven Strategies of Master Negotiators* (Toronto: McGraw-Hill Ryerson, 2002), pp. 7–11.

63. L. L. Putnam and M. E. Roloff (eds.), *Communication and Negotiation* (Newbury Park, CA: Sage, 1992).

64. L. Hall (ed.), *Negotiation: Strategies for Mutual Gain* (Newbury Park, CA: Sage, 1993); D. Ertel, "How to Design a Conflict Management Procedure that Fits Your Dispute." *Sloan Management Review* 32 (Summer 1991), pp. 29–42.

65. Lewicki and Litterer, *Negotiation*, pp. 89–93.

66. J. J. Zhao, "The Chinese Approach to International Business Negotiation," *Journal of Business Communication*, July 2000, pp. 209–37; Paik and Tung, "Negotiating with East Asians"; N. J. Adler, *International Dimensions of Organizational Behavior*, 2nd ed. (Belmont, CA: Wadsworth, 1991), pp. 180–81.

67. Kniveton, *The Psychology of Bargaining*, pp. 100–1; J. Z. Rubin and B. R. Brown, *The Social Psychology of Bargaining and Negotiation* (New York: Academic Press, 1976), Chapter 9; and Brett, "Managing Organizational Conflict," pp. 670–71.

68. A. R. Elangovan, "The Manager as the Third Party: Deciding How to Intervene in Employee Disputes," in *Negotiation: Readings, Exercises, and Cases*, 3rd ed., ed. R. Lewicki, J. Litterer, and D. Saunders (New York: McGraw-Hill, 1999), pp. 458–69; L. L. Putnam, "Beyond Third Party Role: Disputes and Managerial Intervention," *Employee Responsibilities and Rights Journal* 7 (1994), pp. 23–36; Sheppard et al., *Organizational Justice*.

69. M. A. Neale and M. H. Bazerman, *Cognition and Rationality in Negotiation* (New York: Free Press, 1991), pp. 140–42.

70. B. H. Sheppard, "Managers as Inquisitors: Lessons from the Law," in *Bargaining Inside Organizations*, ed. M. Bazerman and R. J. Lewicki (Beverly Hills, CA: Sage, 1983), pp. 193–213.

71. R. Cropanzano, H. Aguinis, M. Schminke, and D. L. Denham, "Disputant Reactions to Managerial Conflict Resolution Tactics," *Group and Organization Management* 24 (June 1999), pp. 124–53; R. Karambayya and J. M. Brett, "Managers Handling Disputes: Third Party Roles and Perceptions of Fairness," *Academy of Management Journal* 32 (1989), pp. 687–704.

72. A. R. Elangovan, "Managerial Intervention in Organizational Disputes: Testing a Prescriptive Model of Strategy Selection," *International Journal of Conflict Management* 4 (1998), pp. 301–35.

73. J. P. Meyer, J. M. Gemmell, and P. G. Irving, "Evaluating the Management of Interpersonal Conflict in Organizations: A Factor-Analytic Study of Outcome Criteria," *Canadian Journal*

of Administrative Sciences 14 (1997), pp. 1–13.

74. K. Downey, "With Its Dispute Resolution Process, Kodak Joins a Trend," *Washington Post,* September 21, 2003, p. F1.

75. C. Hirschman, "Order in the Hearing," *HRMagazine* 46 (July 2001), p. 58; D. Hechler, "No Longer a Novelty: ADR Winning Corporate Acceptance," *Fulton County (GA) Daily Report,* June 29, 2001; S. L. Hayford, "Alternative Dispute Resolution," *Business Horizons* 43 (January–February 2000), pp. 2–4.

CHAPTER 14

1. "Building a Solid Foundation on Value-Driven Principles," *Business Leader* 14 (June 2003), p. 6; "The Greatest Briton in Management and Leadership," *Personnel Today,* February 18, 2003; J. Elder, "The Virgin Knight," *Sun Herald* (Sydney, Australia), November 24, 2002, p. 22; "Redefining Leadership," *Leaders Magazine* 25, no. 4 (2002), pp. 6–7; C. Fox, "CEOs Slipping into Old Habits," *Australian Financial Review,* February 6, 2001, p. 38, p. L11. The story about Mike Abrashoff is reported in "Mike's Story," Grass Roots Leadership website (www.grassrootsleadership.com).

2. R. A. Barker, "How Can We Train Leaders if We Do Not Know What Leadership Is?" *Human Relations* 50 (1997), pp. 343–62; P. C. Drucker, "Forward," in *The Leader of the Future,* ed. F. Hesselbein et al. (San Francisco: Jossey-Bass, 1997).

3. R. House, M. Javidan, P. Hanges, and P. Dorfman, "Understanding Cultures and Implicit Leadership Theories across the Globe: An Introduction to Project GLOBE," *Journal of World Business* 37 (2002), pp. 3–10; R. House, M. Javidan, and P. Dorfman, "Project GLOBE: An Introduction," *Applied Psychology: An International Review* 50 (2001), pp. 489–505.

4. M. Groves, "Cream Rises to the Top, but from a Small Crop," *Los Angeles Times,* June 8, 1998. A recent study also reported that only 3 percent of executives in large firms agreed that their company develops leadership talent quickly and effectively. See H. Handfield-Jones, "How Executives Grow," *McKin-*

sey Quarterly, January 2000, pp. 116–23.

5. C. L. Pearce and J. A. Conger (eds.), *Shared Leadership: Reframing the Hows and Whys of Leadership* (Thousand Oaks, CA: Sage, 2003); R. G. Isaac, W. J. Zerbe, and D. C. Pitt, "Leadership and Motivation: The Effective Application of Expectancy Theory," *Journal of Managerial Issues* 13 (Summer 2001), pp. 212–26.

6. C. L. Cole, "Eight Values Bring Unity to a Worldwide Company," *Workforce* 80 (March 2001), pp. 44–45.

7. M. Callahan, "Key to Success Is Happy Employees, Says Utility's CEO," *Western Star* (Cornerbrook, Newfoundland), May 18, 2002.

8. C. A. Beatty, "Implementing Advanced Manufacturing Technologies: Rules of the Road," *Sloan Management Review,* Summer 1992, pp. 49–60; J. M. Howell and C. A. Higgins, "Champions of Technological Innovation," *Administrative Science Quarterly* 35 (1990), pp. 317–41.

9. Many of these perspectives are summarized in G. A. Yukl, *Leadership in Organizations,* 5th ed. (Upper Saddle River, NJ: Prentice Hall, 2001); R. N. Kanungo, "Leadership in Organizations: Looking Ahead to the 21st Century," *Canadian Psychology* 39 (Spring 1998), pp. 71–82. For a thoughtful review of leadership perspectives in organizational behavior textbooks, see W. B. Snavely, "Organizational Leadership: An Alternative View and Implications for Managerial Education," Paper presented at the Management Education Division of the Midwest Academy of Management, Toledo, Ohio, April 21, 2001.

10. J. Higley, "Head of the Class," *Hotel and Motel Management,* November 2001, pp. 92ff.

11. T. Takala, "Plato on Leadership," *Journal of Business Ethics* 17 (May 1998), pp. 785–98.

12. R. M. Stogdill, *Handbook of Leadership* (New York: Free Press, 1974), Chapter 5.

13. J. Kochanski, "Competency-Based Management," *Training and Development,* October 1997, pp. 40–44; Hay Group et al., *Raising the Bar: Using Competencies to Enhance Employee Performance* (Scottsdale, AZ: American

Compensation Association, 1996); L. M. Spencer and S. M. Spencer, *Competence at Work: Models for Superior Performance* (New York: Wiley, 1993).

14. Most elements of this list were derived from S. A. Kirkpatrick and E. A. Locke, "Leadership: Do Traits Matter?" *Academy of Management Executive* 5 (May 1991), pp. 48–60. Various leadership competencies are also discussed in R. M. Aditya, R. J. House, and S. Kerr, "Theory and Practice of Leadership: Into the New Millennium," in *Industrial and Organizational Psychology: Linking Theory with Practice,* ed. C. L. Cooper and E. A. Locke (Oxford, UK: Blackwell, 2000), pp. 130–65; H. B. Gregersen, A. J. Morrison, and J. S. Black, "Developing Leaders for the Global Frontier," *Sloan Management Review* 40 (Fall 1998), pp. 21–32; R. J. House and R. N. Aditya, "The Social Scientific Study of Leadership: Quo Vadis?" *Journal of Management* 23 (1997), pp. 409–73; R. J. House and M. L. Baetz, "Leadership: Some Empirical Generalizations and New Research Directions," *Research in Organizational Behavior* 1 (1979), pp. 341–423.

15. D. Goleman, R. Boyatzis, and A. McKee, *Primal Leaders* (Boston: Harvard Business School Press, 2002); J. George, "Emotions and Leadership: The Role of Emotional Intelligence," *Human Relations* 53 (August 2000), pp. 1027–55; D. Goleman, "What Makes a Leader?" *Harvard Business Review* 76 (November–December 1998), pp. 92–102.

16. J. D. Mayer, P. Salovey, and D. R. Caruso, "Models of Emotional Intelligence," in *Handbook of Human Intelligence,* 2nd ed., ed. R. J. Sternberg (New York: Cambridge University Press, 2000), p. 396. This definition is also recognized in C. Cherniss, "Emotional Intelligence and Organizational Effectiveness," in *The Emotionally Intelligent Workplace,* ed. C. Cherniss and D. Goleman (San Francisco: Jossey-Bass, 2001), pp. 3–12.

17. J. J. Sosik, D. Potosky, and D. I. Jung, "Adaptive Self-Regulation: Meeting Others' Expectations of Leadership and Performance," *Journal of Social Psychology* 142 (April 2002), pp. 211–32; J. A. Kolb, "The Relationship between Self-Monitoring and Leadership in Student Project Groups," *Journal*

of Business Communication 35 (April 1998), pp. 264–82; S. J. Zaccaro, R. J. Foti, and D. A. Kenny, "Self-Monitoring and Trait-Based Variance in Leadership: An Investigation of Leader Flexibility across Multiple Group Situations," *Journal of Applied Psychology* 76 (1991), pp. 308–15; S. E. Cronshaw and R. J. Ellis, "A Process Investigation of Self-Monitoring and Leader Emergence," *Small Group Research* 22 (1991), pp. 403–20.

18. D. R. May, A. Y. L. Chan, T. D. Hodges, and B. J. Avolio, "The Moral Component of Authentic Leadership," *Organizational Dynamics* 32 (August 2003), pp. 247–60. The large-scale studies are reported in J. Schettler, "Leadership in Corporate America," *Training* 39 (September 2002), pp. 66–73; C. Savoye, "Workers Say Honesty Is Best Company Policy," *Christian Science Monitor*, June 15, 2000; J. M. Kouzes and B. Z. Posner, *Credibility: How Leaders Gain and Lose It, Why People Demand It* (San Francisco: Jossey-Bass, 1993).

19. House and Aditya, "The Social Scientific Study of Leadership."

20. L. L. Paglis and S. G. Green, "Leadership Self-Efficacy and Managers' Motivation for Leading Change," *Journal of Organizational Behavior* 23 (2002), pp. 215–35.

21. R. Jacobs, "Using Human Resource Functions to Enhance Emotional Intelligence," in *The Emotionally Intelligent Workplace*, ed. C. Cherniss and D. Goleman (San Francisco: Jossey-Bass, 2001), pp. 161–63.

22. R. G. Lord and K. J. Maher, *Leadership and Information Processing: Linking Perceptions and Performance* (Cambridge, MA: Unwin Hyman, 1991).

23. W. C. Byham, "Grooming Next-Millennium Leaders," *HRMagazine* 44 (February 1999), pp. 46–50; R. Zemke and S. Zemke, "Putting Competencies to Work," *Training* 36 (January 1999), pp. 70–76.

24. "How No. 1 Big Blue Builds Leaders," *Chief Executive* (U.S.), June 2002.

25. G. A. Yukl, *Leadership in Organizations*, 3rd ed. (Englewood Cliffs, NJ: Prentice Hall, 1994), pp. 53–75; R. Likert, *New Patterns of Management* (New York: McGraw-Hill, 1961).

26. A. K. Korman, "Consideration, Initiating Structure, and Organizational Criteria—A Review," *Personnel Psychology* 19 (1966), pp. 349–62; E. A. Fleishman, "Twenty Years of Consideration and Structure," in *Current Developments in the Study of Leadership*, ed. E. A. Fleishman and J. C. Hunt (Carbondale: Southern Illinois University Press, 1973), pp. 1–40.

27. V. V. Baba, "Serendipity in Leadership: Initiating Structure and Consideration in the Classroom," *Human Relations* 42 (1989), pp. 509–25.

28. M. D. Abrashoff, "Retention through Redemption," *Harvard Business Review* 79 (February 2001), pp. 136–41.

29. P. Weissenberg and M. H. Kavanagh, "The Independence of Initiating Structure and Consideration: A Review of the Evidence," *Personnel Psychology* 25 (1972), pp. 119–30; Stogdill, *Handbook of Leadership*, Chapter 11; R. L. Kahn, "The Prediction of Productivity," *Journal of Social Issues* 12, no. 2 (1956), pp. 41–49.

30. R. R. Blake and A. A. McCanse, *Leadership Dilemmas—Grid Solutions* (Houston: Gulf Publishing Company, 1991); R. R. Blake and J. S. Mouton, "Management by Grid Principles or Situationalism: Which?" *Group and Organization Studies* 7 (1982), pp. 207–10.

31. L. L. Larson, J. G. Hunt, and R. N. Osborn, "The Great Hi–Hi Leader Behavior Myth: A Lesson from Occam's Razor," *Academy of Management Journal* 19 (1976), pp. 628–41; S. Kerr, C. A. Schriesheim, C. J. Murphy, and R. M. Stogdill, "Towards a Contingency Theory of Leadership Based upon the Consideration and Initiating Structure Literature," *Organizational Behavior and Human Performance* 12 (1974), pp. 62–82; A. K. Korman, "Consideration, Initiating Structure, and Organizational Criteria—A Review," *Personnel Psychology* 19 (1966), pp. 349–62.

32. R. Tannenbaum and W. H. Schmidt, "How to Choose a Leadership Pattern," *Harvard Business Review*, May–June 1973, pp. 162–80.

33. For a recent discussion of the contingency perspective of leadership and emotional intelligence, see D. Goleman, "Leadership that Gets Results," *Harvard Business Review* 78 (March–April 2000), pp. 78–90.

34. For a thorough study of how expectancy theory of motivation relates to leadership, see Isaac, Zerbe, and Pitt, "Leadership and Motivation: The Effective Application of Expectancy Theory."

35. M. G. Evans, "The Effects of Supervisory Behavior on the Path–Goal Relationship," *Organizational Behavior and Human Performance* 5 (1970), pp. 277–98; M. G. Evans, "Extensions of a Path–Goal Theory of Motivation," *Journal of Applied Psychology* 59 (1974), pp. 172–78; R. J. House, "A Path–Goal Theory of Leader Effectiveness," *Administrative Science Quarterly* 16 (1971), pp. 321–38.

36. R. J. House and T. R. Mitchell, "Path–Goal Theory of Leadership," *Journal of Contemporary Business*, Autumn 1974, pp. 81–97.

37. M. Fulmer, "Learning across a Living Company: The Shell Companies' Experiences," *Organizational Dynamics* 27 (Autumn 1998), pp. 61–69; R. Wageman, "Case Study: Critical Success Factors for Creating Superb Self-Managing Teams at Xerox," *Compensation and Benefits Review* 29 (September–October 1997), pp. 31–41.

38. M. E. McGill and J. W. Slocum Jr., "A Little Leadership, Please?" *Organizational Dynamics* 39 (Winter 1998), pp. 39–49; R. J. Doyle, "The Case of a Servant Leader: John F. Donnelly, Sr." in *Leadership: Understanding the Dynamics of Power and Influence in Organizations*, ed. R. P. Vecchio (Notre Dame, IN: University of Notre Dame Press, 1997), pp. 439–57.

39. R. J. House, "Path–Goal Theory of Leadership: Lessons, Legacy, and a Reformulated Theory," *Leadership Quarterly* 7 (1996), pp. 323–52.

40. J. C. Wofford and L. Z. Liska, "Path–Goal Theories of Leadership: A Meta-Analysis," *Journal of Management* 19 (1993), pp. 857–76; J. Indvik, "Path–Goal Theory of Leadership: A Meta-Analysis," *Academy of Management Proceedings* 1986, pp. 189–92.

41. R. T. Keller, "A Test of the Path–Goal Theory of Leadership with Need for Clarity as a Moderator in Research and Development Organizations," *Journal of Applied Psychology* 74 (1989), pp. 208–12.

42. Wofford and Liska, "Path–Goal

Theories of Leadership: A Meta-Analysis"; Yukl, *Leadership in Organizations* pp. 102–4; and Indvik, "Path–Goal Theory of Leadership: A Meta-Analysis."

43. C. A. Schriesheim and L. L. Neider, "Path–Goal Leadership Theory: The Long and Winding Road," *Leadership Quarterly* 7 (1996), pp. 317–21. One of the more prominent studies that found evidence against path–goal theory is H. K. Downey, J. E. Sheridan, and J. W. Slocum, "Analysis of Relationships among Leader Behavior, Subordinate Job Performance and Satisfaction: A Path–Goal Approach," *Academy of Management Journal* 18 (1975), pp. 253–62.

44. P. Hersey and K. H. Blanchard, *Management of Organizational Behavior: Utilizing Human Resources*, 5th ed. (Englewood Cliffs, NJ: Prentice Hall, 1988).

45. C. L. Graeff, "Evolution of Situational Leadership Theory: A Critical Review," *Leadership Quarterly* 8 (1997), pp. 153–70; W. Blank, J. R. Weitzel, and S. G. Green, "A Test of the Situational Leadership Theory," *Personnel Psychology* 43 (1990), pp. 579–97; R. P. Vecchio, "Situational Leadership Theory: An Examination of a Prescriptive Theory," *Journal of Applied Psychology* 72 (1987), pp. 444–51.

46. F. E. Fiedler, *A Theory of Leadership Effectiveness* (New York: McGraw-Hill, 1967); F. E. Fiedler and M. M. Chemers, *Leadership and Effective Management* (Glenview, IL: Scott, Foresman, 1974).

47. F. E. Fiedler, "Engineer the Job to Fit the Manager," *Harvard Business Review* 43, no. 5 (1965), pp. 115–22.

48. For a summary of criticisms, see Yukl, *Leadership in Organizations*, pp. 197–98.

49. N. Nicholson, *Executive Instinct* (New York: Crown, 2000).

50. P. M. Podsakoff and S. B. MacKenzie, "Kerr and Jermier's Substitutes for Leadership Model: Background, Empirical Assessment, and Suggestions for Future Research," *Leadership Quarterly* 8 (1997), pp. 117–32; P. M. Podsakoff, B. P. Niehoff, S. B. MacKenzie, and M. L. Williams, "Do Substitutes Really Substitute for Leadership? An Empirical Examination of Kerr and Jermier's Situational Leadership Model," *Organiza-*

tional Behavior and Human Decision Processes* 54 (1993), pp. 1–44.

51. This observation has also been made by C. A. Schriesheim, "Substitutes-for-Leadership Theory: Development and Basic Concepts," *Leadership Quarterly* 8 (1997), pp. 103–8.

52. D. F. Elloy and A. Randolph, "The Effect of Superleader Behavior on Autonomous Work Groups in a Government Operated Railway Service," *Public Personnel Management* 26 (Summer 1997), pp. 257–72.

53. P. Panchak, "Manufacturing in the U.S. Pays Off," *Industry Week*, December 2002, p. 23; J. Kurlantzick, "New Balance Stays a Step Ahead," *U.S. News & World Report*, July 2, 2001, p. 34; A. Bernstein, "Low-Skilled Jobs: Do They Have to Move?" *Business Week*, February 26, 2001, p. 92; G. Gatlin, "Firm Boasts of New Balance of Power," *Boston Herald*, January 24, 2001, p. 27.

54. M. L. Loughry, "Coworkers Are Watching: Performance Implications of Peer Monitoring," *Academy of Management Proceedings*, 2002, pp. O1–O6.

55. C. Manz and H. Sims, *Superleadership; Getting to the Top by Motivating Others* (San Francisco: Berkley Publishing, 1990).

56. C. P. Neck and C. C. Manz, "Thought Self-Leadership: The Impact of Mental Strategies Training on Employee Cognition, Behavior, and Affect," *Journal of Organizational Behavior* 17 (1996), pp. 445–67.

57. G. Chellam, "Haier Story a Smash-Hit," *New Zealand Herald*, September 20, 2003; "Emerging Market Corporates," *The Banker*, July 1, 2003; D. J. Lynch, "CEO Pushes China's Haier as Global Brand," *USA Today*, January 3, 2003, p. 1B.

58. D. Magee, *Turnaround: How Carlos Ghosn Rescued Nissan* (New York: HarperCollins, 2003); B. Littlely, "Everybody Loves Sir Richard," *The Advertiser* (Adelaide, Australia), May 16, 2003; G. Anders, *Perfect Enough: Carly Fiorina and the Reinvention of Hewlett-Packard* (New York: Portfolio, 2003); "The Greatest Briton in Management and Leadership," *Personnel Today*, February 18, 2003, p. 20; K. Freiberg and J. Freiberg, *Nuts! Southwest Airlines' Crazy Recipe for Business*

and Personal Success* (New York: Bantam Doubleday Dell, 1996).

59. B. J. Avolio and F. J. Yammarino (eds.), *Transformational and Charismatic Leadership: The Road Ahead* (Greenwich, CT: JAI Press, 2002); B. M. Bass, *Transformational Leadership: Industrial, Military, and Educational Impact* (Hillsdale, NJ: Lawrence Erlbaum Associates, 1998); J. Seltzer and B. M. Bass, "Transformational Leadership: Beyond Initiation and Consideration," *Journal of Management* 16 (1990), pp. 693–703; J. M. Burns, *Leadership* (New York: Harper & Row, 1978).

60. V. L. Goodwin, J. C. Wofford, and J. L. Whittington, "A Theoretical and Empirical Extension to the Transformational Leadership Construct," *Journal of Organizational Behavior* 22 (November 2001), pp. 759–74.

61. B. J. Avolio and B. M. Bass, "Transformational Leadership, Charisma, and Beyond," in *Emerging Leadership Vistas*, ed J. G. Hunt, H. P. Dachler, B. R. Baliga, and C. A. Schriesheim (Lexington, MA: Lexington Books, 1988), pp. 29–49.

62. R. H. G. Field, "Leadership Defined: Web Images Reveal the Differences between Leadership and Management," Paper presented at the Administrative Sciences Association of Canada Annual Conference, Organizational Behavior Division, Winnipeg, Manitoba, May 2002; J. Kotter, *A Force for Change* (Cambridge, MA: Harvard Business School Press, 1990); W. Bennis and B. Nanus, *Leaders: The Strategies for Taking Charge* (New York: Harper & Row, 1985), p. 21; A. Zaleznik, "Managers and Leaders: Are They Different?" *Harvard Business Review* 55, no. 5 (1977), pp. 67–78.

63. Both transformational and transactional leadership improve work unit performance. See B. M. Bass, B. J. Avolio, D. I. Jung, and Y. Berson, "Predicting Unit Performance by Assessing Transformational and Transactional Leadership," *Journal of Applied Psychology* 88 (April 2003), pp. 207–18.

64. For a discussion on the tendency to slide from transformational to transactional leadership, see W. Bennis, *An Invented Life: Reflections on Leadership and Change* (Reading, MA.: Addison-Wesley, 1993).

65. J. A. Conger, "Charismatic and Transformational Leadership in Organizations: An Insider's Perspective on These Developing Streams of Research," *Leadership Quarterly* 10 (Summer 1999), pp. 145–79; R. J. House, "A 1976 Theory of Charismatic Leadership," *in Leadership: The Cutting Edge*, ed. J. G. Hunt and L. L. Larson (Carbondale: Southern Illinois University Press, 1977), pp. 189–207.

66. Y. A. Nur, "Charisma and Managerial Leadership: The Gift that Never Was," *Business Horizons* 41 (July 1998), pp. 19–26; J. E. Barbuto Jr., "Taking the Charisma Out of Transformational Leadership," *Journal of Social Behavior and Personality* 12 (September 1997), pp. 689–97.

67. R. Khurana, *Searching for a Corporate Savior: The Irrational Quest for Charismatic CEOs* (Princeton, NJ: Princeton University Press, 2002); R. E. De Vries, R. A. Roe, and T. C. B. Taillieu, "On Charisma and Need for Leadership," *European Journal of Work and Organizational Psychology* 8 (1999), pp. 109–33.

68. K. Brooker and J. Schlosser, "The Un-CEO," *Fortune*, September 16, 2002, pp. 88ff.

69. L. Sooklal, "The Leader as a Broker of Dreams," *Organizational Studies*, 1989, pp. 833–55.

70. J. R. Sparks and J. A. Schenk, "Explaining the Effects of Transformational Leadership: An Investigation of the Effects of Higher-Order Motives in Multilevel Marketing Organizations," *Journal of Organizational Behavior*, 22 (2001), pp. 849–69; I. M. Levin, "Vision Revisited," *Journal of Applied Behavioral Science* 36 (March 2000), pp. 91–107; J. M. Stewart, "Future State Visioning—A Powerful Leadership Process," *Long Range Planning* 26 (December 1993), pp. 89–98; Bennis and Nanus, *Leaders*, pp. 27–33, 89.

71. T. J. Peters, "Symbols, Patterns, and Settings: An Optimistic Case for Getting Things Done," *Organizational Dynamics* 7 (Autumn 1978), pp. 2–23.

72. I. R. Baum, E. A. Locke, and S. A. Kirkpatrick, "A Longitudinal Study of the Relation of Vision and Vision Communication to Venture Growth in Entrepreneurial Firms," *Journal of Applied Psychology* 83 (1998), pp. 43–54; S. A. Kirkpatrick and E. A. Locke, "Direct and Indirect Effects of Three Core Charismatic Leadership Components on Performance and Attitudes," *Journal of Applied Psychology* 81 (1996), pp. 36–51.

73. G. T. Fairhurst and R. A. Sarr, *The Art of Framing: Managing the Language of Leadership* (San Francisco: Jossey-Bass, 1996); J. A. Conger, "Inspiring Others: The Language of Leadership," *Academy of Management Executive* 5 (February 1991), pp. 31–45.

74. G. Johnson, "CEOs Who Get It: The Dow Chemcial Co.—Michael D. Parker," *Training* 39 (November 2002), p. 27.

75. Fairhurst and Sarr, *The Art of Framing*, Chapter 5; J. Pfeffer, "Management as Symbolic Action: The Creation and Maintenance of Organizational Paradigms," *Research in Organizational Behavior* 3 (1981), pp. 1–52.

76. L. Black, "Hamburger Diplomacy," *Report on Business Magazine* 5 (August 1988), pp. 30–36; S. Franklin, *The Heroes: A Saga of Canadian Inspiration* (Toronto: McClelland and Stewart, 1967), p. 53.

77. McGill and Slocum, "A Little Leadership, Please?"; N. H. Snyder and M. Graves, "Leadership and Vision," *Business Horizons* 37 (January 1994), pp. 1–7; D. E. Berlew, "Leadership and Organizational Excitement," in *Organizational Psychology: A Book of Readings*, ed. D. A. Kolb, I. M. Rubin, and J. M. McIntyre (Englewood Cliffs, NJ: Prentice Hall, 1974).

78. "Leaders Should 'Walk the Talk': Narayana Murthy," *Indian Express*, September 24, 2003.

79. "Underpaid Women CEOs Say Pay Meets Standards," *Minneapolis St. Paul Business Journal*, July 18, 2003, p. 23; N. St. Anthony, "CEO Led Synovis Back from Brink," *Minneapolis Star Tribune*, February 16, 2003, p. D1; "Most Influential Women & Women to Watch: Karen Gilles Larson," *Minneapolis St. Paul Business Journal*, July 26, 2002, p. S31.

80. E. M. Whitener, S. E. Brodt, M. A. Korsgaard, and J. M. Werner, "Managers as Initiators of Trust: An Exchange Relationship Framework for Understanding Managerial Trustworthy Behavior," *Academy of Management Review* 23 (July 1998), pp. 513–30;

Bennis and Nanus, *Leaders*, pp. 43–55; Kouzes and Posner, *Credibility: How Leaders Gain and Lose It, Why People Demand It.*

81. J. J. Sosik, S. S. Kahai, and B. J. Avolio, "Transformational Leadership and Dimensions of Creativity: Motivating Idea Generation in Computer-Mediated Groups," *Creativity Research Journal* 11 (1998), pp. 111–21; P. Bycio, R. D. Hackett, and J. S. Allen, "Further Assessments of Bass's (1985) Conceptualization of Transactional and Transformational Leadership," *Journal of Applied Psychology* 80 (1995), pp. 468–78; W. L. Koh, R. M. Steers, and J. R. Terborg, "The Effects of Transformational Leadership on Teacher Attitudes and Student Performance in Singapore," *Journal of Organizational Behavior* 16 (1995), pp. 319–33; Howell and Avolio, "Transformational Leadership, Transactional Leadership, Locus of Control, and Support for Innovation."

82. J. Barling, T. Weber, and E. K. Kelloway, "Effects of Transformational Leadership Training on Attitudinal and Financial Outcomes: A Field Experiment," *Journal of Applied Psychology* 81 (1996), pp. 827–32.

83. A. Bryman, "Leadership in Organizations," in *Handbook of Organization Studies*, ed. S. R. Clegg, C. Hardy, and W. R. Nord (Thousand Oaks, CA: Sage, 1996), pp. 276–92.

84. Egri and Herman, "Leadership in the North American Environmental Sector"; B. S. Pawar and K. K. Eastman, "The Nature and Implications of Contextual Influences on Transformational Leadership: A Conceptual Examination," *Academy of Management Review* 22 (1997), pp. 80–109.

85. K. Boehnke, A. C. DiStefano, J. J. DiStefano, and N. Bontis, "Leadership for Extraordinary Performance," *Business Quarterly* 61 (Summer 1997), pp. 56–63.

86. For a review of this research, see House and Aditya, "The Social Scientific Study of Leadership: Quo Vadis?"

87. R. J. Hall and R. G. Lord, "Multilevel Information Processing Explanations of Followers' Leadership Perceptions," *Leadership Quarterly* 6 (1995), pp. 265–87; R. Ayman, "Leadership Perception: The Role of Gender and Culture," in *Leadership Theory and Re-*

search: Perspectives and Directions, ed. M. M. Chemers and R. Ayman (San Diego: Academic Press, 1993), pp. 137–66; J. R. Meindl, "On Leadership: An Alternative to the Conventional Wisdom," Research in Organizational Behavior 12 (1990), pp. 159–203.

88. G. R. Salancik and J. R. Meindl, "Corporate Attributions as Strategic Illusions of Management Control," Administrative Science Quarterly 29 (1984), pp. 238–54; J. M. Tolliver, "Leadership and Attribution of Cause: A Modification and Extension of Current Theory," Proceedings of the Annual ASAC Conference, Organizational Behavior Division 4, pt. 5 (1983), pp. 182–91.

89. L. M. Ah Chong and D. C. Thomas, "Leadership Perceptions in Cross-Cultural Context: Pakeha and Pacific Islanders in New Zealand," Leadership Quarterly 8 (1997), 275–93; J. L. Nye and D. R. Forsyth, "The Effects of Prototype-Based Biases on Leadership Appraisals: A Test of Leadership Categorization Theory," Small Group Research 22 (1991), pp. 360–79; S. F. Cronshaw and R. G. Lord, "Effects of Categorization, Attribution, and Encoding Processes on Leadership Perceptions," Journal of Applied Psychology 72 (1987), pp. 97–106.

90. Meindl, "On Leadership: An Alternative to the Conventional Wisdom," p. 163.

91. J. Pfeffer, "The Ambiguity of Leadership," Academy of Management Review 2 (1977), pp. 102–12; Yukl, Leadership in Organizations, pp. 265–67.

92. Cronshaw and Lord, "Effects of Categorization, Attribution, and Encoding Processes on Leadership Perceptions," pp. 104–5.

93. Six of the Project GLOBE clusters are described in a special issue of the Journal of World Business 37 (2000). For an overview of Project GLOBE, see House, Javidan, Hanges, and Dorfman, "Understanding Cultures and Implicit Leadership Theories across the Globe: An Introduction to Project GLOBE"; House, Javidan, and Dorfman, "Project GLOBE: An Introduction."

94. J. C. Jesiuno, "Latin Europe Cluster: From South to North," Journal of World Business 37 (2002), p. 88. Another GLOBE study of Iranian managers also reported that charismatic visionary stands out as a primary leadership dimension. See A. Dastmalchian, M. Javidan, and K. Alam, "Effective Leadership and Culture in Iran: An Empirical Study," Applied Psychology: An International Review 50 (2001), pp. 532–58.

95. E. Szabo et al., "The Europe Cluster: Where Employees Have a Voice," Journal of World Business 37 (2002), pp. 55–68; F. C. Brodbeck et al., "Cultural Variation of Leadership Prototypes across 22 European Countries," Journal of Occupational and Organizational Psychology 73 (2000), pp. 1–29; D. N. Den Hartog et al., "Culture Specific and Cross-Culturall Generalizable Implicit Leadership Theories: Are Attributes of Charismatic/Transformational Leadership Universally Endorsed?" Leadership Quarterly 10 (1999), pp. 219–56. The Mexican study is reported in C. E. Nicholls, H. W. Lane, and M. B. Brechu, "Taking Self-Managed Teams to Mexico," Academy of Management Executive 13 (August 1999), pp. 15–25.

96. N. Wood, "Venus Rules," Incentive 172 (February 1998), pp. 22–27; S. H. Appelbaum and B. T. Shapiro, "Why Can't Men Lead Like Women?" Leadership and Organization Development Journal 14 (1993), pp. 28–34; J. B. Rosener, "Ways Women Lead," Harvard Business Review 68 (November–December 1990), pp. 119–25.

97. G. N. Powell, "One More Time: Do Female and Male Managers Differ?" Academy of Management Executive 4 (August 1990), pp. 68–75; G. H. Dobbins and S. J. Platts, "Sex Differences in Leadership: How Real Are They?" Academy of Management Review 11 (1986), pp. 118–27. In contrast with these studies, one review cites an unpublished study reporting that women demonstrate more people-oriented leadership and are rated higher than men on their leadership. See M-T. Claes, "Women, Men and Management Styles," International Labour Review 138 (1999), pp. 431–46.

98. A. H. Eagly and B. T. Johnson, "Gender and Leadership Style: A Meta-Analysis," Psychological Bulletin 108 (1990), pp. 233–56.

99. N. Z. Stelter, "Gender Differences in Leadership: Current Social Issues and Future Organizational Implications," Journal of Leadership Studies 8 (2002), pp. 88–99; J. G. Oakley, "Gender-Based Barriers to Senior Management Positions: Understanding the Scarcity of Female CEOs" Journal of Business Ethics 27 (2000), pp. 821ff; A. H. Eagly, S. J. Karau, and M. G. Makhijani, "Gender and the Effectiveness of Leaders: A Meta-Analysis," Psychological Bulletin 117 (1995), pp. 125–45; M. E. Heilman and C. J. Block, "Sex Stereotypes: Do They Influence Perceptions of Managers?" Journal of Social Behavior and Personality 10 (1995), pp. 237–52; A. H. Eagly, M. G. Makhijani, and B. G. Klonsky, "Gender and the Evaluation of Leaders: A Meta-Analysis," Psychological Bulletin 111 (1992), pp. 3–22.

100. A. H. Eagly, M. C. Johannesen-Schmidt, and M. L. van Engen, "Transformational, Transactional, and Laissez-Faire Leadership Styles: A Meta-Analysis Comparing Women and Men," Psychological Bulletin 129 (July 2003), pp. 569–91; M. Sappenfield, "Women, It Seems, Are Better Bosses," Christian Science Monitor, January 16, 2001. R. Sharpe, "As Leaders, Women Rule," Business Week, November 20, 2000; C. D'Nan Bass, "Women May Outdo Men as Sales Managers, Study Says," Chicago Tribune, January 26, 2000.

CHAPTER 15

1. C. Glover and S. Smethurst, "Creative License," People Management, March 20, 2003, pp. 30–33; L. Harrison, "We're All the Boss," Time, April 8, 2002, p. Y10; "The Firm that Lets Staff Breathe," Sunday Times (London), March 24, 2002; A. Brown, "Satisfaction All in a Day's Work for Top 3," Evening News (Edinburgh, Scotland), March 23, 2002, p. 13; L. A. Pappas, "W. L. Gore: A Reputation for Innovation," Wilmington (DE) News Journal, March 17, 2002, p. J55; D. Anfuso, "Core Values Shape W. L. Gore & Associates' Innovative Culture," Workforce 78 (March 1999), pp. 48–53.

2. S. Ranson, R. Hinings, and R. Greenwood, "The Structuring of Organizational Structure," Administrative Science Quarterly 25 (1980), pp. 1–14.

3. J-E. Johanson, "Intraorganizational Influence," Management Communication Quarterly 13 (February 2000), pp. 393–435.

4. "Ford Motor Company Announces Consumer-Focused Organization for the 21st Century," *Auto Channel* (online), October 18, 1999.

5. H. Mintzberg, *The Structuring of Organizations* (Englewood Cliffs, NJ: Prentice Hall, 1979), pp. 2–3.

6. H. Fayol, *General and Industrial Management,* trans. C. Storrs (London: Pitman, 1949); E. E. Lawler III, *Motivation in Work Organizations* (Monterey, CA: Brooks/Cole, 1973), Chapter 7; M. A. Campion, "Ability Requirement Implications of Job Design: An Interdisciplinary Perspective," *Personnel Psychology* 42 (1989), pp. 1–24.

7. A. N. Maira, "Connecting across Boundaries: The Fluid-Network Organization," *Prism,* First Quarter 1998, pp. 23–26; D. A. Nadler and M. L. Tushman, *Competing by Design: The Power of Organizational Architecture* (New York: Oxford University Press, 1997), Chapter 6; Mintzberg, *The Structuring of Organizations,* pp. 2–8.

8. C. Downs, P. Clampitt, and A. L. Pfeiffer, "Communication and Organizational Outcomes," in *Handbook of Organizational Communication,* ed. G. Goldhaber and G. Barnett (Norwood, NJ: Ablex, 1988), pp. 171–211; H. C. Jain, "Supervisory Communication and Performance in Urban Hospitals," *Journal of Communication* 23 (1973), pp. 103–17.

9. V. L. Shalin and G. V. Prabhu, "A Cognitive Perspective on Manual Assembly," *Ergonomics* 39 (1996), pp. 108–27; I. Nonaka and H. Takeuchi, *The Knowledge-Creating Company* (New York: Oxford University Press, 1995).

10. A. L. Patti, J. P. Gilbert, and S. Hartman, "Physical Co-location and the Success of New Product Development Projects," *Engineering Management Journal* 9 (September 1997), pp. 31–37; M. L. Swink, J. C. Sandvig, and V. A. Mabert, "Customizing Concurrent Engineering Processes: Five Case Studies," *Journal of Product Innovation Management* 13 (1996), pp. 229–44; W. I. Zangwill, *Lightning Strategies for Innovation: How the World's Best Firms Create New Products* (New York: Lexington, 1993).

11. For recent discussion of the role of brand manager at Procter & Gamble, see C. Peale, "Branded for Success," *Cincinnati Enquirer,* May 20, 2001, p. A1. Details about how to design integrator roles in organizational structures are presented in J. R. Galbraith, *Designing Organizations* (San Francisco: Jossey-Bass, 2002), pp. 66–72.

12. Fayol's work is summarized in J. B. Miner, *Theories of Organizational Structure and Process* (Chicago: Dryden, 1982), pp. 358–66.

13. J. A. Conger, *Winning 'em Over* (New York: Simon & Shuster, 1998), Appendix A.

14. Y-M. Hsieh and A. Tien-Hsieh, "Enhancement of Service Quality with Job Standardisation," *Service Industries Journal* 21 (July 2001), pp. 147–66.

15. B. Batz, "ORBIS Flying Hospital a Site for Sore Eyes," *Dayton (OH) Daily News,* July 17, 2003; A. Krisnakumar, "A Hospital on Wings," *Frontline* (India), November 23, 2002.

16. J. H. Sheridan, "Lessons from the Best," *Industry Week,* February 20, 1995, pp. 13–22.

17. J. P. Starr, "Reintroducing Alcoa to Economic Reality," in *The Infinite Resource,* ed. W. E. Halal (San Francisco: Jossey-Bass, 1998), pp. 57–67.

18. C. Sittenfeld, "The Factory Powered by People" *National Post,* July 10, 1999, p. D11. This point is also discussed in J. Pfeffer, "Seven Practices of Successful Organizations," *California Management Review* 40 (1998), pp. 96–124.

19. D. D. Van Fleet and A. G. Bedeian, "A History of the Span of Management," *Academy of Management Review* 2 (1977), pp. 356–72; Mintzberg, *The Structuring of Organizations,* Chapter 8; D. Robey, *Designing Organizations,* 3rd ed. (Homewood, IL: Irwin, 1991), pp. 255–59.

20. "BASF Culling Saves (GBP) 4M," *Personnel Today,* February 19, 2002, p. 3.

21. M. D. Parker and G. Johnson. "CEOs Who Get It: The Dow Chemical Co." *Training,* November 2002; S. Ellis, "A New Role for the Post Office: An Investigation into Issues behind Strategic Change at Royal Mail," *Total Quality Management* 9 (May 1998), pp. 223–34.

22. T. Peters, *Thriving on Chaos* (New York: Knopf, 1987), p. 359.

23. L. A. Bossidy, "Reality-Based Leadership," *Executive Speeches* 13 (August–September 1998), pp. 10–15.

24. Q. N. Huy, "In Praise of Middle Managers," *Harvard Business Review* 79 (September 2001), pp. 72–79; L. Donaldson and F. G. Hilmer, "Management Redeemed: The Case against Fads that Harm Management," *Organizational Dynamics* 26 (Spring 1998), pp. 6–20.

25. Mintzberg, *The Structuring of Organizations,* p. 136.

26. S. Lohr and J. Markoff, "You Call This a Midlife Crisis?" *New York Times,* August 31, 2003.

27. M. M. Hamilton, "AES's New Power Center," *Washington Post,* June 2, 2003, p. E1. For a description of AES Corporation's highly decentralized structure, see A. Markels, "Power to the People," *Fast Company* 13 (February–March 1998), pp. 155–65.

28. P. Brabeck, "The Business Case against Revolution: An Interview with Nestlé's Peter Brabeck," *Harvard Business Review* 79 (February 2001), p. 112.

29. Mintzberg, *The Structuring of Organizations,* Chapter 5.

30. B. Victor and A. C. Boynton, *Invented Here* (Boston: Harvard Business School Press, 1998), Chapter 2; M. Hamstra, "McD Speeds Up Drive-Thru with Beefed Up Operations," *Nation's Restaurant News,* April 6, 1998, p. 3; G. Morgan, *Creative Organization Theory: A Resourcebook* (Newburg Park, CA: Sage, 1989), pp. 271–73; K. Deveny, "Bag Those Fries, Squirt that Ketchup, Fry that Fish," *Business Week,* October 13, 1986, p. 86.

31. T. Burns and G. Stalker, *The Management of Innovation* (London: Tavistock, 1961).

32. A. Lam, "Tacit Knowledge, Organizational Learning and Societal Institutions: An Integrated Framework," *Organization Studies* 21 (May 2000), pp. 487–513.

33. Mintzberg, *The Structuring of Organizations,* p. 106.

34. Mintzberg, *The Structuring of Organizations,* Chapter 17.

35. T. Bradner, "Potato Chip Company Starts Small to Ensure Its Success," *Alaska Journal of Commerce,* August 1, 2003.

36. Galbraith, *Designing Organizations,* pp. 23–25; Robey, *Designing Organizations,* pp. 186–89.

37. E. E. Lawler III, *Rewarding Excellence: Pay Strategies for the New Economy* (San Francisco: Jossey-Bass, 2000), pp. 31–34.

38. S. Bunyamanee, "Philips Makes Thailand Financial Hub," *Bangkok Post;* "Nortel Plans 3,500 More Job Cuts," *Canadian Press,* May 29, 2002; M. Hamstra, "McD's to Decentralize US Management Team," *Nation's Restaurant News,* June 2, 1997, p. 1.

39. M. Goold and A. Campbell, "Do You Have a Well-Designed Organization?" *Harvard Business Review* 80 (March 2002), pp. 117–24.

40. T. H. Davenport, J. G. Harris, and A. K. Kohli, "How Do They Know Their Customers So Well?" *Sloan Management Review* 42 (Winter 2001), pp. 63–73. Also see J. R. Galbraith, "Organizing to Deliver Solutions," *Organizational Dynamics* 31 (2002), pp. 194–207; C. Homburg, J. P. Workman Jr., and O. Jensen, "Fundamental Changes in Marketing Organization: The Movement toward a COrganizational Structure," *Academy of Marketing Science Journal* 28 (Fall 2000), pp. 459–78.

41. "Axa Executive Says Global Insurers Must Pool Local Expertise," *Best's Insurance News,* May 1, 2001. The evolution of organizational structures in global organizations is further discussed in J. R. Galbraith, "Structuring Global Organizations," in *Tomorrow's Organization,* ed. S. A. Mohrman, J. R. Galbraith, E. E. Lawler III, and Associates (San Francisco: Jossey-Bass, 1998), pp. 103–29.

42. Robey, *Designing Organizations,* pp. 191–97; A. G. Bedeian and R. F. Zammuto, *Organizations: Theory and Design* (Hinsdale, IL: Dryden, 1991), pp. 162–68.

43. "Tearing Down Silos to Build a Corporate-Wide Communication Plan," *PR News,* July 10, 2000.

44. R. Waters, "SAP America Faces Up to Challenge of Change," *Financial Times* (London), June 13, 2001.

45. J. Belanger, C. Berggren, T. Bjorkman, and C. Kohler (eds.), *Being Local Worldwide: ABB and the Challenge of Global Management* (Ithaca, NY: Cornell University Press, 1999); M. F. R. Kets de Vries, "Charisma in Action: The Transformational Abilities of Virgin's Richard Branson and ABB's Percy Barnevik," *Organizational Dynamics* 26 (Winter 1998), pp. 6–21; Nadler and Tushman, *Competing by Design,* Chapter 6.

46. M. Goold and A. Campbell, "Structured Networks: Towards the Well-Designed Matrix," *Long Range Planning,* 2003 (in press).

47. R. C. Ford and W. A. Randolph, "Cross-Functional Structures: A Review and Integration of Matrix Organization and Project Management," *Journal of Management* 18 (1992), pp. 267–94.

48. H. F. Kolodny, "Managing in a Matrix," *Business Horizons,* March–April 1981, pp. 17–24; S. M. Davis and P. R. Lawrence, *Matrix* (Reading, MA: Addison-Wesley, 1977).

49. K. Knight, "Matrix Organization: A Review," *Journal of Management Studies,* May 1976, pp. 111–30.

50. C. Herkströter, "Royal Dutch/Shell: Rewriting the Contracts," in *Straight from the CEO,* ed. G. W. Dauphinais and C. Price (New York: Simon & Schuster, 1998), pp. 86–93; G. Calabrese, "Communication and Co-operation in Product Development: A Case Study of a European Car Producer," *R & D Management* 27 (July 1997), pp. 239–52; J. L. Brown and N. M. Agnew, "The Balance of Power in a Matrix Structure," *Business Horizons,* November–December 1982, pp. 51–54.

51. C. Campbell-Hunt et al., *World Famous in New Zealand* (Auckland: University of Auckland Press, 2001), p. 89.

52. J. R. Galbraith, *Competing with Flexible Lateral Organizations* (Boston: Addison-Wesley, 1994).

53. R. Bettis and M. Hitt, "The New Competitive Landscape," *Strategic Management Journal* 16 (1995), pp. 7–19; J. R. Galbraith, E. E. Lawler III, & Associates, *Organizing for the Future: The New Logic for Managing Complex Organizations* (San Francisco: Jossey-Bass, 1993).

54. P. C. Ensign, "Interdependence, Coordination, and Structure in Complex Organizations: Implications for Organization Design," *Mid-Atlantic Journal of Business* 34 (March 1998), pp. 5–22.

55. L. Y. Chan and B. E. Lynn, "Operating in Turbulent Times: How Ontario's Hospitals Are Meeting the Current Funding Crisis," *Health Care Management Review* 23 (June 1998), pp. 7–18; M. M. Fanning, "A Circular Organization Chart Promotes a Hospital-Wide Focus on Teams," *Hospital & Health Services Administration* 42 (June 1997), pp. 243–54.

56. R. Cross, "Looking before You Leap: Assessing the Jump to Teams in Knowledge-Based Work," *Business Horizons,* September, 2000; W. F. Joyce, V. E. McGee, and J. W Slocum Jr., "Designing Lateral Organizations: An Analysis of the Benefits, Costs, and Enablers of Nonhierarchical Organizational Forms," *Decision Sciences* 28 (Winter 1997), pp. 1–25.

57. R. Hacki and J. Lighton, "The Future of the Networked Company," *Business Review Weekly,* August 30, 2001, p. 58; A. M. Porter, "The Virtual Corporation: Where Is It?" *Purchasing,* March 23, 2000, pp. 40–48; J. A. Byrne, "The Corporation of the Future," *Business Week,* August 31, 1998, pp. 102–4.

58. J. R. Galbraith, "Designing the Networked Organization," in *Tomorrow's Organization,* ed. Mohrman, Galbraith, Lawler, and Associates, pp. 102; C. Baldwin and K. Clark, "Managing in an Age of Modularity," *Harvard Business Review* 75 (September–October 1997), pp. 84–93; R. E. Miles and C. C. Snow, "The New Network Firm: A Spherical Structure Built on a Human Investment Philosophy," *Organizational Dynamics* 23, no. 4 (1995), pp. 5–18; W. Powell, "Neither Market nor Hierarchy: Network Forms of Organization." *Research in Organizational Behavior* 12 (1990), pp. 295–336.

59 . R. Hacki and J. Lighton, "The Future of the Networked Company," *McKinsey Quarterly* 3 (2001), pp. 26–39; J. Hagel III and M. Singer, "Unbundling the Corporation," *McKinsey Quarterly* 3 (2000), pp. 148–61; T. W. Malone and R. J. Laubacher, "The Dawn of the E-lance Economy," *Harvard Business Review* 76 (September–October 1998), pp. 144–52.

60. J. Vardy, "Mitel Outsources Manufacturing to New Company," *National Post,* September 6, 2001; J. Hagel III and M. Singer, "Unbundling the Corporation," *Harvard Business Review* 77

(March–April 1999), pp. 133–41. For a discussion of core competencies, see G. Hamel and C. K. Prahalad, *Competing for the Future* (Boston: Harvard Business School Press, 1994), Chapter 10.

61. M. A. Schilling and H. K. Steensma, "The Use of Modular Organizational Forms: An Industry-Level Analysis," *Academy of Management Journal* 44 (December 2001), pp. 1149–68.

62. L. Fried, *Managing Information Technology in Turbulent Times* (New York: John Wiley and Sons, 1995); W. H. Davidow and M. S. Malone, *The Virtual Corporation* (New York: HarperBusiness, 1992).

63. C. Taylor, "Agency Teams Balancing in an Ever-Changing Media World," *Media Week*, June 1, 2001, p. 20.

64. G. Morgan, *Imagin-I-Zation: New Mindsets for Seeing, Organizing and Managing* (Thousand Oaks, CA: Sage, 1997); G. Morgan, *Images of Organization*, 2nd ed. (Newbury Park, CA: Sage, 1996).

65. K. Ferdows, "New World Manufacturing Order," *Industrial Engineer* 35 (February 2003), pp. 28–33.

66. C. Meyer and S. Davis, *Blur: The Speed of Change in the Connected Economy* (Reading, MA: Addison-Wesley, 1998); P. M. J. Christie and R. Levary, "Virtual Corporations: Recipe for Success," *Industrial Management* 40 (July 1998), pp. 7–11; H. Chesbrough and D. J. Teece, "When Is Virtual Virtuous? Organizing for Innovation," *Harvard Business Review*, January–February 1996, pp. 65–73.

67. Mintzberg, *The Structuring of Organizations*, Chapter 13; D. S. Pugh and C. R. Hinings (eds.), *Organizational Structure: Extensions and Replications* (Farnborough, UK: Lexington Books, 1976).

68. T. A. Stewart, *Intellectual Capital: The New Wealth of Organizations* (New York: Currency/Doubleday, 1997), Chapter 10.

69. Robey, *Designing Organizations*, p. 102.

70. C. Perrow, "A Framework for the Comparative Analysis of Organizations," *American Sociological Review* 32 (1967), pp. 194–208.

71. Mintzberg, *The Structuring of Organizations*, Chapter 15.

72. Burns and Stalker, *The Management of Innovation*; P. R. Lawrence and J. W. Lorsch, *Organization and Environment* (Homewood, IL: Irwin, 1967); D. Miller and P. H. Friesen, *Organizations: A Quantum View* (Englewood Cliffs, NJ: Prentice Hall, 1984), pp. 197–98.

73. T. Lester, "Country Managers Come Back In from the Cold," *Financial Times* (London), September 25, 2002, p. 18; J. F. Peltz, "Cola Wars," *Hamilton Spectator*, April 13, 2002, p. B1; B. McKay, "Coke Hunts for Talent to Reestablish Its Marketing Might," *Wall Street Journal*, March 6, 2002, p. B4; P. O'Kane, "Coca Cola's Canny Man," *The Herald* (Glasgow), June 18, 2000, p. 3.

74. Mintzberg, *The Structuring of Organizations*, p. 282.

75. R. H. Kilmann, *Beyond the Quick Fix* (San Francisco: Jossey-Bass, 1984), p. 38.

76. J. Child, "Organizational Structure, Environment, and Performance: The Role of Strategic Choice," *Sociology* 6 (1972), pp. 2–22.

77. A. D. Chandler, *Strategy and Structure* (Cambridge, MA: MIT Press, 1962).

78. M. E. Porter, *Competitive Strategy* (New York: Free Press, 1980).

79. D. Miller, "Configurations of Strategy and Structure," *Strategic Management Journal* 7 (1986), pp. 233–50.

CHAPTER 16

1. T. Wanless, "Let's Hear It for Workers!" *Vancouver Province*, June 13, 2002; D. Brown, "Good Ideas Going Wrong," *Canadian HR Reporter*, May 6, 2002, p. 2; D. Mowat, "The VanCity Difference—A Case for the Triple Bottom Line Approach to Business," *Corporate Environmental Strategy* 9 (February 2002), pp. 24–29; D. Grigg and J. Newman, "Corporate Values Can Help Leaders, Workers," *Vancouver Sun*, November 24, 2001, p. E2.

2. T. O. Davenport, "The Integration Challenge; Managing Corporate Mergers," *Management Review* 87 (January 1998), pp. 25–28; E. H. Schein, "What Is Culture?" in *Reframing Organizational Culture*, ed. P. J. Frost, L. F.

Moore, M. R. Louis, C. C. Lundberg, and J. Martin (Beverly Hills, CA: Sage, 1991), pp. 243–53; A. Williams, P. Dobson, and M. Walters, *Changing Culture: New Organizational Approaches* (London: Institute of Personnel Management, 1989).

3. A. Sagie and D. Elizur, "Work Values: A Theoretical Overview and a Model of Their Effects," *Journal of Organizational Behavior* 17 (1996), pp. 503–14; W. H. Schmidt and B. Z. Posner, *Managerial Values in Perspective* (New York: American Management Association, 1983).

4. B. M. Meglino and E. C. Ravlin, "Individual Values in Organizations: Concepts, Controversies, and Research," *Journal of Management* 24 (May 1998), pp. 351–89; C. Argyris and D. A. Schön, *Organizational Learning: A Theory of Action Perspective* (Reading, MA: Addison-Wesley, 1978).

5. "New-Age Banks Bet on Variable Pay Plan," *Business Line* (India), September 22, 2003; "Golden Handshake, the ICICI Bank Way," *Financial Express* (India), July 6, 2003.

6. B. Daly, "Private Lives," *Daily Deal*, July 21, 2003; F. Daniel, "SAS Work-Life Program Creates Winning Balance," *Winston-Salem (NC) Journal*, May 10, 2003, p. D1; M. Fan, "Cary, N.C., Software Firm Posts Steady Growth without IPO," *San Jose Mercury News*, July 29, 2001.

7. A. D'Innocenzio, "Wal-Mart's Town Becomes New Address for Corporate America," *Associated Press*, September 19, 2003; J. Useem, "One Nation under Wal-Mart," *Fortune*, March 3, 2003, pp. 65–78.

8. "Job Satisfaction Means More than Pay," *Business Day* (South Africa), December 6, 2000, p. 14; S. Planting, "Mirror, Mirror . . . Here Are the Fairest of Them All," *Financial Mail* (South Africa), November 24, 2000, p. 48.

9. S. Sackmann, "Culture and Subcultures: An Analysis of Organizational Knowledge," *Administrative Science Quarterly* 37 (1992), pp. 140–61; J. Martin and C. Siehl, "Organizational Culture and Counterculture: An Uneasy Symbiosis," *Organizational Dynamics*, Autumn 1983, pp. 52–64; J. S. Ott, *The Organizational Culture Perspective* (Pacific Grove, CA: Brooks/Cole, 1989), pp. 45–47; T. E. Deal and

A. A. Kennedy, *Corporate Cultures* (Reading, MA: Addison-Wesley, 1982), pp. 138–39.

10. A. Boisnier and J. Chatman, "The Role of Subcultures in Agile Organizations," in *Leading and Managing People in Dynamic Organizations*, ed. R. Petersen and E. Mannix (Mahwah, NJ: Lawrence Erlbaum Associates, in press); A. Sinclair, "Approaches to Organizational Culture and Ethics," *Journal of Business Ethics* 12 (1993), pp. 63–73.

11. M. O. Jones, *Studying Organizational Symbolism: What, How, Why?* (Thousand Oaks, CA: Sage, 1996); Ott, *The Organizational Culture Perspective*, Chapter 2; J. S. Pederson and J. S. Sorensen, *Organizational Cultures in Theory and Practice* (Aldershot, UK: Gower, 1989), pp. 27–29.

12. E. H. Schein, *The Corporate Culture Survival Guide* (San Francisco: Jossey-Bass, 1999), Chapter 4; A. Furnham and B. Gunter, "Corporate Culture: Definition, Diagnosis, and Change," *International Review of Industrial and Organizational Psychology* 8 (1993), pp. 233–61; E. H. Schein, "Organizational Culture," *American Psychologist*, February 1990, pp. 109–19; Ott, *The Organizational Culture Perspective*, Chapter 2; W. J. Duncan, "Organizational Culture: 'Getting a Fix' on an Elusive Concept," *Academy of Management Executive* 3 (1989), pp. 229–36.

13. J. C. Meyer, "Tell Me a Story: Eliciting Organizational Values from Narratives," *Communication Quarterly* 43 (1995), pp. 210–24.

14. K. Frieberg and J. Frieberg, *Nuts!* (New York: Bantam Doubleday Dell, 1998).

15. W. Swap, D. Leonard, M. Shields, and L. Abrams, "Using Mentoring and Storytelling to Transfer Knowledge in the Workplace," *Journal of Management Information Systems* 18 (Summer 2001), pp. 95–114; J. Martin et al., "The Uniqueness Paradox in Organizational Stories," *Administrative Science Quarterly* 28 (1983), pp. 438–53.

16. R. Zemke, "Storytelling: Back to a Basic," *Training* 27 (March 1990), pp. 44–50; A. L. Wilkins, "Organizational Stories as Symbols Which Control the Organization," in *Organizational Symbolism*, ed. L. R. Pondy, P. J. Frost, G. Morgan, and T. C. Dandridge (Green-wich, CT: JAI Press, 1984), pp. 81–92; J. Martin and M. E. Powers, "Truth or Corporate Propaganda: The Value of a Good War Story," in *Organizational Symbolism*, ed. Pondy et al., pp. 93–107.

17. J. Z. DeLorean, *On a Clear Day You Can See General Motors* (Grosse Pointe, MI: Wright Enterprises, 1979).

18. This story is cited in K. Foss, "Isadore Sharp," *Foodservice and Hospitality*, December 1989, pp. 20–30; J. DeMont, "Sharp's Luxury Empire," *Maclean's*, June 5, 1989, pp. 30–33. Also see S. Kemp and L. Dwyer, "An Examination of Organizational Culture—The Regent Hotel, Sydney," *International Journal of Hospitality Management* 20 (March 2001), pp. 77–93.

19. P. S. DeLisi, "A Modern-Day Tragedy: The Digital Equipment Story," *Journal of Management Inquiry* 7 (June 1998), pp. 118–30. Digital's famous shouting matches are also described in E. Schein, "How to Set the Stage for a Change in Organizational Culture," in *The Dance of Change*, ed. P. Senge et al. (New York: Currency/Doubleday, 1999), pp. 334–44.

20. J. M. Beyer and H. M. Trice, "How an Organization's Rites Reveal Its Culture," *Organizational Dynamics* 15, no. 4 (1987), pp. 5–24; L. Smirchich, "Organizations as Shared Meanings," in *Organizational Symbolism*, ed. Pondy et al., pp. 55–65.

21. D. Roth, "My Job at the Container Store," *Fortune*, January 10, 2000, pp. 74–78.

22. L. A. Krefting and P. J. Frost, "Untangling Webs, Surfing Waves, and Wildcatting," in *Organizational Culture*, ed. P. J. Frost, L. F. Moore, M. R. Louis, C. C. Lundberg, and J. Martin (Beverly Hills, CA: Sage, 1985), pp. 155–68.

23. R. E. Quinn and N. T. Snyder, "Advance Change Theory: Culture Change at Whirlpool Corporation," in *The Leader's Change Handbook*, ed. J. A. Conger, G. M. Spreitzer, and E. E. Lawler III (San Francisco: Jossey-Bass, 1999), pp. 162–93.

24. P. Roberts, "The Empire Strikes Back," *Fast Company* 22 (February–March 1999), pp. 122–31. Some details also found at www.oakley.com and americahurrah.com/Oakley/Entry.htm.

25. Churchill apparently made this statement on October 28, 1943, in the British House of Commons, when London, damaged by bombings in World War II, was about to be rebuilt.

26. G. Levitch, "Rethinking the Office," *Report on Business Magazine*, September 2001; T. Kelley, *The Art of Innovation* (New York: Currency/Doubleday, 2001), Chapter 7.

27. T. E. Deal and A. A. Kennedy, *The New Corporate Cultures* (Cambridge, MA: Perseus Books, 1999). Barbara Anderson's statement is cited in B. Nelson, "The Buzz at the Container Store," *Corporate Meetings & Incentives*, June 2003, p. 6.

28. C. Siehl and J. Martin, "Organizational Culture: A Key to Financial Performance?" in *Organizational Climate and Culture*, ed. B. Schneider (San Francisco: Jossey-Bass, 1990), pp. 241–81; J. B. Barney, "Organizational Culture: Can It Be a Source of Sustained Competitive Advantage?" *Academy of Management Review* 11 (1986), pp. 656–65; V. Sathe, *Culture and Related Corporate Realities* (Homewood, IL: Irwin, 1985), Chapter 2; Deal and Kennedy, *Corporate Cultures*, Chapter 1.

29. J. A. Chatman and S. E. Cha, "Leading by Leveraging Culture," in *Next Generation Business Series: Leadership*, ed. Subir Chowdhury (Financial Times–Prentice Hall Publishers, 2003); J. C. Helms Mills and A. J. Mills, "Rules, Sensemaking, Formative Contexts, and Discourse in the Gendering of Organizational Culture," in *International Handbook of Organizational Climate and Culture*, ed. N. Ashkanasy, C. Wilderom, and M. Peterson (Thousand Oaks, CA.: Sage, 2000), pp. 55–70; C. A. O'Reilly and J. A. Chatman, "Culture as Social Control: Corporations, Cults, and Commitment," *Research in Organizational Behavior* 18 (1996), pp. 157–200. For a discussion of organizational culture as social control at the Regent Sydney, see S. Kemp and L. Dwyer, "An Examination of Organizational Culture—The Regent Hotel, Sydney," *International Journal of Hospitality Management* 20 (March 2001), pp. 77–93.

30. B. Ashforth and F. Mael, "Social Identity Theory and the Organization," *Academy of Management Review* 14 (1989), pp. 20–39.

31. S. G. Harris, "Organizational Culture and Individual Sensemaking: A Schema-Based Perspective," *Organization Science* 5 (1994), pp. 309–21; M. R. Louis, "Surprise and Sensemaking: What Newcomers Experience in Entering Unfamiliar Organizational Settings," *Administrative Science Quarterly* 25 (1980), pp. 226–51.

32. G. S. Saffold III, "Culture Traits, Strength, and Organizational Performance: Moving beyond 'Strong' Culture," *Academy of Management Review* 13 (1988), pp. 546–58; Williams et al., *Changing Culture*, pp. 24–27.

33. J. P. Kotter and J. L. Heskett, *Corporate Culture and Performance* (New York: Free Press, 1992); G. G. Gordon and N. DiTomasco, "Predicting Corporate Performance from Organizational Culture," *Journal of Management Studies* 29 (1992), pp. 783–98; D. R. Denison, *Corporate Culture and Organizational Effectiveness* (New York: Wiley, 1990).

34. E. H. Schein, "On Dialogue, Culture, and Organizational Learning," *Organization Dynamics*, Autumn 1993, pp. 40–51.

35. A. Holeck, "Griffith, Ind., Native Takes Over as Steel Plant Manager," *Munster (IN) Times*, May 24, 2003.

36. J. Kotter, "Cultures and Coalitions," *Executive Excellence* 15 (March 1998), pp. 14–15; Kotter and Heskett, *Corporate Culture and Performance*.

37. The features of adaptive cultures are described in W. F. Joyce, *MegaChange: How Today's Leading Companies Have Transformed Their Workforces* (New York: Free Press, 1999), pp. 44–47.

38. B. L. Toffler, *Final Accounting: Ambition, Greed, and the Fall of Arthur Andersen* (New York: Broadway Books, 2003); D. Greising "'Boot Camp' Failed to Teach All They Could Be," *Chicago Tribune*, April 21, 2002, p. C1.

39. C. Fox, "Mergers and Desires II," *Business Review Weekly*, May 11, 2001.

40. D. B. Marron, "Is This Marriage Made in Heaven?" *Chief Executive*, May 2001, pp. 50–52; P. Troiano "Postmerger Challenges," *Management Review* 88 (January 1999), p. 6. For discussion of corporate culture issues in mergers, see M. L. Marks, "Mixed Signals," *Across the Board*, May 2000, pp. 21–26; M. L. Marks, "Adding Cultural Fit to Your Diligence Checklist," *Mergers & Acquisitions*, December 1999; E. H. Schein, *The Corporate Culture Survival Guide* (San Francisco: Jossey-Bass, 1999), Chapter 8; A. F. Buono and J. L. Bowditch, *The Human Side of Mergers and Acquisitions* (San Francisco: Jossey-Bass, 1989), Chapter 6.

41. E. Krell, "Merging Corporate Cultures," *Training* 38 (May 2001), pp. 68–78; J. K. Stewart, "Imperfect Partners," *Chicago Tribune*, March 18, 2001, p. 1.

42. A. Klein, *Stealing Time: Steve Case, Jerry Levin, and the Collapse of AOL Time Warner* (New York: Simon & Schuster, 2003); A. Klein, "A Merger Taken AO-Ill," *Washington Post*, October 21, 2002, p. E1.

43. Marks, "Adding Cultural Fit to Your Diligence Checklist"; S. Greengard, "Due Diligence: The Devil in the Details," *Workforce*, October 1999, p. 68; E. H. Schein, *The Corporate Culture Survival Guide* (San Francisco: Jossey-Bass, 1999). A corporate culture audit is also recommended for joint ventures. For details, see K. J. Fedor and W. B. Werther Jr., "The Fourth Dimension: Creating Culturally Responsive International Alliances," *Organizational Dynamics* 25 (Autumn 1996), pp. 39–53.

44. D. Buckner, "Nortel versus Cisco," *Venture, CBC TV*, January 4, 2000; R. N. Ashkenas, L. J. DeMonaco, and S. C. Francis, "Making the Deal Real: How GE Capital Integrates Acquisitions," *Harvard Business Review* 76 (January–February 1998), pp. 165–76.

45. K. W. Smith, "A Brand-New Culture for the Merged Firm," *Mergers & Acquisitions* 35 (June 2000), pp. 45–50; A. R. Malekazedeh and A. Nahavandi, "Making Mergers Work by Managing Cultures," *Journal of Business Strategy*, May/June 1990, pp. 55–57.

46. A. Levy, "Mergers Spread Despite Failures," *Cleveland Plain Dealer*, August 9, 1998, p. H1.

47. S. F. Walker and J. W. Marr *Stakeholder Power* (New York: Perseus, 2001); S. Silverstein and D. Vrana, "After Back-Slapping Wanes, Mega-Mergers Often Fail," *Los Angeles Times*, April 19, 1998, p. 1

48. "Split Personality," *Baltimore Business Journal*, July 20, 2001, p. 1.

49. J. P. Kotter, "Leading Change: The Eight Steps of Transformation," in *The Leader's Change Handbook*, ed. J. A. Conger, G. M. Spreitzer, and E. E. Lawler III (San Francisco: Jossey-Bass, 1999), pp. 87–99.

50. R. House, M. Javidan, P. Hanges, and P. Dorfman, "Understanding Cultures and Implicit Leadership Theories across the Globe: An Introduction to Project GLOBE," *Journal of World Business* 37 (2002), pp. 3–10; R. House, M. Javidan, and P. Dorfman, "Project GLOBE: An Introduction," *Applied Psychology: An International Review* 50 (2001), pp. 489–505; E. H. Schein, "The Role of the Founder in Creating Organizational Culture," *Organizational Dynamics* 12, no. 1 (Summer 1983), pp. 13–28.

51. E. H. Schein, *Organizational Culture and Leadership* (San Francisco: Jossey-Bass, 1985), Chapter 10; T. J. Peters, "Symbols, Patterns, and Settings: An Optimistic Case for Getting Things Done," *Organizational Dynamics* 7, no. 2 (Autumn 1978), pp. 2–23.

52. A. Effinger, "With Charm, Poise and Attitude Fiorina Rousting Hewlett-Packard," *Seattle-Post Intelligencer*, January 3, 2000, p. E1.

53. "Nature Is Model for Firm's Recycled-Materials Product," *Grand Rapids Business Journal*, February 24, 2003, p. B6; B. Broadway, "Good for the Soul—And for the Bottom Line," *Washington Post*, August 19, 2001, p. A1; N. Hoogeveen, "Reinventing Industry," *Business Record*, April 10, 2001, p. 22.

54. J. Kerr and J. W. Slocum Jr., "Managing Corporate Culture through Reward Systems," *Academy of Management Executive* 1 (May 1987), pp. 99–107; Williams et al., *Changing Cultures*, pp. 120–24; K. R. Thompson and F. Luthans, "Organizational Culture: A Behavioral Perspective," in *Organizational Climate and Culture*, ed. Schneider, pp. 319–44.

55. W. G. Ouchi and A. M. Jaeger, "Type Z Organization: Stability in the Midst of Mobility," *Academy of Management Review* 3 (1978), pp. 305–14; K. McNeil and J. D. Thompson, "The Regeneration of Social Organizations," *American Sociological Review* 36 (1971), pp. 624–37.

56. M. De Pree, *Leadership Is an Art* (East Lansing: Michigan State University Press, 1987).

57. C. Daniels, "Does This Man Need a Shrink?" *Fortune*, February 5, 2001, pp. 205–8.

58. Chatman and Cha, "Leading by Leveraging Culture"; A. E. M. Van Vianen, "Person–Organization Fit: The Match between Newcomers' and Recruiters' Preferences for Organizational Cultures," *Personnel Psychology* 53 (Spring 2000), pp. 113–49; C. A. O'Reilly III, J. Chatman, and D. F. Caldwell, "People and Organizational Culture: A Profile Comparison Approach to Assessing Person–Organization Fit," *Academy of Management Journal* 34 (1991), pp. 487–516.

59. J. Van Maanen, "Breaking In: Socialization to Work," in *Handbook of Work, Organization, and Society*, ed. R. Dubin (Chicago: Rand McNally, 1976), p. 67.

60. D. E. Lewis, "Internships Are Key Résumé Booster," *Boston Globe*, April 13, 2003, p. G1; S. Hirsch, "Software King Builds Young Careers, Too," *Baltimore Sun*, March 9, 2003, p. D1.

61. C. L. Adkins, "Previous Work Experience and Organizational Socialization: A Longitudinal Examination," *Academy of Management Journal* 38 (1995), pp. 839–62; T. N. Bauer and S. G. Green, "The Effect of Newcomer Involvement in Work-Related Activities: A Longitudinal Study of Socialization," *Journal of Applied Psychology* 79 (1994), pp. 211–23.

62. E. F. Holton III, "New Employee Development: A Review and Reconceptualization," *Human Resource Development Quarterly* 7 (Fall 1996), pp. 233–52; G. T. Chao, A. O'Leary-Kelly, S. Wolf, H. J. Klein, and P. D. Gardner, "Organizational Socialization: Its Content and Consequences," *Journal of Applied Psychology* 79 (1994), pp. 450–63.

63. J. T. Mignerey, R. B. Rubin, and W. I. Gorden, "Organizational Entry: An Investigation of Newcomer Communication Behavior and Uncertainty," *Communication Research* 22 (1995), pp. 54–85.

64. B. E. Ashforth and A. M. Saks, "Socialization Tactics: Longitudinal Effects on Newcomer Adjustment," *Academy of Management Journal* 39 (1996), pp. 149–78; C. D. Fisher, "Organizational Socialization: An Integrative View," *Research in Personnel and Human Resources Management* 4 (1986), pp. 101–45; and N. Nicholson, "A Theory of Work Role Transitions," *Administrative Science Quarterly* 29 (1984), pp. 172–91.

65. J. M. Beyer and D. R. Hannah, "Building on the Past: Enacting Established Personal Identities in a New Work Setting," *Organization Science* 13 (November/December 2002), pp. 636–52; H. D. C. Thomas and N. Anderson, "Newcomer Adjustment: The Relationship between Organizational Socialization Tactics, Information Acquisition and Attitudes," *Journal of Occupational and Organizational Psychology* 75 (December 2002), pp. 423–37; H. D. C. Thomas and N. Anderson, "Changes in Newcomers' Psychological Contracts during Organizational Socialization: A Study of Recruits Entering the British Army," *Journal of Organisational Behavior* 19 (1998), pp. 745–67.

66. Van Maanen, "Breaking In," pp. 67–130; L. W. Porter, E. E. Lawler III, and J. R. Hackman, *Behavior in Organizations* (New York: McGraw-Hill, 1975), pp. 163–67; D. C. Feldman, "The Multiple Socialization of Organization Members," *Academy of Management Review* 6 (1981), pp. 309–18.

67. M. K. Gibson and M. J. Papa, "The Mud, the Blood, and the Beer Guys: Organizational Osmosis in Blue-Collar Work Groups," *Journal of Applied Communication Research*, February 2000, p. 68; Ashforth and Saks, "Socialization Tactics"; Bauer and Green, "Effect of Newcomer Involvement in Work-Related Activities."

68. Porter et al., *Behavior in Organizations*, Chapter 5.

69. M. R. Louis, "Surprise and Sensemaking: What Newcomers Experience in Entering Unfamiliar Organizational Settings," *Administrative Science Quarterly* 25 (1980), pp. 226–51.

70. E. Fitzmaurice, "A Hard Lesson," *Sun Herald* (Sydney), March 11, 2001, p. 50.

71. S. Barancik, "Different World, Same Old Stress," *St. Petersburg (FL) Times*, September 3, 2003; A. Daga, "Dial C for Crisis at India's Call Centres," *The Age* (Melbourne, Australia), July 12, 2003.

72. C. A. Young and C. C. Lundberg, "Creating a Good First Day on the Job," *Cornell Hotel and Restaurant Administration Quarterly* 37 (December 1996), pp. 26–33; S. L. Robinson and D. M. Rousseau, "Violating the Psychological Contract: Not the Exception but the Norm," *Journal of Organizational Behavior* 15 (1994), pp. 245–59.

73. D. L. Nelson, "Organizational Socialization: A Stress Perspective," *Journal of Occupational Behavior* 8 (1987), pp. 311–24.

74. Morrison and Robinson, "When Employees Feel Betrayed," p. 251.

75. J. A. Breaugh, *Recruitment: Science and Practice* (Boston: PWS-Kent, 1992), Chapter 7; J. P. Wanous, *Organizational Entry*, 2nd ed. (Reading, MA.: Addison-Wesley, 1992), Chapter 3; A. M. Saks and S. F. Cronshaw, "A Process Investigation of Realistic Job Previews: Mediating Variables and Channels of Communication," *Journal of Organizational Behavior* 11 (1990), pp. 221–36.

76. J. M. Phillips, "Effects of Realistic Job Previews on Multiple Organizational Outcomes: A Meta-Analysis," *Academy of Management Journal* 41 (December 1998), pp. 673–90.

77. Y. Ganzach, A. Pazy, Y. Ohayun, and E. Brainin, "Social Exchange and Organizational Commitment: Decision-Making Training for Job Choice as an Alternative to the Realistic Job Preview," *Personnel Psychology* 55 (Autumn 2002), pp. 613–37; J. P. Wanous and A. Colella, "Organizational Entry Research: Current Status and Future Directions," *Research in Personnel and Human Resources Management* 7 (1989), pp. 59–120.

78. C. Ostroff and S. W. J. Koslowski, "Organizational Socialization as a Learning Process: The Role of Information Acquisition," *Personnel Psychology* 45 (1992), pp. 849–74; N. J. Allen and J. P. Meyer, "Organizational Socialization Tactics: A Longitudinal Analysis of Links to Newcomers' Commitment and Role Orientation," *Academy of Management Journal* 33 (1990), pp. 847–58; F. M. Jablin, "Organizational Entry, Assimilation, and Exit," in *Handbook of Organizational Communication*, ed. F. M. Jablin, L. L. Putnam, K. H. Roberts, and L. W. Porter (Beverly Hills, CA.: Sage, 1987), pp. 679–740.

79. E. W. Morrison, "Newcomer Information Seeking: Exploring Types,

Modes, Sources, and Outcomes," *Academy of Management Journal* 36 (1993), pp. 557–89; Fisher, "Organizational Socialization," pp. 135–36; Porter et al., *Behavior in Organizations*, pp. 184–86.

80. C. Goforth, "Still Recruiting Staff," *Akron Beacon Journal*, July 15, 2001; A.L. Stern, "Bridging the Workforce Shortage," *Trustee*, July 2001, p. 8; D. Francis, "Work Is a Warm Puppy," *National Post*, May 27, 2000, p. W20.

81. S. L. McShane, "Effect of Socialization Agents on the Organizational Adjustment of New Employees," Paper presented at the Annual Conference of the Western Academy of Management, Big Sky, Montana, March 1988.

CHAPTER 17

1. D. Magee, *Turnaround: How Carlos Ghosn Rescued Nissan* (New York: HarperCollins, 2003); C. Dawson, "On Your Marks," *Business Week*, March 17, 2003, p. 52; C. Ledner, "Nissan Motor Co.," *Fast Company* 60 (July 2002), p. 80; Y. Kageyama, "Renault Manager Crosses Cultural Divide to Turn around Nissan," *Associated Press State & Local Wire*, June 25, 2001; A. R. Gold, M. Hirano, and Y. Yokoyama, "An Outsider Takes on Japan: An Interview with Nissan's Carlos Ghosn," *McKinsey Quarterly*, January 2001, p. 95.

2. K. Lewin, *Field Theory in Social Science* (New York: Harper & Row, 1951).

3. K. Naughton, "Bill Ford's Rainy Days," *Newsweek*, June 16, 2003, p. 38; J. McCracken, "Nasser Out; Ford In," *Detroit Free Press*, October 30, 2001; M. Truby, "Ford Revolution Spawns Turmoil," *Detroit News*, April 29, 2001.

4. M. Moravec, O. J. Johannessen, and T. A. Hjelmas, "The Well-Managed SMT," *Management Review* 87 (June 1998), pp. 56–58; M. Moravec, O. J. Johannessen, and T. A. Hjelmas, "Thumbs Up for Self-Managed Teams," *Management Review*, July 17, 1997, p. 42.

5. J. Seifman, "Middle Managers—The Meat in the Corporate Sandwich," *China Staff* 8 (June 2002), p. 7; C. O. Longenecker, D. J. Dwyer, and T. C. Stansfield, "Barriers and Gateways to Workforce Productivity," *Industrial Management* 40 (March–April 1998), pp. 21–28. Several sources discuss resistance to change, including D. A. Nadler, *Champions of Change* (San Francisco: Jossey-Bass, 1998), Chapter 5; P. Strebel, "Why Do Employees Resist Change?" *Harvard Business Review*, May–June 1996, pp. 86–92; R. Maurer, *Beyond the Wall of Resistance: Unconventional Strategies to Build Support for Change* (Austin, TX: Bard Books, 1996).

6. S. D. Green, "EDS Embraces Comms to Help Clean Up Its Business," *PR Week* (U.S.), June 9, 2003, p. 10; D. C. Denison, "Today's CEO Is Not Given Much Time to Produce Results," *Boston Globe*, July 7, 2002, p. E1; P. Mendels, "The Real Cost of Firing a CEO," *Chief Executive* (U.S.), April 2002, pp. 40–44.

7. E. B. Dent and S. G. Goldberg, "Challenging 'Resistance to Change,'" *Journal of Applied Behavioral Science* 35 (March 1999), pp. 25–41.

8. D. A. Nadler, "The Effective Management of Organizational Change," in *Handbook of Organizational Behavior*, ed. J. W. Lorsch (Englewood Cliffs, NJ: Prentice Hall, 1987), pp. 358–69; D. Katz and R. L. Kahn, *The Social Psychology of Organizations*, 2nd ed. (New York: Wiley, 1978).

9. "Making Change Work for You—Not against You," *Agency Sales Magazine* 28 (June 1998), pp. 24–27.

10. M. E. McGill and J. W. Slocum Jr., "Unlearn the Organization," *Organizational Dynamics* 22, no. 2 (1993), pp. 67–79.

11. R. Katz, "Time and Work: Toward an Integrative Perspective," *Research in Organizational Behavior* 2 (1980), pp. 81–127.

12. D. Nicolini and M. B. Meznar, "The Social Construction of Organizational Learning: Conceptual and Practical Issues in the Field," *Human Relations* 48 (1995), pp. 727–46.

13. D. Miller, "What Happens after Success: The Perils of Excellence," *Journal of Management Studies* 31 (1994), pp. 325–58.

14. H. Trinca, "Her Way," *Boss Magazine*, October 9, 2000.

15. P. F. Drucker, "The New Society of Organizations," *Harvard Business Review* 70 (1992), pp. 95–104.

16. J. P. Kotter and D. S. Cohen, *The Heart of Change* (Boston: Harvard Business School Press, 2002), pp. 15–36; T. G. Cummings, "The Role and Limits of Change Leadership," in *The Leader's Change Handbook*, ed. J. A. Conger, G. M. Spreitzer, and E. E. Lawler III (San Francisco: Jossey-Bass, 1999), pp. 301–20.

17. I. J. Bozon and P. N. Child, "Refining Shell's Position in Europe," *McKinsey Quarterly* 2, Special Edition (2003), pp. 42–51.

18. L. D. Goodstein and H. R. Butz, "Customer Value: The Linchpin of Organizational Change," *Organizational Dynamics* 27 (June 1998), pp. 21–35.

19. J. P. Kotter and L. A. Schlesinger, "Choosing Strategies for Change," *Harvard Business Review*, March–April 1979, pp. 106–14.

20. Kotter and Cohen, *The Heart of Change*, pp. 83–98.

21. T. White, "Supporting Change: How Communicators at Scotiabank Turned Ideas into Action," *Communication World* 19 (April 2002), pp. 22–24.

22. J. Conger and K. Xin, "Executive Education in the 21st Century," *Journal of Management Education* 24 (2000), pp. 73–101.

23. J. P. Walsh and S-F. Tseng, "The Effects of Job Characteristics on Active Effort at Work," *Work and Occupations* 25 (February 1998), pp. 74–96; K. T. Dirks, L. L. Cummings, and J. L. Pierce, "Psychological Ownership in Organizations: Conditions under Which Individuals Promote and Resist Change," *Research in Organizational Change and Development* 9 (1996), pp. 1–23.

24. Differences exist between Emery's "Search Conference" model and Weisbord's "Future Search Conference" model. However, we have tried to avoid entering this debate in order to focus readers on the core elements common to both processes. M. Weisbord and S. Janoff, *Future Search: An Action Guide to Finding Common Ground in Organizations and Communities* (San Francisco: Berrett-Koehler, 2000); B. B. Bunker and B. T. Alban, *Large Group Interventions: Engaging the Whole System for Rapid Change* (San Francisco: Jossey-Bass, 1996); M. Emery and R. E. Purser, *The Search Conference: A Powerful Method for Planning Organizational Change and Community Action*

(San Francisco: Jossey-Bass, 1996). For a description of the origins of search conferences, see M. R. Weisbord, "Inventing the Search Conference: Bristol Siddeley Aircraft Engines, 1960," in *Discovering Common Ground*, ed. M. R. Weisbord (San Francisco: Berret-Koehler, 1992), pp. 19–33.

25. R. E. Purser and S. Cabana, *The Self-Managing Organization* (New York: Free Press, 1998), Chapter 7; "Making Organizational Changes Effective and Sustainable," *Educating for Employment*, August 7, 1998; R. Larson, "Forester Defends 'Feel-Good' Meeting," *Washington Times*, November 28, 1997, p. A9; W. Kaschub, "PECO Energy Redesigns HR," *HR Focus* 74 (March 1997), p. 3.

26. N. Cantor, "Affordable Housing Is Key to Build Better Scottsdale," *Arizona Republic*, December 13, 2002, p. 16; P. Botsman, "Government by the People," *Courier Mail* (Queensland, Australia), July 23, 2002, p. 11; C. McCullum, D. Pelletier, D. Barr, and J. Wilkins, "Use of a Participatory Planning Process as a Way to Build Community Food Security," *Journal of the American Dietetic Association* 102 (July 2002), pp. 962–67.

27. For criticism of a recent search conference for lacking innovative or realistic ideas, see A. Oels, "Investigating the Emotional Roller-Coaster Ride: A Case Study–Based Assessment of the Future Search Conference Design," *Systems Research and Behavioral Science* 19 (July/August 2002), pp. 347–55; M. F. D. Polanyi, "Communicative Action in Practice: Future Search and the Pursuit of an Open, Critical and Noncoercive Large-Group Process," *Systems Research and Behavioral Science* 19 (July 2002), pp. 357–66.

28. "Shaping the Future for Tomorrow's Students," *Canada NewsWire*, October 22, 2001.

29. D. Buchanan, T. Claydon, and M. Doyle, "Organisation Development and Change: The Legacy of the Nineties," *Human Resource Management Journal* 9 (1999), pp. 20–37; M. McHugh, "The Stress Factor: Another Item for the Change Management Agenda?" *Journal of Organizational Change Management* 10 (1997), pp. 345–62.

30. T. Joyner, "Merger Toil Replaced Fun in Sun," *Atlanta Journal and Constitution*, August 5, 2001, p. A1.

31. J. Lublin, "Curing Sick Companies Better Done Fast," *Toronto Globe and Mail*, July 25, 1995, p. B18.

32. Nicolini and Meznar, "The Social Construction of Organizational Learning."

33. Kotter and Cohen, *The Heart of Change*, pp. 161–77.

34. E. E. Lawler III, "Pay Can Be a Change Agent," *Compensation and Benefits Management* 16 (Summer 2000), pp. 23–26; R. H. Miles, "Leading Corporate Transformation: Are You Up to the Task?" in *The Leader's Change Handbook*, ed. J. A. Conger, G. M. Spreitzer, and E. E. Lawler III (San Francisco: Jossey-Bass, 1999), pp. 221–67; L. D. Goodstein and H. R. Butz, "Customer Value: The Linchpin of Organizational Change," *Organizational Dynamics* 27 (Summer 1998), pp. 21–34.

35. C. L. Bernick, "When Your Culture Needs a Makeover," *Harvard Business Review* 79 (June 2001), pp. 53–61.

36. D. A. Nadler, "Implementing Organizational Changes," in *Managing Organizations: Readings and Cases*, ed. D. A. Nadler, M. L. Tushman, and N. G. Hatvany (Boston: Little, Brown, 1982), pp. 440–59.

37. B. McDermott and G. Sexton, "Sowing the Seeds of Corporate Innovation," *Journal for Quality and Participation* 21 (November–December 1998), pp. 18–23.

38. J. P. Kotter, "Leading Change: The Eight Steps to Transformation," in *The Leader's Change Handbook*, ed. Conger, Spreitzer, and Lawler, pp. 221–67; J. P. Kotter, "Leading Change: Why Transformation Efforts Fail," *Harvard Business Review*, March–April 1995, pp. 59–67.

39. R. Caldwell, "Models of Change Agency: A Fourfold Classification," *British Journal of Management* 14 (June 2003), pp. 131–42.

40. A. Ellin, "Building a Brand, One Brick at a Time," *New York Times*, June 15, 2003, p. 3.13; "CEOs Talk," *Canadian HR Reporter*, May 19, 2003, p. 15.

41. M. Beer, R. A. Eisenstat, and B. Spector, *The Critical Path to Corporate Renewal* (Boston: Harvard Business School Press, 1990).

42. R. E. Walton, *Innovating to Compete: Lessons for Diffusing and Managing Change in the Workplace* (San Francisco: Jossey-Bass, 1987); Beer et al., *The Critical Path to Corporate Renewal*, Chapter 5; R. E. Walton, "Successful Strategies for Diffusing Work Innovations," *Journal of Contemporary Business*, Spring 1977, pp. 1–22.

43. E. M. Rogers, *Diffusion of Innovations*, 4th ed. (New York: Free Press, 1995).

44. C. Huxham and S. Vangen, "Researching Organizational Practice through Action Research: Case Studies and Design Choices," *Organizational Research Methods* 6 (July 2003), pp. 383–403; D. Coghlan, "Putting 'Research' Back into OD and Action Research: A Call to OD Practitioners," *Organization Development Journal* 20 (Spring 2002), pp. 62–65; P. Reason and H. Bradbury, *Handbook of Action Research* (London: Sage, 2001).

45. V. J. Marsick and M. A. Gephart. "Action Research: Building the Capacity for Learning and Change," *Human Resource Planning* 26 (2003), pp. 14–18.

46. J. Heron and P. Reason, "The Practice of Co-operative Inquiry: Research 'with' Rather than 'on' People," in *Handbook of Action Research*, ed. P. Reason and H. Bradbury (Thousand Oaks, CA: Sage, 2001), pp. 179–88; L. Dickens and K. Watkins, "Action Research: Rethinking Lewin," *Management Learning* 30 (June 1999), pp. 127–40. For a recent application of action research, see K. Ayas, "Managing Action and Research for Rigor and Relevance: The Case of Fokker Aircraft," *Human Resource Planning* 26 (2003), pp. 19–29.

47. M. Beer and E. Walton, "Developing the Competitive Organization: Interventions and Strategies," *American Psychologist* 45 (February 1990), pp. 154–61.

48. For a case study of poor diagnosis, see M. Popper, "The Glorious Failure," *Journal of Applied Behavioral Science* 33 (March 1997), pp. 27–45.

49. K. E. Weick and R. E. Quinn, "Organizational Change and Development," *Annual Review of Psychology*, 1999, pp. 361–86; D. A. Nadler, "Organizational Frame Bending: Types of

Change in the Complex Organization," in *Corporate Transformation: Revitalizing Organizations for a Competitive World*, ed. R. H. Kilmann, T. J. Covin, and Associates (San Francisco: Jossey-Bass, 1988), pp. 66–83.

50. J. M. Watkins and B. J. Mohr, *Appreciative Inquiry: Change at the Speed of Imagination* (San Francisco: Jossey-Bass, 2001); G. Johnson and W. Leavitt, "Building on Success: Transforming Organizations through an Appreciative Inquiry," *Public Personnel Management* 30 (March 2001), pp. 129–36; D. Whitney and D. L. Cooperrider, "The Appreciative Inquiry Summit: Overview and Applications," *Employment Relations Today* 25 (Summer 1998), pp. 17–28.

51. The history of this and other aspects of appreciative inquiry are outlined in Watkins and Mohr, *Appreciative Inquiry*, pp. 15–21. For other descriptions of the appreciative inquiry model, see D. Whitney and C. Schau, "Appreciative Inquiry: An Innovative Process for Organization Change," *Employment Relations Today* 25 (Spring 1998), pp. 11–21; F. J. Barrett and D. L. Cooperrider, "Generative Metaphor Intervention: A New Approach for Working with Systems Divided by Conflict and Caught in Defensive Perception," *Journal of Applied Behavioral Science* 26 (1990), pp. 219–39.

52. G. R. Bushe and G. Coetzer, "Appreciative Inquiry as a Team-Development Intervention: A Controlled Experiment," *Journal of Applied Behavioral Science* 31 (1995), pp. 13–30; L. Levine, "Listening with Spirit and the Art of Team Dialogue," *Journal of Organizational Change Management* 7 (1994), pp. 61–73.

53. M. Schiller, "Case Study: AVON Mexico," in *Appreciative Inquiry*, ed. Watkins and Mohr, pp. 123–26.

54. G. R. Bushe, "Five Theories of Change Embedded in Appreciative Inquiry," Paper presented at the 18th Annual World Congress of Organization Development, Dublin, Ireland, July 14–18, 1998.

55. E. M. Van Aken, D. J. Monetta, and D. S. Sink, "Affinity Groups: The Missing Link in Employee Involvement," *Organization Dynamics* 22 (Spring 1994), pp. 38–54; G. R. Bushe and A. B. Shani, *Parallel Learning Structures* (Reading, MA: Addison-Wesley, 1991).

56. R. Pascale, M. Millemann, and L. Gioja, *Surfing on the Edge of Chaos* (London: Texere, 2000); R. T. Pascale, "Leading from a Different Place," in *The Leader's Change Handbook*, ed. Conger, Spreitzer, and Lawler, pp. 301–20; D. J. Knight, "Strategy in Practice: Making It Happen," *Strategy and Leadership* 26 (July–August 1998), pp. 29–33; R. T. Pascale, "Grassroots Leadership—Royal Dutch/Shell," *Fast Company* 14 (April–May 1998), pp. 110–20.

57. C-M. Lau, "A Culture-Based Perspective of Organization Development Implementation," *Research in Organizational Change and Development* 9 (1996), pp. 49–79.

58. R. J. Marshak, "Lewin Meets Confucius: A Review of the OD Model of Change," *Journal of Applied Behavioral Science* 29 (1993), pp. 395–415; T. C. Head and P. F. Sorenson, "Cultural Values and Organizational Development: A Seven-Country Study," *Leadership and Organization Development Journal* 14 (1993), pp. 3–7; J. M. Putti, "Organization Development Scene in Asia: The Case of Singapore," *Group and Organization Studies* 14 (1989), pp. 262–70; A. M. Jaeger, "Organization Development and National Culture: Where's the Fit?" *Academy of Management Review* 11 (1986), pp. 178–90.

59. For an excellent discussion of conflict management and Asian values, see several articles in K. Leung and D. Tjosvold (eds.), *Conflict Management in the Asia Pacific: Assumptions and Approaches in Diverse Cultures* (Singapore: John Wiley & Sons, 1998).

60. C. M. D. Deaner, "A Model of Organization Development Ethics," *Public Administration Quarterly* 17 (1994), pp. 435–46; M. McKendall, "The Tyranny of Change: Organizational Development Revisited," *Journal of Business Ethics* 12 (February 1993), pp. 93–104.

61. G. A. Walter, "Organization Development and Individual Rights," *Journal of Applied Behavioral Science* 20 (1984), pp. 423–39.

62. Burke, *Organization Development*, pp. 149–51; Beer, *Organization Change and Development*, pp. 223–24.

63. J. P. Sampson Jr., J. G. Lenz, R. C. Reardon, and G. W. Peterson, "A Cognitive Information Processing Approach to Employment Problem Solving and Decision Making," *Career Development Quarterly* 48 (September 1999), pp. 3–18.

64. M. Baumgartner, "A Career with 'Karma,'" *ABC News*, May 3, 2001 (www.abcnews.com).

65. S. Terry, "Job Outlook for Grads: Off Peak, but Not Bleak," *Christian Science Monitor*, May 21, 2001.

66. B. Moses, "Give People Belief in the Future," *Workforce*, June 2000, pp. 134–41.

67. A. Zipkin "Tough Bosses Don't Cut It in Today's Workplace," *San Jose Mercury*, May 31, 2000.

68. B. Moses, "Career Activists Take Command," *Toronto Globe and Mail*, March 20, 2000, p. B6.

69. F. T. McCarthy, "Career Evolution," *The Economist*, January 29, 2000. The survey is reported in Drake Beam Morin, "1999 DBM Career Transition Study," November 2000, www.dbm.com.

70. S. E. Sullivan, "The Changing Nature of Careers: A Review and Research Agenda," *Journal of Management* 25 (May 1999), pp. 457–84; Moses, *The Good News about Careers*.

71. N. Beech and A. Brockbank, "Power/Knowledge and Psychosocial Dynamics in Mentoring," *Management Learning* 30 (March 1999), pp. 7–24; S-C. Van Collie, "Moving Up through Mentoring," *Workforce* 77 (March 1998), pp. 36–40.

APPENDIX A

1. F. N. Kerlinger, *Foundations of Behavioral Research* (New York: Holt, Rinehart & Winston, 1964), p. 11.

2. J. B. Miner, *Theories of Organizational Behavior* (Hinsdale, IL: Dryden, 1980), pp. 7–9.

3. Miner, *Theories of Organizational Behavior*, pp. 6–7.

4. J. Mason, *Qualitative Researching* (London: Sage, 1996).

5. A. Strauss and J. Corbin (eds.), *Grounded Theory in Practice* (London: Sage, 1997); B. G. Glaser and A. Strauss, *The Discovery of Grounded*

Theory: Strategies for Qualitative Research (Chicago: Aldine, 1967).

6. Kerlinger, *Foundations of Behavioral Research,* p. 13.

7. Strauss and Corbin, *Grounded Theory in Practice;* Glaser and Strauss, *The Discovery of Grounded Theory.*

8. W. A. Hall and P. Callery, "Enhancing the Rigor of Grounded Theory: Incorporating Reflexivity and Relationality," *Qualitative Health Research* 11 (March 2001), pp. 257–72.

9. P. Lazarsfeld, *Survey Design and Analysis* (New York: Free Press, 1955).

10. This example is cited in D. W. Organ and T. S. Bateman, *Organizational Behavior,* 4th ed. (Homewood, IL: Irwin, 1991), p. 42.

11. Organ and Bateman, *Organizational Behavior,* p. 45.

12. R. I. Sutton and A. Hargadon, "Brainstorming Groups in Context: Effectiveness in a Product Design Firm," *Administrative Science Quarterly* 41 (1996), pp. 685–718.

CHAPTER ONE

PO1-1 © Richard Hernandez/San Jose Mercury News. Copyright 2002 Richard Hernandez/SanJose Mercury News. All rights reserved

P1-2 © Kenneth Dannemiller/Corbis Saba

P1-3 © LWA-Dann Tardiff/Corbis

P1-4 © AP Photo/Koji Sasahara

P1-5 Courtesy of Toms of Maine

P1-6 © Annette M. Drowlette/ Augusta Chronicle

CHAPTER TWO

PO2-1 Photo courtesy of The Container Store

P2-2 © Apichart Weerawong / AP

P2-3 © Mario Toma/National Post

P2-4 Courtesy of The Warehouse

P2-5 © Whitney Curtis/The Kansas City Star

P2-6 © AP Photo Yonhap

P2-7 © Richmond Times-Dispatch Photo. By C. Blanchard. Used with permission.

CHAPTER THREE

PO3-1 © BBC Photolibrary. Used with permission of Ms. Peruggi

P3-2 © Lynn Ball/Ottawa Citizen

P3-3 © Aimee K. Wiles/Democrat and Chronicle (Rochester, NY)

P3-4 © Michale McAndrews/The Hartford Courant

P3-5 © Middleton Evans

P3-6 © Bill Murphy/The Providence Journal

CHAPTER FOUR

PO4-1 © AP Photo/Elaine Thompson

P4-2 Courtesy of Isle of Capri Casinos

P4-3 © Ohmori Satoru

P4-5 © John Wilcox/The Boston Herald

P4-6 © Rushdy Image/Egypt Today. Used with permission.

CHAPTER FIVE

PO5-1 © H. Lynch/Raleigh News and Observer

P5-2a © Steve Bloom/The Olympian

P5-2b © Steve Bloom/The Olympian

P5-3 Photo courtesy of Encana Corp.

P5-4 © Shawn Michienzi, Riip Saw Inc. Courtesy of CDW

P5-5 © Jean Schiffrin/The Atlanta Journal Constitution.

P5-6 © Simon Clark

CHAPTER SIX

PO6-1 Photo courtesy of Westjet

P6-2 © Steve Lunam/The Sun Herald (Sydney)

P6-3 Photo courtesy of Tien Wah Press

P6-4 © Gary Tramontina/New York Times

P6-5 © J. Tannock/The Marlborough Express. Courtesy of The Marlborough Express.

P6-6 Photo courtesy of Semco

P6-7 Photo courtesy of Sirius Consulting Group

CHAPTER SEVEN

PO7-1 © AP Photo/Vincent Yu

P7-2 © Smiley N. Pool/The Houston Chronicle

P7-3 © Mark Van Manen/ Vancouver Sun

P7-4 © Observer-Dispatch

P7-5 Photo courtesy of The Western Mail

P7-6 Photo courtesy of Ligget Stashower.

CHAPTER EIGHT

PO8-1 © AP Photo/Chris O'Meara

P8-2 © Photofest

P8-3 © The Press Association

P8-4 © AP Photo Natacha/Pisarenko

P8-5 © UK OUT EPA PHOTO PA/John Stillwell

P8-6 © M. Richardson II/The Detroit News

CHAPTER NINE

PO9-1 © AP Photo/Bebeto Matthews

P9-2 © David Joles/Journal Sentinel Inc. Reproduced with permission

P9-3 Photo courtesy of Volvo Car Corporation

P9-4 © H. Darr Beiser, USA Today. Reprinted with permission of The Journal News.

P9-5a All copy, artwork, characters and titles are copyright and Trademark Crossgen Intellectual Property, LLC 2000, 2001, 2002 and 2003. All rights reserved. Reuse and reproduction are prohibited. USED WITH PERMISSION.

P9-5b All copy, artwork, characters and titles are copyright and Trademark Crossgen Intellectual Property, LLC 2000, 2001, 2002 and 2003. All rights reserved. Reuse and reproduction are prohibited. USED WITH PERMISSION.

P9.6 © John Major/Ottawa Citizen

CHAPTER TEN

PO10.1 Photo courtesy of Patchwork Traditional Food Co.

P10.2 Photo courtesy of Jabil Circuits

P10.3 Photo courtesy of Standard Motor Co.

P10.4   Photo by Paul Estcourt ©
New Zealand Herald

P10.5   © Eric Luse/San Francisco
Chronicle

P10.6   Photo courtesy of Straits
Times

CHAPTER ELEVEN

PO11.1   © Mike Kepka/The San
Francisco Chronicle

P11.2   © AP Photo/Erik Lesser

P11.3   © UK Out Epa-Photo/PA
Files/Phil Noble

P11.4   © Mark M. Lawrence/Corbis

P11.5   Photo by The Windsor Star
Group Inc.

P11.6   www.vault.com

CHAPTER TWELVE

PO12.1   © AP Photo/Kenneth
Lambert

P12.2   © Topham/The Image Works

P12.3   © CP/Kevin Frayer

P12.4   © Michael McAndrews/ The
Hartford Courant

P12.5   © AFP/Corbis

P12.6   © Kerris Berrington/News
Limited

CHAPTER THIRTEEN

PO13.1   © AP Photo/David Phillip

P13.2   © AP Photo/L.M Otero

P13.3   © CP/Tannis Toohey

P13.4   © AP Photo/Eric Risberg

P13.5   © Ed Lallo

P13.6   Courtesy of Drum Café.

P13.7   © Reuters New Media Inc./
Corbis

CHAPTER FOURTEEN

PO14.1   © Reuters New Media Inc./
Corbis

P14.2   Photo courtesy of The
Telegram

P14.3   © Tracy Powell

P14.4   © Mark Garfinkel/The Boston
Herald

P14.5   © BBN Publishing

P14.6   © EPA Photo/EPA/ Kim
Ludbrook/Corbis

CHAPTER FIFTEEN

PO15.1   © W.L. Gore & Associates

P15.2   © AP Photo/Ken Bilbert

P15.3   © Minneapolis-St. Paul
Business Journal

P15.4   © T.Bradner/Alaska Journal
of Commerce

P15.5   © AAP/Dave Hunt

P15.6   © AFP/Corbis

CHAPTER SIXTEEN

PO16.1   Courtesy of VanCity

P16.2   Courtesy of Rand Merchant
Bank

P16.3   Courtesy of Four Seasons
Image Library

P16.4   © Reuters New Media Inc./
Corbis

P16.5   © Pierre Roussel

P16.6   © Gideon Mendal/Corbis

CHAPTER SEVENTEEN

PO17.1   © Robert Padgett

P17.2   © AP Wide World

P17.3   © Dean Smith/The Camera
Crew

P17.4a   Reprinted with permission of
The Toronto District School
Board

P17.4b   Reprinted with permission of
The Toronto District School
Board

P17.5   © AFP/Corbis

P17.6   Courtesy of Amanda Troston-
Bloom, Corporation for
Positive Change, Golden CO.

P17.7   © Robert Harbison/The
Christian Science Monitor

658